Ethical issue on developers pulling out of subdivisions, or changing the subdivision in order to sell property in violation of original plans for community (Chapter 21)

Ethical issue on the assessor who reduced the values of property for homeowners in exchange for campaign contributions (Chapter 22)

PRACTICAL TIPS

Verify property boundaries before you buy (Chapter 3)

Tips on the paperwork for filing a lien (Chapter 6)

Ten Steps to an Airtight Prenup – Katie Holmes and Tom Cruise (Chapter 8)

Tips for negotiating a commercial lease (Chapter 10)

How to Avoid Being Turned Down by a Co-Op Board (Chapter 11)

What statutes require buyers to disclose when they sell their homes (Chapter 13)

Avoiding legal problems in foreclosure (Chapter 15)

Practical tip for senior living/age requirement subdivisions – how to maintain the age requirement and be exempt from constitutional and Fair Housing Act issues (Chapter 19)

CONSIDER QUESTIONS

Consider 3.1   How low can the jets at Dobbins Air Force Base fly when the neighbors are affected?

Consider 9.6   What rights do tenants with children have if a registered sex offender moves in next door?

Consider 10.1   Can a tenant hold a landlord to an oral promise on exclusive rights on parking spaces?

Consider 10.7   Is Office Depot as a tenant being undermined in tenant mix with a store called the School Box?

Consider 11.1   What are the rights of one subdivision to make owners of another subdivision pay association fees for use of common facilities?

Consider 13.14   What happens when the square footage on a home is wrong?

Consider 14.1   Cults and undue influence in gaining property for their commune.

Consider 19.1   Can cities and towns seize foreclosed properties by eminent domain and then sell them?

Consider 22.3   What happens if your lawyer doesn't get back from lunch on time to your appeals hearing on your property tax evaluation?

SOUTH-WESTERN
LEGAL STUDIES
IN BUSINESS
ACADEMIC SERIES

REAL ESTATE LAW

TENTH EDITION

Marianne M. Jennings

SOUTH-WESTERN
CENGAGE Learning·

Australia · Brazil · Japan · Korea · Mexico · Singapore · Spain · United Kingdom · United States

SOUTH-WESTERN
CENGAGE Learning·

Real Estate Law, **Tenth Edition**
Marianne M. Jennings

Editorial Director, Business & Economics:
Erin Joyner

Editor-in-Chief: Rob Dewey

Senior Acquisition Editor:
Vicky True-Baker

Developmental Editor: Ted Knight

Editorial Assistant: Tristann Jones

Brand Manager: Kristen Hurd

Marketing Coordinator: Ilyssa Harbatkin

Art and Cover Direction, Production
Management, and Composition: Integra

Senior Media Editor: Kristen Meere

Rights Acquisition Director:
Audrey Pettengill

Rights Acquisition Specialist,
Text and Image: Amber Hosea

Manufacturing Planner: Kevin Kluck

Cover Image: ©istockphoto/Doug
Schneider

For product information and technology assistance, contact us at
Cengage Learning Customer & Sales Support, 1-800-354-9706
For permission to use material from this text or product,
submit all requests online at **www.cengage.com/permissions**
Further permissions questions can be emailed to
permissionrequest@cengage.com

Library of Congress Control Number: 2012950630

ISBN-13: 978-1-133-58655-5

ISBN-10: 1-133-58655-4

South-Western
5191 Natorp Boulevard
Mason, OH 45040
USA

Cengage Learning is a leading provider of customized learning
solutions with office locations around the globe, including Singapore,
the United Kingdom, Australia, Mexico, Brazil, and Japan. Locate your
local office at: **www.cengage.com/global**

Cengage Learning products are represented in Canada by
Nelson Education, Ltd.

For your course and learning solutions, visit **www.cengage.com**

Purchase any of our products at your local college store or at our
preferred online store **www.cengagebrain.com**

Printed in the United States of America
1 2 3 4 5 6 7 16 15 14 13 12

BRIEF CONTENTS

CONTENTS

PREFACE

Since the time that the ninth edition of *Real Estate Law* was published, the traditionally dull, old area of real estate law has continued to occupy the front pages of newspapers and has become a topic of heated debate. Following the housing market collapse, followed shortly thereafter by the economy, housing prices plummeted, and the homeowners who are underwater continue to go through short sales, refinancing, foreclosures, and walking away. The housing market continues to be depressed and the legal issues in foreclosures, refinancing, and walking away have resulted in many case decisions and even more regulatory reforms. Some areas of the country have such "foreclosure blight" that local governments have been fining lenders to force clean-ups and even find local government officials considering eminent domain as a way to take over neighborhoods that have more abandoned than occupied properties. Lenders have been faced with litigation from borrowers as well as from state and federal agencies with regard to their disclosures and timeliness in handling refinancing and sales. This textbook has always been at the forefront of covering current and potential issues in real estate law. The eighth edition covered the potential issues that were evolving because of subprime lending as well as the conduct of the flippers who were buying, selling, and turning over multiple properties at a time, often using the proceeds from the sale of one property for the down payments on several new houses that were closing simultaneously. Chapter 15 in the eighth edition was ahead of its time, sounding a warning about what might happen as the frenzied market continued to climb on a tenuous foundation. The ninth edition dealt with the clean up of those problems. The tenth edition now deals with the complex new laws and regulations on lending, closing, and foreclosure.

It feels as if muddling old real estate law has become the topic on the tip of everyone's tongues. The conversations bring questions: What happens if I just walk away from my mortgage? Who is responsible for abandoned properties and their upkeep? There are also other active areas in real estate. How much power do owners' associations have? Can the city really take my property from me in order to put in a Bass Pro Shop? And, this ARM of mine is still one hefty mortgage, so, can I get out of it? There are market pressures, fast-moving transactions, and even some who would take advantage of those who need help with their mortgage lenders. As a result, there are new laws and regulations affecting everything from loan applications to closing to owners' associations to economic development and takings. Concerns about money laundering continue to affect real estate transactions via the Patriot Act and required disclosures on the transfer of property via escrow agents (see Chapter 16 for more information).

Real Estate Law has been a practical and hands-on study of the laws affecting real property since the time of the first edition in 1984. However, now in its 29th year and tenth edition, *Real Estate Law* charts new territory with its clear and cutting-edge coverage of everything from the basics to the new issues and laws that were passed to grapple with the problems the previous editions noted as percolating into systemic issues.

This edition continues its focus on the three-step approach to understanding the laws that affect real estate:

1. A clear explanation of the applicable laws
2. An example, a case, or a Consider question to help the reader see the application of the law in a particular circumstance
3. Review materials for self-testing on the concepts presented, such as more Consider questions and chapter problems

You find no feudal land systems or archaic terms as a focus of this text. Brokers faced with dual-representation issues need clear discussions of the law and how to apply it. Partners, couples, and putative spouses continue to have their disputes over property with new categories of rights in those relationships. Homebuyers faced with questions about their owners' association need simple explanations of their rights (see Chapter 11). What the tenth edition continues to offer is a format for learning and understanding.

Most real estate books favor a black-letter law approach in which the laws, rules, and terms are presented, but few or no cases and examples help students and professionals grasp the concept and understand how it affects their decisions, rights, and planning.

This is a book that continues to address the real-life situations that those involved in real property transactions encounter. The problems and cases in this and previous editions have been developed through classroom use and experience from 35 years of teaching. This teaching approach allows the students to really understand and grasp the material, and they are able to use their problem-solving skills in their professional and personal real estate transactions. If there ever was a remark I dreaded to hear from a student, it was, "I'll never use this." Each chapter shows students how they will use the material.

Real Estate Law has long been an innovative book that showed that the law of real property need not be a boring subject. Within the pages of the tenth edition the reader will find a case on bedbugs and the landlord's responsibility for them under the warranty of habitability; the *Kelo* case that changed eminent domain forever; a *Countrywide Home Loans* case that focuses on what happens when only one spouse signs the note, but both sign the mortgage; a court's answer to the question—is a walk-in cooler in a convenience store a fixture?; and about those speed bumps in my neighborhood that hurt my car—any remedy for me?; can a mall landlord be held liable for tenants' property being stolen by thieves who broke into the mall; and, finally, what happens when the agent for the buyers starts direct communications with the sellers? And badmouths the sellers' agent?

Readers can study what happens when buyers try to avoid a real estate agent in order to escape paying the agent's commission. They can also learn when minimum-age requirements for housing are valid and what a landlord can do when a tenant is using or selling drugs in the rented property. And what happens when an owners' association tries to foreclose on your property for not paying your fines?

This book does not turn its readers into real estate lawyers; however, it does train the layperson to spot legal issues and important areas in which extra caution, and perhaps legal advice, is warranted. The reader will understand the material, but the ghosts, the baseball players, and the eccentric nude tenant will help make the principles learned endure.

THE REVISED EDITION

As the saying goes, "If it ain't broke, don't fix it." The first through ninth editions of *Real Estate Law* were well received by students and instructors. Indeed, many brokers, agents, developers, and lawyers have found it to be a useful handbook. It has proved to be a successful textbook as well as a practical guide for those in the industry. The tenth edition continues the successful and unique features of previous editions.

However, we do listen when feedback comes, and the complexion of the real estate industry has changed over the 29 years of this book's publication. This edition has the most case updates to date. There are so many cases available, particularly from 2010–2012, that incorporating their drama was needed. The cases chosen for this edition are shorter, easier to read, and memorable. Each case now has a one-line summary to help students remember what the case was about and retain its significance. The chapter on mortgages is practically all new, rewritten to reflect the dramatic shift in regulation in this area. The chapter on land development has, once again, been reorganized and revamped to reflect new issues and the effects of the downturn in real estate development. Impact fees are not the issue they were because development has slowed, but whether a city can force a developer to finish a project is a big legal issue. This edition continues its coverage of the social issues related to real estate ownership, including group homes, social-issue zoning, issues related to the Americans with Disabilities Act, Section 8 housing, environmental issues, and the evolving law on disclosures on so-called meth houses and other property use and location issues.

Real Estate Law, tenth edition, has new materials, updated materials, and some reorganization, but the color, excitement, and interest levels of the first nine editions have only increased. There has, yet again, been substantial rewriting to rid us of the passive voice, which has been reduced slowly but surely through each edition. The reworking brings yet more life to real property. Activism in real estate law issues has brought even more real life to this edition.

ORGANIZATION

The tenth edition carries through the four-part organization. Part 1 covers the basics of real estate law: the nature of real estate and real estate interests, included to provide the students with a richer backdrop earlier in the text. "Land Interests: Present and Future" remains as Chapter 2 so that students have the big picture of the types of ownership and land interests before delving into specific issues related to land ownership, such as easements and liens. Chapter 21 on development is restructured for this edition.

Part 2 focuses exclusively on legal issues related to the types of land ownership. Part 3 remains a collection of all the legal issues involved in all types of transfers of title to property. Part 3 takes the transfer of property from listing agreement to financing to closing of escrow.

Part 4 continues to cover the issues related to land use and development such as zoning, environmental concerns, and constitutional rights and constraints, with the order of the chapters varied slightly to strengthen the flow of the material. The book's chapter on real estate development has changed to reflect the new legal issues that are nearly the opposite of rapid development, or what do we do with all these unfinished projects? Can government step in and help? The structure of the tenth edition still allows instructors to cover chapters as they see fit and even reorder the coverage. Cross-references in all chapters help with such restructuring and can show students how the chapter pieces fit together to supply them with an understanding of all the laws and regulations affecting real property.

TEXT FEATURES

Cases

Very few real estate law books have the benefit of reported cases. The cases used in this edition are new, but continue to offer colorful illustrations of points covered in the descriptive materials. I have rewritten the facts of the cases in order to simplify the court's language and help students attain a clear grasp of the facts before they begin to read and understand the judicial opinion. After the judge's name is listed, the language of the court begins. However, I have also carefully edited the opinions chosen and reduced their length in order to be sure students grasp the point and the court's analysis. There are new cases throughout the tenth edition, many of them with 2011 and 2012 dates.

Case Questions

The restatement of case facts and significant editing help students grasp even the most complex judicial decisions on real property law. However, to be sure that the students understand the case decisions, each case is followed by Case Questions to review facts and findings and to help the students think about what they have read and how to apply it. The Case Questions ensure that the readers understand both the facts of the case and the conclusion of the court. The case questions on existing cases have all been edited and rewritten to encourage students to think more about how the problems in the case could have been prevented or what steps would help as they go forward.

Practical Tips

Highlighted suggestions for avoiding legal problems and litigation in real estate, called Practical Tips, have been updated and appear in each chapter. These Tips include lists, questions, and ways to avoid the problems that caused the litigation in the chapter cases and Consider questions. The Tips provide yet another practical component to the text and increase its value as a handbook.

Consider Questions

Numbered Consider questions, appearing immediately after their applicable text material, help readers grasp the segments of each chapter as they read along. These questions refine reading habits as well as improve comprehension. There are new Consider questions throughout the tenth edition.

Ethical Issues

Continuing this popular feature, this edition includes updated Ethical Issues for each chapter. These real and hypothetical problems allow students to discuss and debate real-world dilemmas that real estate professionals face regularly.

Web Exhibits

First introduced in the sixth edition, the forms that took up great amounts of text space have been omitted from the text and noted with a Web Exhibit designation.

These exhibits are found on the text website; this process enables students and instructors to see the most up-to-date forms that are discussed in the text and frees up the text for coverage of more material. Simply go to the website at www.CengageBrain.com. Directions for accessing your title via CengageBrain are included below.

Charts, Diagrams, and Illustrations

Throughout the book, charts, diagrams, and illustrations aid readers' understanding of the lengthy and complex topics. For example, there are charts and diagrams depicting the relationships of land interests, Article 9 security interests, easements, and the relationships between and among contractors and subcontractors. New to this edition is a diagram on how all of the mortgage transfers affect the rights of parties. This edition also offers even more PowerPoint slides for instructors to use that include the figures from the chapters as well as additional diagrams, problems, illustrations, and charts to help with teaching.

Cautions and Conclusions

Each chapter concludes with Cautions and Conclusions, a feature that wraps up the issues addressed in the chapter. In some chapters, there are precautions, recommendations, or points critical for real estate transactions and professionals in the real world. In other chapters, these are conclusions to be drawn from reading the material covered.

Chapter Problems

Most of the end-of-chapter problems are actual cases, with the case citations. Answers are provided in the *Instructor's Manual/Test Bank*. The cases are short enough to spark interest and yet detailed enough to allow discussion and review of the chapter concepts. Many chapter problems were once cases in the first through ninth editions and have become end-of-chapter review problems as new cases replaced them. Some of the previous cases are found in full in the *Instructor's Manual/Test Bank* so that an instructor could copy and distribute the case to have the students read for purposes of determining the answer to the chapter problems. Each chapter in this edition includes at least one new chapter problem.

Glossary

The glossary of key terms appears at the end of the text and provides short definitions of the terms that are boldfaced in the text.

SUPPLEMENTAL ITEMS

The following supplements to your textbook are available at this text's companion site at CengageBrain.

Accessing CengageBrain

1. Use your browser to go to www.CengageBrain.com.
2. The first time you go to the site, you will need to register. It's free. Click on "Sign Up" in the top right corner of the page and fill out the registration information. (After you have signed in once, whenever you return to CengageBrain, you will enter the user name and password you have chosen and you will be taken directly to the companion site for your book.)

3. Once you have registered and logged in for the first time, go to the "Search for Books or Materials" bar and enter the author or ISBN for your textbook. When the title of your text appears, click on it and you will be taken to the companion site. There you can chose among the various folders provided on the Student side of the site. NOTE: If you are currently using more than one Cengage textbook, the same user name and password will give you access to all the companion sites for your Cengage titles. After you have entered the information for each title, all the titles you are using will appear listed in the pull-down menu in the "Search for Books or Materials" bar. Whenever you return to CengageBrain, you can click on the title of the site you wish to visit and go directly there.

Instructor's Manual

The *Instructor's Manual* was designed to help in lecture preparation and is written by the author. Each chapter is outlined in detail, with examples and illustrations of each of the chapter points. The cases are briefed within the outline as they appear in the text. Answers to all of the Case Questions, Consider questions, and Chapter Problems are provided in the *Instructor's Manual*. Also included are discussion suggestions and resolution for the Ethical Issues.

Each chapter in the *Instructor's Manual* has a list of books and law review articles called Resources. These materials can be used to enhance the instructor's understanding of a topic. They have been updated for this edition.

Some cases that were eliminated from the first through ninth editions to make way for new ones have been added to the *Instructor's Manual* to provide supplemental readings for class use. Interactive learning exercises for each chapter, called In-Class Exercises, are again provided in this edition.

Test Bank

Also written by the author, the *Real Estate Law* Test Bank assists instructors with test preparation by providing sample examination questions. There is a generous selection of true/false, multiple-choice, and essay questions for every chapter. The true/false questions are easier and can be used for a quick review quiz. The multiple-choice and essay questions require the students not only to know the laws and materials covered but to think and apply them to various scenarios that differ from any presented in the cases, Consider questions, and problems in the chapter. This edition offers a still larger menu from which instructors can select questions.

PowerPoint® Slides

A comprehensive set of PowerPoint® Slides (expanded for this edition) will fast-track class preparation by providing ready-made lecture materials. These valuable learning aids also enable students to better synthesize key concepts.

Real Estate Law Website

The website for *Real Estate Law*, at http://www.cengage.com/blaw/jennings, contains all of the teaching supplements, case updates, and links to the Business Law Community Site and the Digital Video Library. Instructors can also access information regarding our custom publishing offerings through this companion website.

DEBTS OF GRATITUDE

Although only my name appears on this book, I cannot claim it as my book alone. As with all achievements in my life, my finished work is the result of the cooperation, work, and sacrifice of many. I cannot name everyone who has helped me in my continuing evolution as an author, but there are those who warrant special note for their efforts in bringing this work to publication:

- Dick Crews, my original editor, who had the educational foresight to see the need for this book and who has been proven correct through the success of eight editions. In 1983, Dick said, "Your book will be around for a long time." Twenty-nine years and counting.
- James Moody, my dad, a never-ending source of stories, fodder, and the right thing to do when buying and selling real estate.
- Vicky True, a longstanding presence in the publishing world and my life as an author, who is now my official editor.
- My patient and tolerant Developmental Editor Ted Knight, who made every step of production painless. His efficiency and responsiveness have been a source of comfort during the period of flying electronic files as we worked together in overlapping phases of production.
- My students, who continue to teach me how to improve *Real Estate Law*.
- The many students around the country and the world who use this book and write to me with questions, suggestions, and insights. It is reassuring to know that there are students who study so hard that they can have a discussion with an author who enjoys seeing their mastery of the material.
- Kris Tabor, my long-suffering friend and assistant, who handles the unenviable tasks of word-processing my scribbles into a polished instructor's manual and test bank.
- The instructors who use *Real Estate Law* and communicate with me via e-mail to update me, correct me, and offer their insights on teaching.
- The reviewers for this edition for their work in offering improvements and suggestions.
- All of the Realtors, developers, lenders, lawyers, and companies that have consented to have their forms and works reproduced in this text in order to make the experience of learning hands-on for the students. Their dedication to education is evidenced by their complete cooperation in granting permission for these items to be used.
- Last, but certainly not least, I am grateful to my husband, Terry, and my children, Sarah, Sam, and John, who sacrifice some of their quality time with me as I hover over the computer. Their "How many chapters do you have left?" keeps me going. I am grateful that they care and are involved. Their presence with me in my office, over the ten editions, has changed from lying on the floor doing their homework as I work, to now actual users of my books as they complete their undergraduate and law degrees. I cherish the time we spent together working toward all of our deadlines. I continue to be grateful for their grounding force in my life. Were it not for my family, I would not be as efficient or as organized. Love and structure are wonderful gifts.

A WORD FOR STUDENTS

In using this book, read the material that describes the law first. Follow that by reading the cases that appear in each section. Answer the Case Questions after each case to make sure that you understood the case and that you grasped the issues and principles of law. Try to solve the Consider questions and Chapter Problems on your own before the instructor gives you the answers. If you can solve all the Consider questions and Chapter Problems, you understand the chapter material. The figures in chart form are designed to streamline ideas and summarize lengthy topics so that you can commit the concepts to memory. The charts are an excellent form of review for examinations and quizzes.

If you would like to consult the Uniform Commercial Code, especially Article 9 on secured transactions, you can go to http://www.nccusl.org or to http://www.law.cornell.edu/ucc/ucc.table.html.

Finally, remember to apply what you have learned when your course is over. Application is the true test of learning. Good luck with the book and its application. Enjoy the color and flavor of real estate law—it is abundant in this book. And I am always happy to hear from you at marianne.jennings@asu.edu.

Marianne M. Jennings

CHAPTER 1

INTRODUCTION AND SOURCES OF REAL ESTATE LAW

Possession is nine points of the law.

Source unknown

The above quote is but one example of an old adage on property ownership. In some areas of real estate law, this old adage remains the guiding principle. While the source of this particular principle of real estate law may be unknown, there are well-known and detailed sources of real estate law, and this chapter answers the question, Where can real estate law be found? One distinguishing feature of real estate law is that its problems are not solved by turning to a single statute or ordinance: A zoning issue cannot be resolved by examining only city ordinances, and a question on adverse possession is not always answered by turning to a statute.

Real estate law is not one simple body of law, as its name implies. Rather, it is made up of different types of laws that have been passed by different bodies at all levels of government. No single governmental body issues laws that are complete or exclusive sources of real estate law. Those who are involved with real estate should be familiar with who and what are involved in the making of real estate law. This knowledge helps to ensure that those involved in real estate transactions do not overlook legal issues, rights, or processes. Knowing the legal issues in a real estate transaction helps prevent major problems, dissatisfaction, and perhaps even litigation.

SOURCES OF REAL ESTATE LAW

If all the sources of real estate law were diagrammed in a scheme depicting their relationships, such a scheme would probably take the pyramidal form depicted in Figure 1.1.

FIGURE 1.1 Sources of Real Estate Law

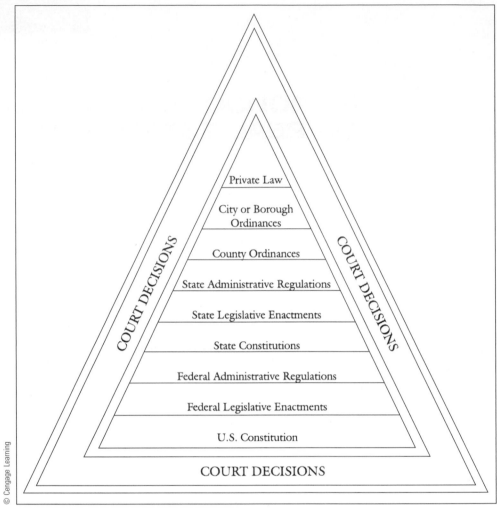

Private Law

City or Borough Ordinances

County Ordinances

State Administrative Regulations

State Legislative Enactments

State Constitutions

Federal Administrative Regulations

Federal Legislative Enactments

U.S. Constitution

COURT DECISIONS

© Cengage Learning

The discussion of these sources of law will begin at the bottom of the pyramid with the United States Constitution. All other sources of real estate law must be consistent with the constitutional rights depicted as the foundation of this pyramid. Court decisions, the final area of discussion, have their surrounding position in the pyramid because court decisions deal with the interpretation and application of all the laws in the pyramid.

The United States Constitution

The **United States Constitution** has several provisions that affect real estate transfers and ownership. The Fourth Amendment affords property owners the right to be secure in their "houses," and from this language has sprung a long series of cases on property owners' rights regarding searches and seizures on their property, as well as the proper issuance and execution of search warrants.

The provisions of the Constitution most relevant to real estate law are two similar clauses found in the Fifth and Fourteenth Amendments. The **Fifth Amendment** prohibits the federal government from depriving any person of "property without due process of law" and from taking private property for public use "without just compensation." The due process provisions have resulted in many cases that deal with obtaining judgments against a person's property and foreclosing on a security interest or mortgage in real property. (See Chapters 5, 15, and 19.) For example, with the sub-prime mortgage market collapse, foreclosure rights have been front and center with homeowners/debtors challenging the right of a lender to foreclose when the lender is not listed as holding the mortgage. (See Chapter 15 for more details and examples). Such challenges are due process challenges by the homeowner/debtors.

The just-compensation provision of the Fifth Amendment relates to land-owners' rights when the government is taking their property for public purposes. This practice, referred to as **eminent domain**, has resulted in a long series of liti-gated cases (Chapter 19) involving questions such as, When is the government actually taking property? and What constitutes just compensation? For example, one issue that the U.S. Supreme Court recently addressed is whether a local gov-ernment has a sufficient public purpose for taking private land when the reason for the taking is economic development. The court issued a decision in a contro-versial and emotional area: When can local governments take private property to allow a different use?

The **Fourteenth Amendment's** language is almost identical to the Fifth Amend-ment, but applies to state governments. The Fourteenth Amendment provides that no state may "deprive any person of ... property, without due process of law." The amendment puts further restrictions on state laws by making it unconstitutional for any state law to interfere with any rights given to citizens in the U.S. Constitution. The Fourteenth Amendment includes the **Equal Protection Clause**, which requires the states to apply the law equally so that all citizens enjoy the same protections, rights, forms of relief, and equal opportunities for land ownership. Racial discrimi-nation cases involving leases, lending, and land purchases and sales have their grounding in the Fourteenth Amendment.

The constitutional foundation of the pyramid sets the parameters for mini-mum rights that cannot be violated by the laws enacted at other levels of govern-ment. Constitutional provisions seem broad and general, but they protect basic and critical rights in real estate ownership, transactions, and processes.

Federal Legislative Enactments

The Constitution establishes a legislative branch of the federal government, which passes laws to carry out the objectives of the Constitution and for the operation of the federal government. Congress, as the legislative branch created in the Consti-tution, can pass statutes, some of which regulate real estate transactions. All Con-gressional enactments are printed in a series of volumes called the **United States Code (U.S.C.)**. The major Congressional enactments affecting real estate transac-tions are discussed in great detail in subsequent chapters, but the following exam-ples illustrate the types of laws found in the U.S.C.

- The **Mortgage Reform and Anti-Predatory Lending Act** was passed in 2010 as part of the Dodd-Frank Wall Street Reform and Consumer Financial Protec-tion Act. The details on the act's protections for mortgagors, including apprai-sals and subprime mortgage loans can be found at 12 U.S.C. §§ 1715 *et seq.* and 15 U.S.C. §§ 1629 *et seq.* and are covered in Chapter 15.
- The **Real Estate Settlement Procedures Act (RESPA)** deals with maximum closing costs and good-faith estimates of closing costs. 12 U.S.C. §§ 2601 *et seq.* (discussed in Chapter 16).

- The **American Recovery and Reinvestment Act of 2009 (ARRA)** provides federal funds to stimulate the economy, including financial assistance for residential mortgagors. 26 U.S.C. §§ 1 *et seq.* (discussed in Chapter 15).
- The **Comprehensive Environmental Response, Compensation, and Liability Act (CERCLA)** is a federal act that authorizes the cleanup of disposal sites for hazardous waste and permits the government to collect cleanup costs from current and former property owners. 42 U.S.C. §§ 9601 *et seq.* (discussed in Chapter 20).

Notice that each of the statutes includes an abbreviation such as "26 U.S.C. § 1" after its name. This abbreviation is referred to as a **citation** or **cite** with the number preceding "U.S.C." being the title or volume number of the United States Code where the statute may be found. The symbol § (or §§ for multiple sections) after "U.S.C." means "section"; it is followed by the section number, which represents the location of the statute within the particular volume. For example, "12 U.S.C. § 2603" would be a cite for a statute that could be found in the 26th volume of the U.S.C., where Section 2603 appears. This particular section describes what is required for a Uniform Settlement Statement for close of escrow. A cite with "U.S.C." in it tells you that a federal law affects the issue, transaction, or property. Using the citation system, you would be able to find the exact language of the statute cited.

Federal Administrative Regulations

For each federal legislative enactment passed by Congress, a new agency is created or an existing agency is assigned to implement and enforce the law. For example, the new laws on mortgage lending and disclosures are enforced by the **Bureau of Consumer Financial Protection (BCFP)**, located within the Federal Reserve. The BCFP is required to develop regulations on credit counseling as well as new disclosure forms for consumer mortgage lending. Like all agencies, the BCFP will be filling in the details for general statutory provisions with procedures, forms, and enforcement.

The Restoring American Financial Stability Act of 2010 was passed by Congress in a general form and was intended to regulate the serious problems that had developed in mortgage lending, particularly in terms of required disclosures in creating the mortgage relationship and in foreclosure processes should the debtor default. The general provision in the statute was expressed as the intent to provide consumer protection in mortgage lending practices and disclosures to consumers (see Chapter 15).

Given the responsibility of enforcement under the act, BCFP has been conducting studies and proposing regulations on the details for disclosing the type of information that fulfills Congressional intent for consumers to have more information about their mortgages and their rights. There are now new disclosure forms as well as requirements for consumer credit counseling agencies that provide assistance to consumers facing foreclosure. The regulations of an administrative agency fill in the details on the Congressional statute's skeletal purpose.

Another example of a federal regulatory scheme is that created by the Environmental Protection Agency (EPA) under authority granted by Congress in CERCLA. CERCLA authorized the EPA to clean up sites contaminated by toxic wastes (42 U.S.C. §§ 9601 *et seq.*; see Chapter 20). The federal regulations fill in the details with a list of 700 substances that are considered toxic wastes that require cleanup and result in liability for the failure to perform the cleanup to rid the land of any of the toxic substances (40 C.F.R. § 302). Congress established the statutory authority and the EPA handles the details and enforcement.

All federal regulations appear in a series of volumes referred to as the **Code of Federal Regulations (CFR)**. When an abbreviation, citation, or cite such as "12 C.F.R. § 226" appears in a book or a real estate document, you know that a federal regulation applies and, using the cite, you could find the regulation. In the example, 12 is the volume number within the CFR, and 226 is the section number of the regulation within that particular volume.

The CFR is a series of paperback volumes that is reprinted every year because of the many changes in administrative agency regulations. In addition, an update to the CFR, called the *Federal Register,* is published each working day and includes changes and proposed changes in existing regulations.

State Constitutions

State constitutions are similar to the U.S. Constitution in that they too provide a framework for state legislative bodies and agencies, and their authority and limits. However, most state constitutions tend to be more detailed than the U.S. Constitution, which emphasizes government structure and powers. For example, California's state constitution has a provision covering *usury,* or charging in excess of a certain maximum interest rate in a credit transaction (Cal. Const. Art. 15, § 1) (see Chapter 15). Five additional examples of provisions from state constitutions are as follows:

1. California—has several sections that provide exemption of certain types of property from taxation, including property used for religious worship or higher education (Cal. Const. Art. 13, § 3).
2. Arizona—allows any person who holds a real estate broker's or salesman's license to draft and fill out any forms related to the sale or leasing of real property, including earnest money receipts, purchase agreements, deeds, mortgages, leases, bills of sale, and other necessary documents (Ariz. Const. Art. 26, §§ 1–3).
3. New Jersey—exempts the real property used exclusively for religious, educational, charitable, or cemetery purposes from taxation (N.J. Const. Art. VIII, § 1, Paragraph 2).
4. Minnesota—makes leases of agricultural lands for longer than 21 years void (Minn. Const. Art. I, § 15).
5. Georgia—covers the requirements for an easement by necessity (Ga. Const. Art. 1, § 3).

These examples illustrate that state constitutions tend to be more specific than the U.S. Constitution and are sources for real estate law in the states.

State Legislative Enactments

Just as at the federal level, the legislative bodies in each state enact laws that affect property rights and transactions, including procedures for obtaining licenses for selling real estate, methods of financing real estate purchases, time periods for adverse possession, and provisions for creating a will or probating an estate. The details of real estate law are found largely in state legislation.

State legislation also contains the so-called uniform laws, a great many of which are important in real estate transactions. Uniform laws are drafted by representatives of industry, academe, and the legal professions. Examples of uniform laws adopted by states that affect real estate transactions include the Uniform Marital Property Act, the Uniform Probate Code, the Uniform Commercial Code, the Uniform Partnership Act, and the Model Residential Landlord/Tenant Act.

These state legislative enactments are found in volumes for each state. In Texas, the legislative enactments are found in *Vernon's Texas Codes, Annotated* (for example, V.T.C.A., *Water Code*, § 1.001). In Illinois, the state statutes are found in *Smith-Hurd's Annotated Illinois Statutes* (for example, S.H.A. Ch. 96, § 4601). Maine's statutes are called *Maine Revised Statutes* (for example, 1 M.R.S. § 2).

State Administrative Regulations

Again, as at the federal level, state legislative bodies also create or assign administrative agencies to enforce legislation. These state agencies also provide the details, forms, and procedures necessary for compliance with state laws. For example, all states have laws on the licensing of real estate agents and brokers. In each state, an agency is responsible for the collection of licensing fees, administration of exams, and the discipline of those agents and brokers who have violated the laws and regulations (see Chapter 12).

County, City, and Borough Ordinances

A great amount of real estate law can be found in the smallest and most local entity, such as a county, city, or borough. For example, most of the laws relating to zoning can be found in the laws passed by local entities and are referred to as **ordinances**. Other topics covered by ordinances on a local level include building permits, building inspections, fire codes, building-height restrictions, noise regulations, and curfews. Many of the battles over economic development, the location of power plants, and even whether a new Walmart store can be built are grounded in the application and interpretation of these local laws. (The zoning discussion appears in Chapter 18. Chapter 21 includes a discussion of economic development issues.)

PRACTICAL TIP

Know how and where to find your state statutes and regulations along with your city and county ordinances. Learn the names of your statutes, regulations, and ordinances, and how they are organized. Request to be placed on mailing lists of state administrative agencies so that you are aware of enforcement actions and proposed rule changes. Check the agendas for city council meetings. When zoning issues appear, you can attend and provide input. Follow legislative sessions and proposed laws through the media or through professional organizations such as the National Association of Realtors.

Private Law

One type of law in the pyramid comes from individuals and landowners: **private law**. Private law consists of those rules and regulations created by landowners. For example, landlords can create and post regulations on the use of common facilities by tenants, such as pools, laundry areas, parking lots, and walkways. (Chapter 9 includes a complete discussion of residential landlord–tenant relationships.) In some instances, private developers have restrictions and covenants on the use of property in their developments. Some residential developments permit only those above the age of 18 years to live as residents in the area. (See Chapter 19 for a complete discussion.) One area of private law that has increased significantly over the past decade is that of homeowners' associations. Litigation by homeowners against their associations almost always involves a question of whether the private rules of the association violate rights given by laws and the constitutions (see Chapter 11 for more discussion).

Private law is also created through contracts for the purchase, sale, lease, or mortgage of real estate. The parties who enter into valid contractual obligations are bound by the terms of the contract as a form of private law. Contractual obligations can be enforced, like public laws, through the courts.

All private law is still subject to the boundaries and rights established in constitutional and statutory sources. A private law related to real estate may not abridge constitutional rights and freedoms. (See Chapter 19 for a full discussion of constitutional rights.)

Court Decisions

The prior discussions of the various sources of law seem complete, and it would be difficult to imagine that much more detail could exist in real estate law. However, the constitutions, statutes, and ordinances are only general statements of the law that leave many terms undefined and also result in questions of application and interpretation. To whom does the law apply? When does the law apply and how is it to be applied? Finding the answers to these questions requires interpretation of law from all levels, a process that is carried out by various courts in the state and federal judicial systems. The role of the courts is to answer the questions of application and to clarify ambiguities in statutes, ordinances, and contracts.

For example, suppose that a state statute requires "good faith" by all parties in performing their contract obligations. The meaning of "good faith" will be established through court cases and judicial interpretation. Is a party acting in good faith when she is unable to obtain financing from one lender and refuses to apply with another lender? Is a broker acting in good faith when he lists a property and then does not advertise or promote its sale? Without case examples and judicial opinions on the definition of "good faith," the statute would be meaningless.

Permanent records of courts' decisions can be found in opinions published in books that far exceed in number the volumes devoted to statutes. These opinions are part of the law in that they give the complete meaning of a statute or ordinance.

In addition to their interpretive function, the courts also have the responsibility of making, applying, and analyzing the **common law**. Common law is law that is not found in any code or statute. The concept of nuisance (see Chapter 4) was developed by the courts to prevent others from interfering with your use and enjoyment of your property. Nuisance examples and the requirements for establishing a nuisance as well as appropriate remedies are found in case law. The law on nuisance comes largely from the courts, not from statutes.

Common law originated in England and continues to exist within case law, changing and growing on a case-by-case basis. Because most American real property concepts can be traced to the English rules on real estate ownership and transfer, common law remains an important source of real estate law.

Reliance on common law or prior court opinions in developing interpretations or resolutions to factually similar problems is also called following **case precedent**. Precedent can be used as a guideline for contracts and transactions that occur after the judicial decision. Once a court has interpreted a particular statute or contract, other parties can use and rely upon the court's interpretation.

For example, all states require that landowners give consent for work or improvement to be done on their property before the person doing that work or improvement can place a lien on that property if the landowner who benefits from the work refuses to pay. "Consent" seems like a simple word and concept, but the following two cases illustrate that "consent" requires a great deal of judicial interpretation. While the rights of landowners and contractors who improve properties are covered in detail in Chapter 7, the following cases illustrate how courts interpret general terms and their application to different sets of facts.

WATERVIEW SITE SERVICES, INC. V. PAY DAY, INC.

11 A.3d 692 (Conn. App. 2010)
Chipping Away at Consent

FACTS

James R. DeVito, a general contractor and partial owner of Waterview Site Services, had a lengthy history of doing business with Salvatore DiNardo, a real estate investor and partial owner of Pay Day, Inc. (Pay Day).

In 2001, Pay Day purchased 575 Asylum Street, Bridgeport, a vacant lot in an industrial area that was unoccupied and overgrown with weeds. DeVito and DiNardo entered into an oral agreement allowing DeVito to occupy the property. DeVito maintained that they both expected that there would be "extensive site improvements" and they would split the cost of those improvements. DeVito's understanding was that after he had made the clean-up that the lot would be used for a rock crushing and processing operation and that in exchange for all his work, the title to the lot would be transferred to a company that DiNardo and DeVito would own in equal shares. DiNardo's understanding was significantly different, and he maintained that he had a straightforward lease agreement that permitted DeVito to use the lot as a contractor's yard or construction yard and that any site work would be credited against rent.

After DeVito (plaintiff) had spent a great deal of time and money to turn the lot into a crushing yard, the relationship with DiNardo went south. DeVito sent invoices for his work to DiNardo. The invoices totaled $269,868.79. DeVito also filed a certificate of mechanic's lien on October 7, 2004, in the same amount. On January 6, 2005, DeVito filed suits seeking (1) foreclosure of the mechanic's lien and (2) damages for unjust enrichment. DiNardo (defendant) filed a counterclaim requesting compensation or a set-off against any recovery for valuable natural resources removed by DeVito without permission.

The lower court ruled in favor of DeVito finding that he had indeed invested substantial sums in time and money in improving the lot. The lower court also ordered foreclosure on the mechanic's lien and also found in favor of DeVito on his unjust enrichment

claim, in the amount of $224,959.24, which represented an adjusted amount after subtraction of $36,000 for the fair rental value of the lot during the time that DeVito was there chipping away at creating a rock-crushing business. DiNardo appealed.

JUDICIAL OPINION
Alford, Justice

The defendant first contends that the court erred in finding that it consented to the site work performed by the plaintiff. It argues that consent for the purpose of the mechanic's lien statute requires that the defendant not only knew that the work was being performed but also agreed that it may be liable for the materials or labor. We agree with the court's finding that the required consent was present for the purposes of foreclosing the mechanic's lien.

As an initial matter, we dismiss the defendant's argument that because the court found no "meeting of the minds" in respect to the contract claims that DeVito filed, individually; it could not in turn enforce the mechanic's lien under the theory of an implied contract. The trial court's finding that there was no meeting of the minds on the contract governing the overall agreement, which controlled use of the property, site work, future dealings and purchase of machinery, among other things, does not preclude a finding of limited consent for the purposes of the mechanic's lien.

General Statutes § 49–33, which governs mechanic's liens, provides in relevant part:

"(a) If any person has a claim for more than ten dollars for materials furnished or services rendered ... in the improvement of any lot or in the site development or subdivision of any plot of land, and the claim is by virtue of an agreement with or by consent of the owner of the land ... then the plot of land, is subject to the payment of the [mechanic's lien]...."

"Under ... § 49–33(a), the consent required from the owner ... is more than the mere granting of permission for work to be conducted on one's property ... or the mere knowledge that work was being performed on one's land.... The consent meant by the statute must be a consent that indicates an agreement that the owner of at least the land shall be, or may be, liable for the materials or labor."

Whether the plaintiff consented to the performance of the defendant's work is a question of fact. Our review of the trial court's factual findings is limited to the question of whether the findings are clearly erroneous.

Because there was no written contract between the parties, the court's conclusion that there was consent for the purposes of foreclosure of the mechanic's lien rested primarily on its assessment of the weight and credibility to be accorded to the witness' testimony. In reviewing the record, we conclude that there is sufficient evidence to support the court's findings. DeVito testified to his belief that there was an agreement that the defendant would be responsible for the cost of site work. DiNardo frequented the property during the period of time the work was being performed and, in fact, explicitly directed certain actions.

He also caused direct payment to be made to sub-contractors for work performed at the site. The court may have credited these pieces of evidence in finding that the defendant consented to being held liable for the payments as required under the statute.

Furthermore, the defendant's position is that it intended to offset the rent by the cost of the site work, which again supports the finding that the defendant consented to being held financially liable for materials and labor used for the site work. In light of this evidence, the court's finding that the defendant consented to the site improvements for the purposes of the implied contract, as required under the mechanic's lien statute, is not clearly erroneous. Accordingly, we affirm the court's decision in favor of the plaintiff.

The judgment is affirmed.

CASE QUESTIONS

1. Is there evidence of consent?
2. What is the significance of DiNardo having visited the property while the work is ongoing?
3. Is consent for a mechanic's lien something different from a "meeting of the minds" for a contract?

LIGHTING AND LAMP CORPORATION V. ATHENS LOFTS, L.L.C.

50 So.3d 1118 (Ala. 2011)
The Enlightened and Unpaid Creditor

FACTS

Between August 2006 and June 2007, Lighting and Lamp Corporation (plaintiff), a supplier of electrical fixtures and supplies, sold Jones-Williams Construction Co., Inc. electrical fixtures and supplies for the Athens Flatts project. Jones-Williams had contracted with Athens Lofts to do the electrical and lighting work for Athens Flatts. Jones-Williams charged those electrical fixtures and supplies to a specific account that Lighting and Lamp had set up for Jones-Williams for the Athens Flatts project. In June 2007, Jones-Williams abandoned the Athens Flatts project before completing its work.

On June 18, 2007, Adam Cohen, a member of Athens Lofts, met with Tim Pearson, Lighting and Lamp's credit manager, and Ronnie Vetrano, the Lighting and Lamp salesman assigned to the Athens Flatts project. Jim O'Brien, a business associate of Cohen's who did not own an interest in Athens

Lofts, attended the meeting with Cohen. At the meeting, Pearson informed Cohen that Jones-Williams owed Lighting and Lamp approximately $119,000 for electrical fixtures and supplies that Jones-Williams had purchased on credit for use on the Athens Flatts project. Pearson and Vetrano said that Cohen orally promised at the meeting that Athens Lofts would pay that amount in full in consideration for Lighting and Lamp's selling Athens Lofts the additional electrical fixtures and supplies needed to complete the Athens Flatts project. Cohen, on the other hand, insists that he did not make such a promise but that he did orally promise that Athens Lofts would pay only for certain electrical fixtures that Lighting and Lamp was holding in its warehouse, which Athens Lofts needed in order to complete the Athens Flatts project, and for any electrical fixtures and supplies purchased after June 18, 2007, for use in completing the Athens Flatts project. O'Brien recalled only a discussion about a payment by Athens Lofts to obtain the release of the fixtures Lamp and Lighting was holding in its warehouse. He did not recall a promise by Cohen to pay in full the approximately $119,000 that Jones-Williams owed.

Between June 18, 2007, and September 24, 2007, Lighting and Lamp allowed the electrician who was completing the electrical work on the Athens Flatts project to charge $33,513.18 worth of electrical fixtures and supplies to the account Lighting and Lamp had set up for Jones-Williams for the Athens Flatts project. During that period, Athens Lofts paid Lighting and Lamp $40,000. On September 24, 2007, Lighting and Lamp began requiring cash payment for all materials it provided for the Athens Flatts project, and Athens Lofts paid cash for all purchases from Lighting and Lamp after that date.

When Jones-Williams abandoned the Athens Flatts project, it had been paid all but $976,414 of the price stipulated for its work in the contract between it and Athens Lofts. Athens Lofts paid subcontractors, suppliers, and laborers over $1,400,000 to complete the work that Jones-Williams contracted to perform.

On November 21, 2007, Lighting and Lamp served Athens Lofts with a notice that it was claiming a materialman's lien, and, on November 27, 2007, it recorded a verified statement of its lien.

On December 10, Lighting and Lamp sued Athens Lofts, Jones-Williams, and several other parties. The trial court entered a summary judgment in favor of Lighting and Lamp on its claims against Jones-Williams and dismissed the claims against all the other defendants except Athens Lofts. In the bench trial for the claims against Athens Lofts, which was largely based on evidence *ore tenus* (oral evidence), the judge entered a judgment in favor of Athens Lofts. Lighting and Lamp appealed.

JUDICIAL OPINION

Bryan, Judge

On appeal, Lighting and Lamp has presented argument regarding three claims: (1) a claim that Cohen's alleged oral promise that Athens Lofts would pay in full the approximately $119,000 Jones-Williams owed Lighting and Lamp made Lighting and Lamp a direct contractor of Athens Lofts and, therefore, Lighting and Lamp is entitled to a full-price lien in the amount owed by Jones-Williams; (2) a claim that Cohen's alleged oral promise that Athens Lofts would pay in full the approximately $119,000 Jones-Williams owed Lighting and Lamp formed a contract between

Athens Lofts and Lighting and Lamp, which Athens Lofts breached by failing to pay Lighting and Lamp that amount in full; and (3) a claim that Cohen's alleged oral promise that Athens Lofts would pay in full the approximately $119,000 Jones-Williams owed Lighting and Lamp created an open account pursuant to which Athens Lofts was obligated to pay that amount to Lighting and Lamp. The factual basis of each of those claims is Cohen's alleged oral promise that Athens Lofts would pay in full the approximately $119,000 Jones-Williams owed Lighting and Lamp; however, the trial court's judgment included an express finding of fact that Cohen did not make such a promise. Consequently, Lighting and Lamp cannot prevail on any of those claims unless the trial court erred in making that factual finding.

The evidence regarding whether Cohen orally promised that Athens Lofts would pay in full the approximately $119,000 Jones-Williams owed Lighting and Lamp was in conflict. Pearson and Vetrano both testified that Cohen made such a promise. In addition, Lighting and Lamp introduced written notes made by Pearson on several occasions on or after June 18, 2007, that tended to prove that Cohen had made such a promise. However, Cohen testified that he did not make such a promise, and O'Brien, a witness who did not have a financial interest in the outcome of the action, testified that he did not recall Cohen's making such a promise. Moreover, the trial court had before it evidence indicating that Lighting and Lamp never requested that Cohen or any other agent of Athens Lofts sign a written agreement obligating Athens Lofts or Cohen to pay in full the approximately $119,000 Jones-Williams owed Lighting and Lamp. The trial court could have found that the absence of such a request was circumstantial evidence tending to prove that Cohen did not orally promise that Athens Lofts would pay in full the $119,000 Jones-Williams owed Lighting and Lamp.

The trial court had the opportunity to observe the demeanor of the witnesses and their apparent candor or evasiveness. As the sole judge of the facts and of the credibility of the witnesses, the trial court could have accepted the testimony of Cohen that he did not orally promise that Athens Lofts would pay in full the approximately $119,000 Jones-Williams owed Lighting and Lamp and rejected the testimony of Pearson and Vetrano that he did make such a promise. Moreover, the trial court could have found that the fact that O'Brien, a witness who did not have a financial interest in the outcome of the action, did not recall such a promise tended to corroborate Cohen's testimony that he did not make such a promise. Furthermore, the trial court could have found that the absence of a request by Lighting and Lamp that Cohen or another representative of Athens Lofts sign a written agreement obligating Athens Lofts to pay in full the $119,000 that Jones-Williams owed Lighting and Lamp was circumstantial evidence tending to prove that Cohen did not make such a promise. Thus, the trial court's finding that Cohen did not make such a promise was supported by credible evidence and was not contrary to the great weight of the evidence. Accordingly, we must accept that finding.

Consequently, we affirm the trial court's judgment in favor of Athens Lofts with respect to those claims.

Affirmed.

CASE QUESTIONS

1. List the facts that differ between this case and *Waterview Site Services, Inc. v. Pay Day, Inc.*
2. What advice would you give to a supplier such as Lighting and Lamp when a customer is not paying or leaves a project?

CONSIDER 1.1   Charles and Shirley McClure bought a condominium in the Villa Parke condominium community and became members of the homeowners' association (VPHOA). Mort Simpson was president of the HOA at the time. Simpson also owns a condominium located in the same complex. Sometime after the McClures purchased the condominium and moved in, the VPHOA raised its monthly dues. The McClures did not pay the increased dues and incurred late fees as a result. The VPHOA was also responsible for having trees cut on some property behind the McClures' condominium. The McClures filed suit when the VPHOA attempted to collect the amounts past due and the late fees and also sought damages for the replacement value of the trees. The McClures then filed a lien on Simpson's condominium to collect for the loss of the trees as well as for the resulting decline in value of their condominium. Would the McClures have consent to place such a lien on Mr. Simpson's condominium? *McClure v. Fisher Attached Homes*, 882 N.E.2d 6 (Ohio 2007).

ETHICAL ISSUE

Evaluate the ethics of the parties in the *Waterview* and *Lighting and Lamp* cases. That is, in one case, there was a clear benefit received by one party, but no legal obligation to pay. In the other case, there was a benefit received and a refusal to acknowledge the benefit. The judicial decisions applied the law in order to resolve the parties' differences. How would you resolve the issue from an ethical perspective? What if the owner of Athens Lofts switched positions and was the owner of Lighting and Lamp? Would he see the resolution of their dispute differently?

JUSTIFICATION FOR STUDYING REAL ESTATE LAW: SOME CAUTIONS AND CONCLUSIONS

Real estate is an industry in which small investments can yield high returns; property appreciation alone exemplifies this profitability. However, the mortgage market collapse in 2008 shows that the significant upside of real estate investment also has a costly downside. Knowing your rights if property values decline is a critical piece of information for purposes of determining the value of a real estate investment. Investment profits are lost if legal difficulties arise with the property or a real estate transaction. A piece of property that doubles in value in two years is not worth much if there is a defect in the title that prevents the owner from selling the property to realize that profit. A new home purchased at a bargain price is a comfort and achievement for a young couple until the announcement that a feed lot is to be constructed only 200 feet from their front door. The purchase of an apartment complex by an overextended corporation is a good tax write-off and cash producer until the corporation learns that the furniture, refrigerators, and stoves did not transfer with the property.

All the errors made in these transactions involve legal issues that could have been avoided if the parties had a basic knowledge of real estate law. The remainder of this book is devoted to providing such knowledge.

As you proceed through the book, think about the questions in the following section. Pay close attention to the Cautions and Conclusions sections in each chapter as you look for answers.

The Most Frequently Asked Real Estate Questions

1. If I move out of my apartment before the lease expires, do I still owe the rent? What if the landlord re-rents the apartment? Will I still owe rent?

2. If a seller backs out of the sale of property, does she still owe the broker the commission?

3. If a buyer backs out of the purchase of property, does the broker still get his commission? What happens to the earnest money deposit?

4. Do all real estate contracts have to be in writing?

5. What if I buy a home and the general contractor has not paid all the subcontractors? Will I have to pay them?

6. If I die without a will, does my property go to the state?

7. If I own a house before I am married, does my spouse own it after we are married?

8. What happens if the value of my property falls below my mortgage amount? Can I walk away?

9. How long does it take to foreclose on a property mortgage?

10. If people cut across my property for a path, am I liable if they are hurt? Can they claim any interest in my property?

11. If the fence on my property is in the wrong place, do I own the property that was accidentally included?

12. Can the EPA require me to clean up or pay for the cleanup of toxic waste on land that I just bought?

13. Is my broker working for me or for the buyer?

14. What happens if my property deed is not recorded?

15. If a property has two mortgages, which mortgage has priority?

CONSIDER 1.2 For each of the frequently asked questions, list the sources of law from the pyramid shown in Figure 1.1 that would be consulted for answers.

KEY TERMS

American Recovery and
    Reinvestment Act of 2009
    (ARRA), 4
Bureau of Consumer Financial
    Protection (BCFP), 4
case precedent, 7
citation, 4
cite, 4
Code of Federal Regulations (CFR), 5

common law, 7
Comprehensive Environmental
    Response, Compensation, and
    Liability Act (CERCLA), 4
eminent domain, 3
Equal Protection Clause, 3
Fifth Amendment, 2
Fourteenth Amendment, 3

Mortgage Reform and
    Anti-Predatory Lending Act, 3
ordinances, 6
private law, 6
Real Estate Settlement Procedures
    Act (RESPA), 3
United States Code (U.S.C.), 3
United States Constitution, 2

CHAPTER PROBLEMS

1. Where would a home buyer turn to find out about rights related to mortgage disclosure terms and foreclosures?

2. Mr. and Mrs. Ralph Williams of Montana purchased an acre of land in a new Florida development called Sunnydale. When the Williamses arrived at Sunnydale,

they did not find the green, lush parcels of which they were told, but instead found property resembling the moon's surface. In determining their rights, to which sources of law should Mr. and Mrs. Williams turn?

3. "Wait a minute," Ella objected. "How can the city take my property to build a Bass Pro Shop? I was here first!" Discuss Ella's rights by helping her with a list of the types of laws that will be involved in answering her questions.

4. When Tom Buttom purchased his home, the builder promised that the neighborhood would consist of single-family dwellings. Tom has just learned that because of economic conditions, the builder will be constructing duplex houses on Tom's street. What sources of law will be helpful to Tom in determining his rights?

5. Jane Jenkins, a licensed real estate agent in New York, will be moving to California. To what sources of law can Jane turn to find the requirements for becoming licensed in California?

6. A deed restriction requires every house in a subdivision to have a "minimum of 2,000 square feet of living space." Although the restriction seems clear, consider the following interpretive problems:

   a. Is a garage part of the 2,000 square feet?
   b. Are porches part of the 2,000 square feet?

   What sources of law would be helpful in determining what is considered to be included in the term "living space"?

7. Ralph and Lillian Palmer owned a dump site in a wooded area in the northern part of Arizona. Cabin owners in the area used the dump site for their trash, and commercial trucks often would bring their loads of trash to the site for a fee. The site has had old batteries, medical refuse, and oil discarded from auto repair shops. The EPA maintains that substances from the site are leaking into the surrounding soil and water supply. What sources of law provide the EPA with its authority?

8. Some isolated parcels within national forests are privately owned. Often, the United States Forest Service will try to arrange exchanges with landowners. With an exchange, the Forest Service will then have a clean parcel and the landowner is given property in an area with development potential near a city or small town. Discuss the types of laws and government agencies that would be involved in such an exchange.

9. Susan Hewitt is a licensed broker in Arizona. She is confused and concerned about her role as an agent for sellers when she lists properties. For example, prospective buyers will often ask her questions about the sellers, their cash needs, their reasons for selling their property, and whether their circumstances require them to sell quickly. What sources of law would help Susan clarify her role with both sellers and buyers?

10. In the summer of 1997, George Klodin, the owner of GVK, approached Patock regarding a construction project on behalf of Colorest, a store also owned by Klodin that sells custom picture frames and radio controlled toys. Klodin wanted Patock to renovate an abandoned building purchased by Klodin in GVK's name so that Colorest could relocate into the renovated building and so that portions of the building could be leased to other tenants.

    While Klodin intended to pay for the entire renovation project with bank loans of $125,000 to $140,000, Patock and GVK did not fix a price for the anticipated work. Patock's president, Jay Patock, testified that there was no fixed price because GVK had only given them a preliminary construction plan. Jay Patock considered it a "time and material job" and that his company would be paid on completion of the project. No hourly rate was discussed and there was no written contract.

    Klodin terminated Patock in November 1997, because he felt that Patock was not doing much work and was behind schedule. He hired Tri-Tech, another construction company, to finish the project. The project was soon completed and Colorest vacated its leased property on January 1, 1998. The only amount GVK paid to Patock was $5,800 in October 1997.

    After its termination, Patock sent a letter to GVK requesting $85,985.16, after crediting the $5,800 received. Patock received no payment or response from GVK, causing it to file a construction lien claim. GVK and Klodin claimed there was no contract and the lien could not be filed without a contract or some form of consent. Who is correct on the lien and why? *Patock Const. Co., Inc. v. GVK Enterprises, LLC*, 858 A.2d 1148 (N.J. Super. 2004).

For research activities related to this chapter, go to our text companion website at www.cengagebrain.com.

CHAPTER 2

LAND INTERESTS: PRESENT AND FUTURE

Those hours when happy hours were my estate,—Entailed, as proper, for the next in line, Yet mine the harvest, and the title mine—....

Edna St. Vincent Millay, *Mine the Harvest: A Collection of New Poems 121* (1954)

The late Senator Burton K. Wheeler of Montana, a leading isolationist of the World War II era, gave [the following answer] when asked in a University of Michigan Law School class in the early 1900s: What is the rule in Shelley's Case? After a moment of thought, Wheeler is said to have responded, "Sir, the Rule in Shelley's case is the same as the rule in any other man's case! The law brooks no favorites!"

Shelley's Tourist Attraction, *7 GREENBAG 175* (2004)

There is no knowing how estates will go when once they come to be entailed.

Jane Austen, *Pride and Prejudice*

There are different levels and types of property ownership or title. Because of land's permanent nature, title can exist in the present or in the future. Land ownership can also be in the form of a partial interest. Possession rights in land can be transferred without an accompanying transfer of title. This chapter explains the types and degrees of land interests and title.

The colorful opening quotes show that land interests' complexity has affected real and literary life. This chapter answers one overarching question: How can an owner hold title to property? That large question includes two subparts: How long can an interest be held? Can interests be transferred? This chapter covers the degree and extent of land ownership. Figure 2.1 summarizes the extent and interrelationships of land interests.

FIGURE 2.1 Land Interests

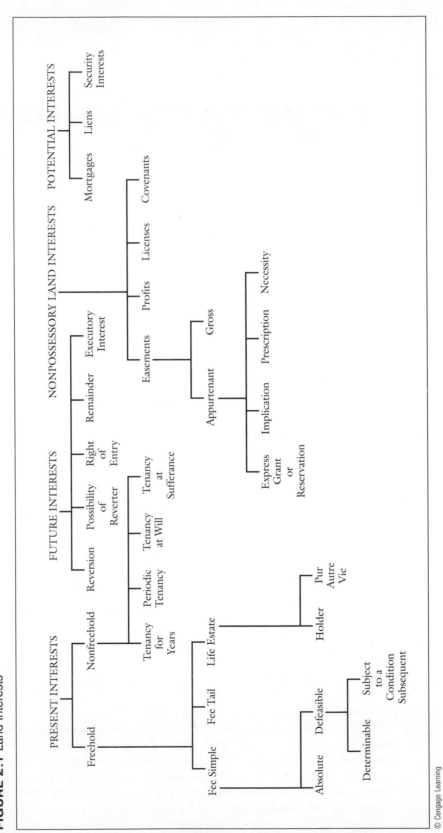

LAND INTERESTS—FREEHOLD ESTATES AND ACCOMPANYING FUTURE INTERESTS

Freehold Estates

The terms **freehold** and **fee**, adopted from English common law, are significant terms in the methods of land ownership. *Freehold* means that an interest in land is uncertain or unlimited in duration. *Fee* means that an interest in land is inheritable. Fee freehold estates are both uncertain or unlimited in duration and inheritable by others when the interest holder dies.

Fee Simple Absolute Ownership

A **fee simple absolute**, often called simply a **fee simple**, is the greatest type of interest in property ownership available. In lay terms, the fee simple absolute estate would be described as absolute ownership. The owners of fee simples are free to transfer their interests to others at any time, including upon death.

At common law, a fee simple estate was created when the transfer or grant made by the owner or grantor read, "To A and his heirs," with "and his heirs" used to indicate the inheritability of the interest. However, in most states, the language requirement of "and his heirs" has been eliminated so that a fee simple can be created simply by using "To A" language.

Fee Simple Defeasible

A **fee simple defeasible** is an interest in land that is uncertain or unlimited in length and that has the potential of being terminated. There are two types of fee simple defeasible estates—the **fee simple determinable** and the **fee simple subject to a condition subsequent**.

Fee Simple Determinables and Possibility of Reverter

This land interest is uncertain in length and inheritable. In a fee simple determinable, the grantor is giving the grantee full title and right to the property so long as the grantee complies with an attached restriction. A fee simple determinable is created with language such as the following: "To A so long as the premises are used for school purposes." The distinguishing characteristic of a fee simple determinable is that A's interest will terminate if the property is not used for school purposes. If A does not comply with the school-use restriction, title to the property reverts to the grantor.

Possibility of Reverter—The Matching Fee Simple Determinable Future Interest

Suppose a grant of real property is made as follows, "To A so long as the property is used for residential purposes." A builds a factory on that land. What happens to the land interest? The rule for fee simple determinable, noted earlier, requires that upon A's violation of the restriction, A's interest terminates and title to the property reverts to the grantor. This potential loss of title is a future interest called the **possibility of reverter**. The grantor and the grantor's heirs hold a possibility of reverter in the property that was created when the fee simple determinable was granted to another.

Possibilities of reverter have some land ownership rights. Under common law, grantors are free to transfer their possibilities of reverter any time while alive (***inter vivos***), and their reverters pass upon their death (**testamentary**) to their heirs or devisees. Many states have now passed statutes regulating the possibility of reverter. In some states, this future interest cannot be transferred or inherited. In others, statutes restrict the possibility of reverter by placing a time limit on validity of the interest—in many states, the maximum is 40 years.[1] Still other states require the grantor or holder of the interest to periodically rerecord a notice that the interest exists. All of these state-enacted statutes are notice systems, which are tremendous helps in land title histories and transfers because future interests affecting titles can be determined without having to examine the granting language in each deed that transferred title to the property. The constitutionality of these title-limiting statutes has been questioned in some court cases, but generally upheld.

Fee Simple Subject to a Condition Subsequent

The second form of fee simple defeasible title is a fee simple subject to a condition subsequent. This interest is created with slightly different language, such as, "To A on the condition that the land be used for school purposes, and if the land is ever not used for school purposes, [the grantor] may re-enter and repossess the land." The fee simple subject to a condition subsequent is similar to a fee simple determinable in that A loses the interest if A violates the restriction. The difference between the two is that the violation of a fee simple determinable restriction terminates A's interest automatically and immediately, whereas violation of a condition subsequent grant requires some action on the part of the grantor (O) before the interest of A terminates. The grantor must take steps, generally through a quiet title action, to show a violation of the restriction and thereby regain title to the property.

Right of Entry/Power of Termination: The Other Matching Future Interest

A fee simple subject to a condition subsequent in the grantee also creates a future interest in the grantor: "To my niece Sally on the condition that liquor never be served on the premises, and should liquor ever be served, I reserve the right to re-enter and take possession of and title to the property." Sally holds the present interest of a fee simple subject to a condition subsequent, but the grantor/uncle holds a future interest called a **right of entry** or **power of termination**. As discussed earlier, the grantor's future interest does not become a present interest automatically. The grantor must take steps to gain title and possession of the property.

At common law, the right of entry could not be transferred *inter vivos* but could be transferred at death. Some states have passed statutes that modify these common law rules. However, at common law and in most states, the grantor can transfer the right of entry to the present interest holder of the fee simple subject

---

[1]For a discussion of the types of state statutes and their validity (such as statutes that cancel, destroy, nullify, or limit enforcement of possibilities of reverter or rights of reentry), see 87 A.L.R.3d 1011. The Uniform Simplification of Land Transfers Act (1976) provides in § 3-409 that a possibility of reverter or right of entry for condition is extinguished 30 years after it or a notice of intent to preserve the interest was most recently recorded. A notice of intent is a statutorily imposed recording requirement for continuing the interest. Without that filing, or recording, as noted in the USLTA, the interest ends.

to a condition subsequent. Such a transfer merges the present and future interests, and the present holder of the fee simple subject to a condition subsequent then holds a fee simple interest. Future interests coupled with present interest are like a math problem: Right of entry + fee simple subject to a condition subsequent = fee simple. In the example, if Sally's uncle conveyed his interest to her, Sally would then have a fee simple. Many states have also passed time limitations and recording requirements for the continuing validity of the future right of entry interest. The restrictions and recording requirements are similar or identical to those described for possibilities of reverter.

Sometimes it is difficult to distinguish between a possibility of reverter and a right of entry because the language used is so similar. When the granting language includes a phrase such as, "grantor shall have the right to re-enter and reclaim the property," the type of future interest created is clear. However, without such clear language the distinction is a fine one, and several judicial rules for interpretation have developed. First, the courts will examine the entire document to determine the grantor's intent. They will also look for certain phrases and words that are key in determining the type of interest. For example, language such as "until," "so long as," or "for so long" indicates a possibility of reverter. Language such as "but," "provided that," or "on the condition that" indicates a right of entry. Many states resolve the issue of which type of interest is created through a presumption in favor of the right of entry, because rights of entry interests require some action on the part of the parties to change title to the property. These statutes eliminate the automatic transfers of a possibility of reverter.

In the following case, the court deals with a question about a fee simple defeasible interest in an easement.

ROGERS V. U.S.

101 Fed.Cl. 287 (Fla. 2011)
Rails to Trails to Reverters

FACTS

Congress enacted the Trails Act to preserve shrinking rail trackage by converting unused rights-of-way to recreational trails. The railroads were granted rights-of-way (easements—see Chapter 5) with the following language in the conveyance:

[Grantor] does hereby remise, release, and forever quit claim unto the SEABOARD AIR LINE RAILWAY... a right of way for railroad purposes over and across the following described parcels of land....

This conveyance is made upon the express condition, however that if the Seaboard Air Line Railway shall not construct upon said land and commence the operation thereon [within] one year of the date hereof of a line of railroad, or, if at any time thereafter the said Seaboard Air Line Railway shall abandon said land for railroad purposes then the above described pieces and parcels of land shall [ipso facto] revert to and again become the property of the undersigned, his heirs, administrators and assigns.

Several landowners (plaintiffs) brought suit challenging the federal government's rails-to-trails program on the grounds that it was an uncompensated taking of their property. The landowners maintained that because the railroad rights-of-way had been unused that title reverted back to them and that the federal government could not take the rights-of-way for trails unless they were paid compensation. The landowners moved for summary judgment.

JUDICIAL OPINION

Williams, Judge

The operation of the Trails Act is subject to the Fifth Amendment to the United States Constitution which provides that private property shall not "be taken for public use, without just compensation." Accordingly, when private property interests are taken by the Government pursuant to the Trails Act, the property owners are entitled to just compensation.

Because property rights arise under state law, Florida law governs whether the landowners have a compensable property interest. In a rails-to-trails case, a taking, if any, occurs when "state law reversionary interests are effectively eliminated in connection with a conversion of a railroad right-of-way to trail use."

The Trails Act prevents a common law abandonment of the railroad right-of-way from being effected, thus precluding state law reversionary interests from vesting. Stated in traditional property law parlance, upon abandonment or termination of a railroad easement, "the burden of the easement would be extinguished, and the landowner's property would be held free and clear of any such burden." By preventing the abandonment and concomitant restoration of a fee simple unburdened by the easement, the Trails Act effects a taking.

In another sense the taking occurs when the government, pursuant to the Trails Act, creates a new easement for a recreational use over land that had

been encumbered by an easement limited to railroad purposes. The statutory imposition of this recreational easement, which otherwise had not been granted, is a taking.

The conveyance grant[ed] Seaboard an easement solely for rail use, and therefore Plaintiffs would have obtained fee simple estates in the corridor upon discontinuance of railroad use if the taking had not occurred. "the conveyance placed an explicit limitation on the use of the property interest conveyed and contained an unequivocal stipulation that title would revert to the grantor upon discontinuance of the use of the parcel for its intended railroad purpose."

The plaintiffs are entitled to compensation because of the taking of their property for trails.

CASE QUESTIONS

1. What type of land interest was granted for the railroad easement?
2. What happened to title to the easement when the railroads quit using the rights-of-way for railroad use?
3. What advice could you give to landowners who have limited use easements that they have granted to others?

CONSIDER 2.1   On July 1, 1926, J. M. Stumbo, Sr., and his wife Della executed a deed that conveyed title to a tract of land located at Harold in Floyd County, Kentucky, to the Board of Education of Floyd County. The deed contained the following language:

> It is further agr ed [sic] that the said Board of Education or their Successors that of [sic] they fial [sic] to erect and maintain a public school building on said property that they will convey the said described property back to J. M. Stumbo for the some [sic] consideration as above mentioned.

The Board paid the Stumbos $500. In meeting the condition contained in the deed, the Board built and operated the Harold Elementary School on the property.

J. M. Stumbo died in 1947. In June 1998, the Board closed the Harold Elementary School, declared the building and property as surplus, and offered it for sale. On October 27, 1998, W. C. Stumbo, on behalf of himself and the other Stumbo heirs, tendered a check for $500 to the Board and requested that the property be reconveyed to the heirs of J. M. Stumbo in accordance with the clause contained in the 1926 deed. The Board refused to convey the property and filed suit seeking to quiet title to the property. Who holds title to the property? What would happen if Kentucky required that holders of future interests record their interests to preserve them and the Stumbo heirs had not recorded their interest? *Stumbo v. Board of Education of Floyd County,* 2001 WL 34800010 (Ky.).

CONSIDER 2.2   Determine what types of future and present interests are created by the following language:

a. "To A so long as the premises are used for church purposes."

b. "To A and his heirs provided that the premises never be used for commercial purposes."

c. "To Cal Trans so long as the land is used for the construction of an off-ramp for access to Harrah's Club Casino."

d. "To Wyndham Development so long as the property is never used for the construction or operation of a Wal-Mart store."

Fee Tail Ownership

The position of **fee tail** interest in Figure 2.1 establishes it as an uncertain or unlimited estate that is inheritable. However, the distinction between fee simple and fee tail is that fee tail is inheritable only by lineal descendants or direct descendants of the grantee. Lineal descendants are children, grandchildren, great-grandchildren, and so on.

Fee tail interests present substantial problems because of the transfer restrictions and because finding lineal heirs can be cumbersome and confusing. To alleviate the problems of fee tail, many states have passed statutes that convert fee tail grants into fee simple absolutes. Thomas Jefferson considered the abolition of the fee tail in Virginia one of his finest accomplishments, something that lessened the "proportion of idle proprietors."[2] Delaware, Maine, Massachusetts, and Rhode Island still recognize the fee tail. However, disentailing, the process of converting from a fee tail to a fee simple, is available in all four states. In most states, creditors are not subject to fee tail restrictions—they can treat the interest like a fee simple.[3] Fee tails created prior to legislative changes are still valid.

Life Estate Ownership
Creation
Another type of freehold estate is the **life estate**, which is an interest in land valid only for the life of the holder or for some other measured life. A life estate is uncertain because it terminates when the person whose life is used as the measure dies. The first type of life estate, a conventional life estate, is created with the language "To A for his life." A's interest will automatically terminate at death. A second type of life estate, measured by a life other than that of the holder, is created by language such as "To A for the life of B" and is called a life estate.

The life estate appears to be an odd method of land ownership, but it is used as an estate planning tool so that estate taxes may be postponed or reduced. For

---

[2]John F. Hart, "A Less Proportion of Idle Proprietors: Madison, Property Rights, and the Abolition of Fee Tail," 58 *Wash & Lee L. Rev.* 167 (2001).

[3]Marianne M. Jennings, "Real Property Could Use Some Updating," 24 *Real Est. L.J.* 103, 107 to 108 (1995).

example, a wife who predeceases her husband might have a will granting her husband a life estate in some property with the provision that the property be given to the children at the termination of the husband's life interest, such as "To my husband for his life, and then to my children in equal shares." The husband holds only a lesser interest for life and will be taxed less, if at all, on his inheritance of the life estate. The distribution will be taxed in full at the time of the children's receipt of the property so that the wife's estate is not taxed twice for transfers to her family.

Some states provide for the automatic creation of legal life estates in certain instances. Dower and curtesy are marital property rights for surviving spouses that entitle them to some portion of their deceased spouse's property. In some states, these marital rights are given to the surviving spouse in the form of a life estate required by statute. (Chapter 8 discusses dower and curtesy rights more fully.)

Rights of Life Tenants

Those who hold life estates, referred to as **life tenants**, have the right of undisturbed possession during the time of their estate. However, life tenants cannot commit waste or destroy the property interest so that the rights of future interest holders are diminished (noted below). For example, cutting timber on the life estate property for the purpose of building fences or for fuel is appropriate conduct for a life tenant; however, cutting timber for commercial sale would be inappropriate because there is a dissipation of the value of the property and the interests of the future holders of title.

While alive, life tenants can transfer their interests, but a transferee's interest lasts only as long as the tenant/transferor is alive. An attempt by a life tenant to convey an interest at death is invalid. Similarly, creditors of the life tenant can have security in the property only until the life tenant's death. States have differing rules for tax liability between and among life tenants and those granted the future interest upon termination of the measuring life.

Reversions

A **reversion** is a future interest in the grantor that is created when the grantor has given someone else a lesser estate. For example, when the grantor makes the grant "To A for life," the present life estate of A will terminate upon A's death. At that point, the land must be transferred to someone, and in this case it will transfer back or revert to the grantor. Throughout A's life estate, the grantor has a future interest called a *reversion*. Other types of conveyances that would give the grantor a reversion include fee tails and the nonfreehold estates. For example, at the termination of any type of tenancy, the land reverts to the grantor.

Remainders

A **remainder** is a future interest created in someone other than the grantor. A remainder also follows a life estate or a fee tail. An example of language creating a remainder would be "To A for life, then to B." B holds the remainder interest, which is a future interest, because the interest becomes possessory only upon the death of A. In this example, the grantor has given to another what would have been a reversion, thereby creating a remainder. There are two types of remainders: vested and contingent.

Vested Remainders

A **vested remainder** is one given to someone identified and in existence who has the immediate right to the land interest upon termination of the freehold estate. In the example "To A for life, then to B," B holds a vested remainder because (1) B is identified and alive at the time of the grant, and (2) B will have the immediate right to the estate upon A's death. B's remainder is an example of one that is absolutely vested.

Two other types of vested remainders that may be created are **vested remainder subject to partial divestment** and **vested remainder subject to complete divestment**. "To A for life, then to the children of B," is a sample grant that can be used to illustrate the types of remainders. This example is one of a vested remainder if B is dead and has one child. However, if B is alive, there is the possibility that B will have additional children during A's life estate. B's child holds a vested interest but could be divested of one-half or two-thirds of the interest should B have one or two more children before A's death. If A dies when B has three children, each child would receive a one-third interest. If A dies when B has one child, that child would receive the full interest. The potential for loss of part of the interest is referred to as *divestment*. The vested remainder created in the example when B is still alive is a vested remainder subject to partial divestment because B stands to lose part of his or her interest.

"To A for life, then to B, but if B is not married, then to C," is an example of a vested remainder subject to complete divestment. At the termination of A's life interest, B, ascertained and in existence at the time of the grant, will have a possessory interest. However, B could lose the interest by not marrying prior to A's death. In this instance, B loses the entire interest if the marriage requirement is not fulfilled at the time of A's death. This type of remainder in B is a vested remainder subject to complete divestment.

Contingent Remainders

A **contingent remainder** is the opposite of a vested remainder. That is, a contingent remainder is one in which the taker of the interest is unascertained or the interest has a condition precedent to its existence and will not pass automatically. An example of a contingent remainder is "To A for life, remainder to the children of B [a bachelor with no children]." It is possible that B may have children at the time of A's death and the children would be entitled to their interest, but at the time of the grant the takers (nonexistent children) are unascertained.

"To A for life, then if B is married, to B," is an example of a contingent remainder because of a condition precedent. In this example, B's interest does not automatically follow A's death, because B must meet the condition precedent of marriage to obtain the interest. There is a fine distinction between a condition precedent contingent remainder and vested remainder subject to a complete divestment. That distinction is that a condition preceding the remainder makes the remainder contingent, whereas a condition following the remainder makes the remainder subject to complete divestment.

When a contingent remainder future interest is created, a reversion or interest in the grantor is also created. If a contingent remainder fails (B is not married or has no children), the interest would revert to the grantor.

All types of remainders are transferable both *inter vivos* and at death. Obviously, a conveyance at death would be invalid if a condition of survival were attached to the remainder.

CONSIDER 2.3   Dr. James Hammons, a physician, died on August 11, 2006. Dr. Hammons provided by will for his wife, Rosa, and his children by a former marriage, Janet and Jillisa. Rosa received a life estate in all of Dr. Hammons's property and Janet and Jillisa received a remainder interest in their father's estate. The will provides, in pertinent part:

> *My said wife during her lifetime shall have the right to sell any property received by her under the terms of this Item and invest and reinvest the proceeds thereof in other property, real or personal, in her absolute discretion.*

> *If my wife does not survive me, then all of my estate of every kind and description and wherever located, including any devise or bequest which may lapse or become void, I give, devise, and bequeath, absolutely and in fee simple, to by daughters, JANET P. HAMMONS and JILLISA S. HAMMONS, to be divided equally between them.*

Janet and Jillisa sought a declaratory judgment that Rosa had only a conditional power to transfer property and, before doing so, must first provide an accounting of her assets. Rosa argued Janet and Jillisa received a contingent remainder because their ability to take is contingent (1) on there being any property left to take, given Rosa's ability to invade the corpus, and (2) on them surviving Rosa. What type of interest was created here? A life estate with a reminder? If so, what kind of remainder? Does Rosa have the right to sell the property or must she preserve the value of the estate? *Hammons v. Hammons,* 327 S.W.3d 444 (Ky. 2010). ■

CONSIDER 2.4   Determine what types of present and future interests are involved in the following grants. Be sure to classify remainders according to their type, vested (partial or complete divestment) or contingent:

a. "To A for life, then to B"

b. "To A for life, then to B and her heirs"

c. "To B for life, then if A is married, to A"

d. "To A for life, then to B's heirs" (B is alive.)

e. "To A for life, then to B, but if B does not survive A, to C"   ■

Executory Interests

In example **e**, "To A for life, then to B, but if B does not survive A, to C," a third party, C, has an interest that does not fit into any of the categories of future interests discussed so far. C holds an **executory interest**, which is a future interest that is not a remainder but is created in one other than the grantor. An executory interest is not vested at the time the grantor makes the grant and is considered to be vested only when the grantee takes possession (in this example, C). An executory interest usually arises in one of three circumstances. The first occurs when a fee simple determinable or a fee simple subject to a condition subsequent is given to two parties at the same time. For example, a grant "To A, so long as the premises are never used for commercial purposes and if they are so used, then to B" creates a fee simple defeasible interest in A and an executory interest in B. B's interest does not follow a life estate and is not a remainder. Further, B's interest is similar to a right of reversion or right of entry, but B is not a grantor; B's interest must be an executory interest.

FIGURE 2.2 Interrelationship of Present and Future Interests

PRESENT INTERESTS	CREATION LANGUAGE OF FUTURE INTERESTS	FUTURE INTERESTS CREATED IN GRANTOR	OTHERS' FUTURE INTERESTS
Fee simple absolute	"To A" "To A and his heirs"	None	None
Fee tail	"To A and the heirs of his body" "To A and the female heirs of her body" "To A and the heirs of his body and his wife J"	Reversion if no heirs	None
Fee simple determinable	"To A so long as the property is used for church purposes"	Possibility of reverter	Executory interest
Fee simple subject to a condition subsequent	"To A on the condition that the property is used for church purposes"	Right of entry/Power of termination	Executory interest
Life estate/holder	"To A for life"	Reversion	Executory interest Remainder

© Cengage Learning

An executory interest also results when the grantor creates a gap between present and future interests. An example would be "To A for life, then one year after A's death, to B." B does not have a remainder because there is no immediate vesting of B's interest. The one-year gap means that B holds an executory interest.

A third type of executory interest results when the grantor creates some future freehold estate, for example, "To A in 10 years." No present interest is created, and the 10-year interest cannot be classified as a grantor's interest because A is not the grantor. The interest is not a remainder because it does not follow another estate. A holds an executory interest. Figure 2.2 summarizes the future interests and their interrelationships with the present interests.

CONSIDER 2.5   Determine what types of estates are created by the following language and examples:

    a. "To A for life"

    b. "To A and his heirs"

    c. "To A"

    d. "To A and B"

    e. "To A and his female bodily heirs"

    f. "To A provided the premises are never used for the sale of liquor"

    g. "To A on the condition that the premises are never used for a dance hall"

h. "To A so long as the premises are used for church purposes"

i. "To my husband, Ralph, for life"

j. "To the trustee for First County Church so long as the premises are never used for the playing of bingo"

k. "To my granddaughter, Alfreda, and all of Alfreda's female issues"

l. "To my daughter, Sara, for the life of my brother, Sam"

m. "To my granddaughter so long as the premises are used for a library for Whitman College"

n. "To my son, John, and his bodily heirs"

o. "To Jess S. Long, and the children of his body begotten, and their heirs and assigns forever"

p. "To A for the period the land is used for a golf course" _____■

SPECIAL RULES GOVERNING INTERESTS IN LAND

Three rules or doctrines that relate to land interests developed as common law in England still apply to the construction and use of future interests: the Rule in Shelley's Case, the Doctrine of Worthier Title, and the Rule Against Perpetuities.

Rule in Shelley's Case

The **Rule in Shelley's Case** applies to grants made with the language "To A for life, remainder to the heirs of A." If the common law rules were followed, A would have a life estate and A's heirs would have a contingent remainder because heirs are unascertainable until the death of A. The Rule in Shelley's Case requires the merger of the present and future interests. Under this rule, A will have a fee simple absolute. Some states have passed legislation eliminating the effect of the Rule in Shelley's Case so that the present and future interests are not merged. The following case illustrates how the Rule in Shelley's Case and the state statutes abolishing it work.

LUSK V. BROYLES

694 So.2d 4 (Ala. Civ. App. 1997)
Shelley's Rule Applied to Andy and Mary Eliza

FACTS

In 1949, Andy Lusk and Mary Eliza Lusk executed a deed conveying certain rights in 130 acres (Parcel One) to Howard Lusk, who was the direct lineal ancestor of Elizabeth Broyles, Charles Lusk, and Homer Lusk (plaintiffs). The deed from Andy and Mary contained the following language:

KNOW ALL MEN BY THESE PRESENTS: That we Andy Lusk and his wife Mary Eliza Lusk...have this day...given, and granted, and by this instrument do give, grant and convey to...Howard Lusk for

and during his natural life and at his death to the heirs of his body per stirpes
[Parcel One]...

To have and to hold the foregoing described lands unto the said Howard Lusk for and during his natural life, and at his death, the right and title to said lands to vest in the heirs at law of said Howard Lusk....

In 1952, Andy and Eliza Lusk executed a deed conveying to Howard an interest in an additional 40 acres of land (Parcel Two). This instrument is a printed form with typewritten additions to render it complete, and reads as follows:

> *KNOW ALL MEN BY THESE PRESENTS, that we, Andy Lusk and his wife, Eliza Lusk, parties of the first part, in consideration of the sum of One Hundred Dollars and other valuable consideration to us in hand paid by R.H. Lusk during his natural life and then to his bodily heirs, party of the second part, the receipt of which is hereby acknowledged, do hereby grant, bargain, sell and convey unto the said party of the second part, the following described property—to-wit:*
>
> *[Parcel Two]*
>
> *It is the intention of the grantors to convey to said R.H. Lusk only a life estate in and to said lands herein described, with the remainder to his bodily heirs.*
>
> *Together with all and singular tenements, hereditaments, rights, members, privileges, and appurtenances thereunto belonging, or in any way appertaining, to have and to hold the same unto the said party of the second part, and to his heirs and assigns, forever; and we hereby warrant the title to the same against all claims whatever.*

In 1994, one year before his death, Howard executed a deed conveying a fee simple interest in Parcels One and Two to himself and Ruth Lusk, his wife (grantee), as joint tenants with right of survivorship.

Upon Howard's death, the heirs (plaintiffs) filed suit for title to the property. The court found for the heirs, and Ruth Lusk appealed.

JUDICIAL OPINION

Robertson, Presiding Judge

In light of these facts, we must consider whether Howard, at the time he executed the 1994 deed to the grantee, possessed a fee simple title to Parcels One and Two or only a life estate, with remainders vested in his bodily descendants (which include the plaintiffs). The grantee contends that the 1949 and 1952 deeds from Andy and Eliza to Howard conveyed common law estates in fee tail, which by operation of statute are converted to estates in fee simple absolute. The plaintiff heirs argue that the deeds instead conveyed life estates to Howard and remainders in fee simple to the heirs of his body, and that Howard therefore could not have conveyed to the grantee anything more

than his own life estates (which necessarily terminate upon his death).

At common law, when an ancestor by any gift or conveyance took an estate of freehold, and in the same gift or conveyance the estate was limited to his or her heirs in fee or in tail, the words "the heirs" were deemed as a matter of substantive law to be words of limitation and not of purchase. See *Wolfe v. Shelley*, 72 Eng. Rep. 490 (1581). This is the famous, or infamous, principle of property law known as the "Rule in Shelley's Case." However, this rule of the common law is not followed in Alabama because it has been superseded by statute. Section 35-4-230, Ala. Code 1975, provides as follows:

> *Where a remainder created by deed or will is limited to the heirs, issue or heirs of the body of a person to whom a life estate in the same property is given, the persons who, on termination of the life estate, are the heirs, issue or heirs of the body of such tenant for life are entitled to take as purchasers by virtue of the remainder so limited by them.*

Thus, the Rule in Shelley's Case would have operated to convert automatically a conveyance of a life estate to a grantee with remainder in fee to the grantee's heirs into a conveyance of a fee in the grantee. However, 35-4-230 alters this arbitrary rule, requiring that a grantor's intent to sever a grantee's life estate interest from the grantee's heirs' remainder interest be honored according to the express terms of the conveyance.

We now turn to the precise language of the 1949 and 1952 deeds themselves to determine whether they may be classified as expressly giving Howard a life estate and his bodily heirs a remainder. The granting clause of the 1949 deed to Parcel One conveys Parcel One to Howard Lusk for and during his natural life. Moreover, the same clause specifically grants Parcel One "to the heirs of his body *per stirpes*" at Howard's death. This language expressly conveys both a life estate to Howard and a remainder interest in his bodily heirs. Similarly, the granting clause of the 1952 Parcel Two deed, while less artfully drafted, conveys Parcel Two to Howard during his natural life, and conveys a remainder interest to his bodily heirs. Indeed, the grantors' intent to do this is evidenced by their statement in the deed that it was their intention "to convey to said R.H. Lusk *only a life estate* in and to [Parcel Two], with remainder to his bodily heirs." Thus, as a matter of law, in 1994 Howard could have conveyed only his life estates in Parcels One and Two to the grantee, which life estates necessarily terminated upon his subsequent death.

The trial court correctly concluded that the grantee held no interest in Parcels One and Two after Howard's death.

Affirmed.

CASE QUESTIONS

1. How does Ruth Lusk claim an interest?
2. Who are the owners of the property if the Rule in Shelley's Case applies and who are the owners if the Alabama statute applies?
3. What language is controlling in determining the intent of the grantors?

PRACTICAL TIP

Verify rights of those who are in possession of property: How long have they been there? What are the terms of their presence? Are they there by lease rights or some other form of grant? What rights do they have for renewal or options?

Doctrine of Worthier Title

The **Doctrine of Worthier Title** applies to grants with the language, "To A for life, remainder to the heirs of the grantor." Following the general future interest rules, A would have a life estate and the heirs would have either a vested remainder or a contingent remainder (depending on whether the grant was *inter vivos* or testamentary). However, under the Doctrine of Worthier Title, A has a life estate, the heirs have no interest, and the grantor holds a reversion. Legislation in some states has eliminated this doctrine or has permitted courts to determine the grantor's true intent in making the grant.

Rule Against Perpetuities

The basic idea of the **Rule Against Perpetuities (RAP)** is to limit the length of time during which grantors may control the transfer, conveyance, and vesting of land interests. The purpose is to ensure that property ownership and transferability is not tied to the grave. However, the rule is arbitrary and applies only to contingent remainders and executory interests.

Generally stated, the rule provides that an interest is good only if it vests no later than 21 years after the death of the last individual who is part of the group of measuring lives for the grant. As noted earlier, a measuring life is the lifetime of individuals named in the grant. Vesting is the absolute right to receive property without conditions. If the 21-year vesting rule is violated by a grant, the grant is lost and title reverts to the grantor or the grantor's estate to be distributed according to the grantor's desires or according to state law if no will exists.

To understand the application of the rule, it is best to explain each portion of it in the context of an example. Here we will use the grant, made in a will, "To my children for life, remainder to any and all of my grandchildren who reach age 21" as the example for working through the rule's application:

Step One—Determine the type of interest involved. The children have a life estate. The grandchildren are unascertained (more could be born during the children's life estate) and therefore hold a contingent remainder. Furthermore, because there is a potential gap between the life estate of the children and the grandchildren (who must be 21), the grandchildren's interest could be classified as an executory interest.

Step Two—Determine whether the RAP is applicable. Because the RAP applies to both contingent remainders and executory interests, the rule is applicable to the grandchildren's interests.

Step Three—Determine when the interest would vest. The interest would vest when the last grandchild reached age 21.

Step Four—Determine the measuring lives in being. At the time of the will's grant, the children are alive and thus would be the measuring lives for purposes of the 21-year rule for vesting.

Step Five—Determine whether all interests will vest within 21 years after the death of the last measuring life. Consider all possibilities of birth and survival. Upon the death of the last child, there can be no more grandchildren. Thus, the longest it can take for a grandchild's interest to vest is 21 years after the death of the last child. (Gestation periods are not included in the 21 years.)

Step Six—Determine if the RAP is violated. Because all grandchildren will have the interest vested within 21 years after the lives in being of the children, the RAP is not violated and the grant is valid.

Because this complex rule could present difficulties in wills and other transfers, some states have passed statutes eliminating the rule or restricting its harsh effects. A Uniform Statutory Rule Against Perpetuities has been adopted in 24

FIGURE 2.3 Summary of the Creation and Rules of Future Interests

FUTURE INTEREST	RELATED PRESENT INTEREST	SAMPLE LANGUAGE OF CREATION	APPLICABILITY OF RULES
Possibility of reverter	Fee simple determinable	"To A so long as the property is used for church purposes"	Some state limitation and filing requirements
Right of entry/ power of termination	Fee simple subject to condition subsequent	"To A on the condition that the property is used for church purposes"	Some state limitation filing requirements
Reversion	Life estate/fee tail	"To A for life" "To A for the life of B"	Doctrine of Worthier Title
Vested remainder	Life estate	"To A for life, then to B"	Rule in Shelley's Case; Doctrine of Worthier Title
Vested subject to partial divestment	Life estate	"To A for life, then to B's children" (B is alive with two children)	Rule in Shelley's Case; Doctrine of Worthier Title
Vested subject to complete divestment	Life estate	"To A for life, then to B but if B is not married, to C"	
Contingent remainder	Life estate	"To A for life, then to B's children" (B is a bachelor) "To A for life, then if B is married, to B"	Rule Against Perpetuities
Executory interest	Life estate Fee simple defeasible Fee tail	"To A for life, then in 10 years to B" "To B in 10 years"	Rule Against Perpetuities

states, and this uniform rule reduces some of the more complicated provisions in the rule such as its application to nonvested interests. In addition, a number of states have abolished the RAP.[4] The RAP is used less frequently because of the generation-skipping tax imposed by federal tax code on estates.

Even in states without such legislation, the effect of the RAP can be avoided simply by placing a **saving clause** in the will or grant of property. A saving clause either provides an alternative for distribution should the grant violate the rule or provides that the grant is to be interpreted so as to avoid violation of the rule.

Figure 2.3, on p. 29, summarizes the future interests, their related present interests, their language of creation, and the rules that govern them.

The RAP causes a great deal of confusion whenever long-term property interests arise. Violation of the RAP in drafting wills and trusts is the largest area of malpractice litigation for estate-planning attorneys. In the following case, the court deals with the confusion of just the simple issue of whether the RAP applies to lease options.

TEXACO REFINING AND MARKETING, INC. V. SAMOWITZ

570 A.2d 170 (Conn. 1990)
Oil and RAP

FACTS

Sam Samowitz (plaintiff) leased property from Texaco Refining and Marketing (defendants) in 1964. The lease term was 15 years with three options to renew for periods of five years each. The lease gave Samowitz

"the exclusive right, at lessee's option, to purchase the demised premises...at any time during the term of this lease or an extension or renewal thereof, from and after the 14th year of the initial term for the sum of $125,000."

On August 14, 1987, Samowitz gave notice via certified mail to Texaco that he desired to exercise his right to purchase the property. Texaco refused to convey the property on the grounds that the RAP was violated, and Samowitz brought suit. The trial court found for Samowitz and Texaco appealed.

JUDICIAL OPINION

Peters, Chief Justice

The defendants rely on the common law rule against perpetuities as their second argument for the unenforceability of the plaintiff's option to purchase their property. The rule against perpetuities states that

"[n]o interest is good unless it must vest, if at all, not later than 21 years after some life in being at the creation of the interest." The defendants maintain that the option in this case did not vest within the time span mandated by the rule.

The trial court determined that the option in the lease agreement did not violate the rule against perpetuities by construing the lease agreement as a series of discrete undertakings, first for an initial fourteen-year term, and thereafter for each renewal term. Because the option could be exercised only within one of these discrete terms, none of which exceeded twenty-one years in length, the court held that the interest in the option would necessarily vest within the time period specified by the Rule Against Perpetuities.

Whatever might be the merits of the trial court's construction of the lease agreement, we prefer to consider a more basic question: do options in long-term leases fall within the jurisdiction of the Rule Against Perpetuities? Our precedents indicate that the rule applies to an unrestricted option to purchase real property; but not to an option to renew the term of a real property lease. We have not, however, previously considered the relationship between the rule against perpetuities and an option to purchase contained in a long-term commercial lease of real property.

---

[4]Alaska Stat. § 34.27.051 (2012) (RAP is 1,000 years long); Del. Code Ann. tit. 25, § 503 (2011) (110 years); Idaho Code § 55-1522 (2012) (eliminates); 765 Illinois Comp. Stat. Ann. 305/4 (West 2012) (eliminates); S.D. Codified Laws § 43-5-8 (Michie 2012) (eliminates); Wis. Stat. Ann. § 700.16 (2012) (30 years).

The defendants have offered no reason of policy why we should extend the ambit of the rule against perpetuities to cover an option to purchase contained in a commercial lease. "The underlying and fundamental purpose of the rule is founded on the public policy in favor of free alienability of property and against restricting its marketability over long periods of time by restraints on its alienation." An option coupled with a long-term commercial lease is consistent with these policy objectives because it stimulates improvement of the property and thus renders it more rather than less marketable. Any extension of the rule against perpetuities would, furthermore, be inconsistent with the legislative adoption of the "second look" doctrine, pursuant to which an interest subject to the rule may be validated, contrary to the common law, by the occurrence of events subsequent to the creation of the interest.

We therefore conclude that an option to purchase contained in a commercial lease, at least if the option must be exercised within the leasehold term, is valid without regard to the rule against perpetuities. This position is consistent with the weight of authority in the United States.

The plaintiff's option in this case was, therefore, enforceable.

Affirmed.

CASE QUESTIONS

1. What land interest did Samowitz have?
2. What does the lower court's basis for its decision indicate about the Rule Against Perpetuities? Explain.
3. Are options to purchase covered by the Rule Against Perpetuities? Why or why not?

CONSIDER 2.6   Determine whether the Rule Against Perpetuities is violated by the following grant made while the grantor is alive: "To my children for life, remainder to any and all of my grandchildren who reach age 21." Be sure to use the six steps in your analysis. ▪

PRACTICAL TIP

The complexities of real estate law and real estate ownership can be confusing, and mistakes about notions of title and interest can be costly. Be certain sellers, buyers, brokers, and lenders understand the implications of various interests in real estate. Legal advice is often necessary to create, clarify, and interpret the form of ownership.

LAND INTERESTS—NONFREEHOLD ESTATES

Nonfreehold estates are limited in duration and noninheritable. Chapters 9 and 10 include detailed coverage of the nonfreehold estates. In lay terms, a nonfreehold estate is a lease.

ECONOMICS OF LAND INTERESTS

Legal rights and responsibilities in land interests are central in the law of real property. However, these protections ensure property ownership, a critical factor in free-market systems. The boxed excerpt "An Economic Theory of Property Rights" by Richard Posner explains the economic rationale for real property rights and protections.

AN ECONOMIC THEORY OF PROPERTY RIGHTS

Imagine a society in which all property rights have been abolished. A farmer plants corn, fertilizes it, and erects scarecrows, but when the corn is ripe his neighbor reaps it and sells it. The farmer has no legal remedy against his neighbor's conduct since he owns neither the land that he sowed nor the crop. After a few such incidents the cultivation of land will be abandoned and the society will shift to methods of subsistence (such as hunting) that involve less preparatory investment.

This example suggests that the legal protection of property rights has an important economic function: to create incentives to use resources efficiently. Although the value of the crop in our example, as measured by consumer willingness to pay, may have greatly exceeded the cost in labor, materials, and foregone alternative uses of the land, without property rights there is no incentive to incur these costs because there is no reasonable assured reward for incurring them. The proper incentives are created by the parceling out among the members of society of mutually exclusive rights to the use of particular resources. If every piece of land is owned by someone in the sense that there is always an individual who can exclude all others from access to any given area, then individuals will endeavor by cultivation or other improvements to maximize the value of the land.

The creation of exclusive rights is a necessary rather than sufficient condition for the efficient use of resources. The rights must be transferable. Suppose the farmer in our example owns the land that he sows but is a bad farmer; his land would be more productive in someone else's hands. The maximization of value requires a mechanism by which the farmer can be induced to transfer rights in the property to someone who can work it more productively. A transferable right is such a mechanism.

An example will illustrate. Farmer A owns a piece of land that he anticipates will yield him $100 a year, in excess of labor and other costs, indefinitely. The value of the right to a stream of future earnings can be expressed as a present sum. Just as the price of a share of common stock expresses the present value of the anticipated earnings to which the shareholder will be entitled, so the present value of a parcel of land that yields an annual net income of $100 can be calculated and is the minimum price that A will accept in exchange for his property right. Farmer B thinks he could net more than $100 a year from working A's land. The present value of B's higher expected earnings stream will, of course, exceed the present value calculated by A. Assume the present value calculated by A is $1,000 and by B $1,500.

Then the sale of the property by A to B will yield benefits to both parties if the price is anywhere between $1,000 and $1,500. At a price of $1,250, for example, A receives $250 more than

the land is worth to him and B pays $250 less than the land is worth to him. Thus, there are strong incentives for the parties to exchange voluntarily A's land for B's money, and if B is as he believes a better farmer than A, the transfer will result in an increase in the productivity of the land. Through a succession of such transfers, resources are shifted to their highest valued, most productive uses and efficiency in the use of economic resources is maximized.

The foregoing discussion suggests three criteria of an efficient system of property rights. The first is universality. Ideally, all resources should be owned, or ownable, by someone, except resources so plentiful that everybody can consume as much of them as he wants without reducing consumption by anyone else (sunlight is a good, but not perfect example—why?). No issue of efficient use arises in such a case.

The second criterion is exclusivity. We have assumed so far that either the farmer can exclude no one or he can exclude everyone, but of course there are intermediate stages: the farmer may be entitled to exclude private individuals from reaping his crop, but not the government in time of war. It might appear that the more exclusive the property right, the greater the incentive to invest the right amount of resources in the development of the property.

The third criterion of an efficient system of property rights is transferability. If a property right cannot be transferred, there is no way of shifting a resource from a less productive to a more productive use through voluntary exchange. The costs of transfer may be high to begin with; a legal prohibition against transferring may, depending on the penalties for violation, make the costs utterly prohibitive.

DISCUSSION QUESTIONS

1. How do property rights serve to protect and "incent" landowners?

2. Why is it sometimes more economically efficient for a property owner to transfer property?

3. What are the three criteria of an efficient system of property rights?

Note: For the answer to the Posner's question on the exclusivity of sunlight, see Chapter 3.
From Richard Posner, *An Economic Analysis of Law.* Little, Brown and Company, 1973. Assigned to Aspen Law and Business, a division of Aspen Publishers, Inc. Reprinted with permission of the author.

CAUTIONS AND CONCLUSIONS

Knowledge of this chapter will be most useful in situations where land titles are being transferred. In the case of a transfer, all parties (buyers, sellers, brokers, agents, and financiers) need to analyze the transfer by checking the following issues:

1. What type of interest does the seller hold?
2. What restrictions are on the transfer? Could the land title be lost?
3. Does the seller have the right and ability to transfer the property? Can the seller transfer full title or simply a lesser interest, such as a life estate?
4. What type of language is being used in the conveyance? Is the buyer getting a fee simple absolute or a life estate? Are restrictions being imposed upon the buyer?
5. What are the implications of other parties' interests in the property in the future?

Land records (discussed in Chapter 14) provide the parties with answers to most of the above questions. Research the answers before any land transaction is completed.

KEY TERMS

contingent remainder, 23
Doctrine of Worthier Title, 28
executory interest, 24
fee, 17
fee simple, 17
fee simple absolute, 17
fee simple defeasible, 17
fee simple determinable, 17
fee simple subject to a condition
    subsequent, 17

fee tail, 21
freehold, 17
inter vivos, 18
life estate, 21
life tenants, 22
nonfreehold estates, 31
possibility of reverter, 17
power of termination, 18
remainder, 22
reversion, 22

right of entry, 18
Rule Against Perpetuities (RAP), 28
Rule in Shelley's Case, 26
saving clause, 30
testamentary, 18
vested remainder, 23
vested remainder subject to
    complete divestment, 23
vested remainder subject to partial
    divestment, 23

CHAPTER PROBLEMS

1. Tom and Doyle Proctor were deeded 20 lots of land in a Florida subdivision with the understanding that they would construct an incinerator on the property. The deed contained no specifics on the incinerator or the Proctors' responsibilities. The developer claims a right of reentry. The Proctors claim the land is theirs as a fee simple estate. Who is correct? *Proctor v. Inland Shores, Inc.*, 373 S.E.2d 268 (Ga. 1988).

2. Buck Ryan Ramsey and Elizabeth Ramsey, his wife, transferred the mineral rights in one of their tracts of land to Joe Grizzle for, "as long thereafter as operations, as hereinafter defined, are conducted upon said land with no cessation for more than ninety (90) consecutive days." Operations were defined to include: "drilling, testing, completing, reworking, recompleting, deepening, plugging back or repairing of a well in search for or in an endeavor to obtain production of oil, gas, sulphur or other minerals, excavating a mine, production of oil, gas, sulphur or other mineral, whether or not in paying quantities." Mr. Grizzle did not begin any kind of operations for over 90 days, and Mr. Ramsey began extracting oil from the tract. Mr. Grizzle filed suit to stop Mr. Ramsey for a violation of his ownership rights? Who is correct? *Ramsey v. Grizzle*, 313 S.W.3d 498 (Tex. App. 2010).

3. Kinney Land and Cattle Company conveyed, by warranty deed, to the state of Kansas 790 acres of land for use as a state park. There was a paragraph in the deed called "Clause of Reversion," which required the state to build and maintain a lake of a minimum of 150 acres. The failure to maintain the lake caused title to "revert to the grantor, successors or assigns." From 1934 to 1970, the state maintained a lake on the property, but the lake was never 150 acres in size. Shareholders of Kinney Land and Cattle have brought suit to quiet title to them in the 790 acres. Will they be given title? *Kinney v. State of Kansas and Kansas Fish and Game Commission*, 710 P.2d 1290 (Kan. 1985).

4. In each of the following, determine what type of present and future interests are created, and also

the applicability of any of the three rules: the Rule in Shelley's Case, the Doctrine of Worthier Title, and the Rule Against Perpetuities.

(G = grantor; L/E = life estate; rem = remainder)

a. G→L/E→   A
→ L/E   A's widow
Rem to A's children at the death of the widow

b. G→L/E→   A

c. G→   A and her heirs on the condition that liquor never be sold on the premises

d. G→L/E→   A→Rem to B and his heirs if B shall survive A

Suppose A (during her lifetime) gave D the right to use the land for 10 years. What type of estate would be created?

e. G→   A so long as liquor is not sold on the premises

Suppose G later left all his interest to A. What type of estate would be created?

f. G→   A when A reaches age 25

g. G→L/E→   A (80 years old) →L/E→ children for life
Rem to grandchildren

h. G→L/E→   A→B and his heirs but if B shall predecease A→C

i. G→L/E→   A→ heirs of A

j. G→L/E→   A→B if B lives to attain the age of 30 years (B is 5 years old)

5. W. E. Collins executed and delivered to the Church of God of Prophecy a warranty deed with the following language:

This transfer or deed is made with the full understanding that should the property fail to be used for the Church of God, it is to be null and void and property to revert to W. E. Collins or heirs.

What types of interests were created in the deed? Do any of the interests violate the Rule Against Perpetuities? *Collins v. Church of God of Prophecy*, 800 S.W.2d 418 (Ark. 1990).

6. Ann Harris, 61, living in Fairfax County, Virginia, experienced brain and spinal cord injuries that rendered her paraplegic and resulted in a seizure disorder. Because she was unable to work, she was facing foreclosure on her home, valued at $600,000. Ms. Harris faced foreclosure on her home because she could no longer meet the terms of a promissory note in the amount of $351,070.51. To prevent fore-

closure, she agreed to refinance her home by transferring her property to her son. The lender had stipulated that, in order to refinance the property, the home must be transferred to Mr. Harris because of Ms. Harris's low income. A deed, dated August 29, 2004, gave Ann's son, Richard Harris, title to the property, after he obtained a loan to pay off the mortgage lien. A month prior to the deed from Ann to Richard, a lease agreement, titled "LEASE" at the top, was entered into between Mr. Harris and his mother by which he purported to convey to her a life estate in the property.

Ann then applied for Medicaid long-term care eligibility ("LTC Services"), which would have enabled her to remain at home while receiving medical services. In March 2005, a social worker began the authorization process. The social worker denied Ann LTC Services because she had recently conveyed property that was an uncompensated asset transfer. Ms. Harris appealed that decision and presented as evidence the amended lease agreement that granted her a life estate in the property. The Assistant Attorney General argued that the agreement did not create a life estate for Ms. Harris, only a lease. Ann and Richard argued that the payoff of the mortgage loan was the compensation and that she received a life estate for the remaining value in her home. In Virginia, however, any freehold, such as a life estate, must be in writing and by deed or will. What interest does Ann hold? What precautionary measures should parties take from this case? *Harris v. Finnerty*, 74 Va. Cir. 551, 2006 WL 3157556 (Va. Cir. Ct. 2006).

7. Richard J. Long and Mary Long, his wife, conveyed by warranty deed dated September 30, 1949, to the Pompey Fire Department a parcel of land (called P-1). The deed, which was properly recorded in the Onondaga County Clerk's Office on November 15, 1949, stated that the grant of the parcel was for the purpose of "erecting thereon a fire house." The deed also included the following language:

In the event that the said premises are no longer used to house a fire department, then and in that event the land and building erected thereon is to revert to Richard J. Long and Mary Long, or their heirs and assigns.

Shortly after the conveyance, a firehouse was erected on P-1. The building is a two-story structure with a cinder-block first floor and a wood-frame second floor. The first floor contains three large bays to house fire trucks and equipment. The building was used continuously from 1950 to 1985 to house the Fire Department. In 1984, the Fire Department acquired another parcel of land (P-2) located about 300 yards from P-1. P-2 had an elementary school

them. The lower court found for the Causbys, and the U.S. government appealed.

JUDICIAL OPINION

Douglas, Justice

The United States relies on the Air Commerce Act of 1926. Under those statutes the United States has "complete and exclusive national sovereignty in the air space" over this country. They grant any citizen of the United States "a public right of freedom of transit in air commerce through the navigable air space of the United States."

And "navigable air space" is defined as "airspace above the minimum safe altitudes of flight prescribed by the Civil Aeronautics Authority." And it is provided that "such navigable airspace shall be subject to a public right of freedom of interstate and foreign air navigation." It is, therefore, argued that since these flights were within the minimum safe altitudes of flight which had been prescribed, they were an exercise of the declared right of travel through the airspace. The United States concludes that when flights are made within the navigable airspace without any physical invasion of the property of the landowners, there has been no taking of property. It is ancient doctrine that at common law ownership of the land extended to the periphery of the universe—*Cujus est solum ejus est usque ad coelum.* But that doctrine has no place in the modern world. The air is a public highway, as Congress has declared. Were that not true, every transcontinental flight would subject the operator to countless trespass suits. Common sense revolts at the idea. To recognize such private claims to the airspace would clog these highways, seriously interfere with their control and development in the public interest, and transfer into private ownership that to which only the public has a just claim.

But the general principle does not control the present case. For the United States conceded on oral argument that if the flights over respondents' property rendered it uninhabitable, there would be a taking compensable under the Fifth Amendment. It is the owner's loss, not the taker's gain, which is the measure of the value of the property taken. Market value fairly determined is the normal measure of the recovery. And that value may reflect the use to which the land could readily be converted, as well as existing use. If, by reason of the frequency and altitude of the flights, respondents could not use this land for any purpose, their loss would be complete. It would be as complete as if the United States had entered upon the surface of the land and taken exclusive possession of it.

The path of glide for airplanes might reduce a valuable factory site to grazing land, an orchard to a vegetable patch, a residential section to a wheat field. Some value would remain. But the use of the airspace immediately above the land would limit the utility of the land and cause a diminution in its value.

We have said that the airspace is a public highway. Yet it is obvious that if the landowner is to have full enjoyment of the land, he must have exclusive control of the immediate reaches of the enveloping atmosphere. Otherwise buildings could not be erected, trees could not be planted, and even fences could not be run. The principle is recognized when the law gives a remedy in case overhanging structures are erected on adjoining lands. The landowner owns at least as much of the space above the ground as he can occupy or use in connection with the land. The fact that he does not occupy it in a physical sense—by the erection of buildings and the like—is not material. As we have said, the flight of airplanes, which skim the surface but do not touch it, is as much an appropriation of the use of the land as a more conventional entry upon it. We would not doubt that if the United States erected an elevated railway over respondents' land at the precise altitude where its planes now fly, there would be a partial taking even though none of the supports of the structure rested on the land. The reason is that there would be an intrusion so immediate and direct as to subtract from the owner's full enjoyment of the property and to limit his exploitation of it. While the owner does not in any physical manner occupy that stratum of airspace or make use of it in the conventional sense, he does use it in somewhat the same sense that space left between buildings for the purpose of light and air is used. The superadjacent airspace at this low altitude is so close to the land that continuous invasions of it affect the use of the surface of the land itself.

The airplane is part of the modern environment of life, and the inconveniences which it causes are normally not compensable under the Fifth Amendment. The airspace, apart from the immediate reaches above the land, is part of the public domain. We need not determine at this time what those precise limits are. Flights over private land are not a taking, unless they are so low and so frequent as to be a direct and immediate interference with the enjoyment and use of the land. We need not speculate on that phase of the present case. For the findings of the Court of Claims plainly establish that there was a diminution in value of the property and that the frequent, low-level flights were the direct and immediate cause. We agree with the Court of Claims that a servitude has been imposed upon the land.

Affirmed.

CASE QUESTIONS

1. What type of business did the Causbys operate and how did the low-flying planes affect that business?
2. Can the use of airspace diminish the value of the surface of the land?
3. What does the court establish as the standard for determining whether a plane is flying too low?

CONSIDER 3.1 Dobbins is a 143-acre military base located approximately fifteen miles northwest of Atlanta in Cobb County, Georgia. Kim Goodman is the owner of property adjoining Dobbins. Ms. Goodman filed suit against the federal government for an uncompensated taking of her property because supersonic jets frequently pass over her property. The F–22, F–16, and F/A–18 are the only types of aircraft that have been stationed at Dobbins in the recent past that are capable of reaching supersonic speeds, and those aircraft do not, except in emergencies, travel at such speeds within the airspace controlled by the Dobbins tower. Aircraft within that airspace are not allowed to travel faster than 250 knots, which is well below the speed of sound.

When an aircraft takes off from Dobbins, its pilot is required under regulation and standard departure procedures to execute the maximum rate of climb in order to reduce aircraft noise over the Fair Oaks neighborhood, where Ms. Goodman lives. Planes passing over Ms. Goodman's property require between 5000 and 7000 feet of departure roll prior to takeoff and therefore become airborne long before reaching the end of the 10,000-foot runway. All planes departing Dobbins are required by regulation to execute the maximum rate of climb following takeoff in order to mitigate noise impacts on the Fair Oaks neighborhood and thus do not travel along the three-degree slope required for arriving aircraft. An air traffic controller at the base testified that most flights departing from Dobbins would pass over the Fair Oaks neighborhood at an elevation of more than 500 feet.

With the exception of Christmas and New Year's Day, when the base is closed, and absent extraordinary circumstances, Dobbins operates seven days a week from 7:00 a.m. until 11:00 p.m. However, different planes have been added to the base operations, including B-52s. In addition, the base does have periodic spurts of intense activity. For example, the base has become a training facility for pilots of all types of military aircrafts. During the period following September 11, 2001, more F-16s were stationed at the base to respond to observation needs. In September 2005, Dobbins became a staging base for Hurricane Katrina rescue and relief operations, which resulted in many additional takeoffs and landings.

Ms. Goodman says that while she did give the government an easement over her property for the takeoff pattern, the additional uses and operating hours entitle her to additional compensation because of the decreased valuation of her property from all the takeoffs and landing. Applying the principles of the *Causby* case, is she entitled to additional compensation? Explain your answer. *Goodman v. U.S.*, 100 Fed. Cl. 289 (2011).

Other uses of airspace can interfere with the land of another. For example, when the eaves of a building or branches from a tree located on one parcel of land hang over onto another landowner's parcel of land, there is a taking of airspace. In the *Causby* case, the court mentioned that a remedy is available for overhang. The property owner affected by the overhang can bring suit for a court order requiring the removal of the eaves or branches, and in some states is even permitted to unilaterally end the invasion by clipping the tree branches.

What Air Rights Can Be Transferred?

The second aspect of air rights deals with the ability of landowners to transfer interests in the air located above their property. The air above property is divided into two areas, the **column lot** and the **air lot**. The column lot comprises everything between the earth's surface and an imaginary plane 23 feet above the surface, and the air lot comprises everything above the 23-foot plane. It is possible for landowners to transfer some interest in their column or air lot.

For example, both the column lot and the air lot could be sold for the construction of a large building. Those constructing the building need only have title to or an easement (see Chapter 4) for small segments of the land surface for the placement of beams or the steel girder foundations of the building. In these types of transfers of column and air lots, landowners retain title to the surface but have conveyed their air rights or a portion thereof, as with Tiffany's and the Trump tower.

There are other examples of large buildings constructed through the use of airspace. In Chicago, the Prudential Mid-America building is built in both the air and column lots above the Illinois Central Terminal. The 52-story Prudential Tower is built in the column and air lots above a shopping mall and restaurants in Boston. In New York, the 59-story Met Life building is built in the column and air lots above Grand Central Station. These examples illustrate that dividing air and surface ownership enables maximum use of real property. Transfers of air rights have become so common that many states are reviewing the Model Airspace Act for possible adoption to govern these transfers. In New York, there is a full regulatory scheme for "transferable development rights" or "TDRs," which governs the declaration and transfer of air rights. Before transferring air rights, the landowner must create a legally defined air space and then convey the interest by deed. Air space deeds are recorded and carry title insurance (see Chapter 13 for more information on deeds and title insurance).

The construction and sale of condominiums is another example of the use and transfer of airspace. When buyers purchase condominiums, they are actually purchasing the airspace located between the walls of their particular units. Ground or surface ownership is not conveyed as part of the title, but the condominium owners do hold real property interests. (See Chapter 11 for a complete discussion of condominiums.)

The Right to Light

Corresponding to the ownership of air as part of a real property interest is the ownership of light. In this era of energy-technology development, the issue of who owns the light is a critical one. Suppose the following hypothetical situation has occurred:

Anna and Beverly are neighbors. Anna has installed a series of solar collectors on the roof of her home. The collectors are positioned so that Anna obtains maximum efficiency in the use of the sun. However, Beverly has decided to plant several trees for backyard shade and within three years of planting, the now-tall trees are interfering with the collection of sunlight by Anna's collectors.

In the absence of any statutory right and under common law, Anna has no right to have the trees removed or seek damages for the blockage of the light unless Anna can establish that Beverly's conduct was malicious, done with the intent of obstructing light from the collectors.

The law has been evolving with a distinction between the right to light and the right to access to the sun for purposes of producing solar power. In the early days of solar technology, a few states, such as New Mexico (N.M.S.A. §§ 47-3-1 *et seq.*) and Wyoming (W.S.A. §§ 34-22-101 *et seq.*), granted a statutory right to sunlight. Under these early statutes, the first user of light for solar energy purposes acquired the right to unobstructed continued use. Now most states, while not moving to a right to sunlight, have **solar easement laws** that protect easements for access.[1] There a number of city ordinances that now have setback requirements that have the effect of prohibiting adjoining landowners from constructing buildings on their properties that would interfere with the sunlight on adjoining properties.[2] California applies the law of easements to solar easements that meet the requirements of the statute (Cal. Civ. Code 801.5). Some states have encouraged zoning as a tool to be used to incorporate solar access considerations.[3] Other states have enacted statutes that permit solar energy users to petition administrative review boards when adjoining landowners refuse to negotiate solar access easements.[4] Arizona, California, Colorado, Florida, Hawaii, Indiana, Iowa, Massachusetts, Nevada, Utah, and Wisconsin make deed restrictions or covenants that prohibit or restrict the installation of solar energy systems void and unenforceable (Cal. Civ. Code § 714).[5] Presently, proposed uniform laws on solar rights and solar energy systems are being developed for use by state legislators in regulating this area of land ownership. However, many states still prohibit the acquisition of a solar easement by a prescriptive taking (a form of adverse possession that occurs through use—see Chapter 4 for more information on prescriptive easements).[6]

---

[1]California, Colorado, Florida, Georgia, Idaho, Illinois (although *O'Neill v. Brown,* 609 N.E.2d 835 [Ill. 1993] held that Illinois was not a solar easement state despite the Illinois Comprehensive Solar Energy Act), Kansas, Kentucky, Maine, Maryland, Minnesota, Missouri, Montana, New Jersey, North Dakota, Ohio, Tennessee, Virginia, and Wisconsin.

[2]Ashland, Or., Mun. Code §18.70.040 (2009); Boulder, Colo., Rev. Code 1981 § 9-9-17(d) (Supp. 2009); and Soldiers Grove, Wis., Ordinances § 2.06 (1980).

[3]Connecticut, Massachusetts, Minnesota, Oregon, and Utah. Note: Oregon affords considerable authority to planning commissions in treating rights for solar systems.

[4]Iowa and Wisconsin.

[5]California also encourages installation of solar devices in new home construction. California Public Resources Code § 25603.5.

[6]Colo. Rev. Stat. § 38-32.5-101 (2008); Conn. Gen. Stat. Ann. § 47-25 (West 2004); Ga. Code Ann. § 44-9-2 (2002); Ky. Rev. Stat. Ann. § 381.220 (2011); Mass. Gen. Laws Ann. ch. 187, § 1 (West 2003); R.I. Gen. Laws § 34-7-3 (1995); Wash. Rev. Code Ann. § 64.04.160 (West 2005); and W. Va. Code Ann. § 2-1-2.

In addition to the property protections that state laws have provided for solar power, the federal government has created a statutory system of incentives to encourage solar power development. The Energy Improvement and Extension Act of 2008 extended the tax credits and incentives for solar energy production. The federal government is also encouraging building construction that maximizes natural light use. The U.S. Green Building Council's 2009 Rating System rewards points toward LEED (Leadership in Energy and Environmental Design) Certification for building designs that meet natural daylight illumination requirements. Natural lighting via skylights and windows means less dependence on electricity for light. However, neighboring buildings or trees limit the ability to construct buildings with natural lighting. Property rights have not yet evolved to a point of balancing the rights to the use of light to conserve energy use with the rights of ownership that include land use that can affect others' access to light. Airspace is now at a premium as its uses become increasingly important in developing alternative energy sources.[7]

CONSIDER 3.2   In 1979, the California Solar Shade Control Act took effect. During 1984–1985, John and Cecilia Zipperer built their solar home in Santa Clara with county permits. In 1991, the county of Santa Clara acquired the adjoining parcel of land, with the trees already on it, and it placed that land in a Parks Reserve. Since 1991, those trees have been growing at the rate of 10 to 15 feet per year. By 2004, the trees were about 100 feet taller than when the county acquired the land.

In 1997, the Zipperers' solar system began to malfunction because the trees on the county's land interfered with the sunlight reaching their solar panels. Despite numerous requests from the Zipperers, and notwithstanding verbal promises by "certain officials and certain individuals that this situation would be corrected," the county did not trim or remove the trees.

In 2002, Santa Clara County adopted an ordinance exempting itself from the Solar Shade Control Act. In 2004, the Zipperers filed suit against the county under the Solar Shade Control Act. Should the Zipperers win? What would they win? *Zipperer v. County of Santa Clara*, 133 Cal.App.4th 1013, 35 Cal.Rptr.3d 487 (Cal. App. 2005).

The courts have undertaken some protection for solar rights through the use of property theories. In *Prah v. Maretti*, 321 N.W.2d 182 (Wis. 1982), the court held, "The law of private nuisance is better suited to resolve landowners' disputes about property development in the 1980s than is a rigid rule which does not recognize a landowner's interest in access to sunlight."

At common law, the **Doctrine of Ancient Lights** provided protection for the use of light. Under the doctrine, anyone who used the light for an uninterrupted period of 20 years was entitled to protection for use of that light, and obstruction was prohibited. However, this doctrine has been rejected by American courts, with most of them following the ruling in the following landmark light-obstruction case.

---

[7]Troy A. Rule, "Airspace in a Green Economy," 59 *UCLA L. Rev.* 270 (2011).

FONTAINEBLEAU HOTEL CORP. V. FORTY-FIVE TWENTY-FIVE, INC.

114 So.2d 357 (Fla. 1959)
Shade Over Miami

FACTS

The Fontainebleau, a luxury hotel, was constructed in Miami facing the Atlantic Ocean in 1954. In 1955, the Eden Roc, another luxury hotel, was constructed adjoining the Fontainebleau and also facing the Atlantic Ocean. Shortly after the construction of the Eden Roc in 1955, the Fontainebleau undertook the construction of a 14-story addition to extend 160 feet in height and 416 feet in length running from east to west. During the winter months, from about two in the afternoon and for the remainder of the day, the shadow of the addition would extend over the cabana, swimming pool, and sunbathing areas of the Eden Roc.

The Eden Roc (Forty-Five Twenty-Five Corp., plaintiff/appellee) brought suit against the Fontainebleau Hotel Corp. (defendant/appellant) to stop construction of the addition after eight stories had been built. The Eden Roc alleged the construction would interfere with its sunlight, cast a shadow, and interfere with the guests' use and enjoyment of the property. The Eden Roc further alleged the construction of the addition was done with malice. The trial court found for Eden Roc. Fontainebleau appealed.

JUDICIAL OPINION

Per Curiam

It is well settled that a property owner may put his own property to any reasonable and lawful use, so long as he does not thereby deprive the adjoining landowner of any right of enjoyment of his property which is recognized and protected by law, and so long as his use is not such a one as the law will pronounce a nuisance.

No American decision has been cited, and independent research has revealed none, in which it has been held that—in the absence of some contractual or statutory obligation—a landowner has a legal right to the free flow of light and air across the adjoining land of his neighbor. Even at common law, the landowner had no legal right, in the absence of an easement or uninterrupted use and enjoyment for a period of 20 years, to unobstructed light and air from the adjoining land.

... [I]t is universally held that where a structure serves a useful and beneficial purpose, it does not give rise to a cause of action, either for damages or for an injunction even though it causes injury to another by cutting off the light and air and interfering with the view that would otherwise be available over adjoining land in its natural state, regardless of the fact that the structure may have been erected partly for spite.

We see no reason for departing from this universal rule. If, as contended on behalf of plaintiff, public policy demands that a landowner in the Miami Beach area are [*sic*] to refrain from constructing buildings on his premises that will cast a shadow on the adjoining premises, an amendment of its comprehensive planning and zoning ordinance, applicable to the public as a whole, is the means by which such purpose should be achieved.

The record affirmatively shows that no statutory basis for the right sought to be enforced by plaintiff exists. The so-called Shadow Ordinance enacted by the City of Miami Beach at plaintiff's behest was held invalid in *City of Miami Beach v. State ex rel. Fontaine bleau Hotel Corp.* It also affirmatively appears that there is no possible basis for holding that plaintiff has an easement for light and air, either express or implied, across defendant's property, nor any prescriptive right thereto—even if it be assumed, *arguendo*, that the common-law right of prescription as to "ancient lights" is in effect in this state. And from what we have said heretofore in this opinion, it is perhaps superfluous to add that we have no desire to dissent from the unanimous holding in this country repudiating the English doctrine of ancient lights.

Reversed.

AFTERMATH: The Eden Roc solved its problem by building a second swimming pool that allowed guests to experience sun and swimming, without the Fontainebleau shadow. Interestingly, in an era in which skin cancer has become an issue, both pools, shaded and unshaded, enjoy guest use, the sun worshippers in the sunny pool and the sun precautionaries in the shaded one. The Marriott Corporation purchased the Fontainebleau, and in 2008 it had a grand re-opening after a remodeling that restored its original 1950s decor.[8]

---

[8]Ruth La Ferla, "Flamboyance Gets a Facelift," *New York Times*, November 2, 2008, SS, p.1.

CASE QUESTIONS

1. Will the court recognize the Doctrine of Ancient Lights? Does the presence of spite make any difference in recognition of a right to light? See *Carlson v. Calusa Golf Inc.*, 498 So.2d 461 (Fla. 1986).

2. Will the court recognize an easement for the sunlight?

3. What remedy does the court suggest? Be sure to recall this case during the discussion of nuisance.

PRACTICAL TIP

Before buying, selling, or listing property, ask the following questions and find answers:

1. *Does the home have solar reliance, passive or active?*
2. *Are the solar components in compliance with the CC&Rs?*
3. *Do the CC&Rs permit installation of solar devices?*
4. *Are there restrictions in the CC&Rs on expansion of solar units?*
5. *Are there obstructions or potential obstructions for the solar units (growing trees; possible construction)?*
6. *Does an easement for light exist?*
7. *Can I get an easement for light?*
8. *Are there statutory protections for light access?*
9. *Is there backup power for the solar panels and system?*

Parties who want to maintain rights to light should do so through private agreements with adjoining landowners who will give them easements for such rights. Some mortgage lenders that are approving loans for properties with solar panels will require solar easements before the mortgage money will be advanced to the borrower. However, in spite of the need for such easements, many parties do not take the time to protect their rights. Recent surveys reveal that 95 percent of all owners of solar energy systems have not obtained easements for the protection of sunlight.

An easement for light should carefully specify the extent of the easement with the following information covered: State the purpose of the easement (for solar panels, windows, or a swimming pool) because the intent of the parties helps courts if interpretation is ever necessary; include the times of day when the sun is to be unobstructed so that rights are clear and the burden on the adjoining land is limited; and list the types of structures (height, width, and so on) that cannot be constructed. Before drafting the agreement, check for compliance with any statutory requirements and/or restrictions. Because light obstructions can come from larger structures located some distance away, a landowner may need easements from more than one adjoining or adjacent landowner.

Homeowners' associations and the covenants, conditions, and restrictions (CC&Rs) for subdivisions should address the issues of type, attachment, and aesthetics of solar units. However, the trend is to rein in homeowners' associations in their exercise of power over homeowners who are seeking permission for solar devices. The associations can ask for reasonable aesthetic changes but cannot impose requirements that make the solar panels cost-ineffective.[9]

ETHICAL ISSUE

While there is no right to light unless some statutory protection applies, individuals and their property values are affected greatly when an adjoining landowner obstructs light. While the obstruction may not interfere with solar access, the obstruction nonetheless affects the character of the property and perhaps its value. What are the ethical issues in a situation in which a new landowner or current owner of a neighboring property undertakes a construction project that interferes with the light of surrounding property owners? How should the conflict between the right to use their property and the rights of adjoining landowners be resolved? Are the issues different when, as in

---

[9]*Palos Verdes Homes Ass'n. v. Rodman*, 182 Cal. App. 3d 324, 227 Cal. Rptr. 81 (1986)

the *Eden Roc* case, the effect will be a loss of business and strength for the competitor/adjoining landowner? Evaluate the following statement, "All landowners assume the risk of changes in the use of surrounding property."

Other Renewable Energy Sources and Ownership Rights

The development of other renewable energy sources has resulted in new air rights issues. Wind energy, through large and small turbines, faces challenges similar to solar energy in that there are competing interests for the airspace wind turbines occupy. Commercial wind energy projects have faced opposition on environmental grounds (disruption of migratory bird populations), national security grounds because of their disruption of military radar systems, and on property rights grounds because the higher the wind turbine, the greater its efficiency, but that intrusion into airspace affects others' rights. In addition, back-to-back turbines, often from competing owners, result in loss of efficiency and energy production.

A wind turbine creates a "wake" of turbulent air that can reduce the wind energy productivity of other turbines behind it for up to half a mile. The wake from an upwind turbine reduces the energy productivity and profitability of a downwind turbine.

Because of these ownership issues, there are already statutes taking effect with regard to wind turbines. There are laws that require a set-back area, or wind buffer zone, to prevent the wake problem. (Minn. Pub. Util. Comm'n, Jan. 11, 2008; http://www.windaction.org/documents/14797). Under these types of laws, wind turbines cannot be placed within quarter-mile-wide bands of property along boundary lines when there is wind energy development on an adjacent parcel.

Other laws affecting wind energy parallel the early solar panel laws; that is, state laws prohibit local governments from passing laws that prevent the development of wind energy in their areas. (Wis. Stat. Ann. § 66.0401)

CONSIDER 3.3 The *Boston Globe* describes it as follows: "It is the largest renewable-energy project ever proposed in the United States, 170 wind turbines able to churn out 420 megawatts of power—enough for a city of 200,000 people—and churn up controversy pitting one environmentalist against another."[10] A dispute over the placement of a wind farm six miles off Cape Cod, Massachusetts, has resulted in a battle among and between homeowners, environmentalists, technology companies, and even the Army Corps of Engineers. Homeowners oppose the wind farm because their view of the ocean changes dramatically. However, others note that the presence of the renewable energy source could help to wean the United States from oil dependence. Long-time researcher and author Wendy Williams has noted that the wind farms are a solution for those who are "actively seeking ways to meet their energy growth requirements without further polluting the atmosphere."[11] But former newscaster, the late Walter Cronkite, once a homeowner in the area,

---

[10]Robert Preer, "Coastal Worries Fuel Local Support for Wind Farm." *Boston Globe,* January 6, 2005, http://www.boston.com.

[11]"Energy collaborative argues for wind farm," Friday, February 14, 2003. http://www.capewind.org.

argued, "Our national treasures should be off limits to industrialization."[12] John Flicker, president of National Audubon Society, has said, "When you look at a wind turbine, you can find the bird carcasses and count them. With a coal-fired power plant, you can't count the carcasses, but it's going to kill a lot more birds."[13] What protections do the wind farm developers have? What protections do homeowners have? What ethical issues do you see in this dispute?[14] ▬▬▬▬■

Right to a View

Several recent cases have raised the issue of the right to a view. Many resort homes, condos in high-rises, homes located near mountains, oceans, or other scenic vistas carry a premium price because of the view from the home's interior. The construction of wind turbines has been met with opposition from landowners who file suit on the basis that the turbines obstruct their view. Without covenants and/or easements, landowners in these premium properties generally do not have any rights when construction on adjoining properties results in obstruction of their view. However, in the following case, the court discusses the issue of "right to a view" when a government entity takes the view away.

BOROUGH OF HARVEY CEDARS V. KARAN

40 A.3d 75 (N.J. Supr. 2012)
The $375,000 View

FACTS

Harvey and Phyllis Karan owned beachfront property on Long Beach Island, New Jersey. The Army Corps of Engineers (Corps) constructed a dune on their property that was part of a system of dunes that will eventually run the length of the ocean side of Long Beach Island. The formerly-spectacular ocean view from the Karans' house (defendants) is now partially blocked by the twenty-two-foot high dune, which occupies one-third of their land. However, their house is now safer from storm damage because the dune was constructed.

The Borough of Harvey Cedars (plaintiff) brought a condemnation action against the Karans. Following a jury trial, the court entered a judgment of $375,000 for the Karans, and the Borough appealed.

JUDICIAL OPINION

Reisner, Judge

The central question on this appeal is whether public construction of an enormous oceanfront beach dune, for which plaintiff condemned an easement on defendants' land, conferred a special benefit on defendants' beach front property in Harvey Cedars.

During the ensuing condemnation trial, both sides' experts agreed that, prior to the taking, defendants' property was worth $1.9 million. However, the jury heard starkly opposing testimony concerning the dune's impact on defendants' ocean and beach view and the diminution in value attributable to the dune easement. Moliver, plaintiff's real estate expert, insisted that any loss of view was *de minimus* [sic] and was only worth $300 in compensation. During cross-examination,

---

[12]Mark Alan Lovewell, "Cronkite Withdraws Ad Against Turbines," http://www.mvgazette.com. August 28, 2003; Katharine Q. Seelye, "Windmills Sow Dissent for Environmentalists," *New York Times*, June 5, 2003, p. C1.

[13]Carl Levesque, "For the Birds: Audubon Society Stands Up in Support of Wind Energy," December 14, 2006, American Wind Energy Association, http://www.awea.org; Greg Chang, "Bird lovers fighting killer windmills," *Arizona Republic*, November 13, 2005, p. A33.

[14]Currently, the Massachusetts environmental agency has given the wind project the green light (http://www.boston.com: "Cape wind project clears state hurdle," March 30, 2007).

however, he admitted that he had never actually gone into defendants' house or out on their second-floor deck in order to see the impact of the dune on their view.

Defendant's expert, Robert Gagliano, testified that the loss of view was significant and reduced the value of the property by $500,000. He also testified that, prior to the construction of the dune, defendants had a strip of private beach on their property, whereas that land was now occupied by a large dune that they could not use for recreation. That added to the property's loss in value.

Mr. Karan gave detailed testimony concerning the 1973 construction of his family's dream house at the shore, with its glass wall facing the ocean, oceanfront decks, and sweeping views of the beach, shoreline and ocean. He also eloquently described the way the twenty-two-foot high dune interfered with that view, including blocking the beach and surf view from the second-floor deck, and transforming the water vista from the dining room into a view of a "wall of sand." The jury was taken to the property for a site visit, during which they observed the view from defendants' house.

The protection afforded to defendants' property by the dune construction is a classic example of a general benefit. While defendant's property may be benefited in somewhat "greater … degree" than its inland neighbors, because it is closer to the ocean and therefore in somewhat greater danger of incurring storm damage, that is not a legally cognizable "special benefit" for purposes of valuation in a condemnation case. The dune construction did not confer special benefits on defendants' land. The project did not permit any new or more lucrative use of the property.

The settlements with other owners were irrelevant to the valuation of defendants' property. The fact that some other homeowners were unwilling to subject themselves to litigation in order to obtain meaningful compensation, or were altruistic enough to give up a portion of their property for the common good, does not mean that defendants were not entitled to pursue just compensation for their property. Contrary to plaintiff's argument, a party's agreement to sign over an easement under threat of condemnation does not represent a compulsion-free transaction between a willing buyer and a "willing" seller.

We find no basis to set aside the $375,000 verdict as excessive.

Affirmed.

CASE QUESTIONS

1. What is the relationship between a benefit received and something taken away in determining a property owner's rights to compensation?
2. What is the relevance of settlements of other landowners with the Borough in determining valuation?
3. How much is the loss of a view worth on oceanfront property?

ETHICAL ISSUE

In 1997, Donald Trump began construction of his Riverside South project in New York City on a railroad yard located between Lincoln Towers and the Hudson River. The first two towers (of 16 planned) blocked the views of the Lincoln Towers residences. One resident noted, "Can you imagine what this man is taking away? Can you imagine somebody taking away the moon?" Another said, "All of a sudden, here was this thing looming up against the sky. You couldn't see the sky. I felt anger—that someone could be allowed to take away your beauty for money." Those in the Lincoln Towers apartments with views of the Trump project have trouble selling their units and overall have fewer prospects view their units. The price difference between a Trump-facing apartment and one facing the river is $50,000. Evaluate the ethical issues in development projects like Trump's.

SURFACE AND SUBSURFACE RIGHTS

This section deals with the second part of this chapter's opening quote, which is the ownership of subsurface rights. Ordinarily, landowners own to the center of the earth, so that mineral rights are included in fee simple absolute ownership. However, landowners are free to convey their subsurface rights as liberally as their air rights. When subsurface rights are conveyed independently of surface rights, there are two different landowners. The owner of the surface rights cannot affect the ownership rights of the subsurface owner. Likewise, the subsurface owner cannot destroy the surface and thereby destroy the surface owner's interest.

Mineral Rights: Oil and Gas Ownership
Nature of Oil and Gas

Oil and gas are petroleum found in liquid and gaseous forms, respectively, beneath the earth's surface. Because oil and gas are not solid like other minerals and will flow from one location to another very readily, this type of property interest presents legal issues not encountered in connection with other subsurface mineral rights.

When oil was first discovered in 1859 at Titusville, Pennsylvania, the courts applied the standard Blackstone adage of "he who owns the surface owns what is beneath the surface as well." However, when a well is drilled and oil and gas are brought to the surface, it is impossible to tell whether they came from directly beneath the landowner's surface or were drawn from another pool under adjoining land. Figure 3.2 illustrates the possible conflicting claims of oil and gas ownership between adjoining landowners.

FIGURE 3.2 Oil and Gas Ownership Issues

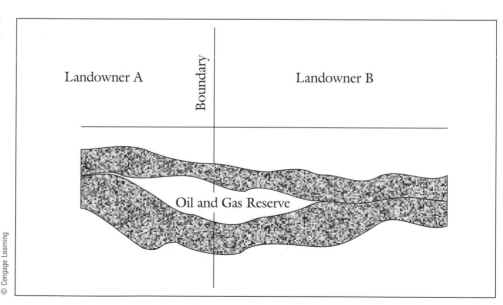

© Cengage Learning

Under Blackstone's rule of subsurface ownership, a landowner pumping oil and gas would be liable to other nearby landowners in the event the well drew oil from reservoirs that extended beneath property owned by others. Such a taking would constitute trespass and would discourage development of the resource. As a result, the courts developed a different rule of ownership for oil and gas rights called the **Rule of Capture**. Simply stated, the rule gives the owner of a tract of land title to all the oil and gas produced by wells located on his or her land even though some of the oil and gas may have migrated from adjoining lands or the well is actually taking oil and gas from a reservoir that stretches across a boundary line onto another's property. This form of ownership protects the driller from liability for trespass so long as the drilling is conducted from his or her property. However, drilling at an angle would be a physical trespass and is not protected under the Rule of Capture.

Two theories are followed under the Rule of Capture. So-called **ownership states** follow the Rule of Capture but provide that the landowner is the owner of the mineral rights that can be lost only if someone else first captures the oil and gas through drilling. The **nonownership states**—which include California, Louisiana, Oklahoma, and Wyoming—provide that no one owns the oil and gas until it has been captured. The difference between these two theories is simply the status of the rights prior to capture. Once capture has occurred, the rights are identical and vest at the same time under either theory.

The Rule of Capture has limits. For example, the rule does not apply after the gas is first captured by someone and stored in a subsurface or surface area. In other words, once the gas or oil has been captured, someone else cannot tap into the storage area and claim ownership under the Rule of Capture. The rule applies to drilling of oil and gas in their natural as opposed to stored states. Also, the Rule of Capture does not apply to what are referred to as "enhanced recovery operations," or "sweeping." These types of processes involve, for example, using high-pressure water systems to drive oil reservoirs from beneath another's property to sweep them into reservoirs on your property so as to capture this oil and gas once it is beneath your land. Again, the Rule of Capture applies to oil and gas located naturally beneath your land or acquired through drilling from your land, and not to recovery initiated by artificial shifting of the minerals. Some states permit recovery for trespass against those who use these "sweeping" techniques to recover oil and gas. Others will not permit a trespass action for "sweeping" if it can be shown that the adjoining landowner would not respond to a reasonable and fair proposal for recovery of the oil and gas. The idea behind this immunity for trespass is to encourage the development of the resource.

The **Doctrine of Correlative Rights** is another limitation on the Rule of Capture that imposes a good-faith requirement that no action will be taken that will cause the destruction of the oil and gas beneath the surface to prevent recovery by adjoining landowners. In other words, landowners cannot use the Rule of Capture to take action that prevents others from capturing the resources beneath their property. This type of action could occur if one landowner allowed a well to burn and drain the oil and gas from an adjoining landowner's subsurface reservoir.

A final limitation on the Rule of Capture is government regulation. Both state and federal governments have oil and gas conservation laws to both prevent waste of these resources and control the extent of drilling. For example, well-spacing regulations limit the number of wells that can be erected according to either a per-acre basis or the amount of space between wells. Also, particularly at the federal level, production limitations control the amount of drilling that can be done. Often referred to as **prorationing rules**, they establish limits on daily, weekly, or monthly production. Prorationing rules can be established either to prevent the early exhaustion of a well or to meet fluctuations in the price of oil and gas in the international markets.

Classification of Oil and Gas Interests

States vary in their positions as to whether oil and gas rights are real or personal property and what type of property interests they are. For example, some states treat oil and gas rights as a *profit a prendre*, or simply the right to enter the land of another and take a part or product of that land (see page 84). Other states have characterized these interests as fee simple determinables that end upon the Rule of Capture ownership by another. Other states have established a separate set of rules for oil and gas rights and the determination of issues such as trespass and suits to resolve title issues. The classification of oil and gas rights as real or personal property also varies and may largely be determined by taxation statutes that control whether the rights would be taxed as real or personal property under the state's revenue system.

> **PRACTICAL TIP**
>
> *Mineral rights are complex and require special details in the sale or lease agreement. The following are questions to be answered: Who owns the mineral rights? Will ownership be exclusive? Can the surface be used? What is included in the mineral rights? Oil? Gas? How and when is payment made? How much will the payments be? What happens upon default?*

Types of Oil and Gas Interests

Acquiring the right to drill for oil and gas can take several different forms. For example, many oil firms will refer to the fact that they own a **fee interest**. This form of ownership simply means that the company owns both the surface and subsurface rights. In other words, the firm has a fee simple in the property where it is drilling.

Other firms own the **mineral rights** or a **mineral interest**. This form of ownership simply means that the subsurface rights have been severed from the surface and air rights, and the company has the right to use the surface to capture the minerals but does not own the surface. This form of ownership grants only an easement on the surface to bring in the equipment necessary for drilling. In Louisiana, this form of ownership is called a **mineral servitude**.

A commonly used term, the **oil and gas lease** is a form of ownership in which a portion of the mineral interest is assigned, usually in exchange for a royalty or share of the profits. A lease is the right to use the surface and remove the oil and gas. The lease could be an interest in perpetuity or one that ends when oil and gas are no longer produced. For example, suppose that farmer Adam has fee simple title to his farm and the subsurface rights. Farmer Adam could sell a mineral interest to ExxonMobil. ExxonMobil could then lease the interest to Xavier Oil Company in exchange for a share of the profits. Farmer Adam could also simply lease his mineral interest to ExxonMobil, and ExxonMobil could use the surface to recover the oil and gas.

The oil and gas lease may also be used to create a **royalty interest**, which is a share of the oil produced from the land. Royalty interests are usually stated in fraction form, such as one-eighth of production. Different amounts and names for royalty interests are used according to whether a landowner, lessee, or mineral interest is involved. Royalty interests are not real property interests. They are very similar to the personal property interest in the form of book royalties.

The various forms of ownership of oil and gas rights have many combinations, and the only limitations seem to be the creativity of those involved in the proposals. Any agreement for oil and gas rights should cover the issues of rights and responsibilities when land ownership is divided in this way between surface and subsurface interests. Damage to the surface by the owner of the subsurface rights is not unusual. But the lease or transfer of subsurface rights can include a provision that the subsurface owner either repair the surface or compensate the surface owner.

Creation of Oil and Gas Interests

Oil and gas interests are considered to be real property interests for purposes of the **Statute of Frauds**, and these interests, regardless of type, must be in writing. The documents should specify the types of minerals that are included in the subsurface transfer if more than oil and gas are conveyed. For example, in *Watt v. Western Nuclear, Inc.*, 462 U.S. 36 (1983), the U.S. Supreme Court reversed all prior gravel cases (pertaining to federal lands) that held that gravel was not a mineral and ruled that gravel is indeed a mineral. In a follow-up decision, *BedRoc Ltd., LLC v. U.S.*, 541 U.S. 176 (2004), the court held that sand and gravel were not valuable minerals in applying state law in a particular interpretation of federal mineral rights. This type of complexity in the judicial rulings is why the parties' agreement is so important in avoiding litigation.

Geothermal Energy

Geothermal resources present an interesting subsurface dilemma because of the difficulty of classifying these resources. **Geothermal energy** consists of steam in rock-surrounded pockets, so some states classify it as a water resource and use their water laws to determine ownership and other rights. Other states classify geothermal resource as an energy resource similar to oil or coal and treat it as a mineral. The federal government classifies geothermal energy as a mineral (*Rosette Inc. v. United States*, 277 F.3d 1222 [10th Cir. 2002] and 25 U.S.C. § 2102[a]). Some states (such as Idaho) have declared that geothermal resources are neither minerals nor a water resource and have developed a specialized scheme of regulation for this interest in real estate. The transfer of geothermal interests requires careful attention to state and federal laws and exact detail in the conveyance.

The federal government also has statutes that affect geothermal energy. The Geothermal Steam Act of 1970 (30 U.S.C. §§ 1001 *et seq.*) regulates permits and use of this subsurface resource, and the Geothermal Energy Research, Development, and Demonstration Act (30 U.S.C. §§ 122 *et seq.*) and Energy Improvement and Extension Act of 2008 (12 U.S.C. § 5201) provide funding and tax credits for development of these resources. Much of this resource is found naturally on federal lands. However, geothermal energy projects use large mirrors to heat water in tubes in order to produce steam that is then a source of energy. The size of these geothermal production facilities is often met with resistance by neighbors because of the appearance and encumbrance of the projects.

Water Rights

The rights to take water from and use water on land are real property interests. The rules of law on the nature and the extent of a landowner's right to use water vary depending on both the type of water source and the geographic region. The rules of law that developed on water rights largely evolved more in the West, where water was scarce. However, Eastern jurisdictions are now facing similar issues because of droughts and localized shortages, particularly in coastal regions where cities face both increased demand and diminished supply because of saline presence. For example, the 68-million-gallon per day diversion of Roanoke River water to meet water supply needs of Virginia Beach, 85 miles away, was a contentious and litigious issue. Likewise, Alabama, Florida, and Georgia have been in litigation as Georgia tries to maintain metropolitan Atlanta's water supply as Alabama and

Florida raise ecological, energy, navigation, power, and recreation interests that result in their downstream locations when Georgia diverts water.[15]

Water Rights: Type of Water

Water rights vary according to the type of water body involved. The first type is surface or navigable waters, or those that flow. Navigable water is defined as water that could be used for navigation regardless of whether it is so used, including natural and artificial lakes, rivers, and streams. Ownership of navigable waters lies with the states as trustees for the public, subject to any federal rights and programs such as dams and water conservation systems built by the Army Corps of Engineers. Two theories of water rights are applicable to these bodies of waters: the Riparian Doctrine and **Prior Appropriation Doctrine**. In the past, most states east of the Mississippi have followed the reasonable use Riparian Doctrine, a doctrine that worked for water-use rights as long as water was plentiful. However, with increased population and new technological processing demands for water, there is a realization of a need for a shift in approach because water is not as readily available. The arid Western states have followed the Prior Appropriation Doctrine.[16] Some states follow a combination of the two theories, with the expectation that more Eastern states will be shifting their approaches to water rights as more conflicts such as in Virginia and Atlanta arise.[17]

The **Riparian Doctrine** is based on sharing, and the Prior Appropriation Doctrine is based on "first in time is first in right," or the first to use the water has first claim to it. Figure 3.3 summarizes and compares the two doctrines. (The figure deals only with water use rights and not with the actual ownership of the land [riverbed] beneath the water.) As noted, water shortages throughout the United States are resulting in increased litigation that finds federal involvement as states sue other states for appropriating water that results in shortages downstream. Federal entities such as the Army Corps of Engineers (hydropower dams) and the Environmental Protection Agency (EPA) (protection of species damaged by reductions in water flows) are intervening in these cases in order to litigate federal rights in interstate rivers and streams. *South Carolina v. North Carolina*, 130 S.Ct. 854 (2010) and *In re MDL-1824 Tri-State Water Rights Litigation*, 644 F.3d 1160 (11th Cir. 2011) *cert.* denied — S.Ct. —, 2012 WL 485675 (2012).

Water Rights: Ownership of Riverbeds

The title to the riverbeds or land beneath surface water is different from the water rights. The state may follow what is known as the **centerline rule**, which provides that the streambed is owned to the center by the abutting landowners.

Water Rights: Private Ponds

Many landowners have private ponds that are within their property boundaries. These ponds are part of their real property interest, and they have all rights in them with the exception of any waters passing through them from upper to lower lands.

---

[15]Robert Haskell Adams, "Water, Climate Change, and the Law: Integrated Eastern States Water Management Founded on a New Cooperative Federalism," 42 *Envtl. L. Rep. News & Analysis* 10433 (2012).

[16]The tax credits were extended as part of the Emergency Economic Stabilization Act, and the tax credits for geothermal were extended again until 2016.

[17]Alaska, Arizona, Montana, Nevada, Utah, and Wyoming.

FIGURE 3.3 Water Rights

THE COMMON LAW RULES OF RIPARIAN WATER RIGHTS COMPARED WITH AND DISTINGUISHED FROM THE DOCTRINE OF PRIOR APPROPRIATION

COMMON LAW RIPARIAN RULES	PRIOR APPROPRIATION DOCTRINE
1. THE DISTINGUISHING FEATURES OF THE COMMON LAW RIPARIAN RULES ARE EQUALITY OF RIGHTS AND REASONABLE USE—There is no priority of rights; the reasonable or permitted use by each is limited by a similar use in every other riparian.	1. THE DISTINGUISHING FEATURE OF THE PRIOR APPROPRIATION DOCTRINE IS FIRST IN TIME IS FIRST IN RIGHT—There is no equality of rights and no reasonable use limited by the rights of others.
2. To be a riparian, one needs only to be an owner of riparian land. Riparian land is land that abuts or touches the water of a lake or stream.	2. To be a prior appropriator, one must do four things: (a) have an intent to appropriate water, (b) divert the water from the source of supply, (c) put such water to a beneficial use, and (d) when applicable, follow the necessary administrative procedures.
3. No one can be a riparian who does not own riparian land.	3. One need not own land to be a prior appropriator. There is one exception—in some jurisdictions such as Arizona, if the appropriation is for irrigation purposes then the appropriator must own arable and irrigable land to which that water right is attached.
4. Riparian lands are lands bordering the stream and within the watershed. Under the natural flow theory, a riparian cannot use water on nonriparian lands. Under the reasonable use theory, a riparian may use water on nonriparian lands if such use is reasonable.	4. The prior appropriator may use the appropriated water on riparian and nonriparian lands alike. The character of the land is quite immaterial.
5. Under the common law riparian rules, the use of water for natural purposes is paramount and takes precedence over the use of water for artificial purposes. Natural uses include domestic purposes for the household and drinking, stock watering, and irrigating the garden. Artificial purposes include use for irrigation, power, mining, manufacturing, and industry.	5. The prior appropriation doctrine makes no distinction between use of water for natural wants and for artificial and industrial purposes.
6. The riparian owner, simply because he owns riparian land, has the right to have the stream of water flow to, by, through, or over his land under the riparian rights doctrine.	6. An owner of land, simply as such owner, has no right to have a stream of water flow to, by, through, or over his land under the prior appropriation doctrine.
7. The riparian has the right to have the water in its natural state free from unreasonable diminution in quantity and free from unreasonable pollution in quality.	7. The prior appropriator has the right to the exclusive use of the water free from interference by anyone, reasonable or unreasonable.
8. The rights of the riparians are equal.	8. The rights of the appropriators are never equal.
9. The basis, measure, and limit of the riparian's water right is that of reasonable use (unless natural flow states: limit use to not interrupting the natural flow).	9. The basis, measure, and limit of the water right of the prior appropriator is the beneficial use to which he has put the water. He has no right to waste water. If his needs are smaller than his means of diversion, usually a ditch, then his needs determine his right. If his ditch is smaller than his needs, then the capacity of his ditch determines his right.
10. The doctrine of riparian rights came to this country from the common law of England, although it seems to have had its origin in French law.	10. The doctrine of prior appropriation is statutory in our Western states, although its origin seems lost in antiquity.

Water Rights: Ground Water

Still another type of water is *percolating* or *groundwater*. This type of water includes all subsurface water other than water that flows in underground streams. The waters included in this group are Artesian waters, aquifers, underground lakes or pools, and waters that seep, ooze, or filter from an unknown source. Sometimes called *groundwater rights* or *overlying rights*, rights in these waters are governed by both the Riparian Doctrine and the Prior Appropriation Doctrine; however, the application of the rules differs because of the nature of the water source.

In the following case, the court discusses the rights of riparian landowners versus government regulation and use of river water.

IN RE OPERATION OF MISSOURI RIVER SYSTEM LITIGATION

421 F.3d 618 (8th Cir. 2005)
When the Mighty Missouri Is Not Enough

FACTS

The Missouri River originates in Montana and runs through North Dakota, South Dakota, Nebraska, Iowa, Kansas and Missouri before emptying into the Mississippi River. In its natural state, the river subjected the surrounding basin to extensive flooding every spring. With the Flood Control Act of 1944 (FCA), Congress authorized the construction of a dam and reservoir system on the upper river to control the flooding. The FCA also envisioned that the reservoirs would provide water for local irrigation projects and steady release into the river during the summer months to support downstream navigation, hydroelectric power generation and lake recreation. The FCA delegated construction and management of the reser and voir system to the Army Corps of Engineers.

A persistent drought in the Missouri River basin has led to a recurring conflict between upstream and downstream water users. In 2002, the Corps planned to release water from Lake Oahe into the river to maintain downstream navigation throughout the summer. South Dakota, fearing a negative impact on the seasonal fish spawn in Lake Oahe and on the reservoir's sport fishing industry, obtained an injunction preventing the Corps from lowering any reservoir in South Dakota until after spawning season. When the Corps decided to lower Lake Sakakawea instead, North Dakota obtained a similar injunction. Not to be outdone, Montana obtained an injunction to prevent releases from Fort Peck Lake. In response, Nebraska obtained an injunction ordering the Corps to make the required releases to support navigation as called for by the Corps' Master Water Control Manual.

The parties appealed all of the injunctions.

JUDICIAL OPINION

Gruender, Circuit Judge

Environmental groups have attempted to force the Corps to operate the system to produce more "natural" river flows to benefit the protected species. The operation of the reservoir system brings the Corps within the provisions of the Endangered Species Act (ESA). Under the ESA, if a government agency concludes that a proposed action may "jeopardize the continued existence" of any protected species or adversely affect its critical habitat, the agency must prepare a Biological Assessment.

[Pursuant to the ESA],the Corps obtained a Biological Opinion finding that the Corps' proposed operation of the reservoir system was likely to jeopardize the continued existence of the three endangered species: the pallid sturgeon, a fish listed as endangered since 1990; the least tern, a migratory bird listed as endangered since 1985; and the piping plover, a migratory bird listed as threatened since 1985.

In an attempt to support downstream water-use interests despite the continuing drought in the basin, the Corps released a draft Annual Operating Plan for 2003 that did not incorporate flow changes recommended in the biological findings.

The states of Missouri and Nebraska and the Nebraska Public Power District argue that the duty of the Corps under the FCA is to maintain river flow sufficient to support uninterrupted downstream navigation. Nebraska and NPPD also argue that the Corps' flow release plan is in conflict with the FCA minimum-flow requirement. Blaske Marine, Conoco-Phillips Company, Ergon Asphalt & Emulsions, Inc., Magnolia Marine Transport Company, Midwest

Terminal Warehouse Company, Inc., MO-ARK Association and Missouri River Keepers argue that a supplemental EIS is required for a contingent summer low flow that the Corps still has the discretion to implement. Finally, the Mandan, Hidasta and Arikara Nation contend that the Corps must operate Lake Sakakawea for the economic benefit of the Nation's members.

The FCA imposes no duty to maintain a minimum level of downstream navigation independent of consideration of other interests. This Court has already addressed thoroughly the balance of interests under the FCA. The FCA does not set forth what level of river flow or length of navigation season is required to make navigation "dominant" over a "secondary" interest, such as recreation. Instead, "the courts can review the Corps's decisions to ensure that it considered each of these interests before making a decision," but "the Act does not provide … a method of deciding whether the balance actually struck by the Corps in a given case is correct or not."

Appellees North Dakota and South Dakota argue that because damage to the recreation industry would have a more dramatic negative economic impact than would damage to the navigation industry, recreation should receive special priority. Nothing in the text or legislative history of the FCA suggests that Congress intended the priority of interests under the FCA to shift according to their relative economic value.

The Corps' balancing of water-use interests is in accordance with the FCA. Therefore, we affirm the grant of summary judgment to the Corps on this claim.

Affirmed.

CASE QUESTIONS

1. Describe the various parties in the case and their interest in the water flow.
2. What is the role of the Army Corps of Engineers? How much power does the Corps have in making decisions?
3. What is the effect of a drought on the Corps' planned releases of water?

CONSIDER 3.4 Shanty Hollow Corporation was issued a permit by the New York State Department of Environmental Conservation to withdraw water from Schoharie Creek for purposes of its snowmaking equipment. Shanty Hollow operates a winter sport recreational area. The Catskill Center for Conservation and Development, property owners along the creek, and anglers brought suit against both the state and Shanty Hollow for excessive withdrawal of water from the creek. What is the result under the Riparian Doctrine? In contrast, what would be the result under the Prior Appropriation Doctrine? *Catskill Center v. NY Dept. of Environ.*, 642 N.Y.S.2d 986 (1996).

Water Rights at the Crossroads

The water rights area of real estate law has proven to be a dynamic one over the past few years because of the role of environmental regulation (see Chapter 20 for more information on environmental regulations on water use). Some scholars have written that the prior appropriation doctrine is often at odds with environmental goals and have encouraged government intervention regardless of water rights. Many state and local authorities have intervened in water-use and water-level issues because of public safety or issues surrounding the flora and fauna in or around the water. Currently, as noted earlier and in the *Missouri River* case, courts are balancing environmental interests with those of adjoining landowners concerned about drought effects due to too-low levels and erosion damage due to levels that are too high.

Development projects that involve water (see Chapter 21 for more information on development) have been subjected to municipal and county reviews for project approval. California courts have noted that the traditional lines of legal reasoning on water rights and use have been changed to broader ones that are based primarily on whether the water use is "reasonable or wasteful" (*City of Barstow v. Mojave Water Agency*, 75 Ca. Rptr.2d 477 [1998]). In issuing permits for use of public waters, states follow either a best-possible-use or maximum-benefit doctrine in making decisions on who will gain access to these waters. Both doctrines require state officials to weigh the economic interests of parties with conflicting interests in land and water use. In many situations, there are emotional issues as developers seek water rights as adjoining landowners oppose their development projects (see Chapter 21 for more discussion of economic development issues and interests).

Thompson on Real Property summarizes the changes in water rights and their relationship to real property as follows: "Although the general rule is that water rights are a species of real property, that designation refers to the right of access to the water while it is in its natural state. Once the right is exercised and water is reduced to possession, it may be considered personal property of the water-right holder. As such, it may become an article of commerce." So the distinction between the traditional laws of real property and the new trends is that the proposed commercial use of water once it is captured pursuant to the legal rights can be regulated by various government entities. These entities now grapple with those who sell their riparian rights, for example, to nonriparians. The issue becomes one of deciding whether to honor the real property origins of water rights and the reliance landowners have placed on that system or to intervene for the sake of allocation of a scarce resource, protection of the environment, and easier commercial transfers. In resolving the issue, states, local governments, and courts have asked whether cities should have higher priorities than the countryside, how federal and state authority applies in water disputes, whether government can intervene for protection of water quality, whether water can be moved to address shortages and allocation proposals and who will do the moving, and what the legal status of water rights should be. For example, in *Long v. Great Spring Waters of America, Inc.*, 2002 WL 31813096 (Cal. App.), the California court dealt with a commerce issue and water use.[18] Since at least 1930, Great Spring extracted water from federal forestlands to bottle and sell for profit. Great Spring had laid pipes, dug trenches, and developed wells with dimensions substantially exceeding those contained in the special use permit. One of Great Spring's bottled-water competitors brought suit on a number of grounds, including the failure of the California regulators to properly control water use. The court held that no permit was required for extraction of water from federal land, and since Great Spring had appropriated the water before anyone else, state law required recognition of its rights. Since the time of the case, California has modified water rights to control such exclusive use.

Water shortages were not an issue at the time the traditional water rights were developed. Intervention may be necessary, and the law is adjusting to permit intervention with private property rights.

ETHICAL ISSUE

Evaluate Great Spring's approach to its water supply. Apply principles of ethics to determine the effects of its business model.

---

[18]The case focused on the antitrust issues in exclusive bottling rights, something that intersected with the water rights.

PROTECTION OF PROPERTY RIGHTS

Trespass

Trespass is defined as the intentional interference with landowners' reasonable use and enjoyment of their property. General examples of trespass include parties' walking across another property owner's land or placing objects on another's land, although trespass can also arise from indirect objects intentionally set in motion by the trespasser. For example, if one landowner were to dam water so that it flooded an adjoining landowner's property, there has been a trespass. Even the simple act of opening shutters so that they extend across a boundary line to an adjoining property owner's land is an act of trespass. Bullets fired across the land of another also constitute trespass. In one unique trespass case, a child hurled a brick at a neighbor. When the neighbor reached across the boundary line and grabbed the child, he committed not only the torts of assault and battery but also that of trespass. A property owner who hires contractors to work on his or her land but does not verify boundaries is responsible if those contractors cross onto neighboring properties and cause harm, such as the destruction of trees.

CONSIDER 3.5   Burlington Northern & Santa Fe Railway Company (BNSF) operated the Livingston Rail Yard in Livingston, Montana, for nearly a century until its closure in 1987. BNSF's operations released hydrocarbons and toxic solvents into the air above the neighboring properties. Several adjacent property owners have filed suit against BNSF for trespass. Could they recover? Why or why not? *Burley v. Burlington Northern & Santa Fe Railway Company,* 273 P.3d 825 (Mont. 2012).

Sometime before 1962, King County built and operated a storm sewer system. Upon its incorporation in 1995, the city of Shoreline took over operation of the system. In 2004, Crystal Lotus acquired two lots in Lake Forest Park, near the Shoreline–Lake Forest Park border. A pipe from the Shoreline stormwater system discharges stormwater onto a lot adjacent to Crystal's lots. Crystal's lots had a swamp-like condition, which an expert concluded was caused by the discharge of stormwater onto the adjacent lot. Crystal filed suit against the city for trespass. The trial court granted summary judgment in favor of the city. On appeal, what should the court decide? *Crystal Lotus Enterprises Ltd. v. City of Shoreline,* 274 P.3d 1054 (Wash. App. 2012).

Nuisance

"Use your own property in such a manner as not to injure that of another [*Sic vere tuo et alienum non laedas*]." **Nuisance** is the unreasonable interference with others' use and enjoyment of their property. Bad odors and excessive noise are generally thought of as nuisances. Pollutants from a factory causing property damage and medical problems can constitute a nuisance. "A nuisance may be merely a right thing in the wrong place, like a pig in the parlor instead of the barnyard."[19]

Nuisances can be classified as private, public, or frequently a cross between the two. A nuisance affecting one property owner or a small group of property owners

---

[19]*Village of Euclid, Ohio v. Amber Realty Co.,* 272 U.S. 365 (1926).

is a private nuisance. For example, a restaurant's storage of garbage bins behind a store is a private nuisance affecting the immediate neighbors. However, the burning of used car materials to salvage metal can create smoke and smells affecting an entire community and would thus be labeled a public nuisance.

The remedies for nuisance usually fall into one of two categories: monetary or equitable relief. **Monetary relief** is compensation for illness and medical expenses or compensation for the reduction in property values because of the nuisance. For example, destruction of plants or paint caused by pollutants would be compensable. **Equitable relief** is injunctive relief where a court orders the nuisance-creating party to cease the nuisance activity. This injunctive relief is used sparingly, because in some circumstances the result will be the closing of a business. In determining whether injunctive relief will be afforded, courts balance the extent of the property owner's harm against the beneficial aspects of the wrongdoer's conduct. The following landmark case deals with a nuisance issue, particularly in balancing landowners' interests against the economic interests of others as well as the interests of the public in a suit where the landowners have requested injunctive relief.

SPUR INDUSTRIES, INC. V. DEL E. WEBB DEVELOPMENT CO.

494 P.2d 700 (Az. 1972)
Moooving to the Nuisance

FACTS

Spur Industries operated a cattle feedlot near Youngtown and Sun City, Arizona (communities 14 to 15 miles west of Phoenix). Spur had been operating the feedlot since 1956, and the area had been agricultural since 1911.

In 1959, Del E. Webb began development of the Sun City area, a retirement community. Webb purchased the 20,000 acres of land for about $750 per acre. In 1960, Spur began an expansion program in which its operating area grew from 5 acres to 115 acres.

At the time of the suit, Spur was feeding between 20,000 and 30,000 head of cattle, which produced 35 to 40 pounds of wet manure per head per day, or over one million pounds per day. And despite the admittedly good feedlot management and good housekeeping practices by Spur, the resulting odor and flies produced an annoying if not unhealthy situation as far as the senior citizens of southern Sun City were concerned. There is no doubt that some of the citizens of Sun City were unable to enjoy the outdoor living which Del Webb had advertised. Del Webb was faced with sales resistance from prospective purchasers as well as strong and persistent complaints from the people who had purchased homes in that area. Nearly 1,300 lots could not be sold. Webb then filed suit alleging Spur's operation was a nuisance because of flies and

odors constantly drifting over Sun City. The trial court enjoined Spur's operations and Spur appealed.

JUDICIAL OPINION

Cameron, Vice Chief Justice

The difference between a private nuisance and a public nuisance is generally one of degree. A private nuisance is one affecting a single individual or a definite small number of persons in the enjoyment of private rights not common to the public, while a public nuisance is one affecting the rights enjoyed by citizens as a part of the public. To constitute a public nuisance, the nuisance must affect a considerable number of people or an entire community or neighborhood.

Where the injury is slight, the remedy for minor inconveniences lies in an action for damages rather than in one for an injunction. Moreover, some courts have held, in the "balancing of conveniences" cases, that damages may be the sole remedy.

Thus, it would appear from the admittedly incomplete record as developed in the trial court, that, at most, residents of Youngtown would be entitled to damages rather than injunctive relief.

We have no difficulty, however, in agreeing with the conclusion of the trial court that Spur's operation was an enjoinable public nuisance as far as the people in the southern portion of Del Webb's Sun City were concerned.

It is clear that as to the citizens of Sun City, the operation of Spur's feedlot was both a public and a private nuisance. They could have successfully maintained an action to abate the nuisance. Del Webb, having shown a special injury in the loss of sales, had a standing to bring suit to enjoin the nuisance. The judgment of the trial court permanently enjoining the operation of the feedlot is affirmed.

A suit to enjoin a nuisance sounds in equity and the courts have long recognized a special responsibility to the public when acting as a court of equity.

In addition to protecting the public interest, however, courts of equity are concerned with protecting the operator of a lawfully [*sic*], albeit noxious, business from the result of a knowing and willful encroachment by others near his business.

In the so-called "coming to the nuisance" cases, the courts have held that the residential landowner may not have relief if he knowingly came into a neighborhood reserved for industrial or agricultural endeavors and has been damaged thereby:

Plaintiffs chose to live in an area uncontrolled by zoning laws or restrictive covenants and remote from urban development. In such an area plaintiffs cannot complain that legitimate agricultural pursuits are being carried on in the vicinity, nor can plaintiffs, having chosen to build in an agricultural area, complain that the agricultural pursuits carried on in the area depreciate the value of their homes. The area being primarily agricultural, and opinion reflecting the value of such property must take this factor into account. The standards affecting the value of residence property in an urban setting, subject to zoning controls and controlled planning techniques, cannot be the standards by which agricultural properties are judged.

*** a party cannot justly call upon the law to make that place suitable for his residence which was not so when he selected it. ***.*

Were Webb the only party injured, we would feel justified in holding that the doctrine of "coming to the nuisance" would have been a bar to the relief asked by Webb, and, on the other hand, had Spur located the feedlot near the outskirts of a city and had the city grown toward the feedlot, Spur would have to suffer the cost of abating the nuisance as to those people locating within the growth pattern of the expanding city.

There was no indication in the instant case at the time Spur and its predecessors located in western Maricopa County that a new city would spring up, full-blown, alongside the feeding operation and that the developer of that city would ask the court to order Spur to move because of the new city. Spur is required to move not because of any wrongdoing on the part of Spur, but because of a proper and legitimate regard of the courts for the rights and interests of the public.

Del Webb, on the other hand, is entitled to the relief prayed for (a permanent injunction), not because Webb is blameless, but because of the damage to the people who have been encouraged to purchase homes in Sun City. It does not equitably or legally follow, however, that Webb, being entitled to the injunction, is then free of any liability to Spur if Webb has in fact been the cause of the damage Spur has sustained. It does not seem harsh to require a developer, who has taken advantage of the lesser land values in a rural area as well as the availability of large tracts of land on which to build and develop a new town or city in the area, to indemnify those who are forced to leave as a result.

Having brought people to the nuisance to the foreseeable detriment of Spur, Webb must indemnify Spur for a reasonable amount of the cost of moving or shutting down. It should be noted that this relief to Spur is limited to a case wherein a developer has, with foreseeability, brought into a previously agricultural or industrial area the population which makes necessary the granting of an injunction against a lawful business and for which the business has no adequate relief.

It is therefore the decision of this court that the matter be remanded to the trial court for a hearing upon the damages sustained by the defendant Spur as a reasonable and direct result of the granting of the permanent injunction. Since the result of the appeal may appear novel and both sides have obtained a measure of relief, it is ordered that each side will bear its own costs.

Affirmed in part, reversed in part, and remanded for further proceedings consistent with this opinion.

AFTERMATH: Del Webb and Spur settled the case with Spur moving and Del Webb paying the costs of $11 million.

CASE QUESTIONS

1. Did Spur create a nuisance?
2. Should it make any difference that Spur was there first?
3. How does the court balance retirement communities and beef production, which are two of Arizona's biggest industries?

DUTIES OF LANDOWNERS

In addition to avoiding the problems of trespass and nuisance, landowners owe certain responsibilities to those entering their property. Those who enter property are classified into one of three categories: trespassers, licensees, and invitees. Traditionally, each category has a different status when on another's property, and landowners owe different degrees of responsibility to those in each category. While these differing categories and duties are discussed here, states are increasingly blending together the responsibilities and degree of care so that the standard becomes one of reasonable care to all those who enter your property, regardless of their classification.

Trespassers

Trespassers are persons on the property of another without permission. Landowners may take the appropriate actions to have trespassers removed, but while trespassers are on their property, landowners have only the responsibility of not intentionally injuring them—that is, landowners may not intentionally injure trespassers or erect mantraps to injure or kill trespassers.

CONSIDER 3.6   Vincent Provenzano had experienced a game of Wiffle ball in a friend's backyard in Greenwich, Connecticut. Later, as he sat with a friend near a vacant town lot discussing the wonder of their Wiffle ball (which was created in Connecticut), they decided to turn the lot, filled with weeds, brush, and poison ivy, into a Wiffle ball field. "If we build it, they will come," the two laughed. The boys and their friends spent three weeks clearing the field, digging holes, pouring concrete, and putting up plywood field barriers. They had a flag and ads for Taco Bell Frutista Freezes on their field boards that they had painted green. The field was an instant success with everyone except those who owned the adjoining lots. The neighbors complained about the noise, the traffic, and the crowds. Lawyers for the city worried about liability. City engineers said the boys had affected the drainage on the lot. The boys have responded, "This is just old-fashioned fun. Maybe people think that's unusual," and "People think we should be home playing 'Grand Theft Auto.'" Discuss the rights and liabilities of all the parties.

Peter Applebome, "Build a Wiffle Ball Field and Lawyers Will Come," *New York Times*, July 10, 2008, L1.

Licensees

Licensees are persons on the property of another who have some form of permission to be there. For example, in most states, fire protectors, police officers, and medical personnel would be classified as licensees. These groups have an implied invitation to a landowner's property so that their services are available to the landowner when needed. It is possible that meter readers would be classified as licensees because the implied invitation arises from the use of the utility or service. In some states, social guests are classified as licensees because, although there may not be an express invitation to all social guests, an implied invitation arises from friendship.

To the licensees, landowners owe a greater duty of care. In addition to the duty not to injure intentionally is the responsibility of warning licensees of any defects of which landowners have knowledge. Thus, landowners must warn of broken steps, cracked concrete, or dangerous animals.

Invitees

Invitees are persons on the property of another by express invitation. Every public place offers an express invitation to all members of the public. Customers are always invitees in places of business. A repair person on the premises to fix a washer or refrigerator is there at the landowner's express request. Invitees are afforded the greatest degree of protection by landowners. Landowners must exercise reasonable care to protect invitees from injury. They owe a duty not only to warn invitees of any defects of which they have knowledge but also to inspect their property for defects and take reasonable steps to correct them. For example, a leaf of lettuce on the floor in the produce section of a grocery store is a hazard for invitees. Grocery store owners are required to periodically check and sweep aisle areas to protect invitees. Figure 3.4 provides a summary view of landowner liability and duty.

FIGURE 3.4 Landowner Duties and Liabilities

TYPE OF PERSON ENTERING PROPERTY	LANDOWNER DUTY	LIABILITY*
Trespasser	Not to intentionally injure	Landowner liable for intentional injury, mantraps, automatic traps, etc.
Licensee	Not to intentionally injure; correct defects aware of	Landowner is liable for intentional injury and any injury caused by known defects
Invitee	Not to intentionally injure; correct defects aware of or should be aware	Above, plus landowner liability for should-have-known-defects

© Cengage Learning

*There are several variations from state to state. For example, some states classify social guests as licensees, whereas others classify them as invitees, hence changing the duties and liability of the landowners. As noted on p. 58, regular trespassers can ripen into licensees.

CONSIDER 3.7 Classify each of the following parties in terms of the landowner's responsibilities. Describe the landowner's duty to each.

a. Paramedic

b. Customer in a department store

c. Marketing researcher doing a door-to-door survey

d. Burglar

Breach of Duty

A landowner's breach of any of these stated responsibilities can result in the imposition of tremendous liability, especially if the trespasser, licensee, or invitee is seriously injured. Landowners must be cautious in exercising their responsibilities and can be further protected through maintenance of adequate insurance.

The following case deals with an evolving and important area of the liability of landowners. The case involves an issue of the landowner's liability to invitees when the invitee is injured by the criminal activity of a third party.

DOUBLE QUICK, INC. V. MOORE

73 So.3d 1162 (Miss. 2011)
Quick Action at the Double Quick

FACTS

On May 17, 2008, Wytisha Jackson was an assistant store manager of a Double Quick convenience store in Shelby, Mississippi. At approximately 7:30 p.m., George Ford, accompanied by his young son, entered Double Quick to make a purchase. Shortly afterward, Cassius Gallion entered the store. Ford and Gallion exchanged words. Gallion left the store first. Then, Ford left the store to pump gas into his car. Because she was worried that Ford and Gallion would fight, Jackson accompanied Ford and helped Ford's son into the car. At the gas pumps, Ford and Gallion again exchanged words. Then, Mario Moore, who had arrived at the Double Quick but had not yet been inside, approached Ford's car, intervened in the argument, and threw a punch at Ford. Mario missed Ford, but struck Jackson, who then returned to the store and called the police. Ford then retrieved a pistol from the trunk of his car and shot Mario. Mario died as result of his injury.

Dorothy Moore, as administrator of Mario's estate, filed suit against Double Quick. Moore argued that Double Quick had neglected to protect Mario from injury and death while he was on the store's premises. Double Quick filed its motion for summary judgment. The trial court denied summary judgment and Double Quick appealed.

JUDICIAL OPINION

King, Justice

Double Quick argued that premises-liability law was applicable, and in order for Double Quick to be liable for the failure to protect Mario from the intentional acts of another, Moore must show that the injury was foreseeable.

To recover damages in a premises-liability action, Moore must show (a) the duty owed to Mario by Double Quick; (b) a breach of that duty; (c) damages; and (d) a causal connection between the breach and the damages, such that the breach is the proximate cause of Mario's injuries.

Generally, in order to determine the duty owed by the business owner, the status of the injured party must be determined. The injured party should be classified as an invitee, licensee, or trespasser. An invitee is a person who enters the premises of another in response to an "express or implied invitation of the owner or occupant for their mutual advantage." A licensee enters the premises "for his own convenience, pleasure, or benefit pursuant to the license or implied permission [.]" A trespasser enters the premises "without license, invitation, or other right."

Under Mississippi law, a property owner is not the insurer of an invitee's safety. Rather, he owes a duty to the invitee to keep the premises reasonably safe and, when not reasonably safe, to warn only of hidden dangers not in plain and open view. Also, the duty owed to a licensee or trespasser is the same—not to willfully or wantonly injure such person.

The parties disagree on Mario's status, but Mario's classification is irrelevant in determining the outcome of this appeal. The issue is not determinative, because even if Jackson and Double Quick owed Mario a higher duty of care, Moore failed to provide evidence that Jackson's action or inaction was the proximate cause of Mario's death.

Proximate cause is defined as the "cause which in natural and continuous sequence unbroken by any efficient intervening cause produces the injury and without which the result would not have occurred." Generally, "criminal acts can be intervening causes which break the causal connection with the defendant's negligent act, if the criminal act is not within the realm of reasonable foreseeability." Thus, in order to establish that Jackson's behavior was the proximate cause of Mario's injury, Moore would have to prove that Mario's injury was reasonably foreseeable.

In premises-liability cases, there are two ways to establish legal causation, or foreseeability, in cases of assault by a third person: the requisite "cause to anticipate" the assault may arise from actual or constructive knowledge of the assailant's violent nature, or actual or constructive knowledge that an atmosphere of violence exists on the premises.

There was no suggestion within the record that Jackson had actual or constructive knowledge of Ford's violent nature. Jackson voluntarily went outside to the gas pumps with Ford. Further, the record does not indicate that an atmosphere of violence existed on the premises of Double Quick. In fact, Moore's attorney conceded during the hearing on the motions for summary judgment that there was no evidence to indicate that Double Quick had a violent atmosphere.

Because Moore failed to prove that the injury was reasonably foreseeable, there is no evidence to suggest that Jackson's behavior was the proximate cause of Mario's injuries. We find that the trial court erred in denying Double Quick's motion for summary judgment. Therefore, we reverse the judgment of the trial court and render a judgment of dismissal in favor of Double Quick.

Reversed.

CASE QUESTIONS

1. What is the difference between a premises liability case and a negligence case?
2. Why does the court not concern itself with determining whether Mario was an invitee?
3. What would establish proximate cause for purposes of attributing liability to Double Quick?

CAUTIONS AND CONCLUSIONS

To avoid problems in this area of the extent of land ownership, parties should take precautions to establish their rights, the scope of those rights, and their liability for injuries that occur on their property. All parties in a sales transaction (seller, buyer, agents, and financiers) should analyze the sale with the following questions:

1. What water is available? Are the water rights protected?
2. Are mineral rights being transferred? What minerals are included? If minerals are not being transferred, who owns them and what do they own? What land-use rights do they have? What are the royalties or payments and who is entitled to receive them?
3. Is light available to the buildings, landscaping, and solar panels? If not, is an easement possible? Will future structures block the light?
4. Are the column and air lots included or have they been transferred? Who owns them?
5. Is air traffic unusually burdensome, close, or noisy?
6. Do any nuisances such as pollution, smell, or insects exist? Can they be remedied?
7. Are there any persons using the property? Do they hold any rights or are they trespassers? This checklist helps buyers understand what they are getting and helps sellers be certain that they are disclosing relevant information about the extent of ownership and transfer.

When a property owner conveys mineral rights, the transaction may be clarified by answering the following questions:

1. What interest is being conveyed? What minerals? Subsurface only? Fee simple interest? Lease? Right of removal?
2. What rights are given on surface use? Will the lessee pay for restoration?
3. How much is the royalty? Are there any other fees to be paid? If no minerals are drawn, is there any payment?
4. Can the land be sold to someone else? Who gets the royalties?
5. Can the mineral rights be transferred to someone else? Will the same restrictions apply?

Property owners are responsible for the way they use their property and may want to answer these questions to limit or eliminate potential liability:

1. Are there significant noises, smells, or other emissions from the property? Do they interfere with others' use and enjoyment of their own property?
2. Are there individuals using the property in an unauthorized manner? Are there trespassers? Are there any mantraps to injure them? Have steps been taken to prevent trespass?
3. Do licensees enter the property? Are there appropriate signs and methods of warning them of dangers?
4. Do invitees enter the property? Are there any dangerous conditions? Have they been remedied? Are periodic inspections done to find and eliminate dangerous conditions?
5. Are nuisances from others affecting the property? Can action be taken to stop the conduct or recover damages?

KEY TERMS

CHAPTER PROBLEMS

1. Arthur and Patricia Pierce own property on a hillside near Seattle. The Northeast Lake Washington Sewer and Water District (District), a municipal corporation providing water and sewer services to 50,000 people, acquired 5.4 acres of residential property adjacent to the Pierces' land. The District applied for a permit to construct a 4.3-million-gallon water storage facility on the site. The District chose the location because the sloping hillside would enable it to obscure the sight of the tank from neighboring residences. The permit was granted with modifications in the tank's location.

   However, the final position of the constructed tank blocked the panoramic view the Pierces had enjoyed of wooded terrain, Lake Washington, Mount Rainier, and the Cascades. The tank was visible from any window in the house.

   After an appraiser issued his opinion that the construction of the tank resulted in a $30,000 reduction in value of the Pierces' property, the Pierces filed suit against the District for nuisance, trespass, negligence, and inverse condemnation. The trial court dismissed the suit for the failure to demonstrate compensable damages and the court of appeals affirmed. The Pierces appealed. Should the Pierces be compensated for the loss of their view? *Pierce v. Northeast Lake Washington Sewer and Water District*, 870 P.2d 305 (Wash. 1994).

2. Osborne, a Little Rock citizen, constructed a massive Christmas lights display. Stretching over several lots, the display included over 1,600,000 lights, complete with reindeer and sleighs, Mickey Mouse driving a steam engine, a musical calliope and a rotating illuminated carousel suspended in the air, and camels and wise men. The spectacle attracted thousands. A handful of neighbors alleged that the display was a private nuisance. They complained of trash on their property, parking on their lawns, vandalism in the neighborhood, traffic hazards, limited access to their own homes, and unreasonable noise and lighting. They filed suit seeking to shut down the display. What should the court do? *Power v. Osborne*, 890 S.W.2d 575 (Ark. 1994).

3. Arizona Revised Statute § 33-439 provides: "Any covenant, restriction or condition contained in any deed, contract, security agreement or other instrument affecting the transfer or sale of, or any interest in, real property which *effectively prohibits* the installation or use of a solar energy device ... is void and unenforceable." William and Joan Madigan and Henry and LaVonne Speak owned homes in the Garden Lakes subdivision in Avondale, Arizona. The Garden Lakes Homeowners' Association's Declaration of Covenants, Conditions, Restrictions and Easements for Garden Lakes includes the following provisions:

   1. All solar energy devices Visible from Neighboring Property or public view must be approved by the Architectural Review Committee prior to installation.

   2. Panels must be an integrated part of the roof design and mounted directly to the roof plane. Solar units must not break the roof ridge line, must not be visible from public view and must be screened from Neighboring Property in a manner approved by the Board of Directors or its designee(s). Roof mounted hot water storage systems must not be Visible from Neighboring Property. Tracker-type systems will be allowed only when not Visible from Neighboring Property.

   The Madigans and Speaks sought approval from the Architectural Review Committee (ARC) to install solar energy devices on the roofs of their homes. The ARC would not approve the panels unless one couple built a very large screen to enclose the system and the other built a large patio cover that would have required covering part of their swimming pool. The costs of adding these aesthetic changes made the use of the solar systems cost-ineffective for the homeowners. Unable to obtain approval, the Madigans and Speaks went forward with their solar panels without ARC approval. The Association brought suit seeking an injunction to have the solar systems removed.

   The Madigans and Speaks defended on the grounds that the ARC restrictions "effectively prohibited" their installation of solar devices in violation of Arizona law. Discuss the Arizona law, its purposes, and whether the Speaks and Madigans must remove their solar systems. *Garden Lakes Community Ass'n, Inc. v. Madigan,* 62 P.3d 983 (Az. App. 2003).

4. Bruce Rankin owns real estate in rural Platt County, Illinois, that is zoned for agricultural use. He has lived there since 1959 and operates a business from his house known as Williams Trigger Specialties. Rankin, a federally registered gunsmith, works on firearm firing mechanisms.

   Also located on the property, which has also been there since 1959, is a firing range. Rankin allows his friends to use the firing range in addition to using it himself. He does not permit strangers to use it. In the last several years, he has also permitted various law-enforcement agencies to use the range for training, practice, and qualification. The Champaign Police Department Strategic Weapons and Tactics (SWAT) team, consisting of 12 people, has used the range 10 to 15 times in the last year.

   Rankin has never charged a fee for use of the range. He has, however, considered putting his range to commercial use at some time in the future. Rankin is almost always present when the range is used by private individuals other than law-enforcement agencies. There has never been an injury or near injury or complaint to Rankin about the range or its use.

   The Kolstads and Hayses lived with the noise from the gunshots, but on October 4, 1988, they became alarmed when the new noise of rapid short bursts of gunfire sounded. Kolstad recognized the noise as the firing of automatic weapons. Both neighbors became concerned about their safety and filed suit for an injunction to halt the use of the property as a firing range. Should the court issue an injunction? Should it be an absolute prohibition on operation of the range or something less? *Kolstad v. Rankin,* 534 N.E.2d 1373 (Ill. 1989).

5. The Great Cove Boat Club had a wharf on the Piscataqua River in Maine. The Bureau of Public Lands, in its work for the preservation of public waterways, entered into lease agreements with private parties so that they could create and operate wharfs, floats, and moorings for public enjoyment. One such 30-year lease resulted in construction of public-access wharfs that flooded the area of the Great Cove's wharf, cutting off access by the owners. Great Cove claimed, as a riparian, that its rights had been violated through the use of the water in such a fashion that its water access rights were destroyed. The Bureau of Public Lands claims that it has the right, as a state agency, to regulate land use and that leasing to parties is part of that regulation to which Great Cove is subject. Is the Bureau correct or have Great Cove's riparian rights been violated? *Great Cove Boat Club v. Bureau of Public Lands,* 672 A.2d 91 (Me. 1996).

6. Bono (Paul Hewson) owns the penthouse in the San Remo, a tony building that overlooks Central Park. Bono purchased the penthouse from Steve Jobs and has neighbors such as Steve Martin, Steven Spielberg, Billy Squier, and a bevy of writers. (Madonna was rejected by the building association in 1989 and not permitted to purchase a unit.) Smoke from the fireplaces of these neighbors and others drifts into Bono's penthouse. One of the Hewsons' children has asthma and the smoke from the fireplaces makes it difficult for the child to breathe. The owners association has been reluctant to ban the fireplaces because owners want the pine-scented experience in the city. Mitch Miller, the host of the 1960s program *Sing Along with Mitch,* said, "If people want fireplaces, let them go live in the country."[20] Is the smoke a nuisance? Does Bono have air rights that could help? Is the smoke a form of trespass? Discuss possible remedies. Be sure to use the doctrine of balancing interests.

7. The City of Spokane (City) has owned and operated Indian Canyon Golf Course, including its driving range, since the 1930s. The Episcopal Diocese of Spokane donated the driving range land to the City. In 1996, the Diocese sold developer Ronald C. McCloskey land at the end of the driving range. Some portion of the property was the driving range rough.

   In the 1960s, the City would retrieve hundreds of golf balls per month from the property. The number increased to approximately hundreds per week until 2000. The City did not seek permission from the Diocese to retrieve the balls. Exact boundaries between the properties were unknown. Initially, machetes were used to clear the underbrush. By the 1970s, City maintenance crews began clearing brush on the subject property two or three times a year with motorized equipment. From around 1985 to 1987, a City employee placed 8 to 10 "No Trespassing" signs on the subject property to keep people from stealing balls.

   When Mr. McCloskey spoke with the City's golf pro about the situation, the pro was surprised the property did not belong to the City. Mr. McCloskey

---

[20]Allen Salkin, "Among the Rich and Famous, A New Dispute Over Air Rights," *New York Times,* May 16, 2007, p. A1.

believed the golf course location would aid in development. Anticipating problems, the City offered to buy the property and discussed screening costs, but the parties could not agree on a price. The City filed an action for injunctive relief and quiet title, alleging a prescriptive easement right to hit golf balls onto the Developers' property and retrieve them. The Developers' counterclaim sought trespass, nuisance, and inverse condemnation damages. Analyze the rights of the parties in the case. *City of Spokane v. Canyon Greens,* LLC, 107 Wash.App. 1005, Not Reported in P.3d, 2001 WL 772498 Wash.App. Div. 3, 2001.

8. Neighbor A has installed a satellite dish on his roof and Neighbor B complains that the dish is unsightly and interferes with the pristine view Neighbor B had enjoyed previously. Neighbor B says the dish interferes with his "line of sight." Neighbor B has petitioned to have the receiving dish removed on the grounds that it is not protected by any solar energy statutes. Neighbor A indicates that there are no prohibitions on the installation of the receivers and no visual impairment statutes that protect Neighbor B. Neighbor A also argues that prohibiting the installation of such receiving dishes impairs technology. Discuss the issues and decide what a court or agency hearing the case should do. *In the Matter of Preemption of Local Zoning or Other Regulation of Receive-Only Satellite Earth Stations,* 59 Rad. Reg.2d (P & F) 1073, 1986 WL 292763 (F.C.C. 1986).

9. At approximately 3:00 A.M., on February 3, 2000, Sonya Winchell was driving two of her friends through a Fort Wayne Taco Bell drive-thru. When Winchell arrived in line, there was one car in front of her at the speaker. Winchell noticed that the occupants of the car, Remco Guy and Ariel Graham, were taking a long time placing their order and then got out of their car. At that point, Winchell yelled out her window, "Can we get moving, we are hungry!" Guy approached Winchell's car, stuck his head in the window, and "started cussing everybody out." Guy removed his head from the window, stuck it back in, and asked, "You got an F-ing problem?" Winchell responded by "drill[ing] him in the nose." Guy then pulled a gun out of his pants and shot Winchell. Winchell survived the shooting, and Guy was convicted of attempted murder. Winchell filed a civil action against Guy and Graham, and against Taco Bell, alleging negligence. Is Taco Bell liable for the injuries that occur on its property? *Winchell v. Guy,* 857 N.E.2d 1024 (Ind. 2006).

10. The U.S. Forest Service has issued a directive that requires the ski resorts to turn over their water rights to the federal government. There has been a long history of legislative, regulatory, and political interactions as to how these water rights came to belong to the ski resorts. A group of ski resorts has filed suit in federal district court in Colorado alleging that the directive is a violation of their Fifth Amendment rights as an "uncompensated taking of private property." Most ski resorts have acquired their water rights from private landowners by following the requirements for transfer of such rights under each state's real estate laws. Some of those water rights have required that the ski resorts put in place considerable infrastructure, such as pipelines, in order to transport the water from the private property to their resorts. The National Ski Association, a trade group with 121 resorts located in 13 states, says that it had to file suit to seek clarification of the directive.

The Forest Service has not yet filed its answer in the case, but a spokesperson explained that the Service is worried that should those water rights become valuable the ski resorts could sell them to someone else and leave the local residents without a source of water.

The ski resort owners also maintain that they were not notified of the proposed directive and given a chance to comment on it, something that is required under the Administrative Procedures Act. They maintain that many of the issues could be resolved without the federal government taking over their water/property rights. What are the two legal bases for the ski resorts' suit against the federal government? What is the concern of the Forest Service about resort ownership of the water rights? Ann Zimmerman, "Water Fight Hits the Slopes," *Wall Street Journal,* March 7, 2012, p. A3.

For research activities related to this chapter, go to our text companion website at www.cengagebrain.com

CHAPTER 4

NONPOSSESSORY INTERESTS IN REAL ESTATE

Good fences make good neighbors.

Robert Frost

Nonpossessory land interests are those that give rights that always fall short of possession of the land. These nonpossessory interests might be labeled *privileges, liberties,* or *advantages.* Nonpossessory interests give their holders some right of entry or use of the land of another. This chapter explains the creation and extent of these nonpossessory interests.

EASEMENTS

An **easement** is a liberty, privilege, or advantage in another's property. It is nonpossessory but can run on in perpetuity. There are many different types of easements and methods for their creation.

Types of Easements: Appurtenant versus Easements in Gross

An **easement appurtenant** is one that attaches to or benefits a particular tract of land. The purpose of an easement appurtenant is to provide benefit to a landowner.

For example, refer to Figure 4.1 and suppose both landowners C and A need access to the street that runs parallel to B's property. The dark strip represents the appurtenant easements held by C and A in B's land and C in A's land that give them access so that they can use and possess their land.

In contrast, an **easement in gross** is not created to benefit any landowner with respect to a particular tract of land; rather, it belongs to the holders regardless of

FIGURE 4.1 Easement Appurtenant

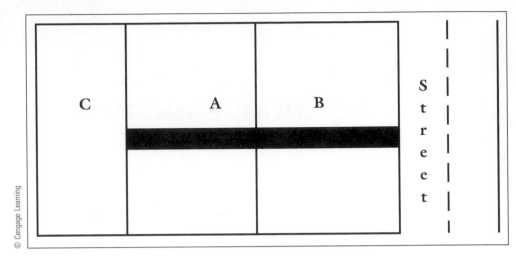

whether they own any adjacent property. Generally, public utilities hold easements in gross through residential property (in the back six or eight feet of the lots, for example) so that cable, electrical, and water lines can be connected to all parcels of the property. At common law, easements in gross were not transferable, but in most states they are now transferable if they are commercial in nature.

Types of Easements: Affirmative versus Negative Easements

The situation diagrammed in Figure 4.1 is an example of an **affirmative easement**, which means that the owner of the easement right can use another's land (the land subject to the easement). In Figure 4.1, A and C have an affirmative easement in B's property. Likewise, C has an affirmative easement in A's property.

A **negative easement** is one in which the holders of the easements prevent other property owners from using their property in a particular way or prevent particular acts by other landowners, such as an easement restricting the heights of buildings on adjoining property. These negative easements, often called *scenic easements*, can have a possible twofold tax advantage. First, the taxpayer/landowner can perhaps take a charitable contribution deduction. For example, a business might grant a neighboring church a negative easement that prevents the blockage of sunlight from the church's stained glass windows. The business can take the value reduction this easement causes in its property as a charitable contribution deduction. Second, the taxpayer/landowner's property taxes can be reduced by the decrease in value brought about by the easement restrictions. An easement that prevents the shading of solar panels (as discussed in Chapter 3) is an example of a negative easement.

Another type of negative easement that has been used extensively over the past few years is the **conservation easement**. A conservation easement is one granted by a landowner who owns property with historical, cultural, or architectural significance. These landowners grant negative easements that will prevent them from tearing down buildings on the property so that their historical significance is preserved. In many cases, again, these easements can be treated as charitable donations. These forms of easements are increasingly being used as governments lack funds to buy or condemn the property. Private landowners accomplish the goal of conservation without the costs being borne by governments and taxpayers.

Recently, conservation easements have been used to preserve farmlands in those areas where development would otherwise force farmers, due to increased property taxes, to abandon their land to further development.[1] The farmers grant to their communities negative conservation easements, often referred to as *purchase and development rights (PDR) contracts*, in which they agree to limit their land uses. In exchange, the communities give the farmers reduced taxes for the promise to preserve their land as natural farmland. The result is a solution to encroaching development as well as to the high taxes faced in agricultural production.

The Parties: Dominant versus Servient Estates

In an easement relationship, the property owned by the easement holder is called the **dominant tenement** or **dominant estate**, and the property through which the easement runs is called the **servient tenement** or **servient estate**. In Figure 4.1, B holds the servient estate for dominant tenants A and C. Since C also has an easement through A's property, A is also a servient estate to C's dominant estate.

Creation of Easements

Easements by Express Grant or Express Reservation

An **easement by express grant** or **express reservation** is one in which the parties actually draw up papers as if transferring an interest in land. Since an easement is a land interest, creation of express easements must comply with all requirements in the state for the conveyance of land interests. Most states' Statutes of Frauds require the conveyance of a land interest to be in writing or evidenced by a record.

Whether an easement is created by express grant or express reservation depends on the physical layout of the land transferred; the two contrasting physical setups for easements are illustrated in Figure 4.2. In both situations, A was the original owner of the full parcel that contained an access route to the street that runs parallel to the tract. In the express grant situation, A retains that portion of the parcel with the access route and must therefore convey to B an easement by express grant. In the express reservation situation, A conveys that portion of the parcel with the access route and must therefore grant himself an easement by express reservation.

The same easement is involved in both circumstances, but the method of acquisition is different. In the deed transferring title to the property conveyed, A would either grant or convey the portion of the parcel B has purchased and would also include a grant to B of the easement for ingress or egress or, in the second circumstances, A would reserve that ingress and egress for himself when B is granted title to the land with that access.

An express easement is not limited to creation in situations of land partition. An express easement may be granted as a separate transaction. For example, a solar easement may be drafted and executed between two neighbors who already own their adjoining parcels of land. They might, for example, create a negative solar easement. The following case deals with an about the scope of an express

---

[1]Some states use negative easements as a means of preserving historic farmlands. *U.S. v. Blackman*, 613 S.E.2d 442 (Va. 2005).

FIGURE 4.2
Express Grant and
Express Reservation
Easement

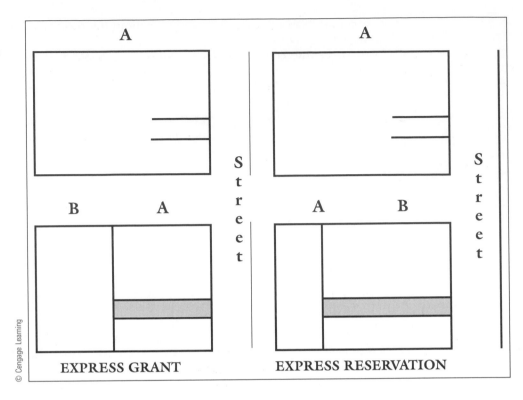

© Cengage Learning

easement and the relationship between dominant and servient estates in an easement relationship.

DIANNE V. WINGATE

84 So.3d 427 (Fla.App. 2012)
Do Speed Bumps on the Easement Get Bumped?

FACTS

Adrian and Charline Wingate (Appellees) own and occupy a home adjoining Gloria Dianne and Freddie L. Wingate's (Appellants) property. On February 1, 1999, Appellant Freddie L. Wingate and his (now deceased) wife, Peggy Ann Wingate (now Peggy Dianne), granted an easement over and across their property, providing ingress and egress to Adrian and Charline, which was recorded. Around October 21, 2009, Freddie and Peggy placed speed bumps across a paved portion of the easement, which is used by Adrian and Charline to gain access to their residence. Freddie and Peggy also placed concrete barriers on either side of the speed bumps to prevent vehicles from going around the speed bumps. The speed bumps have proven dangerous to drivers and their passengers and have

damaged vehicles passing over them. Adrian and Charline demanded summary judgment as well as a permanent injunction restraining Freddie and Peggy from keeping the speed bumps across the easement. The court granted summary judgment and ordered the removal of the speed bumps. Peggy and Freddie appealed.

JUDICIAL OPINION

Ray, Judge

Appellants asserted that the passageway sustained heavy traffic, some motorists used excessive speed, and over time, the posted speed limit signs were regularly ignored and ineffective. Appellants deny that the speed bumps are dangerous and/or substantially diminish Appellees' rights.

Under the terms of the easement, the grantors gave, granted, sold, and conveyed to Appellees, as grantees, "a non-exclusive easement or right of way for ingress and egress, over, along, and across a strip or parcel of land," which is legally described in the agreement. The agreement contained no restrictions and reserved no rights to place speed bumps across the easement. Appellees requested the immediate removal of the speed bumps.

Appellees' counsel argued the speed bumps must be removed because, by their very nature, they impede ingress and egress along the easement, have no reflectors or other warning signs, and substantially diminish Appellees' rights established under the easement agreement. Appellees contended that the placement of a fence along the passageway would be a less intrusive means of protecting people from vehicles crossing the easement, without impeding ingress and egress along the passageway.

Appellants' counsel replied that the speed bumps serve a necessary safety function to reduce speeding and are permitted if they do not unreasonably interfere with the ability to cross over the easement. The trial judge, acknowledging that a factual question may arise as to whether the speed bumps are a substantial interference, found it was not reasonable to place the speed bumps across the easement, where the agreement expressly granted Appellees the rights of ingress and egress. The court noted that the presence of large concrete blocks on both sides of the speed bumps prevents drivers from bypassing them. Although an easement is a real property interest in land, it is a right distinct from ownership of the land itself and does not confer title to the land on which the easement is imposed. The easement holder possesses the dominant tenement, while the owner of the land against which the easement exists possesses the servient tenement. The servient estate owner enjoys all rights to the property, except as limited by the easement, and may use the land burdened by the easement in any manner that does not unreasonably interfere with the lawful dominant use.

Next, in determining the nature and scope of Appellees' rights, we examine the intent of the original parties to the easement, as evidenced by the agreement itself. It is clear that the grantors intended for the grantees to have ingress and egress over the easement property. Where the parties want to keep an easement free of gates, speed bumps, signs, or other obstructions, they can specifically express such intent in their easement agreement. That is not

the case with the instant easement agreement, however, which is silent as to whether the servient estate owners (Appellants) have the right to place speed bumps across the easement.

A similar situation existed in *BHB Development, Inc. v. Bonefish Yacht Club Homeowners Ass'n, Inc.*, 691 So.2d 1174 (Fla. 3d DCA 1997), where a homeowners' association obtained a private right-of-way easement for ingress and egress over a portion of BHB Development's property. Subsequently, BHB Development erected a locked gate across the easement for security purposes and offered keys to the homeowners' association members. The issue was whether the easement allowed BHB Development to install the gate. The trial court issued a final judgment in favor of the homeowners' association, directing BHB Development to remove any gates existing across the easement and forbidding the future installation of gates. The Third District Court stated the general rule as follows:

> [T]he grant of a way without reservation of the right to maintain gates does not necessarily preclude the owner of the land from doing so, and unless it is expressly stipulated that the way shall be an open one, or it appears from the terms of the grant or the circumstances that such was the intention, the owner of the servient estate may erect gates across the way, if they are constructed so as not to interfere unreasonably with the right of passage.

The evidence in *BHB Development* established that having to unlock and open the gate and having to carry a key or have an access code caused inconvenience. The appellate court concluded that the trial court did not err in finding that the locked gate substantially and unreasonably interfered with the homeowners' association's right of passage. The final judgment was affirmed.

As in *BHB Development*, the essential question in this case is whether the speed bumps substantially or unreasonably interfere with the easement holders' right of passage. To conclude as the trial court did, and hold that the speed bumps are impermissible as a matter of law, would effectively grant the easement holders absolute ownership of the easement property contrary to well-established property law.

Whether a particular action by a servient tenement holder constitutes unreasonable interference is ordinarily a question of fact. In resolving the question of reasonableness, significant factors the courts may consider include the number of speed bumps, their height, the spacing between speed bumps, the necessity for their placement in the particular area, and their effect on vehicles and traffic flow. The record reveal[s] the existence of triable issues of fact regarding the speed bumps. Because genuine issues of material fact remain, we reverse summary judgment and remand for further proceedings.

Reversed and remanded.

CASE QUESTIONS

1. Who owns the dominant easement estate?
2. Who owns the servient easement estate?
3. Explain the precedent on easement barriers and the court's requirements for proof of unreasonable interference with an easement owner's rights.

Easements by Implication

An **easement by implication** arises when there is a necessity. Suppose, for example, that in the express grant of Figure 4.2, B's property is landlocked and that crossing A's parcel is B's only method of ingress and egress. Suppose further that the conveyance from A to B makes no provision or express grant in the deed to provide B with an easement. To prevent B from having to hold title to a worthless piece of inaccessible property, the courts developed the doctrine of easement by implication to remedy B's landlocked predicament.

An easement by implication exists if several factors are present. First, there must have been unity of ownership between the two tracts prior to the partition and sale. In this case there was unity of ownership, since A owned the entire parcel prior to the division. Second, there must have been a **quasi easement** at the time of the sole ownership of the parcel. A quasi easement is an access route used by the landowner when the land was not yet divided. Figure 4.2 indicates that A used the road as a means of access, and so a quasi easement existed. The term quasi is used because landowners cannot hold an easement in their own property. Third, the prior quasi easement must have been apparent and used continuously. This requirement is easily satisfied in Figure 4.2 and in most access cases because the road or path is visible. However, visibility is not required to meet the apparent standard in most jurisdictions. For example, sewer-line accesses, although not visible, are apparent because while we may not see sewer lines, we know that people cannot live on property without their presence. Although not shown in the figure, continuous use can probably be assumed in most access cases where, as here, the roadway is the only means of access. Continuous use is normal use and does not require use every day.

The final requirement for an easement by implication is to establish that requiring the dominant estate to obtain access any other way would require unreasonable expense. In Figure 4.2, B's landlocked circumstances indicate that the access through just one parcel is the least expensive and least troublesome method of obtaining access.

There are both easements implied by grant and easements implied by reservation, depending on who holds the dominant estate.

CONSIDER 4.1 For each of the following, determine what type of easement (affirmative, negative, appurtenant, gross) is being created and who will hold the dominant and servient estates:

A. Angela holds an easement that prevents Bill from planting willow trees. (Angela and Bill are adjoining landowners, and Angela obtained the easement because she felt the roots of willow trees would harm her in-ground swimming pool.)

B. Community Cable has just placed television wires along the back wall lines of several neighbors' lots in a new subdivision. The landowners object—they allege a trespass has occurred.

C. Oscar owns a passive solar home (dependent upon window sunlight for heat), and Oscar's neighbor has agreed not to plant trees or shrubs or construct walls on the boundary he shares with Oscar to prevent obstruction.

D. Nordstrom, the retail store, has its name placed on the top of the public parking garage (owned by the city of Scottsdale, Arizona) located next to its store. _____

Easements by Necessity

An **easement by necessity** is one that can arise solely on the basis of necessity, and the requirements of prior use need not be established. However, this type of easement lasts only so long as the necessity continues, whereas an easement by implication may go on in perpetuity. In some states, condemnation procedures are available to assist landowners who need to obtain access to their property. In other states, an easement is automatically given when landlocked property is transferred.[2]

In Figure 4.1, B's circumstances could be changed to require an easement by necessity if the properties were surrounded by water. Then A's only method of access to the street would be through B's land, unless and until a bridge or causeway to B's land was constructed.

Some states have begun to follow doctrines on easements by implication and necessity that are less complex. For example, in *Carter v. County of Hanover*, 496 S.E.2d 42 (Va. 1998), the court found that without any deed restrictions, the "grantor of property conveys everything that is necessary for the beneficial use and enjoyment of the property."

Easements by Prescription

Obtaining an easement by **prescription** is somewhat similar to obtaining title to property through *adverse possession*. However, the term "adverse possession" (discussed in Chapter 13) is inappropriate for easements because easements are non-possessory land interests. An easement by prescription requires the following:

1. *The easement must be used for the appropriate prescriptive period.* The prescriptive period will vary from state to state but generally corresponds to the state's adverse possession period, which ranges from 5 to 20 years throughout the United States.

2. *The use of the easement must be adverse (not permissive).* If the landowner has given the prescriptive taker an oral license, such use is permissive and does not qualify for prescription. The permissive use must be mutually agreed upon—a landowner's posting of permission for use will not prevent prescriptive rights.

3. *The use of the easement must be open and notorious.* In most states, this requirement means that the prescriptive taker must use the property in such a way that a landowner would, under ordinary circumstances, be aware of the use. Because actual knowledge of use is not required, landowners who do not

---

[2]Fla. Stat. § 704.01; see also Restatement *of Property* § 476 and Colo. Const. Art. II § 14. Other states may not have a statute or condemnation procedures but follow strong public policy in favor of an easement. *Big Sky Hidden Village Owners Ass'n v. Hidden Village, Inc.*, 915 P.2d 845 (Mont. 1996).

periodically inspect their property run the risk of having a prescriptive use accumulate.

4. *The use of the easement must be continuous and exclusive.* This requirement forces the prescriptive user to confine use to a particular area. The user is required to use the same strip of land or access route consistently.[3] And parties acting together cannot create a prescriptive easement by ganging up on the property owner to obtain regular use. The prescriptive user must be the exclusive user. One exception is the rule of tacking, which permits those in privity of contract (buyers and sellers) and those who inherit title to land to add their use to that of the seller or deceased in making up the prescriptive period. For example, a father using an easement for five years and then passing his property to his son by will also passes his five years of prescriptive use of the easement.

To stop a prescriptive taking, a landowner may take several prevention steps, most of which are recognized by the majority of states. Written protest is one method of interrupting the prescriptive period, as is physical interruption (for example, the use of a gate). Perhaps court-obtained injunctive relief is the best alternative, because such action provides the landowners with full records for establishing a cutoff of the prescriptive period. The following case deals with multiple issues in the scope of an easement, including whether it was expanded through prescription or implication.

HP LIMITED PARTNERSHIP V. KENAI RIVER AIRPARK, LLC

270 P.3d 719 (Alaska 2012)
Attempted Prescription by Dodging the Owner

FACTS

In 1975, John Todd and Neal Hausam bought 160 acres of undeveloped land that is bordered by the Kenai River to the east and Roberts Subdivision to the north. Todd and Hausam each took an undivided one-half interest in the property and subdivided it into 114 lots known as the Holiday Park Subdivision.

Lot 30—a river-front lot—was drawn nearly twice the size of the other lots to accommodate an easement for the benefit of all Holiday Park property owners. The easement was depicted on the plat as a defined path labeled "30′ BOAT LAUNCH ESM'T" and the plat notes state that "[a]ll roads, airstrip and boat launching area [are] for the use of all property owners in the subdivision."

Todd and Hausam started selling lots in 1976; 12 lots sold between 1976 and 1978, but the partnership was dissolved in 1978 after a disagreement. Todd and Hausam split the remaining lots between them. Todd conveyed his interest in Lot 30 to Hausam.

Todd and Hausam continued to sell lots in Holiday Park, and use of the easement across Lot 30 increased. Some lot owners began parking, camping, and fishing on and around the Lot 30 easement.

In the late 1970s and early 1980s, some Holiday Park lot owners noticed that members of the general public were using the easement to access the river. The owners decided to construct a gate at the top of the easement to prevent unauthorized use; Hausam allowed them to build the gate.

In 1994, Todd sold all of his unsold lots to Holiday Park Limited Partnership (HP Limited), which was owned solely by Todd.

Hausam sent a letter to Holiday Park lot owners on July 2, 2001, informing them that the easement across Lot 30 "was intended and shown on the recorded plat for boat launching for property owners." Hausam also stated that in order to sell Lot 30 that he would begin to enforce the intent on the recorded plat to allow property owners only boat

---

[3] *The Restatement (Third) of Property (Servitudes)* has four theories listed for granting prescriptive easements: (1) sufficiently long use can lead to entitlement; (2) use to perfect a flawed title meets the requirements; (3) long-term use is evidence of a right lost that must be restored; and (4) prescriptive claims arise and can exist but must be advanced within a limited time frame.

launching only across the easement." Hausam then suggested that the lot owners form a homeowners' association and purchase Lot 30 from him. The Holiday Park lot owners chose not to do so. Hausam then constructed a fence along the easement that prevented vehicle access to part of the lot but did not completely enclose the easement area.

Hausam then sold Lot 30 to Voltec International, Inc. in October 2003. Randy Comer, a representative of Voltec, arranged for John Hoback and Fred Schroeder to form the Kenai River Airpark, LLC, which, in May 2004, bought lots in Roberts Subdivision, and three lots—including Lot 30—in Holiday Park. Hoback and Schroeder formed Kenai River Airpark Owners Association, Inc., composed of the owners of 16 lots and one tract in Roberts Subdivision, and the owners of three lots in Holiday Park. Kenai River Airpark transferred ownership of Lot 30 to the Airpark Owners Association on October 11, 2005. The Airpark Owners Association planned to use Lot 30 as a common area "for the benefit of all lot owners in the community."

HP Limited sued Kenai River Airpark and the Airpark Owners Association in June 2007. Their suit alleged that Holiday Park lot owners, including HP Limited, had established an easement by prescription to use Lot 30 for general recreation, including fishing, parking, picnicking, and camping. The Kenai River Airpark and its Owners Association filed a counterclaim.

The superior court ruled that the easement was unambiguously confined to boat launching within the 30–foot wide path depicted on the Holiday Park plat. The court also held that members of the Airpark Owners Association, as the owners of Lot 30, could use the lot so long as their use did not unreasonably interfere with Holiday Park lot owners' enjoyment of the easement. Finally, the court found that HP Limited had not established an easement by prescription because its alleged use did not satisfy the requirements of notoriety and hostility. HP appealed.

JUDICIAL OPINION

Christen, Justice

The Holiday Park plat clearly defines the geographic boundaries of the easement across Lot 30 and the purpose for which it may be used. The plat notes do not add ambiguity to the document; they confirm that the easement is a "boat launching area ... for the use of all property owners in the subdivision." The easement's scope is limited to boat launching within the boundaries depicted on the plat.

HP Limited also argues that easements reserved across the riverfront portions of the lots adjacent to Lot 30 demonstrate that the Lot 30 easement was intended to serve not only as an access route to the river, but also as a walkway easement along the frontage of the river. But HP Limited's counsel conceded during oral argument that the waterfront easements on the lots adjacent to Lot 30 do not appear within the four corners of the Holiday Park plat; in fact, those easements were first reflected in the deeds for the adjacent lots which were recorded a year after the plat was recorded. We conclude that the plat unambiguously limits the scope of the easement across Lot 30 to boat launching within the 30–foot path depicted on the plat.

We have explained that "the land subject to [an] easement is described as a 'servient tenement' and the land enjoying [an] easement [is] the 'dominant tenement.' ... [I]t is not necessary that the two tenements be contiguous or adjoining." Here, because Lot 30 is the lot subject to the easement, it is the servient tenement. Holiday Park's plat notes make clear that the easement is "for the use of all property owners in the subdivision." All of the other lots in Holiday Park are dominant tenements.

"Unless the terms of the servitude ... provide otherwise, an ... easement may not be used for the benefit of property other than the dominant estate." But the Airpark Owners Association is not seeking to use the easement for the benefit of property other than the dominant estate; it seeks to use the servient estate itself for the benefit of its members. "[T]he holder of the servient estate is entitled to make any use of the servient estate that does not unreasonably interfere with enjoyment of the servitude." Because the Airpark Owners Association owns Lot 30, it is entitled to use Lot 30 in any manner that does not unreasonably interfere with the Holiday Park lot owners' use of the boat launch easement.

HP Limited argues that even if the original scope of the express easement was limited, it perfected an easement by prescription to use the designated path and surrounding areas on Lot 30 for general recreation. This argument is based on Holiday Park lot owners' use of the easement between 1976 and 2004.

There are three elements necessary to perfect a prescriptive easement: (1) the use must have been continuous and uninterrupted for at least ten years; (2) the user must have acted as if he were the owner and not merely one acting with permission of the owner; and (3) the use must have been reasonably visible to the record owner." The main purpose of these requirements is to put the record owner on notice of the existence of an adverse claimant."

HP Limited's claim for a prescriptive easement relies largely on how [lot owners] used the easement area over the years. But the lot owners in Holiday Park purchased their properties at different times and used Lot 30 with varying frequency. HP Limited is the only plaintiff in this action, and can only support its claim for a prescriptive easement with evidence of its own use of the easement, or the use of Todd, its predecessor in interest. Any other Holiday Park lot owner seeking to expand the bounds of the express easement by prescriptive use would have to bring his or her own claim and independently satisfy the requirements for a prescriptive easement.

The hostility requirement for a prescriptive easement requires that the "user must have acted as if he were claiming a permanent right to the easement."

Todd testified that he fished on the riverfront of Lot 30 in 1978, 1979, and 1980, but other Holiday Park lot owners testified that they never, or very rarely, saw Todd fishing off of the easement in later years. Todd testified that he also camped on the easement in 1976 and 1977, but he owned the lot during this time and was therefore not acting "adversely" by camping on it. Further, Todd testified that he knew when Hausam was on the lot and that, because he did not like confrontation, he avoided going to Lot 30 when Hausam was around.

Todd's use of Lot 30 was not notorious. The court explained that "by Todd's own testimony he avoided Hausam after they had their falling out in 1978 and he had not seen Hausam in 23 years; that is, until Hausam's deposition was taken in August 2008 in connection with this law suit." The court concluded: "Todd's conduct in avoiding Hausam [was] the antithesis of notoriety." Todd's intentional avoidance of Hausam was inconsistent with an open and notorious use of the property sufficient to put a reasonably diligent landowner on notice.

HP Limited also argues that it established an easement by implication, which expanded the permissible uses of the easement on Lot 30 to include all general recreational activities and broadened the geographic boundaries of the easement.

The first requirement for an easement by implication is a showing that a quasi-easement existed at the time of severance. To establish an easement by implication, there must have been unity of ownership prior to the severance of the title to the land, and the previous owner must have used one part of the land for the benefit of another part.

Prior to 1978, Hausam and Todd each held a one-half ownership interest in Lot 30. They also shared a one-half ownership interest in other unsold Holiday Park lots between 1975 and 1978. Thus, prior to 1978, there was unity of ownership between Lot 30 and other unsold lots in Holiday Park. Because the other unsold lots were benefitted by the easement across Lot 30, Todd and Hausam created a quasi-easement to use the boat launch. Kenai River Airpark argues that the severance of ownership occurred in 1975, when the 160–acre parcel was parceled into 114 lots. But we do not consider the date of parceling to be the date of severance; instead, severance occurs when the lot burdened by the quasi-easement is sold or transferred. In this case severance occurred on May 16, 1978, when Todd conveyed his interest in Lot 30 to Hausam.

To establish an expanded easement by implication, HP Limited also must show that Todd's use of the easement—for purposes other than boat launching within the defined path—was apparent. Todd testified that he camped on the lot for 30 days in 1976 and 1977, but he also testified that he knew when Hausam was on the lot and tried to avoid confrontation after their disagreement. Purposefully avoiding one of the co-owners while using the property is antithetical to an "apparent" use; such hidden use does not establish that the parties intended, or had a reasonable expectation of, an expansion of the easement by implication.

Affirmed.

CASE QUESTIONS

1. What was the significance of Todd's 1978 transfer of his Lot 30 interest?
2. Why does the expansion of the Lot 30 easement by prescription fail?
3. Why does the court discuss the concept of dominant and servient tenements?

CONSIDER 4.2   In the 1960s, the Pothiers sold to the Rickers two Tax Lots 7353 and 7354, property near skiing resorts on Bald Mountain. The Rickers gave their neighbors permission to use an upper path which crossed their property to access Bald Mountain, but were unaware of a lower path (the Path). In 1975, the Rickers sold both lots to Dick Matthews. Sometime during 1975, others in the neighborhood began using the Path, but there was no evidence as to whether Matthews gave permission to use the Path. Matthews sold the property to Fisher in 1978. Fisher lived on the property from 1978 to 1992, during which time he and his family used the Path to access Bald Mountain. Apparently, Fisher gave permission to use the Path to anyone who asked and was friendly to other users. When Fisher moved off the property in 1992, he instructed his tenants, who also used the Path, to allow the neighbors and the public to use it. In 2000, Fisher proposed to develop the portion of his property over which the Path crossed. Hughes, opposed to the development which would have blocked their use of the Path, filed suit to establish a prescriptive right to use the Path. Does he have such a right? *Hughes v. Fisher*, 129 P.3d 1223 (Idaho 2006).

Scope and Extent of Easements

The extent of permissive use of an easement is determined according to the type of easement. If an express easement has been created, determining the extent of the easement is simply a task of interpretation of the deed or contract granting the easement. A court must undertake this task of interpretation and will employ the **rule of reason** in executing its task. The rule of reason prohibits a court from imposing unreasonable burdens when the parties have expressed their desires and intentions in general terms. Under the rule of reason, a court cannot impose a strained construction of the language the parties chose.

For example, if the parties expressly provide for an easement across servient land in a definite location, then the court may not impose a different route for the easement. On the other hand, an express easement for a pipeline that does not specify depth can be interpreted to permit the dominant estate holder to move the pipe to a greater depth because of technological changes and necessities. Likewise, the grant of an easement to use a beach "for the purpose of boating, bathing, fishing, or other recreation" does not include the right to use the beach for the purpose of commercial boat rental. An easement for "foot passage" will not be expanded to permit vehicles, but an easement for "the right to pass" may be properly interpreted to permit vehicular traffic.

The extent, location, and use of a prescriptive easement are determined according to the type of use made during the prescriptive period. For example, a prescriptive right acquired through foot use does not include the right of vehicular use, and a vehicular private prescriptive use does not include an expansion to commercial use.

The task of determining the extent, use, and location of easements is perhaps most difficult in easements by implication. With this type of easement, courts assume that the parties would recognize the normal development of the dominant estate. Normal development is defined according to the initial use of the property. For example, if the dominant estate is used for residential purposes, normal development includes subdivision for numerous residences. However, it is not within normal development for the property to be used as a commercial rock bed with the accompanying use of large trucks. Also, the use of an easement by implication cannot be expanded to benefit properties other than the dominant estate.

However, all types of easements may be enlarged in their scope through prescription. For example, an easement "for the purpose of transporting milk to a factory" may be used for all purposes for a prescriptive period and expand into a general easement once the prescriptive elements are met. The following case deals with the extent and interpretation of an express easement.

BROWN V. CONOCOPHILLIPS PIPELINE COMPANY

271 P.3d 1269 (Kan. App. 2012)
Getting at the Root Cause in an Easement

FACTS

Conoco owns a 10″ high-pressure gasoline pipeline which runs from Paola to Wyandotte County. The pipeline passes through Lonzella Brown's property. The pipeline was laid in 1963 by Conoco's predecessor, Phillips Petroleum Company. That same year, Phillips purchased an easement from the people who owned the property at the time. The easement generally describes the area on the property where the pipelines were to be laid but did not expressly specify the width, length, or location of Phillips' rights for ingress and egress. The agreement merely stated that Phillips had the right to "lay, maintain, operate, inspect and remove" the two pipelines on the property. The easement provided that the landowners were vested with the right to "fully use and enjoy said premises except for the purposes hereinabove granted." The easement was recorded with the Wyandotte County Register of Deeds in 1963. The pipeline has been used continuously since being constructed.

When Mrs. Brown bought the property in 2000, the tree, a 30–year–old pin oak that is 60′ to 70′ tall, was already on the property. Conoco began a tree-clearing project along the 53–mile route of the pipeline from Paola to Wyandotte County. Conoco removed a number of trees in the course of its tree-clearing project. In October 2009, Conoco informed Mrs. Brown that it needed to remove the tree. Brown refused to allow Conoco to do so. Mrs. Brown filed a petition to enjoin Conoco from entering her land and cutting the tree down. Mrs. Brown obtained a temporary restraining order against Conoco. Conoco counterclaimed breach of contract against Brown and for a declaratory judgment confirming its right to remove the tree.

JUDICIAL OPINION

Brazil, Judge

Brown testified that she did not want to lose the tree because it is the only tree in her backyard, it shades her house and yard, and her granddaughter likes to play under it. She called a horticulturist, Phillip Hogan, as an expert, who testified that 80% or 90% of the tree's roots were located within 3 feet of the surface. Hogan testified that tree roots take the path of least resistance, meaning that if they ran into the pipeline, they would go around it because soil is softer than the pipe. He testified that while the top of a tree moves with the wind, tree roots are stable and do not move. He estimated that if the tree was cut down and a new one planted, Brown would be over 90 years old before the replacement tree would reach the current tree's size.

On cross-examination, Hogan admitted the tree's roots could extend over and across the pipeline if the pipeline was located within the first 3 or 4 feet of the ground's surface. He conceded that the pipeline could be damaged by the tree's roots if the pipeline is located close to the surface within a few feet of the tree, much in the same way that tree roots can damage a house's foundation if the house is too close to a tree. He also admitted he did not know the depth at which the pipeline had been buried nor did he know the pipeline's location in relation to the tree. Finally, Hogan admitted he knows nothing about gas pipelines or the safety concerns related to pipelines and tree roots.

Conoco called Michael Kemp, a claims consultant, and Todd Tullio, a regulatory compliance planning manager. Both Kemp and Tullio testified that the pipeline was located about 1 or 2 feet from the edge of the tree. Tullio was unsure of the precise depth at which the pipe had been buried in 1963 but estimated its present location was less than 36″ under the ground's surface. Tullio testified that the close proximity of the tree to the pipeline could damage the pipeline. Tullio explained that the pipeline moves when gasoline is being pumped through it and that the sustained friction between the pipeline and the roots could lead to the loss of the protective coating. The resulting corrosion of the pipeline could lead to a number of different problems, including large or small gasoline leaks, pipeline ruptures, environmental impacts, or possibly an explosion. He also presented pictures showing the effects tree roots can have on pipelines.

Tullio testified that if there were problems with the pipeline on Brown's property, Conoco would be unable to excavate around the pipeline until the tree was cut down because of safety concerns and the inability to access the pipeline due to its close proximity to the tree. He estimated Conoco would be delayed from immediately accessing the pipeline by "at least a couple of days."

He further testified that the tree also impeded Conoco's ability to maintain the pipeline because it interfered with pipeline inspections mandated by federal regulations. Federal guidelines require Conoco to aerially inspect its pipelines 26 times per year. Conoco contracts with an aerial company which navigates the pipeline's route and looks for a variety of things, including dead vegetation, debris, people digging or planting vegetation, and the like. If federal auditors detect shrubs or trees that prevent them from examining the pipelines, they can serve the pipeline company a notice of probable violation (NOPV), which gives the company 160 days to clear the right-of-way or face a fine.

The parties agree that Conoco holds a properly recorded pipeline easement across Brown's property, giving Conoco the right to "lay, maintain, operate, inspect and remove" its pipeline. Once an easement has been formed, the landowner is the servient tenant and the holder of the easement is the dominant tenant. The servient tenant may make any use of his or her property which is consistent with or not calculated to interfere with the use of the easement granted. Courts determine the character and extent of each parties' rights under the easement by examining the language of the grant and the extent of the dominant tenant's use of the easement at the time it was granted. An obstruction or disturbance of an easement is something that wrongfully interferes with the privilege to which the dominant tenant is entitled by making its use of the easement less convenient and beneficial. However, an obstruction or disturbance of an easement is not actionable unless it is of such a material character as to interfere with the dominant tenant's reasonable enjoyment of the easement.

The district court's conclusions are not consistent with its factual findings or the evidence presented. The district court heard undisputed evidence that the close proximity of the pipeline to tree roots can cause significant problems. The testimony that tree roots can damage pipelines was completely uncontested at trial. Brown's expert, Hogan, testified that tree roots travel in the path of least resistance. But by Hogan's own admission, he is not an expert when it comes to tree roots and their impact on pipelines. Furthermore, Hogan admitted the tree's roots could extend over and across the pipeline and that the pipeline could be damaged similar to the way a house's foundation can be damaged by tree roots. If there were any evidence that the tree and the pipeline could coexist in such close proximity, the district court's decision should be affirmed. But the facts of this case simply do not support such a conclusion.

The risk of damage the tree roots could cause to the pipeline alone is sufficient to show that the tree materially interferes with Conoco's privilege to use its easement, let alone the undisputed testimony that the tree causes a significant interference with Conoco's ability to inspect its pipeline. Considering there was no dispute that the tree roots can cause significant harm to the pipeline, the district court's conclusion that the tree did not cause a material interference with Conoco's easement was unsupported by substantial competent evidence.

Brown has not been wronged in this case. There is no dispute that Conoco has the right under its easement to maintain the pipeline. The undisputed facts of this case show that the tree materially obstructs Conoco's reasonable enjoyment of its easement. There is therefore no reason to analyze the above elements. The district court's injunction is vacated and the matter remanded so that Conoco can exercise the privileges it enjoys under the easement.

Vacated and remanded.

CASE QUESTIONS

1. Describe the problems with Mrs. Brown's expert witness.
2. What are Conoco's needs for maintenance of the pipeline?
3. What role did risk play in the court's analysis?

CONSIDER 4.4   John Wescoat owned property adjacent to a 176-acre parcel owned by Shooting Point, L.L.C. Wescoat's property was subject to a recorded easement that was 15 feet wide and 0.3 miles long and provided the only ingress and egress from Route 622 to Shooting Point's parcel.[4] When the easement was granted, both parcels were used for agricultural purposes and the easement was so bucolic and buried among the flora and fauna that it was barely visible to the eye and could not be seen from Route 622.

The parties, as dominant and servient tenements, enjoyed a peaceful coexistence from 1974 until 1999. In 1999, Shooting Point proposed the development of its parcel into 18 lots of approximately 5 acres each, which would surround a serene 50-acre "open-space" preservation. Shooting Point did inform purchasers that the easement for its parcel was limited to the 15-foot width and the plat plan incorporated that limitation.

When Mr. Wescoat learned of the proposed development, he filed suit alleging that such an expanded use of the parcel was "an additional and unreasonable burden" on the easement. From that point forward, the parties' relationship deteriorated as they argued over the true location of the easement and each side placed conflicting markers as to where they felt the easement was located.[5] Mr. Wescoat's son placed his wooden post markers in such a way that there were several 90-degree turns on the easement. The Shooting Point Property Owners Association then brought suit for fewer 90-degree turns.

The trial produced evidence that the presence of the new lot owners would result in 180 trips daily over the easement. In addition, the Wescoats introduced evidence that as more trips occurred on the road, there were more mudholes. The tendency of the lot owners was to drive around those mudholes and the result was that the easement was becoming increasingly wider at many points along the route to Route 622. Can the easement be expanded to accommodate the new land use and its development or is the expansion unjustified under the original terms of its grant? *Shooting Point, L.L.C. v. Wescoat*, 576 S.E.2d 497 (Va. 2003).

Rights and Obligations of Estate Holders in an Easement

Each of the parties in an easement relationship has certain legal responsibilities and rights. The easement owner (dominant estate) must keep the easement on the servient estate in repair. This responsibility of repair exists even if the servient estate owner is responsible for damages or the state of disrepair in the easement. The easement owner has the right to enter the servient land for purposes of repair. Furthermore, the easement owner may improve the easement with pavement or gravel when the easement is a right of passage.

---

[4]The easement is recorded as a metes and bounds description as follows: "[S]aid right-of-way easement to follow the present road leading from Virginia State Highway Route 622 to lands ... known as Shooting Point Farm, said present road running generally in a northerly direction from a point in a turn of said Virginia State Highway Route 622 to a point at or near a corner of a certain woods, thence turning in a generally easterly direction and running along the northern edge of said woods to a point at or near the edge of said woods, thence turning in a generally northerly direction and following along the edge of said woods to a point at or near a corner of said woods, thence turning in a generally easterly direction and running along the edge of said woods until the boundary line separating Shooting Point Farm from the [Wescoat parcel] is reached, at which boundary line the said right-of-way easement terminates." 576 S.E.2d at 498–499.

[5]The overgrown nature of the easement and the metes and bounds description left plenty of room, as it were, for interpretation of the location.

When dealing with easements, follow this checklist for acquiring, maintaining, and protecting an easement:

1. *Be clear in establishing the scope of the easement.*

2. *Specify use limitations in the easement granting language.*

3. *If the dominant tenement is not using the easement, document that the nonuse is not to be taken as abandonment.*

4. *Object to gates, locks, etc. erected by the servient tenement.*

5. *Maintain the easement so as to establish ongoing intent.*

6. *Keep the width and location of the easement clear.*

The owners of servient estates have the right to use their property in any way that does not interfere with the dominant holder's use of the easement. For example, the servient owner may grant more than one easement to more than one party.

Servient estate owners may also construct fences along the easement and install gates so long as there is no interference with the easement owner's use of the easement.

The dominant estate has the right to transfer an easement. An easement is transferred along with the dominant estate even though it is not specifically mentioned in the deed. An "all other appurtenances" clause serves to transfer an easement. Likewise, a servient estate is sold subject to any prior-acquired easements.

Termination of Easements

The termination or extinguishment of an easement occurs in several different ways, depending on the type of easement involved. All easements are terminated when there is one owner for both the dominant and servient estates or when the nonpossessory and possessory interests become united in one owner.

As discussed earlier, an easement by necessity is terminated when the necessity terminates.

All easements can be terminated through abandonment. Abandonment occurs through prescriptive nonuse. Two elements establish abandonment: (1) the easement owner must possess the intent to abandon; and (2) the intent to abandon must be accompanied by conduct indicating the intent to terminate. For example, the owner of a railroad easement who removes the tracks and destroys the shipping factory using the railway has manifested the intent to abandon through conduct. Permitting an easement to fall into a state of disrepair may constitute sufficient conduct manifesting an intent to abandon. For example, allowing an irrigation ditch to become inoperable is an example of disrepair indicating intent to abandon.

CONSIDER 4.5   The Noyeses owned a tract of land that was subject to an easement for "road and utility" purposes for property owners Kaibel, Creech, and Scheffing. The easement, a gravel road, ran from County Road 631, through the Noyes property, across Bob's Creek. Bob's Creek became the crux of the parties' easement dispute because it overflowed in nearly all rainstorms, thereby washing away the dirt and gravel from the ends of the bridge, making the bridge impassable.

During the 1980s, the Kaibels acquired another tract of land and built an access road across that tract of land. The Creeches and Scheffings began using that road with the permission of the Kaibels. The Kaibels, Creeches, and Scheffings then complained to Noyes that the Bob's Creek passageway was impassable and Mr. Kaibel said that he was tired of "messing" with the creek. Noyes asked them to contribute to the cost of installing a culvert pipe, but the parties all declined.

In 1997, thinking that the parties were sufficiently irritated with Bob's Creek that they were no longer interested in passing through, Noyes built a locked gate across the easement. In 1998, Mr. Creech tried to "brushhog" the property, but Noyes appeared and ordered Creech off her property. Creech *et al.* then brought suit seeking an injunction against Noyes to keep her from blocking access to the roadway. Had the easement been abandoned? *Creech v. Noyes*, 84 S.W.3d 880 (Mo. App. 2002).

_____ ■

All easements may be terminated if the servient owner successfully prevents the dominant holder's use of the easement for the required prescriptive period. An easement may be created or terminated through prescription.

Some easements are created for a specific time or purpose and are terminated when the time period expires or the purpose is eliminated. For example, a right-of-way given so long as the dominant land is used for a stable would terminate if the land is used for other purposes.

An easement may be terminated through *estoppel*. Estoppel occurs when the servient owner, believing there has been abandonment, constructs improvements over the easement in reliance upon the abandonment. The idea supporting this theory of termination is that the easement owner should notify the servient land-owner that such improvements interfere with the easement. If the easement owner were not required to object, then the servient landowner would make costly changes only to have them eliminated after completion. Estoppel requires prompt action to minimize expense.

CONSIDER 4.6   Would putting up a gate and posting a "No Trespassers" sign for two years be enough to stop an easement by prescription? *Kessinger v. Matule-vich*, 925 P.2d 864 (Mont. 1996).

_____ ■

PROFITS

A **profit** (or *profit a prendre*) is an easement plus the right of removal. A profit gives the holder the right not only of access to another's land, but also to remove oil, minerals, water, or some other part of the real property (see Chapter 3 for more discussion of oil and gas rights). A profit is not the same as the ownership of sub-surface rights because such ownership is exclusive and unlimited. More than one party can hold a profit in a piece of property, and a profit can be limited by the types of minerals that may be taken, or the time allowed for taking.

A profit is not the sale of personal property, because the landowner does not sever the mineral or soil—the profit owner does. For example, the right to remove coal is a profit, whereas the right to buy coal after removal is the sale of personal property.

A profit can be appurtenant, as in the right to remove water for use on an adjoining tract; or it can be in gross, as when an oil company that owns no prop-erty in the area is given the right to remove oil from a particular parcel.

Apart from these definitional differences, the creation, rights, and obligations of the parties in a *profit a prendre* relationship are governed by the same principles of law discussed in the easement portion of this chapter.

One of the most frequently used profits is one for timber. Timber is consid-ered a part of the real estate but can be severed through the award of a profit in the timber. Under the **Uniform Commercial Code (UCC)** (as adopted in most states), a contract for the sale of timber to be removed by the buyer is considered a contract for the sale of goods, but title to the timber does not pass to the buyer unless and until it is identified or removed from the land.

LICENSES

A **license** is a right to use land in the possession of another, but it passes no land interest and does not alter or transfer property. A license only makes certain conduct on another's land lawful, such as hunting, fishing, or simply being on the property. In many states, a ticket to a football game is a license.

A licensee holds a privilege, and that privilege may be revoked at any time by the landowner. A license may be created by an oral agreement, since it is not an interest in land. If the parties attempt to create an easement by oral agreement, they instead create only a license. Licenses and the legal rights associated with them have re-emerged in the last few years in professional sports and season tickets. In its litigation against StubHub, Inc. over StubHub's listing of its tickets for resale, the New England Patriots alleged that StubHub was engaged in intentional interference with advantageous relations through StubHub's knowing solicitation of ticket holders to violate the terms on which their tickets for access to Patriots home football games are granted (i.e., the license restrictions on transfer of the tickets). Massachusetts' Supreme Court had already held that tickets to entertainment events are revocable licenses, which a venue owner may revoke at any time and for any reason. The Patriots argued that StubHub, by offering season ticket holders' tickets for sale online, was interfering with its license rights. StubHub argued that a ticket was not a license but more like a bearer instrument that could be transferred easily. Not surprisingly, the Patriots continued their winning streak in court. The result is, because 95% of the tickets held to a Patriots game are season tickets, there is no open secondary market for ticket sales to Patriots game. Fans have only the license holder options afforded for selling their tickets. *Yarde Metals, Inc. v. New England Patriot*s, L.P., 64 Mass. App. Ct. 656, 658 (2005); *New England Patriots, L.P. and NPS LLC, Herman v. Admit One Ticket Agency*, 912 N.E.2d 450 (Mass. 2009).

COVENANTS

A **covenant** is a restriction placed in a deed that is, in effect, a nonpossessory interest in land. Covenants restrict or control some aspect of the use of the land. The common law rule on covenants is that they are enforceable against the grantor and grantee but not against any subsequent transferees. For example, a covenant in a grant of land for a railway requiring the construction of a depot and station would be enforceable against the grantee but not against subsequent transferees. For this reason, covenants are not effective in enforcing residential use restrictions. However, **equitable servitudes** may provide a solution. Equitable servitudes are restrictions on the use of land that are enforceable against subsequent transferees in the restricted areas. Sometimes equitable servitudes are called "covenants that run with the land" because they carry through transfers of title to the property.

Equitable servitudes or covenants that run with the land provide residential home buyers with assurance that their neighborhoods will retain their residential character at a certain quality and level. Zoning laws are also helpful in restricting land use and are discussed at length in Chapter 18. The details on covenants and equitable servitudes can be found in Chapter 21.

CONSIDER 4.7   On April 4, 1955, Clarence McKinley received a patent granting him title to 480 acres of land in Carbon County, Wyoming. McKinley also owned an additional piece of land in section 22 that is now held by Seven Lakes. McKinley intended to subdivide the land in sections 22 and 27 and form a small community he called "Woodedge." He created 24 ten-acre plots that were to be sold with the intent that the buyers would erect cabins thereon. McKinley intended to build certain improvements on the land he retained, including a road, a toboggan run, and a lodge; however, such improvements were never completed. Two of the parcels that McKinley conveyed in this manner are now owned by the Maxsons. The deeds from McKinley to the Maxsons' predecessors contained language indicating that the original grantees were also granted a "privilege" to hunt and fish on the lands owned by McKinley. A large portion of the land in the Woodedge area that was subject to the "privilege" is now owned, through various conveyances, by others. Seven Lakes owns the land at issue in section 22 and David Kuhn owns the land in section 27.

The Maxsons filed suit to have their "privileges" to hunt and fish declared a covenant that must be honored. Seven Lakes and Kuhn maintain that the Maxsons held only a profit. Help the court with its analysis of what was granted by McKinley. *Seven Lakes Development Co., L.L.C. v. Maxson*, 144 P.3d 1239 (Wyo. 2006).

CAUTIONS AND CONCLUSIONS

In applying the tools and risks described in this chapter, think through the following questions:

1. Is the property accessible or is it landlocked?
2. If the property is accessible, where is the access and who owns it?
3. If the property is landlocked, how can access be obtained?
4. Where is the access route (or where should it be) located?
5. How large an access route is necessary?
6. What types of uses can be made of the access route?
7. Is the access route recorded in any of the land records?
8. Will the deed in the transaction provide for an easement?
9. What parties are using the property, why, when, and for how long?
10. Who will be responsible for maintenance?

If buyers, sellers, agents, brokers, and financiers would take the time to check land records and physically inspect the property involved, many of the expensive easement litigations noted in this chapter could be avoided. The cases used in this chapter demonstrate the types of strong feelings and reactions that can result from misunderstandings on property use. This expensive hostility might be avoided by thinking through these 10 questions.

KEY TERMS

affirmative easement, 70
conservation easement, 70
covenant, 85
dominant tenement
    (estate), 71
easement, 69
easement appurtenant, 69
easement by express grant, 71

easement by express
    reservation, 71
easement by implication, 74
easement by necessity, 75
easement in gross, 69
equitable servitudes, 85
license, 85
negative easement, 70

prescription, 75
profit, 84
profit a prendre, 84
quasi easement, 74
rule of reason, 79
servient tenement (estate), 71
Uniform Commercial Code,
    (UCC), 84

CHAPTER PROBLEMS

1. Charlotte Minogue and John Monette are sister and brother. Each inherited a home from their father through his last will and testament. Charlotte inherited her father's actual residence at 90 Hawthorne Avenue in Albany, New York. John inherited the contiguous parcel located at 88 Hawthorne Avenue.

   A blacktop driveway, approximately 10 feet wide, runs between the two houses. A survey in 1988 showed the driveway to be located on John's property. A concrete cinder-block garage is located at the rear of Charlotte's two-family home. The driveway had provided access for her father to the garage and to Charlotte and her tenants until John blocked such use in 1988.

   Charlotte filed suit seeking a declaration of easement for ingress and egress over the driveway. Is she entitled to one? What theory could she use? What type of easement might she have? *Minogue v. Monette*, 551 N.Y.S.2d 427 (1990).

2. Granite Properties Limited Partnership owned all of the parcels shown in the diagram below. Between 1963 and 1982, Granite conveyed certain of the parcels, and, in 1982, parcel B was conveyed to Larry Manns and others (defendants). The present status of the parcels is as follows:

   - Parcel A contains a shopping center (built in 1967 and currently owned by Granite). To the north of the shopping center is an asphalt parking lot with 191 feet of frontage on Bethalto Drive.
   - Parcel B is undeveloped and is owned by the defendants.
   - Parcel C contains 5 four-family apartment buildings (owned by a third party).
   - Parcel D contains a health club (owned by a third party).
   - Parcel E contains the Chateau des Fleurs Apartments (owned by Granite).

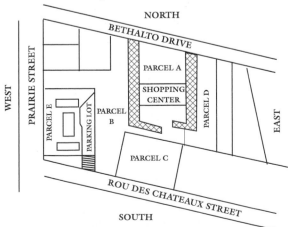

The rear of the shopping center is used for deliveries, trash storage and removal, and utilities repair. To gain access to the rear of the shopping center for these purposes, trucks use a gravel driveway that runs along the lot line between parcel A and parcel B. A second driveway (noted in diagram), located to the east of the shopping center on parcel D, enables the trucks to circle the shopping center and deliver to the stores, including Save-a-Lot Grocery, without having to turn around in the limited space behind the stores. The trucks can thus make a convenient entrance, delivery stop, and exit.

The two pictured driveways existed before Manns purchased the property, and he saw them during an inspection of the land prior to his purchase. There are no references to the driveways in any of the deeds relating to the parcels.

Robert Mehann, owner of the Save-a-Lot grocery store located in the shopping center, testified that groceries, which are delivered to the rear of the store, are loaded by forklift on a concrete pad poured for that purpose. Mehann indicated that there are large, double-steel doors in the back of the store to accommodate items that will not fit through the front door. Mehann testified that semitrailer trucks make deliveries to the rear of the grocery store four days a week, with as many as two or three such trucks arriving daily. An average of 10 to 12 trucks a day, including semitrailer trucks, make deliveries to the grocery store. Mehann further explained that because the area behind the Save-a-Lot building extends only 50 feet to the rear property line, it would be difficult, if not impossible, for a semitrailer truck to turn around in the back and exit the same way it came in. In response to a question as to whether it would be feasible to have trucks make front-door deliveries, Mehann suggested that such deliveries would be very disruptive; pallets that would not fit through the front door would have to be broken down into parts, requiring extra work, and there would not be adequate space in the front of the store to do such work during business hours. Mehann admitted that he had not investigated the cost of installing a front door that would be big enough for pallets of groceries to be brought in by forklift. There would not be enough space to manipulate the forklift around the front of the store, although it could be run between the shelves of food to the back of the store.

Darrell Layman, a partner for Granite, testified that, although it was very difficult, he had seen semitrailer trucks exit the same way they came in. Layman also acknowledged that he had not investigated the cost of expanding the size of the front doors of the building. He also claimed it "would seem impossible" for him to put in any kind of a hallway or passageway that would allow equipment to bring supplies into the store from the front. Layman explained that the delivery trucks follow no set schedule and, therefore, their presence may overlap at times. He stated that he had seen as many as four or five delivery trucks backed up. Layman opined that there was "no way" the trucks could back up and turn around when there were multiple trucks present.

Granite claimed an easement by implication for the shopping center and the parcel E apartment complex. Is there an easement? Is Granite correct that it is an easement by implication? *Granite Properties Limited Partnership v. Manns*, 512 N.E.2d 1230 (Ill. 1987).

3. Christine and Steve Mallock buried their son in a burial plot purchased at Southern Memorial Park, Inc. Each year, the Mallocks conducted a memorial service for their son at his burial plot. On the seventh anniversary of their son's death, the Mallocks went to their son's grave at 11:00 a.m. for the annual service, which generally took 30 minutes. When they arrived, they discovered that a tent and chairs set up for funeral services on the plot next to their son's grave were actually resting on his gravesite. The Mallocks asked Southern's management if the tent and chairs could be moved until they could conduct their service. The managers refused, and the Mallocks went ahead with their ceremony, cutting it to five minutes, after they moved the chairs and tents by themselves.

Southern's managers called the police and had the Mallocks evicted. Southern claims the Mallocks had no rights on the property except for the grave. Their deed for the plot does not award an easement for access. Do the Mallocks have the right to access to the gravesite? *Mallock v. Southern Memorial Park, Inc.*, 561 So.2d 330 (Fla. Ct. App. 1990).

4. American University acquired a parcel of land (Lot 806) from Aetna Life Insurance Company. The university was given a Declaration of Easement and Agreement that provided that the grantor:

conveys to the owners from time to time of [Lot 806 and their] tenants, occupants, guests and business invites, a nonexclusive easement for vehicular parking of not less than 236 automobiles on the parking areas located from time to time upon [Lot 807].

New owners of Lot 807 decided to regulate parking and limit the number of spaces available to American University. Can a private agreement like this or regulations on use change the terms and scope of an easement? *Burka v. Aetna Life. Ins. Co.*, 945 F. Supp. 313 (D.D.C. 1996).

5. In 1962, Temco sold property located at 900 South Wakefield Street to Harvey and Rosabelle Wynn. The purchase contract contains the following provision: "use of apartment swimming pool to be available to purchaser and his family." The Wynns were told that subsequent purchasers of their property would also have use of the swimming pool, which is located in an apartment complex next to the Wynns' home. No reference to use of the swimming pool was made in the Wynns' deed.

In 1969, the Bunns purchased the Wynns' home. The Bunns were told of their right to use the pool but upon moving in were denied access. The Bunns insisted on access but were still denied. They filed suit against the owner of Temco, Offutt, seeking a declaration of the easement rights. Do the Bunns have easement rights? *Bunn v. Offutt*, 222 S.E.2d 522 (Va. 1976).

6. Ten-year-old Joshua Jackson was flying a kite in his friend's backyard and suffered serious injuries when he used an aluminum pole to try to dislodge the kite from an electrical power line that traversed the neighboring property owned by the friend's grandmother, Eve Prince. Jackson filed suit against PG & E, which owned an easement to erect and maintain electrical power lines across the Prince property. The Court of Appeal upheld the trial court's determination that PG & E was immune from liability to Jackson, under the recreational use immunity statute.

Jackson then filed a premises liability action against Prince. The complaint alleges that Jackson was "expressly invited" to use Prince's property, and that Prince knew or should have known that the lines hanging low over her property were high-voltage power lines that posed a hazard to her guests. The complaint further alleges that Prince used a 19-foot-8-inch aluminum pole to shake nut trees, that she left it near the low hanging power lines, and that she "created a foreseeable risk of injury or death should the metal pole be raised near the lines for any purpose."

Prince filed a cross-complaint against PG & E alleging that, based on the easement granted to PG & E and on a statute that requires owners of easements to maintain them in repair, PG & E breached a contractual duty owed to her to maintain its power lines in repair and its failure to do so proximately caused Jackson's injury. Prince seeks indemnity from PG & E for having the power lines too low to the ground. Who is responsible for maintenance of the power lines? Who is liable for the injuries? *Prince v. Pacific Gas & Elec.Co.*, 202 P.3d 1115, 90 Cal.Rptr.3d 732 (Cal. 2009).

7. Pacific Theatres and Supply Company, Limited, acquired title to a lot in Waikiki near Seaside and Kalakaua Avenue. The lot deed also provided:

   TOGETHER with the perpetual right of ingress and egress over the 10-foot strip of land on the Western side of Lot 2-B.

   Consolidated Amusement bought Pacific's lot and has operated a movie theater there since 1936. Waikiki Business Plaza acquired title to an adjacent lot and planned to construct the Plaza Building and set up vendors' booths in the area. Before the vendors began business and during building construction, Consolidated and the Plaza agreed to allow a "pedestrian passageway" for Plaza activities when the Plaza commenced commercial business with the various booths. Consolidated maintains the booths interfere with its easement for theater patrons. Plaza claims that a small passageway is sufficient. Who is correct? Can the easement be reduced by agreement? *Waikiki Business Consolidated Amusement v. Plaza*, 719 P.2d 1119 (Haw. 1986).

8. Asa E. Phillips owned property in Seal Harbor, Maine. His deed included a 20-foot right-of-way over property owned by Kate Gregg and W. Layton Stewart. The right-of-way had long been reduced to a five-foot-wide footpath and was largely overgrown with trees. Gregg and Stewart had placed gates and warning signs along the path to discourage Phillips's use. Phillips brought suit for an injunction to prevent Gregg and Stewart from interfering with his use of his right-of-way. Gregg and Stewart claimed he had abandoned his easement through nonuse. Who is correct? How should the court determine abandonment? *Phillips v. Gregg*, 628 A.2d 151 (Me. 1993).

9. Paul Atkinson purchased land from Donald Mentzel that included an easement across Mentzel's land so that Atkinson could have access to his garage. Atkinson wished to install telephone cable along the easement so that he could more fully use his garage. At the time of the conveyance, the Atkinson property did not have utility service. The easement was described as a right-of-way and including the following:

   The purpose of this easement is to provide access from Lake Shore Drive to the following described real estate and shall allow access for all uses of said property other than retail sales.

   Should Atkinson be permitted to install the telephone cable along the easement? *Atkinson v. Mentzel*, 566 N.W.2d 158 (Wis. App. 1997).

10. The Friersons have a two-story building in Easley, South Carolina that shares a common wall with an adjacent two-story building owned by David and Patricia Watson. An outdoor stairway located on the Watsons' property provides access to the second floor of both buildings. A dispute arose when David Watson began to construct apartments on the second floor of his building and proposed to close off a connecting indoor hallway between the two properties at the top of the stairs located inside the building. The Friersons maintained that they had an easement to use both the outdoor stairway and the indoor hallway for access.

    The Friersons' predecessors-in-interest, E. C., E. O., and D. M. Frierson, purchased the building in 1929 from the "Estate of R. F. Smith, Inc." The 1929 deed, dated January 14 and recorded on January 23, expressly conveyed "an easement in a certain four foot stairway in the back of the building, with right of ingress and egress on said stairway to the second story of said building." On January 21, 1929, two days before the deed was recorded, the parties to the sale executed a "Memorandum of Agreement" that granted an easement for the use of the hallway. The memo was not recorded.

    The Friersons brought suit to stop Watson's construction. The Friersons claimed Watson's construction violated their easement by eliminating the hallway, which denied them access to the second floor of their building.

    The circuit court determined that the Friersons had established an easement for use of the hallway by grant and by prescription and granted the Friersons' motion. David Watson appealed. Who is correct on this easement issue? Explain why. *Frierson v. Watson*, 636 S.E.2d 872 (S.C. App. 2006).

For research activities related to this chapter, go to our text companion website at www.cengagebrain.com

CHAPTER 5

FIXTURES

Is the refrigerator included with the house?

The American Home Buyer

*Every lawyer knows that cases can be found in this field
that will support any proposition.*

Powell, Real Property

A **fixture** is real property that was once personal property. It becomes attached to the real property, and when it does, it becomes a part of it. This chapter answers the following questions: What is a fixture and when does personal property become a fixture? How is the title to a fixture transferred? What rights do creditors have in fixtures?

DEFINITION OF A FIXTURE

Whether a particular item of personal property will become real property depends on several factors discussed in the following sections. No single factor controls; rather, the different factors must be considered together in their entirety in order to determine whether an item is real or personal property. The distinction between real and personal property is critical in two primary areas: First, a fixture passes with title to real property, whereas personal property may be removed prior to the transfer of title to real property. Second, fixtures are subject to the interests of real property creditors, that is, how much the mortgage holder is entitled to on the property and how much belongs to the personal property creditor.

Degree of Annexation Test

The degree of annexation test is the first factor to be considered in determining the status of an item of property, and its purpose is to examine the fixture's degree of attachment. Under the English rule for fixtures, annexation was the controlling factor, and anything attached by mortar, nail, screw, or bolt was classified as a fixture.

Currently, *annexation* is defined as attachment to the realty with a use or purpose related to the realty. A furnace in a home is an example that meets the degree of annexation necessary for a fixture because the furnace cannot function outside the home and the home cannot function without the presence of the furnace (which was once personal property). On the other hand, a ship or boat does not become part of the real property of a dock simply because an anchor is dropped because its attachment to the realty is unrelated. A painting on a wall can be hung on any wall, but the sculptures within building columns are a part of the building and hence meet this annexation test.

The degree of annexation test applies to personal property attached to realty but not to accessions. Accessions are those items of personal property that are used in the construction of a building and become so integrated into the building that their identity is lost. Examples of accessions are lumber, bricks, and beams.

Nature and Use of the Property

The unique nature of the property attached and its necessity in relation to the effective functioning of the building are also factors in determining whether something is a fixture. For example, storm windows are especially built and installed for a particular home and work to help control heat in the home. Likewise, a pipe organ in a church with the pipes serving as decoration for the building has an intricate relation to the building. In a garage, an air compressor that is used to hoist cars for repair is central and necessary to the function of that building.

PRACTICAL TIP

When in doubt, ask! Brokers should verify what is included in a property sale to avoid such items becoming an issue of negotiation and/or contention. Sellers should make their intentions clear and possibly remove any items that could confuse buyers. Buyers should list, count, and verify to be sure they know what they're getting.

Relationship Between Annexor and Premises

Another factor courts examine in determining whether an item is a fixture is what type of land interest the party attaching the personal property (the annexor) owns. The higher the degree of interest in the land, the more likely an item attached by the land interest owner will be treated as a fixture. For example, a small cottage or bungalow placed on cement blocks on the land by a fee simple owner is a fixture. That same bungalow placed on leased land by a tenant will probably retain its characteristics of personal property because the tenant's interest is not permanent.

There are two additional questions to examine in analyzing this factor: (1) Did the tenant intend the item to be a gift to the landlord (that is, did the tenant intend to leave the property at the termination of the lease?); and (2) will removal of the property cause substantial damage? For example, a floor replaced with a new covering by a tenant will be substantially damaged if the covering is removed upon termination of the tenancy. On the other hand, removal of temporary wall bookshelves may not cause irreparable damage and would be classified as a tenant's personal property. The following case deals with an issue of landlord liability that turns on whether a walk-in cooler is a fixture.

GORMAN V. NGO MENG

335 S.W.3d 797 (Tex. App. 2011)
A Shocking Fixture

FACTS

Ngo[1] met Hayden's son when they were both taking air conditioning installation and repair classes. Ngo also owned a convenience store. Ngo quit attending classes and, sometime later, requested that Hayden's son install a walk-in cooler in the store. Because Hayden's son did not have refrigeration experience, Hayden helped his son install the walk-in cooler. Hayden had been licensed to perform HVAC installation and repair, but relinquished the license when he became disabled. Hayden had previously installed between ten and fifteen walk-in coolers and had never experienced any problems with the installations. Hayden had performed some previous work for Ngo.

Ngo purchased the walk-in cooler from his ex-wife. Hayden purchased an air conditioner condenser and modified it to work as a refrigeration unit. Hayden placed the condenser outside the convenience store on a pallet and wired it to the walk-in cooler. Hayden used existing circuits at the store and did not install either an electrical disconnect or a ground on the condenser.

Shortly after the walk-in cooler was installed, customers in the store began complaining they were being shocked when they touched the doors to the walk-in cooler. Further, the lessee of the store was knocked to the floor when he was shocked while mopping the floor next to the cooler. The lessee complained to Ngo at least three times that the walk-in cooler was shocking people.

Each time the lessee complained, Ngo asked Hayden to investigate the problem. Hayden visited the store on three occasions, but the doors to the walk-in cooler did not shock him or show any signs of being energized. After his third trip, Hayden suggested that Ngo hire a licensed electrician to investigate the problem.

Ngo contacted Gorman (his estate and relatives are the appellants), who installed walk-in coolers and freezers, to investigate the problem. Gorman was a licensed electrician with experience installing coolers and condensers.

Using an ohm meter, Gorman determined the cooler doors were energized. Gorman then turned off the breakers to the walk-in cooler and again checked the cooler doors. The cooler doors were no longer energized. Gorman's brother, Gary, did not know whether Gorman turned off the breakers to the condenser outside. The two men went outside the store to check the condenser. Gorman was checking the condenser to "find out where the problem was." There was standing water around the condenser. Gorman asked Gary to hand him a tool. As Gary started to do so, Gorman picked up a control box that was connected to the condenser. The box was energized, and Gorman was electrocuted. Gorman died from his injuries.

Tony Perryman, a licensed professional engineer and journeyman electrician, investigated the walk-in cooler installation following Gorman's death. According to Perryman, Gorman was electrocuted because neither the walk-in cooler nor the condenser was grounded. Perryman said that Gorman would not have been electrocuted if the breaker was off.

The trial court entered a take nothing judgment against Gorman's estate and the estate appealed.

JUDICIAL OPINION

Fillmore, Justice

Chapter 95 governs a property owner's liability for the acts of an independent contractor. The statute applies to a claim (1) against the owner of real property used primarily for business purposes, (2) caused by negligence, (3) that resulted in the death of a contractor, and (4) that arose from the condition or use of an improvement to real property where the contractor constructs, repairs, renovates, or modifies the improvement. Tex. Civ. Prac. & Rem. Code Ann. §§ 95.001(1), (3), 95.002 (West 2005).

It is undisputed that Ngo owned the property, the property was used for business purposes, Gorman was a contractor, appellants' claims are based on Ngo's alleged negligence, and appellants are seeking damages for Gorman's death. Appellants, however, argue chapter 95 does not apply because the condenser was not an improvement to real property, Gorman did not construct, repair, renovate, or modify

---

[1]Ngo was referred to throughout the pleadings and the trial as both Meng H. Ngo and Ngo H. Meng. Ngo testified his name was Meng Ngo. For consistency, the court referred to him as Ngo throughout the opinion.

the condenser, and the condenser was not the improvement on which Gorman was working.

Appellants contend the condenser was not an improvement to the property because it was not annexed to the realty and was not intended to be a permanent addition to realty. Appellants assert that because the condenser "was not mounted and was lying on the pallet upon which it came" and was being used for refrigeration, rather than air conditioning, "the condenser unit was not 'an improvement to real property' as required by Section 95.002."

In *Norris v. Thomas*, 215 S.W.3d 851, 854–55 (Tex. 2007), the Texas Supreme Court addressed whether a sixty-eight foot yacht qualified as a homestead [under] the property code. The court concluded the yacht was not a homestead because it did not rest on land and did not have a requisite degree of physical permanency, immobility, and attachment to fixed realty. The supreme court noted that "personalty does not constitute an improvement until it is annexed to realty." "[T]he annexed object cannot be deemed an improvement to land unless it is intended to be 'a permanent addition to the realty.'"

[A]n improvement includes all additions to the land other than trade fixtures that can be removed without injury to the property. Whether personalty has been affixed to realty depends on (1) the mode and sufficiency of annexation; (2) the adaption of personalty to the use or purpose of realty; and (3) the intention of the owner. The owner's intention is preeminent and the first two factors are evidence of intent.

In this case, Ngo caused a walk-in cooler to be installed in the store. The condenser was placed on a pallet outside the building and was electrically connected to the cooler through the store's breaker box. Hayden modified the condenser to meet the store's need for a refrigeration system. The condenser and cooler were intended to serve the convenience store and to be operated on the premises. We conclude the installation of the walk-in cooler and the condenser evidenced Ngo's intent that the cooler and condenser be annexed to the realty. Accordingly, the condenser was an improvement under section 95. 002(2).

The condenser was connected to the walk-in cooler and was intended to make the walk-in cooler functional. Gorman determined he needed to inspect the condenser in order to determine why the doors of the walk-in cooler were shocking customers of the store. We conclude Gorman was not injured by an improvement separate from the improvement that was the object of his work.

Appellants argue the trial court erred by entering a take nothing judgment in favor of Hayden because Hayden breached his duty to make the premises safe and this breach proximately caused Gorman's death.

In its findings of fact, the trial court found "Hayden also powered down the cooling condensor [sic] and cooler, instructing Ngo and the store owner not to turn on the cooler or condenser until the unit could be inspected by an electrician. Hayden also put a note on the circuit box not to turn the cooler or condensor [sic] back on." Although the power to the condenser and cooler were on when Gorman arrived, "there was no evidence as to who turned the unit on."

The trial court's findings support the conclusions that Hayden took steps to make the premises safe and that, but for someone other [than] Hayden turning on the electricity to the walk-in cooler and the condenser, Gorman would not have been killed. Accordingly, the findings support a conclusion that Hayden exercised "due care" and that appellants failed to prove Hayden's conduct proximately caused Gorman's death. We conclude the evidence is factually sufficient to support the trial court's judgment in favor of Hayden.

We affirm the trial court's judgment.

CASE QUESTIONS

1. Why is it important to determine whether the condenser and cooler were fixtures?
2. How important is intent in the court's decision? Is the relationship of the cooler and condenser to the property important?
3. Make a list of the lessons a property owner might take away from this case.

Intent

The intent of the parties can be the controlling factor in cases where the issue of fixture versus personal property is a close decision, as well as in cases where the parties have reached an agreement (or have placed a provision in their contract or lease) covering the issue of whether an item will be real or personal property.

For example, refrigerators may be included in the sale of residences or apartments, and by the parties' wishes may be considered fixtures. Likewise, washers and dryers may also transfer with the real estate by the parties' agreement.

Trade Fixtures

The term **trade fixture** is a misnomer. Machines, equipment, and other personal property used in a trade or business are called trade fixtures. However, even though their degree of annexation may result in some damage upon removal, trade fixtures do not remain with the property. In the absence of an agreement between the parties, trade fixtures do not pass with the sale of the factory or business location; they remain the property of the business itself. For example, a large printing press bolted to the floor is a trade fixture and thus personal property. Likewise, display counters in stores are attached but are classified as trade fixtures.

CONSIDER 5.1   The Shapleigh, Maine waste transfer station consists of a permanent, large garage-type structure with two levels that are both accessible by automobile. The upper level handles household trash, and the lower level handles recyclable and demolition materials. There are also trash bins outside of the lower level of the building that are used for larger items of trash. These bins are freestanding, have wheels, and are located in a parking lot.

On August 3, 2002, Daniel Sanford went to the waste facility to dispose of some trash. First, he went to the upper level and disposed of household trash. He then drove to the lower level, where an attendant directed him to one of the freestanding bins outside of the building. The door to the bin was closed. Sanford loaded some small, light pieces of scrap wood into the bin and then leaned a heavy piece of plywood against the bin. The attendant told Sanford to place the plywood inside the bin. As he lifted the plywood, Sanford felt a ripping sensation in his left bicep. Sanford testified that several days after the incident, the attendant's supervisor called Sanford and stated that the attendant should have helped him, the bin should have been open, and remedial actions would be taken.

Sanford filed a complaint against the Town alleging negligence in the design, operation, construction, maintenance, and supervision of the transfer station. The Town raised the affirmative defense of immunity under a Maine statute, which provides that "all governmental entities shall be immune from suit on any and all tort claims seeking recovery of damages." The Act creates an exception to immunity when a governmental entity is negligent in "the construction, operation or maintenance of any public building or the appurtenances to any public building." Sanford argued that the trash bin was a fixture and the Town was not immune. Help in the analysis—is the bin a fixture? *Sanford v. Town of Shapleigh*, 850 A.2d 325 (Me. 2004).   ■

Who Wants to Know?

Although the treatises on real property do not list this factor as one to be used in the determination of real versus personal property, the question of "who wants to know" has affected judicial decisions in this area. Application of this factor produces differing results depending on what party seeks to determine the classification for an item of property.

For example, in litigation between a buyer and seller, the buyer is favored because the seller usually presents the form contract and has failed to make all intentions clear in that contract. In an eminent domain valuation procedure, the landowner is favored with a liberal finding of fixtures because the court's concern in these circumstances is just and fair compensation. If a question arises on the application of real property insurance for certain items, the insured will be favored with liberal fixture treatment because of the insurer's failure to clarify coverage provisions. In taxation valuations, assessors are more likely to conclude in favor of finding fixtures because the property value increases when the fixtures are included in the valuation determination.

The following cases are examples of courts applying the various factors used in the determination of whether an item is real or personal property. Note that the courts deal with fixture tests in different ways for different purposes.

CUSTER V. BEDFORD COUNTY BD. OF ASSESSMENT AND REVISION OF TAXES

910 A.2d 113 (Pa. 2006)
A Moveable or Planted Greenhouse?

FACTS

Robert S. Custer owns approximately 97 acres in Cumberland Valley Township, Bedford County, where he operates a nursery business. In March 2001, Custer purchased a used greenhouse for $1,500, disassembled it, transported it by flatbed pickup truck to his property, where he stored it until May 2004, and then reassembled it. The greenhouse is an arch-shaped structure that is 30 feet by 96 feet in size, and is approximately 12 feet high at its highest point. The greenhouse is constructed by 24 vertical pipes on each side. These vertical pipes are inserted two feet into the ground and are connected at the top to arch-shaped pipes. Plastic covering is attached to the arch-ing pipes and serves as a covering for the structure.

Because of the addition of the greenhouse to the property, the Board increased the assessed value of the buildings on Custer's property for the 2004 tax year from $11,124 to $19,978, an increase of $8,854. Custer appealed to the Board contending that the greenhouse should not be assessed because it was not real estate. After the Board denied his appeal, he appealed to the trial court. The trial court affirmed the board's finding and Custer appealed.

JUDICIAL OPINION

Pelligrini, Justice

At the hearing before the trial court, Custer testified that to disassemble the greenhouse and move it to his property, the plastic was removed and then the pieces that held it together were unbolted. After transporting it to his property, he reassembled it without heavy equipment, using only clam shell diggers, shovels and wrenches. He testified that each of the posts/poles was placed two feet into the ground just past the frost line. Custer opined that it was never his intention for the greenhouse to be permanent, but only to serve as a "starter" greenhouse to be replaced in the future by a "better" greenhouse. He stated that if he were to move off the property or quit the nursery business, he would either sell the greenhouse or take it with him. Custer admitted, though, that he had no present intention of moving his business or relocating. As to the greenhouse's purpose, he testified that it assisted him by creating the necessary environment for raising plants going through a "transformation" from seed to plant to shrubbery to make them sellable.

Chattels used in connection with real estate are of three classes: First, those which are manifestly furniture, as distinguished from improvements and not peculiarly fitted to the property with which they are used; these always remain personalty ... Second, those which are so annexed to the property that they cannot be removed without material injury to the real estate or to themselves; these are realty, even in the face of an expressed intention that they should be considered personalty.... Third, those which, although physically connected with the real estate, are so affixed as to be removable without destroying or materially injuring the chattels themselves, or the property to which they are annexed; these become part of the realty or remain personalty, depending upon the intention of the parties at the time of the annexation; in this class fall such chattels as boilers and machinery affixed for the use of an owner or tenant but readily removable.

Regarding the first classification, Custer asserts that the greenhouse is more furniture than an improvement because its purpose was not to enhance the value, beauty or utility of Custer's property or to adapt the property for a new or further purpose. Rather, he argues that the greenhouse was equipment that was necessary, useful and desirable for the purpose of raising plants for his nursery business. "Improvement" has been defined as a "permanent addition to or betterment of real property that enhances its capital value and that involves the expenditure of labor or money and is designed to make the property more useful or valuable as distinguished from ordinary repairs." While the greenhouse may not have been valuable from a monetary perspective ($1,500) or enhanced the beauty of the property from an aesthetic perspective, the greenhouse enhanced the utility of Custer's property by allowing Custer to grow more plants for his nursery business, making it an improvement, not furniture.

Regarding the third classification, Custer contends that because the greenhouse can be removed without harm to it or the property on which it was located, and it was his intention that the greenhouse was to be removed once a new greenhouse was bought or the nursery business failed, it cannot be considered real property.

Custer asserts that because the greenhouse can be removed without any damage to it or the property, it must be personalty. However, in categorizing the canopy as realty rather than personalty, we observed that the degree of attachment necessary to evidence permanence is not high....

"[M]odern construction methods and types of structures allow material that stays for years on a piece of property to be moved with little damage to the property. Acoustic ceiling panels 'affixed' by gravity and removable with no damage to the property are nonetheless taxable as real estate as are door handles and kitchen faucets when attached to a structure." In the case of the greenhouse, each of the posts/poles are placed two feet into the ground, which possesses the requisite degree of "attachment."... [T]here is nothing in the record in the present case suggesting that the greenhouse is an item that was intended to be removed as long as the property was being used as a nursery to grow and cultivate plants. The greenhouse creates the necessary environment for raising plants and will be affixed to the property until it is worn out, the nursery business fails or Custer and his wife no longer occupy the property.... [T]he greenhouse is realty and taxable as real estate.

Accordingly, because the greenhouse is "real estate" the trial court's order is affirmed.

DISSENTING OPINION
Kelley, Senior Judge

I respectfully dissent. Mr. Custer testified that the instant greenhouse was for temporary use in the nursery business until he and his wife could construct a more permanent structure, and that he would take the greenhouse if he should move the business like any other piece of equipment. Mr. Custer's testimony in this regard is supported by the testimony of his wife.

There is simply no objective evidence in the record suggesting that the greenhouse was intended to be permanently affixed to the property so as to become part of the realty. Thus, even if it is assumed that the greenhouse in this case was sufficiently physically attached to the land, requiring an examination of the Custers' intent with respect to the greenhouse, the evidence in this case does not support the determination that the greenhouse was permanently affixed to the realty.

Accordingly, unlike the Majority, I would reverse the trial court's order in this case.

CASE QUESTIONS

1. What effect do you think the "who wants to know" question had on this case?
2. What does the dissenting judge say should be determinative in the case?
3. How does the degree of attachment test apply in this situation?
4. Discuss whether you agree with the majority decision or the dissent, and why.

KOHN V. DARLINGTON COMMUNITY SCHOOL DISTRICT

698 N.W.2d 794 (2005)
The Case of the Procedural Misstep on the Bleachers

FACTS

On September 29, 2000, Elaine Kohn and her then four-year-old daughter, Lori Kohn, attended the homecoming football game at Darlington High School. At about 2:30 p.m. on a glorious Wisconsin Saturday afternoon, young Lori fell through the space at the foot of her seat in the home bleachers to the ground 15 feet below, sustaining injuries. The Kohns brought suit in 2001.

The home team bleachers at Darlington High School were manufactured by Standard Steel Industries, Inc. and purchased by the school for $16,167 in 1969 (Standard was later purchased by Illinois Tool Works [ITW]).

Initially, the Kohns filed suit against Darlington and its insurer for breach of their duty of care to the invitees in the bleachers. Later, however, the Kohns amended their complaint to include ITW as a defendant, alleging that Standard left the bleachers in a defective condition that was unreasonably dangerous and resulted in the accident involving their daughter. Still, the Kohns' suit was dismissed initially because Wisconsin has passed a statute of repose. Under Wis. § 893.89(2), there is a ten-year statute of limitations on recovery for injuries caused by improvements to real property.

Following the dismissal of the Kohns' suit, the Wisconsin Court of Appeals reversed the lower court's dismissal. The court of appeals concluded that the bleachers were not an improvement to real property because there was no evidence that the bleachers were anchored to the ground. The court of appeals held that the Kohns' claims were governed by the three-year statute of limitation on personal injury and product liability actions (within which their 2001 filing date found them), rather than being dismissed under the ten-year period of repose. The Wisconsin Supreme Court then stepped carefully, as it were, into the fray.

JUDICIAL OPINION

Wilcox, Justice

First, do the bleachers in question constitute an "improvement to real property" for purposes of § 893.89 (the statute of repose)? Whether an item is an "improvement to real property" under § 893.89 is a question of law that we review *de novo. Kallas Millwork Corp. v. Square D Co.*, 66 Wis.2d 382, 386, 225 N.W.2d 454 (1975).

No one disputes that the installation of the bleachers at Darlington High School was substantially completed in 1969. The question is whether the bleachers constitute an "improvement to real property" under the statute. If they do, then the "exposure period" ended in 1979, and the Kohns' claims against ITW failed to accrue.

The Kohns contend that the bleachers are not an improvement to real property because they are not anchored in the ground and are portable. The Kohns, like the court of appeals, rely on the "degree of physical annexation" of the bleachers to support their argument. The Kohns further contend that very little effort or expenditure was required to place the bleachers on the ground. They argue that the bleachers are simply "personal property resting upon the real estate" and are not "integral" to the usefulness of the property. Finally, the Kohns assert that the bleachers are not an improvement to real property because they were not specifically designed or manufactured for use at Darlington High School.

ITW argues that the bleachers are permanent as their permanency is a function of their purpose. ITW emphasizes that in the 30 years since they were erected, the bleachers have not been moved, and there is no evidence that they were ever intended to be moved. ITW also focuses on the size of the bleachers and the fact that they enhance the value and usefulness of the property. ITW states that it is significant that the bleachers are specifically adapted to the purpose for which the property is devoted. ITW also argues that the fact that the bleachers theoretically could be disassembled and moved is not dispositive, as most improvements to real estate, including the Eiffel Tower, can be disassembled and moved.

… we conclude that the bleachers here qualify as "permanent" regardless of whether they are anchored into the ground.

We disagree with the Kohns that "the degree of physical annexation" of the alleged improvement is dispositive. While the law of fixtures may focus on the degree of annexation of a chattel to land, courts, applying a commonsense definition to the term "improvement to real property," have "viewed the term 'improvement' as having broader significance than 'fixture' and ha[ve] indicated that the term comprehends all additions and betterments to the freehold, including everything that permanently enhances the value of the premises." Therefore, a given item need not be actually physically annexed to the land in order to constitute a permanent addition to or betterment of property.

We conclude that the bleachers at Darlington High School constitute a "permanent addition to" the Darlington High School stadium and track. First, examining the nature of the bleachers, we note that the home bleachers are a huge structure. They are 15 rows tall, over 100 feet long, and contain a 50-inch-wide walkway elevated 30 inches above the ground. They can seat nearly 1500 individuals. They adjoin a rather large press box and incorporate a wheelchair access ramp. While it is unclear whether they are anchored to the ground, they clearly are not readily moveable.

The Kohns focus on the fact that the bleachers can be disassembled and would not require any excavation to be removed. However, while the bleachers could theoretically be disassembled, that is true of almost any addition to property. Almost any structure that is assembled and installed can be dissembled [sic] and removed, even, as ITW artfully notes, a structure as large as the Eiffel Tower.

While the Kohns rely on the Minnesota Court of Appeals' decision in *Massie v. City of Duluth,* 425 N.W.2d 858 (Minn. App. 1988), that decision is entirely distinguishable and actually beneficial to ITW in light of the distinctions drawn in that opinion. *Massie* involved a 30-foot-tall water slide installed in a shallow lake that was bolted to concrete pads. "The slide was installed at the facility in 1974 and was used during the summers of 1975–83. At the end of each summer, the city would unbolt the slide from its base and apparently store it until the next season." The court concluded that the slide was not an improvement to real property, reasoning:

> The water slide was not a permanent addition to the property. While it was bolted to concrete pads at the bottom of the pond, it was designed to be and was removed every winter for storage.... The slide was a removable piece of playground equipment.... The slide was only used at the Twin Ponds area for three months out of the year and was permanently removed from the area after the 1983 season. There has been no decrease in the capital value of the Twin Ponds facility due to its removal.

Here, in contrast, the bleachers have never been taken apart or moved, much less permanently

removed for an entire season. They are certainly not the equivalent of "a removable piece of playground equipment."

The bleachers ... were never intended to be moved or taken apart. As evidence of this, we again note the length of time they have remained at Darlington High School—over 30 years. The fact that Darlington has constructed a large press box adjoining the bleachers is further evidence of the intent that the bleachers be permanent. Moreover, we note that Darlington has made significant improvements to the bleachers themselves, in the form of a wheelchair accessible ramp, new railings, and new footboards. Further evidence of the intended permanency of the bleachers is the fact that the utility of the stadium and track would be seriously diminished were the bleachers removed. In light of the above analysis, we do not find it significant that the bid contract Standard submitted to Darlington labeled the product as "portable bleachers." As such, we are satisfied that the bleachers constitute "a permanent addition to" the property.

Darlington contracted with Standard to provide the materials for the bleachers and supervise their installation at a cost of $16,167. Thus, the installation of the bleachers clearly involved the expenditure of labor and a significant amount of money. Further, we conclude that the bleachers increase the capital value of the track and football stadium at Darlington High School and make the property more useful or valuable. It seems patently obvious that a football stadium and track with a set of bleachers is more useful and valuable than an empty field and track. Clearly, the school would not be able to attract as many spectators and charge the same admission fee to see a game or meet if there were no bleachers in the stadium, as far less people would be able to have a clear line of vision to the field. Finally, it cannot seriously be argued that the installation of the bleachers constituted "ordinary repairs."[W]e hold that the bleachers at Darlington High School constitute an "improvement to real property" for purposes of § 893.89.

The decision of the court of appeals is reversed.

CASE QUESTIONS

1. Describe the structure, cost, and installation of the bleachers.

2. Why is it important to the Kohns that the bleachers not constitute an improvement to real property?

3. What is the significance of the fact that the contracts for the bleachers described them as "portable"?

4. What is the purpose of statutes of repose?

CONSIDER 5.2   Applying the degree of annexation test, and other fixture tests, to each of the following, determine the likelihood of having the item treated as a fixture.

a. Roger W. Marsh, d/b/a (doing business as) Bestmade Wood Products, constructs wooden cabinets on special order and installs them in homes (usually new homes under construction). He installs the cabinets by placing them in the house and nailing them to the walls and floors. The Department of Revenue wished to collect sales tax from Marsh on the grounds that the cabinets were the sale of personal property. Marsh maintains the property is real estate once installed, he does not receive payment until after installation, and thus he is not liable for sales tax for the sale of personal property. Who is correct? *Marsh v. Spradling*, 537 S.W.2d 402 (Mo. 1976).

b. Is a gasoline pump canopy a fixture, and therefore taxable as realty, or personalty, and not subject to realty tax? *In re Appeal of Sheetz, Inc.*, 657 A.2d 1011 (Pa. Cmwlth.), petition for allowance of appeal denied, 666 A.2d 1060 (Pa. 1995).

c. J. K. S. P. Restaurant, Inc., purchased a prefabricated dining car from Pullman in 1965. The diner was transported in three sections from New Jersey to New York, where it was unloaded, assembled, and installed on a foundation that had been built in the ground. The three sections of the diner were bolted in place. J. K. S. P.'s president stated that the purpose of designing diners in this way was to retain their character and personality and allow for easy removal and movement. Nassau County has included the value of the diner in its assessment of J. K. S. P.'s real property value. Is this correct? *J. K. S. P. Restaurant, Inc. v. Nassau County*, 513 N.Y.S.2d 716 (1987).

d. As a result of an accident in the intersection near its place of business, one of A and A Market's gas pumps was struck and damaged by one of the errant vehicles. A and A is a convenience store/gas station. The total damages to the pump were $17,946.82, and A and A filed a claim with its insurer for the cost of repair. The insurance company has denied the claim because the policy covers personal property for A and A and the pumps are fixtures. Is the insurance company correct? *A and A Market v. Perkin Insurance Company*, 713 N.E.2d 1199 (Ill. App. 1999). ▪

CONSIDER 5.3   Applying the factors for determining what constitutes a fixture and the preceding cases, determine the status of each of the following:

a. Floor-to-ceiling bookcases installed in an apartment by a tenant

b. Automatic garage door opener control

c. Landscaping

d. Electric ceiling fans

e. Stove and refrigerator purchased by the debtor for her mortgaged home (*In re Rolle*, 218 B.R. 636 [Bkrptcy. v. S. D. Fla. 1998])

f. Modular commercial building attached to concrete pad by tenant (*Hot Shots Burgers and Fries, Inc., v. FAS FAX Corp.*, 169 B.R. 920 [E. D. Ark. 1994])

g. Partitions nailed to the floor in an office building

h. Paneled refrigerator (paneled to match kitchen cabinets)

i. Bank vault door

j. Murphy bed (bed that folds into wall)

k. Seats and screens in a theater

l. Ski lifts at a ski resort

m. Storage bins on a farm

n. Display cases in a department store

o. Bus passenger shelter on a sidewalk (*Ali v. City of Detroit*, 554 N.W.2d 384 [Mich. App. 1996])

A Word on Precautions in Fixtures

Once again, the cases in this chapter have demonstrated that emotions and litigation can arise very easily over what appear to be insignificant items. Also, most of the confusion, emotion, and litigation again could be avoided if parties would clearly determine their positions at the outset through written agreements. Figure 5.1 summarizes the questions that should be addressed in various types of land transactions to cover the issue of fixtures.

Attachments

Apart from fixtures, there are many other attachments to land. For example, most property contains trees, bushes, and grasses, which are referred to as *fructus naturales* and are considered part of the real property. When land is sold or mortgaged, these naturally growing elements are simultaneously sold or mortgaged.

FIGURE 5.1 Fixture Analysis

PARTIES	QUESTIONS TO BE ANSWERED
Landlord/Tenant	1. Does the lease contain a provision on what types of attachments the tenant may make and remove? 2. Does the lease contain a provision on payment for damages for removal? 3. Does the lease require prior notification before a tenant attaches property?
Buyer/Seller	1. What items are included with the real property? 2. Are any items specifically excluded? 3. Does the contract list questionable items, such as drapes? 4. Does the contract prevent substitution or removal of fixtures before closing? 5. Is a bill of sale drawn up for questionable items such as washers, dryers, and refrigerators?
Creditor/Attacher	1. Who owns the land where the property is being attached? 2. How permanent will the attachment be? 3. Can removal occur without damage to the property? 4. Are there other creditors with protected interests in the real property?

Some property contains growing crops or *fructus industriales* (or **emblements**). These crops are not treated as part of real property; they are classified as personal property of the tenant who grew them. If a tenant grows crops on leased property, the crops belong to the tenant even though they may not be ready for harvest at the time the tenant's lease terminates. This right of removal of crops planted by a tenant is called the **Doctrine of Emblements**.

CONSIDER 5.4   Phyllis and James Rose were married, but experienced the type of discordance that necessitated their divorce. Phyllis received a judgment of $128,957 from the court in settlement of her marital property rights, a settlement that James neglected to pay. Phyllis reduced the judgment to a lien on their farm that they had jointly owned and operated when marital bliss was greater. After the lien was recorded, but before Phyllis executed on the lien, James planted crops on the property. Just as harvest time approached, the judicial sale of the farm, to satisfy the lien, took place. James demanded that he receive the value of the crops from the sale of the land. Phyllis maintains the crops were part of the real property and could be sold as part of the land. Who is correct and why? *Rose v. Rose*, 2004 WL 830957 (Ohio App. 3 Dist.).

TRANSFER OF TITLE TO FIXTURES AND PERSONAL PROPERTY

If property is classified as a fixture and part of the real property, title to it will pass with the deed transferring title to the property. However, for items not classified as fixtures, some method of transferring title is necessary. Whenever a question exists as to whether an item is real or personal property, a bill of sale should be used to assure complete transfer of title.

CREDITORS' RIGHTS IN FIXTURES

Creditors' rights in fixtures carry some unique complexities. Each state has provisions to protect creditors' interests in personal property that becomes attached to real estate and is then classified as a fixture.

This protection is afforded under **Article 9** of the **Uniform Commercial Code (UCC).** The UCC is a set of laws drafted by a group of scholars, attorneys, and businesspeople with the idea of having state-to-state uniformity in commercial transactions.

Article 9 covers creditors' rights and responsibilities in collateral pledged by debtors for loans. All of the states have adopted some version of Article 9. However, there have been revisions and technical amendments to Article 9 over the years that have been adopted in some states. In 2001, the majority of the states adopted Revised Article 9. These changes are covered in the following sections, and the courts are still struggling with interpretation.[2]

Scope of Article 9

Article 9 of the UCC governs the use of personal property or the use of fixtures as collateral. This book focuses on fixtures because of their relationship to real estate law.

Article 9 permits the creditor to obtain a **security interest** in the collateral, which provides the creditor with certain rights, opportunities, and priorities.

---

[2]The section numbers used are those for Revised Article 9.

Creation (Attachment) of Security Interest (9-203)

There are three requirements for creating a valid security interest: a security agreement, a debtor with rights in collateral, and value given by the creditor.

Security Agreement (9-105)

A security interest begins with the execution of a **security agreement** by the creditor and debtor (9-203). A security agreement has several requirements: (1) It must be evidenced by a record; (2) it must be signed by the debtor (under Revised Article 9, the agreement must be "authenticated," which allows for signing via electronic record); (3) it must contain language indicating that a security interest is being created; and (4) it must contain a description of the collateral that reasonably identifies it. Since fixtures will be attached to real property, a description of the real property involved is helpful in clarifying the identity and location of the property. Form security agreements, available in each state, generally meet all of the requirements for a valid security agreement.

Debtor's Rights in Collateral (9-202)

In some cases, the debtor may already own the collateral and is simply pledging such property as security for a debt. In most fixture cases, however, the creditor is selling goods to the buyer, and the buyer is pledging the purchased goods as collateral. In these cases, the debtor has rights in the collateral at the time of delivery so that the pledge can be properly made. For example, a seller of air conditioners who has the buyer execute a security agreement will have a valid security interest when the buyer takes possession of the air conditioner. The security agreement can be executed in advance and become effective upon the buyer's possession.

Value Given by Creditor (9-203)

The creditor gives value through the binding commitment to extend credit. A creditor may give value in any way that would constitute consideration in a simple contract. In the case of fixtures, the promise to extend credit is most frequently given as value by the creditor.

Once all three requirements are met (authenticated security agreement, collateral interest, and value), the security interest attaches. Just having a security interest gives the creditor certain rights to a superior position over that of other creditors. A secured creditor is always given priority over unsecured creditors. Also, the creation of a security interest entitles the creditor to repossession of the secured property in the event the debtor defaults on payments for the collateral. However, to enjoy the most complete protection available under Article 9, creditors should seek **perfection**, a process of creating notice of a security agreement's existence (see below).

Purchase Money Security Interest in Fixtures (9-103)

Creditors with a **purchase money security interest (PMSI)** obtain more complete protection. A PMSI is given to secure all or part of the purchase price of the item purchased. For example, when a homeowner or business purchases an air conditioner on credit from a seller or manufacturer of such units and the seller or manufacturer takes a security interest, a PMSI exists. The distinction between a PMSI and a security interest is important because the PMSI creditor is entitled to certain priorities in the event the debtor (buyer) defaults on payments for the future.

Perfection of Security Interest (9-301)

Filing a financing statement (9-502) gives the creditor perfection (when fixtures are involved; for other items of personal property, there are other means of perfection). A **financing statement** is a record that will vary from state to state but must include the following items:

1. Names of the debtors and the secured party
2. Signature (authorization under Revised Article 9) of the debtor
3. Address of the secured party from which information can be obtained
4. Mailing address of the debtor
5. A statement describing the items of collateral

Fixture financing statements must be filed in the real estate records. Most of the information required on the financing statement is self-explanatory, but the description item is critical, including a property description for fixtures. While there have been substantial Article 9 changes on perfection, the fixture perfection has remained the same because of the need for filing with real property records.

Filing the Financing Statement

A valid or authenticated financing statement must be filed for fixtures locally, generally at the county level, where land records are kept. Under Revised Article 9, fixture filing remains local, or in property records.[3] For a fixture filing, the legal description of the property is a necessary part of the financing statement because otherwise there is insufficient notice about which property is affected.[4] Security interests for other types of personal property are filed centrally with the idea of creating a national electronic database, similar to the existing Canadian model, in which all types of perfected security interests around the country can be examined.

Upon filing of the financing statement in the proper office, the creditor's interest is perfected. This perfection entitles creditors to priority over subsequent creditors and even priority over some existing creditors. These priorities are discussed in the next section.

Length of Perfection (9-515)

A filing under the UCC is good in most states for a period of five years. However, if the debt is paid prior to that time, the financing statement and security interest can be terminated. If necessary, the creditor may renew the financing statement any time during the final six months of the five-year term and will then receive the protection of perfection for another five years.

General Rules of Priority Among Secured Creditors (9-317)

To determine priorities among creditors in the event of the debtor's default, certain rules and exceptions apply. These general rules are the starting point for determining the priorities in payment rights when a debtor is in default on loans secured by mortgages and security interests in fixtures:

---

[3]Section 9-502 covers "real-property–related financing statements," and requires that goods that are (or are to become) fixtures must be perfected by filing a financing statement in the real property records, which must include a description of the real property.

[4]In *Webb v. Interstate Land Corp.*, 920 P.2d 1187 (Utah 1996), the court held that a fixture financing statement filed without a description of the land on which the sign is located was "totally ineffective to protect its interest in the sign against anyone except a buyer of the sign who saw it affixed." See also *Tustian v. Schriever*, 34 P.3d 755 (Utah 2001).

1. A secured creditor has priority over an unsecured creditor.
2. A perfected secured creditor has priority over an unperfected secured creditor.
3. A perfected secured creditor has priority over subsequent real estate interests. (For example, a filing on January 3 gives the secured party priority over filings occurring later in that month or simply later in time.)
4. A prior real estate interest (mortgage, deed of trust, lien, or judgment) has priority over a subsequently filed security interest.
5. Between perfected secured creditors, the date of filing is controlling, with the first creditor to file having priority.

Exceptions to General Rules

Purchase Money Security Interest (PMSI) Exception (9-324)/(9-334)

A PMSI creditor may take priority over prior real estate encumbrances if the financing statement is filed before the goods become fixtures or within 20 days after they become fixtures. This priority applies even though language in the mortgage provides that all after-attached property and fixtures are subject to the mortgage. To illustrate, suppose that a homeowner has a mortgage on his property, which was filed in August 2008. The homeowner wants to install a solar water-heating system. The homeowner purchases a system from Solar Systems Company on credit, and Solar Systems executes a security agreement and files a financing statement on June 3, 2012. Then Solar Systems installs the water-heating system. Solar Systems (as a PMSI) has priority over the 2008 mortgage holder.

The reason for the PMSI exception is that without some form of special priority for the secured party, creditors would be hesitant to finance improvements and fixtures to existing structures that are still subject to a mortgage. Improvements enhance or maintain property value and thereby protect the mortgagee's collateral. The following case deals with an issue of intent in determining fixture versus personal property as well as priorities.

IN RE WILLIAMS

381 B.R. 742 (W.D. Ark. 2008)
The Homeowner's Credit in the Gutters

FACTS

Charles E. Williams paid for the purchase and installation of a guttering system for his home by Hanke Brothers with a Wells Fargo Home Projects Visa card. Under the terms of this particular Visa card, Williams agreed to pay Wells Fargo a principal amount plus interest in return for payment for the guttering system by Wells Fargo to Hanke Brothers. Wells Fargo made payment, and Hanke Brothers then installed the guttering system. Known as a charge slip contract, the Wells Fargo Home Projects Visa includes the following terms:

Where applicable, you give us a purchase money security interest in any goods, described in this charge slip. We will not claim a security interest

or other lien (except judgment lien) in your principal dwelling. You agree that any property described in this charge slip will remain personal property and will not become a fixture even if attached to real property.

Use of Account: The use of your account by you or anyone permitted by you indicates acceptance of the terms of this agreement. You promise that all purchases made using your account will be for personal, family or household purposes.

Security Interest: To the extent permitted by applicable law, you hereby grant to us and we are retaining a [purchase] money security interest under the Uniform Commercial Code in the merchandise purchased on your account using your special HOME PROJECTS subaccounts until such merchandise is paid in full. You agree to assist us in executing documents necessary to perfect our security interest. If you do not make a minimum payment due on your account by the date on which it is due, we may repossess any merchandise that has not been paid in full.

The instructions for the guttering indicate that the pieces are affixed to the roof with silicone and that screws are used for "Hoods" and "Down-Spouts."

When Williams defaulted on his payments to Wells Fargo and others, he filed bankruptcy. His mortgage company alleged that it had priority in the guttering and that Wells Fargo was no longer a secured creditor because the guttering had become a fixture. Wells Fargo argued that the guttering system is personal property and is a consumer good that did not become a fixture because of the language contained in the charge slip contract. Wells Fargo maintained that because it holds a purchase money security interest in consumer goods, the security interest is automatically perfected upon attachment and no filing is required. Williams argued that the guttering system became a fixture when it was affixed to the house regardless of the contract language; therefore, Wells Fargo was required to file a financing statement, did not do so and does not have a perfected security interest and is an unsecured creditor.

JUDICIAL OPINION

Mixon, Bankruptcy Judge

A fixture is defined as "goods that have become so related to particular real property that an interest in them arises under real property law." To perfect an interest in a fixture, a financing statement must be recorded in the office of the recorder of deeds. The question of whether a type of property constitutes a fixture is usually a mixed question of law and fact.

To determine whether the property is a fixture or remains personal property, Arkansas courts have adopted a three part test: (1) whether the items are annexed to the realty; (2) whether the items are appropriate and adapted to the use or purpose of that part of the realty to which the items are connected; and (3) whether the party making the annexation intended to make it permanent. The intention of the party making the annexation is considered of primary importance. Intention can be inferred from the nature of the chattel, the relation and situation of the

party making the annexation, the structure and mode of annexation and the purpose for which the annexation has been made.

It is well settled that parties can treat as personal property machinery or improvements which would otherwise become a part of the realty, and thus convert it into personal property as between themselves. While this is true, a contract that items remain personalty is only some evidence that the parties intended the item to remain personalty. When the removal of the article from the real estate would do substantial damage to the realty such that the parties could not have intended such a result, the contract will not convert the property to personal property.

Wells Fargo had an agreement with the Debtor that the property purchased was to be treated as personal property even after it was annexed to the real property. It is well settled that parties can agree that an item remain personal property and not become a fixture upon attachment, but only to an extent. When removal of the article would do substantial damage to the realty, where the parties could not have intended this, the contract will not control. Looking at the four factors, [this] Court finds that this contract will control. The nature of the personalty are gutters attached to the roof. Logic dictates that gutters are removable because they wear out and have to be replaced. It is hard to imagine, nor was any evidence offered, that the removal of a guttering system would so harm the property that extensive damage would result.

The agreement provides that the gutters were to be bought for "personal, family, or household purposes" and the type of product involved comes within the definition of a consumer good. The Court therefore finds that the gutters fall within the purview of consumer goods and Wells Fargo's security interest is perfected without filing.

Wells Fargo has a perfected security interest in the guttering system. Wells Fargo's claim of $2,865.00 is allowed as a secured claim.

CASE QUESTIONS

1. What is the importance of the agreement on how guttering purchased with the Wells Fargo card would be classified?
2. If the guttering were classified as real property, what are the consequences for Wells Fargo?
3. How does Wells Fargo become a perfected secured party when it did not file a financing statement?

Construction Mortgage Exception

A construction mortgage is a mortgage used to secure funds in advance for real property improvements. A construction mortgage has priority over fixture security interests for those fixtures that are installed during construction.

Readily Movable Exception

Secured creditors with perfected interests in readily removable office or factory machines or in replaced consumer goods and appliances have priority over conflicting real estate interests. Readily removable office equipment includes items such as fax machines, photocopy machines, and computers. These personal property interests are not real estate and are not subject to a mortgage (a real property interest).

Tenant Exception

Creditors of tenants who have attached fixtures to leased property have priority over other prior and subsequent real estate encumbrances so long as the tenant has the right to remove such items when the lease ends. For example, a secured creditor of a tenant who attaches the financed, movable air conditioner to the landlord's property has priority over a mortgage on the property executed by the landlord.

Good-Faith Purchaser Exception

Good-faith purchasers (9-320) who purchase real property or fixtures in the ordinary course of business will have priority over secured parties so long as they purchase for value. Purchasers of real estate with fixtures covered by security interests are protected regardless of whether the creditor or secured party files the required financing statement.

Default by Debtor and Rights of Secured Party (9-604)

Revised Article 9 includes a specific section for default procedures with regard to security interests in fixtures. The drafters have taken the time to clarify many issues that debtors with fixture collateral raised. First, the secured party can use either the real property remedies (i.e., foreclosure) or the Article 9 remedies (non-judicial but commercially reasonable sale). Second, the secured party can remove the fixture and, while liable for any damage caused by the removal, is not responsible for any diminution in value. Third, the secured party has a choice as to proceeding against the real property itself or the fixture. However, the effect of this new section on fixtures is to overrule all those previous cases which held that the only remedy a secured party with fixture collateral had was the removal of the fixtures.[5] Neither the debtor nor the secured party is responsible for paying any decrease in value caused by the removal of the fixture. For example, if mirrors are removed from a wall, the cost of repair may be $30 for restoring the wall surface. However, the $1,000 decrease in value of the property need not be paid.

---

[5]For example, the case from the seventh edition *Maplewood Bank and Trust v. Sears, Roebuck and Co.*, 625 A.2d 537 (N.J. Super. A.D. 1993) has been superceded by the new provisions of Revised Article 9. See *FGB Realty Advisors v. Bennett*, 672 A.2d 545 (Conn. 1995) for a decision AFTER the revision, i.e., the priority applied only to the swimming pool the creditor had financed through a secondary mortgage.

FIGURE 5.2 Priorities in Fixtures Under Article 9 (9-313)

TYPE OF PARTY	PRIORITY OVER	EXCEPTIONS TO GENERAL PRIORITY RULES
Secured party	Unsecured party, secured party whose interest attached after	Good-faith purchasers
Perfected secured party	Secured party, unsecured party, subsequently filed real estate encumbrances (mortgages, deeds of trust, liens, judgments, security interests)	Good-faith purchasers
PMSI perfected secured party	Secured party, unsecured party, subsequently filed real estate encumbrances Prior perfected security interests and real estate encumbrances if financing statement filed before annexation of the fixture or within 20 days of annexation	Construction mortgages with advancements yet to be made; good-faith purchasers
Construction mortgage	All subsequent encumbrances and security interests	
Secured party for readily removable office or factory machines	No fixture filing required; perfection required	
Secured party for a tenant	Priority over all real estate encumbrances (prior and subsequent) Priority over all real estate encumbrances regardless of perfection so long as tenant holds the right to remove property	
Good-faith purchaser	Prior security interests if purchase is made in the ordinary course of business. For real estate, filing on fixtures gives creditor priority	

© Cengage Learning

CONSIDER 5.5 Edward and Terre Capers bought their home with a purchase money mortgage from Maplewood Bank and Trust. The mortgage was entered into on September 20, 1988, and recorded on October 5, 1988. The original amount of the mortgage was $121,000.

On May 31, 1989, Sears, Roebuck, and Company (Sears) filed a financing statement covering a completely new kitchen for the Caperses consisting of "new countertops, cabinets, sinks, disposal unit, dishwasher, oven, cooktop and hood," all of which had been installed as part of the remodeling … Sears filed a financing statement on the Caperses' property after the Caperses gave Sears a security interest in their home as security for the remodeling of their kitchen on credit.

On August 18, 1989, the Caperses executed a second mortgage on their home to Savings Bank for the sum of $34,000. That mortgage was recorded on August 23, 1989.

When the Caperses defaulted in their payments to Maplewood and Sears, Maplewood declared the entire balance of its loan due. Maplewood filed for foreclosure of its mortgage on November 5, 1989. Sears filed an answer and counterclaim for the amount of its security interest in the kitchen remodeling.

Sears' claim was dismissed because the judge held Sears' only remedy was removal of the kitchen fixtures and work. Maplewood was allowed to foreclose. Sears appealed the dismissal of its claim. How and why would the parties' rights be affected under Revised Article 9? *Maplewood Bank and Trust v. Sears, Roebuck and Co.*, 625 A.2d 537 (N.J. Super. A.D. 1993).

ETHICAL ISSUE

In the *Maplewood* case (Consider 5.5), reexamine the time between when the Caperses entered into the three-credit contracts and their default. Were the Caperses overextended? Is it the creditors' responsibility to decline credit in these circumstances? Why don't laws place limitations on the amount of credit individuals can obtain? Is there an ethical component to the use and extension of credit? What responsibilities should both sides to a credit arrangement have beyond what the law requires?

CAUTIONS AND CONCLUSIONS

Article 9 affords creditors tremendous protection in collateral rights and priorities. However, creditors need to be certain of their positions; the following questions should help ensure them the best position and best available protection for their secured debt:

1. Is there a written security agreement with all of the necessary information?
2. Has value been given?
3. Has the security interest attached?
4. To whose property is the item being attached?
5. What other creditors have interests in that property? Is there a construction mortgage? Have the land records been checked?
6. Is the financing statement complete? Is the legal description included and accurate? Is the collateral sufficiently identified?
7. Has the financing statement been filed and in the correct place?
8. Has the financing statement been filed within the appropriate time limits (20 days on a PMSI)?
9. Is renewal necessary? When?
10. Can removal damage be minimized?

By answering these questions and following through on tasks at the outset, creditors can avoid the problems of forgotten filings, incomplete documents, and the resulting lack of protection.

Before buying real property, check for Article 9 interests. An Article 9 interest that is undisclosed or overlooked opens the door for litigation and liability. The following checklist provides suggestions for buyers, sellers, brokers, agents, and others involved in real estate transactions:

1. Have the records been checked to determine if a perfected security interest exists?
2. If a perfected interest does exist, who is the creditor? What property is covered? How much is owed? What payments are made? Is all of the paperwork proper? Does this creditor have priority?
3. Does an unperfected security interest exist on any items on the property? Who is the creditor? How much is owed? What payments are made? Is all of the paperwork proper?
4. Who will pay the balance due? Will it be paid from sale proceeds? Is the buyer to assume responsibility for payments?
5. Is there a provision in the contract for the disposition of debts and collateral pledges?

KEY TERMS

Article 9, 102
Doctrine of Emblements, 102
emblements, 102
financing statement, 104
fixture, 91

fructus industriales, 102
fructus naturales, 101
perfection, 103
purchase money security interest
  (PMSI), 103

security agreement, 103
security interest, 102
trade fixture, 95
Uniform Commercial Code
  (UCC), 102

CHAPTER PROBLEMS

1. Determine whether each of the following would constitute a fixture. Discuss any further information that would be helpful in making the determination.

   a. A marble monument with a cement foundation in a cemetery
   b. Bookshelves in a library
   c. Wall mirrors installed by a tenant
   d. A furnace that is bolted to the floor in a factory
   e. A hog house (with a cement foundation) on a farm
   f. Ceiling fans in a home
   g. A printing machine in a college copy center

   (*Reynolds v. State Bd. Community Colleges*, 937 P.2d 774 [Colo. App. 1996]).

2. Bill leased an apartment from Windmere Apartments, Inc. Under the lease agreement, Bill is permitted to remove all fixtures installed on the property. Bill arranged to have custom bookshelves placed along one wall (the shelves are attached to the wall). Bill financed the shelves with Carl's Cabinetry, and Carl's filed a valid financing statement for the fixtures on December 1, 2012. Windmere has had a mortgage on the property since 2006.

   a. If Bill defaults, may Carl's remove the shelves?
   b. What obligations does Carl's have?
   c. If Windmere defaults, does its mortgagee get the shelves?
   d. What is the position of Carl's if no filing is made?

3. William and Virginia Britton own a one-acre parcel of land near Detroit's Metropolitan Wayne County Airport. They operate several small industrial businesses in the industrial building located on their land. In 1992, Wayne County began acquiring a total of 550 acres around the airport for expansion purposes. Wayne County offered the Brittons $188,580 for their property. The Brittons disputed the amount for not including the value of their trade fixtures. Listed as trade fixtures were the following: tanks, air compressors, forklifts, scales, storage racks, hose-braiding machines, pipe-threading machinery, hydraulic pumps, grinding machinery, and work tables. It also included such miscellaneous items as a coat tree, an electric clock, a first-aid kit, file cabinets, a refrigerator, a metal folding chair, a flatbed truck, trash drums, and lawn mowers. Should the county be required to compensate the Brittons for these items in a taking of real property? *Wayne County v. Britton*, 563 N.W.2d 674 (Mich. 1997).

4. The Michigan Tax Tribunal held that Michigan National Bank's night depository equipment, drive-up window equipment, vault doors, and remote transactions units, which were physically integrated with the bank's land and buildings, were fixtures and subject to taxation as realty by the city of Lansing. Is the Tax Tribunal correct? Should the drive-up facilities be classified as fixtures or personal property? *Michigan National Bank, Lansing v. City of Lansing*, 293 N.W.2d 626 (Mich. App. 1980); *aff'd* 322 N.W.2d 173 (Mich. 1982).

5. Harry owns Harry's Discount Clothiers, Inc. Harry has a five-year lease on the building in which his store is located. The building had concrete flooring, which was not appropriate for a clothing store, so Harry had parquet flooring installed. The flooring was installed in the same fashion as tile flooring. Determine whether the flooring will be treated as a fixture, trade fixture, or personal property in the following situations:

   a. When the lease terminates, Harry wants to take the flooring with him. What is the result?
   b. Harry purchases the building and then sells it to Bob, who claims that the flooring goes with the building. What is the result?
   c. Harry's fire insurance policy covers personal property but no real property. What is the result?
   d. The county tax assessor wishes to increase the value of the property on the basis of the value added by the floor. What is the result?

6. On January 20, Tom purchased a new hot-water tank for his home from Tanks, Inc. Tanks agreed to carry Tom on part of the price of the tank and took a

security interest in the tank. The tank was then installed. On February 1, Tom borrowed money from First Federal, and First Federal took a second mortgage on the house. On March 1, Fiesta Funtime Pools obtained a judgment against Tom and his house for the unpaid balance due on Tom's pool

a. Who has priority?

b. What would be the result if Tanks had filed a financing statement on January 31?

c. What relation would a first mortgage have in the situation?

d. If Tom defaults to Tanks, what can be done under Article 9?

7. In 1990, the Hogers purchased a furnace and air conditioner from the Kansas Power and Light Company (KPL) to be installed in the Hogers' home. On March 2, 1990, the Hogers and KPL entered into an installment contract and the Hogers executed a promissory note to finance the purchase of the furnace and air conditioner. The furnace and air conditioner were installed on March 20. KPL filed financing statements covering the furnace and air conditioner in Johnson County on March 23, 1990. Capitol Federal, the Hogers' mortgage company, did not receive notice of either the purchase or the installation of the furnace and air conditioner and did not consent to the security agreement. The Hogers defaulted on both the Capitol Federal and the Western Resources loans. Capitol Federal filed a mortgage foreclosure action on December 28, 1992, and named both the Hogers and Western Resources as defendants. A second mortgage holder, Associates Financial Services Company of Kansas, Inc., was also named as a defendant. Western Resources (the successor to KPL) claimed for the $2,887.50 amount the Hogers still owed on their installment contract, claiming a first and prior right to the real estate mortgage foreclosure sale proceeds. How would the foreclosure proceeds be distributed? *Capitol Federal Sav. and Loan Ass'n v. Hoger*, 880 P.2d 281 (Kan. App. 1994).

8. Determine which of the following are improvements to real property:

1. Large steel tubes in a factory used to roll sheet metal
2. Cement block wall
3. Panic doors
4. Storm sewer systems
5. Hardwired smoke detector systems
6. Unfinished stairwell
7. Permanently installed electrical cables
8. Escalators

9. During construction of the Grand Beach Inn, heating and air-conditioning units were installed in the rooms and are part of the walls for each room. The Grand Beach Inn was to be a hotel with individual guest rooms with individually controlled heat and air-conditioning. In a foreclosure on the never-opened inn, the issue of whether the units are included in the real property has arisen. Are the heating and air-conditioning units personal property or fixtures? *Lewiston Bottled Gas Co. v. Key Bank of Maine*, 601 A.2d 91 (Me. 1992).

10. Cliff Ridge Skiing Corporation is in bankruptcy, and a priority dispute has arisen among creditors because of a question as to whether Cliff Ridge's chairlifts are fixtures. The chairlifts were attached to the real property Cliff Ridge had mortgaged to First National Bank. There were concrete pads poured into the realty, towers were bolted to the concrete pads, cables were strung between the towers, and about 100 chairs were attached to the cables. However, one creditor maintains that the chairlifts can be easily removed from the land and sold as a package to another ski resort. Another creditor maintains that the pads, towers, and cables are specifically designed to fit the topography of a particular ski resort and cannot be easily modified for another resort. Who is correct? *In re Cliff's Ridge Skiing Corp.*, 123 B.R. 753, 13 UCC Rep.2d 1309 (Mich. 1991).

For research activities related to this chapter, go to our text companion website at
www.cengagebrain.com

CHAPTER 6

LIENS

The manager of Village Manor Health Care hired Centimark as the project manager for the roof replacement at the health-care complex. Centimark scheduled a meeting between the Village Manor manager and M. Dzen Roofing Company because Dzen was a GAF Master Elite contractor, a group considered to be in the top two percent of shingle roofers in the country. Village Manor chose Dzen as the roof contractor for a total price of $99,000. Dzen then contracted the roofing project out to BHR Construction, which then hired a small crew of independent contractors who then did the new roof. Dzen did give the independent contractors Dzen shirts to wear whilst they were doing the roof. BHR also displayed Dzen signs on the project until the work was completed.

The workmanship on the roof was poor, flashings were missing, and there were considerable defects in the roof and shingles. Village Manor never paid Centimark for the roof. Centimark filed a mechanic's lien against the Village Manor property and then sought to foreclose on the lien. Village Manor counterclaimed for breach of contract, negligence, breach of warranty, negligent misrepresentation, and fraudulent misrepresentation. Can Village Manor escape the lien and the foreclosure?

A **lien** is a special encumbrance that makes real property the security for the payment of a debt or obligation. In some cases, property owners place liens on their property voluntarily as security for a loan. In other cases, creditors have the right to create liens on property because of contracts or work they have performed. This chapter focuses on the second type of lien—the liens of third parties attached for nonpayment.

This chapter answers several questions about liens. What types of liens exist? How are liens created and enforced? How can liens on real property be satisfied and removed from the property? By the end of the chapter, you will be able to answer the question raised in the chapter opening.

TYPES OF LIENS

Statutory Liens

A **statutory lien** is a lien that exists because of an enabling statute. For example, a mechanic's lien is a statutory lien. **Mechanic's liens**, sometimes called *materials and labor liens* or *construction liens*, are created by statutes and allow those furnishing labor and materials for construction and improvement of real property to file a lien against that property for debt or payment security. Mechanic's lien statutes have existed since colonial times and exist now in all states, plus Puerto Rico and the District of Columbia. Some states, like California, afford these liens constitutional protection.[1] There are also state statutes that permit the attachment of a lien on real property when taxes are not paid.

Equitable Liens

An **equitable lien** is created through a mortgage. Sometimes referred to as a **contractual lien**, or voluntary lien, this lien is created to secure repayment of money borrowed to purchase the property or borrowed against the property.

Voluntary versus Involuntary Liens

A **voluntary lien** is one created by both parties; a mortgage is an example. Both parties agree to place a lien on the property as security for the advance of money to purchase the property or simply as security for a loan (see Chapter 15).

An **involuntary lien** is attached to the property but is not done under a contractual arrangement. Tax liens are a form of involuntary liens that are placed on property for satisfaction of property, state, or federal taxes (see Chapter 22).

Judicial Liens

A **judicial lien** arises from some action taken by a court. To collect judgments that have been awarded by the courts, plaintiffs must attach the defendant's property. Plaintiffs can attach wages, bank accounts, equipment, inventory, and, more relevantly here, real property. A judicial or judgment lien allows the sale of defendant's property to satisfy the plaintiff's judgment.

Once a judgment is recorded against real property, it becomes a creditor's lien. If the property is sold, then the plaintiff with the judgment has the priority of a secured creditor in the proceeds from the sale. The priority of the judgment or judicial lien is determined on the basis of "first in time is first in right." If the property is already subject to a mortgage, the judgment plaintiff is a secured creditor with priority after the mortgagee. In some cases, the judgment plaintiff can initiate sale action by foreclosing on the judicial lien. Even without foreclosure, the judgment lien is recorded against the property, and the title cannot be transferred or insured until the judgment has been paid or otherwise resolved between the parties.

Most states permit either the judgment that awards damages or an abstract of the judgment to be recorded in the land records, so that the lien is effective against any property owned by the judgment debtor.

---

[1]Cal. Const. Art. XIV, § 3 (1992) provides "Mechanics, persons furnishing materials, artisans, and laborers of every class, shall have a lien upon the property upon which they have bestowed labor or furnished material for the value of such labor done and material furnished."

Mechanic's and Materials Liens

Mechanic's and **materials liens** arise because companies or individuals have supplied labor, material, or both for the construction, improvement, alteration, or repair of real property or real property structures. This type of lien is the focus of the remainder of this chapter.

The laws on mechanic's liens vary significantly among the states. At one point in the late 1920s, a Uniform Mechanic's Lien Act was proposed. By 1943, the Commissioners on Uniform State Laws withdrew the proposal because "varied conditions made uniformity impossible." However, the purposes of the laws are clear—to prevent unjust enrichment of property owners who do not pay for improvements.

In 1987, the National Conference of Commissioners on Uniform State Laws adopted its Uniform Construction Lien Act. The Act answers three basic questions: Who is entitled to a lien? Who has priority among lien holders? and What are the landowner's rights with respect to payment and liens? The Act has not yet been adopted by any state but its framework is an excellent one for discussing liens. Figure 6.1 summarizes the generic basics of lien rights.

FIGURE 6.1 Basics of Mechanic's Lien Rights

What Property Is Subject to Liens?

- All real property
- Exemptions:

  - Public property
  - Railways
  - Property devoted to public use
  - Property of quasi-public corporations

Who Can Claim Liens?

- Original or principal contractors
- Subcontractors
- Persons supplying labor
- Persons supplying materials

Types of Claims

- Written contracts
- Implied contracts (some states)

© Cengage Learning

CREATION OF MECHANIC'S LIENS

Who Is Subject to Lien?

Any property owner who contracts expressly or by implication with another for the improvement of land or furnishing materials is subject to the provisions of state mechanic's lien provisions. However, the key phrase here is "property owner." Only the property owner or someone acting as an agent or representative of the owner has the authority to contract for improvements that can be the basis for a mechanic's lien. For example, a lessee who has improvements made on leased premises does not have the authority to bind the landlord/property owner for purposes of a lien unless the landlord consents or the lessee is acting as an agent for the landlord. The following case deals with the very common issue of liability among landlord, tenant, and lienor.

R.T.B.H., INC. V. SIMON PROPERTY GROUP

849 N.E.2d 764 (Ind. App. 2006)
When It Comes to Liens, Dick is Not a Good Sport

FACTS

On February 20, 2003, Dick's Sporting Goods, Inc. entered into a lease with Simon Property Group for property Simon owned at the Greenwood Park Mall. The lease was for the express purpose of Dick's demolishing an MCL Cafeteria and Service Merchandise store that were on the property and for constructing a new Dick's store. The lease was for an initial term of 20 years, with options to extend it for a total of 50 years. In order to secure the consent of Simon's mortgage lender for the lease, Simon agreed to complete construction of the new building if Dick's did not do so.

The lease required Simon to pay Dick's a part of the costs associated with demolishing the MCL Cafeteria and constructing a courtyard. Otherwise, Dick's bore the cost of the construction. Simon reviewed and approved the plans for the Dick's store prior to entering into the lease but indicated on the plans, "Landlord's review of contract documents is for design intent and criteria compliance only." The building was to be surrendered to Simon when the lease ended.

Dick's retained S.C. Nestel, Inc., as general contractor for the construction project. Nestel, in turn, sub-contracted window and glass work to McAndrews. McAndrews's (R.T.B.H., Inc. is the corporation with the dba of McAndrews Window & Glass) representative interacted with representatives from Nestel and Dick's during construction of the store. There is no evidence that representatives from Simon ever interacted with any representative of McAndrews during the construction.

The new Dick's store was completed without Simon's intervention. However, Nestel refused to pay McAndrews for its work on the store. Nestel filed a complaint for damages against McAndrews. McAndrews, in turn, filed a counterclaim against Nestel and against Simon, alleging that there was a valid mechanic's lien on the property and that it should be foreclosed. Simon moved for partial summary judgment, alleging that there was no valid mechanic's lien on its property. The trial court entered partial summary judgment for Simon, concluding that there was no valid mechanic's lien as to Simon. McAndrews appealed.

JUDICIAL OPINION
Barnes, Judge

In order for a mechanic's lien to attach to real estate, it is imperative that improvements to the property be made under the authority and direction of the landowner and something more than inactive or passive consent is required. A lien claimant's burden to prove active consent to improvements is especially important when they are requested by someone other than the landowner. Without the landowner's active consent, a lien claimant can only maintain a lien to the extent of his customer's interest in the land. A person about to improve real estate must take notice of the extent of his customer's rights in the land and of the rights of those in possession.

We find this case to be practically indistinguishable from *Stern & Son,* which our supreme court cited with approval in *Gill. Gill,* 810 N.E.2d 1059 (Ind. 2004). There, Gary Joint Venture ("GJV"), a mall owner, leased property to a group of individuals. The express purpose of the lease was to turn the property into a pizza restaurant. A corporation formed by some of the tenants undertook to build the restaurant, and it contracted with Stern & Son for that purpose. GJV approved the construction plans, provided Stern & Son with a set of rules for contractors performing construction work in the mall, and representatives of GJV regularly visited the work site to ensure that the mall's standards were adhered to. The restaurant eventually was completed, but Stern & Son was not paid for its work. It sought to enforce a mechanic's lien against the property. The trial court granted GJV's motion for summary judgment, concluding that no mechanic's lien existed as to GJV's interest in the property.

We first cited the existence of longstanding case law holding that "a lease calling for improvements, even very detailed improvements, will not prove the sort of active consent needed to maintain a mechanic's lien." Next, we noted that GJV's approval of the plans was perfunctory and technical, as was the onsite construction supervision. We stated, "while these facts certainly establish that GJV was aware of the construction, this awareness also does not establish the sort of active consent needed to maintain a mechanic's lien."

Here, the fact that the lease between Simon and Dick's called for the construction of a new building does not mean that Simon actively consented to improvements provided by McAndrews. The only designated evidence in the record is that Simon had no interaction with McAndrews during the course of construction, nor for that matter is there any evidence that Simon had any significant interaction with the general contractor, Nestel. It also appears from the record that Simon's approval of the design plan for the Dick's store was largely technical and perfunctory, as evidenced by the stamp placed on the design by Simon, "Landlord's review of contract documents is for design intent and criteria compliance only." Additionally, evidence that Simon was aware of the construction of the Dick's store, and even McAndrews' involvement in it, is not enough to establish "the sort of active consent needed to maintain a mechanic's lien."

Simon did not receive a direct benefit from the construction of the Dick's store. The benefits it received from the construction of the store were indirect, including some assurance that Dick's would be able to pay the rent required by the lease by its construction and operation of the store, and whatever tangential value the new store would have to Greenwood Park Mall as a whole. The fact that the building would revert to Simon at the conclusion of the lease, which means anywhere from twenty to fifty years in the future, cannot be fairly construed as a primary bargained-for purpose of the lease or a direct benefit to Simon. In any event, it is difficult to conceive that Dick's would physically move the 75,000-square-foot store or intentionally destroy it before the conclusion of the lease; it is natural to expect that Simon would take possession of the structure at that time.

Simon entered into an agreement with its mortgage lender to complete construction of the store if Dick's did not do so. We agree with Simon that this contingency agreement, which contingency never came to pass, is irrelevant to the question of whether Simon actively consented to the improvements provided by McAndrews. The actual facts of this case are that Simon did not participate actively in the construction of the Dick's store and made no payments for any construction to either Nestel or McAndrews.

McAndrews contends that this case is controlled by our opinion in *American Islam Society v. Bob Ulrich Decorating,* 126 Ind. App. 266, 132 N.E.2d 620 (1956). In that case, the American Islam Society owned a hotel and leased it to two individuals. The lease was expressly conditioned upon the lessees making repairs and improvements that were explicitly set forth in the lease. The lessees hired several contractors to perform the required improvements but failed to pay them for their work. Shortly after the work was completed, the lessees defaulted on the lease and possession of the hotel reverted to the Society.

Although there are some superficial similarities between *American Islam Society* and the one before us now, there is a key difference that we noted in the following paragraph:

> *It seems to us on the record herein that the appellant leased its building to tenants of doubtful financial responsibility and that the lease required them to make improvements amounting to several thousand dollars. The lease was surrendered shortly thereafter and the appellants have obtained the benefit of the improvements. The facts illustrate the justice of the rule applied herein. To hold otherwise would permit appellant to unjustly enrich itself at the expense of appellees.*

There is no indication here that the entity to whom Simon leased the property, Dick's, is of "doubtful financial responsibility." The lease is still in effect and it is Dick's, not Simon, who currently is enjoying the direct benefit of the construction performed by McAndrews. Simon has not "unjustly enriched" itself at McAndrews' expense. We conclude that the present case is distinguishable from *American Islam Society.* The trial court correctly concluded that, as a matter of law, McAndrews failed to establish the existence of a mechanic's lien against Simon's ownership interest in the property.

Affirmed.

CASE QUESTIONS

1. Describe the relationships of the parties.
2. What factors point to consent to the lien?
3. What factors indicate that there was no consent?
4. How would you describe the standard for consent now?

CONSIDER 6.1 Max & Benny's was a restaurant operated in a building owned by MCL CDC P21, LLC. On October 4, 2005, Max & Benny's entered into a contract with Stafford-Smith to purchase various commercial kitchen appliances and equipment, which Stafford-Smith was to install in the Max & Benny's restaurant. Stafford-Smith began work in November 2005 and completed work on February 10, 2006. Max & Benny's failed to pay $161,630.46 of the total amount owed to Stafford-Smith.

On May 1, 2006, Stafford-Smith recorded a lien on the premises against Max & Benny's as lessee and "MCL CDC P21, LLC" as owner. Intercontinental Real Estate had purchased the property, with the deed recorded on January 6, 2006. Stafford-Smith discovered that its legal description in the May 1 lien filing was incorrect and it filed a lien on October 3, 2006 with the correct description, which listed IRE and/or Intercontinental Real Estate Corporation as the owner.

Stafford-Smith brought suit to foreclose its lien against Max & Benny's and IRE. IRE says it did not consent to the lien. Illinois requires that when there is a change of ownership that mechanics file their liens within four months of a change of ownership. Stafford-Smith says that its technical error should not allow IRE to benefit from all the equipment and work without paying. The trial court found for IRE, and Stafford-Smith appealed. What should the court do in balancing the interests of the parties? *Stafford-Smith, Inc. v. Intercontinental River East*, LLC, 881 N.E.2d 534 (Ill. App. 2007). ∎

PRACTICAL TIP

Some commercial landlords require contractors to register with them. Upon registration, the contractors are given a statement that limits the landlord's liability and explains that their contracts are with the tenant and not the landlord. For those providing real property improvements, keep checking on ownership of the property and put a clause in the contract on change of ownership.

Any person who can contract and who has authority can subject property to a lien (the party subject to the lien is called the **lienee**). Corporations' properties are subject to mechanic's liens when others provide improvements for those properties. In the absence of a specific statutory provision, no one can impose a lien against the U.S. government or any of the state governments. This governmental exemption prevents the taking of state land for the satisfaction of a mechanic's lien. Construction of schools and public buildings such as courthouses and office complexes is exempt from attachment of mechanic's liens. For quasi-public entities, such as utilities, some states recognize an exemption, while others do not.

Most state lien statutes require that the **lienor** have an underlying contractual arrangement to enforce a lien. However, the degree and type of contractual arrangement varies significantly from state to state: Some states require only an express or implied agreement before a lien may be attached (**consent statutes**). Others require the owner of the property to sign a contract for the work or materials (**contract statutes**). The difference between these contract and consent statutes is that under the contract statutes, the lienor must establish that a contract exists in order to attach a lien. Under the consent statutes, the lienor need only establish that the owner consented through circumstances such as the owner allowing work to continue after seeing that work has begun.

The contract formalities required vary significantly across the states, but the following items are the basic ones that should be included:

1. Amount due under the contract (for labor, materials, and so on)
2. Amount of time within which work is to be completed
3. Amount of time permitted for payments and any schedule of payments
4. Description of the real property involved
5. Description of the work to be completed

6. Signature of the parties. (If the property is community property or held in tenancy by the entirety, then both spouses' signatures are required.)

7. If the property being repaired or improved is consumer property, Regulation Z (12 C.F.R. § 226) requires the following disclosure to be made:

   The buyer may cancel this transaction at any time prior to midnight of the third business day after the date of this transaction.

   Under Regulation Z, the contract must also include cancellation information such as how and to whom cancellation notice must be given.

8. Provisions for breach of the agreement (i.e., nonpayment or nonperformance), such as withholding payment or obtaining another contractor.

> **PRACTICAL TIP**
>
> *When filing a lien, dot your "I's" and cross your "T's," for if one thing is wrong, you lose your lien rights. Check and recheck spelling, addresses, and names.*

It is possible, particularly in construction contracts, to have an open-end agreement so that supplies are purchased as necessary. It is also possible for a contract executed by an agent of the owner to be valid against the owner, so long as the agent held proper authority to enter into the contract. Unincorporated associations, such as churches and foundations, present special problems for lienors. The person who signs the agreement for the nonprofit organization should have some form of authority for the transaction, such as the resolution of the board or officer verification. Without proper authority for the improvements contract, the property of the church or foundation is not subject to a lien. Some states also have special laws that govern contracts with unincorporated associations, typically the structure for nonprofit organizations such as trusts and foundations. Trustees and executors of estates may also have authority to make improvements on real property that is part of the trust or estate, but their authority should be documented by court orders or appointments.

The description of the liened property is critical because the lien is recorded in the real property records. Only an accurate description of the property ensures that buyers, creditors, and others will be put on notice as to what interest is held by whom and in what property. As the following case illustrates, technical compliance with lien filing requirements is a must for a valid lien.

BUCHANAN V. OVERLEY

178 P.3d 53 (Kan. App. 2008)
For Want of an Address, a Lien Is Lost

FACTS

Jerry and Carol Overley contracted with Douglas Buchanan for the construction of a single-family home on land owned by the Overleys in Wichita.

During the course of construction, the Overleys objected to the quality of Buchanan's work. Buchanan refused to make repairs satisfactory to the Overleys, and the Overleys stopped their progress payments to him. Buchanan gave the Overleys written notice of default pursuant to the contract. When the Overleys refused to cure the default, Buchanan filed his mechanic's lien statement.

The Overleys then filed for bankruptcy. The parties later agreed that Buchanan could pursue a state mechanic's lien foreclosure action as an exception from the bankruptcy automatic stay. The Overleys contend Buchanan's lien is invalid due to his failure to include his address on the face of the verified lien statement as required by K.S.A. 60-1102(a). Buchanan did not have his address on the lien form, but he had attached the invoices from all of his subcontractors and suppliers with his address on there. The Overleys argued that Buchanan's address was critical to a valid lien.

The court struck the Overleys' defenses and ordered foreclosure of the mechanic's lien. The Overleys appealed.

JUDICIAL OPINION
McAnany, Judge

The purpose of a mechanic's lien statute is to afford security to any persons or entities furnishing labor, equipment, material, or supplies used or consumed for the improvement of real property under a contract with the owner or the owner's general contractor. While we liberally construe our mechanic's lien statute once a lien has attached, Kansas law requires strict compliance with the procedure prescribed in the statute in order to perfect a mechanic's lien. *Haz-Mat Response, Inc. v. Certified Waste Services Ltd.*, 259 Kan. 166, 170, 910 P.2d 839 (1996).

The statute does not require the filing of any particular form of mechanic's lien statement, only that the requisite information be included. A verified mechanic's lien statement need not be composed of a single document. In fact, K.S.A. 60-1102(a) specifically contemplates the incorporation by reference of information contained in an attachment to the mechanic's lien statement. K.S.A. 60-1102(a)(4) permits the attachment of a promissory note to the claim in lieu of an itemized statement. Nevertheless, Kansas law is clear that a mechanic's lien statement must not only contain the requisite information but also be fully verified.

The problem in the present case arises when we consider whether Buchanan properly verified his address. Here, Buchanan used a preprinted lien statement form that identified the Overleys as the owners, Buchanan as the contractor, the legal description of the property, and the amount claimed for which a lien was asserted. It also specified that "*said labor and materials* and the items thereof, as nearly as practical, are set forth in the bill of items hereto attached, made a part of this statement, and marked Exhibit 'A'." (Emphasis added.) There followed Buchanan's signature and his verification of the truth of his lien statement.

Exhibit A, attached to the lien statement, consisted of a multitude of bills and invoices for labor and materials provided to the project, many of which contained a mailing address for Buchanan in Derby. The contract between Buchanan and the Overleys was a cost-plus contract that obligated the Overleys to "pay for all materials and labor required to construct the residence to the point of occupancy." Buchanan's fee was "a 10% contracting fee" applied to the overall cost of construction. The invoices attached to Buchanan's lien statement, which showed his address, were invoices sent to him by suppliers of labor and materials to the project. The address for Buchanan shown on the invoices was the address used by the suppliers.

The present dispute is typical of those between owners and contractors. An owner who is dissatisfied with the adequacy of the work often stops progress payments to the contractor and demands corrections. When negotiations stall, either the contractor files a mechanic's lien, or the owner hires another contractor to complete the job and files an action against the original contractor for breach of contract, or both. In 1992, the legislature amended K.S.A. 60-1102 to require that the lien claimant provide an address sufficient for service of process. The purpose of the 1992 amendment is to provide the owner with an address in order to perfect service of process on the contractor in, for example, such a breach of contract suit.

Here, an address for Buchanan was contained in the invoices incorporated by reference into the lien statement. There apparently is no contention that the address was insufficient to effect service of process on Buchanan. However, it has long been the law of this state to demand strict compliance with our statutory requirements in order to perfect a mechanic's lien.

This court is duty bound to follow Kansas Supreme Court precedent, absent some indication the court is departing from its previous position.

In summary, the statute requires that the claimant verify the truth of the facts asserted in the mechanic's lien statement. The mechanic's lien statement asserted that the labor and materials supplied to the project were set forth in the attached Exhibit A. Buchanan verified this fact: that the labor and materials supplied to the project were set forth in Exhibit A.

He did not state, nor did he verify, his address for purposes of service of process, as required by the statute. Accordingly, Buchanan failed to comply with the requirements of the statute for perfection of a mechanic's lien.

Because Buchanan failed to strictly comply with the requirements of K.S.A. 60-1102 by not verifying his address sufficient for service of process, the district court erred in holding that the lien was valid.

Reversed.

DISSENTING OPINION
Greene, Presiding Judge

I respectfully disagree. Examining the lien statement itself, there is no question that the "address sufficient for service of process of the claimant" is present at least 21 times on the attachments referenced as Exhibit A and "made a part of [the lien] statement." Jerry and Carol Overley concede as much, but argue that Buchanan failed "to include his address on the face of the lien statement" and failed to verify the address as sufficient for service of process. There is no contention that the address shown on the invoices was incorrect or otherwise inadequate for service of process.

With all due respect to my colleagues, however, I believe they have taken "strict compliance" to a level never before required by our case law and beyond. I believe we should recognize that liens for labor and material are codified within our code of civil procedure and subject to its general rule that its provisions

"shall be liberally construed and administered to secure the just, speedy and inexpensive determination of every action or proceeding."

For all of these reasons, I would affirm the district court.

CASE QUESTIONS

1. Why is the court concerned about the lack of address verification as part of the lien filing?
2. What will be the impact of this decision on owners? On builders and contractors?
3. What advice would you offer builders and contractors?

Who Is Entitled to a Lien?

Who is entitled to place liens on real property varies from state to state but is detailed in the state mechanic's lien statutes. Ordinarily, lien rights exist in mechanics and laborers, but state statutes extend lien rights to others. Some states grant lien rights to contractors, subcontractors, those furnishing materials, those acting in a supervisory capacity, and in some cases, to architects. For each of these categories, lien coverage may be limited or it may require special notice provisions for the landowner or at least that the landowner was aware of the work. In some states, only those who are properly licensed (if licensing is required) are entitled to liens on property. The state courts are continuing to deal with questions about the type of work that is covered by liens. For example, one issue that continues to result in litigation is whether environmental services such as analysis of property use or impact of development are entitled to the lien protections provided for contractors.

One additional issue is critical in determining who is entitled to a lien. The answer to the "Who?" question is in large part controlled by whether the state is a contract state or a consent state, or whether specific provisions have been made for those other than lienors in direct contract with the landowner. The discussion earlier about landlords/tenants and lienors is an important part of "Who?" gets a lien.

To provide payment assurances for subcontractors, suppliers, and laborers not in privity with the landowner, state statutes usually permit them to place a lien on property, provided they meet some notice and other preliminary requirements prior to the time the lien is filed. Basically, the statutes permit them to lien if the property owner is aware of their work.

In some states, it is possible that if all claims (of subcontractors, suppliers, and so on) are pursued and made into liens, the landowner could have liens in excess of the contract price. Other states follow the New York rule and limit the amount of the liens to the contract price less any amounts paid to the general contractor. Figure 6.2 is a summary of state laws on this issue.

FIGURE 6.2 Amounts of Lien Claims by State

RECOVERY ONLY TO EXTENT OF AMOUNT UNPAID TO GENERAL		DIRECT LIEN FOR FULL AMOUNT	
Alabama	Massachusetts	Alaska	New Hampshire
Arkansas	Michigan	Arizona	New Jersey
Connecticut	Minnesota	California	New Mexico
Delaware	Mississippi	Colorado	North Dakota
District of Columbia	Nebraska	Hawaii	Oregon
Florida	New York	Idaho	Pennsylvania
Georgia	North Carolina	Indiana	Rhode Island
Illinois	Tennessee	Kansas*	South Dakota
Iowa*	Utah	Louisiana	Texas*
Kentucky	Virginia	Maryland	Vermont
Maine	West Virginia	Missouri	Washington
		Montana	Wisconsin
		Nevada	Wyoming

© Cengage Learning

* Indicates some variation or limitation

Some states provide an exemption for residential property; that is, the owners of residential property cannot have liens in excess of the contract price with the general contractor. However, courts are also concerned when the homeowners have not paid the full amount to the contractor, and subcontractors have also not been paid. Many subcontractors bring suit on the basis of unjust enrichment in order to recover for the materials and work they have furnished. Courts work to balance the interests of the subcontractors with those of the homeowners. In the following case, the court deals with the application of the residential exemption to a lien by a supplier when the homeowner has made payments to a bankrupt general contractor but did not pay the full amount to that contractor.

ONTIVEROS V. SANCHEZ

3 P.3d 695 (N.M.C.A. 2000)
When Your Contractor Goes Belly-Up, Do You Pay the Subs?

FACTS

Ricardo and Geraldine Sanchez and Nancy Busta-mante (Homeowners) each contracted with William C. Parker, the general contractor, for the construction of their respective homes. The original contracts specified that the Sanchezes would pay $63,000 and Bustamante would pay $73,000 for the completed homes.

Parker purchased building materials, which included doors and windows, from Rawson and hired Ontiveros to install insulation and a heating system (Subcontractors). The services and materials were provided for the homes as contracted for by Parker, and the parties agree that, as a result, value was added to the homes.

Unfortunately for all involved, Parker, the general contractor, declared bankruptcy prior to completing construction of the homes, but after Subcontractors had provided the labor and materials. At the time of bankruptcy, Parker had finished some portion of the work.

Also, at this point in time, the Sanchezes had paid Parker $26,000, or approximately 41 percent of the original contract price, and Bustamante had paid him $45,000, or approximately 62 percent of her original contract price.

Upon Parker's default, the Homeowners completed their homes by other means. Completion of each home ultimately cost the Sanchezes $125,456 and Bustamante $120,851, including the cost of purchasing the land. The post-construction appraisal of the Sanchez and Bustamante homes ultimately exceeded the actual costs of construction by approximately $19,000 and $20,000, respectively. The post-construction appraised value of the Sanchezes' home was $14,000 greater than the pre-construction appraisal.

Both Subcontractors filed suit for unjust enrichment seeking payment for their supplies and services. The district court found the Homeowners liable to Ontiveros Insulation Co., Inc., and Rawson, Inc., Builders Supply (collectively, Subcontractors) for a sum of $13,321.61, plus costs and prejudgment interest.[2]

JUDICIAL OPINION

Armijo, Judge

Subcontractors' suits against property owners are generally not favored. Remedy is instead viewed as best sought from the underlying general contractor. This general disfavor, however, is not required by anything intrinsic to the subcontractor–property owner relationship, but rather is a reflection of the jurisprudence of equity. Simply, equity does not take the place of remedies at law, it augments them; in this regard, an action in contract would be preferred to one in quasi-contract.

The parties agree that the labor and materials added value to the properties. It is axiomatic, however, that courts provide remedy *in quantum meruit* to prevent unjust enrichment. To prove their claim, therefore, it would not be enough that Homeowners were merely enriched at Subcontractors' expense:

That enrichment must also be unjust. The well-founded cautionary rules Homeowners invoke are specific iterations of this basic principle. As a general matter, the limitations are premised on the bedrock principle that it makes little sense to remedy one wrong by inflicting another. The question before us, therefore, is whether the district court abused its discretion in not determining that Subcontractors' action failed because of one of the limitations upon actions for unjust enrichment which Homeowners assert. Homeowners argue, first, that they have paid to the general contractor a substantial portion of the original contract price and that they should not, therefore, be required to pay any further amount. Second, they argue that they did not request or know of the furnished work or materials and should not, therefore, be held liable. We are not persuaded by either argument.

Where a property owner pays to the general contractor "a very substantial part" of the monies due and owing, the subcontractor does not generally have an equitable claim for relief against the property owner. Such payment makes reasonable the presumption that the property owner has already paid for the conferred benefit. It follows, then, that if a defendant has already paid for the benefit, there has been no enrichment, much less unjust enrichment. As such, this limitation upon the action is consistent with the basic rule....

[T]he stipulated record does not indicate what portion of the work remained unfinished upon the general contractor's default, we cannot tell what relation an aggregate payment of 52% on the original contracts bears to what services and materials the general contractor and Subcontractors had provided. The stipulated record does indicate, however, that Subcontractors received no compensation for the approximately $14,000 in work and materials they provided—work which the parties agree—added [*sic*] value to the homes. Moreover, it is clear that, in the aggregate, Homeowners never paid $65,000 out of $136,000 agreed upon in the original contract, but that their homes are now appraised, again in the aggregate, at $40,000 more than they expended. Given the state of the stipulated record, we cannot conclude that it was contrary to logic and reason for the district court's refusal to conclude that Homeowners had already paid for the services and materials Subcontractors had provided.

Finally, we note that while the record discloses no reason why any party should bear the blame for

---

[2]Sadly, both homeowners declared bankruptcy as well and the case was conducted simply for the purpose of determining the subcontractors' rights and priorities for payment in the bankruptcy court.

Parker's bankruptcy, abandonment of the underlying construction contract, or failure to pay Subcontractors, the equities weigh heavily in Subcontractors' favor. Among these considerations, the Subcontractors pursued all possible remedies before turning to the present action. Indeed, but for Homeowners' mortgage defaults and the resulting foreclosure and redemption, Subcontractors could claim an adequate remedy at law without resort to equity. Conversely, by virtue of the foreclosure actions, Homeowners redeemed the properties free and clear of any liens and now live in homes appraised at $19,000 and $21,000 more than expended. As to the work and materials for which Subcontractors now seek compensation, this turn of events has inured directly to their disadvantage and Homeowners' advantage. In light of this record, the district court did not abuse its discretion in providing equitable relief to Subcontractors.

In so holding, we wish to emphasize that recovery on such an action may not be had in every instance where a subcontractor has furnished labor or materials which benefit a third person with whom there is no privity of contract. Our decision today is limited to affirming the propriety of quasi contract as a remedy in a particular factual situation. Each case must be decided according to the essential elements of quasi contract. The most significant requirement for a subcontractor's successful recovery is that the enrichment be unjust. In the present case, Subcontractors exhausted their remedies against the person with whom they contracted, namely, Parker. Despite those efforts, they did not receive any value for the labor and services rendered.

Affirmed.

CASE QUESTIONS

1. What happened with the general contractor?
2. What percentage of the contract price had been paid?
3. Where are the homeowners now and how much are their homes worth?
4. Why does the court make an exception and allow the Subcontractors to recover?
5. What is quasi contract? *quantum meruit*? unjust enrichment?

ETHICAL ISSUE

Evaluate the ethics of the homeowners in this case. Should they have paid the Subcontractors? What additional information would you like to have before discussing the issues of fairness and forthrightness in handling this problem?

PRACTICAL TIP

Mechanic's liens and the sale of residential property are a risky combination. Suppliers and subcontractors should be aware of their lien limitations. Buyers should do background checks on builders and observe the property to be certain lien claims do not arise, even though they may ultimately be defeated. All parties should know their state statutory protections for lien holders and buyers alike.

What Property Is Subject to a Lien?

Once a lien is obtained, it applies to the whole property and not simply the portion of the structure that was the subject of the lienor's work, labor, or materials. The lien attaches to both the building and the lot on which the building is located (subject to the exemptions-noted page). A lienor could lien individual lots in a subdivision for work performed on each of those lots.

There are some lien exemptions. For example, government property is often exempt from liens. See p. 118 for more information on these exemptions. Figure 6.1 provides a visual review of the generic basics of lien rights.

PROCEDURAL ASPECTS OF OBTAINING A LIEN

Because mechanic's liens are statutory, the procedural aspects for creating and enforcing a lien vary from state to state, but the fundamentals are the same. Since the lien is a land interest, it must be recorded in the appropriate governmental land-record office to be valid. In most states, liens are probably filed in the same office as financing statements for fixtures (see Chapter 5). See Web Exhibits 6.1

and 6.2 for sample lien forms. Every lien form in any state always has a place for the legal description of the land.

The times for filing, perfection, and period of validity for liens also differ among the states. Other times that vary include the days allowed for filing a lien and the date that the allowed time period for a lien filing begins. Some statutes begin the 60- or 90-day period for filing the lien on the date the work is completed or on the date the supplies are delivered. Even completion of work is defined differently from state to state: It may mean the end of work, or the completion of the project with the issuance of an architect's certificate.

PRACTICAL TIP

Establish a payment mechanism for the contractor, subcontractors, and suppliers that ensures payment gets to the proper parties. Draws by the general contractor very often do not end up in the hands of the subcontractors and suppliers. Maintain adequate controls over payments so that your funds do not end up in the internal business of the general contractor instead of being paid to the subcontractors and suppliers whose completed work is the basis for the draw.

Many states follow a prenotification procedure, especially for those performing work who do not have a direct contractual relationship with the property owner. Those without a contract who want lien protection must file a preliminary notice within a certain period of time after their work has begun or their supplies have been delivered. This notice is served on the property owner, the contractor (who has a contractual agreement with the property owner), and the construction lender. This notice serves to alert all concerned to the possibility of a lien. Because this notice gives a right to an eventual lien, the party giving the notice must be able to prove that notice was sent, to whom it was sent, and when it was sent. In some states, the notice must be served personally or sent through certified mail. This notice is not a lien; it simply makes all three parties aware of those working on the project, what they are doing, and the supplies and costs involved. The preliminary notice gives only the right to execute a lien in the future. In those states requiring the preliminary notice, failure to give the notice may cost the lienor the right of the lien. There are professional service companies across the states that perform the preliminary notice function for contractors and suppliers.

The time period for which the lien is effective once filed also varies. In some states, the valid lien period is six months (measured from the date of filing). If the owner does not make the necessary payments during the time the lien is effective, then the lienor will bring suit (a form of foreclosure suit) to enforce the lien to satisfy payment due. If the lienor does not bring foreclosure suit within the statutory period of effectiveness, the lien is lost.

CONSIDER 6.2   On September 14, 2006, Roman and Elizabeth Jakimow gave National City Mortgage a mortgage on their property to secure a construction loan. The Jakimows defaulted, and National City filed suit to foreclose its mortgage on September 8, 2008. Hillside Lumber was named as a defendant in the foreclosure suit because Hillside had recorded a mechanic's lien against the property on March 5, 2008. The lien was for $141,188.10 worth of materials furnished to the Jakinows to improve their property and indicated that $65,821.93 was still owed. The lien was signed by Ewa Kulaga. There was no accompanying proof of mailing of the lien to the Jakinows. Hillside filed a counterclaim to foreclose its mechanic's lien.

Kulaga, president of Hillside, testified that on March 5, 2008, Hillside sent the lien by certified mail, with return receipt requested and delivery limited to addressee only, to the owners of the property, the contractor, and National City. A National City representative signed an affidavit indicating that its records did not disclose that it had received the lien. Hillside did not have either the white card evidencing a certified mailing with a tracking number, a copy of the envelope addressed to National City, or a green card evidencing receipt of the lien. The court granted National City's motion for summary judgment and denied Hillside's lien was valid. Did the court make the correct decision in disallowing the lien? *National City Mortg. v. Hillside Lumber, Inc.,* 966 N.E.2d 1076 (Ill.App. 2012). ⬛

PRIORITY OF LIEN INTERESTS

Attachment of Lien

The times and dates of perfection are also important issues in determining priority of recorded liens. In the majority of states, a lien for the construction of a building ordinarily dates back to the commencement of construction. If construction begins on January 1, 2013, and is completed on June 1, 2013, and a lien is filed on July 1, 2010 (assuming a proper filing time), then the priority of the lien dates back to January 1, 2013, when construction began. If new financing (also called permanent financing) were obtained for the building in June, the new lender's mortgage would be second in priority to the contractor's lien, because the contractor's lien has a priority date of the start of construction, or January 1, 2013. This principle is critically important for construction lenders, who must be certain construction has not begun prior to the recording of their mortgage in order not to lose priority. For permanent lenders, this means that all construction costs and subcontractors must be paid and all liens must be satisfied before the lenders record their mortgage or lend the money (so that they are not last in priority behind all those who have worked on the project and who have not yet been paid).

In another group of states, the priority date for liens is the date the particular lienor began work, not the date overall construction began.

In the final group of states, the lien is effective from the date of filing. For example, if the lender records the mortgage before the liens are filed, the lender would have priority because the liens would not date back to the time the construction was begun.

Rights of Purchasers

Whether a good-faith or bona fide purchaser of property will be subject to a pre-existing lien depends on the state's rule on lien attachment. For states that have a rule on attachments dating back to the time construction was commenced, purchasers are subject to liens. In other states, a purchaser would be subject to liens only if the liens were filed and recorded prior to the time of the purchase and transfer of title by deed, along with its recording in the land records (see Chapter 16 for more information on closing and Chapter 14 for more information on deeds and recording). In some states, a residential property exemption does not permit liens on newly constructed residences when the home has been purchased in good faith from a contractor for use as a residence.[3] This exemption protects the buyers even if the priority of liens dates back to the start of the home's construction. There are also the complexities of liens when the owners themselves are constructing or improving existing buildings on their land. Homeowners need to be certain that their general contractor is paying subcontractors and suppliers, and subcontractors and suppliers need to be able to establish their rights with homeowners and the general contractor. The following case deals with an issue of homeowners and problems with payments of subcontractors.

---

[3]Fla. Stat. Ann. § 627.7842(c)

TARLTON V. MILLER'S OF CLAFLIN

227 P.3d 23 (Kan. App. 2010)
When Is a Sub a Sub?

FACTS

The Tarltons (plaintiff) hired Chad Gisick, d/b/a Gisick Construction, to serve as the general contractor in the construction of their new home. They made periodic progress payments to Gisick for work done on the project, apparently based on representations from Gisick but without obtaining lien waivers from the various suppliers. The payment schedule left a remaining balance to be paid to Gisick upon completion of the project. Gisick died in February 2007 before completing the project. His estate was unable to satisfy the outstanding claims of his subcontractors. Miller and S & H filed mechanic's lien statements for unpaid work and materials. Neither Miller nor S & H sent the Tarltons the warning statements required of subcontractors pursuant to K.S.A. 60–1103a(b).

Following Gisick's death, the Tarltons filed an interpleader action with respect to the remaining unspent funds for the project. S & H and Miller counterclaimed for enforcement of their mechanics' liens. The Tarltons moved for cancellation of the liens claimed by Miller and S & H.

The district court ruled that S & H and Miller were subcontractors of Gisick who failed to perfect their liens as subcontractors by giving the statutorily required notice to the owners and struck down their liens. S & H and Miller appealed.

JUDICIAL OPINION

McAnany, Judge

Mechanics' liens are designed to protect unpaid suppliers of labor and materials for real estate construction projects. However, to create a lien a claimant must strictly comply with the applicable statute. One claiming a mechanic's lien has the burden of bringing one's self clearly within the provisions of the statute.

There are different lien perfection requirements for general contractors and for subcontractors. One difference is the requirement in K.S.A. 60–1103a(b) that subcontractors mail to the property owner the warning statement identified in K.S.A. 60–1103a(c) or obtain the owner's signed acknowledgement of that warning and file an affidavit stating that they did so.

There is no question that Miller and S & H did not comply with the statutory requirement that subcontractors give the owners this warning statement. The case turns on whether Miller and S & H were subcontractors of Gisick, the general contractor, or whether they had independent, direct contracts with the Tarltons to supply materials and labor to the project. Whether contracts existed between the Tarltons and these claimants are questions of fact.

First, we must determine who has the burden of proof on the issue of the status of Miller and S & H vis-a-vis the Tarltons. The Tarltons brought this interpleader action against a number of suppliers on the project. They claimed in their petition that S & H and Miller "have or may have claims." The Tarltons tendered into court $13,389.17, "the amount remaining for distribution and payment to the Defendants now making claims." The Tarltons did not ask for affirmative relief with respect to the lien claims of S & H and Miller. The Tarltons denied the allegation that a contractual relationship existed between them and S & H and Miller.

S & H and Miller acknowledged the duty of subcontractors to provide the warning statement described in K.S.A. 60–1103a, but asserted that they were direct contracting parties with the Tarltons and not subcontractors of Gisick, the general contractor.

S & H and Miller have the burden of bringing themselves within the aegis of our mechanic's lien laws. Their lien claims are at risk if they cannot establish what they claimed in their counterclaim: that they are not subcontractors of Gisick but direct contracting parties with the Tarltons. Accordingly, they have the burden of proof on the claim that they had contractual relationships with the Tarltons.

There were at least eight separate documents with different dates wherein [S & H] sold materials to Gisick Construction, who then provided the materials to the plaintiff.... Even though [S & H] attempts at this time to claim Gisick was only an agent of the [Tarltons], the documents make it clear Gisick was the contractor and [S & H] was the sub-contractor.... There was no warning statement sent, and therefore, the lien is defective and ... must be cancelled.

The documents before the court clearly indicated that S & H was a subcontractor of Gisick. Each of the invoices that S & H relies on contains the statement: "Sold To Gisick Const." Nevertheless, S & H maintains on appeal that the Tarltons entered into an oral contract with Gisick, who was the Tarltons' agent for supplying materials for the project. There is no evidence that Gisick was the Tarltons' agent. He contracted to build a home for them, not to serve as their agent. "[W]here the relationship of principal and agent is in issue, the party relying on an alleged agency relationship has the burden of establishing its existence by clear and satisfactory evidence."

The evidence supporting Miller's lien claim consists of two documents attached to Miller's lien statement: an invoice and a sales order form. These two documents are the entirety of the documentary evidence bearing on the issue of Miller's relationship to the Tarltons. The invoice was generated from information contained on the sales order form.

The sales order form lists "Chris and Sara Tarlton" as the customer. However, the "Special Instructions" portion states: "Send to Chad." This apparently refers to Chad Gisick, the general contractor. Send what to Chad and at what location? Clearly not the purchased items of carpet, laminate, and tile. There would be no reason to deliver these items to the general contractor rather than to the job site. After all, Miller was responsible for installation of at least part of the materials, and the flooring in particular. There would be no reason to send these materials to Gisick rather than to the job site. However, if this reference on the document means that the materials should be sent to Gisick, that would tend to prove that Gisick was the contracting party, not the Tarltons.

On the other hand, "Send to Chad" may refer to this sales order form itself, not the materials being sold. If that is the case, then this would also tend to prove that Gisick was the contracting party. Otherwise, why would Gisick have any interest in what particular flooring and tile the Tarltons selected or what they agreed to pay for it?

A notation on the bottom of the sales order form suggests the latter alternative. The form states: "Miller's make no express warranties. We honor and follow factory warranties only. Orders are noncancelable upon manufacturer's acceptance. Please review policies on reverse side of your ticket. Accepted By: X Phone (Chad Gisick)." We find no explanation in the evidence why Miller would obtain Gisick's acceptance of the order if the Tarltons were the contracting parties.

Miller had the duty to come forward with evidence from which one could conclude that it is more probably true than not that the Tarltons were the contracting party, not Gisick. From what meager evidence was provided, we cannot say that Miller met its burden of proof.

Affirmed.

CASE QUESTIONS

1. Why did the court conclude that there was no direct contractual relationship between Miller and S & H and the Tarltons?
2. According to the court, who has the burden of proving that they are entitled to the protections of the mechanic's lien provisions?
3. Develop a list of lessons for homeowners, general contractors, suppliers, and subcontractors that you learn from reading this case.

CONSIDER 6.3   Favalora, a general contractor, was hired by the RC Corporation to renovate a building in New Orleans for use as the dentist office of Dr. Elizabeth Riggs. Favalora contracted with Pioneer, a millworker located in Texas, to fabricate and furnish cabinets, countertops, shelving, and a reception desk at a cost of $24,245.00 to be installed by Favalora. Favalora accepted delivery of the materials on October 4, 2007, and was invoiced by Pioneer the following day. On October 9, 2007, Favalora submitted to the RC Corporation an application for payment of the amount due to Pioneer for materials and supplies, and on October 30, 2007, Favalora received payment for these amounts. However, Favalora failed to settle the account of Pioneer, and in June of 2008, Pioneer filed a lien on the Riggs property. On November 8, 2008, Dr. Riggs agreed to pay Pioneer the sum of $19,905.00 in exchange for Pioneer's release of the lien on the property, reserving all rights against Favalora for the amount of $4,340.00 that was still due under their contract. Favalora refused to pay because Pioneer acted in bad faith in communicating with the owner and securing payment directly. Did Pioneer have the right to communicate with Dr. Riggs? to settle for some payment? *South Texas Pioneer Millwork v. Favalora Constructors, Inc.,* 90 So.3d 1092 (La. App. 2012).   ■

Priority Among Mechanic's Liens

The statutes on the priority among mechanic's liens are widely varied but can be grouped as follows according to attachment times, as discussed earlier:

1. Statutes in which all liens are treated equally, as if all began work at the start of the project
2. Statutes in which liens are given priority according to the time the liens were perfected
3. Statutes in which liens are given priority according to the time individual work began
4. Statutes in which liens are given priority on the basis of the lienor's status

The common law rule, which more than half the states follow, is that all mechanics are on equal footing, as it were, and there is no priority among them. Under common law, all liens go back to the time when construction of the project first began. The reason for this rule under common law was to protect those furnishing labor and materials at the end of a project from always being left without payment or recourse. For example, if first workers or suppliers were given priority, the foundation workers would always be paid but the carpet layers would not.

This method of dating all liens back to the time construction was begun gives all lienors an equal opportunity for recovery. The criteria for determining when construction began varies from state to state, but at common law the construction began with "the first stroke of the ax or spade." Many construction lenders will have the property inspected before a mortgage is recorded, so that they can be assured that no work has begun and that they will have priority over all other lienors who have rights once construction begins.

If there are insufficient funds available to pay lienors on an equal footing, they are paid on a *pro rata* basis. Suppose that there is $15,000 left to be distributed, and the following amounts are due to lienors Akron, Barkley, and Clark:

Akron   = $15,000

Barklay   = $10,000

Clark   = $5,000

Total liens = $30,000

Pro rata distribution is based on proportions. Since the total amount of liens is $30,000, the proportions for the parties are as follows:

Akron   = 15,000 ÷ 30,000, or 1/2

Barklay = 10,000 ÷ 30,000, or 1/3

Clark   = 5,000 ÷ 30,000, or 1/6

Therefore, the $15,000 would be distributed as follows:

Akron   = 1/2 × 15,000 = $7,500

Barklay = 1/3 × 15,000 = $5,000

Clark   = 1/6 × 15,000 = $2,400

In the second group of states, lienor priority is determined by the times each lienor's project or portion of the work began. Again, this method of priorities gives lienors involved with the initial stages of construction a greater chance of payment.

In the remaining two groups of states, lienors are paid according to the time their liens are filed. Laborers may be given special priority over other lienors, or subcontractors may obtain relief after general contractors have been satisfied.

Mechanic's Liens and Fixture Filings

It is possible for an Article 9 UCC fixture filing to have priority over a mechanic's lien. When the security interest is a purchase money security interest (see Chapter 5) and the filing was completed before the item became a fixture or within 20 days after its annexation as a fixture, then the Article 9 interest takes priority, even over previously filed mortgages and (in this case) previously filed or attached mechanic's liens.

Mechanic's Liens and Homestead Exemption

Some states provide for property protection for residential dwellers, called a **homestead exemption**. This exemption provides protection from the attachment of mechanic's liens or at least from the forced sale of property for the satisfaction of a mechanic's lien. Likewise, in those states with dower protection, a mechanic's lien may not attach to a dower or curtesy interest (see Chapter 8), or cause the sale of that interest. The homestead exemption can also preclude foreclosure on a judicial lien.

Mechanic's Liens and Mortgages

As mentioned in the discussion of attachment, whether a mortgage (construction or permanent) will have priority over a mechanic's lien depends on the state's law on the time of attachment. If the priority of liens dates back to the time construction was commenced, then the mortgage must have been recorded prior to that time in order to enjoy priority. If the time of attachment is determined from the date of filing, then the mortgage must have been recorded prior to the time the lien was filed in order to enjoy priority. This priority also applies to mortgages in which the funds are to be advanced in a series of construction draws over a period of time.

TERMINATION OF MECHANIC'S LIENS

Waiver or Release by Agreement

A mechanic's lien may be eliminated by agreement of the parties. The first type of agreement is called a **waiver agreement**, in which a party waives the right (before, during, or after construction) to file a lien for work on materials furnished. Web Exhibit 6.3 is a sample waiver agreement. Some states recognize waivers in original contracts, which make the waiver automatic and enforceable, while other states require the execution of a separate waiver agreement. Waivers executed during and after construction are recognized as valid in all states.

Some states have certain statutory language required for lien waivers. For example, California requires the following language in bold type on the lien waiver:

Notice: This document waives rights unconditionally and states that you have been paid for giving up those rights. This document is enforceable against you if you sign it, even if you have not been paid. If you have not been paid, use a conditional release form. Cal. Civ. Code § 3262(3) and (4).

The purpose of this waiver language is to help subcontractors and contractors understand the distinction between a conditional or limited release and an unconditional release. An unconditional release means that once the signing party is issued a check, all liens are released. Under a conditional or limited release, only the materials and work furnished to the date of the lien are released. The signing party still has lien rights for future work and materials.

Another type of release is the subordination release, which entitles the signing party to a lien, but the lien is secondary to other interests in the property such as those of the construction lender and any other named secured parties. Figure 6.3 provides a visual summary of the issues and rights of parties in mechanic's liens.

LIEN ALTERNATIVES

The complexity of liens and the problems that arise for property owners as well as the cost of enforcement have caused many states to try to resolve construction payment issues by using non-lien methods. A number of jurisdictions[4] now have some form of **stop notice statutes** or **trapping statutes**. These statutes were passed with the subcontractor and supplier interests in mind. Under these statutes, suppliers and subcontractors can give notice to those who are disbursing funds for the project to stop payment to the general contractor until their rights, interests, and payments have been reviewed.

These statutes create many additional issues. For example, what is the liability of the fund holder if payment is not stopped? Also, the result of a stop notice is often that no one is getting paid at all. These relatively new statutes have issues that require resolution through case law.

CONSTITUTIONALITY OF MECHANIC'S LIENS

Several state and federal courts have examined the constitutionality of mechanic's lien statutes. Most have found them to be constitutional so long as there is adequate notice to the landowner of the lien or potential lien. Recent challenges to lien statutes have been grounded in a due process theory that the landowner is being deprived of a land interest without the chance to be heard because there are automatic qualities to the attachment and enforcement of these liens. For example, a lien can attach without a court hearing; the landowner's property and its value are affected and no court will have heard the story from both sides. However, most courts faced with this due process issue have held that no significant property interest is taken, because although the lien decreases the property value, there is a corresponding increase in value for the improvements made. The liens are also upheld because the owner is given a chance to be heard before the amount of the lien is paid or the property is subjected to foreclosure.

---

[4]Alabama, Arizona, California, Colorado, District of Columbia, Florida, Indiana, Louisiana, Michigan, Mississippi, New Jersey, New Mexico, New York, North Carolina, Ohio, Oklahoma, Pennsylvania, Rhode Island, South Dakota, Texas, and Washington.

FIGURE 6.3 Issues in Mechanic's Lien Rights, Waivers, and Collections

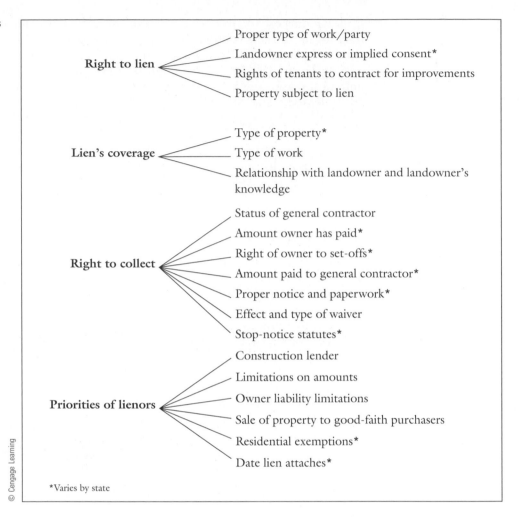

© Cengage Learning

*Varies by state

CAUTIONS AND CONCLUSIONS

The discussions in this chapter affect three parties: property owners, lienors, and lenders. Each group should take appropriate precautions to ensure that liens affect them in only a positive manner.

For property owners, the following questions should be answered:

1. Are licensed, reputable contractors being used?
2. If a general contractor is involved, what guarantees exist for payment of subcontractors and material suppliers? Is there adequate payment supervision?
3. Are there preliminary notice requirements for liens other than those by the general contractor?

For lienors, the following questions should be answered:

1. Who owns the property?
2. Is there a prior mortgage? A construction mortgage?
3. Is preliminary notice of a lien required? If so, how is it properly given?
4. Are there time limits for filing a lien?
5. How long is the lien effective?
6. How long may a lienor wait before foreclosing on a lien?
7. What priorities exist among lien holders?

For lenders, the following questions should be answered:

1. Who owns the property?
2. Is there a prior mortgage? Are there current liens?
3. Has construction or work already begun?
4. Are preliminary notices required?
5. Was the mortgage filed prior to the beginning of the work?
6. Who is the general contractor? What payment supervision is provided?

By assessing their positions and determining their rights and obligations at the outset, property owners, lienors, and lenders can often avoid the pitfalls of liens and enjoy the protections and benefits offered by them. Figure 6.3 provides a summary of the issues in mechanic's lien rights, waivers, and collections.

KEY TERMS

consent statutes, 118
contract statutes, 118
contractual lien, 114
equitable lien, 114
homestead exemption, 130
involuntary lien, 114

judicial lien, 114
lien, 113
lienee, 118
lienor, 118
materials liens, 115
mechanic's liens, 114

statutory lien, 114
stop notice statutes, 131
trapping statutes, 131
voluntary lien, 114
waiver agreement, 130

CHAPTER PROBLEMS

1. In 1977, Chagnon Lumber Company agreed to sell building materials on credit to Stone Mill Construction Corporation. Stone Mill had purchased land and intended to build houses on the property with Chagnon's and other suppliers' materials.

   John and Ann Breiten purchased one of the Stone Mill homes. At closing of the sale, the Breitens were given an affidavit signed by an officer of Stone Mill that stated that the corporation had paid for all materials used in the house. The Breitens paid the purchase price and took title to the house.

   Within 90 days after their last delivery of materials, but after the Breitens' closing, Chagnon filed in court for permission to attach a lien to the Breitens' property.

   The Breitens objected to the lien on the grounds that they had no knowledge that any bills remained unpaid. Are the Breitens correct? Do they have any protection against the lien? *Chagnon Lumber Co., Inc. v. Stone Mill Construction Corp.*, 474 A.2d 588 (N.H. 1984).

2. Carolina Kitchen (CK), a subcontractor, did work for Orndorff Construction Inc. When CK was not paid, it filed a lien (within the 180 days from finishing work — the time-limit for placing a lien in North Carolina). Orndorff then filed for bankruptcy, and CK filed a notice of claim in bankruptcy within 182 days from the time it finished work. Bankruptcy court requires that proof of claims be submitted within all statutory time limits. What should the court do with the lien? *In re Orndorff Const., Inc.*, 394 B.R. 372 (M.D.N.C. 2008).

3. Robert and Janet Barker had signed an installment contract to purchase a home from Roland and Gloria Barker and Eugene and Sandra Barker. Robert and Janet moved into the home in May 1975, and in December 1975, the home was partially destroyed by fire. Robert and Janet moved out of the home for five months so that repairs and restoration could be completed. Robert contracted with Tri-County Builders to repair the house. Robert paid $19,000 of the $20,000 contract price to Tri-County, but Tri-County did not complete the project and also failed to pay Brownsburg Lumber Company (the supplier of the lumber for the home repairs). Brownsburg filed a timely lien notice but notified only Robert and Janet of his supplier role. He did not notify the other Barkers who, under the terms of Robert and Janet's purchase contract, still held title to the house until the full purchase price was paid. Brownsburg filed suit to enforce its lien. Roland and Eugene claim that lien is invalid because they had no notice of Brownsburg's supplier role. Who is correct? Can Brownsburg collect on the lien? *Barker v. Brownsburg Lumber Co., Inc.*, 399 N.E.2d 426 (Ind. 1980); see also *Gravett v. Covenant Life Church*, 841 A.2d 342 (Md. App. 2004).

4. A is a carpenter and has completed the framing of eight homes for G, the general (prime) contractor. Prior to A's work, B had leveled and graded the property; C had put in the foundation; D had staked out the driveways and homes; and E had partially installed the plumbing fixtures. The tasks were completed on the following dates:

   A, November 22, 2012;

   B, August 1, 2012;

C, September 15, 2012;

D, August 15, 2012;

E, August 30, 2012.

All parties properly served a preliminary notice. A construction mortgage was filed August 1, 2012. No one has been paid, and A, B, C, D, and E have all filed liens by December 1, 2012. Who has priority, the mortgage company or the lienors? What order of priority exists among the lienors? What happens if there is not enough money to pay the lienors?

5. Fifteen couples purchased homes in the Green Meadows subdivision, and they had all moved in by August 2012. Two days before Christmas, workmen's liens were filed against the homeowners' properties. Under state law, the filing of the liens dated back to the time construction began, May 2012. The homeowners wish to know their rights. What is the result? Would the result be different in your state?

6. Bank One filed a mortgage on May 31, 1989, on property owned by Sam and Grace Malz. The mortgage secured a $2,400,000 loan Bank One had made to the Malzes for purposes of constructing 10 six-unit buildings on the property. At the time the mortgage on the property was filed, Schalmo Builders, Inc., the contractor hired by the landowner to construct the buildings, had performed soil tests and staked out the locations for the buildings. The Malzes did not pay the builder and defaulted on the loan. The builder foreclosed on its lien and Bank One claimed priority. Who has first claim to the proceeds from the foreclosure sale of the property? *Schalmo Builders, Inc. v. Malz*, 629 N.W.2d 52 (Ohio App. 1993).

7. Allen Betke contracted with Thomas Hake Enterprises, Inc., to construct a home in Carpentersville, Illinois. As construction progressed, Betke was unable to pay, so he arranged for Charlotte Birck and her son, Jason Birck, to buy the house. Charlotte and Jason paid Betke $68,000, and Betke continued to supervise construction and hire subcontractors although Charlotte wrote checks for payment and channeled them through Betke for the contractors, subcontractors, and suppliers.

The house was resold by Charlotte for $175,000 to the Coffmans. However, there were liens on the property from various parties not paid by Betke. The sale could not close until the lien issues were resolved. Charlotte claims she and Jason are not subject to the liens because they had no contracts with the lienors. Is she correct? *Thomas Hake Enterprises, Inc. v. Betke*, 703 N.E.2d 114 (Ill. App. 1998).

8. Morris Plumbing was a general contractor that entered into a Master Work Agreement with Spire Communications to build the infrastructure for a fiber optic network around Atlanta, Georgia. Morris was responsible for directional boring, or digging trenches for the network to be placed underground. Spire eventually fell behind in payments and ultimately had many outstanding purchase orders unpaid. On November 27, 2001, Spire agreed to pay $2,167,366.05 to Morris as a "true-up" of all then-outstanding purchase orders. The settlement was evidenced by an e-mail from Mike Miller of Spire to D. L. Morris, Jr. of Morris Plumbing. In return, Morris agreed that it would continue to work on the network. However, the settlement payments were not made as quickly as Morris wanted and on December 11, 2001, Morris filed a mechanic's lien in the amount of $3.4 million in Fulton County, Georgia. The lien was filed in Fulton County, Georgia, but the work was done in several counties. The lien amount exceeded the amount the parties had agreed was owed. Morris did not file a commencement of work in relation to the lien. In your state, would Morris have a valid lien? *In re Spire Communications, Inc.* 2002 WL 1343463 (Bank. Ct. D. Del. 2002).

9. GRW Engineers, Inc., entered into a contract to furnish architectural and engineering services to Chateau Royale, Inc. Chateau Royale was turning a historic building into a restaurant and hired GRW to prepare plans and specifications for the renovation and conversion. GRW worked on the plan and specs over a period of months. Bills were submitted to Chateau, but not paid. Chateau's attorney finally contacted GRW and said its bills were "out of reason." The attorney then offered GRW $25,000 to settle the account. The original contract amount was $340,000 to $365,000 (depending on some contingencies in the work). GRW refused and filed a lien. Chateau claims GRW did not have the right to lien its property for environmental services. Is Chateau correct? *GRW Engineers, Inc. v. Elam*, 504 So.2d 117 (La. 1987).

10. Go back to the chapter opening problem and think through whether Village Manor should have to pay what Dzen wants for the roof work. *Centimark Corporation v. Village Manor Associates Limited Pshp.*, 967 A.2d 550 (Conn. App. 2009).

For research activities related to this chapter, go to our text companion website at
www.cengagebrain.com

CHAPTER 7

DESCRIBING LAND INTERESTS

*During the subprime mortgage frenzy that ran from 2005 to 2007,
one mortgage underwriter noted that the photo of the property that was being
financed had a number on the house that did not match the address of the property
that was being mortgaged. When she asked the mortgage broker about the
discrepancy, another photograph of the same house with the correct number
appeared on her desk the next day. She turned down the loan, but her supervisor
reversed her decision. Six months later the loan was in foreclosure and when
representatives of the lender went to place a "For Sale" sign on the property they
learned that the property was an empty lot, not a house. The photo was
fraudulent, as was the appraisal of the home and the inspection of the property.*

The introduction illustrates what a difference a legal description—as opposed to just an address—can make. Legal descriptions require precision and detail, but the result is clarity on rights and title. An error in a description of land can have multigenerational impact. And descriptions that do not meet legal requirements cannot pass valid title to property.

This chapter answers the following questions: What are the methods used to describe land? What precautions should be taken in drafting and checking land descriptions?

METHODS OF DESCRIBING LAND INTERESTS

Metes and Bounds

The metes and bounds method is a description technique that uses the boundary lines and marking points in a particular parcel as its basis for identification. **Metes** refers to distance, while **bounds** refers to the direction of the distance to be taken.

A **metes and bounds description** consists of a series of instructions that could be followed to walk out the boundary lines of the land parcel. A permanent beginning point can be natural (such as a stream or river) or artificial (such as a bridge). Monuments are frequently used as starting points for metes and bounds descriptions.

For example, a metes and bounds description of the shaded portion in Figure 7.1 would be as follows:

FIGURE 7.1 Sample Land Parcel for Metes and Bounds Description

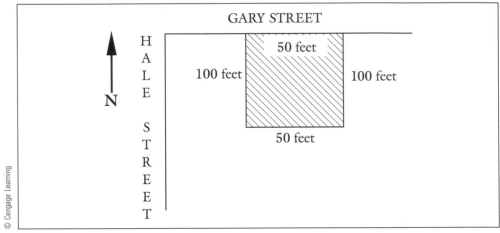

© Cengage Learning

Beginning at a point on the south side of Gary Street, 200 feet east from the corner formed by the intersection of the south side of Gary Street and the east side of Hale Street, then proceeding south parallel to the east side of Hale Street 100 feet; then proceeding east parallel to the south side of Gary Street 50 feet; then proceeding north parallel to the east side of Hale Street 100 feet to the south side of Gary Street; and then proceeding west on the south side of Gary Street, 50 feet or to the beginning point.

Because of their dependency on starting points (which can be moved) and because of the potential for inaccurate measurement, metes and bounds descriptions can result in problems when land is transferred.

The following case deals with the adequacy of a metes and bounds description and the role of additional information in determining whether a description is adequate.

GAUT V. DANIEL

293 S.W.3d 764 (Tex. App. 2009)
Got Description? Gaut Deed?

FACTS

Miguel and Gloria Daniel filed suit against Anna Gonzalez (the administrator of the estate of Alice and Abelardo Garcie, her parents and the original grantors of the 28 acres to the Daniels). The Daniels also sued Lowell and Paula Gaut who claim ownership to 47.71 acres of land (that includes the 28 acres conveyed to the Daniels) that they say they obtained via a warranty deed and as good-faith purchases.

The trial court held that the description of the land in the deed to the Daniels was sufficient to convey title and cancelled the Gauts' deed. The Gauts appealed.

JUDICIAL OPINION
Stone, Chief Justice

The deed in question first generally references the Duval County surveys out of which the 28 acres can be found. None of these surveys are part of the record. The deed also notes the 28 acres as "being out of a called 399.5 acre tract designated as Share No. 6, as set aside to Alice L. Garcia...." It then references several surveys of the partitioned land from which the 399.5 acre tract was taken.

The deed (to the Daniels) provides the following description:

BEGINNING at the NW corner of a 17 acre tract for the place of beginning and NE corner of this 28 acre tract;

THENCE in a southeasterly direction, 1173 feet to point for the SE corner of this 28 acre tract;

THENCE in a southwesterly direction, 760.5 feet to a point for the SW corner of this 28 acre tract;

THENCE in a northwesterly direction 881.2 feet to a point for the NW corner of this 28 acre tract;

THENCE in a northeasterly direction and parallel with Hwy 59, 1388.2 feet to the NE corner of this 28 acre tract and place of beginning.

To be sufficient, a writing conveying title must provide within itself, or by reference to some other existing writing in existence at the time of the deed, the means or information by which the land being conveyed can be identified with reasonable certainty. This has been termed the "nucleus of description" theory. Under this theory, if the deed contains a "nucleus of description," parol evidence may be introduced to explain the descriptive words in order to locate the land. **The essential elements may never be supplied by parol.** The details which merely explain or clarify the essential terms appearing in the instrument may ordinarily be shown by parol. But the parol must not constitute the framework or skeleton of the agreement.

The language above provides no reference to the location of the 17-acre tract mentioned, no means within the deed to locate the tract, and no reference within the deed to any existing extrinsic writing which might assist in determining the location.

1) The distances provided have no identified terminal points; 2) the courses are defined only generally (southeasterly, southwesterly, etc.) without angles, so there are no metes and bounds (defined as boundary lines of land, with their terminal points and angles); 3) the reference to the "northwest corner of a 17-acre tract" does not describe a terminal point because the location of the tract is not identified; 4) the partition deed referenced in the 28-acre deed describes several tracts, one of which (Share 6) is the 399.5 acre tract, providing no information to fix the location of the 28 acres within the acreage; 5) the deed references a survey of the land out of which the 28 acres is taken, but does not provide a clue as to where within it the 28 acres can be found; 6) the only monument referenced—a line parallel with Hwy 59—provides a directional orientation of one boundary line but no information about its location; and 7) the monument the Daniels' surveyor found which he says is the start point, at the edge of 17 acres owned by the Daniels, is not referenced in the deed, and the deed does not make any reference to the Daniels as owners of contiguous acres or state the 17 acres is actually a combination of two tracts.

The Daniels presented parol evidence showing taxing authorities, TxDOT, and oil exploration companies identified the Daniels as the owners of the 28-acre tract. They also introduced photos showing a fence Daniel said he rebuilt and a gate he erected, and testified that "everyone" knew they owned the land. However, none of this evidence is relevant to the sufficiency of the deed because it was not referenced within the deed.

Based on the above, the trial court erred in finding the Daniels' 28-acre deed was sufficient. Because nothing identifies which 28 acres out of the 399.5 are being conveyed, the deed is void. ... [W]e conclude the 1990 deed conveying 28 acres from the Garcias to the Daniels is void for insufficient description, and render judgment in favor of the Gauts.

Reversed.

CASE QUESTIONS

1. Why does the court not allow additional, extrinsic evidence to supplement what is in the deed?
2. What is the problem with the deed description?
3. What happens to the Daniels' rights to the property under this decision?

CONSIDER 7.1   A deed contains the following description:

A certain lot of land situated in the Parish of Lafourche, State of Louisiana, on the right descending bank of Bayou Lafourche, at about one mile above the town of Thibodaux, measuring thirty-five feet front by five hundred forty-five feet in depth, bounded above by land belonging to the Thibodaux Brick Works, now or formerly, below by land of Julia Davis, now or formerly, in front by other property of Lydia Brown, now or formerly, and in the rear by property of Henry Ricks, now or formerly. Together with all the buildings and improvements thereon and all rights, ways, privileges and servitudes thereunto belonging or appertaining. Dickerson v. Davis, 2010 WL 4273178 (La. App. 2010)

Is this a sufficient description to convey title to the land? Explain your answer. ■

PRACTICAL TIP

Physical inspections help verify the accuracy or inaccuracy of descriptions. Compare physical boundaries with deed descriptions.

Plat Map

The **plat map** is probably the most frequently used method for describing property in residential areas. This description method uses a map of a subdivision that is recorded at some state or local agency responsible for property records. Each plat map contains the size and shape of each lot, the numbers of blocks and lots, the names of all streets, indications of alleys and easements, and a list of covenants and restrictions. A sample plat description would be, "Lot 27 of Candlelight Estates IV, as per plat recorded in Book of Maps 30, page 80, in the Office of the County Recorder of Holim County, Utah."

The plat map itself must have certain minimal information to be valid. For example, county and town are critical information. If the deed description relies on an attached map, the map must be labeled with direction, street names, and lot numbers.

CONSIDER 7.2   A deed describes the property as *"the property located at Municipal Address: ——————, City Many, Parish Sabine, Louisiana, Legal description 4.87 acres on Hwy 6, see attached plat...."* The plat map, which was attached, showed only the dimensions of the property and that it was located somewhere on Highway 6. The plat does not show landmarks or adjacent property owners. Is this description sufficient? *Wilson v. Head*, 707 So.2d 127 (La. App. 1998). ■

ETHICAL ISSUE

On June 27, 1996, Will A. Hudson and Betty H. Hudson entered into an agreement with Transamerica Financial Services (Transamerica) whereby Transamerica loaned them $232,610.96. The Hudsons executed a promissory note stating that the loan was secured by certain real estate, and also executed a deed of trust securing the loan with certain real estate listed on an attachment to the deed of trust, "Attachment A." The collateral listed on the promissory note includes four addresses in typeface and four that are handwritten. The face of the note reads, *"THIS LOAN IS SECURED BY ... Real estate located at the following address: 104 & 106 Lord Anson Dr. Raleigh, NC 27610, 1212 Angelus Dr. Raleigh, NC 27601, 3525 Edington Ln. Raleigh, NC 27604, 714, 716, 722 & 724 Woodland Rd."*

Attachment A was not part of the document package the Hudsons executed and the list of properties did not include the "Woodland 501 Road properties as security interest for the loan." However, the Hudsons fell behind on their payments and Transamerica filed for foreclosures on the properties listed as well as the Woodland 501 properties, which had been written into Attachment A. The Hudsons challenged the foreclosure. Transamerica said it understood that all the Hudsons' properties were subject to the mortgage and it modified the description to reflect that. Was it ethical to add the properties unilaterally? Would it affect the validity of the deed? *In re Hudson*, 642 S.E.2d 485 (N.C. App. 2007).

Government Survey
History
Another method for describing a land interest is by the **United States government survey**. This survey was done in 1785 because there was such a vast section of land west of the original 13 colonies with so many conflicting claims of ownership. The purpose of the survey was to provide a uniform system for description based on dividing the vast lands into rectangular segments.

Principal Meridians and Baselines
The geographer for the United States who was assigned the survey task had to develop a system for the survey that would compensate for the Earth's curved surface.

The survey began with **prime** or **principal meridians** and **baselines**. These first guidelines serve as the solution for the curvature of the Earth's surface. The lines were positioned at uniform distances apart so that the curve would not affect the accuracy of the survey. There are 35 prime or principal meridian lines that run north to south, and 32 baselines that run east to west. The meridians are named according to their locations: Chickasaw, Michigan, San Bernardino, and Tallahassee are examples of principal meridians.

Guide Meridians and Parallels
Between each of the baselines and principal meridians, the surveyors placed correction lines to further compensate for the Earth's curved surface. **Guide meridians** were placed between principal meridians, and **parallels** were placed between baselines. These supplementary lines were placed every 24 miles. The result is that the surveyed land is divided into a **grid** of 24-mile squares.

Townships and Ranges
This grid of 24 miles is broken down even further with **township** lines placed every six miles between the parallels and **range** lines placed every six miles between the guide meridians.

Figure 7.2 (on page 140) illustrates these divisions. In the figure, the six-mile squares (townships) are identified by their distances (in the number of squares) from the principal meridian. This distance is labeled as either east or west of the principal meridian. For example, in Figure 7.2, the upper right-hand square is one square west of the principal meridian, or R1W. However, because all squares adjacent to the meridian will have that same label, the townships are further identified according to their distance from the baseline. The upper right-hand square is the fourth square north of the baseline, or T4N.

Each six-mile square or township in Figure 7.2 is further broken down into 36 one-mile squares. Each one-mile square is called a **section**. Sections are numbered in a serpentine fashion starting at the upper right-hand corner and proceeding left (see Figure 7.3 on page 140).

FIGURE 7.2
Twenty-Four-Mile Grid
of U.S. Government
Survey

FIGURE 7.3 Sample
Township

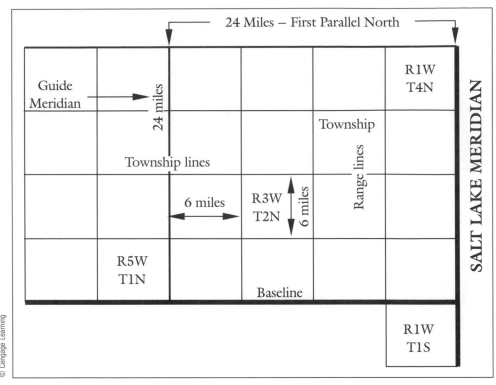

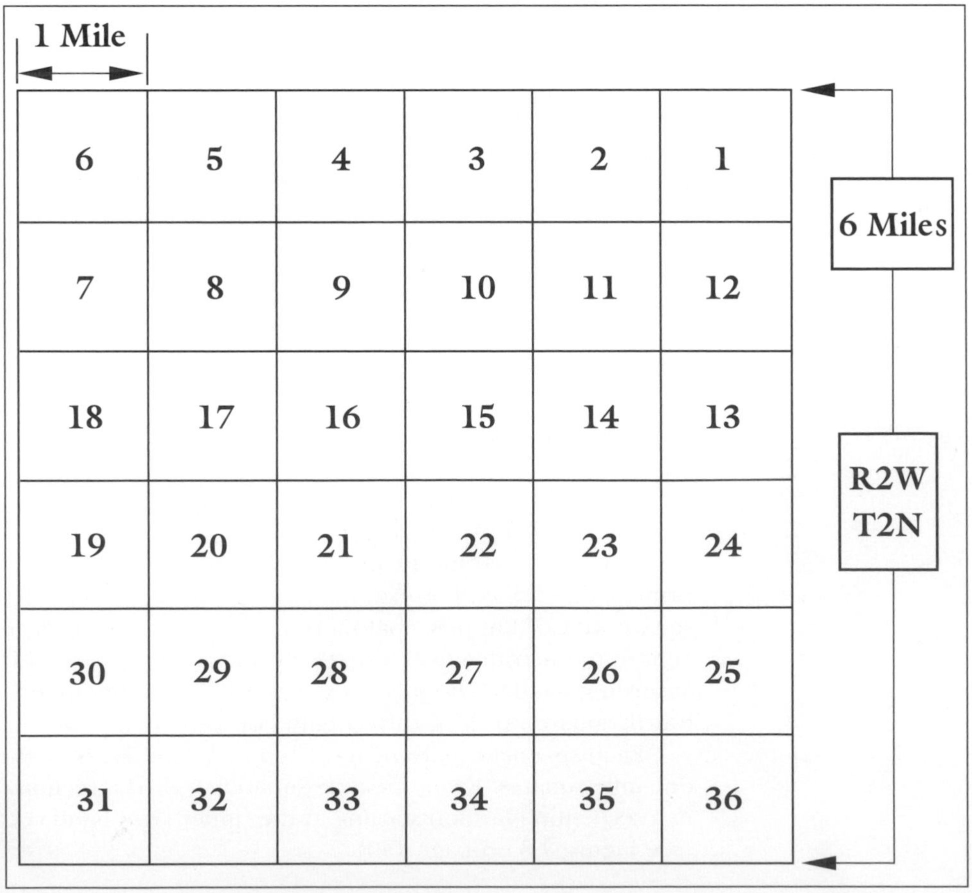

FIGURE 7.4 Sample Section

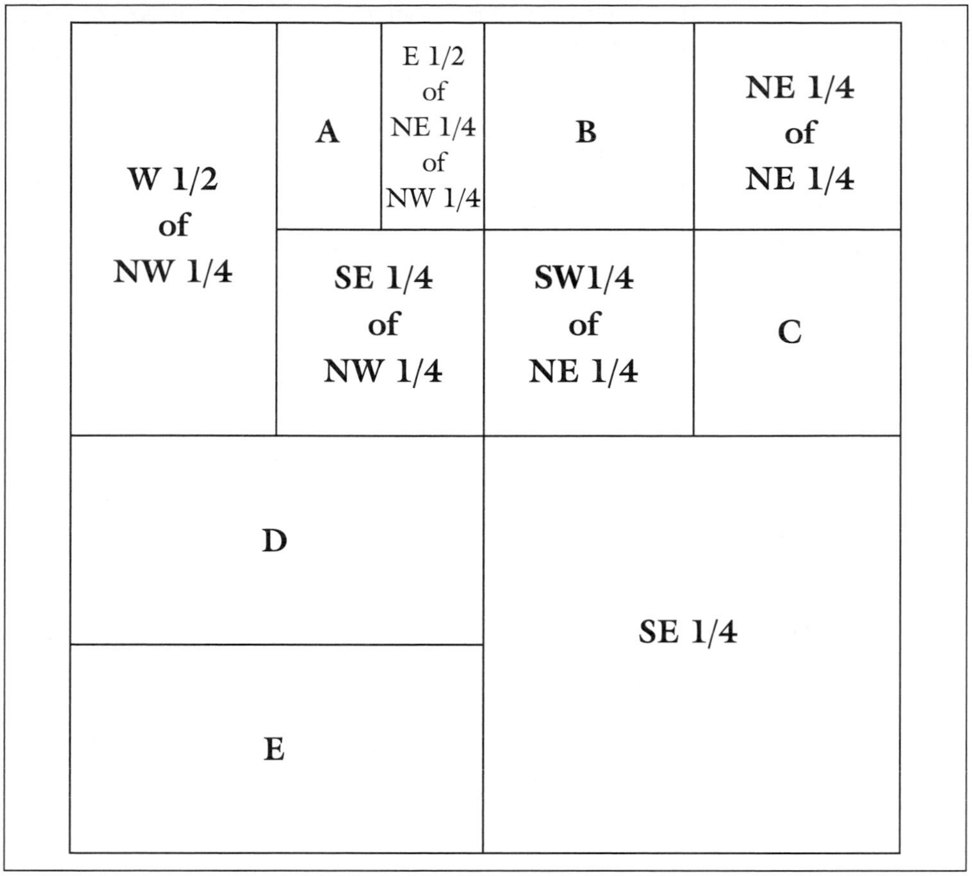

Each section is one mile square, or a total of 640 acres, and each section can be broken down into fractional portions to more precisely describe the land involved. These fractional portions are described according to directional locations. Figure 7.4 is an example of a section with fractional portions labeled. To start, each section can be divided into quarters. The upper right-hand corner is the northeast quarter, and the lower left-hand corner is the southwest quarter. In the same manner, each quarter can be broken into quarters and labeled.

CONSIDER 7.3 Label each of the 21 blank squares in Figure 7.2 according to its location with respect to the Salt Lake Meridian and the baseline.

In Figure 7.4, finish filling in the descriptive names of the unmarked portions (A, B, C, D, and E) of each section.

Description and Size

Pulling together all divisions of the government survey, a sample land description would be "SE 1/4 of Section 12, Township 3 North, Range 2 East of the Salt Lake Meridian, Iron County, State of Utah." The addition of the county and state helps in determining which baseline is involved.

Because the government survey is uniform, it is possible to determine the size of a described parcel of land once the exact description is known. For example, if the land described is the NE 1/4 of a section, then the size of the parcel is 1/4 of 640 acres (the size of a section), or 160 acres. If the land described were the NE 1/4 of the NE 1/4, then the parcel would be 1/4 of 160, or 1/16 of 640, or 40 acres.

CONSIDER 7.4   Frank and Gayle Marek owned property adjacent to property owned by Earl and Sandra Lawrence. The two couples disputed where the boundary lines between their two properties were located. Both couples had title to their property described through deeds that used the government survey in their description portions. The dividing line between their properties in both deeds was described as "the section line dividing Sections 26 and 27." However, the two couples disagreed as to where that line actually was because most people assumed that Three Bear Road was the dividing line, and Three Bear Road did not run along the section line. The court relied on testimony about the assumed boundary line to establish the correct dividing line between the Mareks and Lawrence properties. Was the court correct to do so? Explain why or why not. *Marek v. Lawrence,* 278 P.3d 920 (Idaho 2012).   ∎

ADEQUACY OF DESCRIPTIONS

PRACTICAL TIP

Regardless of the means used for describing the property, make sure the description meets the legal tests for sufficiency under that method.

When properly followed, the three methods of description just discussed are legally sufficient descriptions. However, many other different methods of description are used, some of them legally sufficient and others only creating confusion and causing litigation. The most important criterion in evaluating the legal sufficiency of a description is whether the land is described in such a manner that only one possible tract can be identified from the description.

Description by Popular Name

Often a popular name such as "my ranch, the Double T" is used as a description for conveying land. This type of description may or may not be sufficient, depending on whether the landowner holds one or several tracts of land.

In the following case, the issue of the legal sufficiency of a description by popular name in a contract is addressed. If a description is inadequate for a contract, it is inadequate for a deed.

WADSWORTH V. MOE

193 N.W.2d 645 (Wis. 1972)
Is the Schoolhouse Included with the Farm?

FACTS

L. W. Anacker owned two parcels of land in the town of Stanton, Dunn County. One parcel consisted of a 130-acre farm with a dwelling and a number of other buildings. The other parcel was a one-acre piece of land with a remodeled schoolhouse in which Anacker lived. The schoolhouse was enclosed by a fence and was located 1/8 mile from the other buildings.

After his wife's death in 1962, Anacker became depressed and stopped farming. He lived in the schoolhouse near his daughter, Mabel Moe (appellant).

Anacker decided to sell the farm without the schoolhouse, and the farm was listed for $18,000. Wadsworth (respondent) learned of the listing, and he and Anacker went to a bank and had a real estate option document drawn up. (A standard legal form was used.)

In the blanks provided, the real estate was described as "The L. W. Anacker farm in the town of Stanton." Wadsworth paid Anacker $1,500 for the option and could buy the property by paying an additional $14,000 by January 4, 1968. The contract also provided

> Party of the second part may occupy the land and other buildings from this date forward. Party of the first part may occupy the dwelling and keep possession of the same up to November 1, 1968. Present insurance to be assigned to party of the second part free. The electric stove in the kitchen to remain for party of the second part.

On December 18, 1968, Wadsworth informed Anacker of his intention to exercise the option.

When Mabel Moe learned of the option, she refused to let her father convey title, claiming that the legal description in the option was inadequate.

The trial court entered a judgment for Wadsworth and granted him specific performance. Mrs. Moe appealed.

JUDICIAL OPINION

Wilkie, Justice

An option to purchase real estate which does not conform to the statute of frauds is void and a nullity. To comply with the statute, the contract or memorandum must be reasonably definite as to the property conveyed. Here the trial court determined that the description of the real estate as "the L. W. Anacker farm in the town of Stanton" was not sufficiently definite but that the entire document, considered as a whole together with the stipulation of facts by the parties, did comply with the statute of frauds and was, therefore, valid.

The trial court was entirely correct in deciding that the bare description on the option did not comply with the statute of frauds. When an individual owns more than one parcel of land in the same general locality, the description in the document must be sufficiently definite so that a person might know to a reasonable certainty to which parcel or parcels the document relates.

The trial court did find, however, that although the option description was not sufficient, the whole option when taken together with information in the stipulation of facts was sufficient to meet the statute of frauds. All the terms of a contract may be considered when deciding whether the document conforms to the statute of frauds.

The land description in the option document was admittedly vague as to what constituted the "L. W. Anacker farm." The extent of the land is not shown. The other terms of the option contract do not clear up this ambiguity, neither does the stipulation. The extrinsic evidence shows either that both the farm and all of the schoolhouse land were conveyed; that only the schoolhouse land was conveyed; or that the farm, but not the schoolhouse was conveyed. In short, the contract, even when considered together with this extrinsic evidence, continues to be vague about the extent of the land sold.

In the end, the option contract here does not sufficiently show the extent of the land conveyed and for that reason must be held null and void.

Reversed and remanded for dismissal of the complaint.

CASE QUESTIONS

1. What type of agreement did Anacker and Wadsworth execute?
2. How was the land described? Is the description legally sufficient?
3. Did Wadsworth exercise the option to purchase?
4. What were Mrs. Moe's objections to the agreement?

Description by Street Number

Many times, transfers of residential property have as a description just the street address of the property being conveyed. Although this type of description may be used as a supplement, and is sufficient for a contract, it should not be used in the deed or as the sole description. One reason is that street numbers and names may change. Also, the use of the street address alone does not describe the exact segment of land being transferred.

The following case deals with a description issue in which no real method of description was used and the issue of the deed's validity resulted.

DAVIS V. HINSON

67 So.3d 1107 (Fla. App. 2011)
The Eleven Tenants in Common, One Deed, No Description, and Confusion

FACTS

In July 1983—Geraldine Hinsons' parents recorded a quitclaim deed conveying a tract of approximately 74 acres to Geraldine, her six siblings, and several of the siblings' spouses. The deed named each recipient as tenant in common without a right of survivorship. In September 1989 the tenants in common signed a deed conveying an eleven-acre portion of the 74–acre tract to the Wash and Geraldine Hinson. At the time it was signed, the deed did not include a description of the exact eleven-acre parcel being conveyed.

In August 1990 the Hinsons recorded the September 1989 deed. They attached to the deed a survey describing the exact eleven acres being conveyed. The eleven acres claimed by the Hinsons adjoined a two-acre parcel which they had previously conveyed to Lalisa Davis.

At that time, Davis began to encroach on the boundary separating her two-acre parcel from the Hinsons' eleven-acre parcel. Davis had strewn personal property over the boundary line and built a shed straddling the boundary line.

The Hinsons filed suit against Ms. Davis for quiet title and ejectment. The trial court found for the Hinsons and Ms. Davis appealed.

JUDICIAL OPINION

Hawkes, Judge

Davis claimed the Hinsons lacked standing to bring causes of action to quiet title or for ejectment as they lacked a valid title or possessory interest in the eleven-acre parcel. Davis argued that not all tenants in common had signed the September 1989 deed, thereby invalidating its conveyance of the eleven acres.

During the proceedings below, the Hinsons successfully argued they had a right to possession based on the deed signed in September 1989. We disagree and find this deed did not give the Hinsons legal title to the eleven-acre parcel for the following two reasons:

First, the deed was not signed by all of the owners of the encompassing 74–acre tract. It is undisputed that one of the original tenants in common died before the September 1989 deed was signed, leaving her interest in the property to her surviving children.

One of her children—Rashunn Lewis—did not sign the deed.

Traditionally, when tenants in common convey interest, they convey only their interest in the partial ownership of the complete parcel. "[O]ne cotenant cannot bind another, absent that other's consent, by alienating any specific portion of the estate, since each cotenant owns an interest in the whole which is indivisible except by partition or agreement." Therefore, a cotenant cannot convey exclusive possessory rights to a specific portion of their property unless every cotenant agrees to the conveyance.

Applying these principles here, the September 1989 deed did not give the Hinsons exclusive possessory rights to the eleven-acre parcel as it was not signed by all cotenants with an interest in the land. Because of this, the deed cannot be used to demonstrate valid legal title.

Second, the deed did not convey valid legal title because, at the time it was signed, it did not include a description of the specific eleven acres being conveyed. "To effect a valid conveyance of real property, a deed or other instrument must describe the property such that it is evident that a particular parcel, and not a different or unspecified one, is to be conveyed." A deed which contains a description so vague that a surveyor would not be able to locate the land is considered a nullity.

Here, at the time the deed was signed, it simply stated "this deed was prepared without benefit of abstract; legal description having been furnished by grantors." The exact description of the eleven acres in question was not clarified until one year later, when the Hinsons attached a survey at the time of recording. Because the deed lacked an adequate legal description at the time of signing, it must be considered a nullity and did not convey legal title.

The fact that the Hinsons attached a complete description of the eleven acres at the time of recording does not validate the deed. When parties reform a contract, they must demonstrate that it is the intent of each party to incorporate the changes. There is no evidence in the instant case that the tenants in common each agreed to convey this particular eleven acres to the Hinsons. It does not appear that anyone re-signed the deed after the survey was attached. Without evidence of such mutual agreement, the fact that the survey was later attached to the deed does not correct its omission.

Nor does section 95.231(2), Florida Statutes (2010), cure the deed's defects. The trial court relied on this provision during the proceedings below to address any concerns with the validity of the Hinsons' title. The provision states:

> After 20 years from the recording of a deed or the probate of a will purporting to convey real property, no person shall assert any claim to the property against the claimants under the deed or will or their successors in title.

The trial court found that because the September 1989 deed was recorded in August 1990, and over twenty years had passed since its recording date, Davis was prohibited from contesting its validity. The trial court misjudged this provision's intended effect.

Section 95.231(2) is a curative provision. However, its curative effect extends only to correct technical defects in an otherwise valid deed executed by the person(s) owning the property in question. It cannot validate conveyances made by persons who have no possessory interest in the property. In other words, it cannot be used to create a title where none existed before.

Here, it seems that section 95.231(2) could cure the deed's failure to adequately describe the specific eleven acres being conveyed. This was a mere "technical" defect. But the provision cannot cure the deed's failure to include Rashunn Lewis' signature on the list of grantors. This was not a "technical" defect, but a failure in the chain of title. To find otherwise would mean section 95.231(2) could validate titles in every case where property is conveyed without the full cooperation and agreement of the actual owner. The provision was not meant to apply in such situations, and therefore is inapplicable in this case.

We therefore reverse and remand.

CASE QUESTIONS

1. What was the problem with the signatures on the deed to the Hinsons and why are these signatures important?
2. Why does the attachment of the description by the Hinsons not cure the deed description issue?
3. Explain the Florida statute on deeds after 20 years and why it does not cure the deed to the Hinsons.

General Conveyances

Sometimes a legal description such as "all my real estate" is used. Such a description is inadequate because it does not provide the location, extent, and boundaries of the interest being conveyed.

Impermanent Descriptions

Often, metes and bounds descriptions use a starting point that is impermanent in its character, such as "pile of rocks" or "fences." These types of descriptions create problems because there can be movement or even destruction of the beginning point, thus rendering the description invalid.

INTERPRETATION OF DESCRIPTIONS

In determining the adequacy or meaning of a description, courts follow certain rules that are uniformly applied:

Rule 1: The language of the description is construed against the grantor (seller) of the property and in favor of the grantee. This rule is based on the idea that the grantor drafted the deed and had the opportunity to check it for accuracy.

Rule 2: If there are two descriptions, one ambiguous and one nonambiguous, the nonambiguous description prevails so that a legally sufficient description is found.

Rule 3: Ambiguities may be clarified by reference to other portions of the document and to oral testimony. Outside evidence is permissible for clarification only if there is a latent as opposed to a patent ambiguity in the deed. A latent ambiguity is one that is not apparent to the parties when the deed is written. Examples of latent ambiguities are typing errors or the simple carryover of an erroneous legal description of which the parties are unaware. A patent ambiguity (as in the *Wadsworth* case) can be clarified only by reference to other parts of the deed or document and not by reference to extrinsic evidence.

The following case brings together all of the problems that can arise with a description combining metes and bounds with plat map description, and ambiguities in both creating interpretation issues.

WITHINGTON V. DERRICK

572 A.2d 912 (Vt. 1990)
Dueling Deeds, Warring Neighbors

FACTS

James and Madeline Withington (plaintiffs) and Asa and Vivian Derrick (defendants) dispute the ownership of a piece of land located at the confluence of the parties' properties (as pictured on page 147). On October 10, 1959, in two separate transactions, two brothers, as common grantors, deeded the two pieces of property located in the Village of Wilder, Town of Hartford, Vermont, to the Withingtons and the Derricks. The Derricks' deed provides as follows:

> *Being Lot #36 as delineated on Hazen's Survey and Plan of Lots in the Village of Wilder, so-called, and which lot is bounded on the East by Lot #29, now owned by the grantees herein; on the north by Lot #35, now owned by the Benedicts; on the west by land now of Hoff; and on the south by the street known as Chandler Terrace.*

The phrase in the Derricks' deed describing the western boundary of the property is incorrect: There was no adjacent landowner by the name of Hoff. At the time of the conveyance, people named Haff did own several lots about a block away. Even assuming that the drafter of the instrument was referring to Haff, the Haff property could not possibly have been the western boundary of lot 36. The Withingtons' deed includes the following description:

> *Also an irregular parcel of land described as follows: Beginning at a point marking the southeasterly corner of the Haff premises, and thence proceeding northerly along said Haff premises to the corner of Fern Street; thence easterly along Fern Street to the Benedict premises and St. John premises and the boundary of the right of way to said premises to Lot #36; thence southerly along the westerly boundary of Lot #36 to Chandler Terrace; thence westerly along the southerly*

> *boundary of the premises herein conveyed to the corner of Lot #44 which is the point of beginning.*

This description has two problems. First, the Benedict and St. John deeds do not mention any right-of-way leading to or adjoining their land; however, it is uncontested that a narrow strip of land on the southerly end of the St. John premises separately existed as a right-of-way. Second, the last part of the description does not close the deeded property. Further, Fern Street and Union Street were never accepted as municipal roadways.

The trial court held that the grantors had intended to deed to the defendants the portion of the never-accepted Union Street directly west of lot 36 but that the drawer of defendants' deed has mistaken lot 44 for lot 37 and accordingly named the Hoff (meant to be Haff) property as the western boundary of lot 36. The trial court awarded title to the piece of property at issue to the Derricks, and the Withingtons appealed.

JUDICIAL OPINION
Gibson, Justice

Essentially, only two facts vaguely support the trial court's theory. First, since Union Street was not really a street at the time of the deed, one might infer that the grantors intended lot #36 to include the parcel of land adjoining lot #36 inaccurately marked as a street. Nonetheless, in addition to the fact that this is purely conjecture, we note that the same grantors had granted land in prior deeds (the Benedict and St. John properties) which adjoined, but did not include, Union Street. Thus, there is no reason to assume that Union Street would normally be considered part of one of its adjoining lots simply because it had never been accepted as a street.

Second, the trial court's theory, though attenuated, does provide an explanation of why the description in plaintiffs' deed does not close their property. Nevertheless, since the boundary of the "closing" segment of plaintiffs' land is not in dispute, the fact that plaintiffs' deed description does not close is of little consequence. Where there are several manifest errors and the proffered interpretation hinges on nothing more than speculation, that interpretation cannot prevail without first applying the established rules of construction to determine the intent of the parties.

"In construing a deed, we initially look at the instrument itself, which is deemed to declare the understanding and intent of the parties." Thus, it is the intention expressed by the words of the deed, not the unexpressed intention that the parties may have had, which prevails. Generally, a particular descrip-

tion will govern over a general description, but less significant aspects of a description will "[become] the controlling influence in determining the identity of premises where other parts of [the] description are not sufficiently certain," or are nonexistent. For instance, in *Spiller v. Scribner* 36 Vt. 365 (1863), where the deed described land as "being lots No. 22 and 23" and as "our home farm," this Court held that the disputed land, which was inside the home farm but outside lots No. 22 and 23, was not part of the deeded land because "land conveyed … by clear and well defined metes and bounds … shall prevail … over any general words of description that may have been used in the deed." The Court pointed out that an additional, more particular description could have overridden the reference to specific lot numbers, but that *the description of a lot by reference to*

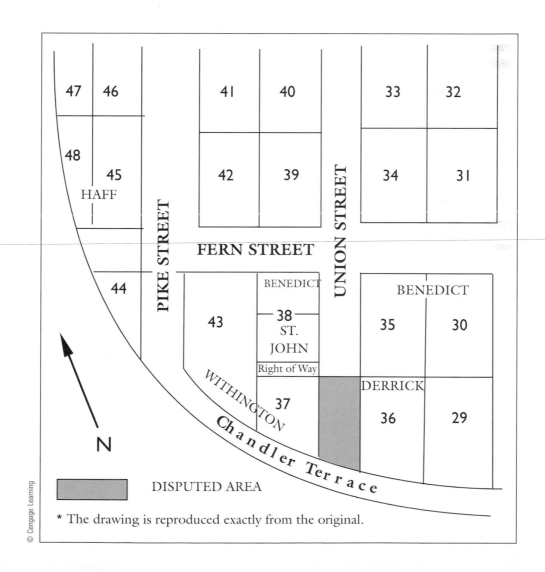

* The drawing is reproduced exactly from the original.

its [number] is a description in its legal effect according to the lines of such lot as surveyed and established in the original division of town, and is just as definite, although not so particular, as it would be if the lines were given, and should receive the same construction and have the same legal effect, in one case as the other, and such description in this case must be the controlling description, and determine the extent of the land conveyed.

In the instant case, the descriptions referring to the land of adjoining property owners are particular descriptions. Further, "[w]here an ambiguity or error exists with regard to the description in a deed, an attached map or survey relating to the ambiguity or error will control."

When there is a conflict between a specific description by metes and bounds and a lot as shown upon a map by which a tract of land is conveyed, the latter provision will control. When a deed the lot intended to be conveyed is properly designated by its number on a recorded plot, but the deed, in attempting to give a more particular description, incorrectly or inaccurately sets forth the dimensions of the same, such designation by lot number will prevail over such other description in the deed.

In the instant case, defendants' deed unambiguously describes their property as "[b]eing Lot 36 as delineated on Hazen's survey and Plan of Lots in the Village of Wilder," and plaintiffs' deed unambiguously describes the disputed property line as continuing "southerly along the westerly boundary of Lot #36." In contrast, the more detailed description of the disputed boundary line in defendants' deed is incorrect and ambiguous. Consequently, the unambiguous description by lot number should prevail over the erroneous reference to an adjoining property owner. The trial court's theory, created in an attempt to reconcile the ambiguities and inaccuracies in the deeds' description, is not supported by any evidence in the record and cannot supplant the plain meaning of the lot descriptions in the deeds.

Reversed and remanded.

CASE QUESTIONS

1. What deed language created the confusion about ownership?
2. To whom does the trial court award title and why? What does the appellate court do?
3. In reviewing the deeds and the ambiguities, what rules does the appellate court follow?
4. What is the significance of the map?
5. What is the significance of "Haff" versus "Hoff"?

CAUTIONS AND CONCLUSIONS

In preparing or proofreading a land description, too much caution is never an issue. A sale of land may have been negotiated to the final detail, but if the deed description is inaccurate, litigation, liability, and other difficulties will result. The following questions should help avoid the difficulties of mistakes, inadequacies, or inaccuracies:

1. Is a legal description used? Is there more than a street address or common description?
2. If a metes and bounds description is used, is a better description available? If not, are permanent beginning points used?
3. If a government survey description is used, are all portions present? Is the prime meridian included?
4. If a plat map is used, is the location of the plat map in the land records accurately identified?
5. If two or more parcels are being conveyed, are they described separately? Are the descriptions distinct and run together?
6. Have two or more persons proofread the description?

The following excerpt from an article by Lewis Kanner lists the important factors to examine when a survey of property is done.

What You Should Know About Surveys

A private survey is more than a sketch of the boundaries of a parcel. A survey is apt to contain, in addition to the legal description of a parcel, information on the status of title to the parcel not disclosed by the usual title examination or title commitment and information on the ability to develop the property. A survey may disclose any of the following:

- Acreage content. The acreage content is important not only for purposes of determining the price of the property but is also important regarding information that must be furnished to many governmental agencies in any permitting process.
- Encroachments on the property. An examination may reveal that encroachments have

ripened into established claims to a portion of the property or may indicate potential litigation that may delay development.

- Encroachments on adjoining property. An investigation may indicate that these encroachments may be a cause for potential litigation with the adjoining property owner.

- Public and private easements not of record. These easements may represent potential matters for litigation or may interfere with the plan of development.

- Undedicated roads. A claim of access across the client's property may be evidenced by an undedicated road. This claim may represent potential litigation or interference in the plan of development.

- Legal access. The survey may indicate that the property in question does not have legal access. If the survey does not reflect a dedicated road adjoining the property, an examination may determine that the property does not have legal access. Your client may therefore have to sue to obtain legal access.

- Gaps between parcels believed to be contiguous. The gaps may prevent your client from developing the parcels as a single parcel.

- The location of utility easements. These easements may interfere with the plan of development and may require relocation to proceed with development.

- The high water line of any water boundary. The high water line may indicate limits of ownership regardless of the legal description.

- Variations in the legal description of the property. Variations must be reconciled with previously utilized descriptions and may represent potential litigation.

- Fences upon the property. Fences may be evidence of adverse claims or boundary lines by agreement or acquiescence contrary to the title information.

- Agricultural use which may be evidence of possession inconsistent with record ownership.

- Historical or archeological sites which, in some areas, may not be disturbed and therefore will interfere with any plan of development.

- Existence of wetlands that may indicate the property cannot be developed.

- Existence of filled lands which may not physically be able to support the planned improvements. Further, an investigation may indicate that the requisite governmental permits to fill the property were not obtained, representing a potential matter for litigation.

Reprinted from "What You Should Know About Surveys," by Lewis Kanner in *The Practical Real Estate Lawyer*, Vol. 5, Issue 5. Copyright 1989 the American Law Institute. Reproduced with the permission of American Law Institute/American Bar Association Continuing Professional Education.

KEY TERMS

baselines, 139
bounds, 135
grid, 139
guide meridians, 139
metes, 135

metes and bounds description, 135
parallels, 139
plat map, 138
prime meridians, 139
principal meridians, 139

range, 139
section, 139
township, 139
United States government
    survey, 139

CHAPTER PROBLEMS

1. Diagram each level of the following descriptions:

   a. SW 1/4 of the SW 1/4 of Section 27, T2N, R3E of the Gila Salt River Meridian.

   b. N 1/2 of the E 1/2 of the E 1/2 of the SW 1/4 of Section 12. How many acres of land does this describe?

   c. NE 1/4 of the NW 1/4 of Section 14, T3N, R4W, Gila Salt River Meridian.

2. Using metes and bounds, describe the property at the junction of Ash and Elm Streets as shown on page 150. What happens if a metes and bounds description is not closed?

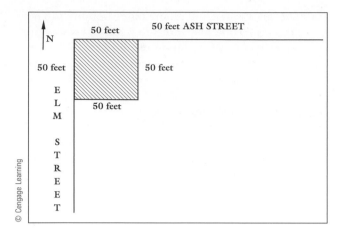

© Cengage Learning

3. Corner Cupboard Craft Shop acquired title to real property from James and Shirley Smith. The legal description in the deed contains a metes and bounds description that contains several distance calls followed by the phrase "more or less" and general directions such as "northwesterly." A plat map is attached to the deed with the metes and bounds description. Is the legal description sufficient to pass title? *Lawyers Title Insurance Corp. v. Nash*, 396 S.E.2d 284 (Ga. 1990).

4. Determine and discuss the legal sufficiency of each of the following descriptions. In the applicable instances, determine if there is a patent or a latent ambiguity.

   a. "The real estate owned by the sellers and located in the town of Oak Grove, now known as the 'Dobie Inn,' and used in the business of sellers."
   b. "My house at Little Chicago."
   c. A metes and bounds description beginning with, "to an iron pipe and a line sighted with a gate marker."
   d. "All my property in Monroe County, Indiana." See *Partnership Props. Co. v. Sun Oil Co.*, 552 So.2d 246 (Fla. App. 1989).
   e. "All my real estate wherever situated."
   f. "My farm, Willamena Estates."
   g. "Two acres in SE corner of SE 1/4 of SW 1/4 of Section 12."

5. The San Antonio Independent School District entered into a lease agreement with South Texas Sports, Inc., for the lease of Alamo Stadium and other tracts of land nearby. The validity of the lease was challenged by several homeowners' associations, including River Road. The homeowners were challenging the lease on administrative grounds, potential nuisance effect, and the insufficiency of the lease agreement itself. The description in the lease was as follows:

That certain tract of land located in Bexar County, Texas, together with all improvements located thereon, such land and improvements being more particularly described and shown on the plot plan attached hereto as Exhibit 'A'.

Exhibit A is a map on which eight tracts of land are marked. Alamo Stadium is not shown as one of the tracts being leased. Is the description along with Exhibit A sufficient for a valid lease? *River Road Association v. South Texas Sports River Road Association*, 720 S.W.2d 551 (Tex. 1986).

6. Joe Tanner, Commissioner of the Department of Natural Resources, brought suit against employees of the Department of Natural Resources (DNR), who were responsible for the management of Sapelo Island. Tanner brought suit because the employees prevented Tanner and others from landing their planes on two lots on Sapelo Island. The DNR employees claimed the state owned the lots (lot 7 and lot 4) and Tanner's claim to any interest or title in the lots was void. DNR claimed that the description in the deed to Tanner was insufficient to pass title. The legal description of lot 4 in the plaintiffs' deed is as follows:

All of that certain lot, tract or parcel of land situate, lying and being in the 1312 District, G.M., McIntosh County, Georgia, at Raccoon Bluff on Sapelo Island, containing Twenty-One (21) Acres, more or less and being Lot (4) Four of the Raccoon Bluff Subdivision of William Hillary. Said property being bounded Northerly by Lot 3, Easterly by Blackbeard Island River; Southerly by Lot 5; and Westerly by the out line [sic] of Raccoon Bluff Tract. This being that same property conveyed to Ben Brown by deed and plat from William Hillary dated July, 1882 and recorded in Deed Book 'U' at Page 298 and 299, to which said deed and plat reference is hereby made for all intents and purposes.

What type of description is this? Do you think it is sufficient to pass title to the property? *Brasher v. Tanner*, 353 S.E.2d 478 (Ga. 1987).

7. Diagram the following: Commencing at a point on the south side of Hale Street, 200 feet from the intersection of the south side of Hale Street and the east side of Gary Street; from thence south ten feet parallel to the easterly side of Gary Street; from thence east five feet parallel to the southerly side of Hale Street; from thence north ten feet parallel to the easterly side of Gary Street; from thence five feet west on the southerly side of Hale Street to the beginning point.

8. Explain why a street address is not a sufficient legal description.

9. On May 20, 2004, TR-One, Inc. and Lazz Development Co., Inc. entered into an agreement giving Lazz the exclusive right and option to buy property described as *"approximately 48 acres of vacant land located at 89 Mount Tom Road, Pawling, New York."* The agreement explained that "[t]he exact size and location of the parcel subject to this option is located primarily in the Village of Pawling and is to be defined and determined by a Survey map to be obtained by Optionee [Lazz] at its expense and which description will be agreed upon by the parties and then added as an exhibit to the contract of sale." The purchase price was $1,600,000 with the ultimate price dependent on the future development of the property. TR-One refused to convey the property because it maintained the description was insufficient. Is the description sufficient for a contract? for a deed? Explain. *TR-One, Inc. v. Lazz Development Co., Inc.,* 945 N.Y.S. 2d 416 (N.Y.A.D. 2012).

10. A deed contains the following description:

Together with an easement for access purposes from State Highway 17 southerly over the existing driveway located on the back lot partitioned and conveyed to Marie Rotter and said easement to extend easterly over the N. 20 feet of the frontage lot partitioned and conveyed to Marie Rotter to the front lot above described of grantee.

Is the description sufficient for legal purposes? *Kampinen v. Bierman,* 617 N.W.2d 908 (Wis. App. 2000).

For research activities related to this chapter, go to our text companion website at www.cengagebrain.com

CHAPTER 8

CO-OWNERSHIP OF REAL ESTATE

You will see him on TV any given Sunday
Win the Superbowl and drive off in a Hyundai
We want prenup! WE WANT PRENUP!

Kanye West, "Gold Digger" (Roc-A-Fella Records, LLC 2005).

Even rappers understand that co-ownership rights can be tricky. Married couples hold title together to their homes. Children inherit a parcel of land from a parent as equal co-owners. Unmarried cohabitants have issues of property ownership and child support, and those about to get married would like to avoid those issues in the event the marriage fails. **Co-ownership** of real estate is common and the issues complex, especially without an understanding of the basic rules and rights of such dual and multiple forms of ownership.

This chapter answers the following questions: How can title be held among several owners? What are the rights of each of the owners? What are the responsibilities of each of the owners? What action or actions may be taken in the event difficulties arise between or among the parties?

METHODS OF CO-OWNERSHIP

There are four methods of co-ownership: tenancies in common, joint tenancies, tenancies by the entirety, and tenancies in partnership. These forms of co-ownership are often intermingled with statutory protections afforded by marital property protections.

Tenancies in Common

When parties hold title to property as tenants in common, they hold separate interests in a single piece of property. The tenants in common may hold equal or unequal shares in the land. For example, two tenants may each hold a one-half interest in a tract of land, or one may hold a one-third and the other a two-thirds portion of the property. Tenants in common may acquire their interests at different times and may convey their interests to others. The conveyances can be made *inter vivos* (while the tenant in common is alive) or by will. For example, if X and Y hold title to a piece of property and X passes away, leaving, by will, his property to sons W and Z, then Y, W, and Z are all tenants in common.

Under a **tenancy in common**, each tenant is entitled to equal possession of the property. To the extent one cotenant has exclusive possession, the other cotenants are entitled to payment for their loss of use. For example, if cotenant A leased the property she owns with B and C to an architectural firm and kept the rent, B and C would be entitled to recover their share of the rental proceeds from A.

In the majority of states, the language necessary to create a tenancy in common is simply "To A and B." When this language is used, A and B will each have a 50 percent interest in the property. To create unequal interests, the amount of ownership must be specified. For example, "One-third of the above described property to my son B and two-thirds of the same to my daughter C" would be the language needed to create a tenancy in common with different shares or interests in the property. (For a discussion of the co-ownership of subsurface rights, see Chapter 3.)

Joint Tenancies

A **joint tenancy** is a form of co-ownership in which the parties hold equal shares and possess unique rights of ownership through survivorship. That is, when one joint tenant dies, title to the property remains with the surviving joint tenants. A joint tenancy interest cannot be given away by will because at the moment of death, title vests in the remaining joint tenants. If A, B, and C are joint tenants and C dies, A and B remain joint tenants and hold title to the property. C's heirs have no rights or interest in the property. If B then dies, A will hold full title to the property and B's heirs have no rights or interest in the property.

An interesting issue that arises in a joint tenancy is whether a joint tenant can make a valid *inter vivos* conveyance of his or her interest. Suppose, for example, that in the A–B–C joint tenancy, C conveys her interest to D. The result is that the unity of title is broken and the joint tenancy is partially severed. The result will be that D becomes a tenant in common with a one-third interest, and A and B remain joint tenants for the remaining two-thirds of the property. Figure 8.1 illustrates the impact of joint tenancy transfers.

The Language of a Joint Tenancy

There are several requirements for the creation of a valid joint tenancy interest. The first requirement is the use of clear language to create a joint tenancy. Some states require the use of the phrase "as joint tenants with right of survivorship." Other states may simply require the use of the term "joint tenants."

Other Requirements for Joint Tenancy Creation: The Unities

There are four other requirements for valid formation. They are referred to as the **unities** of a joint tenancy and they are time, title, interest, and possession.

PRACTICAL TIP

The way title is carried has significant implications for the listing, sale, and purchase of property. Title insurers will not issue policies for property transfers attempted without the consent of all joint tenants. The rights and identity of all co-owners should be determined prior to marketing, buying, or selling property. When a joint tenant passes away, recording the death certificate is necessary in order for title to pass to the surviving joint tenant(s).

FIGURE 8.1 The Severance of a Joint Tenancy

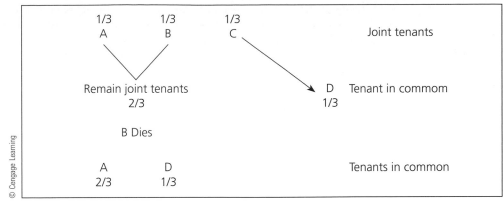

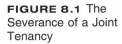

© Cengage Learning

Unity of Time Joint tenants must take their title to the property at the same time. For example, if O conveyed Blackacre to A and B on December 30, 2012, then A and B meet the unity of time requirement because they acquired their interest at the same time. However, if O conveyed half of Blackacre to A on December 30, 2012, and then conveyed the other half to B on June 30, 2013, then A and B are considered tenants in common, not joint tenants, because they acquired their interests at different times.

In some states, this unity of time requirement presents problems when one party owns property prior to marriage and then after marriage wants to make his or her spouse a joint tenant on that pre-owned property. For example, suppose Jane owns a home and upon marrying Bob wants to hold title to the property with Bob as a joint tenant. Jane has a unity of time problem with the creation of the joint tenancy. However, this unity problem can be overcome by setting up what is called a **strawman transaction**. Jane transfers the property to a third party (the strawman), who then transfers the property back to Jane and Bob. Jane and Bob satisfy the requirement of unity of time for joint tenancy through this procedural hoop that satisfies the unity of time. Some states have eliminated the requirement of unity of time in circumstances like Jane and Bob's and have passed statutes that allow couples to create a joint tenancy without a strawman.[1]

CONSIDER 8.1   Terrell Taylor was the owner in fee simple of a 666-acre ranch in Fremont County, Colorado. On March 4, 1991, Taylor executed a warranty deed that conveyed that property from Taylor as sole owner to Taylor and Lucy I. Canterbury as joint tenants.

In 1997, Taylor executed a second deed, this time a quitclaim deed purporting to transfer the property back to himself and Canterbury as tenants in common. The second deed stated, "It is my intention by this deed to sever the joint tenancy created by [the 1991 deed], and to create a tenancy in common." The deed was duly recorded on June 16, 1997—the same day it was executed. Taylor died on August 20, 1999.

Canterbury filed an action to quiet title to the property to herself as surviving joint tenant. In that complaint, she also asked the trial court to set aside the 1997 conveyance and award her damages arising out of Taylor's attempted conveyance. What happens? Who owns the property and how much is owned? *Taylor v. Canterbury,* 92 P.3d 961 (Colo. 2004).

---

[1]For an example of a statute that eliminates the strawman requirement, see *Mass. Gen. Laws Ann.* Ch. 184, §§7-8 (West 2009).

Unity of Title Parties are not joint tenants unless they derive their title from the same source or grantor. For example, if O conveys Blackacre to A and B, A and B can be joint tenants. However, if B then conveys his interest to C, A and C cannot be joint tenants since A derived her title from O and C derived his title from B. A and C are tenants in common.

Unity of Interest This unity requires that joint tenants have equal interests in the property, for example, A and B each holding a one-half interest qualify for joint tenancy. However, if A holds a one-third interest and B holds a two-thirds interest, then A and B can be only tenants in common.

Unity of Possession This requirement holds true for a valid tenancy in common as well. Under unity of possession, the parties must have equal rights to possess the property, and one party cannot dispossess the others of the land. If the land is divided either geographically or by time (into present and future interests; see Chapter 2), then the parties are no longer co-owners, and unity of possession is lost. For example, if O conveys Blackacre to A for life and then to B and C, B and C may be any type of tenants in the future, but they are not joint tenants with A because their interest in the property is divided.

The following case deals with the creation and severance of a joint tenancy when a mortgage is placed on the property.

COUNTRYWIDE HOME LOANS, INC. V. REED

725 S.E.2d 667 (N.C. App. 2012)
Mortgage-in-Law

FACTS

On March 25, 2001, Margaret D. Smith and Mrs. Smith's daughter and son-in-law, Judy and Troy Reed (Defendants), bought a home in Mooresville, North Carolina. Countrywide Home Loans, Inc., (Plaintiff) agreed to finance the purchase of the home and provided a loan of $117,900 to Mrs. Smith. The general warranty deed named the grantees as "Margaret D. Smith and Troy D. Reed and wife, Judy C. Reed Joint Tenants with rights of survivorship[.]" The deed of trust to secure Countrywide's loan and promissory note was prepared in Mrs. Smith's name only and was executed by Mrs. Reed, as attorney in fact for Mrs. Smith, on May 1, 2001. Neither Mr. Reed nor Mrs. Reed signed the deed of trust or promissory note.

The Reeds lived with and cared for Mrs. Smith, such that Mrs. Smith was not required to go to a nursing home. However, by October 2001, the mortgage loan was in default and Countrywide commenced foreclosure proceedings.

On 7 February 2004, Mrs. Smith passed away. After Mrs. Smith's death, the Reeds began corresponding with Countrywide regarding a modification of the loan, such that the loan would be in the Reeds' name. Countrywide drafted a loan modification agreement on June 25, 2004 and sent the agreement to the Reeds. The agreement purportedly "amend[ed] and supplement[ed] (1) the Mortgage, Deed of Trust, or Deed to Secure Debt (the 'Security Instrument')." The Reeds signed the agreement on July 6, 2004.

The Reeds made payments to Countrywide for a short period of time, until approximately August or September 2004. On November 16, 2004, Countrywide notified the Reeds that the loan was in default for nonpayment, but offered the Reeds a chance to cure the default by paying or seeking a loan modification.

In 2006, the Reeds requested that they be considered for a further loan modification. However, this modification was denied because Mr. Reed failed to provide proof of income as required.

On January 23 2009, Countrywide filed a complaint seeking reformation of the deed of trust to reflect the intent of the parties by making the Reeds obligated on the note. The Reeds filed a motion for summary judgment on both of Countrywide's claims. The trial court granted summary judgment for the Reeds.

JUDICIAL OPINION

Thigpen, Judge

The question presented in this appeal is a novel one. The general warranty deed filed on 2 May 2001 created a joint tenancy between Mrs. Smith and Defendants, with right of survivorship. However, the deed of trust, which was filed one minute after the general warranty deed, encumbered the property. Mrs. Smith was the sole obligor on the deed of trust. This Court must determine whether the deed of trust severed the joint tenancy, such that only the portion of the property owned by Mrs. Smith was encumbered, or whether the deed of trust did not sever the joint tenancy, but instead obligated Mrs. Smith and Defendants, thus encumbering the entire property.

N.C. Gen.Stat. § 41–2(a) (2011) permits the creation of a joint tenancy with right of survivorship "if the instrument creating the joint tenancy expressly provides for a right of survivorship." "Upon conveyance to a third party by less than all of three or more joint tenants holding property in joint tenancy with right of survivorship, a tenancy in common is created between the third party and the remaining joint tenant."

North Carolina is considered a title theory state with respect to mortgages, where a mortgagee does not receive a mere lien on mortgaged real property, but receives legal title to the land for security purposes. In North Carolina, deeds of trust are used in most mortgage transactions, whereby a borrower conveys land to a third-party trustee to hold for the mortgagee-lender, subject to the condition that the conveyance shall be void on payment of debt at maturity. Thus, in North Carolina, the trustee holds legal title to the land.

The doctrine of survivorship does not apply to tenancies in common, and upon the death of a person holding property as a tenant in common, the person's share descends to her heirs or is devised as her will provides. "Any joint tenancy interest held by a husband and wife, unless otherwise specified, shall be deemed to be held as a single tenancy by the entirety, which shall be treated as a single party when determining interests in the joint tenancy with right of survivorship."

In this case, because North Carolina is a title theory State, and thus a mortgage is a conveyance, Mrs. Smith severed the joint tenancy when she, as the sole obligor on the deed of trust, filed the deed of trust encumbering the property. After the joint tenancy was severed, Mrs. Smith's interest as a tenant in common was one-half of the property; Defendants' interest, as tenants by the entirety, was also one-half. This is because Defendants are husband and wife; as

such, they held the property "as a single tenancy by the entirety" and were "treated as a single party when determining interests in the joint tenancy with right of survivorship" upon severance of the joint tenancy.

Based on the foregoing, we hold the trial court was correct in concluding that "Troy D. Reed and Judy C. Reed, as Tenants by Entireties, own a one-half undivided interest in the subject real property which is not encumbered by the deed of trust to the benefit of Plaintiff[.]" In other words, the deed of trust executed by Mrs. Smith only encumbered Mrs. Smith's interest in the property—the portion of the property owned by Mrs. Smith as a tenant in common after the severance of the joint tenancy by the filing of the deed of trust. However, we further hold the trial court was incorrect in concluding that "[u]pon the death of Margaret Smith her interest, subject to the deed of trust to the benefit of Plaintiff, vested in Troy D. Reed and wife Judy C. Reed pursuant to the Right of Survivorship as set forth in the deed." The joint tenancy was severed upon the filing of the deed of trust, and Mrs. Smith's interest in the property converted to a tenancy in common, which has no right of survivorship. Lastly, because Mrs. Smith's interest in the property did not vest pursuant to the right of survivorship, we hold the trial court was also incorrect in concluding that "Troy D. Reed and wife Judy Reed own the real property in fee simple absolute[.]"

In summary, Plaintiff is entitled to a judgment as a matter of law on the issue of whether the deed of trust in this case encumbered Mrs. Smith's one-half interest in the property as a tenant in common. We further conclude that the trial court erred by concluding that Mrs. Smith's interest in the property "vested in Troy D. Reed and wife Judy C. Reed pursuant to the Right of Survivorship" and Defendants "own the real property in fee simple absolute[,] subject to Plaintiff's deed of trust." The joint tenancy was severed upon the filing of the deed of trust, and Mrs. Smith's interest in the property converted to a tenancy in common, which has no right of survivorship.

Affirmed, in part, reversed, in part, and dismissed, in part.

CASE QUESTIONS

1. Give a description of the series of events that led to the interrelationships among the parties.
2. What was the effect of Mrs. Smith creating the deed of trust with Countrywide?
3. Explain what the court's decision means for the Reeds and the house, i.e., title, debt, etc.

CONSIDER 8.2   Martha Gallotta owned two parcels of real property with her cousin, Louise Lauriello. One parcel is located on Sackett Street in Brooklyn and the other is located in the Town of Blooming Grove in Orange County. Martha and Louise originally held title to the Brooklyn property as joint tenants. Prior to Louise's death, the form of ownership was changed to a tenancy in common. When Louise died, her will devised her one-half interest in the Brooklyn property to Christopher M. Lauriello and Louis J. Lauriello, who are Louise's heirs, contend that they each now own an undivided 25 percent interest in the Brooklyn property. Who owns what and how much? *Lauriello v. Gallotta,* 873 N.Y.S.2d 690 (2009). ───■

Tenancies by Entirety and Other Survival Marital Property Interests

A **tenancy by entirety** requires the presence of the same four unities as for a joint tenancy plus one additional unity: unity of person. Unity of person requires that the tenants be married.

Tenancy by entirety also carries with it the right of survivorship; spouses are not permitted to dispose of the property by will. Severance of this tenancy requires the signature of the non-severing spouse, and the property itself may be subject to dower and curtesy rights (discussed later in the chapter). Divorce (or dissolution of the marriage) severs the tenancy by entirety. In some states, divorce or dissolution converts the title to joint tenancy; in others, to tenancy in common.

Community property states (see p. 164) follow a set of laws on marital property rights that give spouses a right of survivorship by statute in all assets determined to be marital assets. The spouses have all the survivorship rights of community property but also get the benefits of joint tenancy's ease of transfer upon death of one of the spouses.[2] The use of joint tenancy with right of survivorship in community property estates often caused questions about the underlying character of the property—is it separate or marital property? A newer form of title, **community property with right of survivorship**, allows married couples to hold title unequivocally: The asset is a marital asset and they have rights of survivorship in that asset.

The tax basis for property held as community property with right of survivorship can be stepped up to fair market value at the time one spouse dies, and such a step-up can help minimize estate taxes (see Chapter 17).

Tenancy in Partnership

A **tenancy in partnership** exists either when partners have contributed property to the partnership or when the partnership has purchased property with partnership funds. The partners hold title to such property as co-owners or as tenants in partnership. A tenancy in partnership has the characteristics of a joint tenancy. Upon the death of one of the partners, the remaining partners are entitled to the deceased partner's share. Heirs and devisees of the partner have no rights to the partnership property itself, but they may be entitled to payment for the value of the deceased partner's share or interest in the partnership.

---

[2]See, e.g., A.R.S. § 25–211.

Although laws vary from state to state, a tenancy in partnership has characteristics common to all of the tenancies. Each partner has the right to possession and use of the property for partnership purposes, and one partner cannot dispossess the other partners or the partnership of the property. In many states, transfer of partnership property requires the signature of all partners. Parties who engage in a land transaction with a partner should verify how title is held and whether the partner has authority to transfer the property. (More information on partnerships and limited partnerships can be found in Chapter 21.)

States that have community property as a basis for marital co-ownership (see p. 164 for more discussion) may also have a co-ownership form known as community property with right of survivorship. This form of ownership was created because married persons holding joint tenancies with right of survivorship were faced with questions of whether the property so held was really a marital or community interest.

CONSIDER 8.3   A, B, and C were partners in the operation of a grocery store. The partnership's major assets were the store and the land on which it was located. C has passed away, and the executor of C's estate now wants to sell the estate's one-third interest in the store and the land. A and B claim they now own the land. What is the result?

CREDITORS' RIGHTS AND CO-OWNERSHIP

Because there is more than one method of co-ownership, creditors' rights in property vary. The extent of the creditor's rights in terms of repossession and sale is limited according to the rights of the cotenant. In a tenancy in common, tenants may mortgage, lien, or pledge their share of the property; and in the event of one tenant's default on the underlying debt, the creditor could become a tenant in common or could sell the tenant's portion of the property to satisfy the debt. Tenants may pledge only that portion of the property that they own and a creditor cannot foreclose on the entire property when one of the tenants defaults.

Creditors who accept pledges of property from joint tenants must realize the limitation of their interests. Because the estate is subject to survivorship, it is possible that their security will be lost if their debtors predecease other joint tenants. If a joint tenant defaults on an underlying debt secured by joint tenancy property, the creditor takes possession and title by foreclosure (or other method) and thus becomes a tenant in common.

In a tenancy by the entirety, creditors have no rights in the property unless the underlying debt is a joint debt of the husband and wife. A creditor cannot validly enforce a pledge of the property made unilaterally by one of the spouses.

A creditor taking only a partial property pledge from a co-owner should be aware of problems in priority that may arise if later all tenants pledge their interests to another creditor. In those circumstances, it is possible that the first partial creditor will be second in priority to a later full-pledge creditor.

The following case deals with a creditor's rights on co-owned property.

GAYTON V. KOVANDA

857 N.E.2d 929 (Ill. App. 2006)
Monica the Survivor vs. Louis, Joseph's Creditor

FACTS

Monica and Joseph Gayton, husband and wife, held title to the property at 3524 Riverside Drive, Wilmette, Illinois, as joint tenants with rights of survivorship. On February 2, 2001, Joseph transferred his interest in the property via a quitclaim deed to his wife Monica.

Louis Kovanda was a creditor of Joseph Gayton and had a judgment of $414,000, plus court costs, entered in his favor against Joseph Gayton on November 20, 2003. Joseph Gayton died on November 26, 2003. Kovanda recorded the notice of judgment against the Wilmette property on December 3, 2003.

On March 15, 2004, Monica Gayton filed suit against Kovanda to quiet title to the property. Monica alleged that Kovanda had created a cloud on title by wrongfully recording the judgment as a lien against the property because she was the sole owner of the property and the judgment was against Joseph, who no longer had an interest in the property.

Kovanda filed a counterclaim alleging that Joseph's transfer of his interest in the property to Monica violated the Illinois Uniform Fraudulent Transfer Act.

Monica filed a motion for summary judgment on Kovanda's counterclaim, which the trial court granted. Kovanda appealed.

JUDICIAL OPINION

Karnezis, Justice

In her motion for summary judgment, Gayton argued that even if Joseph's transfer of his interest in the property was fraudulent, Kovanda still had no rights in the property because he did not perfect his judgment against the property prior to Joseph's death.

Assuming that Joseph's transfer of his interest in the property was fraudulent, we must address Kovanda's claim that when a joint tenant fraudulently conveys his or her interest in a property, the conveyance must be avoided and the property restored to a tenancy in common. Kovanda argues Joseph Gayton's voluntary transfer of his interest in the property amounted to an immediate severance of the unities

required to maintain a joint tenancy, thereby extinguishing any rights of survivorship. Therefore, any title that would vest in Joseph Gayton, for purposes of his creditors, would vest in Joseph as a tenant in common and after his death, that interest would be owned by his estate.

A joint tenancy is an estate that two or more individuals hold jointly with equal rights. With joint tenancy comes the right of survivorship, which entitles the last surviving joint tenant to take the entire estate. A joint tenancy can be severed when one tenant voluntarily or involuntarily destroys one of the four unities (interest, time, title, and possession) that are crucial to the creation and continuance of a joint tenancy.

[A]ssuming that Joseph's conveyance of his interest in the property to Monica was fraudulent, the court should treat the property as if the fraudulent transfer had not been made. Therefore, subsequent to Joseph's transfer of his interest to Monica and prior to Joseph's death, Joseph and Monica owned the property in joint tenancy. When Joseph died, the property passed to Monica as a joint tenant through rights of survivorship. It is of no consequence that Kovanda obtained the judgment prior to Joseph's death because a judgment only becomes a lien on the real estate of the person against whom it is entered from the time the judgment is filed with the recorder of deeds in the county in which the property is located. Kovanda did not file the judgment until December 3, 2003, after Joseph ceased to have any interest in the property due to his death. Accordingly, based on the foregoing, we find that the trial court did not err in granting summary judgment for Monica.

Affirmed.

CASE QUESTIONS

1. Give a list of the transactions, issues, and timeline for the case.
2. Did Joseph sever the joint tenancy when he transferred his interest via quitclaim deed to Monica?
3. What is the effect of the fraud in the transfer?
4. Who owns the property and is it subject to the creditor's lien?

ETHICAL ISSUE

Clara Sanders and James R. Newton had lived on farm property in Kentucky together as unmarried cohabitants for some time, with the property being owned by them as joint tenants with right of survivorship. During a party for Sanders's grandchild, Sanders became intoxicated and belligerent, and Newton attempted to restrain her. While doing so, Newton recklessly choked and held Sanders down, resulting in her death. Newton was criminally charged in her death and subsequently pled guilty to reckless homicide, a class D felony. Newton was sentenced to five years' imprisonment, which he has now served.

Sanders' estate filed suit against Newton for wrongful death as well as for the forfeiture of his interest in the farm he had owned with Sanders. A Kentucky statute prohibits someone who murders another from taking property because of the victim's death. The estate moved for the forfeiture because Newton killed Sanders and the statute treats him as if he predeceased Sanders so, under a joint tenancy, Sanders would have gotten all the property, with Sanders' heirs then getting the entire farm. Newton argued that half of the property was his anyway. What should the court do? Why does the court have to be careful about property rights as between murderer and victim? *Newton v. Newton*, 365 S.W.3d 565 (Ky. App. 2011).

Figure 8.2 compares the various kinds of tenancies—their creation, transfer, and creditor relations.

FIGURE 8.2 Comparison of Methods of Co-ownership

CHARACTERISTICS	METHODS OF CO-OWNERSHIP			
Unities	**Tenancy in Common**	**Joint Tenancy with Right of Survivorship**	**Tenancy by the Entireties**	**Tenancy in Partnership**
		1. Time	1. Time	
		2. Title	2. Title	
		3. Interest	3. Interest	3. Interest
	4. Possession	4. Possession	4. Possession	4. Possession
			5. Person (marriage)	5. Person (partners)
Transferability	*Inter vivos*	An *inter vivos* transfer severs tenancy (Severs tenancy)	*Inter vivos* by one spouse invalid One spouse cannot sell	One partner can sell *inter vivos*
	Testamentary transfer	Testamentary transfers are invalid	Surviving spouse takes title	Title goes to surviving partner
Creditors' Rights	Rights survive debtor	Limited to rights of survivorship	Must be debt of husband and wife	Only partnership debts
	Creditor can become tenant in common	Creditor can become tenant in common		

© Cengage Learning

RIGHTS AND RESPONSIBILITIES OF COTENANTS RENTS

In all tenancies, each tenant has the equal right of possession, and nonpossessing tenants are not permitted to collect rent from the tenant who is in possession of the property. However, the possessing tenant does not have the right to exclude the other tenants from the property (see discussion on partition and ouster below). If the tenant in possession is collecting rents and profits from third parties who are using the property, such receipts should be shared with the other tenants. The general rule is that the nonpossessing tenant is entitled to his or her share of the fair market rental value but must also honor the terms of the lease by the tenant in possession.

Expenditures

When cotenants do not pay equal amounts for the purchase of property, most courts have ruled that the shares in the property are not equal and have apportioned title according to the portion of the purchase price contributed.

Some payments are necessary to keep the land or its title clear, such as taxes and mortgage payments. Cotenants are required to share in these expenses according to their proportionate share of title in the property. The proportion of these payments may be offset, in some states, if one of the cotenants has been in exclusive possession.

Expenditures for improvements are made solely at the discretion of the improving cotenant; there is neither a right to require contribution from the other tenants nor a right to offset costs by reducing the portion of mortgages and taxes paid by the improving cotenant. Expenditures for repairs are treated in the same way.

CONSIDER 8.4   X and Y own equal shares of a one-acre parcel of land in the White Mountains of Arizona. Y has built a cabin on it at a cost of $162,000. Y has also managed to rent the cabin for 50 of the 52 weeks in 2012 at $1,000 per week. Mortgage payments on the cabin are $1,120 per month. Utilities vary from summer to winter but average about $190 per month. Taxes on the property are $180 per month with the cabin, but were $140 without it. Insurance is $970 per year. X has demanded an equal share of the profits. Y refuses but says X is responsible for half of the mortgage, utilities, taxes, and insurance. What is the result? Would the result be different depending upon what type of tenancy exists? _____■

Partition and Ouster

Partition is the physical division of co-owned property with the result being that co-owners become adjoining landowners or neighbors. Severance, on the other hand, merely changes the form of co-ownership (as when a joint tenancy is severed, as discussed earlier).

A partition can be made voluntarily when co-owners agree to a geographical division of the property, or it can be made by a court when circumstances require. The following circumstances require the partition of co-owned property: (1) when one tenant has dispossessed the other tenant or tenants and refuses to allow access (ouster), (2) when a tenant refuses to contribute for necessary expenditures, (3) when a tenant refuses to distribute rents and profits earned from exclusive possession (at common law), or (4) when other circumstances arise where the court deems a partition appropriate (such as feuding relatives).

If it is impossible or illogical to physically divide the property, a court may order the property sold and the proceeds divided among the cotenants according to their proportionate interests. For example, if a piece of property has water on only one portion, a division would be unfair but a sale would allow the parties to realize the value of their interests.

CONSIDER 8.5   In 1993, Dr. Nabil and Mrs. Maureen Bell Asterbadi acquired fee simple title to property located at Stone Harbor, Cape May County, New Jersey. The Asterbadis acquired title from the Sheriff of Cape May County, through a foreclosure sale, for $208,000. The sheriff's deed was issued by the Sheriff to grantees "Nabil J. Asterbadi and Maureen Bell Asterbadi, his wife."

The property is a single-family home located in a very desirable area near the Atlantic Ocean. The Asterbadis use the property during summer vacation for their family, and it currently has a value of several million dollars. In addition, the property could be rented and would have a significant income value, possibly $50,000 annually.

On October 4, 1993, a creditor obtained a judgment against Dr. Asterbadi (not Mrs. Asterbadi) in the amount of $2,286,009.97. On August 19, 2003, the judgment was docketed in New Jersey and on May 18, 2005, the Sheriff of Cape May County held a Sheriff's sale of Dr. Asterbadi's interest in the property, at which sale Capital Finance purchased Dr. Asterbadi's interest for $551,100. The Asterbadis have the following questions: Must Mrs. Asterbadi allow Capital to use the property? (Capital would like to lease the property as a time-sharing vacation spot.) What interest does Mrs. Asterbadi have in the property? What happens if Mrs. Asterbadi refuses to allow Capital to lease the property? Will a partition work? *Capital Finance Co. of Delaware Valley, Inc. v. Asterbadi,* 912 A.2d 191 (N.J. 2006).

MARITAL PROPERTY RIGHTS—CO-OWNERSHIP BY MARRIAGE

In every state, there are provisions to protect married persons holding title to property with their spouses. Tenancy by the entirety is one example, and other provisions and protections include dower and curtesy rights in some states and community property rights in other states.

The Common Law—Dower Rights

Under common law, **dower rights** existed for the protection of a widow. The common law rule was that a widow is entitled to a one-third interest for her life in any and all real property her husband owned at any time during their marriage.

Because of probable confusion and complications associated with dower rights, many states have changed dower rights to simply protect a surviving spouse by requiring that one-third to one-half of the deceased spouse's property of any character (real or personal) be given to the surviving spouse. Such statutes help prevent the problem of disinheritance by giving some property to the surviving spouse, but outright instead of in the form of a life estate interest. Some states have homestead exemptions that provide the surviving spouse with a minimum amount of property such as a residence, some personal property, a living allowance, and vehicles. This minimum amount is given to the surviving spouse before any distributions of property and before any creditors' obligations are satisfied.

The Common Law—Curtesy Rights

Curtesy is a surviving husband's protection that, at common law, gave the husband a life estate in all real property owned by his wife during their marriage. However, the **curtesy rights** existed only if there were issue born of the marriage. This right has been modified by the states today, and the above-discussed statutory protections now eliminate common law provisions on dower and curtesy but still protect surviving spouses.

Statutory Marital Law—Community Property

Community property is a system of ownership by spouses that has Spanish origins and exists, in some form, in 11 states, with many others adopting its 50–50 ownership principles. In states where community property is the basis for marital property rights, unless the parties agree and specify otherwise, property is held as community property.

The basic principle governing this system of co-ownership is that both partners in the marriage work for the benefit of the community and do so on an equal basis, and therefore own half of all property acquired during the course of the marriage. This half-ownership principle is true regardless of whether the spouses were employed or unemployed during the course of the marriage.

If community property law is applicable to a marriage relationship, then all property acquired during the course of the marriage is classified as community property and is half-owned by each spouse. However, the spouses may still have some separate property to which they hold complete title. For example, any property owned prior to marriage that is brought into the marriage is separate property. Also, gifts and inheritances received by individual spouses during the marriage are separate property. If, for example, a wife receives an inheritance from her father, the money would be her separate property and would not belong to the community.

Debts are also considered community obligations, and each spouse is responsible for 50 percent of the debts entered into for the benefit of the community.

Those dealing in real estate in community property states need the signature of both spouses for the listing, mortgaging, improvement, or sale of real property. Real estate partnerships operating in these states must obtain a waiver from the spouses of all partners, so that the property can be transferred without the risk of a spouse's interest being exercised at a later time. In noncommunity property states, the same process should be followed for dower and curtesy rights.

One of the benefits of the community property system is that both spouses acquire some property rights during the course of the marriage. In noncommunity property states, marriage for a lifetime does not guarantee a 50 percent share of the property acquired during the marriage. To equalize the states' laws on marital property, the **Uniform Marital Property Act** was drafted, but it has been adopted only in Wisconsin.[3] The purpose of the act is to bring community property principles to noncommunity property states.

---

[3]W.S.A §§ 766.001 to 766.97 (2009).

Extension of Property Rights to Relationships Beyond Marriage

Common Law Marriages

In some states, the basic principles of community property rights have been applied in cases where the parties were not married but lived as husband and wife. The doctrine of common law marriage has traditionally been applied in those relationships that are long-term and that carry the trappings of marriage, such as joint residence, children, and the sharing of property rights. However, common law marriages have imposed a higher standard of proof in terms of obtaining property rights, and perceived injustices can occur prior to the long-term establishment of a common law marriage.

Rights of Unmarried Cohabitants

As a result of the stricter statutory common-law marriage standards not being effective in preventing property rights injustices, courts in community and noncommunity property states have allowed unmarried cohabitants rights in each others' property that is acquired during their cohabitation. Often called an "economic partnership," the cohabitants have property rights when they contribute to living expenses or devote energies toward building the shared habitat and its accoutrements during the period of cohabitation. *Chen v. Hoeflinger*, 279 P.3d 11 (Haw. App. 2012). These property recoveries have been awarded on the basis of contract (express or implied) or quasi-contract agreements between the cohabitants. Often called palimony suits, cohabitants file suit seeking compensation for the time spent in the relationship.[4] However, not all states allow recovery of palimony and courts will not allow palimony or support payments in those cases in which one of the cohabitants is still married to a third party.[5] The following case deals with one court's position on palimony rights and the complexity of property agreements between unmarried cohabitants as well as the risks inherent in these relationships.

WILLIAMS V. ORMSBY

966 NE.2d 255 (Ohio 2012)
I Love You in Exchange for Your Property

FACTS

Amber Williams (appellee) and Frederick Ormsby (appellant) moved into Amber's house on Hardwood Hollow in Medina in May 2004. Amber had received title to the house through her divorce settlement. Frederick began making the mortgage payments in August and paid the 2004 property taxes. He eventually paid the remaining mortgage balance of approximately $310,000. In return, Amber gave Frederick title to the property by executing a quit-claim deed dated December 15, 2004, that was recorded the same day.

Although the couple had planned to marry, they canceled their plans in January 2005 when Frederick's divorce did not occur. They did, however, continue to live together. After a disagreement in March 2005, Amber left the house. As a result of this separation, Amber and Frederick signed a document, dated March 24, 2005, to immediately sell the Medina house and allocate the proceeds.

[4] *Devaney v. L'Esperance*, 949 A.2d 743 (N.J. 2008).
[5] *Combs v. Tibbitts*, 148 P.3d 430 (Colo. App. 2006).

Two months later, the couple tried to reconcile and attended couples counseling. Amber refused to move back into the house with Frederick unless he granted her an undivided one-half interest in the property. On June 2, 2005, they signed a second document, purportedly making themselves "equal partners" in the Medina house and, among other things, providing for property disposition in the event that their relationship ended. Amber then returned to the house, and the couple resumed their relationship. But by April 2007, they were living in separate areas of the house, and although they tried counseling again, Amber ended the relationship in September 2007. The two continued living in separate areas of the house until Frederick left in April 2008.

The next month, Amber and Frederick filed suit against each other. The trial court determined that the March 2005 agreement was supported by consideration but that the June 2005 agreement was not. The court granted judgment to Frederick on Amber's complaint and held that title to the property was vested in him exclusively. Amber appealed.

The Ninth District Court of Appeals reversed the trial court's judgment, concluding that under the facts of this case, "moving into a home with another and resuming a relationship can constitute consideration sufficient to support a contract." Frederick appealed.

JUDICIAL OPINION

Lanzinger, Justice

... [t]he issue is only whether the emotional aspect of resuming a relationship by moving in together can serve as consideration for a contract—separate and apart from the sharing of financial resources and obligations.

Amber argues that the June 2005 agreement is a valid novation of the March 2005 agreement. Because a novation is a new contract, it too must meet all the elements of a contract.

The trial court found that in March 2005, the parties executed a valid, written contract supported by mutual consideration. This agreement provided that the Hardwood Hollow house would be sold, with the first $324,000 of the proceeds to Frederick and the balance to Amber. Both Frederick and Amber specified their separate rights to reside at the subject property until it was sold. Under the March 2005 agreement, Amber assumed responsibility for the real estate taxes if the property was not sold in two

months. The two also were to equally share the costs necessary to operate and maintain the house as long as both were living there. This agreement also detailed who was responsible for certain bills and repairs to the residence.

By resuming the relationship [in June 2005], [Amber] agreed to undertake a way of life that entailed among other things 'providing companionship, and fulfilling each other's needs, financial, emotional, physical, and social, as best as [she was] able,' as well as foregoing other romantic possibilities." Nevertheless, the record does not show evidence of this statement. The June 2005 document states that Amber has "inhabited" the house since 1997. It states that she and Frederick plan to be married and reside there. Apart from stating that Frederick will pay all the expenses for the property, the document makes no mention of fulfilling each other's needs—financial, emotional, physical, social, or otherwise.

Although the June document states that the agreement was made "for valuable consideration," it does not specify what the consideration is. The document does not refer to "fulfilling each other's needs, financial, emotional, physical, and social." The court of appeals supplied those terms on its own. And unlike the March 2005 agreement, which contains mutual obligations and benefits (i.e., both parties had a right to reside at the property and, equally shared costs necessary to maintain the house, with Amber being responsible for real estate taxes starting the second half of 2004), the June 2005 document requires Frederick to pay all expenses, taxes, and insurance costs.

Nonetheless, the court of appeals relied on Amber's reply to a question of whether she had paid Frederick or given him anything of value in exchange for the June 2005 agreement. She stated, "I didn't pay him anything, no. I thought what was of value was the fact that we were sharing all sorts of things. He had my love. He had—I shared my assets with him, too. We were living together as a couple." But this vague statement falls short of establishing that she shared her assets as consideration for the June 2005 agreement and appears to refer to how she had previously shared her assets before entering into the June agreement.

Rather, the evidence demonstrates that the only consideration offered by Amber for the June 2005 agreement was her resumption of a romantic relationship with Frederick. There is no detriment to Amber in the June 2005 document, only benefit. Essentially, this agreement amounts to a gratuitous promise by Frederick to give Amber an interest in property based solely on the consideration of her love and affection. Therefore, the June 2005 document is not an enforceable contract, because it fails for want of consideration.

Because there is no consideration for the June agreement, it cannot extinguish the existing obligations established under the March agreement. Therefore, the June document was not an enforceable novation of the March 2005 agreement.

We hold that merely moving into a home with another while engaging in a romantic relationship is not consideration for the formation of a contract. To

hold otherwise would open the door to palimony claims and invite a number of evidentiary problems.

Judgment reversed.

CASE QUESTIONS

1. What was the difference between the March 2005 agreement and the June 2005 agreement?
2. Describe what the court would have considered to be consideration for the June 2005 agreement.
3. Who gets the house?
4. The dissent in the case indicates its belief that Amber deeded the property to Frederick in an attempt to evade her creditors. Do property rights between unmarried cohabitants create a risk for creditors?

PRACTICAL TIP

Marital and quasi-marital property rights are complex and carry significant impact in terms of real property interests and titles. The status of couples should be verified for both buyers and sellers prior to listing, selling, or buying property. Individuals should have their rights, obligations, and nuptial agreements reviewed by an attorney. The validity of such agreements should be verified according to individual state law.

Domestic Partnerships

Courts are now dealing with the hybrid statutory creation of domestic partnerships. Courts must now hear petitions for dissolution of domestic partnerships, both registered and unregistered, and determine property rights of the domestic partners. Some states have recognized that both gay and straight couples are eligible for property rights under the doctrine of meretricious relationships, whereas other states have held that such doctrines are limited to relationships that appear to be marriages (in those states that do not recognize same-sex marriages). See *Velez v. Smith*, 142 Cal.App.4th 1154, 48 Cal.Rptr.3d 642 (2006) and *In re Domestic Partnership of Ellis*, 76 Cal.Rptr.3d 401 (Cal. App. 4 Dist.). The best protection for property rights is for couples to register under the state's domestic partnership or civil union laws. Those laws afford property rights and protections for domestic partners just as dower and curtesy provided marital property rights automatically at common law.[6]

The following case deals with the difficulties of property rights when the parties are not married.

---

[6]Connecticut, Iowa, Massachusetts, New Hampshire, New York, and Vermont permit gay marriages. California recognized gay marriages for a short period (June 16–November 4, 2008), but Proposition 8 revoked the judicial ruling that allowed the marriages. However, another judicial decision has invalidated the Proposition and the case is headed to the U.S. Supreme Court. Some states recognize gay marriages performed in other jurisdictions, but do not permit them. There are ballot initiatives pending in several states for permitting gay marriages. The Defense of Marriage Act (DOMA), which mandates marriage as being defined as a union between a man and a woman, is a federal law that prohibits the federal government from recognizing same-sex marriages and permits states to refuse to recognize gay marriages. State laws are a patchwork of confusion and are becoming increasingly complex and diverse on domestic partnerships, same-sex partnerships, and same-sex marriages. J. Thomas Oldham, "Lessons from *Jerry Hall v. Mick Jagger*, Regarding U.S. Regulation of Heterosexual Cohabitants or, Can't Get No Satisfaction," 76 *Notre Dame L. Rev.* 1409 (2001). For more detail, see Nan D. Hunter, "Introduction: The Future Impact of Same-Sex Marriage: More Questions Than Answers," 100 *Georgetown Law Rev.* 1855 (2012).

IN RE DOMESTIC PARTNERSHIP OF BRANAM AND BEAVER

202 P.3d 886 (Or. App. 2009)
Captain Beaver Loses His Ship and Just About Everything Else

FACTS

Randy Beaver and Jan Branam moved to Oregon from California in 1996 after the death of Branam's husband, Jim. Beaver had been the captain of a fishing boat owned by Jim, and Branam and Beaver began seeing each other socially after Jim's death.

A captain's license is not necessary for a person to operate commercial fishing vessels, but it is necessary in order to carry members of the public on a vessel. Beaver earned approximately $35,000 per year as a fishing-boat captain. If he gave up his captain's license and later sought to have it reinstated, he would have to start over and fulfill all of the requirements anew.

When Branam and Beaver discussed moving to Oregon and away from Beaver's work as a boat captain in California, Beaver sought assurances from Branam that he would not be "out on the street in a month, in a year, 10 years, 20 years[.]" Beaver also testified, "If I was going to give all that up and move up here I wanted to make sure that I was going to basically have something." He added that "I told her I didn't want to move up here unless I got ... my name on the house to make sure that I at least had a place to live."Branam told Beaver that she had "enough money invested that we'd never have to work again."

Branam inherited some $500,000 from her husband's estate. She used $170,000 of those funds to purchase a home in Oregon, and she put Beaver's and her names on the title to the home. The deed that conveyed the property conveyed it to Branam and Beaver, "not as tenants in common, but with the right of survivorship[.]" Branam testified, "I purchased the house, and his name was on it. I thought we would jointly take care of the house, and then if something happened to me, he'd have at least a place to live." Branam testified that she did not intend to give Branam the money she used to purchase the house. Beaver believed "that if my name was on ... the house, half the house belonged to me." Beaver moved to Oregon with Branam in 1996 and gave up his captain's license. After they moved to Oregon, neither party worked for several years, and Branam gave Beaver a monthly allowance. Branam paid the insurance and taxes for the home and all of the parties' bills. For the first few years, Branam did not ask Beaver to contribute financially to their joint expenses or pay rent. During the parties' cohabitation, Beaver contributed to the household by performing work on the house, including building a fence, building a deck, and gardening. The parties separated in October 2004, and Branam filed a petition for dissolution of domestic partnership. After the parties separated, they had a tenant on the property, and Branam and Beaver each received one-half of the rent from the property.

Before trial, the parties sold the home, netting approximately $262,000 after sale costs. After trial, the court divided the remaining assets so that Beaver and Branam equally shared the appreciated value of the home, but Branam received credit for the payments that she had made to maintain the property after the parties' separation and the purchase price that she had paid for the home. Thus, Branam received $177,801.87 plus 97.6 percent of the interest earned on the proceeds held pending trial, and Beaver received $4,429.60 plus 2.4 percent of the interest. The court concluded that "the mutual intent of the parties ... when the real estate was acquired, was to provide shelter and support for Mr. Beaver while the couple co-habitated [*sic*], but not a portion of Ms. Branam's estate." Alternatively, the court concluded that, even if the intent of the parties was unclear, it was equitable to award Branam the purchase price that she had paid for the home and to divide the appreciated value of the home equally between the parties. Beaver appealed.

JUDICIAL OPINION
Armstrong, P.J.

In the dissolution of a domestic partnership, courts are required to divide property according to the express or implied intent of the parties at the time that they established their partnership. If the court cannot discern the parties' intent, the court may exercise its equitable powers to reach a fair dissolution of the parties' partnership. How the parties held legal title to real property is evidence of the parties' intent, but it is not dispositive.

Here, before purchasing the home, the parties did not discuss what would happen to it if they decided to separate. Both parties agree that Beaver wanted his name on the title to the home before moving to Oregon and leaving his position as a boat captain. That testimony is consistent with the deed to the property, which grants a survivorship right to the parties, and thereby would enable Beaver to remain in the home if Branam died. However, Branam and Beaver did not discuss what would happen to the property if they separated.

Where there is no express agreement of the parties regarding the division of their property in the event of dissolution of their domestic partnership, "courts should closely examine the facts in evidence to determine what the parties implicitly agreed upon."

Joint acts of a financial nature can give rise to an inference that the parties intended to share equally. Such acts might include a joint checking account, a joint savings account, or joint purchases.

Here, the parties took title to the home "not as tenants in common, but with right of survivorship." That language gave the parties concurrent life estates with a contingent remainder to the survivor. Branam and Beaver lived together in the home for nine years. Branam paid all of the household expenses during the parties' cohabitation, such as taxes, insurance, and utilities. Branam also gave Beaver a monthly allowance. Beaver contributed to the upkeep and improvement of the home by performing work on it, such as building a fence, building a deck, and gardening. There is no evidence that the parties maintained joint bank accounts. However, Beaver's testimony that he would not move to Oregon unless his name was on the title, and the fact that Branam put his name on the title when she purchased the home, confirms that the parties intended to share the property equally. The trial court correctly determined that the parties intended to share the property equally.

However, that does not end our inquiry, because we must determine whether Branam should receive credit for the purchase price for the home…. [w]here the parties in a domestic partnership intend to share property equally, the party providing a greater initial contribution to the property will receive credit for that contribution.

Here, Branam and Beaver did not hold themselves out as husband and wife, and accordingly, the presumption of a marital gift does not arise. Furthermore, when asked if she had intended to give Beaver the money that she had used to purchase the home, Branam answered, "No." Because there was no evidence that Branam had intended to make a gift of the purchase price to Beaver, the trial court concluded that "the mutual intent of the parties * * * when the real estate was acquired, was to provide shelter and support for Mr. Beaver while the couple cohabitated, but not a portion of Ms. Branam's estate." We agree.

Branam did not intend to share with Beaver her initial contribution to the purchase of the parties' home. Accordingly, the trial court did not err and properly gave Branam credit for her payment of the purchase price of the home.

Affirmed.

CASE QUESTIONS

1. Is there some inconsistency in a JT/ROS and a finding that the cohabitants did not intend to share property?
2. Does the amount of time in the relationship and reliance play any role in determining property rights?
3. What lessons should cohabitants take away from this decision?

CONSIDER 8.6   Mick Jagger and Jerry Hall lived together for nearly two decades. They had four children together. At the time the couple decided to no longer reside together, Ms. Hall filed for divorce in Britain, citing their wedding ceremony in Bali as proof of their marriage. However, the court found that there was no marriage license and no compliance with Bali law for recognition of marriage there. Does Ms. Hall have any property rights? ____ ■

CONSIDER 8.7   In 1981, William Hurt and Sandra Jennings began living together in New York City. Mr. Hurt was a movie actor, and Ms. Jennings was an accomplished member of a ballet company. In 1982, Ms. Jennings accompanied Mr. Hurt to South Carolina, where he was filming a movie. They lived together as husband and wife during the filming of the movie. Mr. Hurt was still married to another woman at that time, with the divorce becoming final in December 1982.

The relationship was volatile, but Mr. Hurt stated that "as far as he was concerned, we were married in the eyes of God" and "more married than married people." Ms. Jennings gave birth to a child later verified to be Mr. Hurt's. She then filed suit in 1988 seeking to establish her rights in Mr. Hurt's property and earnings. She claimed that Mr. Hurt had promised to support her if she would have his child and give up her career.

Should the court support an award of property and support for Ms. Jennings? *Jennings v. Hurt*, 554 N.Y.S.2d 220 (1990).   ■

Prenuptial, Premarital, or Antenuptial Agreements

In recent years, and particularly with second marriages, many couples have entered into agreements minimizing or waiving their marital property rights. These agreements, called **premarital, prenuptial**, or **antenuptial agreements**, are subject to strict review by courts to determine if they are fair and were entered into voluntarily. Presently, 27 states have adopted the **Uniform Premarital Agreement Act**, or the UPAA, which was passed by the National Conference of Commissioners on Uniform State Laws (NCCUSL) in 1983. The UPAA recognizes these types of marital agreements, and most states that have not adopted the UPAA have passed some form of legislation that recognizes them.[7]

CONSIDER 8.8   Christopher Dargan (husband) had suffered an off-and-on addiction to cocaine for many years. He had several unsuccessful attempts to free himself from his addiction and after several years of marriage, Monica Mehren (his wife) separated after another episode resulting from Christopher's cocaine use. Months later, the parties agreed that Mr. Dargan would return to the family home. Mr. Dargan signed a postmarital agreement promising to grant to Monica Mehren all of his interest in certain of their community property should he use illicit drugs. Subsequently, the parties entered into an "Agreement re Transfer of Property." The agreement recited that Monica "consented to the resumption of marital relations on the condition that [husband] abstain from the deliberate, intentional use or ingestion of any mind altering chemical or substance excluding such use that may be prescribed or approved by a medical doctor. In the event of such deliberate, intentional use or ingestion of mind altering chemicals or substances by [husband], [husband] agrees that he will forfeit all of his right, title and interest in [described property]." They signed the agreement before a notary public.

Unfortunately, Mr. Dargan did not keep his promise. Thereafter, Ms. Mehren filed for divorce, asking that the property described in the agreement be awarded to her as her separate property. Mr. Dargan challenged the postmarital agreement as against public policy and void. Should the court enforce the agreement? *In re Marriage of Mehren & Dargan*, 118 Cal.App.4th 1167, 13 Cal.Rptr.3d 522 (2004).[8]   ■

---

[7]The adopting states are Arizona, Arkansas, California, Colorado, Connecticut, Delaware, District of Columbia, Hawaii, Idaho, Illinois, Indiana, Iowa, Kansas, Maine, Minnesota, Montana, Nebraska, Nevada, New Jersey, New Mexico, North Carolina, North Dakota, Oregon, Rhode Island, South Dakota, Texas, Utah, and Virginia.

[8]There are some states that recognize so-called "covenant marriages." If the parties elect to have a covenant marriage, the statutes creating such marriages "bar divorce except under extreme circumstances like adultery, abandonment, or for 'cruel and barbarous treatment.'" Covenant marriage laws also require couples to participate in premarital and pre-divorce counseling, and "for cases that would correspond to current no-fault divorces, they extend the waiting time to up to two and a half years." *Covenant Marriage Act of 2001*, § 4 (2001 Ark. Acts at 1486). Kristina E. Zurcher, "'I Do or 'I Don't?' Covenant Marriage After Six Years," 18 *Notre Dame J.L. Ethics & Pub. Pol'y* 273 (2004).

HOW TO MAKE YOUR PRENUP WORK

1. Talk about it WAY before the wedding.
2. Make sure each party has a COMPLETE copy of the agreement.
3. Disclose all of your assets BEFORE signing the agreement. Don't ever withhold information about your assets or the extent of your assets.
4. Don't put any time pressure on your spouse-to-be for signing the agreement.
5. Make sure your spouse-to-be has independent legal counsel or signs a waiver.
6. Don't keep changing the prenup before the signature, and if there are changes, follow all the steps above.
7. Put the reasons for the prenup in the agreement, such as your spouse-to-be has his own assets and is able to support himself.
8. Make sure all property is covered in the agreement.
9. Be extra careful with any property you hold jointly prior to the execution of the prenup agreement. Having separate property always makes things easier for a valid prenup.
10. Don't be stingy. Look at your state's marital property rights and provide for your spouse-to-be accordingly. The key is to have the court look at the agreement and conclude that it is fair.
11. Base the prenup provisions on the length of the marriage. Jack Welch's prenup held up in court because he increased the amount his wife would get with each year the marriage lasted.
12. Be careful with clauses related to adultery and personal conduct; they complicate the issues. Focus on the division of the property, not the conduct of the spouses during the marriage.
13. Execute the prenup agreement LONG before your wedding day and the ceremony. Time pressure is always a prenup killer even when the agreement has been in the works for some time prior to the wedding day.
14. Coordinate your will with your prenup. Make sure that your estate plan is in order and that it is consistent with the prenup.
15. Let your families know about the prenup and its provisions. The knowledge of those close to each of you is evidence that it was voluntary and done for valid reasons, such as a second marriage where the spouse's respective children will receive the property.

The area of prenuptial or antenuptial agreements has been clarified by courts and legislation over the past decade. The above box provides a good summary of the areas of concern in these agreements. See also Web Exhibit 8.1 for a sample prenuptial agreement.

The states continue to clarify the requirements for the validity of prenuptial agreements. For example, as a result of a case involving an internationally known sports figure, *In re Marriage of Bonds*, 5 P.3d 815 (Cal. 2000), California clarified its requirements for valid prenuptial agreements by statutes. In that case, Barry Bonds's wife signed a prenuptial agreement in his attorney's offices one day before their wedding, and English was not her native language. While the court upheld the prenuptial agreement, the legislature subsequently passed a statute that requires the parties to a prenuptial agreement to either have their own legal counsel or sign a document that reflects their voluntary waiver of the right to counsel prior to their signing the prenuptial agreement. When prenuptial agreements are done correctly, they can expedite a divorce. For example, actors Tom Cruise and Katie Holmes had an airtight prenuptial agreement that allowed their divorce to be finalized within a few months because there were no disputes over property or funds.

CONSIDER 8.9   Patricia met Joel F. Tamraz in December 1987. At that time, Joel was in the process of purchasing a condominium in Malibu, California, for $220,000. Although Joel initially took title to the property in his name only, before escrow closed he signed a quitclaim deed in which he granted one-third of his separate property interest in the Malibu condominium to Patricia, as her separate property, with title to be held as tenants in common.

Patricia and Joel became engaged in February 1988, and the following month, Patricia moved into the condominium. The parties lived together until September 1996. Thereafter, Patricia lived in Northern California, where she worked for The Gap, Inc. Joel continued to live in the condominium and to maintain his law practice in Los Angeles.

On February 9, 1998, Joel made reservations for the parties to be married on February 14, 1998, in Las Vegas.

On the day before the wedding, Joel faxed an "Antenuptial Agreement," which he had drafted, from his office in Los Angeles to Patricia's place of employment in San Francisco. She was not aware that the facsimile was coming and did not find it in her "in box" until after 4:00 p.m. She contacted Joel and told him that pages appeared to be missing, that she did not understand the terminology. Joel then faxed more pages, including duplicates, that did not appear to be a complete set.

The agreement, dated February 13, 1998, provided that, in the event of divorce, Patricia would receive $20,000 as her full share of the condominium and that she would be required to deed her one-third interest to Joel. The agreement was ten pages long and contained spaces at the bottom of each page for the parties' initials. Joel initialed each page, signed the agreement, and also signed the "Attorney's Certification for Prospective Husband," indicating that he was representing himself. Patricia did not see the version of the agreement signed by Joel until after their marriage. The copy of the agreement initialed and signed by Patricia, and faxed back to Joel, is missing the second page of the agreement, which contained, among other provisions, an express waiver by the parties of the right to any disclosure of the other's property and financial obligations. One page of the agreement signed by Patricia appears to have been cut off by the fax machine and another page is almost completely blank. Patricia signed the "Attorney's Certification for Prospective Wife," adding the handwritten notation, "I understand this agreement."

Prior to receiving the agreement, Patricia had at most two conversations about a premarital agreement. Patricia testified that she relied on Joel's representations and did not read or understand most of the agreement and signed it because she "really loved" Joel and "believed in him" and "believed everything he said." Joel never advised Patricia to seek her own legal advice in regard to the agreement, and she did not do so.

Patricia felt a certain amount of pressure to sign the agreement because she was not convinced that Joel would marry her without the agreement and because everyone at her work knew that she was getting married. She was in "a terrible hurry" when she received the agreement because she had to leave work "within minutes" in order to pick up her luggage in Sausalito and then catch a flight to Las Vegas so that she and Joel could marry the next day. Once in Las Vegas, Joel did not mention the agreement.

Joel, who has practiced law in the state of California since 1967, had drafted other prenuptial agreements for clients and litigated such agreements. He had also previously successfully represented Patricia in helping her to obtain a larger award in her prior divorce.

Joel filed a petition for dissolution of marriage in 2000. Is the agreement valid? *In re Marriage of Tamraz,* Not Reported in Cal.Rptr.3d, 2005 WL 1524199 (Cal. App. 2 Dist.)

Discuss the public policy and ethical issues in prenuptial agreements and in courts upholding their validity. One lawyer has commented, "I've never seen a marriage with a prenuptial agreement last." Why this observation?

Figure 8.3 provides a summary of famous prenuptial agreements and their eventual validity and fallout.

FIGURE 8.3 Prenuptial Agreements of the Rich and Famous

NAME	TERMS	RESULTS
Donald Trump and Marla Maples	No alimony if adultery; child support; limited dollar amount	Prenup honored in divorce; Maples awarded limited amount.
Barry Bonds (San Francisco Giants) and Susann Branco	Agreement (14 pages) signed on the way to the wedding	Appellate court upheld the agreement and Mrs. Bonds was limited to $10,000 per month/per child support and no share of the earnings and property Barry Bonds acquired during their marriage.
Steven Spielberg and Amy Irving	Scrap of paper prenup, but Irving had no lawyer. Gave Irving no interest in Spielberg rights, royalties, revenues, and properties.	Judge set agreement aside for Irving's lack of representation. Spielberg settled for $100 million (4-year marriage).
Melinda and Bill Gates	Unknown	Still married
Jack and Jane Welch	Jane Welch had no interest in Jack Welch's stock, salary, options, and property during the first 10 years of their marriage. After 10 years, they shared in the assets.	Mrs. Welch filed for divorce after 13 years. Public filings in the divorce case caused General Electric shareholders to protest the expenditures and compensation of Welch, GE's retired CEO.

CAUTIONS AND CONCLUSIONS

Whether a party is a seller, buyer, or creditor, the status of property co-owners must be determined. The following are questions to be answered before entering into an obligation regarding the co-owned property:

1. Who are the co-owners?
2. What type of co-ownership exists?
3. Is one co-owner authorized to transfer title or to give a lien?
4. How much of an interest does the co-owner have?
5. Are additional signatures (spouses') required?

KEY TERMS

CHAPTER PROBLEMS

1. On a deed dated November 1, 1928, an acre of land located on Gap Road near Peak Mountain in Rockingham County, Virginia, was conveyed to Add Shoemaker and his wife Bessie Shoemaker with the following provision:

   It is hereby mutually understood and agreed, that the grantees herein named are to have and to hold the said land and tenements as joint tenants, and not as tenants in common.

   Add Shoemaker died intestate (without a will) in 1951 and was survived by Bessie and several children. Bessie, at some point after Add's death, conveyed to Wilmer A. Shoemaker (one of her sons) a 0.542-acre portion of the land she and Add had acquired in the 1928 deed. Bessie died in 1984.

   Wilmer died testate (with a will) sometime before 1988 and by his will devised the 0.542-acre tract of land to Shelby Jean Moubray. Moubray conveyed the tract to David Martin Smith and Vivian Secrist Smith on January 28, 1988.

   On February 19, 1992, Susan Shoemaker Hoover, Catherine G. Shoemaker Smith, Sarah P. Shoemaker Pennington, and Margie C. Shoemaker Hoover (collectively, the Hoovers), the children of Add and Bessie, filed suit against Alvin Shoemaker, Nellie Craun, and Charles Shoemaker, also children of Add and Bessie (collectively, the Smiths). The suit alleged that by the language of the 1928 deed, Bessie and Add were tenants in common only and that upon Add's death his interest in the tract of land should have passed by intestate succession to his children. The children also asked that the land be sold and its proceeds distributed because it was not convenient to partition the land. Are the children right? *Hoover v. Smith*, 444 S.E.2d 546 (Va. 1994).

2. Althea Lynley and Agnes Peach hold title to a 640-acre section in Montana as joint tenants with right of survivorship. The two acquired the property in their younger days with the idea that they would always be there for each other, and that the survivor would carry on with the property's development as a ranch.

   Within five years of their acquisition, Althea married and moved to San Diego, and Agnes was left in Montana, where she married and developed the property with her husband. The title to the property remained the same as it was when the deed was originally recorded. Agnes died in June 1994. Her husband and children assumed they would inherit the land because Agnes's will left everything she owned to them. However, Althea, who returned for Agnes's funeral, claims the land belongs to her. Who is correct?

3. George Herring and his wife had property conveyed to them as "Mr. and Mrs. Herring" with the following language:

   TO HAVE AND TO HOLD unto said parties of the second part, and the Survivor of them, his heirs and assigns forever. It is the intention of this conveyance that said parties of the second part are to be vested with title as joint tenants, with the incident of survivorship, and not as tenants in common; so that upon the death of either said parties of the second part, the entire fee simple absolute title in and to said property shall ipso facto become vested in the Survivor of said parties of the second part.

   Mrs. Herring conveyed her interest in the property to her son from a previous marriage, Clarence Carroll. Mr. Herring brought suit to have the conveyance set aside. During the judicial proceedings, Mr. Herring died and his children, Marshall Herring and Beatrice Midkiff, as Mr. Herring's sole heirs, continued the case, claiming they were entitled to receive title to the property. Mr. Carroll claims the conveyance by Mrs. Herring to him was valid and made him a tenant in common with Marshall and Beatrice. Who is correct? *Herring v. Carroll*, 300 S.E.2d 629 (Ct. App. W. Va. 1983).

4. Barbara Laudig and Robert Laudig were married in 1972. In 1987, Mr. Laudig discovered that Mrs. Laudig was involved in an extramarital relationship. Mr. Laudig left their home, but returned later that year and agreed to stay if Mrs. Laudig would sign a postnuptial agreement. The agreement provided that Mrs. Laudig, in exchange for $10,000, would waive all rights to marital property if she had an extramarital affair anytime during the next 15 years. The agreement was signed by both parties in August 1987.

   In December 1988, Mrs. Laudig renewed her relationship with her former paramour, and Mr. Laudig filed for divorce in May 1989. Mr. Laudig sought to enforce the postnuptial agreement and be awarded all the marital property. Mrs. Laudig objected on the grounds that their postnuptial agreement was against public policy. Who is correct? *Laudig v. Laudig*, 624 A.2d 651 (Pa. 1993).

5. In February 1952, James and Syvilla Ballantyne acquired title, as joint tenants, to a lot in the city of Minot. They lived there in a house located on the lot. On April 10, 1959, James Ballantyne died, leaving a will that purported to devise the lot to his wife, Syvilla, for life, with the remainder to his eight children by a previous marriage. James and Syvilla had no children of their marriage, and the probate court awarded Syvilla a life estate and a remainder to the eight children as part of the final distribution of James's estate.

   Syvilla occupied the home and paid the taxes on it until her death on May 11, 1973. She did not remarry and left a will that did not mention the lot but left the residue of her estate to her sisters and her brother. After Syvilla's death, James's eight children took possession of the property and attempted to sell it. At that time, the discovery of the joint tenancy was made, and Syvilla's sisters brought suit. What interest was created and who owns what and how following Syvilla's death? *Cranston v. Winters*, 238 N.W.2d 647 (N.D. 1976).

6. John Z. DeLorean and Cristina DeLorean entered into an antenuptial agreement on May 8, 1973 (only a few hours before they were married), that provided the following:

   [A]ny and all property, income and earnings acquired by each before and after the marriage shall be the separate property of the person acquiring the same, without any rights, title or control vesting in the other person.

   The marital assets (such as future earnings) could have exceeded $20 million, and practically all of them were in John's name. Without this agreement and considering that the marriage lasted 13 years and resulted in two minor children, Cristina would ordinarily be entitled to 50 percent of the marital assets at the time of divorce.

   On John DeLorean's petition for divorce, Cristina alleged that the agreement was invalid because she was not given full information about the extent of her husband's financial affairs before she signed and because her husband exercised undue influence on her in getting the agreement signed. The trial court upheld the validity of the agreement, and Mrs. DeLorean appealed. Is the agreement valid? *DeLorean v. DeLorean*, 511 A.2d 1257 (N.J. 1986).

   (Note: Mr. DeLorean died at age 80 in 2005. He was acquitted in two criminal trials, one involving charges of conspiring to sell cocaine, and the other for financial fraud. His assets were depleted with a final sale to Donald Trump of his Bedminster estate, a property that is now a golf course.)

7. Robert and Bernice Fick lived together beginning in 1981. In 1984, they were married. Shortly before their wedding, they both signed a prenuptial agreement that had been drafted by Robert. Among other things, the agreement waived both parties' rights to alimony upon divorce. The agreement incorporated by attachment both Bernice's and Robert's financial statements of property ownership and debts. However, Robert's statement was not attached at the time the agreement was signed and was not produced for Bernice until a year after their wedding. In 1989, Bernice filed for divorce and asked that the prenuptial agreement be set aside. Robert maintained that the agreement was valid because Bernice signed voluntarily and was represented by counsel. Bernice says she was misled because Robert did not attach his financials and she signed without complete information. Should the court set aside the prenuptial agreement and award Bernice the alimony and property she is requesting? *Fick v. Fick*, 851 P.2d 445 (Nev. 1993).

8. Carolyn Cummings had been awarded a medical retirement and disability benefits from the state of Alaska during the 1970s. She then met and married Gary Cummings and continued to receive her benefits from Alaska because of her disability. She used the funds to purchase various items for their household, as well as a camp trailer. During an action for divorce, Carolyn claimed that the furnishings and the trailer were her separate property. Gary claimed the commingling of the funds made those items community property. Who is correct? *Cummings v. Cummings*, 765 P.2d 697 (Idaho 1988).

9. Clayton and Margie Gulledge owned a house at 532 Somerset Place (the Somerset property). They had three children: Bernis Gulledge, Johnsie Walker,

and Marion Watkins. After Margie Gulledge died in 1970, Clayton remarried, but the second marriage was not successful.

While the divorce proceedings were pending, and because of his fear of losing the house, Clayton borrowed money from his son, Bernis, in order to pay off the financial demands of the second Mrs. Gulledge. In exchange, Clayton created a joint tenancy of the Somerset property, naming himself and Bernis as joint tenants. Bernis expected, as a joint tenant with right of survivorship, that he would, upon his father's death, take full title to the Somerset property and that his loan to his father would be satisfied.

In 1988, Clayton conveyed his interest in the Somerset property to his daughter, Marion Watkins, "in fee simple tenants in common."

In 1991, Clayton died, survived by his three children. However, Bernis died in 1993 and Johnsie died in 1994. The three estates were consolidated and there ensued quite a battle at the probate court level over the Somerset property. Bernis's personal representative, Deborah Walker, argued that Bernis was the sole owner of the Somerset property at Clayton's death. Marion Watkins argued that Clayton's conveyance to her severed the joint tenancy and she and Bernis were tenants in common at the time of Clayton's death and that she, therefore, owned one-half of the Somerset property. The trial court agreed with Ms. Watkins and Ms. Walker appealed. Who owns what, how much, and why? *Estate of Gulledge,* 673 A.2d 1278 (D.C. 1996).

10. In July 1957, A. Frank Jones and Grace A. Jones, by general warranty deed, conveyed fee simple title to 23 acres of land to Kenneth Quick, Robert Quick, and Robert Bean as joint tenants with right of survivorship (JTWROS). Kenneth Quick died April 27, 1972, and title to the property vested in Robert Quick and Robert Bean as the surviving JTWROS.

On June 14, 1979, Bean executed an oil and gas lease on the property to Paul H. Gerrie & Associates, Inc. On September 15, 1979, Quick gave a similar oil and gas lease to Gerrie. Both leases were recorded on September 20, 1979.

The leases Bean and Quick executed are identical, except the Bean lease contains a typewritten addition that states, *"Should any question of property ownership or royalty dispursements [sic] arise, the Lessor has agreed to accept full responsibility."* The Quick lease does not contain this clause.

After drilling commenced, all royalties were paid to Bean and Quick with each receiving one-half of one-eighth (one-sixteenth) of the royalties from the drilling. These payments continued until Quick died September 25, 1981; after that date, the royalties were paid in the same amount, one-sixteenth each to Bean and the Estate of Quick. In 1992, Bean, through his attorney, Marilyn Bean Jeffers transferred the property to Jeffers. Since 1992, one-sixteenth of the royalties have been paid to Jeffers, and one-sixteenth of the royalties have been held in escrow pending resolution of ownership interests.

Jeffers says title to the property vested in Bean upon Quick's death. She requested the court to quiet title and require Quick's estate to account for funds received as royalties under the lease. Robert Quick's sons and heirs allege that the JTWROS between Bean and Quick was severed by Bean's June 14, 1979, oil and gas lease to Gerrie, and therefore title to the property did not vest in Bean upon the death of Quick, since Bean and Quick held the property as tenants in common. Explain who is correct, who owns how much, and why. *In re Estate of Quick,* 905 A.2d 471 (Pa. 2006).

For research activities related to this chapter, go to our text companion website at
http://www.cengagebrain.com

CHAPTER 9

THE LANDLORD-TENANT RELATIONSHIP

Geoffrey Green lived in a rent-stabilized apartment in New York City. Bedbugs in his apartment forced him and his partner, Dana Shapiro, to sleep with the lights on, and rotate between sleeping in the bedroom, the kitchen, and the living room. They did not use the bedroom between May and August in 2005 and 2006.

Mr. Green testified that from April 2005 through July 2008, he did not have a single full night's sleep during the summer months. Lack of sleep affected Mr. Green's relationship with Ms. Shapiro and his ability to get to work on time.

Mr. Green withheld two months of rent from October 2005 through January 2007 for the prime bedbug months, non-winter months. His landlord brought a forcible detainer action to have him evicted. Mr. Green counterclaimed for his damages from the bedbugs. Mr. Green offered into evidence two zip lock bags containing dead bedbugs. Eviction?

A lease may seem like a simple transaction—the tenant pays the rent and the landlord provides the premises. But both sides have rights and responsibilities, including rent and bedbugs. This chapter answers the following questions: What types of lease agreements exist? What terms should be included in the lease agreement? What rights and responsibilities do each of the parties have? There are several sources of laws and principles for the landlord–tenant relationship, including common law, state statutory provisions, and the **Uniform Residential Landlord Tenant Act (URLTA),** which has been adopted formally in 21 of the states and is also followed in principle in most of the states. This chapter concentrates on residential leases, and Chapter 10 deals with commercial leases.

TYPES OF TENANCIES

The four types of tenancies that existed at common law are *tenancy for years*, *periodic tenancy*, *tenancy at will*, and *tenancy at sufferance*. These tenancies will apply to both commercial and residential leases except when there are specific statutory changes. A lease agreement can provide for its own type of lease and terms.

Tenancy for Years

A **tenancy for years** is created by a lease that will run for a specific period of time. Language used to create a tenancy for years includes "estate for years," "tenancy for a term," or "tenancy for a period." Every tenancy for years has a fixed beginning and ending date and is created by language such as "To A for 7 years" or "To A from 31 March 2012 until 30 June 2015." The lease terminates automatically on the specified ending date.

A tenancy for years that runs for a period longer than one year must have a writing or record to be valid. (See p. 181 on the Statute of Frauds for more details.)

Periodic Tenancy

A **periodic tenancy** has no definite ending date: It continues until one of the parties takes proper legal steps to end the interest. A periodic tenancy can be expressly created, and an example of language used is, "To A on a month-to-month basis beginning 30 June 2012."

However, a periodic tenancy or estate from period to period can be created through the conduct of the parties. For example, suppose that Ruth moves into one of Meryl's Maine beach houses on an oral lease agreement that is to run for 24 months. In Maine, leases that run for longer than one year must be in writing to be enforceable. Because of the writing requirement, the parties do not have an enforceable lease agreement, but once Meryl accepts Ruth's rent, they have created a periodic tenancy by their conduct. Their lease now carries all the rights of a periodic tenancy.

Termination requirements for periodic tenancies are specified by statute in each state, but the key to termination in all states is notice. The type or length of notice will vary, but the requirement of notice is universal. The typical period, both at common law and by state statute on a month-to-month tenancy, is a full period's notice, or one month.

Tenancy at Will

A **tenancy at will** can be created expressly when the parties agree to a lease of property but provide no time period for the lease. Sample language to create a tenancy at will is, "To A at O's discretion or will."

In a tenancy at will, both parties have the right to terminate the tenancy at any time and are not required to provide advance notice. In some states, statutory provisions have changed this freedom and require some form of notice to terminate. In these states, the tenancy at will has been modified to a periodic tenancy by statute.

Tenancies at will can arise in situations with a financed property, where there is a default by the possessing party. For example, suppose Corey leases the land on which her mobile home is located, and her mobile home is financed through a bank. Corey leaves, but the mobile home remains on the leased land. If Corey defaults on her payment and the bank is forced to repossess the mobile home, then the bank, as a creditor in possession, becomes a tenant at will on the land.

Tenancy at Sufferance

This final nonfreehold interest, **tenancy at sufferance**, arises when a tenant from another form of tenancy stays put, or, as the law refers to it, "holds over" on the landlord's property after the original tenancy ends. For example, suppose a landlord leased a bungalow in the Hollywood Hills to Amos Jacobs for two years with a lease termination date of March 31, 2013. Jacobs should vacate the premises by the termination date, but if he remains, he remains there as a trespasser. The landlord may have Jacobs, a holdover tenant, evicted. However, if Jacobs remains on the property without objection from his landlord, and if that landlord accepts rent after March 31, 2013, then Jacobs's lease went from a tenancy for years to a tenancy at sufferance, and finally to a periodic tenancy once the rent is paid and accepted.

The following case deals with an issue of the type of lease and the landlord's attempt to terminate it.

WILSON V. FIELDGROVE

787 N.W.2d 707 (Neb. 2010)
Another Year of Crops Sans Notice

FACTS

Beginning about 1998, Allan Fieldgrove leased farmland to Kenny Wilson (Kenny) under an oral year-to-year lease agreement, with an annual term from March 1 through the end of February each year. Rent was paid in cash. The most recent lease between Allan Fieldgrove and Kenny ran from March 1, 2007, through February 29, 2008. Kenny died on August 4, 2007. Cindy Wilson (Wilson/Appellee) was the sole beneficiary of Kenny's estate. Mrs. Wilson and her sons continued farming the land after Kenny's death. On at least four occasions following Kenny's death, Mrs. Wilson or her sons communicated to Mr. Fieldgrove their intention to continue farming the land in 2008. Mr. Fieldgrove never gave written notice to any member of the Wilson family of his intention to terminate the farm lease before September 1, 2007.

Sometime after Kenny's death, Mr. Fieldgrove prepared to sell the farm at public auction. Upon learning of the upcoming sale, Mrs. Wilson again notified Mr. Fieldgrove that she intended to continue to farm the land in 2008. On January 16, 2008, Mrs. Wilson recorded a document entitled "Notice of 2008 Leasehold Interest" with the county register of deeds, in which she claimed an interest in Fieldgrove's property. On January 18, Mr. Fieldgrove sold the property. On February 20, Mr. Fieldgrove notified Wilson that she and her family were prohibited from entering the property and would be treated as trespassers as of March 1. Mrs. Wilson refused to vacate the property and filed a complaint against Fieldgrove on February 29 seeking a declaration that she was entitled to the leasehold interest. Fieldgrove counterclaimed, alleging slander of title, and he sought to have Wilson removed from the property through a forcible entry and detainer claim.

The court ruled for Mrs. Wilson because Mr. Fieldgrove failed to provide the required 6–month notice of his intention to terminate the lease, so Mrs. Wilson was entitled to possession of the farm until February 28, 2009. Mrs. Wilson then sought summary judgment on Mr. Fieldgrove's slander of title claim. The court granted Mrs. Wilson's motion for summary judgment, and Mr. Fieldgrove appealed.

JUDICIAL OPINION
Connolly, Justice

This appeal presents an issue of first impression: Under a year-to-year lease, is a landlord required to give notice to a tenant's heirs if the tenant dies during the term of the lease?

The parties do not dispute the terms of the oral lease. The sole issue regarding the lease is whether a landlord is required to give notice of termination to the farm tenant's surviving heirs when the tenant dies before the deadline for notice. This issue presents a question of law.

Because the 2008 farming season has already passed, the court's ruling that Wilson had a valid leasehold interest for that year would be moot except that it is relevant to Fieldgrove's claimed damages under his slander of title claim. An action for slander of title is based upon a false and malicious statement, oral or written, which disparages a person's title to real or personal property and results in special damage.

Whether Wilson had a valid leasehold interest depends upon whether Fieldgrove was required to give her notice to quit after Kenny died but before the lease expired. The court found that Fieldgrove did not give Wilson notice to quit. Whether a landlord is required to give notice to quit to a tenant's surviving heir presents an issue of first impression.

Fieldgrove argues that after Kenny died, the lease terminated at the end of the crop year without notice. Courts generally hold that sharecrop farm leases, under which the tenant pays the landlord a share of the crops raised, implicitly include an agreement for the tenant's particular farming skills in which the owner has confidence. In a sharecrop lease agreement, the landlord's receipts directly depend upon the tenant's skills and industry. So, under the common law, a sharecrop agreement is usually considered a personal services contract that does not survive the tenant's death and is not inheritable.

But some courts have found this rule to be abrogated by their state statutes. For example, courts do not agree whether a statutory notice to quit requirement applicable to sharecrop agreements abrogates the common-law rule regarding termination of the lease upon a farm tenant's death. Further, the Kansas Supreme Court has reasoned that the terminate-at-death rule for sharecrop agreements is abrogated under a state statute that subjects the administrator of a tenant's estate to the tenant's liabilities under a lease. Under this statute, the court held that "a lease, including an agricultural sharecrop lease, continues in effect upon the death of the tenant unless the parties have contracted otherwise, and the executor or administrator of the lessee's estate has the fiduciary obligation to see that the lessee's obligations are met."

Nebraska does not have a statutory notice requirement, but we have judicially required a 6–month notice to quit for year-to-year farm tenancies. And we have applied this rule to sharecrop lease agreements. But we need not decide whether the common-law rule regarding termination upon the tenant's death of a sharecrop agreement is abrogated. The lease here is a cash lease agreement. Because Fieldgrove did not share in the fruits of Kenny's labor, we do not construe the lease as a contract for Kenny's personal services.

Outside of contracts for personal services and tenancies at will (or when the common-law rule for sharecrop agreements has been abrogated), the death of the landlord or tenant in a year-to-year lease does not terminate the lease. Instead, a leasehold interest in a tenancy for a term of years or a year-to-year tenancy is considered personal property. And unless the contract provides otherwise, courts have held that a leasehold interest transfers by operation of law to the tenant's personal representative or heir.

Since 1974, in Nebraska, title to both real and personal property passes immediately upon death to the decedent's devisees or heirs, subject to administration, allowances, and a surviving spouse's elective share. But the point of these earlier cases is still relevant: Apart from tenancies at will or leases requiring the tenant's personal services, a tenant's rights and obligations in a leasehold interest survive the tenant's death and pass to his or her heirs, subject to the personal representative's right of possession.

The parties stipulated that Wilson was Kenny's sole heir. We conclude that the leasehold interest passed to Wilson upon Kenny's death.

Under Nebraska law, a year-to-year tenancy can only be terminated by an agreement of the parties, express or implied, or by notice given, 6 months before the end of the current year in the year-to-year tenancy. Generally, in the absence of a different agreement, a yearly lease of farmland begins on March 1 and ends on February 28 of the following year, and the rent becomes due at the expiration of the term. In such a case, a landlord must give notice to terminate by September 1. Here, it is uncontested that neither Fieldgrove nor Wilson gave notice to quit.

In discussing notice requirements under year-to-year tenancies, the Minnesota Supreme Court held that the deceased landlord's estate was required to give the tenant the required notice of its intent to terminate the lease. Absent such notice, the lease continued for the next year. Similarly, the Iowa Supreme Court found that the tenant's death did not terminate the lease agreement. Rather, "[a]bsent receipt of statutory termination of tenancy notice … the widow, as sole surviving beneficiary and executor of her deceased husband's estate, claimed a continuing right to possession and occupancy of the premises for the [next] crop year."

We believe that the reasoning of these cases applies here. We conclude that when a year-to-year farm lease does not terminate upon the tenant's death, the landlord can only terminate the lease by giving notice to quit to the tenant's heirs or personal representative. Fieldgrove failed to comply with this requirement. Wilson, who possessed Kenny's leasehold interest in the property and continued to farm it, was entitled to rely on that lack of notice.

Here, the district court correctly found that Wilson had a valid leasehold interest. Thus, the claim Wilson filed against the property was not false or malicious. And the record lacks any evidence to suggest Wilson filed the claim to slander the title to the property. She believed, rightfully so, that she had a valid interest in the property.

Affirmed.

CASE QUESTIONS

1. What type of lease had the parties created?
2. What time frame was required for giving notice of termination?
3. Was the termination notice required even though the tenant had passed away? Explain the court's reasoning on this issue.

TERMS OF LEASE AGREEMENT

Need for Lease Agreement

Under the Statute of Frauds, a lease that is to run for a period longer than a year must usually be reduced to some form of writing or record. Under E-Sign and relevant state laws, records are defined to include faxes as well as electronically authorized contracts. In some states, the writing or record requirement may be imposed at six months. Residential and commercial leases are subject to the same Statute of Frauds requirements.

To satisfy the Statute of Frauds, the record may be informal—in the form of a letter, memorandum, or series of documents. The basics needed are identification of the parties, the signatures of the parties, a description of the leased premises, the term of the lease, and the amount of the rent. While some real estate transactions (deeds, for example) will still require formal written documents, leases enjoy the new electronic flexibility in documenting lease agreements that fall under the Statute of Frauds. See Web Exhibit 9.1 and 9.2 for samples.

In addition to the minimum requirements for a written lease, there are issues and details that should be covered in the parties' lease agreement and are discussed in the following sections. If the parties do not deal specifically with these issues in a lease agreement, statutory or common law provisions will apply, and the parties may not have the protection or results they expect.

Habitability

At common law, when tenants leased property, the doctrine of *caveat* tenant applied: Tenants leased the premises at their own risk and there were no warranties, covenants, promises, or guarantees that the premises were habitable. Common law did not impose an obligation on the landlord to deliver habitable premises. Without statutory protection, many tenants entered into leases for uninhabitable properties. They were obligated under the lease but faced the difficult task of obtaining repairs and services from the landlord.

To prevent the negative health and safety consequences of this doctrine, particularly in areas where there were housing shortages, most states (with cities imposing additional obligations) enacted laws that require landlords to deliver premises to tenants in habitable condition. The following statutory language is an example of a warranty of habitability requirement.

> *No persons shall rent or offer to rent any habitation, or the furnishings thereof, unless such a habitation and its furnishings are in a clean, safe, and sanitary condition; in repair; and free from rodents or vermin.*

Known as the **implied warranty of habitability**, this protection arose through statute and judicial decisions. The URLTA includes an implied warranty of habitability. The effect of a breach of the warranty of habitability is to make the lease for the uninhabitable premises void. The effect of a void lease is that the tenant need not pay rent. Indeed, a breach of the warranty of habitability is a defense if a landlord brings action for eviction for nonpayment of rent.

Despite statutory protections, tenants should still have a habitability clause in their leases, which may be simple, such as: "Owner (landlord) agrees to deliver premises to tenant in a fit and habitable condition." If the tenant has the opportunity to inspect the premises prior to entering into the lease agreement, a clause may be added to the lease that requires the landlord to make certain repairs and adjustments.

Even in jurisdictions without a statute that applies specifically to leases, some tenants have been excused from performing lease agreements on other grounds. Leases of premises found to have building or fire code violations have been held void, and courts have excused tenants from performing on the grounds of illegality. The key to the cases is that the tenant must have given the landlord notice of the problems and also enough time to bring the premises into a habitable condition.[1] The following case deals with an interesting issue of habitability and answers the question posed in the chapter opening scenario.

BENDER V. GREEN

874 N.Y.S.2d 786 (N.Y. Civ. Ct. 2009)
When Your Landlord Really Bugs You

FACTS

Geoffrey Green lived in a rent-control apartment in New York City. Bedbugs in his apartment forced him and his partner, Dana Shapiro, to sleep with the lights on, and rotate between sleeping in the bedroom, the kitchen, and the living room. They did not use the bedroom between May and August in 2005 and 2006.

Mr. Green testified that from April 2005 through July 2008, he did not have a single full night's sleep. Lack of sleep affected Mr. Green's relationship with Ms. Shapiro and his ability to get to work on time.

Mr. Green withheld rent from October 2005 through January 2007, for the prime bedbugs months, i.e., non-winter months, an amount of $5,665.84. His landlord (Petitioner) brought a forcible detainer action to have him evicted. Mr. Green counterclaimed for his damages from the bedbugs. Mr. Green offered into evidence two Ziploc bags containing dead bedbugs.

The exterminator for the complex did come to spray the building but said that he never saw any live or dead bedbugs in the Green/Shapiro apartment except the specimens that Mr. Green had shown him, in a Ziploc

bag. The exterminator believed that Green and Shapiro (Respondents) may have brought the bedbugs with them from their previous apartment. Theresa Lonng, a neighbor, testified that she had bedbugs in her apartment, but that she also had them in her apartment in the building next door, where she had lived until moving next to Mr. Green and Ms. Shapiro.

JUDICIAL OPINION

Kraus, Judge

RPL § 235-b provides that in all residential lease agreements the landlord warrants that the premises leased are "fit for human habitation" and that occupants "shall not be subjected to any conditions which would be dangerous, hazardous or detrimental to their life, health or safety." "[T]he statute places an unqualified obligation on the landlord to keep the premises habitable throughout the term of the lease, and this obligation may not be waived or delegated." It has been well established that insect infestation is a condition which is considered to adversely impact

---

[1]If the tenant who withholds rent based on allegations of uninhabitable conditions fails to follow procedures under the statute governing summary process actions, including notifying the landlord of the conditions prior to withholding rent, her refusal to pay some or all of the rent due will subject her to eviction proceedings to which she will have no defense; she cannot use the landlord's alleged breach of the habitability warranty as a defense to a notice to quit for nonpayment of rent unless there is compliance with legal requirements. *Jablonski v. Casey*, 835 N.E.2d 615 (Mass. App. 2005).

upon the health and safety of the occupants of a residential premises.

The evidence suggests that the bedbugs were introduced into the Subject Premises, through no fault of the landlord (Petitioner), and in all likelihood by the Respondents themselves. When the Respondents moved in to the Subject Premises there were no bedbugs in the premises for at least one year; and no other tenant in the Subject Building made a single complaint about bedbugs during the entire period in which Respondents alleged the Subject Premises were infested with bedbugs; and no violations for bedbugs placed at any point for any apartment in the subject building, including the Subject Premises, during the relevant period; and Respondents admit that they suffered a bedbug infestation in the apartment they lived in, immediately prior to moving into the Subject Premises; and Respondents acknowledge they travel for work related purposes on a regular basis.

Petitioner did not establish at trial that the presence of bedbugs was caused by any "misconduct" by Respondents. As one commentator has noted:

The world is not only a smaller place for humans, it has become increasingly smaller for bedbugs as well. These opportunistic parasites are known as proficient hitchhikers. They travel from one place to another in luggage and clothing, jumping off at homes and hotels. What is worse is that these resilient pests have been known to survive 500 days without feeding. Wenk & Shafer, Good Night, Sleep Tight, Don't Let the Cimex Lectularis Bite, N.Y.L.J., Jan. 26, 2006, at 4, co. 4. *The same article states that one female is sufficient to lead a local infestation, and that a well fed female can lay up to 500 eggs in a lifetime, which eggs hatch between six to twenty-eight days.*

The Court finds that the presence of bedbugs in the Subject Premises did constitute a breach of the warranty of habitability. The more difficult determination is what, if any, damages Respondents are entitled to as a result of said breach. Once a breach has been established the "parties must come forward with evidence concerning the extensiveness of the breach, the manner in which it impacted upon the health, safety or welfare of the tenants and the measures taken by the landlord to alleviate the violation."

Ms. Lonng, who was readily familiar with bedbugs from her own experience, visited the Subject Premises on at least twenty occasions, and never saw a bedbug. The Exterminator who went to the Subject Premises regularly during the relevant period, sometimes on a weekly basis, never saw a single live bedbug on any visit to the Subject Premises. The only bedbugs anyone saw at the Subject Premises were in ziplock[2] bags, which Respondents had collected, and which were exhibited by Respondent to the Exterminator or Ms. Lonng. Over the three year period, the infestation allegedly took place, Respondents collected approximately twelve bedbugs.

The Court would have expected a three year unabated bedbug infestation to result in evidence similar to that which Ms. Lonng presented regarding her infestation. Other corroborating evidence could have been photographs of stained sheets, or photographs exhibiting the typical bedbug bites in groups of three.

The Court finds that the testimony of the Respondents in this proceeding was not reliable and not consistent with other evidence in the record. For example, the photographs that were offered into evidence, which Respondents alleged depicted bedbug bites, do not appear to have been bedbug bites at all, pursuant to the expert testimony of Eisenberg. Similarly, the testimony that the unabated infestation varied seasonally, was not supported by Eisenberg's testimony that bedbug infestation does not vary seasonally.

Moreover, it is not clear to the Court in what manner Petitioners' response to the complaints was deficient. Petitioner made its Exterminator available to Respondents when as Respondents desired his services. Respondents acknowledged that they took no action beyond what Petitioner had done regarding extermination services. Ms. Green[3] testified because she did not believe that hiring a different exterminator would help. What then should the Petitioner have done?

The Court finds it not credible that tenants would suffer for three years with an unabated bedbug infestation, believing that Petitioner's exterminator was inefficient, and take no action on their own to alleviate the problem. [T]he Court would expect that a tenant might hire their own exterminator, if they believed Petitioner's exterminator was unqualified. Respondents never did.

---

[2] The court uses the terms "zip lock" and "ziplock," perhaps using a trade name for a generic brand or perhaps failing to capitalize and also misspelling the trademark term, "Ziploc." The author does not presume to correct the court or assume that an actual "Ziploc" bag was used to collect the bedbugs.

[3] The court uses the name Ms. Green, but it is assumed this refers to Ms. Shapiro.

Moreover, it seems unlikely to the Court that an unabated bedbug infestation in the Subject Premises would not spread, at any point during the three years, to other parts of the Subject Building. Thus, while the Court credits Respondents' testimony to the extent that the Court finds bedbugs were present to some extent during the period, the Court does not credit Respondents' testimony regarding the length and the extent of the alleged infestation. The Court finds that Respondents' burden to establish the extent of the condition has not been met, and limits the Court in awarding damages to Respondents.

The Court finds that the period for which Respondents are entitled to be an abatement to cover September 2005 through December 2006. The first documented notification to Petitioner regarding the alleged condition was in September 2005. That was the first documented phone call to the Exterminator, and Respondents withheld their rent in September and October of 2005. Based on the log of bites that was kept by Respondents for January 2007 forward, the Court finds Respondents failed to establish the presence of bedbugs from January 2007 forward, and that the bites documented were in all likelihood other insect bites.

The Court finds that Respondents are entitled to a twelve percent abatement in rent, for the period of September 2005 through December 2006 totaling $2724.21. Given the parties' stipulation that there was $5665.84 due at the conclusion of the trial, that leaves $2941.19 remaining due, in unpaid rent, through January 2009. Petitioner is entitled to a final judgment in the amount of $2941.19.

CASE QUESTIONS

1. List the issues that mitigate the landlord's liability even though there is a breach of the warranty of habitability.
2. What lessons should landlords and tenants learn from this case?

CONSIDER 9.1   Linda Schuman had an oral month-to-month tenancy with Ernest and Susan Kobets, d/b/a Lynnleigh Apartments, and had reported to them that pigeons had begun nesting in the broken window casing of her dining room window and in the wall next to the bathroom window. She asked in June 1990 that the holes in the walls be repaired, but the Kobetses were not forthcoming with the repairs.

By July of 1990, Ms. Schuman was experiencing fevers, swollen lymph nodes, and "other maladies." When she was diagnosed with histoplasmosis, she presented her medical bills to the Kobetses for reimbursement. She did not press for payment and her illness passed by the fall of 1990. Histoplasmosis is "a fungus, which is spread by spores that are typically carried in bird excrement, particularly pigeon droppings."

In 1995, the disease appeared again, and Ms. Schuman had to be hospitalized and nearly died. She was taken home to Indiana to be cared for by her mother and forced to postpone her nursing career for one year. She had medical bills of $138,000. Histoplasmosis can reemerge at any time. Ms. Schuman's physicians warned her about the possibility of a lifetime of medical care and treatment for the disease.

Ms. Schuman filed suit against the Kobetses, seeking recovery for all of her medical and related damages. The trial court dismissed all of her claims and the court of appeals affirmed. The Supreme Court affirmed the dismissal except with regard to her claims for breach of the implied warranty of habitability. The trial court granted summary judgment on all claims except the warranty of habitability and the Kobetses appealed. Is this a breach of the warranty of habitability? What is different from the bedbugs case? *Schuman v. Kobets,* 760 N.E.2d 682 (Ind. App. 2002).   ▪

To deal with a mold issue, regardless of statutory requirements, landlords should

♦ *Have the property inspected by a certified mold inspector.*

♦ *Inform tenants of the risks of mold exposure.*

♦ *Provide tenants with information on how to spot and clean molds; some landlords provide tenants with mold test kits.*

♦ *Give tenants information on whom to contact in the event they see signs of growing molds.*

♦ *Have tenants sign off on special forms available from insurers that indicate they were furnished with the mold disclosure and information.*

♦ *Check insurance to be sure there is not a mold exclusion clause that eliminates mold cases as a recoverable issue; landlords can obtain a rider for coverage when mold is excluded but because of litigation (about 10,000 cases per year), the premium can double insurance costs on property.*

Some states have specific statutory requirements on certain conditions in rental property. For example, the presence of lead-based paint in residential property is now highly regulated. In some states, the landlord is required to remove the lead paint and repaint the apartment. In addition to the breach of the warranty of habitability, tenants may have statutory remedies when the habitability issue is one caused by the presence of this type of paint.[4]

Under the Residential Lead-Based Paint Hazard Reduction Act of 1992, 42 U.S.C. §§ 4851–4856, both the EPA and the HUD were charged with disclosure standards for lead paints on their properties. Under the HUD/EPA rules, landlords must disclose to their tenants the presence of lead paint on their leased properties and provide a pamphlet explaining the hazards of lead-based paint (40 C.F.R. § 745.100 *et seq.* and 24 CFR § 35.80 *et seq.*). The effect of the rule has been that landlords are eliminating the lead paint because the disclosure makes properties difficult to rent.

The presence of mold in residential properties has resulted in a new wave of landlord forms and disclosure requirements across the states. For example, in Washington, landlords are required to notify tenants about the health risks of mold and provide information on how to spot mold issues and what to do in the event of any discovery of growing molds. Disclosure is now common practice by landlords and model forms are available. If caught early enough, molds formed because of humidity, condensation, or leaks can be cleaned up easily with just bleach and water. If, however, the molds grow, the spores infiltrate the property and require expertise and decontamination for removal. Most landlords now use inspections by certified mold inspectors prior to the start of leases because of the high health hazard and resulting liability exposure should molds be present.

ETHICAL ISSUE

In some cases, landlords have not been swift to act in making property repairs that are necessary to meet the standards for habitability. Many courts have undertaken creative remedies to this problem of resistance. For example, in Phoenix, Arizona, Sherwin Seyrafi, called a "slumlord" by various news organizations, was charged with misdemeanor violations for the conditions of his various properties and then ordered by a judge, as part of his sentence, to live in one of his properties for 30 days. What is the ethical standard the sentencing judge is applying to the landlord's conduct? Do you agree or disagree with the sentence?

---

[4]However, a recent Rhode Island decision held that the presence of lead is not a public nuisance that entitles property owners and occupants to recover from paint manufacturers. *State of Rhode Island v. Lead Industries, Inc.,* 951 A.2d 428 (R.I. 2008).

CONSIDER 9.2   A 60-unit cooperative apartment building on West 142nd Street in Manhattan was severely damaged by fire on February 7, 1994, and rendered uninhabitable by the Department of Buildings. No action was taken to demolish or renovate the building, and in November 1994, the co-op owners brought suit seeking a court order requiring the Owners Corporation and its managing agent to restore the premises to a safe and habitable condition. However, the property had not been adequately insured, and the Owners Corporation declared bankruptcy on November 23, 1994.

The Owners Corporation defended its inaction on the grounds that the cost of restoration would exceed the market value of the property. The co-op owners maintain that there is a statutory requirement for a landlord to keep his property in a safe and habitable condition. Could the warranty of habitability be used to mandate the reconstruction of a building? Should it be so used? *Bernard v. Scharf,* 656 N.Y.S.2d 583 (Sup. Ct. 1997).

Deposits

Most tenants are required to make some type of deposit when they enter into a lease agreement. The types of deposits include security deposit, cleaning deposit, and prepaid rent.

Security Deposit

The deposit most frequently required is the **security deposit.** Its purpose is to protect the landlord in the event of property damage or to cover lost rent if the tenant leaves before the lease ending date. The money held on deposit as security may be used to cover expenses or damages and may even be specified as liquidated damages in the event of an early termination by the tenant.

In some states, security deposits are regulated to a great extent; in other states, the landlord and tenant can agree on the purpose and effect of the security deposit. For example, under the URLTA, the amount of a security deposit is limited. Section 2.101(a) provides, "A landlord may not demand or receive security, however denominated, in an amount or value in excess of (one) month['s] period."

Once landlords have the tenant's security deposit, they retain it until termination of the lease. There are considerable differences among the states on how landlords may use security deposits received from tenants. The common law rule is that the landlord is a debtor to the tenant for the security deposit and is free to use the funds as if they were the landlord's own. However, some states require landlords to pay tenants a minimum amount of interest (such as 5 percent) for the time the deposit is held. Some states also require landlords to keep the security deposits in special trust accounts and maintain and submit periodic records of their balances and deposits received from tenants.

States also differ in their definitions of what constitutes a security deposit. For example, in some states, prepaid rent is considered part of the security deposit, and in other states, the landlord is not required to follow security deposit procedures on funds labeled prepaid rent.

The security deposit can also double as a liquidated damages provision. A liquidated damage clause is an advance agreement between the landlord and tenant as to how a breach will be determined and what the breach damages will be. The lease may provide that the liquidated damages for breach will be the security deposit. For example, if a tenant leases an apartment for $1,000 per month for a six-month period and abandons the premises at four months, the landlord is entitled, with a proper liquidated damage provision in the lease, to keep the security deposit as damages for early termination by the tenant. When the tenant ends the apartment lease early, the landlord could re-rent the apartment the next day, or the apartment could sit vacant for the remaining two months of the original lease. Because we cannot know in advance how, if, or to what degree the landlord will be harmed by an early termination, an agreement to allow the landlord to keep the security deposit as damages is a valid liquidated damage provision.

In some states and under the URLTA, if the landlord chooses the remedy of keeping the security deposit, then the amount of the security deposit is the total for the landlord's damages. A landlord cannot collect actual damages and keep the security deposit because the result would be an assessment of a penalty for breach against the tenant. Such penalties for breach of residential lease agreements are void. A landlord is not entitled to both liquidated and actual damages. Also under the URLTA, retention of the security deposit requires the landlord to account to the tenant for how much was kept and why.

The following language is an example of the type of clause necessary when the tenant is paying funds taken by the landlord as a security deposit:

> *SECURITY: In order to guarantee Resident's faithful performance of the terms and conditions contained herein, Resident hereby deposits with owner the sum of $ as a security deposit to be applied to the payment of accrued but unpaid rent and any other damages suffered by reason of Resident's noncompliance or breach of any terms and conditions of the Rental Agreement.*

If there are no statutory provisions governing security deposits in the state, the parties should specify in the lease agreement their rights to the security deposit, including procedures and time limitations for its use and return and its effect as a provision for liquidated damages.

Another issue that has arisen with leases is whether the landlord has a duty to mitigate damages by leasing the premises to another tenant. In the absence of an agreement, courts are reluctant to impose such a duty because of the resulting questions that arise, such as whether the landlord was diligent in finding a new tenant, whether the new lease was fair, and whether the costs the landlord incurred in mitigation are recoverable.

CONSIDER 9.3   Barbara Kent and her roommate, Sheila Barnes, have signed a nine-month lease on an apartment. The rent is $1,050 per month, and the roommates were required to make a $1,050 security deposit. At the end of four months, they decide to move to a house closer to their places of employment. The apartment owner is unable to lease the apartment for three months, and the apartment is vacant for that time. Discuss the use of the security deposit to cover damages according to the laws of your state.

Suppose the tenants abandon the leased apartment after performance of three months on a six-month, $1,050-per-month lease, and the landlord is able to rent the apartment for one of the three remaining months, what are the landlord's damages? ____■

Cleaning Deposit

In addition to security deposits, which are intended to secure rental payments, landlords may require tenants to make other deposits. A **cleaning deposit** is a typical lease requirement and may take the form of a nonrefundable fee that all tenants are required to pay. Under the URLTA, a nonrefundable cleaning deposit must be disclosed and provided for in the lease agreement. The following is a sample clause from a lease: "Additionally, Resident hereby pays the sum of $, which is a NONREFUNDABLE redecorating fee." The fees paid may be called cleaning, refurbishing, redecorating, or restoration fees, but they all require advance disclosure of retention under the URLTA.

Some cleaning fees are taken with the idea that they will be used, if necessary, at the time the tenant vacates the premises. The theory behind this type of deposit is that tenants will have greater incentive to keep the premises clean and well-maintained, and not destroy items of property. For example, some leases contain addenda that specify cleaning costs to be assessed if, at the end of the lease and upon the landlord's inspection, particular cleaning tasks are necessary. Specific items such as drapery cleaning or wall repainting may be represented as a dollar amount, so that tenants will know the potential assessments in advance.

Prepaid Rent

Many landlords require tenants to pay the first and last months' rent prior to taking possession of the property. Such a provision is for the protection of the landlord in the event the tenant vacates the premises without paying rent. However, the URLTA and many other states' provisions limit the amount of prepaid rent or total deposits that may be required of the tenant initially, and the limit may be as small as one-and-a-half times the monthly rent. The lease agreement or an addendum to it should specify exactly what amounts are being received from the tenant and the purpose and application of those amounts. These limitations are not applicable in commercial leases. The following case deals with several issues related to the creation of a lease, the start of a lease, the deposits, prepaid rent, and damages if there is a problem with the lease.

FURLAN V. FARRAR

982 A.2d 581 (R.I. 2009)
Maybe I Am Coming to Rhode Island, Maybe Not

FACTS

In August of 2006, Loretta Furlan (plaintiff) called Douglas Farrar (defendant) to inquire about an apartment in Smithfield, Rhode Island that he had advertised as being for rent. Ms. Furlan had been living in Florida, and she intended to move back to Rhode Island. Shortly after placing the phone call to Mr. Farrar, Ms. Furlan asked one or two of her friends to inspect the apartment in her absence. One of those friends reported back to Ms. Furlan that the apartment was "nice and clean." Thereafter, Ms. Furlan and defendant orally agreed that Ms. Furlan would pay $800 as a security deposit and $800 for the first month's rent. On August 25, 2006, Ms. Furlan then sent Mr. Farrar cashier's check in the amount of $1600.

The starting date of the rental period was in dispute. Ms. Furlan contended that the rental period was to begin on October 1, 2006. Mr. Farrar disagreed and asserted that he and Ms. Furlan had agreed that the rental period would begin on September 1.

At some point after having sent the $1600 check to Mr. Farrar, Ms. Furlan called him to inform him that she would be delayed in taking possession of the apartment. The date on which this call was made was also in dispute. According to Ms. Furlan, she placed this call on October 1. The defendant asserts, however, that it was on September 10 and then again in the third week of September that plaintiff called him to inform him of the delay.

On October 6, Ms. Furlan called Mr. Farrar to tell him that she would not be taking the apartment after all, and she asked that he return $800 to her. Mr. Farrar refused to return the money. Approximately one half-hour after her initial phone call to Mr. Farrar, Ms. Furlan called him again to tell him that her brother would be bringing furniture to the apartment. However, Mr. Farrar refused to allow Ms. Furlan to take possession of the apartment.

Ms. Furlan sought damages in Small Claims Court of $800 plus costs. The judge found in favor of Ms. Furlan. Mr. Farrar appealed and had a *de novo* trial in the Superior Court.

The judge in the Superior Court found that the starting date of the rental period was the beginning of September and he also found that the landlord-tenant relationship began when Mr. Farrar received the check for $1600.

The judge then determined that Ms. Furlan was entitled to be awarded the sum of $625—such sum being reflective of the rental value of the apartment from the period from October 6 through October 31, during which period the landlord would not permit the plaintiff tenant to have access to the apartment. However, the trial justice then proceeded to offset that $625 amount by defendant's advertising costs (*viz.,* $339.68), and he accordingly awarded Ms. Furlan $285.32 in net damages, plus costs.

Mr. Farrar appealed.

JUDICIAL OPINION
Robinson, Justice

The defendant is correct in asserting that, with respect to the case at bar, a month-to-month tenancy was created because the oral rental agreement between the parties did not fix a specific term. Unless the rental agreement fixes a definite term, the tenancy is week-to-week in case of a roomer who pays weekly rent, and in all other cases month to month. Moreover, when there is a month-to-month tenancy, rent is payable in equal monthly installments at the beginning of each month.

The trial justice supportably found that the lease term began on September 1, 2006. Thus, $800 of the sum of $1600 that was sent by plaintiff to defendant on August 25 was properly used as September's rent. Moreover, in view of the provisions of the statutes cited in the preceding paragraph, defendant correctly maintains that plaintiff owed him an additional $800 on October 1, 2006 for October's rent. In view of the fact that plaintiff failed to send him an additional check, defendant was entitled to deduct an appropriate amount from plaintiff's security deposit for unpaid, accrued rent.

What distinguishes this case from so many others, however, is the fact that in the instant case rent only accrued until October 6, 2006—on which date the defendant landlord prevented his tenant from having access to the apartment. The trial justice correctly ruled that, because defendant prevented plaintiff and her brother from accessing the apartment after October 6, plaintiff was entitled to the return of her security deposit minus the unpaid, accrued rent for the period from October 1 through October 6.

As for the trial justice's decision to offset plaintiff's damages by the amount that defendant spent on advertising (*viz.,* $339.68), we note that defendant would have had to incur such an expense in any event after the termination of the tenancy. However, there being no cross-appeal as to this issue, we decline to make any definitive ruling about same.

In view of the fact that the plaintiff was under no obligation to pay rent after the defendant denied her access to the apartment on October 6, 2006, we have no occasion to decide whether the plaintiff was required to provide thirty days advance notice in order to terminate the tenancy.

CASE QUESTIONS

1. Explain what type of lease this was and how the court decided that issue.
2. Give an explanation on who gets damages, how much, and why.
3. What lessons should landlords and tenants learn from a case such as this?

Amount of Rent

In addition to specifying the amounts of deposits, the lease agreement should specify the monthly rental fee. The amount of rent becomes more of an issue in commercial leases where landlords are entitled to portions of profits (see Chapter 10). Residential lease agreements should specify how much rent is to be paid, the date the rent is due, to whom the rent is to be paid, and if there are any fees associated with late rental payments. The following is a sample rental fee clause:

RENTAL: The rental shall be $ per month, plus sales tax thereon at the rate in effect from time to time, payable in advance on the FIRST day of each month at the on-site manager's office. An equitable proration of the first month's rent shall be made if the term of this Rental Agreement commences other than on the first day of the calendar month. A late charge of $10.00 per day shall be added as additional rent to any rent payment not paid in full on or before the due date. A $25.00 fee will be charged for all checks returned from the bank unpaid. Management reserves the right to demand that all sums due under the lease be paid in cash and to return any check previously accepted by Management and demand cash.

Rent Control

New York City and San Francisco are examples of cities with **rent controls** that limit the amount of rent landlords can charge to tenants (the *Green* case involved a rent-control lease). Nearly two-thirds of the rental market in both cities is rent-regulated. Under rent regulation, a housing authority sets rates and determines any exceptions. A lease in violation of such rent control or rent stabilization statutes is void. A tenant cannot be evicted for refusal to pay more than the maximum rent permitted by the housing authority (*Washington 921 Ltd. Partnership v. New York State Div. of Housing and Community Renewal*, 912 N.Y.S.2d 846 (N.Y. Sup. 2010)).

In areas where there is a rent-stabilization regime, some landlords have converted their properties to "hotels" and charge higher rates to their occupants. However, rent control provisions also define what constitutes a "housing accommodation," and factors such as length of time of occupation, whether a key is retained on a regular basis by the occupant, what types of belongings the occupant has on the property, and whether the occupant does have a residence other than the occupied property are critical in defining housing. Even though the property owner may call the living area a "hotel," and collect rent on a weekly basis, it may still be subject to rent controls given the factors listed above (*Benroal Realty Associates, L.P. v. Lowe*, 9 Misc.3d 4, 801 N.Y.S.2d 114 (N.Y. Ct. App. 2005)).

Other landlords have tried putting waivers of rent stabilizations in their lease agreements with tenants. These types of waivers are void because they contravene the purpose of rent stabilization, which is providing affordable housing for city dwellers (*Thornton v. Baron*, 4 A.D.3d 258, 772 N.Y.S.2d 326 [2004]).

Still others have tried to circumvent rent controls by arguing that there is a housing shortage. However, courts have not intervened in these debates and deferred to rent control statutes (*Santa Monica Beach, Ltd. v. Superior Court*, 968 P.2d 993 [Cal. 1999]). Some have also argued that such controls on use of property and rent constitute a taking in violation of the due process clause of the U.S. Constitution (see Chapter 19 and *San Remo Hotel L.P. v. City and County of San Francisco*, 41 P.3d 87 (Cal. 2002)).

However, in *Fisher v. City of Berkeley California*, 475 U.S. 260 (1986), the U.S. Supreme Court held that rent control statutes are constitutional as long as landlords are not colluding to fix rents with a resulting cloak for any conspiracy among landlords or between the landlords and the municipality. In other words, the courts do not interfere with rent controls unless there is some private business force trying to monopolize the rental market.

CONSIDER 9.4   In San Francisco and New York, the following discoveries have been made:

a. Two-thirds of residential rental property are under rent controls, and the average rent is $650.

b. The rent for the remaining one-third of properties is $1,500 to $2,000, and the apartments are small, in poor condition, and have a waiting list.

c. Landlords under rent control are converting their properties to commercial facilities or condominiums.

d. There is little tenant turnover in rent-controlled property, with relatives taking leases upon tenants' deaths.

e. Some residents, such as Congressman Charlie Rangel, despite one-residence limits, have more than one rent-controlled apartment that they use for themselves and their families. Others, such as Faye Dunaway, do not meet the standards for being a full-time New York City resident, but hold a rent-controlled apartment anyway.

What explains the price differences and problems? Give the economic analysis.

Lease Term

The portion of the lease agreement that specifies the term may simply state the beginning and ending dates of the lease. However, additional language may be necessary if the tenant wants an option to renew. The option to renew should specify when the option must be exercised, how it is to be exercised, how the rental amount for the option period is to be computed, and the maximum length of the option period.

Attorneys' Fees

In spite of careful drafting and execution of lease agreements, litigation does happen. All leases should include provisions for the payment of costs and attorneys' fees in the event the parties have a dispute that goes to arbitration or is litigated. The following clause is an example of an attorneys' fee provision:

> *In the event legal action is necessary for the enforcement of rights and obligations granted under this agreement, the prevailing party shall be entitled to an award including attorneys' fees and all attendant court costs regardless of the stage to which the legal action proceeds.*

In states where attorneys' fees cannot be collected in contract actions, these clauses are unenforceable.

Rules and Regulations

PRACTICAL TIP

A violation of the rules and regulations imposed by the landlord is also grounds for eviction. Most landlords provide tenants with notice of a violation before proceeding to an eviction.

Particularly in apartment complexes, rules of conduct and for use of the property are necessary for smooth functioning of joint facilities and for each tenant's peaceful enjoyment of the property. Under the URLTA and most state statutes, landlords can promulgate such rules. Section 3.102 of the URLTA permits rules and regulations that promote the convenience, safety, or welfare of the tenants; prevent abusive use of the landlord's property; or provide for a fair distribution of services and facilities held out for the tenants generally. To be valid, these rules of conduct and operation must apply to all tenants, be disclosed to all tenants, and not be applied unfairly. Rules and regulations cannot excuse the landlord from responsibilities or eliminate tenants' rights. Rules and regulations may be incorporated into the lease agreement in two ways:

1. They may actually be written into the section of the lease agreement on the applicability of rules and regulations.
2. They may be incorporated as an addendum or a schedule to the lease agreement or referenced in the lease. If they are referenced, the tenant is entitled to a copy.

The types of rules and regulations that are typical and meet the standards of the URLTA are hours of pool use, use of laundry facilities, parking regulations, and noise and pet restrictions. (A notice of change in the rules should be sent directly to each tenant.)

The following case deals with the reasonableness of a landlord's rule.

BERLINGER V. SUBURBAN APARTMENT MANAGEMENT

454 N.E.2d 1367 (Ohio 1982)
The Fine for a Motorcycle on Your Patio

FACTS

Gary R. Berlinger (plaintiff/appellant) was a tenant in an apartment managed by Suburban Apartment Management (SAM/landlord/appellee). His security deposit was $420, and his monthly rent was $210.

In his lease agreement was the following paragraph:

No animals, birds, pets, motorcycles, waterbeds, trucks, jeeps, or vans shall be kept on the premises at any time.

The rule provided for a $50 fine for each violation. Berlinger had a motorcycle on his patio on October 10, 13, and 24, and November 7, 1979.

SAM notified Berlinger of the violation and the $200 fine. Berlinger did not pay the fine and moved out. SAM kept Berlinger's security deposit for a $200 fine, $210 in rent, and $10.50 in interest. Berlinger objected on the grounds that the fine was excessive and the rule was arbitrary. Berlinger sued to have his security deposit returned. The trial court awarded him $20 based on the following:

Security deposit	$420.00
Plus interest	+$10.50
Subtotal	$430.50
Less rent (for unpaid last month)	$210.00
Less 4 × $50 (four days of motorcycle)	$200.00
Total	$20.50*

Berlinger appealed.

JUDICIAL OPINION

Jackson, Judge

It does not appear that the $50 per diem charge for the presence of a motorcycle was in the nature of a fee for parking or storage. The lease was not modified to permit possession of a motorcycle on the premises. Instead, the charge is in the nature of liquidated damages. It is a matter of common knowledge that motorcycles, if operated loudly, can be objects of great annoyance. This effect is magnified in densely populated places such as apartment complexes. Thus, it is not unconscionable for a landlord to prohibit the bringing of motorcycles on the premises.

A different issue is presented, however, by the liquidated damages clause. To be valid, a provision for liquidated damages must meet three criteria, expressed in the following excerpt from *American Financial Leasing v. Miller* (1974) 41 Ohio App.2d 69, 73, 322 N.E.2d 149 [70 O.O.2d 64] (quoting from 16 Ohio Jurisprudence 2d 155):

[I]t must, according to most cases, appear that the sum stipulated bears a reasonable proportion to the loss actually sustained; that the actual damages occasioned by the breach are uncertain or difficult to ascertain; and most important of all, that a construction of the contract as a whole evinces a conscious intention of the parties deliberately to consider and adjust the damages that might flow from the breach.

---
*The trial court actually miscalculated and hence made the award at $20.00 as opposed to $20.50.

Actual damages occasioned by a breach of the "no motorcycle" provision of the lease are difficult to ascertain. However, the sum of $50 per day (which in a thirty-day month would amount to $1,500) does not bear a reasonable relationship to any loss which might foreseeably be sustained. A court could take judicial notice that the operation of a motorcycle might cause great damage to a landlord, because tenants who object to loud noise might move out. However, no evidence was introduced tending to show the amount of damages which might foreseeably result from the mere presence of a motorcycle.

The liquidated damages clause contained in the Disposition Advice is therefore invalid under the common law and under R.C. 5321.14, and is hereby ordered stricken from the lease.

In the absence of a valid provision for liquidated damages, the appellee was entitled to recover only the monetary equivalent of the actual damages caused by the appellant's breach. Again, however, the appel-lee failed to adduce any evidence tending to show that it sustained actual damages as a result of the presence of the motorcycle on the property, even if the motorcycle was there for one month, as claimed by appellee. In the absence of any evidence on this subject, compensatory damages may not be awarded.

The appellee did prove beyond any doubt that the appellant breached his promise not to bring a motorcycle on the property. The appellee is therefore entitled to judgment on its claim for breach of contract, and an award of nominal damages in the sum of one dollar.

The appellant proved that he was entitled to the return of his security deposit ($420) plus interest ($10.50) less one month's rent ($210), for a total of $220.50.

Reversed.

CASE QUESTIONS

1. What rule was at issue?
2. Was the fine excessive?

CONSIDER 9.5 In January 2002, Mary Jane Nealy entered into a one-year written lease agreement with Southlawn Palms Apartments (SPA). The lease provided that the term would run from January 22, 2002, to January 21, 2003, and would automatically renew on a month-to-month basis at the expiration of its initial term. The lease also provided that SPA could terminate the tenancy for (1) a serious or repeated violation of the terms and conditions of the lease; (2) a violation of federal, state, or local law; (3) criminal activity; or (4) other good cause. SPA had an addendum that listed the rules of conduct for the apartment complex. On April 28, 2004, SPA sent Nealy a "30 Day Notice to Vacate" the premises and listed two reasons for the notice to vacate: (1) "Owner desires possession" and (2) "Undesirable tenant behavior." SPA later filed a forcible detainer action against Nealy, citing "undesirable tenant behavior" as the sole ground for eviction. SPA indicated that "Ms. Nealy breached her lease by violating the rules of Southland Palms Apts. and by violated [*sic*] the Blue Star Addendum. Nealy rode a four-wheeler in the pedestrian areas of the apartment, and there were two reports that Nealy mooned other tenants or maintenance workers." Ms. Nealy points out that "mooning" and the four-wheeler issues were not covered in the addendum rules and that she was not warned about her conduct or given the opportunity to respond to the allegations by the other tenants. Can SPA evict Ms. Nealy? Why or why not? *Nealy v. Southlawn Palms Apartments,* 196 S.W.3d 386 (Tex. App. 2006).

Landlord's Right of Access

Although landlords own the property, tenants have the exclusive rights of possession even as against the landlords so long as a valid lease agreement exists. This principle of exclusive possession was applied at common law and has been codified in many states to protect tenants from landlords' unauthorized entry onto leased premises.

Under Section 3.103 of the URLTA, a landlord can enter a tenant's dwelling if

a. *The tenant consents and the purpose is repair or services; and*
b. *In case of emergency (even without the tenant's consent). Except in emergencies the land-lord must give the tenant at least (2) days' notice and must come at reasonable times.*

In the lease agreement, the parties are free to agree to other terms of entry and arrangements for entry, and in most states these terms will be enforceable so long as the tenant has not been required to give up any statutory rights. With consent required, the tenant must act reasonably.

Assignments and Subleases

Assignments and **subleases** are similar in that they both bring third parties into the landlord–tenant relationship. However, there is a distinction between the two processes: In an assignment, tenants actually transfer their leasehold interests to third parties who will take over all obligations and assume all benefits associated with the original lease. In a subleasing arrangement, the tenants give up only a portion of their leasehold estate. For example, consider a tenant with a three-year lease of a New York City apartment. If while the tenant is studying in Europe for one year—year two of the lease—he has leased the apartment to someone, then he has sublet the apartment. But if the tenant decides to remain in Europe and the third party takes over years two and three completely, then there is an assignment of the lease.

At common law, a lease was freely transferable; both subleases and assignments were permitted and honored. However, landlords and tenants may agree to restrict transfers in their agreements. For example, some leases make any transfer void, although the enforceability of such a provision is questionable. Another type of transfer restriction is a provision that has tenants forfeit their leasehold interests if they attempt to transfer those interests to others. Under this type of provision, the assignment or sublease is not void, but the landlord has terminated both the original party's interest and the subtenant's or assignee's interest. Finally, the lease agreement may simply contain a provision that the tenant promises not to sublet or assign. If the tenant violates the provision and the landlord has resulting damages, the breaching tenant is liable to the landlord for those damages. In some leases, the sublease or assignment is not prohibited, but the tenant is required to obtain the landlord's approval for the transaction. If the landlord does not approve, one of the other types of provisions just mentioned would take effect. The following clause is an example in which prior consent is required: *"Resident may not assign this Rental Agreement or sublet the premises, in whole or in part, without the prior written consent of management."*

This consent to assignment was established as an ongoing right by the 1603 **Rule in Dumpor's Case**, which provided that if the landlord consented to one assignment, all other assignments were also deemed valid. In other words, at common law, once the landlord waived rights to prohibit an assignment, the right to prohibit assignments was lost. Most states have abolished the effect of this rule.

Rights and Responsibilities of Parties to a Lease Assignment

Although an assignment is a complete relinquishment of the tenant's leasehold interest, the tenant's obligations do not end with an assignment. The tenant remains obligated to the landlord; if the assignee does not perform according to the terms of the lease agreement, the original tenant is liable for damages.

The assignee is not responsible for the obligations of the original tenant unless the assignee assumes these obligations. The assumption of responsibilities is not generally a problem since the assignee will be the recipient of the benefits—the right to the leasehold interest. The assignee does have the right to require the landlord to perform according to the terms of the lease agreement, as well as the right to sue in the event of nonperformance.

If an assignee does not perform under the lease or breaches the lease agreement, the landlord can pursue remedies from either the original tenant or the assignee. Although the landlord does not have privity of contract with the assignee, the landlord is still obligated to perform obligations as established by law or by the original parties' lease agreement.

Rights and Responsibilities of Parties to a Sublease

In a sublease, the subtenant becomes a tenant of the original lessee and not a tenant of the landlord. There is no legal relationship between landlord and subtenant and no rights of enforcement by one party against another. Any rights the parties have must be exercised indirectly through the tenant with whom they have a contractual relationship. For example, if a landlord who is required to maintain insurance on the leased premises fails to do so and a subtenant loses property because of it, the subtenant could proceed against the tenant. Although the tenant could then proceed against the landlord for recovery, the subtenant would have no direct cause of action against the landlord because the landlord's obligation to insure is to the tenant and not to the subtenant.

Unconscionability

As with most consumer contracts, leases are subject to judicial standards of fairness in language and bargaining power. Under the URLTA, a rental agreement is unconscionable if the tenant is required to waive any of the rights, remedies, or protections under the act.

Other areas in lease agreements that courts have found to be unconscionable include excessive cleaning deposits, excessive assessment of cleaning fees, excessive security deposit requirements, prohibitions on the right to organize, and waivers of judicial process. The basic standard in all cases is one that looks at the bargaining power of the parties and fairness.

RIGHTS AND RESPONSIBILITIES OF PARTIES TO LEASE AGREEMENT

Both landlords and tenants have required responsibilities of performance as well as mandated rights. The following sections cover those rights and responsibilities.

Responsibilities of Landlords and Rights of Tenants
Maintenance of the Premises

At common law, a lease was a transfer of a land interest with no obligation of maintenance and repair for the landlord once the tenant began the lease period. Just as the doctrine of habitable premises has changed considerably, so has the doctrine governing the landlord's duty of repair. Several theories have now been used by courts or codified by states that require the landlord to keep the leased premises in repair. The theories are (1) constructive eviction, (2) self-help, (3) tort liability, and (4) lease termination.

1. *Constructive Eviction* One theory used to require repairs and thereby ensure the tenant of continued habitability is the doctrine of **constructive eviction**. For this doctrine to apply, the tenant must be able to establish that the landlord had an obligation to repair either through a covenant in the lease agreement or through some statutory or judicially imposed duty. Under URLTA Section 2.104, landlords are required to comply with building codes, make the repairs necessary to keep the leased premises habitable, keep the common areas clean and safe, keep all services and facilities in working order, arrange for trash collection and removal, and supply running water (hot and cold) and heat in winter and according to outside temperatures.

Once the tenant has established that the landlord was responsible for maintenance of the premises, the tenant must also prove that the landlord has failed to perform according to the statute or agreement. Furthermore, whatever the landlord's failure, it must be one that has made it difficult or impossible for the tenant to continue living on the premises. Under the doctrine of constructive eviction, the tenant in these circumstances has no choice but to leave, and this profound act of leaving his or her home excuses the tenant from the lease obligations. The heart of the doctrine is also the greatest problem with the doctrine in a practical sense: The tenant must move out for the doctrine to apply. In areas where housing shortages exist, particularly for low-cost units, this requirement means going from substandard housing to no housing. In some states, the courts have permitted tenants who can establish all of the elements of constructive eviction to fix the problem areas and remain in the leased premises, deducting the cost of the repairs from their rent. The following case presents an interesting example of constructive eviction.

PRACTICAL TIP

When a landlord undertakes the responsibility of providing facilities, he or she must be certain those facilities remain in good repair and that no additional risks are created by the presence of the facilities.

NEWKIRK V. SCALA

935 N.Y.S.2d 176 (N.Y.A.D. 2011)
Something Rotten in the Water

FACTS

Lisa Newkirk and her children rented a home from William Scala (defendant) for the period from December 2003 to December 2004. She paid nine months' rent and made a security deposit. The home's tap water had an overpowering odor from the outset. The home's tap water had a sickening smell that prevented its use for any purpose. The water's stench was so extreme that it made her and her children nauseous, ruined clothes washed in it, and forced them not only to launder clothes, but to bathe and eat, elsewhere. The certified water specialist who first installed the water treatment system at the residence, Bruce Leighton, investigated the situation at Mr. Scala's request and agreed that the water had a "horrible smell," akin to burnt rotting eggs. Mr. Leighton advised Mr. Scala that the odor could be corrected by replacing part of the water treatment system. Despite this information and Ms. Newkirk's repeated pleas, Mr. Scala failed to act. Following Mr. Scala's prolonged failure to correct the problem, Ms. Newkirk and her children moved out in June 2004.

Ms. Newkirk filed suit based on Mr. Scala's breach of the warranty of habitability. The trial court awarded her $10,100 in damages, plus interest, costs and disbursements. Mr. Scala appealed.

JUDICIAL OPINION

Mercure, Acting Presiding Judge

Every residential lease contains an implied warranty of habitability covenanting: "(1) that the premises are 'fit for human habitation,' (2) that the premises are fit for 'the uses reasonably intended by the parties,' and (3) that the occupants will not be subjected to conditions that are 'dangerous, hazardous or detrimental to their life, health or safety'" The warranty is implicated if the premises are unfit for human occupancy and contain "conditions that materially affect the health and safety of tenants or deficiencies that 'in the eyes of a *reasonable person* ... deprive the tenant of those *essential functions* which a residence is expected to provide'" Inadequate plumbing and overpowering odors not only prevent a tenant from making reasonable use of a residence but, indeed, materially affect his or her health and safety.

Giving deference to Supreme Court's assessment of credibility, we conclude that the foregoing [facts] amply supports the court's finding that defendant breached the implied warranty of habitability.

Turning to the amount of damages awarded, "the proper measure of damages for breach of the warranty is the difference between the fair market value of the premises if they had been as warranted, as measured by the rent reserved under the lease, and the value of the premises during the period of the breach" There is no dispute as to the rent charged under the lease and, inasmuch as the breach was severe and persisted throughout plaintiff's occupancy due to defendant's inaction, Supreme Court properly determined that the rental value of the premises was halved.

CASE QUESTIONS

1. Describe what made the premises uninhabitable.
2. Explain how the damages were determined.
3. What advice would you give a tenant in this situation? A landlord?

CONSIDER 9.6   Robert and Barbara Lax (landlords) had Christopher and Melissa Knudsen (tenant/tenants) sign a six-page, 33-paragraph lease on August 1, 2006, for a one-year term. The terms of the lease, which the landlord obtained from an Internet site, were not negotiated by the parties. The lease expressly provided a covenant of quiet enjoyment promising that the tenant "shall ... peacefully and quietly ... enjoy said premises for the term." The lease also stated that, in the event the tenant abandoned the premises before the term ended, the landlord could "hold the tenant liable ... for the rent that would have been payable ... during the balance of the unexpired term."

In January 2007, a Level 3 Sex Offender moved in with the tenants living next to the Knudsens. On January 23, 2007, the Knudsens submitted a written request asking to be allowed to terminate the lease on January 31, 2007, because "... [I]t is our responsibility having three young girls that we feel are potentially endangered of any harm by said sex offender we feel it warrants a release to be granted."

The Knudsens vacated the premises on January 31, 2007, without the landlord agreeing to terminate the lease on that date. The Knudsens filed suit to recover their security deposit, and Lax counterclaimed for the balance of the rent due for the final six months of the contract, which terminated on July 31, 2007. Has there been constructive eviction? Breach of the warranty of habitability? How will courts reconcile the rights of convicted sex offenders to find a place to live with the rights of tenants? *Knudsen v. Lax*, 842 N.Y.S.2d 341 (2007).

2. *Self-help* Common law did not permit the **repair and deduct** self-help method of remedying leased premises in disrepair. However, under the URLTA, this remedy of **self-help** has been adopted by an increasing number of states. Under Section 4.103 of the URLTA, the tenant can make repairs (up to $100) if the landlord does not respond within 14 days of a written demand for repair.

The tenant can then send the landlord an itemized statement on the repair costs and deduct that amount from his rent. Tenants may not make repairs at the landlord's expense if the tenant or family member caused the condition.

Under this section of the URLTA, the tenant is given the statutory right to repair and deduct the cost of property problems that are not self-induced. Before repairing and deducting, the tenant should give notice to the landlord.

3. *Tort Liability* In the absence of the statutorily or judicially imposed self-help right, tenants have another legal theory for recovery from the landlord for correcting problems. In some decisions, the tenant has not been permitted to repair and deduct but has been permitted to repair and recover in tort for the damages caused or alleviated through the tenant's corrective actions. The difficulty with this remedy is that the tenant must take legal action to recover. This remedy provides the tenant with an opportunity for damages and remedies beyond just nonpayment of rent or a reduction in rent.

4. *Lease Termination* A final option available to a tenant faced with a lease of uninhabitable premises is to treat the state of disrepair as constructive eviction, vacate the premises, and regard the lease and the obligation to pay rents as terminated. This right of termination through constructive eviction was a common law right that exists in all states in common law or statutory form. In the event a statute regulates constructive eviction, the tenant must comply with all procedural requirements before vacating the premises.

Retaliatory Action by Landlords

If a tenant exercises any of the rights and remedies afforded by self-help statutes, implied covenants, or tort liability, it is possible that the landlord may, in response to the tenant's action, retaliate with eviction. Because the purposes of these theories would be defeated if landlords used retaliatory eviction, the URLTA and many state statutes provide that landlords may not engage in retaliatory eviction against tenants who choose to exercise their self-help rights. For example, Section 5.101 of the URLTA provides that a tenant cannot be evicted and that a tenant's rental fee cannot be raised or his or her services decreased as a result of any of the following:

1. filing a complaint with housing authorities,
2. organizing or joining a tenant's union, or
3. using self-help procedures and remedies.

If a tenant has engaged in these activities, there is usually a period during which the landlord's eviction would be presumptively retaliatory. For example, the URLTA presumptive retaliatory period is one year after the tenant has engaged in any of the protected activities. The landlord has the burden to establish that the tenant was evicted for reasons other than the exercise of statutorily protected rights. The presumption can be overcome when the tenant has not paid rent or has in some way breached the lease agreement.

Maintenance of the Common Areas

Regardless of any state's position on the landlord's responsibility to maintain individual dwelling units, all states require landlords to maintain the common areas of their leased properties. Common areas are those used by all tenants, such as staircases, halls, and laundry facilities. Although tenants may not be entitled to terminate their leases for disrepair of these areas, the landlord will be held liable for injuries resulting from the disrepair.

Duty to Maintain Premises to Prevent Injuries

The landlord has responsibility and liability for conditions on the leased premises. In many situations, the landlord has dangerous items and structures on the property that can cause injury to tenants even though those structures are not the leased premises and not technically part of the common areas of a building. Perhaps the greatest amount of landlord–tenant litigation in terms of premises liability is related to liability for the acts of third parties that injure tenants. The following is a case that established that the issue of landlord liability for criminal acts of third parties is a question of fact that requires proof of an underlying breach of duty.

YU FANG TAN V. ARNEL MANAGEMENT CO.

170 Cal.App.4th 1087, 88 Cal.Rptr.3d 754 (Cal. App. 2009)
Tragedy When There Aren't Enough Parking Spaces

FACTS

Arnel Management Company (Defendant) manages the Pheasant Ridge Apartments. Pheasant Ridge is a 620-unit, multi-building apartment complex, with over 1,000 residents, situated on 20.59 acres in Rowland Heights, California. Before the gated entrance to the complex are two parking lots; one is a visitor lot, and the other is the parking lot for the leasing office, located on the other side of the road. There are two security gates just past the parking lot. The gates are operated by remote control. Most of the property's parking spaces lie behind these gates by the apartments.

Yu Fang Tang and his wife, Chun Kuei Chang, and their child (Plaintiffs) moved into Pheasant Ridge in July 2002 and received one assigned parking space. Tenants could pay an additional fee for a garage, but Tang chose not to rent one. Tenants with a second car could park in unassigned parking spaces located throughout the complex, or in one of the two lots described, as long as the car was removed from the leasing office lot before 7:00 a.m.

At around 11:30 p.m. on December 28, 2002, Tang returned home and tried to find an unassigned open parking space because his wife had parked the family's other car in their assigned space. Unable to locate an available space, he parked in the leasing office parking lot outside the gated area.

As Tang was parking his car, an unidentified man approached him and asked for help. When Tang opened his window, the man pointed a gun and told him to get out of the car because the man wanted it. Plaintiff responded, "Okay. Let me park my car first." But the car rolled a little, at which point the assailant shot Tang in the neck. The incident rendered Tang a quadriplegic. Tang and Chang filed suit against Arnel for their negligent management of the complex as well as its policy on not having sufficient parking inside the gated area and charging more for such additional spaces. The trial court granted judgment on the pleadings for Arnel and Tang and Chang appealed.

JUDICIAL OPINION

Aldrich, Judge

At the hearing, plaintiffs' expert, UCLA Sociology Professor Jack Katz, looked at police reports, complaints to the police, property management reports, and records of Pheasant Ridge's security service, PacWest Security Services. After excluding from his analysis those prior incidents involving attacks by acquaintances, Professor Katz found 10 incidents he viewed as being "particularly significant warning signs," of which three involved "prior violent incidents." All of the incidents involved a sudden attack without warning, late at night, by a stranger on someone who was on the ungated portion of the premises.

The first example of a violent incident occurred just under two years before plaintiffs' attack and involved an assault with a deadly weapon. A guard, who was patrolling on his bicycle around 1:30 a.m., saw someone standing by the maintenance garage. The guard approached the subject and asked him what he was doing. The subject replied he was waiting for a friend. When the guard asked for identification, the subject retrieved an unknown object from his pocket and swung it at the guard. The guard raised his arm in self-protection and received an [sic] 1.5 inch slash on his forearm.

The second example occurred about a year before plaintiff's attack and before the existing gates at the back of the entrance road were installed. The assailants carjacked a car in Santa Monica with what the victim perceived to be a gun. Finding Pheasant Ridge "a good place to rob somebody" because there was no gate to impede their escape, as they told police later, the assailants came onto the property and robbed a tenant at his parking spot. The assailants committed the robbery by blocking the tenant's car, smashing him on the head, and demanding his valuables. They took the tenant's cell phone and other property.

The third violent incident occurred at 3:55 a.m., nine months before the attack on plaintiff. The incident was "also a violent attack, apparently, by strangers in late nighttime in a parking lot," and may have actually been in the leasing office lot. The assailant suddenly and viciously attacked the tenant in the face causing profuse bleeding.

Professor Katz explained that these three prior incidents all involved "strangers coming in late night, suddenly becoming violent against people they don't know in ungated parking areas." Professor Katz opined that these three incidents "show that the probability is foreseeable … here that people on this property will be attacked at some point by a stranger in open parking areas late at night."

Plaintiffs also presented nearly 80 examples of thefts from garages or cars or thefts of cars occurring on the Pheasant Ridge property. The trial court excluded the evidence of these thefts because they did not involve robberies or violent attacks on people.

'First, the court must determine the specific measures the plaintiff asserts the defendant should have taken to prevent the harm. Second, the court must analyze how financially and socially burdensome these proposed measures would be to a landlord, which measures could range from minimally burdensome to significantly burdensome under the facts of the case. Third, the court must identify the nature of the third party conduct that the plaintiff claims could have been prevented had the landlord taken the proposed measures, and assess how foreseeable (on a continuum from a mere possibility to a reasonable probability) it was that this conduct would occur. Once the burden and foreseeability have been independently assessed, they can be compared in determining the scope of the duty the court imposes on a given defendant. The more certain the likelihood of harm, the higher the burden a court will impose

on a landlord to prevent it; the less foreseeable the harm, the lower the burden a court will place on a landlord.'

Referring to the first step of the analysis, i.e., the specific security measures that plaintiffs proposed defendants should have taken, the record shows that plaintiffs requested minimal changes: Professor Katz recommended (1) moving the existing security gates from the back of the access road, or (2) installing "very similar" gates before the visitor and leasing office parking lots. An additional gate could be "any gate … that would not necessarily impede climbing over it. It wouldn't have spikes or-or [*sic*] be unusually high. It would just define a property boundary…." "[v]ery similar to the gates they have…." Indeed, Professor Katz did not reject swing-arm gates. Any gate could remain open during the day to allow business in the leasing office. Plaintiffs clearly stated they were not asking for the hiring of a guard or for any form of ongoing surveillance or monitoring. Furthermore, because existing fencing extends around almost the entire perimeter of the property, only a "very minor" extension over a "very small area" would be necessary to close the fencing gap, Professor Katz testified, and could be achieved by merely mounding dirt.

The second issue requires the court to analyze how financially and socially onerous the proposed measures would be to the landlord. As plaintiffs observed, their proposed security measures involved a one-time expenditure and did not require ongoing surveillance of any kind, or the expenditure of significant funds. We disagree with the court that the proposed security measures were onerous.

Turning then to the heart of this case, the third element of foreseeability, plaintiffs demonstrated three prior incidents of sudden, unprovoked, increasingly violent assaults on people in ungated parking areas on the Pheasant Ridge premises by a stranger in the middle of the night, causing great bodily injury. Professor Katz opined, based on the three incidents, that "the probability is foreseeable here" of plaintiff's attack because in his experience, "you don't get more than this." The evidence of three vicious criminal assaults in the common areas within two years of plaintiff's attack here is more similar and compelling than the evidence in *Ann M.*, 25 Cal.Rptr.2d 137, 863 P.2d 207 [no evidence landlord had notice of crime on the property], or *Sharon P. v. Arman,* Ltd., 91 Cal.Rptr.2d 35, 989 P.2d 121 [no assaults in 10 years on the premises]. We conclude that plaintiffs presented substantial evidence of prior similar incidents or other indications of a reasonably foreseeable risk of violent criminal assaults on the property so as to impose on defendants a duty to provide the comparatively minimal security measures plaintiffs described.

Reversed.

CASE QUESTIONS

1. List the three areas a court must review before imposing liability on a landlord for a criminal act by a third party on a tenant.

2. What lessons on security precautions should landlords take from the decision in this case?

CONSIDER 9.7   On February 22, 2006, Cynthia Harris drove a friend, Herd Stanley Guice, from New Orleans to his apartment in the Pinewoods Apartments in Watson, Louisiana. The apartment complex, constructed around 1982, was owned and managed by Delta Development Partnership. When Ms. Harris and Mr. Guice arrived at his apartment complex after 8:00 p.m. that evening, it was dark outside. Mr. Guice entered the breezeway where the entrance to his ground-floor apartment was located. His doorway was located beneath the upper floor landing. After setting his small overnight bag down in front of the doorway, Mr. Guice retrieved his keys and opened the door. Leaving the overnight bag in the threshold of the doorway, he walked inside to turn on the apartment's interior and exterior lights, located about nine feet down the entrance hall past a double closet. At about the same time that Mr. Guice reached the light switch, Ms. Harris tripped over his overnight bag and fell, immediately complaining of severe pain in her left ankle. At the time of the accident, no exterior lights were illuminating the breezeway or the apartment doorway.

Ms. Harris sustained a fracture of her left ankle. She filed suit against Mr. Guice, Delta Development, and its insurer for its inadequate lighting at Mr. Guice's complex. Can she recover from them? *Harris v. Delta Development Partnership*, 994 So.2d 69 (La. App. 2008). ∎

CONSIDER 9.8   Barbara Hill was a resident of Casa Blanca Mobile Home Park. Shannon Kearns was a resident of an apartment owned by Fair Plaza Associates. Both Hill and Kearns had month-to-month rental agreements with the property owners.

Hill began complaining in May 1996 about the level of noise from her neighbor's television. The manager of the mobile home park where she lived testified that he was awakened on 15 occasions between the hours of 12:30 and 1:00 a.m. to investigate the TV disturbances. Hill also complained during the day in July about the television set. At that point, the manager served Hill with a 30-day notice of termination on her lease.

Kearns had sent two letters of complaint to the manager of her apartment complex about the noisy neighbors above her. Her manager also sent her a 30-day notice of termination.

Hill and Kearns filed suit alleging that the actions by their landlords were retaliatory and a violation of Uniform Owner–Resident Relations Act (UORRA). Both property owners won at trial, with the court concluding that they had the right to terminate the leases of Hill and Kearns for their complaints about noise. Hill and Kearns appealed. Should Hill and Kearns win? Why or why not? *Casa Blanca Mobile Home Park v. Hill*, 963 P.2d 542 (N.M. App. 1998). ∎

Duty to Comply with Statutes and Regulations: The Americans with Disabilities Act

In addition to compliance with state and federal statutes already discussed, land-lords must also be in compliance with the Americans with Disabilities Act (ADA) (42 U.S.C. §§ 12181–12189). The ADA requires the removal of "architectural bar-riers in places of public accommodation when those barriers are readily removable." While landlords must comply with the ADA, the act does permit the landlord and tenant to allocate the compliance responsibility under the terms of their lease. In residential leases, the landlord makes the accommodations in the common areas, and the tenant makes his accommodations in his individual dwelling. (See Chapter 10 for more details on commercial properties and the ADA.)

Duty to Comply with Statutes and Regulations: Convicts, Registrants, and Leasing

There is a nationwide program, the Crime-Free Multi-Unit Housing Program, that provides a three-step program for reducing crime in multiunit tenant housing. One step is screening out applicants who have a felony conviction.[5] Because of landlords' liability for the actions of tenants, the consideration of convictions is a necessary step to avoiding liability to tenants for criminal activity by someone whose history would have been a relevant consideration prior to leasing. However, if a tenant has an ADA mental disability, eviction for an assault is more compli-cated and requires the landlord to look at reasonable accommodation (*Boston Housing Authority v. Bridgewaters,* 898 N.E.2d 848 (Mass. 2009)). A second step is evicting those who are convicted while residing there. Known as civil collateral sanctions, the effects of a conviction can be far-reaching because of the duties imposed on landlords and the rights of tenants.

The third step in the crime-free program involves employing readily available resources for crime prevention such as tenant involvement, security, and partner-ships with local law enforcement agencies. While landlords cannot refuse to lease to convicts and sex offenders, tenants do have rights when registered sex offenders move into their complexes.[6]

The federal government has addressed the issue of crime by tenants with its public housing guidelines. The Department of Housing and Urban Development follows a policy called "One Strike and You're Out Screening and Eviction Guide-lines for Public Housing Authorities," under which public housing authorities must screen and evict tenants for drug related or "safety threatening" behavior. A drug conviction precludes an applicant from obtaining Section 8 housing. Public hous-ing authorities that receive federal funds must include a lease clause that requires automatic lease termination for any drug or violent criminal activity, even if the activity does not occur on the landlord's property. The following case is a land-mark one that deals with such regulations.

---

[5]*Conviction* is a key term, as opposed to *arrest.* In fact, several states have passed or are considering leg-islation that would seal information on arrests that do not result in a conviction.

[6]For a full discussion of balancing the safety interests versus the rights of convicted felons, see "Council on Crime & Justice, A Balanced Approach Toward Public Accessibility to Arrest Records Not Leading to Conviction" (unpublished legislation, Mar. 2007), available at http://www.pepp.org/new/tan/brief.pdf.

DEPARTMENT OF HOUSING AND URBAN DEVELOPMENT V. RUCKER

535 U.S. 125 (2002)
Eviction Because the Kids and Grandkids Have Marijuana and Cocaine

FACTS

Several young men who are grandsons of William Lee and Barbara Hill (respondents), both of whom were residents on the leases of Oakland Housing Authority (OHA), were caught in the apartment complex parking lot smoking marijuana. The daughter of Pearlie Rucker, who resides with her and is listed on the OHA lease as a resident, was found with cocaine and a crack cocaine pipe three blocks from Rucker's apartment. On three instances within a two-month period, Herman Walker's caregiver and two others were found with cocaine in Walker's apartment. OHA had issued Walker notices of a lease violation on the first two occasions, before initiating the eviction action after the third violation.

After OHA initiated the eviction proceedings in state court against the Hills, Rucker, and Walker, they commenced actions against HUD, OHA, and OHA's director in U.S. District Court, challenging HUD's interpretation of the statute and arguing that the federal statute and HUD regulations do not require lease terms authorizing the eviction of so-called innocent tenants, and, in the alternative, that if it does, then the statute is unconstitutional.

The District Court issued a preliminary injunction, enjoining OHA from terminating the leases of tenants. A panel of the Court of Appeals reversed, holding that HUD regulations and the statutory authority under 42 U.S.C. § 1437d(l)(6) unambiguously permit the eviction of tenants who violate the lease provision, regardless of whether the tenant was personally aware of the drug activity, and that the statute is constitutional. An *en banc* panel of the Court of Appeals reversed and affirmed the District Court's grant of the preliminary injunction. The U.S. Supreme Court granted *certiorari*.

JUDICIAL OPINION

Rehnquist, Chief Justice

... [4]2 U.S.C. §1437d(l)(6) unambiguously requires lease terms that vest local public housing authorities with the discretion to evict tenants for the drug-related activity of household members and guests whether or not the tenant knew, or should have known, about the activity.

That this is so seems evident from the plain language of the statute. It provides that "[e]ach public

housing agency shall utilize leases which ... provide that ... any drug-related criminal activity on or off such premises, engaged in by a public housing tenant, any member of the tenant's household, or any guest or other person under the tenant's control, shall be cause for termination of tenancy."

Regardless of knowledge, a tenant who "cannot control drug crime, or other criminal activities by a household member which threaten health or safety of other residents, is a threat to other residents and the project." 56 Fed. Reg., at 51567. With drugs leading to "murders, muggings, and other forms of violence against tenants," and to the "deterioration of the physical environment that requires substantial government expenditures," 42 U.S.C. §11901(4) (1994 ed., Supp. V), it was reasonable for Congress to permit no-fault evictions in order to "provide public and other federally assisted low-income housing that is decent, safe, and free from illegal drugs."

There are, moreover, no "serious constitutional doubts" about Congress affording local public housing authorities the discretion to conduct no-fault evictions for drug-related crime. The Court of Appeals sought to bolster its discussion of constitutional doubt by pointing to the fact that respondents have a property interest in their leasehold interest, citing *Greene v. Lindsey*, 456 U.S. 444, 102 S.Ct. 1874, 72 L.Ed.2d 249 (1982). This is undoubtedly true, and *Greene* held that an effort to deprive a tenant of such a right without proper notice violated the Due Process Clause of the Fourteenth Amendment. But, in the present cases, such deprivation will occur in the state court where OHA brought the unlawful detainer action against respondents. There is no indication that notice has not been given by OHA in the past, or that it will not be given in the future. Any individual factual disputes about whether the lease provision was actually violated can, of course, be resolved in these proceedings.

CASE QUESTIONS

1. Who was evicted and why?
2. Name the two bases for the challenges to the eviction.
3. What did the Supreme Court decide and why?

CONSIDER 9.9   Lakiasha Harris leased a Section 8 subsidized housing unit in an apartment complex in Cleveland, Ohio. Harris's lease requires Harris to "insure [*sic*] that Resident, household members, family members, guests or other persons, under the residents [*sic*] control, shall not engage in any drug related criminal activity ON or OFF C.M.H.A. premises."

On June 16, 2006, Cuyahoga Metropolitan Housing Authority (CMHA) police came to Harris's apartment to arrest a guest of Harris, Kevin Daniels, on a federal warrant. CMHA police searched Daniels and found a rock of crack cocaine in his pocket. CMHA conducted an inspection of Harris's apartment and found no drugs or drug paraphernalia. Harris testified that she was unaware that Daniels had the cocaine in his possession, and Harris did not interfere with Daniels's arrest.

CMHA began eviction proceedings against Harris based upon violation of her lease: that Harris failed to ensure that her guest did not engage in drug-related criminal activity. Can Harris be evicted? *Cuyahoga Metro. Housing Auth. v. Harris,* 2006 WL 3859205 (Ohio Mun. Ct. 2006).

Liability to Third Parties

In addition to the tenants, other parties may enter the common areas of leased property or the dwelling units of tenants. For injuries occurring to third parties in the common areas, the landlord is liable in the same way as with tenants—that is, landlords are expected to exercise reasonable care in the maintenance of common areas.

The landlord's liability for injury to third parties while the third parties are actually in a dwelling unit varies according to the terms of the lease agreement. If the landlord has accepted the burden of repair and upkeep but fails to meet that burden, then resulting injuries to third parties are the responsibility of the landlord. On the other hand, if the tenant has undertaken the responsibility of repair and upkeep, then such injuries to third parties are the responsibility of the tenant.

Sometimes both the landlord and the tenant are liable. For example, in a case where the landlord is responsible for maintenance and a nonremedied problem exists (such as a loose step), the tenant must warn third parties of the problem until the landlord has the chance to repair. If the tenant fails to warn visitors of the problem during the interim, both landlord and tenant could be held liable.

If the leased premises have code violations, the landlord is responsible for injuries to third parties resulting from such violations. Furthermore, even if the landlord has no statutory or contractual duty to repair, it is his or her responsibility to warn the tenant of any hidden defects and to post notices for third parties who might enter the property.

Today, as noted earlier, landlords may have liability for the failure to provide adequate security or to screen those entering their property.

Use of Exculpatory Clauses

To attempt to avoid liability to both tenants and third parties, landlords frequently include exculpatory or hold-harmless clauses in leases. These clauses provide that the landlord will not be liable for any injuries or damages occurring on the premises because of the landlord's negligence or the negligence of any other parties. Although these clauses can be found in many lease agreements, their legal effect is minimal. In other words, landlords cannot by provisions in agreements hold themselves harmless for injuries caused by their failure to maintain the premises or to comply with building and safety codes. The courts have interpreted such clauses, at least in residential leases, to be unconscionable and unenforceable, or in some decisions, void. Some states have enacted specific statutes that prohibit exculpatory clauses, and in states that have adopted the URLTA, the section on unconscionability has been used to invalidate exculpatory clauses. The following is an example of an exculpatory clause in a residential lease:

> *Lessor and his Agent shall not be liable for any damage or inconvenience to either person or property, that may be sustained by Lessee, his family, invitees, licensees, or guests on or about the premises herein leased, including damage or inconvenience resulting from breakdown or delays.*

Landlords may take two precautions to help reduce their potential liability for injuries caused to tenants and to visiting third parties. The first precaution is for landlords to obtain adequate insurance. The second is to use leases that specify who is responsible for repair and maintenance. A repair and maintenance clause may alleviate the effect of repair and deduct actions by tenants and may also serve to determine who is liable in the event disrepair causes an injury to a third party.

Rights of Landlords and Responsibilities of Tenants

Landlords have several basic rights under the lease agreement that, in turn, constitute the tenants' responsibilities under the agreement. The purpose of leasing property is to have the property produce income; the right of landlords to receive timely rental payments pursuant to the terms of the lease agreement is fundamental.

Tenants have an obligation to make timely rental payments according to the method and place of payment specified by the landlord. If a tenant does not make timely payment, there has been a breach of the lease agreement, and the landlord is permitted to take steps to minimize damages. Under URLTA Section 4.201, the landlord must give the tenant a written notice of nonpayment that states that the lease terminates within a specified period after receipt of the notice if rent is not paid. Although some states have changed the time constraints, the URLTA specifies that if rent is not received within 14 days from the time the tenant receives the notice of nonpayment, the lease will terminate within 30 days from receipt of the notice.

Most states provide specific procedures for having nonpaying tenants evicted from leased premises. Two names for this procedure are **forcible detainer** and **action for dispossession**. A distinct feature of these specialized procedures is that the defenses a tenant may assert are limited, so the landlord is not kept in litigation for long periods while the tenant remains in possession of the property. For example, tenants may assert reasons for nonpayment that are justified under their states' landlord–tenant acts. Under the URLTA, defenses to nonpayment of rent are the landlord's failure to supply heat or water or the tenant's exercise of the right to repair and deduct for maintaining habitability of the premises. However, the right of asserting these defenses for nonpayment is limited to states that have recognized the right of habitability as being interrelated with the payment of rent and the existence of a valid lease agreement. In states not recognizing the doctrine of habitability, uninhabitability is not a defense to a landlord's action for possession.

In seeking to evict a tenant for nonpayment of rent, landlords must be able to establish that they have not waived their rights to timely payment. That is, if they have waited until the eighth day of the month for rent due on the first and have accepted the late payment, they will be bound by the delay period in the future unless they serve tenants with formal notice of the intent to exercise the right to timely payment.

In some states, landlords are afforded other remedies for nonpayment of rent. For example, suppose a tenant abandons the premises and leaves personal property. Some states give the landlord a lien, an interest, or a right to possession of that personal property. Although some landlords attempt the private remedy of changing locks for a truly short dispossession action, the courts have invalidated such conduct on the grounds that the tenant has been denied due process.

In some cases, a tenant stops paying rent upon vacating the premises prior to the expiration of the lease term. The landlord has possession of the premises but no tenant to produce rental income. In these circumstances, the landlord has a right of action for breach of contract against the tenant to collect the lost rents and associated expenses of the property sitting vacant. However, most states do require the landlord to mitigate damages, which means that if it is possible, the landlord must rent the premises and recover from the tenant only for the period during which the apartment was vacant.

Nonpayment of rent is the typical reason for a landlord's action for dispossession, but any breach of the rental agreement by the tenant may result in a termination notice and dispossession action by the landlord. Examples of other breaches include breaking the rules and regulations, failing to maintain the premises according to the lease agreement, and performing illegal activities on the premises.

Tenants are also under obligation to use the landlord's property in such a way that is not destructive of its future value. In the absence of express agreement or permission, tenants cannot destroy vegetation, reconstruct buildings, or destroy existing structures. A tenant's basic right is use without change or destruction. The parties to the lease should agree in advance on the addition of fixtures and what will happen to the fixtures at the end of the lease term, so that their placement or removal is not interpreted to be a waste of the landlord's property.

CONSIDER 9.10   Richard Taylor was a resident of a Kenai low-income housing project known as the Gill Street Apartments and owned by Gill Street Investments. Taylor's apartment badly needed cleaning and exuded a bad odor about which the neighbors complained. Taylor admitted that he left his drapes open and walked around his apartment nude, and his apartment was located near the children's play area in the complex. Taylor was known to sit in his car for extended periods of time and honk his car horn if someone had parked in his parking space, and would continue honking until the car in his place was moved. Taylor was frequently drunk and frightened children when he was intoxicated. Taylor was current in his rent, but Gill Street Investments served him with an eviction notice. Could Taylor be evicted? *Taylor v. Gill Street Investments,* 743 P.2d 345 (Alaska 1987).

CAUTIONS AND CONCLUSIONS

In negotiating a lease, the following factors should be provided for, or at least considered:

1. What is the lease term? Must the lease be in writing? (Usually, leases for longer than one year must be in writing.)
2. When the lease expires, is there an option to renew? Can a month-to-month tenancy then exist?
3. How much notice, if any, is required for termination by both the landlord and the tenant?
4. Are there provisions for attorneys' fees? Does the tenant waive any legal rights?
5. Are pets and children permitted?
6. Are there rules and regulations on noise, pool use, and so on?

7. Is there an exculpatory clause? If so, what is its effect?
8. Who is responsible for maintenance in the dwelling unit and in the common areas?
9. What provision is made for fixture placement and removal?
10. Are assignments and subleases permitted?
11. When may the landlord enter the tenant's dwelling unit without permission?
12. How much is required in deposits? What is the purpose of each deposit? Are deposits refundable?
13. How are utilities paid?
14. Is there a warranty of habitability? Do any items need repair or replacement prior to the beginning of the lease term?
15. Are there late penalties for rental payments?

Although this list does not include all areas that should be covered in the lease, it serves as a checklist for the areas causing both landlords and tenants the most problems and the most litigation.

KEY TERMS

action for dispossession, 205
assignments, 194
cleaning deposit, 187
constructive eviction, 196
forcible detainer, 205
implied warranty of habitability, 181

periodic tenancy, 178
rent controls, 190
repair and deduct, 197
Rule in Dumpor's Case, 194
security deposit, 186
self-help, 197

subleases, 194
tenancy at sufferance, 179
tenancy at will, 178
tenancy for years, 178
Uniform Residential Landlord
    Tenant Act (URLTA), 177

CHAPTER PROBLEMS

1. Louis Varnado, a four-year-old child, sustained serious bodily burns from boiling water being carried in a pot by his grandmother from the kitchen to the bathtub of their apartment. The hot water in the apartment complex did not function and the landlord had not repaired the defective water heater despite complaints from the tenants. As a result, the tenants boiled water in their kitchens and carried it to their bathrooms in order to enjoy warm baths and basin water. Andrea Varnado brought suit against the landlord for her son's injuries, which she says were caused by his failure to repair the water heater. Do you agree? Would you hold the landlord liable? *Bennett M. Lifter, Inc. v. Varnado,* 480 So.2d 1336 (Fla. 1985).

2. Garcia lived in a tenement house in the East Harlem section of Manhattan with his two young children. The paint in one of the rooms and in the bathroom was flaking off the walls, and Garcia's children were eating the paint and the flakes. In spite of Garcia's several complaints, the landlord did not remedy the problem. Garcia then expended $29.53 for materials and $70 for labor to replaster and repaint the walls in the rooms. He brought suit for the recovery of these amounts from his landlord. Could he recover these amounts from his landlord? *Garcia v. Freeland Realty, Inc.,* 314 N.Y.S.2d 215 (1972).

3. Diane LaBorde moved into St. James Place Apartments with her two minor children in 1996. The apartment complex consisted of multiple apartment buildings with a common area between the buildings, which was grassy and wooded. The common area contained tree roots and "quite a few" sawed-off tree stumps, which protruded a few inches from holes in the ground. The same year they moved in, LaBorde's daughter told her that she had tripped and fallen in the common area due to a stump sticking out of a hole in the ground. LaBorde complained about the stump to the apartment complex's on-site manager, Margaret Kern, and assumed that it would be taken care of.

On May 27, 1999, LaBorde discovered a cat tearing into garbage bags on her porch. She had had problems with cats getting into her garbage in the past and became angry. She began chasing the cat through the common area in the hopes that it would leave her garbage alone in the future. While running after the cat, LaBorde's foot hit a stump protruding from a hole in the ground and she fell, injuring her left ankle. LaBorde crawled back to her apartment and called Kern, who took her to the hospital. LaBorde was diagnosed with a sprained ankle. LaBorde filed suit against St. James Place Apartments, its owner, Money Hill Plantation, and their insurer, United National Group Insurance Company. The parties stipulated that LaBorde had $50,000 in damages, but they disagreed on liability. Are any of these parties liable for LaBorde's injury and damages? *Laborde v. St. James Place Apartments,* 928 So.2d 643 (La. App. 2006).

4. Mary Weatherall was a tenant in the Yorktown Townhome complex. She fell on the ice and snow accumulated outside her leased apartment and fractured

her ankle. Can she recover from the landlord for her injury and the landlord's failure to maintain the premises? *Weatherall v. Yorktown Homeowner's Assn.,* 852 P.2d 815 (Okl. 1991).

5. Diana Washington was a tenant in the Related Arbor Court apartment complex. The rules of the complex, given to all tenants at the time they sign their leases, required tenants to maintain utility service to their apartments and also to have their apartments pass periodic health and safety inspections. Ms. Washington did not maintain utility service and, as a result, her apartment did not pass its periodic health and safety inspection. The landlord took steps to have her evicted from the apartment. Ms. Washington defended the forcible detainer action on the grounds that she could not be evicted without notice of these violations. Was notice of the lack of utility service required? Is it possible for a landlord to evict a tenant for rules violations? *Washington v. Related Arbor Court, LLC,* 357 S.W.3d 676 (Tex. App. 2011).

6. Francine M. Fletcher and Michael G. Vazquez were tenants in the house in Scituate, Massachusetts, owned by Stephen F. Littleton. Their children, Paul and Stephen Fletcher, Maria and Dominique Vazquez, and Kristin Lynch, lived in the house with them. On April 4, 1995, while Francine and Michael were out to dinner and the children were at home with a babysitter, a fire broke out inside the living room wall. Maria, Paul, and Stephen were killed in the fire, and Dominique and Kristin were injured. The babysitter was not in any way responsible for the deaths or injuries.

The house, which was built prior to the 1930s, was purchased by Littleton's grandparents in the 1950s, and was later owned by Littleton's parents. They used the house as a summer vacation home until 1977, when they converted it to year-round use. Littleton inherited the house from his parents after their deaths in 1987 and 1988.

When Littleton's parents winterized the house in 1977, they had the walls filled with spray-in insulation but did not change the original wiring. That wiring was of the knob-and-tube variety, commonly used at the time the house was constructed and still frequently in use, but no longer allowed to be used in repairs or new installations. Knob-and-tube wiring creates considerable heat, and the presence of spray-in insulation can prevent the ventilation of that heat and increase the risk of fire. Littleton was not aware of the type of wiring in use in the house, of the presence of the spray-in insulation, or of the potential risk posed by the combination of the wiring and the insulation.

Fletcher and others brought suit against Littleton for wrongful death damages for Littleton's breach of the implied warranty of habitability. Fletcher argued that there was a code violation as well as a failure of Littleton to keep the property in a safe and sanitary condition, and that both were grounds for breach of the implied warranty of merchantability. Littleton defended on the grounds that he was not aware of the wiring and insulation problem. Who is correct? How should the court decide the case and why? *Fletcher v. Littleton,* 859 N.E.2d 882 (Mass. App. 2007).

7. Ella terminated her six-month lease agreement at the end of three months by abandoning her apartment. Her monthly rent was $800. Although the landlord had several opportunities to rent the apartment, he refused, stating, "Why hassle with another tenant when I can sue and collect the $2,400 from Ella?" Is the landlord correct in his assumption?

8. Paul Salmonte leased Richard and Mildred Eilertson's Florida home in 1985. The Eilertsons lived in Houston, Texas, but sometimes returned to inspect the house. The Eilertsons also had an exterminator go to the home on a monthly basis. By May 1986, Salmonte decided that the inspections and extermination were occurring too often and began refusing regular access. The Eilertsons discovered that Salmonte had breached the terms of the lease agreement that prohibited changes in carpeting, wallpaper, and locks, and then went to inspect the home and pets. The Eilertsons noticed that one of their rugs had been moved to the garage and had a car parked on it. They then filed a complaint for eviction for breach of the lease agreement. Could the Eilertsons have Salmonte evicted for violations of the rules? *Salmonte v. Eilertson,* 526 So.2d 179 (Ct. App. Fla. 1988).

9. Adam Armstrong rented Apartment 103-A, located at 441 Kanekapolei Street in Honolulu, from Jack Cione. The apartment was originally part of a two-bedroom unit within a cooperative building called the Waikiki Regent, which was constructed in 1959 and contained nine identical units.

On April 12, 1982, Armstrong's right hand and wrist were injured when a glass panel in the apartment's shower door shattered as he attempted to close it. The shower door was installed when the apartment was originally built and was constructed of three glass panels with hinged aluminum frames on an aluminum track. Safety glass was not used.

Cione says he was unaware of a crack in the door and Armstrong knew the door was difficult to close but never complained to Cione about the problem. Is this a breach of the warranty of habitability? *Armstrong v. Cione,* 736 P.2d 440 (Haw. 1987).

10. Margaret Skinner owned two adjacent parcels of land. She lived on one and leased the other to Bud

Wellington on a month-to-month basis. The Bradys lived on the other side of Wellington. Skinner gave Wellington permission to keep two mules on the property. One was named Martin Luther and the other was named King. King acted like a typical, ornery mule. Basically he did not like anyone and would put his ears back and shy away when anyone got close to him. On the other hand, Martin Luther acted more like a horse than a mule. He was playful and friendly. The mules were docile and neither had ever kicked, bitten, or tried to injure anyone. They were no more dangerous than any other mules, but like other mules, they were unpredictable.

One day Arthur Brady, Jr., who was four years old at the time, was kicked by one of the mules. No one seems to know which mule kicked him. The Bradys filed suit. Is Skinner liable? *Brady v. Skinner*, 646 P.2d 310 (Az. 1982).

For research activities related to this chapter, go to our text companion website at www.cengagebrain.com

CHAPTER 10

COMMERCIAL LEASES

On December 31, 1759, Arthur Guinness signed a lease for the facilities for the St. James Brewery, an unused set of commercial buildings in Dublin, Ireland. The lease was to run for up to 9,000 years for an annual rent of £45. The Guinness Brewery has sold a great deal of beer but paid a total of £11,250 in rent in 250 years since the lease was signed, or about $17,100.

Not everyone can be as lucky as Arthur Guinness when securing a commercial lease, for they are indeed complex beasts. From office space in the Empire State Building to the neighborhood shopping center, commercial leases are also different from residential leases. The statutory provisions and protections discussed in Chapter 9 for residential leases do not carry over to commercial leases. Many states continue to rely primarily on case law for their commercial lease law, interpretation, and protections. While there is a Uniform Commercial Landlord and Tenant Act (UCLTA), it has not been adopted *in toto* by any states.[1] This chapter addresses the following questions: What are the requirements for the formation of a commercial lease? What topics and issues should a commercial lease address? What facts and information should be studied before entering into a commercial lease?

FORMATION OF THE COMMERCIAL LEASE

Negotiations

Commercial leases have additional issues that are often contingent upon business conditions, timely completion of construction, and terms in agreements with other tenants. Potential commercial tenants need complete and accurate information, because good neighbors are perhaps more important in commercial than residential leases. Who are the other tenants? What is the rental amount? How are the other tenants doing in their businesses? In the negotiation stage, the rules for

---

[1]Uniform Commercial Landlord & Tenant Act, 7B U.L.A. 527 (2000).

PRACTICAL TIP

Landlords need to use caution in making oral statements and promises to potential tenants. Tenants need to be careful about relying on landlords' statements and should always check their leases for clauses that apply to representations.

contract formation on misrepresentation and fraud apply. However, relying on leasing agents and landlords for information is risky. In commercial lease negotiations, lessees need independent verification of information such as revenue, customer traffic, net profits, costs, and any other financial information related to the operation of the business. Courts are reluctant to provide relief to tenants who rely on landlords' or their agents' representations about the revenue potential for leased properties.[2]

In addition, most commercial leases include exculpatory clauses that hold landlords not liable for property conditions, issues, and representations on the commercial potential of the leased property. However, when the landlord or landlord's agent has engaged in misrepresentation or fraud in negotiations, the courts have been willing to impose liability even when there is an exculpatory clause. The *Puro v. Neil Enterprises, Inc.* case involves this issue of landlord liability.

PURO V. NEIL ENTERPRISES, INC.

987 A.2d 935 (Vt. 2009)
The Great Antique Rip-Off—After Hours

FACTS

Neil Enterprises (defendant) leases display booths in the Antiques Mall at Quechee Gorge Village (the Mall). Timothy Puro and Steven Yoken are tenants who leased booths at the mall (plaintiffs), The Mall has about 450 booths. Mr. Puro leased a display booth in 2005 to sell coins and currency. Mr. Yoken leased a display booth in 2002 to sell high-end custom jewelry. After closing on September 7, 2005, thieves broke into the Mall through the rear door and quickly stole jewelry and coins from the display booths. The alarm sounded and the security company notified the police. By the time police arrived, the thieves had fled. The Mall contains security cameras, some of which were attached to video recorders, but the images of the thieves were not recorded because the cameras were not operating at the time. The stolen merchandise was never recovered. Mr. Puro lost goods valued at $25,293; Mr. Yoken lost goods valued at $31,698.

Messrs. Yoken and Puro filed suit against Neil alleging negligence and that they were fraudulently induced to lease the display booths by the Mall owner's misrepresentation of the Mall's security system and practices. Neil argued that an exculpatory clause in its agreement with the two tenants, which both signed, precluded any recovery. The clause provides:

shareholders, directors, officers, agents, employees, and staff shall not be held liable for any damages to or loss of property from any cause whatsoever, including but not limited to fire or theft, it being understood that to the extent desired and at [the dealer's] option, that this property shall be insured by the undersigned dealer/licensee.

However, before each of them signed their leases, they discussed security issues with the mall's general manager. The general manager said that the mall had "video cameras everywhere" and that he lived "within minutes of [the Mall], and if anything ever happened [he] would be there first." The manager also stated that the Mall had an alarm system, infrared sensors, and cameras covering every booth at all times. He also described the alarm system as "state-of-the-art."

At the time they signed their leases, the two tenants also received a copy of the "Quechee Gorge Village Dealer Handbook." In a section headed "Security," the handbook included the following:

The Antique Mall is equipped with cameras and customer service personnel who watch over your merchandise. In addition, all dealers, while stocking their booths, are asked to report any suspicious activity to the manager. The building is

---

[2]Allen Blair, "A Matter of Trust: Should No Reliance Clauses Bar Claims for Fraudulent Inducement of Contracts?," 92 *Marquette Law Rev.* 423 (2009).

secured by an alarm system with a direct link to the central office. All doors are alarmed as well as infrared motion detectors in strategic areas. The entire building is covered by a sprinkler system in case of fire. All keys for locks are accounted for on a daily basis. They are signed out and in each business day.

However, the handbook also included the following clause:

"[d]ealers are responsible for their own lost or damaged merchandise. This does happen, and we encourage our dealers to get insurance for the items in their booths."

Neither tenant had obtained insurance for his merchandise.

The superior court granted Neil summary judgment. The tenants appealed.

JUDICIAL OPINION

Per Curiam

Central to this case are defendant's representations to plaintiffs about the presence of security at the Mall. Both plaintiffs received information about the Mall's security system from at least three sources on which they might have relied, in addition to any observations they may have made themselves. First, each spoke with the Mall's general manager, who was in charge of security. Second, each signed an agreement including the exculpatory clause. Third, each received a handbook with information on the Mall's security practices at the time each signed the agreement.

The Mall did, in fact, have security cameras and an alarm system, although plaintiffs argue that important information about the Mall's security was either misrepresented or omitted. Three black and white cameras on the ground floor recorded onto a VCR, but during business hours only. The video footage was retained for seven days, but not routinely reviewed. As they were available, mall staff monitored a rotation of live images from these cameras at the checkout-counter. They additionally monitored unrecorded images from sixteen other cameras that were displayed at the checkout-counter on a screen divided to show views from four cameras at once. The Mall also used nonfunctioning dummy cameras as a theft deterrent. The Mall's exterior was not monitored by cameras.

Along with the cameras, the Mall had an alarm system administered by a security company with infrared motion sensors and sensors on all of the doors. When triggered, the alarm alerted the security company directly, which contacted defendant's security man-

ager and then the police. A loud on-site siren would also sound. There was no signage to indicate the existence of this alarm.

Plaintiffs' first argument on appeal is that the exculpatory clause is invalid as against public policy and cannot bar any of the counts of their action. Plaintiffs present an argument based on the various factors we have used primarily in consumer transactions in evaluating the validity of exculpatory clauses. As the trial court found, however, the parties in this case are business persons with relatively equal bargaining power and were using the clause to determine which party would bear the cost of necessary insurance. We agree with the trial court that the relevant precedent is *Fairchild Square Co. v. Green Mountain Bagel Bakery, Inc.,* 163 Vt. 433, 437, 658 A.2d 31, 33 (1995), where we upheld an exculpatory clause covering fire or casualty loss between a landlord and a commercial tenant. We note additionally that exculpatory clauses relating to security services are routine in business agreements and are virtually unanimously upheld by the courts. We reject plaintiffs' argument that the exculpatory clause is invalid.

We agree with plaintiffs, however, that the exculpatory clause does not bar the fraud, negligent misrepresentation, or consumer fraud counts.

We have not addressed whether an exculpatory clause defeats a claim of fraud in the inducement. We have, however, considered whether a contract for sale of a house, which included a clause that no representation had been made as to the "condition" of the house, would defeat a claim of negligent misrepresentation with respect to the condition of the house. Relying upon decisions from numerous jurisdictions, we held that the "as-is" clause did not defeat the negligent misrepresentation claim.

Whether we view the issue as one of fair construction of the exculpatory clause or implementation of a policy that denies a party the benefit of a fraudulent act, we conclude that the result here is [that] the exculpatory clause does not defeat the fraud or negligent misrepresentation claim.

The decisions from other jurisdictions uniformly support this result, at least as to fraud claims.

Reversed and remanded.

CASE QUESTIONS

1. How effective is an exculpatory clause in a commercial lease? Discuss when it is limited.
2. Make a list of the precautions tenants should take in negotiations as well as in their operations based on what happened that led to this litigation as well as the result.

ETHICAL ISSUE

Suppose that the landlord or the landlord's agent does make some statement about the rental property such as, "This is an ideal location that really brings in the pedestrian traffic," and "The previous tenant did so well on her grosses here." Can a potential tenant rely on these statements? Is there any legal liability for these statements? What ethical responsibilities do landlords and their agents have in discussing income potential on commercial properties with their tenants?

CONSIDER 10.1 Cheung–Loon owns a commercial building in Dallas located at 3317 McKinney Avenue and a parking lot located at 3321 McKinney Avenue. In 2006, Cheung–Loon and Cergon, Inc. d/b/a Primo's Bar and Grille entered into a lease agreement under which Primo's agreed to pay a monthly rental fee for use of the parking lot. Primo's owner said he was told that Primo's would have exclusive use of the parking lot for its customers.

Cheung–Loon began leasing space in its building at 3317 McKinney Avenue to a tenant named Dear Clark. According to Primo's, the employees and patrons of Dear Clark began using the parking spaces in the lot at 3321 McKinney Avenue to such an extent that Primo's customers were excluded from most, if not all, of the lot. Primo's gave notice of a breach of the lease agreement, which did not reference an "exclusive" right to the parking lot. Was there a breach of the lease agreement? How do the oral representations affect your answer to this question? *Cheung–Loon, LLC v. Cergon, Inc.,* --- S.W.3d ----, 2012 WL 1678105 (Tex. App. 2012).

PRACTICAL TIP

Due diligence, or the examination of all aspects of a transaction, is as necessary in commercial leasing as it is in sales of land. Lessees should verify the accuracy of square footage, sales, and income claims. They should look into demographics and planned changes in the area that might affect the sales base. Reliance on rental agents' and landlords' information is misplaced.

The Lease Agreement

As odd as it may seem, many commercial tenants are operating under oral lease agreements. Generally, the statute of frauds requirement for commercial leases takes effect when leases run for more than six months (in some states) or one year (in most states). However, a month-to-month commercial lease would not be covered by the statute even though the lease may run on for years. Regardless of statute of frauds provisions, all commercial tenants should have their lease agreements evidenced by some record. Reliance on oral representations and understandings can be risky because recollections and understandings of oral promises can be fuzzy. See Web Exhibit 10.1 for a sample commercial lease.

TOPICS IN THE COMMERCIAL LEASE

A successful commercial landlord–tenant relationship requires careful attention to details in the lease negotiations and in the lease itself. This section covers the typical provisions in a commercial lease.

The Lease Term

Commercial leases carry peculiarities in terms of start or beginning dates that residential leases will not have. For example, many commercial properties already have tenants with lease agreements before the property is constructed. In the

Phoenix area, a developer who had taken on the responsibility of revitalizing the downtown area had commitments from businesses to be tenants in buildings that were to be constructed based on those commitments. The lease agreements existed before the buildings existed. Such arrangements are also typical with shopping centers and malls. The developer obtains commitments from large or anchor tenants prior to construction of the center or the mall, and the remaining tenants sign on for the yet-to-be-constructed stores on the basis of the anchor tenant's commitment.

In these types of leases, the start date of the leases is tied to completion of construction. However, completion of construction can change as the project progresses. Tenants should have protections for these fluctuations because of resulting problems with planning and inventory holdings. Tenants in malls and shopping centers will want start dates around seasonal swings to avoid opening a business or moving a business to a new location during a slow period in the sales year. For example, retail outlets have highest sales from October through January, so commencing a lease in October would be a profit maximizer. On the other hand, commencing a lease in February begins an obligation during a slow period, with a long wait for increased sales. Relocating a business during peak sales periods hurts the business.

Another beginning-date issue is whether the tenant is allowed to move in before actual completion of the unit or the common areas and, if so, when rent will become due. Because of the uncertainty involved, it is probably best for the parties to put an outside date in the contract: that is, a date by which there must be occupancy or the lease is terminated. With an outside date, the lease provides for contingencies such as noncompletion, bankruptcy, and delays. The developer is not tied to a specific date of completion but has a range, and the tenant has a latest-possible occupancy date for planning purposes. The lease may even provide an option for the tenant to extend the outside date if the date passes and the tenant still desires to continue with the lease.

Premises Condition

The implied warranty of habitability or usability generally does not exist in commercial leases. If a tenant wants a guarantee that the leased premises will be delivered with certain repairs, conditions, or improvements, a warranty for these items must be in the lease agreement. Problems such as faulty heating or air conditioning, leaking roofs, and broken windows should be described in the lease as repairs that are conditions precedent to the tenant's performance under the terms of the lease.

In recent years, the courts have become more helpful to commercial tenants, finding in some instances that the condition of the premises is sufficiently bad to constitute constructive eviction of a commercial tenant.

In addition to the initial condition of the premises, the parties should agree on which party will be responsible for maintenance. The landlord may want to specify that the obligation to repair does not arise until the tenant brings the condition of disrepair to the landlord's attention through a written notice. Some obligations of repair may be imposed upon the tenant, such as keeping trade fixtures in good working condition. For example, many tenants have electronic signs outside their businesses; the obligation of repair and upkeep of those signs belongs with the tenants.

The parties may also wish to make a provision for emergency repairs—an authorization for immediate work in circumstances where the parties are unable to contact each other and the repair is absolutely necessary. Water leaks are an example wherein immediate action may save later costs and damage, and an emergency repair by either party without the other's approval can save money for both. The following case is one of a growing number of decisions affording commercial tenants rights on repairs and habitability.[3]

RICHARD BARTON ENTERPRISES, INC. V. TSERN

928 P.2d 368 (Utah 1996)
When the Elevator Stays Flat: Tenant's Rights

FACTS

On November 21, 1991, Barton and Tsern entered into a lease for the first and second floors of a commercial building in downtown Salt Lake City. Barton agreed to pay rent at the rate of $3,000 per month for the one-year lease. The lease required Tsern to deliver possession of the premises to Barton on December 1, 1991.

Added to the terms of the printed earnest money form were the typed words, "Other than stated in lines 32 and 33, Tenant shall accept the building in 'As Is' condition." The language on lines 32 and 33 required Tsern to repair the building's leaky roof and the freight elevator to "good working order."

Barton's purpose in leasing the building was to establish an antiques dealership. The business inventory included large architectural pieces that, because of the dropped ceiling of the main floor and other limitations, had to be stored on the second floor. For that reason Barton required a freight elevator to transport the large, heavy pieces to the second floor. Barton's need for the elevator was communicated to Tsern repeatedly, both prior to signing the earnest money agreement, when Barton became aware that the elevator was inoperable, and after the lease was executed and Barton took occupancy of the leased premises.

Barton took possession of the ground floor on December 1, 1991, but could not obtain possession of the second floor until December 20, when a holdover tenant finally vacated the floor. The elevator was wholly inoperable, and Tsern had neither repaired the elevator nor entered into a contract to have it repaired. The elevator remained inoperable until January 9, 1992, when Tsern contracted with Kimball Elevator Coto make repairs to the elevator. On Tsern's instruc-

tions Kimball made only those repairs necessary to make the elevator operational in the sense that it would "go up and down." Tsern strictly limited the amount of money he would pay Kimball for repairs to $5,000 and refused to authorize a number of repairs that Kimball stated were necessary to make the elevator operate reliably and safely. Tsern instructed Kimball not to mention the repair limitations to Barton.

The elevator operated from January 9, 1992, until January 24, 1992, when a city inspector ordered it shut down. After Kimball made an additional repair required by the city inspector on February 13, the elevator again operated until March 14. On April 10, a state elevator inspector found that the elevator was not in compliance with state law, directed Tsern to correct nine violations, and ordered the elevator shut down until it could pass a state safety inspection. Tsern refused to spend the $5,552 to make those repairs. On December 10, 1991, Barton suggested a rent abatement because of the difficulties. Tsern suggested a 50 percent rent abatement, but Barton never accepted his proposal.

Barton paid less than the full rent for the months of January and February, and Tsern cashed the checks but maintained that he was entitled to the full rent of $3,000 for each month. Because the elevator operated during the latter part of January and the early part of February, Barton tendered full rent for February on February 1, minus a minor offset for something unrelated to the elevator. On April 15, 1992, Barton filed suit to establish Tsern's legal duty to repair the elevator. Tsern counterclaimed for rent or removal of Barton.

The trial court found that the elevator had not been repaired to "good working order" as required by the lease, and entered judgment against Tsern for the

---

[3]For a case that held there was no right to reduce rent, see *Matte v. Shippee Auto, Inc.*, 876 A.2d 167 (N.H. 2005), in which the court held that because the statute did not allow for rent deductions in commercial leases, it could not allow the tenant damages for the failure to fix a leaky roof.

cost of repairing the elevator to that standard. The court also ruled that although Barton and Tsern had never agreed on the amount of a rent abatement, Barton was entitled to have the rent abated to $2,000 a month. Finally, the court entered judgment against Tsern for attorney fees in the amount of $100,000. Tsern appealed.

JUDICIAL OPINION
Stewart, Associate Chief Justice

In *Union City Union Suit Co. v. Miller*, 162 A.D.2d 101, 556 N.Y.S.2d 864 (1990), a case remarkably similar to the instant case, a commercial lessor failed to repair, and eventually removed, a freight elevator from a leased building in violation of the lease. The court held that the lessor had constructively evicted the lessee from one floor of the building and that the lessee had no obligation to pay rent for the second floor.

Although the fiction of constructive eviction served the useful purpose of ameliorating the harshness of the rule of independent covenants while continuing to use recognized common law vocabulary and concepts, even the doctrine of constructive eviction had limited capacity to achieve fairness. With the evolution from an agrarian to an urbanized, industrialized society, improvements on the land became relatively more important. Improvements such as houses, apartments, office and commercial buildings, and plants and factories came to have greater value to the lessee than did the land itself. These developments have required courts to reassess the doctrines that underlie and define the legal rights and liabilities of parties to a lease.

In 1985, this Court recognized that certain property law rules that historically governed the leasing of land had become obsolete.

… [T]he reality of modern residential leases is that lessees bargain for the use of the structures, facilities, and services attached to the land rather than the land itself, so that the appurtenances to the land are the more important feature of the lease. We held that a contract concept of implied warranty should be extended to residential leases in the form of an implied warranty of habitability and that the covenant to pay rent was dependent on the lessor's compliance with the implied warranty of habitability.

We find that the principles … in the context of residential leases are equally applicable to the commercial context. In addition, several other states have held that under certain circumstances, commercial lessees may withhold rent. One group of states, which includes Texas and New Jersey, holds that

covenants in commercial leases are mutually dependent. Texas offers the most expansive protection for commercial leases; it extends to commercial lessees all protections available to residential lessees, including an implied warranty of suitability that the leased premises are suitable "for their intended commercial purpose." *Davidow v. Inwood North Professional Group—Phase I*, 747 S.W.2d 373, 377 (Tex. 1988). The court in *Davidow* reasoned that a commercial lessee should have the same protections as those accorded a residential lessee and that contract principles rather than medieval property principles should apply. [T]he New Jersey Supreme Court held that "fair treatment for tenants with respect to latent defects remediable by the landlord … require[s] imposition on [the landlord] of an implied warranty against such defects." *Reste Realty Corp. v. Cooper*, 53 N.J. 444, 251 A.2d 268, 273 (1969).

A second group of states does not recognize implied warranties in commercial leases but nevertheless holds that covenants in commercial leases may be mutually dependent. Massachusetts and Indiana hold that the covenant to pay rent and the covenant to repair may be mutually dependent. Both groups of cases recognize that the covenant to pay rent under a commercial lease is dependent on the lessor's compliance with those covenants necessary to provide the lessee with the benefits that were the essence of the bargain as reflected in the lease. This approach relieves a lessee of the obligation to abandon the premises, as is necessary under the fiction of a constructive eviction. Not all breaches of covenants by a lessor, however, justify a lessee in withholding rent. Only a significant breach of a covenant material to the purpose for which the lease was consummated justifies a lessee in abating rent. Temporary or minor breaches of routine covenants by a lessor do not.

Holding Barton liable for the full amount of rent when a significant part of the leased premises was practicably unusable for the purpose for which the premises were leased would be tantamount to requiring that Barton pay for something he could not use. Tsern knew that an operable elevator was essential to Barton's use of the second floor and that the lack of an operable elevator was not simply a matter of inconvenience. Tsern's promise to repair the elevator was a significant inducement to Barton to enter into the lease. Indeed, on several occasions before the lease was signed, Barton explicitly told Tsern that the business required an operable elevator. The absence of an operable and safe elevator had more than a peripheral effect on Barton's use of the premises; it impaired Barton's ability to conduct its business on the premises. It follows that Tsern was entitled to receive rent equal to the value of the premises without an operable freight elevator.

Affirmed.

CASE QUESTIONS

1. Describe the factual situation that led to the landlord–tenant dispute.

2. What is the significance of mutually dependent covenants in a lease?

3. Is the decision of this court in this case a majority or minority view in the United States with regard to commercial leases?

4. What do you conclude commercial tenants have the right to do in Utah when there are problems with their leased premises?

CONSIDER 10.2   Dr. Joseph Davidow entered into a five-year lease agreement with Inwood for medical office space. The lease required Dr. Davidow to pay Inwood $793.26 per month as rent. The lease also required Inwood to provide air-conditioning, electricity, hot water, janitor and maintenance services, light fixtures, and security services. Shortly after moving into the office space, Dr. Davidow began experiencing problems with the building. The air conditioning did not work properly, often causing temperatures inside the office to rise above 85 degrees. The roof leaked whenever it rained, resulting in stained tiles and rotting, mildewed carpet. Patients were directed away from certain areas during rain so that they would not be dripped upon in the waiting room. Pests and rodents often infested the office. The hallways remained dark because hallway lights were unreplaced for months. Cleaning and maintenance were not provided. The parking lot was constantly filled with trash. Hot water was not provided, and on one occasion Dr. Davidow went without electricity for several days because Inwood failed to pay the electric bill. Several burglaries and various acts of vandalism occurred.

Dr. Davidow finally moved out of the premises and discontinued rent payments approximately 14 months before the lease expired. Inwood sued Dr. Davidow for breach of contract. Could Inwood recover? Does Davidow have any defenses? *Davidow v. Inwood North Professional Group—Phase I,* 747 S.W.2d 373 (Tex. 1988).

One additional complication arises when there are repairs to commercial property: business interruption. During renovation, the tenant may experience an interruption of customer traffic or may lose ease of accessibility because of construction blockage or hazards. The following case deals with this issue of a tenant frustrated by construction interruption of business and the limited common law protection available to these commercial tenants.

BIJAN DESIGNER FOR MEN, INC. V. ST. REGIS SHERATON CORPORATION

536 N.Y.S.2d 951 (1989) aff'd, 543 N.Y.S.2d 296 (1989)
Renovation at the Ritz: No Business for Bijan

FACTS

The St. Regis Hotel (defendant), located at Fifth Avenue and 55th Street in Manhattan, was originally built in 1904. In November 1988, the hotel was designated by the Landmarks Preservation Committee as an official New York City landmark. The committee required

that the hotel's heating, ventilating, air conditioning, electrical, plumbing, and fire safety systems be installed or replaced.

Bijan Designer for Men (plaintiff) leases a two-story retail space situated in the St. Regis. Bijan has its own entrance from Fifth Avenue as well as entrances directly from the hotel's lobby and mezzanine. Bijan sells luxury-quality men's apparel and accessories, by appointment only, to a group it describes as "a distinguished and select domestic and international clientele of extremely well-to-do and renowned patrons." Bijan's lease commenced in 1981 for a period of 16 years. Bijan selected the site in the St. Regis because of the hotel's reputation, clientele, layout, security, and ambiance. Both parties expected Bijan to draw clientele from among the hotel's guests.

On June 30, 1988, the St. Regis was temporarily closed to commence the necessary reconstruction and renovation. The work was planned to take 14 to 18 months. The main doors to the hotel lobby were boarded up and access to the hotel lobby involved entering through a defunct restaurant and being cleared by a security guard.

Upon notification of the closure, Bijan informed the St. Regis that its rent would be paid into an escrow account. The St. Regis demanded payment, and Bijan filed suit to prevent the acceleration of rent.

JUDICIAL OPINION

Saxe, Justice

It is the plaintiff's position that by closing the St. Regis, the landlord rendered useless Bijan's contractually provided-for access to the hotel, resulting in an actual partial eviction of Bijan. An actual eviction, whether partial or complete, suspends in its entirety the tenant's obligation to pay rent.

The Defendant relies on paragraph 14.A of the lease, which permits the lessor to, *inter alia*, "make such decorations, repairs, alterations, improvements or additions as lessor may deem necessary or desirable either to the Hotel or the demised premises" and further on provides that "the rent shall in no way abate while the decorations, repairs, alterations, improvements or additions are being made and Lessor shall not be liable to Lessee by reason of loss or interruption of the business of Lessee because of the prosecution of any such work or otherwise."

For its part, Bijan points out that the very first paragraph of the lease promises the tenant that "[t]he first floor of the premises shall have access to the Hotel's main lobby" and also that "[t]he second floor of the premises shall have access to the Hotel's mezzanine." Its position is that this right of access may not be abrogated by the landlord's right to repair. In addition, the tenant contends that the implied covenant of good faith and fair dealing prohibits the actions taken by the landlord.

These motions confront the court with competing policies. Restoration and renovation of an old landmark building should be welcomed and encouraged, and in fact, here, the landlord attempted to contractually provide for that right. On the other hand, the rights accorded a tenant, such as the negotiated-for right of direct access to the hotel lobby, must be carefully protected from undue interference, particularly where, as here, that right provides a substantial economic benefit to the tenant.

Here, the tenant certainly consented to renovations; it is less clear, however, whether that consent was so broad as to permit its right of access to be subsumed or negated by those alterations or improvements.

More recently, in *Broadway Copy Service, Inc. v. Broad-Wall Co.*, 77 A.D.2d 827, 431 N.Y.S.2d 13, where a landlord painted over the clear glass doors leading from the rear of a tenant's store to the building's lobby, it was held as a matter of law that this act did not constitute an actual partial eviction which would excuse the tenant from paying rent. Noting, however, that painting over the glass door prevented prospective customers from knowing the nature of the tenant's business and potentially deprived the tenant of possible sales, the court indicated that the tenant might have a cause of action for compensatory damages.

It is apparent that a landlord's breach of an express or implied lease term does not necessarily result in an actual eviction, but merely gives rise to a cause of action for damages.

The tenant points to several cases in which a landlord's acts constituted an actual partial eviction. For instance, where a landlord sealed and blocked off a freight elevator which opened directly into tenant's store, it was found that this action constituted an actual partial eviction.

When the facts alleged by the plaintiff are viewed in light of the foregoing cases, it is apparent that the plaintiff's theory of actual eviction cannot be supported. The plaintiff agreed to repairs, alterations or improvements either in the store or in the hotel, and that the landlord would not be liable for loss or interruption of Bijan's business due to such work. If extensive alterations made upon consent *within* the leased premises cannot amount to an eviction, I fail to see how extensive renovations made upon consent *outside* the leased premises can be said to constitute an eviction. Moreover, where the exculpatory clause is so broad, for the court to construe the clause to permit extensive work except where the hotel must be closed to customers would constitute a rewriting of the contract by the court. Furthermore, although sealing off contracted-for access has been held to constitute actual eviction, whereas the defendants point out the plaintiff continues to have access to the lobby and mezzanine, albeit a lobby and mezzanine which are part of a hotel undergoing renovations.

It is apparent that the parties, particularly the tenant, did not contemplate that any building renovation might necessitate a lengthy closing of the hotel. I therefore take the opportunity to note that especially where—as here—the value of the leasehold takes into account the presence of the landlord's clientele, tenants are well advised to provide for the eventuality of temporary closing for renovation, or at least to specify some limits to the exculpatory clause concerning repairs.

In the absence of such a provision, Bijan is left with a situation which may clearly have a negative impact on the value of the leased premises, but which just as clearly does not constitute an actual partial eviction.

This is not to say that a tenant in the plaintiff's position is necessarily without recourse. Notwithstanding the exculpatory clause permitting renovations, a right to compensatory damages may exist if the landlord exceeded the rights granted by the lease, and if its actions constitute a breach of another term of the lease, such as a right of access or an implied covenant of good faith or quiet enjoyment.

There was no partial eviction.

CASE QUESTIONS

1. Describe the layout of Bijan's leased premises.
2. Why was the hotel closed? How long was the closure expected to last?
3. What arguments does Bijan make to justify its nonpayment of rent to St. Regis?
4. What protections should have been drafted into the lease?

Condition of the Premises—The Sick Building Syndrome

When Benjamin Franklin was asked to testify about new legal requirements for building ventilation in the 1700s, he offered the following expertise: "I considered [fresh air] an enemy, and closed with extreme care every crevice in the rooms I inhabited. Experience has convinced me of my error. I now look upon fresh air as a friend: I even sleep with an open window. I am persuaded that no common air from without is so unwholesome as the air within a close[d] room that has been often breathed and not changed."[4] Since that statement, we have evolved from a fear that ventilation in buildings brings in disease to one that perhaps the lack of ventilation creates health problems. To combat the **sick building syndrome (SBS)**, there are increasing health and safety regulations focusing on air in buildings as well as a rising trend in litigation related to health hazards being tied to building conditions. The typical hazards are asbestos, lead paint, mold, and PCBs.*

The World Health Organization lists the following as eight common symptoms of SBS: (1) irritation of the eyes, nose, and throat, (2) dry mucous membranes and skin, (3) erythema (dermatitis erythematosa, redness of the skin, inflammation), (4) mental fatigue and headache, (5) respiratory infections and cough, (6) hoarseness of voice and wheezing, (7) hypersensitivity reactions, and (8) nausea and dizziness.

One possible cause of the change in interior conditions has been the decades-long drive to keep energy costs down, which results in the "sealing" of windows and doors to keep cold air out in the winter and hot air out in the summer. There are some dramatic examples of health impacts on employees. For example,

---

[4]Lewis W. Leeds, "Lectures on Ventilation at Franklin Institute," 1866–67 8 (New York: John Wiley and Sons, 1868) (quoting a letter by Benjamin Franklin to Dr. Ingenhaus, Physician to the Emperor at Vienna).

*Many states now have statutes that require property modifications to eliminate risks from these substances and hold property owners liable for injuries that result from tenants' exposure. For example, Maryland has its Reduction of Lead Risk in Housing Act codified in Maryland Code (1982, 2007 Repl. Vol., 2011 Supp.), subtitle 8, §§ 6–801 through 6–852.

Florida's $37 million Polk County Courthouse, a public building constructed in 1987, was evacuated in July 1992 after more than 460 of its 580 employees developed illnesses ranging from coughs to irreversible lung disease that were linked to the building itself. Renovations required to eliminate this telling example of SBS involved gutting the building and replacing air-handling units and vinyl wallpaper.[5]

The EPA and OSHA are working with professional associations to develop construction guidelines and suggestions for existing building modifications in order to minimize the health hazards that seem to occur in these highly contained commercial building settings. Tenants and landlords should provide clauses in their leases that address SBS issues, repairs, costs, and evacuation.

Rent and Rent Terminology

One unique aspect of the commercial lease is its terminology. Rental payments' terms and fees are very different from the flat monthly rates of residential leases. Although some older commercial leases do have flat per-month rates, called **gross rent**, this type of arrangement has been phased out over the past 30 years. Even if it is a part of the lease rent, the tenant will have some form of **escalation clause** that is a formula for extra rent beyond the base rent.

The most common form of commercial lease that has replaced the gross rent lease is the **triple net** or **net-net-net**. Under this arrangement, the tenant pays directly or reimburses the landlord for taxes, insurance, and maintenance expenses for the property, and then pays the landlord a flat rate or **fixed rent** above and beyond the "net" amount paid for taxes, insurance, and maintenance.

For purposes of the triple net lease, *taxes* includes real property taxes and assessments including those on fixtures regardless of whether the landlord or tenant owns them. *Insurance* includes fire, casualty, and liability insurance to cover the tenant's operations. *Maintenance* includes not only maintenance and repair but also operational expenses such as utilities and other services.

Even the fixed rent lease may be subject to adjustment. Many retail centers carry a **Consumer Price Index (CPI) adjustment clause**. This clause ties the flat rate to the CPI and allows the landlord to increase the fixed rent by the amount of increase in the CPI for the year. The lease may provide for a cap or a maximum increase that stipulates the rent will increase by the CPI increase or a maximum of 6 percent.

Some leases contain **specific happenings increase provisions**. For example, a lease may contain a provision that allows a rent increase in the event the developer or landlord is required to pay increased taxes.

As the popularity and hence size of shopping centers have grown, new rent payment ideas have been created to cover the costs of maintaining these large centers. For example, many tenants are responsible for their prorated share of **common area maintenance (CAM)** (sometimes called **operating expenses**).

---

[5]For full details and discussion on SBS, see Gene J. Heady, "Stuck Inside These Four Walls: Recognition of Sick Building Syndrome Has Laid the Foundation to Raise Toxic Tort Litigation to New Heights," 26 *Tex. Tech L. Rev.* 1041 (1995). For particular types of issues, see Walter G. Wright, Jr. and Stephanie M. Irby, "The Transactional Challenges Posed by Mold: Risk Management and Allocation Issues," 56 *Ark. L. Rev.* 295 (2003) and Reid S. Hooper, "Got Mold? Improving Plaintiffs' Toxic Mold Causation Problems with the Introduction of DNA and Mycotoxin Extraction Testing," 42 *Val. U. L. Rev.* 585 (2008).

Operating expenses can be a tricky part of lease negotiations for a tenant. Landlords have included everything from marketing expenses to elevator repairs in the operating expenses for their facilities. Some tenants negotiate out of their CAMs those operating expenses the landlord incurs because of the risks and needs in operating a commercial facility. Such expenses would include the marketing expenses, a type of expense that increases when consumer spending and, as a result, tenant revenues, are down. Other tenants rely on the landlord for promotion of a center or mall that they could not provide for themselves to generate business. Some expenses, such as those related to the elevators, may be capital improvements and should be amortized, as opposed to expensed all at once.

At a minimum, tenants should negotiate full access to the landlord's operating expense records so that they can see what is being included. These expenses can increase the rent substantially. For example, it would not be unusual for a base rent in a commercial building to be $32 per square foot; with expenses, the payment increases to $46 per square foot. Some leases place caps on expenses, with base year restrictions on expenses being no greater than 5 percent above those of comparable properties.

Once the operating expenses are clearly defined, the tenant should negotiate carefully for the percentage of operating expenses he or she will pay. The allocation of operating expenses, or CAM, can be complex, with the following representing one formula:

$$\frac{\text{Rental area of the tenant's premises}}{\substack{\text{Total of all rentable areas on the} \\ \text{property (gross leasable area)}}} \times \substack{\text{Total common area} \\ \text{maintenance costs or CAM}} = \substack{\text{Tenant's} \\ \text{monthly fees}}$$

The language used in the formula is critical. If, for example, the formula used "rented areas" as opposed to "rentable areas," then the effect would be to transfer to the occupying tenants the costs of CAM instead of having the landlord carry those costs until the premises are leased. The definition of even "rentable areas" may need clarification: whether mezzanines, basements, and other areas are included, and the effect of having movable (cart) tenants selling smaller items in a mall.

Shopping center and mall leases usually carry a **percentage rent** that entitles the landlord to a given percentage of the tenant's gross receipts. When drafting a gross-percentage provision, the parties should remember the following details to facilitate collection of the intended fees:

1. A definition of gross sales, including what is and is not included in the computation of gross sales.
2. Record-keeping obligations of the tenant, along with the landlord's right of examination and right to an independent audit of the records.
3. Details of how often the percentage is to be paid, when it is to be paid, and whether the tenant is required to submit periodic reports.
4. A covenant of secrecy for the right of access. The landlord should be subject to suit and damages if information from the sales records is disclosed.

The following case illustrates one issue in these leases: the complexity of determining what constitutes "gross sales."

CIRCLE K CORPORATION V. COLLINS

98 F.3d 484 (9th Cir. 1996); aff'd 127 F.3d 904, cert. den. 522 U.S. 1148 (1998)
Lottery Loot and Leases

FACTS

Circle K Corporation leased property from landowner Frank Collins and agreed to pay rent calculated at 2 percent of "gross sales" on the premises, with some exceptions specified. The lease was a 20-year lease and also provided for a minimum base rent. The lease went into effect in 1975. The lease clause on rent provided as follows:

Lessee shall pay annually as hereinafter provided as additional rent, the amount, if any, by which two percent (2%) of Lessee's "gross sales" (as hereinafter defined) exceeds the guaranteed minimal annual rent plus the sum of the real estate taxes and insurance premiums on the leased premises for such year. Said additional rent is hereinafter referred to as "percentage rent."

The lease defined "gross sales" as follows:

Gross receipts of every kind and nature originating from sales and services on the demised premises, whether on credit or for cash, in every department operating on the leased premises, whether operated by Lessee, or by a Sublessee, or concessionaire excepting therefrom any rebates and/or refunds to customers, refundable deposits on beverage bottles, telephone tolls, gasoline sales, money order transactions, the transfer or exchange of merchandise between the stores of Lessee if any, ... and the amount of any sales, privilege license, excise or other taxes on transactions collected and/or paid either directly or indirectly by Lessee to any government or governmental agency.

In July 1981, Arizona instituted a state lottery. In August 1981, Circle K sent a letter to Collins, advising him that Circle K wished to sell lottery tickets at the store located on Collins's property. At the bottom of the letter was the following statement and a place for Collins to sign:

I, _____ _____, the Lessor (or agent for same) do hereby accept and agree to allow participation in the Arizona Lottery by the Circle K Corporation upon and from the property/ies leased from me. I further agree to exempt and exclude any commissions and computation of sales of Ar-izona Lottery tickets from the calculation of any percentage rentals.

Collins did not sign the letter or return it to Circle K. Circle K began selling lottery tickets and did not pay Collins a percentage rate based on lottery ticket sales. Circle K filed for Chapter 11 bankruptcy in 1990. The bankruptcy court originally held that lottery proceeds were property of the state and should not be included in gross sales, but did include Circle K's commissions from the state for being a lottery agent. The Bankruptcy Appellate panel reversed and included lottery ticket sales in gross sales revenue, and Circle K appealed.

JUDICIAL OPINION

Canby, Circuit Judge

It is a close question whether the Collins lease provides for percentage rent of two percent of Circle K's commissions from lottery sales, or two percent of total ticket sales price. We conclude, however, that the bankruptcy court's view is the correct one: percentage rent should be calculated only on the commissions. The parties have made comparisons to other types of receipts covered or not covered by the terms of the lease, but in our view state-sponsored lottery ticket sales fall into a class by themselves. They are quite unlike the general run of commercial operations mentioned in the lease. The State of Arizona has made Circle K one of its sales agents. State regulations require Circle K to pay over to the state its total proceeds from sales, less commissions and prizes awarded. The commission rate was originally five percent of ticket sales, and is now six percent.

In the hands of the State, lottery proceeds are used for various public purposes in the manner of tax revenues. In its ticket sales, Circle K acts more nearly as a tax collector for the State than as a retailer. It sells chances and takes custody of receipts, in which it has no interest beyond its commission, and remits them to the State. It is paid for its services by commission, and that commission is properly considered a "gross receipt" from "services" performed on the premises. We do not, however, interpret the lease as reaching the total funds received for the State in its calculation of percentage rent.

The only two cases squarely in point agree with this interpretation of similar leases. In *Cloverland Farms Dairy, Inc. v. Fry*, 587 A.2d 527 (1991), the Maryland Court of Appeals dealt with a lease, entered before Maryland authorized its lottery, that contained a clause as broad as the one before us. The lease provided for a percentage rent on "gross sales made in the store." It also provided that in computing "gross sales," the lessee was to take the total amount of sales of every kind made in the store and deduct therefrom the following, to the extent that same are included in such total amount: (1) refunds made to customers, (2) sales, excise and gross receipts taxes, and (3) proceeds from sale of money orders (fee received for issuance of money orders shall not be deducted).

Despite this broad language, the Court held that gross lottery sales did not fall within the percentage rent clause. The Court recognized that reasonable persons "would have thought that the additional rental percentage clause encompassed the sale of any and all items, not expressly excluded, which *Cloverland* would sell in its store in the course of its business activities." Lottery sales did not fall in that category.

The Maryland Court in *Cloverland* relied in part on the only other case cited to us that dealt with the same issue, *Anest v. Bellino*, 151 Ill. App.3d 818, 104 Ill. Dec. 861, 503 N.E.2d 576 (1987). *Anest* held that gross lottery sales did not fall within a percentage rental clause applying to "all gross sales." The Court stated:

Although the restaurant actually handled the money, that portion of the money belonging to the lottery system was not intended by the parties to be included in gross sales. Only the commissions and bonuses belong to the restaurant, and only those amounts increase the restaurant's sales.

Arizona has no decisions in point, but we have no reason to believe that its courts would diverge from these two decisions that are the only ones to have dealt with the lottery issue in connection with percentage rent clauses. The same factors that led Maryland's and Illinois's courts to exclude total lottery sales exist in this case. The money collected by Circle K, except for commissions, belongs to the State. Lottery sales were not part of the Circle K's regular business in the reasonable contemplation of the parties at the time the lease was entered into; they are in a class by themselves. If the parties had foreseen the future legalization of lottery sales, and had addressed the question specifically in the lease, the nature of other exceptions suggests that total proceeds other than commissions would have been excluded from "gross sales." The arguable-comparable activity of money order transactions was so excluded, as were receipts from refundable deposits on beverage bottles, and sales taxes that Circle K collected but transferred to the State. Thus the same kinds of considerations that led to the decisions in *Cloverland* and *Anest* are present here.

We conclude that the term "gross sales" in the percentage rent term of the lease agreement did not include the total sales price of state lottery tickets. "Gross sales" included only the commissions that Circle K received in exchange for its services in selling the tickets. The decision is therefore reversed.

Reversed.

CASE QUESTIONS

1. When was the lease negotiated? How were "gross sales" defined?
2. What have other states done with the issue of lottery sales with respect to rental percentage clauses?
3. Why is the issue of the sale of money orders similar?
4. Is it significant that Collins did not sign the letter on the lottery sales?

CONSIDER 10.3   On June 7, 1968, Sears entered into a "Shopping Center Lease" (lease) with Honey Creek Square, Inc. (Honey Creek), to lease space in its mall, Honey Creek Square Shopping Center.

The lease is a standard Sears form that was modified pursuant to negotiations between Honey Creek and Sears. Rent due from Sears under the lease is based solely on a percentage basis of Sears's net sales made on the Honey Creek Store, with no guaranteed minimum. The monthly amount is calculated according to paragraph 8 of the lease, which reads in pertinent part:

a. *Tenant, in consideration of said demise, does covenant and agree with Landlord to pay as rental for all of said demised premises (including the above mentioned retail store and attached Tire Service Station) a sum equal to three per cent (3%) of so much of "Net Sales" (as herein defined), made by Tenant upon the demised premises during any Lease Year (as herein defined) during the first three (3) years of the term hereinabove provided, as are not in excess of Eight Million Dollars ($8,000,000), and a sum equal to two and one-half per cent (2½%) of so much of such Net Sales made by Tenant upon the demised premises during any Lease Year commencing with the fourth year of said term and continuing thereafter to the end of said term.*

b. *The words "Net Sales" as used herein mean gross sales made upon the demised premises by Tenant and its departmental subleases, concessionaires and licensees occupying space upon said demised premises, but deducting or excluding, as the case may be, the following: (i) sales of departments or divisions not located upon said demised premises; (ii) the amount of all sales, use, excise retailers' occupation or other similar taxes imposed in a specific amount, or percentage upon, or determined by, the amount of retail sales made upon said demised premises; (iii) returns and allowances, as such terms are known and used by Tenant in the preparation of Tenant's profit and loss statements; (iv) delivery, rental, installation and service charges;(v) amounts in excess of Tenant's (or of its sublessees', concessionaires' and licensees'), cash sales price charged on sales made on credit or under a time payment plan; (vi) sales of merchandise ordered through the use of Tenant's catalog order channels, regardless of the place of order, payment, or delivery; (vii) policies of insurance sold on said demised premises and the premiums collected on policies of insurance; and (viii) sales made through the Commercial and Industrial Sales Department of Tenant.*

In December 1981, Sears did not include in net sales the following:

Alteration sales	$ ——
Gift-wrapping sales	$1,262
Bike set-up sales	$112
Auto labor sales	$16,269
Service contract (maintenance agreement) sales	$53,513
Service center sales	$13,217

Sears stated that it had never included income from these categories in its net sales figure, except auto labor, which had been included from November 1977 through September 1981, because of a misunderstanding on the part of its in-store controller. Can Honey Creek recover rent based on the above exclusions from net sales? *Washington National Corporation v. Sears, Roebuck & Co.,* 474 N.E.2d 116 (Ind. 1985).

Security deposits are typical in commercial leases and can be substantial so that the landlord is assured of payment. Because there is no uniform act on commercial leases, the parties should specify the purpose of the security deposit, whether it will be returned, on what grounds it can be retained, and whether there will be any time limits for returning the deposit upon termination of the lease.

Fixtures and Alterations

In most cases, commercial premises consist of walls, a roof, and a door. Generally, very little has been done to improve, finish, or decorate the interior of each retail space. There are substantial cost issues for necessary improvements, alterations, and construction to render the premises usable for a retail operation. Generally, the tenant is responsible for the costs of making the interior ready for operation, because the landlord does not know the needs of the tenant's business or the tenant's business operations. This requirement of completion, plus any restrictions the tenant may have in altering the premises (because of building codes or the landlord's hesitancy or preference), should be covered in the lease. If the landlord wants restrictions on improvements, those limits should be specified.

What happens to all the improvements the tenant has made once the lease is terminated? In other words, are the improvements treated as trade fixtures, or do they become permanent fixtures and property of the landlord? Although legal guidelines determine what a trade fixture is and what remains as the landlord's property (see Chapter 5), intent controls and the parties should address the issue of fixtures.

One common method for addressing tenant alterations in leases is to include a provision in the lease that requires the tenant to obtain prior written approval of the landlord. Under this arrangement, the tenant supplies the landlord with a written proposal that includes specifications for what constitutes a fixture in the proposed alteration and what will remain the property of the tenant as a trade fixture.

Operations

Commercial leases should cover hours of allowable operation as well as the days of closure. For example, many office buildings will be open for operation from 6:00 a.m. until 9:00 p.m. on weekdays, with limited access on Saturdays and Sundays. Many leases list specific holidays on which there will be no access or available amenities. In Arizona, critical portions of office building leases include those days during which the air conditioning for the facility will not be running. In the summer months, the buildings would not be usable on those days.

Shopping center leases contain additional provisions, such as mandatory hours of operation. It does small tenants little good to be open for business if the large tenants in the center have different hours of operation and are not open to attract the foot traffic.

Common Areas
Managing Access

Commercial leases should contain specific provisions on the responsibilities and liabilities for maintenance and safety of the common areas. Businesses and offices will have operational difficulties themselves if the common areas are unsafe, unclean, or simply inaccessible. The landlord should assume responsibility for maintenance and security of these areas. Further, the lease should provide for tenant rights in the event the landlord fails with respect to this responsibility. A critical area in shopping center leases is the availability of parking for those using the tenants' offices and businesses. When there is shared parking among commercial tenants, lease provisions should address overflow issues and accommodations. For example, some tenants have specifically designated spaces in the center parking lot so that customers can gain access.

Managing Free Speech

One of the interesting aspects of shopping center operation is the presence of demonstrators for political causes. Their presence provides an interesting interaction between their First Amendment rights and the rights of the shopping center owners. Currently, there is much litigation and debate over this issue, but the U.S. Supreme Court gave demonstrators certain rights in *Pruneyard Shopping Center v. Robins*, 474 U.S. 74 (1980), and various state and local regulation of such demonstrators' rights remains a topic of constitutional litigation. In the U.S. Supreme Court decision in *Hurley v. Irish-American Gay Group of Boston*, 515 U.S. 557 (1995), the Court held that interference with private speech rights by requiring public accommodation of all views presents First Amendment violations. States must be cautious in mandating speech rights of certain groups on commercial properties.

Twelve of the 17 states that have reviewed the issue of demonstrators' access to shopping centers have permitted the shopping center owners to restrict that access. California, Colorado, New Jersey, Massachusetts (the *Hurley* case)—and Washington permit free speech on commercial properties but do vary in the type of speech allowed. For example, some states permit only the solicitation of signatures for ballot propositions and candidates under the theory that the modern commercial center is the equivalent of the town square where free speech was practiced and protected.[6]

Managing Safety

The liability of commercial landlords and property owners for theft as well as injuries to tenants and tenants' employees by third parties who enter the leased property is an area of increasing litigation. The standard is similar to the residential landlord standard of foreseeability of the conduct of third parties, namely whether there is a history of criminal activity on the property and whether the landlord has provided sufficient security given the level of crime. While landlords are not guarantors of tenant safety, they do have duties with regard to providing security and must be vigilant in affording protections once there has been criminal activity in and around the leased premises. The following case deals with an issue of criminal activity and landlord liability.

PICHARDO V. BIG DIAMOND, INC.

215 S.W.3d 497 (Tex. App. 2007)
Danger from Drive-Aways

FACTS

On the afternoon of November 23, 2002, James C. Luedtke, Jr., and his girlfriend, Heather Roberts, drove into the Diamond Shamrock gas station on White Settle-

ment Road. The attendant activated the pump, and Roberts pumped gas into the vehicle. Roberts hopped in the vehicle, and Luedtke drove away without paying for the gas. As Luedtke drove off, an employee of the

---

[6]For a look at some of the shopping center and free speech cases, see *New Jersey Coalition v. J.M.B. Realty Corp.*, 650 A.2d 757 (N.J. 1994); *Committee For A Better Twin Rivers v. Twin Rivers Homeowners' Ass'n*, 929 A.2d 1060 (N.J. 2007); *Bock v. Westminster Mall Co.*, 819 P.2d 55 (Colo. 1991); *Mazdabrook Commons Homeowners' Ass'n v. Khan*, 2010 WL 3517030 (N.J. Super); *Betchelder v. Allied Stores Int'l, Inc.*, 445 N.E.2d 590 (Mass. 1983) and *Alderwood Associates v. Washington Environmental Council*, 635 P.2d 108 (Wash. 1981). Washington has a later limiting case: *Southcenter Joint Venture v. National Democratic Party Committee*, 780 P.2d 1282 (Wash. 1989).

gas station ran outside and attempted to get the license plate number of the vehicle.

In an effort to escape, Luedtke accelerated the vehicle, ran a red light, and collided with a vehicle driven by Alexis Pichardo, Sr., who had his son, Andrew Warren Pichardo, with him. Peggy Pichardo, Alexis Pichardo, Jr., and Richard Anderson were following Alexis Pichardo, Sr., in a separate vehicle and witnessed the collision. Alexis Pichardo, Sr., and Andrew were injured in the collision.

On November 19, 2004, the Pichardos sued Luedtke; Selma Ann Roberts, the owner of the car Luedtke had been driving; Big Diamond, the believed operator of the gas station; and Diamond Shamrock, the correct operator of the gas station.

Big Diamond and Diamond Shamrock (Appellees) then filed a joint motion for summary judgment, arguing that neither breached a legal duty owed to the Pichardos because Luedtke's actions were not foreseeable, and that any acts or omissions they committed were not a proximate cause of the Pichardos' injuries. The trial court granted the motion for summary judgment. The Pichardos appealed.

JUDICIAL OPINION

Walker, Justice

As a general rule, "a person has no legal duty to protect another from the criminal acts of a third person." An exception is that "[o]ne who controls … premises does have a duty to use ordinary care to protect invitees from criminal acts of third parties if he knows or has reason to know of an unreasonable and foreseeable risk of harm to the invitee." The exception applies, of course, to a landlord who "retains control over the security and safety of the premises."

Likewise, third-party criminal conduct is a superseding cause of damages arising from a defendant's negligence unless the criminal conduct is a foreseeable result of the defendant's negligence. A defendant who seeks a summary judgment on the ground that the defendant has negated foreseeability as an element of proximate cause must prove, however, more than simply that the intervening third-party criminal conduct occurred. The defendant must show the third-party criminal conduct rises to the level of a superseding cause.

If the defendant does this, it has negated the ordinary foreseeability element of proximate cause, and the burden shifts to the plaintiff to raise a genuine issue of fact on foreseeability by presenting controverting evidence that, despite the extraordinary and abnormal nature of the intervening force, there was

some indication at the time that such a crime would be committed.

Big Diamond does not operate store # 723; instead, it is the holder of the alcohol licenses for that facility. Diamond Shamrock owns the land, built the building, and operates store # 723. Based on this unrefuted testimony, it is clear that Big Diamond was not the owner of the property where the gas and dash occurred and therefore could not have owed the Pichardos a duty. Therefore, the trial court properly granted Big Diamond's motion for summary judgment.

The Pichardos argue that Diamond Shamrock knew that it was foreseeable that [not requiring] prepayment for gasoline purchases would in all likelihood result in foreseeable criminal activity such as theft of gasoline, and an attempt by the criminal to run away after the commission of the crime, and the possible injury of third persons such as [the Pichardos].

Here, the accident that injured the Pichardos occurred because Luedtke ran a red light after leaving the Diamond Shamrock gas station. The Pichardos were not invitees at the Diamond Shamrock gas station and the accident did not occur on the gas station premises. Consequently, we hold that the factors utilized to determine the scope of the duty owed by "[o]ne who controls … premises" to "protect *invitees* from criminal acts of third parties" is not applicable here.

[T]he "harm"—Alexis Sr.'s and Andrew's injuries—is a harm different in kind from that which would otherwise have resulted from the alleged negligence of not requiring prepayment for gasoline. Luedtke's actions in running a red light and striking the Pichardos' vehicle appear to be extraordinary rather than normal and appear to be independent of any negligence by Diamond Shamrock in not requiring prepayment for gasoline. Luedtke's action in running the red light is clearly due to his own decision to run the red light, and Luedtke is subject to liability to the Pichardos for his action in running the red light.

Finally, we cannot see how Diamond Shamrock possesses more than possibly a minute degree of culpability for setting Luedtke's running of the red light in motion; the escape of any criminal following unauthorized criminal conduct could involve the running of a red light. Thus, we hold that Diamond Shamrock negated the foreseeability element of proximate cause by conclusively establishing that Luedtke's act of running the red light was a superseding cause of Alexis, Sr.'s and Andrew's injuries. The burden then shifted to the Pichardos to raise a genuine issue of fact on foreseeability by presenting controverting evidence that, despite the extraordinary and abnormal nature of the intervening force, there was some indication at the time that this crime—the running of the red light— would be committed.

The Pichardos presented no such controverting evidence. The record is devoid of any evidence showing that similar accidents had occurred, that the Diamond Shamrock gas station was a frequent victim of gas and dashes, or that the area was crime laden. The record contains no evidence that other crimes or gas and dashes had occurred on the property or in its immediate vicinity, or even that individuals committing a gas and dash frequently run red lights or drive recklessly. Because Diamond Shamrock conclusively negated the foreseeability element of the Pichardos' negligence claim, the trial

court properly granted summary judgment in favor of Diamond Shamrock.

We affirm the trial court's take-nothing summary judgment rendered in favor of Big Diamond and Diamond Shamrock.

CASE QUESTIONS

1. What is the connection between Diamond Shamrock and the injuries the Pichardos experienced?
2. What evidence was missing from the Pichardos' case that was necessary?
3. What does the court say about extraordinary versus normal activity?

CONSIDER 10.4   Sharon P. was an employee at a business located in the Coast Savings building located at 1180 South Beverly Drive, Los Angeles. On Thursday, April 8, 1993, Sharon P. entered the underground parking garage of the building at 11:00 a.m. and parked in her assigned space. While she was leaning back into her car to remove some items from her back seat, a man with a gun who was wearing a ski mask approached her. She was forced back into her car and sexually assaulted.

In the months preceding her attack, the condition of the parking garage had deteriorated. Lights were out (the lights were out in the immediate area of her attack that day), areas of the garage smelled of urine, and security cameras in the garage had not worked for months. In some places there were cots set up where apparently the homeless had moved into the garage.

Sharon P. brought suit against Arman, Ltd., the owner of the building and garage, and APCOA, the manager of the parking garage. APCOA's responsibilities were collection of revenues from those using the garage. The trial court entered summary judgment for Arman and APCOA. Sharon P. appealed. Should she recover? From whom? Discuss the standards for liability of commercial property owners and tenants for injury to those using the property. *Sharon P. v. Arman,* Ltd. 989 P.2d 121 (Cal. 1999) *cert.* denied, 530 U.S. 1243 (2000).

CONSIDER 10.5   One of the difficult issues many shopping center malls face is the presence and access of teenagers to the mall. Referred to as "mall rats," these teenagers often become aggressive and harass tenants and customers alike. They "travel" in groups in the malls and often congregate in intimidating large groups. Their activities can stretch through an entire day. What actions could a landlord take with regard to mall rats? Should a landlord take any action? Do tenants need protection against their presence? Do the mall rats present any security risks?

Americans with Disabilities Act
The Basics of the Law
The **Americans with Disabilities Act (ADA)** (42 U.S.C. § 12007 [1990]) was passed "to provide a clear and comprehensive national mandate for the elimination of discrimination against individuals with disabilities," and to establish "clear, strong, consistent enforceable standards" for "scrutinizing such discrimination."

Section 302 of the ADA provides that "no individual shall be discriminated against on the basis of disability in the full and equal enjoyment of the goods, services, facilities, privileges, advantages, or accommodation by any person who owns, leases (or leases to), or operates a place of public accommodation."[7]

Those who fit the categories of owner, operator, lessee, and lessor must make "reasonable modifications" in "policies, practices, or procedures" that are necessary to allow individuals with disabilities access to their goods, services, or facilities.

> **PRACTICAL TIP**
>
> *In conducting a review of potential leased premises, the tenant should check for access routes, appropriate restroom facilities, automatic doors, drinking fountain heights, and elevators, and should evaluate the costs of compliance.*

ADA Lease Provisions

Without specific provisions on the ADA, legal requirements for access and alterations will be allocated under other lease terms such as those on alterations or repair. The ADA does apply to commercial facilities, referred to as "places of public accommodation" (PPA). Included in the PPA under the ADA would be shopping centers, medical offices, banks, and other professional service office buildings such as those for accountants, lawyers, and architects. The types of requirements for PPA would include the removal of barriers and the presence of paths of entry for those with disabilities. Many of these requirements are met by modifications to property such as automatic doors and ramps.

Tenants should conduct a form of due diligence review of the property to determine ADA compliance. If modifications are required, tenants should negotiate their addition and cost allocation. The lease agreement should allocate the costs of future compliance with the ADA and other laws as well as the cost of upkeep.

CONSIDER 10.6   Jerry Doran is a paraplegic who uses a wheelchair and resides in Cottonwood, California, but has on several occasions visited the 7-Eleven store on North Harbor Boulevard in Anaheim, California. This 7-Eleven store is about 550 miles from his home. Doran filed suit against 7-Eleven under Title III of the ADA seeking injunctive relief for removal of access barriers and also monetary damages.

Doran testified that he had encountered nine barriers at the 7-Eleven store: (1) no van-accessible parking nor any sign denoting such parking; (2) the striping outlining the disabled parking space was faded; (3) no sign designating the location of the wheelchair ramp; (4) the wheelchair ramp was too steep; (5) the store aisles were too narrow; (6) the entry mat obstructed entry to the store; (7) disabled patrons were denied access to the employees-only restroom; (8) the floor space was obstructed by merchandise; and (9) no directional signs indicating the nearest accessible store entrance. Should Doran be given relief in his suit? What could commercial property owners and tenants learn from Doran's list? *Doran v. 7-Eleven, Inc.,* 524 F.3d 1034 (9th Cir. 2008).   ▪

---

[7]Examples of the traditional form of real property accommodations under ADA include sufficient width in aisles and restrooms for wheelchairs (*Pinnock v. International House of Pancakes,* 844 F. Supp. 574 [S.D. Cal. 1993]) and cashiers in liquor stores *Johnson v. Vitale,* 2011 WL 202830 [E.D. Cal. 2011]; permitting guide dogs for the visually impaired (*Crowder v. Kitagawa,* 842F. Supp. 1257 [D. Haw. 1994]), installation of elevators (*Tyler v. City of Manhattan,* 849 F. Supp. 1429[D. Kan. 1994]) and ramps when stairs control access to a store (*Equal Rights Ctr. v. Abercrombie & Fitch Co.,* 767 F.Supp.2d 510 [D. Md. 2010]); resurfacing of streets and sidewalks to remove potholes and ensure smooth surfaces for wheelchairs (*Kinney v. Yerusalim,* 9 F.3d 1067 [3rd Cir. 1993]); reversal of policy prohibiting wheelchairs on the Little League field (*Anderson v. Little League Baseball, Inc.,* 794 F. Supp. 342[D. Ariz. 1992]); and wheelchair accessible slot machines (*Brown v. Showboat Atl. City Propco, LLC,* 2010 WL 5237855 [D.N.J. 2010].)

Landlord's Right of Entry

As in residential leases, tenants have the right to exclusive use of the leased property, but, on occasion, the landlord will need access. The lease should specify the hows and whens of the landlord's access, including when the landlord may enter the tenant's premises and for what purpose; how much notice is required before the landlord may enter, what form that notice must take, and how it is to be delivered; and whether notice provisions may be waived during emergency situations.

Destruction and Damage to Premises

The parties need to make provisions for what would happen to their relationship in the event that an accident or catastrophe destroys the shopping center property. For example, the 2001 destruction of the World Trade Center in New York City left many tenants without office facilities for substantial periods of time. Hurricane Katrina's destruction of most of New Orleans left many businesses without office space. Many tenants had contingency plans for operations. Other tenants filed suit against various government agencies for the interruption of their leases and businesses.

The commercial lease should cover several issues that address disasters: If the premises are damaged or destroyed to the point of being unusable by the tenant, does the responsibility of rent abate? (During the time of nonuse, the lease should make provisions for the tenant to stop paying rent.) May the tenant cancel the lease? At what point are the premises completely destroyed? Allowing the common law to cover these issues invites the ambiguity of the doctrine of impossibility and does not provide the parties with sufficient guidelines for their conduct.

In some cases, the parties incorporate into the lease an obligation of the landlord to rebuild the premises. Because of the unique nature of the shopping center, in which prime location can be the key to a successful business, this obligation to rebuild can be extremely important to the tenant. The tenant may not want to terminate the lease but may want to be back in business as soon as possible and can provide for time limitations on rebuilding. If there is a construction requirement clause in the lease, appropriate insurance to cover reconstruction costs should also be part of the lease covenants.

Breach

The last topic of concern to both parties in the commercial lease is what constitutes a breach and what the damages are in the event of a breach. For the landlord, nonpayment of rent is the major problem because businesses do face fiscal crises. If remedies for nonpayment of rent are not specified, the law affords the same protections in commercial leases as in residential leases. If rental payments are not made in a timely manner, the landlord may bring an action to dispossess the tenant. If the tenant breaches the lease agreement by terminating business prior to the lease expiration date, the landlord may have the responsibility to mitigate the situation by trying to find another tenant, but the parties could specify otherwise and could provide for a liquidated damage figure. In cases of breaches in other areas (such as failure to maintain or failure to grant access), the parties may agree to submit matters to arbitration prior to suit. The following case presents an interesting scenario on access, breach, and damages.

WINCHELL V. SCHIFF

193 P.3d 946 (Nev. 2008)
The Frozen Fish Eviction

FACTS

Calvin Winchell, d/b/a CGL Seafood, Inc. (appellant), owned and operated a wholesale fresh fish business in Las Vegas, Nevada. Winchell's business grew from $36,780 in sales in 1996 to $759,711 in 2000. With such dramatic growth, Winchell was in need of a much larger storage facility for his inventory.

Renate Schiff (respondent) owned a cold storage facility and offered to lease a portion of that space to Winchell. Winchell accepted her offer, and the parties executed a two-year lease agreement. Under the terms of the agreement, Winchell was required to indemnify Schiff and maintain insurance for the mutual benefit of Schiff and Winchell. Additionally, the agreement provided that Schiff and her agents were permitted to enter the storage space at any reasonable time for inspection or maintenance purposes.

A few months before the lease was set to expire (December 2000), while Winchell was out of town, Schiff's property manager, Beryl Duncan, became concerned that Winchell may have abandoned the premises. Having had prior experience with tenants abandoning cold storage units, turning the power off, and leaving unrefrigerated fish behind, Duncan was apparently concerned about whether the electricity had been shut off. Duncan attempted to contact Winchell by telephone, to no avail.

On August 21, 2000, Duncan decided to inspect the storage unit. To gain access into the unit, Duncan hired a locksmith and directed him to drill out and replace the locks. As the locksmith pried the door to the storage unit open, the security alarm was triggered. Duncan directed the locksmith to cut the wires and disable the alarm. Once inside the storage unit, Duncan conducted a preliminary inspection and verified that the electricity was on. The storage unit was full of inventory. Following the inspection, the locksmith secured the storage unit and provided Duncan with the new set of keys.

Winchell returned to Las Vegas on August 23, 2000 and discovered that the locks had been changed. Winchell immediately called Schiff and the police. When Schiff's agent and the police arrived at the storage unit, they found that somewhere between $30,000 and $45,000 worth of inventory had been removed. A review of the alarm records (the locksmith had not dis-

abled the recording portion of the system) revealed that an unaccounted-for entry was made on August 23, 2000. Winchell filed a claim under his insurance policy and received $33,084 in compensation for the lost inventory.

This disruption in Winchell's supply led to the demise of his business in October 2000. Winchell discontinued paying rent, removed the remaining inventory, and vacated the storage unit. Subsequently, Winchell filed suit against Schiff for conversion, breach of quiet enjoyment, breach of contract, and trespass, and he sought compensatory and punitive damages. Schiff counterclaimed for Winchell's early termination of the lease agreement.

The jury awarded Winchell $210,000 in losses for the demise of his business. Schiff was awarded $2,880 for Winchell's failure to pay rent for two months. Schiff appealed.

JUDICIAL OPINION

Douglas, Justice

Evidence showed that Schiff's representatives were the only people who had access to the storage unit after the locks were changed and that it was during this period of Schiff's exclusive control when Winchell's inventory was removed.

From that evidence, the jury could have reasonably inferred that Schiff wrongfully exerted dominion over Winchell's storage unit and inventory, which was in derogation of his rights in the property. Therefore, we conclude that substantial evidence supports the jury's finding that Schiff was liable for conversion.

Schiff alternatively argues that even if substantial evidence supports Winchell's conversion claim, the jury's award of $210,000 must be remitted to reflect Winchell's actual losses. According to Schiff, actual losses must be limited to Winchell's converted inventory, which was valued somewhere between $30,000 and $45,000. We disagree.

During trial, Winchell testified that the fair market value of his business was approximately $500,000. This testimony was supported by documentary evidence in the form of numerous profit and loss statements, and federal income tax returns. ... the injured party should receive full compensation for his actual losses. Additionally, we recognize that the property value is not the sole measure of damages.

Here, the record reveals that the conversion of Winchell's inventory resulted in the demise of his wholesale fresh fish business. No interference can be more serious than one that results in the termination of another's business. Accordingly, we conclude that Winchell is entitled to the value of his lost business and the lost inventory's value as compensation for his actual losses, which the jury determined was worth approximately $210,000 on the day of the conversion.

We now turn to Schiff's argument that the district court abused its discretion by refusing to offset the award of damages by $33,084, the amount Winchell recovered under the insurance policy. [r]egardless of whether Winchell's recovery was from an independent source, he was contractually obligated to make the insurance proceeds available to Schiff for any losses arising from his use of the premises. Therefore, Schiff is entitled to an offset of $33,084, the amount Winchell recovered under the insurance policy.

Winchell contends that the district court erred in granting judgment as a matter of law on his cause of action for breach of the covenant of quiet enjoyment. [T]o prove a sufficient issue for breach of the covenant of quiet enjoyment, the tenant need only provide evidence demonstrating constructive eviction; actual eviction is not required. We conclude that actual eviction is not a prerequisite to a claim for breach of a covenant of quiet enjoyment because such a prerequisite would increase the tenant's suffering by requiring him to await the landlord's eviction before asserting breach of the covenant.

Under the lease agreement, Schiff and her agents were permitted to enter Winchell's storage unit at any reasonable time for the purpose of inspection or maintenance. Relying on this lease provision, the district court found that Schiff's entry into Winchell's storage unit was reasonable. We agree with that conclusion.

Similarly, we conclude that the district court was correct in granting judgment as a matter of law on Winchell's trespass claim because Schiff's entry into the storage facility was reasonable and permitted under the terms of the lease agreement. Winchell provided no evidence suggesting that Schiff's entry was not for the exclusive purpose of inspecting the unit to ensure that the electricity was still running. Accordingly, we conclude that the district court was correct in dismissing Winchell's cause of action for trespass. Accordingly, we conclude that the district court did not abuse its discretion in denying Winchell punitive damages.

Schiff contends that the jury's award of $2,880 was inadequate because the award did not account for the damages resulting from the cleaning, repairing, and re-renting of the storage unit that amounted to $10,339.42. Winchell responded with evidence that Schiff hired independent maintenance staff for the sole purpose of billing Winchell for the cleanup. In addition, Winchell was able to demonstrate that Schiff waited several months before attempting to clean and re-rent the storage unit. Accordingly, we conclude that it was within the province of the jury to reject Schiff's evidence of additional damages. Therefore, the jury's award of $2,880 was not clearly inadequate.

Affirmed in part and reversed in part.

CASE QUESTIONS

1. List what causes of actions the court finds against each party and which it does not.
2. Was the entry by the landlord justified?
3. Does the case create substantial exposure for landlords?

Landlord's Responsibility for Tenant's Conduct

A recent development in commercial leases is one of holding landlords responsible when their tenants are engaged in trademark infringement. For example, many landlords lease properties to stores that sell knock-off goods or goods that the stores are not licensed to sell. Such tenants are often found in outlet malls. To protect their trademarks, some manufacturers have joined together to bring suits against landlords so that landlords are more cautious about their tenants and the tenants' activities. For example, in *Polo Ralph Lauren Corp. v. Chinatown Gift Shop*, 855 F. Supp. 648 (S.D.N.Y. 1994), Polo Ralph Lauren, Rolex Watch USA, and Louis Vuitton brought suit against a landlord who was leasing property to three retailers who were selling goods that infringed on their trademarks for their clothing, watches, and leather goods, respectively. The court held that there was a cause of action against the landlord for its vicarious liability under federal law for facilitating the infringement by the tenants. In *Habeeba's Dance of the Arts, Ltd. v. Knoblauch*, 430 F. Supp. 2d 709 (Ohio 2006), the court held that the landlord (YWCA) could be held liable for contributory infringement for leasing a portion of its facilities to Habeeba's when it knew that Habeeba's was teaching the Habiba form of dancing, a trademarked method that belonged to Habiba, and that such use was likely to cause confusion about ownership of the dance method.

Assignment of Leases

Most states readily permit the assignment of leases by tenants. But in nearly all commercial leases that have been drafted by the developer, assignments are prohibited without approval from the developer. Even if a lease does not contain an assignment prohibition, the type of assignment may be severely limited by the use restrictions clause. Since the tenant remains liable on the lease, the tenant would be responsible for a breach if an assignment were made to a retailer who sold goods that were unauthorized by the use provision.

Commercial leases involve complexities in assignments and subleases because of tenant mix. Many commercial leases have restrictions on assignments or require landlord approval because the landlord would breach his noncompete clauses with other tenants if, for example, an assignment meant there were two drugstores in one shopping center.

SHOPPING CENTER LEASES—SPECIFIC PROVISIONS

A successful shopping center is the result of a careful mix of tenants. To maximize the return on not just the owner's investment but also the profits earned by the individual tenants, the tenants need to complement rather than compete with one another. This section offers background on obtaining that mix.

The Anchor Tenant

Long before a center opens its doors and, in some cases, long before construction of the center begins, the developer or owner negotiates with an **anchor tenant** to begin creating the mix of tenants. The anchor tenant is generally the grocery store in a freestanding center or a major department store for a mall. In the case of a shopping mall, there may be two to five anchor tenants. The anchor tenants are responsible for drawing the majority of the customers to the center or mall and will do a significant amount of advertising that also brings in customers. The terms under which these anchor tenants will come to the center are critical because other tenants and lease terms will be controlled by the demands of the anchor tenant. For example, if a chain drugstore is to be the anchor tenant in a freestanding shopping center, the developer will not be able to lease to a small, locally owned drugstore a smaller space in the center. Likewise, if a discount clothing store is the anchor tenant, it would be difficult to lease the smaller spaces to retail clothing stores.

Commercial leases tend to be significantly longer than residential leases largely because of the degree of investment made by the developer and the time required for recoupment of the investment in the property. Periods of 15 to 20 years for the initial term of the lease are not unusual and are generally accompanied by four to five 5-year renewal options.

A portion of every commercial lease will cover restrictions on the developer's other tenants and future leases. For example, if a center will have a bakery, the bakery tenant will want a clause in the lease that prohibits both the landlord from leasing to another bakery and other tenants from assigning their leases to other bakeries.

One of the difficulties that can arise for a shopping center developer or owner occurs when an anchor tenant is signed and then fails to open for business or opens for business and then fails. Economic twists and turns do affect small retail operations in shopping centers. Because the developer is dependent upon the mix of tenants, and the tenants and their customer traffic are drawn by the anchor tenant, the failure of an anchor tenant to commence operations, even when rent is paid, can be devastating for the center. Likewise, landlords have a right to demand that tenants fulfill their obligations to remain open, despite tougher economic conditions. The *force majeure* clause has made its way into commercial leases. These clauses allow the parties to be excused from performance under the terms of the lease agreement when external events that are not anticipated at the time of the lease agreement result in economic hardship for them. For example, in *Bouchard Transp. Co., Inc. v. New York Islanders Hockey Club, LP,* 836 N.Y.S.2d 654 (2007), the court held that a 30-team league lock-out from a labor dispute was an unanticipated event that excused the parties from their lease obligations where their *force majeure* clause covered "events beyond their control" and listed "labor disputes" as an example of such an event.

The fact that a tenant's business does not do well is not an unanticipated event, and the tenant still owes rent even if it vacant the premises. Some landlords have sought more than just rent and tried to use the courts to force tenants to remain open for business in order to maintain the proper commercial mix of tenants in the shopping center. However, landlords have not been successful in forcing tenants to stay in business. For example, in *Summit Towne Centre, Inc. v. Shoe Show of Rocky Mount, Inc.,* 828 A.2d 995 (Pa. 2003), Summit Towne Centre, Inc., owned and operated Summit Towne Centre, a 550,000-square-foot shopping center with between 20 and 30 tenants, including a number of anchor stores such as K-Mart, Giant Eagle, Sam's Club, and Staples. The Shoe Show of Rocky Mount, Inc. had a lease for a 5,400-square-foot retail unit in the Centre. The lease contained a "use" provision that required it to operate a shoe store as part of the Centre's mix of tenants and also agreed to.

...

> " *keep its Demised Premises adequately illuminated and continuously and uninterruptedly open for business during the same days, nights and hours as any department store or stores located in the Shopping Center and at least, in any event, from the hours of 10:00 a.m. to 9:30 p.m. Monday through Saturday, and 12:00 noon to 5:00 p.m. on Sundays.*"

In 1994, the Shoe Show was not doing well in terms of sales and tried to negotiate an end to its 1992 lease agreement. Summit refused and, despite warnings from Summit, closed on January 30, 2000 and vacated the leased premises. It did, however, continue to pay rent.

Summit sued for an injunction requiring Shoe Show to stay open. The court held that any harm from the closure was speculative and that the Centre continued to operate. Shoe Show was not required to stay open as long as it paid its rent.

In many cases, anchor tenants pay a minimal, or at least lower, amount of rent than the other tenants. If the large spaces in the center go unoccupied, then all of the remaining tenants suffer. Tenants who occupy smaller units in the center do so with the idea that their services and goods will be unique to that center and that the landlord will not reduce their business by leasing to a competing venture in the same center. These ideas of traffic from anchor tenants and noncompetition are marketing tools that must be guaranteed by lease terms.[8]

Business Restrictions

The lessees in the shopping center may want to control the makeup of the center or even the types of merchandise sold by each retailer. Indeed, in some instances, the anchor tenant stipulates that it must review and approve all potential lessees for a center. For example, in some leases, anchor tenants have clauses that disallow the leasing of space to discount merchants. These clauses prevent the anchor tenant from being undersold on certain items because a store in the same center has been leased to a discount merchant of those items.

The issue that arises from these clauses that limit the types of business operations is whether the clauses violate federal or state antitrust laws. Many such clauses have been challenged by the Federal Trade Commission and the Justice Department in an effort to eliminate them.

At this point, it is difficult to determine what clauses do or do not violate antitrust laws. Because the issues of the type of market, location, and competition vary from city to city, the validity of these clauses also varies. But, for the most part, if the clauses are reasonably necessary for shopping center survival, they should be insisted upon by tenants. In the following case, the issue of use restriction is critical.

MARK-IT PLACE FOODS, INC. V. NEW PLAN EXCEL REALTY TRUST

156 Ohio App.3d 65, 804 N.E.2d 979 (Ohio App. 2004)
Selling Baked Goods As a Violation of a Lease

FACTS

In the late 1980s, Wal-Mart Stores, Inc. began to explore the possibility of opening a store in the Scioto County, Ohio area. Wal-Mart retained the services of Leo Eisenberg Co., a nationwide developer and shopping-center manager, to examine the area. Eisenberg found an appropriate location in New Boston. Eisenberg then formed the New Boston Development Company ("NBDC") to build and to later own the shopping center intended to house the new Wal-Mart store. NBDC sought other tenants for the shopping center as well and, on July 27, 1989, entered into a "shopping-center lease" to let 52,628 square feet to Scrivner, Inc., for use as a supermarket. That lease contained the following "exclusive-use" provision:

"Neither Lessor nor any affiliate or related party shall, without Lessee's prior written consent, own,

operate or grant any lease or permit any assignment or sublease for a store (or any portion of a store) in the Shopping Center or any of Lessor's real estate located within 1,500 yards of the Shopping Center which permits a tenant under such lease to *sell or offer for sale groceries, meats, poultry, seafood, dairy products, fruits, vegetables or baked goods,* provided these restrictions shall not be deemed to prohibit a restaurant serving prepared food." (Emphasis added.)

In November of that year, NBDC leased a 112,238-square-foot building and garden center in the shopping center to Wal-Mart. The lease did not include any provision to prohibit Wal-Mart from selling any of the items listed in the above-cited exclusive-use provision, and Wal-Mart sold foodstuffs such as "chips, nuts, beverages, cereal, cookies, canned meats,

---

[8]Recent decisions have some courts implying a covenant of continuing operations, particularly for anchor tenants. When a significant portion of the rent is tied to revenues, courts have held that the tenant must continue operations (*East Broadway Corp. v. Taco Bell Corp.*, 542 N.W.2d [Iowa 1996]).

pasta and other convenience food items." Wal-Mart's lease provided that it could use the demised premises for "any lawful purpose."

On June 14, 1990, Scrivner assigned its leasehold interest to S.M. Flickinger Co., which, on January 9, 1991, entered into a "sublease agreement" subletting the premises to Festival. Fleming is the successor in interest to Flickinger.

In 1992, NBDC decided to sell the shopping center. New Plan expressed interest in acquiring the property and began examining the shopping-center leases. New Plan discovered both the exclusive-use covenant in Scrivner's lease (the property occupied by Festival Foods under the sublease) and the absence of a reciprocal restrictive-use covenant in Wal-Mart's lease. New Plan sent an "estoppel letter" to NBDC and to Fleming asking, among other things, their assurances that there were "no defaults under the terms of the [l]ease." NBDC and Scrivner executed the letter and signified their assent to that representation. Festival, likewise, consented to "execution and delivery of [the] Estoppel Letter." On the basis of those assurances, New Plan acquired the shopping center in early 1993.

In December 1998, Fleming sent a letter to New Plan to notify the company that Wal-Mart was selling foodstuffs at its New Boston store in violation of its assigned lease's exclusive-use provision. Fleming asked that New Plan promptly take action to "ensure that Wal-Mart immediately discontinue the sale of groceries, meats, poultry, seafood, dairy products, fruits, vegetables or baked goods to the public." No action was taken, and Fleming discontinued its rental payments.

Festival filed suit, alleging that New Plan and Fleming had violated the lease's terms by permitting Wal-Mart to sell foodstuffs. The trial court concluded that no breach of the lease's exclusive-use provision occurred by permitting Wal-Mart to sell particular food items. In view of the fact that Wal-Mart was not a "supermarket," and was not primarily engaged in sale of foodstuffs, the court concluded that New Plan did not violate its lease with Fleming. The court granted summary judgment in favor of New Plan.

JUDICIAL OPINION

Abele, Judge

[T]he trial court's interpretation of the contract language is too restrictive. If the lease provision prohibited only the sale of "groceries," then we might agree that the provision could either be construed as meaning "supermarket" or that the term is sufficiently ambiguous to warrant consideration of parol evidence. We note that no case law in Ohio appears to define the term "groceries," but other jurisdictions have, at times, struggled with what is encompassed by that term. Be that as it may, the lease provision at issue here specifies more than just "groceries." It also states that the lessor shall not lease premises to any store that sells "meats, poultry, seafood, dairy products, fruits, vegetables or baked goods...." This language indicates that the parties meant to prohibit not just the sale of "groceries" by supermarkets but also the sale of other specified items by any type of store. For instance, pursuant to the lease, "baked goods" could not be sold by any store, whether that store is a "supermarket" or is another type of store. Had the parties to the lease simply meant to exclude supermarkets, they could have used either that specific term or they could have expressly stated that no other store in the shopping center could sell "groceries." They would not have inserted a litany of other prohibited items. Moreover, by interpreting the exclusive-use provision as prohibiting other supermarkets, we would be forced to ignore the express language of the lease that prohibits any store from selling "meats, poultry, seafood, dairy products, fruits, vegetables or baked goods."

Having concluded that the exclusive-use provision of the lease has a broader meaning than was afforded to it by the trial court, we must now address whether that provision amounted to an illegal restraint of trade. New Plan argued below that if the exclusive-use provision was given its literal meaning, then it would violate state restraint-of-trade laws. The trial court essentially ruled in its March 9, 2001 judgment that the law was not violated because the lease provision prevented letting space only to "supermarkets" or to "store[s] primarily engaged in the sale of foodstuffs." Now that we have given the provision a more expansive reading, consistent with the terminology used therein, it is necessary to revisit the issue of state restraint-of-trade laws.

The gist of New Plan's argument is that by virtue of the exclusive-use provision in the lease, NBDC (its predecessor in interest) and Scrivner (Fleming's predecessor in interest) combined to form an illegal "trust" in restraint of trade. We disagree.

The Ohio Supreme Court recognized years ago that if antitrust laws were construed literally or strictly, no partnership could be formed, no corporation could be organized, no vendor could agree to a reasonable limitation upon his future business, and scores of other activities that have been permitted and approved of in this country for centuries would be banned. Thus, the court held that contracts in restraint of trade are not illegal unless they are unreasonable.

Similarly, in the instant case, the restrictive-use provision prohibits stores only from selling groceries and other specified food items in the shopping center. It did not affect the rest of the New Boston community and, thus, appears to pass muster. Moreover, we believe that the exclusive-use provision satisfies other criteria adopted by courts to determine whether such provisions are reasonable. For example, the federal District Court for the Southern District of Ohio has opined that the factors to examine when determining whether an exclusive-use provision is overbroad are (1) the relevant product and geographic markets, together with the showing of unreasonable impact upon competition in these markets due to the restrictive covenant; (2) the availability of alternate sites for the entity excluded by the operation of such covenant; (3) the significance of competition eliminated by the exclusivity clause, and whether present or future competitors were the parties excluded; (4) the scope of the restrictive covenant and whether it varies depending on the circumstances; and (5) the economic justifications for including the restrictive covenant in the lease. *Child World, Inc., v. S. Towne Centre, Ltd.* (D.C. Ohio 1986), 634 F.Supp. 1121.

Weighing these factors in light of the evidentiary materials submitted below, we are not persuaded that the exclusive-use provision constitutes an unreasonable restraint of trade. As noted previously, this provision pertains only to tenants within that particular shopping center. It does not affect the rest of the community. Our review of the record has found no evidence to suggest that this provision restricted entry of, or prohibited competition by, any grocer or seller of foodstuffs outside the shopping center and in the larger New Boston community. We emphasize that antitrust laws exist for the protection of competition, not competitors, and that the essence of competition is not within a shopping center but between shopping centers.

Affirmed as to summary judgment, but the court dealt with other issues.

CASE QUESTIONS

1. How broad does the court see the lease restriction to be?
2. Given the court's interpretation of the lease restriction, what effect is there on competition?
3. What must landlords be able to establish to enforce a restriction in a shopping center lease?

CONSIDER 10.7   Office Depot had a lease with the District at Howell Mill. A provision in the lease protected Office Depot in terms of exclusivity as an office supply store. However, after Office Depot entered into its lease, the District at Howell Mill negotiated with The School Box to lease premises in the same shopping center. The School Box sells school supplies. Before entering into the lease with The School Box, representatives from the District of Howell Mill met with the Office Depot manager to discuss the product lines of The School Box for conflicting overlap. The manager voiced no objection. Later, Office Depot sought to terminate its lease on the grounds that the exclusivity clause had been violated. Could Office Depot be excused from its lease? What is different about this case from the *Mark-It Place* case? Office Depot, Inc. v. *District at Howell Mill, LLC*, 710 S.E.2d 685 (Ga. App. 2010).

CAUTIONS AND CONCLUSIONS

The commercial lease carries a unique set of legal problems, from antitrust to liquidated damages to store hours. A checklist for commercial lease negotiations is a necessity, and the headings in this chapter can be used as a guideline in making sure that all possible legal issues are covered. As is true with other areas of real estate, an investigation can never be too complete.

The following is a checklist for commercial leases.

1. Amount of rent. If there is a profit-sharing arrangement, specify exact terms. Is it gross or net profit? What percentage? Where is it paid?
2. In the case of a shopping center lease, what competition will be permitted?

3. Who is responsible for maintaining the common areas? Who will carry liability insurance for the common areas?

4. Can the lease be assigned? Is approval for assignment required?

5. Who will make repairs? Who pays?

6. Who will make improvements?

7. Are there mandatory hours of operation?

8. Is there an understanding on fixtures? Who keeps them?

9. What deposits are required? Are they refundable?

10. Is there compliance with all applicable laws, including ADA?

11. How are unforeseen economic setbacks and natural disasters covered under the terms of the lease? What happens if the building is destroyed? Will the landlord be required to rebuild?

KEY TERMS

Americans with Disabilities Act (ADA), 229
anchor tenant, 234
common area maintenance (CAM), 221
Consumer Price Index (CPI) adjustment clause, 221

escalation clause, 221
fixed rent, 221
gross rent, 221
net-net-net, 221
operating expenses, 221
percentage rent, 222

sick building syndrome (SBS), 220
specific happenings increase provisions, 221
triple net, 221

CHAPTER PROBLEMS

1. Walgreens has operated a pharmacy in the Southgate Mall in Milwaukee since its opening in 1951. The current lease, signed in 1971 and carrying a 30-year, six-month term, contains, as had the only previous lease, a clause in which the landlord, Sara Creek, promises not to lease space in the mall to anyone else who wants to operate a pharmacy or a store containing a pharmacy. However, Sara Creek has lost its anchor tenant in the shopping center and has signed a lease agreement with Phar-Mor, a "deep discount" chain, rather than, like Walgreens, just a "discount" chain. Phar-Mor's store would occupy 100,000 square feet, of which 12,000 would be occupied by a pharmacy the same size as Walgreens'. The entrances to the two stores would be within a couple of hundred feet of each other.

   Walgreens filed suit for an injunction halting the opening of the Phar-Mor. Sara Creek indicates that without another tenant in the space, Walgreens' sales will decline dramatically. Sara Creek argues that without the Phar-Mor, Walgreens' sales will drop $2,000,000 and that with the Phar-Mor, Walgreens will lose only $1,000,000 in sales. What do you think of Sara Creek's economic argument? Should those economic issues have a place in deciding whether to enforce restrictive covenants? Should Walgreens be permitted to terminate the lease if no injunction is granted? *Walgreen Co. v. Sara Creek Property Co.*, B.V. 966 F.2d 273 (7th Cir. 1992).

2. Marathon owns and operates the Park Plaza Mall in Little Rock, Arkansas. The mall opened in July 1988, and on March 21, 1989, Boardwalk entered into a ten-year lease agreement with Marathon to operate a Boardwalk Fries restaurant in the mall's food court.

   Boardwalk, with Marathon's approval, sublet the Park Plaza Mall space to Ken Rittmueller and James Tandy as franchisees. Rittmueller and Tandy opened their mall restaurant on May 21, 1989.

   In March 1990, Rittmueller and Tandy closed the mall restaurant and abandoned the premises due to poor sales. Marathon filed suit against Boardwalk for unpaid rents, and Boardwalk filed a third-party claim against Rittmueller and Tandy for the rent.

   Boardwalk claimed that Marathon had misrepresented the sales of other tenants during the lease negotiations. When the annual rent was revealed to be $40,000 for the restaurant space, William Morris, Marathon's leasing agent explained, "Look, this mall is opening gangbusters.... We've got a couple of players in this food court that are going to do more than a million bucks." Jack Csicsek, Boardwalk's vice president for franchising and leasing, Rittmueller, and Tandy all described sales as the "only deciding factor" in their decision to lease in Park Plaza.

   The trial court entered judgment for Marathon, and Boardwalk appealed. What should the court decide and why? *Herring-Marathon Master Partnership B v. Boardwalk Fries, Inc.*, 979 F.2d 1326 (8th Cir. 1992).

3. Hyman Companies, Inc. entered into a lease agreement with the Boston Marriott Copley to place a kiosk in the Marriott Copley for the sale of Hyman's high-end costume jewelry and other merchandise. The lease contained the following clause:

   1. *11. Hotel Alterations. If a major renovation or reconstruction of the Hotel lobby necessitates a relocation or closing of the present Premises, Marriott shall use its best efforts to relocate the Operator's business to a comparable premises (with rentals proportionately abated). If a relocation is not possible, then, in such event, Marriott may terminate this Agreement with sixty (60) days advanced written notice to Operator, provided that Marriott pays Operator on the day it vacates the Premises fifty percent (50%) of its unamortized investment in the Premises, based upon a full amortization over the seven year term of this Agreement.*

   When the Marriott Copley decided to renovate its lobby, it sent a termination notice to Hyman, but the termination notice was sent before Marriott made any effort to find a suitable location. Hyman then assigned its lease to a third party. Marriott claimed the lease was terminated and could not be assigned. Based on what you have learned in the chapter, determine who has what rights in these circumstances. *In re Hyman Companies, Inc.,* 440 B.R. 390 (Bkrptcy Ct. Mass. 2010).

4. On January 17, 1975, A & P entered into a 20-year commercial lease with Jerome Schostak, d/b/a Midland Venture, for property A & P intended to use for operation of a grocery store. The lease provided for a fixed rent of $8,630 per month plus an additional 1 percent of all sales in excess of $10,356,000.00. A & P did not have sufficient sales to owe the 1 percent until 1979. In July 1990, A & P ceased its operations on the property but continued to pay its fixed rent. In November 1990, A & P subleased the store to Dunham's Athleisure Corporation. Dunham's lease provided that it would pay 2 percent of its gross sales in excess of $3,000,000. Dunham also has never had sales sufficient to kick in the percentage portion of rent.

   A & P has simply continued to pay the fixed monthly rent. Midland maintains that A & P owes more because the contract was negotiated with the underlying assumption that A & P would stay in business. Should A & P be required to pay more rent? *Plaza Forty-Eight, Inc. v. Great Atlantic & Pacific Tea Company, Inc.,* 817 F.Supp. 774 (E.D. Wis. 1993). What would happen if a tenant ceased its operations but sublet the premises to another retailer? Would the rent clause require payment on the gross sales of the subtenant? *45-02 Food Corp. v. 45-02 43rd Realty LLC,* 37 A.D.3d 522, 830 N.Y.S.2d 304 (2007).

5. Barry Hinesley worked with Oakshade Town Center's agent and representative, Paul Petrovich, on leasing a suite for operating his business. Hinesley maintains that Petrovich told him that the regional restaurant chain Dos Coyotes, the international coffee shop chain Starbucks, and the international ice cream and yogurt vendor chain Baskin-Robbins would be leasing and occupying suites near the suite Hinesley was to lease. Hinesley said that Petrovich told him that all three chains would commence operations by the end of 1998. Hinesley and Oakshade later executed a lease, dated July 6, 1998, for a 1,200-square-foot space at the Oakshade Town Center Shopping Center for a term of five years.

   Starbucks and Baskin-Robbins never leased space from Oakshade. However, Marble Slab Creamery (an ice cream store) and Common Grounds (a coffee house) did become tenants. Dos Coyotes did become a tenant of Oakshade, but its lease did not commence until December 2000.

   Clause 25.33 of the lease Hinesley signed provides: "Lessor reserves the right to effect such other tenancies in the Shopping Center as Lessor in the exercise of its judgment shall determine to bet [*sic*] promote the interest of the Shopping Center. *Lessee does not rely on the fact nor does Lessor represent that any specific Lessee of* [sic] *type or number of Lessees shall during the term of this Lease occupy any space in the Shopping Center.*"

   Hinesley brought suit to rescind the lease on the basis of the misrepresentations by the landlord's agent on the development of the center and the promised tenants. Does Hinesley have any basis in law for allowing his rescission? Describe the pros and cons of his argument on misrepresentation. *Hinesley v. Oakshade Town Center,* 37 Cal.Rptr.3d 364 (2006).

6. Marc Fiedler is a quadriplegic moviegoer in Washington, D.C., who uses a wheelchair. American Multi-Cinema, Inc. ("AMC") is a nationwide operator of movie theaters, one of which is the Avenue Grand, located on the basement concourse of Union Station, the principal passenger railway terminal in Washington, DC. The only wheelchair seating available to Mr. Fiedler when he attends the Avenue Grand Theater is one of two wheelchair sites situated at the very back of the theater, in the last row of conventional seats farthest from the screen. Fiedler says that by relegating him to inferior seating in the back of the theater when he goes to see a movie at the Avenue Grand, AMC deprives him of full and equal enjoyment of the facilities to which he, as a disabled person, is entitled under the ADA. Fiedler has filed suit against AMC, the company that leases the facilities from the federal government (the owner of Union Station), which is managed by the Department of Transportation, also named as a defendant. AMC argues that the presence of a wheelchair and its occupant in the midst of able-bodied patrons in fear for their own safety could impede a mass

exodus of the theater in the case of an emergency. Such seating would constitute a "direct threat to the health or safety of others," something that excuses ADA compliance. The federal government filed briefs in favor of Fiedler's position. Discuss the ADA issue, AMC's responsibility, and the actions of the federal government in support of a party including it as a defendant in his suit. What is the federal government's exposure in the case? *Fiedler v. American Multi-Cinema, Inc.,* 871 F.Supp. 35 (D.D.C. 1994).

7. David Gotlieb and Taco Bell Corporation entered into a 20-year lease on August 15, 1991, for the purpose of building a Taco Bell restaurant in Brooklyn, New York. There was a due diligence provision in the lease, and Taco Bell was permitted to cancel the lease if it could not obtain the necessary permits for the construction of the fast-food facility. Shortly after the lease was signed, community and religious groups began an organized effort to oppose the construction of the Taco Bell and any other fast-food franchises in the area. Taco Bell worked with community leaders for six months but was unable to make any progress. Taco Bell never applied for the permits but did cancel the lease. Gotlieb objected and sued Taco Bell for lost rents. What are Gotlieb's responsibilities upon Taco Bell's repudiation of the lease? What are Taco Bell's responsibilities? *Gotlieb v. Taco Bell Corporation,* 871F.Supp. 147 (E.D.N.Y. 1994).

8. Elaine Barton entered into a five-year lease with the Mitchell Company for retail store premises for the purpose of operating her patio furniture store. The lease began November 1, 1985. In October 1984, the Mitchell Company leased the space adjoining Ms. Barton's store to Body Electric. Body Electric operated an exercise studio. Loud music, screams, shouts, and yells accompanied the operation of Body Electric during business hours. The intensity and volume of such caused the walls of Ms. Barton's space to vibrate. Paintings fell off the walls. Ms. Barton lost customers and salespeople because of the noise.

Ms. Barton complained of the noise, and Mitchell promised to add insulation to the walls. Nothing was done and the noise levels made it impossible for Ms. Barton to continue her operation. She vacated the premises on August 3, 1985. Mitchell then brought suit against Barton for rent due on the unexpired portion of the lease. Can Mitchell recover the rent? *Barton v. Mitchell Company,* 507 So.2d 148 (Fla. 1987).

9. On September 5, 2006, Pacific Coast Silks, LLC (tenant) and 1247 Realty (landlord) entered into a commercial lease for the seventh-floor at 247 West 36th Street in Manhattan, to be used "for silk garment fabric sales." The building is serviced by a single elevator, which opens directly onto the premises; the only other means of access to the premises is through a stairwell. At the time the lease was executed, the elevator was in the midst of a major renovation that had begun in July 2006, leaving the building without elevator service. It took seven weeks for the elevator to be repaired, and Pacific Coast sought to have the lease ended because of constructive eviction. Pacific Coast had used the property for seven weeks through the stair access and had installed a new wood floor during that time. Has there been constructive eviction? Contrast this fact pattern with the discussion of premises condition in the chapter and note any differences. *Pacific Coast Silks, LLC v. 247 Realty,* LLC 76 A.D.3d 167, 904 N.Y.S.2d 407 (N.Y.A.D. 2010).

10. On August 8, 1994, First Hawaiian Bank notified Colony Surf Development that its consent for any leases of mortgaged property was required under various mortgage agreements between the Bank and Colony Surf Development. On November 15, 1994, the Bank and Colony Surf Development entered into a Restructuring Agreement, which consolidated and restructured Colony Surf Development's debt. Colony Surf began negotiations for JCI to lease the Commercial Space. Colony Surf Development was represented by its agent, Radomile, in those negotiations.

Eventually, on April 27, 1995, Colony Surf Development and JCI entered into a ten-year lease. Radomile executed the lease on behalf of Colony Surf Development. Under the terms of the lease imposed by the Bank, JCI was required to construct, at its sole cost and expense, all interior improvements to the Commercial Space, the hard costs for which were not to be less than $500,000. The requirement was not disclosed to JCI, and the restructuring agreement with the Bank's requirements had not been recorded in the land records. JCI did put in $163,509.20 in improvements, but the Bank required more and claimed JCI was in breach. JCI filed suit for misrepresentation and asked that the lease be set aside. Colony Surf maintains that JCI was not entitled to rely on Radomile. What should the court decide? Is there a misrepresentation that allows the court to set aside the lease? Does it make any difference that the requirement on the expenditures was not public record? *First Hawaiian Bank v. Radomile,* 120 P.3d 1127 (Haw. 2005).

For research activities related to this chapter, go to our text companion website at www.cengagebrain.com

CHAPTER 11

REAL ESTATE COMMUNITIES: MULTIUNIT INTERESTS AND OWNERS' ASSOCIATIONS

Section 12.9. Window Coverings. The largest living room window of each Unit shall have a window covering, the back side of which (i.e., the side of the window covering facing the window pane and visible from the outside of the Building) will be of a color similar to Benjamin Moore #1065.

A sample rule from the CCRs of a condominium association

"There's no question that the financial vigilance of co-op boards contributed to the stability of the Manhattan real estate market during the big economic downturn."
Frederick Peters, president of a New York City real estate agency.[1]

Since the time of Rome, Napoleon, and the Middle Ages, residential housing in limited space has been a struggle. A limited supply of land in those eras generated ownership of floors and "the subdivision of vertical space."[2] France first created multiunit housing and laws in the 1930s. When the supply of surface properties is limited, as discussed in Chapter 3, we turn to the air rights as a way of maximizing property use. Acquiring air rights has resulted in several types of home ownership in a group setting. The condominium, townhouse, cooperative, time-sharing, and recreational lease forms of housing are all answers to the home or second-home ownership dream when land is limited.

Whenever there are property owners in close proximity, as they are in multi-unit housing, they need special rules for the use of their property, as well as rules

---

[1]Vivan S. Toy, "2011: The Year of the Big Turn-Down," *New York Times*, Dec. 29, 2011, p. B1.

[2]Warren Freedman and Jonathan B. Alter, *The Law of Condominia and Property Owners' Associations* 109–24 (1992).

that provide for rights and responsibilities. These special forms of housing create their own communities, with certain statutory controls and a complete set of private laws that govern the community and owner interaction. Understanding how these private governance mechanisms work in housing ownership of all types is important for those who own, sell, or finance these forms of real estate ownership. However, these governance principles for multiunit housing are now a part of single-family subdivisions. Developers of single-family subdivisions are often now required to have **owners' associations** in order to get municipal approval for their projects. These owners' or community associations are now the norm. In 1960, there were an estimated 500 owners' associations in the United States. By 1970, there were 10,000 associations, growing to 36,000 by 1980, 130,000 by 1990, 222,500 by 2000, and by 2011, there were 286,000 owners' associations, meaning that 60 million people, or roughly one in five Americans, were living under the governance of homeowners' associations.[3] In the largest metropolitan areas, more than half of new home sales are connected to an owners' association. With the rise of the gated community and planned housing developments, the regulatory framework for multiunit housing has been adopted and adapted to apply to owners and their housing, in whatever form.

This chapter first examines the forms of multiunit real estate interests and answers the following questions: What are the definitions of and distinctions among condominium, townhouse, cooperative, and time-sharing properties? How is each of the multiunit housing arrangements created? The second part of the chapter examines the governance issues in organized communities, such as in multiunit housing, in single-family housing subdivisions with owners' associations, and in private, gated communities, by looking at the following questions: What laws cover owners' associations? Who is responsible for the common areas? What can owners' associations require and control? What are the rights and responsibilities of associations and owners?

MULTIUNIT HOUSING

The Applicable Laws

Each state has its own statutes to govern each of the types of multiunit real property ownership, and the statutes vary significantly from state to state. This concept of individual ownership of parts of buildings did not exist in the United States until the 1950s because of the relative ease with which a single-family dwelling could be built or purchased. Puerto Rico passed the first applicable laws in 1958 with the adoption of its Horizontal Property Act.

In 1961, Congress authorized the Federal Housing Administration (FHA) to insure mortgages on condominium units; subsequently, the attractiveness of condominiums was substantially enhanced, and state laws were passed. At the end of 1963, 39 states had some form of legislation; by 1969, all states had adopted some form of regulation on condominium and townhouse developments.

The tremendous growth in these multiunit forms of real estate ownership has resulted in some scrambling on the parts of legislatures and uniform law conferences to establish laws on these unique forms of real estate holdings. The uniform laws have not been widely adopted by the states. The oldest uniform law is the **Uniform Condominium Act**, which has been adopted in 12 states. States without the

[3]The National Board of Certification for Community Association Managers, http://www.nbccam.org/.

Uniform Condominium Act may still have legislation on ownership, but it may be referred to as **horizontal property regimes**. In some states, the laws are referred to as **horizontal property acts**.

Laws continue to evolve to address the complex issues that result from these creative forms of ownership. There is a **Model Real Estate Cooperative Act** and a **Model Real Estate Time-Share Act**. The relatively new **Uniform Common Interest Ownership Act** has as its goal to create one type of common ownership by defining a common interest in real property as one in which the owners of individual units also have an interest and/or obligation to pay for maintenance of other land areas This act has met with resistance and concerns about ambiguity and overlapping statutes and, as a result, has not been adopted in any states.

The patchwork approach to legislation on multiunit housing requires covering the principles of law according to the type of units. The following sections provide that coverage.

CONDOMINIUMS

Definition and Characteristics

A **condominium** can take many physical forms: It can be a townhouse, an apartment, or part of a freestanding duplex house. Most states now allow the commercial condominium, with businesses able to enjoy horizontal property ownership in high-rise buildings. Ownership of a portion of a multi-story building allows a business to own real estate and avoid the variability and indefiniteness of lease agreements.

The physical form that the condominium takes, whether patio home or apartment-like unit, has no effect on the owner's legal status or rights. The owner owns a fee simple interest in the actual dwelling unit and is entitled to all the rights of a fee simple holder: The condominium may be sold, leased, or mortgaged and is subject to foreclosure, power of sale, and homestead rights. The owner is also given an undivided joint interest in all the common areas of the building. The owner of a condominium unit in the form of an apartment in a multistory building would have an undivided interest in areas such as the halls, stairs, lobby, and any recreational facilities.

Although the condominium unit owner has an interest in the common areas, only the actual dwelling unit may be mortgaged or pledged, and creditors of the unit owner may foreclose only on a per-unit basis, not on the entire unit. The use and decoration of the unit is controlled by bylaws, CCRs, and owners' associations (see later in the chapter for more discussion).

Creation of a Condominium Development

A condominium development must be created according to statutory processes. If condominium developers do not follow the statutory requirements, they have not created the proper land interests for the owners.

Conversion Restrictions

Because of the large number of conversions of apartments to condominiums, most states have regulations requiring minimum notice periods before conversions can take place. The purpose of **conversion restrictions** is to give tenants the opportunity to decide whether to move or to purchase the condominium unit in which they live. The typical notice requirement under conversion statutes is 120 days. Also, most statutes provide that tenants who decline the opportunity to purchase the condominium unit must be given additional time to find other housing before they are required to end their tenancy. Many conversion statutes require that landlords honor the remainder of the tenants' leases.

Declaration of Condominium or Master Deed

The prerequisite for the creation of a condominium development is the fee simple ownership of a lot or lots of an existing building or buildings. The fee simple ownership may be held by an individual, several individuals, or a corporation. The owner (or owners) begins the condominium development by drafting and recording a master deed or a **declaration of condominium** (called a **declaration of horizontal property regime and covenants** in some states). The **master deed** is, in effect, a description of the subdivision of the building. Every deed to every condominium unit owner will then refer to this master deed for a legal description of the unit. In addition to accomplishing the subdivision of the building, the declaration also covers the following:

1. Legal description of the property
2. Detailed description of the building or buildings making up the complex, and the number of stories, basements, and units
3. Mailing address of each unit and a physical description including the number of rooms, method of access, and other identifiable characteristics
4. Detailed description of the common areas
5. Limitations on the use of common areas
6. Monetary value of the building and each unit
7. How votes are to be assigned—per-unit basis or per-value basis
8. Restrictions on land use: for example, all-adult restrictions
9. Name and address of legal representative for the development
10. Voting procedures
11. Methods for amending the declaration of condominium

In many states, the declaration or master deed for a condominium project may be called a **declaration of covenants, conditions, and restrictions (CC&Rs or CCRs)**.

Regardless of the name, the document that is filed has a certain permanence to it. Only by following amendment procedures can there be variations and changes from the original declaration.

Incorporation

Generally, most condominium projects are incorporated for a number of reasons, including the convenience of having the common areas owned by one entity instead of carrying title in the names of all unit owners, as well as the protection against personal liability of the unit owners for injuries in the common areas (discussed later in this chapter). But corporate ownership also creates a method of governance through shareholder voting (also covered later in the chapter under owners' associations). When disputes arise, there are far more legal precedents in corporate law than there are rights and procedures afforded under a declaration of condominium.

Deeds

Once the master deed is recorded, each unit owner is granted his or her interest through an individual deed. Condominium deeds must meet all requirements of property deeds (see Chapter 12) and should include the following specifics:

1. Legal description (includes a reference to the declaration of condominium and where it is recorded)
2. Mailing address
3. Use restrictions (may be a reference to another document)
4. Title warranties

COOPERATIVES

Nature of Cooperatives

Ownership of a cooperative is different from a fee simple ownership of real estate. A **cooperative** ownership is an undivided joint interest in the land and buildings that make up the cooperative. Ownership is most likely held by the cooperative as a nonprofit organization, with each cooperative unit assigned a certain number of shares in the corporation. A cooperative unit dweller does not own a real estate interest but rather a share or shares in a corporation that owns the entire complex. In essence, the corporation of which the owner is a shareholder is the landlord for all units in the cooperative.

In the following case, the court deals with the issue of the nature of ownership in a cooperative when the owners are in violation of co-op rules and requirements.

HAWAIIAN PROPERTIES, LTD. V. TAUALA

254 P.3d 487 (Haw. App. 2011)
The Tenant "Aloha" Does Not Apply to the Co-Op Owner

FACTS

For many years, Regina P.D. Tauala has lived in unit # 16C of Makalapa Manor Apartments, a Hawaii Cooperative Corporation. The Cooperative was developed in the early 1970's, pursuant to financing insured by the federal Secretary of Housing and Urban Development, acting by and through the Federal Housing Commissioner (HUD), and Tauala's parents bought into the Cooperative in 1971. Her parents received documents that contained the following information about their purchase:

*A subscription for membership in a housing cooperative is more than an application for a place to live. It lends to **your participation in the cooperative ownership** and operation of a housing project.... The cooperative approach to housing **instills a pride of ownership** resulting in a deeper interest in maintaining the property and participating in civic affairs. A cooperative is operated on a demo-*

*cratic basis. It gives the residents a greater insight and appreciation of the democratic process in general. **Cooperative residents normally occupy the premises for longer terms than renters**.... (emphasis in court opinion).*

The cooperative was incorporated as a nonprofit cooperative housing corporation and Tauala's parents received a certificate of membership in the cooperative. Tauala's parents also received an explanation that their payments qualified for real estate tax and mortgage deductions under the Internal Revenue Code.

Tauala's monthly rent was adjusted under a federal assistance-to-the-needy program and was as follows:

Contract Rent	$550
Utility Allowance	$ 97
Assistance Payment	$476
Total Tenant Payment	$171
Tenant Rent	$ 74

However, Hawaii Properties Ltd. (HPL) Senior Property Manager, Francine Martiniz, notified Tauala of a "rent increase" to $624.00 effective February 1, 2007, because her Section 8 rent subsidy program had been terminated.

Tauala refused to pay the increased monthly amount demanded in Martiniz's letter, but continued to make monthly payments of $74.00. Tauala's monthly income, from Social Security, was $623.00. The total amount due because of the rent increase dating back to February 2007 was $4,540.00. Martiniz's notice gave her ten days to pay before her lease would be terminated. Martiniz filed suit for forcible detainer to have Tauala removed.

On November 1, 2007, Tauala filed *pro se* (on her own behalf—she represented herself) a motion to dismiss on the basis that she was an owner of her cooperative unit. The District Court denied the motion. The court then issued judgment for HPL and granted it possession of Tauala's co-op unit. Tauala appealed.

JUDICIAL OPINION

Leonard, Judge

Tauala contends that she was a homeowner, not merely a renter, and therefore, the District Court lacked jurisdiction over this matter.

At first blush, HPL's argument that Tauala was not an owner of the premises—and therefore this is simply a landlord-tenant case over which the District Court had jurisdiction—is appealing. The Cooperative appears to "own" the housing project, Tauala owned only a membership in the Cooperative, *i.e.,* she owned a 1% stock-like interest in the Cooperative corporation, and Tauala occupied the premises pursuant to the terms of the Occupancy Agreement.

The relationship between Tauala and the Cooperative is clearly, and by design, more complex than the typical short-term landlord-tenant relationship in which the lessee is granted "solely the right of possession." [M]embership in the Cooperative was intended to provide a way for low-income and displaced families to: (1) participate in a form of housing ownership; (2) experience the pride of ownership; (3) invest in their housing in a way that will accrue equity; (4) benefit from the same federal income tax advantages as other homeowners; and (5) be able to

sell their interest and right of occupancy. Cooperative members were told that they, collectively, would be their own landlords, they would pay monthly carrying charges (not rent) based on the Cooperative's income and expenses, and they could leave their membership to their loved ones when they died.

Ownership of a cooperative membership, combined with the right to occupy a unit in the cooperative project, is a form of property ownership, even though cooperative owners do not directly hold the title to their properties. This form of home ownership is unlikely to have the economic value of fee simple ownership or a conventional long-term leasehold interest, but it has value and constitutes a right of property beyond mere possession. Indeed, for some low-income families, it may be the only form of home ownership that is economically possible. [W]e conclude that a cooperative member's right to occupy their cooperative unit cannot be cancelled or terminated in a district court summary possession action. The only court that may take cognizance of such actions is the circuit court.

Courts in some other jurisdictions have similarly concluded that members or shareholders in a cooperative apartment corporation hold a unique form of real property ownership, and their relationship to the cooperative is not merely a landlord-tenant relationship. See, e.g., *Kadera v. Superior Court,* 187 Ariz. 557, 931 P.2d 1067 (Ariz.App.1997) (holding that Arizona's landlord-tenant statute did not apply to cooperatives, summary possession proceedings could not be used, and shareholders in a cooperative corporation had an interest in real property, rather than tenants' interest, even though legal title to the land was held by the cooperative). Accordingly, we conclude that the District Court lacked subject matter jurisdiction over HPL's action and, on remand, the District Court must dismiss the case.

Reversed and remanded.

CASE QUESTIONS

1. List the factors that showed Tauala's parents held a property interest, something more than a lease.
2. Explain why there could not be an eviction for the nonpayment of the $624 monthly fee.

Another distinction between cooperative ownership and traditional fee simple ownership is the possibility that the cooperative shareholder may be restricted in the transfer of shares. Although cooperative unit owners may be free to sell their leasehold interests or shares, they may be required to obtain cooperative board approval or even offer their interests first to the corporation. They may also be restricted in how the property can be disposed of upon their death. New York City is filled with urban legends about co-op board denials to potential buyers (see Practical Tip: How To Avoid Being Turned Down by a Co-Op Board). Co-op boards have the right to turn down any buyer, so long as they do not violate the Fair Housing Act (see Chapter 19) by discriminating on the basis of race or religion. As the chapter opening quote noted, the high credit standards of co-op boards helped curb foreclosures in New York City.

ETHICAL ISSUE

Co-op board denials have included one handed to former president Richard Nixon after he resigned in disgrace following the Watergate political scandal. Other celebrities who have been denied by co-op boards include Madonna, Gloria Vanderbilt, Carly Simon, Mariah Carey, Calvin Klein, and Sheik Hamad bin Jassim bin Jaber Al Thani, prime minister of Qatar. The Dakota building, the location of John and Yoko Lennon's home and where Lennon was shot and killed, has other famous occupants (Lauren Bacall, Leonard Bernstein, Rudolph Nureyev, and Mia Farrow). But it is also famous for its public battle with actors Antonio Banderas and Melanie Griffith, who were turned down by the board when they tried to buy a unit. Banderas and Griffith called the decision "arbitrary" and "arrogant" and accused the board of "narrowness of vision." While the actions of the co-op boards in their denials are legal, are they ethical? What reasons could boards give for not wanting actors as residents?

Source: "New York Apartment Buyers Face Powerful Co-Op Boards," *The Epoch Times*, January 27–February 2, 2005, p. 13.

Creation of a Cooperative

The following sections explain the basic documents needed for the creation of a cooperative.

Articles of Incorporation and Evidence of Incorporation

Since ownership of a cooperative is really ownership of an interest in a corporation, the first documents needed are the incorporation papers. Most states do require the filing of articles of incorporation before a certificate of incorporation or corporate charter is issued. The following information is generally required for incorporation:

1. Corporate name
2. Purpose of the corporation (cooperative)
3. Share structure, including voting rights and transferability
4. Name of legal agent or representative
5. Structure of the board of directors and makeup on initial board
6. Provisions for amendment to the articles

Bylaws

The **bylaws** for a cooperative are similar to those for both corporations and condominiums: Their purpose is to specify operating procedures. The bylaws provide the details for meetings, including place, time, notice, quorums, and voting requirements. Finally, the bylaws contain the procedures for transferring ownership rights to cooperative members and usually provide instructions for the proprietary lease.

Proprietary Lease

A **proprietary lease** is very similar to an ordinary lease, covering many of the topics and issues that arise in the landlord–tenant relationship. However, the following factors distinguish the two:

1. *Length* If the proprietary lease provides for a termination date at all, the date will be well into the future. Otherwise, the termination of the lease is tied to the transfer of the tenant's interest in the cooperative corporation.

2. *Rent* A proprietary lease has no provision for rent; instead, the tenant pays a maintenance fee. These maintenance fees can be increased and the lease may even provide for percentage increases according to a cost-of-living scale.

The proprietary lease also covers contingencies, such as the owner's option to sell if maintenance fees increase substantially and the owner's rights if the cooperative unit is uninhabitable for a period of time.

TOWNHOUSES

Nature of Townhouses

The owner of a **townhouse** owns the land on which the townhouse is located, the actual dwelling unit, and an undivided joint interest in the common elements of the development such as a swimming pool or clubhouse. Actual land ownership distinguishes this form of multiunit housing from the others, where there is simply ownership of space.

Creation of Townhouses

As with the other forms of multiunit housing, there are specific requirements for creating townhouse ownership.

Declaration of Covenants, Conditions, and Restrictions

Similar to a master deed or declaration of condominium, the declaration of CCRs is the first step in creating a townhouse development. The CCRs contain all of the rights and responsibilities of the individual owners. Since the CCRs are recorded, everyone is presumed to know their content. Most states now have a requirement that buyers sign off on receipt of a copy of the CCRs. Once recorded, the CCRs serve as constructive notice of the regulations of and restrictions in the development. All-adult restrictions are often part of the CCRs. In the event of a conflict, the CCRs are the final authority for correcting ambiguities or clarifying legal rights.

Articles of Incorporation

The decision to incorporate is discretionary in some states as a more convenient way of holding title. Other states require that a corporation must be formed to hold title to common areas, and each owner is given a certain percentage share of the corporation.

Bylaws

The bylaws deal with the operation of the townhouse development, covering issues such as repairs, maintenance, and compliance with all the CCR provisions. Although the bylaws set up voting procedures, such procedures must be consistent with the articles of incorporation to be valid. The bylaws may also establish various committees to aid in the enforcement of restrictions—an architectural control committee, for example. More details on bylaws appear later in the chapter in the discussion of owners' associations.

Regulations

The purpose of the regulations in a townhouse development is the same as the purpose of those in a condominium development: to keep common facilities in repair and reasonably available to residents in the development.

TIME-SHARING INTERESTS

Nature of Time-Sharing Ownership

In resort areas, the concept of **time-sharing** ownership or recreational ownership has become popular.[4] The owner of a time-share owns a fee simple interest but can exercise the right of possession only for a limited time each year and during the same period of time each year. For example, a time-share may be the right to the use of a two-bedroom apartment in San Diego from June 1 to June 8 every year in perpetuity. This right of use may be transferred *inter vivos* or by will or intestate succession. The limitation on the property is the time of use. In addition to the right to use the dwelling unit, the owner is also given the right to use all common areas, including any recreational facilities such as pools, game rooms, and saunas.

Time-sharing units require clarification of whether a unit owner will always have a particular unit at a given time or whether a unit will simply be available for the buyer's use at the time purchased. The time-share regimen should specify how the time units are divided, the length of each owner's time unit, and whether a specific unit was assigned. A sample length-of-use clause appears below to illustrate the complexity of this task:

> *Week No. 1 is the seven consecutive days commencing at noon on the first Saturday of each year and continues till noon on the following Saturday. Week No. 2 is the seven consecutive days next succeeding Week No. 1. Successive weeks up to and including Week No. 51 are computed in a like manner. Week No. 52 contains the seven consecutive days next succeeding Week 51 together with any additional days not otherwise assigned continuing until the commencement of Week No. 1 of the following year.* From Martin, "Timesharing in Colorado," *11 The Colorado Lawyer* 2804 (1982).

Creation of Time-Sharing Interests

A time-sharing interest may take the form of a recreational lease, a proprietary lease, or a limited fee simple interest. A **recreational lease** is a financing device that allows the lessee to spread out over time the payment for use of another's recreational property. Generally, these recreational leases have rent-escalation clauses that increase the rent according to some scale over the perpetual period of the lease. The lease may be a true lease with a landlord–tenant relationship between the parties, or its character may depend more strictly on the terms of the agreement. Ninety-nine-year leases or those without a specific termination date are more likely to be proprietary leases for a cooperative form of ownership. Leases

---

[4]Many states simply regulate their time-sharing properties through their condominium laws while other states have enacted separate statutes to govern time-sharing projects.

where the rental payment is determined according to a formula that is based on expenses of operation are also more likely to be proprietary leases for a cooperative form of ownership.

Time-sharing interests may also be interests in perpetuity but limited in use to a specified period during each year. It is possible for a time-sharing interest to be a fee simple interest with limited use rights.

The **vacation license** is an arrangement in which the developer retains a fee simple interest in the property and grants licenses for use for certain periods during the year. This type of arrangement is considered the sale of securities by the Securities and Exchange Commission (SEC) and is subject to securities registration requirements.

In some areas, time-sharing owners have developed time-sharing networks in which the owners trade off interests in one location for interests in another. In any of the arrangements, the documents should specify responsibilities and the liabilities for the cost of maintaining the premises.

HYBRIDS

In some states, hybrid forms of ownership can be found under various labels such as **patio homes, garden homes**, and **attached homes**. In these hybrid forms, the owners may own the land and the entire dwelling but will have a party wall agreement for the joint wall between properties. The laws governing these hybrids vary from state to state. In some states, joint wall properties are treated as townhouses, while in others they are labeled condominiums.

MANAGING CLOSE QUARTERS: THE ISSUES OF OWNERS' ASSOCIATIONS

Owners' associations are necessities in condominiums, co-ops, and townhomes, and their creation runs parallel with the conversion or creation of the multiunit interest. However, with the increases in planned communities and gated communities, the creation of an owners' association has also run parallel to a builder's obtaining approval for the creation of a single-family home community and the fee simple ownership buyers will hold. In fact, owners' associations, sometimes called HOAs (for homeowners' associations in single-family neighborhoods) are often called a substitute for zoning in that they regulate the appearance of and types of structures in their communities.

The law on owners' associations is still developing and varies significantly from state to state. However, there are some developing uniform laws, at least portions of which can be found in state statutes. In addition to the provisions in the Uniform Condominium Act and the Model Real Estate Cooperative Act, mentioned earlier, there is also the Uniform Planned Community Act (UPCA) and the Uniform Common Interest Ownership Act that addresses many of the issues of owners' associations that are common to multiunit owners' associations and HOAs. There are three basic issues in all owners' associations: the structure for operating the association or the governance and authority issues, the interpretation and application of rules in the exercise of authority of owners' associations, and, finally, the liability of the association to owners and third parties.

Governance: Running Communities Smoothly and Consistently
How Do You Get an Owners' Association?

An owners' association is created simultaneously with the community.[5] The documents that are part of the creation of a community include the declaration of the land interest (as with the condominium declaration); the plat maps and deeds (including the CCRs); and then a series of documents that serve to create the owners' association as a corporation, including the articles of incorporation and the bylaws. These nonprofit corporation associations have three common characteristics: Every property owner (regardless of the type of ownership) is automatically a member of the association; the individual unit or lot owners hold equal title to the common areas; and all of the individual owners are required to pay annual and/or monthly fees to their associations.

In the initial sale of the units or houses in the communities, the developer/builder holds majority control of the corporation and, as a result, the owners' association. That control is then turned over to owners as the percentage of property owners exceeds the percentage of units or lots owned by the developer/builder. The presence of the corporate structure not only allows that transfer, it provides a means for the association to be run fairly and to take steps that ensure the quality of the community. One writer has described the role of owners' associations as follows: "(1) it maintains common areas; (2) it arranges for delivery of services; (3) it taxes members through regular and special assessments to pay for amenities and services; and (4) it protects neighborhood aesthetics and real estate values by enforcing the declaration."[6] Areas of contention and litigation include determining how much authority the association has and whether the association is acting properly in its contracting and enforcement.

Who Is in Charge? The Association Board

The heart of association governance, as with all corporations, can be found in the articles of incorporation. The articles provide for the election of a board of directors, as elected representatives of the owners charged with the governance of the association and the community. The board will consist of owners in the community. In carrying out its responsibilities, the association board will take care of the four areas of association purposes noted earlier, responsibilities that can include everything from maintenance of common areas to policies on gate access to landscaping decisions.

The association board authority is limited by the powers granted in the declaration. The declaration includes the rights and restrictions that apply to all who purchase units or land in the community, and because the declaration is recorded, those rights and responsibilities run with the land. Under planned community laws now in effect in many states, there are mandatory rights and obligations for all planned communities and they are incorporated by statute.

The declaration can cover everything from the type of roof to the amount of time owners have to get landscaping. For example, a common declaration provision is that owners have 90 days from closing to install landscaping and 60 days from closing to have permanent window coverings such as curtains, blinds, or shutters. Many of the powers necessary for operating an association, including the right

---

[5]For ease of reference, the term "community" as used here includes condos, co-ops, townhomes, and gated and planned neighborhoods.

[6]Brian Jason Fleming, "Regulation of Political Signs in Private Homeowner Associations: A New Approach," 59 *Vanderbilt Law Review* 571, 581 (2006).

of assessment, cannot be put in place by the board after the fact because buyers purchased their interest in reliance on reasonable interpretation of the declaration. Under the association reform statutes being adopted by many states, bylaws and board resolutions creating new rights and obligations that were not in the declaration are subject to a judicial review for reasonableness.

Board Operations: What Can the Board Do and How Much Authority Does it Have?

The board and association can adopt bylaws, or the rules and procedures for running the association/corporation, subject to the powers granted and intent of the association and community formation documents.

The bylaws are generally drafted by the developer but may be adopted by the unit owners once the developer has sold all the units, lots, or houses. The bylaws should contain rules for the following areas:

1. Composition of a governing board or committee for the association, and the methods and requirements for election of its members.
2. Details for meetings, such as place, time, notice, quorum, requirements, and voting processes.
3. Procedures for day-to-day maintenance authorization, equipment replacements, and routine repairs.
4. Amount of any association fees to be collected from unit owners for maintenance of common areas, and so on; the methods for collecting such fees; and the penalties for late payment or nonpayment. (See the following discussion on enforcement for authority of associations for collection.)
5. Procedures for amending the bylaws.
6. Use restrictions, such as adult-only and in-home businesses restrictions and limitations on transfer and rental.

The Board's Role and Authority in Running the Community Rules and Enforcement

The creation of the owners' association, passage of bylaws, and election of a board are the easiest part of running an owners' association. The difficulties come with rules, regulations, and enforcement.

Regulations for a Smoothly Running Community

Regulations are valid if they were adopted in order to keep the community functioning smoothly. Regulations can cover items such as pets and the use of the pool, laundry room, and other recreational rooms and equipment. The bylaws should contain provisions for the development of and amendment to the regulations.

Sources of Rules Enforcement Power: Tools and Areas of Focus

While boards have the authority to propose changes in the bylaws and regulations, they must still follow board processes and procedures and they cannot exceed unreasonably the authority given in the declaration. Any changes to bylaws, regulations, and CCRs must be done correctly under voting procedures provided for in the bylaws and any new restrictions must be reasonable. There are several other areas of considerable contention and litigation in owners' associations, and legal battles result when these contentious issues are not handled properly.

Enforcement tools are limited by both the legal documents of the community as well as, in most states, by statute. If those tools are not established as part of the bylaws, the association cannot use them. An effective homeowners' association is responsible for dealing with issues of noise, property use, property upkeep, and maintenance of the common areas. However, owners' associations frequently end up in litigation because of the need for balance in managing common living conditions and individual property ownership. The amount of litigation related to owners' associations, particularly in condominium developments, has skyrocketed since 1990. Many states have passed Planned Community Acts (PCA) that establish the authority and rights of owners and boards. Listing the rights, responsibilities, and limits of associations and owners in these statutes has served as a way to decrease the contentious litigation surrounding associations as they provide the courts with definitive statutory guidance.

The remedies available to associations include fines and, in cases of public health, where the owner of the house or unit does not maintain sanitary living conditions that rise to the level of nuisance, the association can seek judicial removal of the owner. For example, in *4215 Harding Road Homeowners Ass'n. v. Harris,* 354 S.W.3d 296 (Tenn. App. 2011), the court ordered the removal of a hoarder who resided in a condominium that was so malodorous from trash, food left in the refrigerator, and bugs, that clean-up crews refused to enter the unit and the other owners in the building could no longer live in their units. The property manager spent a year trying to help the owner with maintaining sanitary conditions and even did 38 loads of laundry to remove the dirt and smells from the owner's clothes. The longstanding and good-faith efforts of the association allowed the court to take the position it did of having the owner removed for public health reasons.

The following case deals with issues of changes in the CCRs and the resulting impact on owners as well as the implications of an individual owner's violation of restrictions on leasing.

CAPE MAY HARBOR VILLAGE AND YACHT CLUB ASS'N, INC. V. SBRAGA

22 A.3d 158 (N.J. Super. 2011)
No Slip-Up in HOA Processes

FACTS

The Declaration and CCRs (Declaration) for the Cape May Harbor Village and Yacht Club, a community of 24 single-family homes, were filed in the Cape May County Clerk's office in 1995. Cape May is small and exclusive, consisting of the homes, common areas, and a marina. There are forty boat slips, some of which are owned by homeowners, and others by the Association. The Cape May homes were assessed for local real estate property tax purposes at between $1,181,900 and $1,705,700. Current homes were listed for sale at prices ranging from $2,545,000 to $2,699,000.

Deborah Sbraga (appellant) and her husband purchased a vacant lot in Cape May in June 2000 and built a home on the lot in 2005. Because of a divorce, the property was placed solely in Mrs. Sbraga's name in May 2007. She wished to lease her home.

The Declaration includes the following provisions on leases:

(n) Leases. (i) No Owner may lease less than the entire Lot except that any boat slip appurtenant to a Lot may be leased apart from the Lot.

(ii) Any lease on any Dwelling or boat slip shall be in writing and shall be subject to the provisions of

this Declaration (whether or not such documents have been provided to the tenant); and any failure of the tenant to fully comply with the provisions of this Declaration shall constitute a material default under the lease and be grounds for termination and eviction.

The Declaration could be amended only by a vote of at least 67% of all members of the Association. By the summer of 2009, apparently in the aftermath of her divorce and for financial reasons, Mrs. Sbraga put her home up for sale. Because of the depressed real estate market, obtaining a favorable sale price was difficult, so she decided she would like to lease the property while she was trying to sell it in order to bring in some revenue.

In June 2009, Mrs. Sbraga approached George Via, the President of the HOA (Association), to clarify whether she was permitted to lease her home. Via explained that no one had ever leased any of the homes in the subdivision.

At the Association's annual meeting of August 28, 2009, a proposed amendment was presented to the membership that would prohibit leasing of homes. After a discussion, the amendment was approved by a vote of twenty in favor and three opposed.

Mrs. Sbraga went ahead and leased her home anyway. The Association brought suit seeking an injunction against the lease. Mrs. Sbraga counter-claimed, seeking a declaration that the amendment to the Declaration was void.

The trial court found that the amendment was valid and enforceable, and enjoined the leasing of property. Mrs. Sbraga appealed.

JUDICIAL OPINION
Lisa, Presiding Judge

Appellant argues that the court erred in the manner in which it applied the reasonableness standard when finding that the Association's action to prohibit her exercise of a fundamental property right was legally permissible. Appellant further argues that the amendment to the Declaration, adopted after she took title to the property, cannot be enforced against her. We reject these arguments and affirm.

Via explained that the Association had no one who would be able to enforce violations of the Declaration for the homes. Basically, there had never been any problems with noise or unruly behavior by the owner-occupants of the homes or their families or guests, and the Association members wanted to

keep it that way. It was anticipated that weekly tenants would not be likely to have the same concerns and attitudes about the importance of maintaining a quiet residential neighborhood atmosphere. This community was not a typical seasonal rental area that commonly exists in many New Jersey seashore communities, and the Association members were determined to preserve the stable and non-transient character of their community. Judicial review of the amendment should be guided by the reasonableness standard or the business judgment rule.

The lower court noted that the community was small, exclusive, and had no history of rentals. The court also determined that it was "legitimate" to forecast that having tenants in the community could have an "impact on the neighborhood" and its image, and that members might prefer the community not to have a "transient flavor." Additionally, the court observed that condominium associations and homeowners associations often place restrictions, though perhaps not absolute, on renting. The court conceded the analysis might change if there were a history of homeowners renting, or if the community was larger, with "thousands of homes," or if it was not a "somewhat exclusive community."

Appellant's argument can be simply stated: When she purchased this property, there was no prohibition against leasing, and any subsequently-imposed restriction on leasing cannot apply to her because it would impermissibly deprive her of a valuable property right and constitute a disfavored restraint on the alienation of property. Indeed, appellant urges a *per se* rule in this regard. This position ignores two important considerations. First, although the original Declaration did not prohibit (and indeed contemplated) leasing of homes, it also contained provisions authorizing amendments of its provisions. Therefore, any purchaser was on notice that the provisions in the Declaration were not immutable. Second, the reasonableness rule, by its very nature, requires a fact-sensitive analysis of the restriction on a case-by-case basis, taking into consideration all relevant circumstances.

We agree with appellant that the restriction here is a significant one, in that it does affect a fundamental property right and not some less significant aspect of the manner in which properties are used. The trial court took this into consideration as one of the factors favoring application of the reasonableness standard rather than the business judgment rule.

Applying the Restatement of Property factors, the circumstances in this case support a finding of reasonableness. Those imposing the restraint, namely, the Association members, who are the homeowners in the community, clearly possess an interest in the land they are seeking to protect by enforcement of the restraint. The enforcement of the restraint accomplishes a worthwhile purpose by preserving the stable residential character of the community. The Association members had a rational basis for believing that the peace and tranquility of the community would be disrupted if such rentals were permitted. Leasing to third parties would not likely be employed to a substantial degree by any of the homeowners. This is evidenced by the fact that no homeowner in the history of the community had ever leased his or her home to a third party, and, indeed, some of the homeowners did not even know that leasing was permitted under the original Declaration. Even appellant would be leasing only for the period of time it would take her to sell her home. Thus, the number of persons to whom the alienation is prohibited is small.

Correspondingly, the Restatement of Property factors that would tend to support a conclusion of unreasonableness are not present here (with the same caveat regarding the unlimited duration of the restraint). In particular, the constraint is not capricious. It is founded on a rational basis, a legitimate concern of the Association members, and in accordance with the past practices and customs in the community. Likewise, the restraint was not imposed for spite or malice. There is nothing to suggest any personal animus against appellant, and she has not made any such allegation. The restraint applies equally and uniformly to all homeowners in the community.

Through this analysis, we conclude that in the facts and circumstances of this case, the amendment to the Declaration prohibiting leasing of homes in this community was a reasonable measure.

This brings us to appellant's other contention, namely, that, even if deemed reasonable, the amendment cannot apply to her because it was enacted after she purchased her property. We find no merit in this argument.

Appellant cannot claim a vested and immutable right in one provision of the Declaration, to the exclusion of the applicability of another provision that authorizes amendments to the document. The Declaration provides that all lots in the community "shall be held, transferred, sold, conveyed, leased and occupied subject to this Declaration and all amendments and supplements thereto." Appellant's contention that the amended Declaration cannot be enforced against her because it "serves as a restriction in her chain of title" ignores the fact that the property has been and remains bound by the Declaration and its amendments. There is no new restriction on the title, because the restriction has always existed. As long as the amendment is substantively valid, the fact that the amended restriction was not part of the Declaration extant at the time of appellant's purchase is of no consequence.

Affirmed.

CASE QUESTIONS

1. What supports the argument that the amendment to the Declaration was reasonable?
2. Why do amendments apply to those who purchased their property prior to the amendment?

CONSIDER 11.1   In 1975, Epernay Community Association, Inc., was created as the homeowners' association for Subdivision One, which contains certain recreational areas.

In 1977, a declaration of restrictive covenants was filed for a subdivision known as "Epernay Section 2" ("Subdivision Two"). Epernay Section 2 Community Association, Inc. ("Association Two"), was the homeowners' association for Subdivision Two. In July 1980, Association One and Association Two entered into an "Amended and Restated Recreational Areas Use Agreement," which was recorded later that year. Both subdivisions were constructed by the same company.

Under the Amended Agreement, (1) homeowners in Subdivision Two are required to pay Association One an annual fee to provide for the maintenance of the Recreational Areas, and (2) Association Two transferred to Association One rights and remedies so that Association One can use these rights and remedies to collect the annual fee.

Saad Shaar and Jeanette Shaar are the owners of a lot in Subdivision Two. After Association One sought to assess and collect annual fees, the Shaars filed suit against Association One. The Shaars argue that their CCRs allowed changed only with 75% approval by the owners in the subdivision and no vote was ever taken on the use of the Subdivision One facilities or to require them to pay a fee. Who is correct on the fees and enforcement power and why?

Epernay Community Ass'n, Inc. v. Shaar, 349 S.W.3d 738 (Tex.App. 2011). ▄

Consistent Standards for Association Rule Enforcement

The courts use the following steps to determine whether they will uphold association enforcement actions.

1. Whatever is being enforced must be grounded in law or the association's documents of creation or operation, either at the inception of the association or by vote of the owners, according to proper processes.

2. There must be enforcement authority given in the declaration, in the CCRs, or by statute. A homeowners' association cannot take away due process rights given in the CCRs or by state statutes.

3. The substance of the rule or policy that the association wants to enforce must be valid. In determining validity, the courts use one of the three following tests.

   a. The reasonableness test, which examines both the rule or policy that is to be enforced and how it is to be enforced. The types of rules include everything from restricting hours for common area use to restrictions on pets.

   b. The business judgment rule test, which allows courts to follow corporation law and rely on the governing body of an association to make appropriate choices so long as those choices and decisions are made according to a valid process and in good faith.

   c. The contract law test, in which the courts treat the owners and the governing body as parties to a contract and, absent the usual contract defenses, they are free to contract. Under this test courts do not intervene in association governance.

Associations generally face three types of litigation: rules enforcement, appearance/modification issues, and use issues that carry constitutional questions.

The Requirement of Purpose in Association Rules

Rules must have a purpose tied to benefiting the community; they must be reasonable, and they must be applied in egalitarian fashion. No-pets rules have had considerable push-back from owners, but, if the restrictions are validly adopted, courts will enforce them. Other rules typically found in homeowners' associations (HOAs) and enforced are no street parking, no sheds or other buildings in yards, paint-color restrictions, and architectural control committee reviews and requirements.

PRACTICAL TIP

For avoiding litigation on condominium rules, the following tips are important:

1. *Enforce all the rules quickly and uniformly. Singling out owners for enforcement will give courts a reason for setting aside the rule and the enforcement.*

2. *Try other avenues for enforcement, such as loss of voting privileges, ongoing but minimal fines, and loss of privileges on a temporary basis.*

3. *Be certain the rules are formally adopted and properly recorded as necessary.*

4. *Maintain minutes and records of meetings when rules are adopted so that a court could examine the intent of the owners and their governing body in adopting the rules.*

5. *Include a cost/benefit analysis of the rule in the adoption process.*

6. *Provide somewhere in the rules that attorneys' fees are recoverable when there is litigation.*

CONSIDER 11.2   Wasim Khan lives in a planned townhouse community that is managed by Mazdabrook Commons, a homeowners' association. In 2005, Khan ran for Parsippany Town Council and posted two signs in support of his candidacy at his private residence—one inside the window of his townhouse and another inside the door. Mazdabrook's regulations banned all residential signs except "For Sale" signs. A few days after posting the signs, Khan received a letter from the Board, which stated that a political sign was displayed in his window and ordered its immediate removal. The letter cited the prohibition on signs in the Declaration and assessed a $25 fine for violating that policy. Discuss whether the rule on sign limitations, particularly when an owner is running for office, is reasonable. *Mazdabrook Commons Homeowners' Ass'n v. Khan,* 46 A.3d 507 (N.J. 2012). ▬▬▬▬ ∎

Enforcement of Rules for Appearance and Modification

Another issue of contention in associations is that of changing the appearance or structure of individual units. Many bylaws provide for the creation and operation of an architectural control committee (ACC). The goal of the ACC is to maintain uniformity in the appearance of condominium units. Particularly with regard to freestanding units, similar appearance preserves the value and continuity of the community, and individual owners' changes in colors, structure, or appearance can detract from the overall appearance of the development. The ACC reviews proposed construction changes and then either approves or disapproves them. The ACC can also check the neighborhood to ensure that there are no unauthorized changes or any failures to comply with CCR requirements, such as maintenance and landscaping requirements.

The failure to obtain approval of the ACC for changes that do affect the overall appearance and development scheme of the community usually results in required removal as well as fines and attorneys' fees for the association if suit is required to have the change removed and the fees collected. For example, in *Esposito v. Riviera at Freehold Homeowners Ass'n, Inc.,* 2011 WL 2566171 (N.J. Super. A.D.), the court held that Mr. Esposito's installation, without ACC approval, of a Gothic-like door on his townhome when the community allowed only four types of doors was a violation of the CCRs. Mr. Esposito was assessed over $23,000 for fines and attorneys' fees related to his failure to remove the door.

The following case illustrates the often tense interaction among a condominium owner and her construction project, the association board, and city government.

LASALLE NATIONAL TRUST, N.A. (CARMA McCLURE) V. BOARD OF DIRECTORS OF THE 1100 LAKE SHORE DRIVE CONDOMINIUM

677 N.E.2d 1378 (Ill. 1997), appeal denied, 686 N.E.2d 1163 (1998)
When the Penthouse Is Remodeled, Everyone Is Tense

FACTS

Carma McClure, as a trust beneficiary, was the owner of a penthouse condominium in the Lake Shore Drive Condominiums located at 1100 North Lake Shore Drive. Her condominium consists of units 39A, 39B, and 40B and a roof house on the 41st floor. McClure

had purchased the penthouse on March 20, 1991, for $1.4 million knowing that it was not in good condition. McClure and her husband, James Martin, decided to completely renovate the penthouse. McClure began demolition work in 1991 without first notifying the Board of Directors of the Lake Shore Condominium

(Board/defendant). She also did not obtain the necessary city permits for the demolition.

The demolition resulted in the Board being cited by the city of Chicago for failure to obtain a permit. Also, an elevator cab was damaged, the alarm system in the building was cut off for a day, yard boxes and dumpsters were placed and removed illegally, and two other units in the building were damaged as a result.

McClure paid for the damage to the elevator cab. She also paid $16,552 to Elizabeth Rann, the owner of one of the damaged units as well as the president of the Lake Shore Condominium Association (association). McClure maintained that Rann inflated her damages because of financial difficulty, but that she paid them in order to get construction moving on her penthouse.

Demolition was complete in July 1991. McClure provided the Board and the city with a complete set of plans for the renovation in October 1991. Had the Board approved the plans, the work could have started and been completed in 26 weeks, or in May 1992.

On September 24, 1991, the Board passed a resolution that provided "[a]ll expenses incurred by the Board in connection with the modification by a unit owner to his unit or adjacent living [sic] comment [sic] elements shall be assessed to the unit owner. Expenses which will be assessed include, but are not limited to engineering, architectural and attorney fees and the cost of documents, plans and specifications."

The Board refused to approve McClure's plans unless and until she agreed to assume responsibility for the roof. McClure offered to pay one-third of the cost of replacing the main and machine room roofs if the Board would approve her plans.

Having still not approved the plans in March 1992, the Board proposed to McClure that she pay the Board expenses in reviewing the plans ($10,969); place money in escrow for covering any damages during renovation; repair, replace, and maintain the roof; and have a full-time on-site representative at the penthouse during construction.

Another unit was under renovation at the same time, and its owners were required to sign a similar agreement but were not assessed expenses of review nor required to assume the costs of repairing common elements.

McClure disagreed with many of the proposals but signed an agreement in May 1992 so that she could get her renovation started.

Once renovation began, the building began having infiltration problems. The Board maintained McClure had caused the problems with her construction. McClure said the infiltration was caused by cracks in the side of the building. Because of the infiltration problem, McClure could not finish her renovation in 1992, 1993, or 1994.

The parties were at a standstill until August 1994 when the Board and McClure entered into an agreement whereby she would pay for one-half the cost of installing a new roof. The new roof was installed, but the water infiltration continued. A contractor indicated that the infiltration would not stop until the Board caulked the walls of the building.

McClure then filed suit against the Board on several grounds, including breach of fiduciary duty by the Board in withholding its approval, which amounted to constructive fraud. The trial court found for McClure and awarded her $896,609.52. The Board appealed.

JUDICIAL OPINION
Wolfson, Presiding Judge

The Condominium Declaration provides the Board can be liable to a unit owner only for "any acts or omissions found by a court to constitute gross negligence or fraud." Since there was no claim of gross negligence, and since there were no allegations or evidence of actual fraud, says the Board, there can be no liability....

Condominium boards and board members owe a special duty to apartment owners. The Condominium Property Act provides:

In the performance of their duties, the officers and members of the board shall exercise the care required of a fiduciary of the unit owners.

This fiduciary duty is owed by boards as well as their individual members. The decisions make no distinction between a board and its members when describing fiduciary duty.

The failure of condominium board members to act in a manner reasonably related to their fiduciary duty results in "liability for the Board and its individual members."

The scope of that fiduciary duty can be limited by the declaration. In this case, the relevant part of the Declaration of Condominium is:

"Neither the directors, Board, officers of the Association, Trustee, nor Developer shall be personally liable to the Unit Owners for any mistake of judgment or for any other acts or omissions of any nature whatsoever as such directors, Board, officers, Trustee or Developer, except for any acts or omissions found by a court to constitute gross negligence or fraud."

The first issue we must decide is whether the limitation of liability to acts or omissions that "constitute gross negligence or fraud" applies to McClure's count II. Gross negligence is not an issue in this case, but the Board contends the word "fraud" in the exclusion applies to actual fraud, not to the constructive fraud found by the trial court.

This case concerns a Declaration clause that seeks to exculpate the Board and its members and officers from personal liability except in narrow circumstances. Generally, exculpatory clauses "are not favored and are strictly construed and must have clear, explicit and unequivocal language showing that it was the intent of the parties."

If the Board wanted to limit its liability to actual fraud, it should have said so. Constructive fraud is a well-established doctrine in this State.

Constructive fraud does not require actual dishonesty or intent to deceive. "In a fiduciary relationship, where there is a breach of a legal or equitable duty, a presumption of fraud arises."

Clearly, count II alleges that the Board breached its fiduciary duty to McClure. Where there is a breach of a legal or equitable duty arising out of a fiduciary relationship, a presumption of constructive fraud arises.

McClure placed her confidence in the Board, which, by statute, owed her a fiduciary duty. In return, according to the trial court's findings, the Board virtually held her penthouse for ransom. This Board did not "act in good faith with due regard to the interests of the other."

We conclude the record supports the trial court's findings that: the Board's obstructive acts and lack of cooperation contributed to substantial delays in construction; damages for loss of use of the penthouse apartment, in the form of fair rental value, were recoverable and were properly proved.

Affirmed.

CASE QUESTIONS

1. Prepare an outline of the events in the penthouse renovation project.
2. What did the Board do wrong according to the court?
3. What does the court mean when it states that the Board held McClure's penthouse for ransom?

Tools for Enforcement: Association Fee Collection

In associations, all owners are responsible for the costs of the association, which includes everything from administrative costs to management fees to the maintenance costs for common areas. Owners usually pay monthly fees and perhaps periodic capital assessment payments for special projects such as lighting installation or roof replacement on common area buildings. The amount of these fees may be specified in the declaration or bylaws and may be subject to change upon a vote or according to a formula included in the declaration or bylaws.

Every unit owner is required to pay these fees. In many cases, the fees are paid to the mortgagee, who in turn pays the association (since the mortgagee has an interest in keeping the property, which is held as security, well-maintained).

Collection of these fees, without the help of a mortgage company, can be difficult. There are three tools of enforcement for associations: fines, liens, and, eventually, foreclosure. None of these tools can be used without authorization and their use is restricted by state laws. There have been situations so sympathetic around the country because of extreme enforcement processes by HOAs that state laws now give protection to property owners where the fines and resulting delinquent assessments from associations are less than certain amounts. For example, $1,800 is a typical figure that is a dividing line for what associations can do in their collection efforts against unit owners. For amounts less than $1,800, the association may file a civil action in Small Claims Court. However, the association cannot foreclose on the homeowners' property for unpaid assessments until they exceed $1,800 or the assessments are more than 12 months delinquent.[7] Many states require some

---

[7]Code of Civil Procedure §1365.1.

form of alternative dispute resolution before an association can file suit or impose a lien on owners' property. Some states, such as Arizona, have restricted the right of associations to place liens on property, requiring that there first be a judicial hearing before the lien for association fines, assessments, or penalties can be placed on the owner's property. Still other states have imposed mandatory steps and processes for both liens and foreclosures, requiring notification of owners as the association takes steps to try and collect the amounts due. Those steps also carry time requirements that allow the owners a guaranteed period of time within which they can respond and prevent further action by paying what is due. Some states prohibit foreclosure for association assessments altogether, leaving the association with the power to lien, something that can be collected only out of the proceeds of a sale if the property is ever transferred.

Those who buy properties that carry association liens for nonpayment of fees and dues are also liable for those fees and dues because the obligation runs with the property. *River Oaks Homes Ass'n v. Lounce*, 356 S.W.3d 855 (Mo. App. 2012). In addition, under the Bankruptcy Abuse Prevention and Consumer Protection Act of 2005, pre-bankruptcy owners' association fees and fines are nondischargeable debts in bankruptcy.

In an interesting turn-about in the foreclosure era of 2008–2009, lenders fell behind in their foreclosures on condos, co-ops, and townhomes. Associations had, in the past, waited for lenders to foreclose and then collected their fees as lien holders. However, lenders are delaying foreclosure and allowing the associations "to take them the distance."[8] The foreclosed units present questions as to who is really responsible for the fees: the lender? The mortgage servicing company? The companies holding pooled mortgages? (See Chapter 15 for more information.) With some associations owed as much as $32,000 per unit in back fees, associations have been filing the foreclosure suits; collecting their fees, interest, and costs; and then turning the remainder over to the lenders. The associations have become the workhorses in foreclosure.

Constitutional Issues in Rules Enforcement

There are two frequent constitutional issues that involve owners' associations. The first type of case involves owners who post signs and other materials on their property that are a form of expression. These cases involve issues such as an owner flying a large U.S. flag from his property or the use of a community room for purposes of holding a political rally or for posting political materials on candidates and ballot issues. For the most part, the courts have held that associations are private entities and can impose aesthetic and other restrictions on these forms of speech that would otherwise be protected. However, there is an evolving line of cases that concludes that the private community is now a substitute for the public community and, as such, should be subject to constitutional limitations on the regulation of speech.[9]

The second type of case involves rules passed by owners' associations that prohibit owners from using their properties for certain purposes or impose restrictions on transfer of their properties to certain groups or individuals. In these situations, the homeowners' association, the bylaws, and CCRs often collide with public policy or even antidiscrimination laws. For example, in *Marrick Real Estate, LLC v. Ramirez,*

---

[8]Nick Timirados, "Condo Boards Take On Lenders," *Wall Street Journal*, June 18, 2009, p. A3.

[9]For a discussion of the private versus public regulation, see *Committee for a Better Twin Rivers, v. Twin Rivers Homeowners' Association*, 890 A.2d 947 (N.J. App. 2006).

817 N.Y.S. 2d 210 (2005), the court held that a board did not have the authority to prohibit the operation of a day-care center for adults in one of the condominium units because of the state's interest in promoting such homes and that such an interpretation of the CCRs was too restrictive. CCRs and their enforcement cannot deprive condominium owners of statutory protections or prohibit their exercise of rights. For example, prohibiting the installation of solar panels in a state that provides tax credits for such alternative energy use would be a violation of public policy and such CCRs or board policies would be unenforceable. See *Garden Lakes Community Ass'n, Inc. v. Madigan*, 62 P.3d 983 (Az. App. 2003).

Another use issue involves adult-only covenants in the CCRs. The age restrictions vary and generally limit occupation of units to those above a certain age, with 12, 18, and even 60 being typical ages for such restrictions. These restrictions have been declared constitutionally valid and are covered in Chapter 19.

A final and evolving area in owners' association powers relates to the transfer of property by owners, particularly restrictions on the sale of property to convicted sex offenders. The courts are still working to address this issue.

LIABILITY ISSUES IN OWNERS' ASSOCIATIONS

Owners' Association Liabilities: Management

Because the governing boards of owners' associations often make decisions on contentious issues, impose increases in association fees, and halt construction by individual unit owners for noncompliance with CCRs, they are often defendants in lawsuits brought by unit owners. Courts have had to determine association liabilities, defenses, and immunities. They have borrowed the standards of liability for governing boards from general corporation law.

The boards of owners' associations are protected by what is known in corporate law as the **business judgment rule.** So long as boards act in good faith and for articulated purposes related to the well-being of the property and unit owners, courts will not substitute their judgment for that of the board. Figure 11.1 is a checklist for owners and boards that both should follow in performing their various roles.

FIGURE 11.1 Rules of Thumb for Owners, Owners' Associations, and Boards

1. The CCRs represent property rights and cannot be taken away or changed except in the same fashion that covenants on land parcels are changed or according to procedures outlined in the CCRs themselves.

2. Homeowners' associations and boards govern subject to the CCRs; they do not override the CCRs.

3. Bylaws cannot override CCRs; homeowners' association boards cannot override bylaws or CCRs except by proper process and procedure not in violation of unit owners' property rights.

4. All changes by homeowners' association boards require notice to unit owners and proper vote including raising association fees.

5. CCRs, bylaws, and homeowners' associations cannot pass or enforce rules and restrictions in violation of antidiscrimination laws or public policy.

6. Boards must be consistent in their enforcement of CCRs and bylaws; selective enforcement can be the basis of discriminatory conduct or the loss of protections under the CCRs for lax enforcement.

The following case deals with an issue of whether the board met the standards of the business judgment rule.

DAVIS V. DYSON

387 Ill.App.3d 676, 900 N.E.2d 698 (2008)

FACTS

From 1998 through 2003, Joe Dyson and others served on the board of the Granville Homeowner's Association. Larson Property Management, Inc (LPI) served as the property manager for Granville. Warren Larson, LPI's principal, embezzled $550,000 from the association by forging the signature of Anna Skalka, the director who served as the treasurer for the association, on 100 association checks.

During this period, the directors never reviewed the bank statements for the association nor did they order any type of audit or even a financial review. The embezzlement was not discovered until July 2003 when the on-site manager looked at just one of the bank statements. To add insult and injury to embezzlement, the association did not have a bond covering the Larson crowd. To add outrage to insult, injury, and embezzlement, the directors never sought legal counsel regarding their duties, processes, and responsibilities.

To add expenses to the outrage, insult, injury, and embezzlement, the association had to fork over between $200,000 and $250,000 to pay legal and accounting fees for the investigation to determine exactly how much had been pilfered. The board did obtain $60,000 from an insurer and $4,000 from the bank, but the total uncompensated loss still exceeded $800,000.

Evelyn Davis and other homeowners (plaintiffs) brought suit against former board members (defendants) of the Association. The homeowners sought damages as individuals as well as on a derivative basis and for breach of the business judgment rule. The trial court dismissed the claims and the homeowners appealed.

JUDICIAL OPINION

Gordon, Justice

A fiduciary relationship is a relationship in which "there is special confidence in one who, in equity and good conscience, is bound to act in good faith with due regard to the interests of the other."

As part of this fiduciary duty, directors are required to comply with procedures in the condominium bylaws as well as the strictures of the Condo Act.

[I]n the case at hand, plaintiffs allege that the director defendants have violated the Condo Act and the Association's bylaws by failing to purchase the required insurance to protect the Association against fraud such as was allegedly committed by Larson. [S]uch allegations constitute a valid cause of action for breach of fiduciary duty.

Defendants nonetheless contend that plaintiffs have failed to state a cause of action for breach of fiduciary duty because they did not specifically allege that the board failed to act in the Association's best interest. They cite no other law in support of this proposition.

[I]n the instant case [plaintiffs] have sufficiently alleged a violation of fiduciary duty on the part of the director defendants to survive a motion to dismiss on the pleadings.

Plaintiffs argue that defendants, as former directors, cannot assert the business judgment rule in their defense to bar the current suit. Plaintiffs also contend that the business judgment rule does not apply where defendants have committed a breach of care, as is alleged in the complaint.

Under the business judgment rule, "[a]bsent evidence of bad faith, fraud, illegality or gross overreaching, courts are not at liberty to interfere with the exercise of business judgment by corporate directors." The purpose of this rule is to protect directors who have been diligent and careful in performing their duties from being subjected to liability from honest mistakes of judgment. However, it is a prerequisite to the application of the business judgment rule that the directors exercise due care in carrying out their corporate duties. If directors fail to exercise due care, then they may not use the business judgment rule as a shield for their conduct.

One component of due care is that directors must inform themselves of material facts necessary for them to properly exercise their business judgment. Thus, the business judgment rule is defeated where directors act without "becoming sufficiently informed to make an independent business decision."

Plaintiffs' first contention is that, as the director defendants are only former directors, not current directors, they may not assert the business judgment rule in their favor. Plaintiffs argue that only the Association itself has the power to raise the business judgment rule as a defense with regard to the Association's decision not to bring suit against the defendants. However, this contention is a non sequitur: the former directors are not seeking the protection of the business judgment rule with regard to the current board's decision not to bring suit against them. Rather, these defendants seek it with regard to the actions they took during their tenure as directors. Contrary to plaintiffs' contention, they are not trying to assert the rule on behalf of the corporation, but on their own behalf. The fact that defendants are no longer serving on the board of directors does not preclude them from raising the business judgment rule on their own behalf for the things they did while they were still directors.

… [P]laintiffs allege in their complaint that none of the director defendants reviewed any of the Association's monthly bank statements, which would have enabled them to uncover Larson's embezzlement. Plaintiffs further allege that the director defendants never obtained advice of counsel to learn about their duties regarding insurance coverage, Association finances, or supervision of key personnel. These allegations, when viewed in the light most favorable to plaintiffs could potentially support a finding that the director defendants breached their duty of due care. The "inexcusable unawareness or inattention" is alleged here in the present case.

In addition, plaintiffs allege that the director defendants violated the Condo Act through their failure to purchase proper insurance to protect Association funds. Illegality is one factor that can render directors unable to avail themselves of the protection of the business judgment rule. This is consistent with the general rule of tort law that violation of a statute designed to protect property is prima facie evidence of negligence, which, as discussed above, renders the business judgment rule inapplicable. Therefore, plaintiffs have sufficiently alleged a breach of due care, such that the business judgment rule does not apply to bar plaintiffs' suit at the pleading stage.

Finally, defendants contend that the doctrine of election of remedies precludes plaintiffs from seeking relief from them, as plaintiffs already elected to seek relief in their prior suit against the bank that held the Association funds at issue for its participation in the embezzlement. However, defendants have not shown these actions to be mutually exclusive, nor do they provide any law in their brief in support of this proposition. Accordingly, the argument is waived.

[The court also held that the homeowners could bring a derivative action against the directors on the part of the homeowners, but that they could not bring individual actions against the directors.]

Affirmed in part, reversed in part, and remanded.

CASE QUESTIONS

1. What lessons do homeowners' association directors learn from this case?
2. List the rights of recovery and their bases that homeowners have against their association boards.

Owners' Association Liabilities: Maintenance

A major issue in associations is the liability for injuries occurring in common areas. If the association is a corporation, such as a nonprofit owners' association, then that corporation should carry insurance for liability in the common areas. Ice and snow, jagged walkways, loose rugs, and other hazards have been the cause of many common-area injuries. Regardless of incorporation, the owners are liable together and individually (jointly and severally) for torts in common areas. The corporate organization with insurance simply makes the liability easier to bear, and the premium costs can be part of the assessment to each unit owner.

The liability for injuries occurring in common areas extends to visitors, repairpersons, governmental personnel (such as fire and medical personnel), and any others authorized to be on the premises, including unit owners. The responsibility of maintaining common areas extends to the responsibility for injuries resulting from faulty repair or lack of maintenance.

The following case deals with an issue of condominium associations' liability for harm to third parties in their common areas.

MEDCALF V. WASHINGTON CONDOMINIUM ASS'N

747 A.2d 532 (Conn. App. 2000)

FACTS

Mechelle Medcalf (plaintiff) and a friend, Deborah Michelson, arrived at 1633 Washington Boulevard in Stamford, Connecticut, to visit their friend, Tracy Skiades, who resides at the Washington Heights Condominiums.

Ms. Medcalf parked her car in the street level parking lot and walked to the lobby doors. The lighting in the parking lot was dim. She picked up the intercom and called Ms. Skiades. Ms. Skiades's brother-in-law answered and tried to let Ms. Metcalf in using the electronic buzzer system. The system did not work, so Ms. Skiades indicated she would come down and open the door. As she traveled down to the lobby, Ms. Medcalf was attacked and injured by Kenneth Strickler.

Ms. Medcalf filed suit against Washington Heights Condominium Association and Professional Property Management Company, Inc., its managing agent (defendants). Ms. Medcalf alleged that their failure to maintain the buzzer system was the cause of her assault and injuries. The jury found for Ms. Medcalf and the association and managing agent appealed.

JUDICIAL DECISION

Mihalakos, Judge

The dispositive issue in this appeal is whether there is a causal connection between the assault and the failure of the security system. We conclude that the jury could not reasonably have found that the failure to maintain the intercom security system was the proximate cause of the assault.

The elements in a negligence cause of action are duty, breach of that duty, causation and damages. "The first component of legal cause is causation in fact. Causation in fact is the purest legal application of … legal cause. The test for cause in fact is, simply, would the injury have occurred were it not for the actor's conduct."

The second component is proximate cause. "Proximate cause establishes a reasonable connection between an act or omission of a defendant and the

harm suffered by a plaintiff." "The Connecticut Supreme Court has defined proximate cause as [a]n actual cause that is a substantial factor in the resulting harm…. The substantial factor test reflects the inquiry fundamental to all proximate cause questions, that is, whether the harm which occurred was of the same general nature as the foreseeable risk created by the defendant's negligence." Proximate cause is a question of fact to be decided by the trier of fact, but it becomes a question of law when the mind of a fair and reasonable person could reach only one conclusion. "Lines must be drawn determining how far down the causal continuum individuals will be held liable for the consequences of their actions…. This line is labeled proximate cause." In issues involving proximate cause analysis, this court has held that "an intervening intentional or criminal act relieves a negligent defendant of liability, except where the harm caused by the intervening act is within the scope of risk created by the defendant's conduct or where the intervening act is reasonably foreseeable…. As a general rule, the act of a third person in committing an intentional act or crime is a superseding cause of harm to another resulting therefrom…. In such a case, the third person has deliberately assumed control of the situation, and all responsibility for the consequences of his act is shifted to him." Recovery is barred in a negligence action where there is a lack of causal connection between the defendant's wrongful conduct and a plaintiff's injury.

In *Doe v. Manheimer*, 563 A.2d 699, our Supreme Court was not persuaded that the owner of a property should reasonably foresee that an overgrowth of vegetation would provide an inducement for the commission of a violent crime by a stranger. The court held that the overgrown vegetation was an incidental factor and not a substantial factor that would establish proximate cause.

In the present case, the plaintiff offered no evidence that the malfunctioning intercom system was designed to provide security to a person outside the building. The defendants' failure to maintain the intercom system was inconsequential and was not the proximate cause of the assault. The injury may likely have occurred without any negligence with respect to the intercom system.

The defendants could not have reasonably fore-seen that a malfunctioning intercom system might provide a substantial incentive or inducement for the commission of a violent criminal assault on their prop-erty by one stranger upon another.

We rule that, as a matter of law, the jury could not reasonably have found that the assault on the plaintiff and the resultant injury were within the foreseeable scope of risk created by the defendants' failure to maintain the intercom system. Therefore, the plaintiff failed to establish the necessary causal relationship.

The judgment is reversed.

CASE QUESTIONS

1. What happened and when?
2. What does Ms. Medcalf allege is the cause of her injuries?
3. What is the difference between causation and proximate cause?

CONSIDER 11.3   Rose Stanley, who lives in a condominium project, was at-tacked by Elizabeth Rivera in the common hallway of the complex and pushed into her apartment, where she was stabbed several times and severely injured. Elizabeth Rivera was living in the complex because she was staying with another owner, without required authorization. Stanley filed suit against the condominium board for its failure to provide adequate security. The board defended on the grounds that there had been no other criminal activity on the premises and that Rivera's drug use made her incapable of proper judgment and also introduced a criminal element not affecting other members of the condominium community. Who is correct? What standard should the court apply in evaluating the actions of the condominium board? *Stanley v. Meriden Housing Authority,* 2002 WL 31172927 (Conn. Super. 2002).

Owners' Liability Issues in Associations

Owners of single-family dwellings buy insurance to cover liabilities they may have for injuries occurring on their premises. With single-family dwellings, it is clear that there is liability in ownership and that the liability rests with the homeowner. It is the owner's responsibility to maintain and repair the premises. However, in multiunit housing with common areas, the nature of multiple ownership makes the issues of liability and responsibility less clear.

Contractual Liability of Unit Owners

Three issues of contractual liability for owners are their liability for (1) unpaid bills of the developer, (2) assessment and maintenance fees, and (3) improvement and repair costs of common elements and individual units.

Liability for Unpaid Bills of Developers

A critical point in liability issues arises when control of the development is turned over to the association for operation. This juncture varies—some articles of incor-poration or bylaws provide for a number turnover point (e.g., when three-fourths of all units have been sold), while others provide for an absolute point (when all units have been sold). When control is turned over to the owners, the developer not only is no longer in control but also is no longer responsible for maintenance and repair costs.

One possible problem with turnover is when all construction elements of the development are not owned free and clear (when there are outstanding debts). In most cases, the developer would be responsible for payment of such obligations, since the homeowners' association probably would not have existed at the time of the debt contract. However, there are potential problems in spite of the developer's liability. First, the developer may not be able to pay, and fixtures may be repossessed from the development or liens may result. Second, even if the developer can pay, establishing the developer's liability may take litigation.

Additionally, owners may experience problems with the developer's delivery of promised services and quality of construction, particularly in the common areas. Owners have their various warranties for protection (see Chapter 14), but the association will need to have property inspections of common areas before it takes control so that it can recover from the developer for faulty construction and failed maintenance up to the time the developer turns over control to the association. For example, in gated communities, associations often have the developer make repairs to the private streets before the turnover because of the damage construction vehicles do to the streets. Those costly repairs save the owners the cost of repaving streets.

Tort Liability of Unit Owners

Each owner is responsible for the maintenance and safety of his or her property and liable for any injuries that result from negligence. Owners have insurance on their property to cover such liability.

CAUTIONS AND CONCLUSIONS

Like other real estate purchases, multiunit housing and planned community ownership can be good investments, but study before buying. Consider the following questions that relate to both multiunit housing and owners' associations before investing:

1. What is the structure of the community/building?

2. What is the condition of the property? What repairs are necessary? Who will make the repairs? Who will pay for the repairs?

3. When will the developer turn over control of the building operation? Who or what organization will control the building operation at that point?

4. Is there a provision to opt out (back out) if the units or homes do not sell?

5. Will the developer finish repairs? Are there any outstanding liens?

6. Is there an association? If so, how does it work and is it effective?

7. Are there assessments? If so, how much are they, and do the unit owners pay them?

8. What provisions for operations and restrictions are made in the declaration, charters, bylaws, and regulations?

9. Is there strong board governance and rules enforcement?

10. Are the common areas well maintained?

11. What elements are included in the common areas, and what elements are the responsibility of individual unit owners?

12. How do other unit owners feel about the assessments and how the development is functioning?

13. Are there any pending lawsuits?

14. Is there adequate insurance coverage for the common areas?

15. Are the units rented or owner-occupied?

16. What type of ownership interest is being obtained?

17. Are there restrictions on transferability?

18. Are there use and age restrictions?

19. Are the units subject to architectural control?

The investigation can never be too thorough.

KEY TERMS

CHAPTER PROBLEMS

1. On January 22, 1993, Krag and Erin Kadera (petitioners) purchased one share of stock in Consolidated Cooperative of Scottsdale East, Inc. (respondent), from a former shareholder, paying $21,000 for their share. The Kaderas were required to sign a form designating how they were taking title to their interest, which they did in joint tenancy with right of survivorship.

   When the Kaderas took possession of the unit, they were required to pay a $200.00-per-month "carrying charge." This figure represented a proportionate one-twelfth of the cooperative's annual expenses.

   After the Kaderas moved into their unit, they were served with a Notice of Default, Intention to Terminate Agreement, and Demand for Possession of the Premises. The cooperative, through its manager, alleged that the Kaderas had violated the nonfinancial terms of their occupancy agreement because they had a nonrelative living in their unit and were operating a babysitting service from it.

   On August 16, 1995, the cooperative filed a forcible entry and detainer action seeking to have the Kaderas evicted from their unit. The Kaderas claimed they were not tenants but owners, and could not be evicted under landlord–tenant law. The trial court denied the Kaderas' motion to dismiss and they appealed. What should the appellate court do, and why? *Kadera v. Superior Court and Consolidated Cooperative of Scottsdale East, Inc.,* 931 P.2d 1067 (Az. App. 1996)

2. Roundtree Villas Association, Inc., is a nonprofit corporation whose primary function is to own and administer the common elements of the condominium project called "Roundtree Villas." Roundtree Corporation, Inc., was the original owner of a parcel of real estate that filed a deed under the Horizontal Property Act. Republic Mortgage Investment Services, Inc., was the financier of the project. Mortgage Investment Services, Inc., was an advisory service employed by Republic Mortgage, the lender.

   The condominium project was constructed by Miles and Teal Builders at a time when money was short and sales were slow. Miles and Teal sold what they could and then 4701 Kings Corporation, a company created by Republic Mortgage to accept title to Roundtree Villas in lieu of Republic's foreclosure, took over the property. Shortly after the acquisition, the owners of the units began to complain about problems with the units' roofs and balconies. The lender attempted to remedy the problems, but only with stopgap measures. The problems continued.

   The homeowners' association for Roundtree filed suit against Republic, the lender, and 4701 Kings Corporation for breach of the implied warranty of habitability and sought damages for the repair of the roofs and balconies. The jury entered a verdict against the lender and the lender appealed. Should the lender be held liable? *Roundtree Villas Association, Inc. v. 4701 Kings Corporation,* 321 S.E.2d 46 (S.C. 1984).

3. Melvin R. Luster and Harold E. Friedman formed a partnership to convert the 20 East Cedar property from rental property to condominium units. Deeds to each unit provided purchasers with title for the designated unit plus an undivided percentage of the "common elements." In each sales agreement, the partnership agreed to complete certain repair and rehabilitation work in the building.

   In 1970 (during the conversion process), Luster and Friedman leased a canopy from White Way Electric Sign and Maintenance Company with a down payment of $6,128 and 60 monthly payments of $261.76 each. The canopy was ornamental and was installed at the front entrance of the 20 East Cedar building.

In 1973, the unit owners formed their own association, and Luster and Friedman were relieved of their responsibilities. After the release, the unit owners discovered the liability remaining on the canopy lease as well as several other unpaid expenses incurred by Luster and Friedman in the rehabilitation of the building.

The association brought suit, seeking a complete accounting and monetary relief from Luster and Friedman. The trial court ordered Luster and Friedman to pay for the canopy, and Luster and Friedman appealed. Who is liable? *20 East Cedar Condominium Association v. Luster et al.*, 349 N.E.2d 586 (Ill. 1976).

4. Louis Croce purchased 49 units in the Glenwood Park condominiums at a foreclosure sale in the mid-1970s. Through subsequent acquisitions, he was able to purchase more of the units and now owns 58 of the 60 units in the complex. Mr. Croce sent out a notice to all owners and lessees that he was raising the association fees from $30 to $160 per month. Josephine Artesani, one of the owners, says that she knew of no association meeting in which the increase was discussed. Can Mr. Croce raise the fees in this manner? *Artesani v. Glenwood Park Condominium*, 750 A.2d 961 (R.I. 2000).

5. William B. Miller, an owner of a condominium in San Antonio's Villa Del Sol, has failed to pay his share of common element assessments and owes $3,604.51 in back assessments. The bylaws authorize the directors to enforce the assessments by whatever means necessary. The directors shut off Mr. Miller's electricity. Is this proper under their bylaws? *San Antonio Villa Del Sol Homeowners Association v. Miller*, 761 S.W.2d 460 (Tex. 1988).

6. Puamana was established in 1968 as a Hawaii non-profit corporation. Several owners constructed "pop outs" that encroached onto the common areas owned by Puamana. The term "pop out" refers to an expansion of the dwelling by which the exterior walls are pushed out toward the area beneath the eaves of the building structure.

The Board of Directors of Puamana initially assumed that the "pop outs" remained within the boundaries of the respective units because they did not protrude beyond the drip lines of the eaves. However, the Board subsequently discovered that the unit boundaries coincided with the original position of the exterior walls of the dwellings and that the "pop outs" encroached onto the common areas even though they remained under the eaves.

Dale W. Hillman was one of the unit owners desiring to construct a "pop out," and he proposed to extend nearly all of his 66-foot exterior wall 2.5

feet outward toward the eaves, creating an additional 165 square feet of floor space. The Board rejected Hillman's proposal unless and until the CCRs could be amended to expressly permit encroachments onto the common areas. On October 19, 1999, the Board recorded a document entitled "Amendment of Puamana Declaration, Covenants, Conditions and Restrictions." The amended CCRs authorized the Board to approve "minor encroachments" of up to 200 square feet per unit.

Allan and Barbara Lee and other owners brought suit challenging the authority of the board to amend the CCRs to allow the "pop outs." The Lees also claimed that they enjoyed a scenic view of Kaho'olawe from their third-floor loft, which was blocked when their neighbor, Mark Ciaburri, impermissibly constructed his own third-floor loft.

Did the board have the authority to allow the "pop out" through the amendment? In thinking about your answer, apply the tests of reasonableness and the standards for change from the *Sbarga* case (p. 255). *Lee v. Puamana Community Association*, 128 P.3d 874 (Haw. 2006).

7. The Island House Association, Incorporated, a homeowners' association formed for the operation of the Island House condominiums and villas and assessed each unit for maintenance fees. The association required condominium owners to pay more for maintenance than villa owners because the condominium building was larger, had more units, and required more frequent repairs. The provision for fees was in the bylaws and had been voted on by the owners and approved by a majority. Thiess, a condominium owner, refused to pay his fees and claimed the assessment was inequitable and unfair. How will the court decide this dispute?

8. George E. Western is the owner of a condominium unit in Chardonnay Village. Chardonnay Village Condominium Association, Inc., is the association of condominium unit owners that governs and manages the condominium project. Under the Louisiana Condominium Act, associations are empowered to collect expenses of administration, maintenance, repair, and replacement of the common elements. The condominium declaration of Chardonnay Village authorizes the association to collect the costs of utilities for each unit as well as for common areas.

Western has failed to pay the assessments for the common areas for approximately three years for a total of $4,962.08, which included late fees of $25.00 per month.

On October 1, 1986, the association turned off Western's water supply for failure to pay the assessment.

Western filed for a temporary restraining order to prevent the water turnoff and was awarded such by the trial court. What should be the result? *Western v. Chardonnay Village Condominium Association, Inc.*, 519 So.2d 243 (La. 1988).

9. Donna Marie Morgan lived in the condominium building owned by 253 East Delaware Condominium Association and managed by Joseph Moss Realty. On September 18, 1986, at about 8:30 p.m., Morgan walked from her class at Loyola University's downtown campus to the building, where she entered the lobby. She observed a man talking with the doorman when she first entered the building and was checking her mail. The man followed her onto the elevator.

When the elevator arrived at the tenth floor, the man poked a gun in her back and forced her off the elevator and into the stairwell. He pushed Morgan down to the ninth floor, robbed and beat her with the gun, and caused severe injuries.

Morgan filed suit alleging that Delaware and Moss were negligent for their failure to protect her from criminal acts of unknown parties. Should Delaware and Moss be held liable? *Morgan v. 253 East Delaware Condominium Association*, 595 N.E.2d 36 (Ill. 1992).

10. William and Joan Madigan and Henry and LaVonne Speak owned homes in the Garden Lakes subdivision. The Association recorded a Declaration of Covenants, Conditions, Restrictions and Easements for Garden Lakes ("Declaration"). The Declaration applies to all owners of property within Garden Lakes who purchased a lot after the Declaration was recorded on January 28, 1986. The Madigans and the Speaks purchased their lots after the Declaration and accepted their deeds subject to the following provision in the Declaration:

No improvements, alterations … or other work which in any way alters the exterior appearance of any property or improvements thereon … shall be made or done … unless and until the Architectural Review Committee has, in each such case, reviewed and approved the nature of the proposed work, alteration, structure or grading and the plans and specifications therefor.

The Association established an architectural review committee ("ARC") and architectural review guidelines ("guidelines") that included the following:

a. All solar energy devices Visible from Neighboring Property or public view must be approved by the Architectural Review Committee prior to installation.

b. Panels must be an integrated part of the roof design and mounted directly to the roof plane. Solar units must not break the roof ridge line, must not be visible from public view and must be screened from neighboring property in a manner approved by the Board of Directors or its designee(s). Roof mounted hot water storage systems must not be Visible from Neighboring Property. Tracker-type systems will be allowed only when not Visible from Neighboring Property.

c. The criteria for screening set forth in Section III (M) "Machinery and Equipment," shall apply to solar panels and equipment. Under the "Machinery and Equipment" section, the guidelines provided:

[S]creening or concealment shall be solid and integrated architecturally with the design of the building or structure, shall not have the appearance of a separate piece or pieces of machinery, fixtures or equipment, and shall be constructed and positioned in such a manner so it is level and plumb with vertical building components and shall be structurally stable in accordance with sound engineering principles.

The Madigans and the Speaks installed solar energy devices ("SEDs") on the roofs of their respective homes without ARC or Association approval. These SEDs included solar panels to collect and transfer heat to their swimming pools. The Association sued the Madigans and the Speaks in separate actions, alleging failure to comply with the guidelines and breach of the Declaration. The Association sought permanent injunctions compelling the removal of the SEDs, monetary penalties, and attorneys' fees and costs. The Madigans and Speaks say that the state gives tax credits for these solar panels and that the Association's rules runs contrary to public policy designed to encourage solar energy use. What are the rights of the owners? The Association? The state? *Garden Lakes Community Ass'n, Inc. v. Madigan*, 62 P.3d 983 (Az. 2003).

For research activities related to this chapter, go to our text companion website at www.cengagebrain.com

CHAPTER 12

THE BROKER'S ROLE IN THE TRANSFER OF REAL ESTATE

Terry and Marti Likens listed their home for sale with Remax realtor Carolyn Leiter. Jack Stump is a real estate agent employed by Prickett's Properties who represented Zachary and Holli Gredy. After showing the Likenses' home to the Gredys, the Gredys made an offer to buy the home. During the weeklong negotiations that surrounded the making of the offer, Mr. Stump contacted the Likenses directly—and not through their own agent Ms. Leiter—by phone and email and encouraged them to accept the Gredys' offer. At the time, the Likenses had another offer pending on their home which Ms. Leiter had encouraged them to accept instead. Mr. Stump's e-mails to Marti Likens included his assurances that the Gredys' offer "was a good deal" and his advice that they should "accept" it. Mr. Stump told them that Zachary Gredy was a "financial whiz" and there would be "no reason ... to worry" about a delayed closing. The deal never closed, the Likenses lost the other offer, and they have filed suit against Mr. Stump and Prickett's. Can they recover from someone who is not their agent?[1]

The opening scenario shows the liability issues that brokers and agents face as they try to get deals closed. This business of selling property for others has prickly legal issues at every step. There are ever-evolving dilemmas and questions surrounding the conduct and role of brokers. This chapter answers the following questions: Does the broker represent the seller or the buyer in the transaction? Is the broker responsible for defects the seller fails to disclose? Is the broker entitled to be paid when a sale falls through? What happens if a potential buyer falls through? What is the agency relationship of the broker? What responsibilities and liabilities does the

---

[1] *Schwalb v. Kulaski*, 814 N.Y.S.2d 696 (2006).

broker have as an agent? What ethical constraints should a broker follow? On what areas should a broker focus when listing and selling a property?

NATURE OF BROKER'S/AGENT'S ROLE

Definition

A **broker** is an agent[2] hired either by the owner of a property to aid in its sale or by a potential owner (buyer) to find property suitable for specified needs. A broker is the middle person acting to bring buyer and seller together. Generally, a broker works on a commission basis rather than on salary. That commission is usually specified as some percentage of the sales price and will probably not be paid until the actual sales transaction is complete (see the consideration discussion in this chapter).

Traditional Principal–Agent Concepts versus Principal–Broker Roles

Under the traditional principal–agent relationship, the **agent** works on behalf of the principal, owes a duty of loyalty to the principal, would not breach confidences of the principal, and would not profit at the principal's expense. The principal and the agent are a team, working together with a common interest. However, the nature of property transactions creates flowing, instead of rigid, relationships for the real estate broker. Interactions and methods of conducting business blur the traditional lines and rules of agency. While the industry is still evolving with respect to the role of brokers, there are certain types of broker relationships that are common in the industry. Those types of relationships are discussed in the following section.

THE TYPES OF REAL ESTATE BROKER RELATIONSHIPS

The Listing Agent

The listing agent works directly with the seller to list the property, advertise it, and contribute other marketing services. However, even the listing agent will be involved in showing property to buyers and hence has contact with both the buyer and seller. A Federal Trade Commission survey found that even when the listing agent is the only one involved in a sales transaction, 72 percent of purchasers of real estate still believed that the listing agent represented them and not the seller.

The Dual Agency

Given the confusion of buyers with respect to the role of brokers, many states allow **dual agency** relationships. A dual agency permits an agent to represent both sides in a transaction so long as the parties are aware of the dual representation.

---

[2]Note: The term *broker* is used here in a generic sense to reflect that person hired to represent either the seller or buyer in a real estate transaction. *Broker* and *agent* have distinct meanings in the real estate industry, with differing training and education requirements. A real estate agent must work for a broker but can serve as an agent in the legal sense for seller or buyer. That real estate agent's broker is also a legal agent for the listing seller or the represented buyer. The terms *broker* and *agent* are used interchangeably throughout the chapter.

All states have some form of mandatory disclosure requirements by agents, regardless of the type of agency relationship that the parties have agreed to have. Before buyers or sellers sign with a broker for representation, there must be full disclosure about the broker's role and responsibilities. In addition, the **National Association of Realtors (NAR)**, the professional association for brokers and agents, requires under its code of ethics that NAR members make specific disclosures to all parties.[3]

If the broker does not make these disclosures, the broker will lose the commission or be required to pay back the commission. Web Exhibits 12.1 and 12.2 are sample disclosure forms for Massachusetts and Florida.

In the case of dual representation, the disclosure form, known as a "Consent to Act," must be signed by the parties hiring the broker. Web Exhibit 12.3 is a sample dual representation consent form.

ETHICAL ISSUE

Is it possible for a dual agent to be loyal to both parties? Does one side suffer in a dual agency relationship? Is the dual agent simply protecting information to which the buyer would never gain access if there were separate agents?

The Buyer Broker

It is also possible to have an agency relationship in which the buyer is represented by a broker.[4] The buyer broker may require a nonrefundable up-front fee but is generally paid the bulk of his or her fee as percentage commission from the eventual property sale. Fees are usually in the range of 2 to 3 percent. This type of arrangement raises the question of a conflict of interest because the buyer broker's compensation is tied to the purchase price: Will the buyer broker negotiate the lowest possible price when compensation increases as the price increases? The key to managing this conflict under codes of ethics in the broker profession is disclosure of all terms and all relationships or potential relationships.[5]

The Open Listing Agency

An **open listing** agreement is used when an owner lists the property to be sold with more than one broker. Under this form of listing, not common in residential transactions, the seller owes only one commission to the broker who actually sells the property. The seller also retains the right to sell the property personally, and the seller owes no commission to any broker if the seller actually finds the buyer.

Other brokers are free to solicit listings from sellers who have open listing arrangements with other brokers, and the only commission paid will be to the broker who actually produced the buyer.

---

[3]Standard of Practice 1–12 of the Code of Ethics and Standards of Practice for the National Association of Realtors (effective January 1, 2012) provides that a Realtor may not represent the landlord and tenant or the buyer and seller until there has been full disclosure to and informed consent by both parties.

[4]There is the National Association of Exclusive Buyer Agents (NAEBA), founded in 1995, that is comprised of agents who represent only buyers in real estate transactions. These agents also have their own code of ethics.

[5]Standard of Practice 1–13 of the NAR's code requires the Realtor to disclose the compensation and whether there are any arrangements between the buyer–broker and other brokers.

The Exclusive Agency

An **exclusive agency listing** arrangement is one in which the seller is required to pay a commission to the listing broker if that broker sells the property. However, the seller still retains the right to sell the property independently, and if the seller does sell the listed property, the listing broker earns no commission. If the seller hires another broker, the original broker retains the right to commission and the seller will be obligated for two commissions.

The major distinction between the open listing agreement and the exclusive agency listing agreement is that the open listing permits the seller to list the property with other brokers. Under the exclusive agency listing, sellers should not list with other brokers, because they will still be responsible to the exclusive broker for the commission and may end up paying more than one commission. In both types of listings, the seller may still sell the property independently without being required to pay the commission. See Web Exhibit 12.4 for sample open and exclusive listings.

The Exclusive Right-to-Sell or Exclusive Listing-to-Sell Agency

Under the **exclusive right-to-sell** or **exclusive listing-to-sell** arrangement, the seller agrees to pay a commission to the broker regardless of who produces a buyer. The broker earns the commission even if the seller produces a buyer independently of the broker. This type of listing agreement, which is beneficial to the broker, is the one used most frequently in the real estate industry.

Multiple Listing Agency

The **multiple listing** agreement is not really a form of agency between seller and broker, but rather a service available to brokers who are members of a multiple listing service. An example of a **multiple listing service** is the **MLS**, a network of exclusive right-to-sell listings that affords brokers and sellers a larger market for their properties. Through MLS, broker members are able to show the listed properties of other brokers. The listing broker then shares in the commission if another broker obtains a buyer for the broker's listed property. The split commission is pre-negotiated and determined by the MLS members. Since there is still only one listing agreement, the seller is liable for only one commission. The MLS is a marketing tool that allows brokers to assist one another in finding buyers and gives sellers greater exposure for their properties.

The Subagency

The subagency relationship is a product of MLS arrangements. Under an MLS listing, there is the listing broker (who represents the seller) and then, quite often, the selling broker (who brings the buyers who eventually buy the property). In a subagency, the selling broker is a subagent of the seller because the selling broker derives his or her authority from the listing broker. However, there remains a problem with buyers' perceptions in this type of arrangement—the buyers still feel both brokers work for them. Further, many sellers believe the selling broker works for the buyer rather than for them.[6] In 1993, NAR changed its position

---

[6]Ann Moales Olazábal, "Redefining Realtor Relationships and Responsibilities: The Failure of State Regulatory Responses," 40 *Harvard J. of Legislation* 65 (2003).

that subagents were mandatory agents of the seller, and the result has been a shift to more buyers' agents participating in sales of MLS-listed properties. As a result, the term, "the cooperating broker," is now common. A cooperating broker is one who is working as a subagent of the listing broker and has agreed to a commission arrangement in the event the cooperating broker finds a buyer for the property. All subagents must disclose their relationship and compensation to the seller's agent when they have contact with the property and again if there is an offer or contract on the property. Subagents who are agents of the seller must disclose that information to any prospective buyers. Listing brokers also have obligations to disclose their commission arrangements to cooperating and potentially cooperating brokers.

Net Listing Agency

In the **net listing** agreement, the seller and broker may have any of the previous types of listing arrangements for determining who is entitled to the commission. This arrangement, illegal in residential listing in some states, merely provides a different method for determining the amount of commission the broker is entitled to receive. Generally, the commission is some percentage of the selling price. However, in net listings, the sellers establish a predetermined amount that they must receive from the sale of the property after expenses, insurance, and so on. The broker's commission is anything received above that predetermined amount. For example, if the seller sets the net figure at $40,000, and $41,500 remains after expenses, and so on, the broker receives a $1,500 commission. Again, this form of commission determination may be coupled with an open listing, exclusive agency listing, or exclusive right-to-sell format.

The Designated Agency

A **designated agency** relationship arises when one firm represents both the buyer and seller in a transaction. The broker for the firm designates one salesperson to represent the seller and another salesperson to represent the buyer. The designated agency differs from the dual agency in that two different agents are representing the parties, with the theory being that the representation is more objective. Most states also have disclosure requirements for designated agency arrangements so that sellers and buyers are aware that their agents work for the same broker or agency.

The Nonagent Broker

A **nonagent broker** may be known as a **transaction broker**, **intermediary**, **limited agent**, or **statutory broker**. At least 18 states recognize this relationship, in which brokers represent both buyer and seller in closing a transaction.[7] These types of brokers are simply facilitators for closing. States vary in their requirements for creating a nonagency relationship.

The following case, one that appears as the chapter opening, deals with the intricate issues of agents who interact with both buyer and seller.

---

[7]Ann Moales Olazábal, "Redefining Realtor Relationships and Responsibilities: The Failure of State Regulatory Responses," 40 *Harvard J. of Legislation* 65 (2003).

LIKENS V. PRICKETT'S PROPERTIES, INC.

943 N.E.2d 816 (Ind. App. 2011)
Trust Me—I'm On Your Side

FACTS

Terry and Marti Likens listed their home for sale with Remax realtor Carolyn Leiter. The Likenses signed an agency agreement with Leiter.

Jack Stump is a real estate agent employed by Prickett's Properties who represented Zachary and Holli Gredy. After Mr. Stump showed the Likenses' home to the Gredys, they made an offer to buy home. However, during the weeklong negotiations that surrounded the making of the offer, Mr. Stump explained directly to the Likenses that the Gredys would not have the necessary cash to close for several months but that they would be able to close after concluding certain real estate transactions. Mr. Stump contacted the Likenses not through their own agent Ms. Leiter but by phone and e-mail and encouraged them to accept the Gredys' offer. At the time, the Likenses had another offer pending on their home which Ms. Leiter had encouraged them to accept instead. Excerpts from Mr. Stump's emails to Marti Likens include the following:

"I know I work differently from other realtors—I try to satisfy both sides and keep the 'experience of buying or selling' enjoyable."

"My legal background includes the Naval Legal Court Recording school at Newport, Rhode Island; Naval Legal Officer's school at San Diego, CA and International Law at NETC Mayport, FL."

"I know how to read and write contracts to keep this even for both parties. I'm not sure why other agents can't try to be helpful."

"You did nothing wrong and I told your Dad this morning that the real problem is with your agent … not you!"

"[The Gredys] are finally convinced that your home is the one for them. I'll be getting together with them later today to write the offer. Again, thank you for the opportunity to be of service."

In addition, Mr. Stump advised the Likenses that the Gredys' offer "was a good deal" and that they should "accept" it. Mr. Stump told them that Zachary Gredy was a "financial whiz" and there would be "no reason … to worry" about a delayed closing. Mr. Stump also told the Likenses that the Gredys had "a secret financial deal going on" that he could not disclose

and that it was going to be a cash deal, which was "going to close," "no problem." Mr. Stump also told the Likenses that "Zach…speaks seven languages, he's very smart, his wife is pregnant, they really need to get out of the house that they bought because of the mold…").

On February 28, 2008, the Likenses and the Gredys executed a Purchase Agreement. The first page of the Purchase Agreement lists Leiter as the listing broker and Stump as the selling broker. The final page of the Purchase Agreement provides:

25. ACKNOWLEDGMENTS: Buyer and Seller acknowledge that each has received agency office policy disclosures, has had agency explained, and now confirms all agency relationships. Buyer and Seller further acknowledge that they understand and accept agency relationships involved in this transaction. By signature below, the parties verify that they understand and approve this Purchase Agreement and acknowledge receipt of a signed copy.

The terms of the Purchase Agreement provide that the Gredys would purchase the Likenses' home for $325,000. Closing was to occur on or before September 30, 2008. However, the Gredys were to receive possession on March 15, 2008, and pay the Likenses $2000 per month in rent until closing. In addition, the Gredys were required to place $10,000 in escrow. According to the Counter Offer, the earnest money was to be held by Mr. Stump in the form of a bank letter of guarantee of funds.

The closing did not occur by September 30, 2008, and the bank letter of guarantee of funds turned out to be fraudulent. The Likenses then filed a multi-count complaint against the Gredys, Stump, and Prickett's Properties. As for the Gredys, the Likenses alleged breach of contract for, among other things, failing to close by September 30, 2008, and failing to make rent payments for November and December 2008, pay taxes, and obtain property insurance. The Likenses also alleged that the Gredys committed fraud in remitting the fraudulent bank letter of guarantee of funds and in stating that closing would occur as soon as they sold two of their properties when in fact one property was an office building owned by Zachary's father and the other property was in foreclosure.

As for Mr. Stump, the Likenses alleged two counts: (1) negligence/breach of agency duty and (2) fraud. The Likenses asserted that although Stump was the Gredys' realtor, he "directly communicated with and advised [them] on the purchase/sale of the property" and encouraged them to accept the Gredys' offer because, among other things, the Gredys were "solid buyers." Because of Mr. Stump's direct communications with them, the Likenses alleged that "Stump entered into a constructive agency relationship with [them] throughout the term of the negotiations and transaction." In addition, the Likenses alleged that Mr. Stump failed to ensure that the $10,000 bank letter of guarantee of funds was in fact valid and failed to ascertain the ownership/status of the properties claimed to be owned by the Gredys. Finally, the Likenses alleged that Prickett's Properties was liable for Stump's actions under the doctrine of *respondeat superior*.

Stump and Prickett's Properties filed a motion for summary judgment. The trial court entered summary judgment in favor of Prickett's Properties, Inc. and Jack Stump as to all claims. The Likenses appealed.

JUDICIAL OPINION

Vaidik, Judge

The Likenses argue that contrary to the Gredys' no-duty argument made in the trial court below, Stump owed them a common law duty because "it is clear that Stump went beyond acting as an agent for the Gredys and undertook to advise and coerce [them] into a course of action." In order to establish a common law duty, the Likenses rely on three factors: (1) relationship between the parties; (2) reasonable foreseeability of harm to the person injured; and (3) public policy concerns.

The Gredys respond that pursuant to Indiana statutory law, Stump, as the agent for the buyers in a real estate transaction, owed no duty to the Likenses as the sellers and that this statutory law supersedes any common law to the contrary.

Indiana Code chapter 25–34.1–10 governs real estate agency relationships. The Likenses do not acknowledge this body of statutory law. "Agency relationship" is defined as "a relationship in which a licensee represents a client in a real estate transaction." Ind. Code § 25–34.1–10–0.5. Section 9.5 provides that "[a] licensee has an agency relationship with, and is representing, the individual with whom the licensee is working unless: (1) there is a written agreement to the contrary; or (2) the licensee is merely assisting the individual as a customer without

compensation." According to these sections, Leiter— and not Stump—was the Likenses' agent. That is, the Likenses signed an agency agreement with Leiter, Leiter listed the Likenses' home for sale, and the Purchase Agreement unmistakably lists Leiter as the listing broker and Stump as the selling broker.

Section 11 [states that a] licensee representing a buyer owes no duties or obligations to the seller, except that a licensee shall treat all prospective sellers honestly and not knowingly give them false information. Indiana code § 25–34.1–10–11(c). In addition, a licensee representing a buyer owes no duty to conduct an independent investigation of the buyer's financial ability to perform for the benefit of the seller or to verify the accuracy of any statement, written or oral, made by the buyer or a third party.

Here, the basis of the Likenses' negligence count against Stump is that he directly communicated with and advised them on the sale of their home, failed to ensure that the bank letter of guarantee of funds was in fact valid, and failed to ascertain the ownership/status of the Gredys' alleged properties (which supposedly had to be sold before they could close on the Backwater Road property). Indeed, Stump had a duty to treat the Likenses honestly and not knowingly give them false information. But the negligence count against Stump does not allege any violation of this clearly-articulated statutory duty. Moreover, Section 11 explicitly states that Stump owed no duty to conduct an independent investigation of the Gredys' financial ability to perform for the benefit of the Likenses or to verify the accuracy of any statement, written or oral, made by the Gredys or a third party. Stump therefore had no duty to investigate the bank letter of guarantee or the Gredys' financial ability to pay for the Backwater Road property.

Finally, while Stump's actions in directly contacting the Likenses to encourage them to accept the Gredys' offer may seem inappropriate, Stump, as the buyers' agent, is allowed to provide the Likenses services in the ordinary course of a real estate transaction and any similar services that do not violate the terms of his agency relationship with the Gredys. There is no allegation here that Stump breached his agency relationship with the Gredys. In sum, the Likenses claim that Stump owed them a duty which simply does not exist in Indiana Code chapter 25–34.1–10.

Even if we were to construe the Likenses' argument to be that Stump owed them a separate and distinct common law duty, according to Section 15, "The duties and obligations of a licensee set forth in this chapter supersede any fiduciary duties of a licensee to a party based on common law principles of agency to the extent that those common law fiduciary duties are inconsistent with the duties and obligations set forth in this chapter." Accordingly, the Likenses cannot use common law principles to establish a duty on the part of Stump that does not exist in Indiana Code chapter 25–34.1–10.

Finally, to the extent that the Likenses argue that Stump represented both them and the Gredys at the same time. A "limited agent" is a licensee who, "with the written and informed consent of all parties to a real estate transaction, represents both the seller and buyer … and whose duties and responsibilities to a client are only those set forth in this chapter." In addition, Section 12 provides that a licensee "may act as a limited agent only with the written consent of all parties to a real estate transaction. The written consent is presumed to have been given and all parties are considered informed for any party who signs a writing or writings at the time of entering into an agency relationship with the licensee that contains"

certain specified information. Here, there is simply no evidence of a writing that the Gredys and the Likenses consented to Stump acting as a limited agent for both of them.

Because Stump did not owe the Likenses a duty as the Likenses assert in their complaint, the trial court properly entered summary judgment on the Likenses' negligence claim against Stump. And because Stump is not liable, Prickett's Properties cannot be liable under the doctrine of *respondeat superior*. We therefore affirm the trial court.

Affirmed.

CASE QUESTIONS

1. What does the court mean when it labels Stump's actions "inappropriate"?
2. List the lessons real estate brokers, real estate firms, buyers, and sellers should learn from this case.

ETHICAL ISSUE

Tom Caines is acting as an agent for Luci and Neil Dayton, a couple looking to purchase a home. Tom has located a home in Ventura Canyon that nearly perfectly suits the needs Luci and Neil have described to him. Tom approaches the owner, Mel Cusack, and explains that he is representing Luci and Neil Dayton as buyers. Tom then adds, "Look, you have what they want. You can pretty much get your asking price. It helps me because I am on commission in addition to the fee they paid up front." Has Tom acted ethically? What conflict does Tom have in acting as a buyer broker and earning a commission?

The Internet as an Agent

Stocks, bonds, antiques, and anything eBay sellers can think of have sold well over the Internet. The free-market exchange of information and quick transactions have produced selling booms in everything from books to toys. The idea of matching buyers and sellers of real estate through an Internet database seemed to be a possibility that would eliminate the need for any type of agent or broker. However, since the time of the initial splash of Internet listings, most experts have conceded that agents play a critical role in the buying and selling of real estate, particularly when it comes to homes. The most successful Internet real estate sites are those that partner with agents. Not all real estate buyers are ready to negotiate the purchase of a home without a physical view, and most are not prepared enough to handle the contracting and negotiations by themselves.

Internet listing services are not so different from other types of listings or even the MLS. The seller lists property with the Internet service, which plays the role of the listing broker. Buyers may come to the site with their own agent or broker, or they may use an agent or broker offered by the site. That broker or agent then is entitled to split the commission with the Internet listing service. The laws and codes of ethics provisions on disclosures still apply to brokers acting for sellers and buyers over the many Internet sites for sales of homes. Some brokers and agents are exclusively internet-based, called VOWs, or virtual office websites. When VOWs emerged, the National Association of Realtors (NAR) allowed brokers to opt out of VOW listings, even though its policies prohibited brokers from opting out of listing with other brokers. NAR members also followed a rule of not discussing the availability of VOWs with clients.

In 2005, the Justice Department filed suit against NAR for its anticompetitive rules on opt-out and disclosure with respect to VOWs. In 2009, the Justice Department and NAR settled the litigation with NAR agreeing to eliminate its opt-out provision and provide clients with information about listings on VOWs if there are listings that are not part of MLS.[8]

LISTING AGREEMENTS FOR HIRING BROKERS/AGENTS

The agency arrangement between broker and seller is called a **listing agreement**. State requirements for valid listing agreements vary, but the parties should be cautious about including provisions that specify their rights, duties, and responsibilities. The goal is to cover all fundamentals so that their intentions are made absolutely clear.

Agreements in Writing

Under most state laws and the code of ethics for Realtors®, the agency agreement must be evidenced by a record. In most states where a written listing agreement is required, the absence of some form of a record will cost the broker or salesperson the commission. States now allow faxed agreements as well as electronic communications applications (PDFs) that have been part of the reforms since the federal E-Sign provisions that require parity for electronic forms of communication with paper documents. However, oral agreements for real estate agency contracts remain unenforceable in most states. Even if a broker sells the property pursuant to an oral agreement, the seller need not pay the commission. Exceptions to the writing requirement are rare.

ETHICAL ISSUE

Jeffrey Sisson owned a sports bar and restaurant in Charles City. In early 1999, he contacted Larry Stewart about selling the restaurant. Stewart is a licensed real estate broker in Charles City. Sisson told Stewart he wanted a sales price of around $615,000, and he would pay him 10 percent of the sales price if he found a buyer. However, Sisson did not want Stewart to list the property because he thought he would lose sales and value from the business if the public was aware it was for sale. Stewart agreed to find a buyer, but the parties never reduced the agreement to writing.

---

[8]*U.S. v. National Association of Realtors,* Civil Action No. 05 C 5140 (N.D. Ill.). Both the case and the settlement can be found at: http://www.usdoj.gov/atr/public/real_estate/index.htm

On November 13, 2001, Sisson sold the business to Walter without notifying or involving Stewart. Stewart subsequently learned about the sale and wrote Sisson to inquire about his commission. Sisson replied and asked Stewart for written documentation to verify the agreement. Stewart could not provide documentation in writing.

After trying and failing to resolve the dispute, Stewart filed an action against Sisson for breach of contract in March 2002. Sisson responded by filing a motion to dismiss. He claimed Iowa Administrative Code rule 193E-1.23 (now rule 193E-11.1) barred Stewart's claim. ("All listing agreements shall be in writing, properly identifying the property and containing all of the terms and conditions under which the property is to be sold, including the price, the commission to be paid, the signatures of all parties concerned and a definite expiration date.") The district court dismissed the breach-of-contract claim. Was the result fair? Think of an argument you could make to have the agreement for the 10 percent commission be enforceable. Was Sisson's conduct ethical? *Stewart v. Sisson*, 711 N.W.2d 713 (Iowa 2006).

Signature by Owner

The listing agreement must be signed (according to the state law provisions on electronic communication and statutes on authentication) by the owner of the property. The true or record owner must sign the agreement; if there is more than one owner, all owners must sign. In the case of land owned by a corporation, LLC, or partnership, the officer, director, or partner signing the listing agreement must have the authority to do so.[9] A corporate officer's authority requires a board resolution. The authority of a trustee, executor, administrator, or personal representative can be found in a court order or the letters of administration, along with any restrictions on the authority to transfer title to the property. For example, some executors of estates may have the authority to list the property but not to sell it without prior court approval.

Importance of Careful Drafting and Completion of Standard Form Agreements

Both brokers and sellers should be cautious in drafting the listing agreement, even if drafting consists only of completing forms, so that the type of listing is clear and the commission issue is not clouded with ambiguities. The best way to avoid litigation over who owes how much to whom is to make sure the listing agreement is drafted carefully and unambiguously.

Expiration Date

Most states have some type of law or regulation that requires listing agreements to have a definite expiration date. When an expiration date is required and the listing agreement has none, the agreement is an unenforceable contract, one that does not allow the broker to collect a commission even when that broker produces a sale. Some states impose maximum time limits for listing agreements, with 90 days being a typical maximum length.

Brokers may put a clause in the listing agreement that entitles them to a commission for a certain period of time after the expiration of the listing agreement to cover sales that are post-expiration and made to prospective buyers who were

---

[9]When an individual signs on behalf of a nonexistent LLC, there is no listing agreement. *Barnett v. Saizon*, 994 So.2d 668 (La. App. 2008).

originally introduced to the property during the listing period by the broker who held that listing. A sample post-expiration clause follows:

If within ninety (90) days after the expiration of this listing agreement, a sale is made directly by the broker to any person to whom this property has been shown by you or the broker or an agent of the broker, the same fee shall prevail, unless this listing is renewed or the property is relisted on the same basis with another broker, and in that case, this stipulation shall be void.

Some states have statutory requirements on post-expiration sales. These statutes often require that the broker provide the seller with a list of "protected persons," or those persons to whom the property has been shown, when the listing expires. The broker has documented previous contact and the seller is aware of the broker's claims for a commission on these potential buyers. Many states require that this list be a formal document delivered to the seller within a short time after the expiration of the listing, with 72 hours being a common time limit.

A listing agreement without an expiration date, even in states that recognize the validity of open-ended listings, can be canceled at any time. Such a right of cancellation is often used to avoid paying a commission. However, to prevent commission avoidance, courts still apply an implied duty of good faith in indefinite-duration listing agreements.

The rights of termination under the listing agreements are also important for commission purposes. The listing agreement should cover whether the listing may be terminated, how termination occurs, what type of notice of termination is required, and what damages will be due and owing for termination, if any.

Amount of the Commission

Particularly in multiple listing arrangements, a uniformity in commission rates among brokers that has caused the Justice Department to bring suit alleging a conspiracy among real estate brokers to fix prices. Most listing agreements include language similar to the following to attempt to countermand the allegations of price fixing: "*The commissions payable for the sale, lease, or management of property are not set by any board of Realtors®, multiple listing service, or in any manner other than between the broker and the client.*"

While there has not been a judicial decision directly addressing real estate commissions and their antitrust implications, the United States Supreme Court has ruled in *McClain et al. v. Real Estate Board of New Orleans, Inc. et al.,* 441 U.S. 942 (1980), that real estate brokerage has a sufficient impact on interstate commerce for it to be subject to federal antitrust laws such as the Sherman Act and its prohibition on price fixing. Some states now require that brokers' disclosure forms include language informing consumers that the commission rate is negotiable.

Because the MLS listing enables brokers to tap into an entire community's market, its accessibility is often critical for success in the business. Sales statistics indicate that 80 percent of all residential purchases involve a multiple listing service broker. However, in recent years, these organizations have, like other trade and professional associations, faced review of their anticompetitive effects. Membership restrictions for such organizations are particularly suspect when the result is that those denied memberships, on the basis of unjustified criteria, are effectively barred from the business benefits and activities afforded members.

CONSIDER 12.1   The newly elected president of a professional organization of real estate agents held a dinner at an exclusive country club. He invited his colleagues who would help him manage the organization during his tenure of office. Their discussion at dinner centered around a new membership drive and the organization of committees. The new president then stood up and said the following:

> *My business is dying fast. I have already borrowed $75,000 to keep afloat. If I am going bankrupt at 6 percent, I might as well go bankrupt at 7 percent. I don't care what the rest of you do, that is what I am going to do.*

Has there been an antitrust violation? *U.S. v. Foley*, 598 F.2d 1323 (C.A. Md.1979).   ▉

Because of the Internet, buyers have ease of access to information outside an MLS, and a means for easier and less expensive access to property information. Despite this plethora of information, however, there is still great market power through the MLS, along with relationship issues regarding the use of MLS and the fees associated with it. In *Freeman v. San Diego Ass'n of Realtors*, 322 F.3d 1133 (9th Cir. 2003), *cert*. denied 540 U.S. 940 (2003), the court restricted the power of the MLS services to control pricing on and access to the MLS services.

When Commission Is Due and Owing

Most form listing agreements provide, and the majority of courts hold (in the absence of an agreement to the contrary), that the broker is entitled to the commission when a purchaser who is ready, willing, and able to meet the terms of the listing agreement has been brought to the seller. Actual closing of the deal is not necessary for the broker to collect the commission.[10] However, the listing agreement should spell out this right to a commission, regardless of closing.

Also, the listing agreement must contain all the material terms and conditions for sale of the property, since the broker's entitlement to commission is tied to those terms.

Producing a buyer who is ready and willing simply means that a buyer is ready to purchase according to the seller's listing terms and has made necessary deposits on the property. The *able* portion of the test for earning a commission requires the broker to establish that the buyer had the financial ability, credit, or resources necessary to go through with the transaction.

If the seller contacts the buyer directly and gets the buyer to cancel, this attempt to thwart the transaction still results in the broker earning the commission.

In some states, courts have eliminated the ready, willing, and able standards and now require that the deal actually close before the broker is entitled to a commission. These states are limited, and even in these states the parties must specify a **no deal, no commission clause** in their listing agreement.

---

[10]Some that follow a "no deal, no commission" rule are Oregon, Idaho, Kansas, Massachusetts, and Nebraska. Louisiana remains unclear on its standard, while Vermont and Alaska point to the virtues of "no deal, no commission" even as they adhere to the "ready, willing, and able" standard.

CONSIDER 12.2   What would happen to the broker's commission in a situation in which the property was damaged by fire after the sales contract was entered into but before the transaction closed? Suppose that the sales contract provided that the seller was to carry the risk of loss between the time of the contract for sale and closing, and that the insurer was obligated to pay for the damages caused by the fire. Suppose further that after inspecting the property, the buyer opts to exercise his right to terminate the purchase contract on the grounds that the property could not be delivered in substantially the same condition as it was when the contract was signed. Does this fit into a "ready, willing, and able buyer" situation in which the broker delivered the buyer but the closing did not occur? Or would it be that the buyer was no longer willing? Do we measure from the time the contract is entered into or do we measure from the time of the closing? *Rosepark Properties, Ltd. v. Buess*, 855 N.E.2d 140 (Ohio App. 2006).

Description of Property and Sale Terms

Because the listing agreement will be the basis for advertising the property and a representation of its quality, size, location, and character, brokers must collect and disclose accurate information about the property.

The listing agreement should cover price, method of financing, date the property may be transferred, fixtures included and not included, any conditions for rental or occupancy of the property, any easements or other use restrictions, and any restrictions such as a requirement of court approval. Another important issue for a listing agreement is spelling out what happens to the earnest money if the buyer defaults. The more detailed the listing, the less confusion there will be when an offer comes in and during the process of completing the sale.

Conditions Precedent

A **condition precedent** is a requirement or event placed in a contract that must be fulfilled or should occur before the parties are required to perform their obligations under that contract. Conditions precedent in the listing agreement include court approval for sale of the property or the buyer being able to qualify for financing. With these uncertain future events in the listing agreement, the parties know the contract performance issues before offer and acceptance on the sale of the property.

Liability Limitations

Many brokers insert clauses in their listing agreements limiting their liability to the seller to the amount of commissions they are to be paid under the listing agreement. In some cases, such limitations are effective, but when the seller experiences damages because of the broker's negligence, such clauses may be set aside. (Brokers' duty of care is discussed later in this chapter.) Furthermore, with third parties now able to recover damages directly from brokers, these liability limitations are limited to contract parties, if they are honored at all (third-party liability is discussed later in the chapter).

Other Details

The listing agreement should also contain permission clauses that allow the broker to advertise, place signs on the property, bring prospective buyers to the property,

FIGURE 12.1 Checklist for an Effective Listing Agreement*

1. Name of owner
   a. Are they authorized?
   b. Who holds title?
   c. Is there more than one owner?
   d. Signatures
2. Type of listing agreement
   a. Open
   b. Agency
   c. Exclusive right to sell
   d. Net
   e. Multiple listing
3. Duration of the listing
   a. Length
   b. Extension clause for buyers introduced to the property by the broker
   c. Termination: reasons, methods, notice, damages
4. Entitlement to commission
   a. Ready, willing, and able
   b. No sale, no commission
   c. Fraud or bad faith by the seller
5. Description of the property
   a. Accurate legal description
   b. Correct parcels

6. Selling Terms
   a. Price
   b. Financing
   c. Date of transfer
   d. Good title
   e. Rental or occupancy
   f. Easements
7. Condition precedent
   a. Court approval
   b. Buyer financing
   c. Sale or other property
8. Marketing rights
   a. Advertise
   b. Place sign on property
   c. Showings
   d. Multiple listing
9. Rights upon buyer's default
   a. Earnest money
   b. Effect on listing
10. Liability limitations

© Cengage Learning

*Should be written (i.e., represented by a record).

and use a multiple listing service to market the property. There are also statutory requirements at the state level such as requiring the broker to furnish the owner/seller with a copy of the listing agreement.

Figure 12.1 is a checklist for preparing an effective listing agreement.

RESPONSIBILITIES OF BROKERS/AGENTS

Authority

The listing agreement gives the broker the authority to market the listed property and bring prospective buyers to the seller. Any restrictions and limitations on that authority should be part of the listing agreement. Brokers who engage in conduct beyond the scope of their authority are liable for any damages or obligations that result. For example, a broker who reduces the listing price without the seller's consent would be liable for the price difference. A broker who accepts an offer for a seller without authority to do so would be liable to the buyer and seller for damages caused by the unauthorized agreement.

Antisolicitation Statutes

Some states have enacted antisolicitation statutes that prohibit brokers and agents from soliciting property owners to list their properties for sale. In many cases, these antisolicitation statutes are enacted to prevent "blockbusting," which is the practice of controlling the racial composition of neighborhoods by soliciting listings and sales through use of fear in depicting the neighborhood's racial composition as one that is changing (see Chapter 19 for a more complete discussion).

Antiblockbusting statutes that attempt to restrict access of real estate agents to certain areas for purposes of obtaining listings have not survived constitutional challenges (*New York State Association of* Realtors,® *Inc. v. Shaffer*, 27 F.3d 834 (2nd Cir. 1994). Prohibiting solicitations in certain areas without justification could be challenged as a violation of commercial speech rights.

Duty of Care

A broker is required to exercise care in listing the seller's property, presenting offers, and handling the details of closing.

This duty of care requires the broker to list the property at a reasonable market value figure. Because of commission pay structures, underappraising properties and listing them accordingly can result in rapid, easy sales, complete with the broker's percentage earnings. The listing price should be set according to market comparables with the overarching goal of assisting the seller with the sale of the property that brings a fair return. Brokers should exercise caution in making overzealous statements about sales potential of the property and their abilities, because inflated seller expectations can cause problems for the broker later.

If the seller needs to net a certain minimum from the transaction, the broker's computation of the sales price is even more critical. The broker should take into account all fees and contingencies, and understand every cost associated with the sale, from transfer fees to title insurance to commissions.

The broker's duty of care continues throughout the period of the relationship. Brokers must present all offers to their sellers and provide their expertise in helping sellers evaluate the soundness of those offers, including the hazards or pitfalls, such as the advantages or disadvantages of financing alternatives as well as the risks of contingencies, involved in each offer. Brokers do not advise which offer a seller should take, but they can explain offers' weaknesses and strengths.

In explaining offers, however, brokers should not cross over the fine line between exercising care and practicing law. A broker may explain to a seller the customs and practices of the real estate industry, but not the law. Brokers should refer clients who have questions about legal details or issues to their attorneys.

Brokers should also proofread documents such as the listing agreement, the offer, the contract for the property, and closing documents by checking for errors in figures, descriptions, and dates. In some states, brokers may fill out contracts, but they are under a high duty of care to be sure that all terms are present, carefully drafted, and accurately stated. When brokers use form contracts, offers, and agreements, they should be cautious and be sure that the form language reflects the parties' intentions.

Brokers who prequalify prospective buyers can match properties and sellers with buyers more easily and avoid the problems that arise when a contract falls through because the buyers cannot obtain financing. Also, a broker who knowingly presents an offer from an unqualified buyer exposes himself to liability.

Clauses in listing agreements that try to exculpate brokers for breach of their duty of care are invalid, as they are for accountants, lawyers, engineers, and other professionals. A contract exculpatory clause cannot excuse professionals from liability when they have failed to exercise the standards of care for their profession.

Fiduciary Duty

Once a broker is employed by a principal, that broker is expected to act only in the best interests of the principal, regardless of the negative effects and consequences that may result for the broker. Brokers cannot lead their sellers into unsound transactions for the sake of a commission, and are obligated to tell sellers when problems arise in the negotiation or closing of a transaction. Brokers must be accurate and timely in their disclosures, including any changes affecting the seller's rights or interests.

Most states impose a separate fiduciary duty on brokers with respect to earnest money deposits. Money that belongs to the seller should not be commingled with the broker's own funds. Most states require that deposits be placed in trust accounts or escrow accounts, or else require the establishment of escrow funds within a short time after receipt. Brokers who retain deposits for unreasonable lengths of time may face license revocation or suspension. Sellers and buyers need to use caution in selecting and supervising their real estate agents and brokers because, as the following case indicates, they are responsible for their agents' conduct.

QUEIROZ V. HARVEY

205 P.3d 1120 (Ariz. 2009)
The Phony Escrow Money and the Lost Deal

FACTS

Daniel Harvey listed ten acres of land in Tonopah for sale. Through his agent, Charles Harrison, Ivo Queiroz offered to purchase the land, along with an additional ten acres. The purchase offer called for a $1,000 earnest-money payment and a closing date of February 15, 2005. The proposed purchase price was $150,000, with $68,000 due at closing. Harvey was to finance the balance of $82,000. A counteroffer, faxed the next day and accepted by Queiroz, retained the closing date and the earnest-money requirement, but changed escrow agents. Harrison faxed the contract to the escrow agent on December 10, but sent no earnest money during the following week.

Harvey and his agent became concerned about Queiroz's failure to deposit the earnest money. Repeated efforts to reach Harrison were unavailing.

Finally, on Friday of that week, Harvey's agent told the escrow agent that the contract was canceled. Either that night or the next day, Harrison learned that Harvey had cancelled the contract.

Nevertheless, on the next Monday morning, Harrison took two money orders amounting to $1,000 to a branch of the escrow company. Several hours later, Harvey's written notice of the cancellation arrived at another branch of the escrow agent's office. Harvey's agent returned Harrison's earnest money, informing him that the contract had been canceled.[11]

Queiroz sued Harvey, seeking specific performance of the contract. The superior court found that Harrison had acted inequitably and thus denied Queiroz specific performance. The court determined that Harrison lied about the source of the earnest money, testifying that it was Queiroz's when in fact it

---

[11]The following part of the case relates to a contract issue and could be revisited as part of Chapter 16 studies. The contract called for written notice before cancellation. The superior court concluded that the failure to timely pay the earnest money was a material breach. The court of appeals, however, concluded that payment of the earnest money before the written notice of cancellation had been received cured the breach. See *Queiroz v. Harvey*, 204 P.3d 390, 395 (Ariz. App. 2008). Harvey did not seek review of this holding.

was Harrison's. The court found that in providing the earnest money Harrison either made an undisclosed loan to Queiroz or commingled his own money with Queiroz's funds. The court further found that Harrison's subterfuge went further when he printed his name, rather than signing it, on the purchase offer because he did not have the required earnest-money check, failed to return phone calls, and "raced to the escrow agent to deposit the funds," knowing that Harvey had canceled the contract. Finally, the court found that Harrison had not testified truthfully.

The court of appeals reversed and Harvey appealed.

JUDICIAL OPINION

Ryan, Justice

In this opinion, we address whether a court may consider a real estate agent's inequitable conduct in deciding if the agent's principal is entitled to specific performance of a contract for the sale of real estate. We conclude that the agent's inequitable acts may be imputed to the principal whether or not the principal knew of the agent's misconduct. We granted review because whether an agent's inequitable conduct is chargeable to the principal is an issue of statewide importance and is likely to recur.

A trial court's grant or refusal of specific performance is reviewed for an abuse of discretion. Queiroz does not dispute that specific performance, although a routine remedy in actions involving contracts for the sale of real property, may properly be refused on the basis of unclean hands. Rather, Queiroz argues that a mere agency relationship does not suffice to establish inequitable conduct and that such conduct should not be imputed to an "innocent" principal.

We reject these arguments. Under ordinary principles of agency law, an agent's acts bind the agent's principal. "A representation by an agent made incident to a contract or conveyance is attributed to a disclosed … principal as if the principal made the representation directly when the agent had actual or apparent authority to make the contract or conveyance…." This includes "the circumstances under which representations made by an agent affect a principal's legal position in actions brought to enforce or rescind a contract."

Other courts have similarly concluded that a principal seeking specific performance may be bound by

an agent's inequitable conduct. Principals may not benefit from the inequitable conduct of their agents.

The court of appeals, however, declined to apply this rule. The court concluded that the unclean hands doctrine implicates the moral blameworthiness of the party who seeks equitable relief. Thus, the court held that imputing inequitable conduct of an agent to a principal is not appropriate absent a showing that the principal knew of the agent's misconduct

Queiroz's additional arguments are equally ineffectual. The principles of agency discussed above refute Queiroz's policy argument that we should protect all principals from liability, especially given that without Harrison's acts, the deal here would not have been completed. As between the principal who has retained an unscrupulous agent and an innocent third party who relies on the agent's misrepresentation, it is the third party who deserves protection.

Queiroz also argues that, notwithstanding Harrison's inequitable conduct, Harvey has suffered no harm and thus he should be forced to perform the sale-and-financing contract. This claim, of course, is belied by the transaction, which requires Harvey not only to sell the property, but also to carry the mortgage for Queiroz. Thus, ordering specific performance in this case would effectively place Harvey in a continuing relationship with Queiroz.

Queiroz preserved the issue of whether, assuming Harrison's conduct may be imputed, it was actually inequitable. We defer to the superior court's findings that Harrison's conduct was inequitable and that his statements and actions were dishonest and misleading. Harrison's conduct misled Harvey regarding Queiroz's capacity to go forward with the earnest-money payment and concealed his potential inability to make payments on an ongoing basis.

We vacate the court of appeals' opinion and affirm the judgment of the superior court. Because the contract here requires the prevailing party to be awarded reasonable attorneys' fees, we grant Harvey's request for attorneys' fees.

CASE QUESTIONS

1. What did Harrison do that misled the seller?
2. Why is the court reluctant to award Queiroz specific performance under the contract?
3. Based on what happened in this case, explain why the fiduciary duty of agents is so important.

Duty of Loyalty

A broker may not work both ends of the transaction by representing both parties unless there has been full disclosure and both parties consent to such dual representation. (See earlier clarifications on state variations on duties and types of agencies.)

A broker may not profit secretly from a transaction involving the principal. Brokers must disclose to their clients all they know about all parties involved in the transaction. A broker who wants to buy a listed property or has an ownership interest in a property a buyer is considering must make a full and complete disclosure of these interests. A broker who is a partner, shareholder, or relative of a party to the transaction must disclose those ties as well. If a broker does not make the appropriate disclosure and realizes a secret profit, that profit belongs to the broker's client.

Under dual agency relationships, the duty of loyalty becomes complicated. For example, suppose that a broker representing both buyer and seller knows that the buyer is a credit risk. Does the duty of loyalty require the broker to disclose that to the seller? Does such a disclosure breach the duty of loyalty to the buyer? Most states that permit dual agency also list categories of information the dual agent must keep confidential, such as (1) the seller being willing to take less than the asking price; (2) the buyer's willingness to pay more than the asking price; (3) the motivation of the parties in buying and selling; and (4) the willingness of either party to accept less favorable financing terms. The following case deals with the issues of broker duty and disclosure.

WARREN V. MERRILL

49 Cal.Rptr.3d 122 (Cal. App. 2006)
The Condo Queen and Her Client with Tourette's

FACTS

John Warren (plaintiff and respondent) suffered from Tourette's syndrome and other related neurological disorders affecting his short-term memory and cognitive abilities. His movie set rental business was having financial difficulties and he was also in the process of getting divorced. He met Hildegard Merrill (defendant and appellant) at an open house for a condominium. Merrill, doing business as Calabasas Realty, was the agent for the seller of the condominium. Merrill had acquired her real estate license in 1967 and had been a licensed real estate broker since 1981. She sometimes referred to herself by her professional nickname of the "condo queen." Merrill also held a mortgage broker's license.

Merrill told Warren that the condominium was a good investment and that the seller was motivated to sell. Warren was interested, but he had sustained a $1 million judgment for nonpayment of rent when one of his business ventures collapsed. As a result,

Warren's credit rating was poor. Merrill told Warren he needed a co-borrower with a good credit rating in order to secure a mortgage at a reasonable rate. Merrill suggested her own daughter, Charmaine Merrill, would be the co-owner and co-borrower on the loan. Once the loan/credit hurdle was overcome and escrow closed, Charmaine would execute a quitclaim[12] deed to him to remove her name from title in exchange for $10,000.

As the loan broker, Merrill knew it was important to make a 20 percent down payment in order to secure a reasonable interest rate. Because Warren did not have the money, Merrill offered to defer her commissions of $27,000 and to loan this amount to Warren in order to attain a 20 percent down payment of $77,000. Their entire arrangement was never put in writing.

Merrill wrote up a purchase offer for the condominium with Charmaine and Warren as co-purchasers. Merrill never had Warren fill out a loan application form and Merrill never attempted to secure a loan

---

[12]The court refers to the deed as a "quit-claim deed." However, this terminology is nondistinctive in California for a "quitclaim deed."

with Warren as a co-borrower with her daughter Charmaine. Instead, Merrill applied for and secured a loan in Charmaine's name alone.

Merrill misrepresented facts when she filled out Charmaine's loan application. For example, Merrill stated that the source of the proposed $77,000 down payment was a combination of savings and gifts. The application stated that Charmaine then resided in a condominium at 5800 Kanan Road in Agoura Hills and conducted catering and shuttle businesses out of the residence on Kanan Road, and had been doing so since 2001, earning a monthly income of $7,500 from those businesses. In reality, Charmaine had resided for years in Aspen, Colorado, and had never lived at or conducted a business out of the 5800 Kanan Road residence. Also, the businesses Charmaine conducted had shut down sometime in 1990. Charmaine was instead employed as a waitress in Aspen, Colorado, and periodically conducted her shuttle business there. She otherwise relied on her mother for support. Merrill indicated on the loan application that Charmaine intended the condominium to be her primary residence. Merrill later conceded that she would never have gotten the loan had she been truthful in the loan application. The trial court was so alarmed by Merrill's testimony and her apparent lack of concern about admitting she had committed a form of fraud on the lender that the court recessed the proceedings to permit Merrill to consult with counsel regarding her Fifth Amendment right not to incriminate herself.

How the $77,000 down payment was cobbled together remains a bit of a mystery. According to Warren, he paid the entire $77,000 down payment: (1) By repaying the $27,000 Merrill loaned him toward the down payment; (2) by his and Charmaine's each depositing a check for $10,000 into escrow; (3) by repaying Charmaine this $10,000 by writing two checks of approximately $5,000 each, one to pay toward Charmaine's Chase Platinum credit card balance and the other to pay toward Charmaine's MBNA credit card balance; (4) by writing a check for $30,000 to Merrill's boyfriend again at Merrill's direction.

Merrill also deposited into escrow a check for $30,000 written on her and her boyfriend's investment account at Paine Webber. In exchange for her boyfriend's services, Merrill had Warren write her boyfriend another check for $2,000. But Merrill says she deferred her combined sales commission and loan broker commission of $27,000 to complete the $77,000 down payment. Warren then wrote Merrill a check for $27,000, which Merrill held uncashed until

Warren repaid her this amount. He accomplished repayment of the $27,000 by writing Merrill checks of between $3,000 and $4,000 over the course of about six months. Unbeknownst to Warren, the seller had agreed to credit $6,000 in escrow to defray closing costs, which should have reduced the amount Warren repaid Merrill.

Merrill knew that the lender would not fund the loan request with different people proposed to hold legal title than had applied for the loan. Merrill had Warren sign an amendment in escrow to remove his name from title, explaining that the document was just a formality required to secure the loan and to close escrow. The amendment stated that title would vest solely in Charmaine Merrill. The amendment further stated, "John Warren is no longer a party to this escrow. All monies currently on deposit to this date shall accrue to Charmaine Merrill...."

Escrow closed in October 2001 and Warren moved into the condominium. Merrill did not have Charmaine execute a quitclaim deed to transfer title to Warren after escrow closed.

Warren and/or his attorney made the mortgage payments directly to the lender for several months. However, Warren developed substance abuse problems. He checked into the Betty Ford Center for treatment. He had not made arrangements for someone to handle his personal and financial affairs in his absence. Merrill learned that the homeowners' association was about to foreclose on Warren's unit. A few days before the scheduled foreclosure date, Merrill paid the association the approximately $5,000 then claimed as arrearages to prevent the foreclosure.

Merrill filed an unlawful detainer action to have him removed from the unit. While Warren was still in the Betty Ford Center receiving treatment, Merrill secured a judgment against Warren, got a writ of possession, and evicted him from the premises. She removed all his belongings and placed them either in a storage facility or in the garage of her home in Woodland Hills. Warren's belongings included original artwork, sports memorabilia, the personal papers of his grandfather, the former California Governor and Chief Justice of the United States, Earl Warren, antique furniture, jewelry, medals, and several filing cabinets containing all his business records. Merrill held a lien sale of Warren's personal property and was herself the successful bidder at the sale.

When he left the Betty Ford Center in September 2002, Warren talked to Merrill many times, but she would not permit him to return to the residence. In his last conversation with Merrill, Warren explained that he was desperate and homeless. Over a four-month period, he had stayed with various friends or slept in his car, but was then sleeping in the park and using public facilities to attend to his personal hygiene. Merrill told Warren he just "didn't get it." Merrill informed Warren that he did not owe her any money and directed Warren not to call her anymore. After evicting Warren, Merrill rented the condominium to a series of renters.

Warren filed suit against Merrill, Charmaine, and others. The trial court found that Merrill had acted outrageously and with reckless disregard in perpetrating the fraud on Warren, and made an award of punitive damages of $50,000. The court also entered judgment quieting title in favor of Warren. The court also awarded Warren noneconomic damages in the amount of $15,000 on his causes of action for fraud, breach of fiduciary duty, and ejectment. Merrill agreed to return all of Warren's personal property, and in exchange Warren agreed to pay the storage fees. The court also awarded Warren costs and attorney's fees.

Merrill appealed.

JUDICIAL OPINION

Johnson, Judge

There should be no dispute Merrill owed a fiduciary duty to Warren once she undertook to represent him in the real estate transaction. Merrill herself acknowledged at trial she held a fiduciary position of trust toward Warren. Because she owed Warren a fiduciary duty Merrill further acknowledged she was required to place his interests above her own in the real estate transaction. Nevertheless, she claims there was no evidence of misrepresentation, no evidence of fraud and no evidence of a breach of her fiduciary duties to sustain the court's judgment. She claims this is true because whatever fiduciary duties she owed Warren terminated when he "withdrew" from the escrow.

The record in the present case contains substantial evidence satisfying each of the elements of both constructive and actual fraud. The evidence showed Merrill breached her fiduciary duties toward Warren and committed fraud by deliberately and falsely promising him she would place his name on title to the condominium if he went along with her plan on how to structure the transaction. From the beginning of the transaction she did not intend to perform her promise of placing his name on title. Merrill instead intended to procure the condominium for herself but did not disclose her role as a principal in the transaction. Merrill in fact kept the condominium.

If this was a legitimate transaction, writing checks to third parties would have been wholly unnecessary. However for Merrill's purposes it made it appear, at least superficially, she, and not Warren, had contributed the $30,000 check into escrow, Charmaine had contributed $10,000 into escrow and Merrill had deferred her earned commissions of $27,000 as a credit into escrow (while holding Warren responsible for repayment).

Merrill led Warren to believe he had to sign the amendment in escrow removing his name from the title and gifting his contributions to Charmaine in order to secure financing. Warren obviously trusted Merrill's representation because he signed the amendment. Through these deceptive maneuvers Merrill secured for herself an investment property in her daughter's name by lying to her principal and misappropriating his funds.

In these circumstances it seems preposterous to argue, as does Merrill, Warren "withdrew" from escrow and for this reason she owed him no fiduciary duty and thus could not be guilty of fraud. Instead, it may be more accurate to say Warren was "coerced" into signing the amendment and into "withdrawing" from escrow based on Merrill's representations the loan would not fund and the whole deal would fall apart unless he signed the amendment taking his name off title. If Warren truly "withdrew" from the escrow then all of the money he had contributed to the down payment should have been returned. It was not.

In sum, we agree with the trial court the evidence in this case was more than sufficient to show an egregious violation of the duties of loyalty and undivided interest by a fiduciary toward her principal, as well as a deliberate plan to defraud him out of his down payment and the property.

Merrill argues Warren was not entitled to equitable relief of any sort because he was guilty of unclean hands. She asserts his entire claim for relief was premised on an illegal scheme to conspire to defraud the lender by having Charmaine secure the loan in her name and then fraudulently concealing from the lender Warren's ownership interest in the property. In addition, Merrill points out because of Warren's personal and substance abuse problems he would have lost the property altogether but for her efforts stopping the foreclosure and paying the arrearages.

Although Warren's behavior was far from exemplary, we do not believe under the circumstances he and Merrill were equally at fault. True, Warren agreed to, and acquiesced in, what would have been an improper, if not impossible, plan to use Charmaine as a front in order for him to secure the loan. We note it was Merrill, not Warren, who proposed the "illegal plan." We also note the "illegal plan" never happened and thus Warren never participated in any "illegal scheme." Of course, the "illegal scheme" was not carried out because the fiduciary's own undisclosed plan was to instead take the property for her personal benefit. In the process of carrying out her plan Merrill defrauded her client out of the property and his $77,000 down payment. And she did this to the very person to whom she owed fiduciary duties of loyalty, trust and full disclosure.

In these circumstances the trial court properly weighed the equities and found the doctrine of unclean hands did not automatically bar Warren from receiving relief in this case.

The judgment is affirmed.

CASE QUESTIONS

1. List all of the actions by Merrill that were a breach of her duty of loyalty, the law, or her ethics as a real estate agent.
2. How does the court respond to Merrill's argument that Warren had joined in on the plan to dupe the lender?
3. If Warren did indeed remove himself from the escrow, what should Merrill have done?

LEGAL DUTIES AND RESPONSIBILITIES TO THIRD PARTIES

The broker who lists the property and the buyer of the listed property do not have a direct contractual relationship. However, in some states, the broker may still have liability to the buyer for misrepresentations as to the condition of and defects in the property. This liability is based on the common law tort of misrepresentation, liability that has been expanded dramatically.

Misrepresentation

Misrepresentations about property generally fall into two categories: (1) those made intentionally and (2) those made negligently. Intentional misrepresentation occurs when the broker knows of a fact and then either misstates it to the buyer or simply fails to disclose it. Negligent misrepresentation occurs when (1) the broker failed to make a reasonable effort to determine whether the fact represented was true or false and (2) the buyer justifiably relied on that misrepresentation in purchasing the property.

A broker who makes statements about the property without a sufficient knowledge base may be liable to the buyer under a theory of negligent misrepresentation. An example of negligent misrepresentation occurs when the broker makes statements about the cost of heating, air-conditioning, or electricity, and does so without a statement of cost from the seller or without an actual investigation or verification of the cost.

With negligent misrepresentation, ignorance as to whether a statement is true or false does not allow the broker to avoid liability; it is the broker's responsibility to determine whether information is true or false. When the prospective buyer asks if city sewer, water, and gas are available for the property, the appropriate response for a broker who is uncertain is, "I don't know, but I can check." Brokers are liable for misrepresentations that they make to the buyer orally, for descriptions of the property, for the content in fliers and ads about the property, and for information and photos posted on websites about the property. In short, all marketing materials count for purposes of misrepresentation.

Nondisclosure

Misrepresentation occurs when the broker is aware of the problems or defects in property but fails to disclose that material information to prospective buyers. Cosmetically covered wall cracks and foundation cracks should be disclosed. The traditional water-in-the-basement problem should also be disclosed. The fact that an existing property use violates the city code is another example of a required disclosure.

Sales Puffing

Misrepresentation can result from the sales-puffing techniques of brokers. The classic line given to induce buyers is, "If you are going to do anything, you had better do it quickly because I have another buyer on the line for this property." The statement is innocent enough so long as there is, in fact, another buyer. If no other buyer exists, such statements inflate the value and desirability of the property and constitute misrepresentation to the buyer, who was led to believe the property was in demand. The following case deals with an issue of misrepresentation and whether the broker's language was a basis for a claim by a buyer or was simply puffing.

CAPICCIONI V. BRENNAN NAPERVILLE, INC.

791 N.E.2d 553 (Ill. App. 2003)
Misalignment and Misinformation on the Acclaimed School District

FACTS

In 1998, Dean and Majel Capiccioni (plaintiffs/appellants) moved from Ohio to Illinois and purchased a home in Bolingbrook. Brennan Naperville, a residential real estate brokerage company, and Sharon Clermont, a licensed real estate broker and one of Brennan's agents (defendants), represented the Bolingbrook property's sellers. The sales brochure for the Bolingbrook property listed as one of the home's features "Acclaimed [school] District 204."

The Capiccionis moved into the home, and their three children attended school in District 204 for three years. However, the children were unable to attend District 204 classes during the 2001–2002 academic year after the Capiccionis discovered that their property was actually located in District 365-U. The Capiccionis subsequently sold the property and purchased another home. Their new home was located in District 204.

In June 2001, the Capiccionis filed suit against Clermont and Brennan for giving them false, untruthful, and misleading information. They maintained that they would not have purchased the home if they had known of the true district alignment, that they paid more for the home because of the school district's reputation, and that they had incurred the cost of selling the house and moving in order to be located within the school district boundaries.

The trial court dismissed the Capiccionis' complaint and they appealed.

JUDICIAL OPINION

Callum, Justice

Negligent misrepresentation consists of: (1) a false statement of a material fact; (2) carelessness or negligence in ascertaining the truth of the statement by the party making it; (3) an intention to induce the other party to act; (4) action by the other party in reliance on the truth of the statement; and (5) damage to the other party resulting from such reliance when the party making the statement is under a duty to communicate accurate information.

This court has indicated that negligent misrepresentations of material fact made by a Realtor® "could well be the basis" for a negligent misrepresentation claim.

In *Richmond v. Blair*, 142 Ill.App.3d 251, 256, 94Ill.Dec. 564, 488 N.E.2d 563 (1985), the Appellate Court, First District, decided that such an action can be brought against a Realtor®. In *Richmond*, the plaintiff toured a home with the sellers' real estate broker. The broker informed the plaintiff that the house had experienced water leakage in the basement. When the plaintiff requested assurance that the problem had been fixed, the broker assured her that the home was completely free of water leaks or seepage. The plaintiff purchased the home, and it subsequently flooded. She sued the broker and her employer alleging, *inter alia*, negligent misrepresentation. The trial court granted the defendants' motion to dismiss, and the appellate court reversed and remanded the cause, finding that the plaintiff adequately pleaded the required elements of negligent misrepresentation. The plaintiff alleged that the broker owed to her a duty to be knowledgeable and accurate in her representations about the property; that the broker breached her duty by negligently making statements about the basement without actual knowledge about their truth or falsity; and that the broker's breach proximately caused the plaintiff's injuries.

[R]ealtors occupy a position of trust with respect to prospective buyers and … they owe to them a duty to exercise good faith in their dealings with them, even absent an agency relationship between the parties.

With respect to the second element, plaintiffs alleged in their negligent misrepresentation count that defendants owed to them a duty to use due care in obtaining and communicating information that they knew plaintiffs would rely upon in deciding to purchase the Bolingbrook property; that defendants breached this duty and were negligent in marketing the property as being located in District 204 when it was widely known in the real estate industry that misinformation exists about Bolingbrook school district boundaries; and that Clermont took no action to determine the property's school district. We conclude that plaintiffs properly pleaded negligence.

With respect to the third element—intent—we conclude, as we discussed above, that plaintiffs adequately pleaded this element. They alleged that defendants made the representations in an advertising brochure in the course of selling the Bolingbrook property.

We next address the reliance elements. Plaintiffs contend that they adequately pleaded reliance, where they alleged that they relied on Clermont's false representations and took reasonable steps to confirm the information by contacting District 204 employees.

In the common-law fraud context, the plaintiff's reliance must be justified, i.e., the plaintiff must have had a right to rely. The same requirement applies for a negligent misrepresentation claim. A party is not justified in relying on representations when he or she had ample opportunity to ascertain the truth of the representations before acting.

Here, we conclude that the facts in plaintiffs' amended complaint indicate that plaintiffs would have been entitled to rely on defendants' alleged misrepresentations. Plaintiffs alleged that District 204 employees confirmed that their property was located in the district, and plaintiffs' children were permitted to enroll in District 204 schools for several years. Based on these allegations, we cannot conclude that plaintiffs could not prove a set of facts to establish reasonable reliance. Although plaintiffs' allegations regarding their discussions with school district employees might establish that they did not exclusively rely upon defendants' representations, we cannot conclude, based on the pleadings, that the discussions completely undermine their reliance argument.

Finally, we conclude that plaintiffs properly pleaded damages. They alleged that they were damaged as a direct result of defendants' negligence, in that they purchased a home they would not have otherwise purchased; they paid more for the property than it was worth; the property did not appreciate as much as if it were within the boundaries of District 204; and they paid moving-related expenses associated with the purchase.

For these reasons, we conclude that the trial court erred in granting defendants' motion to dismiss on plaintiffs' negligent misrepresentation count.

Reversed.

CASE QUESTIONS

1. Where did the representation on the schools appear?
2. What is the significance of proximate cause in this case?
3. How does the court handle the issue that the buyers could have checked on the school district themselves?

Safety Standards

A broker may be held liable for conditions on a property that violate codes or are unsafe if the conditions were not disclosed to prospective buyers or remedied prior to the closing of a deal. Brokers should check for hazards while showing the property so that they can note new developments or hazards.

Broker liability for concealment or the failure to disclose material information to potential buyers varies from state to state. In Alaska, the District of Columbia, Illinois, Minnesota, South Carolina, Texas, Utah, and Wisconsin, brokers are even held liable for innocent misrepresentation. Some states impose liability for only intentional or negligent misrepresentation. For example, Washington does not hold brokers liable for innocent misrepresentation because the effect of imposing such liability would be that of a "strict liability" standard for brokers.

"As Is" Clauses

Often property will be sold with a provision in the contract that says it is sold **as is**, meaning that the buyer is taking the property as it stands with all existing defects and no promises of repair. Such a clause would appear to relieve the broker of liability for latent defects and the failure to disclose material information. However, the courts have held that the use of the "as is" clause is not a blanket of immunity for the broker from allegations of fraud. If a broker actively misrepresents the condition of the property or fails to disclose true facts, the "as is" clause will have no effect, and the broker will still be held liable for the silent or affirmative misrepresentation. A dilapidated building sold "as is" will not provide immunity from liability for the broker who failed to disclose that the building had been condemned. The following case presents an interesting issue of nondisclosure by a broker and the presence of an "AS IS" clause in the contract for purchase.

BENTON V. CLEGG LAND CO., LTD

--- So.3d ---, 2012 WL 2362628 (Ala. App. 2012)
That's Just a Little Drought Going on There

FACTS

Sometime before 2002, Curtis Adams and his wife contracted for Don Casey to construct a 10–acre lake on a 646–acre parcel of recreational property in Macon County that Adams and his wife then owned. Casey constructed the lake with a dam on one side; one side of the dam faced the lake, and the other side faced dry land. Subsequent to the construction of the lake, Adams and his wife sold the property to Clegg Land Company in 2002.

Thereafter, Clegg enlarged the existing cabin on the property, built a pole barn, improved the hunting facilities on the property, and improved the roads on the property. Clegg Land Company's owners used the property for hunting and fishing.

Within a year after Clegg purchased the property, Clegg Land Company's owners noticed that the water level in the lake would fluctuate. Casey did some bulldozing and work on the lake, but he informed Clegg's owners that he did not know what could be done to stop the seepage or leak and restored the dirt he had removed to its original location.

Subsequently, Clegg decided to sell the property and listed it for sale with Speaks Land Company for $3,250 per acre. After the property was listed for sale, members of the Clegg family, with the assistance of Harold Dennis, who lived near the property, and Dennis's daughter, put 10,000 to 12,000 pounds of bentonite in the lake near the dam to see if the bentonite would stop the seepage; however, the water level in the lake continued to fluctuate. Clegg did not take any other action to stop the water level from fluctuating.

After the property had been listed for sale for approximately 9 to 12 months, Jason Benton contacted Speaks Land Company and asked to see the property. Jason and his father, Russell, are both experienced in the purchasing of land and own businesses that own land in several states. Tim Speaks, the owner of Speaks Land Company, and Buce, the qualifying real-estate broker for Speaks Land Company's office in Union Springs, met Jason and Russell Benton, at the property on October 11, 2007, when Macon County was experiencing a drought. Jason testified in his deposition that, while Speaks and Buce were showing them the property, he and Russell noticed that the water level in the lake was low and that they asked Speaks and Buce why the water level was low and whether there was a problem with the lake. Jason testified that Speaks and Buce said that the water level was low due to the drought and that there was no problem with the lake.

Jason signed a contract to purchase the property and asked Buce to see if Clegg would agree to sell the property on the terms stated in the contract. The contract listed the purchasers as Jason and Russell and provided that the total purchase price was $1,950,000, that the contract would expire on November 26, 2007, that the sale had to be closed on or before that date, and that time was of the essence. In addition, the contract contained the following provisions:

> "Condition of Property: Neither Seller nor any Agent makes any representations or warranties regarding the condition of the Property. Except as otherwise stated in this Contract or addenda, Purchaser accepts the Property in its present 'AS IS' condition."

The contract also provided:

> "NO ORAL STATEMENT, REPRESENTATION, PROMISE, OR INDUCEMENT SHALL HAVE ANY VALIDITY NOR SHALL BE A PART OF THIS AGREEMENT."

> "DISCLAIMER: The Seller and Purchaser further acknowledge that neither of them have relied upon the representations, covenants, statements, warranties, or advice of any Broker, or agent of any Broker related to the legal and tax consequences of this contract or any other aspect of this contract unless expressly stated herein."

After purchasing the property, Jason and Russell made improvements to the property, which included constructing a lodge beside the lake and constructing two permanent docks on the lake. However, they discovered that the water level in the lake stayed low except for short periods immediately following a heavy rain. Jason testified that, when the water level was low, 30 to 40 feet of shoreline was exposed and the permanent docks were above the head of anyone in a boat on the lake. Russell testified that he and Jason had purchased the property to entertain clients, that they had intended for the lake to be the "jewel" of the property, and that the low water levels made the lake an eyesore rather than a jewel.

Jason and Russell sued Clegg, Speaks Land Company, and Buce, for various forms of fraud through their misrepresentations that the lake was low due to the drought and that there was no problem with the lake.

The trial court entered a summary judgment in favor of Clegg, Speaks Land Company, and Buce. Jason and Russell appealed.

JUDICIAL OPINION

Bryan, Judge

"Where a purchaser's direct inquiry would otherwise impose a duty of truthful disclosure, this Court has held that a purchaser's fraud claim is precluded by language in a sales contract stating that the purchase is 'as is.'"

In the present case, the undisputed evidence established that the property was used real estate that was sold in an arm's-length transaction in which none of the parties to the transaction owed any of the other parties a fiduciary duty. Moreover, there is no evidence indicating that the alleged defect in the lake "affects health or safety."

Therefore, there is no merit in Jason and Russell's argument that Clegg, Speaks Land Company, and Buce had a duty to disclose the existence of the alleged defect merely because they knew of its existence and it was not known or readily ascertainable by Jason and Russell.

Jason and Russell's direct inquiry regarding the lake did impose a duty on Clegg, Speaks Land Company, and Buce to disclose any defects in the lake that were known to them. There was substantial, though not undisputed, evidence before the trial court tending to prove that a defect in the lake existed and that Clegg, Speaks Land Company, and Buce knew of the existence of that alleged defect when Jason and Russell made their direct inquiry regarding the lake. There was undisputed evidence establishing that, in response to Jason and Russell's direct inquiry regarding the lake, Speaks and Buce did not disclose the existence of any defect in the lake and affirmatively represented that the lake was low due to the drought and that there was no problem with the lake. However, it is undisputed that subsequent to Jason and Russell's direct inquiry and Speaks and Buce's response, Jason signed the contract, which contained an "as is" clause. Moreover, although Russell did not sign the contract and argues that he is not bound by the "as is" clause, he admitted that he and Jason had jointly purchased the property, that they had both signed a promissory note to finance the purchase of the property, and that he had signed the closing statement. In addition, he has asserted a breach-of-contract claim against Clegg, Speaks Land Company, and Buce based on the very contract that he contends is not binding on him for purposes of his misrepresentation and suppression claims.

"A party, by his actions and acceptance of the benefits of a contract and by operating under such agreement, may ratify and confirm a contract to which his actual signature is not affixed." Accordingly, we conclude that the "as is" clause in the contract barred Jason and Russell's misrepresentation and suppression claims despite the duty of disclosure imposed on Clegg, Speaks Land Company, and Buce by Jason and Russell's direct inquiry regarding the lake. Therefore, we affirm the summary judgment with respect to the misrepresentation and suppression claims.

The supreme court has held that an "as is" clause in a contract for the purchase of used real estate bars not only the purchaser's misrepresentation and suppression claims but also his or her negligence claims. Therefore, we affirm the summary judgment with respect to the negligence claim.

Jason and Russell argue that the trial court erred in entering a summary judgment with respect to their breach-of-contract claim because, they say, they contracted with Clegg, Speaks Land Company, and Buce to purchase property that was free from any material defect and Clegg, Speaks Land Company, and Buce breached the contract by selling them property that had a material defect. However, assuming, without deciding, that Speaks Land Company and Buce could be liable for breach of a contract to which they were not parties, Jason and Russell's argument has no merit because they did not contract to purchase property that was free from any material defect. They contracted to purchase the property in "as is" condition, and they received the property in "as is" condition. Nonperformance of the contract by the defendant is an essential element of a breach-of-contract claim.

Affirmed.

CASE QUESTIONS

1. How definitive was the evidence that the sellers and agents aware of the defects in the property, i.e., the lake that would not hold water?
2. Why does their knowledge of the problem not make a difference for the buyers in the case?
3. List what lesson you learn from this situation and the court's decision.

Statutory Duties of Disclosure

About one-half of the states have some form of mandatory disclosure statutes that require the seller to disclose varying types of information about the property as part of the listing process. In many states, these disclosure statutes were passed as a result of lobbying efforts by brokers who desired some protection from the increasing liability from the lack of clarity on disclosure responsibilities and resulting liabilities.

Generally called "Residential Property Disclosure Acts," the acts are indeed limited to the sales of residential property and may not apply when residential property is being sold by an owner without the use of a broker. Remedies for the failure to make required disclosures include the right to rescind the purchase contract as well as the usual damage remedies available for misrepresentation or fraud.

Some disclosure statutes are specific, with itemized topics related to structure, plumbing, environmental conditions, foundation issues, and other material types of issues in property transactions. However, other state disclosure statutes are more general, requiring purchasers to disclose whatever information would influence the decision to purchase the property or the price that the buyer would pay. Still another type of state statute simply requires a sworn statement from the seller that the buyer has had all material information disclosed to him or her by the seller.

Both sides enjoy protection under the disclosure statutes. That is, the seller is protected from liability for misrepresentation or fraud when there is compliance with the disclosure statutes, and the buyer enjoys more complete information going into the transaction. In addition, brokers in many states enjoy limited liability when they have complied with the disclosure statutes and required their seller-clients to do the same.

The following case deals with the issues of misrepresentation and its relationship to statutory disclosure requirements.

FULLER V. CROSTON

725 N.W.2d 600 (S.D. 2006)
If It's Fixed – Do I Have to Disclose?

FACTS

In the fall of 2002, Ivan R. Fuller was interested in purchasing a Sioux Falls home owned by James and Patricia Croston, the sole owners of the house since its construction. Fuller received a signed and completed seller's property disclosure statement, as required by SDCL 43-4-38, from the Crostons.

The disclosure statement indicated that the home had not experienced any water penetration problems. However, when the Crostons signed the disclosure statement in November 2002, they were aware of two to three occasions between 1969 and 1977 when water had seeped into the basement. They maintain that they did not include this information in the disclosure statement on the recommendation of their real estate agent, Janey Johnson (a licensed real estate agent), who allegedly advised the Crostons that if they believed the problem was fixed they did not have to disclose it. She denies these allegations. The Crostons, believing that the water problems had been resolved, did not disclose the prior seepage on the disclosure statement. Their disclosure statement also indicated that there were no cracks in the interior walls of the house. However, the Crostons were aware of some cracks in the walls in the basement behind the washer and dryer. They puttied and painted over these cracks two to three years before selling the house to Fuller.

Before signing the purchase agreement, Fuller visited the home with the Crostons. He noticed some flaking on one of the basement walls. When he asked about this, Crostons informed Fuller of a "little bit of water there some time back." They told him that they had experienced some water in the basement on two to three occasions between 1969 and 1977, but they had not experienced any additional water problems since adding a sunroom to the home in 1977. Fuller also noticed some "roughness of the paneling in the family room." The Crostons explained that when they added a sunroom and a garage, they had some water come into the basement. As a result, they did landscaping to seal off the water and also placed wood paneling over the drywall in the basement.

After the conversation with the Crostons about water in the basement, Fuller still offered to purchase the Crostons' home for $158,000. The Crostons accepted this offer and the purchase agreement pro-

vided that Fuller would have 10 days to complete a professional home inspection and notify the Crostons of any unacceptable conditions discovered.

Fuller hired David Kemper of Kemper Inspection Services to perform the inspection. The report noted a small horizontal crack and minor bowing at the north and south foundation walls. The report explained that the north wall had been patched and there was no new cracking. According to the inspection report, this was not unusual and was of no structural significance at the time. The inspection report further indicated some signs of past dampness, which appeared to be old, in the basement.

The cracking and dampness issues raised by the inspection report were not addressed by the addendum because Kemper felt these matters were not significant.

On January 17, 2003, the parties closed the sale on the home. By August 2003, Fuller completely moved into the home. On June 16, 2004, the total rainfall for Sioux Falls was approximately eight inches. According to a FEMA Report, Sioux Falls accumulated a total of 12.74 inches of rain from May 17 to June 16, 2004, a record amount for a 31-day period. At some point during or immediately after this rainfall, Fuller noticed water entering his basement, but could not determine precisely where it was coming in. He stated that the water appeared to be "seeping in around the foundation and the walls." The water created "puddles here and there" until the carpet was largely saturated.

Fuller contacted Roy Johnson, a contractor, to evaluate and remedy the water problem. When Johnson removed some of the paneling in the basement, the "stuff behind the paneling crumbled" in his hands. Johnson advised Fuller that it appeared there had been previous water penetration in the home. He blamed the water infiltration on the existence of cracks in the home's foundation and bowing of the walls. He also told Fuller that there had been major water damage in the past and that frequent water problems would persist unless action was taken. Johnson then installed drain tile around the perimeter of the basement and a sump pump, and reinforced the foundation walls. Fuller also purchased and installed new padding and carpet for the basement.

At about the same time Fuller encountered the water issues, he noticed the garage roof was sagging once again. He contacted Duane Boice, an engineer, to evaluate the roof. Boice advised Fuller that installation of the support beam actually weakened the roof and made it worse. Boice explained that the roof would have to be fixed, or it would collapse. Fuller then hired Able Construction to repair the roof.

Fuller filed suit on the grounds that he was not made aware of the extent of the previous water damage or all of the cracks in the basement walls and that the Crostons were aware of damage behind the paneling.

The circuit court entered summary judgment in favor of the Crostons and the real estate agents (defendants) and Fuller appealed.

JUDICIAL OPINION

Miller, Justice

Crostons admit they had knowledge of previous water damage and a crack in the basement at the time they signed the disclosure statement, and that they did not reveal this knowledge on the disclosure statement. They contend that disclosure of these defects was not necessary. First, they claim their real estate agent (Janey Johnson) advised them not to disclose the prior water penetration because the problems occurred so long ago and were believed to have been fixed. However, the disclosure form mandated by statute simply asks, "have you experienced any water penetration problems in the walls, windows, doors, basement, or crawl space?" Crostons checked "no" to this question. By its plain terms, the question does not ask only for ongoing water penetration problems. Indeed, it is silent as to whether the problems have been fixed or persist. The disclosure statement simply asks if the sellers "experienced" water penetration problems. Crostons [*sic*] own admissions reveal they had.

Second, Crostons contend that disclosure of the crack was not necessary because it appeared insignificant to them. They also claim that their understanding of the question related only to cracks in the sidewalk and driveway. Again, the disclosure form provided in SDCL 44-3-44 asks, "are there any interior cracked walls or floors, or cracks or defects in exterior driveways, sidewalks, patios, or other hard surface areas." The disclosure question does not qualify the cracks in any manner, and it does not ask for significant cracks only. Rather, it asks for cracks in the walls and floors as well as those in the sidewalk and driveway. Based on these facts, viewed in a light most favorable to Fuller, it does not appear Crostons completed the dis-

closure statement truthfully, completely, and in good faith as required by South Dakota's disclosure laws. At the very least, there is a genuine issue of material fact whether they did so.

Despite the absence of completeness and candor in the disclosure statement, Crostons contend that they nevertheless fulfilled the disclosure requirements of SDCL chapter 43-4. They claim that their oral disclosures to Fuller of prior water penetration alleviated any earlier misrepresentation or omission in the disclosure statement. Whether an oral disclosure is sufficient to fulfill South Dakota's disclosure requirements is a matter of first impression.

Again, SDCL 43-4-44 provides a mandatory written form that "shall be used for the property condition disclosure statement." Also, SDCL 43-4-38 requires written amendments to the property condition disclosure statement. That statute provides in relevant part:

> *If after delivering the disclosure statement to the buyer or the buyer's agent and prior to the date of closing for the property or the date of possession of the property, whichever comes first, the seller becomes aware of any change of material fact which would affect the disclosure statement, the seller shall furnish a written amendment disclosing the change of material fact.*

The statutes are otherwise silent as to the issue of oral or written disclosures. This Court has held that "[s]tatutory disclosure statements essentially create a contract between the parties to a land sale." Fuller argues that this contract must be in writing, and that any modifications to the written contract must also be in writing.

The allowance of oral disclosures would defeat the purpose and clear language of the statute requiring written amendments as well as the statute providing the mandatory form. Were we to conclude that oral disclosures were sufficient to satisfy the disclosure statutes, these statutes would effectively be rendered moot. We are not willing to do so. That is the prerogative of the Legislature.

Crostons contend Fuller's knowledge of previous water damage, cracking and roughness in the paneling, which was based on oral disclosures, inspections and observations, defeats their liability. They claim Fuller's knowledge of the defects demonstrates a lack of reliance on the incorrect disclosure statement, and without reliance, the violation of the disclosure statute was not the cause of Fuller's damages.

Whether a lack of reliance on the disclosure statement can defeat a seller's liability is also a matter of first impression in South Dakota.

SDCL 43-4-42 provides in pertinent part, "a person who intentionally or who negligently violates §§43-4-37 to 43-4-44, inclusive, is liable to the buyer for the amount of the actual damages and repairs suffered by the buyer as a result of the violation or failure." This language seems to imply that reliance and causation are necessary elements for a cause of action based on a failure to comply with the disclosure statement requirements.

Several surrounding jurisdictions have discussed whether reliance on the property condition disclosure statement is necessary to create liability. For instance, an Illinois court held, "[a] seller who knowingly makes a false statement is subject to liability under the Act; no exception is made because of a buyer's knowledge of the defect." *Woods v. Pence*, 303 Ill.App.3d 573, 236 Ill.Dec. 977, 708 N.E.2d 563, 565 (1999) (citing 765 ILCS 77/25 (West 1996)). The *Woods* court did provide, however, that a buyer's knowledge was relevant to the amount of damages awarded because any defect of which the buyer was aware would be reflected in the purchase price of the house, thereby reducing those damages. Another Illinois court "reject[ed] defendant's inference that plaintiffs' actual notice of any alleged problems is a bar to their cause of action under the Disclosure Act."

Furthermore, a Nebraska court agreed with the *Woods* analysis and held "the buyer's knowledge of undisclosed damage in a cause of action for failure to provide a disclosure statement is relevant on the extent of damages, but does not provide a total defense." That court held this was "logical and consistent with the obvious purpose of [the] statute, which at its core is to get sellers to give buyers the written disclosure statement." Nebraska's disclosure statute allows for recovery of actual damages, which the buyer has sustained as a result of the violation of the statute.

In this case, Fuller's knowledge is based upon oral disclosures from Crostons and an inspection he hired conducted [*sic*]. By requiring reliance on the disclosure statement, this Court would allow sellers to misrepresent defects in the disclosure statement and cover themselves later by making oral disclosures. Also, this Court would effectively penalize the prudent buyer who conducts an independent inspection and investigation. Anything the buyer learned or was put on notice of would defeat a cause of action for a disclosure-statement violation by the seller. A seller could simply claim the buyer relied on the inspection and investigation instead of the disclosure statement. The legislative intent of protecting consumers would not be upheld if the statutes were construed in such a manner.

Therefore, this Court agrees that a buyer's knowledge of undisclosed damage in a cause of action for violation of the disclosure statutes does not provide a complete defense. However, the buyer's knowledge may be relevant to the amount of damages awarded because any defect of which the buyer was aware would be reflected in the purchase price of the house, thereby reducing damages. This raises a genuine issue of material fact concerning the extent of damages resulting from the violation of the disclosure statutes.

This conclusion, however, should not imply that strict liability results from a seller's nondisclosure under SDCL 43-4-38. Strict liability is not the requisite standard under South Dakota's disclosure statutes, because liability attaches only if the nondisclosure is negligent or intentional. Therefore, a mere nondisclosure without some form of culpability will not result in liability. We hold that a buyer's knowledge does not affect liability and is not a complete bar to the cause of action. However, according to SDCL 43-4-42, a buyer's knowledge is relevant to the extent of damages because recoverable damages are only those suffered "as a result of" the nondisclosure. Damages, therefore, may still be affected by the buyer's knowledge.

Taking the evidence in the light most favorable to Fuller, Crostons assert Johnson told them not to disclose the prior water damage to the home on the disclosure statement. And, as stated earlier, Johnson denies that assertion. Crostons claim she advised them not to disclose because they told her the damage occurred many years ago and was fixed. Johnson, therefore, allegedly was aware of prior water penetration in the home. If that is true, she not only failed to prevent Crostons' nondisclosure, but actually encouraged it. This observation, however, does not end our inquiry. According to SDCL 36-21A-148, a licensee is liable for misrepresentations of the client if the licensee had knowledge of the misrepresentation. Therefore, before Johnson could be held liable, the Court must determine whether the nondisclosure of prior water damage was a misrepresentation by Crostons.

Affirmed in part, reversed in part, and remanded.

CASE QUESTIONS

1. What does the court establish as the law on the failure to disclose preexisting but repaired defects in a home?

2. What does the court establish was the law on oral disclosures that supplements the disclosure requirements?

3. Is there potential liability for real estate brokers who do not advise their clients to make property disclosures?

NOTE: For differing results in cases similar to this in which knowledge did make a difference in the buyer's right to recover from the seller, see, for example, *Sherman v. Elkowitz,* 130 S.W.3d 316 (Tex. App. 2004) (full disclosure of cracks in driveway and presence of termites were sufficient for directed verdict for seller and broker when both were disclosed but buyer later brought suit out of frustration over repairs and costs); *Alires v. McGehee,* 85 P.3d 1191 (Kan. 2004) (no reasonable reliance on seller's statements about the water and the basement); *Funk v. Durant,* 799 N.E.2d 221(Oh. App. 2003) (buyers were aware of problems with basement prior to purchase); and *Alires v. McGehee,* 77 P.3d 1008 (Kan. App. 2003) (leaking basement, but court held the buyers could not rely on statements as a basis for a claim).

ETHICAL ISSUE

John Helm, an architect, designed and built a large home in 1989. Anne Marie Grossman was a co-owner of the home and property with Helm. Because the home was built on hilly terrain, Helm used a pier and grade-beam foundation. Helm and Grossman moved into the home in 1990 and listed it for sale with California Prudential Realty with Marti Gellens-Stubbs as the listing agent.

When Ms. Gellens-Stubbs inspected the property, she noticed hairline stucco cracks, which Helm assured her were only cosmetic. Ms. Gellens-Stubbs did not note the cracks on her portion of the disclosure statement but did write, "property appears to be in good condition … I see nothing to contradict what the seller has mentioned.…" Later, Gellens-Stubbs noticed that the interior paint was peeling near a dining room window. Helm explained that the peeling had been caused by water infiltration during construction, but that the problem had been remedied. Gellens-Stubbs did not note this information either.

Mark and Susan Robinson looked at the home several times in 1991 and noticed the stucco cracks. When they discussed the cracks with their agent, Gracinda Maier, she recommended that they have the home professionally inspected. Helm told the Robinsons that the cracks "were caused by the finish of the house, which is called a Santa Barbara finish, and there was a product called elastomeric that … would alleviate the stucco cracks."

Helm and Grossman accepted an offer of $653,750 from the Robinsons. The purchase contract of May 22, 1991, required Helm and Grossman to furnish the Robinsons with a geological report by Ninyo & Moore. The contract permitted the Robinsons to cancel the agreement if any of the geological reports or testing commissioned by the Robinsons revealed problems they would be unwilling or unable to correct.

On May 24, 1991, Maier added the following to the disclosure statement:

My visual inspection found numerous cracks in the house. Buyer's agent recommends buyer to have property inspected by a professional home inspector and have the land checked by a geologist.

Gellens-Stubbs then added the following:

Stucco cracks on home are cosmetic in nature according to the seller because of finish and type of stucco.

The Robinsons hired Ameritec Home Inspection Service. Robert Brand, an employee, listed the "very old" water stain in the dining room and "normal settling cracking" of the stucco. Brand found no soils-related distress and the report concluded, "the house was very well built ... [and] was not going anyplace...."

A few weeks after moving into the home, as they were attempting to have a swimming pool installed, the entire excavation around the house collapsed. The Robinsons sued Helm, Grossman, Gellens-Stubbs, Prudential, and others for professional negligence and negligent and intentional misrepresentation.

The trial court dismissed the fraud accusations against Prudential and Gellens-Stubbs. The Robinsons appealed. Who should win? Be sure to discuss the law and cases you have studied and consider whether the broker and owner should be held liable. What were the parties' ethical obligations in this situation? *Robinson v. Grossman*, 67 Cal. Rptr.2d 380 (Cal. App. 1997).

Disclosure, Discrimination, and Silence

Brokers and agents have faced increasingly complex issues of disclosure with respect to properties they are listing or showing. Should the fact that a crime has been committed on the property be revealed? Should the fact that someone with HIV/AIDS owned the property previously be revealed? What if there is a registered sex offender living in the neighborhood where the property is located? In some of these disclosure situations, brokers and agents have statutory duties that prohibit them from affirmatively disclosing the information about the property. In other situations, an affirmative duty to disclose is imposed by statute. However, even in those situations in which the information is protected by statute and the broker is prohibited from affirmatively disclosing it, the broker or agent cannot lie in the event the buyer asks a question and the broker or agent has the information. In some states, these disclosure and nondisclosure rules include "shield statutes," which protect the broker from liability for maintaining the statutory silence about the covered subject areas.

The presence or absence of criminal activity on a property or the presence of a released sex offender near a particular property is deemed to be material information because it does affect the value of the property.

NAR has adopted a position on the issue of sex offender information that provides,

all public disclosures should emanate directly from the appropriate law enforcement agency, and no affirmative disclosure duty regarding the location of released sex offenders should be placed on real estate licensees as a result of state public notification programs.

In NAR's position statement, information on sex offenders must come from the government records themselves and not from brokers or agents. Brokers and agents need only respond to questions from buyers by referring them to the public records.

All states currently have some form of statute on the responsibility for disclosure of sex offender information. Some states exempt real estate agents from disclosure, while others include required language in contracts referring buyers to appropriate agencies for information. Still others require brokers and agents to disclose the information if potential buyers ask. Further discussion of these disclosure protections and mandates and the broker's responsibilities and liabilities are found in Chapter 13.

Insurance Protection

Suits against brokers for misrepresentation are a constant in the industry. Actual and punitive damages, for either intentional or negligent misrepresentation by brokers, have been quite large. As noted earlier, a broker may be held liable under a pretense

The following is a checklist for brokers undertaking a new listing and handling prospective buyers of that property:

- *Ask about the property repair record.*
- *Ask about the utilities.*
- *Ask about the condition of appliances, roof, walls, and basement.*
- *Include pertinent information about physical condition in the listing agreement.*
- *Make an independent investigation of the property, carefully looking for recent cover-ups, re-decorating, and hidden defects.*
- *Consider a warranty policy for the home.*
- *Consider having a professional home inspection.*
- *Make no statement that is not based on your firsthand information or knowledge.*
- *Have available a list of addresses and phone numbers for municipal, state, and county offices, so that the prospective buyer may make independent checks on information.*
- *Do not fail to disclose pertinent information, and do not participate with the seller in a nondisclosure scheme.*
- *Take measurements to verify room sizes and square footage.*
- *Follow up on the buyer's questions for which you have no answer or knowledge.*

PRACTICAL TIP

Good or bad, the buyer should have full information about the property. The failure to disclose negative information only leads to litigation against the broker, the agent, and the agency. Negative information finds its way to the surface, as it were, and the resulting liability is significant.

of knowledge even when the broker has no actual knowledge. As a result of the amount of litigation and the size of verdicts and settlements, brokers purchase **errors and omissions insurance** coverage, which is a form of malpractice insurance for brokers, salespeople, and their companies, all of which can be held liable in these types of suits. The amount of coverage available usually begins at $100,000, with a deductible of $1,000 for small claims.

Self-Protection

Perhaps the best protection a broker may obtain against a suit for misrepresentation is preventive protection. Preventive protection includes understanding the property to be sold and all of its defects, restrictions, and limitations.

Web Exhibit 12.5 will link to a seller's disclosure form used by brokers and agents to try to be certain that they know all the material information they are expected to know about a property they have listed. "I didn't know" is no longer a defense for brokers and agents with regard to property conditions and issues affecting the value of the property. Brokers' and agents' liability is determined by whether they *should* have known, not whether they actually *did* know.

LICENSING REQUIREMENTS FOR BROKERS/AGENTS

All states and the District of Columbia have licensing requirements for brokers and agents. Licensing affords protection to the public by requiring real estate practitioners to meet certain uniform standards of competency and practice. Second, licensing protects existing licensees from unscrupulous or illegal conduct by new entrants.

Every state has a statute that establishes licensing requirements for those seeking status as real estate practitioners. In each state statute, some type of administrative agency is created to be responsible for the issuing of licenses to real estate practitioners and will have a title such as the *real estate board, board of real estate, real estate commission,* or *department of real estate.* These administrative agencies are responsible for establishing licensing procedures and qualifications, and for enforcing statutorily imposed licensing procedures and qualifications. Agencies also serve to clarify and interpret applicable legislative provisions. In addition, they are usually responsible for the supervision of licensees, investigations of alleged misconduct, and appropriate disciplinary measures such as license revocation or referrals for criminal prosecution.

Requirements for Obtaining Licenses

Two types of agents may work for the principal buyer or seller in the real estate transaction. Brokers are licensed to operate their own real estate brokerage businesses. A **salesperson** (sometimes called an *agent*) is licensed only to work for a broker, with the broker assuming responsibility for the salesperson's actions. Licensing requirements for brokers are more stringent than those for salespeople, and a salesperson's license is almost universally a prerequisite for a broker's license.

Most state license laws follow the model license law written by the National Association of Real Estate License Law Officials (NARELLO). Each state will have its own variations, but the following list of requirements is part of the NARELLO model.

a. *Educational requirements.* State educational prerequisites for licensing vary from none to an accredited college or university degree.

b. *Experience.* This requirement is limited to broker licenses. Most states require two years' experience as a salesperson or two years' experience in the real estate field as a prerequisite for licensing as a broker.

c. *Examination.* All states require both salespeople and brokers to pass examinations to obtain licensing.

d. *Sponsorship.* About half of the states require candidates for salespeople's licenses to be sponsored by a licensed broker who will be responsible for the salesperson when the license is awarded.

e. *Minimum age.* In most states, the minimum age for licensure is the age of majority in the state (about half of the states list 18 years of age).

f. *Citizenship.* Some states still require U.S. citizenship status as a prerequisite for licensing; however, this requirement with respect to other forms of licensing has been struck down on constitutional grounds.

g. *Residency.* Some states require that license applicants be residents of the state for 30 to 90 days before application may be made. Again, such requirements for other license cases have been subject to constitutional challenges.

h. *Criminal record.* Nearly all of the states have provisions prohibiting licensing if the applicant has been convicted of a felony. However, these states usually limit the length of time for this restriction.

i. *Application.* All states require potential licensees to submit a completed form provided and developed by the regulating agency. Commonly, the application will require the applicant to give character references from persons in the community or from persons already established in the real estate business.

j. *Payment of fees.* All states require the payment of a licensing fee upon original application. Furthermore, a renewal fee is required to be paid at intervals established by the states.

Issuance of Licenses

Once applicants have satisfied the requirements, their state license will be issued. In all states, all licenses must be displayed in the agent's or broker's place of business. Some states also have a requirement whereby licensees must carry pocket cards indicating their licensed status.

Doing Business Without Licenses

Attempting to act as a salesperson or broker without proper licensing is illegal. The licensing of brokers and salespeople is a regulatory scheme, and any contract for commission between an unlicensed salesperson or broker and a seller would also be void. Court enforcement of such a contract is not available. In addition, a fee paid to an unlicensed salesperson or broker may be recovered.

License renewals have become significant over the past few years, with many states requiring evidence of continuing education as well as the payment of license fees. Continuing education requirements may include college course credits as well as professional seminars. Some states require training in fair housing laws for both initial licensing and renewals.

CONSIDER 12.3   Ceas Mortgage Company brought suit against Walnut Hills Associates, Ltd., for an unpaid commission. Ceas alleged that it was a real estate broker for the sale of property to Walnut Hills. Ceas Mortgage did not have a real estate broker's license, but an employee of Ceas who handled the transaction was a licensed broker. The transaction took place in Illinois where the following statute governs the payment of real estate commissions:

> *No action or suit shall be instituted, nor recovery therein be had, in any court of this State by any person, partnership, limited liability company, or corporation for compensation for any act done or service performed, the doing or performing of which is prohibited by this Act to other than licensed brokers or sales persons unless such person, partnership, limited liability company, or corporation was duly licensed hereunder as a broker or salesperson at the time that any such act was done or service performed which would give rise to a cause of action for compensation.*

Should Ceas collect a commission? Is there a legal or ethical obligation to pay the commission? *Ceas Mortgage Co. v. Walnut Hills Associates, Ltd.*, 726 N.E.2d 695 (Ill. App. 2000). ▄

Exemptions from Licensing

All states have some exemptions from the licensing requirement. For example, individuals selling real estate for themselves need not be licensed. In all states, attorneys acting for clients in real estate transactions are not required to be licensed as brokers. Those acting as personal representatives, executors, administrators, or trustees for estates need not be licensed to sell or offer to sell property of the estate. All states also have exemptions for public officials dealing with land and its purchase and sale as part of their official duties and responsibilities.

Professional Organizations

The largest professional association in the real estate industry is NAR. Only those who are members may use the designation **Realtor**®, which is a registered trademark of the association. When used by real estate practitioners, this term indicates that they subscribe to the code of ethics of NAR. NAR also promotes and provides educational opportunities for Realtors®, and local and state chapters often have publications mailed to members that provide updates and information on changes in the field of real estate.

BROKER'S/AGENT'S LEGAL DUTIES AND RESPONSIBILITIES TO STATE

State

Because they are licensed by the state, brokers must also comply with state laws and regulations. Violations can result in penalties that include fines, penalties, and suspension or revocation of license.

Suspension or Revocation of Real Estate License

Each state has its own requirements and penalties for forms of illegal conduct, but certain types of conduct are universally prohibited by the states and usually result in suspension or revocation of license.

1. *Commingling of funds.* All states have some provision prohibiting brokers from commingling clients' funds with their own funds and require the maintenance of separate escrow or trust funds.

2. *Discriminating practices.* Refusing to show property on the basis of a prospect's race, color, sex, or national origin may bring about not only a loss of license, but also the imposition of federal penalties and other state penalties for violations of the fair housing laws. Discriminatory practices include *steering* (where brokers direct certain races to certain areas and away from other areas) and *red-lining* (where sales or listings are agreed to on the basis of the neighborhood racial composition). (See Chapter 19 for a full discussion of these issues.)

3. *Conviction of a felony.* A felony conviction may prevent initial licensing and also result in the loss of license.

4. *Advertising.* Placing media advertising that contains misrepresentations results in disciplinary action in all states. Some states require the written consent of the owner for advertising.

5. *Splitting commissions with an unlicensed party.* Only licensed individuals may split commissions.

6. *Failure to deliver required documents.* Those who fail to deliver required copies of documents to clients, such as purchase contracts and listing agreements, are subject to suspension or revocation.

7. *Failure to submit all offers.* All offers received prior to written acceptance must be submitted to the seller.

8. *Breach of duties to seller and unethical conduct.*

9. *The unauthorized practice of law.* As noted earlier, some states permit brokers to fill in purchase contract forms and closing documents, while other states require attorneys. Brokers who exceed their authorized authority are subject to disciplinary action by both their licensing agency and the state bar.

Rights upon Suspension or Revocation

Constitutional standards of due process for license suspension or revocation are satisfied with administrative proceedings. That is, the licensing agency may conduct appropriate hearings and impose penalties even though such an agency is not a court.

The broker or agent charged with a violation has the right to be informed of the charges and to advance notice of the hearing so that he or she can appear and defend the charges, and present evidence and witnesses. The state, through its agency, must give the broker or agent advance notice of those witnesses who will be called to testify in the hearing, so that the broker or agent can prepare a response or call rebuttal witnesses.

The following case involves a broker's suspension and the issues of fitness for continued licensing.

DEARBORN V. REAL ESTATE AGENCY

53 P.3d 436 (Or. 2002)
Moral Turpitude and Licensing

FACTS

On October 4, 1996, Harold Dearborn (petitioner), then a licensed real estate agent, broker, and designated broker, was arrested at his home. Police officers found small amounts of cocaine and methamphetamine in his home. Police officers were at his home pursuant to an investigation of Dearborn's sexual activities with transients in exchange for drugs. One of the transients with whom he had sexual relations was a 17-year-old. Dearborn was indicted for possession of controlled substances as well as prostitution, endangering the welfare of a minor, and furnishing obscene materials to a minor. Dearborn entered a guilty plea to two counts of possession of a controlled substance, and the other counts were dismissed. He was placed on probation for 18 months, ordered to serve 10 days in jail, perform community service, and pay a $500 fine. He was also ordered to have no contact with juveniles without prior approval from his probation officer.

The Real Estate Commissioner began proceedings to have his broker's license suspended. At the time of the hearing, Dearborn had paid his fine, performed his community service, had his driver's license reinstated (which had been suspended upon the guilty plea), and had his probation changed to unsupervised probation. The Commissioner ordered that Dearborn's license be suspended pending successful completion of the terms of his probation. Upon successful completion of probation, his broker's license would be revoked and he would be issued a limited salesperson's license for two years. Assuming no further difficulties, he could then have an unrestricted license. Dearborn appealed the agency's decision. The Court of Appeals reversed and the Commissioner appealed to the Oregon Supreme Court.

JUDICIAL OPINION
Gillette, Justice

We conclude that there must be a substantial relationship between the conduct at issue and a licensee's real estate activities. We next consider whether the conduct at issue in this case would support revocation of broker's license under one or both of those subsections. We begin with ORS 696.301(26) (1995), which authorizes disciplinary action when a broker is convicted of a crime that is "substantially related" to the broker's fitness to engage in real estate activity.

It is important, at this juncture, to identify which facts are relevant to our analysis. Although the Court of Appeals and the Commissioner appear to have treated all the conduct identified in the Commissioner's findings as relevant to subsection (26), it is clear to this court that only a relatively small subset of that conduct is germane. ORS 696.301(26) (1995) authorizes professional discipline against brokers who have been convicted of a felony or misdemeanor of a specified sort. Evidence pertaining to other, unrelated criminal charges that the court dismissed, or to acts that the authorities discovered in the course of the criminal investigation, do not support revocation or suspension of a license under that subsection.

The Agency suggests that subsection (26) is not so limited. It contends that the provision must be read in the context of ORS 670.280, which provides:

Except as provided in ORS 342.143 or 342.175, no licensing board shall deny, suspend or revoke an occupational or professional license or certification solely for the reason that the applicant or licensee has been convicted of a crime, but it may consider the relationship of the facts which support the conviction and all intervening circumstances to the specific occupational or professional standards in determining the fitness of the person to receive or hold such license or certificate.

The Agency argues that, although it is a more general statute, ORS 670.280 nonetheless modifies ORS 696.301(26) (1995), thereby extending the scope of the latter statute to include conduct and circumstances surrounding the crime and ultimate conviction. That category would include, in the Agency's view, any conduct mentioned in any of the voluminous law enforcement investigative reports that relate to broker's convictions, including discussions of broker's sexual behavior and his pattern of giving drugs to sex partners.

We disagree. Although ORS 670.280 explicitly confers some authority to look at the "facts which support the conviction" and "intervening facts" when applying ORS 696.301(26) (1995), that statute cannot reasonably be read as expanding the scope of subsection (26) to permit imposing a sanction under that subsection for acts extraneous to broker's actual convictions. What the Commissioner may consider … are such facts as the broker's conviction of possession of cocaine and methamphetamine, that both substances are controlled substances, that small amounts of those substances were found in his home, and that he admitted to purchasing and using both substances on more than one occasion. If, in light of those facts, the Commissioner can conclude that broker's crimes were "substantially related" to his trustworthiness or competence to engage in professional real estate activity at the time that he committed them, then the Commissioner had authority to discipline him under section (26).

As the Commissioner acknowledges in his order, however, there is "no evidence" that broker's criminal activities arose out of broker's "use of his position as a real estate licensee." It follows that the Commissioner had no authority to sanction broker under ORS 696.301(26) (1995).

We recognize that the Commissioner offers two justifications in the "Reasoning" section of his opinion that he believes to justify disciplining broker under ORS 696.301(26) (1995). They are: (1) the statement that, when a real estate licensee has used highly addictive drugs (as broker has), there is a risk that the licensee will use his or her access to people's homes to steal prescription drugs, cash, or valuables; and (2) the statement that there is an additional risk that the licensee will use funds held in trust for clients to support his or her drug habit. Those statements miss the mark, because they purport to justify the Commissioner's choice to sanction broker on the possibility that broker might do something in the future that would violate some subsection of ORS 696.301 (1995). As we have explained, however, the Commissioner's right to discipline must arise out of something that a licensee has done, not out of something that a licensee might do. So far as this record discloses, none of broker's criminal acts had anything to do with his real estate activities. None involved clients, real estate, or money entrusted to broker. Without such a nexus,

the Commissioner could not permissibly conclude that broker had violated ORS 696.301(26) (1995). We hold, in short, that the Commissioner erred in concluding that broker's drug possession convictions were "substantially related" to broker's real estate activities.

As noted, the Commissioner explained his decision to revoke broker's license in terms of certain perceived risks to broker's future real estate clients— that, e.g., broker might offer drugs in exchange for sex to a client's children or to other juveniles whom broker might meet through his real estate dealings, that broker might use his access to client's homes to steal prescription drugs, cash, or valuables, or that broker might convert money held in trust for clients to his own use to support his possible drug habit. In doing so, the Commissioner is positing a predictive relationship between broker's past conduct, which the Commissioner acknowledges did not involve real estate activities, and broker's future professional conduct, i.e., the Commissioner is asserting that broker's crimes, sexual behavior, and drug use create or increase the probability that broker will abuse his position as a real estate professional in one or more of the suggested ways.

That is not the question, however. Instead, the question is whether the acts that broker committed, at the time that he committed them, "demonstrated" untrustworthiness, incompetence, or improper dealings with respect to broker's real estate activities. As we have explained with respect to subsection (26), they did not.

The Court of Appeals reversed the Commissioner's order because it found "no factual support in the record to justify the concerns [that the Commissioner] identified" therein. As we have explained, we see the problem somewhat differently, but our analysis leads to the same conclusion: The Commissioner erred.

Reversed.

CASE QUESTIONS

1. Describe the nature of the real estate broker's criminal convictions.
2. Is a criminal conviction grounds for not issuing a license? When is a criminal conviction grounds for revocation or suspension of a license?
3. What mistake did the Commissioner make in issuing the suspension?

RELATIONSHIPS AMONG BROKERS/AGENTS

In this final section, the focus of discussion is on duties and responsibilities among the interrelationships of those acting within the industry.

Broker–Salesperson Relationship

A broker will probably have salespeople working in a common office and should establish the rights of all the agents who will be working together. The office broker should have a contract with each agent that spells out the details of their relationship, including the following:

- Broker will maintain a properly equipped office.
- Salesperson will maintain licensing status (including the payment of fees).
- Broker makes all listings available to agent (salesperson).
- Broker may not dictate which parties salesperson will solicit.
- Salesperson will work diligently for sales and listings.
- Salesperson and broker will abide by the Code of Ethics of the National Association of Realtors®, as well as state, national, and local laws.
- Commission-splitting arrangements will be set and followed.
- Terms for ending relationship are set.
- Arbitration procedures are specified.

Salesperson–Salesperson Relationship

Because there is generally more than one salesperson per office, brokers have rules and regulations governing their interrelationships. For example, most offices have a policy on commission splits for those sales in which more than one agent is involved in getting the deal closed. Offices also have policies on handling walk-ins and the distribution of information about prospects to avoid misunderstandings, resentment, and undercutting.

Broker–Broker Relationship

Often in open listing agreements, the issue of who actually obtained a buyer for a sale—and, hence, who is entitled to a commission—becomes critical. The standard used for determining this is the **procuring cause of the sale standard**. To be entitled to a commission under this standard, the broker need not be the one to obtain the actual sale terms, but must establish that he or she brought seller and buyer together.

Bringing seller and buyer together can result from direct contact or newspaper advertisement. If the broker finds and introduces to the principal a person who is ready, willing, and able to purchase or exchange the property according to the principal's terms, the commission is earned. It is immaterial if the final contract is made without the presence or knowledge of the procuring broker.

The following case deals with a dispute over commissions and the procuring cause of the sale.

ANTRIM, PIPER, WENGER, INC. V. LOWE

159 P.3d 215 (Kan. App. 2006)
Slipping a Deal Past Your Agent

FACTS

On March 31, 2004, David W. Lowe signed a nonexclusive right-to-sell agreement with Einer Johnson, a real estate agent for Antrim, Piper, Wenger, Inc. (Antrim), to sell the Lowes' ranch near Sedan, Kansas. This contract allowed Antrim to list and sell the property for $1,500,000 during a period between March 22, 2004, and August 22, 2004. The commission was to be 5 percent.

On May 19, 2004, Alan Lewis called Johnson to inquire about the ranch. Lewis discovered the property and obtained Johnson's phone number from Antrim's website. The parties disagree over exactly what happened next. Johnson stated that Lewis, who arrived that day in Sedan with his business partner, Murray Logan, told Johnson not to come to the ranch because he just wanted to look around. Nevertheless, Deborah Lowe, David's wife, testified that Johnson told Lewis that he had other arrangements that day and could not show Lewis the property. Johnson then stated that he gave Lewis directions to the ranch, but Lewis seemed confused. After talking to Lewis, Johnson called the Lowes and spoke to Deborah. He told her that people interested in the property were staying at the Ranch Motel in Sedan and that she might want to help them find the ranch. Johnson recommended that Deborah and David go into town to pick them up. Nevertheless, David stated that he did not want to drive to Sedan.

Deborah then called the Ranch Motel and the Ranch Restaurant, which is next to the hotel, and told the waitress to give the Lowes' phone number to two men from Florida when they came in. When Lewis and Logan arrived, the waitress gave them the number. Deborah gave Lewis directions to the ranch. Once they arrived, David showed them around the land. When Lewis decided to buy the property, David wrote a contract for sale, which Lewis signed.

Later that evening, Johnson called and spoke to David, who told him that Lewis and Logan bought the property. Although Johnson offered to write a contract for the sale, David refused his assistance.

On April 12, 2005, the parties closed the sale of the ranch. Despite repeated requests, the Lowes refused to pay Antrim a commission on the sale. In June, Antrim sued the Lowes. The trial court granted the summary judgment to Antrim and the Lowes appealed.

JUDICIAL OPINION

Green, Judge

Because the brokerage contract between Antrim and David was a nonexclusive right to sell, David retained the right to sell his property. Nevertheless, if the agent efficiently produces a buyer who is ready, willing, and able to purchase the property and if the agent is the procuring cause of the deal, the agent is entitled to receive a commission. The agent is not required to introduce the parties or to bring them together personally. Nor is the agent required to procure a binding contract signed by the purchaser. "[I]f [the agent] were otherwise entitled to a commission, the defendant could not defeat that right by closing the deal himself."

Here, despite the fact that the Lowes found the buyers in Sedan, showed them the property, and wrote the contract for sale, the key undisputed fact remains that the Lowes knew that Lewis and Logan had been sent to them through the efforts of Johnson, Antrim's salesperson. Moreover, without Antrim's website listing, Lewis would not have learned of the ranch. Without the website, Lewis would not have called Johnson, and Johnson would not have alerted Deborah to the fact that buyers were in the area. Antrim was the procuring cause (a term apparently used interchangeably with "efficient cause" and "proximate cause") of the Lowes' deal with Lewis. David cannot defeat Antrim's right to a commission by closing the deal himself. Therefore, since the Lowes do not dispute that they sold the property to a purchaser whom they knew was sent to them by Antrim's salesperson, there is no genuine issue of material fact and summary judgment was appropriate.

The Lowes next argue that the agreement allows Antrim to receive its commission only if the contract closed before November 22, 2004. The agreement, which expired on August 22, 2004, stated:

"In addition, if within ninety (90) days after the expiration or termination of this Agreement … Seller *enters into an agreement to sell or exchange said property* to any person … with whom Broker has negotiated for the purchase or exchange of such property during the term hereof, and Seller shall have knowledge of such person and negotiations, Broker shall be entitled to receive the full brokerage fee." (Emphasis added.)

Nevertheless, contrary to Lowes' contentions, the language does not require the sale to be completely closed. It requires only an "agreement to sell or exchange." On May 19, 2004, Lewis signed a contract agreeing to buy the ranch pending a 1031 exchange. This clearly constitutes an agreement to exchange property and fulfills the contract.

The Lowes' other argument asserts that Johnson did not have the permission of Deborah to list and sell the ranch even though she had a one-half ownership interest. The Lowes argue that the trial court abused its discretion since an issue of fact exists on whether Antrim would be entitled to a commission on

Deborah's interest in the property because it never had her consent for the sale.

The Lowes did not raise the issue of Deborah's interest in the property before the trial court. Generally, issues not raised before the trial court cannot be raised upon appeal.

Affirmed.

CASE QUESTIONS

1. What was the key element in finding the real estate agent to be the procuring cause of the sale?
2. Evaluate the ethics of the Lowes in raising Deborah's lack of consent to sell. Evaluate whether there is a legal issue in this defense.

CAUTIONS AND CONCLUSIONS

The real estate broker plays an integral role in the transfer of real estate. The role is not only complex in terms of the knowledge requirements and duties of the broker and agent, it is also complex in its relationships with the many parties involved in real estate transactions. Because of these complexities, brokers and agents should have clear and written agreements on these relationships that cover the following issues: whom the agent or broker represents, how long that relationship will last, how compensation is to be paid, and when that compensation is due. Even relationships between and among agents and brokers in their own firms require written agreements so that issues such as commission arrangements are clear.

All states have statutory requirements for agent and broker licensing and statutory requirements for disclosures to

clients on representation. Brokers and agents should be very careful to comply with the requirements when there is a dual representation of both buyer and seller.

Brokers and agents should be cautious in their descriptions of and representations about the properties they show to potential buyers and the listings they take. Brokers need to verify statements and representations about the property through physical inspection. Full disclosure statutes now impose duties of disclosure on both sellers and their brokers.

Brokers and agents are licensed professionals subject to annual license renewal, as well as reviews of their conduct by agencies and professional groups. They cannot earn commissions without a valid license. That license can be suspended or revoked for misconduct, such as a violation of the law or taking clients' funds.

KEY TERMS

agent, 274
as is, 296
broker, 274
condition precedent, 285
designated agency, 277
dual agency, 274
errors and omissions insurance, 304
exclusive agency listing, 276
exclusive listing-to-sell, 276

exclusive right-to-sell, 276
intermediary, 277
limited agent, 277
listing agreement, 281
multiple listing, 276
multiple listing service (MLS), 276
National Association of Realtors (NAR), 275
net listing, 277

no deal, no commission clause, 284
nonagent broker, 277
open listing, 275
procuring cause of the sale standard, 310
Realtor®, 306
salesperson, 304
statutory broker, 277
transaction broker, 277

CHAPTER PROBLEMS

1. Suppose a broker misrepresented the length of time that a piece of property had been listed. Would such a misrepresentation be a basis for liability? Does the broker harm a seller by such a disclosure? *Beard v. Gress*, 413 N.E.2d 448 (Ill. 1980).

2. On August 29, 2003, Terra Firma Company sought to purchase 3,050 acres of contiguous property in western Monongalia County, West Virginia, for a planned coal preparation facility. Terra Firma hired William Burton as its real estate agent to negotiate the purchase of various tracts of land for Terra Firma.

    Robert and Vickie Morgan owned 173 acres of farm land in Monongalia County and hired a real estate agent, Nancy Kincaid, to sell their farm land. Mr. Burton made an offer on behalf of Terra Firma to purchase the land. However, all of the negotiations regarding the purchase were conducted between Mr. Burton and Ms. Kincaid; the Morgans never met or spoke with Mr. Burton until long after they signed an agreement to sell the land.

    The Morgans were suspicious during negotiations and suspected that Terra Firma might be a coal company or landfill company. They called Ms. Kincaid and asked about the identity of Terra Firma and why it wanted the property. Ms. Kincaid related her own speculation that Terra Firma was a company of investors who were purchasing the property for land development. The Morgans assumed, without further questions or investigation, that Terra Firma intended to develop the land for residential housing. They signed the contract in November 2004.

    On December 14, 2004, at the closing Mr. Morgan said to Mr. Burton, "I want to know if this is a landfill or coal company buying it." Mr. Burton's answer was "rest assured, it is for land development purposes only."

    In March 2005, the Morgans learned from a neighbor that they had sold their land to "Consolidated Coal." The Morgans stopped making rental payments and Terra Firma sent a letter formally terminating the lease. The Morgans filed suit seeking to reform the Real Estate Purchase Agreement to increase the purchase price of the land based on the alleged inequitable conduct of Terra Firma, and on Mr. Burton's alleged breach of his duty as an agent to disclose "all facts known to [Mr. Burton] materially affecting the value or desirability of the property." Can the Morgans be excused from the contract? Do the misrepresentations of the buyer's

    agent affect the contract? *Terra Firma Co. v. Morgan*, 674 S.E.2d 190 (W. Va. 2008)

3. If a real estate broker was convicted of child abuse and is now listed as a registered sex offender could his license be revoked? *Pautsch v. Maryland Real Estate Comm'n*, 423 Md. 229 (Md. 2011)

4. On June 4, 2010, Sioni & Partners. LCC, a real estate broker, and Vaak Properties entered into an "exclusive right to sell agreement" for the property, located at 1135 Boynton Avenue, Bronx, New York, at a price of $6.6 million, with a 3% commission. The agreement stated, "If the broker is able and willing to sell the property at an agreed price, commission of 3% will be paid to the broker." The agreement also stated that "[i]n the event that the price is negotiated and agreed by the seller, the commission also will be negotiated." This agreement was "valid for 3 months, until September 4, 2010."

    Sioni procured a buyer, who made an offer of $6 million. Because the buyer's offer was less than the original $6.6 million asking price, Sioni and Vaak entered into a new contract on September 2, 2010, which provided:

    "The following constitutes and confirms our agreement regarding the proposed sale of the above referenced property …

    "In connection with the proposed contract of purchase and sale, you agree to pay us, and we agree to accept, as compensation for our services as brokers the sum of $160,000 (one hundred and sixty thousand dollars) as compensation, if as and only when title closes."

    They both signed this Amended Commission Agreement. However, above the line for Vaak's signature was handwritten: "subject to attorney modifications & approval."

    The sale closed for $6 million, but despite demands by Sioni for its commission, Vaak never paid because it said the amendment was never approved by its attorney and, therefore, it owed no commission because Sioni was not the procuring cause of the transaction. Was Vaak correct to withhold the payment of the commission? Explain your answer and also provide a list of precautions you learn from this situation. *Sioni & Partners, LLC v. Vaak Properties, LCC*, 939 N.Y.S.2d 57 (A.D.N.Y. 2012).

5. In each of the following hypotheticals, discuss the broker's duties and liabilities.

    ■ A brokerage firm has a property management subsidiary, and its leasing agents are approaching clients in their firm's management subsidiary properties to place them in other properties.

- A broker is a leasing agent for a major anchor tenant and has two listings that will work for the tenant, but only mentions one to the tenant because of his compensation arrangement with the owner of that property.

- A broker accepts a listing on a property located next to land he owns. A buyer approaches the broker about purchasing the broker's land and the broker does not disclose the offer to the listing client/owner of the adjoining land.

- A broker lists a property without results. He then decides to purchase the property. While escrow is pending, he receives an offer on the property for $23,000 more than he has paid. What should the broker do? *Letsos v. Century 21-New West Realty,* 675 N.E. 2d 217 (Ill. App. 1996); *Foley v. Mathias,* 233 N.W. 106 (Iowa 1930); *Reinhold v. Mallery,* 599 A.2d 126 (N.H. 1991); *Baskin v. Dam,* 239 A.2d 549 (Conn. Cir. Ct. 1967).

6. J. Pagel Realty and Insurance Co. acted as real estate brokers for the sale of property owned by Clifton and Mary Morley. The brokers arranged for the sale of a home in Bisbee, Arizona, with the buyers paying for the home with a down payment and a $12,500 note to the Morleys. The phrase, "This note is secured by a mortgage on real property," was crossed off the note. The brokers, as permitted by Arizona law, completed all of the paperwork for the transaction but did not discuss the need for a mortgage to enforce the note. The buyers defaulted on the note and sold the house to another party. The Morleys sued Pagel for damages, claiming that they should have been told of the need for a mortgage. Pagel defended on the grounds that such advice would have been practicing law. Should the mortgage issue have been discussed? *Morley v. J. Pagel Realty & Insurance,* 550 P.2d 1104 (Az. 1976).

7. Lori Hanegan's broker's license was up for renewal in 1994. In Colorado, a broker applying for renewal is required to complete a minimum of "twenty-four hours of credit, *eight of which shall be credits developed by the real estate commission.*" (emphasis added) Ms. Hanegan completed 36 hours of continuing education, but those hours did not include the mandatory eight hours developed by the real estate commission.

Hanegan's failure to take the mandated eight hours was discovered in an audit of licensees' continuing education units. Disciplinary proceedings were initiated and following a hearing, Hanegan was fined $50 and a public censure was recommended. Is the punishment appropriate? *Colorado State Real Estate Commission v. Hanegan,* 947 P.2d 933 (Colo. 1997).

8. Leticia Easton purchased a one-acre parcel of land in the city of Diablo, California, with a 3,000-square-foot home, swimming pool, and a large guest house for $170,000 in May 1976 from the Strassburgers through Valley Realty.

Shortly after Easton purchased the property, there was a massive earth movement and subsequent slides in 1977 and 1978 that destroyed a portion of the driveway. Experts testified that the slides occurred because a portion of the property was fill that had not been properly engineered and compacted. The slides caused the foundation of the house to settle, which in turn caused cracks in the walls and warped doorways. After the damage, the value of the property was set at $20,000. Cost estimates for repairs were $213,000.

Agents Simkin and Mourning represented Valley Realty and inspected the property several times prior to sale. "Red flags" indicated problems, but the agents did not have soil tests done and did not mention to Easton any potential soil problems.

Easton filed suit against the Strassburgers and Valley Realty. Is Valley Realty liable to Easton? Are the Strassburgers liable? *Easton v. Strassburger,* 199 Cal. Rptr. 383 (1984).

9. Kohn is a licensed real estate broker associated with his father's firm, Louis T. Kohn Realty. As managing agent for the Levee Building at the Laclede's Landing area of St. Louis, one of Kohn's responsibilities was to seek tenants for the building. One of the building owners suggested Kohn look into the possibility of Spaghetti Factory's locating a restaurant in the building. The following sequence of events took place:

- *April 1975:* Kohn visited Denver's Spaghetti Factory and presented the idea to the executives.

- *May 1, 1975:* Kohn presented the idea to the Spaghetti Factory home office in Portland.

- *May 22, 1975:* Kohn met with three representatives of the Spaghetti Factory at the Levee Building. The Levee Building was determined to be unacceptable in size. Kohn took the three to Cohn's (defendant/appellee) office to examine his building. Spaghetti Factory executives asked for a floor plan. Kohn, in the presence of Cohn, said he would take care of the details.

- *June 26, 1975:* Kohn and Cohn met, and Kohn indicated he was seeking a tenant for Cohn's building. Cohn said he would go to Portland, but did not go.

- *October 1975:* Kohn and Spaghetti Factory executives met.

- *October 23, 1975:* Cohn and Spaghetti Factory executives met.

- *October 29, 1975*: Spaghetti Factory executives wrote Kohn and declined to lease the Cohn building.
- *September 16, 1976*: Cohn and Spaghetti Factory reached a five-year lease agreement.

Assuming there is no written agreement, could Kohn collect a commission in your state? *Kohn v. Cohn*, 567 S.W.2d 441 (Mo. 1978).

10. Marc and Kristin Glosserman, who are husband and wife, entered into agreements to purchase 2 apartment units, identifying the Corcoran Group Marketing as the "Selling Agent" and listing Douglas Elliman as an "Additional Broker." In late 2009, a year after the couple defaulted on these agreements, Marc's father, Michael Glosserman, purchased the units through his corporation, 15 Madison Ave. LLC. The Corcoran Group filed suit for the commission on the purchase by Mr. Glosserman on the grounds that it was secretly negotiated, closed, and wrongfully not disclosed for the purpose of avoiding having to pay the commission. What should the court do, and why? *Douglas Elliman LLC v. Corcoran Group Marketing*, 940 N.Y.S.2d 595 (A.D. 2012).

For research activities related to this chapter, go to our text companion website at www.cengagebrain.com

CHAPTER 13

THE PURCHASE CONTRACT

People will go to great lengths to get out of a legally binding transaction.

Larry Sorsby, CFO, Hovnanian Enterprises, Inc.[1]

Once the broker brings buyer to seller, when is an enforceable contract for the purchase of real property really formed? And once it is actually formed, are there outs? Bases for cancellation? This chapter provides the insights and information you need on contracts for the sale of real estate: what is required for a valid contract, what it helps to include in a valid contract, and what remedies you have for nonperformance of a valid real estate contract.

COMMON LAW PRINCIPLES OF FORMATION AS APPLIED TO REAL ESTATE CONTRACTS

Although contracts for the purchase and sale of real estate have certain specific requirements, they must still meet the general requirements that all contracts must have for formation. A contract does not exist until there has been an offer, acceptance, and consideration.

Offer

The **offer**, the first step in the real estate transaction, is generally made by the buyer. Listing agreements, advertisements, auction flyers, and notices of public sales are just invitations for offers. These marketing tools make buyers aware of the property and catch the buyer's attention, but they are not offers.

---

[1]Some states have extended the protection to mobile homes, including secondary purchasers of those homes. See *Dinsmore v. Fleetwood Homes of Tenn., Inc.*, 906 N.E.2d 186, 191 (Ind. Ct. App. 2009).

Elements

To be valid, an offer must show a present intent to contract, its terms must be certain and definite, and it must be communicated to the offeree. Most real estate purchase offers are made when the buyer actually fills out, signs, and presents to the seller a form or contract of purchase. The language in such forms has definite evidence of intent to contract: "_____ as seller, agrees to sell to _____ as buyer, and buyer agrees to purchase from seller the following described property ..."

Often, contracts are negotiated not through the use of forms but through very informal procedures. For example, the buyer's offer may come in the form of a letter or memorandum, and we need to find language that shows present intent to contract. Language such as, "I'm considering buying," "Would you consider selling?" or "What would your asking price be?" is not indicative of present intent to contract. These are inquiries or invitations for offers.

Likewise, memoranda or correspondence from seller to buyer that includes language such as, "I might sell," "I'd consider selling," "I'm thinking of offering," or "In December, I'll offer" is too conditional and is not enough for an offer.

Not only must the offer show intent to contract, it must also contain sufficient information and details: the identity of the parties, the description of the property, the price, and the terms (to be discussed in detail). Form purchase contracts list all required information. If one of the basic requirements for formation is missing, then the offer is really just an invitation for an offer or simply a step in the negotiation process.

The final requirement for a valid offer is communication to the offeree. In practice, communication to the offeree comes when the purchase contract form with the buyer's signature is given to the seller or the agent or broker of the seller.

CONSIDER 13.1   Determine if the following language from a letter by Thompson to Hale (the lot owner) meets the requirements for a valid offer:

I am very much interested in your lot, zoned C-2, which is located at the southeastern corner of Gilbert and Southern Roads. If the price is $475,000 or less, I can pay cash. I will need it for construction by 6/1/13.

/s/ Walter Thompson

Termination

An offer is not legally binding and may be revoked or withdrawn at any time prior to acceptance by the offeree (note, as discussed in the section following, that an option is a different type of offer). When an offer is voluntarily withdrawn prior to acceptance, the offeror has not breached any contract, because it was not yet formed, and has no liability for any damages others may have incurred in relying on the offer.

An offer can be limited in time, with a specified ending date, but unless it is an option, it can still be revoked prior to that ending date. The offeror must let the offeree know of the revocation, because the offeree still has the power of acceptance until he or she knows of the revocation. For example, a valid offer may include as one of its terms, "This offer good only until noon on April 5, 2013." This offer would automatically terminate at that time and date unless the offeree accepts prior to that time. Even offers without specific time limits terminate after a reasonable amount of time, although it is probably best for the offerors to withdraw or revoke any long-outstanding offers. What is a reasonable time varies according to the nature and location of the property and the terms of the offer.

The death of either an offeror or the offeree terminates the offer (with an exception noted in the next section, "Options"). At the moment of death, the offer is automatically terminated or withdrawn.

Rejection of the offer by the offeree terminates the original offer. A rejection is a negative response, such as, "No, I'm not interested." But a rejection may be given indirectly. If an offeree makes the acceptance of an offer conditional on certain additional terms and requirements, the acceptance is both a rejection of the original offer and a **counteroffer,** placing the original offeree in an offeror position. The following sequence of excerpts from correspondence illustrates this point.

    a. Offeror: "I will buy Blackacre (legal description) from you for $300,000 cash, to close 6/1/13."

    b. Offeree (counteroffer): "I accept your offer, but must have cash in hand by 5/1/13."

    c. Offeree (original offeror): "That is agreeable."

When the offeree conditioned acceptance on a change in closing date (b), the acceptance was a counteroffer that the original offeror, now an offeree, was free to accept or reject. The contract was formed when the original offeror (now offeree) agreed to the change in terms.

In practice, when brokers and salespeople run between buyer and seller with changes in terms and addenda to the purchase contract, they are engaging in negotiation, and the parties are constantly changing roles as offerors and offerees. The offeree must accept all of the offeror's terms without change or qualification for a contract to be formed. Any change, under the common law rules that apply to all real estate contracts, results in a rejection and a counteroffer.

Options

Requirements

Often, a buyer is unsure about purchasing property and wants time to do research or just to make the decision. However, since an offer may be revoked by the offeror any time prior to acceptance, the opportunity to purchase may pass while the buyer researches and debates the purchase. The buyer would like some type of guarantee that the offer will remain open for a stated period of time. However, simply having the seller include a time provision in the offer ("This offer to remain open until June 15, 2013") is not foolproof, as noted earlier. The offeror can still revoke the offer any time prior to acceptance and with notice of that revocation.

However, if the buyer obtains an option from the seller, this problem is alleviated. An **option** is a contract for time whereby the seller agrees to hold an offer open for a specified period in exchange for consideration (payment). Either a buyer or seller can turn an offer into an option with proper consideration from the offeree.

An option is different from an ordinary offer because the offeree gives consideration to the offeror to keep the offer open. An option is, in effect, a contract for time that is paid for. If an offeror has been paid for an option on property and sells the property to another party, the offeror is in breach of contract and will be required to pay damages to the option holder. The amount of consideration is not important so long as it is actually paid. The following case deals with the issue of consideration in options.

BOARD OF CONTROL OF EASTERN MICHIGAN UNIVERSITY V. BURGESS

206 N.W.2d 256 (Mich. 1973)
For Want of a Dollar, Some Property Was Lost

FACTS

On February 15, 1966, Burgess (defendant/appellant) signed a document that provided Eastern Michigan University (EMU/plaintiff/appellee) a 60-day option for the purchase of Burgess's home. The document, drafted by an agent of Burgess, indicated receipt of "one and no/100 Dollar ($1.00) and other valuable consideration." The dollar was never paid. On April 14, 1966, EMU notified Burgess of its acceptance, but Burgess refused to close and deliver title. EMU brought suit for delivery of the property or specific performance. The trial court found for EMU, and Burgess appealed.

JUDICIAL OPINION

Burns, Judge

Options for the purchase of land, if based on valid consideration, are contracts which may be specifically enforced. Conversely, that which purports to be an option, but which is not based on valid consideration, is not a contract and will not be enforced. In the instant case defendant received no consideration for the purported option of February 15, 1966.

A written acknowledgment of receipt of consideration merely creates a rebuttable presumption that consideration has, in fact, passed. Neither the parol evidence rule nor the doctrine of estoppel bars the presentation of evidence to contradict any such acknowledgment.

It is our opinion that the document signed by Burgess on February 15, 1966, is not an enforceable option, and that Burgess is not barred from so asserting. In the instant case Burgess claims that she never received any of the consideration promised here.

That which purports to be an option for the purchase of land, but which is not based on valid consideration, is a simple offer to sell the same land. An option is a contract collateral to an offer to sell whereby the offer is made irrevocable for a specified period. Ordinarily, an offer is revocable at the will of the offeror. Accordingly, a failure of consideration affects only the collateral contract to keep the offer open, not the underlying offer.

A simple offer may be revoked for any reason or for no reason by the offeror at any time prior to its acceptance by the offeree. Thus, the question in this case becomes, "Did defendant effectively revoke her offer to sell before plaintiff accepted that offer?"

Defendant testified that within hours of signing the purported option she telephoned plaintiff's agent and informed him that she would not abide by the option unless the purchase price was increased. Defendant also testified that when plaintiff's agent delivered to her on April 14, 1966, plaintiff's notice of its intention to exercise the purported option, she told him that "the option was off."

Plaintiff's agent testified that defendant did not communicate to him any dissatisfaction until sometime in July 1966.

If defendant is telling the truth, she effectively revoked her offer several weeks before plaintiff accepted that offer, and no contract of sale was created. If plaintiff's agent is telling the truth, defendant's offer was still open when plaintiff accepted that offer, and an enforceable contract was created. The trial judge thought it unnecessary to resolve this particular dispute. In light of our holding the dispute must be resolved.

An appellate court cannot assess the credibility of witnesses. We have neither seen nor heard them testify.

Accordingly, we remand this case to the trial court for additional findings of fact based on the record already before the court.

Reversed and remanded.

CASE QUESTIONS

1. How much was the consideration? Was the consideration paid?
2. If the option is valid what issue remains to be determined?
3. What advice would you give, based on this case, to those who want to have an option agreement?

CONSIDER 13.2 On February 7, 2013, A entered into negotiations with B for the purchase of B's farm. After consulting with an attorney and having the property appraised, B agreed to sell for $750,000. A and B agreed in writing that in exchange for $1,000 then received from A, B would hold the offer open for nine months. After six months, A wrote B that he was no longer interested in buying the farm. Several days later, A received notice from B that he was negotiating with C to sell the farm for $950,000. A immediately called B, who suggested that if A would agree to pay $875,000 and conclude the deal within 10 days, then B would still be willing to sell to A. A protested that B was driving a hard bargain, but finally agreed by telegram that evening to buy the farm for $875,000 within 10 days. A purchased the farm as agreed and then sought to recover $125,000 from B or alternatively to rescind the purchase (in other words, get out of the contract). What result and why?

Termination

Another distinguishing feature about an option is that, unlike an ordinary offer, it does not terminate with the death of the offeror or the option holder. In other words, the estate of an option holder could elect to exercise the option for the estate. Likewise, the estate of the offeror is required to honor the option if the option holder decides to exercise the right after the death of the offeror.

Another issue in options is what happens when the option holder rejects the option prior to the given ending date. For example, A gives B an option on some property to run from February 1, 2013, to March 2, 2013, and B pays A $1,000 for the option. On February 16, 2013, B notifies A that he is rejecting the offer. The following questions arise: (1) Must A still hold the offer open until March 2, 2013? (2) Is B entitled to a refund of a portion of the option payment? (3) Must A refund a portion of the option payment in order to sell the property prior to March 2, 2013?

The jurisdictions are split on the answers to the questions raised by the option holder's rejection prior to the option's expiration date. One view is that rejection is rejection; that is, an option is an offer that terminates once rejected by the option holder (offeree). The majority view is that a rejection before the option term has no effect on the option; that is, that the option continues until the ending date unless the offeror has materially changed position. Under this view, if the parties agreed to a partial refund and signed a mutual release terminating the option, then the offeror would be free to sell the property to another. Under the first view, release and refund would not be required for the offeror to be free to transfer the property.

In light of the split among the courts on how options are to be handled in the event of rejection prior to their expiration, it is probably best for the parties to put a clause in their option agreement that deals with early rejection and the offeror's and option holder's rights.

The following list of topics is important when negotiating and drafting option agreements:

- Legal description of the property
- Proper names of the parties
- Signatures of the parties
- Length of the option
- Beginning and ending dates of the option period

- Amount of consideration to be paid
- What happens to the consideration if
  a. the option is exercised: Can it be a down payment?
  b. the option expires without acceptance: Does the offeror retain the money?
  c. the option holder rejects prior to expiration: Will there be a prorated refund?
  d. the property is destroyed during the option period?
  e. one of the parties dies?
- Recording of the option in the public records and its removal if not exercised
- Procedures and notifications required for exercise of the option
- All terms or provisions of the sales contract:
  a. marketable title (type of deed, insurance, and so on)
  b. rights of lessees
  c. presence of mortgages and new liens during the option period
- Assignability of the option

Options are not earnest money deposits (the down payments by buyers that accompany offers for buying real property). Earnest money is appropriately named because it is customarily required to show the offeror's good faith and is actually part of the payment for the purchase price. Options generally come from sellers and are promises to hold offers open for periods of time. Payment for an option is not necessarily a payment of part of the purchase price. Furthermore, consideration is required for an option to be valid, whereas earnest money is not required for a valid contract to purchase (although it may be good business practice).

CONSIDER 13.3   In June, 1988, John Simpson granted to his son, D. Bruce Simpson, the right to purchase various parcels of real property that were held initially by John's revocable trust and later by his wife Mildred Simpson's revocable trust. The 1988 option agreement provided that Bruce could exercise the option at any time on or before 20 years from the date of the agreement and contained the following clause: "[i]n consideration for the mutual promises made in this agreement."

When some of the properties were transferred to Mildred's trust in 1993, Bruce executed a waiver of the option only to facilitate the transfer of the properties for estate planning purposes, and Mildred executed a written agreement ratifying and incorporating John's 1988 option agreement. John died in 2002, and Mildred died in 2006. The properties were thereafter administered by John's and Mildred's trusts. In April 2008, Bruce exercised the option on several of the parcels. Bruce then died in March 2009. In April 2009, the personal representative of Bruce's estate completed the purchase of the properties.

Chris, who is John's other surviving son, filed a petition challenging the validity of the 1988 option agreement because of a lack of consideration with the vague clause. Family members testified that the mutual promises were related to John staying in the area, caring for his parents, and running the family fruit farm because Chris had left home and did not want to run the business. Is the option valid and what should the court do about the option and the rights of the parties? *In re John W. Simpson Trust,* 2011 WL 3130327 (Mich.App.).   ◼

Acceptance

Acceptance is conduct by the offeree that indicates a willingness to take the terms of the offer. Acceptance is the second part of the so-called meeting-of-the-minds requirement for formation of a contract. Like the offer, acceptance has certain requirements: (1) It must be by the party with the power of acceptance; (2) it must be absolute, unequivocal, and unconditional; and (3) it must be communicated to the offeror.

Power of Acceptance

The only party with the power of acceptance is the party to whom the offer is made. Offers are not transferable. Options are an exception to this rule. Options, like all nonpersonal contracts, are transferable. An assignment of an option right gives the assignee the right to exercise the option.

Absolute, Unequivocal, and Unconditional Acceptance

This requirement for acceptance was briefly explained in the discussion of termination of offers. The offeree must accept the offer on its terms and must not change those or make acceptance conditional on new or different terms. If the offeree does make any changes in the terms, then there is no acceptance; rather, there is a counteroffer that the original offeror (now offeree) is free to accept or reject.

CONSIDER 13.4   Terry and Marianne Jennings listed their home for sale with Stapley Realty. When the listing agent, Brad Reed, came to the home, he asked if there was anything that was attached to the house that would not be sold with the house. Mr. Jennings pointed to an original Hunter ceiling fan and said it would not stay with the house since he had installed it himself. Reed told the Jenningses that it would be best to remove the fan and replace it with another lighting fixture or fan. They agreed and planned to do the replacement on Saturday. On Friday afternoon, the "For Sale" sign and the lockbox for real estate agent access went on their property. On Saturday morning, another agent taking a couple to another home noticed the Jenningses' house, which had not yet appeared in the multiple listing. He took the couple through it, and that night they made an offer on it. The Jenningses accepted all the terms because they had only 90 days to sell their home and move to another one. Mr. Jennings noted above his signature, "Ceiling fan in family room is not included." The buyers then refused to go through with the sale. The Jennings wish to know if they have any rights. Is there a contract? What happened because of the fan stipulation? _____ ■

Communication of Acceptance to Offeror

The signature on the purchase contract alone is insufficient acceptance: A copy of that agreement must be delivered to the offeror or the offeror's agent for a valid contract to exist. When there is electronic communication (see discussion under the writing requirement that follows), an electronic record is sent when it is properly directed to the system used by the recipient for electronic communication (such as "john.smith@cpan.net"), it is in a form that can be read by the recipient, and only the recipient can control access to the content of the record.

The Timing of Acceptance: When a Contract Is Formed

The timing of an acceptance depends upon the method of communication that the offeror uses. Some offerors give a required means of acceptance. If the offeree uses the stipulated means of acceptance, the acceptance is effective when it is properly sent. For example, if the offeror has required the acceptance to be mailed and the offeree properly mails the letter of acceptance, the acceptance is effective when it is sent. This timing rule for acceptance is called the mailbox rule. If the offeree uses a different means of acceptance, it is considered a counter-offer because the form of acceptance varied from the offeror's terms.

If the offeror does not stipulate a means of acceptance, the offeree is free to use any method for communication of the acceptance. If the offeree uses the same method of communication or, in some states, a reasonable (generally faster) means, the mailbox rule also applies. If the offeree uses a slower method of acceptance, the acceptance is not effective until it is actually received

---

CONSIDER 13.5   Reed Gilmore filed an oil and gas application for Parcel NV-148 in June 1987 with the Bureau of Land Management (BLM). His application was selected in a computerized random drawing. BLM notified Gilmore by an August 26 letter sent certified mail that included the following language:

> Enclosed is the original and two copies of Form No. 3100–11, "Offer to Lease and Lease for Oil and Gas" for your execution. The applicant (or the applicant's attorney-in-fact, as provided by 43 C.F.R. [§] 3112.6–1(a) and (b) [(1986)]), must manually sign and date each copy on the reverse side of the form.

> All copies of the lease form must be properly executed and filed in this office within thirty (30) days from your receipt of this decision, which constitutes a compliance period. Failure to do so will result in the rejection of your offer without further notice.

Gilmore received the letter on August 29, 1987. He signed the copies and sent them certified mail from his office in Kimball, Nebraska, on September 21, 1987, with a return receipt requested. On the morning of September 28, 1987, Gilmore's secretary, Debra Bohac, noticed that she had not yet received the return receipt card. September 28 was the 30-day deadline.

Bohac called the BLM and spoke with Joan Woodin to see if the forms had been received. While there was subsequent disagreement about the full content of the conversation, Woodin and Bohac agreed that Woodin told her the forms had not been received.

Bohac then tried to book a flight for Gilmore to Reno, but there were no flights available that would get Gilmore there before the BLM office closed. Bohac then called the BLM back and spoke with Bernita Dawson, a Land Law Examiner in the BLM. Bohac offered to telefax (fax) the lease forms and maintains that Dawson agreed to take the faxes as acceptance. Dawson denies making such a statement.

Gilmore then sent a telecopy to Robert McCarthy, a Reno attorney, who delivered it to the BLM at 11:15 a.m. on September 28. The mailed originals were received in the BLM office the next day, September 29. BLM informed Gilmore on September 29 that his offer was rejected for failure to comply with the terms. The decision was affirmed by the overall agency and Gilmore filed suit in federal district court. The district court dismissed the case, and Gilmore appealed. What are each of the parties' rights? Was there a contract or did Gilmore fail to accept properly? *Gilmore v. Lujan*, 947 F.2d 1409 (9th Cir. 1991).   ▪

The Timing Rules and the Problem of Multiple Offers

Because of these timing rules, sellers often end up with multiple offers. Because acceptance is effective upon communication to the offeror, an offeror who has made more than one offer may find two acceptances being communicated before one or both of the offers can be revoked. It is a major legal risk for an offeror to have more than one offer outstanding. Consider the following sequence of events as an example:

PRACTICAL TIP

Deal with one party at a time. Multiple offers create confusion and liability. Make sure there is only one outstanding valid offer at a time. Don't extend another offer until an outstanding offer is revoked.

- Day 1: Buyer A submits an offer to seller.
- Day 2: Seller counteroffers to buyer A. Buyer B submits an offer to seller.
- Day 3: Seller counteroffers to buyer B. Buyer A accepts. Before seller can revoke, buyer B accepts.

The seller in the example has formed two valid contracts and would have to convey the property to one buyer and pay damages for breach to the other buyer.

The following case deals with several issues of offer and acceptance, including the problem of more than one offeree.

ANZALACO V. GRABER

970 N.E.2d 1143 (Ohio App. 2012)
Counterproposals, Secondary Offers, Releases, Oh, My!

FACTS

On July 14, 2010, Katherine and Steve Graber, represented by Joseph Keller of Howard Hanna, entered into a purchase agreement with Michael Lee for the sale of their property for $325,000. Under the agreement, Lee was entitled to obtain a general inspection and radon and mold inspections of the property. Within three days after completion of such inspections, Lee was to choose one of the following:

(A) Remove the inspection contingency and accept the property in its "AS IS" present physical condition. If the property is accepted in its "AS IS" present physical condition, then BUYER agrees to sign an Amendment/Removal of Contingency.

(B) Accept the property subject to SELLER agreeing to have specific material defects, that were either previously disclosed in writing by the SELLER or identified in a written inspection report, repaired by a qualified contractor in a professional manner at SELLER's expense; SELLER and BUYER shall have three (3) days from SELLER's receipt of BUYER's written request and copies of inspection reports to agree in writing which material defect(s), if any, shall be corrected by the SELLER at SELLER's expense. If BUYER and

SELLER do not agree in writing within those three (3) days, then this AGREEMENT shall be null and void, and SELLER and BUYER agree to sign a mutual release, whereupon the earnest money shall be returned to the BUYER.

(C) Terminate this Agreement if BUYER's written inspection report(s) or any other source(s) identify material defects NOT previously disclosed in writing by SELLER. If BUYER elects to terminate, BUYER agrees to provide a copy of the written inspection report(s) to SELLER and both parties agree to promptly sign a mutual release, whereupon the earnest money shall be returned to BUYER.

On July 9, 2010, after Lee had the property inspected, Lee invoked option (B). On that date, Lee's realtor[2] sent the Grabers an email in which he identified eight items that he wanted the Grabers to repair or remove. The Grabers refused to make any of the claimed repairs, and on July 21, 2010, Lee presented a counterproposal seeking a $10,000 reduction in the purchase price. The Grabers refused to reduce the price of the home and determined that the contract was null and void.

On July 21, 2010, the Grabers entered into a purchase agreement with William Anzalaco. Both the

---

[2]Note that the court used the term "realtor" incorrectly here. As noted in Chapter 12, "Realtor" is a proper term and refers only to members of the NAR. The court means real estate agent.

Grabers and Anzalaco were represented by Keller. This agreement provided:

> *This X is _____ is not a secondary offer. This secondary offer, if applicable, shall become a primary contract upon BUYER's receipt of a signed copy of the release of the primary contract on or before 7–23–10. BUYER shall have the right to terminate this secondary offer at any time prior to BUYER's receipt of said copy of the release of the primary contract by delivering written notice to the SELLER or SELLER's agent.*

> *[I]f a defect in title appears, SELLER shall have thirty (30) days after notice from BUYER to remove such defect and, if unable to do so, BUYER may either (1) accept title subject to such defect without any reduction in the purchase price or (2) terminate this Agreement, in which case neither BUYER, SELLER[,] nor any REALTOR(S) shall have any further liability to each other, and both BUYER and SELLER agree to sign a mutual release, whereupon the earnest money shall be returned to BUYER.*

On July 22, 2010, the Grabers executed a mutual release and sent it to Lee for his signature. Lee did not execute the release of his purchase agreement with the Grabers. Instead, on July 23, 2010, Lee executed an Amendment to Offer to Purchase and Removal of Contingency, in which he waived his right to a general inspection.

Anzalaco deposited earnest money and the purchase price into escrow, and the Grabers deposited an executed warranty deed for the property. However, the prior purchase agreement with Lee was subsequently deemed a cloud upon the title, and the title company for the transaction refused to issue title insurance.

Steve Graber died on August 3, 2010, and Katherine did not enter into a purchase agreement with Lee. On August 25, 2010, Lee's counsel sent Katherine a proposed complaint for specific performance of his purchase agreement.

On August 31, 2010, Anzalaco filed suit for breach of contract and specific performance against Katherine. Anzalaco alleged that Katherine breached the purchase agreement, and that Howard Hanna and Keller committed fraud and breached their fiduciary duties in this matter.

The trial court entered summary judgment against Lee and against Anzalaco on their claims for breach of contract and specific performance. Lee and Anzalaco appealed.

JUDICIAL OPINION
Kilbane, Judge

On July 16, 2010, Mr. Lee had a home inspection completed. After the inspection, Mr. Lee elected to choose option B. On July 19, 2010, Mr. Lee's realtor sent an email to Ms. Graber's realtor listing eight items that Mr. Lee wanted her to repair. Ms. Graber did not agree to fix any of the items listed by Mr. Lee. In response to Ms. Graber's refusal, Mr. Lee demanded a $10,000 price reduction, which was refused by Ms. Graber as well.

Therefore, under the plain language of this provision, *"If BUYER and SELLER do not agree in writing within those three (3) days, then this AGREEMENT shall be null and void, and SELLER and BUYER agree to sign a mutual release, whereupon the earnest money shall be returned to the BUYER."* This provision operated as a condition precedent to the formation of an agreement once the buyer elected this option.

Moreover, the clear language of this provision does not support Lee's claim that option (B) required the seller to agree in principle to undertake repairs in order for this option to be exercised. Rather, the Buyer was simply permitted, at his discretion, to elect this option.

Although the plain language of option (B) states that, *"If BUYER and SELLER do not agree in writing within those three (3) days, then this AGREEMENT shall be null and void,"* Lee insists that this provision is not effective until the buyer and seller agree in principal that it is necessary to repair specific material defects, and then negotiate the repair of those defects. In rejecting this argument below, the trial court correctly analyzed the issue as follows:

There is nothing in the agreement that required Ms. Graber to agree in principal to undertake repairs before actually receiving a list of repairs from Mr. Lee. It would not make any sense to have a seller agree to do repairs, then receive the actual list of repairs from the buyer in order to negotiate what repairs would be done at the seller's expense.

* * * Rather, [the language in option (B) pertaining to an agreement regarding the repair of defects] spells out the method in which the buyer and seller would negotiate as to what repairs the seller would undertake at her expense. The agreement became null and void once the buyer and seller could not agree on the repairs, which is what happened here.

Lee also insists that the purchase agreement did not terminate through the July 9, 2010 exercise of option (B) because the contract gave him until July 24, 2010 to exercise the inspection provision, and that prior to that deadline, on July 23, 2010, he invoked option (A), and accepted the property "as is." Again, as cogently stated by the trial court, "There is no mechanism under the language of the agreement to allow Mr. Lee to elect a different option once option B became an impossibility." Rather, the July 24, 2010 date is simply the last date for the buyer to obtain an inspection and does not extend the contract once the buyer does so.

Lee also complains that the Grabers acted in bad faith in connection with his purchase agreement by promptly entering into the contract with Anzalaco. The record clearly establishes, however, that the Grabers gave Anzalaco a secondary offer that would only mature into a primary contract upon the release of Lee's purchase agreement. This claim is without merit.

The refusal of the Grabers to make the repairs identified by Lee resulted in the failure of a condition precedent that prevented the parties from entering into an enforceable agreement. Lee's claim for breach of contract lacked merit as a matter of law, and absent an enforceable agreement, Lee's claim for specific performance was likewise without merit.

Further, with regard to Anzalaco's claims for breach of contract and specific performance, the trial court properly determined that there were no genuine issues of material fact and that Katherine is entitled to judgment as a matter of law. The trial court explained:

Because Mr. Lee refused to sign the release [of the primary purchase agreement], the buyer [sic] could not get a signed copy of that release as required under the time frame established by the Anzalaco agreement. Pursuant to this language, the secondary contract could not become the primary contract without the release of the Lee agreement being signed by all parties to that agreement on or before July 23, 2010. As such, there is no valid contract between the parties, and Ms. Graber is entitled to judgment as a matter of law[.]

We concur with this analysis. By application of the ordinary meaning of the common words appearing in the parties' July 21, 2010 purchase agreement, Anzalaco made a "secondary offer." The undisputed facts demonstrate that Lee did not execute a release of the primary contract, so the secondary offer never became a primary contract upon the failure of that condition precedent.

Anzalaco insists, however, that parole [sic] evidence is admissible to demonstrate that his offer became a primary offer. He relies upon Katherine's July 26, 2010 affidavit that she prepared "for the purpose of inducing [the title agency] to issue a title insurance policy or other title evidence" in which she avers that "[t]here are no other contracts, options, or rights to purchase the Property except for the contract being closed."

As noted by the trial court, however, parole [sic] evidence is barred because the terms of "the Anzalaco agreement [are] unambiguous on its face." The parole [sic] affidavit does not alter the unambiguous provisions of Anzalaco's purchase agreement that required "BUYER's [Anzalaco's] receipt of a signed copy of the release of the primary contract on or before 7–23–10," in order to convert Anzalaco's secondary offer to a primary contract. Absent that release, Anzalaco's secondary offer did not mature into a primary contract.

Further, Katherine's ability to deliver clear, marketable title is itself a condition precedent. Under the terms of the parties' agreement, Katherine could not obtain title insurance and Anzalaco had the option to either accept title with the possible reversionary cloud or negate the purchase agreement. Anzalaco offered no evidence that he accepted title subject to that defect as required to proceed with the transaction under the marketable title provision of the agreement. To the contrary, in his response to Katherine's request for admissions, Anzalaco admitted that he would "not accept a general warranty deed from Katherine M. Graber that takes exception for Michael Lee's claims arising from the purchase agreement he entered into with Katherine and Steve Graber."

Affirmed.

CASE QUESTIONS

1. Explain what happened with the Lee offer and acceptance and performance.
2. What was the risk for the title insurer in not writing a policy for the land?
3. Provide your list of advice for parties on outstanding offers and counteroffers and how to handle them, based on what you have learned in this case.

ETHICAL ISSUE

Evaluate Michael Lee's conduct in the situations with the offer and counteroffer and his withholding his signature. Evaluate his conduct in continuing the litigation following the trial court ruling in Katherine's favor.

CONSIDER 13.6   Cynthia has listed her home with We Sell 'Em Realty, Incorporated. Buyer A conveys a written offer of $283,000 to Cynthia on March 1, 2013. Buyer B conveys an offer of $284,000 to Cynthia on March 2, 2008. On March 2, 2013, Cynthia issues counteroffers of $285,000 to both A and B. On the counteroffers, Cynthia adds the following: "This offer good until March 4, 2013, 6 p.m."

Suppose Buyer A accepts on March 3, 2013 (written forms signed), and communicates the acceptance to Cynthia at 7 p.m. that day. Cynthia then contacts Buyer B and says, "I revoke the counteroffer." What is the result?

    a. Suppose that before Cynthia contacts B, B contacts Cynthia and accepts at 2:15 p.m. (written forms signed). What would be the result?

    b. Suppose that B paid Cynthia $500 to hold the offer open until March 4, 2013, 6 p.m. What would be the result?

    c. Suppose same facts as part (b) except that B calls Cynthia at 1 p.m., March 3, 2013, and states, "I reject," whereupon Cynthia receives A's acceptance. What would be the result?

Consideration

The third and final requirement for formation of a valid contract is consideration. **Consideration** is something of value given up by each party to the contract. In most cases involving a sale of real property, consideration is easily established: The seller gives up title to the property, and the buyer gives up money, assumes a mortgage, or both in order to pay for that property.

Consideration need not be money. As noted, the buyer's promise to take over a loan is sufficient consideration. The traditional earnest money deposit received from buyers in a real estate transaction is a form of consideration but is not required for the contract to be valid and binding. Both parties' promises to give something up in the transaction promises constitute sufficient consideration. However, earnest money does demonstrate sincerity and good faith on the part of the buyer and may be used as a source of funds for damages in the event of a problem.

The amount of consideration is not of legal concern to the courts, so long as there is consideration and it passes from one party to the other. A promise to pay $50,000 for property worth $200,000 is valid consideration provided that each party voluntarily agrees to the terms.

The following case deals with the sufficiency of consideration in a real estate purchase agreement.

TRENGEN V. MONGEON

206 N.W.2d 284 (N.D. 1973)
All in the Family: Louis & Margaret & Ernest & Pearl

FACTS

On May 9, 1967, Louis and Margaret Mongeon executed a warranty deed conveying approximately 960 acres of land to their son Ernest and his wife, Pearl (defendant/appellee). The deed contained an acknowledgment of the receipt of $38,400 as consideration for the conveyance. At the same time, the parties entered into an agreement whereby Ernest and Pearl agreed to pay to Louis and Margaret the sum of $1,800 annually for as long as both or the survivor of them shall live. At the time of the agreement, Louis was 87 and Margaret was 83. Ernest's sister, Elaine Trengen (plaintiff/appellant, as guardian for her parents), brought suit seeking to set the deed aside on the grounds of lack of consideration. The trial court found for Ernest and Pearl, and Elaine appealed.

JUDICIAL OPINION

Teigen, Judge

In the present case the consideration is of an indeterminable value. Monetarily, payment of the sum of $1,800 was made in the fall of 1967, and that sum will continue to be payable on or before November 1 of every year for as long as both or the survivor of the plaintiffs shall live. Payments received by the plaintiffs to the present time total $10,800.

… Since adequacy of consideration is not necessary to sustain a deed, and any valuable consideration, however small, is sufficient, the consideration need not equal the value of the property conveyed, especially where no creditor's rights are affected. Indeed, the merely nominal consideration of one dollar, which is frequently recited in deeds, evidences a sufficient consideration. So, where, as compared with the actual value of the property or interest received, the consideration is adequate, the deed will stand, whether such consideration is merely a valuable one without any monetary payment or a valuable one coupled with pecuniary advances.

Adequacy of monetary consideration is not an important element in a conveyance which has for its principal purpose the conferring of a gift or endowment rather than financial gain. The adequacy of consideration is not to be viewed with hindsight, but it should rather be considered from the viewpoint of the parties at the time the deed was executed. The ordinary standard for testing the adequacy of consideration to support a transfer of property is not applicable to a deed conveying realty on condition that the grantee care for the grantor during the remainder of the grantor's life because of the uncertainty of life involved in such agreements. In considering the adequacy of consideration of a promise to care for and support a grantor for the remainder of his life in exchange for a conveyance of land, conditions existing at the time the contract is made are controlling, and subsequent events, such as the early death of the person to be cared for cannot be used to determine the adequacy of the consideration.

The trial court also found that the plaintiff's love and affection for their son Ernest was both a motivating factor and part of the consideration for the transaction.

Natural love and affection has always been held to be sufficient consideration for a deed where the relationship of the parties is such as to justify the presumption that love and affection exists.

The love and affection the plaintiffs (parents) felt toward Ernest is evidenced by the fact that, as stated in the agreement, the land in question had been devised to Ernest by the wills of both Louis and Margaret, and nine days after the land was conveyed to Ernest and the defendant (Pearl), Louis and Margaret executed new wills, each of which contained this provision:

I have purposely omitted my son, Ernest Mongeon, as a devisee or legatee under this Will, for the reason that my [wife, Margaret Mongeon] [husband, Louis Mongeon] and I have made disposition of substantial farmlands to him during our lifetime for a fair consideration … [emphasis added].

We conclude that, in the absence of a finding of fraud or undue influence, the evidence is sufficient to support a finding that there was adequate consideration to uphold the conveyance of the land from the plaintiffs to Ernest and the defendant.

Affirmed.

CASE QUESTIONS

1. What was the relationship between Louis and Margaret and Ernest and Pearl?
2. How much land was conveyed? What was the total price? How was the price to be paid?
3. Of what relevance were Louis's and Margaret's ages at the time of the conveyance?
4. Was there consideration?

SPECIFIC REQUIREMENTS FOR REAL ESTATE CONTRACTS

In addition to meeting the common law requirements just discussed, a valid real estate purchase contract must also meet certain specific requirements that are peculiar to real estate transactions. The following are the requirements: (1) that the contract be in the form of a record, such as a written agreement, (2) that the parties sign or authenticate the contract, and (3) that the description of the property be adequate.

Writing or Record Requirements

The Statute of Frauds requires that real estate contracts be evidenced by a record. The Electronic Signatures in Global and National Commerce Act (E-Sign) requires that electronically signed contracts be given equal legal effect with traditional paper contracts. Under E-Sign, the states can modify the effects of E-Sign if they enact the Uniform Electronic Transactions Act (UETA), which allows electronic signatures, even signatures of notaries for contract formation, in audits, and as evidence in court and other legal proceedings. Called the *rule of parity*, UETA provides that electronic and paper records and signatures are given the same legal effect, with some exceptions. Exceptions include wills and codicils (see Chapter 17), testamentary trusts, and commercial paper such as checks and letters of credit. When consumers are involved in the contracts, they must agree to communication and negotiation via electronic means before they can be bound by electronic records.

However, even with all of the mandates on electronic communication, oral agreements for the transfer of property remain unenforceable. And, standard industry practice for the listing, sale, and purchase of real property is to have all documents and signatures reduced to paper form. While those in the real estate field rely on fax and e-mailed PDF documents, they continue to finalize with paper agreements and signatures.

A contract and its terms may be pieced together from informal exchanges, whether on paper or electronically, as long as all the requirements for formation are met and the necessary elements are present. The following case deals with the complications that can result from electronic communication.

DHILLON V. ZIONS FIRST NATIONAL BANK

462 Fed. Appx. 880, 2012 WL 715273 (11th Cir. 2012)
Sometimes E-Mail Is Not Enough to Form a Contract

FACTS

Gursheel Dhillon, a resident of Tennessee, contacted Zions National Bank about properties it had listed online for sale, a car wash in Cobb County, Georgia, and a retail strip mall in Gwinnett County, Georgia. Dhillon sent an offer to a Zions real estate disposition officer to purchase the car wash for $469,000 and the strip mall for $600,000. Dhillon signed a negotiation agreement provided by Zions, which acknowledged that: (1) "email messages originating from either party or their respective agents during the negotiation process shall be considered verbal in nature and shall not be binding on either party," (2) any "verbal offer, acceptance or agreement … is not a binding agreement until both Parties execute a written contract," and (3) a contract must be signed by both parties to be valid.

The Zions disposition officer e-mailed Dhillon a counteroffer, listing the original asking price for the properties: $525,000 for the car wash and $850,000 for the strip mall. The disposition officer's e-mails included a disclaimer that read in part:

This e-mail may contain a price or other contract term for the sale of real property. The price or other contract term contained in this email is subject to approval by Zions First National Bank's executive management committee or its designee and is not

binding until the executive management committee or its designee provides such approval in writing to the prospective purchaser.

By e-mail, Dhillon accepted the offer and requested information on how to make a deposit. Following Zions' instructions, he sent Zions a $75,000 check. Zions then sent Dhillon a purchase sales agreement, which had not been signed by any Zions official and that had missing terms, including the address or a description of the properties and their purchase price. Dhillon signed the agreement and returned it to Zions, but Zions later refused to sign the agreement and returned Dhillon's deposit.

Dhillon filed suit. The district court granted Zion's motion for summary judgment. Dhillon appealed.

JUDICIAL OPINION

Per Curiam

Dhillon contends that the district court erred by dismissing his breach of contract claim. The Tennessee statute of frauds requires that all contracts for the conveyance of land be in writing and be "signed by the party to be charged therewith." Tenn.Code Ann. § 29–2–101(a)(4)–(5). "A contract must result from a meeting of the minds of the parties in mutual assent to the terms…. In determining mutuality of assent, courts must apply an objective standard based upon the parties' manifestations."

Dhillon argues that two writings attached to his amended complaint show a binding contract: (1) Zions' counteroffer and (2) the purchase sales agreement. The counteroffer was not a binding contract because Zions did not sign it and there was no meeting of the minds to form a contract by e-mail. Dhillon's exhibits to his amended complaint reveal facts—specifically, the e-mail disclaimers—that foreclose any contention that Zions sought to form a valid contract via e-mail. Nor could Dhillon have reasonably expected that the e-mail counteroffer constituted a binding contract because he had already signed the negotiation agreement acknowledging that e-mail correspondence between him and Zions was not a binding agreement and that any contract would have to be signed by both parties.

The purchase sales agreement was not a binding contract either under Tennessee's statute of frauds because the party against whom Dhillon seeks to charge with violating it, Zions, never signed the agreement.

Dhillon argues that two Tennessee cases create exceptions to the traditional statute of frauds and that those exceptions apply in the present case. We disagree. In *Yates v. Skaggs,* 187 Tenn. 149, 213 S.W.2d 41 (1948), the Tennessee Supreme Court considered whether a franchisee could enforce a memorandum amending its earlier contract with its franchisor. Both parties signed the earlier contract, which had no integration clause and had explicitly contemplated further amendments, but only the franchisee signed the memorandum, which the franchisor had prepared. The court held that not all writings to a contract had to comply with

the statute of frauds if the writings can "legally be connected with the agreement which was signed." In the present case, there was no writing signed by both parties and the proposed purchase sales agreement contained an integration clause that explicitly rejected any additions that were unwritten or unsigned.

The second case Dhillon relies on, *Batey v. D.H. Overmyer Warehouse Co.,* 60 Tenn.App. 310, 446 S.W.2d 686, 693 (1969), also is distinguishable from this case. There, the court held that the statute of frauds could not shield a landlord from performing a lease agreement, which the landlord prepared but that only its tenant signed, because the landlord acted in accordance with that lease, renting the tenant the property and depositing his rent checks. In the present case, Zions cancelled negotiations and returned Dhillon's deposit. There was no partial performance by Zions on which Dhillon can hang his lawsuit.

Dhillon's undisputed evidence in the record show[s] that he and Zions did not enter into a contract for the sale of the Georgia properties under Tennessee law. Without a contract, there can be no breach. The district court did not err in ruling that he failed to state a claim for relief on this ground.

Affirmed.

CASE QUESTIONS

1. Explain why there was no electronic formation of a contract, i.e., e-mail.
2. What exceptions does Dhillon try to apply to his situation?
3. Make a list of the lessons we should learn from this case.

PRACTICAL TIP

Always follow up on electronic communications, particularly acceptances, to be sure that the party received the communications and that whoever is accepting an offer truly is the same party who is sending the e-mail. Most lawyers always follow up electronic or fax communication with paper verification to close the loop on proof that the electronic communication was with the correct party and was indeed received.

One of the exceptions to the writing or record requirements for real estate contracts under the Statute of Frauds is the doctrine of part performance. Under this doctrine, a party may be entitled to enforce an oral agreement for the sale of property on the basis of conduct. Under Section 197 of the *Restatement of Contracts,* the party who wants to use the doctrine of part performance to enforce an oral agreement must establish one of the following:

1. that valuable improvements have been made to the property; or
2. that there has been full or partial payment of the purchase price and that the party who has paid money has possession of the property.

Establishing either of these circumstances provides some tangible physical evidence that the parties had an agreement. In other words, if a contract did not exist, why would the improvements have been made, or why was payment accepted but the paying party not permitted to possess the property? While some states do not recognize the doctrine of part performance at all, some

CONSIDER 13.7   Hancock Construction maintained that it had an oral agreement to purchase property from Kempton & Snedigar Dairy. On the basis of the oral contract, Hancock had engineering studies done on the property and arranged to obtain a loan for $292,830. Kempton & Snedigar refused to go through with the contract, alleging a defense of the Statute of Frauds. Hancock brought suit for specific performance relying on the doctrine of part performance. What is the result? *Hancock Construction v. Snedigar Dairy,* 510 P.2d 752 (Az. 1973).   ◼

states recognize variations. For example, some states require possession only, while other states require payment, or improvements, or both.

Signature of Parties

Authentication, through written signature or electronic verification, is required for real estate contracts. In addition to authentication, the parties need to be sure that those who have authenticated have the authority to do so. In the case of joint owners, both parties must authenticate. In many states, both husband and wife must authenticate contracts for the transfer of their property held jointly.

In the case of business organizations such as partnerships, LLCs, LLPs, and corporations, the authenticating parties must have the authority to transfer property and must indicate their capacity. For example, a corporate officer signing for the corporation should have the following signature line:

ABC Company, Inc.
by _____ *Steven Doe, President*
Attest _____ *John Doe, Secretary*

Adequate Description of Property

To satisfy the Statute of Frauds, the property to be conveyed must be adequately described. While a legal description is not required for the purchase contract, it is perhaps the best way to reasonably identify the property and avoid confusion. Without an adequate description, the agreement cannot be enforced. (Chapter 7 provides details on property identification.)

TERMS OF PURCHASE CONTRACTS

Mere compliance with Statute of Frauds requirements may not give the parties enough detail for performance or reflect adequately their intentions.

A complete contract begins with a careful review and inspection of the property. Figure 13.1 is a checklist for buyers to complete before purchasing any property. The following sections cover specific issues that the parties' contract should address.

Property Identification

Most purchase contracts (other than those for acreage) give the street address, followed by a clause such as "and more particularly described as" or "more fully described as," and then the legal description. In many cases,

FIGURE 13.1
Checklist for
Negotiation of Real
Estate Contracts

1. Determine exact boundaries of buildings, driveways, and fences.
2. Determine easements and underground utilities.
3. Determine zoning laws and other governmental regulations applicable to property.
4. Determine future or present uses of surrounding property.
5. Determine quality of available utilities and fire protection.
6. Determine rights-of-way or easements if necessary for use of property.
7. Determine locations of schools, public transportation, churches, and shopping centers.
8. Determine physical condition of building: termites, plumbing, electric, and water in basement.
9. Determine traffic conditions on street and surrounding streets.
10. Determine possible changes in traffic and street structure (such as a proposed freeway).
11. Determine possible nuisances: factories, aircraft, playgrounds, smoke, fumes, and noise.
12. Determine title: judgments and assessments.
13. Determine status of inhabitants (if any).
14. Determine soil suitability if intention is to build.
15. Determine if seller is married or was previously married.
16. Determine utility costs.
17. Determine reputation of builder if new development, verify warranties, approval, conformity with Interstate Land Sales Full Disclosure Act (ILSFDA), bonding, and licensing of builder.
18. Determine if any warranty protection is available.
19. Determine whether any toxic wastes exist or have existed on the property and whether any environmental agencies have actions pending.
20. Determine whether the property is located in a natural hazard area: faults, floodplains, and/or shifting soil.

© Cengage Learning

brokers or salespeople will take the description from the listing agreement; however, the best source for the description is the seller's deed.

Following the legal description, a general protection clause (found in many form contracts) should be inserted:

together with all the right, title, and interest of the seller in and to the land lying in the street in front of or adjoining the above described property, to the center lines thereof respectively.

If there is any personal property that will be conveyed with the title to the real property, that property should be listed in the contract. A clause reading, "together with the following personal property …" may be inserted along with a list of the personal property. Because a deed transfers title to real property only, title to personal property should be handled through a bill of sale, which is in effect a deed for personal property.

The personal property clause is particularly important in the purchase of multiunit dwellings. Since the standards for what constitutes a fixture may vary, it is best to list the property included if there is any doubt. Buyers should verify that the seller actually owns the personal property and whether there are any Article 9 security interests in the property. (See Chapter 5 for a full discussion of security interests.) Identification of the property by serial number provides the buyer with protection against the seller swapping out personal property items prior to closing.

If there are any title limitations such as assessments, easements, or rights-of-way, they should be noted in the contract. A typical provision reads, "subject to rights, rights-of-way, easements, including those for public utilities, water companies, alleys, and streets; assessments and other encumbrances of record." If there are restrictive covenants on the property, they too should be noted. And if the seller needs to reserve or grant an easement, a clause covering and describing that easement issue should also follow the description.

Earnest Money

As discussed earlier, **earnest money** is not required for a valid purchase contract, but it does demonstrate the buyer's good faith. The following phrases provide the necessary information for a security deposit:

1. $1,000.00 earnest deposit payable to Security Title.
2. $1,000.00 cash or check drawn to the order of _____ to be held in escrow by _____.

Financing

This element of the contract is critical. For example, suppose a buyer purchases a home for $310,000, and the earnest money is $1,000 with an additional payment of $49,000 at closing. The remaining amount to be paid is $260,000, and this $260,000 may be paid in a number of ways. The payment methods used most often are (1) assumption of an existing mortgage, (2) purchase money mortgage by the seller, (3) new financing, or (4) any combination of the first three.

Assumption of an Existing Mortgage

In order to pay the remaining $260,000 of the purchase price, the buyer could agree to assume responsibility for the $260,000 mortgage on the property, or take over the seller's payments on the property. (The problems and liabilities of assumption are discussed in Chapter 15.) A sample clause providing for an assumption is as follows:

> *As part of the total purchase price, the Buyer agrees to assume and pay the existing first mortgage on the property described above with (mortgagee) and having an approximate balance of _____ dollars ($ _____.00), with said balance to be established by Seller furnishing a mortgagee's statement with payments of principal, interest, taxes, and insurance of $ _____ per month with an annual interest rate of _____ % and running until _____, 20 _____.*

Some drafters prefer to list the exact balance at drafting and provide for an update at closing. The monthly payments, rate, and ending date of the loan must be accurate.

If approval by the mortgagee is required for an assumption, then a clause stating "subject to the mortgagee's approval" is needed. Furthermore, some states permit the mortgagee to increase the interest rate upon assumption, and the contract should disclose such an increase.

Purchase Money Mortgage by the Seller

In some land transfers, the seller will act as the lender, either by retaining title until the money is paid or by taking a mortgage on the property. In the example, if there were no mortgage to be assumed and the $260,000 still remained to be paid, the seller could finance the buyer's purchase. The language used would be as follows:

As part of the total purchase price, Seller agrees to take a purchase money note secured by a mortgage covering the above described property in the amount of _____ dollars ($ _____.00), with the principal amount of the note being that sum and the rate of interest being _____ % per annum, with both principal and interest payable in the amount of $ _____ on the _____ day of each month beginning on the _____ day of _____, 20 _____, and continuing until _____, 20 _____, when the balance shall be paid in full. It is further agreed that the Buyer will execute the necessary note and mortgage reflecting these terms at or before closing on the property.

The seller may ask the buyer to furnish a balance statement or credit report as a condition to the granting of the note and mortgage. If the seller provides financing on a residential transaction, the seller will need to comply with the federal **Truth-in-Lending Act** and make certain disclosures on financing cost (see Chapter 15).

New Financing

To complete payment of the purchase price, the buyer may agree to obtain new financing for the balance due ($260,000 in the example). At the time the parties agree to the terms of the sale, the buyer's ability to obtain financing may be unknown. This portion of the purchase contract must be phrased as a condition precedent to performance or contingency.

A condition or contingency, known as a condition precedent, is an event that must occur before the parties or one party is obligated to perform under the contract. If a condition precedent never occurs, then the parties are not obligated to perform but are released from their contractual obligations. Although the contract is binding and creates legal obligations, conditions or contingencies control whether those obligations must be performed. Following the collapse of the subprime mortgage market in 2007–2008, lenders increased their standards for borrowers' qualifications. Obtaining a mortgage loan (see Chapter 15 for more discussion) is now more a contingency than it has ever been. These clauses are critical for buyers post-2008 because the chances of not qualifying for a loan are much greater.

At a minimum, such a conditional financing clause should contain the most important terms, such as the principal amount, interest rate, maturity date, amount and frequency of installments, number of points (lender's commitment fee), and source of the financing (bank, trust company, or other source). Also, the clause should place time limitations on the buyer: "The loan application must be made within 14 days of the agreement," plus a maximum time for qualification. The following is a typical conditional financing clause:

This agreement is subject to the Buyer's securing a new first mortgage loan on the property described in this agreement in an amount of not less than _____ dollars ($ _____.00) from (bank, savings and loan, Federal Housing Administration, or other source), principal and interest payable in equal monthly payments of not more than $ _____ at an interest rate of not more than _____ % per annum, said mortgage loan being all due and payable _____ years from date of consummating this agreement.

A conditional financing clause gives the buyer a specified period within which to obtain financing and then gives the seller the opportunity to find financing for the buyer. Carefully drafted time limits and notification requirements are important in condition clauses.

Combinations of Financing Methods

The buyer can pay the purchase price through a combination of the various methods of financing. In the same example of a buyer purchasing a home for $310,000, the financing might be arranged as follows: If the property was already mortgaged for $200,000, the buyer could pay $1,000 earnest money, put $49,000 down, and assume the $200,000 mortgage; and the seller could take a second mortgage and carry the remaining $60,000. The arrangements could be written in the contract as follows:

> *The purchase price of three hundred ten thousand dollars ($310,000) is to be paid as follows:*
>
> a. *$1,000.00 Earnest money to be deposited with ABC escrow in the form of cash or check.*
>
> b. *$49,000.00 Additional down payment to be paid on or before the close of escrow.*
>
> c. *$200,000.00 Approximate balance of first mortgage with California Pacific Mortgage to be assumed by the buyer with monthly payments of principal, interest, taxes, and insurance of $ _____ due and payable on the _____ day of each month and an annual rate of _____%, with final payment being made on _____, 20 _____.*
>
> d. *$60,000.00 Buyer agrees to execute note and second mortgage to seller on the above described property in the amount of $60,000 at a rate of _____ % per annum payable in monthly installments of _____ on the _____ day of each month beginning on the _____ day of _____, 20 _____.*

CONSIDER 13.8   Highlands Plaza, Inc. entered into an agreement to purchase property from Viking Investment Corporation. The purchase was conditioned upon Highlands obtaining a $725,000 mortgage on the property. Highlands was able to obtain the $725,000 only through a first and second mortgage with different institutions, but still sought to go through with the sale. Viking refused on the grounds that the financing condition was not met. Highlands has brought suit for specific performance. What is the result? *Highlands Plaza, Inc. v. Viking Investment Corp.,* 467 P.2d 378 (Wash. 1970).   ____

Property Reports

Often, buyers contract to purchase property before actually knowing the condition (in detail) of the property. However, the contract may require, as conditions precedent to the buyer's performance, expert reports on the property.

Property Condition Reports

One such condition often inserted in the contract is a clean termite report. An example of a termite clause follows:

> *The Sellers shall, at their expense and prior to closing, furnish the Buyers with a certificate from a reputable exterminator (a) certifying that the building(s) are free and clear from infestation and any resulting damage caused by termites or other wood-boring*

insects, and (b) guaranteeing such status for a period of one year from the date of closing. If such infestation or damage is found, buyer shall have the option of terminating all rights and obligations under this contract or requiring the sellers to cure and/or repair any infestation or damage on the property caused by termites or other wood-boring insects.

Another type of report buyers may require is a soil report, particularly in circumstances where buyers are purchasing land for development and construction. The quality of the soil will control the feasibility of constructing homes or other buildings on the property.

In recent years, Phase I, II, and III investigations of environmental issues on properties have been a critical part of pre-closing activity. Buyers begin by checking federal records to determine whether the Environmental Protection Agency (see Chapter 20) has designated the site as a "Superfund" site, a land tract that needs environmental cleanup. Even without that designation, Phase II checks for soil may provide information about contamination that is not yet known to the EPA. Buying property with environmental issues subjects the buyer to liability for cleanup. (See Chapter 20 for discussion of asbestos, radon, and toxic waste.)

Geological reports can provide buyers with information about whether the property is a risk because of its location in a fault or floodplain. Other common, of often required reports, are those that determine the presence of lead paint, radon, or mold. In many states, there are statutory requirements for such inspections.

Federal Disclosure Requirements

In the 1960s, because of an increase in available leisure time and disposable income, land for the construction of recreational, second, or vacation homes became an in-demand commodity. Unfortunately, mail-order lots were offered by less-than-reputable sellers who capitalized on the high demand. Buyers were left with land that was moon-surface quality despite brochures that featured green and lush property. The land they had purchased was raw and undeveloped, often lacking roads, utilities, and water.

Because of the fraud in raw-land sales, Congress passed the **Interstate Land Sales Full Disclosure Act (ILSFDA)** (15 U.S.C. § 1701 et seq.), which regulates sellers of undeveloped properties. The basic purpose of the act is to provide full and accurate information so that buyers are in an equal bargaining position with sellers when making purchase decisions. The ILSFDA is administered by the Office of Interstate Land Sales Registration (OILSR), a division of the **Department of Housing and Urban Development (HUD)**.

Who Is Covered Under the ILSFDA?

The ILSFDA applies only to sales of land involving or affecting interstate commerce—generally, to the sale or lease of 50 or more unimproved lots in interstate commerce. The act defines what constitutes interstate commerce in a negative manner by excluding those sales it does not cover such as sales by court order, sales of cemetery plots, sales in subdivisions with fewer than 25 lots, and sales by government agencies.

The ILSFDA also provides an exemption for intrastate land developers if the developer complies with certain requirements such as an on-site inspection by buyers and disclosures about costs for utilities and roads and when they will be completed. However, if the intrastate-exempt developer advertises the project on

PRACTICAL TIP

Check state and federal regulations on land sales before developing promotional materials, listings, and contracts. Be certain you are in compliance with all filing and disclosure requirements. If you believe an exemption applies, be careful to analyze why you can claim an exemption. Be sure to control when and where ads for the development will appear.

the web, in in-flight magazines, or national publications such as the *Wall Street Journal,* the developer must then comply with ILSFDA.

Content of Filing Reports for Nonexempt Developers

Developers who are nonexempt under the ILSFDA must file a **statement of record** that is a formal disclosure that includes everything from the names of the developers to information about climate, topography, access, and availability of utilities. The statement of record must also cover the buyers' rights of rescission.

In addition to filing a statement of record, the developer must file a copy of the **property report**. Every buyer who signs a contract for purchase of the property must also be given a copy of the property report. The report is really a plain-English version of the information included in the statement of record and is set up in an easily understood question-and-answer format in a more readable manner. The developer cannot give out property reports until HUD has approved the statement of record.

Penalties for Violation of ILSFDA

Developers who fail to comply with ILSFDA disclosure requirements face both civil and criminal penalties. Buyers can recover for fraud or misrepresentation in the property report even without proving their actual reliance on the report. The criminal penalties for willful violations of the Act are $10,000 and/or imprisonment for five years. Civil penalties range from $1,000 to $1,000,000.

Condition of Premises

A contract clause on the property's condition requires the seller to deliver the property in the same condition it is in at the time of the contract. This requirement imposes a duty on the seller to maintain the property as the details of closing are worked out. In addition, any repairs the buyer wants should also be included as conditions of the buyer's performance. The following clause would be appropriate:

> *The Sellers agree to keep the property in the same condition as it exists as of the date of the contract. Sellers further agree to repair the following items: _____ _____*
> *_____. If such repairs are not completed or if the condition of the property has deteriorated, the buyers shall have the option of terminating all rights and obligations under this contract, or having said repairs made, or having conditions corrected at the sellers' expense, or requiring sellers to make said repairs or remedies.*

Implied Warranty of Habitability

Purchasers of new homes have **implied warranty of habitability** protection from builders and vendors. The cases on habitability have given us a body of law with the following warranty protections and standards:

1. It is possible for a new home to be in substantial compliance with building codes and still be uninhabitable.

2. The primary function of a new home is to shelter its inhabitants from the elements. If a new home does not keep out the elements because of a substantial defect of construction, such home is not habitable within the meaning of the implied warranty of habitability.

3. Another function of a new home is to provide its inhabitants with a reasonably safe place to live, without fear of injury to person, health, safety, or property. If a new home is not structurally sound because of a substantial defect of construction, such a home is not habitable within the meaning of the implied warranty of habitability.

4. If a new home is not aesthetically satisfying because of a defect of construction, such a defect does not make the home uninhabitable.

Most states have passed statutes that specifically dictate when warranties are made and also codify the judicially afforded protection of the implied warranties. One critical issue in warranty protection is whether the warranty of habitability extends to purchasers of homes beyond just the original purchaser from the builder. Some states limit the warranty protection to the original buyer. Some states have permitted the extension of the warranty and added a time restriction. That is, the warranty runs for an eight-year or ten-year period regardless of how many buyers have owned the home.[3]

CONSIDER 13.9   In 1992, Mark Cummings entered into a contract with Asilomar, a licensed contractor, to construct a single-family home. Asilomar substantially completed construction by June 2, 1992. Cummings then occupied the home until November 1998, when he sold the property to the Maycocks.

After moving into the home, the Maycocks experienced problems with the residence. They noticed movements in the slab and walls throughout the home, as well as buckling in walls and sagging and cracking of the garage floor. In September 2000, Tom Thomas, a civil engineer hired by the Maycocks to evaluate the property, concluded that the unusual movements in the structure indicated inadequate compaction of the backfill soils during construction.

The Maycocks filed suit against Asilomar in January 2001, alleging negligence and breach of express and implied warranties. Asilomar says that since it did not sell the home to the Maycocks it is not liable, and that there has been too much time that has passed to allow the Maycocks to recover. What should the court do with the suit? *Maycock v. Asilomar Development, Inc.,* 88 P.3d 565 (Az. App. 2004).

The following case presents an interesting issue of both what the warranty of habitability covers as well as whether buyers who are in foreclosure can still proceed to recover for warranty problems.

ARC CONST. MANAGEMENT, LLC V. ZELENAK

962 N.E.2d 692 (Ind. App. 2012)
Mold, Mildew, Mortgage Foreclosure, and a Hanging Warranty

FACTS

John and Cecilia Zelenak entered into a purchase agreement for a newly-constructed home from ARC Construction Management LLC in March 2004. In 2008, the Zelenaks filed suit for breach of the warranty of habitability alleging that the home's windows and doors were not properly installed or were defective when supplied, the lintels remained unpainted, one rafter was missing, there were exposed electrical wires, and the home experienced water intrusion

---

[3]Some states have extended the protection to mobile homes, including secondary purchasers of those homes. See *Dinsmore v. Fleetwood Homes of Tenn., Inc.,* 906 N.E.2d 186, 191 (Ind. Ct. App. 2009).

because of the leaking windows and doors that also resulted in mold and mildew damage to the home. The Zelenaks' son, John, age 8, experienced medical difficulties because of his allergies to the mold and mildew.

In 2010, the Zelenaks' home was taken in foreclosure proceedings. ARC filed a motion to dismiss the Zelenaks' suit because they lacked standing and also because there was a failure to state a claim on the basis of a breach of warranty. The trial court treated the motion to dismiss as a motion for summary judgment and determined that the Zelenaks' case could go forward for them to claim damages from breach of warranty for the time that they lived in the home. ARC appealed.

JUDICIAL OPINION
Barteau, Senior Judge

The builder-vendor of a new home provides an implied warranty of habitability to the first purchaser of the home. The implied warranty of habitability is a warranty that the home will be free from defects that substantially impair the use and enjoyment of the home. A plaintiff must prove that the defect's causation originated in the builder-vendor, and the standard of proof is reasonableness in light of the circumstances. The builder-vendor must be given notice of the alleged breach of warranty and opportunity to cure the defect.

The protection of the implied warranty of habitability also extends to subsequent purchasers of the home, but its scope is limited to latent or hidden defects.

The Zelenaks allege that the windows and doors were installed improperly or were defective when supplied, a rafter was missing, there were exposed electrical wires, and there was water intrusion. These allegations are sufficient to put ARC on notice that the Zelenaks are suing for breach of the implied warranty of habitability. Moreover, the caption of the complaint states that breach of warranty is one of the Zelenaks' claims. The caption here corroborates the fact that the operative facts pleaded in the amended complaint state a claim for breach of the implied warranty of habitability.

A "loss of use and enjoyment" of a home due to alleged defects in construction surely constitutes a "substantial impairment to the use and enjoyment" of a home due to alleged defects in construction.

ARC nonetheless argues that the Zelenaks lost standing to pursue their lawsuit when their home was foreclosed. The judicial doctrine of standing focuses on whether the complaining party is the proper party to invoke the court's power. Courts seek to assure that litigation will be actively and vigorously contested. To have standing, a party must demonstrate a personal stake in the outcome of the lawsuit and must show that he or she has sustained, or was in immediate danger of sustaining, some direct injury as a result of the conduct at issue. The Zelenaks are alleging that they sustained damages as a result of ARC's defective construction of their home. We therefore conclude that they have standing.

Affirmed.

CASE QUESTIONS

1. Explain why the Zelenaks can still recover for breach of warranty even though they have lost their home to foreclosure.
2. How long does the implied warranty of habitability run and to whom?

States that permit disclaimers of the implied warranty of habitability require that the buyers be aware of the limitation. That awareness can come from conspicuous language, actual signing of a disclaimer, or any other type of conduct that shows the buyers knew of the limitation before they purchased the home. Some states permit a disclaimer of the implied warranty only if some other type of express warranty is given in exchange. An example of a disclaimer upheld in a New York case follows:

It is further understood that THE SPONSOR MAKES NO HOUSING, MERCHANT IMPLIED WARRANTY, OR ANY OTHER WARRANTIES, EXPRESS OR IMPLIED, IN CONNECTION WITH THIS

[4]Thomas John Rhoads, "Caveat Venditor: Seller Disclosure in California Residential Real Estate Transactions," 2 *Journal of the Pacific Southwest Academy of Legal Studies in Business* 45 (1996).

PURCHASE AGREEMENT OR THE UNIT, AND ALL SUCH WARRANTIES ARE EXCLUDED EXCEPT AS PROVIDED IN THE LIMITED WARRANTY ANNEXED TO THIS PURCHASE AGREEMENT. THE EXPRESS TERMS OF THE ANNEXED LIMITED WARRANTY ARE HEREBY INCORPORATED IN AND MADE A PART OF THIS PURCHASE AGREEMENT; THEY SHALL SURVIVE THE CLOSING OF TITLE; AND THERE ARE NO OTHER WARRANTIES WHICH EXTEND BEYOND THE FACE THEREOF.

Environmental Contingency Clause

Because of so many issues regarding environmental hazards (see Chapter 20), many contracts now have environmental inspections as conditions precedent to performance. These **environmental contingency clauses** require inspection of the property for problems relating to the presence of toxic waste, radon, asbestos, and other toxins. Some states have statutory disclosure requirements. For example, New York, Rhode Island, and Florida require radon-disclosure notices in residential sales contracts. In some contracts, the cost of reducing an elevated level of radon is charged against the seller at closing. Even developers have soil testing in their purchase contracts so that radon issues are addressed before they purchase undeveloped land.

Risk of Loss

In most jurisdictions, the risk of loss for property damage is with the buyer from the time the purchase contract is executed. Buyers have an insurable interest from the time the contract is executed, and may hold a valid policy on the property even though they do not have title or possession.

However, in most cases, the seller will maintain insurance on the property until closing. To avoid the duplication of insurance and costs, purchase contracts usually provide that the seller will maintain insurance on the property until closing. The buyers can be added to the existing policy along with a notation establishing their interest in the property.

Recording the Contract

The purchase contract need not be recorded to be effective between the parties. However, without recording, liens can be attached and recorded interests would have priority over the buyer's interests. Nonetheless, recording a sales contract is uncommon. One reason for not recording is a very practical one: The contract has conditions and contingencies that might not be met; therefore, it is always subject to the buyer's default. If the recorded contract falls through, the seller is not free to sell to anyone else until a release is signed and the contract is stricken from the records. Without the defaulting purchaser's release, clearing the contract could be an expensive matter requiring a court hearing.

Closing Date and Escrow Instructions

Although the purchase contract establishes the terms of the sale, it does not contain all the details for the execution of documents, transfer of title, and payment of money. The purchase contract will provide an escrow date, such as in the following clause:

1. *Closing shall take place within _____ days of the date of this agreement.*
2. *Closing shall be on _____, 20 __*

In many states, the closing is handled by a third party (see Chapter 16), and a contract is required among the buyer, seller, and third party to properly complete the transaction. Standard forms provide for this type of escrow clause:

> *Buyer and Seller shall execute escrow instructions to fulfill the terms hereof and deliver the same to the escrow agent within 15 days of the date of execution of this agreement.*

Also, if applicable, a simple clause such as "time is of the essence in the performance of this agreement" may be included to indicate the parties' intention that delays mean the contract will not go forward. This type of clause halts the often endless extensions either party could otherwise demand for his or her execution of the contract. Without an indication of the parties' intent on time being of the essence, the courts are likely to permit extensions that may exceed the parties' original intentions on time for performance.

Apportionments

Property is not always transferred at times when taxes, insurance, and rent are due. To be absolutely fair to the parties, amounts paid for six-month or year-long blocks, such as taxes, rent, and insurance premiums, must be apportioned between the buyer and seller as of the date of transfer of title. Specific clauses may be used for the apportionment of each type of fund or a general apportionment clause may be used. The following example of a prorate clause shows the basics of allocation:

> **Taxes** *All taxes due and owing on the property shall be prorated to the date of closing, with the seller paying all taxes due to the date of closing and the buyer paying all taxes due thereafter. Any prepaid taxes shall be prorated in the same manner.*

Marketable Title

The clause on **marketable title** in the purchase contract is a condition precedent to the buyer's performance that requires the seller to deliver a certain quality of title. The clause may be very simple, requiring the seller to furnish a title insurance policy, or it may be demanding and restrictive, by requiring the seller to remove liens or obtain zoning changes. The following are examples of the title clauses:

1. *In the event title to said property herein described is found by a title insurance company to be unmarketable at the time of closing, the purchaser is excused from performance.*
2. *Title to the premises shall be good and marketable and free and clear of all liens, restrictions, easements, encumbrances, leases, tenancies, and other title objections, and shall be insurable as such at ordinary rates by any reputable title insurance company selected by the buyer.*

Marketable title is generally defined as one a prudent person would accept even with full knowledge of all facts about the property. Marketable title is a title that is free from reasonable doubt or controversy and which is not subject to any liens or encumbrances. Marketability is determined on a case-by-case basis. One general standard applied in reviewing the marketability of a title is, Would a prudent person accept this title in exchange for a fair purchase price?

In many purchase contracts, the seller is given time to cure defects in title discovered before closing. For example, if the preliminary title report shows a defect,

FIGURE 13.2
What Affects Marketable Title

AFFECTS MARKETABLE TITLE*	DOES NOT AFFECT MARKETABLE TITLE
Unrecorded easements	Zoning
Easements (unless visible)	CC&Rs
Quiet title litigation pending	Visible easements
Liens	
Leases	
Encroachments	
Mortgages	
Tenancies	
Water rights	
Tax issues	
Disputes among heirs on property rights	
Land contracts	
Prescriptive and adverse possession rights	

*The buyer could agree to accept title subject to any of these and such willingness would be noted in the contract.

the seller may be given an extension on closing of 30 or 60 days to cure the defect. Figure 13.2 provides a list of marketable title issues.

Many states have adopted the **Uniform Marketable Title Act**, which provides that a person who has unbroken record title for 50 years has marketable title. There are certain exceptions to the act, but it was designed to create a 50-year statute of limitations on various title claims and provide a mechanism whereby titles could be cleared of unrenewed and unenforced clouds.

CONSIDER 13.10   The following clause is a marketable title clause in a purchase contract.

Title is to be conveyed free from all encumbrances except: Any state of facts an accurate survey may show, provided same does not render title unmarketable.

A title search revealed that a telephone easement was recorded for the property, and that the height of the sidewalk on the property violated a city ordinance, although a waiver had been obtained for its construction. The title company offered to insure title except for the sidewalk waiver and the telephone easement. The buyers refuse to perform on the grounds of lack of marketable title. What is the result?

Remedies

Liquidated Damages

Many contracts provide that the earnest money or deposit will be used for damages in the event of a breach by one of the parties. That deposit should be large enough to cover damages. The following is an example of such a clause:

> *Should the undersigned Buyer fail to carry out this agreement, all money paid hereunder, including any additional earnest money, shall, at the option of the Seller, be forfeited as liquidated damages and shall be paid to or retained by the Seller, subject to deductions of broker's commission and disbursements, if any. In the event neither party has commenced a law suit within one (1) year after the closing date set forth herein, the broker is authorized to disburse the earnest money as liquidated damages, and if the Seller has not notified the Buyer of election to consider the earnest money as liquidated damages within six (6) months of said closing date, broker is authorized to refund all earnest money to the Buyer.*

In most cases, the courts will enforce the award of the earnest money as a valid **liquidated damages** clause; that is, a clause in which the parties agree on the amount of damages before any breach of contract occurs. However, the seller may not keep the earnest money deposit and collect actual damages in addition. Such double compensation is a penalty and void. Whatever the amount of liquidated damages the parties agree to, it must be reasonable. The courts uphold liquidated damage provisions that reflect the potential loss the seller could or does suffer because of the buyer's breach.

Because of so much litigation over liquidated damage clauses, some states have passed statutes requiring specific language to have an enforceable provision for liquidated damages. Many of these statutes also require that the parties sign or initial the clause in the contract so that a court can be certain the parties were aware of its existence. Still other states require a "second look" at liquidated damages clauses, or a review of reasonableness of the damages provided for in the contract after the breach of contract has occurred.

The following case deals with the issue of appropriate damages when there has been a breach.

PERRONCELLO V. DONAHUE

859 N.E.2d 827 (Mass. 2007)
The $150,000 Deposit As Damages

FACTS

On April 3, 1998, Joseph F. Perroncello (buyer/plaintiff) and Paul J. Donahue, Sr. (as trustee) (seller/defendant) signed a purchase and sale contract for property at 198 Beacon Street in Boston for $2,250,000. The contract contained a clause that provided that *"acceptance of deed by the BUYER shall be deemed to be a full performance and discharge of every agreement and obligation herein contained or expressed."* It also contained a liquidated damages clause providing that if *"the BUYER shall fail to fulfill the BUYER's agreements herein, all deposits made*

hereunder by the BUYER shall be retained by the SELLER and this shall be SELLER's sole remedy at law or in equity." The buyer paid a deposit of $150,000. The sale was to close by May 6, 1998, but the agreement provided that the buyer could seek one 30-day extension (until June 5), which he did, during which time he would be obligated to pay the seller's carrying costs of up to $500 per day. Carrying costs included *"seller's financing costs, taxes, insurance and the like."*

The contract did not include a mortgage contingency clause, and recited that time was of the essence.

As of June 4, 1998, Perroncello had not finalized the mortgage financing he needed to purchase the property. His attorney sent a request to Donahue's attorney seeking an extension of the closing to June 16. Donahue's attorney responded on June 5 with a letter stating that Donahue was ready to deliver the deed on June 5. Perroncello asserts that Donahue told him to continue working with his bank to secure the mortgage and that any correspondence sent by the attorney stating that June 5 was the deadline should be disregarded. On June 12, Donahue's attorney sent written notice to Perroncello's attorney that, no closing having occurred, the contract was breached and the deposit forfeited. Perroncello and Donahue had further discussions and meetings about the real estate through the month of June. On June 23, 1998, the bank approved Perroncello's mortgage, and he notified Donahue. Thereafter, Donahue did not return Perroncello's telephone calls, and put a "For Sale" sign on the property.

On June 30, 1998, Perroncello filed a complaint in the Superior Court for breach of contract, specific performance, deceit, and conversion, and also sought both a restraining order preventing the seller from marketing the property, his $150,000 deposit returned, and a *lis pendens*. Donahue counterclaimed for abuse of process, breach of contract, and unfair and deceptive trade practice.

The trial court granted summary judgment against the seller and the Appeals Court reversed. The buyer appealed.

JUDICIAL OPINION

Cordy, Justice

It is a settled principle that when the purchaser of real property breaches a contract for sale, the seller may retain the property and bring an action for damages or may request specific performance of the contract by offering to perform, and bringing an action for the purchase price. If the purchase and sale contract contains a provision awarding liquidated damages to the seller in the event of the purchaser's breach, that clause will be enforced so long as "at the time the agreement was made, potential damages were difficult to determine and the clause was a reasonable forecast of damages expected to occur in the event of a breach." *Kelly v. Marx,* 428 Mass. 877, 878, 705 N.E.2d 1114 (1999). Liquidated damages clauses providing that a real estate seller may retain the buyer's deposit on breach are a common real estate practice recognized in Massachusetts.

When seeking specific performance of a contract, the seller offers to surrender title to the property and collect the purchase price. In bringing an action for damages on the breach of the contract, the seller proposes to retain the property and have his compensation in damages. While these remedies may not be inconsistent in the sense that they are both premised on the validity of the contract, ordinarily a seller is not entitled to seek both remedies; the retention of a deposit as liquidated damages is an alternative to specific performance, not an additional remedy.

The seller directs our attention to, and the Appeals Court largely relied on, our decision in *Kelly v. Marx, supra.* Such reliance is unwarranted. The *Kelly* case is inapposite. There, the judge permitted the seller to keep the buyer's deposit as liquidated damages following the buyer's failure to tender payment for the real estate. Specific performance was sought by neither party. Rather, after the buyer's breach, the seller found another buyer who purchased the property for $5,000 more than the original contract price. The question presented was whether it was appropriate to enforce the liquidated damages clause of the contract, where the seller ultimately sold the property at a higher price to another party, thereby suffering no loss. We held that the liquidated damages clause was enforceable because potential damages were difficult to determine at the time of the contract formation, and the amount agreed to was a reasonable forecast of damages in the event of a future breach, at that time. In so holding, we rejected the "second look" approach to liquidated damages. We did not imply that liquidated damages could be obtained, in addition to specific performance from the buyer.

Here, the seller sought an order from the judge directing the buyer to purchase the property by September 15, 1998, at the agreed on purchase price, and the buyer complied. The only additional damages the seller was entitled to seek under the contract were for the carrying costs he incurred as a result of the delay between the expected date of performance and the time of actual conveyance. These carrying costs were separately provided for in the contract and ancillary to its performance. The obligation to pay the costs was triggered by the buyer's election to delay the closing for thirty days. This award is not inconsistent with specific performance. *Restatement (Second) of Contracts,* at § 378 comment d ("A party who seeks specific performance or an injunction may … be entitled to damages to compensate him for delay in performance").

The law of contracts is intended to give an injured party the benefit of the bargain, not the benefit of the bargain and a windfall. To award liquidated damages against the buyer for his failure to close and also specific performance to the seller requiring the buyer to acquire the property by a date certain at the contracted price, would violate the fundamental principles of contract law.

The order granting summary judgment to the buyer on the issue of liquidated damages is affirmed.

CASE QUESTIONS

1. List the mistakes the parties made in their purchase contract as well as in their conduct between the time of the contract and the litigation.
2. Does the court distinguish between and among actual damages, specific performance, and liquidated damages?
3. What is the rule on "second looks" on damage clauses in real estate purchase contracts in Massachusetts?

CONSIDER 13.11   On September 4, 1996, Gable Ridge and Barberry Homes entered into a purchase and sale agreement for the sale of 18 undeveloped house lots. Under the agreement, Barberry Homes would purchase the lots from Gable Ridge in three phases, with closing dates on October 21, 1996; June 1, 1997; and October 15, 1997. Six lots were to change hands at the first closing, three at the second, and nine at the third. The total purchase price for the lots was $2,700,000, or $150,000 per lot.

The agreement provided the following if Barberry Homes breached: "If the BUYER shall fail to fulfill the BUYER's agreements herein, all deposits made hereunder by the BUYER shall be retained by the SELLER as liquidated damages and this shall be the SELLER's sole remedy at law and equity."

Before the first closing date, the parties executed an amendment to the agreement. In the amendment, the parties agreed that Barberry Homes would pay $50,000 less than the previously agreed-to price for one of the six lots (Lot 16) set to change hands on the first closing date. The amendment, however, did not lower the total purchase price. Rather, the $50,000 was to be reallocated over the remaining 17 lots being sold, so that the individual lot price for the remaining lots would become $152,942, rather than $150,000.

On October 21, 1996, the parties closed on the first six lots. Barberry Homes paid $100,000 for one lot (Lot 16) and $152,941 for each of the five other lots, for a total of $864,705. In February 1997, Peter Gallipeau, president of Barberry Homes resigned his position. In March 1997, David Carter took over as president of Barberry Homes. On June 1, 1997, the second scheduled closing date under the agreement, Barberry Homes failed to close on the next set of lots. Carter decided not to close on the remaining lots.

Gable Ridge then took Barberry Homes' $50,000 deposit as damages. Barberry Homes says that the $50,000 is a penalty because Gable Ridge was able to sell the lots to others for more than the original agreed-upon contract price. Is Barberry Homes correct? *Carroll v. Barberry Homes, Inc.,* 10 Mass.L.Rptr. 668, 1999 WL 1204020 (Mass. Super. 1999).

Actual Damages

The decision to keep the earnest money as damages is often left to the discretion of the seller. The seller may elect to proceed and collect the actual damages sustained by the buyer's breach. Such damages could include all the monies expended by the seller in preparing for closing, such as the cost of reports. It could also include a commission to the broker or lost rental value if the property remains vacant or if a lease is terminated in anticipation of the buyer's takeover.

Likewise, the buyer may opt to collect actual damages for the seller's breach, which could include the costs of preparation for closing in the form of loan origination or commitment fees, appraisal fees, survey costs, and so on.

The party asking for actual damages has the burden of establishing the amount of the damages and that those damages were a result of the other party's breach.

The **Uniform Land Transactions Act (ULTA)**, drafted for passage by the states in 1975, has several formulas for determining actual damages in the event of a breach of a land sales contract. For example, a seller reselling at a lower price recovers from the breaching buyer the difference in price plus the incidental costs of resale.

Specific Performance

Specific performance is a remedy for buyers that requires the seller to go forward with the transaction according to the terms of the contract.

Generally, specific performance is not awarded to sellers who have breaching buyers; in such cases, sellers are left to the remedies of actual damages or the collection of liquidated damages.

Rescission

Rescission entitles the parties to rescind their agreement and return to the positions they were in before they entered into the contract. The buyer is given back any compensation paid and the seller is no longer obligated to sell the land. Rescission is most commonly used in cases where the seller has misrepresented the property or its condition.

MISREPRESENTATION

Misrepresentation is a defense to the formation of a contract. Misrepresentation occurs when the seller has misled the buyer about the nature or condition of the property. Misrepresentation can be innocent; that is, one party, through misinformation or lack of knowledge, provides the other party with inaccurate and misleading information. Misrepresentation can also be fraudulent, as when one party intentionally provides inaccurate information for purposes of inducing a sale. Finally, misrepresentation can occur because of a party's failure to disclose information that would have affected the purchasing decision. Misrepresentation allows the party affected to rescind the contract. However, all types of misrepresentation require proof of the following:

1. A statement of material fact has been made or omitted—the type of information involved would affect the buying decision.
2. There is reliance on the statement of fact—the buyer uses the fact in making the decision of whether to buy (see earlier discussion under "as is" clauses for disclosures about patent and latent defects).
3. There is detriment—the buyer suffers through loss of property value or cost of repair.

CONSIDER 13.12   Decide whether the following statements would or would not be a basis for misrepresentation in a real estate contract.

a. "The test scores for this area's public schools are the highest in the state."

b. "This roof has a 30-year warranty."

c. "This well could never run dry."

d. "That easement is not recorded, but it's valid."

e. "This property was certified in 2006 as termite-free."

f. "The crime rate is very low here."

g. "The city has no plans for a stadium next to this house."

h. "The value on this house just keeps going up."

i. "Basements in this area don't leak."

The next case illustrates the application of the three elements of misrepresentation in a case in which the misrepresentation was a fraudulent one about a latent defect in the property.

REED V. KING

193 Cal. Rptr. 130 (1983)
The Scene of a Crime As a Residence

FACTS

Dorris Joni Reed (plaintiff/appellant) purchased a house from Robert King through his real estate agents (defendants/respondents). No one informed Reed that a woman and her four children had been murdered in the house 10 years earlier. When Reed learned of the murders, she brought suit seeking rescission and damages. The trial court dismissed the suit and Reed appealed.

JUDICIAL OPINION

Blease, Associate Justice

In the sale of a house, must the seller disclose it was the site of a multiple murder? Neither King nor his agents told Reed that a woman and her four children were murdered there. However, it seems "truth will come to light; murder cannot be hid long." (Shakespeare, *Merchant of Venice*, Act II, Scene II.) Reed learned of the gruesome episode from a neighbor after the sale.

King and his real estate agent knew about the murders and knew the event materially affected the market value of the house when they listed it for sale. They represented to Reed the premises were in good condition and fit for an "elderly lady" living alone. They did not disclose the fact of the murders.

At some point King asked a neighbor not to inform Reed of that event. Nonetheless, after Reed moved in neighbors informed her no one was interested in purchasing the house because of the stigma. Reed paid $75,000, but the house is only worth $65,000 because of its past.

Does Reed's pleading state a cause of action? Concealed within this question is the nettlesome problem of the duty of disclosure of blemishes on real property which are not physical defects or legal impairments to use.

Reed seeks to state a cause of action sounding in contract, i.e., rescission, or in tort, i.e., deceit. In either event her allegations must reveal a fraud. "The elements of actual fraud, whether as the basis of the remedy in contract or tort, may be stated as follows: There must be (1) *a false representation* or concealment of a material fact (or, in some cases, an opinion) susceptible of knowledge, (2) made with *knowledge* of its falsity or without sufficient knowledge on the subject to warrant a representation, (3) with the *intent* to induce the person to whom it is made to act upon it; and such person must, (4) act in *reliance* upon the representation, (5) to his damage."

The trial court perceived the defect in Reed's complaint to be a failure to allege concealment of a material fact. "Concealment" and "material" are legal conclusions concerning the effect of the issuable facts pled. As appears, the analytic pathways to these conclusions are intertwined.

Concealment is a term of art which includes mere non-disclosure when a party has a duty to disclose. Reed's complaint reveals only non-disclosure despite the allegation King asked a neighbor to hold his peace. There is no allegation the attempt at suppression was a cause in fact of Reed's ignorance. Accordingly, the critical question is: does the seller have a duty to disclose here? Resolution of this question depends on the materiality of the fact of the murders.

In general, a seller of real property has a duty to disclose: "where the seller knows of facts *materially* affecting the value or desirability of the property which are known or accessible only to him and also knows that such facts are not known to, or within the reach of the diligent attention and observation of the buyer, the seller is under a duty to disclose them to the buyer." This broad statement of duty has led one commentator to conclude: "'The ancient maxim *caveat emptor* ('let the buyer beware') has little or no application to California real estate transactions.'"

Whether information "is of sufficient materiality to affect the value or desirability of the property ... depends on the facts of the particular case." Materiality "is a question of law, and is part of the concept of right to rely or justifiable reliance." Accordingly the term is essentially a label affixed to a normative conclusion. Three considerations bear on this legal conclusion: the gravity of the harm inflicted by non-disclosure; the fairness of imposing a duty of discovery on the buyer as an alternative to compelling disclosure; and its impact on the stability of contracts if rescission is permitted.

Numerous cases have found non-disclosure of physical defects and legal impediments to use of real property are material. However, to our knowledge, no prior real estate sale case has faced an issue of non-disclosure of the kind presented here. Should this variety of ill-repute be required to be disclosed? Is this a circumstance where "non-disclosure of the fact amounts to a failure to act in good faith and in accordance with reasonable standards of fair dealing[?]"

The paramount argument against an affirmative conclusion is it permits the camel's nose of unrestrained irrationality admission to the tent. If such an "irrational" consideration is permitted as a basis of rescission, the stability of all conveyances will be seriously undermined. Any fact that might disquiet the enjoyment of some segment of the buying public may be seized upon by a disgruntled purchaser to void a bargain. In our view, keeping this genie in the bottle is not as difficult a task as these arguments assume. We do not view a decision allowing Reed to survive a demurrer in these unusual circumstances as endorsing the materiality of facts predicating peripheral, insubstantial, or fancied harms.

The murder of innocents is highly unusual in its potential for so disturbing buyers they may be unable to reside in a home where it has occurred. This fact may foreseeably deprive a buyer of the intended use of the purchase. Murder is not such a common occurrence that buyers should be charged with anticipating and discovering this disquieting possibility. Accordingly, the fact is not one for which a duty of inquiry and discovery can sensibly be imposed upon the buyer.

Reed alleges the fact of the murders has a quantifiable effect on the market value of the premises. We cannot say this allegation is inherently wrong and, in the pleading posture of the case, we assume it to be true. If information known or accessible only to the seller has a significant and measurable effect on market value and, as is alleged here, the seller is aware of this effect, we see no principled basis for making the duty to disclose turn upon the character of the information. Physical usefulness is not and never has been the sole criterion of valuation. Stamp collections and gold speculation would be insane activities if utilitarian considerations were the sole measure of value.

Reputation and history can have a significant effect on the value of realty. "George Washington slept here" is worth something, however physically inconsequential that consideration may be. Ill-repute or "bad will" conversely may depress the value of property. Failure to disclose such a negative fact where it will have a foreseeably depressing effect on income expected to be generated by a business is tortious. Some cases have held that *unreasonable* fears of the potential buying public that a gas or oil pipeline may rupture may depress the market value of land and entitle the owner to incremental compensation in eminent domain.

Whether Reed will be able to prove her allegation the decade-old multiple murder has a significant effect on market value we cannot determine. If she is able to do so by competent evidence she is entitled to a favorable ruling on the issues of materiality and duty to disclose. Her demonstration of objective tangible harm would still the concern that permitting her to go forward will open the floodgates to rescission on subjective and idiosyncratic grounds.

A more troublesome question would arise if a buyer in similar circumstances were unable to plead or establish a significant and quantifiable effect on market value. However, this question is not presented in the posture of this case. Reed has not alleged the fact of the murders has rendered the premises useless to her as a residence. As currently pled, the gravamen of her case is pecuniary harm. We decline to speculate on the abstract alternative.

Reversed.

CASE QUESTIONS

1. What happened in the house? How did Reed discover it?
2. What effect did it have on the value?
3. Is concealment fraud? When?
4. Give examples of other types of disclosures that would be necessary.[5]

CONSIDER 13.13   In 1989, Jeffrey and Patrice Stambovsky bought an 18-room mansion in Nyack, New York, for $650,000. They talked with a local architect who said, "Oh, you're buying the haunted house." The Victorian house has had gifts left by ghosts and the Amazing Kreskin has sought to hold a séance there. The Stambovskys were not given this information before they signed the contract, and they now wish to have their earnest money returned ($32,500). In fact, the house had been written up in *Reader's Digest* in 1977; in the article, the owner described a ghost who looked like Santa Claus. In a description in a house tour book, the house description read: "riverfront Victorian—with ghost." Mr. Stambovsky feels he and his wife are the victims of "ectoplasmic fraud." Is he correct? *Stambovsky v. Ackley,* 572 N.Y.S.2d 672 (1991)[6]. ■

Disclosures, Home Warranty Policies, and "As Is"

The issues related to disclosures, warranties, and resulting liability have resulted in sellers taking several different approaches to their contracts. Some sellers are selling their homes "as is" (see Chapter 12); that is, they are disclosing that there may be defects but that they are not responsible for them, and buyers have been given the opportunity to inspect the property for any problems. In addition, many buyers are purchasing a warranty policy for their homes so that, should problems arise, they will have insurance protection for repairs and renovation.

The earlier discussion of warranties focused on builders and developers and the judicial or statutory requirement of a warranty on construction of the house. This discussion focuses on protection for secondary buyers as when listing signs placed on property offer to buyers, "One-year warranty available." This protection is for the buyer and is a form of insurance that covers defects and problems on the home for one year from closing. Most policies for used homes will run for a period of a year, but varying coverage exists. The buyer should specify in the contract

---

[5]Serial killer Jeffrey Dahmer's apartment building was so stigmatized that a community redevelopment group bought it, razed the building, and, to this day, the lot remains vacant. Likewise, John Wayne Gacy's home, a site of burial for his child victims, was razed. The Ramsey home in Boulder, Colorado, where Jon Benet Ramsey was killed, sold for nearly $2 million less than its value. Likewise, Nicole Brown Simpson's condo sold for $200,000 less than its market value. The Rancho Santa Fe home where the Heaven's Gate cult committed mass suicide sold for less than half its value. Roman Polanski's home, where Charles Manson and his followers killed his actress wife, has never been on the market since the director fled the country following charges that Polanski committed statutory rape in the house. On the other hand, the Miami mansion of Gianni Versace (where he was shot and killed) brought the highest selling price ever in the area. Catherine Rempell, "For Sale: Scene of a Crime," *USA Today,* August 7, 2006. pp. 1A and 2A. "The Scandal Effect," *Wall Street Journal,* August 4, 2006, pp. W1, W6.

[6]The Hudson Valley of New York is infamous for its tales of haunted houses, including the alleged home of Ichabod Crane, Washington Irving's legendary character. Kathryn Matthews, "This Old House Has Ghosts," *New York Times,* October 13, 2006, pp. D1, D4.

what type of protection is sought. Another protection could come through the seller agreeing to warrant the property. A sample seller's warranty clause follows:

> *The Seller warrants that the plumbing, heating, air-conditioning, and electrical systems in the buildings on the property are in good working order and condition, and will be in good working order and condition at the time of closing. In the event such items are not in working order at closing, the Seller agrees to deduct the cost of repair or replacement from the amount due from the buyer at settlement.*

CONSIDER 13.14   Elm Retirement Center, LP, agreed to buy a Scottsdale home based on advertisements for the property that stated that the home had 3,792 square feet of living space. Elm's purchase contract with Callaway, the owner, did not specify the size of the home, but in boldface type provided, "BUYER IS AWARE THAT ANY REFERENCE TO THE SQUARE FOOTAGE OF THE PREMISES, BOTH THE REAL PROPERTY (LAND) AND IMPROVEMENTS THEREON, IS APPROXIMATE. IF SQUARE FOOTAGE IS A MATERIAL MATTER TO THE BUYER, IT MUST BE VERIFIED DURING THE INSPECTION PERIOD." Elm's complaint alleges the home contains only 3,605 square feet and that the difference from the advertised square footage is material. Elm's filed suit for misrepresentation and breach of warranty. Is Elm's entitled to recover? Explain your answer. *ELM Retirement Center, LP v. Callaway*, 246 P.3d 938 (Ariz. App. 2010).

PRACTICAL TIP

Before buying property, talk to the neighbors. Find out about noises and check with others for the history of the property. Have experts check the physical condition of the property for everything from leaky roofs to malfunctioning air conditioners.

PRACTICAL TIP

Issues of disclosure often conflict with sellers' and brokers' duties under the Fair Housing Act (see Chapter 19). In other words, answering a question may result in a pattern of not selling certain properties. Some real estate agents answer buyers' questions about stigmatized (psychologically impacted) property as follows: "It is the policy of our firm not to answer inquiries of this nature one way or the other. In addition, any type of response to such inquiries by me or other agents may be a violation of federal fair housing laws. If you believe that this information is relevant to your decision to buy the property, you must pursue this investigation on your own."

Disclosure in Commercial Property Sales

The sales of commercial properties present additional challenges for brokers and sellers in terms of disclosure, because the buyers will have questions about the level of business activity, profits, and revenues. Sellers and real estate brokers should not make representations about income (see Chapter 10) or provide assurances about future financial performance. Sellers and brokers are best served, as are their buyers, if they refer those buyers to other sources and experts for purposes of determining the potential revenue flow in a commercial property. Sellers should instruct brokers who represent them not to make any representations about income, profits, and revenues. *Homestead Group, LLC v. Bank of Tennessee*, 307 S.W.3d 746 (Tenn. Ct. App. 2009).

Remedies for Misrepresentation

Remedies for misrepresentation include rescission, actual damages, and, if fraudulent, punitive damages. If a real estate agent or broker colludes with a party to defraud or misrepresent, the agent or broker faces license suspension or revocation.

Disclosure Statutes

Because of many problems with innocent and intentional misrepresentation in the sale of property, the National Association of Realtors and other groups worked together to have states adopt disclosure laws. In most states, sellers are required to fill out questionnaires to disclose any known defects, including problems with plumbing, the electrical system, walls, floors, insulation, and the home's foundation. Over half of the states recommend such disclosure. Known as

transfer disclosure statements (TDS), these forms, in the states where they are required, must be presented to potential buyers before they enter into a purchase contract. The result of these mandatory disclosure forms has been growth of real estate inspection firms and the warranty industry that affords buyers protection for defects that arise despite all the caution in inspection and disclosure. In addition to finding defects, the inspections determine compliance with code, for example, the presence of smoke alarms, carbon monoxide detectors, or pool fencing.

The duty of disclosure has also been recognized by many courts regardless of statutory obligations, and all relevant information that would affect a decision to purchase should be disclosed by the seller. An evolving area of disclosure debate is the disclosure required when the property being sold was used as a production facility for methamphetamine, that is, was a so-called "meth lab." Even in those states that protect sellers from failing to disclose criminal activity, the presence of "meth labs" on the property must be disclosed because of possible health risks.[7]

ETHICAL ISSUE

Roberts purchased a home through a real estate agent. When she learned that one of the sellers had died of hepatitis and the other from pneumonia, she suspected that the sellers had AIDS and she brought suit against their estates and the realty for their failure to disclose this psychologically important information about the property. Should Roberts be permitted to rescind the contract? Do you think she has the right to that information about the sellers? If you were the real estate agent, would you feel an obligation to disclose such information? What response is appropriate in those states where the agent is prohibited from disclosing whether the seller had AIDS?

PRACTICAL TIP

Avoid misrepresentation issues:

1. *Don't state unverified information.*
2. *Don't predict the future for property conditions or equipment (e.g., "This air conditioner will last 10 years").*
3. *Get independent confirmation of material information.*
4. *Carefully and visually inspect the property.*
5. *Document what you say and the questions you answer.*
6. *Know the "red flags" of real property (see Chapter 12 and 19).*
7. *Disclose all material issues, defects, and conditions.*

Psychological Disclosure Statutes

A new form of disclosure statute has resulted from cases such as *Reed* and because of additional issues that could have a psychological impact on the buyer and possible resulting reduction in value.[8] More appropriately named "nondisclosure statutes," these laws shield sellers and their agents from liability for the nondisclosure of murder, suicide, or other felonies committed on the property, or that a resident or former resident suffers from AIDS (see Chapter 12 for more discussion of broker/agent responsibilities regarding these types of disclosures). Some states require disclosure for three years and then protect sellers and real estate agents against nondisclosure.

Currently, nearly all states have some form of statute on nondisclosure of information that could have a psychological impact and on liability shields. However, the statutes often leave open the question as to the seller's or agent's response if the buyer specifically asks a question about such activity on the

---

[7]A.R.S. § 32-2156 exempts sellers from liability for failure to disclose criminal activity, but Arizona mandates disclosure if meth labs existed on the property. A.R.S. § 32-101.

[8]For example, Connecticut's statute provides (at Conn. Gen. Stat. 20-329cc) "'psychologically impacted' means ... but is not limited to: (1) the fact that an occupant of real property is, or was at any time suspected to be, infected or has been infected with the human immunodeficiency syndrome, as defined in section 19a-581; or (2) the fact that the property was at any time suspected to have been the site of a homicide, other felony or suicide."

property. Most legal experts agree that if there is a specific question from a buyer, the seller or his agent cannot lie about the property and would be required to disclose such information.

CONSIDER 13.15 Must a seller disclose to a buyer that his neighbors are unusually noisy, that is, that their parties sometimes cause the seller's house to shake? *Shapiro v. Sutherland,* 76 Cal. Rptr.2d 101 (1998). ▬

CAUTIONS AND CONCLUSIONS

To be certain a real estate contract is complete and enforceable, the parties must not only follow the basic contract rules for formation, they must be certain they have covered all the contingencies and issues. This chapter has explained the most common pitfalls in real estate contracts, which include

- the danger of multiple offers and having two parties accept
- the need to have minds meet on all the terms, whether material or immaterial
- contingency clauses so that performance is not required until certain events occur, such as the buyer obtaining financing, the seller being able to deliver marketable title, or experts concluding the property is termite-free
- the need for care in the following:
    a. Details of transfer, such as how the buyer will take title, how the rent and taxes will be apportioned,

who will carry insurance until closing, and how the condition of the property will be preserved.

b. Providing for damages through a liquidated damages clause so that the earnest money becomes the damages for breach.

c. Adequate disclosure about the property's nature and history that will include everything from soil conditions to whether there was a murder there.

d. Federal law compliance with the ILSDFA and the Truth-in-Lending laws.

A contract for the sale and purchase of real estate may seem like a simple exchange of title, but it is a complex transaction with many layers that requires careful negotiation and drafting.

KEY TERMS

acceptance, 323
consideration, 328
counteroffer, 319
Department of Housing and Urban Development (HUD), 337
earnest money, 334
environmental contingency clauses, 341
implied warranty of habitability, 338

Interstate Land Sales Full Disclosure Act (ILSFDA), 337
liquidated damages, 344
marketable title, 342
misrepresentation, 347
offer, 317
option, 319
property report, 338
rescission, 347

specific performance, 347
statement of record, 338
transfer disclosure statement (TDS), 352
Truth-in-Lending Act, 335
Uniform Land Transactions Act (ULTA), 347
Uniform Marketable Title Act, 343

CHAPTER PROBLEMS

1. Eileen Norkunas owns a residence at 835 McHenry Street, Baltimore City, Maryland. Robert and Hope Grove and Robert and Rebecca Cochran approached Ms. Norkunas and expressed their interest in purchasing the property. Assisted by a real estate

agent, the four hopeful buyers gave Ms. Norkunas a handwritten letter of intent together with a check for a $5,000 deposit. The text of the letter of intent is as follows:

3/7/04

LETTER OF INTENT

We, Rebecca Cochran, Robert Cochran, Hope Grove and Robert Grove, Buyers—offer to buy 835 McHenry Street, Baltimore, Md. 21230 for $162,000. Payment by $5,000 check, this date and $157,000 by certified or cashiers funds not later than April 17, 2004.

A standard form Maryland Realtors® contract will be delivered to Seller within 48 hours. Seller to pay only 1/2 normal transfer taxes and a 3% commission to Long & Foster. All other costs of closing to be paid by buyers.

The contract will contain a financing requirement for buyers, but buyers will guarantee closing and not invoke the financing contingency.

We will delete the standard home inspection contingency.

[written in margin:] Buyer to honor Seller's lease and offer tenants any renewal up to 12 months.

The letter of intent was signed by the Groves and the Cochrans under "Buyers," by Ms. Norkunas under "Seller," and by Brian Best under "Agent."

Within a day or so after signing the letter of intent, Ms. Norkunas received a package of documents from the buyers' agent with a cover letter that stated:

Dear Ms. Norkunas,

It was a pleasure meeting you yesterday. Enclosed with this folder are all the documents needed to complete the sale of your home. The basic Real Estate contract, along with a couple of documents I need you to fill out to ratify the contract. The first is a Disclosure/Disclaimer. You can either fill out the first 3 pages (the Disclosure) or you can just sign the last page (the Disclaimer). Also included is a property fact sheet. This is just basic information on the property that needs to accompany the contract. The Groves and the Cochrans are so excited about your home. If you have ANY questions please feel free to call me or have someone near you look over the contract. Rest assure[d] that we want this to go as smooth as possible for you and both the Groves and Cochrans asked me to tell you if there is anything they can do please feel free to ask. I look forward to hearing from you.

You can either fax me the contract and disclaimer back or I[']ll include a Fed-X envelope for you to send back.

Thank you again[.]

The package of documents ("the buyers' offer") contained a number of pre-printed forms, including a form titled "Residential Contract of Sale," published by the Maryland Association of Realtors®, together with 10 or more form addenda. Many of the addenda appear to be forms. Some of the documents had blanks filled in or altered by the buyers. The price and description of the property were the same as in the letter of intent. The form financing contingency had been filled in with details. A separate Property Inspections contingency addendum

was included, but appears to have been struck through as promised in the letter of intent.

Ms. Norkunas never did return the documents to the buyers or their agent. Nor did she otherwise communicate to the buyers or their agent that their offer had been accepted. After a week or so had passed, the buyers were eventually told that Ms. Norkunas was "taking the property off the market."

The buyers filed suit seeking specific performance of the letter of intent. Ms. Norkunas had, in the privacy of her home, signed the documents, striking through two paragraphs relating to the financing contingency, and making some other marks on the documents. At her deposition, Ms. Norkunas explained:

I was probably going through it at the time and kind of getting overwhelmed the more I went through it and questioning parts and kind of scratching out some parts. This was what I thought was going to be my counteroffer. I signed what I thought was going to be a counteroffer, and then it just got so overwhelming, it was too much. It was just too much.

Was a contract formed? Explain how all of the parties' interactions worked in terms of offer and acceptance. *Nortkunas v. Cochran,* 895 A.2d 1101 (Ct. Md. App. 2006).

2. Reese Aherns signed a contract to purchase a mountain home from Mr. and Mrs. Jack Johnson. The contract included the following condition (handwritten in an addendum signed by both parties):

Closing is subject to buyer's inspection of property by him and his designated specialist and complete satisfaction of specialist with property condition.

Aherns's specialist inspected the property and said he thought the roof would need to be replaced in a few years. He also felt some wood near the front of the cabin should be replaced. Aherns demanded that the Johnsons fix these items or he would not close. The Johnsons maintain they did not agree to any repairs; the condition was for Aherns' protection so that he could opt out of the agreement. Aherns has threatened to sue for breach of contract. Who should win?

3. Determine which of the following defects would be covered under the implied warranty of habitability (assuming new-home purchasers):

a. Defective air-conditioning system
b. Use of ungalvanized nails in walls
c. Variations in the color of carpet (one color ordered)
d. Sagging roof
e. Lack of insulation

4. On February 14, 1998, Therese Dorenbach entered into an agreement with Daniel F. Stahr and Georgia A. Stahr to sell them her property at 7800 N.W. 70th Street, Malcolm, Nebraska. The Stahrs were given a right of first refusal in the property next to the purchased property when and if Mrs. Dorenbach received an offer for that adjoining land. Mrs. Dorenbach's real estate broker sent a letter to the Stahrs telling them that once an offer came in, they would be given 24 hours to match or exceed the purchase price.

   On June 27, 2005, Wesley J. Jones submitted an offer to Dorenbach to purchase the property. Jones offered Dorenbach $550,000 for the property, and his offer was conditioned upon his ability to obtain a $400,000 loan. On June 28, Dorenbach accepted Jones's offer. The next day, the Stahrs' agent delivered a purchase agreement to Dorenbach stating that they wished to purchase the property for the same price. The Stahrs offered to pay the purchase price entirely in cash, and inserted the following language in an addendum to their purchase agreement: "Buyer [the Stahrs] reserves the right to assign this contract to a third party prior to closing."

   Dorenbach's attorney informed the Stahrs that their offer was not acceptable, given that the offer provided for the Stahrs to be able to assign the contract to a third party prior to closing. The Stahrs then notified Dorenbach that they would stand on the exercise of their right of first refusal made in response to Jones's initial offer and that they were ready, willing, and able to close on the purchase of the property. Dorenbach did not sell the property to Jones or the Stahrs. The Stahrs filed suit seeking to have the property conveyed to them. Dorenbach says the Stahrs made a counteroffer. Who is correct and why? *Jones v. Stahr*, 746 N.W.2d 394 (Neb. App. 2008).

5. Theresa S. Polk owned 181 acres of land in Polk County, and she listed the property for sale with a real estate agent at a sale price of $1,299,000. On January 24, 2005, Avon made an offer to buy the property. Polk rejected the offer by making counter-offers on February 2 and February 3, 2005. There were some differences between the two counteroffers. However, both counteroffers provided that Avon had until 5 p.m. on February 7, 2005, to accept or reject them: "Seller counters Buyer's offer (to accept the counteroffer, Buyer must sign or initial the counteroffered terms and deliver a copy of the acceptance to the Seller by 5:00 p.m. on 2/7/05)."

   On February 4, 2005, Avon made another offer, which altered the material terms of the counteroffers. Polk did not respond to the February 4 offer, and Avon signed both of Polk's counteroffers and delivered them before the February 7 deadline. Avon also delivered a $25,000 deposit check to Polk's attorney, who accepted the check but eventually wrote "VOID" on it instead of cashing it.

   When Polk refused to perform her duties under the signed counteroffers, Avon filed a suit seeking specific performance.

   Was there a contract formed? In determining the answer, be sure to do a chronological listing of all the back-and-forth between Polk and Avon. *Polk v. BHRGU Avon Properties, LLC*, 946 So.2d 1120 (Fla. App. 2006).

6. Otto and Frank Mattuschek owned a ranch in Montana consisting of 3,540 acres. Carnell, a real estate broker, discovered their interest in selling the ranch, and the following instrument was executed:

PLAINTIFF'S EXHIBIT "A"

APPOINTMENT OF AGENT

I hereby appoint E. F. Carnell of Lewistown, Montana, whose office is located in said City and State, my agent with the exclusive right to sell the following property:

Our Ranch property 3540 acres, T.23 & 22-R-19 & 20-Fergus County Mont.

For the Sum of $30,000.

Conditions and terms of the sale are as follows:

Cash to seller. Possession Dec. 1, 1953, seller retain 5% landowner Royalty. Seller pay 1953 taxes, seller transfers all lease land to buyer.

And I agree to furnish a title as outlined in the following paragraph:

A. An abstract of title showing a good merchantable title to said property together with a warranty deed properly executed.

Said sale may be made for a less amount if hereafter authorized by me; you are further authorized to receive a deposit on the sale price. I agree to pay a commission of $1,000—on the sale price and the commission shall be payable as soon as the sale is made and a down payment has been made, or sale price paid in full at the time of sale, and, or as soon as a binder fee has been collected on the sale, whichever be first.

This authorization is to remain in effect and full force for 30 days and thereafter until revoked by me in writing.

Dated at Lewistown, Montana this 14th day of May 1953—

x <u>Otto Mattuschek</u>
x <u>Frank Mattuschek</u>

Carnell then met Ward, a prospective buyer, and accepted from him a check for $2,500 as a binder. The check looked as follows:

PLAINTIFF'S EXHIBIT B

93-73/921

1st Bank Stock Corporation
First National Bank of Lewistown
Lewistown, Montana, May 20, 1953 No.
Pay To The Order of   *Red Carnell* $2500xx
        twenty five hundred and no/100 Dollars
        s/s E. E. Ward
For down Payment on land
Mattuschek
(Endorsement E. F. Carnell)

At the same time Carnell had the following executed on his letterhead:

PLAINTIFF'S EXHIBIT "C"

(Defendant's Exhibit no. 1)

Real Estate   Fergus Realty City   Property
Insurance   213 Main St. Phone 598   Farms
Rentals   Lewistown, Montana   Ranches
May 20–1953

I hereby agree to buy the Mattuschek place in accordance with the terms of the agreement between E. F. Carnell and the Mattuscheks.
Dated   May 14, 1953.

/s/ E. E. Ward

To Buy or Sell—See "Red" Carnell

Carnell drove to the ranch and advised the Mattuscheks of the sale. They asked if Ward would be willing to lease back the property. When closing was attempted, the Mattuscheks refused to convey the property, and the Wards filed suit seeking specific performance and damages. Is there a contract? Are any damages or remedies appropriate? *Ward v. Mattuscheks*, 330 P.2d 971 (Mont. 1958).

7. Carl and Cleo Nordstrom entered into a contract to purchase 480 acres of farmland from John Lee and Marilee Miller. The purchase price was $480,000. The advertisements for the property described it as "irrigated cropland" and stated that the property had two wells. One advertisement read:

480 acres of Prime Developed irrigation land located northwest of Garden City in Finnery County, Kansas. Two irrigation wells and approximately 14,000 ft. of underground pipe. This land is flood-irrigated and all runs are one-half mile long. THIS IS ONE YOU HAVE TO SEE TO BELIEVE.

Robert Legere, a real estate broker, contacted the Nordstroms and showed them the property. Nordstrom inspected the land, the buildings, and the wells. The Nordstroms paid $15,000 down, sold their home and store in Colorado, and purchased the property and moved in on March 2, 1976.

During the summer of 1976, one of the irrigation wells went dry. On further investigation, Nordstrom discovered that insufficient water was available to supply either well and the farm could no longer be operated owing to its geological limitations.

Nordstrom confronted the defendants with the information, and the defendants offered to drill another well and change the contract payment terms. The Nordstroms refused and brought suit for fraud and misrepresentation seeking rescission

of the agreement. Should they win? *Nordstrom v. Miller*, 605 P.2d 545 (Kan. 1980).

8. The Rosens contracted to purchase from the Luttingers some property in Stamford for $85,000, and paid an $8,500 deposit. The contract contained the following contingency:

subject to and conditional upon the buyers obtaining first mortgage financing on said premises from a bank or other lending institution in an amount of $45,000 for a term of not less than twenty (20) years and at an interest rate which does not exceed 8½ percent per annum.

The Rosens agreed to use due diligence in attempting to obtain such financing. The parties further agreed that if the Rosens were unsuccessful in obtaining financing as provided in the contract, and notified the Luttingers within a specific time, all sums paid on the contract would be refunded and the contract would terminate without further obligation of either party.

In applying for a mortgage that would satisfy the contingency clause in the contract, the Rosens relied on their attorney, who applied at a New Haven lending institution for a $45,000 loan at 8¼% per annum interest over a period of 25 years. The Rosens' attorney knew that this lending institution was the only one that would at that time lend as much as $45,000 on a mortgage for a single-family dwelling. A mortgage commitment for $45,000 was obtained with "interest at the prevailing rate at the time of closing but not less than 8¾%." Since the commitment failed to meet the contract requirement, timely notice was given to the Luttingers, and demand was made for the return of the down payment. The Luttingers' counsel thereafter offered to make up the difference between the 8¾% interest rate offered by the bank and the 8½% rate provided in the contract for the entire 25 years by a funding arrangement, the exact terms of which were not defined. The Rosens did not accept this offer and, on the Luttingers' refusal to return the deposit, an action was brought. Who should win? *Luttinger v. Rosen*, 316 A.2d 757 (Conn. 1972).

9. Eddie L. Bonner sold to Ms. Tommie Lea Davis 20 acres of land located in Vernon Parish, Louisiana, for the sum of $10,000. Mr. Bonner died five days later on November 24, 2004 before the deed was recorded. Mr. Bonner's children filed suit to have the transfer set aside as a sham because Ms. Davis had not paid any of the $10,000 at the time of the transfer and the land was worth much more than $10,000. Ms. Davis responded by explaining that the $10,000 had indeed been paid through the services she had provided to Mr. Bonner over the years including cooking, cleaning, buying him cigarettes, washing his clothes, allowing him to live in her housing, paying his bills when he asked, and, on one occasion, giving him $400, which he then deposited into his bank account. Does Ms. Davis get her land? What are the issues? *Hutsen v. Davis*, 983 So.2d 266 (La. App. 2008).

10. On March 18, 1994, John and Pamela Kelly signed an offer to purchase residential property from Steven and Merrill Marx (defendants) for $335,000. The Kellys gave $1,000 earnest money with the offer.

By early May, 1994, the Kellys and Marxes had signed a purchase and sale agreement and deposited another $16,750. Clause 18 of their agreement provided:

If the BUYER shall fail to fulfill the BUYER'S agreements herein, all deposits made hereunder by the BUYER shall be retained by the SELLER as liquidated damages.

The closing date was set as September 1, 1994, but the Kellys never purchased the property because they were unable to sell their house. The Kellys notified the Marxes on August 9, 1994, that they would not be closing on the transaction.

On August 24, 1994, the Marxes accepted another offer to purchase and eventually sold the property on September 20, 1994, to new buyers for a purchase price of $360,000. The Marxes kept the Kellys' total deposit of $17,750, and the Kellys brought suit to recover it. The trial court granted the Marxes' motion for summary judgment and the court of appeals reversed. The Marxes appealed. What decision should the supreme court make? *Kelly v. Marx*, 705 N.E.2d 1114 (Mass. App. 1999).

For research activities related to this chapter, go to our text companion website at www.cengagebrain.com

CHAPTER 14

METHODS OF TRANSFER AND CONVEYANCE IN REAL ESTATE

A New Orleans lawyer provided the FHA with an Abstract of Title for a client's loan. The abstract traced title back only to 1803 and the FHA demanded a search back to its origins. The lawyer responded:

Your letter regarding title in Case 189156 has been received. I note that you wish to have title extended further than the 194 years covered by the present application. I was unaware that any educated person in this country, particularly those working in the property area, would not know that Louisiana was purchased by the U.S. from France in 1803, the year of origin identified in our application. For the edification of uninformed FHA bureaucrats, the title to land prior to U.S. ownership was obtained from France, which had acquired it by Right of Conquest from Spain. The land came into possession of Spain by Right of Discovery made in the year 1492 by a sea captain named Christopher Columbus, who had been granted the privilege of seeking a new route to India by then reigning monarch, Isabella. The good queen, being a pious woman and careful about titles, almost as much as the FHA, took the precaution of securing the blessing of the Pope before she sold her jewels to fund Columbus' expedition. Now the Pope, as I'm sure you know, is the emissary of Jesus Christ, the Son of God. And God, it is commonly accepted, created this world. Therefore, I believe it is safe to presume that He also made that part of the world called Louisiana. He, therefore, would be the owner of origin. I hope to hell you find His original claim to be satisfactory. Now, may we have our damn loan?

According to Internet legend, the client got the title abstract approved and the loan.

Once you have a contract for the sale of land, you can then proceed to the formal transfer of title, through a deed. However, title to property may be transferred in other ways, including transfer by adverse possession. Regardless of the form the property transfer takes, it must meet minimum legal requirements to be effective. Parties should take care to meet those requirements so that they pass and obtain a title that will remain protected. This chapter answers the following questions: What are the methods for transferring property? What rules and requirements apply to the methods of transfer? What protections are there for title transfer?

TRANSFER OF PROPERTY BY DEED

In England, the transfer of title was originally accomplished by a symbolic ceremony called the **livery of seisin**. In the ceremony, the grantor and grantee stood with witnesses on the property to be transferred, and the grantor gave the grantee some portion of the property such as a clump of dirt or a twig to symbolize the conveyance of the land. The grantor also spoke certain words at the time of this physical transfer to indicate what land and what type of interest, such as simple or fee tail (see Chapter 2), was being conveyed. While lovely and chock full of tradition, this oral ceremony for passing title to land had its drawbacks; there was no record of who owned what parcels and where the boundaries were located (see discussion of adverse possession in this chapter).

With the Statute for the Prevention of Frauds and Perjuries, passed in 1677, England required a written instrument to validly convey title to property. This written conveyance became known as the **deed**. Today, each of the states here in the United States has its own Statute of Frauds and set of requirements for a valid deed.

Requirements for Valid Deed

The general requirements for a valid deed are the following: (1) grantor with legal capacity, (2) signature of the grantor, (3) grantee named with reasonable certainty, (4) recital of consideration, (5) words of conveyance (items 4 and 5 are referred to as the **premises**), (6) habendum or type of interest conveyed, (7) description of land conveyed, (8) acknowledgment, (9) delivery, and (10) acceptance.

Grantor with Legal Capacity: Age and Mental Capacity

States have varying rules for what constitutes mental capacity on the part of the grantor. For grantors who are natural persons, the requirements are a minimum age (the age of majority) and a sound mind. A sound mind, or legal capacity, does not preclude those who are old or eccentric from passing valid title to their property. In order to meet the capacity test, grantors must understand just three things: the legal significance of a deed (an understanding that they are transferring the title to their land), to whom they are conveying their property, and the nature and value of the property they are conveying.

Most grantor competency cases involve issues related to **undue influence** in a confidential relationship. Undue influence consists of obtaining a deed through means that deprive the grantor of choice. A confidential relationship exists when one party places continuous trust in another party and relies on that party for almost everything from management of financial affairs to assistance with day-to-day activities. If mental weakness is accompanied by a factual situation in which the grantor has a confidential relationship with the grantee, most courts find a presumption of undue influence that requires any grantee who was part of that relationship to overcome the presumption.

Typically, a confidential relationship arises in the following circumstances: between parent and child when the parent is elderly; between one who is afflicted or weak (for example, between priest and parishioner); and between one who is younger and stronger and provides care, help, or assistance (for example, between client and attorney). When the stronger party uses the trust gained in the confidential relationship to obtain property or funds, the issue of undue influence arises. If there has been undue influence, the deed that has conveyed the title will be set aside. The following case deals with a question of undue influence.

HOWE V. PALMER

956 N.E.2d 249 (Mass. App. 2011)
The Farm, the Cult, the Deed, and Undue Influence

FACTS

Virgil D. Howe owned a farm through an inheritance from his mother. His wife, Esther, was not on the deed. Howe is a simple man with severe dyslexia and slow mental processing. These issues contributed to a difficult childhood where he was treated harshly and subjected to severe discipline by school administrators, as well as being teased and bullied by his peers and classmates. As an adult, he was easily intimidated and could be made to go along with things he may not really want to go along with.

The Palmers befriended the Howes in the mid-1990s and Palmer became Howe's only friend. Howe confided in Palmer concerning his (Howe's) weak financial position and his fear that he would lose his farm, "his inheritance." Palmer offered to help and advised Howe to pray on it. In the fall of 1998, the Palmers spent one week on the farm with the Howes. The Palmers asked a lot of questions about expenses and about Esther's children from her two previous marriages. After the Palmers spent their "trial" week with the Howes, Palmer told a friend, "[G]ive me a year and I'll have my retirement." Ultimately, the Palmers moved into the Howes' home to share expenses for a period of six months to one year. The inside of the house was cluttered and dirty, and the outside was littered with abandoned and rusting vehicles and other machine parts.

In the spring of 1999, they all started cleaning up the property, but Howe was a somewhat reluctant participant. During "house meetings," Palmer intimidated Howe about the cleaning, forced him to part with items he desired to keep, and yelled at him to keep his word and to speed up his work. Howe became uncomfortable living with Palmer and found it difficult to face him when he came home from his job working on the adjacent farm. Although Palmer professed that he never expected to be paid for the work he did cleaning up the Howe home and property, he decided unilaterally to take a "commission" on the profits of a tag sale they held. Jeanette Palmer kept the balance of the proceeds for household expenses. In addition to the tag sale, more than fifteen tons of "junk" was removed by a junk hauler. Howe never was informed how much, if any, money was realized from that transaction. Howe, fearful of Palmer, did not protest.

Palmer convinced Howe that he owed him $20,000 to $25,000 for his (Palmer's) assistance in cleaning up the property, and that the only way Howe could settle his debt was to sell the farm or convey a fifty percent interest in it to the Palmers. Howe agreed to do so because he "felt like there was no other option." Jeanette Palmer contacted a lawyer, and on March 7, 2000, Howe signed a deed giving the Palmers a fifty percent interest in the property as his joint tenants by the entirety, subject to a life estate for Esther Howe. Although the lawyer inquired as to separate representation for Howe, Howe did not have the money for such representation.

It is unclear exactly when, but at some point in 2000, the parties and Esther Howe decided to create a Christian ministry on the farm, and called it "Shepherds Haven." Through a correspondence course, the Palmers became ministers of Full Gospel International of Pennsylvania. They had a "spiritual board" of four to five people at the farm.

On November 9, 2000, Howe signed a document agreeing to be counseled by Reverend Carol Pomeroy. He also agreed that if he could not "change" himself by March 31, the ministry would be disbanded. Those who wished to continue the ministry to God would leave the farm, and Howe would reimburse them financially for all the time, effort, and work they put into the farm.

Howe's stepdaughter, who was concerned when she learned about the deed to the Palmers, had a discussion with Howe around the time the deed was signed. During the discussion, he told her that he "had been having a bad attitude about everything that was going on at the farm" and asked her to "pray that his attitude would change." He also told her he was "in counseling" with Pomeroy, a friend of the Palmers, and "that he now felt that what was happening out there was okay." The Palmers told Howe that his prior pastor was not "Holy Spirit filled" and, therefore, would not be an appropriate counselor. In addition, they forbade Howe to tell anyone outside of the ministry what went on at Shepherds Haven.

Tensions continued between Howe and Palmer from 2002 through 2005. Palmer told Howe he had the attributes of "Satan," which caused Howe to become depressed. Palmer eventually suggested that Howe ask his boss if he could live in a camper on the boss's farm. On July 16, 2005, Howe packed his things, asked his wife if he could use her trailer, and moved to the neighboring farm. Shortly before he left, he resigned from the board of Shepherds Haven, stating that he had let fear control his life. Palmer made him rewrite the resignation letter eliminating any reference to fear.

Some months later, Howe and his wife reconciled despite the Palmers' efforts to keep them apart by telling Esther that Howe had abandoned her. Esther eventually left the property as well, and the two filed suit to regain title to their property. The trial court rescinded the deed and awarded $60,000 in damages for emotional distress plus interest and costs. The Palmers appealed.

JUDICIAL OPINION

Trainer, Judge

It is well established that the obligations of documents such as deeds, wills, and contracts can be avoided by showing that they were procured by means of fraud or undue influence. Any influence to be unlawful must overcome the free will and eliminate unconstrained action. The nature of fraud and undue influence is such that they often work in veiled and secret ways. The power of a strong will over an irresolute character or one weakened by disease, overindulgence or age may be manifest although not shown by gross or palpable instrumentalities.

Four [factors] are usually present in a case of undue influence: '… an (1) unnatural disposition [is] made (2) by a person susceptible to undue influence to the advantage of someone (3) with an opportunity to exercise undue influence and (4) who in fact has used that opportunity to procure the contested disposition through improper means.'" A claim of undue influence therefore can be made out upon a showing that a third party, here Palmer, "by means of coercion, overpowered the mind of the [victim, here Howe] and caused him to [sign a document] that embodied [Palmer's] 'dominating purpose' rather than the 'wishes of the person signing the instrument,' i.e., [Howe]."

The Palmers do not now contend, nor did they at trial, that there was insufficient evidence to support a finding that the deed was procured by undue influence. Rather, the Palmers argue that even if one of them unduly influenced Howe, the deed should be enforceable by the other because they each have separate enforceable legal rights in the deed. It is well settled, however, that an instrument procured by undue influence is voidable by the person who was unduly influenced. Howe has not ratified the deed, so neither of the Palmers would have any right to its enforcement if the statute of limitations is determined not to prevent the claim of undue influence.

Finally, the evidence warranted a jury verdict on Howe's claim that Palmer had intentionally inflicted emotional distress. Howe was subjected to a concerted, comprehensive, and relentless campaign to overpower his will by the infliction of emotional distress. The Palmers gradually and incrementally exploited each of Howe's personal concerns and weaknesses. They isolated him from his few family members. They alienated him from his church, convincing him of his pastor's spiritual unworthiness while enlisting the aid of another member of the clergy who was apparently complicit, if not in league, with the Palmers. They separated him from the counsel and trust of his wife, eventually convincing him to move away from his farm and his wife and live in a trailer on a neighbor's farm. The Palmers had convinced Howe that he had to convey an interest in his farm to them as joint tenants by the entirety as payment for the cash value of services they rendered in cleaning up the farmhouse and the surrounding property. This pattern of psychological abuse and control, and the resulting fear and intimidation created in Howe, continued relentlessly from 1999 until 2005, when he moved off the farm. A short time later, and despite the Palmers' efforts to prevent a reconciliation, Esther left the farm and joined her husband. Now, out of the control and abuse by the Palmers, and reconciled with his wife, Howe began this action.

These actions were not simple insults or mere displays of anger or overzealousness. Howe suffered several years of torment caused by the intentional, or reckless, conduct of Palmer. The jury were [sic] warranted in finding that Palmer's conduct was extreme, outrageous, and beyond the bounds of decency in a civilized community, and that the distress experienced by Howe was severe.

Affirmed.

CASE QUESTIONS

1. Describe the elements of undue influence
2. List the conduct that the court found to be outrageous and that resulted in a finding of emotional distress as well as undue influence.

Grantor with Legal Capacity: Identification of Grantor

Individual grantors should be identified clearly in the deed. Spelling of the grantors' names is important, and if the grantors have used other names or initials, a separate identity statement can clarify that the grantors with varying names are the same person. For example, "Marianne M. Jennings," "Marianne Jennings," and "Marianne Moody Jennings" are the same person, but the names vary. An identity sheet that the title company records verifies in the public records that the three names are names for the same person. The grantor's name should appear in the deed in the same way the grantor's name appeared as grantee in the instrument conveying title. The identity statement can clarify. For example, "John Edward Doe" is not the same as "J. E. Doe" and would require an additional verification through an identity sheet.

The deed should also give the status of the grantor, such as, "unmarried male" or "single female." On deeds in the eighteenth and nineteenth centuries, single women were referred to as "widow" or "spinster." The term "divorced and not re-married" is used today to clarify the presence or absence of marital rights. Status clauses are assurance that those who execute the deed have proper authority to do so independently. A grantor acting on another's behalf must provide that capacity on the deed. For example, an executor for an estate would have a status description clause: "Paul H. Ramsay as executor for the Last Will and Testament of Mary R. Ramsay, whose will was admitted on [date] in [court] in case [number]."

Grantors need not be individuals; they can also be business organizations, such as corporations. Corporations, partnerships, limited partnerships, LLCs, and LLPs may all hold and convey title. Agents of the business organization will actually execute the deed. Most title companies require a board resolution or other form of agency authority when a business (in whatever form) is transferring property. Documented proof of such authority helps to keep the title chain clear. In the following case, the parties became terribly confused and cost themselves a great deal of time and money because their deeds were executed using the wrong grantor.

An example of a grantor without legal capacity is a charitable organization that is an unincorporated association. In most states, associations such as these have no legal existence and hence may not hold or convey title to property. In these associations, title must be held and conveyed through the association officers or trustees, unless there is a specific state statute authorizing the holding of legal title by unincorporated associations (see footnote h, Figure 14.1, p. 365).

Governmental bodies have no inherent authority to convey title and must have statutory authorization to do so. Agencies must comply with all the guidelines and restrictions in their statutory authorizations.

Executors, guardians, trustees, and administrators have legal authority to convey title on behalf of their estates or protected persons but must do so according to the terms of the will, trust, or court orders, and possibly only with court approval.

PRACTICAL TIP

Nonprofit corporations have played an increasing role in property transfer. Under a HUD program, nonprofits could qualify for low-interest government loans if they had a proven track record of rehabilitation of housing. In areas such as Harlem, nonprofits could qualify for significant federal funds for the purchase, fix-up, and resale of properties there. However, many shell nonprofit corporations were formed for the purpose of obtaining the loan funds without any record or plans for rehabilitation.[1] Real estate speculation using government funds and then reselling quickly, or the practice of flipping, to inflate the price, has resulted in many buyers owning property that is now the subject of litigation and foreclosure by the federal government. Checking the records for the history of a nonprofit grantor is important to assure good title.

Grantor's Signature

A grantor with proper capacity must sign the deed, and if the grantor is not signing as an individual, there must be an indication of any representative or agent capacity. If two persons hold title, both signatures are required. In most states, the signatures of both spouses are required to convey title even in cases where only one holds such title. Those who sign for business organizations, estates, minors, and nonprofits should have some verification of authority.

A party who signs on behalf of a grantor should have a power of attorney. In some states, that power of attorney must be recorded along with the actual deed. The power of attorney should be either a general one, that gives the signer the authority of a general agent, or one specifically authorizing the transfer of real estate or the transfer of the particular parcel.

Grantors who are incapable of signing may place an "X" along with a verification clause to indicate who placed the X. The name may be typed in for the grantor.

In the case of a corporate agent signing for a corporation, many states require that the corporate seal also be placed on the deed. The signature must indicate that the deed is being executed on behalf of the corporation.

CONSIDER 14.1   The following language appears in a deed:

THIS DEED OF CONVEYANCE, made and entered into this 8th day of April, 1975, between LOGAN MIDDLETON, President of the V.T.C. Lines Incorporated, Harlan, Harlan County, Kentucky, party of the first part, and JOHN CHRISTIAN, Evarts, Harlan County, Kentucky, party of the second part.

The signatory portion of the document in its entirety appears thusly:

> */s/ Logan Middleton*
> *Logan Middleton, President*
> *V.T.C. Lines, Incorporated*

The only other reference to the corporate entity is contained in the attestation clause:

> */Subscribed, sworn to, and acknowledged before me by Logan Middleton, President, V.T.C. Lines, Incorporated, to be his own free act and deed, and the act and deed of said corporation on this the 8th day of April 1975.*
> */s/ Mary Alice Hutbank*
> *Notary Public*
> *My Commission Expires: 2/27/79*

Christian is now attempting to convey the property to Johnny Pace. The Johnsons have levied the property as creditors of V.T.C. Lines. Christian claims he is the property owner and that the levy is improper. Using Figure 14.1 and the chapter discussion, determine if title was conveyed to Christian. *Christian v. Johnson*, 556 S.W.2d 172 (Ky. 1977). ▬■

---

[1]Terry Pristin, "Despite Inquiry into Fraud, Buyers Still Seek Harlem Homes," *New York Times*, Jan. 15, 2001, A16.

Figure 14.1 summarizes the types of grantors and the identification and signatures necessary for meeting the requirements for a valid deed.

FIGURE 14.1 Grantor Capacity, Identification, and Signatures

GRANTOR	SAMPLE IDENTIFICATION	SIGNATURE
Individual	"John Edward Doe, a single man" "John Edward Doe, and Mary Frances Doe, his wife." "Eileen Jones Doe, a widow"	"John Edward Doe" "John Edward Doe/Mary Frances Doe" "Eileen Jones Doe"
Incompetent	"John Edwards Doe, a conservator for the estate of Eileen Jones Doe, an adult protected person" (an incompetent)	"Eileen Jones Doe by John Edward Doe, conservator for the estate of Eileen Jones Doe"[a]
Partnership	"ABC Partnership, a partnership organized and authorized to do business under the laws of the state of Arizona."	"ABC Partnership by John Edward Doe, general partner"[b]
Corporation	"LMN Company, Inc.,[c] a corporation incorporated and authorized to do business under the laws of the State of Arizona with its principal place of business in Phoenix"	"LMN Company, Inc., by John Edward Doe, president[d] (corporate seal)"[e]
Executor	"John Edwards Doe, as executor of the last will and testament of Eileen Jones Doe, deceased at Mesa, County of Maricopa, State of Arizona"	"John Edwards Doe as executor of the last will and testament of Eileen Jones Doe"[a]
Minor	"John Edwards Doe, a minor under the age of 18 years"[f]	"John Edwards Doe by Willard Scott Doe, as legal guardian of John Edwards Doe, as minor"
Individual with power of attorney (attorney in fact)	"John Edwards Doe, a single man"	"John Edwards Doe by Willard Scott Doe, his attorney in fact"[g]
Illiterate	"John Edwards Doe, a single man"	"X," with verification clause to indicate who made the "X." Name of grantor should be typed below the "X."
Unincorporated Association[h]	Need individual(s) signatures	"John Doe"

[a]Court approval may be required for transfer.

[b]Authority of partner to convey as general partner should be confirmed.

[c]Use name under which it was incorporated.

[d]Authority to transfer should be verified; board resolution required; check to see if it is an extraordinary corporate transaction (additional approval required).

[e]Should be attested to or verified by corporation's secretary.

[f]Or whatever age of majority happens to be.

[g]Power of attorney must authorize real property transfers.

[h]Nine states have adopted the Uniform Unincorporated Nonprofit Association Act, an act that qualifies nonprofit associations as a legal entity (Alabama, Colorado, Delaware, Hawaii, Idaho, Texas, West Virginia, Wisconsin, and Wyoming). Three states (Arkansas, Iowa, and Nevada) and the District of Columbia have adopted the Revised UUNAA (2008). The signature would be "Tri-City Arts League, by John Doe, President."

Grantee Named with Reasonable Certainty

Grantees must also be identified with reasonable certainty because the usefulness and validity of public land records on land transfers depend on the accuracy of the spelling and identity of grantors and grantees. Accurate spelling is the basis for an effective indexing system for land transactions. Aliases or AKAs (also known as) should be noted on the deed or on a separate, acknowledged form.

The status of the grantee should also be included in the deed. For example, just as with grantors, individuals should be identified as single or married, and corporations should be identified as to their location and place of incorporation. The following case deals with a fascinating issue on the legal capacity of the LLC grantee.

ALLEN V. SCOTT, HEWITT & MIZE

186 S.W.3d 782 (Mo. App. 2006)

FACTS

David and Veronica Allen bought land in Independence, Missouri, during 1994 for $22,000. In January 1998, they listed it for sale with a broker, Chuck Zuvers, asking $88,000. The property remained on the market until May 1999, when Thomas C. Scott contracted to buy it for $90,000. Scott signed the sales contract as "Thomas C. Scott, or assigns" because he was organizing Scott, Hewitt & Mize as a limited liability company and wanted the land deeded to the firm. Scott and his partners planned to list it for sale at a high price, knowing that the price might delay a sale for several years.

At closing, and following Scott's instruction, the Allens deeded the property to "Scott, Hewitt & Mize, LLC." Although Scott and his partners had filed articles of organization for Scott, Hewitt & Mize with the Secretary of State before closing, the Secretary of State rejected the articles because of errors contained in them. Scott corrected the errors, and the Secretary of State issued a certificate of organization to Scott, Hewitt & Mize nine days after closing. Scott, Hewitt & Mize immediately listed the property for sale for more than $1 million.

Approximately 20 days after closing, the Allens, seeing the Scott, Hewitt and Mize listing, tendered a $99,900 check to Scott and asked him to rescind the sale. Scott refused. The Allens sued to rescind the contract, their theory for rescinding the contract being mistake. The circuit court issued summary judgment for Scott, Hewitt & Mize. The Allens appealed.

JUDICIAL OPINION

Spinden, Presiding Judge

We consider first the Allens' argument on appeal that the sale and conveyance should be rescinded because Scott, Hewitt and Mize did not exist until nine days after closing. Even assuming all facts in favor of the Allens, it is wholly irrelevant that Scott, Hewitt & Mize was not organized at the time that the Allens contracted with Scott. The Allens' contract was with Scott. It is of no consequence to the Allens that Scott assigned his interest to an entity that, because of a defect in its organizational paperwork, had not finished the organizational process. The formation issues of Scott, Hewitt & Mize are irrelevant to the Allens' contract with Scott.

Even if this were not the case, Scott, Hewitt & Mize was capable of receiving a valid conveyance despite its not having complete the organizational process. Generally, to be valid, a conveyance requires a grantee in *esse* capable of taking and holding title to property when the conveyance occurs. However, "equitable rights may result in favor of a subsequently formed corporation named as a grantee." The Allens cannot challenge the transfer on the basis that Scott, Hewitt & Mize was not yet a *de jure* entity.

The Allens' petition contended that they should be permitted to void the contract because of their mistake as to the property's value. Value is a matter of opinion—not fact—resting in conjecture. To be a basis for rescinding a contract, a mistake must "relate to the existence or non-existence of a fact, past or present, material to the contract, and not as to a future contingency. The mistake must be as to a matter of fact, not as to a matter resting in mere conjecture or belief."

Property values depend on multiple variables, and a property's value can increase or decrease following sale. The Allens and Scott, Hewitt & Mize agreed on a price that reflected the property's value at the time of contracting. Allowing the Allens to rescind creates a rule whereby sellers could argue mistake after deciding that he or she did not receive a fair deal.

The Allens were not unaware of a fact affecting value. They understood exactly what they were selling. They understood all of the pertinent details surrounding the sale. Their purported mistake was their opinion of what the land was worth. After Scott, Hewitt & Mize bought it from them and listed it for sale at more than $1 million, the Allens simply became dissatisfied with the bargained-for exchange, a risk inherent in any sale.

Affirmed.[2]

CASE QUESTIONS

1. Why was the LLC not formed at the time of the deed transfer?
2. What theory are the Allens using under deed requirements?
3. What does the court find on the Allens' argument on mistake?

The deed should also describe the interests and forms of ownership being conveyed to the grantees. For example, the proper language should be used if the grantees wish to be joint tenants (see Chapter 8). If the grantees are taking unequal shares, then the deed should include the fractional divisions, for example, "one-third to John Edward Doe, a single man, and two-thirds to Jane Elizabeth Doe, a single woman, as tenants in common."

There are statutory presumptions in some states as to how title is taken if the deed does not include a form of ownership for the grantees. For example, in many states, grantees who are married will take the property as tenants by the entireties unless the deed specifies otherwise.

Recital of Consideration

A recital of consideration does not require the parties to actually include the price paid for the land in the deed. In fact, deeds that convey title to real property as gifts generally have a simple recital of consideration, such as, "for the consideration of ten dollars, and other good and valuable consideration" (see Web Exhibit 14.1 for a sample warranty deed and the recital clause). The use of a nominal sum presents no problems for the deed's validity. So long as some consideration was actually paid, the deed's transfer of title may be enforced.

Words of Conveyance

The recital of consideration and words of conveyance portions of the deed are known as the *premises* of the deed. The words of conveyance reflect the grantor's true intent to transfer some title or interest in the property. The words of conveyance can place limits on the title to the property (see discussion of warranties later in this chapter). Standard form deeds use language such as "do hereby grant and convey," "do hereby grant," "do hereby convey and specially warrant," or "do hereby quitclaim." These words determine the warranties or promises made by the grantor to the grantee in the transfer of title.

Habendum: The Type of Interest Conveyed

"*Habendum et tenendum*" means "to have and to hold." The **habendum clause** in a deed declares what type of land interest, such as fee simple, fee tail, or fee simple defeasible, the grantor is conveying. The language used in the habendum clause of the deed is discussed in Chapter 2, similar to these limited examples:

- *Fee simple*: "To A," "To A and her heirs"
- *Fee simple determinable*: "To A so long as the premises are used for a school"

---

[2]For a case that reached the opposite result on an LLC not being able to take title if it is not yet formed, see *Sullivan v. Buckhorn Ranch Partnership*, 119 P.3d 192 (Okl. 2005).

Any restrictions, such as easements or liens, must be included after the habendum clause. These restrictions generally begin "subject to"; for example, "the Carolina Power easement in the four feet along the …"

Description of Land Conveyed

Chapter 7 covered the requirements for an adequate legal description to convey property. The grantee's protection of title is dependent upon this description and it is a key to effective title searches and protection.

Acknowledgment

The **acknowledgment clause** establishes that the act of conveying was indeed done by the grantor. In most states, the deed need not be acknowledged to be valid between the parties to the deed, but acknowledgment is required before the deed can be recorded in the public land records.

Acknowledgment means that the parties have appeared before a notary (or otherwise authorized state official), signed their names, indicated through identification that they are the parties identified in the deed, and that they are executing the deed voluntarily. The acknowledgment format varies from state to state, but generally includes the venue (the county and state), the date, the name of the notary or other official, and that the signature of the person on the deed was indeed the person who appeared before the notary. In most states, the notary must affix some form of seal or stamp. Witnesses may or may not be required for an acknowledgment. In some states, witnesses can serve as a substitute for an acknowledgment.

In the past few years, there have been increasing problems with notarized signatures because the parties did not actually appear before the notary, another individual asked the notary to authenticate the signature, and then problems on the instrument develop. The following case deals with the consequences of such actions taken without a notary being present.

DIVERSIFIED INTERNATL. PROPERTIES, INC. V. LUKACS

2008 WL 5159900 (Ohio App. 5 Dist.)
A Marriage, a Divorce, a Quitclaim, and a Mess

FACTS

In 1987, Tracy Lukacs married David Fillmore. Together they purchased a property located on Kilbannan Court in Dublin, Ohio. In 1991, the parties dissolved their marriage.

On February 17, 2005, Ms. Lukacs signed a quitclaim[3] deed on the Kilbannan property. A notary or witness was not present. Thereafter, Mr. Fillmore had his friend notarize the deed outside of Ms. Lukacs's presence. On February 28, 2005, Mr. Fillmore recorded the deed at the Delaware County Recorder's Office. On April 27, 2005, the parties entered into a separation agreement by which Mr. Fillmore received the Kilbannan property through his corporation, Diversified International Properties (appellee).

On August 9, 2005, Ms. Lukacs retained the services of Kemp, Schaeffer, Rowe & Lardiere Co., L.P.A. (appellant) (KSR&L) to represent her on domestic relations issues. On August 9, 2005, Ms. Lukacs executed a mortgage in the amount of $25,000 in favor of KSR&L for attorney fees. On the same day, KSR&L filed an affidavit attacking the legality of the quitclaim deed to Diversified. The mortgage was recorded on August 11, 2005.

---

[3]The court uses the term "quit claim," but the notion of a "quitclaim" deed is the same in Ohio as it is under the *Restatement of Property*.

On August 20, 2007, Diversified filed an amended complaint for declaratory judgment regarding the quitclaim deed. KSR&L filed a motion to dismiss on November 7, 2007. The trial court found the quitclaim deed was voidable, but not void. Because Ms. Lukacs had conveyed her title in the property to Diversified, the trial court found she had no interest in the property and declared the mortgage to KSR&L a legal nullity.

KSR&L appealed.

JUDICIAL OPINION

Farmer, Judge

[B]ecause the deed was not executed [properly], [it] was defective and legal title did not pass from Ms. Lukacs to appellee. Therefore, what interest did Ms. Lukacs pass to appellee, if any? In *Basil v. Vincello* (1990), 50 Ohio St.3d 185, 553 N.E.2d 602, the Supreme Court of Ohio reinforced the rule that absent fraud, a defectively executed conveyance is valid between the parties.

Therefore, under Basil, appellee *sub judice* has an equitable interest in the Kilbannan property. This specific equitable interest is a contractual one and is enforceable in contract.

Appellant's status is not as a *bona fide* purchaser. It is undisputed appellant was aware of the issues surrounding the validity of the deed at the time of taking the mortgage on the property. Appellant was aware that Ms. Lukacs had signed the deed of her own free will, and the deed was part of Ms. Lukacs's separation agreement. Appellant was clearly aware that an equitable interest in law was created by the deed, but nevertheless proceeded to take a mortgage interest in the property.

"The 'clean hands doctrine' of equity requires that whenever a party takes the initiative to set in motion the judicial machinery to obtain some remedy but has violated good faith by his prior-related conduct, the court will deny the remedy…. The maxim, 'he who comes into equity must come with clean hands,' requires only that the plaintiff must not be guilty of reprehensible conduct with respect to the subject matter of his suit…." Appellant is not a *bona fide* mortgagee and does not have an interest in the property.

This court enters judgment, declaring appellee has an equitable interest in the property which is enforceable in contract, and appellant's mortgage is indeed a legal nullity.

CASE QUESTIONS

1. What type of interest is created when the acknowledgement is flawed?
2. Why does the law firm have unclean hands?
3. What do you think Ms. Lukacs was trying to accomplish?

Delivery

The transfer of title is not complete until the deed has been delivered to the grantee. In most transactions, this step is a simple one: The deed is given in exchange for a consideration. However, **delivery** can be actual or constructive. That is, delivery can occur when the grantor places the deed irrevocably in the hands of a third party or in a location that only the grantee has access to. When delivery is not a direct exchange between grantor and grantee, the intent of the grantor is critical. In delivery to a third party, the grantor must relinquish all control of the deed; otherwise, the intent is not there, and delivery to the grantee has not yet been made. If the deed is placed in escrow with instructions to convey it to the grantee upon receipt of funds, there again is no delivery because a condition is attached. Once the funds are received, then the delivery can take place. Often, grantors execute deeds to grantees and then place them in a safe-deposit box, with instructions to relatives for delivery after the grantor's death. Such a transfer is not delivery and, once death has occurred, title cannot pass without going through proper probate processes. The standards for delivery of deeds are the same as the standards for delivery of gifts (discussed later in the chapter).

CONSIDER 14.2   Holstein wanted his niece to have a parcel of land upon which she could build a home after her completion of law school. Holstein signed and executed a deed for a small parcel that he owned and turned it over to his attorney with instructions that the deed be recorded upon the niece's graduation. Holstein told his niece of the pending gift to inspire her in her last year of law school, but he died before the niece graduated. Both the niece and other heirs claim the parcel. Who wins? ▬▬▬■

In most states, a deed that has been executed, acknowledged, and recorded (discussed later in this chapter) carries a presumption of delivery.

Once delivery has occurred, the grantor's destruction of the deed, change of heart, or even a grant to another grantee do not change the fact that the title has passed.

Acceptance

Although the law does not foist land onto grantees, if the transfer of property is beneficial to the grantee, then acceptance is presumed. This presumption applies even when the grantee has no knowledge of the conveyance. Also, if the grantee has possession of the deed, acceptance is presumed. Likewise, recording the deed presumes acceptance.

TYPES OF DEEDS

The type of deed makes a difference in the grantor's promises about the title. The types of deeds are (1) quitclaim deed, (2) warranty deed, (3) special warranty deed, (4) deed of bargain and sale, and (5) judicial deed.

Quitclaim Deed

A **quitclaim deed** is a deed of no promises. A quitclaim deed makes no bones about it; it does not purport to transfer or convey title to property. A quitclaim deed conveys only any right, title, and interest the grantor may have in the property. But grantors on a quitclaim deed make no promise that they hold any such right, title, or interest in the property. A quitclaim deed is often used as a release for purposes of clearing a cloud on a title or correcting title defects. This form of deed is also used to convey lesser land interests such as life estates. The language of conveyance in a quitclaim is "I (grantor) hereby quitclaim to …" or "I (grantor) hereby remise, release, and quitclaim unto …"

Warranty Deed

Most land transactions require the grantor to transfer title by warranty deed. In most states, a **warranty deed** springs from the language used by the grantor in the words of conveyance, which usually includes "warrant" but by statute may instead include "grant" or "convey."

The warranty deed title describes its purpose. At common law, the grantor who uses a warranty deed gives six warranties: seisin, right to convey, freedom from encumbrances, covenant of warranty, quiet enjoyment, and further assurances. In most states, the warranty or covenant of seisin is a promise that the grantor has title to the property. In other states, the warranty of seisin means that the grantor is in possession of the property. Easements or other noted encumbrances such as liens are not a breach of this warranty.

The right to convey warranty promises that the grantor has the authority to pass title to the property. In states where seisin means only possession, this warranty guarantees the right to transfer more than just possession.

Freedom from encumbrances warrants that the title is free from defects. That is, the grantor warrants that the property is free from both title and physical encumbrances on the property. However, the deed may include a list of any encumbrances that the grantor is passing along, such as an outstanding mortgage or an easement. The types of title defects warranted against (unless specifically listed as excluded) are mortgages, unpaid taxes, assessments, leases, judgment liens, right of redemption, and dower rights. Physical defects warranted against (unless specifically mentioned) are building restrictions, encroachments, easements, profits, party wall agreements, fences, and mineral rights.

The covenant of warranty requires the grantor to compensate the grantee for any losses that result from the grantor's failure to convey title to the property. If a grantee loses title to the conveyed property or is required to pay an amount to retain title, the grantor agrees to identify the grantee for such loss, costs, and expenses.

Under the warranty of quiet enjoyment, the grantor makes the same promise as under the covenant of warranty, which is that the grantor will reimburse the grantee for expenses and losses incurred if a problem with title arises.

The warranty of further assurances requires the grantor to execute documents or institute suits to protect any defects in title that might exist and which the grantee desires corrected.

In the majority of states, these six common law warranties have been combined into the following three basic warranties:

1. The grantor possesses an indefeasible fee simple estate, or the grantor has good title and the transfer is proper.

2. There are no encumbrances against the property except those specifically noted.

3. The grantee shall have quiet enjoyment of the property, and the grantor will warrant and defend title against all claims.

If there is an unbroken chain of warranty deeds conveying title to the property, each grantor is liable to all subsequent grantees on the warranties provided (see Web Exhibit 13.1 for a sample warranty deed).

Special Warranty Deed

A **special warranty deed** offers the same warranties as a warranty deed but limits the time of application. Under a special warranty deed, a grantor's warranties apply only for the period of that grantor's ownership. A grantor who owns property from June 1, 2010, to June 1, 2012, and conveys title with a special warranty deed, would warrant only for that period of ownership and would provide no warranties for defects and encumbrances created or arising prior to or after that time period. In a special warranty deed, the covenants are not listed, and the language used is similar to the following: "Grantor hereby covenants that he has not done anything whereby the above described property has been encumbered in any way whatsoever." Some states allow shortened language in the granting clause, such as "do hereby specially warrant and convey."

Deed of Bargain and Sale

This form of deed is another name, in some states, for a special warranty deed. A **deed of bargain and sale** offers the limited warranty protection of the special warranty deed.

Judicial Deed

A **judicial deed** is a deed executed under court orders. Examples include the deeds of the following: executors and administrators of estates, conservators of estates, guardians of minors or incompetents, and sheriffs. **Sheriffs' deeds** are issued to parties who have purchased properties at foreclosure sales and are issued after the period of the debtor's right of redemption (see Chapter 15). Assuming that all legal procedures have been followed, these deeds serve to convey good title.

CONSIDER 14.3   A deed contained the language, "I, Jacob Smith, of Washington County, warrant and defend unto Christena Smith ... the following real estate ..." Although the deed included all the necessary requirements, the parties are now unclear as to the type of deed given and what warranties, if any, were given. Discuss. *Hummelman v. Mounts,* 87 Ind. 178 (1882).

TRANSFER OF PROPERTY BY ADVERSE POSSESSION

Acquiring title to real property through **adverse possession** (often called **squatter's rights**) can be traced to the Middle Ages. Adverse possession rights arose during that time because there was no proper system for keeping records of land titles, and property owners inevitably lost the documents that established ownership rights. Adverse possession allows owners to prove title through possession for a certain period of time. Even when the American colonies were first settled, the use of adverse possession continued, because recording systems were nonexistent or unsophisticated and important documents were still lost by landowners. Also, adverse possession rights were used by property owners to establish boundary lines on large tracts of land when they themselves were unsure of the exact boundaries of their properties. Boundary disputes were settled by proof of adverse possession. These uses and applications of adverse possession continue today.

Obtaining title to property through adverse possession is similar to obtaining an easement by prescription (discussed in Chapter 4). There is no exchange of a document of title and no closing or deed conveyance under adverse possession. Instead, title is awarded because of certain types of actions related to land. Adverse possession is a statutory doctrine, and the requirements vary from state to state. However, if the statutory requirements are met, title passes as though there had been a conveyance through the traditional methods of deed transfers. The generic requirements for adverse possession are:

- Actual and exclusive possession
- Open, visible, and notorious possession
- Continuous and peaceable possession
- Hostile and adverse possession
- Possession for the required statutory period

The adverse possessor has the burden of proving the coexistence of the requirements, discussed in the following sections.

Actual and Exclusive Possession

Actual and exclusive possession means that the adverse possessor (acquirer) must have sole physical occupancy of the property. The extent of physical occupancy required is determined by the nature of the land. The extent of physical occupancy must correspond with the customary and appropriate uses made on land of that nature and size. The issue of what constitutes possession is a question of fact for a jury, but several common factors help illustrate the standards for customary and appropriate uses.

For residential property, the adverse possessor is required to take up residence in the appropriate structure on the premises; for farmland, the adverse possessor is required to farm the acres sought to be acquired; and for ranch or grazing property, the adverse possessor is required to use the land for the grazing of livestock. In adverse possession of open acreage, such as farm or ranch land, the fencing in of the possessor's acreage is a commonly recognized method of establishing a customary and appropriate use of the property.

Open, Visible, and Notorious Possession

Under this requirement, the adverse possessor must use the property in a manner that is open to the public and sufficient to put those who see the property regularly on notice that there is occupation. This possession must not be secret or clandestine; it must be obvious. Open and visible possession is "calculated to apprise the world that the land is occupied and who the occupant is; and such an appropriation of the land by claimant as to apprise, or convey visible notice to the community or neighborhood in which it is situated that it is in his exclusive use" (*Marengo Cave Co. v. Ross*, 10 N.E.2d 917 [Ind. 1937]). Courts have labeled this element as one of the disseisor (adverse possessor) unfurling a flag over the land and keeping it flying so the owner can see the enemy and the planned conquest.

Continuous and Peaceable Possession

Continuous and peaceable possession requires that the adverse claimant be in possession of the property for the requisite statutory period without being evicted either physically or through court action. The requisite statutory period varies from state to state and is discussed on pages 374–375. This continuity of possession may be established even if the property is used only for certain periods during the year, so long as those periods are consistent and regular.

The doctrine of tacking can be used to establish continuous possession. This doctrine allows a purchaser or someone inheriting a land interest to incorporate the adverse use of the predecessor into meeting the required statutory period. Tacking may be used between predecessor and adverse possessor where there is privity. Privity requires the parties to have a reasonable connection such as a contract, will transfer, or intestate distribution of the predecessor's interest. For example, if A is adversely possessing tract 1 and dies leaving all his property to B after having completed five years on tract 1, B could incorporate those five years in meeting the statutory period of continuous possession.

Hostile and Adverse Possession

This element of adverse possession requires that the adverse possessor establish that the property possession was against the rights of the property's true owner and such action is inconsistent with the title of the true owner. However, the adverse possessor (disseisor) need not establish ill will, bad feelings, or hatred toward the true owner.

The state of mind of the possessor is the issue in establishing this requirement. The appropriate state of mind may be drawn from the concept of either claim of right or color of title. Under claim of right, the possessor claims to be the owner of the property, whether or not such claim has any justification. Under color of title, the possessor has an instrument that is believed to convey title, when in reality such instrument is ineffective or inoperative. Unless specified differently by statute, the claimant may establish hostile and adverse possession under either one of these mental intents. In some states, adverse possession may be established regardless of the presence of either of these two mental states.

Often, factual circumstances arise in which an adverse claim is maintained because there has been a mistake in the placement of a boundary line, and the parties wish to base their claim on that mistaken boundary for the requisite statutory period. Most states find that a mistaken belief about a boundary line is enough to meet the intent requirements for adverse possession.

If a party is given permission by the true title holder to use the property, such permission prevents the user from asserting an adverse claim because permissive use is not hostile and adverse. When the true owner of the property grants a license or easement or gives permission for some other use of property, the user's or possessor's use or possession cannot ripen into an adverse claim.

It is possible for co-owners of property to make adverse claims against one another. Thus, a cotenant may oust others of their possession and gain title by possessing the entire interest for the requisite statutory period.

CONSIDER 14.4   The Kapinskis owned and occupied lot 18 from 1935 to 1950. In 1950, the lot was conveyed to the Wyroskis. The Laurins purchased lot 19 in 1954. The lots were the sites of summer homes. A row of lilac bushes marked the boundary between lots 18 and 19, and the Kapinskis and Wyroskis put in and maintained a lawn and flower bed that bordered the lilacs. A boathouse for lot 18 was also located next to the lilac bushes. Laurin claimed the boundary line was too far on his property and in 1960 brought an action to clear title. The Wyroskis claimed they had obtained title by adverse possession. What is the result? Is there sufficient actual possession? *Laurin v. Wyroski,* 121 N.W.2d 764 (Wis. 1963). ———■

Possession for Required Statutory Period

The possession of the property with the requisite characteristics previously listed must occur for a certain statutory period of time. Although times vary from state to state, the typical adverse period is 20 years. In some states, such as Arizona, the period is as short as ten years (see Figure 14.2). The adverse claimant must maintain possession continuously for the period of time specified by state statute.

FIGURE 14.2 Number of Years Required for Adverse Possession*

STATE	YEARS	STATE	YEARS	STATE	YEARS	STATE	YEARS
Alabama	20	Illinois	20	Montana	5	Rhode Island	10
Alaska	10	Indiana	10	Nebraska	10	South Carolina	10
Arizona	10	Iowa	10	Nevada	5	South Dakota	20
Arkansas	7	Kansas	15	New Hampshire	20	Tennessee	7
California	5	Kentucky	15	New Jersey	30	Texas	3
Colorado	18	Louisiana	30	New Mexico	10	Utah	7
Connecticut	15	Maine	20	New York	10	Vermont	15
Delaware	20	Maryland	20	North Carolina	20	Virginia	25
District of Columbia	15	Massachusetts	20	North Dakota	20	Washington	7
Florida	7	Michigan	15	Ohio	21	West Virginia	10
Georgia	20	Minnesota	15	Oklahoma	15	Wisconsin	20
Hawaii	20	Mississippi	10	Oregon	10	Wyoming	40
Idaho	5	Missouri	10	Pennsylvania	21		

*These figures represent the general time period. Many states have variations depending on issues such as payment of taxes, possession of deed, etc. For example, Texas periods run from 3 to 25 years.

© Cengage Learning

The following case deals with several of the elements of adverse possession and the rights of the parties.

WEINSTEIN V. HURLBERT

45 A.3d 743 (Me. 2012)
Rosa Rugosa and Adverse Possession

FACTS

Richard Hurlbert, Audrey McGlashan, and Hurlbert-McGlashan, LLC (collectively, Hurlbert) has record title to several parcels of land in Owls Head, including a portion of waterfront property known as Cliff Street that extends from the end of Beach Street south and adjacent to the water. Andrew and Melinda Weinstein (collectively, Weinstein) owns property within the "L" created by the intersection of Beach and Cliff Streets, abutting Hurlbert's property. Cliff Street forms the record eastern boundary of Weinstein's property.

Morris and Barbara Coates previously owned the property now owned by Weinstein (the "Weinstein property") that is adjacent to the Cliff Street property. The Coateses acquired the Weinstein property in 1984, and began to maintain the Cliff Street property by mowing the lawn, first themselves, and then by hiring a friend and nearby resident to help. This friend mowed the area before the

Coateses' arrival for the summer months and transplanted rosa rugosa bushes (The rosa rugosa bushes mark the eastern boundary of the area in dispute) in a row along the seaward edge of the lawn area on the Cliff Street property. Barbara Coates maintained and pruned the plantings and gardened on the Cliff Street property. Weinstein argues that the Coates's acquisition of the property in 1984 began the prescriptive period.

When Weinstein acquired the property in 2004, he rebuilt the house and began to occupy it for the summer in 2005. During construction, workers stored building materials on the Cliff Street property. Because the construction and storage of materials damaged the lawn, Weinstein had the area regraded and reseeded. The Weinsteins maintained the Cliff Street property in a manner similar to the Coateses: they mowed the lawn, or hired someone to mow; they pruned the rosa rugosa bushes; and they otherwise kept up the area.

When Hurlbert's predecessor-in-interest posted a notice intended to prevent a prescriptive easement claim, as well as stakes marking the property boundary, Weinstein removed the sign and the stakes. Weinstein's general maintenance ended when Hurlbert began to mow the Cliff Street property in 2009, after having acquired title in 2008. However, between 1984 and 2008, no one other than the Coateses and the Weinsteins maintained the Cliff Street property.

Other members of the community historically used the Cliff Street property but that use diminished in the mid-1980s. Before the mid-1980s, local residents used the property for games of horseshoes and as a place for children to play. Later, children of the family that owned the property abutting the southern boundary of the Weinstein property used the Cliff Street property to cross between their land and the Beach Street area. Boats were infrequently left on the lawn of the Cliff Street property, but this practice was limited after the mid-1980s. The only person who left a boat on the lawn for more than a brief moment during transport was the same friend of the Coateses who planted the rosa rugosa bushes and helped them maintain the Cliff Street property. There was evidence that a prior owner of another portion of Hurlbert's property used the Cliff Street property as a turnaround for his car, but there was no evidence about how often he did this.

The court entered a judgment declaring that Weinstein holds title to the Cliff Street property by adverse possession. Hurlbert appealed.

JUDICIAL OPINION

Levy, Justice

"A party claiming title by adverse possession has the burden of proving, by a preponderance of the evidence, that possession and use of the property was (1) actual; (2) open; (3) visible; (4) notorious; (5) hostile; (6) under a claim of right; (7) continuous; (8) exclusive; and (9) for a duration exceeding the twenty-year limitations period." Because a claim of adverse possession is a mixed question of law and fact, "whether the necessary facts exist is for the trier of fact, but whether those facts constitute adverse possession is an issue of law for the court to decide."

Hurlbert contends that the trial court's decision was at odds with our precedent, particularly with respect to our decision in *Weeks v. Krysa*, 2008 ME 120, 955 A.2d 234. Hurlbert asserts that the Coateses' and Weinsteins' use of the Cliff Street property was no more notorious or hostile than the use at issue in *Weeks*—"casual, seasonal use of an undeveloped waterfront lot," which included recreational use, maintenance of a garden that encroached on to the property, and occasional brush and tree cutting.

Although the trial court distinguished the facts of *Weeks* from those of the present case by concluding that the property was not a "vacant shorefront lot," but instead, "the waterfront lawn of the house now owned by Weinstein" and "a prominent part of the outdoor living space connected specifically to the residence," we cannot agree that the minor factual differences supporting this conclusion are sufficient to establish that the Weinsteins' and their predecessors' use of the property was hostile and notorious. For the full prescriptive period, the adverse use of the property was limited to seasonal lawn mowing, the planting and pruning of several bushes, minimal gardening, a single instance in which building supplies were stored on the property, and removal of a posted notice intended to prevent a prescriptive easement and stakes placed on the property by the record owner.

The "notorious" and "hostile" elements of adverse possession require more. Seasonal grass mowing is not enough. Although more than grass mowing was found to have occurred here, the additional adverse acts were also seasonal, or largely isolated events. Nor were those adverse acts made more compelling by evidence that other neighbors occasionally used the property in a manner consistent with uses typically made of vacant land in a neighborhood. In light of the public policy disfavoring the acquisition of land through adverse possession, Weinstein's use of the property was not sufficiently hostile and notorious to put the true owner "on notice that the land in question is actually, visibly, and exclusively held by a claimant in antagonistic purpose."

Reversed and judgment vacated.

CASE QUESTIONS

1. Why was there not enough hostile and notorious possession?
2. Was there enough possession to put the owner on notice?
3. Does it matter that the use was by a collective group and not a single individual?

CONSIDER 14.5 On April 11, 1946, Lawrence and Pearl Pepka obtained a warranty deed for their residential property, which was Outlot 37 and a portion of Outlot 40 of Big Stone City. In 1991, the Pepkas conveyed their property to their children, holding back a life estate for themselves (see Chapter 2 for more information on life estates).

The Dews' chain of title is somewhat more complex, but involves the remaining two-thirds of Outlot 40 and was eventually conveyed to Thomas C. Dew and Denise A. Dew as husband and wife (the Dews).

The Pepkas believed their driveway on Outlot 40 was on their property, and they used it without the Dews' permission. However, as the Outlot existed at the time of the Pepkas' acquisition, their driveway was actually located well onto the Dews' property. Lawrence Pepka put gravel on the driveway and then later paved it with asphalt. He also mowed the lawn for six feet west of the driveway because he believed that to be the boundary point between his property and the Dews'. Sometime in the 1960s, Lawrence and his son Bernard planted seven evergreen trees along the driveway in the area now disputed. Bernard had received the trees as a gift from a local minister for serving as an altar boy.

The Pepkas did not put up a fence, and the Dews and Pepkas had a good relationship. As the Pepkas aged, Tom Dew helped them maintain their property by mowing their lawn and shoveling their snow. Pearl took the Dews baked goods in exchange for the help. Tom even put up the snow fence for Pearl after Lawrence passed away, and the snow fence was located along what she believed to be the boundary line for their properties.

In 1993, Pearl decided to sell the property. Because of a survey that revealed the true boundary line to be different from that used by the Pepkas, the Dews asserted ownership of the property through the Pepkas' driveway. Pearl attempted to settle the matter and even offered to purchase the disputed strip. When no agreement could be reached, Pearl filed suit to clear title to the strip by adverse possession. The trial court found no disputed facts and declared the Pepkas the owners of the property. The Dews appealed. Discuss what the appellate court should decide and why. *Schultz v. Dew*, 564 N.W.2d 320 (S.D. 1997). ▬▬▬▬▬■

Observations About Adverse Possession

One question often brought out in adverse possession cases is, Who was paying the taxes during the alleged period of adverse possession? Unless a state's statute specifies, the adverse possessor is not required to pay taxes to be allowed to claim title. California's statute, for example, does require the payment of taxes for an adverse claim to be successful. In some states, the failure to pay taxes weakens but does not destroy a claim for adverse possession.

When a title holder is faced with an adverse claimant, the proper method for halting such a claim is to bring a legal action in trespass to have the claimant

PRACTICAL TIP

Even for those who are occupying land with permission, some form of written agreement about their presence can avoid complications and possibly adverse possession. The presence of possession by permissive use should be clarified, if not by agreement, at least by a letter memorializing the arrangement.

removed by court order or injunction. This removal serves to interrupt the claimant's continuous possession and ends the adverse period. Once suit is filed, the claimant's right to possession stops. The clock stops running on the adverse period. Such a proceeding may be brought by seeking an injunction or through a quiet title action in which the court will determine the parties' rights and interests in the property. A **quiet title action** requires that notice be given to all interested in the property in advance of a hearing on the property (as was done with all the heirs in the Williams case). Once title is quieted, any adverse claimant would have to begin anew to establish the requisite statutory period.

TRANSFER OF PROPERTY BY GIFTS

Title to property may be transferred through an *inter vivos* **gift** from **donor** (grantor) to **donee**(grantee); that is, the gift is made while the donor is alive. A *gift* is defined as a voluntary transfer of property by donor to donee where there is no consideration or compensation for the transfer. There are three requirements for passing title by gift. There must be (1) donative intent by the donor or grantor, (2) delivery of the gift, and (3) acceptance by the donee or grantee.

Donative Intent

Donative intent requires proof that the donor intended to pass title absolutely and irrevocably and to relinquish all rights in the property. The best proof of donative intent is a party in possession of a written instrument conveying title.

Delivery

Delivery of a deed can be done through a physical act, or, as noted earlier on delivery of deeds, by proving that the donor intended to part with possession, control, and ownership. In most cases, delivery comes through the simple physical transfer of possession of the written instrument (the deed) from the donor to the donee. Actual delivery occurs when the donee is physically given the deed. **Constructive delivery**, as noted earlier, is tied to exclusive access. For example, if the donor locks the deed in a desk and gives the donee the only key, there has been constructive delivery. Again, a gift is complete if control is relinquished, and the gift fails if the donor maintains control. Joint ownership of a safe-deposit box or delivery of a deed to a third person to hold are transfers of possession, but not a sufficient delivery for purposes of making a gift.

Acceptance

The final requirement for a valid gift is acceptance by the donee. As noted earlier, this element of a gift is presumed unless the donee makes a clear refusal, as by tearing up the deed or refusing to accept the appropriate paperwork.

Gifts may be set aside on some of the same grounds used to set aside apparently valid contracts. For example, a donor (grantor) who executed a deed under duress (force or threat of force or wrongful act) or undue influence may have the gift set aside. Or, in the event of the donor's death, heirs or devisees may petition to have the gift deed set aside on these bases. As noted on p. 360, undue influence exists when a party in a confidential relationship is able to exert great influence over the donor for the party's own benefit to such an extent that the donor feels he has no choice but to convey the land.

CONSIDER 14.6   Mary Blettell was in poor health and went to live with her daughter, Darlene Snider. Herman, Mary's second husband and stepfather to Darlene, continued to live in a house owned by Mary. He was unable to care for Mary, and Mary wanted him to live at the house she owned even though he was not on the title for the property.

Mary instructed Darlene to bring her all the deeds to her property. She signed over the deed to the home where Herman lived and told Darlene to record the deed after Mary died. Darlene then placed the deed in her own safe-deposit box and held onto it for two years until Mary died in 1989. The day after Mary died, Darlene recorded the deed. Herman was not aware of Mary's conveyance to him until after Mary died and Darlene had recorded the deed.

Mary's heirs filed suit, contending that there was not a valid transfer of the property to Herman and that they were entitled to the property as heirs to her estate. The lower court held there had been a valid transfer and the heirs appealed. Who has title to the property? Was there a valid conveyance? *Estate of Mary Blettell v. Snider,* 834 P.2d 505 (Or. App. 1992).

TRANSFER OF PROPERTY BY WILL OR INTESTATE SUCCESSION

Title to property may be transferred upon the death of the title holder by the title holder's will; or, if no will was executed, it may be transferred pursuant to a state statutory scheme of distribution for those dying intestate. The passage of title by will and intestate succession is covered in detail in Chapter 17.

TRANSFER OF PROPERTY BY EMINENT DOMAIN

Eminent domain is the taking of private property by a governmental entity for use for the general public good. Such a taking is permissible and serves to transfer full and complete title to the state if the state provides the existing owners with appropriate compensation. Chapter 19 provides details on eminent domain.

PROTECTION OF TITLE

The discussions of deeds, adverse possession, and other methods of transfer of real estate demonstrate the confusion that can arise with regard to title to property. The deed and the possessory rights are between the parties. However, the issue of third parties and their rights in the land arises if conveyances between grantor and grantee are not documented in the public records. Recording and other forms of public registration are used to protect title and resolve title disputes.

Recording

The process of **recording** as a method of title protection has been practiced in the United States since the days of the colonies. Indeed, the Massachusetts Bay Act of 1634 required records of land transfer to be filed with the court so that an accurate record of land ownership could be maintained. These early acts required the extra work of copying every instrument of conveyance. Every state now has some form of recording act. Although the acts differ, the same topics are covered in each: (1) the documents required to be recorded, (2) the mechanics of recording, (3) a system for maintaining and organizing records, and (4) a method for determining priorities of interests.

Documents Required to be Recorded

All of the recording acts provide that instruments affecting title to land are to be recorded. These instruments include deeds, mortgages, liens, judgments, and, as discussed in Chapter 5, Article 9 financing statements.

The recording of a land-related document affords both protection and public notice. No one can be expected to have actual knowledge or notice about every land transaction. Recording serves to give everyone the chance to verify transactions. Recording is constructive notice of the rights of the parties in the land.

Mechanics of Recording

Recording is accomplished at statutorily designated offices. Offices may be local, such as a county recorder office, or may be a state agency or a town clerk. As discussed in Chapters 3, 4, 5, and 6, other documents such as easements, liens, and fixture filings are recorded in the same place. In most states, recording is accomplished at a county office for the location of the property. Some states may have a separate land records office in counties where the population is large.

The difference between filing and recording is that in filing, the document is retained by the governmental agency. In recording, the document is copied and the copy is retained by the governmental agency in an appropriate organizational system (discussed later in this chapter).

Fees for recording, required in every state, are set according to the type of document and the number of pages in it.

When the fee is paid, the party recording the instrument is given a receipt with the date and time stamped on it. The document being recorded will also have a stamp of date and time. Since many documents are accepted at the same time, each document will also be numbered (the number is sometimes called a fee number) to indicate the exact order of filing. The receipts and time stamps are often critical in establishing title and lien rights in the property. Each document also indicates where in the agency's records it will be filed, such as "Book 425 of Deeds, p. 585" or "Docket 300 of Book of Maps, p. 700."

System for Maintaining and Organizing Records

Every state has some system for organizing land records so that information about title to a piece of property can be readily obtained. The purposes of such recording systems are to provide a method whereby the chain of title for a particular piece of property can be effectively traced and to provide title protection. Chain of title simply provides a history of how a piece of real estate has been transferred over the years between successive owners. To establish ownership of property today, the current owner must establish that the chain of title is unbroken; in other words, that title has been conveyed without any breaks through successive owners.

To be able to trace chains of title, the records must follow an index system. States have either a grantor/grantee system of indexing, a tract system, or both. Most states have a grantor/grantee system, which is easy to understand but more

FIGURE 14.3 Sample Grantor Index

DATE OF RECORDING	GRANTOR	GRANTEE	TYPE OF DOCUMENT	BRIEF LAND DESCRIPTION	DOCKET OR VOLUME	PAGE
4/9/90	American Continental Corporation	Terry H. and Marianne Moody Jennings	Joint Tenancy Deed	Lot 388 of Hohokam Village, Unit Two	14342	913

difficult to use when establishing the chain of title. In a **grantor/grantee index system**, the agency responsible for recording maintains a running index of transactions alphabetized by the grantor's and grantee's names.

Figures 14.3 and 14.4 are sample grantor and grantee index entries. Suppose the Joneses were purchasing lot 388 from the Jenningses. The Joneses could establish the chain of title by first looking for the Jenningses in the grantee index (Figure 14.4) and then verifying the transfer by looking at American Continental in the grantor index (Figure 14.3). To trace further back, they would check American Continental in the grantee index to find its grantor and so on. The docket or volume number and the page number in the index permit the tracing party to turn to the records and actually examine the joint tenancy deed of conveyance.

Although tracing the chain of title seems uncomplicated here, many titles require more thorough searches. Also, the grantor/grantee system of indexing has inherent problems: The use of different names, initials, or married names can cause confusion and an apparent break in the chain of title. (See earlier discussion of grantor and grantee.) Title obtained in other ways, such as by will, may not appear in the land records. Also, some title defects, such as judgments and tax liens, will not appear in the grantor/grantee index.

The second system of indexing, called the **tract index system** (also known as block indexing or numerical indexing), avoids some of the inherent problems of the grantor/grantee system. Many states have both systems, but title companies, which sell insurance for chains of title, use the tract index system to avoid the problems in the grantor/grantee system. Furthermore, tracing the chain of title under the tract index system is much faster than under the grantor/grantee system. Under the tract index system, the entire county is divided into tracts, and the chain of title for each tract is traced back to the time when the land was given in a government grant. Each piece of land is then indexed to a tract, so that every piece of property can have its origins traced quickly to the origination of title.

FIGURE 14.4 Sample Grantee Index

DATE OF RECORDING	GRANTOR	GRANTEE	TYPE OF DOCUMENT	BRIEF LAND DESCRIPTION	DOCKET OR VOLUME	PAGE
4/9/90	Terry H. and Marianne Moody Jennings	American Continental Corporation	Joint Tenancy Deed	Lot 388 of Hohokam Village, Unit Two	14342	913

© Cengage Learning

Method for Determining Priorities of Interests

State recording acts provide a public record of land transfers and interests. Constructive notice serves as notice to the world. Once a document is recorded, everyone has notice of the recorded interest even without seeing a recorded document.

However, without immediate recording of transferred land interests, the door is open for fraudulent conveyances. Unscrupulous grantors have conveyed the same land interests to different parties. Who, then, is entitled to the property, and who is left to collect damages from the fraudulent grantor on the basis of breach of warranty? Three types of state statutes are used for determining rights and priorities in the property: (1) pure race, (2) notice, and (3) race/notice.

1. *Pure Race* North Carolina's statute is a pure race statute and provides as follows:

    § 47–18. Conveyances, contracts to convey, options and leases of land.

    Unless otherwise stated either on the recorded instrument or on a separate recorded instrument duly executed by the party whose priority interest is adversely affected, instruments registered in the public record shall be presumed to have priority based on the order of recordation as determined by the time of recordation. If instruments are recorded simultaneously, then the order of recordation shall be presumed as follows, in order of priority:

    (1) The earliest document number set forth on the recorded instrument.

    (2) The sequential book and page number set forth on the document if no document number is set forth on the recorded instrument.

    A **pure race statute**[4] means first to record is first in right, or the first party to record the instrument in the proper place will hold title to the property. This rule applies even though deeds may have been executed to the parties prior to the time the recording party received the same interests. An example follows:

    - *Day 1*: Grantor conveys Blackacre to A.
    - *Day 2*: Grantor conveys Blackacre to B.
    - *Day 3*: B records interest.
    - *Day 4*: A records interest.

    In a pure race jurisdiction, B takes title as the first to record even though the interest in Blackacre was conveyed first to A.

2. *Notice* Arizona's statute [ARS § 33–412] is an example of a notice statute:

    § 33–412. Invalidity of unrecorded instruments as to bona fide purchaser or creditor

    A. All bargains, sales and other conveyances whatever of lands, tenements and hereditaments, whether made for passing an estate of freehold or inheritance or an estate for a term of years, and deeds of settlement upon marriage, whether of land, money or other personal property, and deeds of trust and mortgages of whatever kind, shall be void as to creditors and subsequent purchasers for valuable consideration without notice, unless they are acknowledged and recorded in the office of the county recorder as required by law.

    B. Unrecorded instruments … as to all subsequent purchasers with notice thereof, shall be valid and binding.[5]

---

[4]Pure race states are Louisiana and North Carolina.

[5]There are some authorities who believe that Arizona is a race/notice state by case interpretation of this statute.

The key to understanding the system of priorities in notice states[6] is the term **good-faith purchaser** or **bona fide purchaser (BFP)**. Under **notice statutes**, the last good-faith purchaser keeps the land interest. However, if a deed is not recorded in a notice state, the purchaser may lose title to a subsequent bona fide purchaser. A good-faith or bona fide purchaser is defined as one who has no knowledge of a prior conveyance, either constructive (no prior recorded interest) or actual (no knowledge of a transfer or sale). A notice example follows.

- *Day 1*: Grantor conveys to A (a BFP).
- *Day 2*: Grantor conveys to B (a BFP).
- *Day 3*: Grantor conveys to C (a BFP).

In this case, since A and B did not record, C takes title. This would be true even if A and B recorded their interests on day 4 before C recorded on day 5. In a notice jurisdiction, the failure to record may cost the parties their interests.

3. *Race/Notice* New York is a jurisdiction following the **race/notice system** of priorities (Real Property § 291):

> *A conveyance of real property, within the state, on being duly acknowledged by the person executing the same, … may be recorded in the office of the clerk of the county where such real property is situated … Every such conveyance not so recorded is void as against any person who subsequently purchases or acquires by exchange or contracts to purchase or acquire by exchange, the same real property or any portion thereof, or acquires by assignment the rent to accrue, therefrom valuable consideration, from the same vendor or assignor, his distributees or devisees, and whose conveyance, contract or assignment is first duly recorded, and is void as against the lien upon the same real property or any portion thereof arising from payments made upon the execution of or pursuant to the terms of a contract with the same vendor, his distributees or devisees, if such contract is made in good faith and is first duly recorded.*

Race/notice statutes entitle the property to go to a good-faith purchaser, but it will go to the good-faith purchaser who is the first to record. An example would be as follows.

- *Day 1*: Grantor conveys property to A (BFP).
- *Day 2*: Grantor conveys property to B (BFP).
- *Day 3*: Grantor conveys property to C (BFP).
- *Day 4*: B records.
- *Day 5*: A records.
- *Day 6*: C records.

In a race/notice jurisdiction,[7] B would take title to the property because B was the first BFP to record the interest; in a notice system, C would take title; and in a pure race system, B would take title. However, if B were not a BFP, in a race/notice

---

[6]Notice states are Alabama, Arizona, and Colorado (race/notice by judicial decisions), Arkansas (except mortgages), Connecticut, Delaware, Florida, Illinois, Kansas, Kentucky, Maine, Massachusetts, Missouri, New Hampshire, New Mexico, Ohio (except mortgages), Oklahoma, Rhode Island, South Carolina, Tennessee, Texas, Vermont, Virginia, and West Virginia.

[7]Race/notice states are Alaska, California, Georgia, Hawaii, Idaho, Indiana, Maryland, Michigan, Minnesota, Mississippi, Montana, Nebraska, Nevada, New Jersey, New York, North Dakota, Oregon, Pennsylvania (except mortgages), South Carolina, South Dakota, Utah, Washington, Wisconsin, Wyoming, and the District of Columbia (where states are listed twice there is some conflict between statute and judicial interpretation).

jurisdiction, A would take title; in a notice jurisdiction, B's status is irrelevant and C would still take title; and in a pure race jurisdiction, B would still take title.

The following case provides a discussion of priorities for title.

IN RE RIVERA

--- P.3d ----, 2012 WL 1994873 (Colo. 2012)
The Creditor Who Loses a Secured Position Over a Street Address

FACTS

In 2006, Anthony E. Rivera ("Debtor") executed a promissory note payable to Norman K. Cygan and Carol S. Cygan ("Defendants"). The promissory note was secured by a deed of trust dated June 29, 2006, on a condominium unit located in Denver. The deed includes the complete street address, including the condominium unit number. The deed of trust does not contain the legal description of the property, but instead describes the encumbered property as: "SEE EXHIBIT A—LEGAL ATTACHED." On July 11, 2006, the deed was recorded in the real property records of the Clerk and Recorder of Denver County, Colorado, and was properly indexed in the grantor–grantee index for the City and County of Denver. However, when the deed was recorded, "Exhibit A" containing the legal description was not attached.

In July 2009, Rivera filed for bankruptcy under Chapter 7 of the Bankruptcy Code. Rivera listed the real property at issue here as an asset. In August 2009, the Cygans filed a motion for relief, seeking to enforce their security interest in the property.

The bankruptcy court granted the motion for relief from the automatic stay in September 2009, and the Cygans began judicial foreclosure proceedings on the property. The parties dispute whether the recorded deed of trust provided sufficient notice of the Cygans' security interest in Rivera's condominium unit.

JUDICIAL OPINION

Marquez, Justice

Because the sufficiency of a property description in a deed is a question of state law, and because the issue of whether a deed of trust that contains no legal description can provide sufficient notice of the encumbrance is one of first impression, the bankruptcy court certified this question to this court.

The bankruptcy court's certified question arose because a bankruptcy trustee stands in the shoes of a bona fide purchaser of real property from the debtor, and may avoid a security interest in the debtor's real property if a hypothetical bona fide purchaser could have acquired that property free and clear of the security interest at the time the bankruptcy case commenced. Under such circumstances, the trustee may recover the deed of trust for the benefit of the bankruptcy estate.

In Colorado, a bona fide purchaser of property is one who pays value, in good faith, without any notice of defect in title. Colorado's race-notice recording statute protects purchasers who acquire an interest in property in good faith without notice of a prior unrecorded instrument or document encumbering that property. In other words, an unrecorded encumbrance on real property has no effect with respect to a subsequent bona fide purchaser who acquires that property without notice of the encumbrance. Conversely, a purchaser who has notice of an encumbrance or defect in title does not qualify as a bona fide purchaser and cannot take the property free and clear of that encumbrance.

We have traditionally recognized three forms of notice: actual notice, constructive notice, and inquiry notice. Actual notice exists when one has actual knowledge of another's claim. By contrast, constructive and inquiry notice operate to impute knowledge to a party under certain circumstances.

Constructive notice is essentially record notice. When a party properly records his interest, the party gives constructive notice to the public of his claim. A properly recorded instrument operates to alert future grantees of the recording party's rights because the law assumes that a grantee will search the index at the county clerk and recorder's office and discover the claim. Thus, the law charges subsequent purchasers with constructive notice of a properly recorded interest, even if they do not locate it.

Inquiry notice likewise operates to impute knowledge to a party under certain circumstances. However, "[u]nlike constructive notice, inquiry notice depends on extrinsic factual inquiry." Inquiry notice arises where a party "becomes aware or should have become aware of certain facts which, if investigated, would reveal the claim of another." "[O]nce there is a duty to inquire, the purchaser 'will be charged with all knowledge that a reasonable investigation would have revealed.'"

Here, the Trustee cannot avoid the Defendants' security interest in the Debtor's property unless, at the time the bankruptcy proceedings commenced, a hypothetical purchaser could have purchased the property in good faith without notice of the Defendants' security interest.

Here, whether a hypothetical purchaser would be charged with constructive notice of the Defendants' security interest depends on whether the interest was properly recorded. We hold that a deed of trust that completely omits any legal description is defectively recorded and cannot provide constructive notice of the encumbrance to a subsequent purchaser.

Colorado's race-notice recording statute provides that "no ... unrecorded instrument or document" shall be valid against a purchaser without notice who records first. This provision is silent with respect to what information the recorded instrument must contain. However, section 38–35–122(1)(a), C.R.S. (2011), provides:

All documents of title relating to real property, including instruments creating a lien on real property, except mechanics' liens and judgment liens, shall include as an aid to identification, immediately preceding or following the legal description of the property, the street address or comparable identifying numbers, if such address or numbers are displayed on the property or any building thereon.

This provision presumes that a valid deed of trust necessarily must contain a legal description because the separately required street address must "precede" or "follow" the "legal description."

This interpretation is consistent both with longstanding practice in Colorado and with the overall purpose and intent of Colorado's recording statutes to render interests in real property "more secure and marketable." § 38–34–101, C.R.S. (2011).

Section 38–24–122, read as a whole, unquestionably elevates the legal significance of a legal description over a parcel's street address. This approach reflects the decidedly increased precision that a legal description provides over a street address. A street address certainly serves as an "aid to identification" in combination with the legal description. But standing alone, a street address may not accurately or fully describe the property interest impacted by a lien. For example, a street address could, in some instances, apply to all or only part of an entire apartment building,

or to all or only part of a sprawling ranch or mountain property. Moreover, in Colorado, an interest in real property might include, for example, subsurface mineral rights, a ditch easement, or a deeded right of way to a ski slope or recreation area—appurtenant rights that will not be reflected in a street address, but that will be evident in a legal description. In short, a legal description, unlike a street address, provides the precise parameters of the encumbered property. Indeed, in this case, the Defendants' security interest (as described in the unrecorded Exhibit A) includes not only the physical area of the condominium unit, but also other property interests, including undivided fractional interests in the condominium and apartment building, the right to use a numbered parking stall and certain common areas, and a common right of way for ingress and egress.

In this case, the deed of trust executed by the Defendants and the Debtor did contain a legal description, in conformity with section 38–35–122. That legal description was contained in an attachment. However, when the deed was recorded, the attachment, Exhibit A, was omitted. Hence, the recorded deed of trust contained a complete and accurate street address, but no legal description of the encumbered property. We conclude that the complete omission of the legal description in the recorded deed rendered the recording defective.

Colorado case law reflects that a recorded instrument containing an erroneous or incomplete legal description may nonetheless provide sufficient notice of an encumbrance so long as the instrument describes the encumbered property with reasonable certainty. Moreover, because the purpose of recording a deed of trust is to provide notice to the public of the recording party's interest, a deed of trust that is recorded without any legal description materially fails to describe the recording party's interest in the property. Such a recording is void and therefore incapable of providing constructive notice of the encumbrance.

Finally, inquiry notice likewise will defeat bona fide purchaser status where a purchaser becomes aware or should have become aware of facts triggering a duty to inquire, and a reasonable investigation would have revealed the encumbrance. However, because the deed of trust in this case was defectively recorded, we cannot conclude that it triggered any duty to inquire. Although a real purchaser might have acquired knowledge of other facts sufficient to trigger a duty to inquire, and a reasonable investigation might have revealed the Defendants' encumbrance on the Debtor's property, such facts are not before us in this hypothetical purchaser setting.

Although today's result may appear severe given the circumstances of this case, real property is an area of the law that demands certainty and dependability, and, standing alone, a street address may not accurately or fully describe the property interest impacted by a lien. Our holding is required by Colorado's recording statutes, is consistent with longstanding practice, and is necessary to protect all future bona fide purchasers who take title to real property without notice of an unspecified encumbrance, the parameters of which are not apparent from the deed of trust's use of only a street address.

DISSENTING OPINION

Coats, Justice

The majority concludes that a recorded deed of trust describing real property by no more than a street address cannot possibly provide sufficient notice of any interest in that property because such a deed would necessarily be "defectively recorded." By "defectively recorded," the majority, of course, does not mean that such a deed could not have been received and entered by the appropriate clerk and recorder, in the manner statutorily prescribed for providing constructive notice to third parties, but rather that it would be inherently so defective as to not even constitute a "deed," or other instrument "affecting the title to real property," within the meaning of the recording statute. In actuality, therefore, the recording statute is only secondarily related to the majority's answer to the certified question. Instead, its conclusion rests primarily on the proposition that such a deed of trust is incapable of conveying, encumbering, or otherwise affecting the title to real property and therefore is not valid against a person with any kind of rights in or to that property, whether he has notice of it or not. I not only consider this proposition of law to be erroneous but in fact the product of somewhat muddled reasoning.

The majority understands section 38–35–122 to require that a deed of trust, in order to be "valid," must contain a "legal description" of the property, by which the majority apparently intends some description more complete or formal than, or at least different from, a street address. The term "legal description" is, however, nowhere defined as a specific statutory term of art. Typically, it refers to a "metes and bounds" description or, with regard to platted property, specification of particular lots of the recorded plat. The term is not so limited, however, and other forms of description, such as description

by natural or artificial monuments or marks, have also been held legally sufficient in the past, we have in fact made clear that no more is required for a valid instrument of conveyance than a description that "identifies, or furnishes the means of identifying, the property conveyed."

As a practical matter, a street address is one form of legal description, analogous to (even if sometimes less complete than) the block and lot number of platted property and is at least as descriptive as the common name for a place or farm or a house on a particular street.

If the legislature had intended by the term "legal description" a specific formula or method of description—something more than simply any description adequately identifying the property at issue—to be mechanically included in every deed, without which the deed would be invalid and unrecordable, one might think it would have specified the required formula or method. It did not do so, however, and instead, virtually every aspect of the statutory scheme dealing with interests in real property and the conveyancing and recording of those interests militates against such a mechanical or formalistic understanding. In its general policy statement regarding titles, the legislature expressly indicates that the purpose of its conveyancing and recording provisions is to render title to real property more secure and marketable, and to that end, laws affecting record title should be construed wherever possible to avoid defeating by technical or strict constructions the record title of a party in possession.

Until today, as the majority appears to acknowledge, we have steadfastly taken this view and found that errors in the description of real property do not necessarily render an offending instrument unrecordable or incapable of constructively providing notice of existing interests. The majority's only basis for declining to apply this principle to instruments describing the subject property solely by street address is its interpretation of section 38–35–122, as invalidating all deeds lacking some other form of legal description.

I therefore respectfully dissent.

CASE QUESTIONS

1. Why does the majority opinion find a street address to be inadequate for meeting the legal description standard?
2. What are the dissent's concerns?
3. What advice would you give to sellers and creditors based on this case?

CONSIDER 14.7 *Day 1:* O conveys to A (BFP).
Day 2: O conveys to B (BFP).
Day 3: A records.
Day 4: B records.
In the above example, who takes title under each of the three types of recording statutes?

Torrens System

Another method of title protection used instead of a recording system is the **Torrens system**—named after Sir Robert Torrens, who introduced it in Australia in 1858. The system is one of land title registration; that is, documents of transfer are not recorded, but title to land is registered once by making an entry reflecting the owner. That owner is then given an official certificate of title. If the owner wishes to transfer title to the land, the certificate and a deed are given to the purchaser. The purchaser then takes these documents to the land registration office where the old certificate is surrendered, a change of ownership is entered, and a new certificate is issued to the purchaser. This system eliminates the need for establishing the chain of title.

Initial registration under the Torrens system requires a form of quiet title action, so that all parties with interests or potential interests may be heard before title is registered.

Title Abstracts

In many states, parties transferring property interests will hire attorneys to trace the chain of title on a piece of property and then issue an opinion on that chain. That opinion, in written form, is called an **abstract of title** and is defined as a concise statement of the substance of documents or facts appearing on the public records that affect the title.

The abstract begins with the legal description of the property, often called a **caption** or **head**, and then proceeds with copies of all documents, in chronological order, affecting title. Acknowledgments and signatures are not included so long as the abstractor views them as being in order and proper.

Part of the abstract also includes the **abstractor's certificate**, which summarizes what the abstractor did not examine. For example, it would be very typical for the abstractor to state that zoning violations may affect the title's marketability but that information on such violations is not available from the recorder's records. The abstractor then directs the users to the appropriate agency for determining whether zoning violations exist.

The buyer's attorney then examines the abstract and issues an opinion that includes a description of the property and time covered by the abstract, who holds title to the property, what defects or imperfections exist, and any recommendations for clearing up these defects and imperfections. The abstract will include summaries of items such as deeds, mortgages, deeds of trusts, *lis pendens* (pending legal action on the property), sheriffs' sales certificates, liens, taxes, assessments, judgments, and bankruptcy petitions.

Title Insurance

Recording and title abstracts still do not provide protection if a title defect arises. Neither system of title protection offers a guarantee that no problems will arise. In most parts of the United States today, **title insurance** affords the property purchaser financial protection in the event certain types of defects arise in the property.

A title insurer may operate in one of two ways. First, it may hire an attorney to do an abstract and then issue insurance on the basis of that opinion. Second, the title insurer may be a complete operation by actually doing the search and abstract and then issuing insurance. Those insurers operating the second type of business maintain a title plant for conducting their operations. A title plant consists of copies of documents taken from the public records. Generally, title companies will organize their records pursuant to a tract index system.

Title insurers issue different policies according to the type of applicant for insurance and the use to be made of the property. For example, there are different policy forms for commercial and residential property. Also, different policies are issued for owners of property and for those who wish insurance as mortgage lenders. Neither policy is issued until the insurance company has had an opportunity to examine the records and establish the chain of title.

Process of Issuing a Policy

Most contracts for the purchase and sale of property have marketable title, often obtained through the purchase and issuance of a title insurance policy, as a prerequisite to closing the transaction. **Marketable title** is a title free of problems in the chain of title, the quality of title, and the seller's right to convey the property. Although the definition of marketable title may vary, adding a requirement that a title insurer issue a policy gives the buyer assurance and financial backing in the event of a problem. A policy will not be issued unless the insurer is reasonably sure that no loss will be incurred.

The seller applies for a policy with a title insurance company. The title company prepares an abstract, and any defects are considered by the title examiner, who decides whether the defects are a risk or whether the property is insurable. If there is a favorable decision, the title insurer issues a preliminary binder that is not a policy but rather a commitment to insure contingent upon the transaction's closing and the title's being delivered to the buyer.

If the company finds defects that make the property uninsurable, the seller may be given the opportunity to correct those defects to make the title insurable. For example, the title abstract will provide a list of all judgments against persons having the same name as the seller. The seller may by affidavit establish that he or she is not the same person as named in those judgments. Tax liens may be removed through payment. When the discovered problems are remedied, the insurer will then issue the preliminary binder.

The fees for preparation of the abstract and issuance of the policy vary. In many states, the fee charged will be based on an escalating scale set by a state regulatory body, which allows the fee charged to increase with the value of the property. The reason for the escalating scale is that a title problem on a more expensive piece of property will cost the insurer more in terms of correction or compensation. In some states, the fees are set by a board composed of industry members and then approved by the state as adopted by the board. Such arrangements have been subject to antitrust scrutiny. In *F.T.C. v. Ticor Title Ins. Co.,* 504 U.S. 621 (1992), the U.S. Supreme Court held that these private board mechanisms for establishing title insurance fees must be subject to adequate state review in order to survive an antitrust charge of horizontal price fixing.

Many companies will physically inspect the property to be insured in order to determine any adverse possession or occupancy not reflected in the public records. Also, when insuring a construction lender, the title insurer must be certain that construction or work has not begun prior to the recordation of the mortgage. As noted in Chapter 6, any start of construction, from the presence of equipment to digging one shovelful of dirt, will place the mechanics in first priority if those acts are done prior to recording.

Coverage Afforded by the Title Policy

Title insurance differs significantly from ordinary fire or auto insurance in covering only defects in title in existence at the time of the transfer. Title insurance does not afford protection for new problems developing after the closing of the transaction and the transfer of title to the buyer.

The Title Policy

The American Land Title Association (ALTA) has developed the most widely used form policies and the ones used by major title insurers.

ALTA issues policy forms for lenders, owners, construction lenders, and leaseholds (for either tenants or landlords). The basic title policy, with the 2006 reforms, expanded greatly the coverage for owners and lenders, and includes the following sections:

1. Insuring clauses (outline the coverage), which cover

   a. failure of title to the property (covers forgery, fraud, unauthorized signatures, electronic recording failure, and a host of other problems that arise in recording titles to property and executing deeds)

   b. defects in title such as liens[8]

   c. lack of right of access

   d. unmarketable title

   e. encroachments (new in 2006)

2. Exclusions (which outline those items not covered) (see the next section)

3. Schedules, generally A and B (which outline the added protections or endorsements purchased by the policy holder)

4. Conditions (requirements for the issuance of the policy, such as removal of liens)

5. Stipulations (certain statements of fact that the parties agree are part of their assumptions for the policy, such as the new definition of what constitutes a "public record")

The ALTA policies also include a unilateral arbitration clause when the amount involved exceeds $2 million. The insurance amount must cover the value of the land when a building is constructed, and not just insurance for the cost of the raw land. Title policy buyers must now purchase title insurance based on the proposed value of the land with completed construction.

---

[8]ATLA estimates (2011) that about 30 percent of residential titles had a defect in them; the most common payout was on liens not discovered in the course of issuing the title policy. The liens involved taxes, unpaid child or spousal support, and first and second mortgages.

The ALTA policy also requires that the title insurer undertake its obligation to defend a title "diligently." This change adds an element of good faith to the title insurer's role in defending claims against the insured property.

Exclusions in Title Insurance Coverage

Exclusions from coverage are listed in what is called schedule B of the policy. Title insurance does not provide protection for facts, rights, or claims that are not noted in the public records but are visible upon inspection. Zoning restrictions are not covered. Additional exclusions from coverage are

- Violations of environmental laws unless recorded in the public records (see Chapter 20 for a discussion of these environmental laws; also, see the *Stewart* case later in this chapter and note that the ALTA revisions have a new definition of "public records").
- Litigation defense costs for items excluded under schedule B exceptions.
- Purchasers who are not bona fide purchasers.
- Problems noted in public records other than those that are part of the property records designated by the state as the proper filing place for matters affecting property (see, again, the *Stewart* case).
- "Unmarketability of title" items (see Chapter 13).
- Problems with title based on usury (see Chapter 15).
- Mechanic's liens (see Chapter 6) that arise from work contracted for and commenced after the date of the policy.
- Eminent domain rights (see Chapter 19) unless there is notice in the public records of eminent domain proceedings prior to the date of the policy.

The Enhanced Title Policy—Special Protection Through Endorsements

Title insurers do offer additional coverage of these and other exemptions for a fee. For example, mechanic's lien protections may be added to a policy.

Other types of endorsements include coverage for violation of protective covenants (see Chapter 21) and violation of zoning laws. The California Land Title Association policy, which is becoming more popular outside California, can include hundreds of endorsements available to title policy purchasers. Sometimes referred to as "the California 100," these endorsements give purchasers a wide choice of options for protections. Some states, such as Texas, do not permit the use of these complex endorsement policies.

Another type of special endorsement would be a successorship and assignment endorsement that allows corporations to transfer the policy protection to subsidiaries or newly formed corporations that result from mergers and consolidations so that the policy rights are not lost to corporate reorganizations.

Who Is Protected Under Title Policy?

The policy affords protection to the insured (or insureds) named in the policy (a mortgagee or buyer). If the mortgagee is protected and a property loss results from a title defect, the insurer will pay the balance due on the mortgage, thereby relieving the owner of liability for the mortgage. However, the owner will lose the property and any existing investment or equity. Title policies are not transferable, and the protection afforded a buyer in one transaction may not be passed along to the next buyer.

CONSIDER 14.8   The Gebhardts, husband and wife, owned a 31.7-acre parcel of property, upon which they held an owner's title insurance policy. In 1995, they discovered that another party was paying property taxes on 4.75 acres of the property. They submitted a claim to their title insurer, demanding that the insurer correct the situation by "negotiating a purchase from the alleged owner (who also has a cloud on title) … and obtaining a quitclaim in favor of [the Gebhardts]." In 1996, before the claim was resolved, the Gebhardts executed, for estate-planning purposes, a special warranty deed conveying all of the property to a Virginia L.L.C. of which they were the sole members. The deed recited a consideration of approximately $161,000.

In 1997, the Gebhardts sued the title insurer for breach of contract for failing to resolve the title dispute. The title insurer refused to pay because the Gebhardts were no longer the policyholders. Mr. Gebhardt said that no consideration changed hands (despite the deed recitation of consideration in the amount of $161,000), and that the only reason for the deed recitation was so that the State of Maryland could "assess the transfer taxes from the individual to the L.L.C."

The Gebhardts argued that they nonetheless remained insured parties under the title policy because the conveyance was, in effect, to themselves, and therefore they still retained an "interest" in the property. Are the Gebhardts correct? *Gebhardt Family Restaurant, L.L.C. v. Nation's Title Ins. Co. of New York,* 752 A.2d 1222 (2000).

The seller is not protected by the purchaser's title insurance policy. The seller remains liable to the buyer for breach of any warranties if defects in title arise. In fact, it is not unusual for a title insurer to pay the buyer the loss resulting from the title defect and then through subrogation proceed against the seller for the seller's breach of warranty to the buyer.

Damages

All title policies have a section dealing with the determination and payment of losses. Under the standard policy, the loss is defined as the least of

1. the actual loss of the insured claimed; or
2. the amount of the insurance set forth in the policy; or
3. if the policy is for a mortgagee, the amount necessary to pay off the mortgage debt.

In addition to actual loss, the title insurer will pay the costs, attorneys' fees, and expenses imposed upon an insured in litigation carried out by the insurer for the insured. The following case deals with the complexities of title insurance and its coverage.

WITKOWSKI V. RICHARD W. ENDLAR INS. AGENCY, INC.

968 N.E.2d 922 (Mass. App. 2012)
A Flood of Title Insurance Questions

FACTS

Brian T. Witkowski (plaintiff) purchased a condominium at the Balmoral Condominium, a property converted in 1984 to a residential condominium from a building originally constructed in 1920. The condominium included eighty-six residential units; four of those, including unit 4 (Witkowski's unit), were located in the basement of the building. The condominium is located in a floodplain area designated by the Federal Emergency Management Agency (FEMA) as an AE flood zone, an area of special flood hazard. Under applicable Federal law, federally regulated lending institutions are forbidden to make any loan secured by improved real estate located in an area of special flood hazard, unless the property is covered for the term of the loan by flood insurance in specified amounts.

Elizabeth Kelley, a paralegal employed by the attorney representing Witkowski's mortgage lender, contacted the management company for the condominium to request proof of flood insurance; she in turn was referred to Richard Endlar Insurance Agency. Kelley transmitted to Endlar a facsimile request for proof of flood insurance on the unit. Endlar responded to Kelley with a request for additional information, including the names and addresses of the prospective purchaser and mortgage lender. Kelley furnished the requested information, and on June 29, 2005, Endlar issued a one-page statement regarding insurance on the condominium. At the top of the page, the statement begins with the words "THIS IS TO CERTIFY THAT"; it then proceeds to identify Witkowski as the unit owner and GMAC Mortgage Corporation as his "[b]ank." Continuing, the document states that the "[a]bove unit owner is insured under the Master Policy issued to: Balmoral Condominium Trust Its Trustees and All Unit Owners, A.T.I.M.A. as follows:"

The document then lists flood insurance issued by "Clarendon National Ins." in the amount of "2500000," and flood insurance issued by "The Hartford" covering the "Building" in the amount of "9800000." A signature appears at the bottom of the page, apparently for the purpose of confirming the information contained therein. Immediately above the signature line, the following legend appears:

> *"The Insured's Name, for the purpose of this insurance, shall be as insurance Trustee for all Unit–Owners collectively. This memorandum is for information only; it is not a contract of insurance but attests that policies as numbered herein, and as they stand at the date of this certificate, have been issued by the Companies. Said policies are subject to change by endorsement, and to assignment and cancellation in accordance with their terms."*

Satisfied with the certificate as proof of the existence of flood insurance on the unit, the attorney for Witkowski's mortgage lender authorized the advance of mortgage funds, and Witkowski closed on his purchase of the unit on July 25, 2005.

Witkowski also purchased a policy of title insurance from First American. Among the risks insured against by the policy is the risk that (as of the date of issuance of the policy) "[y]our Title is unmarketable, which allows someone else to refuse to perform a contract to purchase the Land, lease it or make a Mortgage loan on it." Among the exclusions from coverage under the policy are losses resulting from: *"1. Governmental police power, and the existence or violation of any law or government regulation. ... 2. The failure of Your existing structures, or any part of them, to be constructed in accordance with applicable building codes. This Exclusion does not apply to violations of building codes if notice of the violation appears in the Public Records at the Policy Date."*

The condominium sustained substantial damage as the result of a flood of the Shawsheen River on May 15, 2006. Wisowski's unit was completely destroyed. Approximately one week after the flood, a trustee of the condominium association told the four basement unit owners that their units were excluded from coverage under the association's master policy. Under applicable building codes, because of its location at basement level in a special flood hazard zone, Witkowski's unit cannot be rebuilt for the purpose of human occupancy.

Witkowski filed suit against both Endlar and First American. The trial court granted the insurers summary judgment and Witkowski appealed.

JUDICIAL OPINION

Green, Judge

The record reveals that Kelley communicated to Endlar, on the plaintiff's behalf, the need for a certificate verifying flood insurance coverage for the plaintiff's unit. In response, Endlar furnished a certificate stating that the plaintiff, as owner of unit 4, "is insured" under the master policies issued to the condominium trust including, among other coverage, flood insurance on the building under a policy issued by The Hartford up to a policy limit of $9,800,000. Though the certificate made clear that it is not a contract of insurance, it stated clearly that the listed policies had been issued.

Contrary to the defendant's assertions, the certificate does not contain any express statement that the policies listed thereon are subject to any other conditions or limitations, or that the recipient should review the policies themselves in order to ascertain the scope or existence of coverage. Moreover, though the fact that the policies might contain certain qualifications or limitations may be implicit (since the certificate cannot reasonably be expected to set forth all the terms, conditions, and details of every policy), the exclusion of the plaintiff's unit from coverage entirely is a particularly dramatic limitation in the circumstances. It is one thing to recognize that, in listing the various insurance policies covering the condominium, the certificate does not describe the details of all conditions or limitations of such coverage; it is quite another for an undisclosed exclusion to vitiate the essential purpose for which the certificate was requested. The summary judgment record indicates that the plaintiff's unit (together with the other three basement units) was excluded from coverage under the master flood insurance policy, suggesting that other above-grade units in the condominium were not so excluded. Accordingly, Endlar's contention that the certificate verified flood insurance coverage only for the "building" (but not for the units within the building) rings hollow.

Moreover, the disclaimer that the certificate is not a contract of insurance does not derogate, by its terms or in its context, from the fact that the recipient of the certificate should be entitled to rely on its accuracy, at least concerning the issuance and existence of the policies listed thereon. Particularly in the circumstances attending the request for the certificate, Endlar was aware that the plaintiff (and his mortgage lender) required proof of flood insurance coverage on his unit, and that they would rely on the insurance certificate Endlar furnished to constitute that proof.

The plaintiff's claim accordingly does not rest on a claim of contract, based on the certificate; instead it rests on the contention that the plaintiff relied to his detriment on materially false information furnished by Endlar, in circumstances in which Endlar was aware that the purpose for which the plaintiff had requested the certificate would likely be followed by such reliance. The certificate in the present case was requested for the express purpose of verifying the existence of flood insurance coverage on the plaintiff's unit. On its face, it is somewhat ambiguous, but a reasonable fact finder could construe it to represent that the unit is covered by flood insurance.

On the summary judgment record, construed in the light most favorable to the plaintiff, we conclude that there are triable questions of fact concerning whether the certificate falsely represented that the plaintiff's unit was covered under the master condominium policies of flood insurance, and whether the plaintiff reasonably relied to his detriment on that

representation. The summary judgment dismissing the plaintiff's claims against Endlar accordingly is reversed.

The plaintiff's claim against First American stands differently. The parties acknowledge that the terms of the policy of title insurance are unambiguous; we accordingly construe and enforce them according to their plain meaning. As we have observed, the policy specifically excludes from coverage any losses resulting from governmental regulations (including zoning and building codes). "There is a difference between economic lack of marketability, which concerns conditions that affect the use of land, and title marketability, which relates to defects affecting legally recognized rights and incidents of ownership." Put simply, the fact that Federal flood insurance regulations may restrict the availability of conventional mortgage financing for the unit may affect its value, or even its economic marketability, but it does not constitute a lien or other encumbrance on the property, and does not affect its title.

Our analysis is unaffected by the plaintiff's suggestion that his property should be treated differently by reason of its status as a condominium unit. It is true that the unit exists only as created under, and described in, the condominium master deed. Accordingly, it is also true that the inability to rebuild the unit following its destruction in the May, 2006 flood renders it literally and legally impossible to recreate the unit itself. However, even if we assume (without deciding) that the plaintiff is correct in his contention that the inability to recreate the unit as a legal entity impairs marketability of title to the unit, that condition arose only as a result of the flood in May, 2006, and did not exist on the date the title policy issued. Accordingly, the title policy, which furnishes coverage only for defects in title existing as of the date of its issuance, affords no right or remedy to the plaintiff for any defect in title caused or brought about by the May, 2006, flood. The motion judge correctly entered summary judgment dismissing the plaintiff's claims against First American.

CASE QUESTIONS

1. What happens with the claim against the insurance agency?
2. What happens with the claim against title insurer?
3. Why does the argument that laws and regulation prevent the reconstruction of the condo not convince the court that the title insurer should cover the loss?

ETHICAL ISSUE

In conducting a title search for Fleming before he purchased property, Fleming's attorney discovered a lack of subdivision permit for the dwelling and wastewater system, but failed to inform Fleming. Fleming purchased the property and spent nearly $60,000 getting the problems with the permit resolved. Fleming filed suit against his lawyer for malpractice. Fleming's lawyer maintains that the lack of a permit for a certain use was not a title issue and need not be disclosed. Does Fleming have a cause of action for a defective title? Did Fleming, his estate, or the lawyer have an ethical responsibility to let anyone know of the problem with the property? *Estate of Fleming v. Nicholson*, 724 A.2d 1026 (Vt. 1998).

UNIFORM LAWS AND PROPOSALS

The complications of deeds, title, and recording have produced several uniform acts. Two of them, the Uniform Simplification of Land Transfers Act and the Uniform Marketable Title Act, both drafted for use in 1990, have very limited state adoptions. The Uniform Recognition of Acknowledgments Act, which applies to both deeds and wills, adopted in 16 states, has been withdrawn as a uniform law.

CAUTIONS AND CONCLUSIONS

Transferring title to property requires a great deal of detailed attention to the paperwork and the background of the property itself. Parties involved in a transfer of title by deed should check the following:

1. Does the grantor have the authority to transfer the title to the property?

2. Does the grantor have full and complete title to the property?

3. Is the description for the property accurate?

4. Are there any boundary issues that are evident from a physical inspection of the property?

5. Do the public records reveal any title issues such as judgments or liens?

6. Are there restrictions on the use of the land such as zoning or covenants?

7. Can I obtain title insurance for the property?

8. What will the title insurance cover?

9. How does recording work in my state, and is my title protected if I am first to record my deed?

10. What type of title am I getting, and do I get any warranties with my title?

11. Is there a good chain of title? Do I need a title abstract?

12. Have I checked the rights of those occupying the property, and are there any possible claims for title by adverse possession?

13. Have I proofed the deed for correct spelling and adequate descriptions of the property?

14. Have I met the formal requirements for signature?

The devil is in deeds and these questions should help the parties walk through those potential pitfalls in transferring title.

KEY TERMS

abstract of title, 387
abstractor's certificate, 387
acknowledgment clause, 368
adverse possession, 372
bona fide purchaser
    (BFP), 383
caption, 387
constructive delivery, 378
deed, 360

deed of bargain and sale, 372
delivery, 369
donee, 378
donor, 378
good-faith purchaser, 383
grantor/grantee index
    system, 381
habendum clause, 367
head, 387

inter vivos gift, 378
judicial deed, 372
lis pendens, 387
livery of seisin, 360
marketable title, 388
notice statutes, 383
premises, 360
pure race statute, 382
quiet title action, 378

quitclaim deed, 370
race/notice system, 383
recording, 379
sheriffs' deeds, 372

special warranty deed, 371
squatter's rights, 372
title insurance, 387
Torrens system, 387

tract index system, 381
undue influence, 360
warranty deed, 370

CHAPTER PROBLEMS

1. MGD purchased a policy of title insurance from First American Title Company. The policy generally insured against defects in title to property MGD owned in Tangipahoa Parish, Louisiana that might affect the marketability of the title.

   After MGD purchased the property, they learned that it had been under lease to the United States government during World War II for use as a bombing range. Although the lease had expired years before the purchase, MGD discovered that remnants of bombs were still on the property. Because of the potential hazards from the bombs, officials in Tangipahoa Parish, Louisiana refused to issue permits to develop a residential subdivision on the property. MGD filed a claim with its title insurer because the land could not be sold because the title was unmarketable and the land could not be used for its intended purpose. Is the title insurer liable for a defect in title? *MGD Partners Ltd. Liability Corp. v. First American Title Ins. Co.*, 440 Fed.Appx. 368, 2011 WL 3962568 (5th Cir. 2011).

2. Iver Martin Villa spent most of his life on his family homestead outside of Meeker, Colorado. He married his wife Mary and raised two children, Mary K. Krueger and John Villa, on the ranch.

   Marlyn Ary started working for the Villas as a part-time housekeeper in the mid-1970s. When Mary Villa died suddenly from a brain tumor in 1989, Ary stayed on, providing the same services for Iver Villa. The two became friends.

   In the mid-1990s, Villa's health began to decline. He suffered from multiple ailments, including emphysema, congestive heart failure, and macular degeneration. Ary started acting as Villa's paid caregiver in addition to being his housekeeper. She assisted Villa by administering his medication, reconciling his bank accounts, filling out and helping him sign his checks, reading him his legal and financial documents, and transporting him to his various appointments.

   In 1997, Villa executed a will leaving his estate to Krueger and her children. But in 2001, Villa began construction on a new house, and in April 2003, Villa conveyed an interest in the completed house and the parcel of land it occupied, worth $350,000, to Ary by executing a deed for joint tenancy. After making the conveyance, Villa told multiple people he was worried Krueger would try to overturn it. While in the hospital

in November 2004, Villa wrote Ary a check for $5,000 so she could defend her ownership in court.

   Upon Villa's death in April 2005, Krueger became the personal representative of his estate. She brought suit against Ary, claiming Villa's conveyance of the house, land, and $5,000 were void based on Ary's breach of fiduciary duty and undue influence over Villa as his paid caretaker. Ary denied the claims, asserting the conveyances were gifts from Villa for her years of service. What do you think the court should do? What factors point to capacity? How does undue influence affect capacity? *Krueger v. Ary*, 205 P.3d 1150 (Colo. 2009).

3. Under each of the three types of recording systems, who takes title?
   - *Day 1*: O conveys to A (BFP).
   - *Day 2*: A conveys to B (BFP). B records.
   - *Day 3*: O conveys to C (BFP). C records.

4. Clarence and Lillian Ellison and Clifford and Mary Grace Bearden are adjoining landowners with a dispute regarding the location of the boundary line between their properties. A fence built by the Beardens has separated the two parcels of property for more than 40 years. The Ellisons have raised gardens, cut timber, grazed cattle, and otherwise used the property on their side of the fence for more than 38 years. An error in the location of the fence was discovered, but the Ellisons claimed title to the land up to the fence through adverse possession. The Beardens' son knocked down the southernmost portion of the fence, and the Ellisons filed suit. The trial court found the Ellisons held title to the disputed boundary property and ordered a survey to have the deed reformed. Is this a correct outcome? *Bearden v. Ellison*, 560 So.2d 1042 (Ala. 1990).

5. Prepare a deed on the basis of the following information. Be sure to attach to it any comments on missing information or information that is not necessary.
   a. Land to be conveyed.
   b. Grantors. Mr. and Mrs. Paul S. Smith living in a home on the pictured lot, 4141 Waverly Street, Phoenix, Arizona 85003. They own the property as joint tenants. Mrs. Smith's first name is Helen.
   c. Grantees. Mr. and Mrs. Samuel P. Polk, 3232 Holly Drive, Phoenix, Arizona 85204. They wish to own the property as joint tenants. Mrs. Polk's first name is Janice.

   d. Date of transaction. September 12, 2012.

   e. Amount Polks will pay to Smiths. $252,500.00.

   f. A neighbor of the Smiths, Thomas Jones, is a notary public who will furnish his services for free. His commission expires September 15, 2015.

   g. The Smiths wish to warrant title only for the time they have held the property.

   h. The Smiths have lined up their neighbors, Brad Georges and Bill Daves, to witness the transaction.

   i. A school water pipeline runs through the back two feet of the property. There are no other easements, encumbrances, unpaid taxes, or liens on the property.

   j. The Polks are paying cash.

6. Determine who gets title to the property under each of the three types of jurisdictions in the following circumstances.

   ■ *Day 1*: O conveys to A (BFP).

   ■ *Day 2*: O conveys to B (not BFP).

   ■ *Day 3*: O conveys to C (BFP).

   ■ *Day 4*: B records.

   ■ *Day 5*: A records.

7. Irene Franzen and Joseph and Shirley Cassarino are neighbors. As is often the case, the boundary line between their properties is described one way in their deeds but appears to be physically different. Indeed, part of the Cassarinos' garage is on Franzen's property, and the Cassarinos have used other parts of the area in dispute as a vegetable garden. They have also mowed the yard in the disputed area and planted trees and shrubs. They have so used the land since they moved into their home in 1964. Irene Franzen claims title to the strip of land through her deed. The Cassarinos counterclaim for the land on the grounds of adverse possession. Who holds title to the land strip? *Franzen v. Cassarino*, 552 N.Y.S.2d 789 (1990).

8. In 1968, Colonial Motel Properties, Inc., acquired title to a 7.746-acre tract of land next to land owned by Marathon Petroleum. Colonial decided to expand its motel business by appealing to trailer truck drivers. The southern portion of its acreage and .27 acres of Marathon's property were covered with dirt and gravel for use for parking by the drivers. Since 1970, trucks have parked on this lot. A sign that read as follows was posted: *Free Parking for Colonial Inn Motel Guests Only. All Others $20.00 per night. Violators impounded at owner's expense. All vehicles must register.*

   The motel also employed a security guard for the lot to ensure that all vehicles were registered. The lot, the sign, and the security guard were all visible from Marathon's property.

   In 1985, Marathon was approached by a buyer for its property and the .27 acre encroachment was discovered. Colonial claimed title through adverse possession. Is Colonial correct? *Marathon Petroleum Co. v. Colonial Motel Properties, Inc.*, 550 N.E.2d 778 (Ind. 1990).

9. William Bryant constructed an airstrip on what he believed to be his property. He used the airstrip for landing his plane, but he also permitted other pilots in the area to land there. The airstrip was used for 40 years and was located on land that was primarily used for timber and mining. When Bryant brought suit against the coal mining company that owned the land seeking to establish title to the airstrip by adverse possession, the coal company defended itself by noting that Bryant's use was not exclusive and not sufficiently open and notorious to qualify for a taking by adverse possession. Does Bryant have title by adverse possession? *Bryant v. Palmer Coking Coal Co.*, 936 P.2d 1163 (Wash. App. 1997).

10. Somerset Savings Bank agreed to finance a 72-unit condominium project, and Chicago Title issued a policy for Somerset's $9.5 million mortgage. After the title policy was issued, the city of Revere, Massachusetts, refused to issue a permit for the project because of issues with existing zoning laws, including a railroad right-of-way through the property. Somerset was left with a $9.5 million mortgage on condominiums that would never be built. Somerset brought suit against Chicago Title for its failure to note the zoning issue. The trial court held that the zoning issue was not covered under the policy, the court of appeals reversed on one issue, and Somerset appealed. Who is correct? The title insurance company or Somerset, and why? *Somerset Savings Bank v. Chicago Title Insurance Company*, 649 N.E.2d 1123 (Mass. 1995).

For research activities related to this chapter, go to our text companion website at www.cengagebrain.com

CHAPTER 15

FINANCING IN THE TRANSFER OF REAL ESTATE

Test Your Knowledge

Do you know the meanings of the most commonly used terms in buying a home? Check this list and then take the test at the end of the chapter (pages 445–446).

point	*government loan*	*FHA*
deed of trust	*ARM*	*prepaids*
lock	*caveat emptor*	*conventional loan*
annual percentage rate	*loan-to-value ratio*	*balloon payment*
amortization	*creative financing*	*walk-through*
escrow	*earnest money*	*PITI*
robo-signing	*Fannie Mae*	*MERS*
under-water mortgage	*short sale*	

© Cengage Learning

As this partial list of terms shows, financing the purchase of real property is a complex and critical element of our personal lives, but real estate finance is also a key part of any economy. The events in the mortgage market in 2007 and 2008 affected "Main Street and Wall Street," and also have had an effect on foreclosures and property titles. This chapter discusses the processes, rights, remedies, and obligations in financing the purchase of land.

THE MORTGAGE

Ancient civilizations, such as those in Egypt and Babylonia, pledged property to finance their purchase or simply to secure loans.

The term **mortgage** was not introduced into the English legal system until after the 1066 invasion of England by William I (William the Conqueror). Mortgage is derived from the French word *mort*, which means "dead" or "frozen" (to indicate that the borrower could not transfer the property freely), and *gage*, which means "pledge."

Black's Law Dictionary defines a mortgage as a pledge or security of a particular property for the payment of a debt or the performance of some other obligation, whatever form the transaction may take, but is not now regarded as a conveyance; a written instrument providing security for payment of a debt.

This basic definition applies to all forms of mortgages and mortgage theories. However, the details on the creation, enforcement, and rights of parties do vary among the states.

Parties to the Mortgage

Initially, a mortgage is a two-party relationship. The borrower who is buying or pledging property is referred to as the **mortgagor**. The lender who advances the mortgagor the funds for the loan is referred to as the **mortgagee**. The mortgagor may be borrowing the funds to purchase the property being pledged, called a **purchase money mortgage**.

Subsequent Parties to the Mortgage

After the mortgage is executed, third parties can acquire interests in the mortgage. For example, the mortgagee could sell or assign the mortgage to another lender. In addition, mortgagees often designate mortgage servicing companies to handle the payments from the mortgagor as well as the administration of expenses on the property such as insurance and taxes. One of the problems in the foreclosures that followed the collapse of the real estate market in 2007–2008 was that there were so many third parties involved with mortgages that the rights of the parties in foreclosure became confused and subject to judicial challenges (See pp. 430–431 for more information on this problem).

Title Theory versus Lien Theory

There are three theories of mortgage security: title theory, lien theory, and intermediate theory (a combination of the two).

Title theory states give the mortgagee some type of legal title to the property. This theory is the older of the two and is used primarily in the eastern states. Under title theory, the mortgagee has the right, upon foreclosure, to possession and rents on the property.

In **lien theory** states, the mortgagee has only a lien on the property and is entitled to possession and rents only upon foreclosure. Under this theory, the mortgagor actually holds title to the property. The lien theory is followed by the majority of states west of the Mississippi.

Some states follow an intermediate theory, which is a combination of the title and lien theories. In these states, the mortgagee is entitled to possession and rents upon the default of the mortgagor. However, unlike the lien theory, the mortgagee is not required to wait until after foreclosure; and unlike the title theory where the mortgagee takes the property upon default, the mortgagee in an intermediate state does not hold title until after completion of proceedings that are mandated by statute but fall short of full foreclosure's length and complexity.

The following case shows the complexities of a lender's possession pending foreclosure as it deals with an issue of who is liable for what.

WOODVIEW CONDOMINIUM ASS'N, INC. V. SHANAHAN

917 A.2d 790 (N.J. App. 2007)
Who Pays the Fees When the Condo Owner Walks Away?

FACTS

In April 1997, Keven Shanahan (defendant) bought two units at the Woodview Condominium complex in Millville, New Jersey. The Woodview Condominium Association, Inc. (Association/plaintiff), collected fees on a monthly basis to cover each unit owner's *pro rata* share of expenses for the common areas, including utility charges.

During his ownership, Mr. Shanahan defaulted on his obligation to pay the monthly condominium assessments, which he cured when sued by the Association. On January 11, 2000, Shanahan conveyed title to the two units to Tomas Pratts, Jr., who, in exchange, executed a one-year purchase money mortgage in the amount of $33,000 payable to Shanahan. Pratt also failed to pay the monthly fees, and on January 29, 2001, the Association filed an assessment lien on the units, totaling $3,192.50. In September 2001, Pratts defaulted on his mortgage with Shanahan, and Shanahan assumed control of both units as a mortgagee in possession. Shanahan rented out each unit. Although Shanahan satisfied the Association's assessment liens, he never paid the monthly condominium fees while in possession and control of the units.

As a result, the Association filed suit against Pratt and Shanahan to collect the monthly assessments that were due. Shanahan moved to dismiss on the grounds that he was not personally liable for the accrued fees because he did not hold legal title to the units. The court found for the Association and Shanahan appealed.

JUDICIAL OPINION

Parrillo, Judge

It has long been the view that if a mortgagor defaults in the payment of mortgage debt, the mortgagee has the right to take possession of the mortgaged property, subject to the mortgagor's right of redemption. To be sure, legal title remains in the mortgagor and the mortgagee in possession does not obtain an unfettered interest akin to fee simple ownership. Nevertheless, upon taking possession of the property, the mortgagee in possession has the right to occupy the property as well as the right to lease the property to a third party, and to collect the rent and profits. In addi-

tion, the mortgagee in possession has standing to sue a third party for damage to the property.

Concomitant with the entitlement to profits and rent, mortgagees in possession assume the duties of a provident owner, which requires "management and preservation of the property." This is because although the mortgagee is in possession, legal title remains in the mortgagor, who has the right to redeem the property, and title only passes to the mortgagee at the conclusion of the foreclosure process.

Thus, mortgagees in possession have long been held to "the duty of treating the property as a provident owner would treat it, … of using the same diligence to make it productive that a provident owner would use" and "to keep it in good ordinary repair." Indeed, a mortgagee in possession is liable both for damages to the property while in possession, and in tort for injuries arising from "his actionable fault in utilizing the property or … his failure to perform duties imposed by law upon the owner of the land." Furthermore, "[a] mortgagee in possession may also be subject to prosecution by local governmental authorities for the failure of the mortgaged property to conform to housing codes, health and safety ordinances and other similar regulations." And, mortgagees in possession have been required to "pay taxes as they accrue on the property."

Significant for present purposes, "a mortgagee in possession may be liable for services rendered to him in connection with the property during his occupancy thereof on the basis of an express or implied contract." When a mortgagee goes into possession questions as to his personal liability arising out of his relations with third parties arise. Since he is the person in possession of the premises he is personally liable in tort for injuries resulting either through his actionable fault in utilizing the property or by reason of his failure to perform duties imposed by law upon the owner of the land. Even more clearly he is liable for goods and services furnished to him during his occupancy.

Defendant fully accepted the services either rendered directly or funded by the Association to ensure the premises' habitability and was therefore unjustly enriched by collecting rents without contributing his pro-rata share to their costs.

…[H]ere the mortgagee in possession undoubtedly benefited from services either provided or funded by plaintiff…. [D]efendant here should not be allowed to benefit from the services and goods he has received without having to pay plaintiff his pro rata share of the costs.

Defendant nevertheless argues, through a series of analogies, that he is not personally liable. Comparing condominium fees to realty improvements which the mortgagee has no right to impose upon the mortgagor, defendant posits that requiring him to pay the assessments will impermissibly increase the title holder's cost of redemption. He offers no legal support for this proposition. In any event, the analogy fails because the monthly dues, unlike realty improvements, represent carrying costs necessary to maintaining the property and keeping the rental income flowing.

For all these reasons, we concur in the trial court's ruling holding defendant liable for the outstanding condominium fee assessments accruing during his possession and control of the units. However, a question remains as to whether the judgment is correct in the amount rendered. Since the mortgagee is not entitled to rents or profits accrued before the date of taking possession, it follows, as a matter of course, that defendant is not liable for delinquent condominium fees accruing before he came into possession of the realty…. [I]n the interest of fairness, we deem it appropriate to remand the matter for the limited purpose of determining the date on which defendant became a mortgagee in possession and then appropriately adjusting the amount of the judgment based on that determination.

The judgment is affirmed in all other respects.

CASE QUESTIONS

1. What connection does the court make between right to rents and obligation for maintenance payments?
2. What is the timing issue the court notes, and how is it important to the court's findings?
3. What would be the implications if the mortgagee were not liable for the fees?

CONSIDER 15.1   Bishop Estate is the fee simple owner and was the lessor of two lots of commercial real property located in Kaka'ako, Hawai'i (the Kaka'ako Properties). Bishop Estate leased each lot for a 40-year term. Bishop Estate had pledged the lots in a mortgage to several different lenders and has defaulted on those loans. The lenders have stepped in and are collecting the rents from the two tenants. Bishop Estate objects because there has been no foreclosure. Can the lenders take the rents? Will the answer vary from state to state? *Hawaii Nat. Bank v. Cook*, 58 P.3d 60 (Haw. 2002).

Creation of Mortgage Relationship

Requirement of a Record

As with all real estate transactions, the mortgage must have some form of writing or record. The record is also important because the rights of the mortgagee are protected by public notification of the mortgagee's interest. Recording the mortgage with the appropriate government agency—the same agency where deeds (Chapter 14) and security interests (Chapters 5 and 6) are recorded—provides the public notification. Mortgages are complex land interests, and recorded documents control the parties' interests, rights, and remedies. As is the case with all other written requirements, the documents and signatures can now be electronic.

MERS and Mortgages

The Mortgage Electronic Registry System (MERS) is best described in part of a court opinion that resulted from one of the many cases filed trying to establish parties' rights under the MERS system. In *Jackson v. Mortgage Electronic*, 770 N.W.2d 487, at 490 (Minn. 2009), the Minnesota Supreme Court explained MERS succinctly:

"MERS is an electronic registration system that was created in the aftermath of the 1993 savings and loan crisis. MERS does not originate, lend, service, or invest in home

mortgage loans. Instead, MERS acts as the nominal mortgagee for the loans owned by its members. The MERS system is designed to allow its members, which include originators, lenders, servicers, and investors, to assign home mortgage loans without having to record each transfer in the local land recording offices where the real estate securing the mortgage is located."

Members of MERS, which is incorporated in Delaware, paid membership fees as well as transaction fees to access MERS' records. There was an additional benefit to this centralized electronic recording system which was that many mortgage lenders used MERS as the "mortgagee of record" on the recorded mortgage documents in lieu of the actual mortgagee because, as they believed at the time, listing MERS as the mortgagee facilitated foreclosure without having to run down who held the mortgage interest at the time of the foreclosure. Within MERS, the transfers and transferees were available to members, but only MERS appeared in the publicly recorded documents.

Such a system, however, means that the chain of title in the public records is not present nor traceable without access to MERS. As a result, the chain of title on mortgaged properties is not clear. In fact, some courts have disallowed foreclosure using MERS documents and records because the MERS documentation is separate from the land records in government offices and the right to foreclose could not always be connected to the underlying note or the original mortgagee.

ETHICAL ISSUE

One of the problems with the MERS system was this: Who signs the documents when a mortgage holder wishes to pursue foreclosure? That is, the original publicly recorded owner of the mortgage is no longer the owner, but the owner became MERS when the mortgage was first transferred. It was difficult for those holding the mortgage to determine who actually owned the mortgage and therefore had the right to authorize foreclosure. The mortgages lacked the usual chain of title that would have appeared in the public land records if the transfers had been duly recorded. (See Chapter 13 for more information on recording, title, and chain of title.)

The result was that lenders turned to foreclosure mills, law firms that processed thousands of foreclosures using a technique known as "robo-signing," where an individual with the title of "vice president" for an alleged financial institution signed all the foreclosure documentation. For example, one "Linda Greene, according to MERS foreclosure documentation, was signing as a vice president for foreclosures initiated by twenty different banks, a job she held at all 20 banks at the same time."[1]

Discuss the ethical issues in creating banks, a vice president, and robo-signing mortgage foreclosure documents.

Underlying Debt Requirement

To be valid, a mortgage requires an underlying debt. A mortgage cannot be enforced unless the mortgagor owes some debt to the mortgagee. Generally, that underlying debt is evidenced by a **promissory note**. The promissory note is the actual contractual arrangement between the parties for the loan. Mortgage notes are simple instruments that specify the principal amount, the rate of interest, and

---

[1]David E. Woolley and Lisa D. Herzog, "MERS: The Unreported Effects of Lost Chain of Title on Real Property Owners," 8 *Hastings Bus. L.J.* 365, 378 (2012).

FIGURE 15.1 Promissory Note

$ _____ City, State _____ Date _____, 2013

For value received _____ promises (s)

to pay to _____ or order, at _____

the sum of _____ DOLLARS ($ _____).

Should default be made in the payment of any installment when due, then the whole sum of principal and interest shall become immediately due and payable at the option of the holder of this note, with interest from date of such default at the highest legal rate until paid on the entire unpaid principal and accrued interest.

Should any installment due hereunder not be paid as it matures, the amount of such installment which has matured shall, at the option of the holder of this note, bear interest at 10 percent per annum from its maturity date until paid.

Principal and interest payable in lawful money of the United States of America.

Should suit be brought to recover on this note _____ promise(s) to pay as attorneys' fees a reasonable amount additional to the amount found hereunder.

The makers and indorsers hereof severally waive diligence, demand, presentment for payment and protest, and consent to the extension of time of payment of this note without notice.

This note is secured by a mortgage upon real property.

_____   _____

_____   _____

© Cengage Learning

the payment terms. The note references the underlying mortgage or deed of trust. Figure 15.1 is an example of a note secured by a mortgage.

The promissory note usually contains terms that make it negotiable—a quality that enables the lender to easily transfer and sell the note to third parties. That negotiability permitted financial institutions to bundle mortgages together and sell securities, called mortgage-backed securities, as investment vehicles that helped to fuel a large expansion of the mortgage and real estate markets. Other typical provisions in mortgage notes are discussed later in this chapter. Without an underlying debt, there can be no mortgage and resulting security for a lender and, therefore, no foreclosure. The MERS system complicated this requirement of an underlying debt because the note and the mortgage became separated as the note was used for securitization and bundling of mortgages in the secondary markets. Without a debt accompanying the mortgage, lenders could not foreclose because there was no underlying debt and, hence, no valid mortgage that would allow foreclosure.

The following case deals with this critical issue of whether MERS resulted in a separation of debt and mortgage and, as a result, the issue of the right to foreclose arose.

U.S. BANK, N.A. V. HOWIE

280 P.3d 225 (Kan. App. 2012)
MERS and Mortgages and Lenders and Foreclosure

FACTS

On September 20, 2005, James W. Howie executed a promissory note to U.S. Bank in the amount of $151,600. That same day, James and his wife, Georgia Howie, executed a mortgage granting a security interest in their real property to secure payment of the Note. Under the terms of the mortgage, the Howies were named as "Borrower," U.S. Bank was named as "Lender," and Mortgage Electronic Registration Systems, Inc. (MERS) was named as the mortgagee "acting solely as a nominee for Lender and Lender's successors and assigns."

James died on February 23, 2008, leaving Georgia as the surviving joint tenant with right of survivorship in the mortgaged property. Georgia stopped making payments on the underlying debt and by May 1, 2009, the note was in default. MERS assigned the mortgage to U.S. Bank, and on November 10, 2009, U.S. Bank filed a petition to foreclose the mortgage. Figure 15.2 illustrates the parties' relationships.

Georgia filed a motion for summary judgment. She argued that U.S. Bank could not foreclose against the property under the mortgage because the Note, held by U.S. Bank, and the mortgage, initially held by MERS and later assigned to U.S. Bank, had been irreparably severed.

The district court found that any severance was "cured" by MERS's subsequent assignment of the mortgage to U.S. Bank, thereby permitting U.S. Bank to fore-close on the mortgage. Georgia's motion for summary judgment was denied and she appealed.

JUDICIAL OPINION

Malone, Judge

Generally, a mortgage is unenforceable when it is not held by the same entity that holds the promissory note. However, an exception exists where there is an agency relationship between the holder of the mortgage and the holder of the promissory note. In *Landmark Nat'l Bank v. Kesler*, 289 Kan. 528, 216 P.3d 158 (2009), the Kansas Supreme Court discussed the effect of "splitting" a mortgage from the promissory note:

"'The practical effect of splitting the deed of trust [or mortgage] from the promissory note is to make it impossible for the holder of the note to foreclose, unless the holder of the deed of trust is the agent of the holder of the note. Without the agency relationship, the person holding only the note lacks the power to foreclose in the event of default. The person holding only the deed of trust will never experience default because only the holder of the note is entitled to payment of the underlying obligation. The mortgage loan becomes ineffectual when the note holder did not also hold the deed of trust.'"

Because the parties agree that MERS and U.S. Bank are separate entities, the dispositive issue in

FIGURE 15.2

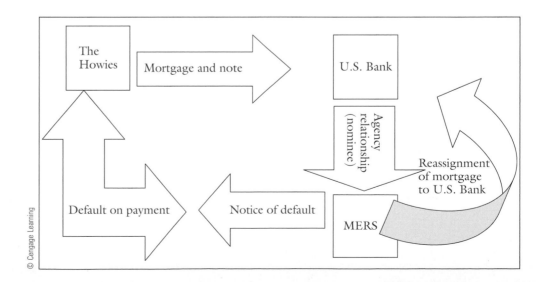

© Cengage Learning

this case is whether MERS, the initial holder of the Mortgage,[2] was acting as an agent of U.S. Bank, the holder of the Note. If so, then the Mortgage and the Note were never severed and U.S. Bank, as the present holder of both, may foreclose on the Mortgage. The only evidence before the district court regarding the existence of an agency relationship between MERS and U.S. Bank was the language of the Mortgage itself, which the parties do not dispute. The Mortgage stated:

> *"Borrower understands and agrees that MERS holds only legal title to the interests granted by Borrower in this [Mortgage], but, if necessary to comply with law or custom, MERS (as nominee for Lender and Lender's successors and assigns) has the right: to exercise any or all of those interests, including, but not limited to, the right to foreclose and sell the Property; and to take any action required of Lender including, but not limited to, releasing and canceling this [Mortgage.]"*

Here, the language of the Mortgage evidences an express agency between MERS and U.S. Bank because it explicitly authorizes MERS to act on behalf of U.S. Bank in all situations related to the enforcement of the Mortgage.

Although the Mortgage uses the term "nominee" rather than "agent," this terminology does not alter the character of the relationship between MERS and U.S. Bank. Georgia acknowledges the language contained in the Mortgage, but she relies on case law to support the proposition that there was no agency relationship between MERS and U.S. Bank. In *Landmark*, the debtor obtained a loan from Landmark National Bank, secured by a mortgage in real property. The mortgage was duly recorded in Ford County, Kansas land records. About a year later, the debtor took out a second loan from Millenia Mortgage Corp., secured by a mortgage in the same real property. The second mortgage named Millenia as the lender and MERS as the mortgagee acting "solely as nominee for Lender … and Lender's successors and assigns." The second mortgage was also recorded in Ford County. At some subsequent time, the second mortgage may have been assigned to Sovereign Bank (Sovereign) and Sovereign may have taken physical possession of the associated promissory note, but the assignment of the second mortgage was not recorded.

Landmark later filed a petition to foreclose its mortgage. Landmark named the debtor and Millenia as defendants but did not serve notice of the petition on either MERS or Sovereign. Since neither of the named defendants answered the petition, default judgment was entered against them, and the secured property was sold at a sheriff's sale. Soon after the sheriff's sale, Sovereign filed an answer to the foreclosure petition, claiming an interest in the property as Millenia's successor in interest. The district court found that Sovereign was precluded from asserting its rights after the judgment had been entered because Sovereign had not recorded its interest in the property.

On appeal, this court agreed with the district court that although the mortgage used the word "nominee," it was clear that MERS was an agent for Millenia. Next, this court found that MERS was not a contingently necessary party because MERS did not have a separate interest, apart from its principal's interest in securing the loan, that would be substantially impaired or impeded absent its participation in the foreclosure litigation. This court specifically noted that MERS did not receive payments on behalf of Millenia or Sovereign and that under the terms of the mortgage, notices of default on superior liens were to go to Millenia, not MERS. Our Supreme Court [held] that the document consistently refers only to the rights of the lender, including rights to receive notice of litigation, to collect payments, and to enforce the debt obligation [and that] the document consistently limits MERS to acting 'solely' as the nominee of the lender.

Landmark does not support Georgia's contention that MERS is not an agent for lenders such as U.S. Bank. Indeed, *Landmark* supports the converse proposition: the fact that MERS has few, if any, rights other than acting on behalf of the lender to secure the lender's rights where necessary indicates that MERS is an agent of the lender.

Georgia also cites *Mortgage Electronic Registration Systems v. Graham,* 44 Kan.App.2d 547, 229 P.3d 420 (2010). In *Graham*, the debtor executed a promissory note in favor of Countrywide Home Loans, Inc. secured by a mortgage held by MERS, "acting solely as nominee for Countrywide." The debtor defaulted on the note and MERS, not Countrywide, brought a mortgage foreclosure action.

[The court] found that, as in *Landmark*, MERS was acting "solely as nominee" for the lender and held no interest in the promissory note. Because there was no evidence that MERS had suffered any injury by the debtor's failure to make payments on the promissory note and there was no evidence that MERS had received permission to act as an agent for the lender, this court held that MERS lacked standing to bring a foreclosure action.

---

[2]Note: The court used "Note" and "Mortgage" capitalized when referring to the specific note and mortgage in this case.

The debtor in *Graham* made the argument that the mortgage was unenforceable because it had been "split" from the promissory note where MERS held the mortgage and Countrywide held the note—precisely the issue before this court.

The court thoroughly examined both *Landmark* and *Graham*. While it found the general principles set forth in *Landmark* to be correct—i.e., that a "split" between a mortgage and a note renders the mortgage unenforceable absent an agency relationship between the holder of the mortgage and the holder of the note—it noted that providing [the debtor with] a copy of its terms and conditions with its lenders as further evidence of the agency relationship.

[Also, the] court relied primarily on the language of the mortgage—language virtually identical to the Mortgage clause herein—to find that the debtor was aware of and understood the relationship between the lender and the mortgagee. Because MERS was acting as an agent of U.S. Bank, the Mortgage and the Note were never severed and U.S. Bank, as present holder of both the Note and the Mortgage, was entitled to foreclose on the Mortgage.

Affirmed.

CASE QUESTIONS

1. What is the significance of the term "nominee" in the mortgage?
2. What is the theory the court uses for allowing U.S. Bank to foreclose despite the separation of debt and mortgage?
3. Explain the effect of severance of the mortgage from the note.

Federal Regulation of Mortgage Debt Instruments

Federal Disclosure Requirements in Mortgage Debt

Federal statutes and regulations require certain specific disclosures in consumer credit contracts, from terms to cancellation. These disclosures, which were mandated by the **Truth in Lending Act (TILA),** and is actually part of the **Consumer Credit Protection Act,** passed by Congress in 1968 (15 U.S.C. § 1601). The Federal Reserve Board was originally delegated the responsibility for enforcing TILA and has promulgated regulations to carry out the details of disclosure, but the new **Bureau of Consumer Financial Protection** (BCFP or Bureau), created under the **Dodd-Frank Wall Street Reform and Consumer Protection Act** (DFCPA), also known as the Wall Street Reform and Consumer Financial Protection Act or the Consumer Financial Protection Act (CFPA), will now assume that enforcement role. Housed within the Federal Reserve, the BCFP now serves the combined roles that the Federal Reserve as well as the FTC and other federal agencies played in dealing with consumer credit laws, regulations, and issues.

Regulation Z(12 C.F.R. § 226) provides the details for credit information and transactions and may be better known than the statute that gave rise to it. Regulation Z applies to both closed-end and open-end transactions. Mortgages are examples of closed-end transactions where the amount of debt is known up-front. Regulation Z requires lenders to make specific disclosures to residential (consumer) mortgage borrowers.

Because of the changes under the **Mortgage Disclosure Improvement Act of 2008 (MDIA),** an amendment to TILA, lenders must furnish more complete and less ambiguous disclosures than were required under Regulation Z and those disclosures must be made within three days after the consumer makes the loan application. A mortgage loan cannot close any earlier than three days after the lender furnishes the specialized mortgage disclosures. The focus of these disclosures is to give consumers a clear idea of how many payments they will make, how much they will be paying to finance the home purchase, and what can happen if they fail to make the payments under the loan.

Federal Debt Rescission Regulations

Although Regulation Z provides for a three-day rescission period for security interests and second mortgages, this rescission period does not apply to

residential mortgage transactions for first mortgages on property being purchased by a consumer for use as a residence. However, the consumer who executes a second note and mortgage on his residence does enjoy the protection of the three-day rescission period. In these types of secondary consumer financings, including home equity loans, the lender must disclose the right of rescission and also provide the consumer/borrower, in written form, the procedures for exercising their right of rescission. Figure 15.3 is a sample right-to-rescission form from the regulations with the new plain-English requirements.

FIGURE 15.3

Sample Rescission Model Form (Home Refinancing or Secondary Mortgage)

NOTICE OF RIGHT TO CANCEL

Your Right to Cancel

You are entering into a new transaction to increase the amount of credit previously provided to you. Your home is the security for this new transaction. You have a legal right under federal law to cancel this new transaction, without cost, within three business days from whichever of the following events occurs last:

(1) the date of this new transaction, which is _____ ; or
(2) the date you received your new Truth in Lending disclosures; or
(3) the date you received this notice of your right to cancel.

If you cancel this new transaction, it will not affect any amount that you presently owe. Your home is the security for that amount. Within 20 calendar days after we receive your notice of cancellation of this new transaction, we must take the steps necessary to reflect the fact that your home does not secure the increase of credit. We must also return any money you have given to us or anyone else in connection with this new transaction.

   You may keep any money we have given you in this new transaction until we have done the things mentioned above, but you must then offer to return the money at the address below.

If we do not take possession of the money within 20 calendar days of your offer, you may keep it without further obligation.

How To Cancel

If you decide to cancel this new transaction, you may do so by notifying us in writing, at _____

(Creditor's name and business address).

You may use any written statement that is signed and dated by you and states your intention to cancel, or you may use this notice by dating and signing below. Keep one copy of this notice because it contains important information about your rights.

If you cancel by mail or telegram, you must send the notice no later than midnight of _____ (Date) _____ (or midnight of the third business day following the latest of the three events listed above).

If you send or deliver your written notice to cancel some other way, it must be delivered to the above address no later than that time.

I WISH TO CANCEL

_____   _____

Consumer's Signature   Date

If the lender makes an error in its required disclosures on APR and other terms of the loan, the consumer is given a three-year right of rescission. Since the time of the mortgage crisis, courts have shifted to a very strict standard for lender compliance on disclosure, a standard the following case illustrates.

IN RE LOWENSTEIN

459 B.R. 227 (E.D. Pa. 2011)
For Want of A $5 Service Charge, a Mortgage Can Be Lost

FACTS

Roger and Lynne Lowenstein (Plaintiffs) refinanced the existing mortgage on their property in 2007 through Countrywide Home loans, Inc. The original principal amount of the loan was $262,400.00. The Lowensteins received a TILA disclosure statement that disclosed the amount financed as $260,526.84. The difference between the principal amount of the loan ($262,400.00) and the disclosed amount financed ($260,526.84) is attributable to various charges assessed in the transaction which were treated as prepaid finance charges, including an underwriting fee of $675.00 and prepaid interest of $920.The total finance charge was disclosed as $722,670.28 and the annual percentage rate was disclosed as 8.183%.

Grateful Abstract, LLC conducted the closing. At the closing, other charges were deducted from the loan proceeds that were not treated as finance charges, but rather as part of the amount financed. The Lowensteins maintain that three of those charges should have been included and disclosed as part of the finance charge rather than the amount financed. The three charges at issue are:

1. a "closing services letter" charge disclosed as being $35.00, but which was assessed twice by mistake, resulting in a total charge of $70.00;
2. a notary fee of $25.00; and
3. a mortgage recording fee of $131.50.

The Lowensteins defaulted on their loan and U.S. Bank, (Defendants), the holder of the note and mortgage sought to foreclose. The Lowensteins, who subsequently declared bankruptcy, sought to have their loan rescinded because of the mistakes in the disclosure. The defendants moved for summary judgment.

JUDICIAL OPINION

Frank, Bankruptcy Judge

TILA is a strict liability statute. The statutory remedies are enforced in favor of the consumer in any case in which the creditor violates the specified provisions of TILA, regardless [sic] whether the creditor's conduct was intentional, negligent, or inadvertent. The technical nature of a violation of the requirements of TILA or Regulation Z is no defense to a TILA claim.

The Plaintiffs assert that the entire $70.00 that they were charged for a "closing services letter" should have been included in the finance charge, not the amount financed. The Defendants concede that the unintended, second $35.00 charge should have been disclosed as a finance charge and that therefore, the finance charge was incorrect. However, the Defendants assert that the intended $35.00 charge for the closing services letter was properly excluded from the finance charge and therefore, that the understatement of the finance charge does not exceed the $35.00 Statutory Error Tolerance.

A closing services letter (also referred to in the literature as a "closing protection letter" or an "insured closing letter") is a contract between the title company and the lender whereby the title insurance company agrees to indemnify the lender for any losses caused by the failure of the title agent to follow the lender's closing instructions.

In consumer credit transactions secured by real property, TILA and Regulation Z provide that certain charges, referred to as "real estate related fees," that might otherwise fit the general definition of a finance charge, are nonetheless excluded from the disclosed finance charge, provided that they are "bona fide and reasonable in amount." The $35.00 charge for the closing services letter is a real estate related fee that TILA excludes from the computation of the finance charge.

Because $35.00 of the $70.00 charge was properly excluded from the disclosed finance charge, the finance charge was understated only by the $35.00 duplicative charge. If no other charges were improperly excluded from the finance charge, the understatement falls within the Statutory Error Tolerance permitted by 15 U.S.C. § 1635(i) and 12 C.F.R. 226.23(h).

Next, the Plaintiffs challenge the exclusion from the disclosed finance charge the $25.00 notary fee.

The notary fee in the Transaction was not paid to the lender (Countrywide). It was paid to a third party, Levin & Associates. Levin & Associates was the attorney for Grateful Abstract, the settlement agent. The fee was paid for the notarization of Plaintiffs' signatures. Their signatures were notarized eight (8) times on the documents memorializing the Transaction.

There is no direct evidence in the record whether Countrywide required some or all of the loan documents to be notarized at closing, but it is fair to assume that the documents were notarized at Countrywide's behest. As a result, Regulation Z § 226.4(a)(2), on its face, suggests that the notary fees are finance charges. However, what Regulation Z giveth with one hand, it taketh away with the other.

In a transaction secured by real property, Regulation Z excludes from the finance the notary fees that are bona fide and reasonable in amount. 12 C.F.R. 226.4(c)(7)(iii); see also 15 U.S.C. § 1605(e)(4). The issue, then, is whether the $25.00 notary charge in the Transaction was bona fide and reasonable in amount.

The Defendants contend that Grateful Abstract could have charged a notary fee of $31, but only charged $25, and therefore, that the $25.00 charge was bona fide and reasonable.

In response, the Plaintiffs acknowledge that the $25.00 charge for eight (8) notarizations falls within the maximum charges permitted by the Pennsylvania statutory notary fee schedule. But they contend that misses the point. They argue (and I agree) that the fact that the $25.00 notary charge did not violate the Pennsylvania statutory notary fee schedule is not, by itself, determinative as to whether the charge may be excluded from the finance charge in the disclosure mandated by TILA.

The Plaintiffs contend that the $25.00 charge for eight (8) notarizations was not reasonable because the only document that needed to be notarized was the mortgage (at a maximum notarization charge of $10.00). The Plaintiffs implicitly suggest that Countrywide went "overboard" by requiring eight (8) signatures to be notarized and that it was not reasonable to do so because only one document, the mortgage, had to be notarized to be legally effective. Because unreasonable notary fees may not be excluded from the finance charge under 12 C.F.R. 226.4(c)(7), the Plaintiffs urge that at least $15.00 of the notary charge be determined to be a finance charge under TILA.

The Plaintiffs did not place the closing documents into the summary judgment record. Consequently, there is nothing in the summary judgment record identifying the documents in the Transaction signed by the

Plaintiffs that were notarized. The Plaintiffs came forward with no evidence regarding prevailing practices regarding the notarization of documents in residential mortgage loan transactions. In particular, the Plaintiffs offered no evidence tending to show that the requirement that their signatures be notarized on multiple documents other than the mortgage is inconsistent "with the prevailing practices of the industry in the locality."

The Plaintiffs have the burden of proof in this adversary proceeding. In response to the Defendants' Motion, it was their burden to come forward with evidence to support the factual underpinnings of their claim. The Plaintiffs failed to meet their burden because they did not produce any evidence that requiring eight (8) notarizations at a cost of $25.00 was inconsistent with industry practice and therefore, was unreasonable. As a result, the Defendants are entitled to a determination that the notary charge was properly excluded from the disclosed finance charge pursuant to 12 C.F.R. § 226.4(c)(7).

The Plaintiffs were charged a mortgage recording fee of $131.50. That fee had two components: $126.50 paid to the Recorder of Deeds and a $5.00 "service charge for using the county's electronic recording system."

The Plaintiffs do not dispute that the $126.50 charge paid to the Recorder of Deeds was properly excluded from the finance charge pursuant to 12 C.F.R. § 226.4(e)(1). They question, however, whether the $5.00 service charge was properly excluded from the finance charge. In response, the Defendants conclusorily characterize the entire $131.50 charge as a "fee prescribed by law and paid to a public official for the purpose of recording a mortgage."

I find that there is a disputed issue of fact regarding the $5.00 service charge because the [record] is ambiguous regarding the precise nature of the charge and is susceptible to being read to in a manner that could support either side's position in this proceeding.

At the same time, the Declaration's characterization of the fee as a "service charge" creates a significant ambiguity and implies that the $5.00 fee was paid to some entity other than the Recorder of Deed. The use of the term "service charge" (particularly without identifying the payee) implies that the $5.00 fee may have been paid to Countrywide or its agent as an additional charge for accessing the county electronic recording system (similar to the "service charge" assessed by agencies that sell tickets on-line for entertainment and sporting events)—as opposed to being a separate fee paid to a government official other than the Recorder of Deeds. If the fee was retained by Countrywide or a related private entity, the charge cannot be excluded from the finance charge under 12 C.F.R. § 226.4(e)(1).

That factual issue involves a nominal loan charge of $5.00 for a mortgage recording fee "service charge." However, because the Statutory Error Tolerance in this proceeding is only $35.00 and it is undisputed that the finance charge was understated by $35.00 in TILA disclosures provided to the Plaintiffs, a finding that the $5.00 mortgage recording fee "service charge" is a finance charge would result in the determination that the erroneous finance charge disclosure exceeded the Statutory Error Tolerance and

that there was a material violation of TILA, giving rise to an extended right of rescission.

Motion for summary judgment denied.

CASE QUESTIONS

1. Why does the court allow summary judgment on the issues of the closing letter and the notary fees?
2. What is different about the recording fees?
3. If the $5.00 went to Countrywide, then what is the effect on the Lowenstein mortgage?

ETHICAL ISSUE

Evaluate the ethics of the Lowensteins in their efforts to be released from her debt obligation.

Federal Debt Credit Advertising Regulation

Regulation Z also regulates the advertisement of the credit terms by lenders. Regulation Z defines an **advertisement** as "a commercial message in any media that promotes, directly or indirectly, a credit transaction." Regulation Z also covers electronic types of messages. Lenders must advertise accurately and must also make some mandatory disclosures when they use **triggering language**. Triggering language includes any statements about down payments, the number of payments, time for repayment, the amount of each monthly payment, and finance charges. If a lender hits a triggering term, it must then make additional disclosures. Two examples of down-payment triggering language are "total move-in costs of $1,000" or "as low as 10 percent down." The phrase "30-year loan" is an example of a triggering term because it indicates the repayment period. "Payable in monthly installments of $750" is triggering language related to the amount of the payments. Triggering language related to the finance charge includes "total cost of credit is…" and "$190,000 mortgage with two points." However, general language such as "no down payment," "years to repay," and "monthly installments to suit your budget" may be used without triggering additional disclosure requirements.

CONSIDER 15.2 Do the following advertisements contain any triggering language requiring further disclosure?

(a) NEW LISTING—Exciting three-bedroom home. Excellent Northeast Mesa location. Pool and tennis court. Low rates and low down payment.
(b) 10% DOWN, 6½% INTEREST LOAN—Country style two-bedroom and guest house.

Federal Regulation of Home Equity Loans

Because interest paid on home mortgages is deductible and credit and funds were so readily available, home equity lines of credit were aggressively marketed between 2005 and 2007. Lenders urged consumers to pay off their credit card debt with a home equity loan. High levels of borrowing on homes placed borrowers at risk when property values declined, because the amount they owed often exceeded the reduced value of their property. At the end of 2008, lenders placed stringent requirements on the standards for home equity loans as well as on borrowing levels. Regulation Z requires that home equity loan disclosures spell out the following:

1. That the line of credit or home equity loan creates a security interest in their home and that they could lose their home if the obligation is not repaid.
2. That they need to consult a tax advisor on the deductibility of the interest.
3. The full cost of the loan or line of credit (application fees, points, and annual fees).
4. All the standard Regulation Z disclosures.
5. The three-day right of rescission.

In 2011, the Federal Reserve Board developed special disclosure requirements for what are called high-rate, high-fee mortgages or home equity loans (also called Section 32 mortgages). These loans include mortgage and home-equity loans at interest rates more than 8%–10% above Treasury security rates or that involve fees or points more than the greater of $592 or 8% of the total loan amount. Section 32 mortgage disclosures are in addition to the Regulation Z disclosures for other mortgages and have certain prohibitions such as no balloon payments, no higher interest rates if the mortgagor defaults, and negative amortization mortgages.

Federal Regulation of the Decision to Extend Credit for Real Property Financing

The federal government regulates lenders more extensively now in their decisions to extend credit for the owner's purchase of real property.

Qualifying Borrowers and Verifying Appraisals

Because of the fraud that occurred in the mortgage markets prior to 2007, there have been both statutory and regulatory changes that increase lender requirements as they make the decision to write a mortgage. Ironically, one of the cornerstones of the new laws and regulations is the requirement that lenders verify the income of borrowers through a third party with the preferred method being obtaining copies of the borrower's tax returns. The factors that a lender must review (factors that were once good lending practices) include: verification of employment, credit history, current obligations, debt-to-income ratio, financial resources other than home equity, and generally speaking, a good, hard look at their ability to repay the mortgage loan.

New also are the requirements for appraisals of the property, which now include a physical visit to the property. The physical visit is the result of so much fraud committed as appraisers submitted photos of properties with changed house numbers so as to lead lenders to believe that raw land was actually a dwelling. In addition, those who conduct the appraisal must be independent. That is, the appraiser must not have been paid by either the lender or the mortgagor to come up with a figure that will allow the loan to go forward. Even the withholding of payment to an appraiser following the appraiser's low figure on a property can be construed as an attempt to influence the appraiser. (15 U.S.C. § 1639e)

Equal Credit Opportunity Act

Mortgage lenders are also subject to the provisions of the **Equal Credit Opportunity Act (ECOA)** (15 U.S.C. § 1691), which prohibits lenders from refusing loans or discriminating in lending on the basis of sex, marital status, race, religion, or national origin. Penalties for violations include private suits as well as fines. Under the ECOA, lenders must base their decisions on issues of creditworthiness that can be substantiated, and not on race, sex, religion, and other protected class groupings under the act.[3]

The application of the ECOA to real estate loans is slightly different from its application to other credit arrangements because, as a practical matter, the real estate lender will generally need the signature of the spouse for the mortgage or deed of trust to ensure protection of its security in real property for the loan. Marital property rights can deprive a lender of one-half of the security in a piece of land if a spouse did not sign necessary documents. A mortgage creditor cannot usurp state marital property rights. So, requiring a spouse's signature for a real estate loan is not necessarily a violation of the ECOA.

Fair Housing Act, Community Reinvestment Act, and Home Mortgage Disclosure Act: The Three Well-Intentioned Laws That Contributed to the Economic Crisis of 2008

The Fair Housing Act prohibited discrimination in lending, including extending mortgage loans. In fact, the Home Mortgage Disclosure Act required lenders to report the data on their borrowers to show lending by race. However, despite the federal mandate against discrimination, lending data showed that loan approval rates were higher for white applicants than for minority applicants. As a result, Congress passed the **Community Reinvestment Act (CRA) of 1977.** This federal law required bankers and other lenders to show that they were making mortgage loans that reflected the diversity in their communities and that their lending programs were reaching first-time homebuyers as well as those who had struggled in obtaining mortgage loans in the past. Lenders were given a mandate to approve more loans for low-to-moderate income applicants (known as LMIs).

From 1977 through 1992, the CRA remained a topic in discussion of social responsibility among banks and in business ethics, but there was little done at the federal level to enforce the law. In 1992, The Boston Federal Reserve Bank released a study (one whose methodology has since been questioned) that concluded there was discrimination by lenders on the basis of race in their decisions to extend mortgage loans. As a result, bank regulators required audits of lenders to determine whether their loan portfolios included CRA loans and whether the banks had programs of outreach to LMI and minority borrowers. Many banks were defendants in Justice Department suits that alleged discrimination in lending.[4]

Fannie Mae, the quasi-public corporation that guaranteed federal loans (see p. 417), was also encouraged to expand its role in seeing that those who had traditionally been unable to qualify for loans had access to mortgage loans. In order to meet the congressional mandates on expansion of the home mortgage market, Fannie Mae loosened its standards for guarantee and purchase of mortgage loans. Fannie allowed up to 97 percent of the purchase price to be loaned, often waived down-payment requirements, and agreed to accept increasingly larger numbers of LMI mortgage loans. The increasing subprime mortgage market attracted not only those borrowers whom the CRA public policy was intended to benefit

---

[3]The application of the ECOA has been extended in some jurisdictions from consumer transactions to commercial transactions. *Bagley v. Lumbermens Mut. Cas. Co.,* 100 F. Supp.2d 879 (N.D. Ill. 2002).

[4]The U.S. Supreme Court has ruled that state attorneys general can also enforce against lenders state laws that prohibit discrimination in lending and include requirements that lenders reach out to LMI borrowers. *Cuomo v. Clearing House Ass'n, LLC,* 557 U.S. 519(2009).

but also served as a financing vehicle for speculators and flippers. Because the government-guaranteed market for mortgages was expanding so quickly, the lenders who did conventional types of mortgage loans changed their standards for lending in order to compete and attract more LMI loans themselves.

The incentives and laws expanded the availability of mortgage credit to LMI applicants. The latest figures (2011 Federal Financial Institutions Examination Council) indicate that African-Americans and Latinos received 25.8% of all LMI loans. However, that group also accounted for 32.9% of the foreclosures and 64% of foreclosures involve subprime mortgages.

In addition to the new disclosures on subprime loans, the federal government now limits compensation to mortgage brokers as a means of disincentivizing mortgage brokers from steering clients into higher priced loans. The Loan Originator amendment to Regulation Z prohibits the payment of yield spread premiums, a compensation system that tied what the broker was paid to the rate or terms of the mortgage the broker was able to "sell" to the borrower. Commissions are now paid on the loan amount, not the interest rate or terms. (16 U.S.C. § 1639a) (See Chapter 16 for more information.)

Debtor's Rights in Mortgage Credit Transactions: Bad Faith

Lenders who are not cautious in handling loan applications and decisions have been held liable to credit applicants for their bad faith. Lenders have an obligation of good faith and fair dealing and are liable to buyer/borrowers for negligence in responding to loan applications. Lenders are liable for the lack of timely approval or the withdrawal of an approval for financing already issued. Because of significant tightening in the credit markets, lenders are increasingly cautious with applicants and are informing them of the risk of a decline before the process begins. The "credit crunch" has nearly eliminated the possibility of bad faith because lenders are so cautious in even accepting applications.

Debtor's Rights on Interest Rates: Usury

Most states have laws fixing the maximum interest rates that may be charged legally. If the lender charges a rate in excess of that statutory maximum, that is **usury**. The usury rate varies significantly from state to state and also according to changes in the economic climate and the type of credit transaction involved.

Although most lenders would never use an interest rate that exceeds the statutory maximum, they may step into usury accidentally with fees on top of the loan interest, such as financier's charges and points. However, some of these fees and charges may be made without making the loan usurious. Examples of charges that would not be included in interest rate computations include the costs of getting the loan closed—any costs actually incurred in developing the paperwork or doing credit checks. An example of a charge that would be included would come from a **Brundage clause,** which requires the borrower to pay any tax that may be imposed on the lender's mortgage. In some states, the loan will be usurious if the tax plus the interest charged exceeds the statutory maximum.

The penalties for charging a usurious rate vary from state to state. In some states, the lender forfeits all interest and recovers only the principal. In others, the lender forfeits only that amount of interest above the maximum. In yet other states, the entire contract is void, and the lender forfeits both interest and principal. Usury laws are experiencing a wave of reforms as states limit interest rates on subprime loans (see below), payday loans, title loans, and other lending forms that have traditionally captured the LMI borrower.

Debtor's Rights: Subprime Loans and Predatory Lending

Troubled credit history is a problem for debtors when they want to buy a home. Nonetheless, when there is bad credit repentance and lender redemption, the latter can be profitable. From 1996 to 2007, there was significant growth in the subprime mortgage market. The subprime mortgage market is defined to include those borrowers with a FICO (Fair Isaac Co.) score below 620. The median FICO score is 720, with a perfect score being 850.

The subprime home mortgage market was 5 percent of the mortgage market in 1997, but it grew to 20 percent of the mortgage market by 2007 (from $35 billion to $1.3 trillion), and subprime loans represented about 60 percent of the mortgages used for bundling and sale in the secondary securities market for mortgage-backed investments. The 2011 foreclosure rates on subprime loans were 14.28 percent, versus 2.5 percent on regular loans. There are pockets of subprime difficulties. For example, in Cleveland, 84 percent of the foreclosures are on properties with subprime loans. These high default and foreclosure rates on subprime mortgages carried both a primary and secondary market impact starting in early 2007. First, subprime lenders collapsed under the weight of their foreclosure portfolios in a soft real estate market. With the increasing foreclosures and resulting collapses, the ratings agencies, whose analysts had given an investment grade rating to the mortgage-backed investment instruments, began a process of systematically downgrading the collateralized debt obligations (CDOs) and other mortgage-backed instruments. Because of this downgrade, investment firms, under mark-to-market accounting, had to write down their value on their books. The result was that the stock market lost one-half of its value. The ripple effect of the market drop was an economic downturn that resulted in additional foreclosures, now among the conventional, low-risk mortgages, because the borrowers had less income or were layoff casualties of a general business slowdown and many business closures. What began as a well-intentioned mortgage program designed to help LMI homebuyers proved to be destructive when defaults began.

The Subprime Role of Mortgage Brokers, Mortgage Lenders, Flippers, and Speculators

The subprime mortgage market did not grow without the help of mortgage professionals, as well as home investors who were trying to reap the profits from a real estate market that seemed to climb endlessly. The easier standards and a growing real estate market brought "**flippers**" into the markets. Flippers are those who were buying homes and then turning around and selling them in a growing real estate market that allowed substantial gains in a short time. Flippers often misrepresented whether the mortgage was for their primary residence. These flippers, also called *speculators*, also misrepresented the sources of their down payments, which were likely to be the proceeds from the closings on other properties that were occurring simultaneously with their new purchases. As housing markets have begun to recover in 2012, flippers are re-emerging, trying to purchase properties at low prices with the hope of profitable sales as the markets continue to improve.

ETHICAL ISSUE

"We made so much money, you couldn't believe it. And you didn't have to do anything. You just had to show up,"[5] commented Kal Elsayed, a former executive at New Century Financial, a mortgage brokerage firm based in Irvine, California. With his red Ferrari, Mr. Elsayed enjoyed the benefits of the growth in the subprime mortgage market. However, those risky debtors, whose credit histories spelled trouble, are now defaulting on their loans. New Century Financial is under federal investigation for stock sales and accounting irregularities as it tries to deal with his portfolio of $39.4 billion in subprime loans. "Subprime mortgage lending is easy," is the comment of mortgage brokers and analysts—until the market changes. What are the ethical issues in subprime mortgage loans? Do the lenders fill a market niche? What could or should they have done differently? Why do you think so many of the subprime lenders experienced financial collapse in the 2006–2007 period?

Business Practices in the Subprime Market

The business practices of the subprime lenders have been largely curbed, as noted earlier, through new federal disclosure requirements as well as changes in the compensation systems for mortgage brokers. With so many subprime loans in default, the industry practices came to light and an extended period of increasing regulation began in 2007.

More than half the states have adopted the guidelines promulgated by a national group of bank supervisors and mortgage regulators for supervision of subprime lenders. The same group proposed a nationwide licensing and standards system for mortgage brokers, a program adopted by the federal government in its **Secure and Fair Enforcement of the Mortgage Licensing Act of 2008 (SAFE Mortgage Licensing Act).**[6] **Mortgage brokers,** or loan originators, as SAFE refers to them, must either be licensed or registered as brokers. These processes require background checks and annual filings. The Secretary of HUD is charged with overseeing the state efforts on license and registration, and is authorized to develop a national system if the states fail to develop a system of licensing and regulation or neglect to continue with a system of regulation.

State laws, known as "Homeowner Security Protection Acts" or "High Cost Home Loan Acts" or "Home Loan Protection Acts," take various approaches to protecting consumers from predatory lending practices.[7] Some states limit charges or interest rates. Other states limit foreclosures or refinancings within certain time frames. Some, such as Cleveland's ordinance, simply prohibit predatory practices, making such activity a criminal misdemeanor. Cleveland's ordinance, like so many of the anti-predatory statutes, has been judicially challenged by lenders who have argued that the regulation of home loans is preempted by the extensive federal regulation of both home mortgages and consumer credit.[8] Cleveland's ordinance was held to be preempted by Ohio's laws on predatory lending. *Am. Financial Servs.*

---

[5]Julie Creswell and Vikas Bajas, "A Mortgage Crisis Begins to Spiral, and the Casualties Mount," *New York Times,* March 5, 2007, pp. C1, C4.

[6]12 U.S.C. § 5101 (as amended, July 2008).

[7]For a summary of the state legislation on predatory lending practices, see Therese G. Franzén and Leslie M. Howell, "Predatory Lending Legislation in 2004," 60 *Business Lawyer* 677 (2005).

[8]Am. Fin. Servs. Ass'n v. City of Cleveland, 824 N.E.2d 553 (Ohio Ct. App. 2005); *City of Dayton v. State,* No. 02-CV-3441 (Ohio Ct. Common Pleas Aug. 26, 2003); 813 N.E.2d 707 (Ohio Ct. App. 2004) *Am. Fin. Servs. Ass'n v. City of Oakland,* 23 Cal. Rptr. 3d 453 (Cal. 2005); and *Mayor of New York v. Council of New York,* 780 N.Y.S.2d 266 (N.Y. Sup. Ct. 2004).

Assn. v. Cleveland, 858 N.E.2d 776 (Ohio 2007). However, states are free to impose more stringent regulations on lenders and brokers than what is required by federal laws and regulations. (See Chapter 19 for more discussion of the constitutional issue of preemption.)

Debtor's Rights with Recording

A mortgage need not be recorded to be valid. However, an unrecorded mortgage gives rights only between the borrower (mortgagor) and the lender (mortgagee). In order to protect the mortgagee against others' rights or to give the mortgagee priority in relation to other creditors, the mortgage must be recorded in the appropriate government office. Recording the mortgage gives the lender priority over subsequently recorded and unrecorded land interests. (See discussion of priorities in Chapter 14 and later in this chapter.)

Terms of the Mortgage

Additional terms in the mortgage agreement, beyond just the basic requirements, protect and define the rights of the parties. The same provisions can often be found in the underlying promissory note.

> **PRACTICAL TIP**
>
> *A "prior forbearance" clause is one that allows the lender to accelerate a loan when payment is late even if late payments have been made in the past. Under a prior forbearance clause, the lender does not need to reinstate his or her right to prompt payment before declaring the loan in default and accelerating the loan for the full amount due.*

Acceleration Clause

An **acceleration clause** permits the mortgagee to accelerate the maturity date of the note if the mortgagor defaults. The second paragraph in Figure 15.1 is a typical example of an acceleration clause. Virtually all mortgage notes contain an acceleration clause because without them, the mortgagee's only recourse for default would be a suit to collect the payments missed or a partial foreclosure for the amount of those missed payments. The mortgagee would be required to bring suit each time there was a default. Acceleration clauses are valid in all states and are also permitted in government-insured loans for real estate.

One of the common issues with acceleration clauses is whether the lender can accelerate the loan when the lender has a history of allowing late payments. Suppose, for example, that your mortgage payment was due on the first of each month. You have never paid before the 15th of the month and have occasionally paid a late penalty. Your mortgage company has always accepted your late payments. One month you pay on the 16th of the month, with the late fee, and the lender declares you in default and accelerates your loan. In some states, the lender could not take such action until it gave notice that timely payment was now reinstated as a requirement under the mortgage. States that follow this principle of reinstatement of timeliness do not allow lenders to accelerate and foreclose until the late payment *after* reinstatement of timely performance. Lenders eliminate the problems of late payments, timeliness in reinstatement, and acceleration by putting a clause such as this in their mortgages:

> *Holder may exercise this option [to accelerate] during any default by maker regardless of any prior forbearance.*

Interest Acceleration Clause

This clause increases the interest rate to either the maximum amount permitted by law or some other amount when some event, such as a default, occurs. Many subprime loans had **interest acceleration clauses**. However, under the new laws, these interest acceleration clauses have been curbed.

Balloon Payment Clause

Usually, a mortgage is amortized over a certain number of years so that the full amount of the mortgage loan and the interest are paid when the term of the mortgage has expired. For example, after 30 years of a typical residential 30-year mortgage, the mortgagor will have paid the full amount of the debt and interest due on the mortgage.

Under a mortgage with a balloon payment, the mortgagor is still required to make periodic installment payments, but those payments do not fully amortize the amount of the loan; hence, the mortgagor will be required to pay the balance of the amount due at the end of the mortgage term. The lump sum due at the end of the mortgage term is called a **balloon payment**. These types of balloon payments are typical in commercial and subprime loans. Government-insured loans cannot include balloon payment provisions. Balloon payments have now been prohibited in certain types of consumer mortgage loans. Where balloon payments are permitted, there are new disclosure requirements including this warning to consumers, "There is no guarantee that you will be able to refinance to lower your rate and payments." During the real estate boom, many lenders and mortgage brokers represented that a balloon payment was not a problem because the mortgagor/borrower could simply choose to refinance the home. However, following the market crash, refinancing was not an option for most facing a balloon payment because their properties were not worth the amount of their mortgage and/or their income situations had changed. Those with balloon payments that came due after 2007 generally lost their homes.

Prepayment Penalty Clauses

The mortgagee has the right to earn the interest on the money invested in the mortgage loan for the term of the loan. Unless the note or the mortgage specifically provides, the mortgagor has no right to prepay the loan before the end of the mortgage term.

The penalty is compensation for the lender for having to find a new investment outlet and incurring the expenses of finding and making that reinvestment. The penalty may apply only during the first 5 to 10 years of the mortgage, or may run for the full mortgage term. The Federal Reserve Board has suggested the following disclosure in consumer mortgages:

> *Prepayment: If you pay off early, you*
>
> ☐ *may* ☐ *will not have to pay a penalty.*
>
> ☐ *may* ☐ *will not be entitled to a refund of part of the finance charge.*

All states allow prepayment penalties; however, certain types of government-insured loans prohibit them.

Late Payment Clause

Late payment clauses are usually included in mortgage documents, promissory notes, or both. These clauses allow the mortgagee to charge a late fee for payments received a certain number of days after the due date. Late payment clauses are legal in all types of loans. Acceptance of a late payment may or may not waive the right to acceleration.

Due-on-Sale Clause

The **due-on-sale clause** is a provision in the mortgage agreement that is similar to the acceleration clause. The difference is that it takes effect upon the attempted sale of the property by the mortgagor to a buyer who will take over mortgage payments.

The due-on-sale clause gives the mortgagee the right to call the entire balance of an indebtedness due and payable if the borrower sells the mortgaged property.

As interest rates increase, a due-on-sale-clause helps the mortgagee because mortgage notes at older, unprofitable rates can be eliminated with the funds reinvested at higher rates. However, the clauses do create problems for mortgagors trying to sell property when interest rates are high. If the buyer cannot take over an existing loan and the cost of borrowing is prohibitive, then the seller's pool of buyers is small.

Although there was much confusion and debate over the validity of due-on-sale clauses during the economic downturn of the early 1980s, the issue was settled when the U.S. Supreme Court held in *Fidelity Federal Savings and Loan v. de la Cuesta*, 458 U.S. 141 (1982), that the clauses were valid and could be enforced in federally related mortgage loans. State laws declaring the clauses invalid were preempted by the federal law.[9]

Following the Supreme Court's decision, Congress enacted the Garn–St. Germain Depository Institutions Act of 1982 (called the Garn Bill; 12 U.S.C. § 226), which provides that states may not restrict the enforcement of due-on-sale clauses with respect to real property loans except to protect home buyers who relied on due-on-sale restrictions and reasonably believed they had assumable loans.

Types of Mortgages

Government-Insured Mortgages—FHA and VA Mortgages

The acronyms **FHA** and **VA** are terms that signify a government-backed loan, which means that if the borrower defaults on repayment of the loan, the lender can recover the loan amount from the federal agency insuring the loan. The FHA and the Veterans Administration (VA), respectively, serve as the insuring agencies for these types of loans.[10]

These loans have restrictions, most of which are imposed for the protection of the mortgagor. For example, the interest rate on such loans is set by the federal government, and the borrower must qualify for the loan through the government agency. Also, the terms of the mortgage and note are regulated by the federal government, and certain types of clauses are prohibited. Both FHA and VA carry maximum loan amounts, so these loans are not available for higher-priced residences. Also, the borrower is required to pay the premium for the government insurance, which is a fixed percentage of the outstanding balance for the life of the loan. There may also be down-payment minimums required on government loans.

Traditionally, the federal government also provided a secondary market for VA and FHA mortgages through quasi-public entities or **government-sponsored entities (GSEs)** such as the **Federal National Mortgage Association (FNMA or Fannie Mae)** and the **Federal Home Loan Mortgage Corporation (FHLMC or Freddie Mac)**. Fannie and Freddie purchased blocks of government-insured mortgages and, in some cases, conventional mortgages. They then bundled those mortgages and sold mortgage-backed securities as a way of financing their purchase of more

---

[9]However, not all state regulation of mortgage lending is preempted. In *Cuomo v. Clearinghouse Ass'n., LLC*, 557 U.S. 519 (2009), the court held that state attorneys general could obtain records and file suit against federal lenders for discrimination in lending.

[10]Under the FHA Modernization Act of 2008, the FHA is undergoing changes. The agency is to establish a pre-home purchase counseling program and test alternative means for determining which buyers are qualified to receive home mortgages. In addition, FHA is to expand the protections of RESPA (see Chapter 16) to manufactured homes.

mortgages. Fannie and Freddie have struggled since the 2008 economic collapse. Their mortgage acquisition zeal during the subprime market left them with securities portfolios that resulted in substantial losses. The result was that the two were insolvent and required a federal bailout. Under the **Housing Economic Recovery Act (HERA) of 2008**, Congress created the **Federal Housing Finance Agency (FHFA)**. This new agency acts as a receiver or conservator charged by Congress with the liquidation of Fannie Mae, Freddie Mac, and their affiliates. Fannie Mae and Freddie Mac are now in conservatorships.[11]

Federal Regulatory Agencies for Mortgage Lending

The longstanding system of federal regulation of mortgage banking has been turned upside down with the government takeover of Fannie and Freddie. The **Federal Deposit Insurance Corporation (FDIC)**, the organization that worked us through the savings and loan collapses of the late 1980s and early 1990s, remains the stalwart of oversight for financial institutions.

Ironically, Congress passed the **Financial Institutions Reform, Recovery, and Enforcement Act (FIRREA) of 1989** to reform the federal thrift industry for its excesses on loans to unqualified individuals on overvalued properties. FIRREA also established standards for real estate appraisals, as well as internal controls for federal financial institutions on their appraisals and evaluations of the qualifications of their appraisers, because of the role appraisers played in the overvaluation of so many properties that led to inflated savings and loans portfolios and, ultimately, their collapses. The very reforms implemented to correct excesses in lending during the 1980s and 1990s were ignored in the home mortgage industry, and those excesses and then some returned.

Conventional Mortgages

The **conventional mortgage** is a mortgage made by a private lender that is not insured by a government agency and, therefore, not subject to the government restrictions on loan structure. Conventional mortgages are offered by the same institutions offering FHA and VA loans.

Purchase Money Mortgage

The purchase money mortgage is one in which the mortgagor is using the borrowed funds to buy the property that will serve as the security for the loan. Most residential mortgages are purchase money mortgages. Pledging your home in order to borrow money for a college education is not a purchase money mortgage.

Straight Term Mortgages or Interest-Only Mortgages

A **straight term mortgage**, now known in the decade from 1998 to 2008 as the "interest-only mortgage," and another subprime mortgage feature, is a mortgage in which there is no amortization of principal over the loan period. The borrower makes only interest payments and then repays the unpaid principal, along with any accrued interest, at the end of the term (usually three to five years). For those of you reading closely, this is a form of a balloon payment. "Interest-only mortgages" allowed buyers who might not

---

[11]The former CFO of Fannie Mae, David Kellerman, a young man who had taken over the position after the ouster of those who had "subprimed" Fannie, was found dead in his home on April 22, 2009, an apparent suicide victim. The subprime market's tentacles have reached far and wide into many organizations, industries, and lives.

qualify to afford the high-priced homes of this era. By making only interest payments, their monthly housing costs were lower. In the subprime market, the interest-only loans were typical and the repossession/foreclosure rates high once the balloon payment came due. The **interest-only mortgage** is known as one of the creative financing techniques (see the discussion later in the chapter).

Subordinate or Wrap-Around Mortgages

A **subordinate mortgage** (or **wrap-around mortgage**) is one in which sellers act as lenders for their buyers who cannot afford a loan from a commercial lender because of high rates. This type of mortgage is discussed in the alternative financing section of this chapter.

Piggyback Mortgage

This type of mortgage was also part of the subprime market. A home buyer/borrower structures an 80 percent loan, one in which the borrower/home buyer puts down 20 percent and qualifies for a conventional or government mortgage at a lower rate and without the cost of mortgage insurance. However, straightaway, the buyer/borrower then puts a second mortgage on the property (usually at a much higher interest rate) to recoup the 20 percent down. The money from that loan is then used to purchase yet another property. The property is mortgaged to its full value without the first lender being aware of the **piggyback mortgage**. And the buyer has now linked properties together, all with the hope of being able to "flip" or sell the property quickly and for a gain (if the market remains on an upswing). These types of mortgages have become an impossibility because of increased oversight and regulation on the sources of borrowers' down payments.

Anaconda or Dragnet Mortgages

An **anaconda mortgage** or **dragnet mortgage** secures all items of indebtedness that the mortgagor may, at any time during the period of mortgage, owe to the mortgagee. Under a dragnet mortgage, a lender could acquire all the mortgagor's debts at a discount and then collect 100 percent through the mortgage transaction.

Adjustable or Variable Rate Mortgages

The **adjustable rate mortgage (ARM)** has a fluctuating interest rate throughout the life of the loan, the loan's rate being tied to some index such as the FHA rate, the Treasury Securities Index, or Treasury Bill rates. The rates fluctuate according to the terms of the note or loan agreement. Because so many ARMs were part of the subprime industry, there are now new regulations on everything from the index used for determining the adjustable rate (AR), to the frequency of adjustment, to rate caps, to which rate is used for qualifying the borrower for the mortgage loan. A newer form of an ARM is the **hybrid adjustable rate mortgage,** which is a mortgage that begins with a fixed rate but then can change in the future to an adjustable rate through a reset provision in the note.

Regulation Z has mandatory disclosure forms for ARMs and hybrid ARMs that have been greatly simplified. The H-4 disclosures forms (found at 12 C.F.R. § 226, Appendix H) require full disclosure of the following information along with examples of how the homeowners' payments will be affected with changes in interest rates.

1. The beginning interest rate
2. How that rate and your payments will be determined

3. Where you can find information about the index or rate the lender will use
4. How much your interest rate can change
5. How often your interest rate can change
6. When and how you will be notified of the rate change and new payment
7. Time requirements for notice and the beginning of a new payment
8. Instructions for computing your payment: "To see what your payments would be, divide your mortgage amount by $10,000; then multiply the monthly payment by that amount. (For example, the monthly payment for a mortgage amount of $60,000 would be: $60,000 ÷ $10,000 = 6; 6 x _____ = $_____ per month.)"

Negative Amortization Mortgages (NAM)

One of the tools lenders used during the housing boom in order to get buyers qualified for larger homes and, as a result large mortgage amounts, was the **negative amortization mortgage**. A negative amortization mortgage is one that allows the lender to lower monthly payments for mortgagors in the initial years by adding on the interest accumulated but unpaid to the amount of principal owed. Under a NAM, the mortgagor/borrower actually has a higher mortgage at the end of five years of payments. With declining property values and increasing principals under NAMs, the problem of under-water mortgages was greater. The special disclosures on NAMs including required statements about the need to consult with a financial adviser on the tax effects of a NAM

Reverse Mortgages

With a retired population on the rise, and most with large amounts of equity in their homes, lenders have found profits high in the **reverse mortgage** business. Reverse mortgages allow retired homeowners to supplement their retirement income by borrowing on the equity in their homes. In a reverse mortgage, the mortgage company agrees to loan the homeowners a sum that will be distributed to them in monthly payments over a specified term, or until their death. The owners do not repay the loan; repayment comes when they die and the house is sold. The reverse mortgagee is repaid the principal amount of the loan plus interest from the proceeds from the sale of the house. As of 2012, one in ten reverse mortgages are in foreclosure, and their regulation was the focus of a CFPB report released in July 2012 on the risks of reverse mortgages. The high foreclosure rate is generally the result of the homeowners' failure to pay taxes and insurance, a requirement that is part of their reverse mortgage. New regulations will focus on advertising content, the lump-sum pay-out to mortgagors, and confusion in disclosure terms.

Commercial Mortgages

The focus of this chapter has been primarily on residential mortgages, but commercial buildings are also financed through mortgages. However, commercial loans involve additional issues such as what happens to the lessees in the building and whether there will be assignment of rents presently or in the event of a default. Commercial lenders must also perform due diligence on prior and current uses of the property for purposes of environmental issues and liabilities (see Chapter 20).

Rights and Responsibilities of Mortgagor and Mortgagee

If the parties fail to specify all the necessary terms of their relationship, the law does step in to provide certain rules for governing the relationship.

Rents and Leases

The rights of the parties for rents from the property will vary (as discussed earlier) according to whether the property is located in a title or a lien theory state. In the title theory states, the mortgagee has the right to the rents upon execution of the mortgage. In the lien theory states, the mortgagee is not entitled to rents or possession until after default and foreclosure.

One issue in commercial property mortgage defaults is that of the tenant's rights. Tenants of mortgaged property have rights that vary according to when the lease was executed. For those leases that antedate the mortgage, the mortgagee is required to honor the tenant's rights, even when the mortgagee forecloses. In a post-dated lease, the mortgagee is permitted to terminate the lease simply because of the mortgagor's default. Of course, the mortgagor and the mortgagee could have a clause in the lease that made tenants' rights subject to all mortgages.

Both tenants and mortgagees should scrutinize documents carefully. For example, a tenant who leases property after the mortgage exists should check the mortgage for termination and cancellation provisions. A mortgagee taking a mortgage on property subject to existing leases should review the leases prior to execution of the mortgage.

Property Covered by the Mortgage

Unless otherwise specified, the mortgage covers all property (houses, buildings, fixtures, easements) on the land described in the mortgage. The mortgage covers all buildings, fixtures, easements, and any other items classified as real property. The mortgagee should specify any questionable items that might be construed as personal instead of real property. The following clause is an example of a thorough inclusion clause that would follow the legal description of the property in the mortgage agreement.

> *TOGETHER with all articles and fixtures used in occupying, operating, or renting the building on the premises, including but not limited to gas and electric fixtures, radiators, heaters, washers, driers, engines and machinery, boilers, ranges, elevators, escalators, incinerators, motors, bathtubs, sinks, pipes, faucets, and other heating and plumbing fixtures, air-conditioning equipment, mirrors, cabinets, refrigerators, stoves, fire prevention and extinguishing devices, furniture, shades, blinds, curtains, draperies, drapery and curtain rods, rugs, carpets and all other floor coverings, lamps, wall hangings and pictures, and all replacements thereof and additions thereto from this point on and such additions and replacements shall be deemed to form a part of the realty and are thus covered by the lien of this mortgage.*

This clause also includes an **after-acquired property clause**, a provision that serves to add to the mortgage coverage any buildings, fixtures, or other attachments that are made after the mortgage is attached.

Persons Covered by the Mortgage

One of the issues that has emerged in all of the foreclosures of the past few years is that the precision in mortgage paperwork has not been, well, all that precise. In many cases, the mortgages on property owned by husbands and wives were not signed by both spouses. Whether the lender can foreclose on the full property remains a question that is determined on a case-by-case basis unless state statutes are passed. The following case is one that made national news because of the outcome for the mortgagors.

CITIMORTGAGE, INC. V. DANIELSON

771 N.W.2d 653 (Iowa App. 2009)
A Payment and a House Free and Clear

FACTS

Matthew and Jamie Danielson were beneficiaries of the housing boom, he as a contractor and she as a mortgage broker. When the market slowed, they decided to downsize from their lifestyle of a $600,000 home on Saylorville Lake, a car lot, and several cars to go with it all. Well, "decided" may be charitable. The couple lost the Saylorville home to foreclosure and the lender (her employer), First Horizon, had to sell the lake home for $339,500.

Following the forced downsizing was the Danielsons' 2007 purchase of an 1800-square-foot, 3-bedroom, 2 ½-bathroom home in Ankeny, Iowa. However, Mrs. Danielson's credit was shot because she was the mortgagor on the Lake house and approaching her employer for another loan after the embarrassing default was not an option. So, Mr. Danielson applied for the mortgage for the Ankeny home, an amount of $320,228, which was 100 percent of the value of the home plus $50,000 the couple borrowed to remodel the basement. But the best part of the story is to come—the closing was completed at a food court in the local mall. Mr. Danielson, with his son in tow, met his mortgage broker, Jason Larson, at the food court on May 24, 2007.

Mr. Danielson had asked Larson when he called 45 to 50 minutes before the food-court meeting if his wife needed to be present. Larson indicated that she did not need to be there. Matt attempted to call Jamie anyway because she handled the couple's finances and was employed as a loan originator for a mortgage banker. He was unable to reach Mrs. Danielson and attended the closing alone with Larson.

At the closing, described as "rushed," Larson had Mr. Danielson sign a large packet of documents that included two uniform residential loan applications. One application appears to have been generated by One Source Mortgage while the other was generated by Citimortgage. Both loan applications identify Larson as the interviewer and indicate the application was taken by telephone. Mr. Danielson and Larson signed both applications at the mall closing. The applications refer to Mr. Danielson as "unmarried" and as a "[s]ingle man." Mr. Danielson also signed a promissory note in the amount of $320,228 at the

May 24 closing. The note is payable to Citimortgage and secured by a purchase money mortgage on the Danielsons' home. The mortgage, which contains a homestead exemption waiver clause, identifies the borrower as "Matthew D. Danielson, a single man."

Because Mr. Danielson's business went south after just one payment on the home, Citimortgage initiated foreclosure proceedings in December 2007 against Mr. Danielson who consulted an attorney. The attorney raised the scepter of Iowa's statute that renders a mortgage signed by only one spouse on jointly owned marital property as void. The Danielsons then filed a counterclaim to quiet title to the property, seeking an order from the court that Matthew's mortgage with Citimortgage is void under Iowa Code § 561.13, which required the signature of both spouses in order to have any kind of attachment to the couple's marital property.

The trial court held that the mortgage was void and Citimortgage appealed.

JUDICIAL OPINION

Doyle, Judge

Homestead rights are jealously guarded by the law. One way in which the legislature has sought to protect homesteads is through Iowa Code section 561.13, which invalidates encumbrances of the homestead not signed by both spouses "unless and until the spouse of the owner executes the same or a like instrument." If Section 561.13 is not satisfied, the transaction is invalid as to both the husband and the wife.

Section 561.13 was not satisfied in this case because the mortgage encumbering the parties' homestead was signed only by Matthew, who was married to Jamie at the time of the encumbrance. The mortgage is therefore invalid and void as to both Matthew and Jamie.

Citimortgage attempts to avoid the harsh effect of section 561.13 in this case by asserting Matthew procured the mortgage by fraudulently misrepresenting his marital status, which it contends should result in the imposition of an equitable mortgage. The district court denied this claim, finding there was "not one piece of evidence to indicate Mr. Danielson knowingly or with any intent to defraud gave false information to anyone throughout this transaction." Citimortgage claims the district court erred in so concluding.[12] We do not agree.

Our supreme court has recognized in "other circumstances that 'courts of equity are bound by statutes and follow the law in [the] absence of fraud or mistake.'" It is a well-settled principle of equity that misrepresentations amounting to fraud in the inducement of a contract, whether innocent or not, give rise to a right of avoidance on the part of the defrauded party. Here, however, Citimortgage attempts to use the Danielsons' supposed fraud in procuring their mortgage to enforce that mortgage rather than avoid it.

The evidence presented at trial establishes, as the district court found, that "everyone involved who actually had a role in this actual transaction ... knew that Mr. Danielson was married." Matthew and Jamie toured the home together with their real estate agent, the builder, and the builder's real estate agent before Matthew agreed to purchase it. They also met with those individuals on several other occasions to discuss matters related to the purchase of the home. The warranty deed prepared by the attorney for the builder's real estate agent originally referred to Matthew as "a married person," though someone later changed that deed to identify him as "an unmarried person." Matthew, whom the district court found to be credible, testified that Larson "absolutely" knew he was married. He specifically asked Larson before the closing if his wife needed to be present, and Larson said no. Matthew nevertheless attempted to contact her on his way to the closing. In light of the foregoing, we do not believe the record reveals any intent on Matthew's part to induce Citimortgage to act on the basis of the representations in the closing documents regarding his marital status.

Indeed, it appears Citimortgage approved Matthew for the loan before receiving a signed copy of his loan application. Matthew did not sign the loan applications prepared by Larson until the closing on May 24, 2007. Yet Citimortgage issued a commitment letter to Matthew on May 16 advising him that his application for a mortgage had been approved. No evidence was presented as to what information Citimortgage relied on in approving the loan to Matthew and preparing the mortgage that identified him as a "single man." We cannot see how Citimortgage could have justifiably relied on the representations contained in the loan applications and the mortgage itself regarding Matthew's marital status in agreeing to loan him $320,228 on May 16 when those documents were not executed until May 24. Finally, even if we were to assume for the sake of argument that Matthew fraudulently induced Citimortgage to enter into the mortgage by representing that he was not married, there is no evidence present in the record from which we could conclude that Jamie had any part in that supposed fraud.

[T]he purpose of the homestead laws is to provide a margin of safety to the family, not only for the benefit of the family, but for the public welfare and social benefit which accrues to the State by having families secure in their homes.

While it may be tempting for courts to fashion remedies deemed to be fair and just under the particular circumstances of a case, "the law has defined those concepts and must dominate the decision making process." We are thus bound to apply section 561.13 to invalidate the mortgage in this case as it did not contain the signatures of both spouses and Citimortgage did not establish any fraud on the part of either spouse in obtaining the mortgage.

We therefore affirm the judgment of the district court dismissing Citimortgage's petition to foreclose its mortgage on the property and declaring that mortgage to be void under section 561.13.

Affirmed.

AFTERMATH: Shortly after the decision, the Iowa legislature passed a law that indicated the signature of both spouses as not required when there was a purchase money mortgage involved, the property was the couple's homestead and the non-signing spouse lived there. In addition, in *JP Morgan Chase Bank National Association v. Hawkins,* 798 N.W.2d 349 (Iowa App. 2011), a court held that the homestead protection was never intended to apply to purchase money mortgages. Can a Danielson case ever happen again in Iowa?

CASE QUESTIONS

1. Why is the mortgage void?
2. What kinds of actions do you anticipate married couples would take as well as lenders because of this decision?

---

[12]12 U.S.C. § 5201 et seq.

ETHICAL ISSUE

Evaluate the ethics of the Danielsons in owning their home free and clear after just one payment.

Transfers and Assignments by Mortgagor

In many mortgage arrangements, the mortgagor will not remain in possession or use of the property for the entire term of the mortgage. In both residential and commercial transactions, the original mortgagor may need to sell or transfer the mortgaged property. The following sections cover the methods of transfer and the rights and duties of the parties.

The Assumption

In many cases, the original mortgagor's interest rate is lower than the rates available at the time the transfer of the property becomes necessary. If the buyer can purchase the property by agreeing to assume the responsibility for repayment of the original mortgage, the seller will have a much better chance of being able to sell the property at a good price.

The following factual example illustrates how this method of transferring the mortgage debt as part of the purchase price of the property works:

Hal Wood purchased a small home for $275,000 in 2004. In 2012, Hal had to sell the home. Hal had a mortgage balance of approximately $265,000 on the home, and he advertised to sell the home for $298,000. Bob Freeman has made an offer to purchase the home for $295,000, with Bob paying Hal $30,000 cash and agreeing to assume responsibility for repayment of the $265,000 mortgage.

The following diagram illustrates the transfer:

FIRST MORTGAGEE ⇆ *HAL WOOD, MORTGAGOR*
↓
BOB FREEMAN, BUYER

The transaction is a simple assignment of contract benefits and a delegation of contract duties. Bob will enjoy the benefits of residing in the property but will assume responsibility for the mortgage payments. The transaction is referred to as an **assumption**, or, frequently, as a **cash-to-mortgage sale**, since Bob is paying enough cash down to be able to assume the mortgage.

An assumption does not relieve the original mortgagor (Hal) of liability under the mortgage arrangement. The mortgagor remains liable for repayment of the debt and, if the buyer defaults, the mortgagor must still pay the mortgage debt. The mortgagee has the right to enforce repayment against either one of the parties and always retains the right of foreclosure in the event both parties default (discussed later).

The only way the mortgagor can be relieved of liability under the mortgage agreement is if the mortgagee consents to a release. Many mortgages require a release once the mortgagee has qualified or is satisfied with the purchaser and has consented in writing to the transfer and assumption.

Many mortgages are subject to a due-on-sale provision (discussed on p. 416), which effectively prevents the mortgagor from transferring the rights available under the mortgage.

The Subject-to Sale

In a sale of property by a mortgagor to a buyer in which the buyer takes *subject to* the existing mortgage, the mortgagor remains personally liable on the mortgage; the buyer undertakes no personal responsibility for payment of the mortgage; and the property remains subject to the foreclosure. In a **subject-to sale**, the seller continues to be responsible for the payments on the mortgage. The mortgagee's rights are not affected by a transfer of property subject to its existing mortgage. The subject-to sale can be used very effectively in some of the alternative financing techniques discussed later in the chapter.

Refinancing

In some property sales where the cash-to-mortgage balance is too high for the buyer, the buyer will need to finance the purchase of the property by borrowing the money under a new note secured by a new mortgage. This new mortgage is called **refinancing** the purchase of the property. The original mortgagee is paid the full amount due on the mortgage, the seller gets the cash difference between the sale price and the mortgage balance, and the new mortgagee puts a new mortgage on the property. The seller is no longer liable and the old, original mortgagee no longer has any rights in the property.

Transfers and Assignments of Mortgages by Mortgagees

Many property owners are confused when they receive notification that their mortgage has been sold. Some believe that their loan or credit rating will be affected by such a transfer. MERS was a result of the very fluid transfer of residential mortgages. As noted earlier, one of the problems that resulted from the frequent transfers is establishing the right to foreclose in the event of a default, especially when the underlying debt (note) is separated from the mortgage itself.

Upon an assignment of a mortgage loan, the mortgagor's rights remain the same. The change in payment place occurs only after the new mortgagee notifies the mortgagor of the change for future payments. Under the new federal regulations, there are requirements for timely notification so that mortgagors are clear where to send payments and inquiries, and have the ability to make contact when they are experiencing payment difficulties. Many work-outs and foreclosures were delayed post-2007 because mortgagors were not clear who actually held their mortgages.

Satisfaction of Mortgage

Once the debt underlying the mortgage is repaid, the mortgage ends through the execution and recording of an agreement called a **satisfaction of mortgage**. The satisfaction of mortgage requires only an adequate description of the property and the signature of the mortgagee (usually notarized). The satisfaction of the mortgage is recorded with all other land interests and, when recorded, clears the mortgage lien in lien states or vests title in the mortgagor in title states. All states have some type of statutory penalty for mortgagees who wrongfully refuse to execute a release or satisfaction of the mortgage. The penalty can be a one-time sum or a weekly fee that continues until the title is cleared by the mortgagee.

Foreclosure

Default of the Mortgagor

Foreclosure is a mortgagee's right when the mortgagor defaults. A **default** occurs when the mortgagor fails to comply with some provision of the mortgage. The most common form of default occurs when the mortgagor fails to make timely payments. However, any breach of the mortgage or note, or violation of any of the other provisions of either, is a default. For example, most mortgagees require the mortgagor to maintain hazard insurance on the property and to make timely payments of taxes and assessments. Failure to comply with these provisions is a default.

If the mortgagor causes destruction, devaluation, or general decline of the property, known as *waste*, the mortgagee may declare a default.

The mortgage agreement should define default. In other words, the mortgage should include a list of the triggers for default. All states afford remedies for mortgagees upon the mortgagor's default, but very few state statutes specify what a default is. The mortgage acceleration clause will also be tied to violations of the mortgage terms and the resulting default. A typical trigger for a default and acceleration is a failure to maintain hazard insurance.

Avoiding Foreclosure: Refinancing, Restructuring, and Modifying

This option finds the mortgagor changing the mortgage loan and/or its repayment. Refinancing means that the mortgagor, through the original lender or a new one, refinances the full amount of the mortgage. Generally, refinancing means a lower interest rate or a fixed interest rate in lieu of an ARM. Restructuring or modifying a mortgage loan means that the mortgagor returns to the original lender and requests what is often called a **workout**. The parties are trying to work out an alternative other than foreclosure.

A workout can involve an extension of the loan repayment and amortization period; a temporary suspension of loan payments; a reduction or elimination of accrued future loan interest; additional security; a reduction in the loan's principal; personal guarantees from officers or directors; or additional or new control on borrower operations, cash disbursements, or accounts receivables.

Many lenders use the workout period as a way to avoid **lender liability** suits that are usually brought as counterclaims by borrowers in foreclosure actions. These counterclaims often allege malice or bad faith on the part of the lender in dealing with an ailing borrower who can establish that recovery and repayment were possible. Many lenders have borrowers waive these liability claims as part of the workout conditions. The key for lenders in avoiding liability in a workout is avoiding coercion and misrepresentation. Having the mortgagor sign workout agreements that spell out all conditions, consequences, and costs helps avoid liability. However, the liability of a lender for taking the necessary steps for supervision of a troubled borrower is now very rare. *Gavin v. Sovereign Bank*, 2008 WL 2622839 (D.Mass. 2008).

In an upside-down market, lenders are more willing to restructure and modify because some payment is better than an idle property for sale in a glutted market in which credit is frozen. In fact, the extent of the problem properties during an economic downturn has resulted in growth in the loan servicing industry. This is an industry that works with a lender to mitigate the damages to investors who hold mortgage-backed securities by trying to work with the mortgagors/borrowers in order to obtain some payments so that the mortgage loans are not taken as a write-off loss. The loan servicer creates a loss mitigation plan that can involve sales of homes, refinancing of homes, deeds in lieu of foreclosure, or even the full sales of the mortgage-backed instruments so that another company can take over all the mortgage issues.

In these situations where there are unemployed mortgagors and/or mortgagors underwater, the mortgagor's goal is generally getting a lower payment. That can be achieved through a lower interest rate, a fixed interest rate, a longer period for repayment, a breather period of a few months with no or reduced payments, or a reduction in principal. Mortgage servicers must report on loss mitigation plans to the Secretary of the Treasury. The result is that mortgage modifications, short sales, and sales of mortgage-backed securities now have an additional regulatory hurdle to clear before these properties can be sold or refinanced.

Amidst all the new regulations the parties must still be careful to meet the contracts basics in their deals. Because these new terms with the original mortgage lender are simply a modification of the contract, there must be a mutual agreement as well as new detriment on both sides. The lender accepts less, but the mortgagor has to agree to something new as well. That something new could be a new checking account opened at the lender, automatic deduction of payments from that account, and a host of other changes that are simple and can serve to make the modification valid. Bank of America has been restructuring all of the loans it acquired from Countrywide that have large increases in interest rates about to take effect.

Government refinancing programs have been available since 2008 and include special interest rates for homeowners who are **underwater** (owe more on their mortgages than their property is worth) as well as for members of the armed services who are on active military duty. The Home Affordable Refinance Program (HARP) has been expanded since the 2008 market collapse and is available to homeowners whose loans are backed by Fannie Mae and Freddie Mac. The **Hope for Homeowners Act of 2008** established the authority for FHFA to help homeowners restructure, refinance, and modify their loans. Homeowners must meet certain specific requirements to qualify for this assistance, but those qualifications have been eased since 2008 in order to allow more homeowners who are under water to qualify for refinancing.

The **Troubled Asset Relief Program, or TARP**, a program that authorized the Secretary of the Treasury to purchase troubled assets from financial institutions, has provided lenders and borrowers with government restructuring. The goal of these programs was reducing or avoiding foreclosures, a process that reduced property values and continued to fuel a decline in property values.

Avoiding Foreclosure: Just Walking Away, Sometimes with Stuff from the House

Facing foreclosure, mortgagors who have loans that exceed their property value often have a sense of hopelessness and "nothing to lose." These mortgagors simply leave the property, something that is likely in an underwater mortgage because they have so little to lose. Their credit rating is affected, but they no longer have the payments or the worries of maintenance. In some cities, mortgagors who have abandoned their homes have stripped the property of everything from the stove to the copper plumbing. Some states have increased the criminal charges and penalties for stripping properties. The federal government has set up special task forces to try to stop the stripping of properties by mortgagors.

Most mortgage agreements require the mortgagor to maintain the property in livable condition, but again, desperate times bring desperate actions. Also, taking items from the mortgaged property is not theft unless and until title has been taken back through the foreclosure process. Stripped and abandoned properties bring down the value of neighborhoods and result in increased crime levels. Areas with high levels of abandoned properties now unoccupied and held by lenders that are unable to sell them have been labeled "foreclosure ghettos." In cities with high foreclosure rates, "walk-aways" and stripping have resulted in urban blight in certain areas. Cities are passing ordinances that require lenders to maintain the abandoned properties, or are actually taking back the properties through eminent domain so that the abandoned homes do not become drug houses or residences for the homeless. In some cities, blocks of foreclosed homes have been razed in order to curb crime in these abandoned areas.

Avoiding Foreclosure: Deed in Lieu of Foreclosure

Under this option, the mortgagor simply surrenders the deed to the property to the lender. There is still an impact to the mortgagor's credit rating, but there is always a notation of this good-faith effort to return the property in good condition. A deed in lieu is akin to a white flag of surrender.

Chances are that before foreclosure occurs there have been substantial efforts to work with the mortgagor to correct the default. On government-insured loans, the average duration of default before foreclosure is initiated is 6 months. If the mortgagor tries to correct the default—in most cases by making up back payments—the average default period before foreclosure is 10 months. The lender/mortgagee also works with the borrower before foreclosure. The lender/mortgagee encourages the mortgagor to try to sell the property in an effort to salvage any equity interest it may have in the property. In an upside-down market, sales are just not possible.

After the default period efforts, from workouts to sales, have failed, the parties may still reach an agreement to avoid the costs and delays of foreclosure. The parties agree that the mortgagor will quitclaim the property to the mortgagee. This transaction is called a **deed in lieu of foreclosure**. When the deed is signed over by the mortgagor, the underlying debt is canceled. Perhaps one of the most famous deed-in-lieu-of transactions occurred in 1994 when Sears turned over the deed to the Chicago Sears Tower (now the Willis Tower) to a trust set up for the benefit of all the mortgage holders on the property. After facing mounting costs and years of declining real estate values, Sears walked away from the financings and cost involved.

Some states require the mortgagee to pay something to the mortgagor (in addition to canceling the debt) in order to be a *bona fide* and protected purchaser. Many mortgagors simply pay an additional $500 so that the mortgagee is a purchaser for value and entitled to full protection as a transferee. The transaction must also be free of coercion and the mortgagee must be able to prove that the mortgagor acted voluntarily. To avoid difficulties and questions about voluntariness, particularly if the mortgagor subsequently declares bankruptcy, the parties should sign an agreement explaining their transaction or at least have the mortgagor execute an affidavit explaining the reason for the transfer and the consideration being paid for it.

Processes of Foreclosure

Foreclosure follows state law, and each state has different procedures for the mortgagee to follow in exercising foreclosure rights. There are two basic groups of foreclosure proceedings: judicial foreclosure and strict foreclosure.

Judicial Foreclosure

Under **judicial foreclosure**, required in about 40 percent of the states, the mortgagee is required to bring suit to have the rights of the parties established. The court then has the power, following its findings, to order the sale of the property to satisfy the debt due. In order to pass good title to the property, the judicial foreclosure sale must follow all procedural requirements. The failure to follow these steps (a critical part of the mortgagor's due process) means that the foreclosure may be set aside.

1. *Filing the Petition.* For judicial foreclosure, the petition is usually filed in the state and county where the property is located. The petition must include the factual basis for the foreclosure action, including the dates and amounts of all defaults, the exact amount of principal due on the underlying debt, and the relief requested, such as a judicial sale.

2. *Notifying Required Parties.* Once the petition is filed, it must be served on all parties who will be affected by the foreclosure. Other parties could include tenants, second or junior mortgagees, holders of mechanic's liens, secured creditors under UCC Article 9, any government agencies with tax claims, and any other lienors. A search of the land records will give the names of those who should have a notice of foreclosure.

3. *Filing a Notice of Action (**Lis Pendens**).* Court backlogs and statutory waiting periods mean that it may be some time before the foreclosure sale actually occurs. But public notification of the pending foreclosure prevents others from further burdening the property between the filing of the petition and the actual sale of the property. Also, the public notice gives lienors and potential lienors notice that any lien amount on the property in foreclosure is not likely to bring proceeds sufficient enough to help with their repayment. The notice that a mortgage foreclosure action has been filed is called a *lis pendens*. The notice is filed under all parties' names to ensure that others can pull up the information if they search the records.

4. *Foreclosure Trial or Hearing.* The proof required at a foreclosure is that there has been a default and that the mortgage agreement authorizes judicial action and sale. Generally, the hearing is a formality, with the mortgagor rarely appearing to challenge the action.

5. *Order of Foreclosure.* Once the court finds that the foreclosure is appropriate, it orders foreclosure. In strict foreclosure states, the order has a definitive time for final sale, such as a three- or four-month period. If the mortgagor is not able to pay the amount due within that time, the order provides for a sale of the property. Once the sale has occurred, the mortgagor loses forever all interest in the property and the right to reacquire the property. In other states, the court orders a sale for as soon as possible, but the mortgagor is still given one last chance to redeem the property interest. For a statutory period ranging from six months to a year after the foreclosure sale, the mortgagor may pay the full amount due and regain title to the property (even if the property has in fact been sold). This right to pay the debt after the judicial sale is referred to as the **statutory right of redemption**. The effects of the statutory period are twofold: (1) the mortgagee is required to wait before closing the case file completely and (2) the purchaser of the property is required to wait before actually obtaining full and complete title.

6. *The Sale Logistics.* A foreclosure sale is held as a public sale or as a private sale for which there has been published notice. The sale is carried out by an officer of the judiciary, such as a sheriff, and is an auction, with the property being transferred to the highest bidder. In strict foreclosure states, the purchaser is given a **sheriff's deed**, which serves to convey title but does not include any warranties of title. The deed is only as good as the judicial

procedures were proper. In statutory redemption states, the purchaser is given some type of document, such as a certificate of sale, but the purchaser cannot be given title to the property until the statutory redemption period has passed. At the end of the statutory redemption period, the purchaser is also given a sheriff's deed (also called a **judicial deed**, see Chapter 14).

7. *The Soldiers and Sailors Civil Relief Act (50 U.S.C. § 501).* As originally passed, this federal law, known as the **Soldiers and Sailors Civil Relief Act (SSCRA)**, postponed or prevented foreclosure on the homes of military personnel while they were on active duty. The protections for military personnel were expanded during the first Gulf War in 1991 and require courts to postpone foreclosure proceedings if the default of the mortgagor results from a pay reduction because of induction into the armed services.[13]

The SSCRA, as amended, provides additional protections for military personnel including: an upper limit of 6 percent interest on a home mortgage loan during the time of active service and for three months after that active service ends; statutory redemption cannot require payment of interest for the period of the mortgagor's active military service (i.e., the period does not begin until active service terminates); and delayed civil proceedings so long as the mortgagor is on active duty. The wars in Afghanistan and Iraq in 2001 and 2003 resulted in amendments to this law to cover National Guard reservists who were called to active duty for 30 days or more and experienced economic hardship. Called the Servicemembers Civil Relief Act of 2003, the military personnel who were deployed in Operation Iraqi Freedom also enjoyed protection in other areas of property law, from eviction for nonpayment of rent without a hearing to being excused from their car leases upon being sent to active duty. In 2011, the Relief Act was again amended to prohibit foreclosure on the properties of active-duty service members as well as provide special programs for refinancing for the homes of members of the military.

Challenges to Foreclosure

Prior to the subprime crisis, most challenges to foreclosure proceedings focused on the way the sale was conducted. The challenges centered on adequate advertising of the sale as well as the bids and price paid. However, the low-price complaint is seldom a basis for setting aside the sale. Pre-subprime foreclosure challenges that were successful were based on lapses in procedures.

In the subprime foreclosures of 2008–2012, the challenges were based on the nature of the loans and whether the party bringing the foreclosure was actually a lender or assignee entitled to bring foreclosure actions. A lawyer known as "The Foreclosure Angel" created a foundation with a purpose of challenging foreclosures on subprime mortgages. Those challenges were largely based on the issues discussed earlier with relation to MERS.

Mortgage Work-Out Firms

On the other side of foreclosures, there have been law firms and lawyers who specialize in work-outs and mortgage renegotiations. However, not all these experts are truly experts and mortgagors faced with losing their homes have paid substantial up-front fees to these experts, only to lose both the fee and their homes. Currently, several states and the federal government are moving to enact

---

[13]The act has been expanded to cover leases, including real property and auto leases.

standards and licensing for foreclosure assistance companies. The Federal Trade Commission (FTC) rules prohibit these companies from charging you until they actually present an offer from your lender that you accept. Known as Mortgage Assistance Relief Scams (MARS), the FTC has a list of advertising come-ons that signal a potential fraud by someone who presents himself as an expert in foreclosure:

"Stop foreclosure now!"

"Get a loan modification!"

"Over 90% of our customers get results."

"We have special relationships with banks that can speed up the approval process."

"100% Money Back Guarantee."

"Keep Your Home. We know your home is scheduled to be sold. No Problem!"

CONSIDER 15.3   Edward Knudsen owned a nine-acre ranch, adjacent to a country club, that was appraised at $900,000. Knudsen's monthly mortgage payments of $4,008 became too burdensome, and he defaulted. The mortgage company, after public notice, sold the ranch for $214,460—a mere $5.66 more than the mortgage on the property. Has the mortgage company acted properly?

Strict Foreclosure or Foreclosure by Power of Sale

Many states permit mortgagees to sell the property upon the mortgagor's default without court proceedings. This **power of sale** is a characteristic of the deed of trust financing arrangement (discussed later).

Under this method of foreclosure, a rather quick and nonjudicial sale may be held. The following are the typical procedures the mortgagee must follow to execute a valid sale.

1. *Notice and Advertisement.* The mortgagee must furnish notice to all interested parties (the mortgagor, secondary or junior creditors, lienors, and so on) and also advertise or publish notice of the impending sale, including time and place of the sale. In some states, this notice is such a critical part of this process that this method of foreclosure is referred to as **foreclosure by advertisement**. Many states have time requirements on the notice, such as the notice and advertisement be given 90 days prior to the date of sale.

In many states, the ease of the power of sale is not without some cost to the mortgagee: The mortgagee loses the right to a deficiency action by exercising the power of sale. In other words, the mortgagee is entitled to a speedy foreclosure; but if the sale does not bring enough to satisfy the debt, the mortgagee cannot collect the deficiency. Challenges to these sales are successful when the mortgagee has not complied with the process requirements, including notice.

2. *Right of Redemption.* An additional distinction between the power of sale and foreclosure procedures is that under the power of sale, the debtor loses the statutory redemption period. The debtor has time only up until the sale to redeem the property. Once the property is sold, the buyer gets full title to

the property, and the debtor does not have a redemption period (as under judicial foreclosures). The power of sale process is swift, clean, and permanent.

3. *The Soldiers and Sailors Civil Relief Act.* This act applies to the power of sale foreclosure as well. Procedures must simply be postponed for all those who qualify. The postponement runs for the period of active service.

The following case provides some insight into the complexities of mortgages and the relationship between lender and borrower as well as the effect of layered mortgages.

HULL V. NORTH ADAMS HOOSAC SAVINGS BANK

730 N.E.2d 910 (Mass. App. 2000)
When the Marriage and the Property Values Go South

FACTS

Before his marriage to Kathleen Hull, M. Harry Hull (Harry) had a variety of real estate investments, including one acquired in 1985 and located at East Quincy Street and another also acquired in 1985 at Millard Avenue. The Quincy Street property had a first mortgage to the sellers and the Millard Avenue property had a first mortgage to North Adams Bank.

Following his marriage to Kathleen, Harry conveyed the properties to himself and Kathleen as tenants by the entirety and subject to the mortgages. Immediately upon conveyance to them jointly, the two used the properties to obtain an additional property, located on Yale Street, subject to a mortgage. The Hulls lived in a rental unit in the Millard Avenue property. The following diagram illustrates the Hulls' complex mortgage relationships.

By 1988, and still more mortgages later, the marriage was over and Harry had all loans in default. The banks threatened foreclosure, and Kathleen borrowed $15,000 from her parents to bring the payments on the properties current.

Harry filed for divorce in 1989 and conveyed his interests in the East Quincy and Yale properties to Kathleen, subject to the mortgages. Kathleen also agreed to assume the payments for these properties. The divorce court awarded her the Millard Avenue property.

Kathleen fell into arrears trying to make payments on all three properties and asked the bank to separate them out. The bank maintained that the liens were indistinguishable and filed for foreclosure shortly after Kathleen filed suit to have her rights under the mortgages determined and for the bank's bad faith in its refusal to separate the loans and properties.

The jury at the trial court awarded Kathleen $300,000, and the trial court judge granted the bank's motion for judgment *non obstante veredicto*, or judgment *n.o.v.,* Kathleen appealed.

JUDICIAL OPINION

Kass, Judge

We have laid out the facts in some detail and at some length to test the correctness of the grant of judgment *n.o.v.* Kathleen's primary contention is that the bank owed her a duty to explain that she was not liable on Yale Street. Failing to do so, she says, saddled her with operating and attempting to maintain mortgage

Millard Avenue		East Quincy Street	Yale Street
1985 loan (to Harry)	1st mortgage (from Harry)	1st mortgage (from Harry & Kathleen)	1st mortgage (from Harry)
1986 loan (to Harry & Kathleen)	2nd mortgage (from Harry & Kathleen)		
1988 loan (to Harry)	3rd mortgage (from Harry)		

© Cengage Learning

service on all three properties, a burden that was her undoing. The jury found (by special verdict) that the bank's insistence on payment of mortgages on all three properties was a failure on the part of the bank to exercise good faith in the bank's dealings with Kathleen and that this inflicted $300,000 in damages on her.

The facts do not admit of the finding of failure by the bank to exercise good faith; the question of damages falls by the wayside with that conclusion. Although Kathleen was not on the Yale Street mortgage note in October, 1988, when the bank first asked her for payment on that property along with the other two loans, she had already acquired an undivided interest in the primary security for that note, i.e., the Yale Street property, by deed from Harry dated February 16, 1988. In addition, the Yale Street loan from the bank was cross-collateralized by a third mortgage loan on Millard Avenue. Consequently, a default on Yale Street triggered a default on Millard Avenue. In turn, a default on Millard Avenue caused a default on East Quincy Street because those two properties had been mortgaged to the bank together to secure the September 9, 1986, loan. On the basis of the loan documents between the bank and the Hulls, the bank was quite within its rights in asking that the loans involving all three properties be made current, on pain of foreclosure if they were not.

Had there been any doubt about Kathleen's interest in Yale Street, that was resolved by her accepting sole title to it on May 31, 1989, with a proviso in the deed that the grantee, by accepting the deed, assumed and agreed to pay the mortgage to the bank. She then became personally liable on the Yale Street debt. She also acquired the title to the Millard Avenue and East Quincy Street properties.

Between the time of Kathleen's acquisition of sole title to the three properties on May 31, 1989, more than five years went by before the bank foreclosed on the three loans in November, 1994. The forbearance of the bank did not work a waiver of its rights as a mortgagee under the loan documents nor was it inequitable for the bank to exercise its contractual rights under the governing documents.

It follows that the judge correctly allowed the motion for judgment n.o.v.

Affirmed.

CASE QUESTIONS

1. Why did the bank treat all the loans as one?
2. Did Kathleen agree to assume personal liability? Were all the properties subject to foreclosure?
3. Does Kathleen still owe the money if she wants to keep the property?

Proceeds and Priorities upon Foreclosure

Very often, when a mortgagor defaults, more than one creditor has an interest in the property. The priority of the parties will determine rights of foreclosure and will also determine who will be entitled to payment first upon sale of the mortgaged property at a foreclosure sale. The priority of the various creditors will determine the order of distribution of the proceeds from the sale of the property.

Recorded Interests

As mentioned earlier, a mortgage is valid even if not recorded, but only as between mortgagor and mortgagee. An unrecorded mortgage takes last position against any interests in the mortgaged property that are recorded either prior to the mortgage execution or subsequent to it.

If a mortgage is recorded, the general rule for priority of interests is "first in time is first in right." That is, the mortgage recorded first will enjoy priority over junior or second mortgages recorded later in time. Generally, the same rule applies for the priority of mortgage interests over other recorded land interests such as lien or security interests: If the mortgagee recorded the mortgage prior to the recording of these other interests, then the mortgagee will have priority. There are exceptions, as discussed in Chapters 5 and 6. For example, purchase money security interests (PMSIs) in fixtures take priority over previously recorded mortgages if the PMSI is recorded before annexation of the fixture to the land or within 20 days after its annexation; and mechanics' liens take priority over previously recorded mortgages if work on the land began before the mortgage was recorded. In addition, the MERS issues have resulted in breaks in the chain of title in the public records, something that can result in confusion regarding priorities.

Applications of Proceeds from Foreclosure

The determination of priority among the various interest holders is the preliminary step in determining who will or will not be paid in the event foreclosure on the property becomes necessary. It is very likely that a foreclosure sale will bring only a minimal amount—perhaps simply the amount of the outstanding debt. However, the order of the distribution of funds is as follows:

1. Payment of the costs of sale: court costs, fees, notice and publication costs, and so on

2. Payment of the mortgage debt having first priority

3. Payment of any junior liens, claims, or mortgages in the order of their priority

4. If there is any surplus, it is distributed to the mortgagor

There are some exceptions to the general priority rule of first in time is first in right (see discussion in Chapter 14). One such exception is the priority of liens for federal and state taxes. Although a mortgage recorded prior to the filing of the tax lien will enjoy priority, the expenses associated with foreclosure may be subordinate to the tax lien.

The foreclosure sale extinguishes all mortgages and liens on the property regardless of whether the sale proceeds were sufficient to cover all of them.

CONSIDER 15.4   M gave a mortgage to C1, who recorded the mortgage that day (May 30, 2013) at 8 a.m. in the county recorder's office. M had previously given a mortgage to C on May 15, 2013, which C recorded at 11 a.m. on May 30, 2009. Who, between C and C1, has priority?

CONSIDER 15.5   A foreclosure sale on a parcel of property took place on September 11, 2012. The amount received from the sale is $175,000. The following list indicates the parties holding interests in the property sold. Distribute the funds according to the priority of the parties.

- First Federal: balance of $132,000 due on note secured by mortgage recorded January 21, 2000
- Great Western: balance of $8,000 due on note secured by mortgage recorded October 16, 2001
- Federal tax lien: balance of $22,000 due, with notice of lien recorded on January 5, 2001
- First Federal's costs and expenses of foreclosure: $5,000
- Judgment lien against the property owner for $10,000 recorded December 23, 1997
- American Finance: purchase money security interest in solar water heater, filed before attachment on December 1, 2001, in the amount of $3,000

Postforeclosure Remedies—The Deficiency Judgment

In many cases, the sale of the mortgaged property at a foreclosure sale does not bring enough to satisfy the mortgage debt and foreclosure expenses. Many states allow a **deficiency judgment**, or allow the mortgagee to seek a personal judgment against the mortgagor to collect what the foreclosure process did not bring.

In some states, courts grant a personal judgment against the mortgagor at the same time the decree of foreclosure is entered. In other states, an action for deficiency cannot be brought until the foreclosure sale is held and the exact amount of the deficiency is known. In yet other states, deficiency judgments are not permitted in certain types of mortgages, particularly in purchase money mortgages for residential property.

Statistics indicate that deficiency actions, particularly in the case of residential purchase money mortgages (even where permitted), are not frequently used because of the unseemliness of taking more from debtors who just lost their homes to foreclosure.

In some states, mortgagees must take certain steps before they are permitted to pursue a deficiency judgment. One common prerequisite is establishing that they have exhausted the foreclosure remedy. In some states, if the mortgagee pursues a personal judgment on the note against the mortgagor, that mortgagee loses the right of foreclosure. In other states, the mortgagee bidding for the property must make it clear that it intends to pursue a deficiency. For example, when a bank bid in a foreclosure sale and took back the property without exercising its rights for the deficiency (because the bank's bid was less than the mortgage amount), the bank could not later seek to recover the insurance checks paid to the mortgagor for damage to the property. *Option One Mortg. Corp. v. J.P. Morgan Chase & Co.*, 940 N.Y.S.2d 225 (N.Y.A.D. 2012).

The Uniform Nonjudicial Foreclosure Act

The Uniform Nonjudicial Foreclosure Act (UNFA) has been promulgated by the National Conference of Commissioners on Uniform State Laws. The goal of the Act is to enhance negotiated foreclosures while providing prompt relief and protections, particularly for residential debtors. Perhaps its most attractive provision is that foreclosure sales would be handled not through the courts, but through the use of a real estate broker and a listing, just as with the sale of nonforeclosure properties. The act's elimination of the public auction, the typical type of sale in both judicial and nonjudicial foreclosure, should increase the sale proceeds. One goal of the UNFA, a mutually beneficial one, is to preserve property value and bring as much in sales proceeds as possible.

The UNFA would also bring uniformity to redemption periods, a problem with a national investment market because it is unclear how long it will take, with properties in various states, before the purchaser at a foreclosure public sale has title to the property.

ETHICAL ISSUE

Would you accept an approved mortgage loan that you knew was stretching your budget?

What are the moral hazards of mortgage bailouts? Re-default rates are 55 percent with those defaults occurring within 6 months after restructuring.

What are the risks in highly leveraged personal finance?

Who are the stakeholders in mortgages?

DEEDS OF TRUST

The typical mortgage involves only two parties: the mortgagor and the mortgagee. The **deed of trust** (also known as the "trust deed form of securing debts with real property") is a type of mortgage or security agreement that involves three parties. The property owner (buyer/trustor) conveys title to a third party (trustee) who then holds title for the benefit of the lender (beneficiary).

This three-party financing arrangement holds several advantages for the lender. First, the lender in most states has the right of foreclosure in the event of default without judicial process (called the *power of sale*). The power of sale requires only notice to the trustor and publication of the proposed sale date. Although there is a statutory minimum waiting period before the sale can take place, that waiting period is much shorter than that required for foreclosure. This simple notice and private sale is also much cheaper than judicial foreclosure.

A second advantage for the lender is that the lender's involvement can be kept secret, since only the trustee's name need appear in the records.

Another advantage is that the deed of trust facilitates the borrowing of large sums. Sales of bonds and other debentures by corporations to many parties can be secured by one deed of trust on corporate property, which will be held by a third party.

Relationship to Mortgages

Even though a deed of trust may be used instead of a mortgage to secure an underlying debt, the rights and relationships of the parties, with the exception of foreclosure, remain the same. That is, the trustor still has the obligations of timely payment, nonwaste, insurance, and so on. Furthermore, the deed of trust contains the same types of clauses and provisions as mortgages.

The lender must use the correct language to set up a deed of trust, or in many states, the arrangement will be treated as a mortgage. Perhaps the most important part of the deed of trust instrument is that the parties spell out the separation of title, with a named trustee.

The power of sale characteristic of the deed of trust eliminates or limits redemption rights of the trustor/borrower. Under the deed of trust, the borrower is usually given a right of reinstatement, which is the right to pay the amount due and owing the trustor at any time prior to the time of the sale (thereby redeeming the property). Reinstatement must take place prior to the sale. Under a deed of trust, once the sale takes place, all of the borrower's rights end. Under a mortgage, the period of redemption actually begins at the time of the sale and runs for six months to a year afterwards.

In some states, reinstatement requires the trustor to pay only the amount due in back payments plus costs and expenses. In other words, when the power of sale is exercised, the right of reinstatement may be exercised without the trustor paying the full, accelerated amount of the loan then due. This type of provision permits borrowers to reinstate more easily.

Duties and Responsibilities of the Trustee

The trustee in a deed of trust financing arrangement acts for the benefit of both parties. The trustee is the administrator responsible for carrying out the financing arrangement according to the terms set forth.

In many states, a statute specifies what parties are permitted to serve as trustees in a financing arrangement. In all states recognizing this form of financing, the trustee must be someone other than the lender. Typically, those authorized to serve as trustees are lawyers, brokers, title insurers, and escrow companies.

When conflicts arise between the parties or when a default has occurred, the trustee must adhere to the provisions of the trust agreement and conduct a sale pursuant to the terms of the agreement and any statutory procedures in the state where the property is located.

Advantages of the Deed of Trust Upon Default

One of the advantages of this form of lending and security is that most courts have held that its nonjudicial foreclosure method—the power of sale exercised by the trustee—can proceed without concerns about the separation of the security from the debt because the trustee is always the legal title holder. The MERS issues do not affect foreclosure under a deed of trust, or, as it is often referred to, a nonjudicial foreclosure.

CONSIDER 15.6   Fill in the chart to indicate the distinctions between mortgages and deeds of trust. Be sure to list under the mortgage sections the provisions applicable in title theory and lien theory states.

	Number of Parties	Title	Remedies upon Default	Right of Redemption
Mortgages				
Deeds of Trust				

© Cengage Learning

INSTALLMENT LAND CONTRACTS

The **installment land contract** is an alternative to a mortgage or a deed of trust as a method of financing the purchase of property. The installment contract is used frequently when the buyer is unable to obtain financing, when the buyer cannot come up with a large-enough down payment, or when interest rates are very high. Often called a **contract for deed** or a **long-term land contract**, the installment contract is also used to finance the purchase of property in areas where lenders have been reluctant to lend.

Each state has different statutes and regulations for land contracts, but all states follow a basic formula for this method of financing. The installment land contract is not a purchase contract with earnest money. Rather, the installment land contract is an agreement that covers the rights and responsibilities of the parties for the life of the debt, which is being carried by the seller and repaid by the buyer. The installment land contract, unlike the purchase contract, is not executed until closing.

The Forfeiture Aspect

One of the unique features of the installment land contract is that in some states the seller has a very strong remedy in the event of the buyer's default: **forfeiture**. In other words, some states provide that a buyer who defaults under an installment contract will forfeit all interest acquired in the property to the seller, and the forfeiture occurs without judicial process according to time periods established by statute. All states require the seller to give some form of notice of default to the buyer/borrower that includes a statement of the intent to exercise forfeiture rights.

The amount of notice and grace period for installment contracts varies. For example, some states provide that if a defaulting buyer has paid less than 20 percent of the property's purchase price, then that buyer's interest is forfeited within 30 days after the notification of the default. The 30 days is a grace period that allows the buyer to redeem the property by paying what is then due and owing. The length of the grace period varies according to the amount the buyer has paid in to the seller; in some states it may last up to a year.

A seller who wants to keep forfeiture rights must be cautious in accepting late payments from the buyer. If the seller has been accepting late payments, the forfeiture provisions cannot be invoked unless the seller provides the buyer with notice of the reinstatement of timely payments. Some states still require a form of foreclosure proceedings for a forfeiture of an interest held under an installment contract. In these states, the courts require sellers to give buyers a chance for redemption rather than subject them to the time limits of strict forfeiture.

Title Problems

A clean title is the secret to the stability of the mortgagee's security. However, in an installment contract, no third party is involved in the financing. The parties have only to deal with each other, and there is a good chance that the title check will slip. Tax liens and other deficiencies lessen the value of the land for the buyer and the extent of security for the seller.

Furthermore, without the involvement of a third-party lender, many buyers neglect to record the installment contract, and their rights are at risk for anything recorded after the fact. The time span of the contract is also a challenge in terms of preserving title.

For the seller of the property, recording the land contract can present problems if the buyer defaults and forfeits all interest in the property. The seller would have a recorded land contract as a defect on the title to the property, and a quiet title action would be required to remove the cloud of the forfeited contract from the records.

Tax Consequences

One of the benefits of using the installment contract is that the seller may defer recognition of gain made on the sale of the property to the buyer. By meeting certain Internal Revenue Service regulations, the seller avoids having to report an entire gain on the sale of property in one year. The specific tax benefits available in installment sales are discussed in Chapter 22.

Regulation Z Application

The seller in an installment contract must comply with certain disclosure requirements if Regulation Z (12 C.F.R. § 226) is applicable to the property sale. Many lots for second or resort homes are purchased on an installment basis and Regulation Z applies (see Appendixes D and E). The seller must also disclose all minimum requirements for a closed-end transaction under Regulation Z. (Minimum disclosure requirements, discussed earlier, include such information as the amount of the payments, the number of payments, the annual percentage rate, and so on.)

SUBDIVISION TRUSTS

The **subdivision trust** is available only in a limited number of states. This method of financing is a three-party arrangement that involves a trust relationship, but the parties have different roles from those in the deed of trust financing arrangement. Both the buyer and the seller are beneficiaries of a trust managed by a third-party trustee. The seller transfers title to the property to the trustee, and the buyer and seller execute a note or other contract that contains the payment terms governing the parties' relationship.

In addition, the parties will execute a trust agreement that assigns duties and responsibilities to a trustee, who will hold title to the property. The trust agreement determines when the trustee may take action and how payments are to be made. The diagram shows the subdivision trust relationship.

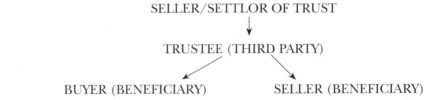

If the buyer defaults on the payments due, the trust agreement gives the trustee the right of sale of the property, or perhaps a right of reconveyance of title to the seller with a forfeiture of the buyer's interest in the property. This method of financing permits the seller quick relief in the event of a buyer default.

Typically, the subdivision trust is used by developers (buyers) with great ideas but little cash for the development of land parcels. Under this arrangement, the buyer and seller have the protection of a third party holding title, and the benefit of having the trust continue once the developer is able to sell or lease the development. Both buyer and seller share in the profits obtained as the development is completed and sold. The seller not only is paid a certain amount for the property, but also collects a certain portion of the development profits after the buyer begins to earn on the investment.

An example of a subdivision trust arrangement is when a farmer sells a substantial portion of prime-location real estate to a shopping center developer. During the construction of the shopping center, the farmer would take minimal or no payments for the property. Upon completion of the shopping center, the leasing of the property, and the collection of rents and perhaps percentages of the sales of tenants, the farmer would collect the purchase price of the property, an additional share of the profits received for a certain period of time, or both. The relationship is shown in the diagram.

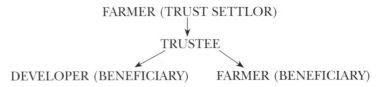

In states that recognize the subdivision trust method of financing, the rules on foreclosure, redemption, power of sale, and reinstatement rights are simply inapplicable. Rather, the parties are governed only by the law of trusts. In these states, the parties have provisions in their trust agreements for the trustee to follow in the event of nonpayment or any other form of default.

© Cengage Learning

ALTERNATIVE FINANCING METHODS

During economic downturns, price increases and high interest rates create financial barriers to the purchase and ownership of real estate. Those barriers include large down payments and high monthly payments, which effectively shut out many willing buyers. To break down those barriers, many lenders, sellers, buyers, and brokers have developed financing methods that combine traditional methods, create new methods, and often combine these two. The following sections cover some of the new and combined financing methods.

Shared-Appreciation or Equity-Participation Financing Mortgages

The **shared-appreciation mortgage** or **equity-participation financing** is a creation of the commercial lender that involves a trade-off: The lender offers lower monthly interest rates in exchange for a share in the appreciation of the property, pledged as security. Under this approach, the lender will finance a loan at, say, 7 percent as opposed to 8 percent, and, upon the borrower's sale of the property, will receive some percentage of the profit made—usually no more than 40 percent. The lender enjoys a gain on the transfer of the property, and the buyer enjoys the benefit of lower monthly payments by giving up a portion of the property appreciation.

Wrap-Around Mortgages

This type of financing arrangement is used in the purchase of property that already has financing not subject to a due-on-sale clause upon transfer. The wrap-around mortgage is similar to an assumption except that the seller is involved more and gets more security.

For example, suppose that a residence is being sold for $285,000, and there is an existing mortgage balance of $250,000 on the property. The buyer can afford to put $20,000 down. In an assumption, the buyer would then assume the $250,000 obligation, and the seller would take a second mortgage on the property to come up with the remaining $15,000 difference. Under a wrap-around arrangement, the buyer simply takes title to the property subject to the mortgage. The buyer is given a loan by the seller for $285,000, which is secured by an all-inclusive mortgage. The seller will continue to make the payments on the $250,000 loan, and the buyer will make payments to the seller on a full $285,000 at a lower-than-market rate. The seller keeps that portion of the buyer's monthly payment that is above the amount due on the $250,000 mortgage.

One way the seller can make a profit on the transaction is to charge a higher rate on the entire wrap-around mortgage. If the $250,000 original mortgage is at 7 percent, the seller could carry the full $285,000 at 8 percent, and would make 8 percent on $35,000 and an additional 1 percent on the original $250,000 obligation.

Exchange or Trades

In a property exchange, the parties involved swap the equity in their properties as a means of purchasing each other's property. This type of financing is used more commonly in commercial transactions and when consumers have second homes that they use as investment properties (a 1031 exchange). When employees in the same firm are being transferred to each other's respective locations, each needs a house in the other's location, and the equities are simply swapped as a means of purchase.

The primary concern of the parties using a property exchange is that the equities are even. If the equities in the exchanged properties are not even, one of the parties must pay the other the difference in cash. When an individual sells one second residence and buys another, the IRS has strict timing requirements as well as the requirement that the proceeds move from escrow to escrow, not through the owner's accounts.

Lease-Purchase Agreements

If it is difficult for the buyer to obtain financing, and if the seller does not want to carry the buyer's purchase, then the parties may enter into an agreement of sale along with a lease agreement. The purchase agreement will have a delayed closing date.

The parties will agree to the purchase price and to a future date for closing the sale when financing will be more reasonable. Usually, the buyer will make a deposit toward the down payment and will also make monthly rental payments to the seller. The amount of the monthly rental payments will cover at least the underlying mortgage debt, and it may exceed that amount as a benefit to the seller carrying the lease or as partial payment of the eventual down payment that will be required.

With the **lease-purchase mortgage**, the buyer has a definite purchase price locked in at the current market price as well as the opportunity to wait for better loan terms. The seller enjoys the tax benefits of leasing the property (discussed in Chapter 22) and has a sale guaranteed at some future date. The seller also has the generally afforded remedy of retaining the buyer's deposit in the event the sale falls through or the buyer terminates the lease.

A variation of this method of financing is the lease with an option to buy. Under this type of arrangement, the parties do not actually enter into a purchase contract, but the buyer is given the right to exercise an option to purchase at any time during the period of the lease. The parties' agreement may also provide that the rental payments may be used toward the down payment if the option to purchase is exercised.

The Broker, Regulation Z, and Alternative Financing

Alternative methods of financing carry with them complexities that require the assistance of brokers and lawyers. In addition, these methods of financing may carry hidden legal pitfalls for the broker assisting a seller or a buyer.

The broker who is regularly involved in the arrangement of credit must meet all of the Regulation Z disclosure requirements. "Regularly involved in credit arrangements" means that the broker has participated in the arrangement of credit for "more than 5-secured by a dwelling" financing arrangements, or for more than 25 transactions in which a dwelling was not used as credit. A financing arrangement is one that involves more than four installments.

Brokers should also consult with an attorney to determine whether the acts of individual salespeople in arranging credit transactions can be attributed to them as part of the "regularly involved in credit arrangements." A broker may also be required to make disclosures if the salespeople working in the same office have met the criteria for the firm as a whole.

CAUTIONS AND CONCLUSIONS

The many complexities and loopholes of all the methods of financing discussed in this chapter are potentially costly to one or both of the parties to the transaction. It is important that all parties involved in the financing arrangement for the purchase of real property consider the following questions before entering into an agreement, so that problems and pitfalls can be avoided initially rather than encountered during the course of performance.

- Is there some form of security for loan repayment?
- What constitutes default under the agreement? Is it defined?
- Are late payments permitted? Can the acceptance of late payments cause rights to be waived?

- Have I complied with all federal disclosures on consumer loans?
- Are there other secured interests in the property?
- Who has priority?
- May the security instrument be recorded for protection?
- If there is a default, will the debtor be given some type of grace period?
- What happens if the property is transferred?
- What tax benefits or implications exist?
- Does the written document (or documents) reflect all desires and intents?

KEY TERMS

CHAPTER PROBLEMS

1. A purchased B's home through a cash-to-mortgage arrangement with A assuming B's $140,000 Federal Housing Administration (FHA) loan. Three months after the purchase, A has lost his job and is unable to meet the monthly payments. The mortgagee has turned to B for the payments, and B protests, claiming he is no longer liable on the underlying mortgage note. The mortgagee, complying with proper procedures, forecloses on the property and sells it for $125,000. The mortgagee is now interested in obtaining a deficiency judgment and has therefore sued both A and B. Has the mortgagee acted properly under the circumstances? Is B correct about his liability? Is a deficiency judgment possible under the circumstances? Would it make any difference if a deed of trust arrangement were involved?

2. The following summarizes the sequence of events involved on a parcel of property located in Nevada and owned by the Lundgrens:

   - *November 30, 1970*: The Lundgrens executed a note in favor of Nevada Wholesale Lumber in the amount of $7,767.44, secured by a deed of trust, with Title Insurance and Trust Company as trustee.
   - *May 8, 1972*: The Lundgrens, without notifying Nevada Wholesale, conveyed fee simple title to Rampart Corporation.
   - *December 6, 1972*: The Lundgrens executed a second note to Nevada Wholesale for $12,126.99. The note was secured by a dragnet clause in the November 30, 1970, deed of trust.
   - *January 16, 1973*: Rampart Corporation executed a note and deed of trust to Myers Realty.
   - *February 7, 1973*: Nevada Wholesale recorded a notice of default and election to sell the property.
   - *February 12, 1973*: Nevada Wholesale filed suit on the $12,126.99 note.
   - *June 28, 1973*: Default judgment was awarded Nevada Wholesale on suit and the land was attached.
   - *August 17, 1973*: Myers Realty filed notice of foreclosure on its deed of trust from Rampart Corporation.

   Assuming the sale of the property does not bring enough to satisfy all parties in the transactions, who has priority? *Nevada Wholesale Lumber Co. v. Myers Realty*, 544 P.2d 1204 (Nev. 1976).

3. W. J. Minderhout has entered into a lease agreement with Coast Bank under which Minderhout will lease an office building (worth $200,000) from Coast for rental payments of $25,000 per year. The agreement also provides that at the end of the 10-year lease period established in the agreement, Minderhout will have the option to purchase the building for $40,000. Minderhout wishes to know if the arrangement is a mortgage or a lease and what rights both he and Coast will have in the event he defaults on the lease payments. *Coast Bank v. Minderhout*, 392 P.2d 265 (Cal. 1964).

4. Seven Palms Motor Inn obtained financing from Commerce Mortgage Company for the purchase of a motel. Commerce secured the purchase through a duly recorded mortgage on the property, which contained an after-acquired property clause. Seven Palms then contracted, through a security agreement perfected by the filing of the financing statement, with Sears, Roebuck and Company for the purchase of drapery rods, drapes, and matching bedspreads for each of the rooms in the motel. Seven Palms defaulted and Commerce foreclosed. Sears claimed priority in the items it furnished, since the items were personal property. Commerce claimed the items were fixtures and were covered by the mortgage. What was the result? *Sears, Roebuck & Co. v. Seven Palms Motor Inn, Inc.*, 530 S.W.2d 695 (Mo. 1975).

5. Leon Zeibert had given his nephew, Alan Sloane, large amounts of cash over the years. Zeibert maintained that Sloane and his wife, Gloria, had signed a mortgage on their home as security for the loans. However, Zeibert did not have a copy of the note.

   Zeibert claimed priority over other creditors of Sloane in a state receivership proceeding. First American Bank objected to Zeibert's claim of a mortgage. The lower court held that there was no mortgage because Zeibert's cash advances were gifts not intended to be secured by a mortgage. Zeibert appealed. What should the appellate court do and why? *First American Bank of New York v. Sloane*, 651 N.Y.S.2d 734 (Sup. Ct. App. 1997).

6. Lynley and Samuel Crabtree purchased their first home in 1996 for $195,000. Their purchase was financed by Western Mortgage and secured by a deed of trust. Two years later, the Crabtrees decided to put in a swimming pool. They were given a loan by Valley National Bank for pool construction. The loan was secured by a second deed of trust. In 2002, the Crabtrees sold their home to John and Julia Gardner. The Gardners assumed the Western Mortgage. The Crabtrees agreed to carry the Valley pool loan in the form of wrap-around financing. Valley was not notified of the sale of the property.

Both of the Gardners were victims of layoffs in their companies, and they fell behind on all their payments. Western has begun foreclosure proceedings. The property is worth $214,000. The Gardners owe $7,000 in back payments. The mortgage amount due is $189,000. The pool loan balance is $10,000. The expenses of the sale are $7,000 (including a real estate agent's commission). The property is sold for $212,000. How will the amounts be distributed?

7. Stuckenberg, through a straw party, purchased a ranchette-style apartment building with five apartments under one roof. Stuckenberg purchased the property with funds from a note signed with First Federal, which was secured with a deed of trust on the property. Paragraph 7 of the deed of trust provided:

   First Federal shall have power and authority to take possession of the said real estate and to manage, control, and lease the same and collect all rents, issues and profits therefrom for the purpose of paying the note secured by the deed of trust.

   The full amount of the loan was due in February 1969, and Stuckenberg defaulted on both the January and February 1969 payments. After the default, First Federal notified Stuckenberg's son of its intention to exercise its rights under paragraph 7 and requested information on the tenants, the rental amounts, and the rental due dates. First Federal then sent to Stuckenberg, his attorney, and all the tenants a notice of First Federal's rights under paragraph 7 and its intent to exercise those rights. A management corporation was hired by First Federal, and personal service of the letter was given to three of the five tenants in the building (the other tenants could not be reached). Can First Federal collect the rents and take over the property in this manner? *In re Stuckenberg*, 374 F.Supp. 15 (Mo. 1974).

8. Michael McKinney bought a five-bedroom home near Baltimore, Maryland, for $1,000,000 in October 2007. Mr. McKinney put 30 percent down and financed the remaining $700,000. He is current on his $4,400 payments, which are one-half of his monthly income. The value of his property has dropped $130,000. Mr. McKinney says, "People like me are cut out of the process. Why are people in some parts of the country being penalized by a limit that doesn't reflect reality in many areas?" Evaluate whether Mr. McKinney qualifies for help from any of the federal programs created following the subprime crisis.

Nick Timiraos, "Homeowners Size Up Housing-Aid Plan," *Wall Street Journal*, March 5, 2009, p. A4.

9. Explain what you should know if you got a foreclosure notice from MERS.

10. Dynamic Development Corporation (Dynamic) is a developer that builds and sells residential and commercial property. In May 1985, Mid Kansas Federal Savings and Loan Association of Wichita (Mid Kansas) loaned Dynamic $803,250 for the construction of 10 "spec" homes in a subdivision Dynamic owned in Prescott, Arizona. There were 10 separate loans made, with a note and deed of trust (see p. 436) on each of the 10 lots.

By January 1986, Dynamic needed additional funds to complete the homes, and Mid Kansas loaned another $150,000, which was secured by a second note and deed of trust on seven of the lots for the spec homes that had not been sold.

The first and second notes were both due in the summer of 1986. Two more lots were sold and released from the deeds of trust. In fall 1986, Mid Kansas notified Dynamic that the five remaining properties would be sold at a trustee's sale if the total debt owed was not paid. Dynamic could not pay the loan amount but did sell one additional lot and applied the proceeds to the loans.

Mid Kansas gave notice of a trustee's sale on the four remaining lots. At the time of the sale, Dynamic owed Mid Kansas $102,000 on the second note and $425,000 on the first note. Mid Kansas foreclosed on the second notes and bought the properties for a credit balance at the sale. Mid Kansas never foreclosed on the first notes, but brought suit, waiving the security, against Dynamic for the deficiency. Can the deficiency be collected? *Mid Kansas Federal Savings and Loan Association of Wichita v. Dynamic Development Corporation*, 804 P.2d 1310 (Az. 1991).

For research activities related to this chapter, go to our text companion website at www.cengagebrain.com

A QUIZ ON HOME BUYING TERMS

Take this quiz to see if you understand the language of buying and financing a home. The answers are at the bottom of p. 446.

1. **Point**
    (a) The time for closing
    (b) The Treasury rate
    (c) One percent of the value of the loan
    (d) An upfront escrow charge for closing the loan

2. **Deed of trust**
    (a) Another name for a will
    (b) A temporary financing arrangement
    (c) A three-party means of creating security in the property being purchased
    (d) The title to the land given to the buyer upon closing

3. **Lock**
    (a) What the real estate agent puts on properties listed for sale
    (b) The date for closing
    (c) A lender commitment for a loan interest rate
    (d) A time after which foreclosure can occur

4. **Annual Percentage rate**
    (a) The same as APR or the real cost of a loan
    (b) Illegal now under post-2008 reforms
    (c) Not permitted in home mortgage loans
    (d) The same as the finance charges

5. **Amortization**
    (a) The process of paying off a mortgage loan over a predetermined time
    (b) Late penalty in a mortgage
    (c) The same as an adjustable rate mortgage
    (d) The same as the annual percentage rate

6. **Escrow**
    (a) Another name for a deed of trust
    (b) The process for passing title to property from seller to buyer
    (c) The collateral for a mortgage loan
    (d) A form of secured lending

7. **Robo-signing**
    (a) Central signing process permitted under new mortgage reforms
    (b) Signing through an internet site
    (c) Signing during the escrow process
    (d) Signing of all mortgage foreclosure documents by one person

8. **Government loan**
    (a) A mortgage loan from the U.S. government
    (b) A mortgage loan from a state or local government
    (c) A mortgage loan through a subsidized government program
    (d) A mortgage loan insured by the federal government

9. **ARM**
    (a) Annuity reversed mortgage
    (b) Adjustable rate mortgage
    (c) Annualized revenue mortgage
    (d) Accounting reversal mortgage

10. *Caveat emptor*
    (a) A form of deed when the purchase is financed
    (b) A form of a deed of trust
    (c) Let the buyer beware
    (d) Let the seller beware

11. **Loan-to-value ratio**
    (a) The amount of the loan on a property over the value of the property
    (b) An underwater mortgage
    (c) The value of the property over the amount of the loan on the property
    (d) The amount of the loan in relation to the buyers' income

12. **Creative financing**
    (a) Financing that does not meet federal standards
    (b) Financing that involves something other than a 30-year mortgage loan
    (c) A form of subprime financing
    (d) Financing that requires the seller's giving a loan

13. **Earnest money**
    (a) The down payment on a house
    (b) Extra payments on principal paid by the mortgagor
    (c) The payment made at the time a purchase contract is signed
    (d) Money required beyond the down payment on federally insured mortgages

14. **Fannie Mae**
    (a) A candy company on the East Coast
    (b) The Federal National Mortgage Association
    (c) A non-existent federal agency
    (d) The same as Freddie Mac

15. **Short sale**
    (a) A sale of a mortgaged property for an amount less than the mortgage
    (b) A sale that goes through very quickly through a short process
    (c) A sale that requires a 40% down payment
    (d) A sale of property when there is no mortgage on that property

16. **FHA**
    (a) The same as Fannie Mae
    (b) The Federal Home Association
    (c) The Federal Housing Administration
    (d) The Financing Homes Association

17. **Prepaids**
    (a) A mortgage loan in which the interest is paid in advance
    (b) The payment of utilities and taxes in advance of the closing on the property
    (c) Expenses on the property that must be paid by the seller prior to closing
    (d) Subprime loans

18. **Conventional loan**
    (a) Subprime loan
    (b) Negative amortization loan
    (c) Loans that does not have federal insurance
    (d) Illegal after 2008 federal reforms

19. **Balloon payment**
    (a) The pay-off of a mortgage loan through a large payment at the end of the loan period
    (b) An initial large payment required before closing on the property
    (c) Payment due when there is a default on the mortgage
    (d) Payment due every five years under a subprime mortgage

20. **Walk-through**
    (a) Advance class on mortgage lending required by the Consumer Financial Protection Bureau
    (b) Process of closing on a property
    (c) Paperwork disclosures that must be reviewed prior to closing
    (d) Inspection of property by buyer prior to closing

21. **PITI**
    (a) Priorities in the interest
    (b) Principal interest Taxes and insurance
    (c) Prime interest together with income
    (d) Process income taxes internally

22. **MERS**
    (a) Mortgage Equity Reform Statute
    (b) Mortgage Equivalent Repossession Security
    (c) Mortgage Electronic Recording System
    (d) Mediated Electronic Reform System

A score of 22 means you understand real estate law. A score of 15 or above means you are probably ready to buy a home. If you score less than 15, do a little more studying before you buy a home.

Answers

1-c, 2-c, 3-c, 4-a, 5-a, 6-b, 7-d, 8-d, 9-b, 01-c, 11-a, 12-b, 13-c, 14-b, 15-a, 16-c, 17-b, 18-c, 19-a, 20-d, 21-b, 22-c

CHAPTER 16

CLOSING THE DEAL

"It ain't over until it's over."

Attributed to Yogi Berra

The penalty for illegally giving or receiving a kickback, which is covered in Section 8 of RESPA, is:

- Up to 90 hours of community service
- Loss of real estate license
- Requirement to attend a RESPA education program
- A fine of up to $10,000 or up to one year in prison or both

Under RESPA, a real estate professional may give in return for the referral of real estate settlement service business:

- A thank you
- A thing of value
- A kickback
- A fee

> From the RESPA quiz on the website of the National Association of Realtors© (Answers appear at the end of the chapter)

Closings are tricky things. Escrow is not simple, and a contract for purchase of real property does not mean the deal is done. Closing is a legal and logistical challenge. Buying property isn't the same as buying Junior Mints at the grocery store. That transaction is simple, done face-to-face with title and payment passing at the same time. However, a piece of property is not as neat and compact as a box of candy, even a theater-size box. The issues of others' interest in the land, financing, and property inspections must all come together somewhere, sometime, and somehow—"It ain't over until the closing." This chapter covers all the issues related to closing a real estate transaction: How is a closing done? What documents are

447

necessary for closing? What parties will be involved in closing? What are their responsibilities during the closing process?

THE NATURE OF CLOSING

Where?

The nature of a closing varies from state to state, and even within states. In some states, a closing is held at the government office responsible for recording land documents, such as the county clerk, county recorder, or recorder of deeds. The closing may be held after the government office closes (or the document recording for that day ends) so that the problems of multiple conveyances and title confusion covered in Chapter 14 do not arise. Depending on the state, some closings are held in title company offices, some at an attorney's office with the attorney representing one of the parties, and some at escrow companies established exclusively for the purpose of handling the documents, funds, and people necessary for the transaction to close.

What?

In some states, closing is a formal process in which the parties gather in a room for signing and exchanging documents. In other states, a designated party, such as an escrow agent or title company, gathers the necessary documents and signatures, and sets a date for closing.

Regardless of the method or place, there is one consistent factor among all the states' methods of closing: getting all the conditions for closing met. Regardless of how, the closings all occur at the same time: when all parties have fulfilled their obligations under the contract and the closing agreement or escrow instructions.

Who?

The closing or **escrow** setup generally involves three or four parties. The buyer and seller who set up the escrow arrangement are the first two parties. If there is a lender involved in either the financing or assumption of financing of the property, the lender is also a party to the transaction. The final party is an independent party (as noted above) who handles the collection of necessary documents and the actual transfer of funds and title.

While the term *escrow* is used throughout the remainder of the chapter, it is used for convenience. Regardless of the method for closing, the parties must designate an agent to handle the preparation for the closing. The agent selected, regardless of name, has the same obligations as an escrow agent. Further, the parties must establish a contractual relationship with this third party regardless of how the physical closing takes place.

State law dictates who the third party can be, such as an escrow company, attorney, or title company. In some states, insurance companies and certified public accountants are permitted to handle closings.

An escrow agent should be carefully screened because the agent will handle title and funds. Background checks on the proposed agent have become quite common, complete with references and a history of the agent or company.

THE CLOSING SETUP

Requirements for Setting Up the Escrow or Closing

Valid and Enforceable Contract for Purchase and Sale of Real Estate

An escrow is not valid without an underlying contract between the parties. Without such a purchase contract, the escrow agent is carrying out an agency relationship that has no binding effect on either of the parties, since there is no direct contractual relationship between them. Many parties believe they can move more quickly by going directly to escrow instructions, but such a timesaving step can be costly in that there is no enforceable contract between buyer and seller—only an agency contract between the escrow agent and buyer and seller. The two can be combined, as when the parties sign a "Purchase Agreement and Escrow Instructions."

Deposit of Deed with an Agent

A valid escrow requires irrevocability, which means that the parties are not permitted to withdraw their funds and documents at will, but only if the provisions in their contract and escrow instructions are not met. If the seller is free to revoke the deed at any time or if the buyer is able to withdraw the funds at any time, the agent's responsibilities would be frustrated, liabilities complicated, and the deal never closed. The seller must deposit a validly executed deed with the escrow agent as the first step of irrevocability.

Valid Escrow Instructions

Even the irrevocable deposit of the deed with the third party will not create an escrow unless the agent and the parties execute a contract, called **escrow instructions**, which will direct the agent on the hows, whens, and whats of closing the property transaction. The escrow agent can do only what is prescribed in the escrow instructions; without instructions, the third party has no authority to consummate a sale.

Contents of Escrow or Closing Instructions

Mandatory Matters

Because the escrow involves the transfer of a land interest, the agent's authority must be documented by a record. In addition, escrow instructions should include these mandatory items:

1. Name of the agent, third party, or depository
2. Names of the buyer (buyers) and seller (sellers) and their proper designation (partnership, corporation, married couple, single person, and so on)
3. Legal description of the property to be transferred
4. Purchase price of the property
5. Conditions of transfer and payment
6. Allocation of expenses, costs, insurance, taxes, assessments, and so on
7. Signatures of the buyer and seller

Recommended Provisions

The minimum requirements do not always provide for the contingencies that arise in closing a property transaction. The parties are wise to include additional provisions. Although many states and regions have customs that might apply when the escrow instructions lack provisions, disputes over such customs can mean expensive and time-consuming litigation.

Allocating Costs   The escrow instructions should specify who will pay which costs associated with closing the transaction. Again, there are many customs for such allocations, but it is easier and legally binding to list such cost breakdowns as part of the escrow instructions. The following list covers the typical costs of closing:

1. Escrow fee
2. Fees for title search, title abstract, title insurance, and attorneys' work associated with such
3. Recording fees for the deed, mortgage, deed of trust, and any other documents required
4. Mortgage transfer or release fees
5. Loan origination fees
6. Inspection reports (including termite, condition of property, and environmental)
7. Appraisal or survey fees
8. Credit report fees
9. Loan discount points
10. Other attorneys' fees, such as for drafting documents

By agreeing on allocation of costs in advance, the parties avoid confusion and delay in closing. However, the parties should not violate any lender restrictions on closing costs. For example, with certain government-insured loans, federal regulations specify which party must pay which costs. With some government loans, the seller is required to pay the loan discount points.

Closing fees are often a sticky point for the parties. Someone—an attorney, a title company, or an escrow firm—will collect a fee for closing the transaction. In the case of title companies used as escrow agents, there is a fee for both the closing and the title insurance policy. In many states, those fees are set by statute or regulation; that is, the title companies' fees are regulated. In some of those states, the fees are established by a board composed of members of the title industry in that state. (See Chapter 14 for more details on this fee issue as it relates to title insurers.)

PRACTICAL TIP

An increasing number of closing agreements include mandatory arbitration clauses. These clauses are helpful in situations in which the parties disagree over compliance with the conditions as the escrow deposit sits in limbo. Arbitration is often faster than litigation.

Prorating Prepaids   As noted in Chapter 13, prorating insurance, property taxes, and other fees paid annually or semi-annually is part of the transfer process. Escrow instructions should spell out *pro rata* formulas for allocation. The formulas follow one of two general theories. Theory 1 breaks the year into 360 days with 12 months of 30 days each. Theory 2 holds that the year consists of 365 days and prorates prepaids on a daily basis of 1/365th of the total annual cost. Suppose, for example, that the seller had paid a $360 insurance premium in January for a 6-month period to run through the end of June. Assuming the closing took place on March 15, in the example above, under theory 1, the seller would receive a credit of $210, or 3 months at $60 plus a half-month at $30. Under theory 2, the seller would receive a credit of $1.97 per day ($720 ÷ 365). Taking the number of days from March 15 to June 30, the total credit would be $210.79 (107 × $1.97).

Sale of Personal Property   The seller should furnish the escrow agent with a bill of sale if the transfer of personal property, such as washers, dryers, and refrigerators,

CONSIDER 16.1   A seller has prepaid both taxes and insurance on the property about to be transferred. The taxes are $6,000 per year, and the insurance premiums are $1,200 per year. The seller prepaid both in January for the entire year through December 31. The closing on the property will take place on March 15, and the parties wish to know what formulas can be used to prorate these prepaids. Explain the results to them under both the 360-day–year and the 365-day–year formulas. ━━━━━■

is part of the transaction. The bill of sale should describe the property being transferred, including model number and serial number if available. If furniture is being transferred, as in the sale of an apartment complex, the description should be specific and include the size, color, and purpose of the furniture; for example, "one 96-inch green-and-yellow plaid living-room sofa." The bill of sale should also warrant that the seller has title to the property and is authorized to transfer title, and that there are no liens or encumbrances on the transferred property.

Documents to be Delivered by Each Party

There are other documents that both seller and buyer must deposit for the closing. The following list is not comprehensive but shows the layers of detail needed for a closing.

1. By the seller
   a. Title documents: abstract, opinion, and insurance
   b. Most recent tax bill
   c. Insurance policies
   d. Plans and specifications for original construction and modifications
   e. Warranties on any appliances, heating systems, and so on
   f. Uniform Commercial Code (UCC) bulk sale affidavit for business transfer (where applicable—Article 6 on Bulk Sales has been repealed in some states)
   g. Soil, termite, and other property condition reports, including reports from environmental agencies
   h. Keys
   i. Notes, mortgages, deeds of trust, UCC Article 9 security agreements, and financing statements
   j. List of tenants and copies of leases
   k. Building code inspection and compliance

2. By the buyer
   a. Earnest money check
   b. Loan commitment
   c. List of defects to be remedied prior to closing
   d. Corporate authorization if corporate buyer is involved

3. By the lender

    a. Mortgage, deed of trust, and promissory note

    b. Truth-in-Lending statement (see Chapter 15)

    c. Real Estate Settlement Procedures Act (RESPA) statement (see later in chapter for discussion)

    d. Required forms if Federal Housing Administration (FHA) or Veterans Administration (VA) loan is availed

    e. Required inspections if FHA or VA loan is involved

Cancellation of Escrow

> **PRACTICAL TIP**
>
> *The escrow agent must follow the instructions as the parties drafted them. An escrow agent is not in a position to make a "close enough" decision. Either the documentation and requirements have been met or they have not. Any change in the conditions requires a modification of the instructions signed by both parties. The parties together must make a "close enough" decision. One party cannot talk an escrow agent into deviating from the instructions.*

The escrow agent can consummate the transaction only when conditions specified in the instructions are met. If those conditions are not met, the parties are excused from their performance under the contract and the escrow is canceled.

Many states have provisions for cancellation, but it is best for the escrow instructions to specify when and how cancellation occurs. The cancellation clause should cover three issues. First, the escrow instructions should include the grounds for cancellation. The grounds may be a simple statement such as "if either party fails to comply with the terms hereof," or some items may be spelled out, such as the failure of the seller to supply a clean soil report. Second, the instructions should make clear the procedures for cancellation. The cancellation notice requirements could include, for example, that the cancellation be in writing and how notice is communicated (personally, through the escrow agent, or by mail). Third, the cancellation clause should include time elements: when the cancellation takes effect and whether the other party will be allowed a time to comply with a missed requirement before the cancellation takes effect.

Cancellations, Contingencies, and Contract Performance

Complex issues on contract provisions and contingencies often create confusion in the closing process. The following sections highlight some key issues.

Relationship Between Purchase Contract and Escrow Instructions

In the majority of real estate transactions, the parties have used both form purchase contracts and escrow instructions. One difficulty with such form agreements is that they are not carefully cross-compared and may include contradictory terms. Often, the contract may have a remedy or procedure different from that remedy provided in the escrow instructions. The question becomes, Which document is controlling? Some states hold that the escrow instructions control, since they were executed later in time and can be viewed as superseding the contract. Other states hold that the contract is better evidence of the parties' intent, since the escrow agreement is merely a set of instructions to a third party and not the parties' original agreement.

The following older case remains a landmark one for the majority view among the states on the relationship between purchase contracts and escrow instructions.

ALLAN V. MARTIN

574 P.2d 457 (Az. 1978)
How Many Times Do I Need to Cancel Before the Deal is Canceled?

FACTS

Kirby and Felicienne Allan (defendants/appellants), both licensed real estate agents, approached George and Pamela Martin (plaintiffs/appellees) about purchasing the Martins' property, which was located in Mesa, Arizona. The Martins wished to sell the property to obtain funds to complete and move into a home they were building in the mountains. The parties entered into a purchase and sale contract, which provided that escrow would close on or before July 31, 1974. The Martins needed the funds by that date so that their mountain home could be completed and they could be in it before cold weather began. Escrow instructions were prepared by a title company and signed by both parties.

The closing did not take place on July 31, but the Martins agreed to a 15-day extension. The Martins checked with the title company on August 15, the last day of the extension, and discovered that the money necessary to purchase their property had not been deposited into escrow. The Martins sent a telegram to the Allans that read, "Due to delay in the sale to you of our home we will no longer sell as the contract expired 7-31-74." The Allans received the telegram on August 15.

The next day, the Martins signed a "13-day letter," which instructed the title company to cancel the escrow if the Allans did not comply with the escrow instructions within 13 days from the date of the letter. The 13-day provision for notice and compliance was part of the escrow instructions. The Martins indicated that they believed the 13-day notice was given only for the purpose of canceling the escrow. The Allans complied within the 13 days, but the Martins refused to sell. The Martins brought suit seeking cancellation of the contract. The trial court found for the Martins, rescinding the contract and awarding them $1,000 in damages. The Allans appealed.

JUDICIAL OPINION

Hays, Justice

A contract to sell real estate and an escrow arrangement are not the same thing. There must exist a binding contract to sell the real estate which is the subject of the escrow, or the escrow instructions are unenforceable. An escrow primarily is a conveyance device designed to carry out the terms of a binding contract of sale previously entered into by the parties. Therefore, the escrow instructions are not a part of the underlying real estate sales contract and the terms of the instructions cannot alter or modify the sales contract unless the parties specifically and clearly state such alteration or modification in writing with specific reference to the fact it changes the original contract.

The appellants (Allans) base their appeal almost entirely upon a fine print form provision in the escrow instructions:

Cancellation

16. If either party, who has duly performed hereunder, elects to cancel these instructions because of the failure of the other party to comply with any of the terms hereof within the time limits provided herein, said party so electing to cancel shall deliver to Escrow agent a written notice to the other party and Escrow agent demanding that said other party comply with the terms hereof within thirteen days from the receipt of said notice by Escrow agent or that these instructions shall thereupon become canceled.

This term clearly applies only to the procedure for canceling the escrow instructions; it has nothing to do with how and under what circumstances the real estate contract may be rescinded. The time for performance of the contract was the date designated in the contract for the close of escrow. The latest date agreed upon by the parties was August 15, 1974. The sales contract stated that time was of the essence, and appellees [Martins] informed appellants that the time for the closing of the transaction was very important to them. The latest date for closing was a bargained-for term, clearly material in this case. The cancellation provision in the escrow instructions cannot be construed to permit the appellants to perform their contract obligation any later than August 15, 1974.

On August 15 the appellant still had not complied with the sales contract; the money to purchase the property had not been delivered to the escrow agent. When time for performance is material to a contract and one party fails to perform by the contract deadline date, the other party may treat the contract as ended. Thus, when the purchase price was not paid into escrow on the last day agreed upon for closing, the appellees had the legal right to refuse to convey their property and to cancel the contract. They notified appellants they were exercising this right by telegram on August 15.

When appellees exercised their right to treat the contract as ended, the escrow instructions became unenforceable because there was no longer a binding contract to sell the property which was the subject of escrow. The "thirteen day letter" canceling the escrow then became only a formality to prove that the escrow was now void. The fact that the quoted provision on cancellation of the escrow instructions gives a party thirteen days to comply with the terms of the escrow does not mean that one may belatedly comply with the breached sales contract when the nonbreaching party has given notice that he elects to treat the contract as ended. Nothing in the escrow instructions can revive an already dead underlying contract.

Appellants also urge that by signing the "thirteen day letter" appellees elected the escrow cancellation remedy and thus are bound to convey the property because appellants met their obligations under the escrow within thirteen days. As explained previously, this is incorrect because the escrow was already void at the time the letter was issued and also because the escrow cancellation procedure does not apply to a sales contract.

Affirmed.

CASE QUESTIONS

1. What was the original closing date as provided in the purchase contract? Why was a timely closing important to the Martins?
2. What happened when closing did not occur on the original closing or second closing date?
3. What is the significance of the "13-day letter" in the escrow instructions? Is the 13-day provision controlling?

CONSIDER 16.2   On September 11, 2005, John and Sharon Rebeske entered into a contract with ITC Homes, Inc. for the construction of a custom house on a lot in Unit 29 of a subdivision known as Santa Rita Estates located near Vail, Arizona. The Rebeskes made an initial escrow deposit of $5,000. The Sales Contract provided for an additional $20,000 deposit when the parties agreed on a final price for the custom house.

On October 9, 2005, the parties agreed on a price of $475,000, and the Rebeskes paid an additional $20,000 for a total escrow deposit of $25,000. ITC asked for a release of the $25,000 from escrow, and the Rebeskes signed the release. After that point, ITC did not proceed with the construction of the home. Indeed, ITC declared bankruptcy. The Rebeskes sought to have their $25,000 deposit returned because although they had signed the release, the terms of their purchase contract required that construction begin and proceed through certain phases before any funds could be released from escrow. The Rebeskes' position as creditors in the bankruptcy is higher if their claim is for an error made by the escrow company. If the release was effective, they are simply unsecured creditors of ITC. Are they entitled to the return of their $25,000? Which controls, the release or the contract?

In re ITC Homes, Inc., 2007 WL 3287589 (Bkrptcy. D. Ariz. 2007).

Mutual Cancellation Provisions

In addition to a unilateral cancellation clause, the parties may want a procedure for cancellation by mutual agreement. The escrow instructions should then cover the distribution of funds and costs in the event of cancellation. All the provisions should be consistent with the sales contract, but the escrow instructions can address their intent to have the escrow instructions control. For example, the following clause would allow the escrow instructions to control in the event of a conflict:

In the event of any conflict in the provisions of these escrow instructions and the underlying sales agreement, it is the intent and desire of the parties that the terms of these escrow instructions be controlling.

Contingencies for Closing

Contingencies vary significantly from transaction to transaction, but spelling out carefully all the contingencies is an important part of escrow instructions. There are several types of contingencies that show up in both residential and commercial transactions. For example, a requirement that the seller establish compliance with building codes and zoning restrictions may be a contingency. As discussed in Chapter 13, delivery of marketable title is yet another contingency to closing. The most common contingency is that of the buyer's obtaining financing.

Other contingencies include the assignment of all lease and service contracts associated with the property, furnishing a favorable pest report, providing evidence of repair of items agreed to, furnishing of an architect's certificate of completion on a newly constructed building, providing a final property inspection, verifying boundaries with a survey, and, for business sales, furnishing audited financial statements. The number and types of contingencies are limitless, but in drafting the escrow instructions, the parties should think through their interests that require protection before money and title change hands.

Once the contingencies are established, then the escrow agent and the parties must honor how those contingencies play out or they risk confusing their rights under the contract and the escrow timing as well as damages. The following case illustrates what can happen when conduct gets in the way of contingencies.

REGAL REALTY SERVICES, LLC V. 2590 FRISBY, LLC

878 N.Y.S.2d 363 (2009)
When Obtaining a Loan Is a Condition — Are We There Yet?

FACTS

Regal Realty Services (Plaintiff) entered into a contract on March 7, 2007, for the purchase of real property from defendant 2590 Frisby. The contract terms provided for a purchase price of $3,050,000, with a down payment of $152,500 to be held in escrow by Frisby's attorney.

The balance of the purchase price was to be secured by Regal through a mortgage. Section 16 of the contract required Regal to obtain, within 30 days, a written mortgage commitment in the amount of $2,182,500, or such lesser sum as Regal would be willing to accept.

If Regal failed to secure the mortgage by the 30th day after the contract signing (the Commitment Date), both parties had a mutual option to cancel the contract on written notice, and in the event of such cancellation, the down payment was to be refunded. This mortgage contingency period would expire on the earlier of the date Regal received a mortgage commitment or five days after the Commitment Date, unless the parties agreed to an extension.

Section 17 of the contract provided that its terms could only be modified or changed in writing.

Regal's initial mortgage application was to HSBC, and was rejected. Although the exact date of denial is unclear, there was a verbal communication of the denial in the beginning of April 2008. The reason for the denial had nothing to do with the marketability of title or condition of the premises. Regal wanted to cancel the contract, suggesting that the denial took place before the mortgage contingency expiration date in the contract of sale. Regal advised Frisby's attorney of the rejection and, upon Frisby's suggestion, it applied to Frisby's current mortgagee, Hudson Valley Bank, for financing.

In August 2007, the parties attempted to renegotiate the terms of sale and amend the contract.

Although the initial draft prepared by Frisby noted that the mortgage contingency in section 16 of the original contract had expired on April 11, 2007, Regal objected to that provision and it was removed from the final rider to the contract. That rider, executed on August 23, raised the purchase price to $3,075,000 and added a payment option in the form of a purchase money note and second mortgage.

A mortgage commitment letter was issued by Hudson Valley Bank on August 20, 2007, three days prior to the execution of the rider. That commitment was for $2,135,000, which was less than Regal was willing to accept for purchasing the property. The commitment was extended to September 29.

On September 21, 2007, Frisby's attorney sent notice to Regal's counsel that Regal was in default of the contract and set a "time of the essence" closing for October 22. Regal's lawyer wrote back to Frisby's lawyer on October 15, indicating that it was terminating the contract, and demanding return of the down payment. The next day, Regal's lawyer sent another letter, objecting to the October 22 closing date, and pointing out that the "condition precedent" of section 16 of the contract had not occurred, thus entitling Regal to a refund of the deposit.

Frisby's counsel responded on October 17, stating that the mortgage contingency provision had expired by its terms six months earlier, and that as of April 13 the contract ceased to be conditioned upon the issuance of a mortgage commitment. This letter further objected to Regal's demand for a return of the down payment.

The October 22 "time of the essence" closing date passed without a closing taking place. Litigation commenced, and Frisby moved for summary judgment, asking that it be able to keep the deposit as liquidated damages pursuant to the terms of the contact.

Regal also moved for summary judgment, arguing that since Frisby was working "hand in hand" with Regal to obtain a mortgage from Hudson Valley Bank, that constituted a waiver of the mortgage contingency clause, thus entitling Regal to a return of its deposit. In response, Frisby argued the contract by its terms could not be orally modified, that Regal never requested an extension of the mortgage contingency clause, and that other than the rider of August 23, 2007, no modifications were made to the original contract.

The motion court denied both motions, finding issues of fact including whether Frisby, by its actions, extended or waived the mortgage contingency clause. The parties appealed.

JUDICIAL OPINION

Friedman, Presiding Judge. Sweeny, Catterson, Renwick, Freedman, Judges

There is a fundamental concept that "a written agreement that is complete, clear and unambiguous on its face must be enforced according to the plain meaning of its terms."

The mortgage contingency clause of the contract of sale expired by its terms on April 12, 2007. Based upon the unambiguous terms of section 16 of the contract of sale, plaintiff, when notified by HSBC of the denial of its initial financing application, could have cancelled the contract or requested an extension of time to obtain financing through Hudson Valley, but did neither. In either event, section 17 required any changes to be in writing.

Plaintiff's claim that Frisby's actions in assisting with financing from Hudson Valley led it to believe that Frisby had waived the terms of section 16 requires reliance on parol evidence to alter the terms of the written contract. This "ignores a vital first step in the analysis: before looking to evidence of what was in the parties' minds, a court must give due weight to what was in their contract." Evidence from outside the four corners of an unambiguous document as to the parties' intentions is generally inadmissible to vary the writing.

This is particularly so where, as here, section 17 unequivocally provided that "This Agreement may not be changed or terminated orally or in any manner other than by written agreement executed by Seller and Purchaser." Additionally, section 28 of the contract provided that "No failure or delay of either party in the exercise of any right given to such party hereunder or the waiver by any party of any condition hereunder for its benefit (unless the time specified herein for exercise of such right, or satisfaction of such condition, has expired) shall constitute a waiver of any other or further right nor shall any single or partial exercise of any right preclude other or further exercise thereof or any other right." Frisby's failure to declare immediately, on April 13, 2007, the day after the mortgage contingency expired, that the contract was no longer contingent on financing did not prevent it from doing so later. On the other hand, plaintiff's failure either to cancel the contract or obtain an extension to obtain financing by April 12 did preclude it from seeking to attempt, as it did here, to cancel the contract some six months after the contingency expired.

Plaintiff's failure to comply with the terms of section 16 resulted in the expiration of the financing contingency. Its inability to subsequently obtain what it considered sufficient financing from Hudson Valley Bank led to Frisby's declaration of a time-of-the-essence closing, giving plaintiff 30 days to close or be in default. Plaintiff's failure to close on the law day placed it in default and subjected it to the liquidated damages clause in the contract. The validity of such liquidated damages provisions has long been established in this State.

Judgment entered in favor of defendant, Frisby.

CASE QUESTIONS

1. What is the danger of the parties' helping each other to meet a failed contingency?
2. Given the court's decision, what should the lawyers have done when the loan denial was first communicated?
3. Can a written contract and escrow agreement that requires written modification be modified through conduct?

RESPONSIBILITIES OF THE LENDER IN CLOSING—THE REAL ESTATE SETTLEMENT PROCEDURES ACT

Lenders involved in property transfers must furnish the promissory note, the Truth-in-Lending disclosures statement, and also the mortgage or deed of trust to be recorded to protect the lender's interest. However, the **Real Estate Settlement Procedures Act (RESPA)** (12 U.S.C. § 2601 *et seq.*), if it applies, imposes some additional disclosure requirements. RESPA and its regulations, originally promulgated by the **Department of Housing and Urban Development (HUD)**, are now under the CFPB, housed within the Federal Reserve Board. Referred to collectively as Regulation X, RESPA and its related regulations place strict controls on the closing process. Those controls were refined and expanded following the 2008 market collapse.

Purpose of RESPA

The Real Estate Settlement Procedures Act was passed by Congress in 1974 in reaction to evidence that buyers of residential property were surprised at closings with additional fees and expenses that were not disclosed to them in advance. The result was that neither buyers nor sellers could meet these substantial additional costs, or if they could meet them, there was a loss on the expected return on the sale. RESPA was passed to provide more effective advance disclosure to home buyers and home sellers of settlement costs, to eliminate kickback or referral fees that tend to increase the costs of settlement services, and to reduce the amounts buyers are required to pay into escrow for taxes and insurance. In 2009, HUD, after receiving 12,000 comment letters, substantially reformed RESPA procedures, partially in response to abuses that came to light in the post-subprime mortgage era (see Chapter 15 for more information).[1] Those changes were challenged by several factions of the real estate industry, but the changes have been upheld.

Application of RESPA

RESPA applies to "federally related mortgage loans," which includes first and second mortgages, refinancings, home equity loans, and lines of credit using a home as security for the loan. The required RESPA information (discussed later) must be furnished at the time the lender makes a commitment to offer any of these types of loans. RESPA does not apply to loans for commercial transactions.

---

[1]The changes to the disclosure requirements were so substantial that they were phased in over a nine-month period in 2009.

Disclosures Under RESPA

Buyer's Information Handbook

When a RESPA lender receives a loan application, the lender must give the applicant what is now called a Special Information Booklet within three days. The handbook may be printed by the lender or purchased from the CFPB. Written by the CFPB, the handbook includes explanations of RESPA, the selection of an escrow agent, the role of the real estate broker, and the lender's responsibilities. It also contains sample disclosure forms and explanations for fees charged.

Good Faith Estimate of Settlement Costs

RESPA requires lenders to give a good faith estimate (known as a GFE) of the charges expected at closing. Figure 16.1 is an example of a form that meets the requirements for the GFE.

RESPA requires the lender to estimate only those figures that the lender "anticipates the buyer will pay at settlement based upon the lender's general experience as to which party normally pays each charge in the locality." Under the 2009 reforms, there can be changes in individual line-item charges, but the final settlement charges cannot exceed the GFE by more than 10 percent in total. The GFE corresponds with the CFPB (formerly **HUD-1**) Settlement Statement that is used at closing. These mirror-image documents allow borrowers to see costs of their loans from start to closing.

How Much Can the Lender Be Off in the GFE?

The new RESPA rules spell out the margins for error on lender disclosures. There is some variation based on the nature of the fees, for example the loan originator's fee (including processing and underwriting fees) has a zero tolerance rule on disclosure because the lender should know its fee. Likewise, state, local, and property transfer taxes must be exact. When the borrower locks in an interest rate, there is no room for changing the GFE. The following are zero tolerance figures when there is a loan lock: the credit or charge for the interest rate chosen (i.e., yield spread premium or discount points) while the interest rate is locked; and the adjusted origination charge while the interest rate is locked.

When the loan is not locked then these charges do fall into the margin-for-error category, but are covered under the *ten percent tolerance category*. Fees in the ten percent group may increase or decrease, but they cannot increase by an amount greater than 10 percent above the GFE total figure.

Finally, there are some fees that are not subject to any restrictions on increase, such as when the borrower is selecting his or her own escrow agent or title insurer. The lender is unable to determine those costs at the time of the GFE and is, therefore, no restricted on resulting increases because of the companies chosen by the borrower.

Post-Subprime Lending Disclosures Under GFE   The 2009 RESPA reforms, designed for greater "clarity and transparency," have changed the one-page GFE into a three-page document. While the form still calls out the loan origination charges and settlement costs, it is also designed to afford loan and market transparency on loan costs. The new GFE form is a plain-English form that features a question-and-answer format designed to address the lack of disclosure issues that surrounded the subprime mortgage market before 2008. Borrowers have information specifics called out for them with questions such as "Can your interest rate rise?" The lender must then disclose the maximum rate and when the rate change can occur. Other questions that must be answered include whether there is a

FIGURE 16.1 Good
Faith Estimate (GFE)

OMB Approval No. 2502-0265

Good Faith Estimate (GFE)

Name of Originator		Borrower	
Originator Address		Property Address	
Originator Phone Number			
Originator Email		Date of GFE	

Purpose

This GFE gives you an estimate of your settlement charges and loan terms if you are approved for this loan. For more information, see HUD's *Special Information Booklet* on settlement charges, your *Truth-in-Lending Disclosures*, and other consumer information at www.hud.gov/respa. If you decide you would like to proceed with this loan, contact us.

Shopping for your loan

Only you can shop for the best loan for you. Compare this GFE with other loan offers, so you can find the best loan. Use the shopping chart on page 3 to compare all the offers you receive.

Important dates

1. The interest rate for this GFE is available through [_____]. After this time, the interest rate, some of your loan Origination Charges, and the monthly payment shown below can change until you lock your interest rate.

2. This estimate for all other settlement charges is available through [_____].

3. After you lock your interest rate, you must go to settlement within [__] days (your rate lock period) to receive the locked interest rate.

4. You must lock the interest rate at least [__] days before settlement.

Summary of your loan

Your initial loan amount is	$
Your loan term is	years
Your initial interest rate is	%
Your initial monthly amount owed for principal, interest, and any mortgage insurance is	$ per month
Can your interest rate rise?	☐ No ☐ Yes, it can rise to a maximum of %. The first change will be in .
Even if you make payments on time, can your loan balance rise?	☐ No ☐ Yes, it can rise to a maximum of $
Even if you make payments on time, can your monthly amount owed for principal, interest, and any mortgage insurance rise?	☐ No ☐ Yes, the first increase can be in and the monthly amount owed can rise to $. The maximum it can ever rise to is $.
Does your loan have a prepayment penalty?	☐ No ☐ Yes, your maximum prepayment penalty is $.
Does your loan have a balloon payment?	☐ No ☐ Yes, you have a balloon payment of $ due in years.

Escrow account information

Some lenders require an escrow account to hold funds for paying property taxes or other property-related charges in addition to your monthly amount owed of $[_____].
Do we require you to have an escrow account for your loan?
☐ No, you do not have an escrow account. You must pay these charges directly when due.
☐ Yes, you have an escrow account. It may or may not cover all of these charges. Ask us.

Summary of your settlement charges

A	Your Adjusted Origination Charges *(See page 2.)*	$
B	Your Charges for All Other Settlement Services *(See page 2.)*	$
A + B	Total Estimated Settlement Charges	$

Good Faith Estimate (HUD-GFE)   1

FIGURE 16.1
Continued

Understanding
your estimated
settlement charges

*Some of these charges
can change at settlement.
See the top of page 3 for
more information.*

Your Adjusted Origination Charges

1. **Our origination charge**
   This charge is for getting this loan for you.

2. **Your credit or charge (points) for the specific interest rate chosen**
   - ☐ The credit or charge for the interest rate of [____] % is included in "Our origination charge." (See item 1 above.)
   - ☐ You receive a credit of $[_____] for this interest rate of [____] %. This credit **reduces** your settlement charges.
   - ☐ You pay a charge of $[_____] for this interest rate of [____] %. This charge (points) **increases** your total settlement charges.

   The tradeoff table on page 3 shows that you can change your total settlement charges by choosing a different interest rate for this loan.

A	Your Adjusted Origination Charges	$

Your Charges for All Other Settlement Services

3. **Required services that we select**
   These charges are for services we require to complete your settlement. We will choose the providers of these services.

Service	Charge

4. **Title services and lender's title insurance**
   This charge includes the services of a title or settlement agent, for example, and title insurance to protect the lender, if required.

5. **Owner's title insurance**
   You may purchase an owner's title insurance policy to protect your interest in the property.

6. **Required services that you can shop for**
   These charges are for other services that are required to complete your settlement. We can identify providers of these services or you can shop for them yourself. Our estimates for providing these services are below.

Service	Charge

7. **Government recording charges**
   These charges are for state and local fees to record your loan and title documents.

8. **Transfer taxes**
   These charges are for state and local fees on mortgages and home sales.

9. **Initial deposit for your escrow account**
   This charge is held in an escrow account to pay future recurring charges on your property and includes ☐ all property taxes, ☐ all insurance, and ☐ other [_____].

10. **Daily interest charges**
    This charge is for the daily interest on your loan from the day of your settlement until the first day of the next month or the first day of your normal mortgage payment cycle. This amount is $[_____] per day for [____] days (if your settlement is [_____]).

11. **Homeowner's insurance**
    This charge is for the insurance you must buy for the property to protect from a loss, such as fire.

Policy	Charge

B	Your Charges for All Other Settlement Services	$

A + B	Total Estimated Settlement Charges	$

Good Faith Estimate (HUD-GFE) 2

FIGURE 16.1
Continued

Instructions

Understanding which charges can change at settlement

This GFE estimates your settlement charges. At your settlement, you will receive a HUD-1, a form that lists your actual costs. Compare the charges on the HUD-1 with the charges on this GFE. Charges can change if you select your own provider and do not use the companies we identify. (See below for details.)

These charges **cannot increase** at settlement:	The total of these charges **can increase up to 10%** at settlement:	These charges **can change** at settlement:
■ Our origination charge ■ Your credit or charge (points) for the specific interest rate chosen *(after you lock in your interest rate)* ■ Your adjusted origination charges *(after you lock in your interest rate)* ■ Transfer taxes	■ Required services that we select ■ Title services and lender's title insurance *(if we select them or you use companies we identify)* ■ Owner's title insurance *(if you use companies we identify)* ■ Required services that you can shop for *(if you use companies we identify)* ■ Government recording charges	■ Required services that you can shop for *(if you do not use companies we identify)* ■ Title services and lender's title insurance *(if you do not use companies we identify)* ■ Owner's title insurance *(if you do not use companies we identify)* ■ Initial deposit for your escrow account ■ Daily interest charges ■ Homeowner's insurance

Using the tradeoff table

In this GFE, we offered you this loan with a particular interest rate and estimated settlement charges. However:

■ If you want to choose this same loan with **lower settlement charges,** then you will have a **higher interest rate.**
■ If you want to choose this same loan with a **lower interest rate,** then you will have **higher settlement charges.**

If you would like to choose an available option, you must ask us for a new GFE.

Loan originators have the option to complete this table. Please ask for additional information if the table is not completed.

	The loan in this GFE	The same loan with lower settlement charges	The same loan with a lower interest rate
Your initial loan amount	$	$	$
Your initial interest rate¹	%	%	%
Your initial monthly amount owed	$	$	$
Change in the monthly amount owed from this GFE	No change	You will pay $ **more** every month	You will pay $ **less** every month
Change in the amount you will pay at settlement with this interest rate	No change	Your settlement charges will be **reduced** by $	Your settlement charges will **increase** by $
How much your total estimated settlement charges will be	$	$	$

¹ For an adjustable rate loan, the comparisons above are for the initial interest rate before adjustments are made.

Using the shopping chart

Use this chart to compare GFEs from different loan originators. Fill in the information by using a different column for each GFE you receive. By comparing loan offers, you can shop for the best loan.

	This loan	Loan 2	Loan 3	Loan 4
Loan originator name				
Initial loan amount				
Loan term				
Initial interest rate				
Initial monthly amount owed				
Rate lock period				
Can interest rate rise?				
Can loan balance rise?				
Can monthly amount owed rise?				
Prepayment penalty?				
Balloon payment?				
Total Estimated Settlement Charges				

If your loan is sold in the future

Some lenders may sell your loan after settlement. Any fees lenders receive in the future cannot change the loan you receive or the charges you paid at settlement.

 Good Faith Estimate (HUD-GFE) 3

Source: www.hud.gov.

prepayment penalty, whether there is a balloon payment, and whether the loan balance can increase. The GFE also features a chart that allows the borrower to shop around and compare lending terms. The lender must keep the terms given in the GFE available for ten business days in order to allow the borrower to shop those terms against other lenders. (See Figure 16.1.)

Mortgage Brokers, YSPs, and the GFE   Two groups have been particularly hard hit by the GFE reforms. Under the new GFE, lenders must disclose the yield spread premium (YSP). The YSP is the difference between the lowest mortgage rate the borrower qualifies for and the rate the mortgage broker is able to obtain. The better the credit rating of the borrower, the lower the interest rate for that borrower. But the higher the interest rate, the greater the rebate to the mortgage broker. With this rebate incentive on higher interest rate loans, some mortgage brokers were able to steer borrowers into mortgages that carried higher interest rates but, perhaps initially at least, had lower payments and made them seem appealing to those borrowers. Under the new GFE, the YSPs for mortgage brokers must be disclosed, again with the purpose of giving borrowers the chance to shop around for the best loans for their needs. The GFE chart also allows the borrower the opportunity to compare the full costs of all loans in a form that contrasts the costs of lower initial payments with the true cost of the loan over its full term. Original lenders are not required to disclose their YSPs.

Homebuilders, Volume Discounts, and GFE   The issue of volume discounts continues to be a contentious one in the real estate industry. Are such volume discounts a "kickback" that violates RESPA? (See p. 465 for more discussion.) Some service providers, such as lenders and closing agents, offered volume discounts to builders who referred their homebuyers to particular service providers. In *Yeatman v. D.R. Horton, Inc.,* 577 F.3d 1329 (11th Cir. 2009) the buyers' purchase agreement with D.R. Horton builders gave the Yeatmans the option of receiving a discount on their closing costs on the house, provided they used DHIM as their mortgage lender (with DHIM being an affiliate of D.R. Horton). The court held that giving buyers an option but not requiring them to use the affiliate is not a RESPA violation.

GFE and RESPA Penalties

While originally Congress provided buyers/borrowers with a private right of suit for falling short of GFE requirements, that provision was eliminated, and federal courts have held that there is no private cause of action for the violation of the RESPA's GFE. Rather, enforcement is handled by the CFPB (*Altman v. PNC Mortgage,* 850 F. Supp.2d 1057 [E.D. Cal. 2012]). In addition, loan applicants cannot use state tort laws to recover for RESPA/GFE disclosures because such suits would circumvent the "no private right of suit" mandate of RESPA. (*Morrison v. Brookstone Mortg. Co., Inc.,* 415 F. Supp.2d 801 [S.D. Oh. 2005]) and (*Munoz v. Financial Freedom Senior Funding Corp.,* 567 F. Supp.2d 1156 [C.D. Cal. 2008]).

RESPA Disclosures Relating to Assignments

RESPA has been expanded to require certain disclosures when there is an assignment, sale, or transfer of the loan or the servicing of a loan account. At the time of the loan application, the lender must disclose to the one borrower(s) whether the loan may be transferred, and how often loans are transferred.

There are also paperwork requirements for these disclosures, including the borrowers' signatures as well as notification when there is a transfer. Notifications of transfers must be made within 15 days after the effective date of the transfer.

RESPA and the Settlement Statement and Advance Disclosure

The old RESPA **Uniform Settlement Statement** has now been replaced with the **Uniform Settlement Statement (USS)**. With the change of jurisdiction to the CFPB, the HUD-1 prefix has been dropped. Borrowers must be given a copy of their USS at least one day in advance of the settlement.

A sample USS appears at Web Exhibit 16.1. All of the charges listed on the form must be disclosed. In cases of outside payment, such as for pest inspection, the cost must still be noted on the USS but will be followed by the abbreviation **poc (paid outside closing)**.

The USS is not required if the buyer is to pay one flat fee at closing, as long as the fixed fee is given to the buyer as a dollar amount at the time of the loan application. This exemption applies when the buyer is purchasing a new home from the developer, who is offering fixed closing costs as an incentive for purchase.

Prohibited Conduct Under RESPA

RESPA was also passed to eliminate the kickback and referral costs, which were increasing the cost of closing for buyers. The following sections cover the prohibited fees and relationships.

Kickbacks and Unearned Fees

Prior to the passage of RESPA, it was common practice for escrow agents to pay fees for business referred to them by lenders, brokers, and salespeople. Such fees were paid as percentage commissions. RESPA prohibits giving or accepting "any fee, kickback, or thing of value" for the referral of business. Cash payments, special discounts, stock, and special prices are all prohibited. One of the areas of intense class action litigation has focused on YSPs. As noted earlier, these fees must now be disclosed, but they are not considered a violation of RESPA's anti-kickback provisions. (*Schuetz v. Banc One Mortg. Corp.*, 292 F.3d 1004 [9th Cir. 2002], cert. denied, 537 U.S. 1171 [2003]).[2]

FREEMAN V. QUICKEN LOANS, INC.

132 S.Ct. 2034 (2012)
A Quick Fee for Quicken

FACTS

Three married couples (Petitioners) in this case obtained mortgage loans from Quicken Loans, Inc. (Respondent). In 2008, they filed suit against Quicken for violation of RESPA because Quicken charged loan discount fees of $980 and $1,100 to the Freemans and the Bennetts, respectively, but did not give them lower interest rates in return. The Smiths'

---

[2]For a contra view, see *Culpepper v. Inland Mortg. Corp*, 132 F.3d 692 (11th Cir. 1998). However, the case here reflects a view of more of the federal circuits, although there are strong dissents in the cases. This issue may need to be resolved ultimately by the U.S. Supreme Court. However, the U.S. Supreme Court did deny *certiorari* in this case.

allegations focus on a $575 loan "processing fee" and a "loan origination" fee of more than $5,100.

The Federal District Court found that there was no violation of RESPA because the fees were not split. A divided panel of the Fifth Circuit affirmed. The couples appealed.

JUDICIAL OPINION

Scalia, Justice

The question in this case pertains to the scope of § 2607(b), which provides that "[n]o person shall give and no person shall accept any portion, split, or percentage of any charge made or received for the rendering of a real estate settlement service … other than for services actually performed." The dispute between the parties boils down to whether this provision prohibits the collection of an unearned charge by a single settlement-service provider—what we might call an undivided unearned fee—or whether it covers only transactions in which a provider shares a part of a settlement-service charge with one or more other persons who did nothing to earn that part.

When Congress enacted RESPA in 1974, it included a directive that HUD make a report to Congress within five years regarding the need for further legislation in the area. Among the topics required to be included in the report were "recommendations on whether Federal regulation of the charges for real estate settlement services in federally related mortgage transactions is necessary and desirable," and, if so, recommendations with regard to what reforms should be adopted. The directive for recommendations regarding the desirability of price regulation would make no sense if Congress had already resolved the issue—if § 2607(b) already carried with it authority for HUD to proscribe the collection of unreasonably high fees for settlement services, i.e., to engage in price regulation.

By providing that no person "shall give" or "shall accept" a "portion, split, or percentage" of a "charge" that has been "made or received," "other than for services actually performed," § 2607(b) clearly describes two distinct exchanges.

The phrase "portion, split, or percentage" reinforces the conclusion that § 2607(b) does not cover a situation in which a settlement-service provider retains the entirety of a fee received from a consumer. It is certainly true that "portion" or "percentage" can be used to include the entirety, or 100 percent. But that is not the normal meaning of "portion" when one speaks of "giv[ing]" or "accept[ing]" a portion of the whole, as dictionary definitions uniformly show. Aesop's fable would be just as wryly humorous if the lion's claim to the entirety of the kill he hunted in partnership with less ferocious animals had been translated into English as the "lion's portion" instead of the lion's share. As for "percentage," that word can include 100 percent—or even 300 percent—when it refers to merely a ratable measure. But, like "portion," it normally means less than all when referring to a "percentage" of a specific whole ("he demanded a percentage of the profits").

Petitioners also appeal to statutory purpose, arguing that a prohibition against the charging of undivided unearned fees would fit comfortably with RESPA's stated goal of "insur[ing] that consumers … are protected from unnecessarily high settlement charges caused by certain abusive practices." It bears noting that RESPA's declaration of purpose is by its terms limited to "certain abusive practices"—making the statute an even worse candidate than most for the expansion of limited text by the positing of an unlimited purpose.

In order to establish a violation of § 2607(b), a plaintiff must demonstrate that a charge for settlement services was divided between two or more persons. Because petitioners do not contend that respondent split the challenged charges with anyone else, summary judgment was properly granted in favor of respondent. We therefore affirm the judgment of the Court of Appeals.

CASE QUESTIONS

1. What does the language of the statute indicated is the meaning of portion with regard to unearned fees kept by a single lender?
2. List the other factors the court deems important in determining whether the "unearned fees" restriction applied to a single lender.
3. What should borrowers do when they review the fees in the Uniform Settlement Statement?

---

[3]In response to concerns about YSPs, HUD created the **Guaranteed Mortgage Package (GMP)** that would give a RESPA liability exemption to lenders who package all of the settlement services required by the lender and guarantee the cost as well as the interest rate up front to the borrower. Following universal real estate industry hooting, the proposal was withdrawn.

CONSIDER 16.3   Security Escrow kept $250,000 in an account with South-western Savings and Loan at no interest. Southwestern was a substantial residential mortgage lender in the area and had all of its borrowers use Security Escrow to close their residential purchases. Would this no-interest account present any problems under RESPA? ▬

Requiring the Use of a Specific Title Company

RESPA also prohibits sellers from requiring "that title insurance be purchased by the buyer from any particular title company." This provision stopped the practice of developers receiving substantial discounts in their title policies in exchange for the promise to send all of their purchasers to the title insurer for their policies. Prohibitions on kickbacks also apply to referrals on refinancings, lines of credit, and home equity loans.

RESPA Penalties on Kickbacks

Unlike the disclosure sections of RESPA, the prohibition sections contain specific penalties for violation. The penalty for violating the kickback section is a fine of $10,000, one year of imprisonment, or both; plus liability to the harmed party in the amount of three times the kickback paid or received; plus court costs and attorneys' fees. The penalty for requiring the use of a particular title company is three times the amount charged for the title insurance (paid to the buyer), plus court costs and attorneys' fees. The treble recovery is permitted even if the charge for the policy was reasonable and conformed to charges acceptable within the area.

Controlling Business Arrangement and RESPA

One of the more intricate RESPA issues that Regulation X addresses is a referral by a real estate agent, lender, or attorney of a buyer/borrower to a mortgage company or title firm in which the real estate agent, attorney, or lender owns an interest. There is no kickback or referral fee for the business sent, but the agent, attorney, or lender does enjoy the benefit of higher earnings and perhaps dividends from the title company or mortgage firm. Under Regulation X, a referral by someone who owns a 1 percent or greater interest in the company receiving the referral must make a disclosure to the buyer/borrower. These referrals are not prohibited under RESPA, but the buyer must be furnished with the following information:

1. That the referring party owns a controlling interest in the provider
2. An estimate of the charges the provider will make
3. A statement that use of the provider is not mandatory

A separate piece of paper must be used to make this disclosure and it must be provided no later than the time of the referral. Web Exhibit 16.2 is a sample Affiliated Business Arrangement Disclosure Statement form.

Those real estate firms that provide in-house computerized loan origination services must disclose not only their charges for such services, but also any interests they hold in the service or any mortgage firms included in the databases.

CONSIDER 16.4   Amy and Peter Haug obtained a mortgage loan and, under the terms of their GFE and USS, paid $50 for a credit report, $300 for an appraisal, and $25 for document delivery services in connection with the loan. The Haugs discovered that their lender, Bank of America, obtained their credit report from a third-party vendor for less than $15, and that the appraisal and document delivery services from a third-party vendor cost significantly less than the amount they were charged. The Haugs brought suit alleging that the overcharges constituted a "split of fees" or "unearned fees" in violation of Section 8(b) of RESPA. Are the Haugs correct? *Haug v. Bank of America, N.A.,* 317 F.3d 832 (3rd Cir. 2003). ———■

ETHICAL ISSUE

In 2003, HUD settled a civil complaint brought against 13 attorneys in New York for violating RESPA. HUD alleged that the lawyers improperly referred their clients to title companies they formed, earning payments based solely on the volume of business referred.

As principal shareholders, the attorneys received referral fees from the title company that they established. As part of the agreement, the title company was required to file amended tax returns for the prior three years.

The attorneys had established Covenant Abstract Company, Inc., and two affiliated title companies, Citation Abstract Company and Titlewaves Abstract. The attorneys agreed to pay $200,000 for the settlement of the RESPA allegations and to divest themselves of any interest in a title company for three years.

How would the federal government know of the arrangement? How would it learn of the ownership? Aren't the lawyers in technical compliance with RESPA? Evaluate the lawyers' conduct from an ethical perspective. ◢

RESPA Consumer Rights on Questions on Mortgage Accounts

Consumers' RESPA rights continue through to the servicing of their loans. If they make a written inquiry on their loan, the mortgage service provider must acknowledge the request within 20 days and take action on it within 60 days. The mortgage service provider must do an investigation that results either in a credit to the consumer's account for any errors or a full explanation that answers the consumer's question or dispute. Violations of these sections of RESPA carry civil class action remedies of up to $1,000 for each litigant, not to exceed $500,000 or 1 percent of the net worth of the loan service company, whichever is less.

Limitations on Escrow Deposits Under RESPA

RESPA also eliminates excessive prepaids and deposits that were once required of buyers before escrow could close. Lenders required the prepaids and deposits to be certain that the property was insured and that no tax liens would arise after closing. For the buyer, the prepaids were a form of forced savings, but they also created difficulties because coming up with the cash necessary for closing prevented home ownership for too many. RESPA limits the amount for deposits that the lender may require at escrow, and also limits the amount that the lender requires as monthly payments for taxes and insurance.

At escrow, the maximum payment is calculated as the amount that would normally have been paid into escrow from the date the charge would have been last paid until (but not including) the date of the first full mortgage payment, plus the equivalent of two-months' payment (actually, the wording of the statute is "one-sixth of 12 months"). For example, suppose annual taxes on the property are $1,200 (or $100 per month), due on April 30. Closing on the property will occur on July 15, and the first full mortgage payment will be made on September 1. Under RESPA, the maximum deposit would be $600, computed as follows: $100 would be paid on

May 1, June 1, July 1, and August 1 before the first full mortgage payment is due, for a total of $400. The two-month cushion is $200, so the total is $600.

After settlement, RESPA prohibits the lender from requiring large monthly deposits for taxes and insurance. Monthly payments for taxes and insurance are limited to one-twelfth of the amount that will become due during the year on such charges. About one-third of the states have regulations that require lenders to pay borrowers the interest on their escrow accounts earned during the year.

There are no civil or criminal penalties in RESPA for violation of these deposit limitations, but there have been several suits by harmed buyers in which federal district courts have taken jurisdiction and have held that the buyers do have a civil remedy.

CONSIDER 16.5   The Calhouns are purchasing property. The taxes on the property are $1,200 per year, and the insurance is $600 per year. Both taxes and insurance are due on June 30. Closing on the property will take place on September 15, with the Calhouns' first mortgage payment due on November 1. How much is the lender permitted to be paid at closing? How much may the lender require in monthly deposits? ▬■

ESCROW AGENT'S RESPONSIBILITIES

The difficulty with the role of the escrow agent is that the relationship is not a true agency, since both parties' interests are carried forth by a single agent. The unique position of the agent in closing has duties and responsibilities spelled out in the escrow instructions.

Escrow Agent's Duty to Follow Instructions

The escrow agent must follow the directions and limitations in the escrow instructions. The agent can do no more and no less than what is specified in that agreement, because the escrow agent holds only the authority given in the escrow instructions. Escrow agents who exceed their authority are liable for any resulting harm. For example, if an agent is required to pay all tax liens on the property before turning funds over to the seller but fails to do so, the agent is liable to the buyer for the amount of the tax liens.

The escrow agent often faces the same difficulties the buyer and seller face, namely, which document controls the closing? In the absence of a specific provision, the agent must follow only the escrow instructions, because that is the only agreement to which the escrow agent is a party. The following case illustrates this principle of limiting the duties of the agent to the escrow instructions.

EAST HILLS CONDOMINIUMS LTD. PARTNERSHIP V. TRI-LAKES ESCROW, INC.

280 S.W.3d 728 (Mo. App. 2009)
When the Condo Subcontractors Are Left Holding the Bag: Who Pays?

FACTS

In early 1993, East Hills Condominiums Limited Partnership (Respondent) decided to create a 136-unit condominium development in Branson, Missouri, which was located in six buildings. East Hills hired Killian Construction ("Killian") to be the general contractor on the Foothills project. Great Southern Savings Bank ("Great Southern") supplied the financing for the project, and Tri-Lakes Escrow, Inc. (appellant) served as the escrow agent.

On August 18, 1993, the parties entered into the "FOOTHILLS CONDOS-EAST HILLS DEVELOPMENT ESCROW DISBURSAL CONTRACT," which was a four-way contract between East Hill as "Owner," Killian as "Contractor," Great Southern as "Lender," and Tri-Lakes as "Agent." The Agreement provided "for disbursals of the proceeds of that certain loan ... in the amount of $6,779,373.00 to be used in the Foothills construction." The agreement also provided:

> Before payment shall be due ... [Killian] shall submit to [Tri-Lakes] individual 'Contractor's Request for Payment Certificate', ... executed by or on behalf of each general contractor, subcontractor, workman or materialman upon whose behalf payment is requested, together with the certificate of the Architect certifying the amount due upon said application for payment.
>
> Thereafter, [Tri-Lakes] shall provide [Killian] with individual 'Waiver of Lien,' for each general contractor, subcontractor, workman or materialman, in substantial form as that shown on Exhibit 'D', attached hereto and made a part hereof ... which Waiver upon due execution and presentation to [Tri-Lakes] shall be paid.

By early January of 1994, problems had arisen on the Foothills project such that Killian "pull[ed] off" the project on January 10, 1994, and ceased construction. Thereafter, Tri-Lakes was notified by numerous subcontractors and vendors that they had not been paid for their work on the project, although Killian had received its funds from Great Southern via Tri-Lakes. East Hills asked Tri-Lakes for the lien waivers that corresponded with its disbursements to the various contractors and materialmen.

Leora Zook-Piatt ("Ms. Zook-Piatt"), Tri-Lakes's "[s]enior construction disbursal officer," testified that she had the lender approve the disbursements and that she had collected lien waivers equal to the amount she disbursed to contractors and materialmen. However, Ms. Zook-Piatt said that she placed the lien waivers in a box in preparation for her deposition, and that was the last time she saw the lien waivers. No one has been able to locate the box or the lien waivers. Saliently, Ms. Zook-Piatt stated that she had no way of knowing if the money she paid to Killian was, in fact, used to pay the vendors and subcontractors on the Foothills project.

East Hills had to pay contractors and materialmen $501,305, including $29,938 to General Electric (GE) for washers and dryers it had furnished to Killian for the condo project because GE had not been paid and had not signed a lien waiver.

The trial court found that Tri-Lakes had breached the parties' escrow agreement and held Tri-Lakes liable for the $501,305, including the amount due to GE. Tri-Lakes appealed.

JUDICIAL OPINION

Barney, Judge

Appellant breached an express trust and breached the Agreement by failing to obtain lien waivers and properly disburse money. "... [A]s a direct and proximate result of [Appellant's] failure to properly account for the personal property in the form of funds placed into [Appellant's] hands for [Respondent], all pursuant to the ... Agreement, [Respondent] has been damaged...." Appellant "made an express and written promise to pay money pursuant to [the Agreement] for the benefit of the subcontractors and material providers on the [Foothills project]" and ... the Agreement, "[t]he [p]ayment [a]pplications and supporting documents represented the obligations for which [Appellant] undertook to ensure proper payment to the proper parties...." Appellant then "breached the obligation to pay the vendors, subcon-tractors and suppliers by failing to ensure that the payments made were for the benefit of the subcontractors and suppliers ..." such that there was damage from non-payment. Further, East Hills had to negotiate with the vendors and subcontractors who had not received payment and had to pay out of pocket to settle those claims. [Those out-of-pocket costs are the measure of damages for the breach.]

Appellant argues that because washers and dryers are not the type of items which could be subject to a mechanic's lien this amount should have been excluded from the award because "the evidence does not support the trial court's judgment that [Appellant] should pay [Respondent] for them as a consequence of a failure to obtain lien waivers that [Mr. Sawhill] acknowledged would never have been given in the first place."

"When interpreting any contract, a court must follow the terms of the contract as written if those terms are plain, unequivocal, and clear." "Only if a contract is determined to be ambiguous will a court then look to parol evidence in order to determine the parties' intent." Here, as already stated, the cause of action tried to the court was based on Appellant's breach of the Agreement by paying out monies without obtaining the proper lien waivers. The trial court heard the evidence in this matter and awarded damages to Respondent for Appellant's clear breach of this Agreement.

There is no mention in the Agreement of a provision which allowed discretion on Appellant's part in obtaining these lien waivers only for items that might be subject to a mechanic's lien suit. Appellant failed to produce a lien waiver in relation to the monies paid to General Electric. This was a breach of the Agreement and it matters not, under the clear wording of the Agreement, whether the items purchased from General Electric could have been subject to a mechanic's lien suit in the future. The trial court did not err in including the payment to General Electric in the award of damages.

The judgment of the trial court is affirmed.

CASE QUESTIONS

1. What lessons does this case offer on recordkeeping?
2. Are washers and dryers the type of property that permit the attachment of a mechanic's lien?
3. What should have been done when all the mechanics and materialmen began emerging as unpaid?

Escrow Agent's Fiduciary Responsibilities

Along with the duty of following instructions, the escrow agent also has the responsibility to act only in the best interests of the parties to the transaction. The agent cannot jeopardize either party's rights by closing for the sake of earning the closing fee if the required terms and conditions of the instructions have not been met. An escrow agent who breaches this fiduciary responsibility must reimburse anyone who suffers a loss as a result.

Embezzlement of deposited funds by the escrow agent is definitely a breach of fiduciary duty, but the problem is that usually the agent has disappeared or has squandered the funds. This lack of remedy leaves the parties to the underlying sales contract to determine who will absorb the loss of the embezzled funds. The risk of loss will be determined according to the degree of compliance with the contract contingencies. That is, if the buyer has complied with all contingencies and the money has been deposited with the agent, then title to the money technically belongs to the seller, who would absorb the loss. Likewise, if the money has been deposited but the contingencies necessary for transfer have not been completed (e.g., the buyer does not qualify), title to the funds (and hence the risk of loss) would revert to the buyer. The following case deals with the issue of misconduct by an escrow agent.

BAKER V. STEWART TITLE & TRUST OF PHOENIX, INC.

5 P.3d 249 (Az. App. 2000)
The Lawyer, the Escrow Agent, and a Lot of Embezzlement

FACTS

Ben Friedman, an attorney, obtained investments from Baker and others (plaintiffs) for a number of limited partnerships he created. However, the limited partnerships were a scam for Friedman to reap secret profits.

Friedman would find a property, and, using a fictitious name, buy it through an escrow established at a title company. While the escrow for the property was open, he would create a limited partnership and solicit investors for the down payment. After the escrow closed, he would then sell the property to the partnership for a far greater price than the purchase price he had paid to the seller of the property. By using fictitious names and shell entities, he was able to conceal the fact that he was making substantial gains each time a partnership was created.

However, Friedman required assistance in making these transactions work. He had that help from

Bonnie DeAngio, an employee of Stewart Title & Trust (defendant/appellee). Ms. DeAngio handled at least eight of the Friedman escrows, and on at least one of the escrows she notarized the signature of a fictitious person on a deed of trust. On another escrow, she helped Friedman impersonate a fictitious buyer in a face-to-face meeting with the seller. DeAngio also handled the transfer of the properties to the limited partnerships, and the affidavits of value in these transfers showed that the fictitious buyer, whom DeAngio knew to be Friedman, was receiving the profits from the transfer. Following each closing and transfer, an associate of Friedman's, Tom Lynch, paid DeAngio several hundred dollars.

There is no evidence to indicate that Stewart Title knew of DeAngio's fraudulent actions. DeAngio did leave Stewart Title and went to work for Chicago Title, where she continued her work for Friedman.

When the limited partnerships failed, all of the investors (plaintiffs/appellants) filed suit against Stewart Title alleging its liability for the fraud of its employee. The trial court granted Stewart Title summary judgment on this issue as well as their racketeering claim (alleged violation of federal RICO statutes). The investors appealed.

JUDICIAL OPINION

Berber, Judge

An employer is vicariously liable for the negligent or tortious acts of its employee acting within the scope and course of employment. Conduct falls within the scope if it is the kind the employee is employed to perform, it occurs within the authorized time and space limits, and furthers the employer's business even if the employer has expressly forbidden it.

Here, DeAngio's actions fell within the scope of her employment because she typically notarized documents and opened and closed escrows. Opening escrows using fictitious names by itself is legal; DeAngio's opening of these escrows was thus not wrongful unless she knew that Friedman was acting with intent to defraud.

DeAngio's more apparent wrongful actions involved notarizing documents for Friedman that she knew he had signed under fictitious names and then concealing his fraudulent signature. Tom Lynch gave her cash after these closings. When Friedman was asked in his deposition, "So basically, anything that you asked her to do with respect to the defrauding of the investors, she [DeAngio] did?" He answered

"yes." He also described her as "a very important facilitator" in his schemes. Though Stewart Title argues that appellants cannot show that DeAngio knew of Friedman's actions, the parties' depositions suggest that she may well have knowingly engaged in misconduct while at Stewart Title by notarizing signatures she knew to be false.

Stewart Title further claims that it would have received escrow fees, collection account fees and title insurance fees even if DeAngio had acted legitimately and, further, that the increase in purchase prices of properties due to her malfeasance did not affect its fees. Nevertheless, DeAngio's activity benefitted and furthered the business of Stewart Title because of the repeat business that she generated with Friedman. In fact, DeAngio stated that Stewart Title encouraged its escrow officers to procure new clients and develop business with existing clients. These clients would usually follow the escrow officers when they changed employment. Generating such benefits may suffice for liability. Due to DeAngio's conduct furthering its business, Stewart Title may incur vicarious liability. Whether Stewart Title would have received the same fees if she had acted properly is irrelevant.

The appellants claim that DeAngio is liable for conspiracy to defraud and, therefore, Stewart Title incurs liability under *respondeat superior* for all fraud-based claims. We address Stewart Title's liability for conspiracy as it applies to each group of plaintiffs and to each summary judgment.

The preliminary issue is whether DeAngio herself is liable for conspiracy. "For a civil conspiracy to occur two or more people must agree to accomplish an unlawful purpose or to accomplish a lawful object by unlawful means, causing damages."

However, the central issue remains whether Stewart Title could be liable under *respondeat superior* for DeAngio's acts in furthering the Friedman conspiracy. We find no case that holds an employer liable for its employee's acts to perpetuate a conspiracy to defraud under *respondeat superior*. The absence of such case law may result from the term "conspiracy" generally indicating vicarious liability for concerted action. If Stewart Title is liable for conspiracy through respondeat superior, two layers or "double" vicarious liability would result: DeAngio would be liable for a concerted action she did not personally perform and Stewart Title would be further liable. The nexus between Stewart Title and all the appellants thereby becomes too remote.

Reversed and remanded.

CASE QUESTIONS

1. Explain what scheme to defraud existed and what the title company employee's role in it was.
2. What is *respondeat superior,* and how does it apply in this case?

3. Will the title company be held liable for the problems with the investment?
4. Do you think DeAngio understood what she was doing?

Escrow Agent's Duty of Care

The escrow agent has a duty to exercise reasonable care and skill during the closing. An escrow agent is expected to understand and comply with title procedures and recording requirements. In other words, the agent is held to the professional standards of those who are involved in real estate transactions. The following case illustrates the difficulties an escrow agent can encounter as a result of an oversight.

BOATRIGHT V. TEXAS AMERICAN TITLE COMPANY

790 S.W.2d 722 (Tex. 1990)
When Flip Transactions Flop

FACTS

Philip and Linda Boatright negotiated for the purchase of 2.013 acres of land from Meadowbrook, Ltd. The Boatrights paid cash and executed a note payable to Meadowbrook for $63,200. A deed of trust secured the note, and Meadowbrook executed a general warranty deed to the Boatrights. Texas American Title acted as escrow agent for this transaction.

The Boatrights immediately entered into a "flip transaction," meaning that they immediately found a buyer for the property. Akro-Tex was the buyer, and Texas American was again designated as the escrow agent. Akro-Tex paid $33,000 cash and executed two promissory notes: (1) one for $63,200 and (2) one for $36,025. The escrow agreement provided that the notes would be secured by deeds of trust, and the Boatrights executed a general warranty deed. However, the warranty deed failed to mention the Akro-Tex lien. Only the deed of trust for the $63,200 note was recorded by Texas American. Unknown to the Boatrights, the $36,025 deed of trust was never recorded.

Akro-Tex made only three payments on the $36,025 note and defaulted. The Boatrights hired Harold F. Harris to pursue collection of the note. The lack of the recorded deed of trust was then discovered, and the Boatrights had additional difficulties in their relationship with Meadowbrook as a result of the default and lack of deed of trust. The Boatrights sued Texas American for breach of fiduciary duty. The trial court granted a judgment notwithstanding

the verdict for Texas American, and the Boatrights appealed.

JUDICIAL OPINION
Fuller, Justice

When an escrow agent undertakes to act in an escrow relationship with the parties by performing such actions as preparing the escrow papers, advising both parties and accepting and cashing checks, a fiduciary duty arises between the escrow agent and both parties.

Donald R. Conoway, senior vice president and general counsel for Southern, testified that title companies such as Texas American perform escrow functions in the ordinary course of their business and agreed that they hold critical real estate documents and money in escrow.

Dan Oliver, an attorney offered as an expert by the Boatrights, testified that title companies acting as escrow agents owe a fiduciary duty to both closing parties. He testified that he would not perform a closing without the deed of trust and that a breach of fiduciary duty occurred to the seller if the escrow agent in the title company failed to deliver one of the two deeds of trust. Texas American admitted that a deed of trust covering the $36,025.00 note was never recorded.

Patricia Sweisthal, an escrow officer with Texas American that handled the Boatright-Akro-Tex transaction agreed that it is part of the function of an escrow officer to match the real estate documents just to see that everything has been done. She could not swear there was ever a deed of trust for the $36,025.00 note. She was asked: "And part of your responsibility as an escrow officer is seeing that you have the proper deeds of trust securing the notes involved?" She agreed and was then asked: "That much was not done?" She answered: "Evidently not." There was sufficient evidence before the jury to find Texas American negligent. The elements needed to provide negligence, duty, breach and injury were presented.

Gerald Anthony Colbert, a real estate broker, testified that all of the papers, including the deeds of trust were present at the closing. Texas American was to forward the documents to Akro-Tex.

There was sufficient evidence for submission of the issues as to the negligence of Texas American for jury determination and sufficient evidence to justify the jury's findings as to Texas American's negligence and the actual damages suffered by the Boatrights. We also find there was evidence that supported the jury's finding that Texas American was grossly negligent in failing to see that all supporting documents were executed and properly recorded, thereby indicating a conscious indifference as to the Boatrights' welfare.

The trial court should have entered judgment for the Boatrights against Texas American.

Reversed.

CASE QUESTIONS

1. Describe the series of sales and deeds of trust.
2. What is a "flip transaction"?
3. What document was missing and in what transaction? What was the effect of the missing document?
4. Is the escrow agent a fiduciary for both parties? Was the escrow agent negligent here?

Escrow Agents and the USA Patriot Act

Any time large sums of money are part of transactions, there is the potential that those types of transactions could be used for money laundering. Until 2002, federal laws that were designed to curb money laundering were applicable to just financial institutions. With the passage of the USA Patriot Act following the September 11, 2001, terrorist attacks on buildings in the United States, Congress expanded the money laundering protections to escrow agents, title companies, and others involved in closing real estate transactions, the types of transactions in which large sums of money change hands.[4] Section 352 of the USA Patriot Act applies to anyone involved in real estate closings and requires them to develop effective internal controls on the use and source of funds coming into the organization for real estate closings. Part of effective internal controls is an independent audit. In addition, employees must receive training on compliance and how to spot money-laundering schemes. The companies must also have a designated compliance officer to oversee these functions and requirements.

The USA Patriot Act requires those who close real estate transactions to use due diligence in preventing their transactions from being used for money-laundering purposes. One of the industry's best practices is to require that buyers provide copies of account statements that show the source of the funds they are using as either a deposit (if over $10,000) or down payment. For example, if a buyer were making a $120,000 down payment from his or her bank account, the closing agent would ask for a copy of the bank account statement as well as an affidavit from the account holder that explains the source of the $120,000 in the account, and something that could verify the source as the sale of another piece

---

[4]The real name of the act is "Strengthening America by Providing Appropriate Tools Required to Intercept and Obstruct Terrorism Act of 2001," and the specific provisions that apply to real estate transactions, known as the International Money Laundering and Anti-Terrorist Financing Act of 2001, amended the Bank Secrecy Act of 1970 ("BSA") and can be found codified at 12 U.S.C. §§ 1829b, 1951–1959 and 31 U.S.C. §§ 5311–5322 (2001).

of property, a distribution of a gift from an estate, or the payment of royalties or dividends. Without this direct linkage with fund sources, closings have been used as a means for laundering money for terrorist organizations.

In addition, escrow agents are required to obtain IRS disclosure forms from the parties so that the transfer and payment of funds can be communicated to the IRS. The disbursement of funds is a taxable event in many closings and government access to the information, for purposes of compliance as well as in monitoring the flow of cash in our economy, an issue critical to curbing the funding of terrorist organizations.

CAUTIONS AND CONCLUSIONS

The devil is once again in the details. Closing a property transaction is a matter of careful attention to the paperwork and timing. When preparing to close on a property ensure the following:

1. Be sure you have all the necessary paperwork.

2. Make sure the paperwork is signed by someone with authority.

3. Make sure the paperwork is dated.

4. Make sure the paperwork has all the blanks completed.

5. Make sure that you have placed deadlines and timelines in your closing agreement.

6. Be sure to choose a reputable company and parties for handling the closing.

7. Be sure that you have complied with all the required paperwork for federal and state laws in the closing documents.

8. Make sure your escrow and closing instructions are detailed enough for the agent to handle all issues and handle them so that your risk is minimized.

9. Be sure you are clear on the relationship between your contract and the closing agreement or escrow instructions.

10. Keep copies of all closing documents.

11. Make sure you comply with RESPA and the USA Patriot Act.

KEY TERMS

Department of Housing and Urban Development (HUD), 457
escrow, 448
escrow instructions, 449

Guaranteed Mortgage Package (GMP), 464
HUD-1 Settlement Statement, 458
poc (paid outside closing), 463

Real Estate Settlement Procedures Act (RESPA), 457
Uniform Settlement Statement (USS), 463

CHAPTER PROBLEMS

1. Herbert Walsh is the owner of valuable commercial/industrial acreage located near a municipal airport. Sam Stanton is interested in purchasing the property and informs Walsh that he has deposited $25,000 with First American Escrow, along with signed escrow instructions to purchase the property for a total cash price of $750,000. If Walsh signs the escrow instructions, do the parties have an enforceable contract?

2. Nedzad and Danijela Krzalic and other property purchasers brought a class action suit against Republic Title, the closing agent in their purchase of a home, for charging them $50 for recording their mortgage yet paying the county recorder only $36. The Krzalics claim that the $14 difference pocketed by the defendant represented the receipt of a portion of a charge other than for a service actually performed, and so violated Section 8(b) of RESPA.

The trial court dismissed the suit and the Krzalics and others appealed. How should the court decide the case? *Krzalic v. Republic Title Co.*, 314 F.3d 875 (7th Cir. 2002)

3. Dearborn paid United Financial Mortgage $100 rent for every closing that it conducted at United's office that involved United as a lender. Dearborn paid $300 rent for every closing that involved another lender. Is this a RESPA violation?

Lawyers Title Ins. Corp. v. Dearborn Title Corp., 118 F.3d 1157 (7th Cir. 1997); remanded at 22 F. Supp.2d 820 (N.D. Ill. 1998).

4. Jerry and Jacqueline Benis filed a loan application with Union Bank, seeking to refinance the first mortgage on their home. Besides their first mortgage with Wells Fargo, they had two outstanding mortgages with Fifth Third Bank. The title opinion identified three outstanding mortgages on the property: (1) a mortgage to Fifth Third, recorded on May 25, 2001, to secure the original principal amount of $140,000, (2) a mortgage to Prospect Bank (assigned to Wells Fargo), recorded on October 28, 2002, to secure the original principal amount of $275,000, and (3) a mortgage to Fifth Third, recorded on January 7, 2003, to secure the original principal amount of $52,000. Union Bank asked Fifth Third to subordinate its February 2003 mortgage, and it agreed to do so. On closing, in August 2003, the title company paid off the Wells Fargo loan, but did not pay off the original Fifth Third loan. The escrow company assumed that the loan was subordinated.

   Several years later, the Benises defaulted on their Union Bank loan and the $191,000 in foreclosure proceedings went to pay off the Fifth Third bank mortgage of $140,000 because it had first priority. With expenses, Union Bank received nothing. Combining your knowledge of mortgage priorities with your knowledge of closing and escrow agent responsibilities discuss who has liability for what happened and why. *Union Sav. Bank v. Lawyers Title Ins. Corp.*, 946 N.E.2d 835 (Ohio App. 2010).

5. Jeff and Kathy Briggs obtained a mortgage loan from Madison Equity Mortgage Company, Inc. Madison Equity lent the Briggses funds that they used to refinance their residence. Madison Equity is a mortgage broker, and once the loan had been made to the Briggses, Madison transferred the loan to Countrywide Funding Corporation in exchange for a $528.75 payment. Countrywide maintains that the payment is simply a yield spread premium all lenders pay to brokers and that the Alabama state legislature has authorized such payments from lenders to brokers. The Briggses maintain that the fee is a kickback that violates RESPA. Who is correct? Do you think state law or federal law will govern the payment? *Briggs v. Countrywide Funding Corp.*, 931 F. Supp. 1545 (M.D. Ala. 1996).

6. Prepare a good faith estimate of closing costs and a settlement statement from the following information:

   - *Sales price:* $70,000
   - *Term of loan:* 30 years
   - *Loan:* $63,000; 90 percent FHA loan; $450 origination fee; 2 percent discount
   - *Principal and interest:* $652
   - *FHA insurance:* 1 percent
   - *Location of property:* 5730 E. Grand Ave., Mesa, AZ 85203, Maricopa County
   - *Tax information:* $1,200 per year for city, county, and state taxes; taxes due July 1, 2013
   - *Estimated settlement date:* June 15, 2013, with first payment on August 1, 2013

   What additional information is needed to complete the good faith estimate and USS or former HUD-1 settlement statement?

7. Which of the following loans and lenders would be subject to RESPA?

   a. A loan for a single-family dwelling
   b. A loan for the purchase of one condominium unit for use as a residence in a complex consisting of 450 such units
   c. A loan secured by a second mortgage for the construction of a swimming pool in the backyard of a residence
   d. A loan for the purchase of a cooperative that was formerly an apartment
   e. Refinancing a home mortgage to take advantage of lower interest rates
   f. Home equity line of credit with funds to be used for a child's college education costs
   g. A loan for the purchase of a mobile home (*Campbell v. Machias Sav. Bank*, 865 F. Supp. 26 [D. Me. 1994])

8. Anita Oginsky and others purchased property, mostly as investments, in Costa Rica from Paragon. The properties were to close using Charles L. Neustein, P.A. as the escrow agent. Charles L. Neustein, a Florida lawyer, had served as a North Miami Municipal Judge and the brochures and other materials sent to investors emphasized Neustein's judicial experience. The escrow instructions provided that upon payment of the full amount of the purchase price, Neustein was to convey title to the property to the investors. Paragon was actually a group of 16 entities engaged in a Ponzi scheme. However, Neustein was not conveying title once the investors had met all the payment requirements. When the Ponzi scheme was uncovered, the investors also discovered that Neustein had turned the funds over to Paragon, but had not received the deeds from Paragon. Discuss Neustein's liability to the investors. *Oginsky v. Paragon Properties of Costa Rica, LLC*, 784 F.Supp.2d 1353 (S.D. Fla. 2011).

9. William R. Bliss agreed to sell George P. Salemo, Jr. (and later his nominee, Catherine Salemo, his wife)

a piece of residential property in the Phoenix area for $795,000. U.S. Life Title Company of Arizona was employed as the escrow agent for the transaction. Written escrow instructions were executed and delivered to U.S. Life Title.

The buyer's agent gave a certified check for $114,023.80 to U.S. Life Title at the time of closing. The certification was forged, and Chase Manhattan Bank, on which the check was drawn, refused payment. Before the forgery was discovered, U.S. Life Title delivered the closing documents, including the deed, from Bliss to Salemo, and disbursed $74,422.28 to Bliss. U.S. Life Title recorded a *lis pendens* and brought suit against Salemo for the amount of the forged check. The suit was later amended to include Bliss as an additional defendant on the grounds of an indemnity provision in the escrow instructions.

After the forgery was discovered on October 22, Bliss purchased a home from the Tillotsons and as part payment assigned the note he had received from Salemo. That note was secured by a deed of trust on the property. Tillotson foreclosed on the deed of trust and resold it to Bliss, who in turn sold it to another buyer for $755,000. Thus, Bliss received $49,745 from Salemo through escrow and $74,422.28 at closing, and then recovered the property that he had sold. Bliss therefore received benefits of $310,000 to $375,000 from the various transactions. Who will bear liability for the forgery? *U.S. Life Title v. Bliss*, 722 P.2d 356 (Az. 1986).

10. From September 1975 through May 1979, Graham Mortgage Corporation provided Rose Hill Realty, Inc., with interim financing of Rose Hill's purchase, rehabilitation, and resale of Detroit-area residences. For each loan it received, Rose Hill agreed to refer to GMC two mortgage loan applicants from its brokerage business, in addition to referring the purchaser of the rehabilitated house. In turn, GMC, when making FHA or VA mortgage loans to purchasers of the rehabilitated residences sold by Rose Hill, charged Rose Hill fewer points than it charged other sellers. To recoup the income lost through the reduction in points charged to Rose Hill, GMC increased the points charged to buyers of residences referred to Rose Hill and financed by FHA or VA loans.

Richard E. Chapin, executive vice president and director of GMC; Thomas P. Heinz, a vice president and manager of GMC; and Manford Colbert, president of Rose Hill Realty, were charged along with GMC with violations of Section 8(a) of RESPA (kick-backs section).

GMC moved at the trial court to have the indictment dismissed on the grounds that the making of a mortgage loan is not "a real estate settlement service." Is this correct? *U.S. v. Graham Mortgage Corp.*, 740 F.2d 414 (6th Cir. 1984).

For research activities related to this chapter, go to our text companion website at www.cengagebrain.com

ANSWERS FOR OPENING CHAPTER QUIZ

1. One year in prison and $10,000. Penalties for violation of Section 8 of the Act may include a fine of up to $10,000 or up to one year in prison, or both.

2. Nada, nothing, except a thank-you. RESPA prohibits any person from giving or receiving a fee, kickback, or "a thing of value" for referring business to a mortgage broker, banker, or title company. Saying "thank you" is not considered a thing of value for purposes of the Act.

CHAPTER 17

TRANSFERRING REAL ESTATE AFTER DEATH: WILLS, ESTATES, AND PROBATE

*Let's talk of graves, of worms, and epitaphs; Make dust our paper,
and with rainy eyes Write sorrow on the bosom of the earth.
Let's choose executors and talk of wills.*

William Shakespeare, King Richard II, Act III, Scene 2

- *Malcolm Forbes left $1,000 each to owners of nine New York restaurants, including Lutece, the Four Seasons, and Mortimer's; and $1,000 each to 30 motorcycle clubs.*
- *Bob Fosse left $25,000 to be divided among 66 friends, including Dustin Hoffman, Liza Minnelli, and Neil Simon, "to go out and have dinner on me."*
  - *Cole Porter left his clothes to the Salvation Army.*
- *Lillian Hellman gave her Toulouse-Lautrec poster to Mike Nichols.*
- *Jim Morrison left everything to his wife, who died three years later, so Morrison's estate went to his father-in-law.*
  - *Philip, fifth Earl of Pembroke, used his will to get back at a friend: "I give to the Lieutenant-General Cromwell one of my words ... which he must want, seeing that he hath never kept any of his own."*
    - *John Lennon's will disinherited anyone who contested it.*
  - *Judy Garland left $250,000 to each child to be paid in two installments, at ages 25 and 35, but the probate located only $40,000 in assets and $1,000,000 in debts.[1]*

---

[1]Sources: Stephen M. Silverman, *Where There's a Will* (HarperCollins 1991) and Jeff Stryker, "Poison-Pen Wills: They Couldn't Resist: Oh, One Last Thing," *The New York Times*, May 31, 2000, WK 7.

Death is inevitable, but what happens to your property can be dictated by you or by the law. The law of wills and estates determines who gets what when you die.

The list with odd wills and estates raises questions about your property and what happens to it when you die. Can a will direct any disposition of property? Can you disinherit a spouse, children, or other relatives? How are creditors paid? What if there are insufficient assets to pay the creditors? Will taxes be paid first? If there is no will, what happens to your property? This chapter answers these questions and others about your property and its transfer and disposition upon death.

LAW OF WILLS, ESTATES, AND PROBATE

In all areas of real estate law, we have seen significant variations from state to state. This degree of variation is greatly exaggerated in the law of wills, estates, and probate—so much so that it would take an entire series of texts to fully explain it all. So, this chapter deals with the subject in general terms.

However, there is a uniform law in the area, called the **Uniform Probate Code (UPC)**, which has been adopted in some form by about one-third of the states.[2] Its provisions are noted throughout the chapter.

INTESTATE ESTATES

If a person dies without a valid will or fails to dispose of certain items of property in a will, the person is said to have died **intestate** or partially intestate. In the case of an intestate death, the property of the decedent is distributed according to the state's law on **intestate succession**. The method of distributing the intestate's property follows different formulas in different states, but in all states, intestate distribution is tied to the decedent's familial situation at the time of death.

Intestacy with Surviving Spouse

Generally, each state statute begins by attempting to have the decedent's property go to the closest living relatives. All state intestacy statutes focus first on surviving spouses, leaving all or some portion of the property to the surviving spouse. In some states, the surviving spouse will share the amount of the estate with any surviving children. As early as 1670, England's statute of distribution gave one-third of the intestate's property to the surviving spouse and two-thirds to the surviving children.

Under the UPC, the surviving spouse of the intestate will inherit the entire estate if no parent survives the decedent and there are no surviving children or their descendants. However, if there are surviving children, they are all children of the surviving spouse, and the surviving spouse has no other children, the surviving spouse will still receive the full estate. This last portion comes from the "Cinderella" problem. The theory is that a surviving spouse left with children from two marriages might favor the children from a previous marriage and shortchange the decedent's children.

---

[2]Not all states have the same version of the UPC. The 17 states that have adopted some version of the UPC are: Alaska, Arizona, Colorado, Florida, Hawaii, Idaho, Maine, Michigan, Minnesota, Montana, Nebraska, New Mexico, North Dakota, South Carolina, South Dakota, South Carolina, and Utah. The remaining 33 states have adopted parts of the UPC. The predominant form of the UPC continues to be the 1969 version, but the more recent 1999 and 2003 versions have seen states adopting various sections and integrating it with the 1969 version.

Certain marital property rights in some states may supersede intestate formulas for distribution. For example, in community property states (see Chapter 8), the surviving spouse would always be entitled to his or her one-half of all community assets. The more complex the family relationships, the greater the need for a will to clarify desires with respect to family members. Most states do not include domestic partners in their intestate distribution statutes.[3] Also, federal tax laws do not recognize domestic partners for purposes of the marital/life estate tax benefits (generation-skipping trusts).[4] However, domestic partners in those states that do not recognize same-sex marriage would still be able to execute valid wills leaving their property to their family members as they define that family, thereby bypassing the intestate succession definitions for purposes of order of inheritance.

Intestacy with No Surviving Spouse but with Descendants

Under the UPC, if a decedent has no surviving spouse, the estate property will pass to his or her descendants. The UPC uses the term "descendants" to refer to children, grandchildren, and other direct lineal descendants of the intestate decedent. The UPC follows the policy that, where possible, property should pass to future generations and not back to older generations. The terms and amounts of distribution among the descendants are covered later in this chapter.[5]

Intestacy with No Surviving Spouse and No Descendants

If the decedent has no surviving spouse or descendants, the estate property goes back to the decedent's parents in equal shares. If there is one parent, that parent will receive the full estate.

If the decedent has no surviving spouse, no descendants, and no parents, the property is then inherited by the descendants of the parents, or, in lay terms, the brothers and sisters of the decedent and their descendants (the decedent's nieces and nephews).

If there are no descendants of the parents, the grandparents of the decedent inherit the property, with one-half going to the maternal grandparents and one-half going to the paternal grandparents. Likewise, the descendant rules apply here, so if the grandparents are deceased, their descendants (or the aunts and uncles of the decedent) would inherit the property.

---

[3]Some courts have clarified state intestate succession laws by holding that their property rights are limited to spouses who are of the opposite sex, thereby concluding that intestate succession laws are not applicable to unmarried couples or domestic partnerships. *Storrs v. Holcomb*, 168 Misc. 2d 898, 645 N.Y.S.2d 286 (Sup. Ct. 1996). Changes in marital status laws will now affect intestate distributions in states that permit same-sex unions.

[4]The Defense of Marriage Act, 1 U.S.C.A. § 7, provides that "[i]n determining the meaning of any Act of Congress ... the word 'spouse' refers only to a person of the opposite sex who is a husband or a wife."

[5]Some courts have expanded same-sex partner rights to make the surviving partner a parent for purposes of issues such as intestate distribution as well as visitation and other parental rights. See, e.g., *Elisa B. v. Emily B.* P.3d 660, 666 (Cal. 2005) (lesbian who helped raise partner's children, but did not adopt, is considered a parent to the children); In re *the Parentage of L.B.*, 122 P.3d 161 (Wash. 2005) (a de facto [same-sex] parent stands in legal parity with an otherwise legal parent, whether biological, adoptive or otherwise); *V.C. v. M.J.B.*, 748 A.2d 539 (N.J. 2000) (finding that a former domestic partner, who was not a biological parent, is entitled to child visitation rights). But see In re *Bonfield*, 780 N.E.2d 241 (Ohio 2002) (concluding that a cohabiting same-sex partner of biological mother was not a parent). For more details, see Roger Severino, "Or For Poorer? How Same-Sex Marriage Threatens Religious Liberty," 30 *Harvard Journal of Law and Public Policy* 939 (2007).

CONSIDER 17.1

Ralph married Cora in 1959. Ralph and Cora had two children, Steven and Alice. Cora died in 1969, and Ralph married Susan in 1973. Ralph and Susan had two children, Alan and Erica. Ralph has just died intestate and his estate is valued at $800,000. How would Ralph's property be distributed under the intestacy laws of your state? How would it be distributed under the UPC?

Ron, a single young man, has just passed away. Survivors include his parents, a brother, a sister, both sets of grandparents, and two uncles. How would Ron's property be distributed under the laws of intestacy of your state? How would it be distributed under the UPC?

Intestacy with No Surviving Relatives

All states have some provision for the destiny of the decedent's property when a decedent has no surviving relatives. At some point in all of the state statutes, the property will go to the state or some public fund, or will **escheat** to the state. The degree to which a state statute permits distant relatives to inherit varies. Under the UPC, the property will escheat if there are no lineal descendants of the maternal or paternal grandparents; the UPC does not permit second or collateral heirs to inherit.

The escheat provisions of state intestate statutes are often referred to as **laughing heir statutes**, because an escheat occurs before distant heirs, who may not have known the decedent, inherit the decedent's property despite feeling no grief but, rather, the joy of a windfall.

Intestacy Terminology and Special Provisions

The following sections cover the terms and special provisions that are used in intestacy statutes to determine how property is distributed.

Per Stirpes versus *Per Capita* Distribution

The formulas for distribution of intestate property were developed because there were often many relatives who would be heirs of an intestate decedent. A question that arises is, Who gets how much?

There are basically three theories for distribution of intestate property. Under a *per capita* theory, the parties take an equal share. Under a *per stirpes* theory, the parties take by degree of relationship. Under the UPC theory (for which there are pre- and post-1999 and 2003 versions that result in different distributions even across UPC states, since not all states have adopted the 1999 or 2003 modifications), the results for distribution are somewhat of a cross between *per capita* and *per stirpes*, often called a "right of representation theory."

The best way to understand these theories of distribution is by an example, complete with variations. Suppose that G is the intestate grandfather (decedent) and he has three children: A, B, and C. C has two children, Y and Z. B has one child, X. A has no children. The family relationships are diagrammed as follows:

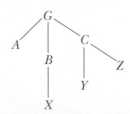

Suppose that all three children have survived G. In this case, all three systems reach the same solution: A, B, and C take one-third each.

Suppose that one child, C, predeceases G. The other two children survive G. Under a straight *per capita* distribution, A, B, Y, and Z each take one-fourth of the estate. Under *per stirpes* and the UPC, A and B take one-third each and Y and Z have one-half of one-third, or one-sixth of the estate of G for each.

Suppose that all three children predecease G. Under the *per capita* and pre-1999 and post-1999/2003 UPC, the result is the same: X, Y, and Z each take one-third of the estate. However, under the *per stirpes* method, X takes one-half, and Y and Z each take one-half of one-half, or one-quarter.

Suppose A and B predecease G, but C survives G. Under the old UPC, which is the same as *per stirpes* distribution, the result would be that C and X would each take one-half of G's estate. The result is the same under a *per capita* distribution because there are only two surviving heirs. Under the revised UPC (*per capita* at each generation), the solution is often debated. One view is that C would take one-half of the estate, with the remainder (one-half) combined into a single share and distributed equally among the surviving grandchildren of G (with the exception of C's children), so that X would get one-half of the estate. Another view is that after C's one-half interest, the remaining one-half is distributed equally among all the grandchildren so that X, Y, and Z would receive one-third of one-half of the estate, or one-sixth of G's estate.

CONSIDER 17.2   H and W were married in 1959. They had four children, A, B, C, and D. H died in 2012 and left all of his property to W. W passed away two months ago, intestate. A had died in 2011 but had three children, X, Y, and Z. B, C, and D are alive at the time of W's death. B has one child, R; and C has two children, T and S. How would the property of W be distributed in your state? How would the property be distributed by *per stirpes* distribution under the UPC?   ■

Relatives by Marriage

In most states, relatives by marriage other than the surviving spouse are not entitled to receive property through intestate distribution. Stepchildren, nieces, nephews, and spouses of predeceased children are all part of this excluded group.

Half-Blood Relatives

No state has a provision that absolutely excludes half-blood relatives of the intestate from taking a share under the statutory scheme of distribution. Many states and the UPC treat a half-blood relative the same as a full-blood relative. Other states have provisions requiring half-blood relatives to take a lesser proportion of the estate than full-blood relatives.

Posthumous Heirs

At common law and under all state statutes and the UPC, children born after the intestate's death are still treated as heirs.

Some states stipulate that the **posthumous** or **afterborn heir** must be born within 10 months of the decedent's death in order to be treated as an heir. Because of scientific developments, there are now heirs being born years after the decedent has passed away. One writer has noted, "Modern reproductive technologies have enabled physicians and scientists to intervene in the procreative process in infinite ways. The ability to conceive a child after the death of one or both of the parents has become a reality."[6] Some states do not permit any such posthumous relatives to take property under intestate distribution; other states stipulate that these relatives must be at least in the embryonic stages of development at the time of the intestate's death to be eligible to take property. The Uniform Status of Children of Assisted Conception Act (USCACA) is a relatively new uniform law that addresses the issues of science meeting probate law, but only three states have adopted it.[7] Courts had a difficult time with application of Social Security benefits for children both conceived and born after the beneficiary had died. However, in 2012, the U.S. Supreme Court held that twins who had been conceived in vitro after their father had died were not entitled to Social Security death benefits through their father. The court held that the Social Security Administration should follow state intestate and probate laws in determining the eligibility of posthumous children for Social Security benefits.[8]

Illegitimate Children

Under the UPC and in all states, illegitimate children who have not been adopted by anyone are treated as natural children of their mothers and are entitled to inherit from their mothers and their mothers' relatives. Unless legitimized, these children are not treated as the natural children of their fathers. Paternity suits establish the right of the child to inherit once the determination of paternity is made judicially or the father acknowledges paternity. The late actor Heath Ledger had acknowledged that he had a daughter with actress Michelle Williams. However, his will predated the birth of his daughter, and he did not change his will. His daughter would have a claim on his estate under U.S. law.

Adopted Children

The legislative trend has been for adopted children to be treated as the natural children of the parents adopting them. The UPC also follows this doctrine for purposes of intestate distribution.

CONSIDER 17.3   When Hank Williams, Sr., the country-western singer, died in 1953, he left a single living heir: his son, Hank Williams, Jr. In the month before his death, however, Williams, Sr., entered into an agreement with Bobbie Jett regarding the care of a child that Jett was then carrying. Under the agreement, Jett surrendered all parental rights in the child and Williams, Sr., without specifically claiming the child as his own, undertook to raise and support it. This child was born five days after Williams, Sr.'s, death. The child, now an adult, is Cathy Louise Deupree Adkinson. After her birth, pursuant to the agreement between Williams, Sr., and Jett, Adkinson's mother, Adkinson was adopted by Lillian Stone, the mother of Williams, Sr. Upon Mrs. Stone's death two years later, however, Adkinson was placed in foster care and eventually adopted out of the Williams family. Adkinson's adoptive parents did not tell Adkinson of her connection to Williams, Sr.

In 1967, the Williams family petitioned the Montgomery Circuit Court for final settlement of the estate of Williams, Sr. At this time, the trustees of the estate advised the court of Adkinson's potential claim on the estate, in light of the agreement between Williams, Sr. and

---

[6]Benjamin C. Carpenter, "A Chip Off the Old Ice Block," 21 *Cornell J. of Law & Public Policy* 347 (2011); Julie C. Fletcher, "The Inheritance Mess With Texas ART Children: The Simple Fix," 4 *Estate Planning and Community Property Law Journal* 1 (2011); and Brandon S. Mercer, "Embryo Adoption: What Are the Laws," 26 J. Juvenile Law 73 (2006).

[7]North Dakota, Florida, and West Virginia. The law is becoming more complicated as states have now passed laws allowing for embryo adoption and new uniform laws, such as the Uniform Status of Children of Assisted Conception Act are also passed.

[8]*Astrue v. Capato ex rel. B.N.C.*, 132 S.Ct. 2021 (2012); *Beeler v. Astrue*, 651 F.3d 954 (8th Cir. 2011).

Adkinson's mother. Because Adkinson's adoptive parents chose not to participate in the distribution, the court appointed a guardian to represent Adkinson's interests. As a result of proceedings held in 1967 and 1968, the court ruled that Williams, Jr., was the sole heir to the estate and that, according to state law, Adkinson, as an illegitimate child who had been twice adopted, was not entitled to inherit from Williams, Sr., even if she were found to be his natural child. The guardian *ad litem* appealed this ruling on behalf of Adkinson, but the trial court denied permission to appeal. In 1975, the Williams estate was closed.

Sometime after 1974, when she reached the age of majority, Adkinson discovered her connection to the Williams family and the possibility that she might be the natural child of Williams, Sr. In 1985, Adkinson wrote Williams, Jr., demanding a share in the renewal copyrights of her father's songs. Anticipating litigation over the renewal copyrights, Williams, Jr., filed suit to re-establish his property rights through the estate. Who is the rightful heir? Are the songs included as his inheritance? Should the estate be re-opened? *Stone v. Williams,* 766 F. Supp. 158 (S.D. N.Y. 1991); *Stone v. Gulf American Fire & Casualty Ins. Co.,* 554 So.2d 346 (Ala. 1989); *Williams v. Adkinson,* 792 F. Supp. 755 (M.D. Ala. 1992), *cert. den.* 508 U.S. 906 (1993).

Aliens

Aliens are entitled to receive property through intestate distribution. Their citizenship is not an issue in their right to inherit.

Convicts

A convict is permitted to inherit property and have it distributed through intestate succession at the time of death. Convicts' property does not escheat to the state.

Murder

Under the UPC and in most states, an heir convicted of murdering (intentionally and feloniously) the intestate is not entitled to the intestate share of property that ordinarily would be awarded.[9] State provisions vary as to the type of conviction required before the inheritance is lost. The following case deals with an issue of murder and inheritance.

IN THE MATTER OF THE ESTATE OF MORRIS P. VAN DER VEEN

935 P.2d 1042 (Kan. 1997)
Slayer Statutes and Killer Inheritances

FACTS

On or about April 30, 1993, Kent Van Der Veen murdered his parents, Morris and Deanne Van Der Veen. Kent was 19 years old at the time and had fathered a child two years earlier who had been legally adopted by persons not identified in the court proceedings. Morris and Deanne were not aware of the existence of Kent's child prior to their deaths.

The 1989 joint will of Morris and Deanne Van Der Veen provides for the following distribution of their estate after debts and obligations are paid:

Upon the death of the survivor of us, each of us hereby gives, devises, and bequeaths all of the rest, residue, and remainder of our property of every kind, character, and description, and

---

[9]The 2003 version of § 2-803 of the UPC provides: "An individual who feloniously and intentionally kills the decedent forfeits all benefits under this Article with respect to the decedent's estate, including an intestate share, an elective share, an omitted spouse's or child's share, a homestead allowance, exempt property, and a family allowance. If the decedent died intestate, the decedent's intestate estate passes as if the killer disclaimed his [or her] intestate share."

wherever located, unto our children, Laura Ann Van Der Veen and Kent Phillip Van Der Veen, equally and per stirpes.

Kent Van Der Veen was disqualified from inheriting any portion of his parents' estate under Kansas's slayer statute. Kent's child, the biological grandchild of Morris and Deanne, petitioned to inherit one-half of her biological grandparents' estate. The grandchild is identified in the case only as "D.B.B." The trial court denied the grandchild any interest in the estate, and the grandchild appealed.

JUDICIAL OPINION

Allegruccci, Justice

In their will, the Van Der Veens bequeathed one-half of their estate to each of their children, Laura and Kent. It is agreed that Kent is statutorily disqualified from inheriting property from his parents. At all pertinent times, it has been provided by statute:

> *No person convicted of feloniously killing, or procuring the killing of, another personal shall inherit or take by will[,] by intestate succession, as a surviving joint tenant, as a beneficiary under a trust or otherwise from such other person any portion of the estate or property in which the decedent had an interest. K.S.A. 1996 Supp. 59-513.*

This appeal challenges the district court's determination that the statute prevails over the express terms of the Van Der Veens' will, resulting in D.B.B.'s being disinherited. The argument made on behalf of D.B.B. by her guardian *ad litem* is that the language of her grandparents' bequest to their children, "equally and per stirpes," must be construed to give what would have been Kent's share, if he had not been disqualified, to his heir, D.B.B. D.B.B.'s guardian *ad litem* further argues that D.B.B.'s adoptive status is irrelevant because K.S.A. 59-2118(b) provides that "[a]n adoption shall not terminate the right of the child to inherit ... through the birth parent."

Appellee Laura Van Der Veen counters that the language of 59-2118(b), on which D.B.B. relies, was added in 1993 and became effective after the Van Der Veens' deaths. If the effective date of the amendment does not prevent it from applying in the present case, appellee further argues, the statute should be construed to restrict inheritance "through the birth parent" to instances where the birth parent has died. In other words, it should be interpreted so as to exclude inheritance through a birth parent who is alive but disqualified. In appellee's words, the statute should be

interpreted so that the disqualified killer is treated as if he never existed rather than as if he had died.

We first address whether D.B.B.'s adoption affects her right to inherit from her biological grandparents. There is no doubt that the legislature intended that 59-2118(b), at all pertinent times, permitted an adoptee to inherit from and through his or her biological parents.

In that enactment, the sentence, "An adoption shall not terminate the right of the child to inherit from or through the birth parent," was added to 59-2118(b).

The Court of Appeals in [*In re Estate of Hirderliter*, 882. P.2d 1001 (Kan. 1994)] concluded that the 1993 amendment to 59-2118 merely codified existing law so that the rule should be given effect whether decedent died before or after the effective date of the statutory amendment, July 1, 1993.

We find the Court of Appeals' rationale persuasive and conclude that D.B.B.'s adoption would not bar her from inheriting from or through her biological parent.

We next consider whether Kent's being barred from inheriting from his parents prevents the inheritance from passing through him to his child. This was the basis for the trial court's decision and has not been decided by the appellate courts of this state. The question has arisen in other jurisdictions, however, and has been pondered by commentators, scholars, and the National Conference of Commissioners on Uniform State Laws.

With regard to the UPC, the Tennessee Court of Appeals, in *Carter v. Hutchison*, 707 S.W.2d 533, 537 n. 10 (Tenn. App. 1985), noted:

> *A vast majority of states enacting the forfeiture statutes have patterned them after the model statute proposed by Dean Wade in 1936, see J. Wade, [Acquisition of Property by Willfully Killing Another— A Statutory Solution, 49 Harv. L. Rev. 715, 753–55 (1936)], or the Uniform Probate Code. Thus, in twenty-nine states there is a statutory presumption that the victim's property passes to his estate as if the slayer had predeceased the decedent. Four states provide for forfeiture but are silent as to distribution. Tennessee is among ten states that provide for forfeiture and for distribution to the decedent's heirs through the laws of intestate succession. The eight remaining states without statutes have forfeiture provisions by court decision.*

It appears that Kansas is one of the few states that does not expressly provide for distribution of the forfeited share.

Turning to the present case, it is clear that under either version of the UPC, appellee would take one-half of the estate of her parents. The other half would be taken by her disqualified brother's minor child.

The disposition of the slayer's share is one of four issues identified as unresolved by 59-513 and discussed in a 1984 law review article. Kuether, *Barring the Slayer's Bounty: An Analysis of Kansas' Troubled Experience, 23 Washburn L. J.,* 494, 495, 519–26 (1984).

Professor Kuether undertook to show why two possible objections to considering the slayer to have predeceased the victim were not significant. The first is that the slayer might act in order to benefit his heirs. He suggests that "[t]his will be rare since it is a very costly gift by the slayer." Furthermore, to bar all taking by representation and any antilapse with the exceptional slayer in mind would be unjust and typically contrary to the victim's intent. The second "is Kansas' traditional position that those who take by representation take subject to the equities against their ancestors." Kuether's analysis why this principle is not applicable in the case of a slayer/beneficiary is convincing. He states that the principle was developed in cases where an heir claims through a person who was indebted to the decedent. The shares of the other beneficiaries were reduced by the amount of the indebtedness. In contrast, the other beneficiaries' shares have not been reduced by the slayer's killing the decedent. In fact, their benefits have been accelerated. Thus, just treatment of the other beneficiaries does not demand that the slayer's heirs be disqualified or penalized. To illustrate this proposition in the circumstances of the present case, we need only look at appellee's situation. She would take one-half of her parents' estate if they had died from natural causes, and she would take the same if Kent is disqualified for killing their parents and his share passes as if he predeceased them. In contrast, if Kent's child were

disqualified because Kent killed his parents, the innocent child would be penalized, and appellee would take twice what the testators intended and what she expected.

We conclude that the better rule where the slayer's heir or heirs are wholly innocent would be to dispose of the disqualified slayer's share as if the slayer predeceased the victim(s).

The Van Der Veens intended for their daughter to take one-half of their estate. Their knowledge of Kent's troubled nature is reflected in a provision of the Van Der Veens' will that nominates Laura to serve as Kent's guardian and conservator. Nonetheless, they bequeathed one-half of their estate to him. There is nothing in the instrument from which the court could conclude that the Van Der Veens intended for Laura to receive the entire estate in the event of Kent's incapacity or disqualification. By extension, it may reasonably be inferred that they would not have intended for Kent's innocent child to be disqualified in order for Laura to receive the entire estate.

Appellee invites the court to speculate that the Van Der Veens would not have intended for their unknown, illegitimate grandchild to share in their estate. We decline the invitation and note there is no factual support in the record for such a speculation.

Reversed.

CASE QUESTIONS

1. What is a "slayer statute"?
2. What does the court find about adopted children inheriting from their biological parents?
3. What does the court find about grandchildren of murderers inheriting the barred murderer's share of an estate?
4. Is Laura's position different from what it would have been if the inheritance by the grandchild were disallowed?

ETHICAL ISSUE

What ethical and public policy issues exist in the dilemma of slayers, beneficiaries, and decedents? What concerns are courts and legislators trying to address with slayer statutes? For more information on slayer statutes see, Karen J. Sneddon, "Should Cain's Children Inherit Abel's Property? Wading Into the Extended Slayer Rule Quagmire," 76 *Univ. Mo. K.C. Law Rev.* 101 (2007).

Advancements

At common law, the doctrine of **advancements** required that any gifts made by the intestate while alive to his or her heirs had to be subtracted from that heir's share of the intestate estate. For example, suppose three heirs were entitled to receive equal shares of a $90,000 estate. If one heir had received $10,000 as an *inter vivos* gift, that heir would get only $20,000 under the doctrine of advancements. The remaining two heirs split the extra $10,000. Some states still follow the doctrine, but it is recognized under the UPC only if the intestate indicated in writing that the gift was an advance.

Property Interests Not Passing by Intestate Succession

Some land interests do not transfer by intestate distribution because of their characteristics. These interests, which were discussed in Part I, are life estates, joint tenancies by the entireties, and rights under dower and curtesy (discussed in Chapter 8). These interests automatically pass title at the time of death and are not distributed under intestacy rules. Life insurance benefits also pass to beneficiaries named in the policy, not by the laws of intestacy.

Simultaneous Death

In cases of accidents and air disasters, husbands and wives, who would ordinarily receive each other's estates, often perish together or die under circumstances where it is impossible to tell who predeceased the other. Some states have survival period requirements before an heir may inherit through intestate distribution. Under the UPC, heirs must survive by 120 hours before they are permitted to inherit. Survival clauses make intestate distribution easier. For example, a husband might survive his wife in an auto crash by only a few hours or a day and then pass away. In the absence of a survival provision, the property of the wife would pass to her husband's estate, which would in turn pass according to the remaining rules of intestate succession. With a survival provision, the property of each would be directly distributed to those next in line.

Some states have passed a uniform law related to the UPC, the **Uniform Simultaneous Death Act (USDA)**, which provides that if a married couple dies under circumstances where it is impossible to determine the order of their deaths, then property of each spouse is distributed as if the other spouse had predeceased them. The wife's property would be distributed as if she died without a surviving spouse and the husband's property would be distributed in the same manner. Perhaps the most famous application of this provision was in the case of the deaths of John Kennedy and Carolyn Bessette-Kennedy in a plane crash. Their estates would have gone to each other, but because of their simultaneous deaths, and no children, his estate went, not to his wife because she had died simultaneously, but according to his will provisions, to the children of his sister, Caroline Kennedy Schlossberg.

WILLS

Purpose of a Will

A **will** is a series of written instructions that sets forth what is to be done with the decedent's property upon death. Property transfers under a will take place only after the death of the testator.

A will reflects the wishes of the decedent and can expedite the distribution of property. Under the UPC, probate procedures require a minimal number of court appearances and substantially reduce paperwork, court costs, and attorneys' fees.

A will can also name who will be responsible for handling and distributing the property, who should be appointed as guardian for minor children, who will make funeral arrangements, and the type of funeral arrangements. Wills can also create trusts to protect the income of minor children and to minimize estate taxes.

Requirements for a Valid Will

The requirements for executing a valid will vary from state to state as significantly as intestate distribution rules. However, all of the states have provisions on these basic requirements: writing, testamentary capacity, signature, witnesses, and acknowledgment.

Writing

Like all other documents conveying interests in real property, a will is generally required to be in writing. The writing requirement is true for wills even if the testator is not disposing of any real property in the will. A few states do recognize oral or **nuncupative wills**, but such wills are often limited to the disposal of personal property and must be created when the testator is near death. In many states, the nuncupative will requirements are similar to the requirements for gifts in contemplation of death (gift *causa mortis*). Electronic forms of wills and faxes, the type of documentation now permitted in other areas, still will not serve as a writing because of the need for notaries and other attestations on wills. In fact, the most frequently litigated issue in estate distributions is whether the document submitted for probate actually constitutes a will. The following sections discuss the validity of such will substitutes.

Holographic Will   Most wills are thought of as formally typed documents drafted by attorneys, backed by blue paper, and written in very formal language. However, other types of writings can qualify as wills that have none of those characteristics. Many states and the UPC recognize the holographic will as valid. The **holographic will** is a will that is written entirely in the handwriting of the testator and signed by the testator. Former Chief Justice Warren Berger had a 176-word holographic will in which he left his property to his children. Some states now permit holographic wills to be placed on a preprinted form.

Some states require that the holographic instrument be witnessed to be valid, while others recognize the will as valid so long as it is signed. One problem with the holographic will, particularly in states where the will need not be witnessed, is establishing the authenticity of the handwriting and the signature as that of the testator. The long-lasting probate battle over the will of billionaire Howard Hughes resulted because there were several purported holographic wills submitted to the court, all of which had different property distributions.

CONSIDER 17.4   The following language was found in a holographic will left in the residence of William P. Avery and Deborah Smalling, who were unmarried but lived together in the house they had built with their earnings and savings:

> *I would like Deborah to have my home and property to maintain and keep with the hope that she may find the comfort and independence that has been denied me. She has been my love and faithful consort and has given me untold support and happiness. Words fail me.*
>
> */s/William P. Avery*

Does this qualify as a holographic will? Does the language have any ambiguities? Would the will also pass to Deborah the 32 acres of land on which the house sat? *Smalling v. Terrell*, 943 S.W.2d 397 (Tenn. App. 1996).

Contracts to Make Wills and Joint or Mutual Wills   Husbands and wives often enter into contracts to make joint or mutual wills that will serve to dispose of the property belonging to the two in a certain way. The idea behind the contract to make a will is to bind the spouse so that the agreed-upon distribution cannot be changed by the surviving spouse. The contract to make the wills is not a will. However, once the wills are executed, the terms of both the agreement and the wills can be enforced. To be enforceable, a contract to make a will must be supported by consideration. Husbands and wives offer consideration through their mutual relinquishment of the right to distribute their property according to their desires. Theoretically, each party is bound even after the death of one of the parties to the agreement. In practice, these contracts cause litigation.

A **joint will** is the same will executed by different parties as their own will. **Mutual wills** are the separate wills of parties that are reciprocal in their provisions and are probably based on a mutual agreement, understanding, or contract to make a will. States vary in their recognition of the validity of joint wills, but all states recognize mutual wills. Because of their nature, mutual wills are also often the subject of will contests. One of the issues often arising in the case of a mutual will is whether its provisions can be revoked. The provisions can be revoked with the mutual consent of the parties. Unilateral revocation usually brings litigation by the heirs or potential heirs.

Content of the Writing   There are no requirements for specific provisions in a valid will (with the exception of execution requirements discussed later). However, all wills should clearly explain the testator's intentions and desires for the distribution of his or her property and the handling of the testator's affairs upon death.

Generally, wills can be broken down into the following topics, although the topics and their content may vary from state to state and according to the needs of the testator's family.

1. *Declaration clause*: Declares the age, capacity, and residence of the testator and that the document is a will.
2. *Definition clause or clauses*: Lists wife, husband, children, and so on. Defines terms such as *children* and *issue*.
3. *Funeral and burial arrangements clause*: If desired, specifies funeral procedures.
4. *Debt clause*: Provides for payments of all debts, estate and inheritance taxes, and so on.
5. *Appointment clause or clauses*: Appoints the party responsible for the administration of the estate. May also specify the powers of the appointed person.
6. *Gift clause or clauses*: Disposes of the estate property, by either specific dispositions or a general disposition.
7. *Execution and signature clauses*: See the discussion later in this chapter.

Testamentary Capacity

There are two requirements for **testamentary capacity**: age capacity and mental capacity.

1. *Age Capacity* Every state has a statute that fixes the minimum age requirement for executing a valid will. In most states, the age of testamentary capacity is the age of majority, which in most states is 18. The age requirement must be met at the time the will is executed.
2. *Mental Capacity* Many wills begin their declaration clause with "I, being of sound mind …" This clause establishes the mental capacity requirement for

the execution of a valid will, which is that the testator must be of sound mind. Mental capacity is not synonymous with intelligence, logic, or distributing property only to relatives. Rather, mental capacity requires proof that the testator understood the following at the time the will was executed:

a. The nature or extent of his or her property

b. What persons would be the natural recipients

c. What disposition is being made of the property

d. The relationship between items a to c

e. How to form an orderly distribution of property

Eccentricity or old age alone do not establish a lack of testamentary capacity. A famous quote from a capacity case is, "[a] man may believe himself to be the supreme ruler of the universe and nevertheless make a perfectly sensible disposition of his property, and the courts will sustain it when it appears that his mania did not dictate its provisions."[10] In other words, it takes a great deal to establish a lack of testamentary capacity. Each case on testamentary capacity presents a different set of factual circumstances and requires the court to apply each of the five factors listed according to the familial situation of the individual testator. The following case presents a typical pattern in testamentary capacity cases.

MAIMONIDES SCHOOL V. COLES

881 N.E.2d 778 (Mass. App. 2008)]
Capacity v. Confusion vs. Caring

FACTS

After an 11-month struggle with esophageal cancer, Leonard R. Brener died on December 8, 2001, at age 85. He had never married. He had no children. He had a long and successful career as a stockbroker. The value of his estate approximated $8 million. Several nieces and nephews survived him. He had originally left nearly all of his estate to the Carroll Center for the Blind, the Perkins School for the Blind, and Beth Israel Deaconess Medical Center, Inc. The gifts to these nonprofit organizations during Brener's life and through his will were made through detailed living, testamentary, and pour-over trusts. Brener said he did not understand all aspects of the trusts. During the last five weeks of his life he was hospitalized and drafted and executed the final version of his will, which made one niece and her husband the primary beneficiaries of his estate. The nonprofit organizations (contestants) sought to have the will set aside for lack of testamentary capacity.

During those five weeks of terminal illness, Brener spoke of suicide by jumping out of the window, complained of depression, and often complained to his lawyer that he did not understand all the estate planning tools that were being used in his will. The staff at the hospital testified that Brener did not seem confused and was aware that he was dying and wanted to be sure his affairs were in order.

The lower court held that there is a presumption of mental capacity that the nonprofits were not able to overcome with testimony from either a doctor or those who had daily contact with Brener. The nonprofit organizations appealed.

JUDICIAL OPINION

Sikora, Judge

The motion judge correctly applied the standard for testamentary capacity and not the more demanding test for contractual capacity. First, Brener's trust

---

[10]*Gulf Oil Corp. v. Walker*, 288 S.W.2d 173, 180 (Tex. Civ. App. 1956) (quoting *Fraser v. Jennison*, 3 N.W. 882, 900 (1879)).

instruments were not complex, even though they disposed of property worth millions of dollars. They did not require contractual capacity for their intelligent creation and execution.

The record shows that Brener suffered severe depression accompanied by thoughts of suicide in February of 2001. The contestants do not dispute that Brener had the requisite mental capacity to name them beneficiaries in the first trust amendment on March 14, 2001. No evidence appears that Brener was senile or delusional or that he did not recognize his family and friends. Dr. Welch's promise to expand on his affidavit at trial could not forestall a motion for summary judgment.

On October 28, 2001, a nurse wrote in her report that Brener was "alert and oriented, but depressed." He complained that he was not going to last long and should jump out of the window. During her deposition, a social worker testified that Brener had been mentally alert and not confused about the identity of his family members. Acknowledging that she had mentioned that Brener was confused, she explained that she had meant that Brener was a sick man moving from one setting to another with insufficient time to get used to his new surroundings and without the knowledge of next events. She spoke to Brener after he had made the statements about death and jumping out of the window and attributed the statements to depression.

On October 26, 2001, Brener told the attending physician that he wanted to be "full code," meaning that he wished to be resuscitated in the event the procedure was necessary to maintain, or bring him back to, life. There is no evidence that Brener ever attempted to commit suicide or that any physician or caretaker ever put him on any suicide watch.

The record shows that Brener suffered severe depression accompanied by thoughts of suicide in February of 2001. The contestants do not dispute that Brener had the requisite mental capacity to name them beneficiaries in the first trust amendment on March 14, 2001. No evidence appears that Brener was senile or delusional or that he did not recognize his family and friends.

In sum, the contestants' evidence is insufficient to defeat the presumption that Brener had the requisite mental capacity to execute the second trust amendment.

CASE QUESTIONS

1. Why was this case so important to the nonprofit organizations?
2. Can a will be valid if the person executing the will is depressed?
3. What types of behaviors would result in a finding of no testamentary capacity?

CONSIDER 17.5 Burnell Young died on December 18, 1995, leaving a will that left all of his property to his daughter, Martha Young. Freeman Young, his son, challenged the validity of the will on the grounds that Burnell could not read. Should a will be set aside because the testator cannot read? *Succession of Young*, 692 So.2d 1149 (La. App. 1997).

CONSIDER 17.6 Dr. Albert Blakes had separated from his wife Alyce 12 years before his death. Despite the separation, Blakes continued to provide Alyce with financial support. Additionally, Blakes maintained his relationship with his stepson Richard and treated him as one of his children. Blakes was diagnosed with malignant melanoma about one year before his death. During that year, Blakes underwent various treatments for his cancer. By January or February of 1999, Blakes's condition was classified as stage four, indicating that the cancer had spread within his body. His condition continued to deteriorate and on May 20, 1999, he was admitted to the hospital suffering from confusion and dehydration.

On May 25, 1999, William Podsednik, Blakes's friend, was informed by Reeta Parlin (a nurse from Blakes's medical practice with whom Blakes was romantically involved) that Blakes wanted to make a will. Podsednik testified that he was generally aware of how Dr. Blakes wanted to dispose of his property from conversations during past years. Podsednik specifically asked Blakes what he wanted to do about Richard, to which Blakes responded, "Nothing." Podsednik relayed what he believed to be Blakes's wishes to attorney Jack Garbo.

Based on information provided by Podsednik, Garbo prepared a will for Blakes. Podsednik then brought the will to the hospital on May 26, 1999, for Blakes's signature. Podsednik, two witnesses, and a notary were present when Blakes executed the will in the afternoon. During the will execution, Blakes got tired and asked to finish the next day. Parlin and Podsednik urged Blakes to continue, and he completed the signing. Garbo never spoke directly to Blakes about the will he prepared, and did not go to the hospital to supervise its execution. Blakes died at midnight on May 26, 1999. Among other things, the will purported to leave Blakes's interest in his medical practice to his partner Dr. Sharon Rae, and the remainder of his estate to his three biological children. The will left nothing to his wife Alyce and stepson Richard Blakes. Is the will valid? *In re Estate of Blakes*, 104 S.W.3d 333 (Tex. App. 2003).

_____

PRACTICAL TIP

Get a will. Get a will while your mind is clear. Get a will that reflects your intent. Get a formal will that is witnessed and notarized. The estate of billionaire philanthropist Brooke Astor was tied up in probate for five years as multiple parties fought over whether her will was valid and whether she had capacity at the time it was executed.

Signature

All states require, as part of the formal prerequisites for a valid will, that the will be signed by the testator. The signature requirement is straightforward when the testator is able to sign. However, there are circumstances when the testator, because of disease or hospital equipment, is unable to personally sign the will. In these circumstances and under the UPC, the testator may direct someone else to sign the will so long as the testator acknowledges the will and is present at the signing of it.

Those who are unable to write may still authenticate a will by placing an *X* on the signature portion of the will, witnessed by others as being placed by the testator.

The signature of the testator should appear at the end of the will to make clear what portions and provisions were intended to be included in the will. As a matter of practice or law, the testator should also initial each page of the will to prevent pages from being added or altered after the execution occurs.

Witnesses

The witness requirements for a valid will vary from state to state. The number of witnesses required for a valid will is either two or three; under the UPC, the requirement is two. In addition, some states require that the witnesses be disinterested parties; that is, the witnesses must not be beneficiaries under the will. The UPC does not impose this requirement of having disinterested witnesses.

Many states also specify the manner in which the witnesses witness the transaction. For example, some states require that all of the witnesses be present in the same room at the time the testator signs the will, and that the witnesses sign in the presence of the testator and in the presence of one another. Other states and the UPC do not require the witnesses to actually witness the signing by the testator so long as the testator indicates the signature is authentic before the witness signs.

CONSIDER 17.7   George Baxter Gordon executed a will that provided that the Church of Christ of New Boston, Texas, would receive a substantial amount of his property. The will was executed with two members of the church serving as witnesses for the will. Upon Gordon's death, several heirs contested the admission of the will to probate on the grounds that the witnesses were interested parties. What was the result? *In re Estate of Gordon*, 519 S.W.2d 902 (Tex. 1975).   ▬▬▬■

Acknowledgments

Many states and the UPC provide all testators with the opportunity to execute a **self-proving will**. In a self-proving will, the signatures of the testator and the witnesses are notarized following a clause that is a form of affidavit for the parties. If the proper acknowledgment procedures are followed, then the will enjoys a presumption that it was validly executed. Figure 17.1 is an example of an acknowledgment clause used in a UPC state. The clause follows after the testator and witness signatures.

Will Contests

The validity of a will may be challenged by anyone who might have an interest in the estate of the decedent—someone named in the will or an heir omitted from the will. Some of the grounds for such challenges include the testator's lack of testamentary capacity or the failure to meet the requirements for signatures or witnesses.

FIGURE 17.1
Sample Will
Acknowledgment

STATE OF _____   )

SS. ACKNOWLEDGMENT/AFFADAVIT   )

County of _____   )

We, _____ , _____ , and _____ , the Testator and the witnesses, respectively, whose names are signed to the foregoing instrument, being first duly sworn, do hereby declare to the undersigned authority that the Testator signed and executed the instrument as his Last Will and Testament and that he signed willingly, and that he executed it as his free and voluntary act for the purposes therein expressed, and that each of the witnesses, in the presence of the Testator, signed the will as witness and that to the best of their knowledge the Testator was at that time eighteen or more years of age, of eighteen or more years of age, of sound mind, and under no constraint or undue influence.

Testator _____

Witness _____

Witness _____

Subscribed and sworn to and acknowledged before me by _____ , the _____ , Testator, and subscribed and sworn to before me by _____ , and _____ , witnesses, this _____ day of _____ , 20 _____

Notary _____ , My Commission Expires _____

One frequent reason wills are set aside is that there has been **undue influence** in its execution. When undue influence is raised in a will contest, the party challenging the will does not dispute the valid execution of the will, but rather raises the defense that the will was not executed of the testator's own free will and choice—that someone else influenced the testator in an unfair manner to execute the will.

Undue influence is a difficult concept to define. There need not be force to establish undue influence, but there must be something more than advice, persuasion, and kindness. The following elements are required to be able to set aside a will on the grounds of undue influence:

1. The testator must be established as a person who could be subject to undue influence.
2. A party must be shown to have had the opportunity to exercise undue influence.
3. A party must have been disposed to exercise undue influence.
4. There must be a will that reflects the results of undue influence.

Undue influence, like testamentary capacity, is based on the factual circumstances. Classically, undue influence occurs when an elderly party becomes dependent on a friend or relative for assistance in day-to-day living, then executes a will leaving all or the majority of his or her estate to that person while other relatives are ignored in the testamentary disposition.

Relationships of dependency and trust are called *confidential* relationships. In many states, there is a presumption that undue influence was involved in the execution of a will if there is a confidential or fiduciary relationship between the testator and the party who is a major beneficiary and who also procured the execution of the will.

The following case deals with an issue of undue influence.

IN RE MELTER

273 P.3d 991 (Wash. App. 2012)
My Brother's Keeping It All

FACTS

Mary Virginia Melter and John R. Melter had three children: Mary Jane, John D., and William. John was 8 years older than William, the youngest child.

In May 2002, Mary Jane died of cancer. Virginia's husband became ill shortly thereafter and died in July 2002. The closely timed deaths of Virginia's only daughter and husband left her in a vulnerable state, physically and emotionally. Shortly after, John died and Virginia was unable to live on her own.

Following John R.'s funeral and interment in Washington, William traveled to Florida to stay with his mother and help prepare for her move to the Pacific Northwest. All of her possessions, including her car and furniture, were shipped to William's home in Kent. During the couple of months William spent with Virginia in Florida, he influenced her, in her weakened state, to make significant changes to her estate plan. In a new will—her second, executed in September 2002—Virginia bequeathed her Florida home to William; left only $5,000 to Jennifer Winkler, Mary Jane's only child; and left the balance of the estate in equal shares to John and William. William obtained a power of attorney from his mother and took over management of her financial affairs. He did not tell his brother, John, about the new will. When asked by John for copies of their parents' wills, he failed to provide them.

In early October 2002, William flew with Virginia to Spokane, Washington. He left her to stay temporarily with John and his wife Sandra, while William traveled with his wife to a family wedding in Hawaii. William brought Virginia's legal documents with him from Florida, having promised to deliver them to John, but then failed to do so, telling John he had inadvertently left them on the plane. William got the documents to John only after several years had passed and John was unaware of the will changes until he did so.

William suffered a serious heart attack in Hawaii and his extended recovery delayed Virginia's move to Kent. With the passage of time, she became comfortable living with John and Sandra and decided to make her home with them instead. Among reasons for her change of heart was that she would have been required to live in a retirement home in Kent, since William's was a tri-level home whose stairs she was unable to navigate. She could get around in John's home, in which she had her own bedroom and bathroom. She had not wanted to live in a retirement home, preferring to live with one of her sons.

Virginia was aware that she had executed legal documents during the time William spent in Florida in the fall of 2002. She was either not certain as to their substance or reluctant to acknowledge it, but whatever the case, there is evidence that by late 2002 she wished to change her will.

In December 2002, John helped arrange for his mother to meet with Spokane attorney Steve Jolley, who drafted a revocable trust and a new will—her third—which she executed in December. The trust and will left Virginia's estate to her two sons, in equal shares, with John being named her successor trustee under the trust and personal representative of her estate. William was named alternate trustee and alternate personal representative. Virginia also executed a durable power of attorney in favor of John.

John informed William that his mother had executed a new will, that it left her estate to the two sons equally, and that John was named personal representative and had been appointed his mother's attorney in fact.

At this point, John began a course of conduct to influence Virginia's execution of a fourth will several months later. The relationship between the two brothers became increasingly hostile. John drafted a letter to attorney Jolley that was signed by Virginia, requesting that Mr. Jolley prepare a fourth will that would disinherit William. Mr. Jolley declined the engagement to prepare the fourth will for reasons not relevant here. He referred John to another law firm, Trankenbolz & Rohr.

John arranged for Virginia to meet with attorney Pamela Rohr in May 2003. At the time of the meeting with Ms. Rohr, Virginia was disappointed and upset with William for a number of reasons that she was able to clearly articulate to Ms. Rohr. Virginia had

testamentary capacity at the time, was aware of her assets, knew the objects of her bounty and was clear about how she wanted her estate distributed. She clearly articulated her reasons for wanting to disinherit William. Ms. Rohr drafted and Virginia executed Virginia's fourth will, specifically disinheriting William, bequeathing 99 percent of her estate to John, and bequeathing the remaining 1 percent to her granddaughter Jennifer Winkler. Virginia revoked the trust that had been prepared by Mr. Jolley.

For the remaining 4 1/2 years of her life, Virginia lived with John and Sandra. John spent a great deal of time and energy directing his mother's estate affairs. He transferred substantially all of her assets to himself and his wife before Virginia's death on March 21, 2007. Her estate had amounted to some $617,000 after the sale of her Florida home in April 2005. At the time of her death only $11,000 remained, in a joint tenancy account with John. William did not learn of the existence of the fourth will or become aware of John's transfers of assets until their mother's death.

John and his wife took excellent care of his mother during the years she lived with them. Virginia benefited from an excellent quality of life with them; they were solicitous of her and assured she had good medical care.

On the other hand, John, like William, criticized the other to their mother; drawing her into a hostile family situation they created by their arguing over how her estate would be handled and which of them would be in charge. Virginia was estranged from William during the years she lived with John.

William challenged the fourth will on the grounds of coercion and undue influence. The trial court concluded that the serial transfers of virtually all of Virginia's assets to John and her fourth will were invalid. The trial court determined that Virginia's third, December 2002 will, should control the disposition of her estate. John and Sandra appealed.

JUDICIAL OPINION
Siddoway, Judge

A will is presumed valid. It may be disregarded when a will contestant presents clear, cogent, and convincing evidence that the will was the product of undue influence.

John testified that he was only a scrivener of his mother's wishes and request, but in light of the trial court's finding that John was not credible, we disregard his testimony bearing on this and other findings challenged on appeal.

William argues that the trial court was free (as it apparently did) to disbelieve John's testimony that he was merely relaying his mother's request and conclude the opposite: that he was the source of the requested changes.

Where, as here, the standard of proof is clear, cogent, and convincing evidence, it is especially clear that the court's adverse view of John's credibility cannot satisfy William's burden of production.

Undue influence has been described as "'tantamount to force or fear which destroys the testator's free agency and constrains him to do what is against his will.'"

Viewed in the light most favorable to William, the evidence established that John stood in a confidential relation to his mother; that he facilitated creation of the will by making the contact with Mr. Jolley that led to the referral to Ms. Rohr, made the appointment with Ms. Rohr, and drove his mother to the appointment; and that he was bequeathed virtually her entire estate under that will. Nonetheless, these facts alone do not satisfy William's burden of [proof].

John's evidence is sufficient to rebut the presumption and satisfy his burden of restoring evidentiary equilibrium for similar reasons. He established to the satisfaction of the trial court that Virginia "was disappointed and upset with William for a number of reasons which she was able to clearly articulate to attorney Rohr," that she "had testamentary capacity when she executed the will[,] was aware of her assets, knew the objects of her bounty, ... was clear about how she wanted her estate distributed," and "clearly articulated her reasons for wanting to disinherit William," and that John and his wife "took excellent care of his mother and provided her with a comfortable home." This evidence was a sufficient counterbalance to William's reliance on the presumption.

William's evidence falls short of key elements commonly found in decisions recognizing undue influence. William has not demonstrated that John's role in facilitating creation of the May 2003 will was one that interfered with Virginia's free will or prevented the exercise of her judgment or choice.

What William did establish to the trial court's satisfaction was that John bore equal responsibility with William for a contentious relationship that contributed to Virginia's and William's estrangement. William established to the court's satisfaction that John could not meet his burden of proving Virginia's informed approval of his asset transfers during her lifetime. But on matters bearing on the validity of the fourth will, William proved, at most, that John may have had the opportunity to exert influence over Virginia.

Because the trial court's undue influence determination was its sole basis for invalidating the fourth will, its invalidation of the fourth will must be reversed. In light of the validity of the fourth will, William has no standing to challenge lifetime transfers of his mother's assets.

We reverse.

CASE QUESTIONS

1. Who had the burden of proof on undue influence?
2. What did the court find was established by the evidence?
3. Explain what happens to Virginia's property and why.

CONSIDER 17.8 Bill Cruxton died in November 1992. He was widowed, childless, and past 80. In his will, he left $500,000, the bulk of his estate, to a 17-year-old waitress who had been kind to him as part of her job as a waitress at Dink's Restaurant in Chagrin Falls, Ohio. Cruxton had lunch and dinner there every day for 13 months preceding his death. He was very public about leaving the money to her because he knew that her father had died and that she wanted to attend college. Cora Bruck, Cruxton's 86-year-old sister, is challenging the will as Cruxton's only relative. Cruxton left her only sufficient funds to cover her funeral expenses. Mark Fishman, Bruck's attorney, has stated, "Mr. Cruxton's longtime friends all agree that this was not the same guy. The Bill Cruxton that they knew was a very conservative and down-to-earth guy. This is the last thing they would have expected from the true Bill Cruxton." Are there valid grounds for challenging the will?[11]

---

[11]This real situation became the basis of a 2007 movie, *Waitress*, starring Keri Russell.

Disinheritance and Limitations on Distribution

Most states have provisions that prevent **disinheritance** of certain family members. In fact, all states have some protections for the surviving spouse. Although a will may purport to disinherit a surviving spouse, the surviving spouse will be entitled to one or more of the following depending on the state's system of property allocation between husband and wife.

1. *Dower:* In some states, the wife is entitled to a certain portion of her husband's estate. If she is not provided for in the will, she will still receive her statutory dower percentage.

2. *Curtesy:* In some states, the husband is entitled to a portion of the wife's estate, and the result will be the same as in the dower situation above.

3. *Community property:* In community property states, the surviving spouse is entitled to half of the community property even if the testator spouse has attempted to disinherit by the terms of the will.

4. *Homesteads, exemptions, and family allowances:* Most states have some provision that requires that the home and often specific personal property (usually furnishings) pass to the family (spouse and children) of the decedent. These items are thus given to the family regardless of disinheritance provisions in the will. Also, many states provide for an allowance to be given to the spouse and children of the decedent for the purposes of support during the probate of the estate.

In some cases, the surviving spouse has been provided for in the will but would be entitled to receive more under the afforded statutory protections. Under these circumstances, many states permit the surviving spouse to elect whether to take what was provided under the will or to take the statutory share as provided by the applicable protections. The election must be formally filed as part of the probate proceedings, usually within a certain limited period.

Relatives other than the surviving spouse may be disinherited. As noted earlier, testators who disinherit relatives generally have their wills challenged, especially when their intentions and motivations are not clear.

CONSIDER 17.9   James G. Newkirk left his wife and daughter in 1951. Shortly thereafter, he met Pauline Knight and began living with her; they held themselves out as husband and wife in all places where they resided. In 1952, Newkirk executed a will that left all of his property to Pauline and made no provision for his wife or daughter except the following clause:

> *Third: I have a daughter, Joan Janick, who is married, and for whom I have heretofore provided, and I do not wish her to participate in my will.*

Newkirk died in 1964, and Pauline presented the will for probate. Newkirk's daughter challenged the will on the grounds of undue influence because the will had been made less than a year after Newkirk left and was made at a time when he was still married and had a child to provide for. What was the result? *In re Estate of Newkirk*, 456 P.2d 104 (Okl. 1969).

Tortious Interference with Expectation of Inheritance

A new theory for will contests has emerged. Many heirs who are left out or whose inheritances are challenged by other heirs are using **tortious interference with expectation of inheritance** as a basis for contesting a will. Perhaps the most famous case involving tortious interference with expectation of inheritance involved a former Playmate of the Year, the late Anna Nicole Smith (aka Vicki Lynn Marshall). Ms. Smith's husband, 90-year-old J. Howard Marshall, II, a wealthy oil company owner, died leaving a $1.6 billion estate. Ms. Smith was given $90 million, not from Mr. Marshall's estate, but rather from Mr. Marshall's son, for what Ms. Smith proved was his interference with the execution of a will by the late Mr. Marshall that would have allowed her to be an heir.[12] A California bankruptcy court awarded her the damages from her husband's son.[13] The son appealed the jurisdictional issues, challenging the federal court's authority to grant the tortious interference claim when a Texas probate court had jurisdiction over the estate. The U.S. Supreme Court sided with Ms. Smith and sent it back to the bankruptcy court to determine her rights. The bankruptcy judge then went with the Texas court's interpretation of intent and Ms. Smith took nothing from the estate or her late husband's son. Ms. Smith did challenge her husband's trusts (there were seven) in Texas courts, but she was awarded nothing from them, per his expressed intention.

The U.S. Supreme Court's decision in the case confirms that this tort is an action outside of probate created to prevent fraud in the execution of wills; some state legislatures and more courts are developing statutes and precedent that provide a right to recover for such interference. Nearly a majority of the states recognize the tort, with the remaining states either unclear in their acceptance of the tort or not yet taken a case or passed legislation to address the issue. Hesitation on allowing this tort as a means of recovery stems from concern that the role of the probate courts in distributing property according to the testator's intention.[14]

Living Wills

The term **living will** has been a part of a national dialogue since 2004, when the country was gripped by the legal saga of Terri Schiavo, a woman in a persistent vegetative state whose husband had won the right to withhold food because of his belief that she would not want to live in such a condition.[15] A living will is a document that verifies the wishes of the testator to be taken off artificial life-support systems when there is no reasonable prospect of recovery. States that recognize living wills have statutory requirements for their validity. For example, disinterested witnesses and specific language are required in many states. Whatever requirements a state has must be followed if the living will is to be valid. Web Exhibit 17.1 is a sample living will form.

The **Uniform Rights of the Terminally Ill Act**, as approved by the Conference on Uniform Laws and endorsed by the American Bar Association, provides a comprehensive statement of law regarding the rights of the terminally ill. This act gives legal rules for living wills, authorization of appointment of

---

[12]*In re Marshall*, 253 B.R. 550, 553 (Bankr. C.D. Cal. 2000). Ms. Smith's real name is Vickie Lynn Marshall. She was married to Mr. Marshall for 14 months before he passed.

[13]*Marshall v. Marshall*, 547 U.S. 293 (2006). Sadly, Ms. Smith passed away from drug ingestion in February 2007. She was not alive in 2011 when the Supreme Court affirmed the bankruptcy court's denial of her claim against the estate. *Stern v. Marshall*, 131 S.Ct. 2594 (2011).

[14]Jared S. Renfroe, "Does Tennessee Need Another Tort? The Disappointed Heir in Tennessee and Tortious Interference with Expectancy of Inheritance or Gift," 77 *Tenn. L. Rev.* 385 (2010).

[15]*Bush v. Schiavo*, 885 So.2d 321 (Fla. 2004).

an agent to make healthcare decisions, rules for determination of which family members may make decisions on healthcare for the incapacitated, and rules on immunities and liabilities of healthcare givers in cases covered under the act. Living wills under the act are labeled "Declaration Relating to the Use of Life-Sustaining Treatment."

In *Cruzan v. Director, Missouri Dept. of Health*, 497 U.S. 261 (1990), the Supreme Court required that the right to be removed from life-support systems is valid if the individual evidenced a desire to exercise that right in advance of illness or disability. The court also ruled that the decision can be made by others for the individual, according to requirements and standards established by the states. Most states now have laws that establish the procedures for allowing others to make the decision for those who are in a coma or, as in the Schiavo matter, in a persistent vegetative state. Known as "absence of advance directive statutes," these laws provide authority to spouses, parents, and children to petition a court for withdrawal of life support and life-sustaining systems if they can provide proof "supported by clear and convincing evidence that the decision would have been the one the patient would have chosen had the patient been competent or, if there is no indication of what the patient would have chosen, that the decision is in the patient's best interest."[16] The original *Schiavo* (851 So.2d 182 [Fla. App. 2003]) case on the Florida lack-of-advance-directive statute provides insight into how these statutes are applied, with strong deference to the statements and testimony of those closest to the patient.

PRACTICAL TIP

The living will must be done cautiously, methodically, and with a full understanding of the laws that apply.

Living Trusts

One of the more popular property transfer forms over the past five years is the **living trust**. The living trust is a revocable trust established during the testator's life. It can be revoked at any time and the testator still retains control of the trust assets. However, upon the testator's death, the trust property passes according to the provisions of the trust and probate is avoided.

These trusts must be executed formally and can involve large amounts of paperwork for compliance with the tax laws. While touted as a tax-avoidance device, there is nothing accomplished with a living trust that cannot be done through a will and the use of joint tenancy ownership (see Chapter 8).

Revocation of Wills

A will can be revoked in several different ways: (1) by physical destruction of the document, (2) by execution of a subsequent document, or (3) by operation of law.

Revocation by Physical Destruction

Revocation occurs when there is mutilation or destruction of the will by either the testator or by someone acting at the testator's request. In addition to the physical destruction of the document, the testator must have intent to destroy the will. The degree of destruction varies across states. For example, some states recognize crossing out portions of a will as a revocation of those portions of the will, whereas other states treat such an act as a destruction of the entire will.

---

[16]F.S.A. § 765.401 (2003).

The types of acts sufficient for physical destruction include cutting, tearing, burning, and writing *void* or *canceled* across the will. If there are copies of the will, some states provide that the destruction of one of the copies constitutes revocation of the will, while other states require the destruction of the original.

Revocation by Execution of a Subsequent Document

A will can be revoked by the subsequent execution of another instrument. A second will serves to revoke a prior will. An addition to a will (called a **codicil**), which may contain provisions inconsistent with the original will, also serves to revoke certain portions of the will. Revocation by a subsequent document is valid only if the subsequent document is executed with the same formalities required for the execution of the original will.

Generally, a subsequent will contains a clause that provides that the testator "hereby revokes any prior wills and codicils." However, such a clause is not required. The will that is latest in time of execution serves to revoke prior wills.

In jurisdictions that recognize holographic wills, a holographic will or codicil can serve to revoke a prior formally executed will so long as the holographic instrument complies with all validity requirements.

CONSIDER 17.10   Charles Uhl executed a will in 1946, found in his safe-deposit box after his death. The will contained several interlineations and markings made by Uhl in colored pencil, including a notation in the left-hand margin of the first page that stated, "Revise whole mess."

Uhl's sister visited him while he was alive and they found the will. His sister told him the will would not be valid and Uhl replied, "The will is still good and is good anywhere. Oh, nuts! I am going to make a new one. I will get it done. Don't worry about it."

When the will was offered for probate, the sister objected because her share was small and she contended the will had been revoked. What was the result? *In re Estate of Uhl,* 81 Cal. Rptr. 436 (1969).

Revocation by Operation of Law

Most states have provisions that require the revocation or partial revocation of a will when the testator's family circumstances change between the time of the will's execution and the testator's death. For example, many states provide that divorce automatically serves to revoke a will at least with regard to property left to the former spouse. In other states, marriage after the execution of the will entitles the new spouse to at least an intestate share of the property.

Perhaps one of the most common partial revocations of wills occurs when testators have children after execution of the will but before death. Children born or adopted after will execution are called **pretermitted** children. Many states provide that these children are entitled to receive the amount they would have received through intestate succession.

PROBATE

Purpose of Probate

Probate includes all legal proceedings required to accomplish the passing of title of the decedent's property to those for whom it was intended. Probate involves determination of the existence of a valid will and defenses to the will, the existence of heirs if no will exists, the proper construction of the will, the collection of the decedent's assets, the payment of debts, and the distribution of the estate. The procedures and terminology vary from state to state, but the following sections cover the basic processes.

Appointment of Party to Administer Probate

In every state, some party or parties is appointed to carry out the administrative details involved in probate. If the decedent died intestate, the party is often called an **administrator** or **administratrix**. If the decedent died testate, the party is often called an **executor** or **executrix**. Under the UPC, the party is called a **personal representative** regardless of whether the decedent died testate or intestate.

No matter which name applies, the probate administrator is responsible for all transfers, payments, and distributions of the estate. In many cases, because of the substantial sums and valuable property in an estate, the administrators are required to post a bond for the duration of the probate. Under the UPC and in most states, the bond requirement can be waived in the testator's will or by statute, particularly in cases where the sole beneficiary will act as the personal representative. Waiving the bond can mean a substantial savings in the cost of administering the estate.

Who serves as the probate administrator (when not specified in the will) is provided for by state statute. If the party appointed in the will is unable to serve or if the decedent died intestate, the court follows the state statute that specifies who qualifies and in what order for serving as a probate administrator. In many states, the surviving spouse has first priority for appointment.

Application for or Opening of Probate

Probate proceedings are opened when an application or petition is filed, generally with the probate division or probate court located in the area where the decedent lived. However, other courts may have jurisdiction. For example, if the decedent owned property in a second state, the probate court in that area would also have jurisdiction for probate. In the case of an estate located in multiple jurisdictions, one probate court will serve as the court for hearings, petitions, and so on, and the other courts will then recognize those proceedings for purposes of property distribution and carrying out that court's orders.

Parties who can petition for probate include heirs, devisees, persons entitled to appointment as personal representatives, and creditors. Basically, any party with an interest in the estate can open probate.

The application or petition will attach any (and all) wills if the decedent died testate. The petitioner must serve notice upon potential heirs and interested parties that application has been filed, and the notice includes a hearing date. Because the purpose of the hearing is to determine the validity of the will, anyone who wants to challenge the will must prepare to present evidence at the hearing on the will's admission to probate. Many of the cases in this chapter involved appeals from hearings where wills were challenged.

Collection of Assets

Once the will is admitted to probate or the finding of intestacy has been made, the administrator or personal representative must collect the estate's assets. Most states and the UPC require the personal representative to file an inventory with the court within a certain period after appointment. The inventory is sent to heirs and devisees. The administrator is fully accountable for all assets and also fully responsible for collecting any funds due to the estate and all property the decedent owned.

Determination and Payment of Debts

In addition to collecting and reporting assets, the personal representative must determine whether valid debts exist and if they should be paid. Most states require the publication of a notice of probate in a public newspaper to alert creditors to file a claim with the estate. For example, under the UPC, the personal representative is required to publish notice of the opening of probate once a week for three weeks in a newspaper of general circulation. Creditors then have four months from the time of first publication to file a claim with the estate or have their claim forever barred from collection.

Once the personal representative receives a creditor's claim, the personal representative reviews it and makes the decision to allow or disallow it. If a claim is disallowed, the creditor always has the opportunity to bring an action against the estate to have a judicial determination on the claim's validity.

Distribution of Estate

Whether the decedent died testate or intestate, probate determines who will be entitled to what portions of the estate after creditors' claims, taxes, and administrative expenses have been paid.

In the case of intestacy, the court will hold a hearing or trial for the adjudication of heirs. In the case of a testate estate, the court may still be required to construe the provisions of an ambiguous will. In interpreting a will, the court's primary rule is to follow the intent of the testator. If intent is not clear from the document itself, the court may use extrinsic evidence to clarify the intentions of the testator.

After the determination of heirs and the interpretation of the will, the property is distributed to the appropriate parties. Different terms describe the types of gifts given to heirs of the decedent. A gift of real property is called a **devise** and the recipient a **devisee**; a gift of money is called a **legacy** and the recipient a **legatee**; a gift of personal property is called a **bequest** (general term that includes legacies).

Occasionally, the distribution of gifts is impossible. For example, a testator may have left a specific item of property or a legacy to an heir who has predeceased the testator. In the absence of the testator's provision or a state statute that permits such a gift to go to the heirs of the predeceased recipient, the gift will **lapse**, become part of the residuary estate, and revert to those who are entitled to that portion of the estate. If there is no clause devising the residuary estate, the specific gift would be distributed according to the laws of intestacy.

Also, there are times when a testator has left a specific item of property to an heir and, although the heir is still in existence, the property is not. For example, a testator may have left a "2009 Honda Accord to my nephew Ralph." If the testator does not own the Honda Accord at death, the gift adeems or fails completely. This doctrine of **ademption** will apply regardless of the intention of the testator.

Closing of Probate

Once all of the preceding steps are complete, the personal representative can close the estate. Closing the estate may require a hearing or, as under the UPC, may be done through an informal filing of a closing inventory and accounting.

PRACTICAL TIP

Will contests, even among families with the best of feelings, are not uncommon. Clarity in language is critical. Careful drafting avoids confusion and will contests.

Once the proper procedures are complete, the estate is closed and cannot be reopened to relitigate creditors' and heirs' claims. Closing an estate operates as an estoppel for future actions unless there has been fraud or misconduct in the administration of the estate or a failure to follow the statutory processes.

Estate Tax Implications

The transfer of property from the decedent to the heirs may involve tax issues on parts of the estate and the heirs. The estate may be taxed at both the federal and state levels. States vary significantly in their laws on computation of the estate's value as well as in tax rates. At the federal level, the amount of tax due on an estate subject to taxation is computed according to tables provided by the federal government, and certain deductions are allowed before the taxable value is actually determined. For example, the federal government allows a marital deduction for a probate transfer of property between spouses, a deduction that consists of the entire amount of the estate. Currently, the federal estate tax is on an annual increasing exclusion schedule.[17] Estates valued below the federal exclusion are not required to pay federal estate taxes.

The federal laws also provide estate tax exemptions for family-owned businesses when the death of one of the principals in that business occurs. The time limitation for filing a federal estate tax return is nine months, which can be extended upon an estimation of no tax or a payment of the amount estimated to be due.

At the state level, there may be inheritance taxes in addition to estate taxes. An inheritance tax is one that applies to heirs, requiring them to pay a certain percentage of the amount they receive from an estate. The inheritance tax is an obligation of the heir, not the estate.

CAUTIONS AND CONCLUSIONS

There are two ways to die: intestate and testate. If you die intestate, there are laws in each state to provide for the distribution of your estate. Those laws can be complex and may not distribute your property according to your desires. The other way to die, testate, is preferred. The execution of a will not only assures that your property is distributed in the way in which you would like to see it distributed, it can also save time and money in the administration of your estate.

A will should be executed with witnesses and at a time when those witnesses can verify that the will is done voluntarily and with a clear-enough presence of mind to understand what property is being given away in the will and who the beneficiaries are.

When executing codicils or new wills, use great caution to be certain that the right will and your correct intentions are carried out by the valid document.

Living wills provide for withdrawal from life support or life-sustaining processes.

The probate process is a series of mandatory notices and hearings that ensure the correct and orderly distribution of the decedent's property.

---

[17]The issue of estate tax has become a political one, with a strong movement for elimination of the so-called "death tax."

KEY TERMS

CHAPTER PROBLEMS

1. On August 9, 1983, Mr. Emmett King was taken to the emergency room at Halifax Memorial Hospital with a leaking abdominal aneurysm. He was in extreme pain and suffering from shock from the loss of blood. He was given considerable pain medication including meperidine (Demerol), morphine, and diazepam (Valium). Meperidine and morphine both may decrease mental awareness.

   He was placed on a respirator with an intratracheal tube and taken to intensive care. At about 1:00 p.m., Delores King, one of King's daughters, visited him with Jeff Crowder, King's grandson. Jeff went to the waiting area and asked Patsy West and Rhoda Joyner to come and witness a codicil that King was executing. When they arrived, Delores read the codicil to King and asked him if he understood that he was giving Jeff his business and the real property on which it was located. King nodded that he did. Delores helped guide King's hand across the document for a signature. Patsy and Rhoda signed as witnesses. The witnesses indicated that Mr. King was aware of them and what was happening. The codicil was executed at 1:00 p.m., and King died at 2:15 p.m. Dr. Richard Frazier, King's doctor, said that King was in a semi-coma during most of the morning and had been sedated. Dr. Frazier believed that King would have been incapable of knowingly executing the document.

   Prior to the execution of the codicil, King's wife, children, and grandchildren received his estate. With the codicil, Jeff got most of it. The trial court found the will and codicil to be valid, and Thomas King, a son, appealed. Is the will/codicil valid? Discuss all issues. *In the Matter of the Will of Emmett J. King*, 342 S.E.2d 394 (N.C. 1986).

2. In 1984, Alexander Tolin executed a will under which the residue of his estate was to be devised to his friend Adair Creaig. The will was prepared by Steven Fine, Tolin's attorney, and executed in Fine's office. The original will was retained by Fine, and a blue-backed photocopy was given to Tolin.

   In 1989, Tolin executed a codicil to the will that changed the residuary beneficiary from Creaig to Broward Art Guild, Inc. The codicil was also prepared by Fine, who retained the original and gave Tolin a blue-backed photocopy of the original executed codicil. Tolin died in 1990.

   Six months before his death, he told his neighbor, Ed Weinstein, who was a retired attorney, that he had made a mistake and wished to revoke the codicil and reinstate Creaig as the residuary beneficiary. Weinstein told Tolin he could do this by tearing up the original codicil. Tolin handed Weinstein a blue-backed document that Tolin said was the original codicil. Weinstein looked at the document—it appeared to him to be the original—and gave it back to Tolin. Tolin then tore up and destroyed the document with the intent and for the purpose of revocation.

   Some time after Tolin's death, Weinstein spoke with Fine and found out for the first time that the original will and codicil had been held by Fine. Tolin had torn up the blue-backed copy that had been given to Tolin at the time of execution. The document that Tolin tore up was an exact photocopy of the will.

   Tolin's personal representative petitioned the court to have the will and codicil admitted to probate. Creaig filed a petition to determine if there had been a revocation of the codicil. Had there been a revocation of the will? *In re Estate of Tolin*, 622 So. 2d 988 (Fla. Dist. Ct. App. 1993).

3. The heirs of Vern V. Walls filed a will contest alleging that the last will and testament of Vern V. Walls was the result of undue influence by Cyril DeClercq

(brother of Kathryn Walls, Vern's predeceased wife) and Floyd DeClercq (nephew of Kathryn).

Vern V. Walls died on March 31, 1986, at the age of 79. Kathryn had died two months earlier after a long illness. Walls and Kathryn had one child who had predeceased them at age 14. Walls was survived by several brothers and sisters. Cyril is Kathryn's brother. Prior to Kathryn's death, Vern's and Kathryn's wills provided that on the death of the survivor, their estate would be divided equally between the Walls heirs and the DeClercq heirs.

On March 15, 1986, Vern, then in the hospital for emphysema, executed a new will that directed the bulk of Vern's estate, valued at approximately $300,000, be given to the DeClercq heirs. Only $34,000 in cash bequests were given to the Walls heirs.

Harold Tenney, the original lawyer for the 1985 wills, testified that he represented Vern on a roof problem subsequent to the will execution but that their relationship terminated over the roof problem. Donald G. Baird, Cyril's lawyer, drew up the new will as well as a power of attorney from Vern to Cyril. He was contacted by Cyril to handle these matters for Vern. Is there undue influence? *In the Matter of the Estate of Walls*, 561 N.E.2d 344 (Ill. 1990).

4. William and Margaret Pearl Phillips, husband and wife, executed a joint will for the disposition of their property. The will contained the following clause:

It is the intention of the testators that the surviving testator shall have the right by codicil to change the bequests of equal division referred to said testator's heirs, but may not change the bequests to the heirs of the first deceased testator.

William died first. Margaret drafted a codicil that changed the distribution of the property to William's heirs. Upon her death, William's heirs challenged the admission of the will to probate on the grounds that the codicil violated a joint contract to make a will. What is the result? *In re Estate of Philips*, 195 N.W.2d 486 (Wis. 1972).

5. D. W. Elmer died testate, and a provision in his will was as follows: *"THIRD: I make no provision for my brothers, Jake N. Elmer, Henry Elmer, nor for my sisters, Lena Elmer, Rachel Martell, and Marie Brown, all of whom are financially so fixed that they can well live without any benefits from my estate."*

Unfortunately, D. W. did not dispose of all of his property under the provisions of the will. To whom will the property be given? *In re Estate of Elmer*, 210 N.W.2d 815 (N.D. 1973).

6. On February 13, 1956, Philip Bogner made his last will and testament. One portion of the will gave a one-half interest in some real and personal property to his daughter Helen Bogner Fallgren and her husband, Curtis Fallgren. At the time of the execution of the will, Helen and Curtis were married and had eight children. From 1946 to 1956, Curtis was employed by Philip and received a salary of $5,800 as well as a furnished home.

In 1956, the Fallgrens moved to Oregon to run a poultry ranch that had been purchased using a loan on an insurance policy Philip had purchased for Helen. Philip repaid that loan when it became evident the Fallgrens would not. Sometime thereafter, a physician and Helen told Philip that Curtis had been involved in depraved moral conduct including incestuous relationships with one of his daughters and that such activity had continued for a number of years.

Helen obtained a divorce from Curtis in 1965 on the grounds of infidelity and returned home to North Dakota with her children to live with her father. Bogner told several people including a family counselor, his sister, and one of his employees that he was going to disinherit his son-in-law. Bogner died on September 3, 1968, and portions of his will read as follows:

THIRD: To my daughter, Helen Bogner Falgren and her husband Curtis Falgren, or to the survivor of them …

SIXTH: I appoint my daughter, Helen Bogner Falgren, to be my Executrix under this Will, and if she fails or ceases to act, I appoint Curtis Falgren Sr., husband of my daughter, Helen Bogner Falgren, to be the Executor and successor Trustee of the trust hereinabove provided. If my daughter does not survive me, or dies before a grandchild of mine attains the age of 21 years, without having appointed a guardian of the persons and estates of my grandchildren, I appoint Curtis Falgren, Sr. to be guardian of the persons of such grandchildren and their estates.

Lines had been forcefully drawn through the references to Curtis. The obliterations did not exist at the time the will was originally executed. Has there been an effective revocation? *In re Estate of Bogner*, 184 N.W.2d 718 (N.D. 1971).

7. John C. Ramsey, Sr. (Senior), executed a will in the last months of his life that left the bulk of his estate to Melody Taylor, his paramour. Senior's relationships with his son and grandsons were strained and his will included the following clause:

I have intentionally provided significant, yet smaller amounts for my son and grandsons because they have for several years alienated my affections by being irresponsible, contentious, and constantly seeking financial support from me rather than providing for themselves.

I have made provisions for MELODY J. TAYLOR because MELODY J. TAYLOR provides me care and support.

Senior was suffering from cancer and renal failure, and his pain was extraordinary. His doctors prescribed high doses of morphine, which Melody administered. Senior died from an overdose of morphine.

John Ramsey, Jr. (John II), Senior's son, challenged the validity of the will on the grounds of undue influence as well as felonious killing of a testator by a beneficiary. The trial court found there was undue influence and refused to admit the will to probate. Melody appealed. *Ramsey v. Taylor*, 999 P.2d 1178 (Or. App. 2000).

8. Slusarenko's (the decedent) first wife, Juanita Slusarenko, died in 1986. Around early 1988, Jack met Wilma, a woman 26 years his junior. In April 1988, Jack wrote that he had been sad since Juanita's death, but that he had been spending time with Wilma and she took his mind off his pain. He added that his children "seem to resent me keeping company with her. But [I] think I have my life to live & I'm a lot happier now since I met her."

Jack and Wilma married in March 1990. Jack did not tell his children ahead of time, and tensions soon developed between Wilma and the children. According to Jack's friend Rosa Howton, Wilma did not encourage Jack to be with his family and "seemed to want to keep Jack in a box." Jack and Wilma also had a turbulent relationship. Jack complained to his children and his friends about Wilma's cooking, her failure to get a job or help with the farmwork, and her spending. After Jack and Wilma married, the house and yard were extremely dirty and ill-maintained. Jack and Wilma separated and reconciled in 1991, separated again in 1997, divorced in January 1998, and remarried in December 1998.

Between 1986 and 1998, Jack made five different written estate plans. In late 1998, Jack and Wilma began seeing attorney David Gallaher. Gallaher's 13 years of private practice included a good deal of estate planning and work on many mental commitment cases. When Gallaher realized that Jack wanted to talk about a will, he explained that he would be representing Jack and that he needed to speak with Jack alone. Gallaher met with Jack for a little over half an hour on the first visit and had five or six total meetings with him in November and December. Although Wilma came along to the meetings, Gallaher preferred to talk with Jack alone.

Jack told Gallaher that he loved and had no ill will toward his children but wanted to use his assets to ensure that he would be taken care of. Jack told Gallaher that his children were successful, implying, without expressly stating, that the children did not need an inheritance. Jack did not want to tell his children about the change in his estate plan until it was done.

In the 1998 will, Jack left all of his property to Wilma or, if she predeceased him, to his church.

Jack and Wilma did not obtain a marriage license until after all of the documents pertaining to the will were executed. Wilma testified that Jack was still in the hospital when the documents were signed but that they got married as soon after that as possible. On December 22, Jack and Wilma remarried.

At that same time, Jack signed a bargain-and-sale deed (the 1998 deed) transferring the farm from himself individually to himself and Wilma with a right of survivorship. Jack died in July 2000. Wilma sought to enforce the 1998 will and claimed to be the sole beneficiary of his estate and the sole owner of the farm. Ronald J. Slusarenko, Louise Hofer, Patricia D. Shaver, Donald L. Slusarenko, Terri J. Eisele, and David Slusarenko, all but one of Jack's children from his first marriage, challenged Jack's will and deed to Wilma because of undue influence.

The trial court found that Jack had capacity and that there had been no undue influence. The children appealed. Is the will valid or not? Explain whether any of the grounds for challenging a will apply and why. *In re Slusarenko*, 147 P.3d 920 (Or. App. 2006)

9. Wilma has passed away intestate and is survived by the following relatives: her mother, Catherine; her sister, Chris; her granddaughter, Elizabeth (daughter of Wilma's deceased daughter Jill); a grandson, Joe (son of Wilma's living daughter Buddy); daughter Buddy; and a single daughter, Diane. Who is entitled to Wilma's estate?

10. Egon Engers II murdered his mother, Dorothy Engers. Dorothy died testate and her Last Will and Testament left specified personal property to her two children, Egon and a daughter, Laura Jo Jones (formerly Engers), and the estate residue to a testamentary trust. In that Egon murdered his mother he is disqualified from taking any interest in her estate by Oklahoma's slayer statute, 84 O.S.Supp.1994, § 231. However, unbeknownst to Dorothy and Laura, Egon had an illegitimate son, Jason Kyle Hulett, a minor, who now wishes to inherit what his father would have inherited from his mother were he not barred by the statute that precludes a murderer from inheriting from his victim. Laura objects because her mother's will did not acknowledge the existence of such a child and because it would be against public policy to allow the relatives of murderers to inherit. Who is correct? Does Jason have an interest in his grandmother's estate? *Hulett v. First Nat. Bank and Trust Co. in Clinton*, 956 P.2d 879 (Okl. 1998).

**For research activities related to this chapter, go to our text companion website at
www.cengagebrain.com**

CHAPTER 18

ZONING

Property is in its nature timid and seeks protection, and nothing is more gratifying to government than becoming a protector.

John C. Calhoun, March 21, 1834

Local laws that control land use are grouped into one term that describes their effect: **zoning.** The zoning on a piece of property can affect its value, price, and marketability. This chapter answers the following questions: What is zoning? What types of zoning exist? What terms are used in zoning and zoning procedures? Are all forms of zoning constitutional? Is it possible to change or make exceptions to zoning requirements?

PURPOSES

Each community is divided into areas, districts, or zones in which certain activities are permitted and others prohibited. Zoning laws classify property areas and permissible activities. Zoning controls building heights and whether apartments or single-family dwellings may be constructed in any area. Zoning sometimes prohibits construction altogether, such as when homes on a mountainside are prohibited. Zoning is a method of controlling community development. Zoning follows and enforces a **general** or **master plan** for the community so that the community develops in an orderly fashion. Zoning and a master plan prevent the problems and nuisances that result when, for example, residential areas are next to factories.

Zoning laws are, for the most part, local governmental ordinances. Cities and towns act under an enabling statute. In most cases, the enabling statute is based on the **Standard State Zoning Enabling Act**, which was drafted by the U.S. Department of Commerce in the 1920s. This act authorizes local governmental entities to pass zoning laws that "lessen congestion...promote safety...prevent overcrowding... avoid undue concentration of population...and promote health and general welfare."

AUTHORITY

"Promot[ing] health and general welfare" is a broad grant of authority to local government that is grounded, as it were, in the police power clause of the U.S. Constitution (Section 8, cl. 1), which provides that governments exist for the promotion of the health, safety, morals, and general welfare of people. Zoning laws passed for the general welfare purpose fit within this constitutional framework.

To meet the constitutional standard of police power, zoning laws passed must serve some public health, safety, or morals interest. In addition, zoning laws cannot be arbitrary or discriminatory. (These issues are discussed later in the "Methods" section.) Another constitutional issue that arises is whether zoning use restrictions constitute a taking without due process of law as required under the Fourteenth Amendment, an issue covered in Chapter 19.

In the *Village of Euclid, Ohio v. Ambler Realty Co.,* 272 U.S. 365 (1926), the U.S. Supreme Court recognized zoning as constitutional in general, a permissible exercise of police power. Any decreases in land values that result from zoning are not takings that require compensation (see Chapter 19).

METHODS

Generally, zoning begins with a master plan that divides the geographical area (county, city, or town) into districts with varying shapes that will supervise safety, traffic flow, and so on. Once these districts are created, the government entity then passes ordinances for each district. While the zoning standards can vary from district to district, all districts have the same procedural rules and regulations for exemptions and variances. The following sections address the types of rules and regulations in a zoning structure.

Use Restrictions

Use restrictions can be classified into four general categories: residential, commercial or business, industrial, and agricultural. These categories can have subcategories, as when residential is divided into R-1 for single-family dwellings, R-2 for duplex houses, and R-3 for apartments or mobile homes. Industrial districts may be classified according to the nature of the noise, waste, activity, danger, odor, and so on. When subcategories are created, the number 1 is usually associated with the most restrictive land use, as in the example of R-1, which includes generally only single-family dwellings.

Zoning classifications may be cumulative or noncumulative. In a **cumulative classification**, the lesser restricted areas allow all of the activities permitted in more restrictive areas. If cumulative zoning existed in the R-1 example above, then R-2 districts would allow single-family dwellings to be included along with R-2 duplex houses, and R-3 districts would allow single-family dwellings and duplex houses, along with R-3 apartments and mobile homes. Some sample classifications are listed below:

1. Residential, single-family
2. Residential, multiple-family
3. Residential, apartment
4. Commercial, office
5. Commercial, business
6. Industrial

For example, an area zoned commercial could have residential uses within it under cumulative zoning. However, the reverse does not apply, and no industrial or commercial activity would be permitted in residential areas.

In a **noncumulative classification**, only the activities specified by the applicable zone are permitted. For example, in R-2 areas, there would be no single-family dwellings. An area zoned industrial or commercial in a noncumulative system cannot have residences. Noncumulative zoning prevents nuisance actions by prohibiting homes and apartments in industrial areas.

Limitations on Use Restrictions

In developing their zoning systems, local governments are constrained by constitutional protections. One of the issues raised repeatedly in challenging zoning ordinances is single-family dwelling limitations, particularly in areas where housing costs are high and, with zoning, less costly forms of housing are not available for a significant portion of the population. Courts have held zoning laws that strictly control the use of manufactured homes to be valid as long as the community is able to show that reasonable housing is available for various income ranges. *Mississippi Manufactured Housing Ass'n v. Board of Sup'rs of Tate County*, 878 So.2d 180 (Miss. App. 2004); *cert. denied, Assoc. v. Bd. of Super.*, 878 So.2d 67 (Miss. 2004).

Changes in Use Restrictions

One of the zoning issues that has resulted from the halt in residential developments has been the petitions by developers to change the use restrictions on their land in order to use the land for developing, generally, denser and cheaper housing. These changes in uses, also known as reclassifications, are permitted if the governing body, such as the city, is able to show that the zoning restrictions were either a mistake or that there is a public need that has resulted from a change in the character of the area. The following case deals with an issue of justification for a change in zoning classification.

GARDNER V. CITY OF TUPELO

76 So.3d 204 (Miss. App. 2011)
From Hay to PUD: Big Lots to Townhomes

FACTS

Wilson Coleman owned 45 acres of residential property that he had intended to develop as a large-lot residential area. However, when the real estate market took a down-turn, Mr. Coleman filed a "Request for Rezoning" with the City of Tupelo's Department of Planning and Community Development to have his property rezoned from large-lot residential to a planned unit development (PUD) consisting of single-family homes and a retirement community.

The Planning Department reviewed the request and issued a report recommending that Coleman's request for rezoning be approved. The City Council held a public hearing regarding the rezoning request. Thomas Gardner appeared at the hearing and opposed the rezoning. However, the City Council voted to approve Coleman's request. The trial court affirmed the City Council's decision. Gardner appealed.

JUDICIAL OPINION

Irving, Presiding Judge

Gardner asserts that there is insufficient evidence that the character of the neighborhood has changed or that public need calls for rezoning. Before a zoning board may reclassify property from one zone to another, there must be proof that "(1) a mistake in the original zoning occurred; or (2) a change in the character of the neighborhood occurred that justified rezoning, and a public need existed for the rezoning."

At the outset, we note that the City of Tupelo contends that the City Council's decision to approve Coleman's request for a PUD does not constitute rezoning, and, therefore, its decision should not be evaluated under the "change or mistake" rule discussed above. The City asserts that PUDs do not eliminate the existing zoning ordinances; instead, PUDs supplement the ordinances with "additional regulations and development restrictions." However, the City cites no Mississippi case law in support of its argument, and we are aware of none. In fact, the Mississippi Supreme Court has consistently categorized PUD designations as rezoning and has evaluated such designations using the "change or mistake" rule. This issue is without merit.

[T]herefore, this Court's analysis will focus on whether there was sufficient evidence that the character of the neighborhood had changed and that rezoning satisfied a public need. There is no bright-line rule as to what constitutes sufficient evidence of change in a neighborhood's character or public need. However, there must be enough evidence for the zoning board to reach an informed decision.

[O]ur supreme court has provided some guidance stating that, at a minimum, a zoning board should consider evidence such as "maps showing a change [in a neighborhood's character] or recent rezoning in the area, statistics or other evidence of growth in the neighborhood, and charts showing the quantity of construction [in the area]," or other comparable evidence.

The City argues that the rezoning is justified based on the changing character of the area. Specifically, the City points out that Toyota plans to build a plant near the rezoned property and that a private school had recently been built in the area. However, the record contains no evidence as to how either the Toyota plant, which will be located seven miles from the property, or the school has changed the character of the neighborhood. Furthermore, this Court has held that the potential for future development does not constitute evidence of a change in a neighborhood's character.

In this case, the City's rationale for its decision to rezone the property is based on speculative future changes in the neighborhood's character. The City argues that the character of the neighborhood has changed because a Toyota plant will be built seven miles from the property and because a school has been built near the property. Additionally, there is no quantification of how the Toyota plant will impact the rezoned property. Instead, Coleman merely alluded to anticipated future growth in the area following the plant's completion. Likewise, there was no evidence as to how the recently built private school had changed the neighborhood.

Finally, we note that the report issued by the City's Planning Department describes the area as "rural in character with hayfields, pastures, and large[-]house lots." Also, in the report's analysis of whether the changes in the neighborhood warranted the rezoning, the Planning Department concluded that such changes were "not applicable." Based on the report's description of the area, we can only interpret this to mean that such changes did not exist.

The record before this Court simply does not support a change in the neighborhood's character that warrants rezoning. Insufficient proof of such a change leads this Court to conclude that the City Council's decision was arbitrary and capricious.

While an inquiry into public need is unnecessary given our holding that Coleman failed to present the City Council with clear and convincing evidence of a change in the neighborhood's character, we pause briefly to note that even the evidence presented to the City Council regarding public need was insufficient to justify rezoning. At the hearing, the City Council heard testimony that the proposed residential development would assist in attracting retirees to Tupelo, which promotes itself as a certified retirement community. However, there was no evidence of an existing public need for a new retirement community. The City Council also heard testimony that demographic trends indicate that people prefer living in higher-density neighborhoods, like Coleman's proposed development. However, there was no presentation of empirical data supporting the existence of such trends. The only concrete evidence presented to the City Council regarding public need consisted of testimony from Pat Falkner, the city planner. Falkner opined that based on projected population growth, future housing needs would require the construction of approximately 450 houses each year and that currently only 120 to 130 houses are being built annually. However, Falkner provided no estimate of when the City's increased housing needs would occur.

Based on our review of the record, we are unable to find any evidence upon which the City Council could rely upon to justify rezoning the property. Without a change in the neighborhood's character or an existing public need, this Court must conclude that the City Council's decision was arbitrary and capricious.

Reversed.

CASE QUESTIONS

1. What does the developer say justifies the change and what is the court's problem with the evidence related to that justification?
2. What evidence did the city present on public need and what was the problem with that evidence?
3. List the two requirements for a city's change to an existing zoning classification.

CONSIDER 18.1 The Panola County Board of Supervisors rezoned a five-acre parcel owned by Chris Aldridge from an agricultural to an industrial classification and also granted a special exception to Aldridge to operate a recycling facility/junkyard on the property. Lent Thomas, a neighbor, appealed on the grounds that the county board had no reason for the change. Aldridge argued that the County made a mistake in its zoning, but there was no evidence related to how there was a mistake. There was evidence that there are numerous businesses that have developed along the highway where Aldridge's land is located on adjoining properties. Some are industrial; some are commercial. Some are supply companies. There are many retail sales locations for automobiles as well as lumber supply companies, schools, and private homes, including some farms. Aldridge's property had been used for a number of years as a concrete plant.

The evidence also showed that the county was in need of another junkyard because there was currently no place for solid waste within 10 miles of Aldridge's proposed junkyard. Determine whether the County acted properly in changing the use and allowing the operation of the junkyard. *Thomas v. Board of Sup'rs of Panola County,* 45 So.3d 1173 (Miss. 2010). ▬▬▬▬ ∎

Intensity Zoning

Intensity zoning regulates location and size of structures on land. Intensity regulations generally take the following forms:

1. Building-height limitations
2. Setbacks for buildings (minimum distance between the street or sidewalk and the structure)
3. Minimum lot sizes (may be total square feet or minimum length and width)
4. Maximum structures per area (often called *density*—specifies, for example, the number of houses that may be built in an R-1 tract)
5. Floor area ratios (sets a maximum amount of floor area per lot; for example, a 10-to-1 ratio would permit a 10-story building to occupy an entire lot or a 20-story building to occupy half the lot).

Aesthetic Zoning

The purpose of **aesthetic zoning** is to control or improve the beauty of an area. Zoning that is purely aesthetic is not valid in a majority of the states. However, if aesthetic controls can be tied to or coupled with a health or welfare purpose, then they are valid. Courts recognize the public interest in aesthetic controls and uphold such zoning. For example, an aesthetic zoning ordinance that prohibits construction of homes on the side of a mountain to preserve the beauty of the mountain is not a stand-alone reason for upholding the ordinance. However, the city or county could show that there is great risk in constructing homes on the mountainside because of possible slides, destruction of the homes, injury to others, and the need for city safety and rescue equipment. With this explanation, the ordinance becomes a valid exercise of police power for safety reasons, not just aesthetic ones.

Aesthetic zoning has been used to preserve historical towns and portions of cities by controlling the type of architecture, its repair, and alteration.[1] These types of zoning ordinances are valid because they preserve historical areas as well as the resulting tourist business.

The following case deals with an issue of zoning aesthetics.

CATSIFF V. McCARTY

274 P.3d 1063 (Wash. App. 2012)
The Legal Tentacles of Zoning on the Inland Octopus Toy Store

FACTS

In 1991, the city of Walla Walla enacted a sign ordinance as part of a coordinated downtown revitalization plan to further central business district (CBD) renovation and to preserve and restore its historic resources. The 1991 sign code's stated purpose was to improve the city's visual quality and limited wall signs to 25 percent of a wall area. In addition, no combination of sign areas may exceed 150 square feet per street frontage and signs cannot extend higher than 30 feet above grade.

In March 2004, Robert Catsiff opened the Inland Octopus toy store on Main Street. He applied for, and was issued, a sign permit. In February 2010, desiring to change business locations, Mr. Catsiff leased 7 E. Main Street and told the owner he wanted to paint a wall sign depicting a hiding octopus on the exterior back wall of his store. In late April 2010, Mr. Catsiff painted a wall sign depicting an octopus hiding behind a rainbow over the rear entrance of the store. He did not apply for a permit before painting it. In September, Mr. Catsiff painted on the store front an octopus hiding behind several buildings with a rainbow above the buildings. The front sign exceeds the city's height and width limits.

Acting Walla Walla City Manager, Tim McCarty, issued a notice of civil violation to Mr. Catsiff and his landlord regarding both signs on October 14, 2010, for violating the city's sign code permitting requirements, and the sign size and height requirements of the sign code and the downtown design standards. At the violation hearing, Mr. Catsiff stipulated factually to his violations, but asserted the regulations were unconstitutional. The city's hearing examiner concluded he violated the WWMC by failing to get sign permits and further ruled the front sign constituted a continuing violation of the size and height requirements of both the sign code and the downtown design standards.

Mr. Catsiff appealed to the superior court and the court rejected Mr. Catsiff's constitutional claims and affirmed the hearing examiner's decision. Mr. Catsiff appealed.

JUDICIAL OPINION

Brown, Judge

The issue is whether the trial court erred in deciding the city's sign-and-height code restrictions did not violate Mr. Catsiff's free speech rights under the state and federal constitutions.

First, Mr. Catsiff incorrectly contends the octopus signs on his business were not commercial speech. The Supreme Court has said commercial speech is "expression related solely to the economic interests

---

[1] *Brick Haus, Inc. v. Board of Adjustment,* 723 N.W.2d 452 (Iowa App. 2006).

of the speaker and its audience." The octopus signs meet both formulations.

Mr. Catsiff named his toy store "Inland Octopus." He designed a store logo depicting an octopus hiding behind inland buildings. He displayed images of his Inland Octopus logo and rainbows on his original storefront and in advertising for his store. Mr. Catsiff admits he used an octopus on his storefront to convey "[t]hat its [sic] a wonderful experience to come into my store and a wonderful place to buy toys." Since the purpose of the sign was economic, the sign would be characterized as commercial speech.

Second, because the city restricted commercial speech, we must decide whether, as Mr. Catsiff contends, the city met its burden of justifying the restrictions because they were narrowly tailored to protect the city's substantial interest in traffic safety and aesthetics.

Walla Walla's wall sign size and height restrictions do not limit what a business owner may say or depict in a wall sign. The requirements in the sign code regulate size and placement.

The city satisfies the reasonableness test. The legislative history shows the city carefully considered its sign size and height restrictions. Its sign code was a product of its stated policy of "working with downtown businessmen to develop a workable sign code specifically for the downtown area." A building improvement guide was commissioned which recommended a "sign should not dominate; its shape and proportions should fit your building just as a window or door fits." It suggested "[s]ome types of signs are not appropriate, including … oversized signs … applied over the upper facade." The city used those considerations when choosing its sign size and height limitation in 1991, and it continues to rely on them. The city's consideration of such issues demonstrates rea-

sonable legislative balancing based on local study and experience which satisfies any calibration duty.

Here, the sign code purpose section states, "The purpose of this section is to accommodate and promote: sign placement consistent with the character and intent of the zoning district; proper sign maintenance; elimination of visual clutter; and creative and innovative sign design. To accomplish this purpose, the posting, displaying, erecting, use, and maintenance of signs shall occur in accordance with this Chapter." Mr. Catsiff argues the purpose section is inadequate because it does not use the words "aesthetics" or "traffic safety." But, the section analogously discusses "visual clutter." The sign code manifests its interest in traffic safety where it explains it does not apply to a "sign which is not visible to motorists or pedestrians on any public right-of-way." Notably, the city has provided a legislative history showing the wall sign size and height restrictions were adopted as part of a comprehensive plan to address aesthetics and traffic control. Thus, the city has demonstrated a legitimate regulatory interest in adopting its sign restriction ordinances.

In sum, the city shows its restrictions were content neutral, reasonable, and supported by a legitimate regulatory interest. We hold the city has met its burden of showing the ordinances are lawfully justified.

Affirmed.

CASE QUESTIONS

1. List the three factors the court lists that must be used in determining whether a sign code is legal.
2. What are the purposes of the Walla Walla sign restrictions?
3. What advice would you offer a business owner such as Mr. Catsiff?

CONSIDER 18.2   Nestled in the Mount Washington Valley, the town of Conway, New Hampshire, historically has been a tourist destination for activities in the White Mountain National Forest. Route 16 links the villages of Conway and North Conway and offers striking views of the mountains and ledges to the west. Substantial commercial development, primarily along this highway, has rendered part of the town a shoppers' mecca. Hundreds of signs draw tourists in the day and evening hours to the shopping centers, lodging facilities, and restaurants clustered in the villages of Conway and North Conway.

In 1982, the town of Conway passed a zoning ordinance requiring all property owners to obtain a permit from the town zoning officer before erecting a sign. The same zoning ordinance prohibited signs "illuminated from within," but allows signs illuminated by external lights.

Michael Asselin, the owner of Mario's, a restaurant on Route 16, purchased a sign that was illuminated from within and erected it on his property. The town notified Asselin that the sign was in violation of the ordinance. Asselin challenged the authority of Conway to regulate commercial speech (his sign) solely for the purpose of "preserving scenic vistas" and "retaining the character of a country community." Is Conway's restriction of the types of signs for its businesses covered as permissible zoning? *Asselin v. Town of Conway*, 628 A.2d 247 (N.H. 1993).   ▪

Telecommunications, Aesthetic Zoning, and NIMBYs

Cellular phone service is now the preferred method of communication. Many individuals opt not to have landlines, and the result is an increasing number of wireless tower sites needed to accommodate this new form of telecommunications. However, the sites for those towers continue to be problematic for local zoning boards. The so-called NIMBYs, an acronym for "not in my back yard," along with the BANANAs (build absolutely nothing anywhere near anything) and the NoWIMPs (not with my property), were vocal presences at local zoning hearings when telecommunications companies applied for approval for locating cellular phone towers. Responding to active and vocal constituencies, local authorities created blocks for cellular telecommunications companies and their towers.

Congress intervened with Section 332(c) of the Telecommunications Act of 1996, which covers "Mobile Services."[2] The federal law does not preempt local zoning authority over tower locations, but it does place some limitations on local governments in decisions on siting that relate to discreet presence factors. For example, state and local governments cannot engage in unreasonable discrimination among "providers of functionally equivalent services." If they allow telephone wires and cables, then they must allow towers. The Act also prevents state and local governments from prohibiting "the provision of personal wireless services."

To prevent stalling, the Act requires state and local governments to respond within a reasonable time to tower-siting requests. Denials require written reports that include "substantial evidence" supporting that denial. If the denial is based on health claims, the state and local authority must provide something more than community hysteria in its report. There must be scientific and medical evidence to support a denial based upon health claims. For example, a denial on the basis of aesthetics violates the standards of the Act. Telecommunications companies are entitled to expedited judicial review of the denial. The following case deals with the limitations on local zoning authorities when there is an issue of telecommunications structures.

---

[2]47 U.S.C.A. § 332(c).

CROWN COMMUNICATION OF NEW YORK V. DEPARTMENT OF TRANSPORTATION

824 N.E.2d 934 (N.Y. 2005)
The Crowning Towers—Public Objection

FACTS

In 1997, the New York State Police and the Department of Transportation (DOT) (collectively, the State) entered into an agreement with Crown Communication to construct and operate telecommunications towers on state-owned lands and rights-of-way. Under the agreement, Crown could license space on the towers to localities and commercial wireless providers, and the State could co-locate its own communications equipment on the towers.

After Crown identified two potential locations for towers on state-owned property within the City of New Rochelle (the City), the State approved construction of both towers.

In June 2000, Crown and the State gave a public presentation to the Mayor and City Council regarding the purpose and intended use of the two proposed towers. At this meeting, the City voiced no objection to the siting or construction of the towers, and Crown offered space on the facilities to the municipality for use by its public safety agencies. DOT performed an environmental review of both sites. DOT's study found that neither the replacement tower nor the maintenance yard tower would result in any significant adverse environmental or aesthetic impact.

Crown proceeded with the construction of the towers and entered into license agreements with a number of commercial wireless telecommunications providers to lease space on the towers for their equipment. During construction, the City issued a stop work order, contending that the towers were subject to the City's zoning laws and that Crown must apply for a special permit from the City's Planning Board.

The Supreme Court determined that Crown need not comply with local zoning requirements. The Appellate Division also determined that the wireless telecommunications providers are not subject to local zoning regulation and affirmed. The parties appealed.

JUDICIAL OPINION

Graffeo, Justice

In this case we are asked whether the installation of private antennae on two state-owned telecommunications towers is exempt from local zoning regulation.

Under the particular facts and circumstances of this case, we conclude that the commercial telecommunications providers involved in this state project are not required to make applications for special permits.

The City argues that, although the towers themselves are exempt from regulation, no justification exists to extend such immunity to the installation of commercial equipment on the towers. Specifically, the City asserts that it has the right pursuant to its zoning authority to evaluate whether private antennae are necessary to close cellular telecommunications coverage gaps or should be placed elsewhere, and to require some form of aesthetic camouflaging of equipment. In response, Crown and the State contend that the private carriers are entitled to share in the immunity already enjoyed by the state-owned towers. They claim that the State's plan envisions a public-private partnership and that the joint use of its towers facilitates the State's public safety and environmental goals.

…[T]he State submitted evidence of numerous benefits the government's use of the towers would afford the public, which Supreme Court took into account in finding the towers immune from local regulation under the balancing test. For example, the State is currently in the process of developing its telecommunications infrastructure in anticipation of establishing a Statewide Wireless Network (SWN), which will replace outdated systems with a state-of-the-art digital land mobile radio network designed to permit interagency and intergovernmental communications across the state in emergency situations. Consultants retained by the State Police have indicated that in order to operate in the higher frequency range, it will be necessary to construct three to four times the approximately 150 existing state-maintained radio sites. The State has therefore reserved space on the replacement and maintenance yard towers for anticipated SWN use when the network becomes operational.

Additionally, DOT has developed an Intelligent Transportation System (ITS), which monitors traffic flow, weather and road conditions. DOT's Director of Traffic Engineering and Safety stated that the collection of such data aids DOT and public safety entities in being able to "respond to emergency situations, manage and divert traffic, and provide real-time traffic information to motorists," thereby improving the safety of the traveling public and reducing travel times.

Finally, the State has followed a policy of offering space on its towers to local public safety authorities and offered such space on the two towers to the City in this case. Currently, Westchester County has placed antennae on the replacement tower for use by its Department of Public Safety.

… [W]e agree with the Appellate Division that the installation of licensed commercial antennae on the towers should also be accorded immunity because co-location serves a number of significant public interests that are advanced by the State's overall telecommunications plan. At this time, there are apparently more private than public antennae on the towers, but the presence of commercial equipment does not exclusively serve private interests. The private antennae will improve the availability of 911 emergency cellular calls made by the public, thereby promoting the public safety interest central to construction of the State's towers. Significantly, the co-location of public and private equipment also eliminates the need for the proliferation of telecommunications towers, an important environmental and aesthetic public concern. Furthermore, profits derived from licensing space to wireless providers will ultimately aid in financing the construction of the State's telecommunications infrastructure plan.

The fact that the wireless providers will also realize profit from their services does not undermine the public interests served by co-location. In sum, the public and private uses of the towers are sufficiently intertwined to justify exemption of the wireless providers from local zoning regulations.

The order of the Appellate Division should be affirmed.

DISSENTING OPINION
Ciparick, Justice

Because I do not believe the exemption from local zoning regulation accorded to the state-owned telecommunications towers should be applied to the private telecommunications providers here, I respectfully dissent.

The State's immunity from local zoning requirements should not be extended to the private providers. The State has not preempted this area and there is no indication that the local zoning regulations would conflict with the State's purposes. Thus, I would reverse the order of the Appellate Division and reinstate the order of Supreme Court.

CASE QUESTIONS

1. Why is the presence of private users an issue in the case?
2. What test does the court apply in determining whether the towers are exempt from local ordinances?
3. What is the focus of the dissenting justice's opinion?

ETHICAL ISSUE

What interests are the zoning boards balancing as they make the decision to site a telecommunications tower? What economic issues are at stake? One city council member said that not allowing the towers would sentence his city to being a second-class citizen in the business world. What does he mean by that? Who is affected by the tower sitings? What arguments can be made in their favor? What arguments against?

Exclusionary Zoning

Exclusionary zoning controls who comes into the community and in what numbers. Antigrowth ordinances are invalid if they are a permanent block to any use of the land. Restrictions on the rate of development so that services and governmental organization can grow to meet needs serve a legitimate public interest and are permissible forms of regulation.

An area of contention in zoning ordinances and processes has been that of the exclusion of religious structures and church buildings and developments. In 2000, Congress passed the Religious Land Use and Institutionalized Persons Act

NIMBYs protest about other issues such as the location of waste and nuclear depositories, utility plants, and even Wal-Marts. Before applying for zoning approval, applicants should be aware of the psychological impact and likely outcry from the type of facility they propose. Working with the NIMBYs before application for zoning approval may be the key to obtaining approval. For example, some telecommunications companies have turned their cellular towers into works of art that rally the NIMBYs and the community to their side.

(RLUIPA). RLUIPA requires that local government land use regulation on religious organizations meet a standard of strict judicial scrutiny.[3] The federal protections have engendered emotional battles over local zoning and federal control. Cases under the law include church expansions, the creation of church educational facilities, the use of single-family residences for church facilities, and church use and alteration of storefront properties.

Interim Zoning

It may take a city or town some time to perform a study and develop a master plan. In the time it takes for such study and planning, developers may develop segments to frustrate the plan and enjoy the protections of nonconforming use. To alleviate this problem, cities and towns may adopt **interim** or **hold zoning** to prevent uncontrolled development before a comprehensive plan and ordinances are adopted. The interim zoning may be as simple as a requirement of approval before construction or development begins. This prior approval gives the city or town government control before permanent zoning takes effect.

Social Issue Zoning

Zoning provisions that battle social issues through land use controls are known as **social issue zoning**. For example, zoning ordinances have been used to disperse adult theaters and bookstores. In *Young v. American Mini Theaters*, 427 U.S. 50 (1976), the U.S. Supreme Court held that zoning ordinances may classify these types of businesses differently from other movie houses and bookstores for safety purposes, thus upholding the disbursement treatment required by the ordinances. In *City of Renton v. Playtime Theaters, Inc.*, 475 U.S. 41 (1986), the U.S. Supreme Court held that zoning restrictions on adult bookstores are valid under the First Amendment so long as nothing prevents such businesses from locating in other areas of the city. In the following case, a federal appellate court faces the issue of alternative availability.

HOLD FAST TATTOO, LLC V. CITY OF NORTH CHICAGO

580 F.Supp.2d 656 (N.D. Ill. 2008)
The Tattoo Parlor That Left a Legal Mark

FACTS

Hold Fast Tattoo wishes to open a tattoo studio on North Sheridan Road in the City of North Chicago and has obtained a prospective lessor at its desired location. In accordance with North Chicago's zoning ordinance, Hold Fast Tattoo applied for a special use permit to operate a tattoo studio at that location. On June 21, 2007, the Zoning Board of Appeals of North Chicago recommended approval of the permit to its city council. The proposal was discussed at two council meetings, on July 9, 2007, and July 16, 2007, and

Hold Fast Tattoo's (plaintiff) request for a special use permit was ultimately denied. The city council informed Hold Fast that its special use permit was denied because it was "not the kind of business" the council wanted in North Chicago. Hold Fast filed suit.

JUDICIAL OPINION

Moran, Senior District Judge

Plaintiff argues that its right to draw tattoos is protected by the First Amendment Free Speech Clause.

---

[3]42 U.S.C. § 2000cc(a)(1) (2000).

The nature of the right to draw tattoos is a question that has not been directly addressed by the Seventh Circuit nor the Supreme Court. However, we are persuaded by related authority, as well as the decisions of numerous other courts, that the act of tattooing is not constitutionally protected free speech.

The First Amendment protects speech. It also protects expressive conduct, as long as the conduct is "sufficiently imbued with elements of communication to fall within the scope" of the First Amendment. To determine whether an activity warrants First Amendment protection, the court must determine whether there was intent to convey a particularized message and whether there is a great likelihood that the message would be understood by those who view it.

The act of tattooing fails the first prong of this test because the act itself is not intended to convey a particularized message. The very nature of the tattoo artist is to custom-tailor a different or unique message for each customer to wear on the skin. The act of tattooing is one step removed from actual expressive conduct, which is similar to a sound truck, which enables each customer to express a particularized message, but the sound truck vehicle itself is not expressive. Similarly, the tattoo artist's daily work may be used by customers to convey a message, but it is not protected by the First Amendment in and of itself. Because the act of tattooing fails the first prong of the test for First Amendment protection, there is no "message" to be understood by viewers and tattooing must also fail the second prong. Therefore, this court agrees with other courts that have held the act of tattooing is not an act protected by the First Amendment.

Where no fundamental right or suspect class is at issue, "legislation is presumed to be valid and will be sustained if the classification drawn by the statute is rationally related to a legitimate state interest."

Here, Hold Fast Tattoo has not alleged the violation of a suspect class or a fundamental right, so the challenged legislation is presumed valid and will be upheld if the statute's classifications are rationally related to a legitimate state interest…. The special use permit required by North Chicago's zoning ordinance is substantially related to its municipal planning goals. In the motion to dismiss plaintiff's complaint, defendant sets forth numerous municipal planning goals that are advanced by the requirement of a special use permit for plaintiff's business: character, stability, or intended development of the City's central business district; suitability of the location to the proposed use; necessity and desirability of a proposed use in a particular location; and protection of the health and/or safety of the community…. [W]e find defendant's zoning ordinance could be rationally related to a legitimate state interest.

The complaint contains a portion of a sentence that alleges the zoning ordinance "unreasonably requires Plaintiff to submit to controls not imposed on other similarly situated businesses or properties." In order to bring a class of one equal protection claim, a plaintiff must allege that (1) he has been intentionally treated differently from others similarly situated and (2) there is no rational basis for the difference in treatment, or that the differential treatment is due to a "'totally illegitimate animus' toward the plaintiff by the defendant." We cannot conceive of how Hold Fast Tattoo can satisfy the second prong of this test because the grounds for it do not appear in the complaint.

The only deprivation that is alleged in the complaint here is the right to the "use and operation" of plaintiff's business. Plaintiff does not allege, nor can we find a component of the due process clause or an Illinois state law that gives a legitimate claim of entitlement to perform the act of tattooing. Therefore, since plaintiff has not alleged the deprivation of a protectable interest, the procedural due process allegation fails before we can reach the second required prong of this claim.

Plaintiff claims that the zoning ordinance enacted by defendant is an unlawful exercise of the state's police power, both as applied to plaintiff and on its face. "It is well-established [sic] that, as an exercise of the police power, a zoning ordinance is presumed to be constitutionally valid." A party challenging the ordinance must show "that the ordinance is clearly arbitrary and unreasonable, having no substantial relation to the public health, safety, morals, or general welfare."

Here, defendant's zoning ordinance requires a special use permit for certain uses, to meet municipal planning goals that protect the health and/or safety of the community. As discussed above, the zoning ordinance is rationally related to a legitimate state interest.

Plaintiff's complaint is dismissed.

CASE QUESTIONS

1. Why is the ordinance not a violation of the First Amendment?
2. What legitimate government interest(s) is/are satisfied with the prohibition on tattoo parlors? Does it matter that 33 percent of the U.S. population now have one or more tattoos?

CONSIDER 18.3   In 1995, the city of Long Beach passed an ordinance that amended its existing adult entertainment zoning ordinance by prohibiting adult entertainment businesses within 300 feet of a residential zoning district, 1,000 feet of any public or private school, 600 feet of any city park, 500 feet of a church, and 1,000 feet of another adult entertainment business. Seung Chung Lim and his corporation, Fluffy, Inc., challenged the constitutionality of the newly amended ordinance. He and Fluffy, Inc., own and operate two adult entertainment businesses located within 300 feet of residential districts. The district court found the ordinance to be valid, and Mr. Lim appealed. What are the constitutional issues? Discuss the likely outcome of the case. *Lim v. City of Long Beach*, 217 F.3d 1050 (9th Cir. 2000).

ETHICAL ISSUE

The city of Southborough, Massachusetts, passed a zoning ordinance that prohibited the operation of abortion clinics within the town. Framingham Clinic attempted to establish a clinic that would perform first-trimester abortions and challenged the ordinance. Is the regulation permissible? *Framingham Clinic, Inc. v. Board of Selectmen*, 367 N.E.2d 606 (Mass. 1977). Would it be constitutional for a city to restrict protestors outside abortion clinics? What if the city could establish that the protests caused congestion and noise? *Madsen v. Women's Health Center, Inc.*, 512 U.S. 753 (1994).

Group Home Zoning Provisions

One social zoning issue that has emerged over the past few years is the concept of group homes for those recovering from addiction, those with terminal illnesses or mental or physical disabilities, and those who are on supervised release from prison. This area continues to be one of confusion, contention, and litigation. However, the following case from the U.S. Supreme Court continues to be the overarching guide on how requests for and zoning related to such group homes in residential areas should be resolved.

CITY OF EDMONDS V. OXFORD HOUSE, INC.

514 U.S. 725 (1995)
A Family or Recovering Residents?

FACTS

In the summer of 1990, respondent Oxford House opened a group home in the city of Edmonds, Washington (City), for 10 to 12 adults recovering from alcoholism and drug addiction. The group home, called Oxford House–Edmonds, is located in a neighborhood zoned for single-family residences. Upon learning that Oxford House had leased and was operating a home in Edmonds, the City issued criminal citations to the owner and a resident of the house. The citations charged violation of the zoning code rule that defines who may live in single-family dwelling units. The occupants of such units must compose a "family," and family, under the City's rule, "means an individual or two or more persons related by genetics, adoption, or marriage, or a group of five or fewer persons who are not related by genetics, adoption, or marriage." Oxford House–Edmonds houses more than five unrelated persons, and therefore does not conform to the code.

Oxford House relied on the Fair Housing Act, which declares it unlawful "[t]o discriminate in the sale or rental, or to otherwise make unavailable or deny, a dwelling to any buyer or renter because of a handicap of... that buyer or renter." The residents of Oxford House–Edmonds "are recovering alcoholics and drug addicts and are handicapped persons within the meaning" of the Act.

The District Court granted summary judgment to the City. The Court of Appeals reversed and remanded, and the City and the group home appealed.

JUDICIAL OPINION

Ginsburg, Justice

Discrimination covered by the FHA includes "a refusal to make reasonable accommodations in rules, policies, practices, or services, when such accommodations may be necessary to afford [handicapped] person[s] equal opportunity to use and enjoy a dwelling." §3604(f)(3)(B). Oxford House asked Edmonds to make a "reasonable accommodation" by allowing it to remain in the single-family dwelling it had leased. Group homes for recovering substance abusers, Oxford urged, need 8 to 12 residents to be financially and therapeutically viable. Edmonds declined to permit Oxford House to stay in a single-family residential zone, but passed an ordinance listing group homes as permitted uses in multifamily and general commercial zones.

On May 17, 1993, the State of Washington enacted a law providing

No city may enact or maintain an ordinance, development regulation, zoning regulation or official control, policy, or administrative practice which treats a residential structure occupied by persons with handicaps differently than a similar residential structure occupied by a family or other unrelated individuals. As used in this section, "handicaps" are as defined in the federal fair housing amendments act of 1988 (42 U.S.C. Sec. 3602).

Wash. Rev. Code § 35.63.220 (1994).

The United States asserts that Washington's new law invalidates ECDC § 21.30.010, Edmonds' family composition rule, as applied to Oxford House–Edmonds. Edmonds responds that the effect of the new law is "far from clear."

The sole question before the Court is whether Edmonds' family composition rule qualifies as a "restrictio[n] regarding the maximum number of occupants permitted to occupy a dwelling" within the meaning of the FHA's absolute exemption. In answering this question, we are mindful of the Act's stated policy "to provide, within constitutional limitations, for fair housing throughout the United States." Land-use restrictions designate "districts in which only compatible uses are allowed and incompatible uses are excluded. These restrictions typically categorize uses as single-family residential,

multiple-family residential, commercial, or industrial. In particular, reserving land for single-family residences preserves the character of neighborhoods, securing "zones where family values, youth values, and the blessings of quiet seclusion and clean air make the area a sanctuary for people." *Village of Belle Terre v. Boraas*, 416 U.S. 1 (1974). To limit land use to single-family residences, a municipality must define the term "family"; thus family composition rules are an essential component of single-family residential use restrictions.

Maximum occupancy restrictions, in contradistinction, cap the number of occupants per dwelling, typically in relation to available floor space or the number and type of rooms.

Turning specifically to the City's Community Development Code, we note that the provisions Edmonds invoked against Oxford House, ECDC §§ 16.20.010 and 21.30.010, are classic examples of a use restriction and complementing family composition rule. These provisions do not cap the number of people who may live in a dwelling. In plain terms, they direct that dwellings be used only to house families. Captioned "USES," ECDC §16.20.010 provides that the sole "Permitted Primary Us[e]" in a single-family residential zone is "[s]ingle-family dwelling units." Edmonds itself recognizes that this provision simply "defines those uses permitted in a single family residential zone."

A separate provision caps the number of occupants a dwelling may house, based on floor area:

Floor Area. Every dwelling unit shall have at least one room which shall have not less than 120 square feet of floor area. Other habitable rooms, except kitchens, shall have an area of not less than 70 square feet. Where more than two persons occupy a room used for sleeping purposes, the required floor area shall be increased at the rate of 50 square feet for each occupant in excess of two.

ECDC § 19.10.000.

Edmonds nevertheless argues that its family composition rule, ECDC § 21.30.010, falls within § 3607(b)(1), the FHA exemption for maximum occupancy restrictions, because the rule caps at five the number of unrelated persons allowed to occupy a single-family dwelling. But Edmonds' family composition rule surely does not answer the question: "What is the maximum number of occupants permitted to occupy a house?" So long as they are related "by genetics, adoption, or marriage," any number of people can live in a house. Ten siblings, their parents and grandparents, for example, could dwell in a house in Edmonds' single-family residential zone without offending Edmonds' family composition rule. Family living, not living space per occupant, is what ECDC §21.30.010 describes. Defining family primarily by biological and legal relationships, the provision also accommodates another group association: Five or fewer unrelated people are allowed to live together as though they were family. This accommodation is the peg on which Edmonds rests its plea for §3607 (b)(1) exemption. Had the City defined a family solely by biological and legal links, § 3607(b)(1) would not have been the ground on which Edmonds staked its case. It is curious reasoning indeed that converts a family values preserver into a maximum occupancy restriction once a town adds to a related persons prescription "and also two unrelated persons."

This curious reasoning drives the dissent. If Edmonds allowed only related persons (whatever their number) to dwell in a house in a single-family zone, then the dissent, it appears, would agree that the §3607(b)(1) exemption is unavailable. But so long as the City introduces a specific number—any number (two will do)—the City can insulate its single-family zone entirely from FHA coverage. The exception-takes-the-rule reading the dissent advances is hardly the "generous construction" warranted for antidiscrimination prescriptions.

Edmonds additionally contends that subjecting single-family zoning to FHA scrutiny will "overturn Euclidian zoning" and "destroy the effectiveness and purpose of single-family zoning." This contention both ignores the limited scope of the issue before us and exaggerates the force of the FHA's antidiscrimination provisions. We address only whether Edmonds' family composition rule qualifies for § 3607(b)(1) exemption. Moreover, the FHA antidiscrimination provisions, when applicable, require only "reasonable" accommodations to afford persons with handicaps "equal opportunity to use and enjoy" housing.

The parties have presented, and we have decided, only a threshold question: Edmonds' zoning code provision describing who may compose a "family" is not a maximum occupancy restriction exempt from the FHA under § 3607(b)(1). It remains for the lower courts to decide whether Edmonds' actions against Oxford House violate the FHA's prohibitions against discrimination set out in §§ 3604(f)(1)(A) and (f)(3)(B).

For the reasons stated, the judgment is affirmed.

DISSENTING OPINION

Scalia, Thomas, and Kennedy, Justices

Consider a real estate agent who is assigned responsibility for the city of Edmonds. Desiring to learn all he can about his new territory, the agent inquires: "Does the city have any restrictions regarding the maximum number of occupants permitted to occupy a dwelling?" The accurate answer must surely be in the affirmative—yes, the maximum number of unrelated persons permitted to occupy a dwelling in a single-family neighborhood is five. Or consider a different example. Assume that the Federal Republic of Germany imposes no restrictions on the speed of "cars" that drive on the Autobahn but does cap the speed of "trucks" (which are defined as all other vehicles). If a conscientious visitor to Germany asks whether there are "any restrictions regarding the maximum speed of motor vehicles permitted to drive on the Autobahn," the accurate answer again is surely the affirmative one—yes, there is a restriction regarding the maximum speed of trucks on the Autobahn.

The majority does not ask whether petitioner's zoning code imposes any restrictions regarding the maximum number of occupants permitted to occupy a dwelling. Instead, observing that pursuant to ECDC §21.30.010, "any number of people can live in a house," so long as they are "related 'by genetics, adoption, or marriage,'" the majority concludes that §21.30.010 does not qualify for § 3607(b)(1)'s exemption because it "surely does not answer the question: 'What is the maximum number of occupants permitted to occupy a house?'" The majority's question, however, does not accord with the text of the statute. To take advantage of the exemption, a local, state, or federal law need not impose a restriction establishing an absolute maximum number of occupants; under §3607(b)(1), it is necessary only that such law impose a restriction "regarding" the maximum number of occupants. Surely, a restriction can "regar[d]"—or "concern," "relate to," or "bear on"—the maximum number of occupants without establishing an absolute maximum number in all cases.

CASE QUESTIONS

1. What is the nature of the group home in this case?
2. What federal and local laws are in conflict?
3. What must the local law do to avoid conflict with the federal law?
4. What is the dissent's point?
5. What would you say is the rule for group homes and zoning?

CONSIDER 18.4   Harry Eichlin appealed the decision of a New Hope Borough Zoning and Hearing Board decision to grant a zoning permit to Buck Villa, Inc. (BVI), for use of a single-family dwelling as a group home for eight unrelated HIV-infected persons. Section 218(3) of the Ordinance defines the term "family" to include:

A home for no more than eight unrelated persons which is sponsored and operated by a non-profit group, organization, or corporation for a group of persons to live together in a single communal living arrangement where the residents permanently live together as the functional equivalent of a traditional family in a non-profit dwelling unit maintaining a non-transient common household with single cooking and dining facilities and sharing a permanent unity of social life. This shall be referred to as a "family group home". Groups contemplated by this use include, but are not limited to, the handicapped, the elderly, and the disabled, but excludes halfway houses for ex-convicts and for drug or alcohol rehabilitation, or for licensed personal care homes or any other use specifically provided for in this Ordinance. A family group home may have no more than two residential managers living at the home in addition to the residents. Residential managers are agents or employees of the agency or organization sponsoring and operating the group home.

New Hope Borough Zoning Ordinance No. 1933-2, art. 1 §1(3)

Applying the *Edmonds* case, determine whether the ordinance is valid and whether the group home can remain. *Eichlin v. Zoning Hearing Board of New Hope Borough*, 671 A.2d 1173 (Comm. Ct. Pa. 1996).   ▬■

ZONING AS A TAKING

Many who have had their permissible land uses restricted by zoning have raised the issue of whether such regulation constitutes a "taking" under the U.S. Constitution's Fifth Amendment, which would require that they be compensated for the loss in value of their land. (See Chapter 19 for additional details on eminent domain and just compensation.) Moratoria on development, a form of local regulation that allows government infrastructure the chance to "catch up" with expanding housing and population base by prohibiting, for example, construction of multiunit housing for six months, expanded during the real estate boom market. However, such moratoria are not automatically a taking of property and are subject to review based on individual situations and controls.[4] One **takings issue** that has been the focus of litigation relates to restrictions on beachfront and **wetlands** development. In the following landmark case, the U.S. Supreme Court faced the issue of a "taking" because of development restrictions on wetlands.

PRACTICAL TIP

Over the past few years, many wetlands cases have brought challenging developmental restrictions. Property purchasers considering coastal property should check not only local zoning, but state and federal restrictions as well prior to purchasing.

---

[4]*Tahoe-Sierra Preservation Council, Inc. v. Tahoe Regional Planning Agency*, 535 U.S. 302 (2002).

LUCAS V. SOUTH CAROLINA COASTAL COUNCIL

505 U.S. 1003 (1992)
No Beach Houses Here on the Beach

FACTS

In 1986, David H. Lucas (petitioner) paid $975,000 for two residential lots on the Isle of Palms in Charleston County, South Carolina. Lucas intended to build single-family homes on the lots. In 1988, South Carolina's legislature enacted the Beachfront Management Act. The effect of the act was to prohibit Lucas from erecting any permanent habitable structures on his two lots. Lucas filed suit challenging the legislation as a taking under the Fifth and Fourteenth Amendments, which requires that he be compensated. The trial court found that the law rendered Lucas's land valueless. The South Carolina Supreme Court reversed, and Lucas appealed.

JUDICIAL OPINION

Scalia, Justice

Prior to Justice Holmes' exposition in *Pennsylvania Coal Co. v. Mahon*, 260 U.S. 393, 43 S.Ct. 158, 67 L.Ed. 322 (1922), it was generally thought that the Takings Clause reached only a "direct appropriation" of property.

Justice Holmes recognized in *Mahon*, however, that if the protection against physical appropriations of private property was to be meaningfully enforced, the government's power to redefine the range of interests included in the ownership of property was necessarily constrained by constitutional limits. If, instead, the uses of private property were subject to unbridled, uncompensated qualification under the police power, "the natural tendency of human nature [would be] to extend the qualification more and more until at last private property disappear[ed]." These considerations gave birth in that case to the oft-cited maxim that, "while property may be regulated to a certain extent, if regulation goes too far it will be recognized as a taking."

We have, however, described at least two discrete categories of regulatory action as compensable without case-specific inquiry into the public interest advanced in support of the restraint. The first encompasses regulations that compel the property owner to suffer a physical "invasion" of his property. In general (at least with regard to permanent invasions), no matter how minute the intrusion, and no matter how weighty the public purpose behind it, we have

required compensation. For example, in *Loretto v. Teleprompter Manhattan CATV Corp.*, 458 U.S. 419, 102 S.Ct. 3164, 73 L.Ed.2d 868 (1982), we determined that New York's law requiring landlords to allow television cable companies to emplace cable facilities in their apartment buildings constituted a taking, even though the facilities occupied at most only 1½ cubic feet of the landlords' property.

The second situation in which we have found categorical treatment appropriate is where regulation denies all economically beneficial or productive use of land.

As we have said on numerous occasions, the Fifth Amendment is violated when land-use regulation "does not substantially advance legitimate state interests *or denies an owner economically viable use of his land.*"

On the other side of the balance, affirmatively supporting a compensation requirement, is the fact that regulations that leave the owner of land without economically beneficial or productive options for its use—typically, as here, by requiring land to be left substantially in its natural state—carry with them a heightened risk that private property is being pressed into some form of public service under the guise of mitigating serious public harm.

We think, in short, that there are good reasons for our frequently expressed belief that when the owner of real property has been called upon to sacrifice *all* economically beneficial uses in the name of the common good, that is, to leave his property economically idle, he has suffered a taking.

Under Lucas's theory of the case, which rested upon our "no economically viable use" statements, that finding entitled him to compensation. Lucas believed it unnecessary to take issue with either the purposes behind the *Beachfront Management Act*, or the means chosen by the South Carolina Legislature to effectuate those purposes. The South Carolina Supreme Court, however, thought otherwise. In its view, the *Beachfront Management Act* was no ordinary enactment, but involved an exercise of South Carolina's "police powers" to mitigate the harm to the public interest that petitioner's use of his land might occasion. By neglecting to dispute the findings enumerated in the Act or otherwise to challenge the legislature's purposes, petitioner "concede[d] that the beach/dune area of South Carolina's shores is an extremely valuable public resource; that the erection of new construction, *inter alia*, contributes to the erosion and destruction of this public resource; and that discouraging new construction in close proximity to the beach/dune area is necessary to prevent a great public harm."

It is correct that many of our prior opinions have suggested that "harmful or noxious uses" of property may be proscribed by government regulation without the requirement of compensation. For a number of reasons, however, we think the South Carolina Supreme Court was too quick to conclude that that principle decides the present case.

("[T]he problem [in this area] is not one of noxiousness or harm-creating activity at all; rather it is a problem of inconsistency between perfectly innocent and independently desirable uses."). Whether Lucas's construction of single-family residences on his parcels should be described as bringing "harm" to South Carolina's adjacent ecological resources thus depends principally upon whether the describer believes that the State's use interest in nurturing those resources is so important that *any* competing adjacent use must yield.

When it is understood that "prevention of harmful use" was merely our early formulation of the police power justification necessary to sustain (without compensation) *any* regulatory diminution in value; and that the distinction between regulation that "prevents harmful use" and that which "confers benefits" is difficult, if not impossible, to discern on an objective, value-free basis; it becomes self-evident that noxious-use logic cannot serve as a touchstone to distinguish regulatory "takings"—which require compensation—from regulatory deprivations that do not require compensation. *A fortiori* the legislature's recitation of a noxious-use justification cannot be the basis for departing from our categorical rule that total regulatory takings must be compensated. If it were, departure would virtually always be allowed.

Where the State seeks to sustain regulation that deprives land of all economically beneficial use, we think it may resist compensation only if the logically antecedent inquiry into the nature of the owner's estate shows that the proscribed use interests were not part of his title to begin with. This accords, we think, with our "takings" jurisprudence, which has traditionally been guided by the understandings of our citizens regarding the content of, and the State's power over, the "bundle of rights" that they acquire when they obtain title to property. It seems to us that the property owner necessarily expects the uses of his property to be restricted, from time to time, by various measures newly enacted by the State in legitimate exercise of its police powers; "[a]s long recognized, some values are enjoyed under an implied limitation and must yield to the police power."

In the case of land, however, we think the notion pressed by the Council that title is somehow held subject to the "implied limitation" that the State may subsequently eliminate all economically valuable use is inconsistent with the historical compact recorded in the Takings Clause that has become part of our constitutional culture.

On this analysis, the owner of a lake bed, for example, would not be entitled to compensation when he is denied the requisite permit to engage in a landfilling operation that would have the effect of flooding others' land. Nor the corporate owner of a nuclear generating plant, when it is directed to remove all improvements from its land upon discovery that the plant sits astride an earthquake fault. Such regulatory action may well have the effect of eliminating the land's only economically productive use, but it does not proscribe a productive use that was previously permissible under relevant property and nuisance principles.

As we have said, a "State, by *ipse dixit*, may not transform private property into public property without compensation...." *Webb's Fabulous Pharmacies, Inc. v. Beckwith*, 449 U.S. 155, 164, 101 S.Ct. 446, 452, 66 L.Ed.2d 358 (1980). Instead, as it would be required to do if it sought to restrain Lucas in a common law action for public nuisance, South Carolina must identify background principles of nuisance and property law that prohibit the uses he now intends in the circumstances in which the property is presently found. Only on this showing can the State fairly claim that, in proscribing all such beneficial uses, the *Beachfront Management Act* is taking nothing.

The judgment is reversed.

CASE QUESTIONS

1. What did Lucas purchase and for how much? When?
2. When was the law on beachfront construction passed?
3. Does South Carolina allege an important public purpose?
4. What is the distinction between this case and one in which a landowner is required to remove a business because it is a nuisance?
5. What implications does this case have for government preservation of wetlands properties?

PROCEDURAL ASPECTS

Adoption of Zoning Regulations

As already stated, local governments obtain their authority for zoning from an enabling act, and most states have adopted some form of the Standard State Zoning Enabling Act. This act consists of nine basic sections, summarized as follows.

- *Section 1—Grant of Power*: In this section, the governmental unit is given the authority to zone on the basis of a need to preserve health, safety, morals, and the general welfare of the community.

- *Section 2—Districts*: In this section, the governmental unit is given the authority to divide its area of jurisdiction into any size, shape, and number of districts for purposes of regulating activities or structures in those districts.

- *Section 3—Purposes in View*: This section requires the governmental unit to exercise its power under Section 2 pursuant to a master plan designed to provide all areas with adequate safety protection, schools, water, sewage, parks, and all other amenities.

- *Section 4—Method of Procedures*: In this section, the governmental unit is authorized to establish procedures for adopting and amending zoning regulations.

- *Section 5—Changes*: This section specifies that changes in zoning may be made but can be stopped if 20 percent or more of the owners of lots in the area in question oppose the change. The 20 percent may also include those who own lots within a certain distance of the area subject to the change. The distance (in feet) is left blank, to be determined by the adopting governmental unit.

- *Section 6—Zoning Commission*: This section establishes the right of the governmental unit to appoint a **zoning commission** to set up the original zoning plan on the basis of studies of the area.

- *Section 7—Board of Adjustment*: The purpose of this section is to allow the local governments to set up a **board of adjustment** that can, in cases and circumstances they deem appropriate, make exceptions to the zoning regulations in particular areas, so long as the exceptions are in keeping with the idea of the master plan and basic district division. These exceptions are called **variances** under the act.

- *Section 8—Enforcement*: In this section, the local governmental body is authorized to call zoning violations misdemeanors and to provide for penalties of either fines or imprisonment. Also, the local governmental body is authorized to bring suit to stop construction or use of property that is in violation of the zoning regulations—in other words, to seek an injunction for violative activity.

- *Section 9—Conflicts*: This section serves to clarify which set of laws will govern in the event that two governmental units have established zoning for the same area—for example, if a county has adopted zoning for the county, but the cities within the county have adopted their own zoning ordinances. This section provides that city ordinances will be controlling to the extent to which they are stricter than the county ordinances.

Today, although the Standard State Zoning Enabling Act is still the law in the majority of states, it provokes some dissatisfaction. The American Law Institute has drafted a Model Land Development Code that some states have adopted as a supplement. Although there may be slight variations, zoning control must meet the basic requirements and follow basic procedures to guarantee due process.

Exceptions from Zoning Regulations

Section 7 of the Standard State Zoning Enabling Act provides for a board of adjustment that can grant exceptions or variances for uses that differ from assigned zoning. An application for a variance must show two things:

1. That an undue hardship results if the ordinance is enforced
2. That the granting of the variance will not be excessively disruptive of the surrounding land or the master plan

Factors considered by boards in granting variances include the effect of the use on surrounding land, the benefit to the public of the varied use, whether the property is different in its surface character from other property in the district, whether loss results without the variance, and whether the master plan's purposes would be defeated through the grant of the variance.

One of the most frequently approved variances involves an exception to building-height restrictions. It may be economically beneficial to the community and not a burden on surrounding property to permit a large business to build a multi-story building in a district zoned for single-story buildings.

Another exception to a zoned use is **special permit**. A special permit allows an exception for the construction of a church or school in a residential area provided certain restrictions or conditions are met. A variance or special permit is, more or less, a matter of opinion.

If a variance or special permit is denied, there is a right of judicial review on the grounds of abuse of discretion, constitutionality, or arbitrariness. Figure 18.1 (on p. 527) summarizes the procedural aspects of zoning.

Nonconforming Uses

A **nonconforming use** is a grandfather-clause protection in zoning used when a zoning ordinance now prohibits a use that already existed. An example would be a store or business operating in an area that has just been zoned residential. Because of *ex post facto* issues, these grandfathered uses remain (although see Chapter 19 for more discussion of economic development and takings issues).

For a nonconforming use to be immune from zoning, it must be in existence at the time the zoning is passed. Furthermore, the nonconforming use cannot be expanded beyond the use at the time the zoning was passed.

A right to nonconforming use can be lost if the nonconforming activity is abandoned or if the nonconforming building is destroyed by fire or natural events. The zoning ordinances specify a time period for abandonment as well as what constitutes destruction for purposes of ending a nonconforming use.

Recently, many local governments, in an effort to carry out their community planning objectives, have sought to eliminate nonconforming uses over time and have passed ordinances that require amortization of nonconforming uses. These amortization sections require nonconforming uses to be eliminated over a specified period—usually five years. Amortization periods allow landowners some time to convert their property to appropriately zoned activities or buildings.

FIGURE 18.1 Zoning Process

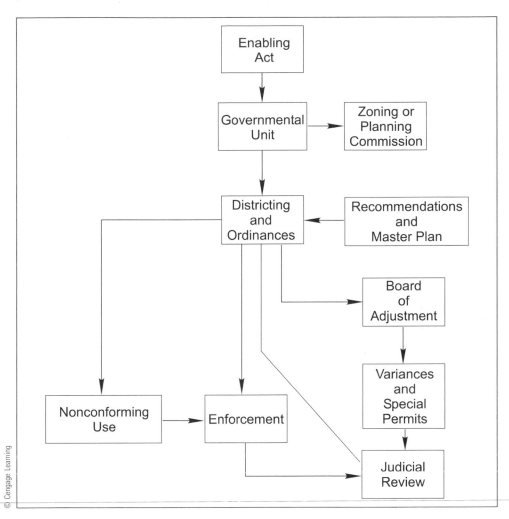

The following case deals with an issue of a continuing nonconforming use.

IN RE HALE MOUNTAIN FISH AND GAME CLUB, INC.

969 A.2d 691 (Vt. 2009)
The Zoning Trap for Trap Shooters

FACTS

The Hale Mountain Fish and Game Club had a nonconforming use permit that exempted it from the state and local wetlands regulations that controlled noise levels in and around the protected wetlands area. The Club had been in existence for decades prior to the enactment of the 1970 noise regulations. However, neighbors began to complain that the level of activity and noise at the Club had increased substantially since 1970 and that because of the change in use, the Club should now be required to apply for use change permits.

When the neighbors filed a complaint, the Permit Board held a hearing to determine whether the Club had exceeded its permissible use that had been grandfathered in and protected. Based on the testimony of Club members whose memberships began prior to 1970 and continued afterwards, and some evidence of clay pigeons and spent ammunition at the site, the Permit Board determined that the Club's activities have broadened but that the intensity of use has remained about the same over the years. For example, the trap shooting area, rifle range, and pistol range accommodate approximately the same number of users now as they did prior to 1970. Additionally, the Board found that shifting from private to town snow-plowing has not affected the number of users at the Club in winter. According to the Board, although the Club has engaged in various marketing efforts to increase participation, those efforts have done little more than maintain participation at pre-1970 levels. Neighbors offered no comparative testimony about pre-1970 membership and usage levels, and what they alleged were "increased" levels in later years. The Board found the members' testimony more persuasive for that reason. From a decision in favor of the Club, the neighbors appealed.

JUDICIAL OPINION

Per Curiam

This is the second time that we have considered neighbors' appeal of the Board's decision. In neighbors' first appeal, we held that the Board's initial decision regarding whether the Club need apply for an Act 250 permit insufficiently addressed whether, "since 1970 when Act 250 became law," changes made to the Club increased the intensity of use of the Club and resulted in greater noise emanating from the Club's property. *In re Hale Mountain Fish & Game Club, Inc.*, 2007 VT 102, ¶¶ 9-11, 182 Vt. 606, 939 A.2d 498. We also held that the Board needed to address, in greater detail, the impact of the Club's improvements on nearby streams and wetlands. Therefore, we issued a remand order that required the Board to make additional findings and conclusions on these critical issues. Although it took no new evidence, the Board reviewed prior witness testimony with these issues in mind and filed supplemental findings supporting its original conclusion that a general Act 250 permit was unnecessary. We affirm.

On this second appeal, neighbors first assert that the Board's factual findings are not supported by sufficient evidence. In addition to generally disagreeing with the Board's factual findings, neighbors also argue that the Board erred in relying on the testimony of several of the Club's witnesses instead of their own testimony

The Board, as a trier of fact, determines the credibility of witnesses and weighs the persuasive effect of evidence; this function is committed to its sound discretion. Where, as here, a party contests the sufficiency of the evidence supporting the Board's factual findings, our standard of review is deferential. We will uphold the Board's findings if they are supported by substantial evidence, i.e., "such relevant evidence as a reasonable mind might accept as adequate to support a conclusion."

The Board rejected neighbors' testimony, and accepted that of the Club's members, on legitimate

grounds; therefore, we cannot say that the Board's factual findings, which were based on the testimony, were not supported by substantial evidence. The factual issue before the Board was whether there had been a "substantial change" to a pre-existing project. Because the Club has existed since the 1940's, the most salient testimony was that given by longstanding members of the Club with knowledge of the Club's activities over time. Neighbors' testimony was limited to activity occurring after they moved near the Club, which generally was after 1970, and in some cases not until the late 1980s. Although the testimony of the Club's members did not account for every month and year of the Club's existence, when considered in relation to the Board's original findings, their testimony and the additional physical evidence provided sufficient support for the Board's conclusion. The Board acknowledged that there had been changes in the Club's activities and membership over the years, but the level of intensity of the members' use and the concomitant noise, neighbors' principal complaints, could not be said to have increased over pre-1970 levels.

Furthermore, on appeal, "[w]e will affirm the Board's legal conclusions when they are rationally derived from a correct interpretation of the law and supported by the findings." Here, the Board concluded that there were some substantial changes made to the property that required an Act 250 permit; however, according to the Board, all of the changes were discrete and did not require permitting the entire project. The Board discussed these changes in detail in its original decision. Increases in noise and intensity of use [must be] directly connected to substantial changes made at that club. Similar facts were absent, in the Board's view, in this case. Applying consistent and correct legal principles to each matter, the Board here determined that factual distinctions between the matters compelled different legal results.

As noted previously, our standard of review of the Board's decision is deferential. Neighbors have not demonstrated a basis on which to overturn either the Board's factual findings or the Board's legal conclusion that the Club has not made a substantial change to a pre-existing project that would subject the entire project to an Act 250 permitting process.

Affirmed.

CASE QUESTIONS

1. What do neighbors need to show to cause the nonconforming use to be lost?
2. Why was the testimony of the Club members given greater weight?

ETHICAL ISSUE

Ralph Horowitz owned land in the Los Angeles area that had been zoned for manufacturing and warehousing. When he acquired the land, it had not been used for those purposes since 1992, when about 350 local residents had begun a communal garden there. The garden, complete with fruit-bearing trees, had been praised by the Los Angeles mayor as a wonderful community touch among the industrial plants and warehouses. Among the gardeners and their supporters were Danny Glover, Laura Dern, Joan Baez, and Daryl Hannah. Mr. Horowitz had to seek judicial help to get the gardeners removed from his property. He even had the sheriff postpone their removal until they could harvest their seasonal gardens. Ms. Hannah sat in one of the garden trees for days to resist the execution of the court order for removal. Ms. Hannah was removed from a tree by police, who had to employ the help of a fire truck ladder from one of the nearby stations. Ms. Hannah, upon her removal, made the following statement to the media: "I'm very confident this is the morally right thing to do, to take a principled stand in solidarity with the farmers." Some violence broke out as police removed other protestors who had chained themselves to a walnut tree in the garden. The gardeners said they wanted Mr. Horowitz to commit the land to an urban garden.

What are their rights? What are Mr. Horowitz's rights? Evaluate the ethics on both sides of the use of the land.

CAUTIONS AND CONCLUSIONS

From the information and cases in this chapter, it is not difficult to see that the issue of zoning can be controlling in the value of property and is certainly controlling in the use to be made of property. Before purchasing land or beginning construction, make a zoning check. In addition, check surrounding tracts and plats to see the effects of growth and expansion and also the resulting effect on property values. Finally, evaluate the master plan to determine any future problems and possible changes or variances that might affect the land's value. When it comes to the issue of zoning, there can never be enough research.

KEY TERMS

aesthetic zoning, 511
board of adjustment, 525
cumulative classification, 508
exclusionary zoning, 516
general plan, 507
hold zoning, 517
intensity zoning, 511

interim zoning, 517
master plan, 507
nonconforming use, 526
noncumulative classification, 509
social issue zoning, 517
special permit, 526

Standard State Zoning
   Enabling Act, 507
takings issues, 522
variances, 525
wetlands, 522
zoning, 507
zoning commission, 525

CHAPTER PROBLEMS

1. The city of Philadelphia's Department of Licensing and Inspections denied Midnight Sessions, Ltd., a permit for the operation of an exotic dance club because of a history of disturbances and crime when such dance clubs operated. The city, through police department records, was able to establish that there was an increase in noise, trash, drug activity, loitering, and public urination in every area where an exotic dance club was given a permit for operation. In addition, the clubs attracted between 3,000 and 5,000 patrons on weekend event nights, and after the show many of those patrons roamed the surrounding neighborhoods in a state of drunkenness. Could the city prohibit the clubs altogether?

Midnight Sessions, Ltd. v. City of Philadelphia, 945 F.2d 667 (3rd Cir. 1991).

2. The city of Treasure Island Florida has 7500 permanent residents, but during the winter season, its population doubles. To cope with the influx, Treasure Island has zoning for resident dwellings and zoning for tourist dwellings. With this separation, permanent residents need not suffer through the parties and happiness that the tourists bring with them during their stays.

   Schwarz owned operated six half-way houses for recovering addicts and alcoholics who have finished their residence rehabilitation programs and are easing back into work and society. The half-way houses were located in the residential zoning areas of Treasure Island. Following several complaints by neighbors about noise and drinking and drug use, the city cited Schwarz for zoning violations because the turnover of residents in the home exceeded the limit for residential zoning. Schwarz filed suit on the grounds that the restriction on the use of his homes was a violation of the Fair Housing Act and unconstitutional discrimination against those who are recovering from substance abuse. The city won its case at the trial court level. What should the court of appeals do with the case? *Schwarz v. City of Treasure Island*, 544 F.3d 1201(11th Cir. 2008).

3. Edward Salib owns a Winchell's Donut House franchise within a designated redevelopment area of Mesa. To attract customers, Salib displays signs affixed to his store windows that advertise his products. On August 5, 2002, after giving Salib several warnings, a Mesa code enforcement officer ordered Salib to remove his window signs because their display violated Mesa's Sign Code which Mesa had enacted the prior November. Salib's display violated Sign Code 11-19-6, which prohibited businesses from covering more than 30 percent of their windows with signs.

   In March, 2003, the Sign Code was amended to define "window" to include a series of neighboring windows not separated by more than six inches. The effect of the amendment was to allow larger signs because the 30 percent would be measured against a larger area.

   On January 8, 2003, Salib filed suit against Mesa alleging the Sign Code violates his free speech rights under the Arizona and U.S. Constitutions. He asked the court to declare the Sign Code unconstitutional and enjoin Mesa from enforcing it. The trial court granted summary judgment in favor of Mesa. Salib appealed. Explain what the court should do with the case and why. *Salib v. City of Mesa*, 133 P.3d 756 (Az. App. 2006).

4. The Township of Brady has zoning restrictions on the number of animals that can be kept on properties in certain areas. More pigs are permitted per acre than cows. A farmer has brought suit alleging that the zoning restriction is arbitrary and not based on a public welfare basis. Township officials say that pig waste does not smell as much as cow waste and hence they permit more pigs than cows. Is the zoning restriction valid? *Richardson v. Township of Brady*, 218 F.3d 508 (6th Cir. 2000).

5. The Madison County Livestock and Fair Association owns a tract of land that has been used as the location for county fairs. The tract is now located in an area in which zoning changes prohibited such uses. The use of the tract as a fairgrounds has been a nonconforming use. The Association filed for a permit to build a race track on the tract. Neighbors objected because they said that such a proposed use could not be grandfathered in under the nonconforming use. Are they correct? *Perkins v. Madison County Livestock & Fair, Ass'n.*, 613 N.W.2d 264 (Iowa 2000).

6. SprintCom, Inc., began erecting a cell phone tower on leased residential land. It had obtained a construction permit from Stark County, Ohio, but had not obtained a zoning certificate or conditional use permit. When residents tried to stop the construction, SprintCom claimed it was not subject to zoning restrictions under the Federal Telecommunications Act. The city and county maintained that the federal law did not exempt SprintCom from the procedural requirements of local government. Who is correct and why? *Weckbacher v. Sprintcom, Inc.*, Slip Copy, 2006 WL 2459077 (Ohio App. 5 Dist.).

7. 35 Club L.L.C. began operating a business called "XXXV Gentlemen's Club" in the Borough of Sayreville, New Jersey. The business has been described as an "all-nude gentlemen's cabaret." N.J.S.A. 2C:34–6 (a) prohibits the operation of a sexually oriented business within 1,000 feet of a public park or residential zone. The city issued a permanent injunction against its operation in that location. The Club conceded that its location violated the statute, but argued that there was no location in Sayreville where it could operate its business without violating the statute. How should the court deal with this argument? *Borough of Sayreville v. 35 Club L.L.C.*, 33 A.3d 1200 (N.J. 2012).

8. The Stoyanoffs sought to build a home of an ultra-modern design in Ladue, Missouri. The home was to be built in a neighborhood in which all of the homes were of two-story conventional architectural design such as Colonial, French, or English.

The city of Ladue has a zoning ordinance that requires that a proposed structure conform to certain minimum architectural standards of appearance and conformity with surrounding structures, and that unsightly, grotesque, and unsuitable structures, detrimental to the stability of value and the welfare of surrounding property, structures, and residents, and to the general welfare and happiness of the community, be avoided, and that appropriate standards of beauty and conformity be fostered and encouraged.

Can the city stop construction of the Stoyanoff home? *State of Missouri Ex Rel. Stoyanoff v. Ladue*, 458 S.W.2d 305 (Mo. 1970).

9. Bernard Smookler and his wife purchased a 123-acre tract of land at the intersection of Jolly and Meridian Roads in Wheatfield Township in 1968. Ninety acres were used for agriculture, and 1.5 acres were rented to a tenant for residential use. Two years later, they requested a zoning change from rural agricultural to mobile home park with a 300-foot strip for commercial zoning. The planned mobile home park would be called Wheatfield Acres Mobile Home Park, would include five units per acre, and would have 535 total units.

The 1970 census put the population of Wheatfield Township at 1,117 with 325 housing units. There is no master plan for the township, which is 36 square miles with 18,297 acres and only about 5 percent developed. Three residential areas are in the township, with most of them located in the northern part. The proposed park would be in the northwest section. At the time of the application, Wheatfield had one commercial development: a gas station along Interstate 96. The township had no police or fire department and relied on the adjoining cities, counties, and the state for such services. There are no mobile home parks in the township and nothing that could be characterized as low-cost housing, but there has been some discussion of creating mobile home parks.

The Zoning and Planning Commission denied the Smooklers' application, stating that the area would be better for residential use; that there would be an added burden to police and fire services, and to the schools; and that there would be no benefit to the surrounding community.

The Smooklers appealed the commission's decision to the trial court. There the Smooklers and the commission stipulated that there would neither be traffic problems nor any problems with the sanitary or sewage systems. The Smooklers alleged at the trial court that the decision of the commission was evidence of a preconceived scheme to eliminate or prohibit mobile home parks. Can zoning be used in this way to control population growth? *Smookler v. Township of Wheatfield*, 232 N.W.2d 616 (Mich. 1975).

10. The Houghtalings are the owners of a travel business known as "Pleasure Cruises." Pleasure Cruises is operated out of the Houghtalings' home on East Liberty Street in Medina, Ohio. Mr. Houghtaling had installed a metal replica of an anchor on the lawn of their home in 1997. The anchor is seven and one-half feet in height and the crossbar is six feet long. Two lights were added to the ends of the crossbar a few months later.

In May 1997, the Medina City Planning Director, Richard Grice, sent a letter asking the Houghtalings to remove the anchor. The letter stated that the anchor violated City Zoning Code 1113.07.

The Houghtalings appealed Grice's decision to the board. The board ordered the sign removed. Lower courts found for the Houghtalings and the board appealed. How should the court decide the case? *Houghtaling v. City of Medina Board of Zoning Appeals*, 731 N.E.2d 733 (Ohio App. 1999).

For research activities related to this chapter, go to our text companion website at www.cengagebrain.com

CHAPTER 19

CONSTITUTIONAL ISSUES IN REAL ESTATE

Supreme Court Justice Sandra O'Connor is stepping down. She didn't want to resign—she just wants to make sure she's home so nobody can seize her house.[1]

Jay Leno's comment in his monologue after the U.S. Supreme Court issued its eminent domain decision in *Kelo v. City of New London*

Owning and transferring title to real property also includes certain constitutional rights that entitle property owners to certain guarantees with regard to their property ownership. This chapter discusses the constitutional protections for real property owners and purchasers.

LAND TITLE AND CONSTITUTIONAL ISSUES—EMINENT DOMAIN

The right of a governmental body to take title to property for a public use is called **eminent domain**. This right is found in the Fifth Amendment to the Constitution as well as in certain state constitutions. Private individuals cannot require property owners to sell their property, but governmental entities can require them to transfer title for public projects for the public good. The Fifth Amendment provides that "property shall not be taken for a public use without just compensation." A governmental entity can exercise eminent domain only when three standards come together: the taking is for a public purpose, there is a taking (as opposed to use regulation), and the owner is given just compensation.

---

[1]"Notable and Quotable," *Time*, July 18, 2005, p. 21.

Public Purpose

Eminent domain requires proof of a government purpose. "Public purpose" brings to mind taking land for highways and schools. However, government purposes for eminent domain extend much further. The following uses are considered public purposes: the condemnation of slum housing (for purposes of improving city areas), the limitation of mining and excavation within city limits, the declaration of property as a historic landmark, and economic development. That last purpose has created a firestorm of judicial, legislative, and public controversy over the last few years. The following case was the U.S. Supreme Court decision that changed the eminent domain landscape, as it were.

KELO V. CITY OF NEW LONDON

545 U.S. 469 (2005)
Little Pink Houses vs. Big Companies

FACTS

In 1978, the city of New London, Connecticut, undertook a redevelopment plan for purposes of creating a redeveloped area in and around the existing park at Fort Trumball. The plan had the goals of achieving all the related ambience a state park should have, including the absence of pink cottages and other architecturally eclectic homes. Part of the redevelopment plan was the city's deal with Pfizer Corporation for the location of its research facility in the area. The preface to the city's development plan included the following statement of goals and purpose:

to create a development that would complement the facility that Pfizer was planning to build, create jobs, increase tax and other revenues, encourage public access to and use of the city's waterfront, and eventually "build momentum" for the revitalization of the rest of the city, including its downtown area.

The redevelopment plan included detailed and extensive documentation on its socioeconomic impact. The affected property owners, including Susette Kelo, live in homes and cottages (15 total) located in and around other existing structures that will be permitted to stay in the area for the proposed new structures that will consist of primarily private land developers and corporations. In fact, the city was assisted by a private, nonprofit corporation, the New London Development Corporation (NLDC), an entity the city created, in the development of the economic plan and the ferrying of it through the various governmental processes, including that of city council approval. The central focus of the plan was attracting Pfizer to the Fort Trumbull area (where the homeowners and their properties were located) with

the hope of the economic boost and benefits a major corporate employer can bring to an area.

Kelo and the other homeowners (petitioners) whose homes would be razed to make room for Pfizer and the accompanying and resulting economic development plan filed suit challenging New London's legal authority to take their homes. The trial court issued an injunction preventing New London from taking certain of the properties but allowing others to be taken. Following an injunction, the property owners who were denied relief appealed and the city cross-appealed. On appeal, the landowners were held subject to eminent domain.

The appellate court found for New London on all the claims, and the landowners (petitioners) appealed.

JUDICIAL OPINION

Stevens, Justice

Two polar propositions are perfectly clear. On the one hand, it has long been accepted that the sovereign may not take the property of A for the sole purpose of transferring it to another private party B, even though A is paid just compensation. On the other hand, it is equally clear that a State may transfer property from one private party to another if future "use by the public" is the purpose of the taking; the condemnation of land for a railroad with common-carrier duties is a familiar example. Neither of these propositions, however, determines the disposition of this case.

As for the first proposition, the City would no doubt be forbidden from taking petitioners' land for the purpose of conferring a private benefit on a particular private party. Nor would the City be allowed to take property under the mere pretext of a public purpose, when its actual purpose was to bestow a private benefit. The takings before us, however, would be executed pursuant to a "carefully considered" development plan.

The disposition of this case therefore turns on the question whether the City's development plan serves a "public purpose." Without exception, our cases have defined that concept broadly, reflecting our longstanding policy of deference to legislative judgments in this field.

In *Berman v. Parker*, 348 U.S. 26, 75 S.Ct. 98, 99 L.Ed. 27 (1954), this Court upheld a redevelopment plan targeting a blighted area of Washington, D.C., in which most of the housing for the area's 5,000 inhabitants was beyond repair. Under the plan, the area would be condemned and part of it utilized for the construction of streets, schools, and other public facilities. The remainder of the land would be leased or sold to private parties for the purpose of redevelopment, including the construction of low-cost housing.

The owner of a department store located in the area challenged the condemnation, pointing out that his store was not itself blighted and arguing that the creation of a "better balanced, more attractive community" was not a valid public use. Writing for a unanimous Court, Justice Douglas refused to evaluate this claim in isolation, deferring instead to the legislative and agency judgment that the area "must be planned as a whole" for the plan to be successful. The Court explained that "community redevelopment programs need not, by force of the Constitution, be on a piecemeal basis—lot by lot, building by building."

"We do not sit to determine whether a particular housing project is or is not desirable. The concept of the public welfare is broad and inclusive.... The values it represents are spiritual as well as physical, aesthetic as well as monetary. It is within the power of the legislature to determine that the community should be beautiful as well as healthy, spacious as well as clean, well-balanced as well as carefully patrolled. If those who govern the District of Columbia decide that the Nation's Capital should be beautiful as well as sanitary, there is nothing in the Fifth Amendment that stands in the way."

Those who govern the City were not confronted with the need to remove blight in the Fort Trumbull area, but their determination that the area was sufficiently distressed to justify a program of economic rejuvenation is entitled to our deference. The City has carefully formulated an economic development plan that it believes will provide appreciable benefits to the community, including—but by no means limited to—new jobs and increased tax revenue. As with other exercises in urban planning and development, the City is endeavoring to coordinate a variety of commercial, residential, and recreational uses of land, with the hope that they will form a whole greater than the sum of its parts. To effectuate this plan, the City has invoked a state statute that specifically authorizes the use of eminent domain to promote economic development. Given the comprehensive character of the plan, the thorough deliberation that preceded its adoption, and the limited scope of our review, it is appropriate for us to resolve the challenges of the individual owners, not on a piecemeal basis, but rather in light of the entire plan. Because that plan unquestionably serves a public purpose, the takings challenged here satisfy the public use requirement of the Fifth Amendment.

[P]etitioners urge us to adopt a new bright-line rule that economic development does not qualify as a public use. Putting aside the unpersuasive suggestion that the City's plan will provide only purely economic benefits, neither precedent nor logic supports petitioners' proposal. Promoting economic development is a traditional and long accepted function of government. There is, moreover, no principled way of distinguishing economic development from the other public purposes that we have recognized. In our cases upholding takings that facilitated agriculture and mining, for example, we emphasized the importance of those industries to the welfare of the States in question. It would be incongruous to hold that the City's interest in the economic benefits to be derived from the development of the Fort Trumbull area has less of a public character than any of those other interests. Clearly, there is no basis for exempting economic development from our traditionally broad understanding of public purpose.

Petitioners contend that using eminent domain for economic development impermissibly blurs the boundary between public and private takings. Again, our cases foreclose this objection. "The public end may be as well or better served through an agency of private enterprise than through a department of government—or so the Congress might conclude. We cannot say that public ownership is the sole method of promoting the public purposes of community redevelopment projects." It is further argued that without a bright-line rule nothing would stop a city from transferring citizen A's property to citizen B for the sole reason that citizen B will put the property to a more productive use and thus pay more taxes. Such a one-to-one transfer of property, executed outside the confines of an integrated development plan, is not presented in this case. While such an unusual exercise of government power would certainly raise a suspicion that a private purpose was afoot, the hypothetical cases posited by petitioners can be confronted if and when they arise. They do not warrant the crafting of an artificial restriction on the concept of public use.

Just as we decline to second-guess the City's considered judgments about the efficacy of its development plan, we also decline to second-guess the City's determinations as to what lands it needs to acquire in order to effectuate the project. Once the question of the public purpose has been decided, the amount and character of land to be taken for the project and the need for a particular tract to complete the integrated plan rests in the discretion of the legislative branch.

The judgment of the Supreme Court of Connecticut is affirmed.

DISSENTING OPINION

O'Connor, Justice, joined by Justices Scalia, Thomas, and Rehnquist

Under the banner of economic development, all private property is now vulnerable to being taken and transferred to another private owner, so long as it might be upgraded—i.e., given to an owner who will use it in a way that the legislature deems more beneficial to the public—in the process. To reason, as the Court does, that the incidental public benefits resulting from the subsequent ordinary use of private property render economic development takings "for public use" is to wash out any distinction between private and public use of property—and thereby effectively to delete the words "for public use" from the Takings Clause of the Fifth Amendment. Accordingly I respectfully dissent.

Where is the line between "public" and "private" property use? We give considerable deference to legislatures' determinations about what governmental activities will advantage the public. But were the political branches the sole arbiters of the public-private distinction, the Public Use Clause would amount to little more than hortatory fluff. An external, judicial check on how the public use requirement is interpreted, however limited, is necessary if this constraint on government power is to retain any meaning.

Even if there were a practical way to isolate the motives behind a given taking, the gesture toward a purpose test is theoretically flawed. If it is true that incidental public benefits from new private use are enough to ensure the "public purpose" in a taking, why should it matter, as far as the Fifth Amendment is concerned, what inspired the taking in the first place? How much the government does or does not desire to benefit a favored private party has no bearing on whether an economic development taking will or will not generate secondary benefit for the public. And whatever the reason for a given condemnation, the effect is the same from the constitutional perspective—private property is forcibly relinquished to new private ownership.

CASE QUESTIONS

1. What is different from this case and a case in which property is taken for a freeway?
2. What is the concern of the dissent about the decision?
3. Why does the majority state that the courts should be reluctant to get involved in local government eminent domain activities?

The Post-Kelo Impact

The impact of the *Kelo* case has been substantial. The decision unleashed new uncertainty in the minds of landowners and paved the way for legislative reforms that curb eminent domain powers at the state and local levels. Following the November 2006 and 2008 general elections, one-half of the states had passed ballot propositions limiting the exercise of eminent domain, adopted constitutional amendments restricting economic development eminent domain, or passed legislation with similar limitations.[2]

---

[2]The states that adopted reforms, whether through legislation, ballot proposition, or judicial decision (although the degrees of post-*Kelo* reforms in these states vary in strength) are: Alaska, Arizona, Arkansas, California, Florida, Georgia, Michigan, and New Hampshire, along with Alabama, Colorado, Hawaii, Idaho, Indiana, Illinois, Iowa, Kansas, Kentucky, Louisiana, Maine, Maryland, Minnesota, Mississippi, Missouri, Montana, Nebraska, Nevada, North Carolina, New Jersey, North Dakota, Ohio, Oregon, Pennsylvania, Rhode Island, South Carolina, South Dakota, Utah (had reform prior to *Kelo*), Tennessee, Texas, Vermont, Washington, West Virginia, Wisconsin, and Wyoming, passed legislation limiting eminent domain reforms. In November 2005, the U.S. House of Representatives passed "The Private Property Rights Protection Act of 2005" (also known as House Resolution 4128) by a vote of 376 to 38. The bill died in the Senate. In 2006, President George W. Bush signed Executive Order 13406 called, "Protecting Property Rights of the American People," which prohibited the taking of private property for purposes of economic benefit to another private party.

Ms. Kelo's home and 15 others were razed. Pfizer merged with Wyeth in 2009 and closed all company operations in New London. The Fort Trumball area has no houses, no research park, no businesses, and is now undeveloped land. However, after Hurricane Irene, in 2010, officials from New London announced that residents could use the Fort Trumball area for dumping their branches and fallen trees. The location that once had Ms. Kelo's and others homes is now a landfill.

CONSIDER 19.1   Bailey's Brake Service, a bit of an eyesore at a main intersection near the faltering downtown area of Mesa, Arizona, was a family-founded, owned and operated business that had been open in its existing location since 1970. Lenhardt's True Value Hardware store was also a longstanding Mesa business with a location south and east of Bailey's and a desire for a better location as well as a professed desire to revitalize Mesa's downtown area. The Lenhardt's had purchased the property abutting Bailey's but felt that the street-facing Bailey's property was necessary for its location.

The city fathers and mothers were in favor of condemnation of the Bailey use, a taking by eminent domain, followed by a "reissuing" of the once Bailey property to Lenhardt's for its construction of a new retail establishment on the site. The Baileys challenged the city's taking in the Superior Court as unconstitutional, but the court held that the taking was constitutional as part of the city's plan for redevelopment and revitalization of the area. The Baileys appealed. Applying the *Kelo* decision, what should the appellate court do? *Bailey v. Myers,* 76 P.3d 398 (Az. Ct. App. 2003). ▪

Taking or Regulating

A governmental entity is required to pay a landowner compensation when there has been a **taking** of the property. A taking occurs when a landowner is deprived of any use of the property. In the landmark case of *Pennsylvania Coal v. Mahon*, 260 U.S. 393 (1922), the U.S. Supreme Court established standards for what constitutes a taking. A Pennsylvania statute prohibited the mining of coal under any land surface where the result would be the subsidence of any structure used for human habitation. The subsurface owners, the coal companies, brought suit challenging the statute as a taking without compensation. The court held that the statute was more than regulation and, in fact, was an actual taking of the subsurface property rights.

Technology has brought many new and subtly different issues in takings. In *Loretto v. Teleprompter Manhattan CATV Corp. et al.*, 458 U.S. 419 (1982), the U.S. Supreme Court grappled with an eminent domain claim for a cable television box on the roof of an apartment complex. A New York statute required landowners to allow the cable boxes, but the court held that a permanent physical occupation authorized by the government is a taking even with the public interest of cable access being served. The owners of the buildings with the cable boxes were entitled to compensation for the use of their land.

In some situations, government use of the land is not occupation but a right of way. The following case is a landmark one on the complex interrelationships among the public, landowners, and government regulation for the public good.

NOLLAN V. CALIFORNIA COASTAL COMMISSION

483 U.S. 825 (1987)
A Beach House in Exchange for a Public Easement

FACTS

James and Marilyn Nollan own a beachfront lot in Ventura County, California. A quarter-mile north of their property is Faria Park, an oceanside public park with a public beach and recreation area. Another public beach, known as "the Cove," lies 1,800 feet south of their lot. A concrete seawall approximately eight feet high separates the beach portion of the Nollans' property from the rest of the lot.

The Nollans originally leased their property with an option to buy and had only a small bungalow (504 square feet) located on the lot. The Nollans' option to purchase was conditioned on their promise to demolish the bungalow and replace it. To do that, the Nollans had to apply for a coastal development permit from the California Coastal Commission. They filed for such a permit and proposed construction of a three-bedroom home similar to other residences in the area.

The Nollans were informed that their application was on the calendar and that the staff had recommended approval provided that the Nollans allow a public easement to make it easier for the public to get to the Cove and Faria County Park.

The Nollans filed suit in the Ventura County Superior Court asking it to invalidate the easement condition. The court agreed and remanded the matter to the commission for a full hearing. The commission found that the new house would block the view of the beach and also inhibit the public psychologically from using the beach.

The Nollans filed another suit and said the condition constituted a taking of their property. The trial court agreed and remanded to the commission. The commission appealed, and the appellate court reversed. The Nollans appealed to the U.S. Supreme Court.

JUDICIAL OPINION

Scalia, Justice

Had California simply required the Nollans to make an easement across their beachfront available to the public on a permanent basis in order to increase public access to the beach, rather than conditioning their permit to rebuild their house on their agreeing to do so, we have no doubt there would have been a taking. To say that the appropriation of a public easement across a landowner's premises does not constitute the taking of a property interest but rather,

"a mere restriction on its use," is to use words in a manner that deprives them of all their ordinary meaning. Indeed, one of the principal uses of the eminent domain power is to assure that the government be able to require conveyance of just such interests, so long as it pays for them. Perhaps because the point is so obvious, we have never been confronted with a controversy that required us to rule upon it, but our cases' analysis of the effect of other governmental action leads to the same conclusion. We have repeatedly held that, as to property reserved by its owner for private use, "the right to exclude [others is] one of the most essential sticks in the bundle of rights that are commonly characterized as property."

Given, then, that requiring uncompensated conveyance of the easement outright would violate the Fourteenth Amendment, the question becomes whether requiring it to be conveyed as a condition for issuing a land use permit alters the outcome. We have long recognized that land use regulation does not affect a taking if it "substantially advance[s] legitimate state interests" and does not "den[y] an owner economically viable use of his land."

The Commission argues that among these permissible purposes are protecting the public's ability to see the beach, assisting the public in overcoming the "psychological barrier" to using the beach created by a developed shorefront, and preventing congestion on the public beaches. We assume, without deciding, that this is so—in which case the Commission unquestionably would be able to deny the Nollans their permit outright if their new house (alone or by reason of the cumulative impact produced in conjunction with other construction) would substantially impede these purposes, unless the denial would interfere so drastically with the Nollans' use of their property as to constitute a taking.

The Commission argues that a permit condition that serves the same legitimate police-power purpose as a refusal to issue the permit should not be found to be a taking if the refusal to issue the permit would not constitute a taking. We agree. Thus, if the Commission attached to the permit some condition that would have protected the public's ability to see the beach notwithstanding construction of the new house—for example, a height limitation, a width restriction, or a ban on fences—so long as the

Commission could have exercised its police power (as we have assumed it could) to forbid construction of the house altogether, imposition of the condition would also be constitutional. Moreover (and here we come closer to the facts of the present case), the condition would be constitutional even if it consisted of the requirement that the Nollans provide a viewing spot on their property for passersby with whose sighting of the ocean their new house would interfere. Although such a requirement, constituting a permanent grant of continuous access to the property, would have to be considered a taking if it were not attached to a development permit, the Commission's assumed power to forbid construction of the house in order to protect the public's view of the beach must surely include the power to condition construction upon some concession by the owner, even a concession of property rights, that serves the same end. If a prohibition designed to accomplish that purpose would be a legitimate exercise of the police power rather than a taking, it would be strange to conclude that providing the owner an alternative to that prohibition which accomplishes the same purpose is not.

The evident constitutional propriety disappears, however, if the condition substituted for the prohibition utterly fails to further the end advanced as the justification for the prohibition. [H]ere, the lack of nexus between the condition and the original purpose of the building restriction converts that purpose to something other than what it was. The purpose then becomes, quite simply, the obtaining of an easement to serve some valid governmental purpose, but without payment of compensation. Whatever may be the outer limits of "legitimate state interests" in the takings

and land use context, this is not one of them. In short, unless the permit condition serves the same governmental purpose as the development ban, the building restriction is not a valid regulation of land use but "an out-and-out plan of extortion."

We are left, then, with the Commission's justification for the access requirement unrelated to land use regulation. The Commission [believes] that the public interest will be served by a continuous strip of publicly accessible beach along the coast.

The Commission may well be right that it is a good idea, but that does not establish that the Nollans (and other coastal residents) alone can be compelled to contribute to its realization. Rather, California is free to advance its "comprehensive program," if it wishes, by using its power of eminent domain for the "public purpose," but if it wants an easement across the Nollans' property, it must pay for it.

It is quite impossible to understand how a requirement that people already on the public beaches be able to walk across the Nollans' property reduces any obstacles to viewing the beach created by the new house. We therefore find that the Commission's imposition of the permit condition cannot be treated as an exercise of its land use power.

Reversed.

CASE QUESTIONS

1. What was the proposed use of the Nollans' land?
2. If the Commission could not have the condition, were they willing to grant the permit?
3. What arguments did the Commission make? Why does the court reject them?

In 2010, the U.S. Supreme Court handled a different coastal property owner issue. In *Stop the Beach Renourishment, Inc. v. Florida Department of Environmental Protection*, 130 S.Ct. 2592 (2010), the court held that when the state of Florida undertook a beach restoration project that added beachfront property to existing homeowners' lands, the state's dedicating the restored and expanded beaches to public use was not a taking that required that the homeowners be compensated. The owners' property lines were their original property lines and any extension of the beach achieved through the state's project constituted public lands and not a taking of their private rights of way to the ocean.

Just Compensation

The final requirement for the proper exercise of eminent domain is **just compensation**. The issue of just compensation is a difficult question of fact. The compensation for the owner is not measured by the governmental entity's gain. In *United States v. Miller*, 317 U.S. 369 (1943), the Supreme Court held that, in cases where it can be determined, fair market value is the measure of compensation. And in *United States ex rel. T.V.A. v. Powelson,* 319 U.S. 266 (1943), the Supreme Court defined fair market value to be "what a willing buyer would pay in cash to a willing seller."

Problems in applying these relatively simple standards include peculiar value to the owner, consequential damages, and greater value of the land because of the proposed governmental project. Basically, the issue of just compensation becomes an issue of appraisal, which is affected by all the various factors involved. One of the current issues in eminent domain is the delay in the government taking, something that leaves the property owners in limbo, without the ability to either develop or lease the property. The following case deals with both the government's and owner's rights as eminent domain stalls and value is affected.

POTOMAC DEVELOPMENT CORP. V. DISTRICT OF COLUMBIA

28 A.3d 531 (D.C. 2011)
The Slow Eminent Domain Pitch

FACTS

Since the 1970s, the Potomac Development Corporation, South Capitol Associates, and 1625 Capitol Street S.W., LLC (appellants/landowners) have owned and managed two pieces of real estate in the 1500 and 1600 blocks of South Capitol Street, S.W. in the District of Columbia. These properties are within two blocks of the Nationals' ballpark. Because of their location near the ball park, these properties were worth significantly more than they would be as simply properties suitable for industrial warehouses.

On June 21, 2005, the District of Columbia Department of Transportation (DDOT) informed the three landowners by letter that the replacement of the Frederick Douglass Memorial Bridge (also known as the South Capitol Street Bridge) required that their properties be taken for purposes of building the approaches to the new bridge. The letter indicated that they would be part of an early acquisition program and that they should expect to have formal action taken in January 2006.

Dreams turned to dust and the best laid plans of the wizards of government central resulted in no action in May 2006, January 2007, and January 2008. Each time the landowners queried DDOT, they were given another promise. The situation would stay in a holding pattern of promises of formal processes and missed deadlines on those promises until 2008 when DC officials hired an appraiser to determine the value of the properties. The appraiser did not have an appraisal until 2009. There was one more glitch when the city learned that the appraiser was coming in with numbers that were too high. So the city fired the appraiser before he revealed his numbers. DC officials hired another appraiser in June 2009, but he had not yet visited the properties as of October 2009.

At this point, the three property owners gave up and filed suit against the city alleging in their complaint that because of the threat of imminent eminent domain, they could not develop or profitably use the properties or sell them to other developers. The complaint described the landowners' situation as one in which they were "in a long-term holding pattern with short-term leases." One property had two tenants under leases that permitted termination on three months' notice, and another property remained vacant and unleased. Before the announced condemnation in 2005, the landowners had been able to lease their properties to generate sufficient income to pay taxes, maintain the properties, and (when feasible) generate net income, awaiting a time when the properties might become more valuable.

The damages portion of the complaint was based on comparable sales. Properties in the area were worth $56 per buildable square foot in mid–2005, $65 per buildable square foot in early 2006, $100 per buildable square foot in late 2006, and between $95 and $117 per buildable square foot in mid–2008. The total damage claim was $34 million based on the number of buildable square feet of the properties and a fair market value of $100 per buildable square foot.

The lower court granted DC its motion to dismiss, concluding that a delay of 5 years was not an unreasonable delay and that the landowners had not lost all value of their property and, as such, were not entitled to compensation. The landowners appealed.

JUDICIAL OPINION

Epstein, Judge

The landowners had brought what is characterized as a "delay-based" taking claim, a claim based on the notion that the actions of the 'taking" governmental body results in a *de facto* or "regulatory" taking.

Whether delay is extraordinary depends on its length and the reasons for it. No categorical rule establishes how long governmental action must preclude use of property before a taking occurs. In assessing the reasons for the delay, courts may consider whether the government acted in good faith, and some courts have been reluctant to find extraordinary delay in the absence of bad faith by the government.

The economic impact of the governmental action in a *de facto* taking case must be severe because "even a substantial reduction of the attractiveness of the property to potential purchasers does not entitle the owner to compensation under the Fifth Amendment."

Before an agency breaks ground on any significant project, whether or not it would require any taking, the agency should be able to get input from the community, which requires advance notice. Early public announcement may also benefit targeted property owners by enabling them to avoid wasteful investment; as appellants acknowledge, property owners may not want to make substantial investments if an impending taking would prevent them from realizing a reasonable return. A lax standard for delay-based taking claims would discourage timely announcement and "encourage hasty decision-making."

Appellants make no claim that the District knew any prediction was false at the time it made the prediction, and they did not allege fraud. Appellants admit that when the District made these predictions, it was planning to replace the Frederick Douglass Memorial Bridge and genuinely intended to take their properties for that public purpose.

Equally important, appellants make no factual allegations concerning the reasons why the District did not meet the schedule it initially described, much less that the reason or reasons for the delay were illegitimate. In fact, appellants acknowledge that the timing of the announcement of the planned taking "may have had any number of reasons behind it," and that reasons for delay such as "budgetary restraints, administrative priorities, planning needs and the like" are wholly legitimate.

Appellants allege that the fair market value of their and other properties near Nationals Park increased substantially during the period of delay, and the District had every reason to move as quickly as possible if delay would cause the amount of just compensation to increase. It would be at best speculative to infer from the facts alleged by appellants that the District needlessly or arbitrarily pushed back its initial schedule even though rising real estate values made delay costly to the District.

Moreover, at oral argument, appellants stated that if the District had told them that it did not know when the planned taking would occur, appellants would have no claim that a *de facto* taking occurred in the interim, and for a substantial part of the four-year period of delay, appellants knew from the District's communications and non-communications that the timing of the actual taking was uncertain at best. However, appellants allege no facts reasonably implying that it is extraordinary for the planning of a public works project of the magnitude of the replacement of the Frederick Douglass Memorial Bridge to take four years from public announcement to institution of formal eminent domain proceedings. For any major capital project like this one, planning is complex and time-consuming, environmental and other reviews take time to complete, and funding takes time to secure, especially when the District and federal governments face fiscal constraints. Appellants do not identify any comparable project in the District or in other jurisdictions that moved more quickly, much less make any factual allegations reasonably suggesting that projects of this scale ordinarily get underway in substantially less than four years.

The second problem that appellants contend supports their delay-based taking claim is that the District replaced the first appraiser because it thought his appraisals would be too high. Although the District hired a new appraiser within a month, the new appraiser allegedly had to start from scratch, delaying the appraisal process by a longer period. Appellants, however, do not allege that but for replacement of the appraiser, the District could or would have initiated formal eminent domain proceedings before appellants filed this lawsuit, so this allegation does not support a claim that the delay was extraordinary or unjustified. To the extent the District's replacement of the original appraiser is suspicious, it would be suspicious regardless of the timing of initiation of eminent domain proceedings. As the trial court observed, appellants have a remedy for any illegitimate decision to replace the appraiser—calling the first appraiser as a witness in the eminent domain case to testify that the properties are worth more than the District claims. In any event, this allegation does not support a plausible inference that the District acted improperly or in bad faith.

It is reasonable to infer from the facts alleged by appellants that the Sword of Damocles hanging over these properties reduced their short-term income-generating potential to a small fraction of what it would otherwise have been. Appellants admit that their "long-term holding pattern" leaves them able to enter into "short-term leases," and they in fact leased one property under an indefinite lease permitting termination on three months' notice. However, appellants allege that the impending taking reduced the income from the short-term lease for one property that they were able to negotiate to a level sufficient only to diminish their losses. As the District points out, appellants acknowledge that it was not always feasible in the three decades they owned the properties to generate a net income, and appellants do not allege that they attempted to find any short-term tenants for the other property that stands vacant and unleased. But appellants allege that the rent generated by any short-term lease in these circumstances would be artificially and substantially depressed by the District's actions.

It is no answer, as the District suggests, that appellants could have found a buyer because any buyer would be assured that it would receive just compensation in the event of a taking. It is plausible to infer from appellants' factual allegations that any potential purchaser while the properties remain in limbo could not make any more productive use of the properties than appellants themselves were able to make, so the only effect of the sale would be to substitute the purchaser for appellants as the plaintiff in a taking case. If the District's actions left appellants' properties with no economic value to any owner except the value of a just compensation claim against the District, the properties have no economic value for purposes of [this] analysis.

However, appellants allege that the fair market value of the properties actually increased during the period of delay, so their ability to realize their long-term investment-backed expectations improved: based on sales or bona fide offers on comparable parcels, appellants contend that the fair market value of their properties increased from $50–65 per buildable square foot to over $100 between 2005 and 2009—that is, from roughly $20 million to $34 million. Because just compensation is generally measured at the time of the taking, appellants would have gotten about $14 million less if the District had taken their properties in 2006 before the delay began than in 2009 after the process became prolonged.

Although the impending taking adversely affected appellants' ability to develop or sell the properties and the short-term value of the property, the fact remains that these long-term investors benefitted from a substantial increase in property values around Nationals Park. Appellants therefore have not alleged facts indicating a "deprivation significant enough to satisfy the heavy burden placed upon one alleging a regulatory taking."

The judgment below is affirmed.

CASE QUESTIONS

1. How does the court respond to the property owners' argument that they are in limbo and unable to lease or sell their properties?
2. What is the court's reasoning regarding the four years of delay by the District of Columbia?
3. Explain how just compensation will be determined in this case.

CONSIDER 19.2   The U.S. Energy Department located its now-failed supercollider project in Ellis County, Texas. Generally, land prices in the area had been $500 to $800 an acre. However, during the two years preceding the announcement of the now-defunct project, as anticipation about the area getting the supercollider project grew, land began selling for as high as $7,000 an acre. The U.S. government's policy is to pay "fair market value" for the land that it needs. How was the fair market value for the nearly 7,000 acres taken by eminent domain for the project determined?   ∎

CONSTITUTIONAL ISSUES IN LAND-USE RESTRICTIONS

The use of land is restricted through zoning requirements (Chapter 18), future interests (Chapter 2), and covenants or restrictions in deeds that control the use of the property being transferred (Chapter 21). Restrictions on land use are

PRACTICAL TIP

Many racially restrictive covenants can still be found in the chain of title for property. Although they are often used for sensational effect, as when the title to the late Chief Justice William Rehnquist's Arizona land was revealed in the newspaper, when his Senate confirmation was pending, as having a racial restriction, they are simply invalid and unenforceable. No one can control the language in deeds used prior to the time of their ownership.

subject to judicial scrutiny. All three forms of restrictions have met with constitutional challenges, discussed in the following sections.

Zoning

Constitutional challenges to zoning have already been discussed in the *Nollan* case and in Chapter 18.

Annexation

The decision to annex property to a city is a difficult one that is marked by strong emotions on both sides of the issue. The U.S. Supreme Court has dealt with the issue of whether a city's annexation process violated the federal Voting Rights Act. In *City of Pleasant Grove v. United States*, 479 U.S. 462 (1987), the court held that the decision on annexation cannot be based on race.

Future Interests

Although fee simples determinable and fee simples subject to conditions subsequent do restrict the use and transferability of property, the courts have not intervened in these land interests unless the restrictions have violated any constitutional rights. Racial restrictions violate constitutional rights. In *Capitol Federal Savings and Loan Association v. Smith*, 316 P.2d 252 (Colo. 1957), the Colorado Supreme Court, in a decision followed by other courts, held that racially based fee simples determinable are unconstitutional.

ETHICAL ISSUE

Consider the following excerpts from insurance memos during the 1950s and 1960s, prior to civil rights laws in the United States.

> *Non-whites present special insurance problems traceable to their generally less favorable living conditions and greater instability of the family among them.*

—From a Met Life internal memo on insurance underwriting in 1964

> *I am concerned about the likelihood that if we continue to write business extensively in certain portions of cities, such as Washington, Baltimore, Detroit, Chicago and New York, where the proportion of the total population that is colored is increasing, we may, say in ten years, wind up with a serious handicap....*[3]

—Edward A. Lew, Internal memo Actuary and statistician, MetLife, 1959

Both documents emerged in a racial discrimination suit filed in 2001 in a federal district court in New York City. Were the actions of the companies legal? Were they ethical?

---

[3]Scott Paltrow, "Old Memos Lay Bare MetLife's Use of Race to Screen Customers," *Wall Street Journal*, July 21, 2001, A1, A10.

All-Adult Covenants

In many areas, particularly in retirement communities, owners impose a restrictive covenant that allows only persons above the ages of 18 or 21 to reside in a particular area: an **all-adult covenant**. The validity of these all-adult covenants and communities has been an issue before the courts, and the following case is one of those judicial reviews.

TAYLOR V. RANCHO SANTA BARBARA

206 F.3d 932 (9th Cir. 2000)
The 55+ Only Mobile Home Park

FACTS

Michael Shawn Taylor, aged 41, bought a mobile home that was located in the Rancho Santa Barbara mobile home park, which rents the lot under the privately owned unit to qualified renters. Taylor applied for a rental agreement. His application was rejected because of his age. As published in park rules, Rancho Santa Barbara restricts occupancy to persons 55 years old or older, and thus Taylor found that he had 14 years to wait before he could move into his unit.

When Taylor learned that spaces would not be rented to persons under 55 years of age, he sued in the district court to challenge as unconstitutional the state and federal statutes that permit park operators to enforce age restrictions. The court dismissed his claim.

The federal Fair Housing Act and California's Mobilehome Residency Law permit otherwise qualified mobile home parks to refuse to rent to tenants aged under 55 years. Taylor challenges these laws as inconsistent with the equal protection accretions to the Fifth Amendment, for 42 U.S.C. § 3607(b)(2) (C), and the Fourteenth Amendment, for California Civil Code § 798.76.

JUDICIAL OPINION

Goodwin, Circuit Judge

We apply rational-basis review to the challenged legislation. Age classifications are not constitutionally suspect, and legislative distinctions based upon age warrant only traditional rational-basis review.

Under rational-basis review, a legislature "need not actually articulate at any time the purpose or rationale supporting its classification. Instead, a classification must be upheld if there is any reasonably conceivable set of facts that could provide a rational-basis for the classification."

Under the current version of the FHA, a community can qualify for the housing-for-older-persons exemption provided that "at least 80 percent of the occupied units are occupied by at least one person who is 55 years of age or older." 42 U.S.C. § 3607(b)(2)(C)(i) (1996). Rancho Santa Barbara qualifies for the exemption as currently enacted.

The housing-for-older-persons exemption bears a rational relationship to the government's legitimate interest in preserving and promoting housing for older persons. Congress reasonably determined that older persons have a particular need for an affordable "safe, supportive environment." Many live on fixed incomes, have particular health needs, and may no longer need a home big enough for a large family.

The housing-for-older-persons exemption permits exempted communities to reduce costs. The exemption permits communities to exist in areas less appropriate or desirable for younger people. Sites typically lack schools or day care facilities. Parks can thrive relatively far from employment centers. The land can be acquired at low cost, and often might otherwise go underused.

In the city of Hemet, 50 percent of its housing is 55-and-over communities. Removing the seniors-only status and requiring these communities to absorb families with children will result in a dramatic shortage of classroom space, and [affect] the tax-base. Demographics are such that the financing of new school construction, in a city that was planned as a retirement community, would not be possible.

The exemption also allows exempted housing communities to offer facilities more appropriate for older persons than for children. For example, communities can devote fewer resources to ensure quiet privacy and child safety. They can build thinner walls, smaller units, and tinier yards. Conversely, communities can devote more resources to facilities and services for older persons. Even though the FHA does not require such facilities, the exemption might rationally promote enhanced services.

That Congress drew the line at age 55—rather than at age 35 or 65 or 67—does not violate equal protection. The selection of age 55 accommodates those who retire early and those who desire to relocate prior to reaching retirement or very old age, when moving might be more difficult. Furthermore, even though the selection of age 55—or any age—might be over and underinclusive on the margin, legislatures are given leeway under rational-basis review to engage in such line drawing.

Taylor contends that the California scheme is even more arbitrary than the federal scheme—and thus even more clearly violative of equal protection—because it allows discrimination against those under 55 in mobile home housing while prohibiting the same discrimination in all other forms of housing. We reject this claim, because the exemption of mobile home parks is rationally related to the legitimate interest of promoting affordable housing for older persons.

By providing this benefit, California conceivably promotes the supply of mobile home parks for older persons. As discussed above with respect to older persons' housing in general, the exemption allows mobile homes to exist in more remote areas and be tailored towards the needs of older persons.

Mobile home parks offer several distinct characteristics that make such housing a particularly desirable option for many older people. Mobile home parks offer small units sitting on small lots, necessarily offering limited privacy and limited room for children. Additionally, mobile home parks are particularly adaptable to inexpensive land away from schools and major economic centers. The parks can be built on minimally improved land, without producing sufficient revenue to make them a viable occupant of more expensive real estate.

Furthermore, mobile homes as a class usually are less expensive than other types of housing, which makes them marketable to persons living on fixed incomes during, or in preparation for, retirement. According to Taylor's own submissions, a two-bedroom mobile home in the area around Santa Barbara sells for roughly $50,000, whereas a comparable two-bedroom condominium in the same area sells for roughly three times as much. Providing a special housing benefit to older persons is neither irrational nor illegitimate.

According to a survey taken shortly before passage of the FHAA, 72 percent of mobile home park residents in California were age 55 or older. Those demographics support the contention that mobile home parks offer distinguishing features making them particularly attractive to older people. Given all of this, California did not act arbitrarily or irrationally by giving disparate treatment to mobile home parks for older persons.

We hold that the challenged legislative schemes do not deprive the plaintiff of equal protection under the laws, because the legislative schemes are rationally related to legitimate state interests. Affirmed.[4]

CASE QUESTIONS

1. Give a description of the history of housing protections for those who are aged 55 and above.
2. Explain the public policy reasons for allowing the age restrictions.

CONSTITUTIONAL ISSUES IN TRANSFER OF PROPERTY

One of the major issues in the transfer of property is discrimination against certain buyers. The Fair Housing Act, passed in 1968 (42 U.S.C. § 3601 *et seq.*), provides that it is

> *unlawful to refuse to sell or rent after the making of a bona fide offer, or to refuse to negotiate for the sale or rental of, or otherwise make unavailable or deny, a dwelling to any person because of race, color, religion, sex, familial status, or national origin.*

The basis for this statutory regulation is the Equal Protection Clause of the Fourteenth Amendment. As discussed in Chapter 1, the Fourteenth Amendment ensures that all citizens are treated equally under state laws.

---

[4]The federal circuits are in agreement with this California decision that all-adult covenants are constitutional. See *Taylor v. Rancho Santa Barbara*, 206 F.3d 932 (9th Cir. 2000).

The Fourteenth Amendment is the basis for many of the racial, religious, and national origin discrimination cases.

The Fair Housing Act applies not only to sellers of properties, but also to real estate brokers and salespeople, mortgage lenders, property insurers, and property appraisers. The following sections cover application of the Fair Housing Act.

Application of the Fair Housing Act

The Fair Housing Act applies to residential housing and prohibits discrimination in selling, renting, lending, or insuring residential property on the basis of race, color, religion, sex, handicap, family status, or national origin. Some states may have additional classes protected under state law.

A handicap is defined as it is under the Americans with Disabilities Act (see Chapters 10 and 11 on leases). A *handicap* is a mental or physical impairment that limits one or more major life activities. Examples of impairment protected under the Fair Housing Act include impairments in sight, mobility, and hearing. Mental illness, heart disease, cancer, cerebral palsy, multiple sclerosis, diabetes, AIDS, HIV, and treatment for substance abuse are also protected. Smokers and current drug users are not protected.

There are some Fair Housing Act exemptions. The owner exemption applies when an owner is selling his or her own home, does not use a real estate agent or broker, does not own more than three single-family homes, and does not use any form of discriminatory advertising. Another owner exemption applies to the owner of a residential dwelling in which he or she also resides and that has four or fewer units that are leased to others. There is also a religious exemption for religious organizations. These organizations can discriminate on the basis of religion in selling and leasing residential properties. Another exemption covered earlier in the chapter is for senior housing, or housing for senior citizens exclusively. There are a substantial number of requirements for senior housing, such as having 80 percent or more of the units occupied by at least one resident who is aged 55 or above.

Types of Discriminatory Conduct Under the Fair Housing Act
Advertising

Brokers, agents, and even newspapers that run residential property ads must use caution in their descriptive terms so that the ads do not suggest limitations on availability of the property to certain protected classes. For example, language that suggests the property is "great for a mature person" would be discriminatory. To comply, brokers and agents should try to describe the property, not potential buyers or lessees, or the seller or the neighbors. The following is an excerpt from a HUD memo offering guidelines for advertising real property.

1. Race, color, national origin. *Real estate advertisements should state no discriminatory preference or limitation on account of race, color, or national origin. Use of words describing the housing, the current or potential residents, or the neighbors or neighborhood in racial or ethnic terms (e.g., white family home, no Irish) will create liability under this section.*

   However, advertisements which are facially neutral will not create liability. Thus, complaints over the use of phrases such as master bedroom, rare find, and desirable neighborhood should not be filed.

2. Religion. *Advertisements should not contain an explicit preference, limitation, or discrimination on account of religion (e.g., no Jews, Christian home). Advertisements which use the legal name of an entity which contains a religious reference (for example, Rose-lawn Catholic Home), or those which contain a religious symbol (such as a cross), standing alone, may indicate a religious preference. However, if such an advertisement includes a disclaimer (such as the statement, "This Home does not discriminate on the basis of race, color, religion, national origin, sex, handicap, or familial status"), it will not violate the Act. Advertisements containing descriptions of properties (apartment complex with chapel), or services (kosher meals available) do not on their face state a preference for persons likely to make use of those facilities, and are not violations of the Act.*

   The use of secularized terms or symbols relating to religious holidays such as Santa Claus, Easter Bunny, or St. Valentine's Day images, or phrases such as "Merry Christmas" or "Happy Easter," or the like does not constitute a violation of the Act.

3. Sex. *Advertisements for single-family dwellings or separate units in a multi-family dwelling should contain no explicit preference, limitation, or discrimination based on sex. Use of the term master bedroom does not constitute a violation of either the sex discrimination provisions or the race discrimination provisions. Terms such as "mother-in-law suite" and "bachelor apartment" are commonly used as physical descriptions of housing units and do not violate the Act.*

4. Handicap. *Real estate advertisements should not contain explicit exclusions, limitations, or other indications of discrimination based on handicap (e.g., no wheelchairs). Advertisements containing descriptions of properties (great view, fourth floor walk-up, walk-in closet), services or facilities (jogging trails), or neighborhoods (walk to bus stops) do not violate the Act. Advertisements describing the conduct required of residents ("non-smoking," "sober") do not violate the Act. Advertisements containing descriptions of accessibility features are lawful (wheelchair ramp).*

5. Familial status. *Advertisements may not state an explicit preference, limitation, or discrimination based on familial status. Advertisements may not contain limitations on the number or ages of children, or state a preference for adults, couples, or singles. Advertisements describing the properties (two bedroom, cozy, family room), services and facilities (no bicycle allowed), or neighborhoods (quiet streets) are not facially discriminatory and do not violate the Act.*

For additional guidance on advertising, see the *HUD Advertising Guide* reproduced in the *Fair Housing Handbook*, which identifies the red flags—the practices and language that may result in FHA violations

---

CONSIDER 19.3   Evaluate the following language and determine whether there is a violation of the Fair Housing Act in running an ad with these terms.

   a. "Spacious 1- & 2-bedroom apartments in quiet mature complex. No pets, please."

   b. "2-person limit."

   c. "Adults pref."

   d. "No children."

   e. "Mature Christian handyman wanted to share house."

   f. "Ideal for professionals."

   g. "Mature setting."

   h. "For one person."

i. "Within walking distance."

j. "Handyman's dream."

k. "No alcoholics."

l. "Female tenant wanted."

m. "Near church."

n. "Desirable neighborhood."

o. "Call Betsy."

p. "No pets."

Blockbusting

Blockbusting, a violation of the Fair Housing Act, is a method of controlling the racial composition of neighborhoods and is usually attributed to the actions of real estate brokers or salespeople. For example, in *United States v. Mitchell*, 327 F. Supp. 476 (N.D. Ga. 1971), a real estate agent went from house to house in a neighborhood informing the residents that "negroes were coming into the neighborhood" and that houses should be sold as quickly as possible. All of the white residents in the neighborhood sold their homes, and the neighborhood became all-black. Mitchell was convicted of violating the Fair Housing Act.

Steering

Steering is another violation of the FHA that is generally attributed to real estate brokers and salespeople. It is an attempt to direct buyers to specific sections of town that are labeled as either "white" or "black" areas. In *Zuch v. Hussey*, 394 F. Supp. 1028 (E.D. Mich. 1975), salespeople found to have violated the Act made statements such as, "Do you read the newspapers? Even the police are afraid to live in the area, and they are supposed to protect the rest of us," and "You wouldn't want that home–the coloreds have moved in pretty good there." In the same case, salespeople discouraged black buyers from buying in white areas by temporarily taking homes off the market. Through these tactics (which were declared illegal), several real estate firms were able to maintain racially segregated neighborhoods in the Detroit area for a time. The following case deals with the extent of liability for FHA violations by brokers and agents.

MEYER V. HOLLEY

537 U.S. 280 (2003)
Is the Broker His Discriminatory Agent's Keeper?

FACTS[5]

Emma Mary Ellen Holley is African-American, her husband, David Holley, is Caucasian, and their son, Michael Holley, is African-American. The Holleys (Respondents) visited Triad Realty's office during October 1996 in Twenty-Nine Palms, California, where they met with Triad agent Grove Crank and inquired about listings for new houses in the range of $100,000 to $150,000. Crank showed them four houses in the area, all above $150,000. In mid-November 1996, the Holleys located a home on their own that happened to be listed by Triad. In response to the Holleys' inquiry about the

---

[5]Some of the facts were added from the lower court opinions in the series of cases surrounding this final decision, such as *Holley v. Crank*, 258 F.3d 1127 (9th Cir. 2001).

home, Triad agent Terry Stump informed them that the asking price for the house was $145,000. The Holleys expressed interest in purchasing the home and offered to pay the asking price and to put $5,000 in escrow for the builder to hold the house until April or May 1997 when they closed escrow on their existing home.

Stump told the Holleys that their offer seemed fair, as did the builder, Brooks Bauer, when Mrs. Holley called him with the same offer. Bauer did express, however, that the offer would have to go through Triad. Later, Stump called Mrs. Holley to tell her that more experienced agents in the office, one of whom was later identified as Grove Crank, felt that $5,000 was insufficient to get the builder to hold the house for six months. The Holleys decided not to raise their offer and Triad never presented the original offer to Bauer. One week later, Bauer inquired at Triad about the status of the Holleys' offer. Crank then allegedly used racial invectives in referring to the Holleys, telling Bauer that he did not want to deal with those "n------s" and called them a "salt-and-pepper team." The Holleys eventually hired a builder to construct a house for them, and Bauer later sold his house for approximately $20,000 less than the Holleys had offered.

Bauer and the Holleys filed suit against David Meyer, the office broker, and Crank and Triad for violations of federal and state fair housing laws. The District Court dismissed all claims other than the Fair Housing Act claim. It also dismissed the claims against Meyer in his capacity as officer of Triad because (1) it considered those claims as assertions of vicarious liability, and (2) it believed that the Fair Housing Act did not impose personal vicarious liability upon a corporate officer.

The Ninth Circuit reversed those determinations. Meyer sought *certiorari* and the U.S. Supreme Court granted his petition.

JUDICIAL OPINION

Breyer, Justice

The Fair Housing Act forbids racial discrimination in respect to the sale or rental of a dwelling. 42 U.S.C. §§3604(b), 3605(a). The question before us is whether the Act imposes personal liability without fault upon an officer or owner of a residential real estate corporation for the unlawful activity of the corporation's employee or agent. We conclude that the Act imposes liability without fault upon the employer in accordance with traditional agency principles, i.e., it normally imposes vicarious liability upon the corporation but not upon its officers or owners.

The Fair Housing Act itself focuses on prohibited acts. In relevant part the Act forbids "any person or other entity whose business includes engaging in residential real estate-related transactions to discriminate," for example, because of "race." 42 U.S.C. § 3605(a). It adds that "[p]erson" includes, for example, individuals, corporations, partnerships, associations, labor unions, and other organizations. It says nothing about vicarious liability.

Nonetheless, it is well established that the Act provides for vicarious liability. This Court has noted that an action brought for compensation by a victim of housing discrimination is, in effect, a tort action. And the Court has assumed that, when Congress creates a tort action, it legislates against a legal background of ordinary tort-related vicarious liability rules and consequently intends its legislation to incorporate those rules.

The Ninth Circuit held that the Fair Housing Act imposed more extensive vicarious liability—that the Act went well beyond traditional principles. The Court of Appeals held that the Act made corporate owners and officers liable for the unlawful acts of a corporate employee simply on the basis that the owner or officer controlled (or had the right to control) the actions of that employee. We do not agree with the Ninth Circuit that the Act extended traditional vicarious liability rules in this way.

For one thing, Congress said nothing in the statute or in the legislative history about extending vicarious liability in this manner. And Congress' silence, while permitting an inference that Congress intended to apply ordinary background tort principles, cannot show that it intended to apply an unusual modification of those rules.

For another thing, the Department of Housing and Urban Development (HUD), the federal agency primarily charged with the implementation and administration of the statute, 42 U.S.C. § 3608, has specified that ordinary vicarious liability rules apply in this area. And we ordinarily defer to an administering agency's reasonable interpretation of a statute.

Neither does it help to characterize the statute's objective as an "overriding societal priority." We agree with the characterization. But we do not agree that the characterization carries with it a legal rule that would hold every corporate supervisor personally liable without fault for the unlawful act of every corporate employee whom he or she has the right to supervise. Rather, which "of two innocent people must suffer," and just when, is a complex matter. We believe that courts ordinarily should determine that matter in accordance with traditional principles of vicarious liability—unless, of course, Congress, better able than courts to weigh the relevant policy considerations, has instructed the courts differently.

The Ninth Circuit did not decide whether other aspects of the California broker relationship, when added to the "right to control," would, under traditional legal principles and consistent with "the general common law of agency," establish the necessary relationship. But in the absence of consideration of that matter by the Court of Appeals, we shall not consider it.

Respondents also point out that, when traditional vicarious liability principles impose liability upon a corporation, the corporation's liability may be imputed to the corporation's owner in an appropriate case through a "'piercing of the corporate veil.'" *United States v. Bestfoods*, 524 U.S. 51. The Court of Appeals, however, did not decide the application of "veil piercing" in this matter either. It falls outside the scope of the question presented on certiorari. And we shall not here consider it.

The Ninth Circuit nonetheless remains free on remand to determine whether these questions were properly raised and, if so, to consider them.

The judgment of the Court of Appeals is vacated, and the case is remanded for further proceedings consistent with this opinion.

CASE QUESTIONS

1. When is vicarious liability for violation of the FHA imposed?

2. What does the Court do with the issue of piercing the corporate veil?

3. What conclusions can you draw about broker liability under FHA for the acts of his or her agents?

PRACTICAL TIP

With this new standard on vicarious liability under the FHA, brokers and their companies should take steps to prevent liability. First, the office should have clear policies on discrimination and provide training on the FHA. Second, the broker may have to perform occasional checks or audits on offers and how they are processed. Finally, agents should be reminded of their obligation to present all offers from buyers to sellers.[6]

Redlining

Redlining, yet another FHA violation, is the refusal by a lender to lend or an insurer to insure on property because of its location within a predetermined geographic area. The name for this practice arose because lenders and insurers were literally drawing red lines on maps around areas in which property loans and insurance should not be made or should be made on less-than-favorable terms. The Fair Housing Act and many state statutes prohibit redlining; in many cases, they require lending institutions to submit loan figures so that an agency can verify the institutions' lending records. For example, federal institutions are required to submit loan figures under the Home Mortgage Disclosure Act (12 U.S.C. §§ 2801 *et seq.*). As noted in Chapter 15, the Community Reinvestment Act (CRA) of 1977 (12 U.S.C. §§ 2901 *et seq.*) imposes an affirmative obligation on federal financial institutions to meet the community's loan needs regardless of property location or area condition. The demand on lenders for expanded numbers of loans to LMI borrowers was a contributing factor to the subprime mortgage market collapse.

Redlining can occur in a number of different ways. The most obvious is when lenders openly refuse to make loans in particular areas. Other, more subtle processes still classified as redlining include the arbitrary variation of loan application processes and loan terms. For example, redlining can consist of requiring a higher down payment, higher closing costs, minimum loan amounts, lowered percentage of loan amount to appraised value, or underappraisal of property. During the housing bubble, there were many redlining suits filed against lenders who offered different sets of lending terms based on either the race of the applicants or the location of the property. To recover in these suits, the plaintiffs had to be

---

[6]There are a number of differing decisions on vicarious liability of principals for the acts of their agents related to the Fair Housing Act. See, e.g., *Padilla v. Yoo*, 633 F. Supp.2d 1005 (N.D. Cal. 2009), *Lebron v. Rumsfeld*, 764 F.Supp.2d 787 (D.S.C. 2011), and *Colon v. Zydell*, 635 F. Supp. 2d 264 (W.D.N.Y. 2009).

able to show that terms presented and used were done along racial lines. For example, it would be unconstitutional to offer only ARMs to a certain racial group as opposed to offering options on fixed-rate loans. *Grimes v. Fremont General Corp.,* 785 F.Supp.2d 269 (S.D.N.Y. 2011).

CONSIDER 19.4   Great Eastern Bank has been sued by several members of the Navajo Tribe for redlining on home loans located on the reservation. Great Eastern has supplied statistics indicating that over 75 percent of all home mortgage loans on reservation property end in default and foreclosure. Is Great Eastern's statistic a valid basis for denying future reservation loans? ▪

Redlining is also an issue in setting appraisal values. In *United States v. American Institute of Real Estate Appraisers,* 442 F. Supp. 1072 (Ill. 1977); affirmed 590 F. 2d 242 (8ᵗʰ Cir. 1978), appraisals done after taking race and national origin into account were held to be violative of the Fair Housing Act.

Section 8 Housing and the Fair Housing Act

One of the complex issues in the area of fair housing arises when there is an intersection of several federal statutes that provide housing rights. For example, the so-called "Section 8 housing program" now places low-income families in mainstream housing and does so through rent vouchers. Landlords who participate in the program were once required by HUD regulation and federal statute to take all the Section 8 tenants sent their way, with the only limitation being HUD's restrictions on the number of Section 8 tenants within a particular apartment complex or area. Known as the "take one, take all" provisions, the impact on landlords and properties was substantial, and the requirement was repealed by Congress. A landlord need not take all Section 8 tenants, but the decision not to rent must be based on something other than receipt of public assistance.[7]

Zoning and the Fair Housing Act

Another constitutional issue that has emerged in fair housing relates to zoning provisions that cover group homes. In *U.S. v. City of Baltimore,* 845 F.Supp.2d 640 (D. Md. 2012), the U.S. Department of Justice brought suit against the city of Baltimore for its zoning provisions that required proposed group homes (and other types of businesses such as adult bookstores, rehab centers, rest homes, pharmacies, and hospitals) to apply for conditional use permits, a process that takes around six weeks to complete. Baltimore's code dealt with all applications for conditional uses for rehab facilities as application for "non-bedridden alcoholics." The court held that such a broad classification in the city's zoning laws, without a showing of dangers presented by such a classification, was a violation of their constitutional rights because the city had required special review of the group without showing that such increased scrutiny was necessary.

---

[7]*Becker v. Our Lady of Angels Apartments, Inc.,* 192 F.3d 601 (6th Cir. 1999). See also, *Commission on Human Rights and Opportunities v. Sullivan,* 939 A.2d 541(Conn., 2008).

The Americans with Disabilities Act and the Fair Housing Act

Both the Fair Housing Act and the laws and regulations on Section 8 housing prohibit discrimination on the basis of disability. One form of discrimination is the refusal of a landlord to make reasonable accommodations for tenants with disabilities. For example, a landlord must provide a tenant with multiple sclerosis an assigned parking space despite the usual "first-come, first-serve" policy because of the tenant's difficulty with walking and incontinence, and the space he or she needs for negotiating getting in and out of the car.

Courts are often faced with yet another wrinkle as ADA intersects with FHA as it intersects with Section 8 housing recipients. For example, in *Salute v. Stratford Greens Apartments*, 136 F.3d 293 (2nd Cir. 1998), Richard Salute and Marie Kravette both had disabilities but were also qualified to receive Section 8 housing assistance. They were denied an apartment at the Stratford Greens Garden Apartments because the owner refused to take Section 8 tenants. Salute and Kravette filed suit alleging that they were refused an apartment because of their disabilities. The court found for the landlord, holding that because "the Section 8 program is voluntary and nonparticipating owners routinely reject Section 8 tenants, the owners' 'non-participation constitutes a legitimate reason for their refusal to accept Section 8 tenants and … we therefore cannot hold them liable for … discrimination under the disparate impact theory.'" Not all courts have followed this line of reasoning in such cases. Resolving the conflicting rights of landlords to refuse to rent to Section 8 tenants along with the protections of FHA and ADA has resulted in differing views among the federal courts. The perfect storm of federal laws and rights will require U.S. Supreme Court resolution.

CONSIDER 19.5   Henry W. Geter, II, rents an apartment at a complex named "The Cloisters," which is located on Michigan Avenue, N.E., in the District of Columbia. Geter's lease began on March 28, 2003, and ran for one year with rent payments of $1,325 due on the first day of each month. After several months, Geter suffered complications from diabetes and had both feet amputated. Based on his disability, Geter was awarded disability benefits from the Social Security Administration ("SSA") beginning in November 2003 "on or about the second Wednesday of each month." On October 26, 2003, Geter presented the SSA notice of award to property manager Connie Fletcher and requested that his monthly payment date and rent "be adjusted to reflect the comments of the filing received from the Government, with the reassignment of the rent to $890."

On February 16, 2007, Geter received a Notice to Cure Violation of Tenancy or Vacate for "continually and habitually paying [his] rent late." He was given the option of curing the violation by "paying the full amount of the rent due" by March 31, 2007, or vacating the premises on or before April 1, 2007. Geter responded by claiming, in part, housing discrimination based on his disability. He renewed his request for reasonable accommodations by changing the due date of his monthly payments from the first of the month to the 15th of the month and reducing his monthly rent payment to $890. Geter then filed suit for a violation of the Fair Housing Act. Did the landlord violate the FHA? Discuss why or why not. *Geter v. Horning Bros. Management*, 537 F.Supp.2d 206 (D.D.C. 2008). ■

Another FHA/ADA issue that has resulted in significant litigation involves emotional support animals and apartment complex/HOA restrictions on pets. The apartment and HOA rules cannot prohibit the animals, but they can require medical documentation for the need for the animals. The rules can also impose requirements on the owners when the animals are in common areas. The decisions require reasonable accommodations for the animals. *Stevens v. Hollywood Towers and Condominium Ass'n,* 836 F.Supp.2d 800 (N.D. Ill. 2011).

Penalties Under the Fair Housing Act

The Fair Housing Act is enforced through civil suits by individuals and through complaints filed by state agencies, HUD, or special interest groups on behalf of protected classes. Even testers, or individuals sent out to pose as potential buyers or renters, can bring actions for violations. Administrative law judges assigned to hear complaints brought by HUD have the authority to issue injunctions to halt an activity. They also have the authority to assess fines and penalties which range from $10,000 to $50,000, depending upon the nature of the violation and the violator's past history of violations. Individuals can recover damages for emotional distress, mental anguish, and any other damages resulting from the discrimination.

Many cases brought by HUD are settled through a consent decree that requires a remedy for the disparity in housing opportunities. Compliance with the consent decree terms is critical because the courts have upheld fines against officers and government officials when they fail to comply with the requirements of the decree. In *Spallone v. United States,* 493 U.S. 265 (1990), the city of Yonkers, New York, was charged with engaging in a pattern and practice of housing discrimination. The city signed a consent decree but by 1988 the requirements of the decree to remedy past housing discrimination had not been met, and a federal district court held city council members in contempt and imposed a daily fine. The U.S. Supreme Court eventually reversed the contempt holding and the fines against the individuals as a violation of some portions of the First Amendment, but did uphold sanctions against the city for failure to comply. The case made clear the authority of the federal government to collect fines from municipalities.

Due Process and Real Property

Throughout the preceding chapters, the concept of due process has crept into the discussion. For example, mortgage foreclosures are a huge group of due process rights. With respect to real property taxes, landowners must be given opportunities to be heard on the valuations of their properties. Tax sales require advance notice to the property owner and an opportunity for redemption. All of these protections are afforded through the Fifth and Fourteenth Amendments' due process clauses of the Constitution. Due process protections may be satisfied through judicial or administrative proceedings, as long as there is the opportunity to be heard.

CAUTIONS AND CONCLUSIONS

This chapter discussed only a few issues of constitutional law affecting real property rights. The opportunities for constitutional challenges to real property rights and procedures are as limitless as the field of constitutional law. Basically, the areas of constitutional law affecting real property are concerned with fairness, the deprivation of rights in existing property, or the right to own property. Constitutional protections offer security for property owners holding title and provide potential property owners the opportunity to purchase.

KEY TERMS

all-adult covenant, 544

blockbusting, 548

eminent domain, 533

just compensation, 539

redlining, 550

steering, 548

taking, 537

CHAPTER PROBLEMS

1. The Laufmans attempted to purchase property in an area of Cincinnati that was changing in racial composition from white to black. Oakley Building and Loan denied the Laufmans' loan application on grounds that the neighborhood was declining and they would not have sufficient security by taking a mortgage on the property located there. The Laufmans filed suit alleging that Oakley Building and Loan had violated the Fair Housing Act. Is there a violation? *Laufman v. Oakley Building & Loan Co.*, 408 F. Supp. 489 (Ohio 1976).

2. What would happen if the state took private property for the purposes of building an overpass that resulted in directing traffic to a newly developed area to the benefit of its developer and away from existing businesses? How would the *Kelo* case apply? *County of Hawai'i v. C & J Coupe Family Ltd. Partnership*, 198 P.3d 615 (Haw. 2008).

3. William G. Haas & Company purchased land and procured a site permit from the city of San Francisco for the construction of a high-rise project. The site permit was later invalidated because of violations of the Environmental Quality Act and because of the rezoning of the property, which prohibited high-rise projects in the area. Haas brought suit claiming the rezoning and the imposition of other land-use restrictions diminished the value of his property to such an extent that the regulations constituted a taking. What was the result? *Haas v. San Francisco*, 605 F.2d 1117 (9th Cir. 1979).

4. Midwestern Indemnity refused to write insurance policies for homes located in neighborhoods that were predominantly black. Midwestern's reasons were high theft, vandalism, and arson rates in the areas, and company officials had the areas marked on maps in their offices. Several black homeowners brought suit, alleging the insurer was redlining. Midwestern maintains that insurers are not subject to the Fair Housing Act. What is the result? *Dunn v. Midwestern Indemnity*, 88 F.R.D. 191 (S.D.Ohio 1980).

5. Brigid Healy has resided in Apt. 3B at 30 Eastchester Road, New Rochelle, New York, since December 1, 1996. The parties had a written lease initially that was entered into on November 1, 1996, with the lease to commence December 1, 1996, and end one year later. In connection with this lease, Healy entered into a Housing Assistance Payment (HAP) Contract with the City of New Rochelle as the Section 8 Administrator. HAP was to pay the Landlord, under the Section 8 program, a subsidy of $607 per month; Healy had the responsibility to pay the balance of the rent.

The lease was renewed for additional periods, and the proportion of the rent paid through the Section 8 program subsidy was periodically adjusted so that as of November 1, 2001, of a total contract rent of $986, tenant was to pay $7 and the Administrator was to pay $979 to the Landlord. The lease as renewed was to end by its terms on November 30, 2001.

Several months prior to the November 30 termination date, the Landlord notified the Administrator's Section 8 office that the Landlord "no longer wish[ed] to accept the Section 8 Program" and that the Landlord "will be terminating the tenant's lease when it expires (11-30-01)." However, HAP continued to pay the rent, and rent for December 2001 and January 2002 had been paid, but Healy did not pay her portion of the rent for those months. Now the landlord wishes to evict Healy for nonpayment of rent. Can Healy be evicted for nonpayment of rent, or does Section 8 Housing protection apply? Can the landlord simply decide not to rent to Section 8 tenants? *30 Eastchester LLC v. Healy*, 2002 WL 553709 (N.Y. City Ct. 2002); see also *Rosario v. Diagonal Realty LLC*, 803 N.Y. S.2d 343 (N.Y. 2005).

6. Robyn Halprin owned a home in The Prairie Single Family Homes of Dearborn Park subdivision in Chicago, Illinois. Robyn was engaged or married to Rick Halprin, who is Jewish. On January 8, 2001, Rick became a co-owner of the home.

Problems began around November 2, 2000, when Robyn was not elected to one of two vacant Director seats on the Association's Board, and the board refused to inform Robyn how many proxy votes had been cast in the election. Robyn believed that the board strategically used proxies to maintain control of Association elections. The Association also refused Robyn's December 2000 requests for documents pertaining to matters such as the Association's spending practices and conduct of its Board elections.

At some time between December 20, 2000, and January 10, 2001, a board member vandalized Robyn's home by writing with a red marking pen on a stone wall the phrase "H-town property." Robyn says that "H-town" is a shorthand version of the derogatory slang term "Hymie Town," which refers to places where Jewish persons reside.

The relationships deteriorated and, as a result of these disputes, Robyn and her husband filed a suit for violation of the Fair Housing Act ("FHA"). Would the FHA apply to treatment of tenants and home-owners *after* they have taken possession of the property? *Halprin v. Prairie Single Family Homes of Dearborn Park Ass'n.*, 208 F. Supp.2d 896 (N.D. Ill. 2002).

7. In 1927, W. T. Shore and T. C. Wilson gave property to the city of Charlotte "so long as the property was used for municipal parks, golf courses, or playgrounds for whites only." Several black citizens have brought suit, alleging the restriction is unconstitutional. What type of interest was created, and what is the result?

8. Bradley Winker owned a duplex dwelling unit in Brookings, South Dakota. The duplex was located in an "R-2" residential zoning area that permits two-family dwellings but limits the number of unrelated adults who may constitute a "family." An inspection of one unit in the duplex on November 8, 1994, revealed the presence of at least four unrelated adult college students residing in one unit of the duplex. Brookings filed a complaint against Winker, charging him with a violation of the Brookings ordinance that restricts the number of unrelated adults per unit. Winker sued, challenging the Brookings ordinance as a violation of the due process and equal protection clauses with its restrictive definition of family. Is the zoning restriction valid or unconstitutional? Be sure to refer to cases in this chapter and Chapter 18 to help you analyze the question. *City of Brookings v. Winker*, 554 N.W.2d 827 (S.D. 1996).

9. The Montgomery Newspapers, Inc., ran ads for rental properties in their six newspapers with the following language:

 a. "mature person"
 b. "ideal for quiet and reserved single and/or couple"
 c. "professional male ... only"
 d. "quiet mature setting"

 Do any of these phrases violate the Fair Housing Act?

 Fair Housing Council of Suburban Philadelphia v. Montgomery Newspapers, 141 F.3d 71 (3rd Cir. 1998).

10. Bert and Cleone Reece own an apartment building near Logan Field in Billings, Montana. Their policy was to refuse to rent any of their apartments to single women who did not have cars. Further, they did not consider alimony or child support in determining whether a woman could meet monthly rental payments. Do their policies create any constitutional problems? *United States v. Reece*, 457 F. Supp. 43 (Utah 1978).

For research activities related to this chapter, go to our text companion website at www.cengagebrain.com

CHAPTER 20

ENVIRONMENTAL LAW

By the shores of Gitche Gumee,
By the shining Big-Sea-Water, ...
How they built their nests in summer,
Where they hid themselves in winter,
How the beavers built their lodges,
Where the squirrels hid their acorns,
How the reindeer ran so swiftly,
Why the rabbit was so timid

Henry Wadsworth Longfellow, *"Hiawatha's Childhood"*

This chapter discusses land use and answers the following questions: What types of governmental regulations affect property use and ownership rights? Who is responsible for enforcing governmental regulations? What are the penalties for violation of the regulations? In the event of conflicts between common law rights and governmental regulations, which group of laws will control?

STATUTORY ENVIRONMENTAL LAW: AIR POLLUTION REGULATION

Early Legislation

The first legislation dealing with the problem of air pollution, the Air Pollution Control Act, was passed in 1955, but it lacked enforcement teeth. Federal regulation in this area continued to be ineffective until the Air Quality Act of 1967 which authorized the then Department of Health, Education, and Welfare to oversee the states' adoption of air quality standards and the implementation of those plans. Still, by 1970 no state had adopted a comprehensive plan.

1970 Amendments to the Clean Air Act: New Standards

Because the states did not take action concerning air pollution, Congress passed the 1970 amendments to the original **Clean Air Act** (42 U.S.C. § 7401) with amendments providing the first real authority for enforcement. Under the act, the **Environmental Protection Agency (EPA)** was authorized to establish air quality standards; once those standards were developed, states were required to adopt implementation plans to achieve the federally developed standards. These **state implementation plans (SIPs)** had to be approved by the EPA, and adoption and enforcement of the plans were no longer discretionary but mandatory. To obtain EPA approval, the SIPs had to meet deadlines for compliance with the EPA air quality standards.

1977 and 1990 Amendments

With the 1977 amendments came authority for the EPA to regulate business growth by mandating air quality standards. The EPA developed two categories for determining business growth. **Nonattainment areas** include those areas with existing, significant air quality problems, the so-called dirty areas. Today, the number of nonattainment areas has been reduced significantly. In some categories, nonattainment areas have been eliminated. The second classification, called **prevention of significant deterioration (PSD) areas,** provides the EPA with a means for monitoring and preventing increased pollution in these designated spots.

The EPA is authorized under the 1990 amendments to pay $10,000 rewards to people who provide information leading to criminal convictions or civil penalties. The penalties for violations are now substantial.

New Forms of Control: EPA Uses Economic Forces

For nonattainment areas, the EPA developed its **emissions offset policy**, which imposes three requirements before a new facility can begin operation in a nonattainment area: (1) The new facility must have the greatest possible emissions controls; (2) the new facility operator must have all its other operations in compliance with standards; and (3) the new facility's emissions must be offset by reductions from other facilities in the area.

In evaluating permission for the new facility, the EPA follows the **bubble concept**, which examines all the air pollutants in the area as if they came from a single source. If a new plant will have no net effect on the air in the area (after offsets from other plants), the EPA allows the new facility to operate. This bubble concept now applies in PSD areas. PSD regulations give the EPA the right to review proposed plant constructions and modifications before they can be started. Facility operators must establish that air quality will not experience any significant effects and that emissions will be controlled with appropriate devices.

In *Environmental Defense v. Duke Energy*, 549 U.S. 561 (2007), the U.S. Supreme Court supported the EPA's PSD role in plant modifications, even when those modifications are not major ones. Duke Energy had begun implementing modifications to one of its coal-fired electricity plants without first seeking EPA approval. Duke was relying on past EPA procedures that had required approval for major modifications only. An environmental group brought suit against the company to require EPA approval and the agency agreed. The Court held that the EPA was acting within the authority granted to it by Congress and that requiring permits for all modifications was not beyond the agency's authority under the Clean Air

The purchase of a particular tract of land may be tied to the buyer's being able to obtain the necessary emissions permits, as available under the 1990 amendments to the Clean Air Act. The Chicago Board of Trade deals with emissions permits in much the same way in which it sells other commodities. The first trading in these emissions permits occurred on March 30, 1993, with a permit for emission of one ton of sulfur dioxide selling for between $122 and $450. Environmental groups currently own about 10 percent of all emissions permits. In 2006, the carbon credits market also emerged. Companies and individuals can purchase, from companies that specialize in renewable energy sources, credits for their own carbon emissions as a means of offsetting their contributions to global warming. Under Cap and Trade, this market would increase in activity and price.

Act. The Court also held that the EPA could step up its standard for permit requirements to one that goes beyond best available technology (BAT) to **maximum achievable control technology (MACT)**, a standard not controlled by cost alone.

New Forms of Control: EPA Regulations and Global Warming

In *Massachusetts v. EPA*, 549 US 497 (2007), the Court held that the Clean Air Act mandated EPA action on greenhouse gases and global warming. With this decision and the change of administration in 2009, the EPA has begun developing new regulations under the Clean Air Act.

These regulatory changes have resulted in challenges by states and businesses with the EPA experiencing losses in six of those challenges because the regulations went beyond the EPA's statutory authority. For example, the Cross-State Air Pollution Rule (the Transport Rule) was enacted by the EPA in 2011 and was promulgated to address downwind pollution, i.e., pollution that drifts from one state to others. The Clean Air Act authorizes the EPA to require the upwind states to reduce omissions that were causing the problems downwind, something that drew on the bubble concept. Upwind states (there are 28) must prevent sources within their borders from emitting federally determined "amounts" of pollution that travel across state lines and "contribute significantly" to a downwind State's "nonattainment" of federal air quality standards.[1]

Sometimes called the "good neighbor" provision, the Transport Rule limits emissions from upwind States' coal- and natural gas-fired power plants. Those power plants generate the majority of electricity used in the United States, but they also emit pollutants that affect air quality. Several groups and businesses filed suit against the EPA challenging the Transport Rule, *Eme Homer City Generation, L.P. v. EPA*, --- F.3d ----, 2012 WL 3570721 (C.A.D.C.) as *ultra vires*. The impact of the rule has been the shut-down of many coal-fired utility plants.

The court found that under the Transport Rule, upwind states may be required to reduce emissions by more than what they had contributed to a downwind state and that state's resulting nonattainment of EPA standards. The court also found that the EPA was using the good neighbor provision to impose massive emissions reduction requirements on upwind states without regard to the limits imposed by the statutory text. In addition, the Clean Air Act grants to the states the initial opportunity to implement reductions required by EPA under the good neighbor provision. However, the EPA did not allow the states to exercise this statutorily provided initial opportunity to implement the required reductions. Instead, the EPA designed Federal Implementation Plans and imposed them on the states.

The court concluded that such steps were *ultra vires* because they "transgressed statutory boundaries." The court noted that while Congress could decide to alter the statute to permit or require the EPA's approach but that unless and until

---

[1]The 28 states involved in EPA nonattainment actions are: Alabama, Arkansas, Florida, Georgia, Illinois, Indiana, Iowa, Kansas, Kentucky, Louisiana, Maryland, Michigan, Minnesota, Mississippi, Missouri, Nebraska, New Jersey, New York, North Carolina, Ohio, Oklahoma, Pennsylvania, South Carolina, Tennessee, Texas, Virginia, West Virginia, and Wisconsin.

Congress does so, the agency must follow the statute, "It is not our job to set environmental policy. Our limited but important role is to independently ensure that the agency stays within the boundaries Congress has set. EPA did not do so here." This case and others will be heard on appeal to the U.S. Supreme Court.

New Forms of Control: EPA and Small Businesses

The impact of the 1990 Clean Air Act amendments was more substantial on smaller businesses, such as dry cleaners, paint shops, and bakeries, because the definition of a major source of pollution was changed from those businesses emitting 100 tons or more a year to those emitting 50 tons or more per year. Many dry cleaners impose an environmental surcharge on their customers to cover the cost of emissions compliance.

New Forms of Control: EPA and Market Forces

The **Clean Air Act Amendments of 1990** also resulted in an exchange for the buying and selling of EPA permits for sulfur dioxide emissions. If, for example, a utility has an EPA permit to discharge one ton of sulfur dioxide per year, but its equipment permits it to run "cleaner" so that it discharges less than the one ton, the utility can sell the emissions savings portion of its permit to another utility.

CONSIDER 20.1   Do you think that emissions permits are real or personal property? What issues do you see arising if the permits are classified as real property? What concerns arise if the permits are classified as personal property? What issues do you see with the sale of carbon credits?

CONSIDER 20.2   Union Electric Company is an electric utility company servicing St. Louis and large portions of Illinois and Iowa. It operates three coal-fired generating plants in metropolitan St. Louis that are subject to sulfur dioxide restrictions under the state of Missouri's implementation plan. Union Electric did not seek review of the implementation plan, but applied for and obtained variances from the emissions limitations. When an extension for the variances was denied, Union Electric challenged the implementation plan on the grounds that it was technologically and economically infeasible and should therefore be amended. Will Union Electric succeed in having the plan amended? What in the Clean Air Act provides the response to Union? *Union Electric Co. v. EPA*, 427 U.S. 246 (1976).

STATUTORY ENVIRONMENTAL LAW: WATER POLLUTION REGULATION

Early Legislation

The **Rivers and Harbors Act of 1899** was the first federal water pollution statute and it prohibited the release of "any refuse matter of any kind or description" into navigable waters in the United States without a permit from the Army Corps of Engineers. Decades later, in 1965, the **Water Quality Act** created both the first federal law on water quality as well as the **Federal Water Pollution Control Administration (FWPCA)**. Because the act contained few expeditious enforcement procedures, only about half of the states had developed their zones and standards by 1970, and none of the states were engaged in active enforcement of those standards.

Present Legislation

The 1972 passage of the **Federal Water Pollution Control Act of 1972** (33 U.S.C. § 1401) was the first meaningful and enforceable federal water legislation. In 1977, the act was renamed the **Clean Water Act** and moved water pollution regulation from local to federal control. Federal standards and requirements for water discharges were established nationwide.

The ranges of discharges permitted per industrial group are referred to as **effluent guidelines**. The EPA has developed a permit system based on standards for effluent discharge around three categories of pollutants: **conventional, nonconventional,** and **toxic pollutants**.

All discharges into the waterways require a **National Pollution Discharge Elimination System (NPDES)** permit from the EPA. This type of permit is required only for direct dischargers, or **point sources**, and is not required of plants that discharge into sewer systems (although these secondary dischargers may still be required to pretreat their discharges). Obtaining a permit requires EPA and state approval as well as public hearings.

The permits also impose requirements on the permit holder. If the plant is going to release a conventional pollutant, the EPA can require it to pretreat the substance with the **best conventional treatment (BCT)**. However, the EPA can also require the **best available treatment (BAT)** standard, which is the highest standard imposed. Until 2009, the standard for requiring BAT was solely consideration of environmental effects and not the economic effects on the applicant. However, in *Entergy Corporation v. Riverkeeper, Inc.,* 556 U.S. 208 (2009), the U.S. Supreme Court held that the EPA can use cost–benefit analysis to allow variances from those standards. In the case, Entergy's cost of bringing cooling water intake structures to the higher level the EPA requires for new structures would have been 9 times its existing costs. The court held that the additional benefit achieved was too small to justify the cost of bringing the cooling water facilities to current standards.

CONSIDER 20.3   Inland Steel Company applied for a permit from the EPA under the Federal Water Pollution Control Act of 1972. Although Inland was granted the permit, the EPA made the permit modifiable as new standards for toxic releases and treatment were developed. Inland claimed that the modification restriction on the permit was invalid because the EPA did not have such authority and also because Inland would be subject to every technological change or discovery made during the course of the permit. Inland filed suit. Was the restriction invalid? *Inland Steel Company v. Environmental Protection Agency,* 574 F.2d 367 (7th Cir. 1978).

In 1986, Congress passed the **Safe Drinking Water Act** (42 U.S.C. §300f), which provided for the EPA to establish national standards for contaminant levels in drinking water. The states are primarily responsible for enforcement and can have higher standards than the federal standards, but they must at least enforce the federal standards for their drinking water systems.

In 1990, Congress passed the **Oil Pollution Act (OPA)** (33 U.S.C. §1251). The act was passed in response to large oil tanker spills, such as the one resulting from the grounding of the *Exxon Valdez* in Prince William Sound, Alaska, that resulted in a spill of 11 million gallons of crude oil that coated 1,000 miles of Alaskan coastline. By the summer of 2010, the *Exxon Valdez* oil spill seemed to be a relatively small environmental disaster, despite its scope, because of the April 2010 explosion and subsequent 90-day leak from BP's Deepwater Horizon rig in the Gulf Coast. Over 200 million gallons of oil flowed into the Gulf before the well was capped on August 3, 2010. BP was required to establish a recovery fund of $20 billion for damages to property as well as for payment of lost income to affected businesses and individuals.

STATUTORY ENVIRONMENTAL LAW: SOLID-WASTE DISPOSAL REGULATION

During the 1970s, two major toxic waste debacles resulted in federal regulation of toxic waste disposal. In 1978, "Love Canal," as it came to be called, made national news as 80,000 tons of hazardous waste were found in the ground in an area that was primarily residential and included an elementary school. Epidemiological studies of cancer and illness rates in the area led to the discovery and eventual cleanup. Also, in Sheppardsville, Kentucky, an area that came to be called "Valley of the Drums," 17,000 drums of hazardous waste leaked tons of chemicals into the ground and water supply before their removal.

The emotional reaction to these two problem areas and the public outcry resulted in the passage of the **Toxic Substances Control Act (TOSCA)** (15 U.S.C. § 601) in 1976 and authorized the EPA to control the manufacture, use, and disposal of toxic substances.

Also passed by Congress in reaction to dangerous dumping practices was the **Resource Conservation and Recovery Act of 1976 (RCRA)** (42 U.S.C. § 6901). The two goals of the act are to control the disposal of potentially harmful substances and to encourage resource conservation and recovery. A critical part of the act's control is the requirement that manufacturers obtain a permit for the storage or transfer of hazardous wastes so that the location of such wastes can be traced through a detailed permit system.

CERCLA and the Superfund

In 1980, Congress passed the **Comprehensive Environmental Response, Compensation, and Liability Act (CERCLA)** (42 U.S.C. § 9601), which authorized the president to issue funds for the cleanup of areas that were once disposal sites for hazardous wastes. Under the act, a **Hazardous Substance Response Trust Fund** was set up to provide funding for cleanup. If funds are expended in such a cleanup, then, under the provisions of the act, the company responsible for the hazardous wastes can be sued by the federal government and required to repay the amounts expended from the trust fund. Often called the **Superfund**, the funds are available for governmental use but cannot be obtained through suit by private citizens affected by the hazardous disposals. Under the **Superfund Amendment and Reauthorization Act**, the EPA can recover cleanup funds from those responsible for the release of hazardous substances.

CERCLA Lender Liability

One of the more intriguing issues that resulted from CERCLA liability was whether a lender has the responsibility of cleanup because it took back property due to a foreclosure sale or a deed in lieu of foreclosure. The **Asset Conservation, Lender Liability, and Deposit Insurance Protection Act of 1996** provides a specific exclusion for lenders in that the definition of "owner/operator" does not include someone who "holds indicia of ownership primarily to protect his security interest." This provision has been called the "secured lender exemption" from CERCLA liability. However, a lender can lose its status if it "actually participate[s] in the management or operational affairs of a vessel or facility." A lender can do the following and still not be subject to environmental liability:

- Monitor or enforce terms of the security agreement
- Monitor or inspect the premises or facility
- Mandate that the debtor take action on hazardous materials
- Provide financial advice or counseling
- Restructure or renegotiate the loan terms
- Exercise any remedies available at law
- Foreclose on the property
- Sell the property
- Lease the property

CERCLA—Four Classes of Liability Rules

Four classes of parties can be held liable under CERCLA. The present owners and operators of a contaminated piece of property comprise one group. While *owner* is self-explanatory, *operator* includes those who lease property and then contaminate it, such as those who lease factories, operate storage facilities, and so forth. The owners and operators at the time the property was contaminated form the second group. This group brings under CERCLA jurisdiction those who were responsible for the property contamination, as opposed to present owners who had the problem deeded to them. For example, many gas stations have been converted to other businesses. Suppose that one of the underground gas tanks once used by the gas station has been leaking hazardous materials into the surrounding soil. Not only would the present owners be liable; so also would be all those who owned the gasoline station previously. The final two groups consist of those who transport hazardous materials and those who arrange for the transportation of hazardous materials. Virtually no liability exemptions are available to those who fit into these four groups. The following case deals with an interesting interpretation of CERCLA liability.

BURLINGTON NORTHERN RAILWAY / SHELL OIL CO. V. U.S.

556 U.S. 599 (2009)
Am I My Customer's Keeper? I'm Only the Arranger

FACTS

In 1960, Brown & Bryant, Inc. (B & B) began operating an agricultural chemical distribution business (the Arvin facility). B & B opened its business on a 3.8-acre parcel of former farmland, and then expanded operations onto an adjacent 0.9-acre parcel of land owned jointly by the Atchison, Topeka & Santa Fe Railway Company and the Southern Pacific Transportation Company (Railroads). Wastewater and chemical run-off from B & B's operations seeped into the groundwater.

B & B purchased its chemicals from Shell. Shell would arrange for delivery and when the product arrived, it was transferred from tanker trucks to B & B's bulk storage tank. During each of these transfers leaks and spills could—and often did—occur.

In the late 1970s Shell took steps to encourage customers to handle its products safely. Shell provided distributors with safety manuals and offered a voluntary discount program for customers that improved their bulk handling and safety facilities. Later, Shell required customers to obtain inspections for self-certification of compliance with laws and regulations. Despite improvements to its facilities under these Shell programs, B & B remained a "'[s]loppy' [o]perator."

In 1989, the EPA designated B & B's land as a Superfund site. However, B & B went bankrupt that year. By 1998, the federal, state, and local governments (governments) had spent more than $8 million in cleanup costs at the B & B site.

In 1991, the EPA ordered the Railroads to conduct cleanup processes. The Railroads did so, incurring expenses of more than $3 million in the process. The parties ended up in court seeking a determination of their share of cleanup liability. The U.S. District Court held that both the Railroads and Shell were responsible parties (PRPs) under CERCLA: the Railroads because they were owners and Shell because it had "arranged for" the disposal of hazardous substances through its sale and delivery of chemicals. The court apportioned the Railroads' liability as 9 percent of the Governments' total response cost. The court held Shell liable for 6 percent of the total site response cost.

Shell and the governments appealed. The Ninth Circuit held that Shell, as an arranger, was involved in the disposal of a hazardous substance and held Shell and the Railroads jointly and severally liable for the Governments' clean-up costs.

The Railroads and Shell appealed.

JUDICIAL OPINION

Stevens, Justice

...an entity could not be held liable as an arranger merely for selling a new and useful product if the purchaser of that product later, and unbeknownst to the seller, disposed of the product in a way that led to contamination. Less clear is the liability attaching to the many permutations of "arrangements" that fall between these two extremes—cases in which the seller has some knowledge of the buyers' planned disposal or whose motives for the "sale" of a hazardous substance are less than clear.

The Governments assert that by including unintentional acts such as "spilling" and "leaking" in the definition of disposal, Congress intended to impose liability on entities not only when they directly dispose of waste products but also when they engage in legitimate sales of hazardous substances knowing that some disposal may occur as a collateral consequence of the sale itself. Shell was properly found to have arranged for the disposal. Shell was aware that minor, accidental spills occurred during transfer...

[t]he evidence does not support an inference that Shell intended such spills to occur. To the contrary, the evidence revealed that Shell took numerous steps to encourage its distributors to reduce the likelihood of such spills

Although Shell's efforts were less than wholly successful, given these facts, Shell's mere knowledge that spills and leaks continued to occur is insufficient grounds for concluding that Shell "arranged for" the disposal. Accordingly, we conclude that Shell was not liable.

[T]he [district] court found that the volume of hazardous-substance-releasing activities on the B & B property was at least 10 times greater than the releases that occurred on the Railroad parcel. The Railroad parcel contributed to no more than 10% of the total site contamination, some of which did not require remediation.

The fact that no spills on the Railroad parcel required remediation lends strength to the District Court's conclusion ... any miscalculation on that point is harmless.

For the foregoing reasons, we conclude that the Court of Appeals erred by holding Shell liable as an arranger under CERCLA. Furthermore, we conclude that the District Court reasonably apportioned the Railroads' share of the site remediation costs at 9%. The judgment is reversed.

CASE QUESTIONS

1. Where do you think the term "arranger" fits in the categories of those who are responsible for cleanup costs under CERCLA?
2. What do you think the practical effect of this decision will be on companies who own Superfund sites? Does the complexity of analysis for liability help companies in clean-up cases?
3. What do you think will happen to government agencies in their efforts to seek reimbursement for their cleanup efforts?

CONSIDER 20.4   Grand Auto Parts Stores receives used automotive batteries from customers as trade-ins. Grand Auto drives a screwdriver through spent batteries and then sells them to Morris Kirk & Sons, a battery-cracking plant that extracts and smelts leads. Tons of crushed battery casings were found on Kirk's land. The EPA sought to hold Grand Auto liable for cleanup. Can Grand Auto be held liable? *Catellus Dev. Corp. v. United States*, 34 F.3d 748 (9th Cir. 1994). ———————— ■

CERCLA and Corporate Liability

CERCLA liability has also been extended to corporate board members and corporate successors and officers where a company is purchased by another firm. Those who merge or buy corporations also buy into CERCLA liability—liability under CERCLA continues after a transfer of ownership. The U.S. Supreme Court ruled in *United States* v. *Bestfoods*, 528 U.S. 810 (1999) that a parent corporation is not automatically liable under CERCLA for a subsidiary corporation's conduct, but may be responsible if the subsidiary is simply a shell. In other words, CERCLA's liability of parent corporations for the actions of their subsidiaries is governed by corporate law on piercing the corporate veil (see Chapter 22). Under the *Bestfoods* case, liability of the parent corporation for actions of a subsidiary results if the parent operates or controls the operation of the subsidiary.[2]

CERCLA and Buying Land

PRACTICAL TIP

Due diligence is necessary not only when buying property but also when buying companies with land holdings. Liability under CERCLA transfers via land ownership or corporate ownership.

The best safeguard against CERCLA liability is screening the property carefully before buying it or accepting it as collateral. The lender and any purchaser of a piece of property should conduct a *due diligence review* of the property. A due diligence review has three phases. Phase I consists of a search to determine whether evidence of past or current environmental problems is present on the property. Evidence reviewed in a Phase I search would be private and public records, aerial photographs, and a site inspection. If Phase I reveals some concerns, the parties proceed to Phase II, which consists of chemical analysis of soil, structures, and water from the property. If Phase II finds the presence of contaminants, the report for Phase II estimates the cost of cleanup. Phase III is the actual cleanup plan.

New Developments under CERCLA

CERCLA Challenges

Companies have been grounding challenges to CERCLA in the basic administrative law principle of an arbitrary and capricious action of an EPA demand for cleanup of a site when the demand for cleanup is not linked to any danger. For example, the EPA was challenged in *U.S.* v. *Broderick Investment Co.*, 200 F.3d 679 (10th Cir. 1999) on its costly clean-up demands that required that the cancer rate in the area be reduced to 1 in 100,000, a rate higher than in non-Superfund sites. However, because a day-care center was planned for the land, the court upheld the clean-up standards as neither arbitrary nor capricious.

---

[2]The work of Professors Cindy A. Schipani and Lynda J. Oswald is an excellent resource for discussions on parent liability for CERCLA violations, as well as a history of the development and scope of CERCLA. See, e.g., Lynda J. Oswald and Cindy A. Schipani, "CERCLA and the 'Erosion' of Traditional Corporate Law Doctrine," 86 *Northwestern Law Review* 259 (1990). Their work was referred to in the *Bestfoods* case.

PRACTICAL TIP

When negotiating for environmental hazard insurance, be sure to cover both known and unknown hazards. Be sure to cover on-site and off-site hazards so that the issue of, for example, lead creeping into the water supply from adjoining land is covered for the contractor who builds on clean land.

Insurers and CERCLA

Another judicial issue that continues to evolve is whether property insurance can be used to cover CERCLA liability. Courts are left with interpretation issues on these policies. Ambiguities in the meaning of the term "pollution" in a policy are construed against the insurer and in favor of coverage for the property owner. One court has held that there is no other way to interpret "pollution" other than to include CERCLA liability. *Sulphuric Acid Trading Co., Inc. v. Greenwich Ins. Co.*, 211 S.W.3d 243 (Tenn. App. 2006). CERCLA coverage is available, but it is a policy rider and requires additional premiums. Many insurers exclude coverage without a specific rider.

CERCLA and The Self-Audit

The EPA encourages companies to self-identify problem lands and areas in exchange for reduced fines. The EPA and the company work together to solve problems and be certain cleanup is done where warranted. Self-audits also help companies to be more accurate in their disclosures to shareholders and analysts.

PRACTICAL TIP

Companies have hired executive-level managers such as vice presidents for environment or vice presidents for health, safety, and environment to manage a staff of in-house professionals who do everything from supervising a company's current activities to investigating past activities to determine environmental problems. These problems are then reported to the EPA and the company and agency work together to solve the problem and ascertain that cleanup is done where warranted. These self-audits and disclosures also help the companies be more accurate in their disclosures in materials for shareholders and analysts.

Under the EPA's program, **Incentives for Self-Policing, Disclosure, Correction, and Prevention of Violations**, those companies that come forward voluntarily, having met certain conditions, will have their penalties reduced for any violations uncovered. The conditions for reduced penalties are:

1. The violations were uncovered as part of a self-audit or due diligence done on property.
2. The violations were uncovered voluntarily.
3. The violations were reported to the EPA within 10 days.
4. The violations were discovered independently and disclosed independently, not because someone else was reporting or threatening to report.
5. There is correction of the violation within 60 days.
6. There is a written agreement that the conduct will not recur.
7. There can be no repeat violations or patterns of violations.
8. There is no serious harm to anyone as a result of the violation.
9. The company cooperates completely with the EPA.

The EPA will reduce fines and penalties by 75 percent if substantially all the conditions are met. The EPA will also not recommend criminal prosecution to the Department of Justice. The documents related to the audit can be protected by the attorney/client privilege, even those that are disclosed to the EPA. The clarification of the privilege has resulted in most companies taking advantage of the EPA's self-reporting protections.

CERCLA and Brownfields

CERCLA has been so effective that designated Superfund sites, as of 2010, that remained undeveloped totaled 425,000. Called "**brownfields**," these sites are defined by the EPA as "real property, the expansion, redevelopment, or reuse of which may be complicated by the presence or potential presence of a hazardous substance, pollutant, or contaminant." Brownfields often contribute to urban blight and are barriers to economic development and revitalization.[3]

The Small Business Liability Relief and Brownfields Revitalization Act allows 75 federal agencies to work together in the *Federal Partnership Action Agenda* to provide funding for proposals to clean up and use these brownfields (42 U.S.C.A. §9601). EPA rules now provide a process for application to become an "innocent land-owner," someone who seeks to develop the Brownfield but wants an exemption from CERCLA exposure. That designation then allows the applicant to obtain federal funding for purposes of cleaning up and developing the Brownfield.

ETHICAL ISSUE

The Superfund has been used quite frequently since its inception. The result is that more funding is needed to keep it going. Congress has proposed expanding the tax used for funding to include all manufacturers. When expansion of the funding sources for the Superfund has been proposed in Congress, the businesses not currently subject to the Superfund tax have opposed additional impositions on them. Do these firms have an obligation to assist in the cleanup? Can some firms claim that they do not affect the environment? Is the cleanup a general business obligation?

State Regulation of Hazardous Waste

Many states have their own regulatory schemes to provide mechanisms and funding for cleanup, and penalties for failure to follow their requirements. All 50 states have some form of hazardous waste regulation, and the definitions of hazardous wastes as well as the penalties vary. Arizona includes garbage in its definition, and Oregon establishes fines on the basis of a fee per animal destroyed as a result of the waste. The death of one mountain goat due to hazardous waste will cost the violator $3,500 in Oregon.

Some states impose mandatory disclosure requirements in certain real estate transactions. Some states also have regulations that cover other types of transfers, such as stock sales, that might result in the indirect transfer of property. The purpose of these disclosure statutes is to have the seller reveal the types of activities that have occurred on the premises. The goal is to either have the parties then agree to have cleanup done prior to closing, or force the selling party into a cleanup because the disclosure of environmental hazards can permit a rescission of the sales agreement.

STATUTORY ENVIRONMENTAL LAWS: ENVIRONMENTAL QUALITY REGULATION

As part of its environmental control scheme, Congress also passed an act that regulates what its own governmental entities can do in the use of their properties. The **National Environmental Policy Act (NEPA)** of 1969 (42 U.S.C. § 4321) was passed to require federal agencies to take into account the environmental impact

---

[3]For more information about brownfields, go to http://www.epa.gov/brownfields/about.htm.

of their proposed actions and to prepare an **environmental impact statement (EIS)** before taking any proposed action.

An EIS must be prepared and filed with the EPA whenever an agency sends a proposed law to Congress and whenever an agency will take major federal action significantly affecting the quality of the environment. The information required in an EIS is as follows:

1. The proposed action's environmental impact
2. Adverse environmental effects (if any)
3. Alternative methods
4. Short-term effects versus long-term maintenance, enhancement, and productivity
5. Irreversible and irretrievable resource uses

Examples of federal agency actions that have faced the issue of preparation of EISs include the Alaskan oil pipeline, the extermination of wild horses on federal lands, the construction of government buildings, the NAFTA treaty, and highway construction. In 2008, the U.S. Supreme Court held there was an exigency exception to the EIS requirements in a case in which Navy training that was necessary for national defense would have been unduly delayed and the resulting harm from the Navy's use of sonar was not irreparable. *Winter v. National Resources Defense Council*, 555 U.S. 7 (2008).

The following case involves an issue of whether an EIS was required.

SIERRA CLUB V. UNITED STATES DEPARTMENT OF TRANSPORTATION

753 F.2d 120 (D.C. 1985)
Jetting into Jackson Hole

FACTS

In 1983, the Federal Aviation Administration (FAA) issued two orders amending the operations specifications for Frontier Airlines, Inc., and Western Airlines, Inc. These amendments gave the airlines permanent authorizations to operate Boeing 737 jet airplanes (B-737s) out of Jackson Hole Airport, which is located within the Grand Teton National Park in Wyoming. These two airlines are the only major commercial carriers that schedule flights to and from Jackson Hole.

Private jets have flown into the airport since 1960. Western Airlines has been flying into Jackson Hole since 1941. The airport is the only one in the country located in a national park, and Congress has continually funded expansions and improvements of the once single-dirt-runway airport.

In 1978, Frontier applied for permission to fly B-737s into the Jackson Hole Airport. The FAA released its EIS on the application in 1980. The EIS found that B-737s were comparable with C-580 propeller aircraft (the type then being used by Western and Frontier) for noise intrusion, but were substantially quieter than the private jets using the airport. The study also showed that fewer flights would be necessary since the B-737 could carry more passengers and that different flight paths could reduce noise. Based on this EIS, Frontier was given the right to use B-737s for two years. When Frontier applied for permanent approval, the FAA used the 1980 EIS statement and found that with flight time restrictions, the impact would not harm the environment.

The Sierra Club (Petitioner), a national conservation organization, brought suit for the failure to file an EIS for the 1983 amendments and for the use of national park facilities for commercial air traffic without considering alternatives.

JUDICIAL OPINION

Bork, Circuit Judge

We do not think the FAA violated NEPA by failing to prepare an additional EIS. Under NEPA, an EIS must be prepared before approval of any major federal action that will "significantly affect the quality of the human environment." The purpose of the Act is to require agencies to consider environmental issues before taking any major action. Under the statute, agencies have the initial and primary responsibility to determine the extent of the impact and whether it is significant enough to warrant preparation of an EIS. This is accomplished by preparing an Environmental Assessment (EA). An EA allows the agency to consider environmental concerns, while reserving agency resources to prepare full EIS's for appropriate cases. If a finding of no significant impact is made after analyzing the EA, then preparation of an EIS is unnecessary. An agency has broad discretion in making this determination, and the decision is reviewable only if it was arbitrary, capricious or an abuse of discretion.

This court has established four criteria for reviewing an agency's decision to forego preparation of an EIS. First, the agency must have accurately identified the relevant environmental concern. Second, once the agency has identified the problem, it must take a "hard look" at the problem in preparing the EA. Third, if a finding of no significant impact is made, the agency must be able to make a convincing case for its finding. Last, if the agency does find an impact of true significance, preparation of an EIS can be avoided only if the agency finds that changes or safeguards in the project sufficiently reduce the impact to a minimum.

The first test is not at issue here. Both the FAA and Sierra Club have identified the relevant environmental concern as noise by jet aircraft within Grand Teton National Park. The real issues raised by Sierra Club are whether the FAA took a "hard look" at the problem, and whether the methodology used by the agency in its alleged hard look was proper.

We find that the FAA did take a hard look at the problem. The FAA properly prepared an EA to examine the additional impact on the environment of the plan. The EA went forward from the 1980 EIS. The 1980 EIS, which was based on extensive research by Dr. Hakes of the University of Wyoming, noise testing by the FAA, and data derived from manufacturer information, showed that noise intrusions of B-737 jets over the level caused by C-580 propeller aircraft amounted to only 1 dbl near the Airport and decreased in proportion to the distance from the Airport. The agency, exercising its expertise, has found that an increase this minute is not significant for any environment. In addition, the EIS and Hakes studies were based on a worst case scenario, and it was determined that if certain precautions were taken the actual noise levels could be diminished greatly.

Petitioner argues that because Jackson Hole Airport is located within national parkland a different standard—i.e., individual event noise level analysis—is mandated. Both individual event and cumulative data were amassed in preparing the 1980 EIS on which the EAs were based. The fact that the agency in exercising its expertise relied on the cumulative impact levels as being more indicative of the actual environmental disturbance is well within the area of discretion given to the agency. We agree with petitioner that although noise is a problem in any setting, "airplane noise is a problem fundamentally inconsistent with the type of recreational experience Park visitors are seeking" and should be minimized. Here the FAA found that a cumulative noise increase of 1 dbl or less is not significant—even for the pristine environment in which Jackson Hole Airport is located.

Given all of these facts, we think the FAA was not required to prepare yet another EIS before granting permanent authorizations for the use of B-737s.

The orders of the FAA are hereby affirmed.

CASE QUESTIONS

1. Who is involved in the case?
2. What is the basis for the appeal?
3. What has the FAA allowed? Will the authorizations stand?

STATUTORY LAW: OTHER FEDERAL ENVIRONMENTAL REGULATIONS

In addition to the previously discussed major environmental laws, many other specific federal statutes protect the environment.

Surface Mining

The **Surface Mining and Reclamation Act of 1977** (42 U.S.C. §6907) requires those mining coal to restore land surfaces to their original conditions and prohibits surface coal mining without a permit.

Noise Control

Under the **Noise Control Act of 1972** (42 U.S.C. §4901), the EPA, along with the FAA, can control the amount of noise emissions from low-flying aircraft for the protection of landowners in flight paths.

Pesticide Control

Under the **Federal Environmental Pesticide Control Act**, the use of pesticides is controlled. All pesticides must be registered with the EPA before they can be sold, shipped, distributed, or received. Also under the act, the EPA administrator is given the authority to classify pesticides according to their effects and dangers.

OSHA

The **Occupational Safety and Health Administration** (OSHA) is responsible for workers' environments. OSHA controls the levels of exposure to toxic substances and requires safety precautions for exposure to such dangerous substances as asbestos, benzene, and chloride.

Asbestos

Buildings that contain asbestos materials remain a problem for buyers, sellers, and occupants. The **Asbestos Hazard Emergency Response Act (AHERA)**, passed in 1986, required all public and private schools to arrange for the inspection of their facilities to determine whether their buildings had asbestos-containing materials. Schools are required to develop plans for containment, but other buildings are not regulated. Questions such as the impact of the release of asbestos from the walls when tenants, employees, and others hang photos and other objects by nailing them into the walls remain. The issues of the degree of harm and the cost of replacement continue to be debated among property owners.

Endangered Species

In 1973, Congress passed the **Endangered Species Act (ESA)**, a law that has been a powerful tool for environmentalists in protecting certain species through their advocacy of restrictions on commercial use and development when the habitats of certain species are interfered with. Under the act, the Secretary of the Interior is responsible for identifying endangered terrestrial species, and the Secretary of

Commerce identifies endangered marine species. In many instances, litigation deals with which species should or should not be on the list. Once a species is on the list, its critical habitat cannot be disturbed by development, noise, or destruction.

The following case is one that gave federal agencies broad authority in protecting endangered species.

BABBITT V. SWEET HOME CHAPTER OF COMMUNITIES FOR A GREAT OREGON

515 U.S. 687 (1995)
Lumberjacks v. Spotted Owls

FACTS

Two U.S. agencies halted logging in the Pacific Northwest because it endangered the habitat of the northern spotted owl and the red-cockaded woodpecker, both endangered species. Sweet Home Chapter (respondents) is a group of landowners, logging companies, and families dependent on the forest products industries in the Pacific Northwest. They brought suit seeking clarification of the authority of the Secretary of the Interior and the Director of the Fish and Wildlife Service (petitioners) to include habitation modification as a harm covered by the Endangered Species Act (ESA).

The federal district court found for the Secretary and Director and held that they had the authority to protect the northern spotted owl through a halt to logging. The court of appeals reversed. Babbitt, the Secretary of the Interior, appealed.

JUDICIAL OPINION

Stevens, Justice

Section 9(a)(1) of the Endangered Species Act provides the following protection for endangered species:

Except as provided in sections 1535(g)(2) and 1539 of this title, with respect to any endangered species of fish or wildlife listed pursuant to section 1533 of this title it is unlawful for any person subject to the jurisdiction of the United States to—(B) take any such species within the United States or the territorial sea of the United States[.] 16 U.S.C. §1538(a)(1).

Section 3(19) of the Act defines the statutory term "take":

The term 'take' means to harass, harm, pursue, hunt, shoot, wound, kill, trap, capture, or collect,

or to attempt to engage in any such conduct. 16 U.S.C. § 1532(19).

The Act does not further define the terms it uses to define "take." The Interior Department regulations that implement the statute, however, define the statutory term "harm":

Harm in the definition of 'take' in the Act means an act which actually kills or injures wildlife. Such act may include significant habitat modification or degradation where it actually kills or injures wildlife by significantly impairing essential behavioral patterns, including breeding, feeding, or sheltering. 50 C.F.R. §17.3 (1994).

We assume respondents have no desire to harm either the red-cockaded woodpecker or the spotted owl; they merely wish to continue logging activities that would be entirely proper if not prohibited by the ESA. On the other hand, we must assume *arguendo* that those activities will have the effect, even though unintended, of detrimentally changing the natural habitat of both listed species and that, as a consequence, members of those species will be killed or injured. Under respondents' view of the law, the Secretary's only means of forestalling that grave result—even when the actor knows it is certain to occur—is to use his §5 authority to purchase the lands on which the survival of the species depends. The Secretary, on the other hand, submits that the §9 prohibition on takings, which Congress defined to include "harm," places on respondents a duty to avoid harm that habitat alteration will cause the birds unless respondents first obtain a permit pursuant to §10.

The text of the Act provides three reasons for concluding that the Secretary's interpretation is reasonable. First, an ordinary understanding of the word "harm" supports it. The dictionary definition of the verb form of "harm" is "to cause hurt or damage to: injure." *Webster's Third New International Dictionary* 1034 (1966). In the context of the ESA, that definition naturally encompasses habitat modification that results in actual injury or death to members of an endangered or threatened species.

Respondents argue that the Secretary should have limited the purview of "harm" to direct applications of force against protected species, but the dictionary definition does not include the word "directly" or suggest in any way that only direct or willful action that leads to injury constitutes "harm." Moreover, unless the statutory term "harm" encompasses indirect as well as direct injuries, the word has no meaning that does not duplicate the meaning of other words that §3 uses to define "take." A reluctance to treat statutory terms as surplusage supports the reasonableness of the Secretary's interpretation.

Second, the broad purpose of the ESA supports the Secretary's decision to extend protection against activities that cause the precise harms Congress enacted the statute to avoid. As stated in §2 of the Act, among its central purposes is "to provide a means whereby the ecosystems upon which endangered species and threatened species depend may be conserved."

Third, the fact that Congress in 1982 authorized the Secretary to issue permits for takings that §9(a)(1)(B) would otherwise prohibit, "if such taking is incidental to, and not the purpose of, the carrying out of an otherwise lawful activity," 16 U.S.C. §1539 (a)(1)(B), strongly suggests that Congress understood §9(a)(1)(B) to prohibit indirect as well as deliberate takings. The permit process requires the applicant to prepare a "conservation plan" that specifies how he intends to "minimize and mitigate" the "impact" of his activity on endangered and threatened species, 16 U.S.C. §1539(a)(2)(A), making clear that Congress had in mind foreseeable rather than merely accidental effects on listed species.

The Court of Appeals made three errors in asserting that "harm" must refer to a direct application of force because the words around it do. First, the court's premise was flawed. Several of the words that accompany "harm" in the §3 definition of "take," especially "harass," "pursue," "wound," and "kill," refer to actions or effects that do not require direct applications of force. Second, to the extent the court read a requirement of intent or purpose into the words used to define "take," it ignored §9's express provi-

sion that a "knowing" action is enough to violate the Act. Third, the court employed *noscitur a sociis* to give "harm" essentially the same function as other words in the definition, thereby denying it independent meaning. The canon, to the contrary, counsels that a word "gathers meaning from the words around it." The statutory context of "harm" suggests that Congress meant that term to serve a particular function in the ESA, consistent with but distinct from the functions of the other verbs used to define "take." The Secretary's interpretation of "harm" to include indirectly injuring endangered animals through habitat modification permissibly interprets "harm" to have "a character of its own not to be submerged by its association."

When it enacted the ESA, Congress delegated broad administrative and interpretive power to the Secretary. The task of defining and listing endangered and threatened species requires an expertise and attention to detail that exceeds the normal province of Congress. The proper interpretation of a term such as "harm" involves a complex policy choice. When Congress has entrusted the Secretary with broad discretion, we are especially reluctant to substitute our views of wise policy for his. In this case, that reluctance accords with our conclusion, based on the text, structure, and legislative history of the ESA, that the Secretary reasonably construed the intent of Congress when he defined "harm" to include "significant habitat modification or degradation that actually kills or injures wildlife."

In the elaboration and enforcement of the ESA, the Secretary and all persons who must comply with the law will confront difficult questions of proximity and degree; for, as all recognize, the act encompasses a vast range of economic and social enterprises and endeavors. These questions must be addressed in the usual course of the law, through case-by-case resolution and adjudication.

Reversed.

CASE QUESTIONS

1. Is habitat modification harming endangered species?
2. Does the Court's interpretation mean no intent is required to violate ESA?
3. Did Congress intend to give the secretary authority to shut down an industry?
4. What ethical issues arise from this case?

Since the time of these head-on confrontations, the logging and paper industries have adopted a "Sustainable Forestry Initiative." The Initiative, adopted by 200 members of the American Forest and Paper Association, supports eco-friendly logging. The Nature Conservancy supports the Initiative, which has had the effect of negotiated solutions to the issue of logging versus environmental protection. No further legislation has been needed at the federal level because of the cooperation between and among these groups.

In the following case, the U.S. Supreme Court interpreted the Endangered Species Act as also permitting lawsuits by landowners who are affected by the statute's application.

BENNETT V. SPEAR

520 U.S. 154 (1997)
Suckered into a Dam

FACTS

The Fish and Wildlife Service issued an opinion on the operation of the Klamath Irrigation Project and the project's impact on two varieties of endangered fish. The Klamath Project is one of the oldest of the federal reclamation projects and is a series of lakes, rivers, dams, and irrigation canals in northern California and southern Oregon. The opinion concluded that the operation of the project might impact on the Lost River Sucker (*Deltistes luxatus*) and Shortnose Sucker (*Chasmistes brevirostris*), species of fish that were listed as endangered in 1988. The opinion further provided for alternative means of operation for the project that included the maintenance of minimum water levels in certain portions of the project.

Brad Bennett and other ranchers (petitioners) operate their ranches within the areas designated to receive less water pursuant to the biological opinion issued. Bennett filed suit alleging that the opinion was incorrect in its conclusions on the impact of the project on the two species of fish and that the opinion failed to take into account the resulting economic impact of lessening the water levels. Bennett's complaint alleged that the ESA and the Administrative Procedure Act (APA) required the federal government to take his interests into account in making the determination as to what to do about the project. The federal district court dismissed the complaint and the court of appeals affirmed the dismissal. Mr. Bennett appealed.

JUDICIAL OPINION

Scalia, Justice

We first turn to the question the Court of Appeals found dispositive: whether petitioners lack standing by virtue of the zone-of-interests test. Although petitioners contend that their claims lie both under the ESA and the APA, we look first at the ESA because it may permit petitioners to recover their litigation costs, and because the APA by its terms independently authorizes review only when "there is no other adequate remedy in a court."

The question of standing "involves both constitutional limitations on federal-court jurisdiction and prudential limitations on its exercise."

Numbered among these prudential requirements is the doctrine of particular concern in this case: that a plaintiff's grievance must arguably fall within the zone of interests protected or regulated by the statutory provision or constitutional guarantee invoked in the suit.

We have made clear, however, that the breadth of the zone of interests varies according to the provisions of law at issue, so that what comes within the zone of interests of a statute for purposes of obtaining judicial review of administrative action under the "generous review provisions" of the APA may not do so for other purposes.

The first question in the present case is whether the ESA's citizen-suit provision, set forth in pertinent part in the margin, negates the zone-of-interests test (or, perhaps more accurately, expands the zone of interests). We think it does. The first operative portion of the provision says that "any person may commence a civil suit"—an authorization of remarkable breadth when compared with the language Congress ordinarily uses. Even in some other environmental statutes, Congress has used more restrictive formulations, such as "[any person] having an interest which is or may be adversely affected," or "any person having a valid legal interest which is or may be adversely affected ... whenever such action constitutes a case or controversy." And in contexts other than the environment, Congress has often been even more restrictive. In statutes concerning unfair trade practices and other commercial matters, for example, it has authorized suit only by "[a]ny person injured in his business or property."

Our readiness to take the term "any person" at face value is greatly augmented by two interrelated considerations: that the overall subject matter of this legislation is the environment (a matter in which it is common to think all persons have an interest) and that the obvious purpose of the particular provision in question is to encourage enforcement by so-called "private attorneys general"—evidenced by its elimination of the usual amount-in-controversy and diversity-of-citizenship requirements, its provision for recovery of the costs of litigation (including even expert witness fees), and its reservation to the Government of a right of first refusal to pursue the action initially and a right to intervene later. Given these factors, we think the conclusion of expanded standing follows.

It is true that the plaintiffs here are seeking to prevent application of environmental restrictions rather than to implement them. But the "any person" formulation applies to all the causes of action authorized by §1540(g)—not only to actions against private violators of environmental restrictions, and not only to actions against the Secretary asserting underenforcement under §1533, but also to actions against the Secretary asserting overenforcement under §1533. The Court of Appeals therefore erred in concluding that petitioners lacked standing under the zone-of-interests test to bring their claims under the ESA's citizen-suit provision.

By the Government's own account, while the Service's Biological Opinion theoretically serves an "advisory function," 51 Fed. Reg. 19928 (1986), in reality it has a powerful coercive effect on the action agency:

> The statutory scheme … presupposes that the biological opinion will play a central role in the action agency's decision-making process, and that it will typically be based on an administrative record that is fully adequate for the action agency's decision insofar as ESA issues are concerned … [A] federal agency that chooses to deviate from the recommendations contained in a biological opinion bears the burden of 'articulat[ing] in its administrative record its reasons for disagreeing with the conclusions of a biological opinion,' 51 Fed.Reg. 19, 956 (1986).

A Biological Opinion of the sort rendered here alters the legal regime to which the action agency is subject. When it "offers reasonable and prudent alternatives" to the proposed action, a Biological Opinion must include a so-called "Incidental Take Statement"—a written statement specifying, among other things, those "measures that the [Service] considers necessary or appropriate to minimize [the action's impact on the affected species]" and the "terms and conditions … that must be complied with by the Federal agency … to implement [such] measures."

The Service itself is, to put it mildly, keenly aware of the virtually determinative effect of its biological opinions. The Incidental Take Statement at issue in the present case begins by instructing the reader that any taking of a listed species is prohibited unless "such taking is in compliance with this incidental take statement," and warning that "[t]he measures described below are nondiscretionary, and must be taken by [the Bureau]." Given all of this, and given petitioners' allegations that the Bureau had, until issuance of the Biological Opinion, operated the Klamath Project in the same manner throughout the twentieth century, it is not difficult to conclude that petitioners have met their burden—which is relatively modest at this state of the litigation—of alleging that their injury is "fairly traceable" to the Service's Biological Opinion and that it will "likely" be redressed—i.e., the Bureau will not impose such water level restrictions—if the Biological Opinion is set aside.

Whether a plaintiff's interest is "arguably … protected … by the statute" within the meaning of the zone-of-interests test is to be determined not by reference to the overall purpose of the Act in question (here, species preservation), but by reference to the particular provision of law upon which the plaintiff relies. It is difficult to understand how the Ninth Circuit could have failed to see this from our cases. As we said with the utmost clarity in National Wildlife Federal, "the plaintiff must establish that the injury he complains of … falls within the 'zone of interests' sought to be protected by the statutory provision whose violation forms the legal basis for his complaint."

The Court of Appeals erred in affirming the District Court's dismissal of petitioners' claims for lack of jurisdiction. Petitioners' complaint alleges facts sufficient to meet the requirements of Article III standing, and none of their ESA claims is precluded by the zone-of-interests test. Petitioners' § 1533 claim is reviewable under the ESA's citizen-suit provision, and petitioners' remaining claims are reviewable under the APA.

Reversed.

CASE QUESTIONS

1. Can those affected by the protection of an endangered species bring suit under the ESA?
2. How does the Court deal with the issue raised by the government that the opinion is only an opinion and not government action?

3. The Court's opinion was unanimous. Do you agree that both sides in an environmental case, those representing the interests of the species and those representing economic interests, should have the right to challenge a finding by the federal government?

Eminent Domain ESA

A new issue that arose under ESA is whether restrictions on land use that are imposed pursuant to the ESA constitute a taking for purposes of eminent domain. Several cases have now held that ESA restrictions are neither takings nor compensable claims. *Seiber v. U.S.*, 364 F.3d 1356 (4th Cir. 2004).

Standing Under ESA

In a 2009 decision, the U.S. Supreme Court limited somewhat the ability of individuals and groups to bring suit under the ESA and other environmental protection statutes. In *Summers v. Earthland Institute*, 555 U.S. 488 (2009), the U.S. Supreme Court held that the claim that the plaintiffs would be using various national parks around the country at some point in the future was not sufficient standing to bring suit to halt the U.S. Forest Service's policies and regulation on forest clearing. The decision means that those who bring such challenges must have an "active, ongoing dispute" that is specific to the activity.

STATE ENVIRONMENTAL LAWS

In addition to the federal enactments, 30 states have enacted some form of environmental laws and have established their own environmental policies and agencies. Some states may require new industrial businesses to obtain a state permit along with the required federal permits for the operation of their plants. As noted earlier, all 50 states have some form of hazardous waste regulation.

ENFORCEMENT OF ENVIRONMENTAL LAWS

Federal environmental law can be enforced through criminal sanctions, penalties, injunctions, and suits by private citizens. In addition to the federal enforcement rights, there are common law remedies such as nuisance or trespass that can be used to protect property and property rights.

Parties Responsible for Enforcement

The EPA is responsible for enforcement of the major environmental laws on air and water pollution, solid-waste disposal, toxic-substance management, and noise pollution. The EPA promulgates specific standards and seeks remedies and sanctions for violations. The EPA works with state EPAs on enforcement issues.

The **Council on Environmental Quality (CEQ)** was established in 1966 under the National Environment Protection Act and is part of the executive branch. Its role is that of policy-maker. The CEQ formulates national policies on the quality of the environment and makes recommendations to lawmakers regarding its policy statements.

In addition to these agencies, other federal agencies such as the Atomic Energy Commission, the Federal Power Commission, the Department of Housing and Urban Development, the Department of the Interior, the Forest Service, the Bureau of Land Management, and the Department of Commerce have specific areas for which they have enforcement authority. All federal agencies that deal with the use of lands, water, and air are involved in compliance with and enforcement of the environmental laws.

ENFORCEMENT OF ENVIRONMENTAL LAWS

Criminal Sanctions for Violations

Most of the federal statutes discussed above carry criminal sanctions for violations. See Figure 20.1 for penalties. The following case deals with criminal sanctions for environment violations by a subdivision developer.

U.S. V. AGOSTO-VEGA

617 F.3d 541 (1st Cir. 2010)
What a Waste!

FACTS

Braulio Agosto-Vega Agosto was the owner and principal officer of a closely-held family corporation, Mansiones de Hacienda Jiménez, Inc. (Mansiones), a real estate development company which he used to develop a housing project in Río Grande, Puerto Rico called Mansiones de Hacienda Jiménez.

The development began selling units in 2003, with the first purchasers moving into their residences in the summer of 2004. Almost immediately, several of the new homeowners began to experience frequent overflows of raw sewage from the septic tanks located in front of their houses. These tanks would become completely full, often in a matter of days, and raw sewage would routinely overflow into the front yards, onto the sidewalks, and into streets, where it would then drain into the storm sewers. Raw sewage would also bubble up inside the homes through the toilets, the bath tubs, and the sink drains. As would be expected, the septic tank issue became contentious and was the subject of numerous meetings, telephone calls, and correspondence between the homeowners individually, the Homeowners Association, and Agosto, his representatives, and his lawyers.

Although at first Agosto paid reputable companies to dispose of the waste, he soon turned to Mansiones employees. They would use a hose to suction the raw sewage from the septic tanks and either discharge the wastewater directly into storm drains that emptied directly into Jiménez Creek through an underground pipe, or into a large tank truck registered to Agosto Motors (another company owned by Agosto), which

would then be emptied into the storm drains, onto land adjacent to the Creek's basin, or into the Creek itself. The Creek is a tributary of the Espíritu Santo River, a major river on the northeastern coast of Puerto Rico, which empties into the Atlantic Ocean.

In March and April of 2005, after receiving multiple complaints, the Puerto Rico Environmental Quality Board (EQB) and the U.S. Environmental Protection Agency (EPA) investigated the allegations regarding the discharges into the Creek. The investigation revealed that thousands of gallons of raw sewage had been discharged into the Creek. These discharges caused the water in the Creek, at times, to turn black and reek of sewage.

On May 11, 2005, Agosto and Agosto's brother, Juan, were indicted by a federal grand jury and charged with engaging in a conspiracy to violate the CWA, as well as three counts of aiding and abetting in the unlawful discharge of raw sewage from a point source into waters of the United States, namely the Creek. Agosto Motors was charged with two of the three counts of aiding and abetting alleged in the indictment. Juan pleaded guilty prior to the trial.

After a sixteen-day trial, which lasted intermittently through July 24, 2008, Agosto and Agosto Motors (appellants) were convicted on all counts. Agosto and Agosot Motors appealed.

JUDICIAL OPINION

Torruella, Circuit Judge

The CWA prohibits the "discharge of any pollutant" without a permit issued pursuant to the National

Pollutant Discharge System administered by the EPA or approved state agencies. The knowing violation of this prohibition is a felony. The CWA defines the discharge of a pollutant as "any addition of any pollutant to navigable waters from any point source," and includes as pollutants, "sewage, … sewage sludge, … [and] biological materials … discharged into water. The term "navigable waters" is defined as "waters of the United States, including the territorial seas."

Agosto claims that there is no direct evidence that he knew of the discharges, that he was ever present when discharges occurred, that anyone ever told him about the discharges, or that he knowingly directed or approved the discharges. Agosto argues that there is no direct evidence of actual knowledge on his part, and that the case against him is entirely circumstantial. However, even assuming arguendo that this contention is correct, it is well-established that "[k]nowledge may be proven by circumstantial evidence alone;" indeed, "it frequently cannot be proven in any other way."

The jury reasonably could have found that Agosto was fully aware of the raw sewage problem at the Mansiones development, and that he knew and understood its severity. There was evidence presented at trial that Agosto visited the development at least several times a week throughout periods when raw sewage routinely overflowed from the septic tanks onto the front lawns, sidewalks and streets of the homes his company had constructed and sold. Furthermore, as an experienced businessman, Agosto was likely cognizant of the fact that he was ultimately responsible for the solution to this intractable nuisance. The jury could have concluded this from the fact that Agosto engaged homeowners directly and through intermediaries and representatives, and attended several meetings and discussions with his legal counsel.

For a time, Agosto was able to provide a legal solution to this situation by paying the municipality or hiring reputable contractors (through his corporations) to remove the sewage from the premises. However, by October 2004, for whatever reason, Agosto stopped using these third parties and instead proceeded to employ his own workers, providing them with an old military truck with a 3000-gallon tank (which was registered to Agosto Motors) for the purpose of suctioning off the raw sewage from the septic tanks and surroundings.

It is not reasonable to think that Agosto had expectations that these polluted liquids would somehow evaporate from inside the truck's tank. The logical conclusion is that these pollutants would have to be disposed of in some way. A photograph which forms part of the government's case provides part of the answer. It shows the truck dumping sewage into the storm sewers of the project's streets. There was also testimony from several eyewitnesses establishing that the truck dumped raw sewage into these sewers, or into the Creek itself, on numerous occasions. It is uncontested that these sewers empty into the Creek, which in turn flows into the Espíritu Santo River and thereafter into the Atlantic Ocean. This evidence provides resounding proof of violations of the federal environmental laws.

Since it is undisputed that raw sewage continued to overflow the septic tanks, and because Agosto and his closely-held companies, Agosto Motors and Mansiones, had to continue to remove it to appease the homeowners, and equally important, to be able to continue with the sale of additional homes in the Mansiones development. The jury could have reasonably concluded that the dumping of sewage by the employees not only took place, but that this activity could not have happened without the direction, knowledge and approval of a person who was an active participant in the day-to-day operations of Mansiones and Agosto Motors and was their *de facto* chief executive officer: Agosto. Additionally, but critically, as the principal owner of the Mansiones project, Agosto was the person who stood the most to gain economically, and conversely to lose if things went sour and the sewage was not disposed.

One additional piece of damning circumstantial evidence came from Agosto's brother, Juan, who was the person whom Agosto indicated was acting on his behalf in managing the housing project. With respect to the illegal sewage discharges, Juan testified that "the land belonged to [Agosto]" and that Juan was "just following orders."

In light of all this, there was undoubtedly sufficient circumstantial evidence to establish by proof beyond a reasonable doubt: (1) the existence of a conspiracy between Agosto, his brother Juan, and others to dispose of raw sewage into the Creek, without the appropriate permits, (2) that several overt acts were performed by members of the conspiracy in furtherance of its objectives, and (3) that Agosto had knowledge of these illegal actions.

CASE QUESTIONS

1. Of what significance is the abandonment of the professional service providers and the use of employees to handle the waste?
2. Why is the company held liable in addition to Agosto?
3. What is the significance of circumstantial evidence in proving intent?

CONSIDER 20.5   In 1994, Edward Hanousek, Jr., was employed by the Pacific & Arctic Railway and Navigation Company as the roadmaster of the White Pass & Yukon Railroad. Hanousek supervised a rock-quarrying project at a site known as "6-mile," which is located on an embankment 200 feet above the Skagway River, six miles outside of Skagway, Alaska. During rock removal operations, a backhoe operator employed by Hunz & Hunz, an independent contractor retained before Hanousek was hired, accidentally struck a petroleum pipeline near the railroad tracks. The operator's mistake caused the pipeline to rupture and spill between 1,000 and 5,000 gallons of oil into the river.

Hanousek, who was off duty and at home when the accident occurred, was indicted and convicted under the Clean Water Act for negligently discharging oil into a navigable water of the United States. He was fined $5,000 and sentenced to sequential terms of six months' imprisonment, six months in a halfway house, and six months of supervised release. Hanousek appealed his conviction, arguing that it violated his due process rights to convict him for discharging oil negligently. What are the standards for criminal liability under the CWA? What concerns should employees and companies have about a case such as this one? *Hanousek v. U.S.,* 528 U.S. 1102 (2000). ────■

FIGURE 20.1 Penalties for Violation of Federal Environmental Laws

ACT	PENALTIES	PRIVATE SUIT
Clean Air Act	$25,000 per day, up to 1 year imprisonment; 15 years for willful or repeat violations $10,000 rewards	Citizen suits; authorized EPA suit for injunctive relief
Clean Water Act	$25,000 per day, up to 1 year $50,000 and/or 3 years for violations with knowledge; $100,000 and/or 6 years for subsequent violations	Citizen suits; authorized EPA suit for injunctive relief
Resource Conservation and Recovery Act (Solid Waste Disposal Act)	$250,000 and/or 15 years imprisonment for intentional violation; $1,000,000 for corporations $50,000 and/or 5 years for others	Citizen and negligence suits after EPA refuses to handle
Hazardous Substance/ Response Trust	Fund for cleanup	EPA suit for injunctive relief and reimbursement of trust funds
Oil Pollution Act	$25,000 per day, or $1,000 per barrel $3,000 per barrel if willful or negligent $250,000 and/or 5 years for failure to report	Private actions in negligence

Civil Liability for Violations
Injunctive Relief

Although the criminal sanctions imposed on violators may be costly, adjoining landowners may just want to stop the polluting activity. As indicated in Figure 20.1, under each federal statute, the EPA has the authority to bring suit for injunctive relief. In seeking injunctive relief, the EPA asks the court to order a business to stop an activity or other violation of one of the acts. In addition to the EPA's power to seek injunctive relief, each federal act (except NCRA) allows private citizens to bring suit for damages for violations and also for obtaining injunctive relief.

Common Law Relief

In spite of the complex federal regulatory scheme, the elimination of pollution has frequently come through private suits based on the common law doctrine of nuisance. Nuisance was covered in Chapter 3. However, **nuisance** is applied by courts to allow landowners living near contaminated sites to recover for damages to their property as a result of the contamination. Other theories that can be used to challenge uses of land include negligence and trespass (see Chapter 3 for more details).

Group Suits—The Effect of Environmentalists

Private suits have had the most effect in terms of obtaining compliance with environmental regulations or abating existing nuisances affecting environmental quality. The reason for their success may be the ultimate outcome of the litigation—possible business shutdowns and, at the least, significant damages and costs.

In some cases, environmental groups that have the organizational structure and funding bring these suits. In some cases, the environmental groups are formed to protest one specific action, such as Citizens Against the Squaw Peak Parkway. Other groups are national organizations that take on environmental issues and litigation in all parts of the country. Examples of these national groups include the Sierra Club, the Environmental Defense Fund, Inc., the National Resources Defense Council, and the League of Conservation Voters. These groups have been successful in bringing private damage and injunctive relief suits, and in forcing agencies to promulgate regulations required under the federal laws.

CAUTIONS AND CONCLUSIONS

The implications of environmental laws on real property transactions are tremendous. Anyone seeking to purchase property for industrial use must be familiar with the air quality standards and release permit requirements in the area to determine if industrial use is possible, and if it is possible, if it will be more costly because of environmental constraints. Due diligence is required before property is sold. That due diligence includes a look at the property as well as at how it has been used. Property owners must also be diligent in voluntary audits and disclosure to the EPA to minimize liability. There are government and private mechanisms for enforcement of environmental laws, including citizen suits under both statutory and common law.

KEY TERMS

CHAPTER PROBLEMS

1. In 1976, Swainsboro Print Works (SPW), a cloth-printing facility, entered into a "factoring" agreement with Fleet Factors Corporation (Fleet) in which Fleet agreed to advance funds against the assignment of SPW's accounts receivable. As collateral for these advances, Fleet obtained a security interest in SPW's textile facility and all of its equipment, inventory, and fixtures.

   In August 1979, SPW filed for bankruptcy under Chapter 11 (the corporate-reorganization chapter). The factoring agreement continued until early 1981, when Fleet ceased advancing funds because SPW's debt to Fleet exceeded Fleet's estimate of the value of SPW's accounts receivable. On February 27, 1981, SPW ceased operations and began to liquidate its inventory. Fleet continued to collect the accounts receivable assigned to it under Chapter 11. In December 1981, SPW was adjudicated a bankrupt under Chapter 7, and the bankruptcy trustee assumed title and control of SPW's facility.

   In May 1982, Fleet foreclosed on its security interest in some of SPW's inventory and equipment and contracted with Baldwin Industrial Liquidators (Baldwin) to conduct an auction of the collateral. Baldwin sold the material "as is" and "in place" on June 22, 1982, with buyers assuming the responsibility for removal of the materials.

   On August 31, 1982, Fleet contracted with Nix Riggers (Nix) to remove the unsold equipment in consideration for leaving the premises "broom clean." Nix had performed its work in the facility by the end of December 1983.

   On January 20, 1984, the EPA inspected the facility and found seven hundred 55-gallon drums containing toxic chemicals and 44 truckloads of material containing asbestos. The EPA incurred costs of $400,000 in cleaning up the SPW facility. On July 7, 1987, the facility was conveyed to Emanuel County, Georgia, at a foreclosure sale from SPW's failure to pay state and county taxes.

   The government sued Fleet and the two principal officers and stockholders of SPW to recover the costs of cleaning up the hazardous waste.

   Can Fleet be held liable under CERCLA? *United States v. Fleet Factors Corp.,* 901 F.2d 1550 (11th Cir. 1990).

2. The FAA changed the flight path approaches to Phoenix Sky Harbor Airport. Residents of Cave Creek, Arizona, complained that the change resulted in a significant increase in noise for their neighborhoods as well as over areas of pristine desert flora and fauna. The residents wanted the flight path implementation delayed because no EIS had been filed. The FAA maintained that its change of

flight path involved no construction of relocation and, as such, did not require an EIS. Who is correct? Discuss why. *Town of Cave Creek, Arizona v. F.A.A.* 325 F.3d 320 (D.C. 2003).

3. Reynolds Metal has been held to the same technological standards in its pollution control for can manufacturing plants as those applied to aluminum manufacturers. Reynolds claims that the processes are different and that the technology is not yet available for can manufacturing. Does Reynolds have a point? *Reynolds Metals Co. v. EPA*, 760 F.2d 549 (D.C. 1985).

4. Sullivan's Ledge, once a popular swimming and hiking area located near New Bedford, Massachusetts, has become little more than an industrial dumping ground for scrap rubber, waste oils, gas, combustion ash, and old telephone poles. The sludge became so toxic, the refuse so thick, and the stench so overwhelming that the city closed the area in the 1970s.

   The EPA identified a number of business entities and their successors as responsible for the cleanup of the area. Acushnet Company entered into a consent decree with the EPA but then filed suit seeking financial contribution from Mohasco Corporation and others including American Flexible Conduit (AFC), New England Telephone & Telegraph Company (NETT), and Ottaway Newspapers, Inc. The defendant companies said that their actions were a very small part of the sludgy mess and that Acushment was primarily responsible for the pollution.

   The trial court found that there was insufficient evidence to find these companies liable under CERCLA and granted them summary judgment. Acushnet appealed. Should the companies be held liable to Acushnet for their contribution to the pollution? For how much? *Acushnet Company v. Mohasco*, 191 F.3d 69 (1st Cir. 1999)

5. Kelley Technical Coatings is an industrial paint–manufacturing company which operates two plants in Louisville, Kentucky. Arthur Sumner was the vice president in charge of manufacturing operations for Kelley. Sumner oversaw the manufacturing process at both plants, including the storage and disposal of hazardous wastes. He was also responsible for environmental regulatory compliance, and submitted the necessary paperwork to the state environmental authorities to register Kelley as a generator of hazardous waste.

   Kelley generated hazardous wastes in its manufacturing process, including spent solvents, such as toluene, ethyl benzene, xylene, and methyl ethyl ketone; excess and unusable paint, paint resins, and other paint ingredients which contained, among other things, toxic heavy metals such as chromium, lead, cadmium, and nickel; and paint sludge. Kelley

accumulated hundreds of drums of these waste materials and stored them in drums behind one of its plants. Kelley never applied for a permit to store or dispose of its hazardous wastes on-site.

In July 1992, when the Kentucky Department of Environmental Protection inspected the Kelley plants, there were between 600 and 1,000 drums behind one of the plants. The drums had been stored on-site for more than 90 days, and in some cases for many years. Some of the drums had rusted and were leaking on the ground.

Between 1986 and 1989, Sumner had arranged for a licensed hazardous waste disposal company to remove and dispose of some of the drums containing hazardous wastes. From late 1989 to July 1992, however, no drums of hazardous waste were shipped off-site. Instead, in an effort to save money, Kelley contracted with a hazardous waste disposal company to come on-site and drain the liquids from the drums. After the bulk of the hazardous wastes were drained off, employees were directed to pour off any rainwater that had collected into the drums onto the ground and to consolidate the remaining residue into one drum. The consolidation process resulted in the spilling of hazardous substances onto the ground.

Both Kelley and Sumner were convicted under the RCRA. They appealed their convictions on the grounds that they did not have the *mens rea* required for conviction under the RCRA statute. Are they correct? Are they criminally responsible? *U.S. v. Kelley Technical Coatings, Inc.*, 157 F.3d 432 (6th Cir. 1998).

6. Albert J. Hubenthal leased approximately 55 acres of property in Winona County, Minnesota, to start a worm-farming operation. Shortly thereafter, he began to collect large amounts of material, including waste paper, cardboard, used tires, scrap wood, scrap metal, leather, and other building materials that he contends were essential to the worm-farming operation.

The county attorney filed suit seeking to compel Hubenthal to clean up the property on the grounds that it was a public nuisance. After a hearing, the lower court enjoined Hubenthal from storing solid-waste material that could be a "source of filth and sickness" and from maintaining a junkyard. The order gave Hubenthal 30 days to clean up, which he failed to do. Two months after the order was issued, county officials took three days to remove the materials accumulated from Hubenthal's farm. Hubenthal filed suit for trespass and violation of his due process rights. Is it a nuisance? Can the government clean it up? *Hubenthal v. County of Winona*, 751 F.2d 243 (8th Cir. 1984).

7. From July 7, 1944, to December 16, 1980, Herschel and Nellie McLeod owned a 117-acre piece of land in the town of California, Maryland, in St. Mary's County (referred to as the "California Maryland Drum site" or "CMD site"). During this period of ownership, Maryland Bank & Trust (MB&T) loaned money to the McLeods for the operation of their two businesses: Greater St. Mary's Disposal, Inc., and Waldorf Sanitation of St. Mary's, Inc., which were both trash and garbage businesses. The record indicates that MB&T was aware of the nature of the businesses, but it is unclear when it acquired its awareness.

   From 1972 to 1973, the McLeods permitted the dumping of hazardous wastes on their property, including lead, chromium, mercury, zinc, and ethylbenzene.

   In 1980, the McLeods' son, Mark, obtained a loan from MB&T and purchased the 117 acres from his parents. Mark failed to make payments, and MB&T instituted foreclosure proceedings in 1981 and bought the property at a sale in May 1982.

   The EPA discovered the hazardous waste problems and conducted a cleanup of the site at a cost of $551,713.50. The EPA then demanded payment from MB&T. When payment was refused, the EPA brought suit to collect the cost of the cleanup. Can EPA collect from MB&T? *United States v. Maryland Bank & Trust Co.,* 632 F. Supp. 573 (D. Md. 1986).

8. Frezzo Brothers, Incorporated, is a Pennsylvania firm engaged in mushroom farming at a location near Avondale. To produce their mushrooms, Guido and James Frezzo (the two family members responsible for the operation of the business) used a growing medium that consisted of fermented hay and horse manure. White Clay Creek, which flowed alongside of the Frezzo operation, was considerably polluted, and upon analysis the pollutants were found to consist mainly of horse manure. There had been no rain in the area, and the Environmental Protection Agency charged the Frezzos and their corporation with willfully discharging manure into the stream. The Frezzos claim the right to use the stream as riparians, and the United States government claims environmental regulations will control over common law rights. Would discharging manure into a stream be a violation of any environmental laws? *United States v. Frezzo Brothers, Inc.,* 602 F.2d 1123 (3rd Cir. 1979).

9. First Capital Life Insurance Company made a loan of $7,300,000 to Schneider, Inc., in 1986. The loan was secured by a mortgage on real property located in Allegheny County, Pennsylvania. Schneider failed to make payments in 1988, and in 1989, First Capital declared the loan in default. First Capital then sent representatives to the property to conduct an environmental inspection. Schneider employees refused to grant access to the property. There was no provision in the mortgage regarding such inspections upon default. Combining your knowledge from Chapter 15 on financing and this chapter on environmental liability issues, determine whether First Capital should be permitted access to the property prior to foreclosure. *First Capital Life Insurance Co. v. Schneider, Inc.,* 608 A.2d 1082 (Pa. 1992).

10. Attique Ahmad owns a Spin-N-Market in Texas, a convenience store and gas station. One of the Spin-N-Market's gasoline tanks developed a leak. Jewel McCoy of CIT Environmental Services inspected the tank and said it needed to be drained and then pumped. McCoy gave Ahmad the cost of draining, but Ahmad suggested he would do it himself despite McCoy's warning about violations of the law. Ahmad rented a pump at the local hardware store and pumped over 5,000 gallons into a manhole near his store (4,690 of those gallons were gasoline). The gasoline made its way to the storm sewer system and then a creek, as well as the city sewage treatment center. While firemen were working to divert the gasoline, the treatment center and two nearby schools had to be evacuated. Ahmad was charged with violation of the Clean Water Act and was convicted of two charges. Ahmad appealed. Should the conviction stand? Explain why or why not. *U.S. v. Ahmad,* 101 F.3d 386 (5th Cir. 1996).

For research activities related to this chapter, go to our text companion website at www.cengagebrain.com

CHAPTER 21

LEGAL ISSUES IN LAND AND ECONOMIC DEVELOPMENT

Plans get you into things, but you got to work your way out.

Will Rogers

If a builder builds a house for a man and does not make its construction firm, and the house which he has built collapses and causes the death of the owner of the house, the builder shall be put to death.

Hammurabi's Code

Real estate planning and development are not easy tasks. In fact, real estate development requires knowledge from the other 21 chapters of this book along with an understanding of some new areas of law. From interaction with zoning and planning commissions to negotiations with lenders for financing to bids with contractors, a developer faces law at every turn in the complex maze of real estate development.

This chapter covers the stages of real estate development and the laws that apply and affect those stages of development. From construction law to syndication requirements to zoning and planning constraints, development requires constant interaction and compliance with the law. Figure 21.1 on p. 584 provides a flowchart look at the process of land development.[1]

---

[1]Real estate development is a creative endeavor that involves entrepreneurial skills. Developers approach projects in a different order. Developers may first seek government approval for annexation or may even work with state and local governments for support, tax exemptions, and joint projects before even acquiring the land. The order in this chapter may be different from the order of development.

FIGURE 21.1 Steps in Land Development

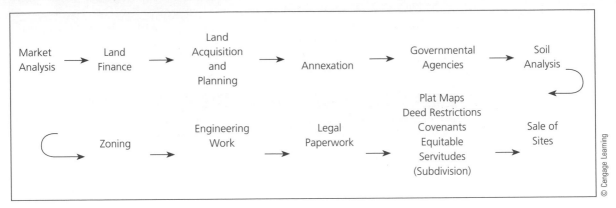

LAND ACQUISITION

Market Analysis

Because the value of real estate has declined so much since 2006, the idea of beginning a new real estate development seems to be a pipe dream. With so many homes now on the market either for sale or in foreclosure, buyers have many choices and significant room for price negotiation. However, the development process is a lengthy one, and markets do turn around. In fact, many cities and towns are trying to attract developers with special tax and joint-investment projects in order to stimulate economic development. Developers may vary the order of the development process in these times—they may have government approval and support before they actually invest in land. Even with a government friendly environment, there remain other prerequisite tasks such as feasibility determinations and whether, even with government support, there is market potential.

Before acquiring land or deciding on how land should be developed (single family, condominium), a developer should know the economic status and physical needs of those in the area. For example, during 2009, Arizona had one of the highest foreclosure rates in the nation. However, a developer conducted a market study and found that there was pent-up demand on the part of first-time buyers who were looking for simple, starter homes. The developer purchased an existing subdivision that was in foreclosure and then developed three different homes for the subdivision, all smaller in size and simple in upgrades. Within weeks of opening the subdivision for sale, the developer had sold 23 homes. The market study was correct and the new development met a need. These preliminary marketing studies indicate what forms of housing will sell. For example, areas with a concentration of families need subdivisions with larger, single-family homes. In that same area, townhouses and condominiums might not sell. In college towns, on the other hand, smaller housing units sell because investors and students need that type of unit for rental properties or temporary residences.

In some situations, developers find bargains in acquiring failed developments, often called ghost developments. However, the original zoning approvals for the failed subdivision may not address current market needs. In these situations, the developer does need to obtain approval for changing the zoning from, for example, single-family homes, to townhomes. In these zoning change applications, city councils often require the developer to put in parks or swimming pools as a condition for the rezoning. *Town of Huntington v. Beechwood Carmen Bldg. Corp.,* 920 N.Y.S.2d 198 (N.Y.A.D. 2011)

Governmental Analysis

Developers must work closely with governmental agencies at all steps of their project, sometimes even before buying the land.

Annexation

In some cases, no land parcels that are large enough for subdivision are located within city limits. However, the developer will have a difficult time selling properties in the subdivision if the city emergency and utility services are not available. So, the developer proceeds with the steps required for annexation.

The process of **annexation** is similar to a change in zoning and follows the same process that any change in zoning would require. The public hearing required allows objections, feedback, and questions (see Chapter 19). There is a trade-off with annexation versus a subdivision outside city and town limits. No annexation means fewer regulations and restrictions; the developer spends less money in this initial phase. However, the developer must still find a way to provide the usual government services, such as trash pickup and street cleaning. The developer must pay a private contractor to perform those functions. Those contracts are generally longer-term contracts because the service contractors cannot commit to having the equipment and staffing necessary unless there will be a return on that substantial up-front investment required to provide services for a subdivision.

An issue that continues to evolve when developers proceed with subdivisions outside city limits is what happens to service providers if and when the subdivision is annexed to the city. Developers who have located subdivisions outside city limits contract for services such as waste removal and street cleaning. When the city annexes the property, those contracts are often no longer valid. The contracting companies that have lost their contracts have often filed suit claiming a taking by eminent domain for which they seek compensation. Whether these service providers will get compensation remains a matter of judicial determination, and court decisions differ. The following case shows one court's position on the interrelationships among cities, developers, and service providers when annexation is post-contract.

EXPRESS DISPOSAL, LLC V. CITY OF MEMPHIS

2008 WL 5396242 (Tenn. Ct. App.)
Trashing a Contract: Does Annexation Do That?

FACTS

Express Disposal had a contract with Berryhill, Tennessee, a small community outside of Memphis, for garbage collection from the residences there. However, Memphis annexed Berryhill, effective January 1, 2007. In October 2006, the city of Memphis sent notice of the annexation to Express, along with a reminder that a Memphis ordinance prohibited private companies from collecting residential trash within the city unless the city granted a permit.

Express filed suit against the city on the grounds that it had negotiated its fees for trash removal from Berryhill based on its assumption that it would have a longstanding agreement with Berryhill for the services. Express alleged that the annexation and result-

ing prohibition of collection constituted a taking by the city of Memphis, a taking that entitled Express to compensation. The trial court dismissed the complaint and Express appealed.

JUDICIAL OPINION
Highers, Presiding Justice

"Eminent domain" refers to a proceeding initiated by the government to obtain property through condemnation, while, "'[i]nverse condemnation' is the popular description of a cause of action against a governmental defendant to recover the value of the property which has been taken in fact by a governmental defendant even though no final exercise of the power of eminent domain has been attempted by the government." Because Express Disposal seeks compensation for a governmental "taking" although Memphis has instituted no eminent domain proceedings, we classify Express Disposal's cause of action as one for inverse condemnation.

In support of its contention that the "taking" of its ability to service residences in Berryhill "does not differ in any manner from eminent domain wherein a highway is built on or through a person's property." Express Disposal cites two Tennessee cases. We do not find these cases demonstrate a right in Tennessee to receive just compensation for a "taking" of the ability to conduct business in a certain area.

First, Express Disposal cites *Duck River Electric Membership Corporation v. City of Manchester*, 529 S.W.2d 202 (Tenn. 1975). In *Duck River*, the city of Manchester sought to condemn the property of a public non-profit electric membership corporation, which supplied electricity to the city's residents, in order that the city could take over supplying electricity. Express Disposal contends that our Supreme Court, in *Duck River*, held that although the city had the exclusive power to control utilities—thus, allowing the city to exercise eminent domain—the city was required to "pay just compensation to those utility providers that were prevented from operating in the area pursuant to Article I, § 21 of the Tennessee Constitution." However, we find Appellant's reliance on *Duck River* misplaced. While our Supreme Court held that the displaced utility provider was entitled to just compensation, such payment was to compensate for the loss of the utility's real property as well as its "personal property including poles, conductors, anchors, guy wires, lightning arresters, transformers, street lights, and numerous other items of equipment used in an electrical distribution system." Thus, *Duck River* did not allow just compensation for any taken intangible "property" rights.

Express Disposal also relies on *Forked Deer Electric Cooperative, Inc. v. City of Ripley*, 883 S.W.2d 582 (Tenn. 1994) in support of its claim for compensation for its lost ability to service residential customers in Berryhill. Again, we find Express Disposal's reliance unfounded. In *Forked Deer*, the Forked Deer Electric Cooperative lost at least a portion of its existing customer base when the town of Halls awarded to another cooperative, an exclusive franchise to deliver power within the town's city limits. Forked Deer sued alleging inverse condemnation, and the United States District Court for the Western District of Tennessee found that the exclusive franchise had "'taken away Forked Deer's right to serve its members without formal condemnation proceeding[s],' [and that] such action was in the nature of an inverse condemnation, and therefore constituted a taking under the Fifth Amendment [of the United States Constitution]." However, the only issue certified to our Supreme Court was the calculation of the compensation formula.

We find several reasons why *Forked Deer* lacks precedential value in this case. First, *Forked Deer* involved a taking without just compensation under the Fifth Amendment to the United States Constitution, rather than Article I, section 21 of the Tennessee Constitution. Second, our Supreme Court, in *Forked Deer*, did not find that Forked Deer's lost right to service its customers constituted a "taking," but instead only answered the question certified to it concerning calculation of compensation. Finally, Tennessee Code Annotated section 6-51-112(a) requires that compensation be paid to electric cooperatives whose property and service rights are "taken" through annexation; however, our State's statutes afford no similar protection to displaced garbage collectors.

Based on the foregoing authority, we find no support for Express Disposal's contention that Memphis' appropriation of garbage collection services for Berryhill residences constituted a taking, such that just compensation is required. Thus, we affirm the dismissal of Express Disposal's Complaint for failure to state a claim upon which relief could be granted.

CASE QUESTIONS

1. What is the distinction between and among the cases cited and the Berryhill situation?
2. What lessons should developers, those who buy homes in private subdivisions, and those in city government take from this decision?

Interstate Land Sales

If a developer is selling unimproved lots, the Interstate Land Sales Full Disclosure Act (ILSFDA; 15 U.S.C. § 1701 *et seq.*) will apply. HUD requires statements of record and property reports (see Chapter 14).

Federal Loan Approvals for Sales

If the developer is selling single or multiunit housing units, Federal Housing Administration (FHA) and Veterans Administration (VA) financing for buyers help increase sales. The FHA and VA must approve the subdivision before buyers can obtain this government-backed financing.

The Cost of Development—Impact Fees

Since the 1980s, local governments have been requiring developers to bear some of the infrastructure costs that result from new housing developments such as the cost of new schools and additional fire and police personnel. Often called **impact fees**, these special assessments cover the costs of expanded government services required because of new subdivisions.

Impact fees have not set well with developers and have been a continuing basis for judicial challenge each time cities and counties implement a new type of fee. For example, impact fees for constructing schools seem to be fairly well-sanctioned by the courts, but development fees for expansion of roads and highways still create judicial controversy. Developers use several theories to challenge impact fees, including the city or town's lack of statutory authority as well as the constitutionality of a tax assessed without proper process. The cases are split in terms of both authority and constitutionality, with many towns and cities going back to the drawing board, as it were, to find a way to impose the fees to cover the additional costs of expansive growth.[2] In *Mayor and Bd. of Aldermen, City of Ocean Springs v. Homebuilders Ass'n of Mississippi, Inc.*, 932 So.2d 44 (Miss. 2006), the court dealt with the issue of Mississippi cities and towns imposing higher impact fees on developers as a means of rebuilding schools, parks, fire and police departments, and other services and infrastructure in the post–Hurricane Katrina redevelopment effort. The court found that although the need was great, there was no state authority allowing cities and towns to impose and collect such fees. However, the following case is a decision in which public good could justify impact fees against a developer not necessarily responsible for the additional costs.

UPTON V. TOWN OF HOPKINTON

945 A.2d 670 (N.H. 2008)
Expanding a Turnpike In Order to Build a Residential Development

FACTS

In August 2006, Barry O. Upton (petitioner) applied to the planning board of the Town of Hopkinton, New Hampshire, for subdivision approval. He proposed replacing the existing single-family residence on his property and creating four new residential lots. The board considered the application at public hearings in September, October, November, and December

---

[2]For decisions that recognize impact fees as valid, see *Caparco v. Town of Danville*, 886 A.2d 1045 (N.H. 2005); *McCarthy v. City of Leawood*, 894 P.2d 836 (Kan. 1995); *Idaho Bldg. Contractors Ass'n v. City of Coeur d'Alene*, 890 P.2d 326 (Idaho 1995) (valid as a tax, but city had no authority for impact fees); *City of Dunedin v. Contractors and Builders Ass'n of Pinellas County*, 312 So.2d 763 (Fla. App. 1975) (but Florida is all over the maps on these impact fees, depending upon the county and the nature of the fees, with some struck down, e.g., *Broward County v. Janis Development Corp.*, 311 So.2d 371 [Fla. App. 1975]). For cases in which impact fees were held invalid, see *Citizens' Alliance for Property Rights v. Sims*, 187 P.3d 786 (Wash. App. 2008); *Cranberry Tp. v. Builders Ass'n of Metropolitan Pittsburgh*, 621 A.2d 563 (Pa. 1993); *Country Joe, Inc. v. City of Eagan*, 560 N.W.2d 681 (Minn. 1997); and *New Jersey Builders Ass'n v. Mayor and Tp. Committee of Bernards Tp., Somerset County*, 108 N.J. 223, 528 A.2d 555 (1987).

2006. In addition, the board took a site walk of the property, and reviewed comments from the Town's consultant engineer, fire chief, public works director, and road committee, as well as from the Town of Bow, the City of Concord, and the Central New Hampshire Regional Planning Commission.

Among the concerns raised was "access to the development should [the] … Turnpike be closed due to flooding." The flooding was estimated to occur approximately 500 feet from Upton's development. The fire department, for instance, was concerned about responding to an emergency should the Turnpike be closed. There was also concern about school bus access to the subdivision in the event that the Turnpike was closed. The Turnpike had been closed for flooding three times in 2005 and three times in 2006. The public works director estimated that "any time [the town] receive[s] 2 inches of rain the road needs to be closed temporarily due to its elevation and its location through a wetland." When the Turnpike is closed, residents must travel through Bow and Concord to access their properties. Even when the Turnpike is not closed, the chief of the fire department noted that this particular location "has one of the furthest response times."

Additionally, the Central New Hampshire Regional Planning Commission opined that Upton's development would result in an additional 38 to 40 vehicle trips per day, which might "warrant road upgradings in Hopkinton." The commission observed that "based on the origins and destinations of trips from the subdivision's residents, … the majority of trips may be along [the] … Turnpike heading generally northerly towards I-89 or to center Hopkinton or Contoocook."

At the November hearing, a majority of the board believed that Upton needed to address "the issue of safety as a result of the condition of [the] … Turnpike," perhaps by paying for a portion of the cost of improving the road.

At the December hearing, the board considered what was needed to improve the Turnpike. The Town's consultant engineer and Upton's experts agreed that installing a box culvert was necessary and that it would cost between $250,000 and $300,000. The board voted to approve the subdivision with the condition that Upton bear one-third of the cost of installing a box culvert.

Upton appealed to the superior court arguing that the proposed project and fees did not bear a rational nexus to his proposed subdivision. The trial court found to the contrary, and Upton appealed.

JUDICIAL OPINION
Duggan, Justice

Impact fees "can only be required to the extent that [they] bear a 'rational nexus' to the needs created by the project being constructed by the landowner." Thus, the amount of an impact fee must be "a proportional share of municipal capital improvement costs which is reasonably related to the capital needs created by the development, and to the benefits accruing to the development from the capital improvements financed by the fee." Only a municipality that has passed an impact fee ordinance may assess an impact fee.

[T]he Town's ordinance against imposing impact fees to pay for upgrades to existing facilities and infrastructures applies only when the need for such upgrades is not "reasonably related" to the new development. As long as the need for the upgrade is "reasonably related" to the new development, both the statute and the Town's ordinance allow the Town to assess an impact fee to help pay for it. Where the improvements are required solely because of the development, it may be permissible for a municipality to require the subdivider to bear the total cost of improvements. Where, as here, the improvements are not required solely because of the development, the Town may only require the subdivider to bear "a proportional share" of their cost. Only when the need for the improvements bears no reasonable relationship to the proposed development is the municipality prohibited from requiring the subdivider to pay for a portion of the cost of the improvements.

In the instant case, the record supports the board's determination that the need for the improvements to the Turnpike was reasonably related to the petitioner's proposed development. Based upon the evidence before it, the board reasonably could have found that the addition of four more residences on the Turnpike made it necessary to upgrade it now. The board could reasonably have determined that "[e]xposing more households to the risk that emergency vehicles would be unable to respond when their services were required" magnified the Turnpike's existing hazard, and made it imperative that the Turnpike be improved now. Although the Turnpike's condition existed before the petitioner submitted his subdivision application, "a planning board must consider current as well as anticipated realities when ruling on a request for subdivision approval." Accordingly, we hold that the board had the authority to require the petitioner to pay a portion of the cost of improving the Turnpike.

The petitioner next asserts that the board erred when it found that one-third of the cost to improve the Turnpike represented his proportional share. In assessing a developer's proportional share of the cost of an improvement, "[n]o single factor can be determinative." Factors relevant to determining a developer's proportional share of the cost for road improvements may include, but are not limited to: (1) the standard to which the town currently maintains the road; (2) the frontage of the proposed subdivision; (3) the potential traffic increase necessitated by the proposed subdivision; (4) the character and potential for development of the neighborhood served by the road; and (5) the number of residences presently fronting on or normally trafficking these roads.

The petitioner contends that the board erred because it relied exclusively upon the fact that his development would nearly double the number of homes on the Turnpike to justify the fee assessed. The record does not support this contention. In calculating the petitioner's proportional share, the board also considered evidence concerning the character of the neighborhood served by the Turnpike and the Turnpike's current condition. Specifically, the board observed that school-aged children lived in some of the residences on the Turnpike, and noted that the Turnpike in Hopkinton was a scenic gravel road that was closed because of flooding three times in the last year. Elsewhere, the Turnpike is paved. The board also examined the additional distance that emergency vehicles must travel to access Turnpike residences when it is closed, and the response time of emergency vehicles to properties on this portion of the Turnpike.

For all of the above reasons, therefore, we hold that the trial court did not err when it upheld the board's decision to condition its approval of the petitioner's subdivision upon his paying one-third of the cost to improve the Turnpike.

Affirmed.

CASE QUESTIONS

1. Why does the town believe the improvements to the Turnpike are necessary?
2. What does the case offer as insights for developers of even small subdivisions?

CONSIDER 21.1   In 2003, the City of Lincoln, Nebraska enacted an ordinance conditioning the issuance of a building permit for new residential development on the payment of "impact fees," intended to offset the expenses associated with providing municipal services to the new development. The "Impact Fee Ordinance" (the Ordinance) provided that

> any person who applies for a building permit for a development or who applies for any other permit for a development where a building permit is not required, or who seeks to engage in a development for which no permit is required, shall pay a water system impact fee, water distribution impact fee, wastewater impact fee, arterial street impact fee, and neighborhood park and trail impact fee unless the type of development described in the permit or to be engaged in is specifically exempted, waived or subsidized by this ordinance, or unless the type of development described in the permit or to be engaged in is not located in an impact fee benefit district for the above-described impact fees.

The Home Builders Association of Lincoln has filed suit challenging the authority of Lincoln to impose such fees. Determine what the court should do and why. *Home Builders Ass'n of Lincoln v. City of Lincoln*, 711 N.W.2d 871 (Neb. 2006). ____

Use or Deed Restrictions

In addition to zoning requirements and limitations, developers are subject to the existing covenants on land that pass, or run with the land, through deed restrictions. Chapter 2 covered use restrictions in fee simple defeasible grants. Deed restrictions that may hamper development include those that have clauses restricting the use of the land for a park. The following case illustrates that, in revitalization projects, a grantor's restriction on land use controls developers' plans as well as government authority in working jointly with developers.

WHITE V. METROPOLITAN DADE COUNTY

563 So.2d 117 (Fla. 1990)
The Tennis Tournament vs. the Deed Restriction

FACTS

In 1940, several members of the Matheson family deeded three tracts of land located on the northern portion of Key Biscayne to Dade County. The 680 acres came to be known as Crandon Park. In the recorded deeds, the grantors expressly provided:

This conveyance is made upon the express condition that the lands hereby conveyed shall be perpetually used and maintained for public park purposes only; and in case the use of said land for park purposes shall be abandoned, then and in that event the said grantor, his heirs, grantees or assigns, shall be entitled upon their request to have the said lands reconveyed to them.

Since the time of the original grant, several amendatory deeds have been issued by the grantors to allow ancillary uses such as the construction of public roads, public utilities, and a firehouse. However, the grantors did refuse to allow the building of a cable satellite dish.

In 1986, the Dade County Board of County Commissioners entered into an agreement with Arvida International Championships, Inc. (Arvida), and the International Players Championship, Inc. (IPC), to construct a permanent tennis complex on the property. The complex consisted of 15 tennis courts, service roads, utilities, and landscaping, and took up 28 acres. The agreement with Arvida and IPC provided that for two weeks each year the complex would become the site of the Lipton International Players Championship Tennis Tournament (Lipton tournament).

In February 1987, the first Lipton tournament was held before approximately 213,000 people. A permanent clubhouse was then erected, with plans calling for a 12,000-seat stadium. The facilities are closed to the public for periods of time before and after the Lipton tournament (three weeks before and one week after) for site preparation and dismantling. When additional parking space became necessary, the grantors' heirs refused to give consent for more parking, and a suit resulted seeking an injunction against the Lipton tournament on the grounds that the deed restriction was violated and the master plan for Dade County was violated because the park was designated as an "environmentally sensitive parkland." The trial court found for Dade County, and the grantors' heirs and environmental groups (appellants) appealed.

JUDICIAL OPINION

Gersten, Judge

Appellant/heirs first contend that the construction of the tennis complex violates the deed restriction. As previously stated, the deed provides that the "lands hereby conveyed shall be perpetually used and maintained for public park purposes only."

"In construing restrictive covenants the question is primarily one of intention and the fundamental rule is that the intention of the parties as shown by the agreement governs, being determined by a fair interpretation of the entire text of the covenant." Similarly, "the terms of dedications of land for park purposes where the lands are conveyed by private individuals are to be construed more strictly than is the case where the lands are acquired by the public body by purchase or condemnation."

Appellant/heirs argue that it was the intent of the Matheson family to limit the use of Crandon Park to passive activities such as picnicking, swimming, and the like. We glean no such intention from the language of the deed. Further, the Florida Supreme Court has adopted a very broad definition for what a "park" encompasses. The court has stated:

[A] park is considered not only as ornamental but also as a place for recreation and amusement. Changes in the concepts of parks have continued and the trend is certainly toward expanding and enlarging the facilities for amusement and recreation found therein.

The court further explained that the permissible uses for a public park include:

[T]ennis courts, playground and dancing facilities, skating, a swimming pool and bathhouse, horseshoe pitching, walking, horseback riding, athletic sports and other outdoor exercises ... golfing and baseball ... parking facilities ... provided always that a substantial portion of the park area remains in grass, trees, shrubs and flowers, with seats and tables for picnicking, for the use by and enjoyment of the public.

We conclude that the construction of the tennis complex did not violate the "public park purposes only" provision of the deed restriction.

Appellant/heirs next argue that turning the tennis complex over to a commercial operator violates the deed restriction. We do not agree. Florida courts have consistently ruled that commercial benefit does not defeat a park's purposes.

Finally, appellant/heirs contend that the operation of the Lipton tournament violates the deed restriction because it deprives the public of the use and enjoyment of Crandon Park, including the use and enjoyment of tennis facilities. We are persuaded by this argument and rule that the holding of the Lipton tournament violates the deed restriction because it virtually bars the public uses of Crandon Park during the tournament, and does bar public use of the tennis complex, for extended periods of time.

In ruling that the holding of the Lipton tournament violates the deed restriction, we note that a distinction must be made between "park purposes" and "public purposes." Assuming *arguendo* that the Lipton tournament is an economic success which brings innumerable benefits to Dade County and its citizens, such an undeniable public purpose is not consistent with a deed restriction mandating the narrower "public park purposes only."

In addition, the word "only" in the deed restriction at issue further buttresses our ruling that the operation of the Lipton tournament, as presently constituted, violates the restriction.

Dade County contends that the tennis complex is consistent with the "public park purposes" restriction provided for in the deed. In support, Dade County argues that the complex is open to the public when the tournament is not being held, the site of the tennis complex utilizes less than 5 percent of Crandon Park, and that a valid park purpose is served by "spectating." Dade County also points to the benefits derived by Dade County from having the Lipton tournament in Dade County.

Here, the public, in fact, is deprived from using these tennis facilities for a period of three to four weeks during the Tournament Period. Further, under the contract as to the 1987 tournament, Arvida had the right to exclude the public for as long as five months.

Dade County argues that the use of the property as a tennis complex is better than its previous use as a dump. While we agree that a tennis complex in a public park, is better than a dump in a public park, we note that the County's previous use of the site as a dump, was also in violation of the deed restriction. We do not congratulate Dade County for shifting from one impermissible use to another.

Finally, Dade County argues, and we agree, that it is well settled that "equity abhors a forfeiture," that "such restrictions are not favored in law if they have the effect of destroying an estate," and that they "will be construed strictly and will be most strongly construed against the grantor."

Appellants/heirs, however, clearly represented to the court and the trial court that they were not seeking a reversal. What appellant/heirs want is a declaratory judgement [*sic*] that the present use of the park is in violation of the deed restriction and an injunction to prevent any further erosion of the "public park purposes only" deed restriction.

We therefore declare Dade County to be in violation of the deed restriction. We reverse the trial court order as to the deed restriction, and remand for entry of an order enjoining Dade County from permitting the Lipton tournament to proceed as it is presently held. Our ruling does not prevent Dade County from using the tennis complex for tennis tournaments. It merely seeks to insure that in holding such tournaments, public access to the rest of Crandon Park is not infringed; and use of the tennis complex is not denied to the public for unreasonable periods of time.

We reverse the trial court order on this point and remand for entry of an order enjoining any further development at the site.

CASE QUESTIONS

1. What type of land interest was created with the grant to Dade County?
2. How does the court interpret the "park only" requirement?
3. Of what significance is the fact that the public cannot use the courts before, during, and after the tournament?

GOVERNMENTAL APPROVAL

Zoning

Even property that is already designated for residential zoning may need to be changed for its density. Some cities limit the number of housing units per acre, and if the developer is planning a condominium development or single-family dwellings on minuscule lots, the density restrictions may need to be waived. (See Chapter 18 for a discussion of obtaining zoning variances.)

ETHICAL ISSUE

Suppose that a member of the city council who is scheduled to vote on a particular zoning application is the beneficiary of a family trust that owns property in the area near where the proposed project will be built. The effect of the project going forward will be a substantial increase in value of the surrounding properties. Should the city council member participate in the discussions and vote on the zoning for the proposed project? What issues do you see in such a scenario?

Protests of Residents Exercising Rights

Developers not only deal with cities and government agencies, they must also work with various types of interest and watchdog groups that exist to preserve parks, historic buildings, beachfront and coastal zones, and, generally speaking, the environment. Their support may be necessary for approval by the governmental bodies.

Because of these third-party groups and their political power, many developers have found that presenting a more extensive **master-planned community**, reached through negotiations with agencies and third-party groups, allows for faster processing. Developers now propose larger-scale projects that are actually community development as opposed to subdivision creation; this larger-scale and integrative approach is sometimes referred to as a **planned unit development (PUD)**.[3] The community plan envisions parks, commercial and office facilities, and a completely pre-planned layout. To obtain approval for the concept, the developer may be required to guarantee the use of the land in a certain way and thus may present a full package of covenants that will govern the community. For example, the developer may agree that certain areas will remain as parks for the planned community, or that only single-family residences will be constructed in certain areas of the community.

The Uniform Planned Community Act has been adopted in several states. The primary purpose of this act is to help establish structures, policies, and procedures that recognize the powerful private lawmaking bodies that exist within these communities and their fundamental impact on property rights and property owners. Increasing litigation involving homeowners and homeowners' associations has resulted in increasing legislation to cover the various issues and procedures in planned communities. (See Chapter 11 for more information on HOAs.)

---

[3]Some states have rural cluster developments in which housing is grouped close together, but the community has preserved open park-like areas that cannot be developed in the future.

Master Communities, Foreclosure, and Blight

Master communities, or common interest developments (CIDs), do make it easier for developers to obtain approval because the cities and towns can see the economic benefits of having these new population centers in their areas. However, the collapse of the mortgage market has revealed a new risk for developers who have undertaken CIDs or even just community revitalization. When there are a substantial number of foreclosures in one area, what is known as the "broken windows" problem often results.[4] Abandoned properties, foreclosed properties, and properties that have been stripped (see Chapter 15 for more information) result in security concerns because of abandoned properties as well as maintenance issues on homes and the private parks and roads in the development. These abandoned properties then become focal points for crime, such as when they become drug houses or when they are simply the targets of vandalism, including arson. Those who live in neighborhoods that are next to the high-foreclosure area must often pay higher insurance rates because of increased risk, and the loss of the tax base in abandoned properties means that the taxes for those in the surrounding neighborhoods increase substantially.

These high-foreclosure neighborhoods become difficult for cities and towns to manage in terms of assigning patrols, curbing crime, and preserving the value of occupied homes in the area. Some cities and towns are even grappling with the problems of mosquito infestation in the swimming pools of the abandoned homes because the pools have not been maintained. Cities and towns have undertaken a number of initiatives to hold lenders and developers accountable for the abandoned homes in these high-foreclosure areas. HUD has adopted a Neighborhood Stabilization Program that offers grants to cities and towns to provide them with the funds necessary to fix up the properties, add additional enforcement mechanisms, and even purchase some of the properties to shore up the value and the condition of the properties. In the nonprofit sector, there is now help for cities and towns from the National Vacant Properties Campaign that attempts to work with local governments in helping them to solve the problems of the foreclosure neighborhoods.[5]

Stalled Developments

Following the 2008 bank collapses, additional federal regulation and economic conditions found developers scrambling to obtain the financing necessary to finish their subdivisions and CIDs. Banks were simply not willing to risk loans in a real estate market that was down and showing few signs of recovery. As a result, even without foreclosures, cities and counties were left with abandoned subdivisions and other development projects. In an effort to avoid these abandoned eyesores, cities and counties have often tried to provide special deals, discounts, and incentives to have developers finish the projects. As well intentioned as these government efforts are, the authority to do so cannot be spun from whole cloth. The actions must be authorized legislatively and cannot result in favoritism to certain

---

[4]George L. Kelling and James Q. Wilson, "Broken Windows: The Police and Neighborhood Safety," *The Atlantic Monthly*, March 1982. Dr. Wilson argued that there is a correlation between law enforcement's failure to enforce "quality of life" laws and the increased likelihood of violent crimes in a particular neighborhood. Dr. Wilson advocated fixing the windows first. Former New York City mayor Rudy Giuliani followed Dr. Wilson's theory. Mr. Giuliani removed the "squeegee guys" from the city streets as a first step in restoring safety to city streets. The symbolism and appearance—in the experience and research of both men—make a difference in the quality of life in a city or town.

[5]National Vacant Properties Campaign, http://www.vacantproperties.org.

developers. Because of taxpayer objections, courts have had to make decisions on developer rescues, using strict statutory and constitutional applications and interpretations. The following case involves a challenge to a city's aid to a developer experiencing difficulty finishing a project.

TURKEN V. GORDON

224 P.3d 158 (Ariz. 2010)
When CityNorth Goes South

FACTS

CityNorth was to be the commercial core of a planned community development north of Phoenix that was known as Desert Ridge. CityNorth's developer, NPP CityNorth LLC, was struggling with completion and sought help from government entities for completion. The city of Phoenix was concerned because without the completed luxury hotels, stores, restaurants, and office occupants, the hoped-for tax revenues were pie-in-the-sky. However, CityNorth was very close to the city of Glendale and Glendale wanted to inch CityNorth into its city boundaries because it too could see tax revenue potential. As a result, the competition to woo the developer with promised deals for either annexation or staying put began.

Phoenix was able to seal the deal for CityNorth when the Phoenix City Council passed an ordinance that allowed the city to pay for a parking facility provided a consultant could show that the tax revenues from the development would exceed what the city would dole out for the parking structure. Not surprisingly, a consultant did indeed find that the tax revenues would tower, as it were, over the city funds dished up for the parking garage.

The ordinance/agreement provided that NPP would build the parking garage but, for the next 45 years, would set aside 2,980 spaces for the use of the general public and 200 spaces for commuters. The city would pay for the garage when NPP built at least 1.02 million square feet of retail space as well as the garage itself. The payments would run for 11 years and could not exceed $97.4 million.

When taxpayers got wind of the ordinance/agreement, there was a mini-revolution. Meyer Turken, the leader of the taxpayer pack, brought suit alleging that the agreement violated the Gift Clause of the Arizona Constitution:

Neither the state, nor any county, city, town, municipality, or other subdivision of the state shall ever give or loan its credit in the aid of, or make any donation or grant, by subsidy or otherwise, to

any individual, association, or corporation, or become a subscriber to, or a shareholder in, any company or corporation, or become a joint owner with any person, company, or corporation…

The trial court granted the city's motion for summary judgment. The court of appeals reversed and the city appealed.

JUDICIAL OPINION

Hurwitz, Vice Chief Justice

[The Gift Clause] represents the reaction of public opinion to the orgies of extravagant dissipation of public funds by counties, townships, cities, and towns in aid of the construction of railways, canals, and other like undertakings during the half century preceding 1880, and it was designed primarily to prevent the use of public funds raised by general taxation in aid of enterprises apparently devoted to quasi public purposes, but actually engaged in private business.

Our cases interpreting the Gift and Tax Clauses have struggled to define "public purpose." In a seminal Tax Clause case, we noted that "[p]ublic purpose is a phrase perhaps incapable of definition, and better elucidated by examples."

Our cases also emphasize that although determining whether governmental expenditures serve a public purpose is ultimately the province of the judiciary, courts owe significant deference to the judgments of elected officials.

We adhere to that straightforward approach today. When a public entity purchases something from a private entity, the most objective and reliable way to determine whether the private party has received a forbidden subsidy is to compare the public expenditure to what the government receives under the contract. When government payment is grossly disproportionate to what is received in return, the payment violates the Gift Clause.

No party questions that payments by the City under the Parking Agreement would serve a public purpose. The parties agree that providing parking is a legitimate public purpose and that the City could have erected a parking structure of its own without violating the Gift Clause.

The City contends that the Parking Agreement also serves several indirect public purposes. It argues that because NPP may have been unable to complete its planned retail component absent the Agreement, the transaction will serve to increase the City's tax base. The City also asserts that the Agreement will produce denser development, decreased pollution, and employment opportunities for city residents.

In taking a broad view of permissible public purposes under the Gift Clause, we have repeatedly emphasized that the primary determination of whether a specific purpose constitutes a "public purpose" is assigned to the political branches of government, which are directly accountable to the public.

In this case, we cannot conclude that the City Council "unquestionably abused" its discretion in determining that the Parking Agreement had a public purpose.

When public funds are used to purchase something from a private entity, finding a public purpose only begins the constitutional inquiry. [We are required] to examine the "consideration" received from the private entity. The Gift Clause is violated when that consideration, compared to the expenditure, is "so inequitable and unreasonable that it amounts to an abuse of discretion, thus providing a subsidy to the private entity."

The term "consideration" has a settled meaning in contract law. It is a "performance or return promise" that is "bargained for ... in exchange for the promise of the other party." In other words, consideration is what one party to a contract obligates itself to do (or to forbear from doing) in return for the promise of the other contracting party.

Under contract law, courts do not ordinarily examine the proportionality of consideration between parties contracting at arm's length, leaving such issues to the marketplace. In contrast, our Gift Clause jurisprudence quite appropriately focuses on adequacy of consideration because paying far too much for something effectively creates a subsidy from the public to the seller. The potential for a subsidy is heightened when, as occurred here, a public entity enters into the contract without the benefit of competitive proposals.

[T]he superior court viewed the relevant consideration as not only the value of the parking places obtained by the City, but also indirect benefits, such as projected sales tax revenue. The court erred in that analysis. Although anticipated indirect benefits may well be relevant in evaluating whether spending serves a public purpose, when not bargained for as part of the contracting party's promised performance, such benefits are not consideration under contract law. Analysis of adequacy of consideration for Gift Clause purposes focuses instead on the objective fair market value of what the private party has promised to provide in return for the public entity's payment.

A hypothetical illustrates the point. Assume that a municipality must repair a sewer line. If the line is not repaired, disease will likely break out and spread quickly, causing deaths and significant public health care expenditures. Several competent contractors are willing to do the repair for $5,000. Under the City's reasoning, the municipality could pay a contractor $5 million without violating the Gift Clause because the indirect benefits from the repair-saved lives and avoided health care costs-exceed the $5 million payment.

The Gift Clause prohibits subsidies to private entities, and paying far more than the fair market value for the repair plainly would be a subsidy to the contractor. We therefore turn to the consideration provided for in the Parking Agreement. To be sure, the City's obligation to make payments under the Agreement does not commence until NPP has developed a specified amount of retail space. However, the Agreement makes plain that NPP has no contractual obligation to build the retail component, characterizing retail construction as "a condition precedent of the City's obligation to pay the Use Payment and not a covenant of the Developer."

As the City notes, the payments for the parking spaces under the Agreement are based on the taxes generated at the development. But the Agreement does not obligate NPP to produce a penny of tax revenue for the City. Rather, the duty of CityNorth and its tenants to pay taxes arises from law applicable to all, not out of contract.

In short, the only consideration flowing to the City from NPP under the Parking Agreement is the right to use the parking spaces. [The] relevant inquiry is whether the amount the City has agreed to pay for use of those spaces is grossly disproportionate to what it will receive.

The Parking Agreement obligates the City to pay up to $97.4 million for the parking spaces. The City argues that its payments cannot be a gift or subsidy under the Gift Clause, because they will be offset by tax revenues from the CityNorth project. But this argument misses the point. Once collected, these tax revenues are public funds. Whether the subsequent expenditure of those funds is consistent with the Gift Clause depends on what the City receives in return under the Parking Agreement.

The Constitution requires that the consideration received by the City not be grossly disproportionate to the amount paid to the private entity. The statute imposes a separate and additional requirement— municipalities entering into tax incentive agreements must certify that the anticipated increase in tax revenues exceeds the proposed expenditure. A.R.S. § 9-500.11(D)(1). Thus, the remaining question is whether the $97.4 million that the City has promised to pay far exceeds the value of the parking places promised in return. Turken has conceded that $97.4 million might well be a fair payment for exclusive use of 3,180 spaces over the next 45 years. The Parking Agreement, however, gives the City exclusive use of only 200 spaces. Nothing in the Agreement prevents CityNorth customers from filling up the other 2,980 spaces when other members of the public might most want to use them.

We find it difficult to believe that the 3,180 parking places have a value anywhere near the payment potentially required under the Agreement. The Agreement therefore quite likely violates the Gift Clause. However, because the superior court viewed projected sales tax revenue and other indirect benefits as consideration, it never separately addressed the value of the parking places. We are not finders of fact, and our intuitions as to proportionality, however strong, cannot substitute for specific findings of fact. Thus, under normal circumstances, we would be constrained to remand to the superior court.

A remand, however, is not necessary in this case. Although "[n]ormally our decisions in civil cases operate retroactively as well as prospectively," "[w]hether

an opinion will be given prospective application only is a policy question within this court's discretion."

We today overrule no prior decision. But we recognize that the consideration prong has been widely misunderstood during the past two decades and that our cases have never squarely addressed that issue. The able trial judge believed that indirect benefits satisfied the consideration prong and no party appears to have directly argued to the contrary below. Moreover, various *amici* (friends of the court) have claimed that a number of public–private transactions were entered into under a similar misapprehension.

[M]unicipalities may have understood the "public benefit" language to suggest a broader view of "consideration." [W]e did not mean to suggest that something that is not consideration under contract law is somehow transformed into such for Gift Clause purposes.

[W]e understand how that notion might have been mistakenly inferred from language in our opinions. We therefore believe it appropriate to limit today's clarification of the consideration test to transactions occurring after the date of this opinion.

[W]e vacate the opinion of the court of appeals. [W]e affirm the superior court's dismissal of Turken's Gift Clause claim.

CASE QUESTIONS

1. Why do city governments want to step in and help developers finish projects?
2. What is the concern addressed through gift clauses in state constitutions?
3. Why does the court allow the city's deal to go through even though it finds a violation of the gift clause?

CONSIDER 21.2   Erling "Curly" Haugland challenged the City of Bismarck's implementation of an urban renewal plan and use of tax increment financing to fund urban renewal projects as a violation of North Dakota's constitutional provision, known as the gift clause. Bismarck had undertaken a decades-long project under statutory authority given to cities and towns. Section 40–58–04, N.D.C.C. authorizes a municipality to use private and public resources to facilitate the development of industrial or commercial properties, to eliminate and prevent the development or spread of slums and urban blight, and to rehabilitate slum and blighted areas by encouraging voluntary rehabilitation and by compelling repair of deteriorated or deteriorating structures and redevelopment of those areas.

Haugland claimed Bismarck's renewal plan created an illegal and perpetual downtown renewal area, which continues to keep redeveloped property within the renewal area as a resource for completion of the plan as a whole. Haugland also claimed Bismarck improperly used excess tax increment funds for its "CORE Incentive Program," which resulted in gifts to some property owners within the renewal area for facade and signage, housing incentives, technical assistance, revolving loans, and payments for subsurface infill of vaults below the public right-of-way within the renewal area. Discuss what the North Dakota court should decide with regard to its gift clause and the special funding of certain merchants and property owners. *Haugland v. City of Bismarck,* 818 N.W.2d 660 (N.D. 2012).   ▬

Time Limits for Development

Some faltering projects have been taken over because of the "failure to develop." Because of economic constraints, stalled development projects have also become eyesores and drains for communities. Cities and towns are now passing and using time-limit statutes to stop developers from dragging out the time for construction and requiring progress in CIDs. For example, many cities allow developers only one extension of time for submission of their subdivision plans. The courts have ruled that the city's refusal to grant extensions after the statutory limit is neither arbitrary nor unconstitutional, even when it means that the developer loses financing and the ability to carry forward with the project. The time limits serve a public purpose of not having undeveloped land create problems with non-use. *Dry Creek Partners, LLC, v. Ada County Com'rs, ex rel. State,* 217 P.3d 1282 (Idaho 2009).

Registering the Properties

Most cities and towns begin their stabilization and reclamation plans with some form of a registry. Local officials develop resources for finding and mapping the abandoned homes so that they can develop plans for remedying the decline. Some local governments have partnered with colleges and universities to use students through their course projects to identify the properties and then develop their ideas for remedies.

Working on the Properties

Some cities and towns are contacting lenders and developers to seek their cooperation in solving the problem of blight. That contact can result in a request for the developer or lender to take the property back. In some situations in which the developer or lender helped the buyers engage in mortgage fraud, the local governments are using prosecutions to force settlements that move the property from abandonment and disrepair to restoration and perhaps ownership in the hands of a qualified buyer or leased to qualified tenants. Other cities and towns are using code violations and eminent domain proceedings to take back properties that lenders have allowed to remain abandoned. The constitutionality of this process depends upon compensation to the lender or developer for the properties taken.

Code Violations

Using either existing code provisions or new ones promulgated in response to the abandoned properties crisis, some cities and towns are using code enforcement officials to issue violations to lenders and developers. The unavailability of the owner/borrower means that the violations shift to the equitable title holder, the lender, or the developer. The city or town then has a bit of a hammer over these third parties because the choice of paying for the code violations or either surrendering or repairing the property usually finds them doing the latter just because it is so much cheaper.

Goodwill

Some developers are simply stepping up to help in their subdivisions that are now experiencing the problems of abandonment. They are doing so because of a desire to maintain their reputations with the affected cities and towns. When the real estate market is better and developers once again require approval for new subdivisions, their response to this crisis creates a sense of community, responsibility, and accountability that will render their future approval processes less arduous.

Taking Over the Mortgages

A new idea that has emerged to resolve both the underwater and foreclosed mortgaged properties comes from venture capitalists who have offered to buy the mortgages using eminent domain by the government entity. Using government-backed bonds, the mortgages would then be refinanced and bundled and sold as mortgage-backed securities. Cities and counties are exploring the idea in order to eliminate foreclosure blight. However, some question whether there is the appropriate level of "public purpose" present in such a large taking of private contracts (the mortgages) related to property.

LAND FINANCE

Financing a real estate development is often not as simple as going to the bank and obtaining a mortgage loan.[6] A developer may have to be more creative and bring together a pool of investors to finance the project. These investors will want something more than interest as a return on their funds; they will want to join in on the profits made from the development project. **Real estate syndication** is a generic term for the process of investor ownership of real estate projects. Real estate syndication allows developers to acquire nontraditional funding for a project through groups of individual investors. Syndication can be something as simple as pooling funds to buy an apartment complex, or as complicated as the development of raw land into a planned community or commercial complex. The following sections cover some basics of the various forms of syndications.

The Basics of Real Estate Syndication

The primary party in a real estate syndication is the entrepreneur or syndicator. Those who invest in the syndicate are referred to as *unit purchasers*. The form of the syndicate may be a partnership, a corporation, a limited liability company (LLC), or a real estate investment trust (REIT).

Syndication Forms—General Partnerships

A **general partnership** is a form of doing business that can be used for syndication so that all profits and losses flow through to the individual partners. Their personal assets are all subject to the creditors of the partnership. Governed by the **Uniform Partnership Act (UPA)**, this law has been adopted in 49 states so that partnership structures are fairly clear for purposes of national syndication.

---

[6]Again, the order of obtaining financing can vary. A developer may have soft commitments before even approaching the local government for approval.

There is a difference between co-ownership of property and a partnership. The distinction is that partners co-own property for the purpose of generating profits and one partner can agree to sell the property. Joint venturers hold property as tenants in common and consent of the co-owners is required for sale of the property. In many of the failed developments, the absence of a formal partnership agreement has left the courts with litigation that raises the question of whether the parties are truly partners or simply co-owners. That distinction controls when, why, and how the property may be sold, something that has created rifts and resulting litigation. *Kay Inv. Co., L.L.C. v. Brody Realty No. 1, L.L.C.,* 731 N.W.2d 777(Mich. App. 2006).

The Internal Revenue Code (IRC) recognizes partnerships as an aggregate of the partners only and permits each partner to report his or her share of the partnership's income, gains, and losses. In a real estate investment, this attribute of partnership taxation enables the partners or unit owners to enjoy the full benefit of deductions for depreciation.

Syndication Forms—Limited Partnership

A limited partnership is a form of doing business and syndication governed by the **Uniform Limited Partnership Act (ULPA)** and the **Revised Uniform Limited Partnership Act (RULPA)**.

A **limited partnership** is a partnership with a slight variation in the liability of those involved. There are two types of partners in a limited partnership: There must be at least one **general partner** and one **limited partner**. General partners have the same liability as all partners in a general partnership—full and complete personal liability for all partnership obligations and losses. Limited partners' liability is limited to the amount of their capital contributions. Their personal assets are not placed at the risk of the limited partnership's success. The most they can lose is the amount of their investment.

A limited partnership is a statutory creature. Unlike a general partnership, which can be formed with an agreement or **articles of partnership**, a limited partnership must be created formally with a public filing of the document of creation, often called the **articles of limited partnership**. The articles must be filed with a public office, generally the secretary of state in the state where the limited partnership is created and will do business.

The principal advantages of a limited partnership is that limited partners have only limited liability, and the income and losses, just as with a general partnership, flow through to the individual partners' income tax returns. If the limited partners comply with the rules for limited liability, their liability is limited to the amount of their capital contribution.

In many limited partnerships, the general partner contributes an undeveloped piece of property, and the limited partners furnish the money for its development. Limited partners are known in lay terms as *silent partners* and must not create the impression that they are involved in firm management and so fully liable as general partner/managers are.

The following case involves an interesting issue of a slipshod arrangement for development and the resulting liability.

PRACTICAL TIP

A checklist for those interested in getting into syndication:

1. Check the current market value of the properties involved.
2. Check current leases, rental fees, payment histories, and terms.
3. Check the property and syndicator's expenses.
4. Perform a cash flow analysis.
5. If there are vacancies, why? How does the market look?
6. Check title, taxes, assessment, public records.
7. Check on the tax implications.
8. Check the zoning.
9. Check for environmental issues, liability, and targets.
10. Check terms of underlying loan agreements, mortgages, deeds of trust, and other contracts.
11. Determine whether state and federal securities laws apply to the syndication.
12. Check the background and experience of the syndicator(s).
13. Review the paperwork for the syndication structure and, if applicable, of the syndicator.
14. Are salespeople licensed real estate agents? Are they licensed securities dealers?
15. Verify brokerage fees and other commissions for sales of interest in the syndication.

BYKER V. MANNES

641 N.W.2d 210 (Mich. 2002)*
The Partner Who Didn't Quite Understand Liability

FACTS

In 1985, David Byker (plaintiff) was doing accounting work for Tom Mannes (defendant). The two talked about going into business together because they had complementary business skills. Mr. Mannes could locate certain properties because of his real estate background, and Mr. Byker could raise money for their property purchases. Indeed, the parties stipulated the following as part of the litigation process in this case:

> [T]he Plaintiff ... and Defendant ... agreed to engage in an ongoing business enterprise, to furnish capital, labor and/or skill to such enterprise, to raise investment funds and to share equally in the profits, losses and expenses of such enterprise.... In order to facilitate investment of limited partners, Byker and Mannes created separate entities wherein they were general partners or shareholders for the purposes of operating each separate entity.

They also stipulated that they had investment interests in five real estate limited partnerships. With regard to these partnerships in which they invested over a nine-year period, they shared equally in the commissions, financing fees, and termination costs. The two also personally guaranteed loans for these investments from several financial institutions.

The business relationship between the parties began to deteriorate after they created Pier 1000 Ltd. in order to own and manage a marina. Shortly after the creation of Pier 1000 Ltd., the marina encountered serious financial difficulties. To address these difficulties, the parties placed their profits from another partnership, the M & B Limited Partnership II, into Pier 1000 Ltd. and borrowed money from several financial institutions.

When Mr. Mannes refused to make any additional monetary contributions, Mr. Byker continued to make loan payments and incurred accounting fees on behalf of Pier 1000 Ltd., as well as on behalf of other business entities. Mr. Byker also entered into several individual loans for the benefit of Pier 1000 Ltd.

These business transactions were performed without Mr. Mannes's knowledge. The marina was returned to its previous owners in exchange for their assumption of Mr. Byker's and Mr. Mannes's business obligations. At this point, the business ventures between Mr. Byker and Mr. Mannes ceased.

Mr. Byker then approached Mr. Mannes to obtain his share of the payments required as a result of the losses from the various businesses. Mr. Mannes testified that he was "absolutely dumbfounded" by the request for money.

Mr. Byker then filed suit for the payments, saying that the two had entered into a partnership. Following a bench trial, the court determined that the parties had created a general partnership that included all of the business entities. The Court of Appeals reversed that decision. Mr. Byker appealed.

JUDICIAL OPINION

Markman, Justice

"[T]here is no necessity that the parties attach the label 'partnership' to their relationship as long as they in fact both mutually agree to assume a relationship that falls within the definition of a partnership."

In determining whether a partnership exists, the focus is not on whether individuals subjectively intended to form a partnership, that is, it is unimportant whether the parties would have labeled themselves "partners." Instead, the focus is on whether individuals intended to jointly carry on a business for profit regardless of whether they subjectively intended to form a partnership.

Whether Michigan partnership law, M.C.L. § 449.6(1), requires a subjective intent to form a partnership or merely an intent to carry on as co-owners a business for profit is a question of law.

At present, partnership is defined as "an association of 2 or more persons, which may consist of husband and wife, to carry on as co-owners a business for profit...." This definition, as well as its

---

*This case created a bit of a tussle between the Michigan Court of Appeals and its Supreme Court. Following this decision and remand, the Court of Appeals found that there was no partnership because the parties had to be aware of it to be liable, thus defying the Michigan Supreme Court. On appeal, the Michigan Supreme Court reversed the Court of Appeals, 668 N.W.2d 909 (Mich. 2003), not offering an opinion but explaining it was reversing for the reasons stated in the dissenting opinion at the Court of Appeals on the second round.

predecessors, was modeled after the definition of partnership set forth in the 1914 UPA.

In 1994, however, the UPA definition of partnership was amended by the National Conference of Commissioners. The amended definition stated that "the association of two or more persons to carry on as co-owners a business for profit forms a partnership, whether or not the persons intend to form a partnership."

Although Michigan has not adopted the amended definition of partnership as set forth in § 202 of the Uniform Partnership Act of 1994, we believe nonetheless that M.C.L. § 449.6 is consistent with that amendment.

… [I]f the parties associate themselves to "carry on" as co-owners a business for profit, they will be deemed to have formed a partnership relationship regardless of their subjective intent to form such a legal relationship. The statutory language is devoid of any requirement that the individuals have the subjective intent to create a partnership. Stated more plainly, the statute does not require partners to be aware of their status as "partners" in order to have a legal partnership.

Further, the Court of Appeals emphasis upon subjective intent as being of "prime importance in ascertaining whether a partnership exists," belies the absence in the statute of even a reference to such "intent" as a factor for consideration. Indeed, M.C.L. § 449.7, entitled "Rules for determining existence of a partnership," contains a listing of items to be specifically considered in this process and the subjective intent of the parties is conspicuously absent.

Although the provisions of M.C.L. § 449.6(1) set forth the standard for determining whether a partnership has been formed, we note that the Court of Appeals relied heavily on several of our earlier cases that, in the Court's view, focused this inquiry on whether the parties mutually intended to form a partnership. However, upon further examination of these cases, we respectfully disagree with the Court of Appeals. Rather, we find that, despite language that could potentially lead to such a conclusion, these cases, in fact, contemplated an examination of all the parties' acts and conduct in determining the existence of a partnership.

Pursuant to this common law, individuals would be found to have formed a partnership if they acted as partners, regardless of their subjective intent to form a partnership.

If parties intend no partnership the courts should give effect to their intent, unless somebody has been deceived by their acting or assuming to act as partners; and any such case must stand upon its peculiar facts, and upon special equities.

It is nevertheless possible for parties to intend no partnership and yet to form one. If they agree upon an arrangement which is a partnership in fact, it is of no importance that they call it something else, or that they even expressly declare that they are not to be partners. The law must declare what is the legal import of their agreements, and names go for nothing when the substance of the arrangement shows them to be inapplicable.

Thus, one analyzes whether the parties acted as partners, not whether they subjectively intended to create, or not to create, a partnership.

Accordingly, we believe that our prior case law has, consistent with M.C.L. § 449.6(1), properly examined the requirements of a legal partnership by focusing on whether the parties intentionally acted as co-owners of a business for profit, and not on whether they consciously intended to create the legal relationship of "partnership." We emphasize, however, that any future development of case law regarding partnership in our state must take place in accord with the provisions of the Michigan Partnership Act.

With the language of the statute as our focal point, we conclude that the intent to create a partnership is not required if the acts and conduct of the parties otherwise evidence that the parties carried on as co-owners a business for profit. Thus, we believe that, to the extent that the Court of Appeals regarded the absence of subjective intent to create a partnership as dispositive regarding whether the parties carried on as co-owners a business for profit, it incorrectly interpreted the statutory (and the common) law of partnership in Michigan.

Accordingly, we remand this matter to the Court of Appeals for analysis under the proper test for determining the existence of a partnership under the Michigan Uniform Partnership Act.

CASE QUESTIONS

1. What type of relationship did Mr. Byker and Mr. Mannes have?
2. What does the court say about the intent of the parties?
3. Is Mr. Mannes liable to Mr. Byker for the payments Mr. Byker made with regard to their investments?

Syndication Forms—Corporations

Nature and Creation

The corporation form of syndication has the advantages of limited liability and unlimited duration. Partnerships are subject to dissolution when a partner withdraws, goes bankrupt, or dies. Limited partnerships have the same problems with regard to their general partners, but corporations can go on in perpetuity regardless of the investors' status.

State laws on corporation are not as uniform as those on partnerships and limited partnerships. However, the **Model Business Corporation Act (MBCA)** and **Revised Model Business Corporation Act (RMBCA)** are adopted in about one-third of the states. Many other states have portions of these model acts or use them as models for their own laws.

A corporation is also a statutory creature and must be created formally by public filing of a document known as the **articles of incorporation**. These articles must be published, and once formed, a corporation must file annual reports and keep separate books and records for the corporate transactions, even when there is just a single shareholder. A corporation is known as a *fictitious person*, with all the rights of an individual (except taking the Fifth Amendment). The owners or shareholders own a percentage of this entity, but that entity has a legal existence that allows it to take and hold title to real property, obtain a loan to purchase property, and give a mortgage on that property to secure the corporate debt under that loan.

Taxation Issues

One benefit of partnership structure that is lost when investors form a "C" corporation is the ability of the investors to directly deduct losses from their income. However, the IRC does permit corporations to elect **Subchapter S** or **S corporation** status. With an S corporation, the shareholders have the protection of limited liability and the benefit of direct deduction of losses. This direct deduction of losses is critical in real estate corporations because of the depreciation deductions for real property.

Subchapter S structure is limited to certain types of corporations, and the Subchapter S election must be made before the taxable year ends and filed with the IRS. There are limits on the number of shareholders, classes of stock, and income sources for S corporations.

Syndication Forms—Limited Liability Companies

Nature and Creation

A relatively new business structure that is popular in real estate syndication is the **limited liability company**, or **LLC**. Now permitted in all states and the District of Columbia, this form of business organization is a business entity that offers the limited liability of a corporation but permits the tax advantages of a partnership. The IRS permits the flow-through handling of LLC income and losses in the same manner as those of partnerships, limited partnerships, and S corporations. The owners of an LLC are called *members*, and the members or owners then report their portion of the income or losses on their individual tax returns.

An LLC is also a statutory creature, complete with filing requirements, with most states mandating the use of the words "limited liability company" or the letters "LLC" or "LC" following the company's name.

Operating Agreement

The members manage their LLC through an operating agreement. An operating agreement would be equivalent to the bylaws of a corporation or a partnership agreement. The members can specify that they will manage the LLC together, or they can delegate that responsibility to a managing member, called a *manager*. However, all the LLC members enjoy limited liability. The owners, managers, and members of an LLC do not have personal liability for the debts of the LLC itself.

Taxation Issues

LLCs offer the best features of all business forms when the owners wish to enjoy the tax benefits of flow-through income and losses. In real estate investments, the flow-through aspect is often a critical feature for investors provided their liability exposure is limited to their investment. With an LLC, real estate investors can enjoy flow-through benefits, limited liability, and a voice in management without losing that protection.

Syndication Forms—Limited Liability Partnerships

The newest form of business structure is the **limited liability partnership**, or **LLP**. An LLP is a partnership with unique statutory protection for all its members. Not all states have LLP statutes, but those that do have strict formal requirements for the creation of an LLP, yet another statutory creature. If the LLP formation requirements are not met, the owners have just a general partnership with full personal liability for all the partners. If the LLP is formed correctly, all partners have limited liability, with no personal liability exposure except to the extent of the capital contribution. The LLP has the flow-through characteristic for income, with losses and profits flowing through to the partners. All partners or a designated partner can manage without risking personal liability exposure.

Syndication Forms—Investment Trusts

Nature and Creation

Real estate investment trusts (REITs) and **mortgage investment trusts (MITs)** are legislative creatures that permit small investors access to the returns a diversified portfolio of real estate can provide. Instead of being a limited partner or a shareholder, the investor owns a beneficial interest in a trust. The idea for this form of real estate syndication originated in Massachusetts more than a century ago, and remains popular today because of the tax benefits this form of investment provides for investors as well as the access to capital it provides for real estate developers.

A REIT is set up as any other trust is: with a trust agreement or declaration of trust. As discussed in Chapter 15, a trust separates legal and equitable title. In a REIT, the trustee holds legal title to the property to be developed and is also responsible for the management of the properties in the trust, which is really a portfolio of real estate investments. Each investor, as a beneficiary, holds equitable title to the property, or at least a percentage of those properties. A **trust certificate** given to each beneficiary reflects the level and amount of the investor's ownership. Investors are not involved in the management of the properties or the portfolio; they allow the trustee to handle the real estate investments.

REIT owners/beneficiaries are not personally liable for the obligations of the trust; their liability is limited to the trust assets. Beneficiaries vote for the management of the trust in that they elect the trustees. The trustees owe a fiduciary duty to the beneficiaries and the trust, and must act with the best interests of the trust and its beneficiaries as a priority.

Taxation Issues

If a trust qualifies for REIT treatment, then the REIT is taxed only on undistributed income and gains. If the income or gains are distributed to the beneficiaries, there are no taxes to the trust. REITs avoid the double taxation of corporations. The beneficiaries are taxed as individuals on the current or accumulated income; however, they are not entitled to the benefit of individual deduction of trust losses. To qualify as a REIT for purposes of these tax benefits, the REIT must have predominantly passive income from real property. REITs must follow the 85/95 rule. First, 85 percent of a REIT's gross income must consist of income from the following sources: (a) rents from real property; (b) interest from mortgage loans; (c) gain from the disposition of real property or mortgage loans (other than inventory); (d) dividends from or gains from disposition of shares in other REITs; (e) abatements and refunds of real property taxes; (f) income from foreclosure property; (g) commitment fees received as consideration for entering into agreements to make mortgage loans or to purchase or lease real property; and (h) income from qualifying temporary investments of new capital. Second, at least 95 percent of the REIT's gross income must consist of the following: (1) income that satisfies the 85 percent income test; (2) dividends; (3) interest; and (4) gains from the disposition of stock or securities.[7] If a REIT falls short on these specific IRS requirements, then the REIT is taxed as a corporation (26 U.S.C. § 4981).

Figure 21.2 provides a chart comparison of the various forms of real estate syndication.

Securities Issues in Finance and Syndication

While general partnerships do not involve any sales of securities because the general partners all have debt, work, and contribution responsibilities, limited partnership interests, interests in REITs, share ownership in corporations, and interests in LLCs have been included as forms of securities for the purposes of the application of federal securities laws. Unless exempted, all sales of securities must be registered with both state and federal governments. When registration is required for the sale of interests in whatever form of syndication chosen, syndication becomes more expensive because of the complicated paperwork involved in the registration process. Some real estate syndications are small and structured to fit exemptions from the complicated and costly federal securities registration. However, many REITs are structured as publicly traded securities so that investors can buy and sell their REIT interests on national exchanges, an attractive flexibility that brings wider pools of capital to real estate development projects. For example, many of the malls around the country are owned by REITs. Even if these smaller arrangements are exempt under federal law, the developers may have to register the sale of interest as securities under state law.

CONSIDER 21.3 Francine Weiss and a number of other Maryland residents invested in the BJV real estate syndication. After she and the others lost most of their investment, they sued the principals in the syndication. During the course of the lawsuit they discovered that the property interests they purchased were at prices two to two-and-one-half times their actual market value. The BJV principals claim that the prices charged were to permit Francine and the other investors a greater tax break by allowing them more to depreciate. How could Francine and the others have avoided the loss of their investment? *Weiss v. Lehman*, 713 F. Supp. 489 (D.D.C. 1989).

[7]This explanation comes from Jack H. McCall, "A Primer on Real Estate Trusts: The Legal Basics of REITS," 2 *Transactions: Tenn. J. Bus. L.* 1 (2001).

FIGURE 21.2 Forms of Real Estate Syndication

	GENERAL PARTNERSHIP	LIMITED PARTNERSHIP	LIMITED LIABILITY COMPANY (LLC)	LIMITED LIABILITY PARTNERSHIP (LLP)	CORPORATIONS*	S CORPORATIONS OR SUBCHAPTER S CORPORATIONS
Creation	No formality required	File a certificate of limited partnership with appropriate state office	File articles of organization with appropriate agency	Registration of LLP filed with state government	File articles of incorporation with appropriate agency	File articles of incorporation with appropriate agency
Liability	Unlimited liability of each partner for firm debts	General partners: unlimited liability for firm debts Limited partners: no liability beyond amount of investment	All members are liable for LLC debts to the extent of their capital contributions and equity in firm. No personal liability beyond such	No liability for partners beyond their contributions and equity in firm, except unlimited personal liability for their wrongful acts and those of persons whom they supervise	Limited liability except: watered shares corporate veil pierced	Limited liability except: watered shares or when corporate veil pierced
Management	All partners according to their partnership agreement or the UPA or RUPA	General partners according to their partnership agreement or according to the ULPA or the RULPA; Limited partners cannot be managers	By members of firm, who may delegate authority to managers	All partners according to their partnership agreement or state law	Officers and board	Officers and board
Dissolution	As set forth in the partnership agreement for the UPA or RUPA	As set forth in the partnership agreement or the ULPA or RULPA	As set forth in LLC statute or articles of organization	As set forth in partnership agreement by state law	Major corporate transaction (shareholder beverage)	Major corporate transaction (Vote)
Control/Transfer	Can transfer interest, but not partner status	More easily transferred	No admission without consent of majority	No admission without consent of majority	Shares (with reasonable restrictions) are easily transferred	Restrictions on transfer to comply with S Corporation IRS regulations
Taxes	Partners pay taxes on individual returns after profits and losses of partnership flow through to them	Same as partnership (flow-through)	Flow-through treatment	Flow-through treatment	Corporation pays taxes; shareholders pay taxes on dividends	Shareholders pay taxes; take losses; flow-through

*S or Subchapter S Corporations formed under state law; tax status election (Small Business Job Protection Act of 1996).

© Cengage Learning 2014

LAND IMPROVEMENT AND CONSTRUCTION

The development, once financed, moves to the physical work of construction.

Legal Paperwork for Development and Construction

The developer must provide a subdivision or plat map with easements, roads, and lots clearly indicated. The plat map, which has been recorded, will be used as a reference point for descriptions of all lots to be sold in the subdivision. (See Chapter 7 for more detail on plat maps and their importance in legal descriptions.)

In addition to the plat map, the developer will record restrictions or **protective covenants** for the subdivision. These covenants, or **deed restrictions**, cover all of the architectural and use requirements for the subdivision such as minimum square footage, restrictions on in-home business operations, restrictions on the types of animals that may be kept on the lots, restrictions on dividing lots and selling smaller portions of them, and restrictions on the types of structures that may be erected in addition to the dwelling units.

Deed restrictions are based on the common law concept of covenants. At common law, covenants were restrictions placed in the deed from the grantor to the grantee. This problem of direct contact between grantor and grantee, or *privity*, is solved with a clause in the deed that transfers title subject to all the restrictions that have been recorded for the subdivision. Most deed restrictions (covenants) are now subject to statutory requirements if they are to be valid. For example, most states now require that the developer have buyers sign statements that they have received a copy of the deed restrictions and that they understand that their use of the property is subject to those restrictions. Title companies cannot close on subsequent transfers of the property unless and until buyers receive a copy of the deed restrictions and also sign off on them. In many areas, buyers are given a notebook with the deed restrictions that is sent via certified mail so that the developer can prove receipt by the buyer of the deed restrictions.

Even without the statutory deed restriction delivery requirements, the pattern of development can be binding. If the covenants and restrictions are visible by looking at a subdivision or area, courts will uphold them. For example, a buyer who sees the same roofing material in a subdivision is required to honor that restriction. An obvious scheme of development is binding on buyers. To protect those who already own homes in the subdivision, the common law doctrine of **equitable servitudes** exists. An equitable servitude is a restriction on land use that exists because of the nature of the subdivision or area. Under this doctrine, buyers of land within a partially developed subdivision are required to use the land purchased in a manner consistent with the plan of development in existence at the time of their purchase. The basis for the doctrine of equitable servitude is notice; a party who purchases land in an area where a common scheme of development is obvious is bound to abide by the development scheme.

In addition, a developer who pulls out of a subdivision prior to its completion may face claims of misrepresentation because the existing property owners purchased under the assumption that the subdivision would be completed with certain forms of construction. Both the doctrine of equitable servitudes and the remedy of misrepresentation serve to protect homeowners from declines in property values in the event a developer decides not to complete a subdivision and sells the lots to others. On the other hand, there are the issues of changed circumstances and what should be done when the restrictions are ignored and development and uses proceed as if the restrictions did not exist.

Some experts see a shift from governmental control of land use through zoning to private control through the use of covenants and deed restrictions. These new structures are called *residential community associations, common interest communities, residential private government,* and *gated communities.* Whatever the name, these areas, created by developers in the initial recorded documents for the development of the community, are self-contained units of private law governance, created and sustained through covenants.

The following case deals with an interesting issue of the enforceability of developer promises, covenants, and, as has been usual over the past few years, changed circumstances.

AMERICAN DREAM AT MARLBORO, L.L.C. V. PLANNING BD. OF TP. OF MARLBORO

35 A.3d 1198 (N.J. 2012)
A Lot at Risk

FACTS

American Dream at Marlboro, L.L.C., (plaintiff; ADM) acquired Beacon Road Associates, L.L.C., an entity that sought the approval of the Marlboro Township Planning Board in the 1990s for its proposed development, Beacon Woods I.

The development involved a series of building lots for homes on both sides of a roadway, to be named Haven Way, which ended in a cul de sac. There was a lot located near the end of Haven Way that had only fifty feet of frontage on the roadway and that was to be reached by a long driveway, a configuration referred to as a flag lot. Although the flag lot was of sufficient size to meet criteria, Beacon needed township approval because of a municipal ordinance that generally limited subdivision of flag lots. As part of the approval process, Beacon agreed to a deed restriction whereby the flag lot would not be subdivided in the future. The Planning Board's 1995 resolution granting preliminary major subdivision approval was specifically conditioned on the inclusion of a restriction in the deed for the flag lot that would preclude its further subdivision.

In 1997, Beacon, having failed to file the deed restriction relating to the flag lot, returned to the Planning Board for final approval. In June 1997, when the Planning Board granted final approval for the amended application, it continued to include the requirement that the flag lot be subject to the deed restriction to prevent its further subdivision.

In September 1997, ADM, which was then the contract purchaser of the proposed development, entered into an agreement with the Township to serve as the developer of the project. That agreement included ADM's agreement to be bound by all of the terms and conditions in the 1995 and 1997 Planning Board resolutions. The deed restriction relating to the flag lot was never recorded.

Instead, in 1998, ADM entered into a contract to purchase a tract of land behind the flag lot, which it then sought to merge with the flag lot for the purpose of creating a new six-lot subdivision at the end of Haven Way, the previously approved cul de sac, to be called Beacon Woods II. The tract that ADM planned to acquire included an easement that could be used to access the tract through a nearby major roadway, but as part of the Beacon Woods II plan, ADM intended to abandon that easement. In its place, ADM intended to transform the flag lot's driveway into a new road, to be called Sandra Court, that would lead from Haven Way to a second cul de sac development.

During the concept plan approval process, ADM did not reveal that the flag lot was required to be deed-restricted against further subdivision, but instead described its new plan as involving the "reconfiguration of one existing lot."

In March 1999, Patricia Cleary (defendant) entered into a contract with ADM to purchase one of the properties in the originally approved development. The lot she chose, designated as lot 20.09, was near the end of Haven Way. According to the original proposal for the development, her lot backed onto the existing flag lot and was next to the driveway that was proposed to serve the flag lot. She contends that ADM did not reveal to her that the flag lot was subject to the deed restriction prior to the time when she closed on her property in January 2001. ADM's marketing materials relied on the new configuration of the expanded development, and ADM felt there was no need to make Ms. Cleary aware of the original flag lot plan.

In October 1999, the Planning Board approved ADM's application for the new Beacon Woods II subdivision. After the final major subdivision approval was approved on February 21, 2001, and memorialized in an April 4, 2001, resolution, ADM closed on its purchase of the additional land, and vacated the easement that had provided that parcel with separate access to a nearby road other than Haven Way.

In 2002, when ADM entered into an agreement to sell Beacon Woods II to another developer, ADM realized that it had failed to reserve the easement that it needed to cross defendant's property and to construct Sandra Court, the proposed public roadway leading from the cul de sac to the new part of the development. When negotiations to secure Ms. Cleary's consent to the easement failed, ADM redesigned the roadway so as to obviate the need for her agreement. In 2003, ADM submitted an application to the Planning Board seeking to amend the final subdivision approval, apparently for this purpose. Ms. Cleary appeared and objected at every opportunity. Eventually, the contract between ADM and the new developer was terminated as a result of the inability to resolve Ms. Cleary's dispute.

In 2006, ADM returned to the Planning Board and requested that it act on the 2003 application for an amendment to the final subdivision approval. Early in 2007, the Planning Board advised ADM that its prior approvals had expired and it rejected ADM's assertion that the 2003 application had been approved by default.

ADM filed suit seeking a declaration that the 2003 application had been approved by default. Ms. Cleary filed a counterclaim seeking a declaration that the flag lot was prohibited from being subdivided because of the earlier-imposed deed restriction.

The trial court concluded that ADM had failed to demonstrate that it was entitled to be relieved from the deed restriction and granted summary judgment in favor of Ms. Cleary. The appellate court reversed and remanded. The supreme court granted certification.

JUDICIAL OPINION

Per Curiam

We begin with the observation that the parties do not dispute before this Court that the Planning Board lacked the power to eliminate the previously imposed, but never-recorded deed restriction on the flag lot. Instead, they concede that it is the courts that have the "equitable power to modify or terminate" such a restriction. Therefore, this Court need only consider the standards that the trial court must apply when considering an application to eliminate a deed restriction based on changed circumstances and the manner in which the proofs should be evaluated.

The essential test that applies to such a claim of changed circumstances requires the applicant to demonstrate that it has become "'impossible as a practical matter to accomplish the purpose for which'" a servitude or restrictive covenant was created.

The doctrine of changed circumstances is narrowly applied and "the test is stringent: relief is granted only if the purpose of the servitude can no longer be accomplished." That is, when a "servitude [is] terminated under this rule, it is ordinarily clear that the continuance of the servitude would serve no useful purpose and would create unnecessary harm to the owner of the servient estate."

Although we agree with the appellate panel that the trial court misapplied these governing standards, and that as a result the matter must be remanded for further proceedings, we modify the panel's judgment because its independent factual analysis unduly constricted the scope of the proceedings that are appropriate on remand. We so conclude for two reasons.

First, the appellate panel believed that the Planning Board only imposed the deed restriction because of a concern about further development of the flag lot. That interpretation of the record was essential to the panel's conclusion. Our review of the opinion of the trial court, however, reveals that the trial court apparently agreed with defendant's assertion that the Planning Board had additional reasons for imposing the deed restriction, but failed to identify them in concluding that plaintiff could not meet its burden. Because that aspect of the trial court's reasoning was not fully explicated, the appellate panel did not consider whether there were other reasons that retain vitality, relying instead on the single reason the panel had identified. Because the evaluation of the existence and continuing validity of such other reasons must weigh in the balance of whether the deed restriction's "purpose … can no longer be accomplished," the trial court should not be foreclosed on remand from further explanation of its findings and further exploration of the alternate reasons for the imposition of the deed restriction.

Second, as defendant pointed out, the elimination of a deed restriction is an exercise of the inherent equitable powers of the court. That being so, defendant's assertion that plaintiff acted with unclean hands in its applications to the Planning Board and her assertion that the allegedly changed circumstances are of plaintiff's own making should have been considered.

The judgment of the Appellate Division is affirmed and the matter is remanded to the trial court.

CASE QUESTIONS

1. What does this case teach developers about the timing of approvals?
2. Of what importance is the recording of deed restriction?
3. What impact does the non-disclosure of the deed restrictions to Ms. Cleary have on the case?

CONSIDER 21.4   Shalimar Estates is a residential land development consisting of 134 acres in Tempe, Arizona. The development consists of a golf course and adjacent residential lots. The golf course is an integral part of the development, and the lots were sold to buyers with the sales representations that there would always be a golf course and that their homes would always overlook a golf course. There were, however, no deed restrictions on the use of the golf course property. The original developer sold the property, and the developers planned to eliminate the golf course to maximize the property value. The homeowners have brought suit on the basis of the representations made to them. Can they win? *Shalimar Association v. D.O.C. Enterprises, Ltd.,* 688 P.2d 682 (Az. 1984).

ETHICAL ISSUE

When there are economic downturns, some developers simply walk away from their projects, leaving unfinished homes and subdivisions without functioning homeowners' associations. Some developers continue their developments but according to a different plan, with smaller homes or lots, different from what the original purchasers thought they were getting in their community. List those who are affected by developers' responses to economic downturns. Explain their ethical obligations in these situations and focus on the ethics of developers walking away.

CONSTRUCTION STAGE

Terminology and Parties

Understanding the names and roles of the parties in the construction project is helpful in determining rights and obligations, summarized in the list that follows:

1. The **owner** owns the land on which the building is being constructed.

2. The **construction lender** finances the project during the construction period.

3. The **permanent lender** or **lender** carries the mortgage on the property once construction is completed. (The permanent lender pays the construction lender's loan once construction is complete.)

4. The **general contractor** or **prime contractor** or **builder** is responsible for the coordination of the construction.

5. The **architect** may work with the general contractor or owner in making sure the building is constructed properly.

6. The **subcontractors** (usually a large group) perform individual projects for the construction. Subcontractors are responsible for separate jobs such as the electrical system, the heating and cooling system, and the roof.

7. The **suppliers** (a form of subcontractor) do no actual construction work but are usually a large group consisting of all businesses that supply materials for use in the construction project.

8. The **surety** or sureties stand as **guarantors** for either payment or performance according to the terms of the owner's contract or the contracts of subcontractors and suppliers.

9. The **insurer** for the owner, the contractor, or any other party stands liable in the event of destruction of the project during its course.

10. The **governmental supervisor** is the party who must be consulted or who must inspect as the project progresses.

Assurance in Construction—Bonds

One of the procedures an owner or developer can use to lessen the chances that a construction project will come to a disastrous end is to require certain types of bonds by the contractor. Three types of bonds are involved in construction projects. The first is the **bid bond**, which is a guaranty by a bonding company that a contractor will actually complete the contract at the bid price. If the contractor does not perform according to the terms of the bid and at the bid price, the contractor is liable for damages to the owner. However, these damage claims are of little comfort if the contractor has not performed because it is out of business or has filed for bankruptcy. The bonding company or surety will be liable to the owner when these financial collapses occur.

A **performance bond** is a guaranty by a bonding company that a project will be completed. If a contractor stops work on a project, the performance bond company is required to pay whatever is necessary to get the project completed. This amount, sometimes referred to as the **penal sum**, is usually equal to the contract price. Under a performance bond, the bonding company usually has the option of completing the construction itself or hiring another company to do the project.

The final form of bond, the **payment bond**, is one that offers insurance that the subcontractors will be paid. Under this type of bond, the bonding company agrees to pay subcontractors if the general contractor does not pay their claims. This type of bond serves as a means for preventing liens on the property by subcontractors. Many bonding companies issue a combination performance and payment bond. This combination bond usually gives the owner less protection because amounts paid to subcontractors will reduce the obligation amount for performance.

Formation of Construction Contracts

The formation of construction contracts is nearly standardized procedure. The owner sends out a **bid notice**, which is an invitation for offers. General contractors then have the opportunity to bid on the project. Before bidding, general contractors invite subcontractors to submit offers for subcontract work.

The subcontractors' submission of bids to the general contractor for their portion of the work is an offer. The general contractor's submission of a bid with the incorporated subcontractors' bids to the owner is also an offer.

Some companies use a process known as reverse bidding. This method requires those submitting proposals to place them on the Internet, where other competitors can see the price. Those who are interested in the project can then submit a lower bid in the hope of winning the contract.

Some construction organizations fear that reverse bidding may be compromising quality and safety in the contractors' effort to win bids. Others fear that there could be collusion among those who are bidding. That is, they could work together and agree on pricing so that someone who is ensured the bid with one customer then intentionally holds back in the next project, allowing the next contractor their "turn." Some companies use reverse bidding in projects only for the purchase of merchandise. Do you see any other ethical issues in reverse bidding?

Once all the bids are submitted, the owner reviews the bids from the general contractor, makes a decision, and notifies the chosen general contractor. Upon that notification, there is a contract between the owner and the general contractor.

Figure 21.3 summarizes the flow of legal events in the formation stage of the construction contract.

To avoid subcontractors' revoking their offers before the general contractor is awarded the project and at any time prior to acceptance, a general contractor has several alternatives. First, in the invitation for bids, the general contractor could specify that once submitted, a bid is irrevocable. Second, the general contractor could make acceptance automatic upon the owner's acceptance of the general contractor's bid. Finally, the courts have used the doctrine of promissory estoppel to require subcontractors to perform according to their bids once the general contractor has relied upon the bids. Reliance occurs once the general contractor uses the subcontractors' bids in the bid to the owner/developer.

CONSIDER 21.5   Gordon, a general contractor, was submitting bids to the city's port authority to construct a bridge in the city. Coronis submitted a bid to Gordon as subcontractor for the structural steel work. Gordon incorporated the Coronis bid in his bid to the port authority. After the city had accepted Gordon's bid, but before Gordon notified Coronis, Coronis revoked its bid and refused to perform. Gordon had to hire another subcontractor, Elizabeth Iron Works, to do the steel work at an additional cost of $53,000. Gordon has sued Coronis to recover the $53,000. What is the result? *E. A. Coronis Assoc. v. M. Gordon Constr. Co.,* 216 A.2d 246 (N.J. Super. 1966).

FIGURE 21.3 Legal Relationships in the Bidding Process

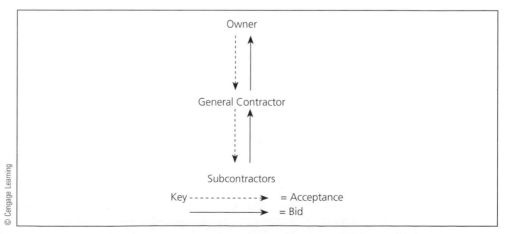

Payment and Payment Assurances in Construction Contracts

Because of the large number of parties involved and the need for money to flow down from its source to the general contractor, subcontractors, and suppliers, payment of the parties is a major issue in the construction contract and in construction litigation. Indeed, the payment problem is the basis for the mechanic's lien system (see Chapter 6).

General contractors are entitled to payment as their work is completed and may stop performance if payment is not made, so work stoppage is a means of security for them. General contractors usually have the benefit of a three-party arrangement, whereby the funds are held by a third party (examples of third parties used are lenders, architects, escrow companies, attorneys, trustees, and banks) and released upon the architect's certification of adequate completion. With the three-party system, the general contractors know the funds exist—it is simply a matter of performance to have them released.

Owners can also use the three-party system to ensure performance by the general contractor. Most standard contracts permit withholding a certain amount of the contract amount to cover defective work, late performance, or the general contractor's failure to pay subcontractors and suppliers. The withheld amount is typically 10 percent of the contract price and also 10 percent of each installment made during the construction period.

General contractors can also protect themselves against the subcontractors for the owner's nonpayment through the use of a **flow-down clause**. Under a flow-down clause, the general contractor is not required to pay the subcontractors until the owner has paid the general contractor.

Contract Price

Usually, the price in a construction contract is fixed and covers the entire project. Other forms of pricing include **unit pricing**, in which the contract is broken down into units. For example, excavation could be one unit in a project. Framing could be another unit. The overhead costs for the project would be divided among the units according to the amount of time or cost involved in each unit. The unit system makes the payment division easier. Another form of pricing that leaves many variables and can create problems is the **cost-plus formula**, in which the general contractor recovers whatever the cost of construction is along with a predetermined percentage or amount for profit. The difficulty with the cost-plus system is determining which costs are reimbursable as project costs and which are the general contractor's cost of doing business: personnel salaries, equipment, and other overhead items.

After the price or price formula is determined and construction begins, two possible problem areas may affect the price paid for the project by the owner: changed circumstances and work-order changes.

Changed Circumstances

The general contractor's bid on a project is based on assumptions about the project location, soil content, weather analysis, and other variable factors. If significant, unanticipated changes occur in those assumptions, the general contractor's costs will increase. With these cost increases, the issue arises of whether the price of completion will also increase. A clause in standard form contracts provides for price increases when (1) there are concealed conditions below the surface of the ground or concealed conditions in any existing structure at variance with those conditions indicated by contract; and (2) there are unknown physical conditions of an unusual nature at the site, differing materially from those ordinarily encountered and generally recognized as part of the work provided for in the contract. Other conditions that are considered unusual and unknown are unseasonal or unusually bad weather conditions, labor problems, and material shortages. Even without a changed-circumstances provision in the contract, the contractor is entitled to obtain an increased price if costs are greater because of misrepresentation of conditions by the owner in the bid information, the negotiations, or the contract.

PRACTICAL TIP

Change-order procedures should be placed in the construction contract and followed. Variation from the process will result in the adoption of that process as the parties' agreed-upon means of procedure. Further, confusion and error result when others believe the change-order process remains the same as in the written agreement. Often, the time saved by not following the process results in greater expense and litigation later.

Change Orders

The second type of situation in which a contractor may increase the project price is through a **change order**. Because of circumstances or preferences, the owner may wish to change plans and specifications that represent additional costs to the contractor.

A change order may be necessary for several reasons. The change may be needed simply because the owner or developer sees the project as it progresses and perceives that it does not look the same as it did in conception or on paper. Zoning changes may have been approved after the time the contract is negotiated but before construction begins or before a building permit has been issued for the plans that now violate the zoning laws. In the case of shopping centers, a change may be necessary to keep an anchor tenant or attract another tenant. There may be facilities missing. A typical change-order clause spells out the hows and costs of the modification. The more changes, documents, and supplements, the greater the likelihood of delay and error. The following case deals with an issue of changing circumstances and changes in construction.

DUGAN & MEYERS CONSTR. CO., INC. V. OHIO DEPT. OF ADM. SERVS.

864 N.E.2d 68 (Ohio 2007)
The Really Expensive Change Orders

FACTS

In 1997, Dugan & Meyers submitted a successful competitive bid to serve as the lead contractor for the construction of three buildings to be part of the Fisher College of Business at OSU: an undergraduate building, a resource center, and an executive-education building. Dugan & Meyers and the department, which served as the authorized contracting agent for OSU, executed a written contract in which the department agreed to pay Dugan & Meyers $20,932,500 and Dugan & Meyers agreed to complete construction work according to plans and specifications prepared by the associate architect, Karlsberger Companies.

The contract provided that Dugan & Meyers was to complete the work "on or before 660 consecutive days, following the date set forth in the Notice to Proceed, unless an extension of time [was] granted by the Director [of the department] in accordance with the Contract Documents."

Construction progressed virtually on schedule during the first year. By June 1998, however, the project began to fall behind schedule. By February 1999, it was apparent that the project was unlikely to be completed in time to ensure completion of that portion of the project that was needed for fall 1999 classes. Dugan & Meyers did not make any written requests for extensions of time after January 1998.

Attempts to bring the project back on schedule failed, and OSU ultimately relieved Dugan & Meyers of its responsibilities as lead contractor. According to the referee's report, the undergraduate building was completed in time for fall classes in September 1999 and the last of the three buildings was completed on January 16, 2000, six months after the modified deadline.

Dugan & Meyers sought payment from OSU for services rendered under the contract. In determining the amount due, OSU deducted the amount paid to Gilbane, the substitute contractor, for completing the lead-contractor duties. OSU also assessed Dugan & Meyers liquidated damages based on 188 days of delay in completion. OSU determined the liquidated damages by apportioning responsibility for the 188 days of delay between three subcontractors and Dugan & Meyers, and charged Dugan & Meyers for its contribution to the project delay. Dugan & Meyers filed suit seeking $3.4 million under the contract.

After a 17-day trial, a Court of Claims referee found that "the principal cause of the delay in completion of [the project] was the existence of an excessive number of errors, omissions and conflicts in the design documents furnished to bidders by the state and incorporated into [Dugan & Meyers's] contracts." He further observed that the "state offered no expert or lay testimony to rebut [Dugan & Meyers's] evidence that the design documents were incomplete and inaccurate and constituted the underlying cause of the delay in achieving project completion." The referee recommended that Dugan & Meyers be awarded additional damages for the "cumulative impact" of the excessive number of design changes needed during construction. OSU appealed. The Court of Appeals reversed because Dugan & Meyers had not requested an extension as they were required to do. Dugan & Meyers appealed.

JUDICIAL OPINION

Moyer, Chief Justice

… [E]ven if the plans had required more changes than originally contemplated, the contract established a detailed procedure to be followed for all changes. In order to hold in favor of Dugan & Meyers, we would need, first, to find that the state had implicitly warranted that its plans were buildable, accurate, and complete, and, second, to hold that the implied war-

ranty prevails over express contractual provisions. To do so would contravene established precedent, which we will not do.

Next, we reject Dugan & Meyers's argument that it was excused from complying with the specific change-order procedure for requesting extensions because the state had actual notice of the need for changes to the deadline, and therefore any failure to comply with procedure was harmless error. The record lacks evidence of either an affirmative or implied waiver by the department or OSU of the change-order procedures contained in the contract. Dugan & Meyers has not convinced us that its failure to request extensions was harmless to OSU. To the contrary, Dugan & Meyers agreed that the contract language stated that failure to provide written notice "shall constitute a waiver by the Contractor of any claim for extension or for mitigation of Liquidated Damages." The court of appeals correctly concluded that Dugan & Meyers "has not demonstrated that it was entitled to disregard its obligations under that part of the contract and to claim … that OSU unreasonably withheld liquidated damages for delay in completing the project."

Affirmed.

CASE QUESTIONS

1. What mistake did Dugan & Meyers make in handling the contract?
2. How does the fact that OSU's specifications were incorrect relate to the final decision in this case?

Substantial Performance by Contractor

Construction contracts present the unique problem of how to determine when the contractor has performed well enough to satisfy the terms of the contract. Because of the nature of construction, perfection is not possible, and variations between plans or specifications may be required as problems with soil, weather, and other elements arise during construction. Contractors enjoy the slack afforded by the doctrine of **substantial performance**, which provides that a contractor may recover for completed projects in spite of variations between the plans and the actual finished product.

The following questions are the test for substantial performance:

1. For practical purposes, is the construction just as good?
2. Was the minor breach by the contractor nonmalicious?
3. Can the owner be compensated for the substitution or error made by the contractor?

An example of substantial performance is when the wrong color scheme or cabinet work is installed in a home or office. The owner may not be as happy, but the error meets the three criteria, and the contractor will be paid the contract price less an adjustment for the owner to be compensated or have the work redone.

Substantial performance does not excuse a contractor for errors in construction and poor workmanship.

In home construction, the contractor is required for one year (in most states) to repair or replace faulty construction problems under the implied warranty (see Chapter 13).

Compliance with Building Codes

One of the critical requirements for adequate performance by a contractor is that the structure complies with state and local building codes. Building codes may restrict building height, ceiling height, window placement, fire sprinkler systems, exits, lighting, and materials. Contractors must be familiar with building codes and will be liable for their failure to meet the codes.

Compliance with the Americans with Disabilities Act

Both in the new construction of buildings and under the retrofit requirements of the Fair Housing Act (see Chapter 19), the issue of access and usability for those with disabilities is now a critical part of construction. Buildings constructed after 1988 must have access and accommodations for those with disabilities. The ADA requires all existing buildings to be accessible and that facilities accommodate those with disabilities.

CAUTIONS AND CONCLUSIONS

Real estate development is a complex process that involves all areas of real estate law. The three steps in development are land acquisition, land finance, and land improvement and construction. In all three steps, there are individual rights and governmental regulations. In land acquisition, developers must consider the zoning laws, the planning components of local governments, impact fees, and the rights and interests of those affected by the proposed development.

Developers need to work more closely with cities and towns to be certain that their projects do not fall into disrepair through foreclosures and abandonment. In addition, in the post-collapse of the real estate market, cities and counties are working with developers to help finish projects through joint financing and other efforts.

In land finance, the developer must consider the sources of funds available and how best to structure the financing in terms of tax, liability, and management is-

sues. At times, a developer's choice for financing may also involve the sale of securities and require compliance with federal and state laws on the sale of securities. In land improvement and construction, the developer must be aware of private land-use restrictions such as covenants and create a plan consistent with those restrictions. In addition, the entire body of construction law—with its protections for payment and performance—comes into play as buildings are constructed.

Developers must work their way through a complex process for the creation of a successful project. One key to success is to carefully review and follow all the laws affecting everything from securities sales to construction bonds. Good developers work with policy-setters, lawmakers, neighbors, contractors, and regulators to be certain that their project is not just successful but in compliance with the law and well received by members of the community.

KEY TERMS

CHAPTER PROBLEMS

1. A wishes to put together a syndicate for the purpose of purchasing and operating two apartment complexes. A feels she can best sell the syndicate interests if the investors are able to directly deduct the depreciation losses that will result from the first three years of operation. What form of syndication will allow A's investors to take such deductions?

2. Burr, a general contractor, was bidding on a plant project for General Motors. Burr had two bids from electrical subcontractors. One was from Corbin-Dykes, and the other from White Sands. White Sands agreed to do the project for $4,000 less than Corbin-Dykes's bid if it could do the work in conjunction with another project it had in the area. Burr used Corbin-Dykes's bid and was awarded the project. However, Burr contracted with White Sands because it could do the work in the same amount of time at $4,000 less. Corbin-Dykes brought suit on the grounds of promissory estoppel and sought to force Burr to pay them. What was the result? *Corbin-Dykes Electric Co. v. Burr*, 500 P.2d 632 (Az. App. 1972).

3. Explain when a deed restriction imposed on a development can be set aside.

4. In 1948, the Phipps family devised real property to Palm Beach County. The deed provided in part that the conveyed premises were to be used only as a "public park and public bathing beach and recreational area … and for no other purpose." Although the 1948 deed did not contain a reverter clause, it did provide that this recreational use restriction "runs with the land in perpetuity and upon any breach or threatened breach thereof, the Grantor, its successors or assigns, or any person being a resident of Palm Beach County, Florida, may bring any appropriate action therefor."

   Nine years later, in October 1957, Palm Beach County conveyed the property to the Town of Palm Beach. This 1957 deed did not reiterate the specific restrictive public recreation language of the 1948 deed, but instead provided that the conveyance was "subject to easements, covenants, limitations, reservations and restrictions of record."

   At the time of the 1948 conveyance, a caretaker's shack existed on the property. In 1964, the shack was expanded to a fire station complex and then expanded again in 1979. The Town now seeks to replace the old fire station with a new one on a different site within the same property. The new proposed fire station will constitute approximately 1.7 percent of the approximately 714,000 square feet of the property.

   In an effort to prevent construction of this new fire station, Anthony Martin, a resident of Palm Beach County, sued the Town seeking enforcement of the 1948 deed restriction. Can Martin enforce the deed restriction and prevent construction of the firehouse? *Martin v. Town of Palm Beach*, 643 So.2d 112 (Fla. App. 1994).

5. Jesse and Michele Knight were interested in buying a lot in a subdivision in the Manor Estates. They went to the sales office and talked with Mr. David Goates. They explained that they were interested in buying a lot and building a home with a basement apartment that they could then rent out for income purposes. Goates was unclear about whether the apartment would be permitted, but stated that he had friends who had such apartments even when the deed restrictions prohibited them.

   The Knights purchased a lot and built their home with the basement apartment, which they then rented. There was a deed restriction prohibiting such use in the subdivision. The Knights claim that Goates is guilty of misrepresentation, and they did not know about the recorded restrictions. Will the Knights be permitted to rent their basement? *Secor v. Knight*, 716 P.2d 790 (Utah 1986).

6. Century Homes has been involved in a subdivision development of luxury homes for three years. The market for these large, expensive homes is no longer active, and Century is selling the remaining lots to builders who will be building small, inexpensive homes. Prior to Century's sales of the lots, the smallest home in the subdivision was 2,500 square feet. One builder is planning a 1,500-square-foot home. The existing homeowners wish to know if they have any protections. What is the result?

7. George D. Warner and other property owners in Terry Cove Subdivision, Unit One, a subdivision in Orange Beach, Alabama, filed suit against Orange Beach Marina, Inc., seeking an interpretation of restrictive covenants applicable to the Terry Cove Subdivision, Unit One. A proposed use involved the further subdivision of the lots for the development of a high-quality condominium project that would include 40 single-family residential units arranged in a circular fashion around a private yacht basin or marina with a yacht club, health club, tennis courts, and guardhouse.

   The restrictive covenant read as follows:

   1. Nothing but a single [family] private dwelling or residence of not less than 900 sq. ft. living area designed for occupancy of families shall be erected on any lot in these units of said subdivision with the exception of those lots or tracts that shall be designated by the said Dot-Dot Corporation [the developer of the subdivision and original fee owner of the subdivision property]. Dot-Dot Corporation shall be the sole authority to designate any area for commercial venture.

   2. No residence of any kind of what is commonly known as "boxed," "pilings," or "sheet metal" construction shall be built on said tract unless the same shall be covered over upon all the outside walls with lumber, weather-board, brick, stone or other materials with the exception of wet or dry marinas on locations as designated by the said Dot-Dot Corporation.

   The Trial Court found that the proposed development by Orange Beach violated the restrictive covenants, and that the restrictive covenants could not be amended without the consent of the Terry Cove property owners. Can the restrictive covenants be ignored? *Orange Beach Marina, Inc. v. Warner*, 500 So.2d 1068 (Ala. 1986).

8. The city council of Pell City, Alabama commissioned a study on its sewer system, and the study concluded that because of the age of the system and continuing back-ups of sewage, especially during rainstorms, that a substantial portion of the system needed to be replaced. The city council assessed service fees against all property owners, including developers. The fees per unit of housing that were assessed on the developers were substantially higher than those assessed to existing property owners. For example, hospitals were assessed on the basis of their building size. The developers filed suit challenging the constitutionality of the service fees. Determine the developers rights by reviewing the purpose of impact/service fees and the rights of government entities to assess such fees. *St. Clair County Home Builders Ass'n v. City of Pell City*, 61 So.3d 992 (Ala. 2010)

9. James Broward was developing a project in Palm Beach County, Florida. The project was one for 65 luxury condominiums. When the construction contract was awarded to Warren Construction, Inc., each condominium was to have a balcony. When construction was nearly 50 percent completed, the planning commission withdrew its approval for the balconies on the condominium and ruled that the building must have a flat face. The planning commission found that balconies tend to become storage places for occupants and take on a look that is not pleasing aesthetically. Broward wishes to know his rights and whether the timing of the withdrawal of approval is legal. Offer Mr. Broward some advice. Suppose Mr. Broward decides to go ahead and remove the balcony from the construction plans. He calls to notify the foreman at Warren Construction. Is this oral notification sufficient? What if there are additional costs in changing the building from having balconies to being flat-faced? Can Warren demand more money for the changes?

10. The city of North Las Vegas adopted an ordinance requiring payment of a fee when an applicant applied for a city building permit. The fee proceeds were earmarked for the funding of fire protection and emergency medical services within the city. Southern Nevada Homebuilders Association (SNHBA) filed a complaint asserting that the ordinance was invalid. SNHBA then filed a motion for summary judgment on the grounds that the city's special building permit fees constituted an unlawful tax that substantially benefited those who were not subject to the payment of such fees. The district court granted summary judgment and the city appealed. Should the city prevail? Provide the backdrop on impact fees as part of your answer. *Southern Nevada Homebuilders Association, Inc. v. City of North Las Vegas*, 913 P.2d 1276 (Nev. 1996).

**For research activities related to this chapter, go to our text companion website at
www.cengagebrain.com**

CHAPTER 22

TAX ASPECTS OF REAL ESTATE OWNERSHIP AND TRANSFER

Taxes are what we pay for a civilized society.

Oliver Wendell Holmes, Jr.

The power of taxing people and their property is essential to the very existence of government.

James Madison

There are three major types of taxes affecting land ownership and transfer.[1] Property tax is an annual assessment based on the value of the property. Real estate ownership and property transfer can provide tax breaks, such as a deduction for the mortgage interest paid on a residence. Finally, estate, gift, or inheritance taxes (or all three) are paid when property is transferred after the death of its owner (see Chapter 17). The purpose of this chapter is to give a general overview of the taxes that affect and involve real estate ownership and transfer. This chapter answers the following questions: What is property tax? How is the amount of property tax determined? What happens if property taxes are not paid? Can the amount of the property tax be contested? What effects on income does the sale of property have? Can owning property offer income tax deductions and credits? Are there any exemptions for gains made from the sale of property?

---

[1]Most states also have transfer taxes (see Chapter 16 for references to these taxes in discussion of closings). In addition, there are estate taxes at the federal and state levels that affect the transfer of property at death (see Chapter 17 for more information). There are also tax issues in *inter vivos* gifts of property, commonly referred to as *gift taxes*, that are established under the Internal Revenue Code.

PROPERTY TAXES

Property taxes have been documented from as early as 596 B.C., when the city of Athens levied a tax on the property owners who lived in that city. Roman taxes applied to both real and personal property. During the reign of England's Henry II, there was a 10 percent tax rate on all "rents and movable properties." In 1697, England levied its first "land tax." When the colonists arrived in North America, they brought poll, property, and faculty (income earning capacity) taxes with them.

The purpose of levying the various forms of taxes was to support the government. Property taxes in the United States currently account for 85 percent of the tax revenues of local governments and finance about half of all local government expenditures. As property tax rates have increased, the issue of valuation has become a critical one for landowners. Property taxes are a sure thing: There is always property to tax even when there is no income, and nonpayment has the remedies of a lien or sale of the property (discussed later in the chapter).

Property tax rates are an emotional issue that often bring out ballot initiatives that limit rates or control valuation and/or the right of taxation. California, with its Proposition 13, was the first state to undertake property tax reform through the ballot box. These citizen initiatives on tax limitations are frequent and constitutionally valid. Because of high property values during the period from 2004 through 2006, assessed values for homes rose dramatically. With the decline in values beginning in 2007, new taxpayer initiatives have emerged for further reduction in assessed values because of the depressed real estate market and economic recession.[2] In the following landmark U.S. Supreme Court case, a new home buyer challenged the constitutionality Proposition 13 because of its resulting effect on her costs of home ownership.

NORDLINGER V. HAHN

505 U.S. 1 (1992)
The California Prop 13 Tax Revolt

FACTS

Stephanie Nordlinger lived in a rented apartment in Los Angeles, never owning any real property until 1988, when she purchased her first home in the Baldwin Hills neighborhood of Los Angeles County for $170,000.

In early 1989, Nordlinger (petitioner) received an assessed value notice for her property from the Los Angeles County Tax Assessor (Hahn/respondent) that reassessed the home upward to $170,100. The new assessed value resulted in a tax increase of $453.60, or 36 percent, to $1,701. Nordlinger later learned from talking with her neighbors that she was paying five times more in taxes than some of her neighbors who had owned their homes since 1975. For example, an identical house one block away from Nordlinger's had an assessed valuation of $35,820 and a resulting annual tax of $358.20.

This disparity resulted because of the voter passage of California's Proposition 13 (Title XIIIA), a tax-limiting proposal. The maximum amount that any pre-1976 homeowner's assessed value could be increased per year was 2 percent. The amount of the assessed value adjustment was limited to per-year inflation, but the maximum was 2 percent. A pre-1976 owner of a $2.1 million Malibu home paid only a few dollars more than Nordlinger in property taxes. Nordlinger paid her taxes under protest and filed suit against the assessor on the grounds that her tax was unconstitutional. The trial court dismissed the complaint and the court of appeals affirmed. The California Supreme Court rejected all such tax

---

[2]Jeff D. Opdyke, "Homeowners Wage a Tax Rebellion," *Wall Street Journal*, April 28, 2007, p. B1.

challenges, and Nordlinger appealed to the U.S. Supreme Court.

JUDICIAL OPINION

Blackmun, Justice

The Equal Protection Clause does not forbid classifications. It simply keeps governmental decision-makers from treating differently persons who are in all relevant respects alike.

As a general rule, "legislatures are presumed to have acted within their constitutional power despite the fact that in practice their laws result in some inequality."

Accordingly, this Court's cases are clear that, unless a classification warrants some form of heightened review because it jeopardizes exercise of a fundamental right or categorizes on the basis of an inherently suspect characteristic, the Equal Protection Clause requires only that the classification rationally further a legitimate state interest.

As between newer and older owners, Article XIIIA does not discriminate with respect to either the tax rate or the annual rate of adjustment in assessments. Newer and older owners alike benefit in both the short and long run from the protections of a 1% tax rate ceiling and no more than a 2% increase in assessment value per year. New and old owners are treated differently with respect to one factor only—the basis on which their property is initially assessed. Petitioner's true complaint is that the State has denied her—a new owner—the benefit of the same assessment value that her neighbors—older owners—enjoy.

We have no difficulty in ascertaining at least two rational or reasonable considerations of difference or policy that justify denying petitioner the benefits of her neighbors' lower assessments. First, the States have a legitimate interest in local neighborhood preservation, continuity, and stability—*Euclid v. Ambler Realty Co.*, 272 U.S. 365, 47 S.Ct. 114, 71 L.Ed. 303 (1926). The State therefore legitimately can decide to structure its tax system to discourage rapid turnover in ownership of homes and businesses, for example, in order to inhibit displacement of lower income families by the forces of gentrification or of established, "mom-and-pop" businesses by newer chain operations. By permitting older owners to pay progressively less in taxes than new owners of comparable property, the Article XIIIA assessment scheme rationally furthers this interest.

Second, the State legitimately can conclude that a new owner at the time of acquiring his property does not have the same reliance interest warranting protection against higher taxes as does an existing owner. The State may deny a new owner at the point of purchase the right to "lock in" to the same assessed value as is enjoyed by an existing owner of comparable property, because an existing owner rationally may be thought to have vested expectations in his property or home that are more deserving of protection than the anticipatory expectations of a new owner at the point of purchase. A new owner has full information about the scope of future tax liability before acquiring the property, and if he thinks the future tax burden is too demanding, he can decide not to complete the purchase at all. By contrast, the existing owner, already saddled with his purchase, does not have the option of deciding not to buy his home if taxes become prohibitively high. To meet his tax obligations, he might be forced to sell his home or to divert his income away from the purchase of food, clothing, and other necessities. In short, the State may decide that it is worse to have owned and lost, than never to have owned at all.

Petitioner and *amici** argue with some appeal that Article XIIIA frustrates the "American dream" of home ownership for many younger and poorer California families. They argue that Article XIIIA places start-up businesses that depend on ownership of property at a severe disadvantage in competing with established businesses. They argue that Article XIIIA dampens demand for and construction of new housing and buildings. And they argue that Article XIIIA constricts local tax revenues at the expense of public education and vital services.

Certainly, California's grand experiment appears to vest benefits in a broad, powerful, and entrenched segment of society, and, as the Court of Appeal surmised, ordinary democratic processes may be unlikely to prompt its reconsideration or repeal. Yet many wise and well-intentioned laws suffer from the same malady. Article XIIIA is not palpably arbitrary, and we must decline petitioner's request to upset the will of the people of California.

Affirmed.

CASE QUESTIONS

1. Discuss and compare Nordlinger's property taxes with those in her neighborhood and other California areas.

2. What two reasons does the Court give as a rational basis for the difference in treatment of homeowners?

3. How does the Court respond to Nordlinger's point about the American dream?

---

*Friends of the court; aka interested parties who filed briefs in the case.

Assessment

A tax **assessment** estimates the value of land for the purposes of taxation. The amount of tax is calculated on an assessment rate, such as $10 per $1,000 valuation. This ratio is called a *millage rate*; one mill equals 1/10th percentage of the assessed value, and the assessed value of property for tax purposes is generally 35 to 50 percent of the property's market value. Property owners pay at the same rate but in different amounts depending on the assessed value of their property. For example, if the tax rate is $10 per $1,000 of valuation and a property is valued at $300,000, then the tax would be $3,000. However, someone with property valued at only $100,000 would pay property tax of $1,000.

Real property taxes are ***ad valorem* taxes** because the amount of tax increases with the property value. Property taxes are not based on the ability to pay or on the amount of government services received. *Ad valorem* taxes are constitutional so long as the uniform rate structure is applied.

In some states, only fee holders are subject to the *ad valorem* tax on real property, whereas other states tax leasehold interests as well as some form of real-property interests. Because of statutory limitations on tax rates, some local governments have become creative in collecting new revenues. For example, some states now collect transfer fees as a property tax when title to property changes hands. These additional taxes, beyond the traditional *ad valorem* property taxes, are constitutional so long as the system is uniform across all transfers, with the transfer tax determined according to a formula. *C. R. Campbell Construction Co. v. City of Charleston*, 481 S.E.2d 437 (S.C. 1997).

Each taxing entity has a tax **assessor** or other official prepare a list of all properties and owners, a list known as a **property tax roll.** Once the list is completed, the assessor (who is usually an elected official) determines valuations for all properties on the list (see discussion in the next section).

ETHICAL ISSUE

John Noguez was the Los Angeles County Assessor. He is now on leave from his position as an investigation looks into allegations that he revalued homes in Beverly Hills and Brentwood to lower values in exchange for campaign contributions from the home and business owners. An appraiser for the county has already been arrested on felony charges of lowering property values by a total of $172 million. Tax agent Ramin Salari is alleged to have worked for his clients for these reductions, and members of Mr. Salari's family contributed $10,000 to Mr. Noguez's election campaign. Tax agents who work for businesses and homeowners to reduce their valuations are generally paid 25 to 35 percent of the amount of the reduction they achieve in appealing to the county assessor. Tax agents are largely unregulated and there is little transparency in their efforts with county officials, including appraisers and assessors. Evaluate the ethics of the government employees, tax agents, and home and business owners in participating in a plan to make donations in exchange for lower valuations.

Methods of Valuation for Assessment

The assessment of property involves a great deal of discretion, and assessors are never without criticism because all home and business owners must pay them—

there is no escaping the taxes or fudging the values because the government entities determine the tax rate. Property taxes per year range from $7,544 in Passaic County, New Jersey to $235 in Webster County, West Virginia and $202 in Union Parish, Louisiana, with the U.S. average for annual home property taxes at $1,981.[3] After New Jersey, the top five real property states are New Hampshire, New York, Rhode Island, Massachusetts, and Connecticut. The states with the lowest property taxes, after Louisiana, are Alabama, Arkansas, Mississippi, South Carolina, and West Virginia.

The timing of an assessment can affect the assessment figure. In many areas, assessments are done not on an annual basis but rather biennially or as infrequently as every three or four years. In some cases, raw land is being assessed, but a subdivision or some other type of development is imminent because of surrounding property usage. Some assessments will value the property as if it were capable of being in use at the time (the highest and best-use concept) and will, of course, cause a higher tax on the property. Sometimes, this type of future value assessment serves to force development because the owner of raw land cannot afford the assessed value tax.

There are three different approaches for valuation of property. The **market approach** bases the value of the property on an analysis and correlation of actual transaction prices. The assessor examines sales and purchases of property similar to the one being assessed.

Under the **income approach,** the value of the land is based upon prospective income that the land produces. In using this approach, the assessor can examine net income, net operating income, gross or net rental income, and gross or net cash flow. In this category, assessors often determine the highest and best use of the property as the basis for valuation, such as its potential use as a casino versus a country club, with the latter capable of generating much higher revenues. *Snider v. Casino Aztar/Aztar Missouri Gaming Corp.*, 156 S.W.3d 341 (Mo. 2005).

The third, known as the **cost approach,** is based on what it would cost to replace the buildings on the property. The assessor examines information such as the total replacement cost of the building and then subtracts out factors such as deterioration of the premises and whether the facility is obsolete.

PRACTICAL TIP

Changes and limitations in property taxes have taken effect all around the country. When a listing agreement or property owner provides information on current taxes, be sure to check the valuation rates and procedures to be certain you know the full tax costs associated with the property.

Under any of the formulas, the task of assessment is complex, with room for disagreement about the numbers used and the projections in those formulas where some estimating is involved. Lawyers who specialize in assessment appeals assist clients in appealing the value assessed to their properties. Going into the appeal, landowners should understand that the assessor's findings are presumed to be valid and the burden of proof on errors in valuation rests with the landowner.

The following case deals with one of the more complex valuation issues that confront appraisers today, one that deals with property transfer rights such as air rights and other components of land ownership, known as TDRs, or transferrable development rights. (Refer to Chapter 3 for a discussion of the extent of land interests and the components that could be transferred as land rights without surrendering all rights in the property.)

[3]These are 2010 figures, the latest available, from The Tax Foundation www.taxfoundation.org.

MITSUI FUDOSAN (U.S.A.), INC. V. COUNTY OF LOS ANGELES

268 Cal. Rptr. 356 (1990)
The Tax Value of Air Rights

FACTS

The County of Los Angeles adopted a redevelopment plan for the Central Business District Redevelopment Project. The plan limited Mitsui Fudosan (U.S.A.), Inc. (Mitsui), to a maximum floor area ratio of six square feet of building area to one square foot of parcel area. However, Mitsui could exceed that level through transfer of other unused floor area ratios from other parcels within the project area. Making use of these so-called *transfer development rights (TDRs)*, Mitsui, in 1983, purchased from several adjacent land-owners at a cost of $8,209,000 sufficient TDRs to permit it to construct an additional 490,338 square feet of building area, more than doubling the density originally permitted.

Beginning in the 1984–1985 tax year, the county assessor increased Mitsui's base assessment by $8,209,000 to reflect the value of the TDR transactions. This resulted in increased taxes of $266,821.10 for the 1984–1986 tax years. Mitsui paid the taxes under protest and appealed to the county appeals board. The appeals board labeled the issue a legal question and summarily denied the application. The trial court granted Mitsui's motion for summary judgment and ordered a refund. The county appealed.

JUDICIAL OPINION

Gates, Associate Justice

The word "land" is not specifically defined by the Revenue and Taxation Code or related property tax regulations. However, no purpose would be served by attempting to force relatively recent three-dimensional land use concepts such as TDRs into one of the cubicles reserved for traditional interests in real property. Virtually since its inception it has been the law of this state that "[t]he sort of property in land which is taxable under our laws is not limited to the title in fee."

Whether or not TDRs are actually embodied within the definition of air rights, which already have been classified under the heading "land," or represent something entirely separate, they are appropriately viewed as one of the fractional interests in the complex bundle of rights arising from the ownership of land. As the density in urban areas increases, diminishing the number of sites available for new construction, the ability to exploit air space in various ways to achieve vertical expansion becomes essential. Property rights which evolve as a means of furthering such goals are properly subject to taxation.

The transactions in the instant case bear all the hallmarks of a transfer of real property. The owners of the donor parcels received valuation consideration, over eight million dollars, in fact, in return for divesting themselves of a portion of their own property interests, interests which are now possessed and owned by Mitsui.

In addition, in conjunction with the conveyances escrows were opened, escrow instructions and purchase and sale agreements were executed, title reports and insurance issued, property surveys were obtained and covenants restricting development were recorded against the donor parcels.

We find unpersuasive Mitsui's suggestion that it merely purchased some type of "zoning variance." As the County quite correctly observes, "[i]n a typical situation of rezoning, an owner does not negotiate with nearby property owners for the acquisition of property rights. A change in zoning does not entail title reports, sales contracts, brokerage commissions, etc." The mere fact that future zoning changes might diminish the value of a TDR is essentially irrelevant since the same fate could befall any property purchased for purposes of development.

The transactions here under review were intended to, and did, involve the transfer of a most significant present, beneficial property interest. The terms of that transfer, as well as the price paid by Mitsui, amply supports an inference that the entire fee interest in the TDRs was transferred. In the absence of substantial and convincing evidence to the contrary, the assessor was entitled to rely upon the purchase price for purposes of determining their full cash value.

The judgment is reversed.

CASE QUESTIONS

1. What additional assessment was made against Mitsui?
2. Are TDRs property? Why or why not? Explain their characteristics.
3. What is the significance of increasing urbanization?

CONSIDER 22.1   The Villard Houses, located in Manhattan, and leased by the Archdiocese from the royal Brunei family of Borneo, are known as a fine evocation of the Italian Renaissance. In 1974, the Archdiocese leased the airspace above the Villard Houses to Harry Helmsley, who, with the help of his wife, Leona, built the Palace Hotel around these brownstones and architectural wonders. However, the 99-year-lease held by the Archdiocese expired in 2001. With the hotel in the airspace, the Brunei family and the Archdiocese battled for control. The Helmsleys bowed out by selling the hotel to one of the princes in the Brunei family for $202 million. The Archdiocese has offered to rent the airspace to the prince for $9 million because it has factored in the value of the Villard Houses. The prince is willing to pay $4.5 million for the airspace because he maintains that the value of the Villard Houses should not be included in his airspace.[4] How should property taxes be allocated on these land interests? Should the value as a whole be assessed against both owners?

Environmental Issues and Assessment

EPA mandates on cleanups (see Chapter 20) have resulted in questions about the valuation of polluted property. Hazardous waste on the property and a government mandate for cleanup have some effect on the value of the property. The following case addresses this issue.

MATTER OF COMMERCE HOLDING CORP. V. BOARD OF ASSESSORS OF THE TOWN OF BABYLON

673 N.E.2d 127 (N.Y. App. 1996)
The Value of Polluted Property

FACTS

Commerce Holding Corporation owns a parcel of industrial property in the town of Babylon in Suffolk County. The property, purchased by Commerce in 1984, consists of 2.7 acres of land improved with a one-story industrial building that is presently divided into 37 rental units. A former tenant on the property performed metal-plating operations on the premises and discharged wastewater containing copper, lead, cadmium, zinc, and other metals into on-site leaching pools, ultimately resulting in severe subsurface contamination.

As a result of the contamination, the property was designated as a Superfund site in 1986, making the owner strictly liable for its cleanup. In 1988, Commerce entered into a consent decree with the EPA to remediate the site.

From 1986 to 1991, assessors for the Town valued Commerce's property at between $1.5 million and $2.6 million each year. Commerce filed timely challenges to each yearly assessment on the grounds of excessive valuation. The lower court held that the

value of the property has declined because of environmental issues, and the Town appealed.

JUDICIAL OPINION
Ciparick, Justice

In a hearing before Supreme Court, real estate experts for both Commerce and the Town primarily used the income capitalization method to determine the value of the property as if unaffected by contamination, and then subtracted a cost to cure from that value. Specifically, Commerce's expert valued the property by using an income capitalization approach, with a sales approach for the land only, and then subtracted from the property's value in each year the total remaining cost to cure all the contamination. The outstanding cost to cure was calculated in 1991 dollars, trended back to account for inflation in each of the prior years, and reduced by any sums actually spent on remediation that particular year. By contrast, the Town's expert valued the property in an

[4]Charles V. Bagli, "The Church, the Royals and Rent at the Palace," *New York Times,* December 29, 2000, A19.

uncontaminated state based on comparable sales data "blended" with an income capitalization approach, and then subtracted from the property's value only the amount actually expended by Commerce in the year the costs were incurred.

The cardinal principle of property valuation for tax purposes, set forth in the State Constitution, is that property "[a]ssessments shall in no case exceed full value." The concept of "full value" is typically equated with market value, or what "a seller under no compulsion to sell and a buyer under no compulsion to buy" would agree to as the subject property's price. In view of this market-oriented definition of full value, the assessment of property value for tax purposes must take into account any factor affecting a property's marketability. It follows that when environmental contamination is shown to depress a property's value, the contamination must be considered in property tax assessment.

The Town nevertheless asks this Court to adopt a per se rule barring any assessment reduction for environmental contamination. Otherwise, the Town contends, polluters would succeed in shifting the cost of environmental cleanup to the innocent taxpaying public in contravention of the public policy of imposing remediation costs on polluting property owners and their successors in title.

Whatever the merits of the Town's argument, the "full value" requirement is a constitutional mandate that cannot be swept aside in favor of the asserted environmental policy. As the State Board of Equalization and Assessment has recognized, the public policy "argument, while possessing superficial appeal, runs afoul of the requirement found in … New York's Constitution, that real property may not be assessed at more than its full (fair market) value." The high courts of Massachusetts and New Jersey have ruled likewise, concluding that statutory and constitutional full value requirements cannot be subordinated to environmental policy concerns.

The Town's contention that assessment reductions for environmental contamination will encourage landowners to delay remediating their property, this policy argument cannot eviscerate the constitutional directive. Moreover, the Town's concern appears to be overstated; whatever tax benefit Commerce might obtain by deferring implementation of remedial measures pales in comparison to Commerce's potential liability for failure to take appropriate remedial action, including severe penalties under CERCLA and $2,000 in daily penalties for noncompliance with the consent order.

We also reject the Town's argument that because Commerce, by consent order, has agreed to pay the cleanup costs even if it sells the property, the property's market value would be unaffected by the presence of contamination. This contention is belied by the reality that a purchaser of the site, on notice of the environmental contamination, nevertheless would be liable for the cleanup costs under CERCLA. Moreover, that Commerce has agreed to remediate the property does not resolve the question of whether, and to what extent, the contamination in fact affects the value of the land. As Commerce's expert opined, a buyer of the property would have demanded an abatement in the purchase price to account for the contamination notwithstanding the existence of the consent order. Whether a property owner's agreement to pay the cleanup costs would affect the property's value in a given case is a factual matter for the assessment board, but it cannot be said, as a matter of law, that the existence of the consent order in this case precluded an assessment reduction.

While it is not possible to prescribe any one method to assess the effects of environmental contamination, there are certain factors that should be considered. These include the property's status as a Superfund site, the extent of the contamination, the estimated cleanup costs, the present use of the property, the ability to obtain financing and indemnification in connection with the purchase of the property, potential liability to third parties, and the stigma remaining after cleanup.

Against this backdrop, we cannot say that the methodology here employed was erroneous as a matter of law. The valuation of Commerce's property was accomplished by the use of the income capitalization approach to determine the value in an uncontaminated state of this income-producing property, combined with a downward environmental adjustment in the amount of outstanding cleanup costs. While cognizant of the potential of this valuation method to overstate the effects of environmental contamination, we nevertheless conclude that cleanup costs are an acceptable, if imperfect, surrogate to quantify environmental damage and provide a sound measure of the reduced amount a buyer would be willing to pay for the contaminated property.

In conclusion, we hold that based on the record in this case, the reviewing court properly considered the effects of environmental contamination in assessing the value of Commerce's property and applied an acceptable valuation technique.

Affirmed.

mortgage or deed of trust, the mortgagee or trustee or an assigned servicing agent generally pays the taxes for the property owner through monthly withholdings included in mortgage payments and disclosed in the loan agreement.

Tax Liens

Because property tax is not a personal obligation but rather a property obligation, the nonpayment of the tax allows a lien on the property. Once the tax is not paid, the enforcement agency can execute and file a lien upon the property. Each state's statutes must provide procedures for translating nonpayment of property taxes into a lien. In some states, nonpayment results in an automatic lien on the property without any filing or recording. In these states, title cannot be cleared or insured until the tax records are checked to be sure there are no property tax delinquencies.

The effect of a **tax lien,** in most states, is to make all other liens and mortgages inferior and to give the tax lien first priority for payment. The tax lien may be removed only by payment of the tax due plus any delinquencies and statutory penalties that accrue due to nonpayment. (See Chapter 6 for a discussion of other liens.)

Tax Sales

The authority to foreclose on a lien or sell property to pay delinquent taxes must also be provided for in the statutory process and authority. The key factor in the **tax sale** of real property is due process. Before a tax sale can be valid, property owners must be notified and allowed an opportunity to respond.

Due process does not require judicial proceedings prior to the tax sale. Although the procedures for tax sales vary from state to state, they usually begin with notice, delivery of notice to the property owner, and the publication of notice of sale.

When the sale is held, anyone may bid, because the sale must be a public one. The proceeds from the sale are applied first to satisfy the taxes due, interest accrued during nonpayment, any applicable penalties, and the costs of the sale. After those amounts have been satisfied, payment goes according to priorities of the secured parties. (See Chapters 5, 6, 13, and 15 for a complete discussion of priorities.)

In most states, the tax sale is not a final resolution of the property owner's rights, for the delinquent property owner usually has a right of redemption. This right may be exercised in two ways, but whichever method a state follows, the purchase of property at a tax sale does not result in full and complete title. The rights obtained by a buyer at a tax sale are subject to the property owner's right of redemption.[5]

Under one method of redemption, the buyer is given a deed to the property, but the deed conveys only defeasible title. At any time during the statutory redemption period, the title of the buyer can be defeated if the property owner is able to pay all amounts due in taxes, interest, penalties, and costs. Once the statutory period expires, the defeasible title becomes full fee simple title. The statutory period varies from state to state from six months to six years.

Under the other method of redemption, the buyer at a tax sale is given only a certificate of sale, which is simply evidence of the purchase. Once the redemption period has expired, the buyer is given a deed to the property.[6]

---

[5]*Simon v. Cronecker*, 915 A.2d 489 (N.J. 2008).

[6]*Grivas v. Smith*, 915 A.2d 489 (N.J. 2008).

Under either method, the deed given is called a **tax deed** and is issued by the appropriate tax agency or official in the jurisdiction. The tax deed, like a sheriff's deed, has no warranties either express or implied; the buyer's title is only as good as the agency's or official's compliance with the requirements for a valid tax sale. If there is noncompliance, the buyer runs the risk of having the sale set aside by a property owner who has been denied due process. The following U.S. Supreme Court decision deals with an owner's appeal of a tax sale and whether the notice given met due process standards.

JONES V. FLOWERS

547 U.S. 220 (2005)
The Duty of the Government to Find Property Owners Who Owe Taxes

FACTS

Gary Jones (petitioner) purchased his home in Little Rock, Arkansas, in 1967. Gary and his wife spent 26 blessed years of bliss in the home, but, in 1993, they called it quits. Gary moved out of their North Bryan Street home, but his wife[7] remained there. Southern gentleman and court orders being what they are, Jones continued making the mortgage payments on the home until 1997, when the 30-year mortgage on the property was paid off, and Jones owned the property free and clear of that long-term obligation that had been used to secure the house. Jones assumed that his obligations on the marriage and home were fulfilled, so the taxes went unpaid.

By 2000, the Commissioner of State Lands in Arkansas was trying to notify Jones of his delinquency and his right of redemption. The letter indicated that if Jones did not remedy the delinquency, the property would be sold on April 17, 2002. Pursuant to statutory procedures, the Commissioner sent a certified letter to Jones at the North Bryan Street address. No one was home to sign for the Commissioner's letter, and no one appeared at the post office to claim it. The letter was returned to the Commissioner as "unclaimed."

Two weeks prior to the noticed date of sale, the Commissioner published a notice of sale of the North Bryan Street house, but there were no takers in this public offer.[8] The Commissioner then undertook the process of a private sale via bid. Enter Linda Flowers, who submitted her bid for $21,042.15.[9] The Commissioner tried mailing the notice once again at the North Bryan Street address and, once again, the post office returned the letter "unclaimed."

When the 30-day post-redemption period expired, Ms. Flowers served an unlawful detainer notice on the North Bryan Street occupants, one of whom was Jones's daughter, who managed to get the notice to Jones, and all in just a few days.

Jones then filed suit against the Commissioner challenging the sale on the grounds of a lack of adequate notice. Flowers and the Commissioner moved for summary judgment, contending that the notice provisions of the Arkansas statute satisfied the state constitutional requirements. The trial court granted summary judgment for Flowers, and the state and the Arkansas Supreme Court affirmed. The U.S. Supreme Court granted *certiorari* because of conflicts in the circuits on the requirements of notice on property sales.

JUDICIAL OPINION
Roberts, Chief Justice

Due process does not require that a property owner receive actual notice before the government may take his property. Rather, we have stated that due process requires the government to provide "notice reasonably calculated, under all the circumstances, to apprise interested parties of the pendency of the action and afford them an opportunity to present their objections."

We do not think that a person who actually desired to inform a real property owner of an impending tax sale of a house he owns would do nothing when a certified letter sent to the owner is returned unclaimed. If the Commissioner prepared a stack of letters to mail to delinquent taxpayers, handed them to the postman, and then watched as the departing postman accidentally

---

[7]The missus is never named in the court opinion, being referred to only as "his wife."
[8]The notice was published in the state's largest circulation newspaper, the *Arkansas Democrat Gazette.*
[9]To add insult to divorce and other injuries, the property was valued at $80,000 at the time of the Flowers deal.

dropped the letters down a storm drain, one would certainly expect the Commissioner's office to prepare a new stack of letters and send them again. No one "desirous of actually informing" the owners would simply shrug his shoulders as the letters disappeared and say "I tried." Failure to follow up would be unreasonable, despite the fact that the letters were reasonably calculated to reach their intended recipients when delivered to the postman.

By the same token, when a letter is returned by the post office, the sender will ordinarily attempt to resend it, if it is practicable to do so.... This is especially true when, as here, the subject matter of the letter concerns such an important and irreversible prospect as the loss of a house. Although the State may have made a reasonable calculation of how to reach Jones, it had good reason to suspect when the notice was returned that Jones was "no better off than if the notice had never been sent."

[I]f a feature of the State's chosen procedure is that it promptly provides additional information to the government about the effectiveness of notice, it does not contravene the *ex ante* principle to consider what the government does with that information in assessing the adequacy of the chosen procedure. After all, the State knew *ex ante* that it would promptly learn whether its effort to effect notice through certified mail had succeeded. It would not be inconsistent with the approach the Court has taken in notice cases to ask, with respect to a procedure under which telephone calls were placed to owners, what the State did when no one answered. Asking what the State does when a notice letter is returned unclaimed is not substantively different.

We think there were several reasonable steps the State could have taken. What steps are reasonable in response to new information depends upon what the new information reveals. The return of the certified letter marked "unclaimed" meant either that Jones still lived at 717 North Bryan Street, but was not home when the postman called and did not retrieve the letter at the post office, or that Jones no longer resided at that address. One reasonable step primarily addressed to the former possibility would be for the State to resend the notice by regular mail, so that a signature was not required. The Commissioner says that use of certified mail makes actual notice more likely, because requiring the recipient's signature protects against misdelivery. But that is only true, of course, when someone is home to sign for the letter, or to inform the mail carrier that he has arrived at the wrong address. Otherwise, "[c]ertified mail is dispatched and handled in transit as ordinary mail," and the use of certified mail might make actual notice

less likely in some cases—the letter cannot be left like regular mail to be examined at the end of the day, and it can only be retrieved from the post office for a specified period of time. Following up with regular mail might also increase the chances of actual notice to Jones if—as it turned out—he had moved. Even occupants who ignored certified mail notice slips addressed to the owner (if any had been left) might scrawl the owner's new address on the notice packet and leave it for the postman to retrieve, or notify Jones directly.

Other reasonable follow-up measures, directed at the possibility that Jones had moved as well as that he had simply not retrieved the certified letter, would have been to post notice on the front door, or to address otherwise undeliverable mail to "occupant." Most States that explicitly outline additional procedures in their tax sale statutes require just such steps. Either approach would increase the likelihood that the owner would be notified that he was about to lose his property, given the failure of a letter deliverable only to the owner in person. That is clear in the case of an owner who still resided at the premises. It is also true in the case of an owner who has moved: Occupants who might disregard a certified mail slip not addressed to them are less likely to ignore posted notice, and a letter addressed to them (even as "occupant") might be opened and read. In either case, there is a significant chance the occupants will alert the owner, if only because a change in ownership could well affect their own occupancy. In fact, Jones first learned of the State's effort to sell his house when he was alerted by one of the occupants—his daughter—after she was served with an unlawful detainer notice.

Jones believes that the Commissioner should have searched for his new address in the Little Rock phonebook and other government records such as income tax rolls. We do not believe the government was required to go this far. An open-ended search for a new address—especially when the State obligates the taxpayer to keep his address updated with the tax collector—imposes burdens on the State significantly greater than the several relatively easy options outlined above.

We hold that when mailed notice of a tax sale is returned unclaimed, the State must take additional reasonable steps to attempt to provide notice to the property owner before selling his property, if it is practicable to do so. Under the circumstances presented here, additional reasonable steps were available to the State. We therefore reverse the judgment of the Arkansas Supreme Court.

DISSENTING OPINION

Thomas, Scalia, and Kennedy, Justices

In Arkansas, approximately 18,000 parcels of delinquent real estate are certified annually. Under the Court's rule, the State will bear the burden of locating thousands of delinquent property owners. These administrative burdens are not compelled by the Due Process Clause. Here, Arkansas has determined that its law requiring property owners to maintain a current address with the state taxing authority, in conjunction with its authorization to send property notices to the record address, is an efficient and fair way to administer its tax collection system. The Court's decision today forecloses such a reasonable system and burdens the State with inefficiencies caused by delinquent taxpayers.

Moreover, the Court's proposed methods are no more reasonably calculated to achieve notice than the methods employed by the State here. Regular mail is hardly foolproof; indeed, it is arguably less effective than certified mail. Certified mail is tracked, delivery attempts are recorded, actual delivery is logged, and notices are posted to alert someone at the residence that certified mail is being held at a local post office. By creating a record, these features give parties grounds for defending or challenging notice. By contrast, regular mail is untraceable; there is no record of either delivery or receipt. Had the State used regular mail, petitioner would presumably argue that it should have sent notice by certified mail because it creates a paper trail.

Interestingly, the Court stops short of saddling the State with the other steps that petitioner argues a State should take any time the interested party fails to claim letters mailed to his record address, namely searching state tax records, the phonebook, the Internet, department of motor vehicle records, or voting rolls, contacting his employer, or employing debt collectors. Here, the Court reasons that because of the context—the fact that the letter was returned merely "unclaimed" and petitioner had a duty to maintain a current address—the State is not required to go as far as petitioner urges. If 'title to property should not depend on factual vagaries,' then it certainly cannot turn on 'wrinkles' caused by a property owner's failure to be a prudent ward of his interests. The meaning of the Constitution should not turn on the antics of tax evaders and scoff-laws. Nor is the self-created conundrum in which petitioner finds himself a legitimate ground for imposing additional constitutional obligations on the State.

CASE QUESTIONS

1. What is the significance of an *ex ante* evaluation of due process?
2. What additional steps will Arkansas need to take to meet the standards of this decision?
3. What is the dissent's concern with the majority's decision?

CONSIDER 22.4   Sawmill Creek, LLC, a Wyoming entity, purchased property in Marion County, Indiana. No one at Sawmill Creek noticed, but when the deed was recorded, it was recorded under the name of "Saw Creek Investments, LCC," with the mailing address being listed as the Indianapolis business address for Bill Simpson, the manager of Sawmill Creek, LLC. Mr. Simpson later relocated his offices and sent a notice to the Marion County Auditor under the name Sawmill Creek, LLC. That change was never recorded because the auditor could not find the company in its register. The taxes went unpaid, and the auditor sent notices of delinquency as well as a notice of tax sale three times to the original Indianapolis address. With all notices being "return to sender," and "no response," the auditor went ahead and sold the property. Sawmill Creek sought to set aside the sale on the grounds of a lack of notice and failure of due process, citing the *Flowers* case. Is Sawmill correct, or did the auditor do all that he could to serve notice? *Marion County Auditor v. Sawmill Creek, LLC,* 964 N.E.2d 213 (Ind. 2012).

PRACTICAL TIP

Make sure that you notify the assessor when your billing address changes and be sure to use the same name that appears on your deed in your notification so that the address change can be logged with the proper property.

INCOME TAX AND REAL PROPERTY

Although income tax is a personal tax and is tied not to ownership of property but to earning of income, real estate ownership and transfer does affect the net income of an individual.

Home Interest Deduction

The **Internal Revenue Code (IRC)** permits home mortgage interest as a personal deduction, along with the mortgage interest from one other residence that the taxpayer uses as a second home under IRC definitions. The IRC also allows taxes paid on those properties as a personal deduction. The amount of debt that qualifies for the interest deduction is limited. An original home loan interest is deductible only to the extent of the fair market value of the home. These interest deduction limitations were designed to prevent manipulation of the real estate tax benefits. For example, this provision prevents someone from borrowing more than the home's value in order to have deductible interest, such as buying a home for $280,000 and financing $300,000. However, during the real estate boom that ran from 2005–2007, many homeowners did carry almost 100 percent financing or first-mortgage financing with a second mortgage being the source of the down payment. This high-leverage approach to home mortgages exacerbated the problems and foreclosures for homeowners when property values declined.

For purposes of deductibility of interest, there are two types of home mortgage debt: **acquisition indebtedness** and **home equity indebtedness.** The IRC has upper limitations on both types of debts for purposes of deducting the interest (26 U.S.C. §163[1]). Any interest paid in excess of these amounts is considered personal interest and is subject to the phase-out rules of the now completely nondeductible credit card and other loan interest.

Because of economic changes, many homeowners are now refinancing their residences to lower monthly payments, change from ARMs to fixed rates, and generally restructuring their mortgage loans (see Chapter 15 for more information on the government programs available for such restructuring).

Installment Sales

The IRC limits the use of the installment sales method of reporting income from property sales. Although the restrictions on installment sales do not apply to personal residence sales (hence the wrap-around mortgage remains a popular means of financing [see Chapter 15]), they do apply to business sales. The deferral of gains is the tax benefit in installment sales, and that deferral is still available for installment sales of personal use (residence) property.

Sales of Property and Basis

The key figures for determining whether there is taxable income (gain) when real property is transferred are basis and sale price. If you buy your home, your basis is its cost to you. Cost includes the purchase price and certain settlement or closing costs. Generally, your purchase price includes your down payment and any debt, such as a first or second mortgage or notes you gave the seller in payment for the home. If you build, or contract to build, a new home, your purchase price can include costs of construction. If the person who sold you your home paid points on your loan, you may have to reduce your home's basis by the amount of the points. Your basis can increase by the value of improvements that you make if those improvements will last longer than one year. The cost of additions, swimming pools, landscaping, and alarm systems could be added to your basis.

For commercial properties, the basis is, again, the cost in terms of price paid or construction costs, plus improvements, but less the **depreciation** taken over the life of the property. Depreciation is a business expense for wear and tear on the building, and it is subtracted from the value of the property for purposes of determining the property's basis.

To determine the gain on a property sale, the expenses of the sale and the basis are taken from the selling price to arrive at the figure. An example using numbers follows:

Gain Realized Calculation

Selling price of property	$297,000
Less selling expenses	–3,000
Amount realized	$294,000
Basis of property	
Cost	$275,000
Depreciation	–10,000
Improvements	+2,000
Adjusted basis	$267,000
Gain realized	$27,000

Residential Property Sales, Basis, and Exclusions

The basis for residential property is computed in the same way just discussed. However, depreciation is not available for homeowners, and the computation of gains for residential property is very different from commercial property or property held for investment. If a taxpayer sells a principal residence (the IRC provides specific requirements for this) the taxpayer is exempt from paying taxes on the gain from the sale of that residence, up to certain limits that are provided in the Internal Revenue Code. The basis is as described beginning p. 633.

Depreciation Issues in Real Estate

Property depreciation can be computed using the straight-line method (the value of the property is divided by the number of years it will be used and it is then depreciated at that rate for each of those years); the sum-of-the-years digits method (the number of years of property use are added together and then used as a denominator in a fraction applied each year); or the double-declining balance method (more depreciation is taken in the early years and less as the property ages). However, the IRC requires the **Maximum Accelerated Cost Recovery System (MACRS)** method for real estate if the real property was placed into use after 1986.

Under MACRS, real estate is depreciated over time periods that are dictated by the type of real estate. The classifications of property for depreciation do have some public-policy purposes. For example, properties used for solar, geothermal, or wind energy production can be depreciated as five-year properties. Furniture and appliances in rental properties can also be depreciated over a five-year period. Apartment buildings are subject to a period of 27.5 years, while farm buildings have a 20-year depreciation life. The tax code also contains depreciation tables that provide the annual depreciation figure for property values at given year rates.

Property Exchanges

Investment properties can be exchanged in a process named after the IRC provision that governs it, the **1031 exchange.** An exchange of like-kind property (commercial for commercial or residential for residential) results in a gain only if cash or other property is actually received by the taxpayer. For example, suppose that Taxpayer A owns a cabin that is worth $420,000, but that was purchased for $63,000 about 15 years earlier. Taxpayer A wants to upgrade and build a newer cabin, at a cost of $435,000. If Taxpayer A sells the first cabin, closes on the new cabin within 180 days of selling that cabin, and if the money is transferred from the first cabin escrow directly to the new cabin escrow, then Taxpayer A owes no capital gains tax on the gain made in the sale of the first cabin (the $420,000 less the cost of $63,000 plus any improvements made to that cabin). And, Taxpayer A's basis is now the price of the new cabin, a stepped-up basis gained through the exchange. Under recent revenue clarifications, the 1031 exchanges can be used only if the owner rented out the property for at least 14 days during certain periods required under the IRC.

Capital Gains

When real property is sold, the money made above basis and costs is known as a **capital gain** if the seller has owned the property for "more than 12 months."[10] In 1997, Congress established a cap of 20 percent on the amount of tax on capital gains.[11] With tax reforms expected and tax breaks expiring, the capital gains rate is a focus of continuing political debate. Capital losses in sales of real property can be used to offset capital gains, but cannot be used to offset regular income.

Housing Tax Credits

The IRC provides tax credits for certain types of real estate purchase, and use. For example, tax credits for **low-income housing** provide incentives for developers to construct, for example, apartment complexes that will accept Section 8 (low income voucher program) tenants. These Section 8 credits, as they are often called, can be claimed annually for a 10-year period and can generate one of the few remaining significant tax savings in owning real estate. Qualifying for the credit requires that rent in such projects be set according to formulas established by the federal government. HUD sets rents by the market rates. In other words, strict rent controls apply when this credit is available to low-income housing developers. Further, the credit is not available to owners with buildings that are in violation of local health, safety, and building codes. In addition to federal tax credits, state and local governments also provide tax benefits for developers who construct low-income housing. From 2009–2012, the federal government provided tax

[10]There was a wrinkle during 1997 and 1998 that required an 18-month holding period, but the 12-month period was restored by the IRS Restructuring and Reform Act of 1998.

[11]That rate is 10 percent for those in the 15 percent bracket. A special lower rate of 18 percent applies (for those in higher tax brackets) to transactions after December 31, 2000, if the asset sold was held for more than five years.

credits and other special programs for homebuyers in certain income ranges as well as to existing homeowners with underwater mortgages in order to ease the debt burden associated with owning real property.

Real Estate Investment, Passive Income, and Deductions

The depreciation deductions for real property can be substantial. Prior to tax reform in 1986, many real estate investors were taking their large depreciation deductions from their real property investments and deducting them from their other income. The result was that many taxpayers showed little income, no income, or, in many cases, paper losses because of the extensive depreciation deductions.

This rather large loophole in the tax code was closed when the IRC was amended to make a distinction between passive and active income and losses. **Active income** exists when the taxpayer "materially participates" in the business, as in those situations where the taxpayer earns a wage from the business or owns the business as a sole proprietor. **Passive income** results from partnership earnings from real estate investments. Indeed, the federal tax laws include a presumption that all income from real estate partnerships is passive. Since most real estate investments are in the form of limited partnerships, the extra benefit for real estate investors of being able to use their real estate losses to offset other income is not available. The losses, often called **suspended** or **passive losses,** may be carried forward indefinitely but cannot be used to reduce other income. For example, a loss on a real estate investment could not be taken against the active salary income of the individual investor.

At-Risk Rule

Real estate investment activities are subject to the **at-risk rules.** Real estate investors are at risk for only those borrowed funds for which they have personal liability. The amount a taxpayer has at risk is the initial capital contribution plus any borrowed amounts as long as the taxpayer has personal liability for repayment or has pledged property that is not used in the activity as collateral for the loan. Even these two tests will not put the taxpayer at risk if the lender is also involved in the activity in some way other than as a creditor. Again, interest losses cannot be taken in real estate syndications when the syndicating entity or partnership was the lender for the operating partnership. Investors are not really at risk when the syndicator is the lender.

If the taxpayer is not at risk, the losses must be taken from that activity and not from other income. Again, the losses can be carried forward indefinitely.

CAUTIONS AND CONCLUSIONS

A practical note for the discussion on property taxes is to verify taxes and do a title search to determine whether there are any tax liens on the property. Looking into assessment and valuation provides insight into the value of the property as well as into the tax costs of ownership.

Buyers and sellers should always investigate the tax consequences of their real estate transactions before entering into contracts. In some cases, the sale may be structured to maximize benefits. In the case of property ownership, checking for all possible deductions provides for a greater return on the property investment.

Those who own property should monitor assessment and watch for notices on valuation as well as any delinquency. Following the tax activity on your property is an important part of maintaining ownership and preventing liens.

No property transaction should be completed without a tax-effect investigation—both on the property and on the income of the parties involved.

KEY TERMS

CHAPTER PROBLEMS

1. Galena Oaks Corporation constructed apartment units for the purpose of renting them. Because of a factory shutdown in the area, most of the tenants left and the apartments were difficult to rent. Galena sold the units and treated the gain as a capital gain. The IRS claims the gain is ordinary income. What is the result? *Galena Oaks Corp. v. Scofield*, 218 F.2d 217 (5th Cir. 1974).

2. Otis and Ethel Wade are considering purchasing a second home in the Catskills. The home will be an A-frame cabin, and they plan to spend six to ten weeks plus five to six weekends there per year. Currently, the Wades own a home in New Rochelle and have paid off 10 years of their 30-year mortgage. They wish to finance the purchase of the cabin but are concerned that the interest may no longer be deductible. Offer Otis and Ethel an explanation of the deductibility of interest payments on second homes.

3. Indiana's tax sale statute requires that the notice of sale be sent to the property owners' "last known address." The Auditor of Marshall County sent Urbano and Irma Elizondo a notice of sale, which was returned by the post office for an incorrect address. However, the auditor had access to the Elizondos' current address through public records. No follow-up mailing was made. When the Elizondos protested the sale, the statute of limitations had expired. They claim they were denied due process because they did not receive the notice. Are they correct? *Elizondo v. Read*, 556 N.E.2d 959 (Ind. 1990).

4. Roberta Hathaway is a limited partner in a partnership that runs a shopping center. The center had a loss of $600,000 during its first year because tenants were hard to find. Roberta's share of the loss is $50,000. She will have personal income of $62,000. Can she take the loss? If so, how much?

5. Suppose that Hathaway was a limited partner in a HUD low-income housing development. Would the result be different?

6. In October 2002, Washington, D.C. officials were notified by the Washington Area Sewer Authority that residential water supplies had tested above the Environmental Protection Agency's 'action' level for lead contamination. Homeowners in the D.C. area sought to have their property values reduced because their water might be contaminated. What should the court do in determining whether the valuation should be done with or without the contamination issue? What if someone told a landowner that he believed there was oil beneath his property? Does the owner have to tell the assessor about the find? *Tolu Tolu v. District of Columbia*, 906 A.2d 265 (D.C. 2006).

7. Ellen Libbey Andrew purchased a thirty-five-acre parcel of land in 1998, and her property is located within a subdivision that contains thirty-five-acre and twenty-acre parcels. By 2010, nineteen of the subdivision parcels had improvements and seventeen were vacant. All of the parcels are subject to a perpetual conservation easement, established in 1990 for the preservation of wildlife habitat, a restriction that permits building areas of up to two acres on each subdivided parcel for residential purposes.

    Ms. Andrew constructed a residence on her parcel, receiving a certificate of occupancy in August 2009. Through the 2009 tax year, based on the perpetual conservation easement, Ms. Andrew's parcel was classified as agricultural land. However, based on the completion of her residence, the county assessor changed the classification of taxpayer's parcel for the 2010 tax year to residential land. That reclassification increased her valuation, as well as her taxes, substantially. Ms. Andrews has filed suit to set aside the valuation. Explain what her rights are and what presumptions about the assessor's valuation exist. *Andrew v. Teller County Bd. of Equalization*, 284 P.3d 172 (Colo. App. 2012).

8. Glenda Johnson purchased her home in 1997 for $145,000. In 1990, she added a swimming pool that

cost $20,000. Her landscaping cost her $2,800, and her draperies and shutters were $3,100. In 2013, Glenda decided to sell her home because she had found a larger home in a better neighborhood. She was able to sell her house for $293,000. What will she owe in taxes on this sale? Can you compute her basis?

9. Cecos International, Inc. was the owner and operator of a former hazardous waste facility now subject to an EPA cleanup and litigation regarding liability. Cecos has proposed deducting the cost of the cleanup from the valuation, which would render the property valueless. The assessor has proposed simply a reduction in fair market value. Which method should be followed? *Vogelgesang v. Cecos International, Inc.,* 1993 Ohio App. Lexis 1478 (Ohio App. March 15, 1993); *Microsemi Corp. of Colorado v. Broomfield County Bd. of Equalization,* 200 P.3d 1123 (Colo. App. 2008).

10. Dade County's property appraisal adjustments board assessed the value of the property of the Bath Club, which brought a trial court action challenging the assessments. The trial court refused to reduce the assessments, and the Bath Club appealed on several grounds, one of which was that the board's authority to appoint special masters to take testimony and make recommendations denied procedural due process since taxpayers could not appear and offer testimony. Are the taxpayers correct? *Bath Club, Inc. v. Dade County,* 394 So.2d 110 (Fla. 1981).

For research activities related to this chapter, go to our text companion website at
www.cengagebrain.com

The United States Constitution

Article I

Section I

All legislative Powers herein granted shall be vested in a Congress of the United States, which shall consist of a Senate and House of Representatives.

Section 2

The House of Representatives shall be composed of Members chosen every second Year by the People of the several States, and the Electors in each State shall have the Qualifications requisite for Electors of the most numerous Branch of the State Legislature.

No Person shall be a Representative who shall not have attained to the Age of twenty five Years, and been seven Years a Citizen of the United States, and who shall not, when elected, be an Inhabitant of that State in which he shall be chosen.

Representatives and direct Taxes shall be apportioned among the several States which may be included within this Union, according to their respective Numbers, which shall be determined by adding to the whole Number of free Persons, including those bound to Service for a Term of Years, and excluding Indians not taxed, three fifths of all other Persons. The actual Enumeration shall be made within three Years after the first Meeting of the Congress of the United States, and within every subsequent Term of ten Years, in which Manner as they shall by Law direct. The Number of Representatives shall not exceed one for every thirty Thousand, but each State shall have at Least one Representative; and until such enumeration shall be made, the State of New Hampshire shall be entitled to choose three, Massachusetts eight, Rhode Island and Providence Plantations one, Connecticut five, New York six, New Jersey four, Pennsylvania eight, Delaware one, Maryland six, Virginia ten, North Carolina five, South Carolina five, and Georgia three.

When vacancies happen in the Representation from any State, the Executive Authority thereof shall issue Writs of Election to fill such Vacancies.

The House of Representatives shall chuse their Speaker and other Officers; and shall have the sole Power of Impeachment.

Section 3

The Senate of the United States shall be composed of two Senators from each State, chosen by the Legislature thereof, for six Years; and each Senator shall have one Vote.

Immediately after they shall be assembled in Consequence of the first Election, they shall be divided as equally as may be into three Classes. The Seats of the Senators of the first Class shall be vacated at the Expiration of the second Year, of the second Class at the Expiration of the fourth Year, and of the third Class at the Expiration of the sixth Year, so that one third may be chosen every second Year; and if Vacancies happen by Resignation, or otherwise, during the Recess of the Legislature of any State, the Executive thereof may make temporary Appointments until the next Meeting of the Legislature, which shall then fill such Vacancies.

No Person shall be a Senator who shall not have attained to the Age of thirty Years, and been nine Years a Citizen of the United States, and who shall not, when elected, be an Inhabitant of that State for which he shall be chosen.

The Vice President of the United States shall be President of the Senate, but shall have no Vote, unless they be equally divided.

The Senate shall chuse their other Officers, and also a President pro tempore, in the Absence of the Vice President, or when he shall exercise the Office of President of the United States.

The Senate shall have the sole Power to try all Impeachments. When sitting for that Purpose, they shall be on Oath or Affirmation. When the President of the United States is tried the Chief Justice shall preside: And no Person shall be convicted without the Concurrence of two thirds of the Members present.

Judgment in Cases of Impeachment shall not extend further than to removal from Office, and disqualification to hold and enjoy any Office of honor, Trust or Profit under the United States: but the Party convicted shall nevertheless be liable and subject to Indictment, Trial, Judgment and Punishment, according to Law.

Section 4

The Times, Places and Manner of holding Elections for Senators and Representatives, shall be prescribed in each State by the Legislature thereof; but the Congress may at any time by Law make or alter such Regulations, except as to the Places of chusing Senators.

The Congress shall assemble at Least once in every Year, and such Meeting shall be on the first Monday in December, unless they shall by Law appoint a different Day.

Section 5

Each House shall be the Judge of the Elections, Returns and Qualifications of its own Members, and a Majority of each shall constitute a Quorum to do Business; but a smaller Number may adjourn from day to day, and may be authorized to compel the Attendance of absent Members, in such Manner, and under such Penalties as each House may provide.

Each House may determine the Rules in its Proceedings, punish its Members for disorderly Behaviour, and, with the Concurrence of two thirds, expel a Member.

Each House shall keep a Journal of its Proceedings, and from time to time publish the same, excepting

such Parts as may in their Judgment require Secrecy; and the Yeas and Nays of the Members of either House on any question shall, at the Desire of one fifth of those Present, be entered on the Journal.

Neither House, during the Session of Congress, shall, without the Consent of the other, adjourn for more than three days, nor to any other Place than that in which the two Houses shall be sitting.

Section 6

The Senators and Representatives shall receive a Compensation for their Services, to be ascertained by Law, and paid out of the Treasury of the United States. They shall in all Cases, except Treason, Felony and Breach of the Peace, be privileged from Arrest during their Attendance at the Session of their respective Houses, and in going to and returning from the same; and for any Speech or Debate in either House, they shall not be questioned in any other Place.

No Senator or Representative shall, during the Time for which he was elected, be appointed to any civil Office under the Authority of the United States, which shall have been created, or the Emoluments whereof shall have been encreased during such time; and no Person holding any Office under the United States, shall be a Member of either House during his Continuance in Office.

Section 7

All Bills for raising Revenue shall originate in the House of Representatives; but the Senate may propose or concur with amendments as on other Bills.

Every Bill which shall have passed the House of Representatives and the Senate, shall, before it become a Law, be presented to the President of the United States; If he approve he shall sign it, but if not he shall return it, with his Objections to that House in which it shall have originated, who shall enter the Objections at large on their Journal, and proceed to reconsider it. If after such Reconsideration two thirds of that House shall agree to pass the Bill, it shall be sent, together with the Objections, to the other House, by which it shall likewise be reconsidered, and if approved by two thirds of that House, it shall become a Law. But in all such Cases the Votes of both Houses shall be determined by Yeas and Nays, and the names of the Persons voting for and against the Bill shall be entered on the Journal of each House respectively. If any Bill shall not be returned by the President within ten Days (Sundays excepted) after it shall have been presented to him, the Same shall be a Law, in like Manner as if he had signed it, unless the Congress by their Adjournment prevent its Return, in which Case it shall not be a Law.

Every Order, Resolution, or Vote to which the Concurrence of the Senate and House of Representatives may be necessary (except on a question of Adjournment) shall be presented to the President of the United States; and before the Same shall take Effect, shall be approved by him, or being disapproved by him, shall be repassed by two thirds of the Senate and House of Representatives, according to the Rules and Limitations prescribed in the Case of a Bill.

Section 8

The Congress shall have Power To lay and collect Taxes, Duties, Imposts and Excises, to pay the Debts and provide for the common Defense and general Welfare of the United States; but all Duties, Imposts and Excises shall be uniform throughout the United States;

To borrow Money on the credit of the United States;

To regulate Commerce with foreign Nations, and among the several States, and with the Indian Tribes;

To establish an uniform Rule of Naturalization, and uniform Laws on the subject of Bankruptcies throughout the United States;

To coin Money, regulate the Value thereof, and of foreign Coin, and fix the Standard of Weights and Measures;

To provide for the Punishment of counterfeiting the Securities and current Coin of the United States;

To establish Post Offices and post Roads;

To promote the Progress of Science and useful Arts, by securing for limited Times to Authors and Inventors the exclusive Right to their respective Writings and Discoveries;

To constitute Tribunals inferior to the supreme Court;

To define and punish Piracies and Felonies committed on the high Seas, and Offenses against the Law of Nations;

To declare War, grant Letters of Marque and Reprisal, and make Rules concerning Captures on Land and Water;

To raise and support Armies, but no Appropriation of Money to that Use shall be for a longer Term than two Years;

To provide and maintain a Navy;

To make Rules for the Government and Regulation of the land and naval Forces;

To provide for calling forth the Militia to execute the Laws of the Union, suppress Insurrections and repel Invasions;

To provide for organizing, arming, and disciplining, the Militia, and for governing such Part of them as may be employed in the Service of the United States, reserving to the States respectively, the Appointment of the Officers, and the Authority of training the Militia according to the discipline prescribed by Congress;

To exercise exclusive Legislation in all Cases whatsoever, over such District (not exceeding ten Miles square) as may, by Cession of particular States, and the Acceptance of Congress, become the Seat of the Government of the United States, and to exercise like Authority over all Places purchased by the Consent of the Legislature of the State in which the Same shall be, for the Erection of Forts, Magazines, Arsenals, dock-Yards, and other needful Buildings;—And

To make all Laws which shall be necessary and proper for carrying into Execution the foregoing Powers, and all other Powers vested by this Constitution in the Government of the United States, or in any Department or Officer thereof.

Section 9

The Migration or Importation of such Persons as any of the States now existing shall think proper to admit, shall not be prohibited by the Congress prior to the Year one thousand eight hundred and eight, but a Tax or duty may be imposed on such Importation, not exceeding ten dollars for each Person.

The Privilege of the Writ of Habeas Corpus shall not be suspended, unless when in Cases of Rebellion or Invasion the public Safety may require it.

No Bill of Attainder or ex post facto Law shall be passed.

No Capitation, or other direct, Tax shall be laid, unless in Proportion to the Census or Enumeration herein before directed to be taken.

No Tax or Duty shall be laid on Articles exported from any State.

No Preference shall be given to any Regulation of Commerce or Revenue to the Ports of one State over those of another; nor shall Vessels bound to, or from, one State, be obliged to enter, clear or pay Duties in another.

No Money shall be drawn from the Treasury, but in Consequence of Appropriations made by Law; and a regular Statement and Account of the Receipts and Expenditures of all public Money shall be published from time to time.

No Title of Nobility shall be granted by the United States: And no Person holding any Office of Profit or Trust under them, shall, without the Consent of the Congress, accept of any present, Emolument, Office, or Title, of any kind whatever, from any King, Prince or foreign State.

Section 10

No State shall enter into any Treaty, Alliance, or Confederation; grant Letters of Marque and Reprisal; coin Money; emit Bills of Credit; make any Thing but gold and silver Coin a Tender in Payment of Debts; pass any Bill of Attainder, ex post facto Law or law impairing the Obligation of Contracts, or grant any Title of Nobility.

No State shall, without the Consent of the Congress, lay any Imposts or Duties on Imports or Exports, except what may be absolutely necessary for executing its inspection Laws: and the net Produce of all Duties and Imposts, laid by any State on Imports or Exports, shall be for the Use of the Treasury of the United States; and all such Laws shall be subject to the Revision and Control of the Congress.

No State shall, without the Consent of Congress, lay any Duty on Tonnage, keep Troops, or Ships of War in time of Peace, enter into any Agreement or Compact with another State, or with a foreign Power, or engage in War, unless actually invaded, or in such imminent Danger as will not admit of delay.

Article II

Section 1

The executive Power shall be vested in a President of the United States of America. He shall hold his Office during the Term of four Years, and, together with the Vice President, chosen for the same Term, be elected, as follows:

Each State shall appoint, in such Manner as the Legislature thereof may direct, a Number of Electors, equal to the whole Number of Senators and Representatives to which the State may be entitled in the Congress: but no Senator or Representative, or Person holding an Office of Trust or Profit under the United States, shall be appointed an Elector.

The Electors shall meet in their respective States, and vote by Ballot for two Persons, of whom one at least shall not be an Inhabitant of the same State with themselves. And they shall make a List of all the Persons voted for, and of the Number of Votes for each; which List they shall sign and certify, and transmit sealed to the Seat of the Government of the United States, directed to the President of the Senate. The President of the Senate shall, in the Presence of the Senate and House of Representatives, open all the Certificates, and the Votes shall then be counted. The Person having the greatest Number of Votes shall be the President, if such Number be a Majority of the whole Number of Electors appointed; and if there be more than one who have such Majority, and have an equal Number of Votes, then the House of Representatives shall immediately chuse by Ballot one of them for President; and if no Person have a Majority, then from the five highest on the List the said House shall in like Manner chuse the President. But in chusing the President, the Votes shall be taken by States, the Representation from each State having one Vote; a quorum for this Purpose shall consist of a Member or Members from two thirds of the States, and a Majority of all the States shall be necessary to a Choice. In every Case, after the Choice of the President, the Person having the greatest Number of Votes of the Electors shall be the Vice President. But if there should remain two or more who have equal Votes, the Senate shall chuse from them by Ballot the Vice President.

The Congress may determine the Time of chusing the Electors, and the Day on which they shall give their Votes; which Day shall be the same throughout the United States.

No Person except a natural born Citizen, or a Citizen of the United States, at the time of the Adoption of this Constitution, shall be eligible to the Office of President; neither shall any Person be eligible to that Office who shall not have attained to the Age of thirty-five Years, and been fourteen years a Resident within the United States.

In Case of the Removal of the President from Office, or of his Death, Resignation, or Inability to discharge the Powers and Duties of the said Office, the Same shall devolve on the Vice President, and the Congress may by Law provide for the Case of Removal, Death, Resignation, or Inability, both of the President and Vice President, declaring what Officer shall then act as President, and such Officer shall act accordingly, until the Disability be removed, or a President shall be elected.

The President shall, at stated Times, receive for his Services, a Compensation, which shall neither be encreased nor diminished during the Period for which he shall have been elected, and he shall not receive within that Period any other Emolument from the United States, or any of them.

Before he enter on the Execution of his Office, he shall take the following Oath or Affirmation:—"I do solemnly swear (or affirm) that I will faithfully execute the Office of President of the United States, and will to the best of my Ability, preserve, protect, and defend the Constitution of the United States."

Section 2

The President shall be Commander in Chief of the Army and Navy of the United States, and of the Militia of the several States, when called into the actual Service of the United States; he may require the Opinion, in writing, of the principal Officer in each of the executive Departments, upon any Subject relating to the Duties of their respective Offices, and he shall have Power to grant Reprieves and Pardons for Offenses against the United States, except in Cases of Impeachment.

He shall have Power, by and with the Advice and Consent of the Senate, to make Treaties, provided two thirds of the Senators present concur; and he shall nominate, and by and with the Advice and Consent of the Senate, shall appoint Ambassadors, other public Ministers and Consuls, Judges of the supreme Court, and all other Officers of the United States, whose Appointments are not herein otherwise provided for, and which shall be established by Law: but the Congress may by Law vest the Appointment of such inferior Officers, as they think proper, in the President alone, in the Courts of Law, or in the Heads of Departments.

The President shall have Power to fill up all Vacancies that may happen during the Recess of the Senate, by granting Commissions which shall expire at the End of their next Session.

Section 3

He shall from time to time give to the Congress Information of the State of the Union, and recommend to their Consideration such Measures as he shall judge necessary and expedient; he may, on extraordinary Occasions, convene both Houses, or either of them, and in Case of Disagreement between them, with Respect to the Time of Adjournment, he may adjourn them to such Time as he shall think proper; he shall receive Ambassadors and other public Ministers; he shall take Care that the Laws be faithfully executed, and shall Commission all the Officers of the United States.

Section 4

The President, Vice President and all Civil Officers of the United States, shall be removed from Office on Impeachment for, and Conviction of, Treason, Bribery, or other high Crimes and Misdemeanors.

Article III

Section 1

The judicial Power of the United States, shall be vested in one supreme Court, and in such inferior Courts as the Congress may from time to time ordain and establish. The Judges, both of the supreme and inferior Courts, shall hold their Offices during good Behaviour, and shall, at stated Times, receive for their Services, a Compensation, which shall not be diminished during their Continuance in Office.

Section 2

The judicial Power shall extend to all Cases, in Law and Equity, arising under this Constitution, the Laws of the United States, and Treaties made, or which shall be made, under their Authority;—to all Cases affecting Ambassadors, other public Ministers and Consuls;—to all Cases of admiralty and maritime Jurisdiction;—to Controversies to which the United States shall be a Party;—to Controversies between two or more States;—between a State and Citizens of another State;—between Citizens of different States,—between Citizens of the same State claiming Lands under Grants of different

States, and between a State, or the Citizens thereof, and foreign States, Citizens or Subjects.

In all Cases affecting Ambassadors, other public Ministers and Consuls, and those in which a State shall be Party, the Supreme Court shall have original Jurisdiction. In all the other Cases before mentioned, the supreme Court shall have appellate Jurisdiction, both as to Law and Fact, with such Exceptions, and under such Regulations as the Congress shall make.

The Trial of all Crimes, except in Cases of Impeachment, shall be by Jury; and such Trial shall be held in the State where the said Crimes shall have been committed; but when not committed within any State, the Trial shall be at such Place or Places as the Congress may by Law have directed.

Section 3

Treason against the United States, shall consist only in levying War against them, or in adhering to their Enemies, giving them Aid and Comfort. No Person shall be convicted of Treason unless on the Testimony of two Witnesses to the same overt Act, or on Confession in open Court.

The Congress shall have Power to declare the Punishment of Treason, but no Attainder of Treason shall work Corruption of Blood, or Forfeiture except during the Life of the Person attainted.

Article IV

Section 1

Full Faith and Credit shall be given in each State to the public Arts, Records, and judicial Proceedings of every other State. And the Congress may by general Laws prescribe the Manner in which such Acts, Records and Proceedings shall be proved, and the Effect thereof.

Section 2

The Citizens of each State shall be entitled to all Privileges and Immunities of Citizens in the several States.

A Person charged in any State with Treason, Felony, or other Crime, who shall flee from Justice, and be found in another State, shall on Demand of the executive Authority of the State from which he fled, be delivered up, to be removed to the State having Jurisdiction of the Crime.

No Person held to Service or Labour in one State, under the Laws thereof, escaping into another, shall, in Consequence of any Law or Regulation therein, be discharged from such Service or Labour, but shall be delivered up on Claim of the Party to whom such Service or Labour may be due.

Section 3

New States may be admitted by the Congress into this Union; but no new State shall be formed or erected within the Jurisdiction of any other State; nor any State be formed by the Junction of two or more States, or Parts of States, without the Consent of the Legislatures of the States concerned as well as of the Congress.

The Congress shall have Power to dispose of and make all needful Rules and Regulations respecting the Territory or other Property belonging to the United States; and nothing in this Constitution shall be so construed as to Prejudice any Claims of the United States, or of any particular State.

Section 4

The United States shall guarantee to every State in this Union a Republican Form of Government, and shall protect each of them against Invasion; and on Application of the Legislature, or of the Executive (when the Legislature cannot be convened) against domestic Violence.

Article V

The Congress, whenever two thirds of both Houses shall deem it necessary, shall propose Amendments to this Constitution, or, on the Application of the Legislatures of two thirds of the several States, shall call a Convention for proposing Amendments, which, in either Case, shall be valid to all Intents and Purposes, as Part of this Constitution, when ratified by the Legislatures of three fourths of the several States, or by Conventions in three fourths thereof, as the one or the other Mode of Ratification may be proposed by the Congress; Provided that no Amendment which may be made prior to the Year One thousand eight hundred and eight shall in any Manner affect the first and fourth Clauses in the Ninth Section of the first Article; and that no State, without its Consent, shall be deprived of its equal Suffrage in the Senate.

Article VI

All Debts contracted and Engagements entered into, before the Adoption of this Constitution, shall be as valid against the United States under this Constitution, as under the Confederation.

This Constitution, and the Laws of the United States which shall be made in Pursuance thereof; and all Treaties made, or which shall be made, under the Authority of the United States, shall be the supreme Law of the Land; and the judges in every State shall be bound thereby, any Thing in the Constitution or Laws of any State to the Contrary notwithstanding.

The Senators and Representatives before mentioned, and the Members of the several State Legislatures, and all executive and judicial Officers, both of the United States and of the several States, shall be bound by Oath or Affirmation, to support this Constitution; but no religious Test shall ever be required as a Qualification to any Office or public Trust under the United States.

Article VII

The Ratification of the Conventions of nine States, shall be sufficient for the Establishment of this Constitution between the States so ratifying the Same.

Amendment I (1791)

Congress shall make no law respecting an establishment of religion, or prohibiting the free exercise thereof; or abridging the freedom of speech, or of the press; or the right of the people peaceably to assemble, and to petition the Government for a redress of grievances.

Amendment II (1791)

A well regulated Militia, being necessary to the security of a free State, the right of the people to keep and bear Arms, shall not be infringed.

Amendment III (1791)

No Soldier shall, in time of peace be quartered in any house, without the consent of the Owner, nor in time of war, but in a manner to be prescribed by law.

Amendment IV (1791)

The right of the people to be secure in their persons, houses, papers, and effects, against unreasonable searches and seizures, shall not be violated, and no Warrants shall issue, but upon probable cause, supported by Oath or affirmation, and particularly describing the place to be searched, and the persons or things to be seized.

Amendment V (1791)

No person shall be held to answer for a capital or otherwise infamous crime, unless on a presentment or indictment of a Grand Jury, except in cases arising in the land or naval forces, or in the Militia, when in actual service in time of War or public danger; nor shall any person be subject for the same offense to be twice put in jeopardy of life or limb; nor shall be compelled in any criminal case to be a witness against himself, nor be deprived of life, liberty, or property, without due process of law; nor shall private property be taken for public use, without just compensation.

Amendment VI (1791)

In all criminal prosecutions, the accused shall enjoy the right to a speedy and public trial, by an impartial jury of the State and district wherein the crime shall have been committed, which district shall have been previously ascertained by law, and to be informed of the nature and cause of the accusation; to be confronted with the witnesses against him; to have compulsory process for obtaining Witnesses in his favor, and to have the Assistance of Counsel for his defense.

Amendment VII (1791)

In Suits at common law, where the value in controversy shall exceed twenty dollars, the right of trial by jury shall be preserved, and no fact tried by a jury, shall be otherwise reexamined in any Court of the United States, than according to the rules of the common law.

Amendment VIII (1791)

Excessive bail shall not be required nor excessive fines imposed, nor cruel and unusual punishments inflicted.

Amendment IX (1791)

The enumeration in the Constitution, of certain rights, shall not be construed to deny or disparage others retained by the people.

Amendment X (1791)

The powers not delegated to the United States by the Constitution, nor prohibited by it to the States, are reserved to the States respectively, or to the people.

Amendment XI (1798)

The Judicial power of the United States shall not be construed to extend to any suit in law or equity, commenced or prosecuted against one of the

United States by Citizens of another State, or by Citizens or Subjects of any Foreign State.

Amendment XII (1804)

The Electors shall meet in their respective states and vote by ballot for President and Vice President, one of whom, at least, shall not be an inhabitant of the same state with themselves; they shall name in their ballots the person voted for as President, and in distinct ballots the person voted for as Vice-President, and they shall make distinct lists of all persons voted for as President, and of all persons voted for as Vice-President, and of the number of votes for each, which lists they shall sign and certify, and transmit sealed to the seat of the government of the United States, directed to the President of the Senate;—The President of the Senate shall, in the presence of the Senate and House of Representatives, open all the certificates and the votes shall then be counted;—The person having the greatest number of votes for President, shall be the President, if such number be a majority of the whole number of Electors appointed; and if no person have such majority, then from the persons having the highest numbers not exceeding three on the list of those voted for as President, the House of Representatives shall choose immediately, by ballot, the President. But in choosing the President, the votes shall be taken by states, the representation from each state having one vote; a quorum for this purpose shall consist of a member or members from two-thirds of the states, and a majority of all the states shall be necessary to a choice. And if the House of Representatives shall not choose a President whenever the right of choice shall devolve upon them, before the fourth day of March next following, then the Vice-President shall act as President, as in the case of the death or other constitutional disability of the President—The person having the greatest number of votes as Vice-President, shall be the Vice-President, if such number be a majority of the whole number of Electors appointed, and if no person have a majority, then from the two highest numbers on the list, the Senate shall choose the Vice-President; a quorum for the purpose shall consist of two-thirds of the whole numbers of Senators, and a majority of the whole number shall be necessary to a choice.

But no person constitutionally ineligible to the office of President shall be eligible to that of Vice President of the United States.

Amendment XIII (1865)

Section 1

Neither slavery nor involuntary servitude, except as a punishment for crime whereof the party shall have been duly convicted, shall exist within the United States, or any place subject to their jurisdiction.

Section 2

Congress shall have power to enforce this article by appropriate legislation.

Amendment XIV (1868)

Section 1

All persons born or naturalized in the United States and subject to the jurisdiction thereof, are citizens of the United States and of the State wherein they reside. No State shall make or enforce any law which shall abridge the privileges or immunities of citizens of the United States; nor shall any State deprive any person of life, liberty, or property, without due process of law; nor deny to any person within its jurisdiction the equal protection of the laws.

Section 2

Representatives shall be apportioned among the several States according to their respective numbers, counting the whole number of persons in each State, excluding Indians not taxed. But when the right to vote at any election for the choice of electors for President and Vice President of the United States, Representatives in Congress, the Executive and Judicial officers of a State, or the members of the Legislature thereof, is denied to any of the male inhabitants of such State, being twenty-one years of age, and citizens of the United States, or in any way abridged, except for participation in rebellion, or other crime, the basis of representation therein shall be reduced in the proportion which the number of such male citizens shall bear to the whole number of male citizens twenty-one years of age in such State.

Section 3

No person shall be a Senator or Representative in Congress, or elector of President and Vice President, or hold any office, civil or military, under the United States, or under any State, who, having previously taken an oath, as a member of Congress, or as an officer of the United States, or as a member of any State legislature, or as an executive or judicial officer of any State, to support the Constitution of the United States, shall have engaged in insurrection or rebellion against the same, or given aid or comfort to the enemies thereof. But Congress may by a vote of two-thirds of each House, remove such disability.

Section 4

The validity of the public debt of the United States, authorized by law, including debts incurred for payment of pensions and bounties for services in suppressing insurrection or rebellion, shall not be questioned. But neither the United States nor any State shall assume or pay any debt or obligation incurred in aid of insurrection or rebellion against the United States, or any claim for the loss or emancipation of any slave; but all such debts, obligations and claims shall be held illegal and void.

Section 5

The Congress shall have power to enforce, by appropriate legislation, the provisions of this article.

Amendment XV (1870)

Section 1

The right of citizens of the United States to vote shall not be denied or abridged by the United States or by any State on account of race, color, or previous condition of servitude.

Section 2

The Congress shall have power to enforce this article by appropriate legislation.

Amendment XVI (1913)

The Congress shall have power to lay and collect taxes on incomes, from whatever source derived, without apportionment among the several States, and without regard to any census or enumeration.

Amendment XVII (1913)

The Senate of the United States shall be composed of two Senators from each State, elected by the people thereof, for six years; and each Senator shall have one vote. The electors in each State shall have the qualifications requisite for electors of the most numerous branch of the State legislatures.

When vacancies happen in the representation of any State in the Senate, the executive authority of such State shall issue writs of election to fill such vacancies: *Provided,* That the legislature of any State may empower the executive thereof to make temporary appointments until the people fill the vacancies by election as the legislature may direct.

This amendment shall not be so construed as to affect the election or term of any Senator chosen before it becomes valid as part of the Constitution.

Amendment XVIII (1919)

Section 1

After one year from the ratification of this article the manufacture, sale, or transportation of intoxicating liquors within, the importation thereof into, or the exportation thereof from the United States and all territory subject to the jurisdiction thereof for beverage purposes is hereby prohibited.

Section 2

The Congress and the several States shall have concurrent power to enforce this article by appropriate legislation.

Section 2

This article shall be inoperative unless it shall have been ratified as an amendment to the Constitution by the legislatures of three fourths of the several States within seven years from the date of its submission to the States by the Congress.

Amendment XIX (1920)

The right of citizens of the United States to vote shall not be denied or abridged by the United States or by any State on account of sex.

Congress shall have power to enforce this article by appropriate legislation.

Amendment XX (1933)

Section 1

The terms of the President and Vice President shall end at noon on the 20th day of January, and the terms of Senators and Representatives at noon on the 3d day of January, of the years in which such terms would have ended if this article had not been ratified; and the terms of their successors shall then begin.

Section 2

The Congress shall assemble at least once in every year, and such meeting shall begin at noon on the

3d day of January, unless they shall by law appoint a different day.

Section 3

If, at the time fixed for the beginning of the term of the President, the President elect shall have died, the Vice President elect shall become President. If a President shall not have been chosen before the time fixed for the beginning of his term, or if the President elect shall have failed to qualify, then the Vice President elect shall act as President until a President shall have qualified; and the Congress may by law provide for the case wherein neither a President elect nor a Vice President elect shall have qualified, declaring who shall then act as President, or the manner in which one who is to act shall be selected, and such person shall act accordingly until a President or Vice President shall have qualified.

Section 4

The Congress may by law provide for the case of the death of any of the persons from whom the House of Representatives may choose a President whenever the right of choice shall have devolved upon them, and for the case of the death of any of the persons from whom the Senate may choose a Vice President whenever the right of choice shall have devolved upon them.

Section 5

Sections 1 and 2 shall take effect on the 15th day of October following the ratification of this article.

Section 6

This article shall be inoperative unless it shall have been ratified as an amendment to the Constitution by the legislatures of three fourths of the several States within seven years from the date of its submission.

Amendment XXI (1933)

Section 1

The eighteenth article of amendment to the Constitution of the United States is hereby repealed.

Section 2

The transportation or importation into any State, Territory, or possession of the United States for delivery or use therein of intoxicating liquors, in violation of the laws thereof, is hereby prohibited.

Section 3

This article shall be inoperative unless it shall have been ratified as an amendment to the Constitution by conventions in the several States, as provided in the Constitution, within seven years from the date of the submission hereof to the States by the Congress.

Amendment XXII (1951)

Section 1

No person shall be elected to the office of the President more than twice, and no person, who has held the office of President, or acted as President, for more than two years of a term to which some other person was elected President shall be elected to the Office of the President more than once. But this Article shall not apply to any person holding the office of President when this Article was proposed by the Congress, and shall not prevent any person who may be holding the office of President, or acting as President, during the term within which this Article becomes operative from holding the Office of President or acting as President during the remainder of such term.

Section 3

This article shall be inoperative unless it shall have been ratified as an amendment to the Constitution by the legislatures of the several States, as provided in the Constitution, within seven years from the date of the submission hereof to the States by the Congress.

Amendment XXIII (1961)

Section 1

The District constituting the seat of Government of the United States shall appoint in such manner as the Congress may direct:

A number of electors of President and Vice President equal to the whole number of Senators and Representatives in Congress to which the District would be entitled if it were a State, but in no event more than the least populous State; they shall be in addition to those appointed by the States, but they shall be considered, for the purposes of the election of President and Vice President, to be electors appointed by a State; and they shall meet in the District and perform such duties as provided by the twelfth article of amendment.

Section 2

The Congress shall have power to enforce this article by appropriate legislation.

Amendment XXIV (1964)

Section 1

The right of citizens of the United States to vote in any primary or other election for President or Vice President, for electors for President or Vice President, or for Senator or Representative in Congress, shall not be denied or abridged by the United States or any State by reason of failure to pay any poll tax or other tax.

Section 2

The Congress shall have power to enforce this article by appropriate legislation.

Amendment XXV (1967)

Section 1

In case of the removal of the President from office or of his death or resignation, the Vice President shall become President.

Section 2

Whenever there is a vacancy in the office of the Vice President, the President shall nominate a Vice President who shall take office upon confirmation by a majority vote of both Houses of Congress.

Section 3

Whenever the President transmits to the President pro tempore of the Senate and the Speaker of the House of Representatives his written declaration that he is unable to discharge the powers and duties of his office, and until he transmits to them a written declaration to the contrary, such powers and duties shall be discharged by the Vice President as Acting President.

Section 4

Whenever the Vice President and a majority of either the principal officers of the executive departments or of such other body as Congress may by law provide, transmit to the President pro tempore of the Senate and the Speaker of the House of Representatives their written declaration that the President is unable to discharge the powers and duties of his office, the Vice President shall immediately assume the powers and duties of the office as Acting President.

Thereafter, when the President transmits to the President pro tempore of the Senate and the Speaker of the House of Representatives his written declaration that no inability exists, he shall resume the powers and duties of his Office unless the Vice President and a majority of either the principal officers of the executive department or of such other body as Congress may by law provide, transmit within four days to the President pro tempore of the Senate and the Speaker of the House of Representatives their written declaration that the President is unable to discharge the powers and duties of his office. Thereupon Congress shall decide the issue, assembling within forty-eight hours for that purpose if not in session. If the Congress, within twenty-one days after receipt of the latter written declaration, or, if Congress is not in session, within twenty-one days after Congress is required to assemble, determines by two-thirds vote of both Houses that the President is unable to discharge the powers and duties of his office, the Vice President shall continue to discharge the same as Acting President; otherwise, the President shall resume the powers and duties of his office.

Amendment XXVI (1971)

Section 1

The right of citizens of the United States, who are eighteen years of age or older, to vote shall not be denied or abridged by the United States or by any State on account of age.

Section 2

The Congress shall have power to enforce this article by appropriate legislation.

Amendment XXVII (1992)

No law varying the compensation for services of the Senators and Representatives shall take effect until an election of representatives shall have intervened.

The Fair Housing Act
42 U.S.C. § 3601 *et seq.* (Excerpts)

Sec. 3601.—Declaration of Policy

It is the policy of the United States to provide, within constitutional limitations, for fair housing throughout the United States.

Sec. 3602.—Definitions

As used in this subchapter—

(a) "Family" includes a single individual.

(b) "Person" includes one or more individuals, corporations, partnerships, associations, labor organizations, legal representatives, mutual companies, joint-stock companies, trusts, unincorporated organizations, trustees, trustees in cases under title 11, receivers, and fiduciaries.

(c) "Handicap" means, with respect to a person—

   (1) a physical or mental impairment which substantially limits one or more of such person's major life activities,

   (2) a record of having such an impairment, or

   (3) being regarded as having such an impairment, but such term does not include current, illegal use of or addiction to a controlled substance (as defined in section 802 of title 21).

(d) "Familial status" means one or more individuals (who have not attained the age of 18 years) being domiciled with—

   (1) a parent or another person having legal custody of such individual or individuals; or

   (2) the designee of such parent or other person having such custody, with the written permission of such parent or other person.

The protections afforded against discrimination on the basis of familial status shall apply to any person who is pregnant or is in the process of securing legal custody of any individual who has not attained the age of 18 years.

Sec. 3603.—Effective Dates of Certain Prohibitions

(a) Application to certain described dwellings Subject to the provisions of subsection (b) of this section and section 3607 of this title, the prohibitions against discrimination in the sale or rental of housing set forth in section 3604 of this title shall apply:

   (1) Upon enactment of this subchapter, to—

      (A) dwellings owned or operated by the Federal Government;

      (B) dwellings provided in whole or in part with the aid of loans, advances, grants, or contributions made by the Federal Government, under agreements entered into after November 20, 1962, unless payment due thereon has been made in full prior to April 11, 1968;

      (C) dwellings provided in whole or in part by loans insured, guaranteed, or otherwise secured by the credit of the Federal Government, under agreements entered into after November 20, 1962, unless payment thereon has been made in full prior to April 11, 1968: Provided, That nothing contained in subparagraphs (B) and (C) of this subsection shall be applicable to dwellings solely by virtue of the fact that they are subject to mortgages held by an FDIC or FSLIC institution; and

(D) dwellings provided by the development or the redevelopment of real property purchased, rented, or otherwise obtained from a State or local public agency receiving Federal financial assistance for slum clearance or urban renewal with respect to such real property under loan or grant contracts entered into after November 20, 1962.

(b) Exemptions

Nothing in section 3604 of this title (other than subsection (c)) shall apply to—

(1) any single-family house sold or rented by an owner:

Provided, That such private individual owner does not own more than three such single-family houses at any one time: Provided further, That in the case of the sale of any such single-family house by a private individual owner not residing in such house at the time of such sale or who was not the most recent resident of such house prior to such sale, the exemption granted by this subsection shall apply only with respect to one such sale within any twenty-four month period: Provided further, That such bona fide private individual owner does not own any interest in, nor is there owned or reserved on his behalf, under any express or voluntary agreement, title to or any right to all or a portion of the proceeds from the sale or rental of, more than three such single-family houses at any one time: Provided further, That after December 31, 1969, the sale or rental of any such single-family house shall be excepted from the application of this subchapter only if such house is sold or rented

(A) without the use in any manner of the sales or rental facilities or the sales or rental services of any real estate broker, agent, or salesman, or of such facilities or services of any person in the business of selling or renting dwell-

ings, or of any employee or agent of any such broker, agent, salesman, or person and

(B) without the publication, posting or mailing, after notice, of any advertisement or written notice in violation of section 3604(c) of this title; but nothing in this proviso shall prohibit the use of attorneys, escrow agents, abstractors, title companies, and other such professional assistance as necessary to perfect or transfer the title, or

(2) rooms or units in dwellings containing living quarters occupied or intended to be occupied by no more than four families living independently of each other, if the owner actually maintains and occupies one of such living quarters as his residence.

Sec. 3604.—Discrimination in the Sale or Rental of Housing and Other Prohibited Practices

it shall be unlawful—

(a) To refuse to sell or rent after the making of a bona fide offer, or to refuse to negotiate for the sale or rental of, or otherwise make unavailable or deny, a dwelling to any person because of race, color, religion, sex, familial status, or national origin.

(b) To discriminate against any person in the terms, conditions, or privileges of sale or rental of a dwelling, or in the provision of services or facilities in connection therewith, because of race, color, religion, sex, familial status, or national origin.

(c) To make, print, or publish, or cause to be made, printed, or published any notice, statement, or advertisement, with respect to the sale or rental of a dwelling that indicates any preference, limitation, or discrimination based on race, color, religion, sex, handicap, familial status, or national origin, or an intention to make any such preference, limitation, or discrimination.

(d) To represent to any person because of race, color, religion, sex, handicap, familial status, or national origin that any dwelling is not available for inspection, sale, or rental when such dwelling is in fact so available.

(e) For profit, to induce or attempt to induce any person to sell or rent any dwelling by representations regarding the entry or prospective entry into the neighborhood of a person or persons of a particular race, color, religion, sex, handicap, familial status, or national origin.

(f) **(1)** To discriminate in the sale or rental, or to otherwise make unavailable or deny, a dwelling to any buyer or renter because of a handicap of—

   (A) that buyer or renter,

   (B) a person residing in or intending to reside in that dwelling after it is so sold, rented, or made available; or

   (C) any person associated with that buyer or renter.

(2) To discriminate against any person in the terms, conditions, or privileges of sale or rental of a dwelling, or in the provision of services or facilities in connection with such dwelling, because of a handicap of—

   (A) that person; or

   (B) a person residing in or intending to reside in that dwelling after it is so sold, rented, or made available; or

   (C) any person associated with that person.

(3) For purposes of this subsection, discrimination includes—

   (A) a refusal to permit, at the expense of the handicapped person, reasonable modifications of existing premises occupied or to be occupied by such person if such modifications may be necessary to afford such person full enjoyment of the premises except that, in the case of a rental, the landlord may where it is reasonable to do so condition permission for a modification on the renter agreeing to restore the interior of the premises to the condition that existed before the modification, reasonable wear and tear excepted.

   (B) a refusal to make reasonable accommodations in rules, policies, practices, or services, when such accommodations may be necessary to afford such person equal opportunity to use and enjoy a dwelling; or

   (C) in connection with the design and construction of covered multifamily dwellings for first occupancy after the date that is 30 months after September 13, 1988, a failure to design and construct those dwellings in such a manner that—

      (i) the public use and common use portions of such dwellings are readily accessible to and usable by handicapped persons;

      (ii) all the doors designed to allow passage into and within all premises within such dwellings are sufficiently wide to allow passage by handicapped persons in wheelchairs; and

      (iii) all premises within such dwellings contain the following features of adaptive design:

         (I) an accessible route into and through the dwelling;

         (II) light switches, electrical outlets, thermostats, and other environmental controls in accessible locations;

         (III) reinforcements in bathroom walls to allow later installation of grab bars; and

         (IV) usable kitchens and bathrooms such that an individual in a wheelchair can maneuver about the space.

(4) Compliance with the appropriate requirements of the American National Standard for buildings and facilities providing accessibility and usability for physically handicapped people (commonly cited as "ANSI A117.1") suffices to satisfy the requirements of paragraph (3)(C)(iii).

(5) **(A)** If a State or unit of general local government has incorporated into its laws the requirements set forth in paragraph (3)(C), compliance with such laws shall be deemed to satisfy the requirements of that paragraph.

Sec. 3605.—Discrimination in Residential Real Estate-Related Transactions

(a) In general

It shall be unlawful for any person or other entity whose business includes engaging in residential real estate-related transactions to discriminate against any person in making available such a transaction, or in the terms or conditions of such a transaction, because of race, color, religion, sex, handicap, familial status, or national origin.

(b) "Residential real estate-related transaction" defined

As used in this section, the term "residential real estate-related transaction" means any of the following:

(1) The making or purchasing of loans or providing other financial assistance—

(A) for purchasing, constructing, improving, repairing, or maintaining a dwelling; or

(B) secured by residential real estate.

(2) The selling, brokering, or appraising of residential real property.

(c) Appraisal exemption

Nothing in this subchapter prohibits a person engaged in the business of furnishing appraisals of real property to take into consideration factors other than race, color, religion, national origin, sex, handicap, or familial status.

Sec. 3606.—Discrimination in the Provision of Brokerage Services

After December 31, 1968, it shall be unlawful to deny any person access to or membership or participation in any multiple-listing service, real estate brokers' organization or other service, organization, or facility relating to the business of selling or renting dwellings, or to discriminate against him in the terms or conditions of such access, membership, or participation, on account of race, color, religion, sex, handicap, familial status, or national origin.

Sec. 3607.—Religious Organization or Private Club Exemption

(a) Nothing in this subchapter shall prohibit a religious organization, association, or society, or any nonprofit institution or organization operated, supervised or controlled by or in conjunction with a religious organization, association, or society, from limiting the sale, rental or occupancy of dwellings which it owns or operates for other than a commercial purpose to persons of the same religion, or from giving preference to such persons, unless membership in such religion is restricted on account of race, color, or national origin. Nor shall anything in this sub-chapter prohibit a private club not in fact open to the public, which as an incident to its primary purpose or purposes provides lodgings which it owns or operates for other than a commercial purpose, from limiting the rental or occupancy of such lodgings to its members or from giving preference to its members.

Sec. 3613.—Enforcement by Private Persons

(a) Civil action

(1) (A) An aggrieved person may commence a civil action in an appropriate United States district court or State court not later than 2 years after the occurrence or the termination of an alleged discriminatory housing practice, or the breach of a conciliation agreement entered into under this sub-chapter, whichever occurs last, to obtain appropriate relief with respect to such discriminatory housing practice or breach.

(b) Appointment of attorney by court

Upon application by a person alleging a discriminatory housing practice or a person against whom such a practice is alleged, the court may—

(1) appoint an attorney for such person; or

(2) authorize the commencement or continuation of a civil action under subsection (a) of this section without the payment of fees, costs, or security, if in the opinion of the court such person is financially unable to bear the costs of such action.

(c) Relief which may be granted

(1) In a civil action under subsection (a) of this section, if the court finds that a discriminatory housing practice has occurred or is about to occur, the court may award to the plaintiff actual and punitive damages, and subject to subsection (d) of this section, may grant as relief, as the court deems appropriate, any permanent or temporary injunction, temporary restraining order, or other order (including an order enjoining the defendant from engaging in such practice or ordering such affirmative action as may be appropriate).

(2) In a civil action under subsection (a) of this section, the court, in its discretion, may allow the prevailing party, other than the United States, a reasonable attorney's fee and costs. The United States shall be liable for such fees and costs to the same extent as a private person.

APPENDIX C

The Truth-in-Lending Act
15 U.S.C. § 1601 *et seq.* (Excerpts)

15 U.S.C.A. § 1635

§ 1635. Right of rescission as to certain transactions

(a) Disclosure of obligor's right to rescind

Except as otherwise provided in this section, in the case of any consumer credit transaction (including opening or increasing the credit limit for an open end credit plan) in which a security interest, including any such interest arising by operation of law, is or will be retained or acquired in any property which is used as the principal dwelling of the person to whom credit is extended, the obligor shall have the right to rescind the transaction until midnight of the third business day following the consummation of the transaction or the delivery of the information and rescission forms required under this section together with a statement containing the material disclosures required under this subchapter, whichever is later, by notifying the creditor, in accordance with regulations of the Bureau, of his intention to do so. The creditor shall clearly and conspicuously disclose, in accordance with regulations of the Bureau, to any obligor in a transaction subject to this section the rights of the obligor under this section. The creditor shall also provide, in accordance with regulations of the Bureau, appropriate forms for the obligor to exercise his right to rescind any transaction subject to this section.

(b) Return of money or property following rescission

When an obligor exercises his right to rescind under subsection (a) of this section,

he is not liable for any finance or other charge, and any security interest given by the obligor, including any such interest arising by operation of law, becomes void upon such a rescission. Within 20 days after receipt of a notice of rescission, the creditor shall return to the obligor any money or property given as earnest money, down payment, or otherwise, and shall take any action necessary or appropriate to reflect the termination of any security interest created under the transaction. § 1637a. Disclosure requirements for open end consumer credit plans secured by consumer's principal dwelling

(a) Application disclosures

In the case of any open end consumer credit plan which provides for any extension of credit which is secured by the consumer's principal dwelling, the creditor shall make the following disclosures in accordance with subsection (b) of this section:

(1) Fixed annual percentage rate

Each annual percentage rate imposed in connection with extensions of credit under the plan and a statement that such rate does not include costs other than interest.

(2) Variable percentage rate

In the case of a plan which provides for variable rates of interest on credit extended under the plan–

(A) a description of the manner in which such rate will be computed and a statement that such rate does not include costs other than interest;

(B) a description of the manner in which any changes in the annual percentage rate will be made, including–

  (i) any negative amortization and interest rate carryover;

  (ii) the timing of any such changes;

  (iii) any index or margin to which such changes in the rate are related; and

  (iv) a source of information about any such index;

(J) An itemization of any fees imposed by the creditor in connection with the availability or use of credit under such plan, including annual fees, application fees, transaction fees, and closing costs (including costs commonly described as "points"), and the time when such fees are payable.

(4) Estimates of fees which may be imposed by third parties

  (A) Aggregate amount

    An estimate, based on the creditor's experience with such plans and stated as a single amount or as a reasonable range, of the aggregate amount of additional fees that may be imposed by third parties (such as governmental authorities, appraisers, and attorneys) in connection with opening an account under the plan.

  (B) Statement of availability

    A statement that the consumer may ask the creditor for a good faith estimate by the creditor of the fees that may be imposed by third parties.

(5) Statement of risk of loss of dwelling

  A statement that–

  (A) any extension of credit under the plan is secured by the consumer's dwelling; and

  (B) in the event of any default, the consumer risks the loss of the dwelling.

(6) Conditions to which disclosed terms are subject

  (A) Period during which such terms are available

    A clear and conspicuous statement–

    (i) of the time by which an application must be submitted to obtain the terms disclosed; or

(ii) if applicable, that the terms are subject to change.

(C) an explanation of how the amount of any minimum monthly or periodic payment will be determined under each such option, including any differences in the determination of any such amount with regard to the periods described in clauses (i) and (ii) of subparagraph (A).

(9) Example of minimum payments and maximum repayment period

  An example, based on a $10,000 outstanding balance and the interest rate (other than a rate not based on the index under the plan) which is, or was recently, in effect under such plan, showing the minimum monthly or periodic payment, and the time it would take to repay the entire $10,000 if the consumer paid only the minimum periodic payments and obtained no additional extensions of credit.

(10) Statement concerning balloon payments

  If, under any repayment option of the plan, the payment of not more than the minimum periodic payments required under such option over the length of the repayment period–

  (A) would not repay any of the principal balance; or

  (B) would repay less than the outstanding balance by the end of such period,

  as the case may be, a statement of such fact, including an explicit statement that at the end of such repayment period a balloon payment (as defined in section 1665b (f) of this title) would result which would be required to be paid in full at that time.

(11) Negative amortization

  If applicable, a statement that–

  (A) any limitation in the plan on the amount of any increase in the minimum payments may result in negative amortization;

  (B) negative amortization increases the outstanding principal balance of the account; and

  (C) negative amortization reduces the consumer's equity in the consumer's dwelling.

(13) Statement regarding tax deductibility
A statement that–
(A) the consumer should consult a tax advisor regarding the deductibility of interest and charges under the plan; and
(B) in any case in which the extension of credit exceeds the fair market value (as defined under Title 26) of the dwelling, the interest on the portion of the credit extension that is greater than the fair market value of the dwelling is not tax deductible for Federal income tax purposes.

§ 1638. Transactions other than under an open end credit plan

(a) Required disclosures by creditor

For each consumer credit transaction other than under an open end credit plan, the creditor shall disclose each of the following items, to the extent applicable:

(1) The identity of the creditor required to make disclosure.

(2) **(A)** The "amount financed", using that term, which shall be the amount of credit of which the consumer has actual use. This amount shall be computed as follows, but the computations need not be disclosed and shall not be disclosed with the disclosures conspicuously segregated in accordance with subsection (b)(1) of this section:
   (i) take the principal amount of the loan or the cash price less down payment and trade-in;
   (ii) add any charges which are not part of the finance charge or of the principal amount of the loan and which are financed by the consumer, including the cost of any items excluded from the finance charge pursuant to section 1605 of this title; and
   (iii) subtract any charges which are part of the finance charge but which will be paid by the consumer before or at the time of the consummation of the transaction, or have been withheld from the proceeds of the credit.

(B) In conjunction with the disclosure of the amount financed, a creditor shall provide a statement of the consumer's right to obtain, upon a written request, a written itemization of the amount financed. The statement shall include spaces for a "yes" and "no" indication to be initialed by the consumer to indicate whether the consumer wants a written itemization of the amount financed. Upon receiving an affirmative indication, the creditor shall provide, at the time other disclosures are required to be furnished, a written itemization of the amount financed. For the purposes of this subparagraph, "itemization of the amount financed" means a disclosure of the following items, to the extent applicable:

(3) The "finance charge", not itemized, using that term.

(4) The finance charge expressed as an "annual percentage rate", using that term. This shall not be required if the amount financed does not exceed $75 and the finance charge does not exceed $5, or if the amount financed exceeds $75 and the finance charge does not exceed $7.50.

(5) The sum of the amount financed and the finance charge, which shall be termed the "total of payments".

(6) The number, amount, and due dates or period of payments scheduled to repay the total of payments.

(14) In the case of any variable interest rate residential mortgage transaction, in disclosures provided at application as prescribed by the Bureau for a variable rate transaction secured by the consumer's principal dwelling, at the option of the creditor, a statement that the periodic payments may increase or decrease substantially, and the maximum interest rate and payment for a $10,000 loan originated at a recent interest rate, as determined by the Bureau, assuming the maximum periodic increases in rates and payments under the program, or a historical example illustrating the effects of interest rate changes implemented according to the loan program.

(15) In the case of a consumer credit transaction that is secured by the principal dwelling of the consumer, in which the extension of credit may exceed the fair market value of the dwelling, a clear and conspicuous statement that–

(A) the interest on the portion of the credit extension that is greater than the fair market value of the dwelling is not tax deductible for Federal income tax purposes; and

(B) the consumer should consult a tax adviser for further information regarding the deductibility of interest and charges.

(b) Form and timing of disclosures; residential mortgage transaction requirements

(i) state in conspicuous type size and format, the following: "You are not required to complete this agreement merely because you have received these disclosures or signed a loan application."; and

(ii) be provided in the form of final disclosures at the time of consummation of the transaction, in the form and manner prescribed by this section.

(C) In the case of an extension of credit that is secured by the dwelling of a consumer, under which the annual rate of interest is variable, or with respect to which the regular payments may otherwise be variable, in addition to the other disclosures required by subsection (a), the disclosures provided under this subsection shall do the following:

(i) Label the payment schedule as follows: "Payment Schedule: Payments Will Vary Based on Interest Rate Changes".

(ii) State in conspicuous type size and format examples of adjustments to the regular required payment on the extension of credit based on the change in the interest rates specified by the contract for such extension of credit. Among the examples required to be provided under this clause is an example that reflects the maximum payment amount of the regular required payments on the extension of credit, based on the maximum interest rate allowed under the contract, in accordance with the rules of the Bureau. Prior to issuing any rules pursuant to this clause, the Bureau shall conduct consumer testing to determine the appropriate format for providing the disclosures required under this subparagraph to consumers so that such disclosures can be easily understood, including the fact that the initial regular payments are for a specific time period that will end on a certain date, that payments will adjust afterwards potentially to a higher amount, and that there is no guarantee that the borrower will be able to refinance to a lower amount.

15 U.S.C.A. § 1638a

§ 1638a. Reset of hybrid adjustable rate mortgages

(a) Hybrid adjustable rate mortgages defined

For purposes of this section, the term "hybrid adjustable rate mortgage" means a consumer credit transaction secured by the consumer's principal residence with a fixed interest rate for an introductory period that adjusts or resets to a variable interest rate after such period.

(b) Notice of reset and alternatives

During the 1-month period that ends 6 months before the date on which the interest rate in effect during the introductory period of a hybrid adjustable rate mortgage adjusts or resets to a variable interest rate or, in the case of such an adjustment or resetting that occurs within the first 6 months after consummation of such loan, at consummation, the creditor or servicer of such loan shall provide a written notice, separate and distinct from all other correspondence to the consumer, that includes the following:

(1) Any index or formula used in making adjustments to or resetting the interest rate and a source of information about the index or formula.

(2) An explanation of how the new interest rate and payment would be determined, including an explanation of how the index was adjusted, such as by the addition of a margin.

(3) A good faith estimate, based on accepted industry standards, of the creditor or servicer of the amount of the monthly payment that will apply after the date of the adjustment or reset, and the assumptions on which this estimate is based.

(4) A list of alternatives consumers may pursue before the date of adjustment or reset, and descriptions of the actions consumers must take to pursue these alternatives, including–

  (A) refinancing;

  (B) renegotiation of loan terms;

  (C) payment forbearances; and

  (D) pre-foreclosure sales.

(5) The names, addresses, telephone numbers, and Internet addresses of counseling agencies or programs reasonably available to the consumer that have been certified or approved and made publicly available by the Secretary of Housing and Urban Development or a State housing finance authority

15 U.S.C.A. § 1639

§ 1639. Requirements for certain mortgages

(2) New disclosures required

  (A) In general

    After providing the disclosures required by this section, a creditor may not change the terms of the extension of credit if such changes make the disclosures inaccurate, unless new disclosures are provided that meet the requirements of this section.

  (B) Telephone disclosure

    A creditor may provide new disclosures pursuant to subparagraph (A) by telephone, if–

    (i) the change is initiated by the consumer; and

    (ii) at the consummation of the transaction under which the credit is extended–

      (I) the creditor provides to the consumer the new disclosures, in writing; and

      (II) the creditor and consumer certify in writing that the new disclosures were provided by telephone, by not later than 3 days prior to the date of consummation of the transaction.

(3) Modifications

  The Bureau may, if it finds that such action is necessary to permit homeowners to meet bona fide personal financial emergencies, prescribe regulations authorizing the modification or waiver of rights created under this subsection, to the extent and under the circumstances set forth in those regulations.

§ 1639a. Duty of servicers of residential mortgages

(a) In general

Notwithstanding any other provision of law, whenever a servicer of residential mortgages agrees to enter into a qualified loss mitigation plan with respect to 1 or more residential mortgages originated before May 20, 2009, including mortgages held in a securitization or other investment vehicle–

(1) to the extent that the servicer owes a duty to investors or other parties to maximize the net present value of such mortgages, the duty shall be construed to apply to all such investors and parties, and not to any individual party or group of parties; and

(2) the servicer shall be deemed to have satisfied the duty set forth in paragraph (1) if, before December 31, 2012, the servicer implements a qualified loss mitigation plan that meets the following criteria:

  (A) Default on the payment of such mortgage has occurred, is imminent, or is reasonably foreseeable, as such terms are defined by guidelines issued by the Secretary of the Treasury or his designee under the Emergency Economic Stabilization Act of 2008.

  (B) The mortgagor occupies the property securing the mortgage as his or her principal residence.

(C) The servicer reasonably determined, consistent with the guidelines issued by the Secretary of the Treasury or his designee, that the application of such qualified loss mitigation plan to a mortgage or class of mortgages will likely provide an anticipated recovery on the outstanding principal mortgage debt that will exceed the anticipated recovery through foreclosures.

(b) No liability

A servicer that is deemed to be acting in the best interests of all investors or other parties under this section shall not be liable to any party who is owed a duty under subsection (a)(1), and shall not be subject to any injunction, stay, or other equitable relief to such party, based solely upon the implementation by the servicer of a qualified loss mitigation plan.

(c) Prohibition on steering incentives

(1) In general

For any residential mortgage loan, no mortgage originator shall receive from any person and no person shall pay to a mortgage originator, directly or indirectly, compensation that varies based on the terms of the loan (other than the amount of the principal).

(2) Restructuring of financing origination fee

(A) In general

For any mortgage loan, a mortgage originator may not receive from any person other than the consumer and no person, other than the consumer, who knows or has reason to know that a consumer has directly compensated or will directly compensate a mortgage originator may pay a mortgage originator any origination fee or charge except bona fide third party charges not retained by the creditor, mortgage originator, or an affiliate of the creditor or mortgage originator.

(B) Exception

Notwithstanding subparagraph (A), a mortgage originator may receive from a person other than the consumer an origination fee or charge, and a person other than the consumer may pay a mortgage originator an origination fee or charge, if–

(i) the mortgage originator does not receive any compensation directly from the consumer; and

(ii) the consumer does not make an upfront payment of discount points, origination points, or fees, however denominated (other than bona fide third party charges not retained by the mortgage originator, creditor, or an affiliate of the creditor or originator), except that the Bureau may, by rule, waive or provide exemptions to this clause if the Bureau determines that such waiver or exemption is in the interest of consumers and in the public interest.

(d) Liability for violations

(1) In general

For purposes of providing a cause of action for any failure by a mortgage originator, other than a creditor, to comply with any requirement imposed under this section and any regulation prescribed under this section, section 1640 of this title shall be applied with respect to any such failure by substituting "mortgage originator" for "creditor" each place such term appears in each such subsection.

(2) Maximum

The maximum amount of any liability of a mortgage originator under paragraph (1) to a consumer for any violation of this section shall not exceed the greater of actual damages or an amount equal to 3 times the total amount of direct and indirect compensation or gain accruing to the mortgage originator in connection with the residential mortgage loan involved in the violation, plus the costs to the consumer of the action, including a reasonable attorney's fee.

§ 1639c. Minimum standards for residential mortgage loans

(a) Ability to repay

(1) In general

In accordance with regulations prescribed by the Bureau, no creditor may make a residential mortgage loan unless the creditor makes a reasonable and good faith determination based on verified and documented information that, at the time the loan is consummated, the consumer has a reasonable ability to repay the loan, according to its terms, and all applicable taxes, insurance (including mortgage guarantee insurance), and assessments.

(2) Multiple loans

If the creditor knows, or has reason to know, that 1 or more residential mortgage loans secured by the same dwelling will be made to the same consumer, the creditor shall make a reasonable and good faith determination, based on verified and documented information, that the consumer has a reasonable ability to repay the combined payments of all loans on the same dwelling according to the terms of those loans and all applicable taxes, insurance (including mortgage guarantee insurance), and assessments.

(3) Basis for determination

A determination under this subsection of a consumer's ability to repay a residential mortgage loan shall include consideration of the consumer's credit history, current income, expected income the consumer is reasonably assured of receiving, current obligations, debt-to-income ratio or the residual income the consumer will have after paying non-mortgage debt and mortgage-related obligations, employment status, and other financial resources other than the consumer's equity in the dwelling or real property that secures repayment of the loan. A creditor shall determine the ability of the consumer to repay using a payment schedule that fully amortizes the loan over the term of the loan.

(4) Income verification

A creditor making a residential mortgage loan shall verify amounts of income or assets that such creditor relies on to determine repayment ability, including expected income or assets, by reviewing the consumer's Internal Revenue Service Form W-2, tax returns, payroll receipts, financial institution records, or other third-party documents that provide reasonably reliable evidence of the consumer's income or assets. In order to safeguard against fraudulent reporting, any consideration of a consumer's income history in making a determination under this subsection shall include the verification of such income by the use of—

(A) Internal Revenue Service transcripts of tax returns; or

(B) a method that quickly and effectively verifies income documentation by a third party subject to rules prescribed by the Bureau.

§ 1639d. Escrow or impound accounts relating to certain consumer credit transactions

(a) In general

Except as provided in subsection (b), (c), (d), or (e), a creditor, in connection with the consummation of a consumer credit transaction secured by a first lien on the principal dwelling of the consumer, other than a consumer credit transaction under an open end credit plan or a reverse mortgage, shall establish, before the consummation of such transaction, an escrow or impound account for the payment of taxes and hazard insurance, and, if applicable, flood insurance, mortgage insurance, ground rents, and any other required periodic payments or premiums with respect to the property or the loan terms, as provided in, and in accordance with, this section.

§ 1639e. Appraisal independence requirements

(a) In general

It shall be unlawful, in extending credit or in providing any services for a consumer credit transaction secured by the principal dwelling of the consumer, to engage in any act or practice that violates appraisal independence as described in or pursuant to regulations prescribed under this section.

(b) Appraisal independence

For purposes of subsection (a), acts or practices that violate appraisal independence shall include—

(1) any appraisal of a property offered as security for repayment of the consumer credit transaction that is conducted in connection with such transaction in which a person with an interest in the underlying transaction compensates, coerces, extorts, colludes, instructs, induces, bribes, or intimidates a person, appraisal management company, firm, or other entity conducting or involved in an appraisal, or attempts, to compensate, coerce, extort, collude, instruct, induce, bribe, or intimidate such a person, for the purpose of causing the appraised value assigned, under the appraisal, to the property to be based on any factor other than the independent judgment of the appraiser;

(2) mischaracterizing, or suborning any mischaracterization of, the appraised value of the property securing the extension of the credit;

(3) seeking to influence an appraiser or otherwise to encourage a targeted value in order to facilitate the making or pricing of the transaction; and

(4) withholding or threatening to withhold timely payment for an appraisal report or for appraisal services rendered when the appraisal report or services are provided for in accordance with the contract between the parties.

§ 1639f. Requirements for prompt crediting of home loan payments

(a) In general

In connection with a consumer credit transaction secured by a consumer's principal dwelling, no servicer shall fail to credit a payment to the consumer's loan account as of the date of receipt, except when a delay in crediting does not result in any charge to the consumer or in the reporting of negative information to a consumer reporting agency, except as required in subsection (b).

§ 1639h. Property appraisal requirements

(a) In general

A creditor may not extend credit in the form of a higher-risk mortgage to any consumer without first obtaining a written appraisal of the property to be mortgaged prepared in accordance with the requirements of this section.

(b) Appraisal requirements

(1) Physical property visit

Subject to the rules prescribed under paragraph (4), an appraisal of property to be secured by a higher-risk mortgage does not meet the requirement of this section unless it is performed by a certified or licensed appraiser who conducts a physical property visit of the interior of the mortgaged property.

(2) Second appraisal under certain circumstances

(A) In general

If the purpose of a higher-risk mortgage is to finance the purchase or acquisition of the mortgaged property from a person within 180 days of the purchase or acquisition of such property by that person at a price that was lower than the current sale price of the property, the creditor shall obtain a second appraisal from a different certified or licensed appraiser. The second appraisal shall include an analysis of the difference in sale prices, changes in market conditions, and any improvements made to the property between the date of the previous sale and the current sale.

(B) No cost to applicant

The cost of any second appraisal required under subparagraph (A) may not be charged to the applicant.

(3) Certified or licensed appraiser defined

For purposes of this section, the term "certified or licensed appraiser" means a person who–

(A) is, at a minimum, certified or licensed by the State in which the property to be appraised is located; and

(B) performs each appraisal in conformity with the Uniform Standards of Professional Appraisal Practice and title XI of the Financial Institutions Reform, Recovery, and Enforcement Act of 1989, and the regulations prescribed under such title, as in effect on the date of the appraisal.

Real Estate Settlement Procedures Act 12 U.S.C. § 2601 *et seq.* (Excerpts)

2601. Congressional Findings and Purpose

(a) It is the purpose of this chapter to effect certain changes in the settlement process for residential real estate that will result—

(1) in more effective advance disclosure to home buyers and sellers of settlement costs;

(2) in the elimination of kickbacks or referral fees that tend to increase unnecessarily the costs of certain settlement services;

(3) in a reduction in the amounts home buyers are required to place in escrow accounts established to insure the payment of real estate taxes and insurance; and

(4) in significant reform and modernization of local recordkeeping of land title information.

2602. Definitions

For purposes of this chapter—

(1) the term "federally related mortgage loan" includes any loan (other than temporary financing such as a construction loan) which—

(A) is secured by a first or subordinate lien on residential real property (including individual units of condominiums and cooperatives) designed principally for the occupancy of from one to four families, including any such secured loan, the proceeds of which are used to prepay or pay off an existing loan secured by the same property; and

(B) (i) is made in whole or in part by any lender the deposits or accounts of which are insured by any agency of the Federal Government, or is made in whole or in part by any lender which is regulated by any agency of the Federal Government, or

(ii) is made in whole or in part, or insured, guaranteed, supplemented, or assisted in any way, by the Secretary or any other officer or agency of the Federal Government or under or in connection with a housing or urban development program administered by the Secretary or a housing or related program administered by any other such officer or agency; or

(iii) is intended to be sold by the originating lender to the Federal National Mortgage Association, the Government National Mortgage Association, the Federal Home Loan Mortgage Corporation, or a financial institution from which it is to be purchased by the Federal Home Loan Mortgage Corporation; or

(iv) is made in whole or in part by any "creditor", as defined in section 1602(f) of Title 15, who makes or invests in residential real estate loans aggregating more than

$1,000,000 per year, except that for the purpose of this chapter, the term "creditor" does not include any agency or instrumentality of any State;

(2) the term "thing of value" includes any payment, advance, funds, loan, service, or other consideration;

(3) the term "settlement services" includes any service provided in connection with a real estate settlement including, but not limited to, the following: title searches, title examinations, the provision of title certificates, title insurance, services rendered by an attorney, the preparation of documents, property surveys, the rendering of credit reports or appraisals, pest and fungus inspections, services rendered by a real estate agent or broker, the origination of a federally related mortgage loan (including, but not limited to, the taking of loan applications, loan processing, and the underwriting and funding of loans), and the handling of the processing, and closing or settlement;

(4) the term "title company" means any institution which is qualified to issue title insurance, directly or through its agents, and also refers to any duly authorized agent of a title company;

(5) the term "person" includes individuals, corporations, associations, partnerships, and trusts;

(6) the term "Secretary" means the Secretary of Housing and Urban Development;

(7) the term "affiliated business arrangement" means an arrangement in which (A) a person who is in a position to refer business incident to or a part of a real estate settlement service involving a federally related mortgage loan, or an associate of such person, has either an affiliate relationship with or a direct or beneficial ownership interest of more than 1 percent in a provider of settlement services; and (B) either of such persons directly or indirectly refers such business to that provider or affirmatively influences the selection of that provider; and

(8) the term "associate" means one who has one or more of the following relationships with a person in a position to refer settlement business: (A) a spouse, parent, or child of such person; (B) a corporation or business entity that controls, is controlled by, or is under common control with such person; (C) an employer, officer, director, partner, franchisor, or franchisee of such person; or (D) anyone who has an agreement, arrangement, or understanding, with such person, the purpose or substantial effect of which is to enable the person in a position to refer settlement business to benefit financially from the referrals of such business.

2603. Uniform Settlement Statement

12 U.S.C. § 2603. Uniform settlement statement

(a) The Bureau shall publish a single, integrated disclosure for mortgage loan transactions (including real estate settlement cost statements) which includes the disclosure requirements of this section and section 2604 of this title, in conjunction with the disclosure requirements of the Truth in Lending Act that, taken together, may apply to a transaction that is subject to both or either provisions of law. The purpose of such model disclosure shall be to facilitate compliance with the disclosure requirements of this chapter and the Truth in Lending Act, and to aid the borrower or lessee in understanding the transaction by utilizing readily understandable language to simplify the technical nature of the disclosures. Such forms shall conspicuously and clearly itemize all charges imposed upon the borrower and all charges imposed upon the seller in connection with the settlement and shall indicate whether any title insurance premium included in such charges covers or insures the lender's interest in the property, the borrower's interest, or both. The Bureau may, by regulation, permit the deletion from the forms prescribed under this section of items which are not, under local laws or customs, applicable in any locality, except that such regulation shall require that the numerical code prescribed by the Bureau be retained in forms to be used in all localities. Nothing in this section may be construed to require that that part of the standard forms which relates to the borrower's transaction be furnished to the seller, or to require that that part of the standard forms which relates to the seller be furnished to the borrower.

(b) The forms prescribed under this section shall be completed and made available for inspection by the borrower at or before settlement by the person conducting the settlement, except that (1) the Bureau may exempt from the requirements of this section settlements occurring in localities where the final settlement statement is not customarily provided at or before the date of settlement, or settlements where such requirements are impractical and (2) the borrower may, in accordance with regulations of the Bureau, waive his right to have the forms made available at such time. Upon the request of the borrower to inspect the forms prescribed under this section during the business day immediately preceding the day of settlement, the person who will conduct the settlement shall permit the borrower to inspect those items which are known to such person during such preceding day.

§ 2604. Special information booklets

(a) Distribution by Bureau to lenders to help borrowers

The Bureau shall prepare and distribute booklets jointly addressing compliance with the requirements of the Truth in Lending Act and the provisions of this title, in order to help persons borrowing money to finance the purchase of residential real estate better to understand the nature and costs of real estate settlement services. The Bureau shall distribute such booklets to all lenders which make federally related mortgage loans.

(b) Form and detail; cost elements, standard settlement form, escrow accounts, selection of persons for settlement services; consideration of differences in settlement procedures

Each booklet shall be in such form and detail as the Bureau shall prescribe and, in addition to such other information as the Bureau may provide, shall include in clear and concise language–

(1) a description and explanation of the nature and purpose of each cost incident to a real estate settlement;

(2) an explanation and sample of the standard real estate settlement form developed and prescribed under section 2603 of this title;

(3) a description and explanation of the nature and purpose of escrow accounts when used in connection with loans secured by residential real estate;

(4) an explanation of the choices available to buyers of residential real estate in selecting persons to provide necessary services incident to a real estate settlement; and

(5) an explanation of the unfair practices and unreasonable or unnecessary charges to be avoided by the prospective buyer with respect to a real estate settlement.

Such booklets shall take into consideration differences in real estate settlement procedures which may exist among the several States and territories of the United States and among separate political subdivisions within the same State and territory.

(c) Estimate of charges

Each lender shall include with the booklet a good faith estimate of the amount or range of charges for specific settlement services the borrower is likely to incur in connection with the settlement as prescribed by the Bureau.

(d) Distribution by lenders to loan applicants at time of receipt or preparation of applications

Each lender referred to in subsection (a) of this section shall provide the booklet described in such subsection to each person from whom it receives or for whom it prepares a written application to borrow money to finance the purchase of residential real estate. Such booklet shall be provided by delivering it or placing it in the mail not later than 3 business days after the lender receives the application, but no booklet need be provided if the lender denies the application for credit before the end of the 3-day period.

(e) Printing and distribution by lenders of booklets approved by Bureau

Booklets may be printed and distributed by lenders if their form and content are approved by the Bureau as meeting the requirements of subsection (b) of this section.

§ 2605. Servicing of mortgage loans and administration of escrow accounts

(a) Disclosure to applicant relating to assignment, sale, or transfer of loan servicing

Each person who makes a federally related mortgage loan shall disclose to each person who applies for the loan, at the time of application for the loan, whether the servicing of the loan may be assigned, sold, or transferred to any other person at any time while the loan is outstanding.

(b) Notice by transferor of loan servicing at time of transfer

(1) Notice requirement

Each servicer of any federally related mortgage loan shall notify the borrower in writing of any assignment, sale, or transfer of the servicing of the loan to any other person.

(2) Time of notice

(A) In general

Except as provided under subparagraphs (B) and (C), the notice required under paragraph (1) shall be made to the borrower not less than 15 days before the effective date of transfer of the servicing of the mortgage loan (with respect to which such notice is made).

(3) Contents of notice

The notice required under paragraph (1) shall include the following information:

(A) The effective date of transfer of the servicing described in such paragraph.

(B) The name, address, and toll-free or collect call telephone number of the transferee servicer.

(C) A toll-free or collect call telephone number for (i) an individual employed by the transferor servicer, or (ii) the department of the transferor servicer,

that can be contacted by the borrower to answer inquiries relating to the transfer of servicing.

2607. Prohibition Against Kickbacks and Unearned Fees

(a) Business referrals

No person shall give and no person shall accept any fee, kickback, or thing of value pursuant to any agreement or understanding, oral or otherwise, that business incident to or a part of a real estate settlement service involving a federally related mortgage loan shall be referred to any person.

(b) Splitting charges

No person shall give and no person shall accept any portion, split, or percentage of any charge made or received for the rendering of a real estate settlement service in connection with a transaction involving a federally related mortgage loan other than for services actually performed.

(c) Fees, salaries, compensation, or other payments

Nothing in this section shall be construed as prohibiting (1) the payment of a fee (A) to attorneys at law for services actually rendered or (B) by a title company to its duly appointed agent for services actually performed in the issuance of a policy of title insurance or (C) by a lender to its duly appointed agent for services actually performed in the making of a loan, (2) the payment to any person of a bona fide salary or compensation or other payment for goods or facilities actually furnished or for services actually performed, (3) payments pursuant to cooperative brokerage and referral arrangements or agreements between real estate agents and brokers, (4) affiliated business arrangements so long as (A) a disclosure is made of the existence of such an arrangement to the person being referred and, in connection with such referral, such person is provided a written estimate of the charge or range of charges generally made by the provider to which the person is referred (i) in the case of a face-to-face referral or a referral made in writing or by electronic media, at or before the time of the referral (and compliance with this requirement in such case may be evidenced by a notation in a written, electronic, or similar system of records maintained in the regular course of business); (ii) in the case of a referral made by telephone,[1] within 3 business days after the referral by telephone, (and in such case an abbreviated verbal disclosure of the existence of the arrangement and the fact that a written disclosure will be provided within 3 business days shall be made to the person being referred during the telephone referral); or (iii) in the case of a referral by a lender (including a referral by a lender to an affiliated lender), at the time the estimates required under section 2604(c) of this title are provided (notwithstanding clause (i) or (ii)); and any required written receipt of such disclosure (without regard to the manner of the disclosure under clause (i), (ii), or (iii)) may be obtained at the closing or settlement (except that a person making a face-to-face referral who provides the written disclosure at or before the time of the referral shall attempt to obtain any required written receipt of such disclosure at such time and if the person being referred chooses not to acknowledge the receipt of the disclosure at that time, that fact shall be noted in the written, electronic, or similar system of records maintained in the regular course of business by the person making the referral), (B) such person is not required to use any particular provider of settlement services, and (C) the only thing of value that is received from the arrangement, other than the payments permitted under this subsection, is a return on the ownership interest or franchise relationship, or (5) such other payments or classes of payments or other transfers as are specified in regulations prescribed by the Secretary, after consultation with the Attorney General, the Secretary of Veterans Affairs, the Federal Home Loan Bank Board, the Federal Deposit Insurance Corporation, the Board of Governors of the Federal Reserve System, and the Secretary of Agriculture. For purposes of the preceding sentence, the following shall not be considered a violation of clause (4)(B): (i) any arrangement that requires a buyer, borrower, or seller to pay for the services of an attorney, credit reporting agency, or real estate appraiser chosen by the lender to represent the lender's interest in a real estate transaction, or (ii) any arrangement where an attorney or law firm represents a client in a real estate transaction and issues or arranges for the issuance of a policy of title insurance in the transaction directly as agent or through a separate corporate title insurance agency that may be established by that attorney or law firm and operated as an adjunct to his or its law practice.

(d) Penalties for violations; joint and several liability; treble damages; actions for injunction by Secretary and by State officials; costs and attorney fees; construction of State laws

(1) Any person or persons who violate the provisions of this section shall be fined not more than $10,000 or imprisoned for not more than one year, or both.

(2) Any person or persons who violate the prohibitions or limitations of this section shall be jointly and severally liable to the person or persons charged for the settlement service involved in the violation in an amount equal to three times the amount of any charge paid for such settlement service.

(3) No person or persons shall be liable for a violation of the provisions of subsection (c)(4)(A) of this section if such person or persons proves by a preponderance of the evidence that such violation was not intentional and resulted from a bona fide error notwithstanding maintenance of procedures that are reasonably adapted to avoid such error.

(4) The Bureau, the Secretary, or the attorney general or the insurance commissioner of any State may bring an action to enjoin violations of this section. Except, to the extent that a person is subject to the jurisdiction of the Bureau, the Secretary, or the attorney general or the insurance commissioner of any State, the Bureau shall have primary authority to enforce or administer this section, subject to subtitle B of the Consumer Financial Protection Act of 2010.

Glossary

A

Abstract of title   A concise statement of the substance of documents or facts appearing on the public land records that affects the title to a particular tract.

Abstractor's certificate   A summary by the abstractors of what was and was not examined in the title review.

Acceleration clause   Provision in note, mortgage, or deed of trust that provides for the acceleration of the due date of the loan; generally results in the full amount of the loan being due upon default such as nonpayment.

Acceptance   Action of offeree in agreeing to terms of an offer that results in a binding contract.

Acknowledgment   Notary signature and seal; appears on deeds and some contracts as well as on wills.

Acknowledgment clause   Language that precedes notary verification of signatures and identification of signatories.

Acquisition indebtedness   For tax purposes, determination of qualified residential interest; the amount of debt entered into for purchase of a primary or secondary residence.

Action for dispossession   Court proceeding by landlord to have tenant removed from property; generally brought for nonpayment of rent or destruction of landlord's premises.

Active income   For income tax purposes, income earned as wages or other forms of compensation for work/services performed.

Ad valorem tax   Tax based on value that increases as value increases. Property taxes are *ad valorem* taxes.

Ademption   In testate distribution, the failure of a gift if the property is no longer owned by the testator at the time of death.

Adjustable rate mortgage (ARM)   A type of mortgage with a rate that changes according to some interest-rate index.

Administrator   Male party responsible for the probate of an intestate estate.

Administratrix   Female party responsible for the probate of an intestate estate; antiquated.

Advancements   Common law doctrine that subtracts amounts of *inter vivos* gifts from an heir's share of decedent's estate (still followed in some states).

Adverse possession   Method of acquiring title to land by openly taking possession of and using another's property for a certain period of time.

Advertisement   Under Regulation Z, public disclosure of credit terms.

Aesthetic zoning   Zoning that regulates the appearance of property and exists for beautification purposes or architectural uniformity.

Affirmative easement   An easement that involves the use of another's property; e.g., a right of access.

After-acquired property clause   Mortgage, note, or security interest provision that provides that the security for the loan includes the existing property and any property added after the note; mortgage security interest is attached to newly acquired property.

Agent   One who acts on another's behalf. In real estate, the agent is the party who works to bring the buyers and sellers of real estate together in exchange for payment (generally a commission).

Air lot   That portion of the airspace from 23 feet above the Earth's surface to the heavens.

Air Pollution Control Act   The original federal act relating to air pollution; provided for studies but did little to control air pollution (1955).

Air rights   Property ownership rights in the air above the surface.

All-adult covenant   Deed restriction that limits residency in a particular area to certain ages and prohibits residency of children less than a certain age.

American Recovery and Reinvestment Act (ARRA) of 2009
Federal law that provided funding for infrastructure and had the goal of economic recovery.

Americans with Disabilities Act (ADA)   1990 federal law prohibiting discrimination on the basis of disability and requiring reasonable accommodation by employers and landowners.

Anaconda mortgage   (also known as a **dragnet mortgage**) Mortgage covering all debt owed by the mortgagor to the mortgagee.

Anchor tenant   The tenant in a shopping center that leases the largest space and will draw the greatest amount of traffic; e.g., grocery store in a plaza or major department store in a mall.

Annexation   Taking in an area of land as part of a governmental unit (city, town, or county). Many subdivisions are annexed before they are developed.

Antenuptial agreements   Premarital contracts in which the spouses-to-be waive their interests in each other's properties that will be accumulated during the course of the marriage.

Architect   Participant in the construction process; may oversee quality of subcontractors' work and issue lien waivers.

Article 9   Section of the Uniform Commercial Code that governs security interests in personal property and fixtures.

Articles of incorporation   Document used to create a corporation.

Articles of limited partnership   Document used to create a limited partnership.

Articles of partnership   Document used to create a partnership.

As is   Clause in contract that waives any warranty protection.

Asbestos Hazard Emergency Response Act (AHERA)   Federal law that mandates inspection of facilities receiving federal funds to determine presence of asbestos and asbestos fibers.

Assessment   Process whereby a tax amount is assigned to a parcel of real estate on the basis of the value of the parcel.

Assessor   Public official responsible for the valuation and assessment of real property and the subsequent collection of taxes.

Asset Conservation, Lender Liability, and Deposit Insurance Protection Act of 1996   Federal law that clarifies the liability of lenders on real property pledged as security for a loan.

Assignments   Process of transferring contract rights to another; e.g., assignment of a mortgage or lease.

Assumption   Process whereby a buyer of real property agrees to assume responsibility for payments on an existing mortgage on the property.

At-risk rules   Under the Internal Revenue Code, a restriction on taking losses that requires those taking the loss to have funds at risk in the operation of the business.

Attached homes   A form of multiunit housing; each generally has common walls with other homes.

B

Balloon payment   Provision in a mortgage or mortgage note that calls for the payment of a large lump sum at the end of the mortgage period.

Balloon payment clause   Clause in mortgage that requires a large payment at one time to satisfy the debt obligation.

Baselines   In the United States Government Survey, the major east–west guidelines.

Basis   Property owner's cost of property; used for computing gain or loss on the sale of property.

Bequest   A gift of personal property by will.

Best available treatment (BAT)   The highest standard the EPA can impose for the control of water pollution.

Best conventional treatment (BCT)   A standard for water pollution control that requires a firm to follow the best commonly used treatment methods; a standard that is lower than best available treatment.

Bid bond   Guarantor of bid submitted on construction project that guarantees bidder will do work at price bid.

Bid notice   Call for bids on a project by a contractor.

Blockbusting   Illegal racial discrimination practice wherein real estate brokers attempt (by encouraging listings and sales in a neighborhood) to change the racial composition of a neighborhood.

Board of adjustment   Governmental entity (usually at city or county level) that is responsible for approving variances and adjustments.

Bona fide purchaser (BFP)   Good faith purchaser.

Bounds   See *Metes and bounds description.*

Broker   Party who is licensed to handle property listings.

Brownfields   Land sites that are undeveloped due to contamination and/or designation as a Superfund site.

Brundage clause   Provision in a mortgage that calls for the mortgagor to pay all taxes on the property.

Bubble concept   EPA concept of examining all air pollutants in an area as if they came from a single source; this concept is used in making a decision regarding the possibility of a new plant in the area.

Builder   See *General contractor.*

Business judgment rule   Standard for imposing liability on directors of corporation; they must give time and thought to decisions.

Bylaws   In multiunit housing, the document governing the details of operation; voting rights of members, meetings, notices, etc.

C

Capital gain   The amount of a net gain made on the sale of property; carries a special lower tax rate.

Caption   The legal description in an abstract.

Case precedent   Doctrine of *stare decisis;* examining prior decisions to reach decisions in present cases.

Cash-to-mortgage sale   Sale of real property in which the buyer pays the difference between the sales price and the mortgage balance and then takes over the mortgage (assumption).

Centerline rule   Rule that provides landowners with adjoining streams and rivers ownership of the land beneath these waters to the centerline of the river or stream.

Change order   In construction contracts, a change in work, design, or materials.

Citation   Legal shorthand referring to cases, statutes, regulations, and ordinances.

Cite   See *Citation*.

Clean Air Act   One of the original air pollution statutes that gave HEW authority to monitor interstate pollution problems.

Clean Air Act Amendments of 1990   First major revisions to Clean Air Act with coverage of acid rain and vehicle emissions and provision of new deadlines for SIPs.

Clean Water Act   Major federal statute on water pollution that gave the federal government authority and control.

Cleaning deposit   The amount in a lease that a tenant is required to pay prior to commencement of the lease to cover the cleaning of the premises when the tenant has gone; under URLTA, the lease must state if this deposit is nonrefundable.

Code of Federal Regulations (CFR)   Compilation of regulations of federal agencies.

Codicil   An addendum to a will.

Column lot   Portion of air rights from the surface of the Earth to 23 feet above the surface.

Common area maintenance (CAM)   Fee charged to tenant in commercial leases to pay costs of maintenance of sidewalks in shopping and other commercial centers; fee is often a pro rata share of expenses based on that paid in other commercial projects.

Common law   Uncodified law found in cases or in the history of real property.

Community property   Method of married persons' co-ownership of property; limited to certain states.

Community property states   States that have marital property systems based on the Spanish system.

Community property with right of survivorship   Relatively new form of marital property ownership that has a couple owning the property subject to their marital interests while alive, with automatic vesting in surviving spouse upon death of one spouse.

Community Reinvestment Act (CRA)   Federal law establishing record-keeping requirements for lenders' investments in inner-city areas.

Community-Right-to-Know substance   Federal disclosure law requiring notification of presence of toxic substance on property, including items such as asbestos.

Comprehensive Environmental Response, Compensation, and Liability Act (CERCLA)   The Superfund; a program for private payment by polluting industries for cleanup of toxic waste.

Condition precedent   In a contract, a requirement before the contract can be performed; e.g., delivering marketable title or qualifying for financing.

Condominium   Form of multiunit housing in which the owner owns the area between the walls and ceiling.

Consent statutes   Statutes that permit the attachment of a lien if the property owner consented to the work done by the lienor even though there was no direct contract with the owner.

Conservation easement   A negative easement given by a property owner that provides that the property will not be used in such a way as to destroy a historic site on the property.

Consideration   The detriment given by each party to the contract; *e.g.*, the land conveyed by the seller and the money paid by the buyer.

Construction lender   Party serving as financier for a project during construction.

Constructive delivery   Delivery other than direct delivery to the person; delivering by precluding access by all others.

Constructive eviction   Process whereby a tenant is forced to leave leased premises because the premises are in a state of disrepair and uninhabitable.

Consumer Price Index (CPI) adjustment clause   Clause that allows for rent increases when the CPI changes.

Contingent remainder   Future interest that follows a life estate and that is not certain to follow or has unknown takers.

Contract for deed   Another name for an installment contract; financing transaction in which seller carries the buyer and holds onto title until the buyer has paid in full.

Contract statutes   With references to liens, statutes that require lienors to have a direct contractual agreement with property owners to be able to place a lien on property on which work was performed.

Contractual lien   Liens that arise because of a contractual agreement between the lienor and the owner of the liened property.

Conventional mortgage   Mortgage not insured by a government agency.

Conventional pollutants   One of the categories of water pollutants of the EPA; subject to the least amount of restriction and regulation.

Conversion restrictions   Laws that regulate the conversion of leased premises into multiunit houses to afford protection for the existing tenants.

Cooperative   Form of multiunit housing in which a corporation owns the property and owners of the shares in the corporation live in each of the units.

Co-ownership   Label given to ownership of property by more than one person.

Cost approach   Tax appraisal method that bases value of the property on its original cost plus costs of improvement.

Cost-plus formula In construction, a method of pricing in which the contractor charges all costs plus a profit margin.

Council on Environmental Quality (CEQ) Established in 1966 by the National Environment Protection Act as part of the executive branch of government and given the responsibility of formulating national policies on the quality of the environment and making recommendations to lawmakers based on its policies.

Counteroffer Offer made in response to offeror by the offeree; can occur by a change in the offeror's terms.

Covenant Promise in a deed that affects or limits the use of the conveyed property.

Cumulative classification Zoning system that permits higher uses in lower-use areas; e.g., residential uses in commercially zoned areas.

Curtesy rights Right of husband to a life estate in all real property owned by his wife during their marriage provided they had children.

D

Declaration of condominium Master deed for condominium project; the document recorded to reflect the units involved on the real property. See also *Declaration of horizontal property regime and covenants.*

Declaration of covenants, conditions, and restrictions (CC&Rs or CCRs) The restrictions and limitations on the use and construction of land.

Declaration of horizontal property regime and covenants Another name for the declaration of condominium; multiunit housing is often referred to as *horizontal housing regimes.* The master deed recorded to reflect the existence of the multiunit housing and the location and number of units on the property.

Deed Instrument used to convey title to real property.

Deed in lieu of foreclosure Process of borrower's/property owner's/mortgagor's surrendering title to property to prevent lender's foreclosure.

Deed of bargain and sale A deed with warranty protection limited to the time of the grantor's ownership; see *Special warranty deed.*

Deed of trust Security interest in real property in which title is held by a trustee until the borrower and occupant of the land repays the beneficiary (lender) the amount of the loan.

Deed restrictions Provisions usually recorded for subdivisions; the CCRs; restrictions on the use, development, and construction of the premises.

Default Failure to comply with mortgage or promissory note requirements; generally a failure to pay or obtain insurance.

Deficiency judgment Judgment against the mortgagor or borrower after foreclosure sale, requiring payment of the amount due on the loan that was not obtained through sale of the mortgaged property.

Delivery Requirement for gifts and transfers of property by deed that mandates some form of actual or constructive possession by the grantee.

Department of Housing and Urban Development (HUD) Federal agency responsible for regulation of interstate land sales and other federal acts affecting real property.

Depreciation Wear and tear on property; can be deducted each year and used to offset income earned on income-producing property; greatly limited under Tax Reform Act.

Designated agency Agency relationship in which seller names agent to act on his/her behalf in closing transaction.

Devise Gift of real property by will.

Devisee Recipient of real property gift by will.

Disinheritance Process of leaving an heir out of a will; not giving anything to someone who would ordinarily receive a share of the estate if there were an intestate distribution.

Doctrine of Ancient Lights Theory that originated in England that provides right to light if so used for 20 years or more; this prescriptive form of rights is no longer followed in the United States.

Doctrine of Correlative Rights Term in oil and gas law that limits recovery of oil and gas in situations where others' rights or deposits would be destroyed.

Doctrine of Emblements In landlord/tenant relationship, the right of the tenant to remove crops from the leased premises even after the lease expires if the tenant is responsible for their production.

Doctrine of Worthier Title Principle of common law that gives a grantee the full fee simple title when the grant is made "to grantee with remainder to the heirs of the grantee;" the two estates are merged into a fee simple estate for the grantee.

Dominant estate A property owner who holds an appurtenant easement in another's property; the land enjoying the benefit of an easement through another's property.

Dominant tenement See *Dominant estate.*

Donee Recipient of a gift.

Donor One who makes a gift.

Dower rights Rights of widow in husband's estate; not applicable in all states.

Dual agency Agency relationship in which broker represents both the buyer and the seller.

Due-on-sale clause Clause in mortgage or mortgage note that requires full payment of the loan when the property is sold; in effect, a prohibition on assumptions.

E

Earnest money Deposit given by buyer on signing a contract for the purchase of property.

Easement Right to use another's property for access, light, and so on.

Easement appurtenant   Easement that benefits a particular tract of land; generally an access easement or right-of-way.

Easement by express grant   Easement given in a deed by the original landowner to provide a means of access for the purchaser of one part of the land.

Easement by express reservation   Easement reserved in a deed by the original landowner to provide a means of access across a purchaser's land.

Easement by implication   Easement that arises based on need because of previous use of the property in the same manner when the property was owned in a single tract.

Easement by necessity   Easement given by circumstances that require it; the property is inaccessible or unusable without it.

Easement in gross   An easement that does not benefit a particular tract of land; e.g., utility easements that run through all parcels of land in an area.

Effluent guidelines   EPA standards for release of materials into waterways.

Emblements   With regard to leases, the right of the tenant to harvest growing crops even after the lease has terminated if the tenant was responsible for growing the crops.

Emergency Economic Stabilization Act   Federal law passed in the fall of 2008 as a means of stabilizing financial firms with federal funds infusion.

Eminent domain   Process of governmental entity's taking title to private property for public purposes.

Emissions Offset Policy   EPA policy of requiring a reduction of other pollution sources in the area to allow the operation of a new plant and source of emissions.

Endangered Species Act (ESA)   Federal law that affords protection for habitats of species designated as endangered; requires biological evaluation of impact of development and projects on species population.

Environmental contingency clauses   Provisions in contracts that provide buyers with the right to rescind the contract if environmental hazards that cannot be cleared arise during the course of a due diligence search.

Environmental impact statement (EIS)   Report required to be filed when a governmental agency is taking action that will have an effect on the environment; e.g., construction of a dam by the Army Corps of Engineers.

Environmental Protection Agency (EPA)   Governmental agency responsible for the enforcement of environmental laws.

Equal Credit Opportunity Act (ECOA)   Federal law prohibiting discrimination in credit decisions.

Equal Protection Clause   Part of the Fifth and Fourteenth Amendments to the Constitution; requires that laws apply equally to all.

Equitable lien   Lien created as a result of a mortgage arrangement; also referred to as a *contractual lien*.

Equitable relief   Court remedies that require parties to perform certain acts or specifically perform a contract.

Equitable servitudes   Restriction on land use arising because an area has a common scheme or development that puts buyers on notice that particular uses and construction are required or prohibited.

Equity-participation financing   Creative financing technique in which the lender will share in the appreciation of the property and will be entitled to a portion of the equity on sale of the mortgaged property.

Errors and omissions insurance   Professional liability insurance for brokers and agents.

Escalation clause   Clause generally in a lease, providing for increasing rent.

Escheat   Process whereby property of a decedent is given to the state because no heirs are available.

Escrow   Process whereby details of property transfer, payments, and deed conveyance are handled by a third party.

Escrow instructions   Contract between buyer, seller, and escrow agent for the closing of escrow on a property transfer.

Exclusionary zoning   Zoning that prohibits certain types of businesses, activities, or housing in certain areas.

Exclusive agency listing   Listing agreement that requires the seller to pay the commission to the broker only if the listing broker sells the property; the seller may sell the property independently and not be required to pay a commission.

Exclusive right-to-sell/listing-to-sell   Listing that requires the seller to pay the broker/agent a commission regardless of who obtains a buyer for the property.

Executor   Male party responsible for the probate of a decedent's estate pursuant to the decedent's will.

Executory interest   Future interest that is not a remainder and not an interest in the grantor.

Executrix   Female party responsible for the probate of a decedent's estate pursuant to the decedent's will.

F

Federal Consumer Credit Protection Act   Federal law requiring disclosures, billing practices, and rights in consumer credit transactions.

Federal Deposit Insurance Corporation (FDIC)   Federal agency that regulates savings and loan institutions.

Federal Environmental Pesticide Control Act   Federal law regulating the manufacture, containment, labeling, transportation, and use of pesticides.

Federal Home Loan Mortgage Corporation (FHLMC or Freddie Mac)   Federal/quasi private corporation that provides secondary mortgage market support.

Federal Housing Finance Agency (FHFA) Federal oversight agency for government housing and subsidies.

Federal National Mortgage Association (FNMA or Fannie Mae) Government corporation that purchases mortgages on the market.

Federal Water Pollution Control Act of 1972 Federal law that was the first anti–water pollution law with enforcement and details.

Federal Water Pollution Control Administration (FWPCA) Originally the agency responsible for developing and enforcing water pollution control; merged into EPA in 1975.

Fee An inheritable interest in land.

Fee interest In oil and gas ownership, owner owns both the surface and subsurface rights.

Fee simple Highest land interest; full title; right to convey or transfer by will or mortgage without restriction.

Fee simple absolute Another term for a fee simple.

Fee simple defeasible A fee simple estate that can be lost by violation of a condition or use restriction placed in the transfer by the grantor.

Fee simple determinable Full title to land so long as certain conduct is avoided; e.g., "To A so long as the premises are never used for a bar."

Fee simple subject to a condition subsequent Full title provided that there is compliance with a condition; e.g., "To A upon the condition that the property is used for school purposes."

Fee tail Full title restricted in its passage to direct descendants of the owner.

FHA Federal agency that provides a market for lower-rate consumer home mortgages and governs the terms and conditions for those loans if the lender desires to sell loans through FHA.

Fifth Amendment Provision in United States Constitution that provides guarantee of due process.

Financial Institutions Reform, Recovery, and Enforcement Act (FIRREA) of 1989 Federal law that followed the savings and loan debacle; implements controls on bank lending practices on real estate, including appraisals.

Financing statement Document filed to protect a security interest; must contain information about the parties and a description of the collateral.

Fixed rent In shopping center and commercial leases, rental standard of paying net rent (after utility costs or other fees specific in lease).

Fixture Personal property that becomes attached to and is so closely associated with real property that it becomes a part of the real property.

Flippers Housing investors who sell one property and use the proceeds as the down payment on another property closing at the same time.

Flow-down clause Clause in a construction contract that does not require the general contractor to pay subcontractors and suppliers until the owner has paid the general contractor.

Forcible detainer Action by landlord for rent; requires tenant to pay or be evicted by court order.

Foreclosure Process of selling mortgaged property to satisfy the debt owed by the defaulting mortgagor.

Foreclosure by advertisement (notice of sale) Creditor's remedy of sale by providing public notice; used in deeds of trust.

Forfeiture Loss of rights; in a contract for deed, the loss of all interest in the property for nonpayment.

Fourteenth Amendment Application of due process rights to the states (including the Equal Protection Clause), which requires uniform application of laws and nondiscrimination; applied in cases in which land conveyances attempt to include racial restrictions.

Freehold An interest in land that is uncertain or unlimited in duration.

Fructus industriales Vegetation that grows on property as result of work of owner or tenant; i.e., crops.

Fructus naturales Vegetation that grows naturally on property; not the result of efforts of the owner or tenant.

FWPCA See *Federal Water Pollution Control Administration.*

G

Garden homes Form of multiunit housing; usually a townhouse that includes a small enclosed yard or patio.

General contractor In a construction project, the party responsible for the construction; can hire subcontractors and suppliers but bears ultimate responsibility; has direct contractual relationship with owner, construction lender, or both.

General partner Investor with full personal liability for partnership debt.

General partnership Voluntary association of two or more persons as co-owners in a business for profit.

General plan Development plan and zoning areas as developed by city or county; provides zoning designations for all areas within the municipality or county.

Geothermal energy Form of energy that is the result of naturally formed pockets of hot steam; can be a mineral right.

Good-faith purchaser Buyer who buys property with no knowledge (constructive or actual) of any title defects, liens, or other problems other than those specifically disclosed by the seller; also called *bfp* or *bona fide purchaser.*

Grantor/grantee index system Method of record keeping for land transactions; all transactions are recorded under the name of both the grantor and grantee to permit title to be traced according to the transfers among parties.

Grid The 24-mile square created between each guide meridian and parallel in the United States Government survey.

Gross rent   Flat rent in commercial lease; no percentage of profits.

Guarantors   Parties who agree to stand liable if a debtor defaults.

Guide meridians   Vertical lines placed every 24 miles on the United States Government Survey; intersect with parallels to create 24-mile squares used for describing land parcels.

H

Habendum clause   Clause in deed indicating the type of land interest being conveyed; in mineral lease, a clause that establishes the length of the lease, the grounds for termination, and drilling delay penalties.

Hazardous Substance Response Trust Fund   Fund created under federal environmental laws; known as the Superfund for use in cleanup of toxic waste.

Hold zoning   Interim zoning adopted prior to the time of the finalized general plan.

Holographic will   Will entirely in the handwriting of the testator and signed by the testator (valid in some states).

Home equity indebtedness   Consumer debt secured by residence of debtor; includes mortgage, other loans, and lines of credit.

Home Mortgage Disclosure Act   Federal law mandating disclosure on consumer loans for second mortgages on residential property.

Homestead exemption   Debtor protection that entitles the debtor to a certain amount in real property that is exempt from attachment by creditors.

Horizontal property acts or regimes   Multiunit housing laws that govern forms of housing such as condominiums, cooperatives, and townhouses.

Housing Economic Recovery Act of 2008 (HERA)   Federal law that provides assistance for homeowners in the renegotiation of their mortgage loans.

HUD-1 Settlement Statement   Federal document that includes specific disclosures on the funds required for closing a sale of property.

I

Impact fees   Fees paid by developers for schools and other public facilities needed because of additional population developer brings in with project.

Implied warranty of habitability   Implied warranty given by contractors of new homes to buyers; between landlord and tenant, the landlord's guaranty that the premises are fit for habitation and, if not, will be put into that condition.

Incentives for Self-Policing, Disclosure, Correction, and Prevention of Violations   EPA guidelines for company's voluntary audit for and disclosure of environmental violations.

Income approach   Tax appraisal method that bases value of the property on the income generated by the property.

Installment land contract   A contract for deed; method of selling property in which the seller serves as the financier for the buyer and the purchase; seller holds onto title until there has been payment in full under an installment payment plan.

Insurer   Party who indemnifies for loss.

Intensity zoning   Zoning laws that control the number of structures or degree of occupancy in a given area.

Inter vivos   During the life of; while alive; e.g., an *inter vivos* gift.

Inter vivos **gift**   Gift made while the donor is still alive.

Interest acceleration clauses   Clauses in notes that increase interest in the event of default.

Interest-only mortgage   Mortgage that requires initial payments that cover only the interest on the mortgage with no payments to principal.

Interim zoning   Hold zoning; temporary zoning before general plan is developed.

Intermediary   Another name for a statutory broker.

Internal Revenue Code (IRC)   Federal law governing income taxation.

Interstate Land Sales Full Disclosure Act (ILSFDA)   Federal law regulating the sale of property across state lines; requires advance filing of sales materials, mandatory disclosure of certain information, and prohibitions on promises about the land's future development.

Intestate   Death without a will.

Intestate succession   Statutory method for distributing the property of one who dies without a will (intestate).

Invitees   Parties who are specifically invited to enter another's property or are members of the public in a public place.

Involuntary lien   Lien that does not result from a contractual arrangement; e.g., a tax lien or a judicial lien.

J

Joint tenancy   Method of co-ownership that gives title to the property to the last survivor.

Joint will   Will made in conjunction with another's will; requires distribution of property in a certain way regardless of who dies first.

Judicial deed   Deed given by court after litigation of rights in the subject property.

Judicial foreclosure   Foreclosure accomplished by filing a petition with the proper court; not a power of sale.

Judicial lien   Lien on property that is the result of a judgment; lien to collect a court judgment.

Just compensation   In eminent domain, the requirement that landowners whose property is taken for public purposes be adequately paid for the loss of that property.

L

Lapse   In probate of a will, what happens when beneficiary dies prior to testator; the gift ends.

Laughing heir statutes   Statutes that limit the degree of relationship of relatives who can inherit property from an intestate; causes property to escheat to the state before a remote relative would inherit an intestate's estate.

Lease-purchase mortgage   Financing method that permits potential buyers to lease property for a period with an option to buy.

Legacy   Gift of money by will.

Legatee   Beneficiary/donee of gift of money by will.

Lender   See *Permanent lender.*

Lender liability   Doctrine that makes lenders liable for the lack of timely approval or withdrawal of an approval for financing already issued.

License   Revocable right to enter another's property.

Licensees   Parties who enter another's land with express or implied permission; e.g., a social guest.

Lien   Interest in real property that serves as security for repayment of a debt.

Lien theory   One theory of mortgages that gives the mortgagor title to the property and the mortgagee a lien on the property as security for debt repayment.

Lienee   Person whose property is subject to a lien.

Lienor   Party who places a lien on real property.

Life estate   Interest in land that lasts for the life of the grantee.

Life estate *pur autre vie*   Life estate that lasts for the length of some measuring life other than that of the grantee.

Life tenants   Those who hold a life estate in property.

Limited agent   Agent whose authority is limited in time or scope.

Limited Liability Company (LLC)   Business entity that is a cross between a corporation and a partnership.

Limited Liability Partnership (LLP)   Business entity that has limited liability for all partners (except for professional negligence of each).

Limited partner   Investor in limited partnership whose maximum liability is his/her capital investment.

Limited partnership   A partnership with at least one general partner in which limited partners can purchase interest, be liable only to the extent of their interests, and not risk personal liability.

Liquidated damages   Damages that are specified in formula or in amount in the written and signed agreement of the parties; must be reasonable.

Lis pendens   "Suit or action pending"; document recorded with the land records to indicate a suit involving the land is pending; filed in mortgage foreclosures and quiet title actions.

Listing agreement   Contract between a broker and landowner for the broker's services in helping to sell the owner's property.

Livery of seisin   English ceremony for passage of title; involved a physical transfer of a clod of earth between grantor and grantee.

Living trust   Trust created by settlor who is alive.

Living will   Term for authorization to take testator off life-support equipment recognized in many states but must use appropriate or required language and be formally executed.

Long-term land contract   See Contract for deed.

Low-income housing   Under Tax Reform Act of 1986, special housing category affording investors special tax treatment.

M

Market approach   Tax appraisal method that bases value of the property on prices of similar properties.

Marketable title   Form of title generally required to be delivered in the sale of property; property is free from liens and there are no defects in title other than those noted or agreed to.

Master deed   In a condominium development, the document recorded to reflect the location of the project and the individual units.

Master mortgage   Single mortgage document recorded for all loans and referenced to save recording fees.

Master plan   General plan for zoning.

Master-planned community   Large development project that involves construction of all facilities as well as housing.

Materials liens   Liens on property for the amount due for materials furnished to the owner or to others performing work on the land.

Maximum Accelerated Cost Recovery System (MACRS)   Under federal tax law, a method of depreciation.

Maximum achievable control technology (MACT)   Term under Clean Air Act Amendments of 1990; establishes standards for pollution control on utilities and other targeted industries for scrubbers and other antipollution devices.

Mechanic's liens   Liens placed on real property to secure amount due to those who performed work or supplied materials for improvements or other projects on the land.

Metes   See *Metes and bounds description.*

Metes and bounds description   Method of land description that begins with a permanent object and then through distances and directions describes the parcel of land.

Mineral interest   Ownership right to minerals on property; could also be a lease.

Mineral rights   Subsurface rights in property; the rights to mine minerals; also known as *mineral interest.*

Mineral servitude   Easement across the surface of the land for access to the land.

Misrepresentation   Giving incorrect or misleading information to a party in contract negotiations or failing to disclose relevant information; inaccurate information that would affect the buying or selling decision.

Model Business Corporation Act (MBCA)   Uniform law on corporations adopted in approximately one-third of the states.

Model Real Estate Cooperative Act   Model act on co-ops.

Model Real Estate Time-Share Act   Model act on time-share real property interests.

Monetary relief   Form of remedy for contract or trespass that awards money damages for breach.

Mortgage   Pledge of property as security for a loan.

Mortgage brokers   Agents who match borrowers with mortgage companies.

Mortgage Disclosure Improvement Act   Federal law that imposes additional requirements on the nature of mortgage payments, the interest rates, and any changes over the course of the mortgage loan.

Mortgage investment trusts (MITs)   Real estate syndication method that provides investment opportunity in pool of mortgages.

Mortgage Reform and Anti-Predatory Lending Act   Federal law that regulates subprime, title, and other types of high-interest/high-default/high-repossession rate loans; provides requirements for disclosures and processes for consumers who obtain these types of loans.

Mortgagee   Lender or party who holds the mortgage lien.

Mortgagor   Borrower or party occupying land that is mortgaged.

Multiple listing   A listing that appears on more than one broker's inventory of homes.

Multiple listing service (MLS)   A specific multiple listing service that is nationwide and to which most brokers subscribe.

Mutual wills   Wills of parties that are reciprocal in their distribution; usually based on a contract to make a will; generally enforceable.

N

National Association of Realtors (NAR)   Professional organization of brokers and agents; has standards for admission and maintenance of membership.

National Environmental Policy Act (NEPA) of 1969   Act that requires federal agencies to do an EIS before they approve a project.

National Pollution Discharge Elimination System (NPDES)   Permit system that requires EPA approval for water discharges.

Negative easement   An easement that prohibits a property owner from doing something that affects the property of another; e.g., a solar easement is a negative easement.

Net listing   Type of listing that allows the broker to collect as a commission any amount received that is above the figure set as the seller's net take on the sale of the property.

Net-net-net   See *Triple net*.

No deal, no commission clause   Provision in listing agreement that requires a sale of property to close before any commission is due and owing to the broker.

Noise Control Act of 1972   Environmental statute regulating noise levels, disclosure requirements, and precautions.

Nonagent broker   Broker who sells property via multi-listing but is not the listing broker.

Nonattainment areas   In environmental regulation, those areas that have not reached acceptable levels of pollution; highly regulated.

Nonconforming use   In zoned areas, a use that does not comply with the area's zoning but that existed prior to the time the zoning was effective.

Nonconventional pollutants   Second in line in terms of water pollution dangers; EPA can require higher pretreatment standards for nonconventional pollutants.

Noncumulative classification   Method of zoning in which use in a particular area is limited to the zoned use; e.g., industrial zones cannot include residential buildings and apartment areas cannot include single-family dwellings.

Nonfreehold estates   Type of land interest that is certain and definite in duration, such as a lease for a period of time.

Nonownership states   Method for oil and gas ownership that disallows ownership of oil and gas until they have been captured through drilling.

Notice statutes   Form of recording statute that gives later bona fide purchasers priority in the case of multiple purchases if the previous purchasers fail to give notice by recording their transactions.

Novation   Original parties to a contract and a new third party agree to substitute the third party for the performance of the agreement.

Nuisance   Use of property so as to interfere with another's use and enjoyment of property; e.g., bad smells and loud noises.

Nuncupative wills   Oral wills; not valid in all states.

O

Occupational Safety and Health Administration (OSHA)   Federal agency responsible for assuring safety in the workplace.

Offer   Initial communication in contract formation that, if accepted, results in the formation of a contract.

Oil and gas interest   Form of ownership in which a portion of a mineral interest is assigned.

Oil and gas lease   Transfer of rights to remove oil and gas in exchange for payment to landowner; generally payment is in the form of royalties.

Oil Pollution Act (OPA)   Federal law that requires companies to bear the cost of cleanup for an oil spill and also imposes civil and criminal penalties for certain types of spills.

Open listing   Listing that pays a commission to whichever broker or salesperson sells the property; permits the owner to list with more than one broker and be liable for only one commission.

Operating expenses   In commercial leases, the costs of running the property; variable and defined by lease.

Option   Right (which has been paid for) to purchase property during a certain period of time.

Ordinances   Laws passed on a local level of country, state, or city governments.

Owners' associations   Corporations or other organized entities that have private laws that control the architecture, use, and modification of property within a subdivision or multiunit housing development.

Ownership states   Method for oil and gas ownership right determination that states mineral rights can be lost only if someone first captures the oil and gas by drilling.

P

Paid outside closing (POC)   Costs not paid through escrow or closing.

Parallels   Horizontal guidelines in the United States Government Survey.

Passive income   Income from investments for income tax purposes.

Passive losses   Losses resulting from passive activity; under the 1986 Tax Reform Act, there are limitations on taking passive losses, i.e., passive losses can be taken only from passive income and not from wages and other income, as many taxpayers had done in the past to maximize the benefits of real estate ownership.

Patio homes   Form of multiunit housing that generally include a closed-in yard or patio area.

Patriot Act   Federal law with many provisions designed to curb terrorist activities; impacts real estate transactions because of disclosure requirements imposed on escrow agents regarding transfer of title and deposits of cash; imposes new disclosure and signature requirements for buyers and sellers.

Payment bond   In construction, a bond on the general contractor to ensure payment to subcontractors and suppliers; i.e., if the general contractor does not pay, the surety will pay.

Penal sum   Sum bonding company must pay to have project completed if contractor fails to perform.

Per capita   Method of allocation of intestate property among heirs; basic principle is that each heir gets an equal share.

Per stirpes   Method of distributing property to heirs whereby those closer in relation to the decedent get greater shares.

Percentage rent   Rent for commercial properties expressed as a percentage of net or gross income.

Perfection   Process of gaining priority on an Article 9 security interest; requires a filing of a financing statement to give public notice of the creditor's interest.

Performance bond   Bond on general contractor that guarantees performance; if the general contractor does not perform, the surety will provide performance or payment for damages resulting from noncompletion of the work.

Periodic tenancy   Temporary possessory interest in land that runs on a period-to-period basis, such as a month-to-month lease.

Permanent lender   Once construction is complete, the lender who will carry the permanent financing on the project; pays the construction lender and assumes priority.

Personal representative   Party responsible for the probate of a will under the Uniform Probate Code; formerly referred to as an *executor*.

Piggyback mortgage   A mortgage on top of another existing mortgage that incorporates both payments.

Planned unit development (PUD)   Subdivision that includes a development of a full community.

Plat map   Method of land description that relies on a recorded map of a subdivision, with each deed making reference to the map and the particular lot being transferred.

poc (paid outside closing)   Costs not paid through escrow or closing.

Point sources   Discharge points where water leaves land and runs into streams, rivers, and so on.

Possibility of reverter   Future interest in the grantor that follows a fee simple determinable.

Posthumous or afterborn heir   Heir born after the death of the decedent.

Power of sale   In a deed-of-trust financing arrangement, the right of the trustee to sell the property on default by the trustor/borrower.

Power of termination   Future interest in the grantor that follows a fee simple subject to a condition subsequent.

Premarital agreements   Contracts that serve to waive marital property rights of the spouses; must be voluntary and carefully drafted.

Premises   The words of conveyance in a deed; e.g., "do hereby grant and convey."

Prenuptial agreements   Agreements in advance of marriage that alter statutory marital property rights.

Prepayment penalty clause   Clause in mortgage or promissory note that requires the mortgagor to pay an additional charge for paying off the loan early.

Prescription   Process of acquiring an easement through adverse use of the easement over a required period of time.

Pretermitted A testator's child conceived prior to but born after testator's death.

Prevention of significant deterioration (PSD) areas Part of 1977 Clean Air Act amendments establishing emission standards for clean areas to prevent pollution.

Prime contractor General contractor on a project.

Prime meridians The key vertical lines in the United States Government Survey.

Principal meridians See *Prime meridians.*

Prior Appropriation Doctrine Water allocation policy of first to use the water gets the rights to that water.

Private law Laws between individual parties; e.g., landlord's rules and regulations or the terms of a contract.

Probate Process of collecting the assets of a decedent; paying the decedent's debts, determining the decedent's heirs, and distributing property to the heirs.

Procuring cause of the sale standard Standard of determining commission among brokers under an open listing agreement.

Profit Rights of removal in another's property; shorthand for *profit a prendre.*

Profit a prendre Right to enter another's land for the purpose of removing soil, water, minerals, or another resource.

Promissory note Two-party debt instrument that, in real estate, is generally secured by a mortgage or deed of trust or some other interest in real estate.

Property report Summary of facts about undeveloped land required to be given to purchasers (part of ILSFDA).

Property tax roll Assessor's formal records of parcels of land; the valuation and assessment.

Proprietary lease Interest of cooperative owner in a dwelling unit.

Prorated Allocation of prepaid insurance, taxes, and rent; generally done at close of escrow between buyer and seller.

Prorationing rules Rules that limit oil and gas production at the well site.

Protective covenants In development, covenants regarding nature and/or use of structures.

Psychological disclosure statutes Statutes that require disclosure of events on property that create psychological reactions in buyers and affect market value; e.g., the fact that a home has been the site of a murder or that those who lived there were infected with the AIDS virus; some statutory limitations apply.

Purchase money mortgage A mortgage used to secure a debt for the funds used to buy the mortgaged property.

Purchase money security interest (PMSI) Under Article 9 of the UCC, a security interest given to a lender who financed the purchase of the property that is the collateral.

Pure race statute Recording priority statute that awards title (in the event of multiple conveyances) to the first purchaser to record.

Q

Quasi-easement A right-of-way as it existed when there was unity of ownership in a parcel of land.

Quiet title action Court action brought to determine the true owner of a piece of land.

Quitclaim deed Deed that serves to transfer title if the grantor has any such title; there are no guarantees that the grantor has any title or good title.

R

Race/notice system State recording statutes that award title to the first *bona fide* purchaser to record his/her title when there are conflicting claims of ownership in the property.

Range In the United States Government Survey, the lines placed vertically every 6 miles between the guide meridians.

Real estate investment trusts (REITs) Form of real estate syndication in which investors hold trust interests and enjoy profits of trust's real estate holdings.

Real Estate Settlement Procedures Act (RESPA) Federal statute regulating disclosure of closing costs in advance and prohibiting kickbacks for referring customers to title companies.

Real estate syndication Group investment in real estate in the forms of trusts, partnerships, and corporations.

Realtor® Trademark/name used by the National Association of Realtors (NAR) to refer to one of its members.

Recording Process of placing a deed or other document on the public records to give notice of a transaction or interest in the land.

Recreational lease In multiunit housing, a lease that runs for a short period of time during each year; sometimes called *time-sharing.*

Redlining Practice of targeting certain areas or neighborhood as high-risk areas for loans or insurance, or requiring lower valuation.

Refinancing Negotiating a new loan for real estate; generally done to obtain a lower rate or, in the case of a sale, to allow a buyer to be able to purchase a property.

Regulation Z The Federal Reserve Board's regulations on disclosures in all types of credit transactions.

Remainder Future interest in someone other than the grantor; a remainder follows a life estate.

Rent controls Statutory maximums for rents on residential property.

Repair and deduct A tenant's right to repair leased premises when the landlord fails to do so and to deduct the cost of the repairs from his/her rent.

Rescission Right to treat a contract as if it never existed; rescind contract rights; generally appropriate in cases of fraud and misrepresentation.

Residential mortgage transactions Mortgages for the purchase of property to be used primarily as a residence for the buyer.

Resolution Trust Corporation (RTC) Defunct federal agency that handled savings and loan cleanup.

Resource Conservation and Recovery Act (RCRA) of 1976 Federal law regulating hazardous waste and garbage that requires record-keeping and controls amounts of garbage.

Resource Recovery Act Part of the federal environmental statutory scheme on the cleanup of property contaminated with toxic substances.

Reverse bidding Process of using the Internet for contractors to submit bids online and the bids go down from opening bid.

Reverse mortgage A form of mortgage that enables retired individuals to draw the equity from their homes in the form of a monthly payment. No payments or finance charges are due on the loan underlying the mortgage until the owner dies.

Reversion Future interest in grantor that results after life estate terminates and no remainder interest was given.

Revised Model Business Corporation Act (RMBCA) Model act on corporations; adopted in about one-third of states.

Revised Uniform Limited Partnership Act (RULPA) New uniform law updating ULPA.

Right of entry Future interest in grantor that results when the grantee fails to honor the condition placed on the grant of a fee simple subject to a condition subsequent.

Riparian Doctrine In water rights, governs the landowner who adjoins water; a theory that entitles all riparians to use of their water; does not allow one riparian to use all of the water.

Rivers and Harbors Act of 1899 A federal statute that attempted to regulate dumping in rivers and harbors; a predecessor to today's environmental statutes; still used.

Royalty interest Interest landowner retains upon leasing of oil well.

Rule Against Perpetuities (RAP) Rule that prohibits the control of estates from the grave; provides a duration cap on contingent remainders and executory interests.

Rule in Dumpor's Case English rule that provides that if a landlord consents to one assignment of the lease by the tenant, the landlord consents to all subsequent assignments; most statutes have abolished by statute the effects of this rule.

Rule in Shelley's Case Common law rule that merges future and present interests in A when grant is "To A for life, remainder to A's heirs"; has been abolished in many states.

Rule of Capture In mineral rights, a first-in-time-is-first-in-right philosophy in which the first to take subsurface minerals has title regardless of property boundary lines.

Rule of reason In easements, the standard followed in making decisions regarding the expansion of easement use; in antitrust, a standard for determining non per se violations.

S

S corporation Another name used for a Subchapter S corporation.

Safe Drinking Water Act 1986 amendment to Clean Water Act that establishes minimum standards for drinking-water purity; states must adopt federal minimums or their own higher standards.

Satisfaction of mortgage Payment of full loan amount by mortgagor.

Saving clause Provision for alternative distribution of property being willed away; can be a defense to the Rule Against Perpetuities.

Section In the United States Government Survey, 1-mile squares in townships.

Secure and Fair Enforcement of the Mortgage Licensing Act of 2008 (SAFE Mortgage Licensing Act) Federal law that imposes additional requirements on mortgage brokers.

Security agreement Under Article 9, the contract that gives the creditor a lien in the personal property or fixture; makes it the collateral for the loan.

Security deposit In the lease, the amount of money prepaid by the tenant to secure performance of the lease; often provides the amount of liquidated damages if the tenant does not perform.

Security interest Creditor's right in collateral under Article 9; the lien on the personal property or fixture.

Self-help Remedy for tenants with premises in disrepair; the right to repair defects on the property and then seek reimbursement.

Self-proving will A will that is acknowledged or notarized and thereby enjoys presumption of validity.

Servient estate Land through which an easement runs or that is subject to the easement.

Servient tenement Land through which an easement runs or that is subject to the easement.

Shared-appreciation mortgage Method of creative financing in which the lender charges a lower interest rate in exchange for the right to a return of a portion of the equity, including the increased value, of the home.

Sheriff's deed Form of title given to a buyer at a mortgage foreclosure sale; carries no warranties.

Sick building syndrome (SBS) Conditions in building that cause respiratory and other ailments in occupants; causes vary from lack of ventilation to use of various materials; EPA and OSHA have developed guidelines and standards for ventilation and remediation.

Social issue zoning Use of zoning to control influences in the community; e.g., the prohibition of adult theaters near residential districts.

Solar easement laws Negative easements that prevent the servient estate from doing anything that would block the sunlight access of the dominant estate.

Soldiers and Sailors Civil Relief Act (SSCRA) Federal law that provides time restrictions on foreclosures involving those in active military service.

Solid Waste Disposal Act Initial federal act on waste disposal that provided states with money for research on solid-waste disposal.

Special permit Exception to zoning uses provided by a board of adjustment.

Special warranty deed Deed that provides warranty of title only for the period during which the grantor owned the property; see *Deed of bargain and sale.*

Specialty trust A trust created for a specific purpose; e.g., a corporate trust created to expand the firm's real estate holdings.

Specific happenings increase provisions In commercial leases; provisions that result in increase in rental fees.

Specific performance Equitable remedy that requires a party to a contract to perform the contract promise or promises.

Squatter's rights A lay term for adverse possession or prescription.

Standard State Zoning Enabling Act Standard act adopted by most jurisdictions to govern the development and enforcement of a zoning plan.

State implementation plans (SIPs) All state and local laws and ordinances that make up the state's air pollution control plan.

Statement of record Under ILSFDA, the disclosure document filed with HUD before any sales of underdeveloped land can occur.

Statute of Frauds Statute dictating what types of contracts must be in writing to be enforceable.

Statutory broker Term used in some states to describe a broker who represents both buyer and seller; special disclosures required to serve in this capacity.

Statutory lien Right in land created by statute as a means of ensuring payment for work, materials, or other obligations.

Statutory right of redemption Specified period of time after foreclosure sale for buyer to redeem property by paying full amount of debt, interest, and costs associated with foreclosure.

Steering Form of racial discrimination in which brokers or salespeople direct interested purchasers away from and toward certain neighborhoods to control racial composition.

Stop notice statutes Statutes that allow subcontractors and materials suppliers to record a document and/or give service or notice of their rights to payment to the owner or general contractor so that disputed payment issues are resolved before there is double payment or end of funding.

Straight-term mortgage Mortgage with fixed interest rate for a set number of years.

Strawman transaction Transaction that is artificial and non-permanent; generally used to satisfy the unities required for creating a joint tenancy.

Subchapter S corporation A special form of corporation under the Internal Revenue Code that allows the protection of limited liability but direct flow-through of profits and losses.

Subcontractors Workers hired by the general contractor on a project to complete certain portions of the project.

Subdivision trust Form of financing in which seller and buyer are trust beneficiaries, and a third party acts as trustee. Seller and buyer will share in the profits of land development after the seller has paid for the property.

Subject-to sale A transfer of real property in which the buyer takes the property subject to an existing mortgage but does not agree to assume responsibility for the mortgage payments.

Subleases Arrangements in which a tenant leases rental property to another, and the tenant becomes landlord to the subtenant.

Subordinate mortgage Mortgage with a lesser priority than a preexisting mortgage.

Substantial performance Construction doctrine that requires good-faith completion of a project, but not necessarily perfection.

Superfund The fund created by the federal government to sponsor cleanup of toxic waste disposal sites.

Superfund Amendment and Reauthorization Act Federal law establishing cleanup funding, policies, and liability for toxic wastes.

Surety One who stands as a guarantor for an obligation, as in a payment or performance bond.

Surface Mining and Reclamation Act of 1977 Federal law that regulates surface mining and the required cleanup afterwards.

Suspended losses For tax purposes, losses that exceed passive income and are carried forward to future years' passive income.

T

Taking Term used to describe the government action of taking private property for permanent public purposes.

Takings issues Under Fifth Amendment, constitutional protections in eminent domain.

Tax deed Form of title given in the event property is sold to satisfy taxes; carries no warranties.

Tax lien Lien placed on property for amount of unpaid taxes.

Tax Reform Act (TRA) Federal law (1986) that substantially changed real estate income tax issues.

Tax sale Foreclosure sale on property for nonpayment of taxes.

Telecommunications Act of 1996 Federal law that includes regulation of local zoning for location of cellular phone towers; section of this federal law was passed to limit the local resistance to placement of the towers because the local objections were impeding the progress of the cellular network.

Tenancy at sufferance   Tenancy wherein the tenant is on the property of the landlord but has no right to be and may be evicted at any time.

Tenancy at will   Tenancy wherein the tenant remains as long as both parties agree; either party may terminate at any time and without notice.

Tenancy by entirety   Method of co-ownership that is a joint tenancy between husband and wife.

Tenancy for years   Tenancy for a stated period of time.

Tenancy in common   Simplest form of co-ownership; unless otherwise stated, the presumed method of ownership for multiple landowners.

Tenancy in partnership   Form of co-ownership in which the parties are partners; similar to joint tenancy in that the partners have a right of survivorship.

Testamentary   Disposition by will.

Testamentary capacity   The requisite mental capacity needed to make a valid will; a person's need to understand who his/her relatives are and how the property will be distributed by his/her will.

Time-sharing   Form of multiunit housing in which owners own the unit for a limited period of time during each year.

Title insurance   Insurance that pays damages to the buyer of property in the event certain title defects arise.

Title theory   Theory of mortgage law that puts title in the mortgagee and possession in the mortgagor.

Torrens system   System for recording land titles designed to prevent the selling of the same parcel of land to more than one person.

Tortious interference with expectation of inheritance   New tort that allows recovery if potential beneficiary can demonstrate that another deprived him/her of an inheritance.

Townhouse   Form of multiunit housing in which the owner owns the area in the unit and also owns the land on which the unit is located.

Township   Term in the United States Government Survey for the 6-mile squares formed between the guide meridians and the parallels.

Toxic pollutants   EPA classification for the worst form of water pollutants.

Toxic Substances Control Act (TOSCA)   Federal law regulating the manufacture, labeling, and distribution of toxic substances.

Tract index system   Form of land record that keeps history of title through identification of transactions with the particular tract.

Trade fixture   Personal property that is attached to real property but is used in the operation of a business; remains the tenant's property; a misnomer in that it is personal property.

Transaction broker   Broker used for a sale who is not the listing broker.

Transfer development rights   In areas in which building heights are limited, the right to sell air rights for purposes of business expansion and construction; i.e., a company not using all of its height expansion allowance can transfer the right to build in the airspace to another company.

Transfer disclosure statement (TDS)   In some states, a form that provides information about the residential property being transferred: length of ownership, date of construction, construction and improvements, etc.

Trapping statutes   Another name for stop notice statutes.

Trespass   Invasion of the property of another by a person or object.

Trespassers   One who is on the property of another without permission.

Triggering language   In credit advertisements, language describing credit terms that will require full and complete disclosure of all credit terms under Regulation Z.

Triple net   Form of commercial lease rental formula; tenant pays taxes, insurance, and maintenance and fixed rent above these amounts.

Troubled Asset Relief Program   Federal program that purchases underwater properties to provide relief to real estate markets.

Trust certificate   In a real estate trust, the evidence of ownership given to each trust holder.

Truth-in-Lending Act   Name given to federal statutes and regulations concerning credit terms and their disclosure.

Truth-in-Lending laws   General term applied to series of federal laws and regulations that require disclosures and procedures in consumer credit transactions.

U

Undue influence   The use of a confidential relationship to gain benefits under a will or contract.

Uniform Commercial Code (UCC)   Uniform statute adopted in most states that governs commercial transactions; Article 9 deals with security interests in fixtures.

Uniform Common Interest Ownership Act   Uniform law on multiple-ownership issues.

Uniform Condominium Act (UCA)   Uniform law adopted in some states governing ownership, rights, and obligations in condominium interests.

Uniform Land Transactions Act (ULTA)   Uniform act with provisions governing land contracts.

Uniform Limited Partnership Act (ULPA)   Uniform act governing formation, operation, and dissolution of limited partnerships.

Uniform Marital Property Act   Uniform law that provides for ownership of property by married persons and means of division of property in the event of divorce or death.

Uniform Marketable Title Act   Former law on what is required to deliver marketable title in sale.

Uniform Partnership Act (UPA)   Uniform statute adopted in most states governing the creation, operation, and dissolution of partnerships.

Uniform Premarital Agreement Act   Uniform law adopted in some states that governs the drafting and execution of premarital agreements.

Uniform Probate Code (UPC)   Uniform law adopted in about one-third of the states governing the distribution of intestate property, the making of wills and probate, and administration of estates.

Uniform Residential Landlord Tenant Act (URLTA)   Uniform law governing residential leases.

Uniform Rights of the Terminally Ill Act   Proposed uniform law on the rights of the terminally ill to refuse treatment; would establish rules for electing refusal of treatment.

Uniform Settlement Statement (USS)   Under RESPA, the required form for showing how money was paid and distributed at close of escrow.

Uniform Simultaneous Death Act (USDA)   Uniform law designed to allow direct distribution to heirs next in line when husband and wife die simultaneously (or within 5 days of each other).

Unit pricing   Means of costing in construction that divides contract into units for prices and payment.

United States Code (U.S.C.)   Compilation of all federal laws.

United States Constitution   Framework for federal government.

United States government survey   National survey of land.

Unities   In co-ownership, the presence of requirements on creation; i.e., the interests must have been created at the same time, with the same title and interest, and with equal possession rights.

Usury   Charging interest rates in excess of the statutorily allowed maximums.

V

VA   Veteran's Administration.

Vacation license   Form of time-sharing interest ownership.

Variances   Approved uses of land outside the scope of an area's zoning.

Vested remainder   A remainder that will automatically take effect when the life estate ends.

Vested remainder subject to complete divestment   A remainder that can be completely lost if the terms of vesting are not met; not automatic on termination of the life estate.

Vested remainder subject to partial divestment   A remainder that can be partially lost as other remaindermen develop, i.e., more children are born during the life estate.

Voluntary lien   A lien created because of a contract (as opposed to a tax lien, which is involuntary).

W

Waiver agreement   In liens, a document that waives the right of a supplier or laborer to lien the property; generally given in exchange for payment.

Warranty deed   Deed that conveys title and carries warranties that the title is good, the transfer is proper, and there are no liens and encumbrances other than the ones noted.

Water Quality Act   One of the predecessors to today's federal water pollution control statutory scheme.

Water rights   System of priority for water use.

Wetlands   Protected areas near water; formerly known as *swamps.*

Will   Legal document that transfers property rights from testator to named beneficiaries.

Workout   In commercial real estate loans, the process of adjusting loan repayment because of borrower's financial difficulties.

Wrap-around mortgage   Mortgage in which seller carries the buyer with a second mortgage that encompasses the first mortgage and requires a payment that covers both mortgages.

Z

Zoning   Process of regulating land use by designating areas of a community for certain uses.

Zoning commission   Governmental agency responsible for developing the zoning plan.

CASE INDEX

Note: Page numbers with "n" indicate footnotes.

SUBJECT INDEX

Note: Page numbers with "f" indicate figures; those with "n" indicate footnotes.